GAY
AMERICAN
HISTORY

*Lesbians and
Gay Men
in the U.S.A.*

BY THE AUTHOR

Resistance at Christiana: The Fugitive Slave
    Rebellion, Christiana, Pennsylvania, September
    11, 1851
Coming Out!: A Documentary Play About Gay
    Life and Liberation in the U.S.A.
Gay American History: Lesbians and Gay Men in
    the U.S.A.

CO-AUTHOR WITH BERNARD KATZ

Black Woman; A Fictionalized Biography of
    Lucy Terry Prince

GENERAL EDITOR

Homosexuality: Lesbians and Gay Men in Society,
    History and Literature

GAY
AMERICAN
HISTORY

LESBIANS AND GAY MEN
IN THE U.S.A.

A Documentary by
JONATHAN KATZ

THOMAS Y. CROWELL COMPANY

Established 1834/NEW YORK

The author's research in Gay American history is ongoing; he would much appreciate learning of any additional documented sources. Communications may be sent to him in care of his agent, Raines and Raines, 475 Fifth Avenue, New York, N.Y. 10017.

Copyright acknowledgments will be found on page 565.

Designed by S. S. Drate

Index by James D. Steakley

Manufactured in the United States of America

Library of Congress Cataloging in Publication Data

Katz, Jonathan.
    Gay American history: Lesbians and gay men in the U.S.A.

    Bibliography: p.
    Includes index.
    1. Homosexuality—United States—History.
2. Lesbianism—United States—History. I. Title.
HQ76.3.U5K37 1976   301.41'57'0973   · 76-2039
ISBN 0-690-01164-4
    0-690-01165-2 (pbk.)

1 2 3 4 5 6 7 8 9 10

For my people,
with love,
in struggle—
and in honor
of two pioneers,
JEANNETTE HOWARD FOSTER
(author of *Sex Variant Women in Literature*)
and
HENRY HAY
(a founder of the Mattachine Society).

CONTENTS

VI

NOTE

♀ In books about both male and female homosexuality, references to Lesbianism are often subsumed under the general category of "homosexuality"—and lost. In the present volume, Lesbian-related material is dispersed unequally within the parts, and not always readily identifiable by title—thus difficult to locate at a glance. For this reason, a female sign is here placed beside the title of each text containing the most substantial references to women-loving women. However, since brief, important references are not so tagged, the interested reader is advised to consult the index for a complete list of Lesbian-related items.

ITEMIZED TABLE OF CONTENTS

II. TREATMENT: 1884–1974

♀ III. PASSING WOMEN: 1782–1920

IV. NATIVE AMERICANS/GAY AMERICANS: 1528–1976

V. RESISTANCE: 1859–1972

VI. LOVE: 1779–1932

LIST OF ILLUSTRATIONS

INTRODUCTION

We have been the silent minority, the silenced minority—invisible women, invisible men. Early on, the alleged enormity of our "sin" justified the denial of our existence, even our physical destruction. Our "crime" was not merely against society, not only against humanity, but "against nature"—we were outlaws against the universe. Long did we remain literally and metaphorically unspeakable, "among Christians not to be named"—nameless. To speak our name, to roll that word over the tongue, was to make our existence tangible, physical; it came too close to some mystical union with us, some carnal knowledge of that "abominable" ghost, that lurking possibility within. For long, like women conceived only in relation to men, we were allowed only relative intellectual existence, conceived only in relation to, as deviants from, a minority of—an "abnormal" and embarrassing poor relation. For long we were a people perceived out of time and out of place—socially unsituated, without a history—the mutant progeny of some heterosexual union, freaks. Our existence as a long-oppressed, long-resistant social group was not explored. We remained an unknown people, our character defamed. The heterosexual dictatorship has tried to keep us out of sight and out of mind; its homosexuality taboo has kept us in the dark. That time is over. The people of the shadows have seen the light; Gay people are coming out—and moving on—to organized action against an oppressive society.

In recent years the liberation movements of Lesbians and Gay men have politicized, given historical dimension to, and radically altered the traditional concept of homosexuality, as well as the social situation, relations, ideas, and emotions of some homosexuals. Those of us affected by this movement have experienced a basic change in our sense of self. As we acted upon our society we acted upon ourselves; as we changed the world we changed our minds; sexual subversives, we overturned our psychic states. From a sense of our homosexuality as a personal and devastating fate, a private, secret shame, we moved with often dizzying speed to the consciousness of ourselves as members of an oppressed social group. As the personal and political came together in our lives, so it merged in our heads, and we came to see the previously hidden connections between our private lives and public selves; we were politicized, body and soul. In one quick, bright flash we experienced a secular revelation: we too were among America's mistreated. We moved in a brief span of time from a sense that there was something deeply wrong with us to the realization that there was something radically wrong with that society which had done its best to destroy us. We moved from various forms of self-negation to newfound outrage and action against those lethal conditions. From hiding our sexual and affectional natures, we moved to publicly affirm a deep and good part of our being. Starting with a sense of ourselves as characters in a closet drama, the passive victims of a family tragedy, we experienced ourselves as initiators and assertive actors in a movement for social change. We experienced the present as history, ourselves as history-makers. In our lives and in our hearts, we experienced the change from one historical form of homosexuality to another. We experienced homosexuality as historical.

Documents of our history, the history of Lesbians and Gay men in the United States—including related heterosexual attitudes and acts—are for the first time brought together in this anthology. These selected materials of homosexual American history are organized into six chronologically arranged topical sections. Part I, "Trouble: 1566–1966," contains documents covering four hundred years of homosexual oppression and self-oppression, records of this society's conflict with Gay people, and Gay people's socially induced conflict with themselves. Part II focuses on the history of the "Treatment" and mistreatment of Lesbians and Gay men by psychiatrists and psychologists, 1884–1974. Part III, "Passing Women: 1782–1920," reprints accounts of women who dressed and worked and lived as men—maintaining intimate relations with others of their own sex. Part IV, "Native Americans/Gay Americans: 1528–1976," presents observations on various forms of male and female homosexuality among the first inhabitants of this continent. Part V concerns "Resistance" to the oppression of homosexuals, 1859–1972, including individual isolated acts, and the early history of the organized homosexual emancipation movement in America. Finally, Part VI, "Love," presents documents of intimate relations between people of the same sex, 1779–1932. Extensive notes and topical bibliographies are included for those interested in pursuing this history further.

In researching and selecting these documents, the attempt was made to present, overall, material about Lesbians and Gay men equal in quality and quantity, although this was not possible within each section. The decision to deal in this book with both male and female homosexuals required special research efforts sensitive to the fact that the Lesbian experience has received less attention than that of Gay men, Lesbian persecution has been closely associated with the oppression of all women, and the fact that the social situation and history of Lesbians have differed from that of male homosexuals and are reflected in different types of sources. In selecting Lesbian materials, special attention was paid to those documents which reflect on issues raised by the recent women's liberation and Lesbian-feminist movements; the male-dominated structure of power and the sexual division of labor; the various forms of male chauvinism; the socially determined character of "masculinity" and "femininity" and of male and female sex roles; the influence of sexism on the lives of women; and, of course, the particular character of Lesbian oppression, resistance, and love. The one section devoted entirely to persons of a particular gender, Part IV, "Passing Women," presents material which throws new light on these feminist issues.

This collection includes accounts of a wide range of Gay lives and life-styles, from a great variety of sources, and covers a period of more than four hundred years. My research focused on uncovering and presenting enough significant evidence to demonstrate that the heretofore suppressed, hidden history of homosexual Americans does exist, and to insure that, like Gay Americans today, its existence can no longer be denied. The focus here on primary sources, the reprinting of the earliest available accounts in chronological order, is based on a felt need to get back to the language, content, and original temporal sequence of these documents, to cut through that thick, years-old encrustation of interpretation and evaluation which has hidden and distorted the Gay American historical experience. Most of the documents in this anthology are reprinted here for the first time. And for the first time they are treated not as unique and purely personal curios, but as fragments of an ongoing, though previously unrecognized, group experience, the history of which is only beginning to be pieced together from many separate sources.

As an arbitary criterion, the older a document, relative to the other material available on a topic, the more likely it was to be favored for reprinting. The focus of these selections is away from purely theoretical formulations; the emphasis is on those documents which reveal some aspect of the American homosexual experience as it was actually lived. Documents were selected which allude to some recurring theme, contain some larger resonance, or suggest some meaning transcending an immediate event or particular personality. Emphasis was placed on those documents which permit the authentic voice of a speaker to come through with the greatest force and clarity, whether this was the rarely heard voice of the individual Gay person, or the more often heard voice of the heterosexual bigot.

The focus here is on the homosexual experience in the United States, a national emphasis intended to bring this history home with the most impact and to avoid the overly general, diffuse, and amorphous quality of previous international sexual-historical surveys. This American focus is also intended to suggest the possibilities of detailed, in-depth research and to emphasize the influence of a particular national setting on the historical forms of homosexuality found within it. The documents here reveal and record as much about heterosexual acts and attitudes toward homosexuals as they do about Gay life itself.

Particular attention was paid to documenting the experience of ordinary Gay people. No particular effort was made to document the lives of homosexuals creative or famous, a past Gay concern arising from heterosexuals' denunciation of homosexuals as non-procreative and infamous. Those well-known individuals who do appear here do so because the content of their lives or work was felt to contribute some insight into those aspects of the Gay American experience upon which this book does focus: homosexual oppression, resistance, and love.

The documents here were discovered by hard labor and a certain dogged, one-track, single-minded, obsessive persistence. Communication with Gay people proved to be an important source of leads to materials once read, heard about, or rumored to exist. Friends, neighbors, relatives, lovers, fellow researchers, correspondents, and groups before whom I spoke all supplied clues to elusive evidence. The existing bibliographies on homosexuality were collected, and a chronological and topical survey was made to discover what types of sources and documents previous researchers had already discovered. I attempted to find any passing references to American homosexual history in previously published sources, wanting to avoid duplication of labor and to proceed from what was already known. Inquiries to the Institute for Sex Research in Indiana brought valuable information, primarily in the form of bibliographies on requested topics and photocopies of rare items unavailable elsewhere. I rummaged through library card-catalogs and walked through library stacks, pulling out likely books and consulting indexes. A printed "Appeal for Help" describing my research was distributed at every, even unlikely, opportunity. And always file cards were kept, containing detailed notations of references, dates, topics, locations of items, and even unproductive sources. I moved through libraries like a detective, a tracer of missing prisons, following up clues, following trails from footnote to footnote, an explorer in an unknown land.

Among the sources consulted, and from which documents were derived, are foreign language books and periodicals, especially the materials produced by the German homosexual emancipation movement between 1897 and 1930; a number of these foreign language texts appear here, translated for the first time. Other sources are records of insane asylums, universities, and churches; articles in medical, psychiatric, psychological, and legal journals; legal appeals court records; periodicals, ephemeral handouts, and other publications of the early American homosexual emancipation movement; reports of local, city, and state governments, and of the federal government; reports of travelers, missionaries, explorers, anthropologists, sociologists, penologists; passing references in histories, biographies, autobiographies, diaries; artworks (Black blues, cowboy poems, engravings, photographs); and literary works (novels, short stories, poetry, plays). Such literary sources must be mentioned as an especially important source for the historical study of American Lesbianism. The novel, short story, poetry, and drama are creative forms in which Lesbians have been portrayed, and Lesbianism developed as a subject, even while it was excluded from other, more traditional historical sources. Such literary materials, quite apart from their artistic merit, are rich and valuable materials for the study of Lesbianism in different social-historical settings. In using literature as social document, the main point, of course, is to avoid assuming any necessary correlation between the fictional representation and actual, historical society. Such factors as an author's gender, sexual orientation, life-style, personal history, intended audience, and type of publisher will deeply affect the extent to which any literary creation accurately reflects its time; only by comparing such artistic work with other sources can its meaning and validity as a historical document finally be judged.

The research for this book uncovered a number of original documents, indicating that such Gay history materials can be found if a search is made for them. Among the previously unpublished manuscripts printed here are the love letters from Almeda Sperry to Emma Goldman, dating to 1912, and the documents of the 1846 hearing in the matter of Edward McCosker, an Irish policeman of New York City accused of making advances to men. Research on women who spent part of their lives disguised as men led to the recovery of a group of documents concerning Lucy Ann Lobdell. The discovery of Lobdell's previously forgotten autobiography, published in 1855, provides her own account of her early life and reasons for adopting male attire; to my surprise and pleasure, Lobdell's book also turned out to contain an explicit feminist appeal. Two medical journal articles that were discovered discuss Lobdell's later life, mental disturbance, and commitment; one report includes a short biography of her female lover. A friend, James Steakley, by chance knew that the insane asylum to which Lobdell had been committed in 1883 still existed (a homosexual acquaintance had committed suicide there in the 1960s). Investigation revealed that Lobdell's eighty-year-old asylum records were indeed extant, and permission to use them was obtained. Research on other "passing women" also brought to light a psychiatrist's report of 1920 containing a female life history which reads like a short story. Although the subject of this article is referred to only as "H," research based on internal evidence led to the discovery of this woman's identity and of capsule comments about her accompanying several photographs (including her baby picture) which appeared in her college yearbook in 1911.

Among other discoveries made during the research for this book was the original charter of the Chicago-based Society for Human Rights, issued by the state of Illinois in

1924; this charter documents the existence of the earliest known homosexual emancipation organization in the United States, founded by Henry Gerber. Another major discovery was a group of twelve previously unknown essays by this same Henry Gerber, some on the subject of homosexuality, originally published in an obscure, mimeographed literary periodical in 1934. An article, "In Defense of Homosexuality," published in 1932, was also discovered to have been written by Gerber under a pseudonym.

The present book also includes what may be termed "created documents," five interviews taped by myself with Lesbians and Gay men whose personal experiences are of some special significance in Gay American history. Included are interviews with Henry Hay, founder of the first Mattachine Society; Barbara Gittings, a founder of the Lesbian rights organization, the New York Daughters of Bilitis; and Alma Routsong, author of the Lesbian-feminist novel *Patience and Sarah*. Also included are interviews with a young man who, in the mid-1960s, received electric shock treatment to "cure" his homosexuality, and another man jailed as a result of the antihomosexual witch-hunt in Boise, Idaho, in 1955–56. These taped reminiscences indicate the value of oral history recordings in the further development of Gay history.

In any future Gay history research the importance of exactly and fully specifying sources cannot be overemphasized, the practice has so rarely been observed in the past. The exact specification of sources has nothing to do with academic ritual, but is a necessity if each researcher is to be enabled to begin where the last one left off, and Lesbian and Gay male history is to develop and become a cooperative endeavor.

Despite the bigot's association of homosexuality and subversion, Gay people, of course, include persons of every political persuasion. Since the 1950s, however, when American homosexual emancipationists began to speak out, the most vocal have been the most establishment oriented. Therefore, a bit of Gay American history I did not set out to find, but stumbled upon nevertheless, is the existence of a little-known anti-capitalist, prosocialist (or at least radical) tradition among a small but significant group of homosexual emancipation pioneers, American as well as English and German. The newly unearthed writings of Henry Gerber suggest such a political orientation, as does the Communist affiliation of Henry Hay and some other founders of the original Mattachine Society. Among the earliest public defenders of homosexuality in America was anarchist Emma Goldman, long a staunch anticapitalist, pro–working-class advocate. In 1957, Black left-wing political activist and playwright Lorraine Hansberry enthusiastically (though anonymously) supported the emerging American Lesbian liberation movement. After 1969, when some Gay activists put forth a radical, left-leaning interpretation of homosexual oppression, they unknowingly followed in an old tradition. In England, in 1891, even that upper-class homosexual emancipationist John Addington Symonds wrote to Edward Carpenter that the "acknowledgment" and "extension" of homosexuality "would do very much to further the advent of the right kind of socialism." From the mid-1890s onward, Edward Carpenter publicly espoused socialism, homosexual emancipation, and feminism. In 1896, Fabian socialist George Bernard Shaw was one of the few to publicly defend Oscar Wilde, who had himself earlier expounded on the benefits of socialism for the "soul." The radical tradition among Gay people and their supporters is an intriguing subject for future research.[1]

Although this anthology is intended for general readers of all sexual persuasions, my research and selections have been particularly concerned with that material I hoped would be most useful to Gay women and men in our present struggle to create a positive, rounded sense of self, to establish unalienated ways of relating, and to abolish those social institutions that deny us. In making these selections I relied primarily on my own emotional and intellectual reaction to the material, my sense of what was most significant. I trust my response will often parallel some similar reaction in others. Paradoxically, by focusing on what seems most interesting to me and on what I hope will prove interesting to other Gay people, by thus presenting an individual and authentic Gay viewpoint, this book should also be most illuminating for heterosexuals.

Although the viewpoint upon which this work is based is authentically Gay, it is only one of many Gay viewpoints. Because there has been no previous single volume on homosexual American history, and because such a limited range of Gay people have had access to the means of mass communication, there is a danger that what I present and say here will be taken as "the Gay viewpoint." The selections here, the topical organization, value judgments, and brief analytical comments are my own; other Gay people may or may not agree with them. I have no desire to speak for all Gay men, much less for any Lesbian. This book indicates the existence of many Gay voices, many Gay lives, many homosexualities. It is intended to raise questions, not answer them. This work contains historical materials whose implications can be the subject of prolonged and creative discussion in the years to come. Meanwhile, more hard research and much careful intellectual analysis need to be undertaken. This book, I hope, is only a beginning.

On the one hand, the aim of my research, while physically most ambitious, was intellectually quite modest—to simply recover and present a significantly large, wide-ranging collection of historical documents concerning six selected aspects of Gay American history. I make no claim to completeness; this work is not definitive. I had no intention of writing an all-encompassing, analytic, narrative history of Gay American life. After several years of research, working alone, with quite meager financial resources, I was able to uncover evidence of a vast, subterranean world of same-sex relations, coexistent with the ordinary historical universe. I now believe it will one day be possible to write a comprehensive, analytical, narrative chronicle of the homosexual American experience, but only after Gay history is legitimized, after it becomes a cooperative enterprise, after more research is undertaken and more evidence collected. For the time being, I think, we must still be wary of analytical generalizations based on the limited evidence at hand. Gay people have for a long time been oppressed by generalizations based on unrepresentative samples. It will require years of additional detailed historical detective work and analysis to bring to light the myriad, subtle, and far-reaching implications of the Gay American experience, to set it firmly within the larger framework of American history. Here only a minimal attempt has been made to suggest the all-important social and temporal context of those documents presented. The attempt here is to make a start at recovering from the depths a previously submerged aspect of American social life.

On the other hand, I will be pleased if this book helps to revolutionize the traditional concept of homosexuality. This concept is so profoundly ahistorical that the very existence of Gay history may be met with disbelief. The common image of the homosexual has been a figure divorced from any temporal-social context. The concept of homosexuality must be historicized. Ancient Greek pederasty, contemporary homosexual "marriages," and Lesbian-feminist partnerships all differ radically. Beyond the most obvious fact that homosexual relations involve persons of the same gender, and include feelings as well as acts, there is no such thing as homosexuality in general, only particular historical forms of homosexuality. There is no evidence for the assumption that certain traits have universally characterized homosexual (or heterosexual) relations throughout history. The problem of the historical researcher is thus to study and establish the character and meaning of each varied manifestation of same-sex relations within a specific time and society. The term "situational homosexuality" has been applied to same-sex relations within prison and other particular institutional settings. The term is fallacious if it implies that there is some "true" homosexuality which is *not* situated. All homosexuality is situational, influenced and given meaning and character by its location in time and social space. Future research and analysis must focus as much on this conditioning situation as on the same-sex relations occurring within it.

The prevailing notion of homosexuality as a purely psychological phenomenon has limited discussion, focusing research almost exclusively on three areas: the causation, character, and treatment of homosexuality as a psychosexual orientation disturbance. Almost no research has been undertaken on the history of homosexuals as a social group living in a hostile environment, on the effect on homosexuals of, for instance, a changing sexual division of labor and roles, or on the character, causation, and treatment of heterosexuals' seemingly obsessive antihomosexuality. The supremacy of the psychological model has meant that the existence of homosexuals as a people with our own history, traditions, and culture has not been explored. The dominance of the psychological model has meant that this model itself was not seen as a historical invention. A temporal perspective emphasizes that homosexuality was once thought of by theologians as essentially a moral issue, a sin; by legislators as a legal problem, a crime; only later, by a rising class of medical entrepreneurs, as a psychological phenomenon, a psychic disturbance. If the traditional psychological model is to be transcended, homosexuality must be reconceived as a historical, social, political, and economic phenomenon, as well as a psychological one. The psychological-psychiatric professionals must be divested of their power to define homosexuals; Gay people must acquire the power to define ourselves.

The traditional concept of homosexuality also has begun by consistently assuming a basic negative value judgment. This condemnatory approach has assured that every conceivable undesirable human character trait has, at one time or another, been attributed to homosexuals as a group. Every unpleasant trait displayed by a particular Gay person within a specific social-historical setting has at some time been ascribed to all homosexuals, to homosexuality itself. Homosexuals have long evoked deep emotions and extreme judgments from heterosexuals. Homosexuals have long felt their own deep feelings and sense of themselves at stake when confronted by some searing manifestation of heterosexual bigotry. Homosexuality is still emotion-provoking and value-laden; lives are inevitably affected by any pronouncement on the subject. To pretend to a cool, objective stance regarding Gay history, to ignore its political and personal implications, is only to hide one's feelings and judgments and fail to confront an inevitable aspect of an emotionally charged subject. Here I have tried to state my own evaluations and feelings with clarity, candor, and boldness. I have not been concerned with presenting a "good image" of homosexuals to heterosexuals—a defensive strategy which limits what Gay people can know of themselves. Thus, those who wish to confirm their stereotypes may find materials here to feed their prejudice. Others more open-minded will see in these same documents materials for an investigation and analysis of that human-political phenomenon hidden behind the traditional stereotype and mask.

One failing of traditional, ethnocentric, antihomosexual researchers is their inherent inability to see themselves in time, as historical, their own moral judgments as relative, making such investigators too sure of themselves, the victims of a self-righteousness incompatible with profundity of intellectual inquiry. Antihomosexual proponents have held sway for so long, with such force and moral certitude, that little dialectical play of argument and counterargument has occurred, insuring that the level of intellectual discourse about homosexuality has been abysmally low. Reading the pronouncements on the subject, one is repeatedly struck by the sheer stupidity of a great many authors.

Knowledge of the present book's mode of production will clarify its character. This work is the creation of an independent writer-researcher, with minimal funding, unaffiliated with those academic institutions which usually subsidize historical research. I say this not by way of apology, but simply as explanation. Only recently have the first two Ph.D. theses on homosexuality been permitted in the history and political science departments of American universities. The writers were both warned that they were risking their academic careers by taking up this topic; both went ahead nevertheless. I know of two other recent instances in which a history department and an English department did not allow theses on homosexual subjects; another German department Ph.D. candidate was discouraged from writing on homosexual literature because the topic would impair future teaching prospects. Researching the present work without capitalization from academia took considerable ingenuity, and could not have been accomplished without the valuable voluntary assistance of a number of Gay people and a few heterosexuals, all named in the acknowledgments. This book is significantly not a product of academia; it does not play it safe; it is rough at the edges, radical at heart.

I began this research late in 1971 with only a presumption—that Gay American history must exist. That year, as an outgrowth of my involvement in the Gay Activists Alliance of New York, I conceived the idea of a documentary play, part historical, part literary, which would convey some of the new ideas and feelings about Gay life and liberation in the United States arising from the current emancipation efforts of Lesbians and Gay men. This play, *Coming Out!*, was first produced in June 1972 as part of the annual commemoration of the Stonewall Resistance. The play was revised and revived for the same occasion in the summer of 1973. The contract for the present book was agreed upon that summer, and signed in September 1973; the main body of the manuscript was delivered two years later, on October 1, 1975. I am satisfied with the accomplishment. I am aware, however, of what might be done if future Gay history research were properly funded.

I have a vision, the dream of receiving that substantial financing needed to support, without strings, a team of Lesbian and Gay male researchers; together we would establish what seems most important for our people and others to learn about our past, decide how best to recover that information, and work cooperatively to actually discover and disseminate our forgotten history. Perhaps this book will contribute to the realization of that dream.

Knowledge of Gay history helps restore a people to its past, to itself; it extends the range of human possibility, suggests new ways of living, new ways of loving. The study of homosexual history suggests a new basis for a radical critique of American society. The study of homosexual social life raises questions about the sexual division of labor and power; the manifestations of male domination and female oppression; the character of same-sex relations, and indirectly of relations between the sexes; the nature of "masculinity" and "femininity"; the influence of socially assigned sex roles; the character of family life and marriage; the role of the religious, legislative, judicial, medical, and psychological professions in the social creation of pain; and the various effects of sexism on the quality of social life. Finally, the study of the Gay past raises the question of whether this society can accommodate the demands of America's dispossessed for power and control over the machinery by which they make their lives.

Most Gay people now see the ending of homosexual oppression in America as a matter of law reform, of obtaining civil rights, and of fitting into this society as it is constituted. Others, myself among them, see the movement for Gay law reform and civil rights as only the present form of a much larger struggle by Gay people and others for power and control over those social institutions which most affect our lives. In this view, Gay liberation is part of that national and worldwide organization and activity for radical social change in which each group, starting from a sense of its own particular oppression, is struggling for the democratic control of that society in which all work, live, and try to love.

Jonathan Katz
New York City,
September 1, 1976

I

TROUBLE
1566-1966

Introduction

During the four hundred years documented here, American homosexuals were condemned to death by choking, burning, and drowning; they were executed, jailed, pilloried, fined, court-martialed, prostituted, fired, framed, blackmailed, disinherited, declared insane, driven to insanity, to suicide, murder, and self-hate, witch-hunted, entrapped, stereotyped, mocked, insulted, isolated, pitied, castigated, and despised. (They were also castrated, lobotomized, shock-treated, and psychoanalyzed, a history documented in Part II.) Homosexuals and their behavior were characterized by the terms "abomination," "crime against nature," "sin," "monster," "fairies," "bull dykes," and "perverts." The vicious judgments such terms expressed were sometimes internalized by Lesbians and Gay men with varying results—from feelings of guilt and worthlessness, to trouble in relating to other homosexuals, to the most profound mental disturbances and antisocial behavior. External judgments internalized became self-oppression; reexternalized this might result in behavior destructive to the self and others. Heterosexual society conditioned homosexuals to act as the agents of their own destruction, to become victims of themselves. But always, finally, they were oppressed, situated in a society that outlawed and denied them.

When simply working, living, and loving, homosexuals have been condemned to invisibility. The present documents of trouble indicate that homosexuals, like heterosexuals, have sometimes made sexual nuisances of themselves, sometimes indulged in sexual relations with youths below a reasonable age of consent, sometimes committed coercive sexual acts, sometimes been neurotic, sometimes insane, sometimes murderous, sometimes seducers. But unlike heterosexuals, Gay people have been burdened by a pernicious myth equating homosexuality per se with its most negative manifestations. If heterosexuals were known by their child-molesters the situation would be analogous. Such anti-Gay myth is still perpetuated by the mass media's reference to a "homosexual murderer"; one never hears of a "heterosexual murderer," but simply "the killer of Miss

X." Historically, only when homosexuals were in jail, on trial, in psychiatric treatment, or caught in some compromising situation—in some sort of trouble—have they come to public attention and their stories been recorded. These documents of homosexuals in trouble are those which have fed antihomosexual myth, those examples which have been generalized to give credence to antihomosexual bigotry. Particular homosexuals in difficulty have been taken to represent homosexuals in general; heterosexuals in difficulty have represented only themselves. Yet for history to ignore the plight of Gay people in trouble would be to ignore what can now be seen as a major aspect of homosexual oppression.

The documents here concerning males include the earliest known case of a homosexual being put to death in America, that of a Frenchman, murdered in 1566 by the Spanish military authorities in St. Augustine, Florida, a victim of the imperial rivalry between Spain and France. These documents also record executions for sodomy in colonial America: Richard Cornish, executed in Virginia about 1624, and William Plaine, executed in New Haven in 1646. Also in 1646, Jan Creoli, a Black living on Manhattan Island, then part of the Dutch New Netherland Colony, was condemned to be choked to death, then burned to ashes. (The ten-year-old Black on whom the crime had been committed was also punished.) In the same colony in 1660, for a homosexual rape, Jan Quisthout Van Der Linde was sentenced to be "tied in a sack and cast into the river," a punishment quite as grotesque as the crime.[1] In reference to the capital punishment for homosexuality and other forms of nonprocreative sex, Governor William Bradford reports an exchange of views in 1642 among the elders of the Massachusetts Bay Colony and those of Plymouth on the fine points of the theological question, What sodomitical acts are to be punished with death? The subject had become a matter of practical concern with the outbreak of various forms of such "wickedness."

With the American Revolution there seemingly began a move away from capital punishment for such crimes as sodomy. Between 1777 and 1779 Thomas Jefferson and a group of liberal reformers suggested a revision of Virginia law eliminating the death penalty for sodomy—they proposed, instead, castration. In 1778 a lieutenant in George Washington's army was dishonorably discharged for attempted sodomy on the person of another soldier. In Maryland, in 1810, one Davis was found guilty of assault and attempted sodomy upon one W.C., a male, nineteen years of age; Davis was sentenced to four months in jail, fifteen minutes in the pillory, and was fined $500; he appealed this verdict to a higher court—one of the earliest legal appeals involving an American sodomy trial. Other early, precedent-setting sodomy cases were appealed in 1873 in Massachusetts, and in 1878 in the Montana Territory.

An early report of homosexuality in American prisons dates to 1824–26 and concerns what is termed the "prostitution" of "juvenile delinquents" with older male prisoners. Male prostitution is also a prominent aspect of the reports, dating from 1892, of the homosexual underworld in American cities. These reports also include descriptions of Black male homosexual transvestites, homosexual activity at steam baths, newspaper solicitations, and street life, and they preserve examples of the period's homosexually relevant slang.

One of the earliest reports of an alleged homosexual discharged from a civil service position dates to 1846; the case involves an Irish New York City policeman charged with making improper advances to other males while on duty. An early case of a minister being separated from his church because of homosexual activity dates to 1866; the clergyman was Horatio Alger, Jr., and the activity was allegedly with two "boys" in the parish from which Alger immediately departed, traveling to New York City and becoming, in time, a popular writer, ironically enough, of boys' books. Dr. A. M.

Hamilton reports in 1896 on a case—allegedly the "first in this country"—arising "in connection with the civil rights" of a homosexual male to dispose of his property as he saw fit. On the basis of his homosexuality the family of Henry Palmer, a wealthy businessman of New Brunswick, New Jersey, questioned his soundness of mind. Although Dr. Hamilton testified to his absolute certainty of Palmer's sanity, the court found Palmer "insane," based on his admission of homosexuality. One student's encounter with heterosexuality, homosexuality, and homophobia at Amherst College dates to 1915–16: interestingly, although this student found homosexual advances disturbing, in retrospect, the antihomosexual bigotry of poet-teacher Robert Frost appears to have made a more negative impression.

Lesbianism in America is referred to in a few early documents. Among the earliest references is John Cotton's 1636 proposal to the Massachusetts Bay Colony that homosexual relations between women be placed on a par with male homosexuality as a capital offense. The theological debate of 1642 includes the Plymouth Colony's Rev. Charles Chauncy mentioning in passing the punishment by death of "unnatural lusts of men with men, or women with women." In 1656 the New Haven Colony actually enacted into law a statute prescribing the death penalty for Lesbianism, as well as male homosexuality. Moreau de St. Méry's brief, tantalizing observation concerning "unnatural pleasures" sought by American women with other women dates to the 1790s.

Bertrand Russell's reminiscence of an 1896 trip to Bryn Mawr College presents a brief glimpse into the troubled relations between the College's president, Helen Carey Thomas, and a teacher named Mary Gwinn, then being wooed and won by a dashing male suitor named Alfred Hodder. The triangular relation between Thomas, Gwinn, and Hodder also fascinated Gertrude Stein, who closely followed reports of its development, and finally cast it into fictional form in one of her earliest short novels, *Fernhurst*, written in 1904 or 1905, but not published until 1971, after her death. In his 1896 medical journal article on "The Civil Responsibility of Sexual Perverts" Dr. A. M. Hamilton discusses the case of a rich young woman whose family had consulted him for advice. The subject of their concern had gone to live with a woman doctor with whom she was infatuated; the young woman had withdrawn large amounts of money from her bank, coincidentally with her doctor friend's construction of a large house. When Hamilton confronted the young woman with the idea that she was the passive victim of a domineering female extortionist, she defiantly challenged him to find her of unsound mind. Hamilton admits this would have been difficult.

An 1897 newspaper report headed "She dislikes men and dogs" describes the legal troubles of Augusta Main, a "spinster farmer near Berlin, N.Y.," who had opened fire on a male trespasser. Although nothing in this report indicates any especially romantic liaisons with other women, the story does reveal that even in harvest time Main avoided male help and "hires strapping young women." A Massachusetts newspaper story of 1901 reports the suicide of a young woman whose intimacy with an older, married woman had caused their respective families to oppose and frustrate their relation.

Three documents on Lesbianism in prison date to the years 1913–29. Margaret Otis's 1913 report of intimate relations between young white and Black women in reform school presents a picture of one aspect of working-class Lesbianism in early twentieth-century America. Kate Richards O'Hare's comments on Lesbianism in the Missouri State Penitentiary are based on her own observations while incarcerated there in 1919–20. Charles A. Ford's 1929 report on "Homosexual Practices of Institutionalized Females" discusses in more detail a prison population much like that written about earlier by Otis.

A group of newspaper accounts dating to 1926–27 relate the history of the reaction to the opening on Broadway of a play, translated from the French, titled *The Captive*, concerning a young woman's "twisted relationship with another woman." Although Brooks Atkinson's review of this "tragedy" emphasizes how well the production conveys the "loathsomeness" of Lesbianism, the very presentation of such a previously unmentionable subject caused puritanical outcries from conservative members of the public, upon which city and state politicians were quick to capitalize. The production of *The Captive* and several other sexually suggestive plays resulted, in 1927, in the New York State legislature's passage of a bill outlawing homosexuality as a subject for the state's stages—a law that remained on the books until 1967.

Chris Albertson's recent biography of Bessie Smith (1972) describes the Black blues singer's Lesbian relations and her conflicted marriage to Jack Gee, providing an uncensored view of Smith's husband-trouble in the mid-1920s. Among the documents of the antihomosexual, anti-Communist witch-hunts of the 1950s is a firsthand account of one Lesbian's personal experience at the hands of the inquisitors—a story with an ironic ending. In 1960 Fannie Mae Clackum won her almost ten-year battle against the United States Air Force, which had discharged her on the grounds of Lesbianism, "under conditions other than honorable." Clackum's case, and that of *Louisiana* v. *Mary Young and Dawn DeBlanc* in 1966–67, are two of the relatively rare, Lesbian-related legal actions in American history. Young and DeBlanc are the principals in a case which established the legal precedent that "oral copulation by and between two women constituted 'unnatural carnal copulation'" under the Louisiana statute outlawing such conduct.

These documents portray Lesbians and Gay men enmeshed in a variety of difficult situations, an oppressed and troubling presence, with whom America has yet to deal with justice.

1566: GONZALO SOLÍS DE MERÁS;
The French Interpreter to Be Put to Death Secretly

The imperialistic conflict between French Lutheran and Spanish Catholic colonialists over the possession of Florida led to the murder, in 1566, by the Spaniards, of an allegedly treasonous French Lutheran interpreter, said to be "a great Sodomite." In this case the victim's homosexuality is associated with, though seemingly secondary to, the subversiveness of his nationality and the heresy of his Lutheranism; the medieval connection of heresy with homosexuality is suggested. The primary work documenting this incident is a "Memorial" of the Adelantado, governor and captain-general, Pedro Menéndez de Avilés, one of the pioneering Spanish conquerors and explorers of Florida. This "Memorial" is written by Menéndez's brother-in-law, Gonzalo Solís de Merás, probably in 1567, a year after the event described. The document is difficult to understand, both because of its style and the great number of individuals named in it. For the reader's convenience, among these are:

the Adelantado, Pedro Menéndez de Avilés,
Alonso Menéndez [Marqués], the Adelantado's nephew,
Vasco Zabal, a Spanish ensign,
Guillermo, a French Catholic working for the Spaniards,
the Cacique Guale, or chief of an American Indian clan of the Guale area,
the son of the cacique, interestingly said to "love" the French Lutheran inter-
     preter "very much,"
the French Lutheran interpreter, said to be living with two sons of the cacique,
Estébano de las Alas, Spanish captain at Santa Elena.

Alonso Menéndez [Marqués], the Adelantado's nephew, and [ensign] Vasco Zabal had told him [the Adelantado] that the French interpreter who was there [at Guale] was a Lutheran and a great Sodomite; that when the Adelantado had departed thence for Santa Elena, he [the interpreter] went to the Indians [telling them] they should kill them [the Spanish]; and that through Guillermo [a French Catholic working for the Spaniards] he could inform himself of what was happening in this [matter], so that he [Guillermo] could speak with 2 Indians with whom he [the interpreter] was living, one of whom they said was the cacique's [chief's] eldest son.

The Adelantado made inquiries with great secrecy; and learning that it was the truth, and that they saw him [the interpreter] spit on the cross many times before the Indians,* scoffing at the Christians, he spoke with Alonso Menéndez [Marqués], his nephew, and with Vasco Zabal, the ensign of the royal standard, who knew this and had seen it, and told them that it was not well to leave that cacique and his people disconsolate, since they wanted to become Christians, and that it would please him [the Adelantado] greatly if they would remain there, as before.

Vasco Zabal replied that he would sooner the Adelantado had him beheaded, than be left there.

Alonso Menéndez [Marqués] said that he would much regret staying, but since his lordship ordered it, he would do so, on condition that that Frenchman should be killed, or the Adelantado would take him with him; for otherwise nothing could be accomplished, and the Indians would slay him [Menéndez] and those who remained with him; that the son of the cacique had more authority than his father, and loved that interpreter very much; that if they [the Spaniards] killed the interpreter [openly], the Indians would be angered and again break out in war. This reasoning appeared very good to the Adelantado, and because he trusted Guillermo, and held him to be a Catholic, he called him: he told him to tell that interpreter that he should go with him to Santa Elena, for they can go there in a canoe in 2 or 3 days, by a river, without putting out to sea; that Estébano de las Alas [the Spanish captain at Santa Elena], who was a very good captain and liberal, would make him many presents; and that he would bring back a gift to his cacique, for the Cacique of Santa Elena had sent word to him to send for it. The interpreter was pleased at this, and without knowing that the Adelantado knew it, he [the interpreter] came to beg him to give him a letter for Estébano de las Alas so that he might know him, and to give him a hatchet, because he wished to set out to get the present which the Cacique of Santa Elena was to send to his Cacique

* While the Indians were worshipping the cross, he spat on it, and committed other heinous sins."2

15

Guale. The Adelantado told him to give him paper and ink, that he would write the letter at once; and so he did, writing one very favorable to the interpreter, and giving it to him.

Then Cacique Guale dispatched that interpreter in a canoe, with 2 of his Indians, that they might go and return immediately. The son of the cacique showed much sorrow because the interpreter was going, and prayed him, weeping, to return at once. The Adelantado sent a soldier with a letter to Estébano de las Alas in order that he might have that interpreter killed with great secrecy, as he was a Sodomite and a Lutheran; and if he returned alive, the Indians of Guale who desired to be Christians, would not as quickly become so; that he might greatly entertain the two Guale Indians who went with the interpreter; that Orista should do likewise, giving them a handsome present, sending another to Guale, and offering him his friendship; and that Estébano de las Alas should feign great regret because the interpreter did not appear, [saying] that as he was a false Christian, he must be hiding in the woods so as not to return to Guale, and so that if some ship should come from his country, he might go back on board of her. And therefore Estébano de las Alas had him garroted with great secrecy, and the two Indians returned to Guale; and the Adelantado had already departed for San Mateo and St. Augustine, leaving in Guale his nephew, Alonso Menéndez [Marqués], and the 4 Christians who were with him: he took away Vasco Zabal.[3]

c. 1624–25: Virginia Colony;
The Execution of Richard Cornish
"Hanged for a rascally boy wrongfully"

About 1624–25 a ship's master, Richard Cornish, was executed in the Virginia Colony for an alleged homosexual attack on one of his stewards, a crime that Cornish's brother later denied. The testimony against Cornish, and reports of his brother's defense, are recorded in the surviving *Minutes of the Council and General Court of Colonial Virginia. . . .*[4] The exact dates of these Council meetings are unknown, but the testimony is presented here in the same (seemingly correct) order as it appears in the published *Minutes.*

The Council and General Court that executed Richard Cornish was the ruling body of the Virginia Colony. As historian Edmund S. Morgan points out, the Council

consisted almost entirely of the men holding large numbers of servants. . . . These men, with a more than average interest in controlling the labor force, were thus enabled to maintain their personal ascendancy not only over their servants but over all lesser men.[5]

Council members met every challenge to their authority with the rigor of an absolute government. As these documents suggest, the execution of Richard Cornish was intricately involved with colonial class politics. The major testimony in the case follows.

1.

William Couse [or Cowse], aged 29 years or thereabouts, sworn and examined sayeth, that the 27th day of August last, past about one or 2 of the clock in the afternoon, being aboard the good ship called the Ambrose, then riding at anchor in James River, Richard Williams, also [known as] Cornish, master of the said ship called the Ambrose, being then in drink, called to this examinee to lay a clean pair of sheet into his bed, which this examinee did, and the said [Richard] Williams went into the bed, and would have this examinee come into the bed to him, which this examinee refusing to do, the said Richard Williams went out of the bed and did cut this examinee's cod piece, . . . , and made this examinee unready [unsteady?], and made him go into the bed, and then the said Williams also Cornish went into the bed to him, and there lay upon him, and kissed him and hugged him, saying that he would love this examinee if he would now and then come and lay with him, and so by force he turned this examinee upon his belly, and so did put this examinee to pain in the fundament, and did wet him, and after did call for a napkin which this examinee did bring unto him, and [Cornish did] sayeth that there was but one man aboard the ship, which was Walter Mathew, the boatswain's mate, being [passage missing]. And further sayeth that he was for 3 or 4 days after, and that after this, the next day after, in the morning, the said Williams also Cornish said to this examinee, "Though [I did] play the fool with you yesterday, make no wonder." Further he sayeth that after this, many times, he [Cornish] would put his hands in this examinee's cod piece and played [with him] and kissed him, saying to this examinee that he would have brought them [sic] to sea with him, if he had [passage missing] him, that would have played with him. And after this examinee being called and refusing to go he . . . [took?] him before the mast and forbade all the ship's company to eat with him, and made this examinee cook for all the rest.[6]

2.

Walter Mathew, sworn and examined sayeth, that [he] being in the storage room in William Cowse's cabin, the master called the boy [Cowse] into his bed cabin, both being locked in the great cabin. . . . William Cowse replied that he would not—saying further that, if he did so, it would be an overthrow to him both in soul and body, and alleged the scripture to him [the master]. But of what it was that the Master did urge him to [do] he [Mathew] knoweth not, nor heard not the boy [Cowse] cry out for help after this. This examinee went forth of his cabin upon the deck and heard no more, but when William Cowse came forth of the cabin this examinee asked him what the matter was between the Master and him. . . . [Cowse] replied he would keep that to himself till he came into England, but after told this examinee that the Master would have buggered him, or to that effect, but did not confess that the Master did the fact.[7]

The above testimony resulted in Richard Cornish's execution. After this the Virginia Court called several witnesses to an incident in Canada in which Cornish's brother, Jeffery, had sworn revenge for his relative's death—the injustice of which one, Edward Nevell, reportedly emphasized.

3.

Nicholas Roe sworn and examined sayeth that he remembereth at Canada, . . . being at Dambrell's Cove, Jeffery Cornish came aboard the ship called the Swan and demanded [of] this deponent the cause of his brother's execution, saying that [he] hath been told his brother was put to death wrongfully, and that he would be revenged of them that were the occasion of it.

And further sayeth that whilst Jeffery Cornish and this examinee were in talk, Mr. Nevell came in [the] place and told the said Jeffery Cornish that he was at the trial of his brother, and at his execution also, and that he would say more concerning his execution than this deponent could do, after which this deponent was called down into the hold, so that what other conversation was betwixt them—concerning that he knoweth not. The said Cornish and Nevell remaining upon the deck talking together—and more he cannot depose.

John Giles sworn and examined sayeth that he heard Jeffery Cornish swear and say that he would be the cause of the death of those that were the cause of putting his brother to death, this deponent being aboard their own ship called the Swan, . . . but that Edward Nevell or another told the said Cornish he was put to death wrongfully, he cannot say.

Christopher Knollinge sworn and examined sayeth, that being ashore at Dambrells Cove in Canada, Jeffery Cornish came unto him, and demanded of him what he could say concerning his brother being put to death, saying that some of [those aboard] the Swan should tell him that his brother was put to death wrongfully, and [J. Cornish] said that he would spend his blood for his brother, to be revenged of them that did it, but this deponent, asking the said [J.] Cornish who told him so [that his brother was wrongfully executed], he [J. Cornish] refused to tell him, and more he cannot say.[8]

4.

William Foster, sworn and examined sayeth, that he, this deponent, demanded of Mr. Nevell at Canada, being aboard the Swan, wherefore Mr. [Richard] Cornish was hanged, unto whom Nevell answered, and said, "he was hanged for a rascally boy wrongfully," and that he [Foster] hath heard Mr. Nevell say so divers times.[9]

5.

Thomas Crispe, gentleman, by the oath he hath formerly taken, affirmeth that Jeffery Cornish did say that Edward Nevell should tell him that his brother suffered death wrongfully, and the said Thomas Crispe wished the said Jeffery Cornish to take heed what he said, for sure the Governor would do no wrong or injustice to any man, for that he [Jeffery Cornish] shall be answerable for what he doth. Thereupon the said Jeffery Cornish did vow that he would be the death of the Governor if ever he came for England.[10]

6.

Arthur Avelinge, sworn and examined sayeth, that he being at Dambrells Cove in Canada aboard the Swan, one who come aboard asked Mr. Nevell wherefore Mr. [Richard] Cornish was put to death. Then Edward Nevell answered "he was put to death through a scurvy boy's means, and no other came against him." Then the other men replied, "I have ill luck my brother should come to such an end."

It is ordered that Edward Nevell for his offence shall stand on the pillory with a paper on his head showing the cause of his offence in the market place, and to lose both his ears, and to serve the Colony for a year, and forever to be incapable to be a freeman of the country.[11]

Several witnesses testify to another, later incident, this time at Edward Fisher's house in the Virginia Colony, involving dissension over Richard Cornish's execution.

7.

James Hickmote, sworn and examined sayeth, that one Saturday night, being the fourth of February, 1625, being at the house of Edward Fisher in James City, one Peter Marten being in company and falling in talk concerning Richard Williams also Cornish that was executed for buggery, the said Marten then commending the said Cornish for an excellent mariner and skillful artist, Thomas Hatch, being also in company, said that in his conscience he thought the said Cornish was put to death wrongfully, whereupon this deponent [James Hickmote] said, "You were best take heed what you say, you have a precedent before your eyes the other day, and it will cost you your ears if you say such words." To which the said Thomas Hatch replied, "I care not for my ears, let them hang me if they will."

Sara Fisher the wife of Edward Fisher sworn and examined affirmeth as much as Mr. James Hickmote hath upon his oath formerly delivered.

Anthony Jonnes sworn and examined sayeth that he heard Thomas Hatch say that Richard Cornish was put to death wrongfully, and that he did not care for his ears.

It is ordered that Thomas Hatch for his offence shall be whipped from the fort to the gallows and from thence be whipped back again, and be set upon the pillory and there to lose one of his ears, and that his service to Sir George Yardly for seven years shall begin from the present day, according to the condition of the duty boys, he being one of them.[12]

1629: FRANCIS HIGGESON;
"5 beastly Sodomiticall boyes"

The Rev. Francis Higgeson's journal of his voyage to New England in 1629 on board the ship *Talbot* records the discovery of sodomical activity among the first

American immigrants while on their way to the new land. Higgeson's diary of June 23, 1629, reads:

This day we examined 5 beastly Sodomiticall boyes, which confessed their wickedness not to bee named. The fact was so fowl we reserved them to bee punished by the governor when we came to new England, who afterward sent them backe to the company to bee punished in ould England, as the crime deserved.

Sodomy was then a crime for which an Englishman over fourteen might be hanged.[13]

♀ 1636: JOHN COTTON; "Unnatural filthiness"

In the colonial era, as Louis Crompton points out, the English buggery statute was not taken to apply to sexual relations between two women. "No doubt," says Crompton, "this reflected the fact that the Old Testament prescribed the death penalty for male homosexuality but made no reference to Lesbianism. On the other hand, church canonists interpreting the traditions of Roman law as they bore on sodomy regularly included Lesbian acts as meriting capital punishment. . . ."

In 1636, the Rev. John Cotton was asked by the General Court of Massachusetts to draw up a group of laws for the colony. In his proposed legislation Cotton innovatively includes Lesbianism along with male homosexuality as "sodomy," a capital crime:

Unnatural filthiness, to be punished with death, whether sodomy, which is carnal fellowship of man with man, or woman with woman, or buggery, which is carnal fellowship of man or woman with beasts or fowls.[14]

Cotton's proposals were not adopted.

♀ 1642: GOVERNOR WILLIAM BRADFORD; "Sodomy and buggery . . . have broke forth in this land"

Governor Bradford's history *Of Plymouth Plantation*, in a chapter on events of 1642, discusses how "wickedness" did that year break forth.

Marvelous it may be to see and consider how some kind of wickedness did grow and break forth here, in a land where the same was so much witnessed against and so narrowly looked unto, and severely punished when it was known, as in no place more, or so much, that I have known or heard of; insomuch that they have been somewhat censured even by moderate and good men for their severity in punishments. And yet all this could not suppress the breaking out of sundry notorious sins (as this year, besides other, gives us too many sad precedents and instances), especially drunkenness and uncleanness. Not only incontinency between persons unmarried, for which many both men and women have been punished sharply enough, but some married persons also. But that which is worse, even sodomy and buggery (things fearful to name) have broke forth in this land oftener than once.[15]

Among the causes of such outbreaks of wickedness in New England Bradford lists: (1) "our currupt natures"; (2) the Devil may be angrier at the churches here because of their greater holiness, purity, and strictness; (3) wickedness is more repressed here so that when it breaks out it does so more violently than elsewhere; and (4) evils are more likely to be discovered here because the churches and magistrates are more watchful, the population smaller. Elsewhere, Bradford points out that the colonists' need for "labour and service" made them "glad to take such as they could," and brought to this country "many untoward servants," both men and women. Bradford accuses profit-seeking traders of transporting to the New World any who "had the money to pay them," and so sending "unworthy persons."[16]

Bradford reports that in March 1642 the theological authorities of Plymouth received a letter from the governor of the Massachusetts Bay Colony, Richard Bellingham, asking their advice on how to punish "heinous offenses in point of uncleaness," specifically a case of heterosexual "sodomy" involving the rape of two little girls, and a case of bestiality. In May 1642 Bradford answered the Massachusetts governor, passing along to him the written opinions of three Plymouth theologians in answer to the question, "What sodomitical acts are to be punished with death?" The answers include references to male homosexuality, and one to Lesbianism:

Rev. John Raynor writes "that carnal knowledge of man or lying with man as with woman," including penetration, "was sodomy, to be punished with death. . . ." "It seems also," says Raynor, "that this foul sin might be capital," though there was no penetration, but only contact and movement causing ejaculation. His authority is the Bible.[17]

Rev. Ralph Partridge thinks it "probable that a voluntary effusion of seed," caused by one man lying with another, even without penetration, is the sin forbidden by the Bible, to be punished with death. But of this opinion Partridge is not confident.[18]

Rev. Charles Chauncy, quoting the Bible, writes that adultery, rape, abortion, incest, bestiality, sodomy, and "all presumptuous sins" are to be punished by death. He also reasons that if "unnatural lusts of men with men, or women with women . . . be punished with death, then . . . natural lusts of men towards children under age are so to be punished."

Interestingly, the two heterosexual rapist-child-molesters got off with a fine and whipping; their offense was not found to be a capital one.[19]

After presenting these opinions Bradford describes the execution in 1642 of Thomas Granger, a teen-ager discovered in an act of bestiality (or "buggery"). The horror of the ritualistic trial and punishment Bradford details now seems far worse than the crime. Bradford then adds:

Upon the examination of this person and also of a former that had made some sodomitical attempts upon another, it being demanded of them how they came first to the knowledge and practice of such wickedness, the one confessed he had long used it in old England; and this youth last spoken of said he was taught it by another that had heard of such things from some in England when he was there, and they kept cattle together. By which it appears how one wicked person may infect many, and what care all ought to have what servants they bring into their families.[20]

1646: JOHN WINTHROP;
The Execution of William Plaine
"A monster in human shape"

The first governor of the Massachusetts Bay Colony, John Winthrop, writes in his *History of New England*:

Mr. Eaton, the governour of New Haven, wrote to the governour of the Bay, to desire the advice of the magistrates and elders in a special case, which was this: one Plaine of Guilford being discovered to have used some unclean practices, upon examination and testimony, it was found, that being a married man, he had committed sodomy with two persons in England, and that he had corrupted a great part of the youth of Guilford by masturbations, which he had committed, and provoked others to the like above a hundred times; and to some who questioned the lawfulness of such filthy practice, he did insinuate seeds of atheism, questioning whether there was a God, etc. The magistrates and elders (so many as were at hand) did all agree, that he ought to die, and gave divers reasons from the word of God.* And indeed it was *horrendum facinus* [a dreadful crime], and he a monster in human shape, exceeding all human rules and examples that ever had been heard of, and it tended to the frustrating of the ordinance of marriage and the hindering the generation of mankind.

1646: New Netherland Colony; Jan Creoli,
"Condemned of God . . . as an abomination"

The *Calendar of [Dutch] Historical Manuscripts* reports the following proceedings in 1646, on Manhattan Island, New Netherland Colony—a report significant for its reference to Black homosexuality, and for its use of the word *faggots* (for kindling) in a situation involving punishment for homosexuality.

June 25. Court proceedings. Fiscal [public prosecutor] vs. Jan Creoli, a negro, sodomy; second offense; this crime being condemned of God (Gen., c. 19; Levit.,

---

* The margin informs us "he was executed at New Haven."[21]

c. 18: 22, 29) as an abomination, the prisoner is sentenced to be conveyed to the place of public execution, and there choked to death, and then burnt to ashes. . . .

And on the same date the *Calendar* lists:

Sentence. Manuel Congo, a lad ten years old, on whom the above abominable crime was committed, to be carried to the place where Creoli is to be executed, tied to a stake, and faggots piled around him, for justice sake, and to be flogged; sentence executed. . . .[22]

♀ 1655: New Haven Colony;
"If any woman change the naturall use . . ."

In 1655, the New Haven Colony published a body of laws which generally followed the model of the Massachusetts Bay Colony's Body of Liberties, approved in 1641. But the New Haven sodomy statute is unique among colonial laws for including Lesbianism, heterosexual anal intercourse, and masturbation among the crimes punishable by death.

If any man layeth with mankinde, as a man lyeth with a woman, both of them have committed abomination, they both shall surely be put to death. Levit. 20. 13. And if any woman change the naturall use into that which is against nature, as Rom. 1. 26. she shall be liable to the same sentence, and punishment, or if any person, or persons, shall commit any other kinde of unnaturall and shamefull filthines, called in Scripture the going after strange flesh, or other flesh than God alloweth, by carnall knowledge of another vessel then God in nature have appointed to become one flesh, whether by abusing the contrary part of a grown woman, or child of either sex, or unripe vessel of a girle, wherein the natural use of the woman is left, which God hath ordained for the propagation of posterity, and Sodomiticall filthinesse (tending to the destruction of the race of mankind) is committed by a kind of rape, nature being forced, though the will were inticed, every such person shall be put to death. Or if any man shall act upon himself, and in the sight of others spill his owne seed, by example, or counsel, or both, corrupting or tempting others to doe the like, which tends to the sin of Sodomy, if it be not one kind of it; or shall defile, or corrupt himself and others, by any kind of sinfull filthinesse, he shall be punished according to the nature of the offence; or if the case considered with the aggravating circumstances, shall according to the mind of God revealed in his word require it, he shall be put to death, as the court of magistrates shall determine.[23]

1777–79: THOMAS JEFFERSON;
"Sodomy shall be punished by castration"

In the autumn of 1776, Jefferson and other leading citizens began a thorough-going revision of Virginia law. The intent was to reform the entire structure of law, stripping it of all former monarchical and aristocratic aspects, bringing it into conformity with republican principles. This revision, however, was never embodied in any enactment.

In the "Plan Agreed upon by the Committee of Revisors at Fredericksburg," January 13, 1777, Thomas Jefferson was among those liberals who suggested that "Rape, Sodomy, Bestiality . . . be punished by Castration," rather than, as earlier, by death.[24]

As finally written, bill number 64, authored by Jefferson himself and "Reported by the Committee of Advisors, 18 June 1779," adds polygamy to the list.

Whosoever shall be guilty of Rape, Polygamy, or †Sodomy with man or woman shall be punished, if a man, by castration, if a woman, by cutting thro' the cartilage of her nose a hole of one half inch diameter at the least.

A note to the above "Sodomy" reference explains:

†Buggery is twofold. 1. with mankind, 2. with beasts. Buggery is the Genus, of which Sodomy and Bestiality are the species.[25]

1778: GEORGE WASHINGTON;
The court-martial of Lieutenant Frederick Gotthold Enslin

Washington's general orders for March 10, 1778, report the general court-martial of Lieutenant Frederick Gotthold Enslin for attempted sodomy.

At a General Court Martial whereof Colo. Tupper was President (10th March 1778) Lieutt. [Frederick Gotthold] Enslin of Colo. Malcom's Regiment tried for attempting to commit *sodomy*, with John Monhort a soldier; Secondly, For Perjury in swearing to false Accounts, found guilty of the charges exhibited against him, being breaches of 5th. Article 18th. Section of the Articles of War and do sentence him to be dismiss'd the service with Infamy. His Excellency the Commander in Chief approves the sentence and with Abhorrence and Detestation of such Infamous Crimes orders Lieutt. Enslin to be drummed out of Camp tomorrow morning by all the Drummers and Fifers in the Army never to return; The Drummers and Fifers to attend on the Grand Parade at Guard mounting for that Purpose.[26]

1788: HELEN H. TANNER;
Homosexuality in the Spanish Army in Florida

Helen Hornbeck Tanner's history, *Zéspedes in East Florida*, describes the problems of the area's first governor, Vicente Manuel de Zéspedes y Velasco, who served St. Augustine from 1784–90. During this period, Spain, England, and France all had imperialistic designs on the province. In 1783, Spanish troops retook Florida from the British at the end of the American Revolution. The control of these Spanish troops, stationed in St. Augustine, became a problem for Governor Zéspedes, especially when a high church official, Fray Cyril de Barcelona, arrived in July 1788 to investigate the religious and moral life of the province. Tanner writes:

The key to the basic social problem is in one simple statistical comparison for the year 1788. While the garrison maintained about four hundred soldiers, for the most part unmarried, there were in the entire province only fifty-five unmarried women between the ages of sixteen and forty. The large proportion of the military spent their time exclusively in masculine society, drinking, carousing and gambling illegally in St. Augustine wineshops catering to their trade. Those who found favor with the limited feminine element naturally made the most of their good fortune, often creating problems for Father Hassett. The parish priest did his best to assure the future of illegitimate children by securing reliable godparents, usually leading members of the community. . . .

Governor Zéspedes was unpleasantly aware of the growing sexual irregularity in the small community, and attempted in several ways to correct the situation during Fray Cyril de Barcelona's lengthy stay in St. Augustine. When the rising incidence of homosexuality among the soldiers included little boys, offenders were prosecuted and sent to Havana for trial. Zéspedes was still waiting for the arrival of a legal official to handle infractions of the law in East Florida. Until he had this assistance, he adopted the policy of taking testimony and sending the prisoners and indictments to Havana to await the decision of the *auditor de guerra* in Cuba. The boys, sons of Spanish, Minorcan and English parents, were remanded to the corrective attention of their families with the exception of one unfortunate orphan who was sent away because there was no one responsible for him in St. Augustine. Perhaps the town became a better community without him, but it is doubtful if he found a therapeutic environment in Havana.[27]

♀ 1793–98: MOREAU DE ST. MÉRY;
The "unnatural pleasures" of American women

A French lawyer and politician, Moreau de St. Méry, lived in America from 1793 to 1798, most of the time in Philadelphia. His brief comment is one of the earliest known observations concerning Lesbianism in this country, and not surprisingly it also involves a negative moral judgment. "Although in general one is conscious of widespread modesty in Philadelphia," says St. Méry,

the customs are not particularly pure, and the disregard on the part of some parents for the manner in which their daughters form relationships to which they, the parents, have not given their approval is an encouragement of indiscretions which, however, are not the result of love, since American women are not affectionate.

St. Méry later adds:

I am going to say something that is almost unbelievable. These women, without real love and without passions, give themselves up at an early age to the enjoyment of themselves; and they are not at all strangers to being willing to seek unnatural pleasures with persons of their own sex.[28]

1810: Davis versus Maryland;
"Seduced by the instigation of the Devil"

A contemporary appeals court record indicates that in September 1810 one Davis was indicted in the Court of Oyer and Terminer in Baltimore County, Maryland,

for assaulting, and attempting to commit *Sodomy*, on the body of W. C. The indictment contained two counts. The *first* stated, that *Davis*, not having the fear of God before his eyes, but being moved and seduced by the instigation of the Devil, . . . with force and arms . . . in and upon one W. C., a youth of the age of 19 years, in the peace of God, and of the state of *Maryland*, . . . did make an assault, and him the said W. C., then and there did beat, wound, and illtreat . . . [intending] that most horrid and detestable crime, (among christians not to be named,) called *Sodomy*, with him the said W. C., and against the order of nature, then and there feloniously, wickedly and devilishly, . . . to the great displeasure of Almighty God, contrary to the act of assembly in such case made and provided, and against the peace, government, and dignity of the state. The second count stated, that the said *Davis* . . . [did assault W. C. intending] to have a venereal affair, . . . that sodomitical, detestable, and abominable sin, (among christians not to be named,) called *Buggery*. . . .

[Davis] having appeared, filed a suggestion, on oath, that he could not have a fair and impartial trial in the court of oyer and terminer, . . . and prayed the court to order and direct the record of the proceedings to be transmitted to the judges of an adjoining county court, there to be tried, &c. This prayer the court refused. . . . [Davis] having pleaded not guilty, the case was tried, and a verdict of guilty was found against him.[29]

Davis's counsel then appealed, asking the court to reverse his guilty verdict on several grounds, among them:

"That the facts charged in the indictment" were not "indictable by the laws of this state."

"That the indictment is insufficient, inasmuch as it does not charge . . . [Davis] with an intent to have carnal knowledge of the body of W C."

That the indictment was wholly insufficient "to authorize the court to pass judgment" on Davis.

Justice Charles Scott overruled the motion, "and rendered judgment on the verdict," commanding that Davis should be imprisoned in the gaol of *Baltimore* county, from the 9th of January 1811, until the 9th of April 1811, and that he stand in the pillory on the third Saturday of January . . . for the space of fifteen minutes, between the hours of 12 and 1 o'clock of the same day, and that he also pay to the state the sum of $500, for his fine laid upon him for the offence aforesaid, according to the act of assembly in such case made and provided, and that he be committed to prison until he pays the said fine, &c.[30]

Davis took this verdict to an even higher court, the Maryland Court of Appeals, where his lawyers argued his case on technical legal grounds. One of the presiding judges, adding his concurring opinion to that of the court, declared: "The crime of sodomy is too well known to be misunderstood, and too disgusting to be defined, farther than by naming it." With one of the ten appeals justices dissenting, the original judgment against Davis was affirmed.[31]

1824–26: LOUIS DWIGHT;
"The sin of Sodom is the vice of prisoners . . . "

A printed broadside, in the form of a letter dated Boston (in handwriting), April 25, 1826, signed by Louis Dwight, is apparently directed to a government official. The earliest known document discussing homosexuality in this country's prisons, this broadside argues for the amelioration of conditions for those young prisoners "prostituted to the lust of old convicts." Dwight states:

Since October, 1824, I have visited most of the prisons on two routes, between Massachusetts and Georgia, and a large number of Prisons besides, in the New England States and New York. Juvenile Delinquents have been subjects of particular consideration, in all these visits; and I have found melancholy testimony to establish one general fact, viz. THAT BOYS ARE PROSTITUTED TO THE LUST OF OLD CONVICTS.

I am aware, that the mere suggestion of this subject, is so revolting, that we should gladly omit the further consideration of it; but if we would meet the evil and remove it, we must give our attention to the facts.

I have seen boys in Prison, of a very tender age, who had no natural deformity, who were among the most unnatural and deformed objects, which I ever saw. The peculiar skin, the strained and sunken eye, the distorted mouth and head, and the general expression of the countenance; as if God had impressed the mark of the beast upon them, for unnatural crime; were things, which I did not understand, till I learned, that the SIN OF SODOM IS THE VICE OF PRISONERS, AND BOYS ARE THE FAVORITE PROSTITUTES.

Perhaps I ought to stop here, believing, that the mere suggestion of the subject is enough; but as facts are more effectual in producing conviction, than opinion, I will add the following testimony on the subject.

I have seen and conversed with two convicts, who had a controversy concerning a boy, in one of our Penitentiaries, in which one of them received thirteen wounds from the other, who thrust a knife or dirk into his breast and side. Without implicating him, in the guilt of such abomination, I asked one of the men, if he ever knew a boy retain his integrity in a Penitentiary? He said, *"Never."* I asked another convict the same question, concerning the same Penitentiary, when speaking of the same crime, and he made the same reply.

Another witness, who is a respectable man, now living in society, who was four years in a Penitentiary, not above alluded to, writes in answer to my question on this subject, as follows: "I have known boys, of as much apparent diffidence as any in society, who in consequence of a criminal association with the profligate and vile, have, in less than three months, become so perfectly brutalized, as publicly to glory in every species of abomination." "Sodomy," says he, "is said to be constantly practised among them. I have frequently heard them make their boast of it. Boys are said to be kept and rewarded; and I have frequently heard them say, they were forced to give up their *Kinshon*, (which is the name given to a boy thus prostituted,) for want of funds."

Another witness, of character similar to the one last mentioned, whom I know intimately, and for whom I have great regard, whose excellent conduct and character for three years, entitle his testimony to credit, who was three years in a Penitentiary, wrote to me, that what he saw in regard to this thing was simply this: "when a boy was sent to Prison, who was of a fair countenance, there many times seemed to be quite a strife between old grey headed villains, to secure his attention. Numerous presents were given for this purpose; and if it could be obtained, no art was left untried, to get the boy into the same room and into the same bed. A strong attachment would immediately seem to follow. Meals and every dainty would be shared together, and they would, in many cases, afterwards, seem to have an undivided existence. They would suffer the most severe punishment, rather than criminate their mate, or technically *Kinshon*, in any thing."

With the testimony of this witness, that of the Superintendent, in the same Penitentiary, given to me in conversation, coincided almost *verbatim.*

In a Penitentiary not alluded to in either of the above statements, the Superintendent showed me a man, who, it was supposed, had been guilty of Sodomy. This man had been in that Prison fifteen years; and without accusing him, I inquired whether he had ever known any Prisoners guilty of this crime. He mentioned the names of two, who, he said, "were eternally at it; first one and then the other." He also mentioned the names of two others, who, he said, "took turns, as near as they could find out." He acknowledged, that the attempt had been made upon him; but denied, that he ever submitted to the horrible abuse.

I will only add to this testimony, the following conversation which I had with a boy, in the Penitentiary last mentioned: "Was the crime ever committed upon you? Yes, Sir! By whom? Pat, an Irishman! Why did you submit? He choked me! He was stronger than I! Why did you not complain? I did, in the room! but they said if I told of it, they would punish me! Who said so? They all said, I must not tell any thing out of the room! Did Pat effect his object? Yes, Sir."

The above I believe to be a true statement of facts.

In the language of the Governor of Massachusetts, *nature and humanity cry aloud for redemption from this dreadful degradation.*

Should the above contribute, in any degree, to the conviction, that it is important and humane to separate Juvenile Delinquents from hardened offenders, in our Public Prisons, it would afford me great pleasure.[32]

1846: New York City Police Department; "In the Matter of Complaint against Edward McCosker"

The extremely rare documents that follow were discovered among the voluminous manuscript materials in the archives of the City of New York, by a young scholar researching the history of the city's police. The fact that such unindexed archival materials are especially difficult to locate lends them a special interest; their early date, relative to other known homosexually relevant documents, adds to their interest. They are reprinted here for the first time. These materials document the charges at a hearing before the mayor of New York City concerning the case of a young Irishman, Edward McCosker, alleged to have made sexual advances to other males while on duty as a New York City policeman. McCosker denied the charges, and it is possible he was framed. The documents date to just one year after the founding of the city's police department.

In the context of the present struggle for Gay rights in the area of civil service employment, the reprinting of these documents takes on a charged and controversial political character. Antihomosexual bigots have argued in the mid-1970s that to allow homosexuals employment in the New York City Police Department would give license to such behavior as that with which McCosker was charged in 1846. The present depth and pervasiveness of such antihomosexual argument unfortunately requires that such myths be refuted. It should be unnecessary to say that if the charges against McCosker were true, these documents would still not indicate anything about the prevalence or likelihood of such behavior. The charges against McCosker must be seen in the context of an antihomosexual society in which examples of homosexual misconduct are more likely to be recorded and labeled as such than equivalent heterosexual acts. How many heterosexual policemen, for instance, made advances toward women without finding this behavior later used as grounds for serious complaint, much less for dismissal—and had their cases documented for posterity?

On February 20, 1846, the captain of the First Patrol District sent a report to the mayor of New York City concerning policeman Edward McCosker, charged with:

Indecent conduct while on duty. Violent, course, and insolent language and behavior

Specification.

That on the morning of the 15th Feby. while one Thomas Carey was making water in Cedar St. he was accosted by . . . McCosker, who said there was a great deal of grinding going on [in] that neighborhood. Carey asked him where and he directed him around in Temple St. and walked around with him, and when he got there, McCosker commenced indecently feeling his privates, and made use of indecent language to him, and asked Carey to feel his (McCosker's) privates, at which Carey became indignant at such conduct and reprimanded him severely, saying he was a "pretty officer," and words to that effect. McCosker then most grossly abused said Carey making use of very profane and blackguard language, threatening to take him to the Station House, . . . which attracted the attention of the Roundsman Mr. Pierson who came up and enquired the cause of the disturbance, and got the above facts from Carey—also on or about the 12th day of January last said McCosker committed the same indecent assault on one Michael O'Brien of 137½ Washington St. under similar circumstances.[33]

At a hearing before the mayor of New York, several witnesses testified as follows:

Edward McCosker being examined[:] on the morning of the 15th, . . . between 1 & 2 o'clock, I came up Thames St. from Trinity Place and on getting opposite Temple St. I saw Carey and a female standing close by to the City Hotel. I went around and came back again and they were still there. I watched them a while, and presently they moved off; I then went around the block and I met Carey in Cedar St. making water. I went up to him and tapped him on the shoulder, and said to him "what are you doing around here at this hour of the night with the woman?" He said "What woman?" He then became abusive and made use of very indecent language to me; then I arrested him and threatened to take him to the Station House; he followed me to Thames St. and continued his abuse until Mr. Pierson came up; after some more talk Mr. Pierson told him to go home; Policeman Simons also came up, but would not help me take Carey to the Station House; Mr. Pierson again advised me to let him go, which I did. I was perfectly sober; I deny knowing O'Brien who has also made charge against me, and did not commit the act as stated by him.

Thomas Carey (sworn) resides at No. 21 Rose St.; on the morning of 15th February last, between 12 & 1 o'clock, saw Policeman McCosker and spoke to him, as I was making water against a wall; he made use of very gross, indecent language to me, and directed me around the corner in Thames St.; he there indecently took hold of deponent by the privates and at the same time requested the deponent to feel his privates, at which deponent became enraged and called him names, that he was a "pretty policeman" and words to that [effect]; he [McCosker] abused deponent and called deponent names. Shortly after [that] Sargeant Pierson came up, and deponent stated the aforesaid facts to him.

Cross Ex. I was going home at that time of the night. I had been in Washington St. to see a friend; I was alone. I had been drinking that night; did not keep account how much I had drank, probably 3 or 4 glasses of beer; don't recollect whether I drank anything else; I was not so much intoxicated as but what I knew where I was; after I told him he was a pretty policeman he told me to go home; McCosker did not accuse me of following after a woman; he threatened to take me to the Station House; he [McCosker] rapped his club on the ground [to call for help]; after Mr. Pierson came up McCosker told Pierson to take me in. Pierson told me to go home, he said to me "you have been drinking."

Joseph D. Pierson (sworn); is a Sergeant and was on the rounds on the night of 15th Feby. and saw some person standing near the Shady [tavern] in Thames St.

On approaching there heard very loud language; on getting up to them saw Policeman McCosker who exclaimed "it is a God damned shame," and told deponent that the man Carey had abused him; Carey told deponent that McCosker had abused him. McCosker then made use of very profane language to Carey who was accusing McCosker of having committed an indecent assault on him. McCosker then took hold of Carey by the collar and threatened to take him to the Station House; Carey was a little intoxicated but knew what he was about; deponent told Carey to go home, and deponent then left him. Shortly after Carey followed deponent and told deponent the facts as stated in his affidavit. Carey said to McCosker "lay down your club and I will lick you."

Timothy H. Simons (sworn); is a Policeman; was on duty night of 15 Feby.: deponent was attracted by the rap of a Policeman to a corner opposite the Shady [tavern] in Thames St. When I got there saw Policeman McCosker and Mr. Carey there. These were using loud and violent language to each other. McCosker asked my assistance to take the man, and laid his hands on Carey and said "I'm damned if I don't take you to the Station House." From what I heard from the parties I thought it was a blackguard scrape; shortly after the mob dispersed I went away. I thought McCosker was intoxicated which was the reason I did not assist him as it was likely that McCosker might have assaulted Carey, as for Carey to assault him. Carey told McCosker if he would lay down his club he would lick him. I think McCosker said he had asked Carey something about some women.

James Rees (sworn). Keeps the Shady [tavern] on Limber & Thames Sts. On the night of 15th Feby. I heard some raps of policemen and saw policeman McCosker and Mr. Carey. The latter was calling McCosker "a damned son of a bitch, if you lay down the club I will lick you." McCosker said "if you don't stop I will take you to the Station House"; after that Policemen Pierson & Simons came up. Mr. Pierson advised him to go home; after it was dispersed I went in the house; McCosker was not intoxicated to my knowledge. I did not hear McCosker charge Carey with being with a woman that night.

Michael O'Brien (sworn) of No. 135 Washington St.; is not acquainted with policeman McCosker (non-present) but met him on or about the night of the 12th day of January, about 6 weeks ago. I am setting on a spar at the corner of Rector and Washington P[lace]. He came up to me and spoke to me and asked me what I was doing there; and after talking sometime about females, he put his hands two or three times towards deponent's privates in a very indecent manner and making very indecent expressions, and finally put his hands on deponent's privates; after awhile he asked me to go over to the Porter House of Dennis Mullins, where he treated me to a glass of beer. . . . I afterwards left him.—I am a Tobacconist. Is a single man. Policemen Johnston & McCloud asked me about this complaint; . . . I heard that policeman McCosker was going to sue Carey for slander in making such charge against him; is confident that Edward McCosker non-present is the man . . . alluded to.

An additional witness testified against McCosker.

Bernard Campbell one of the policemen of the 1st District being duly sworn deposes and says that one night in the month of January deponent went on his post in Washington Street and that while patroling his beat in company with policeman Edw. McCosker, said Cosker commenced talking about women and said to deponent "don't you feel stiff now?" and put his hand in deponent's pantaloons and endeavored to feel deponent's privates; deponent told him to go away and asked him what he meant; he said "nothing", he "only wanted to feel if he [deponent] was stiff"; deponent then took hold of his hand and pushed him away. Further deponent saith not.

An unsigned lawyer's brief, included among the records of McCosker's hearing before the mayor of New York, argues in defense of McCosker. It suggests that there may have been a conspiracy to frame McCosker on the part of several policemen of the First Patrol District, as well as on the part of Thomas Carey and Michael O'Brien. The brief argues that Carey and O'Brien were "intimate acquaintances," and that on the night of McCosker's alleged proposition, Carey had "just left O'Brien." The brief argues that Carey had been drunk, and *did want to fight*" McCosker, despite Carey's testimony to the contrary. Contradictions in Carey's testimony should "shake confidence" in it, the brief says, arguing that in a court of law Carey's testimony "would be *excluded* altogether" as might O'Brien's. The brief also asks the mayor to notice O'Brien's testimony that McCosker had propositioned him:

At one moment he [O'Brien] was grossly insulted by the proposition of McCosker and he looked upon him as a *brute*, yet this same man would go and *drink* with him. *If a man whose views change so quick upon a subject so vital* to a man's *finer feelings*, I am confident that little if any confidence can be placed upon any statements he may be pleased to make.

The brief also includes the affidavits of three witnesses who testified to McCosker's good character. One of these follows.

Francis Donnelly of said [New York] city being duly sworn deposes and says that he is a policeman of the first ward of the city of New York; that he is well acquainted with Edward McCosker above named; that deponent has been in the habit of sleeping with said McCosker for the last three months, and that said McCosker never to deponent's knowledge acted indecent or indelicate; that deponent never knew said McCosker to be guilty of any improper conduct, nor did he ever hear that he was guilty of any such conduct until he heard the charges preferred against him by Carey and O'Brien.

The mayor of New York decided:

1st Patrol District.

In the matter of Charges against
Edward McCosker
Policeman.

Dated 20th day of Feby 1846

Decision

The . . . charges are substantiated by the evidence. It is ordered and adjudged that Edward McCosker be and he is hereby dismissed from office as Policeman of the First District. . . .

1866: Unitarian Church, Brewster, Massachusetts;
Horatio Alger Accused
"Gross immorality and a most heinous crime"

Horatio Alger, the famous nineteenth-century author of numerous books for boys, is known as a major ideologue of the American dream of individual success within the capitalist marketplace. He was also deeply concerned with ameliorating the oppressive conditions of homeless, abandoned boys whom he saw struggling to survive in the streets of New York City. Alger's philanthropic efforts on these boys' behalf succeeded to some extent in arousing public concern about a great social evil and in instituting reforms to better the situation of these young people. That Alger's interest in boys arose out of a homosexual impulse (specifically the pederastic attraction of older to younger) seems confirmed by the recent discovery and publication of the following documents concerning the thirty-four-year-old Alger's confrontation by the Unitarian Church of Brewster, Massachusetts, where he officiated as minister. The fact that Alger's popular boys' books, and his concern for child welfare, arose out of pederastic feelings violently condemned by the same society that made him a hero is an irony whose complexity requires a detailed, subtle analysis.

In 1866, a special parish investigating committee of the Unitarian Church of Brewster, Massachusetts, reports:

We learn from John Clark and Thomas S. Crocker [two boys] that Horatio Alger, Jr. has been practicing on them at different times deeds that are too revolting to relate. Said charges were put to the said Alger and he did not deny them. He admitted that he had been imprudent and considered his connection with the Unitarian Society of Brewster dissolved.

Another Brewster church committee immediately wrote to Unitarian headquarters in Boston, communicating the feelings of an "outraged community,"

That Horatio Alger, Jr. who has officiated as our Minister for about 15 months past has recently been charged with gross immorality and a most heinous crime, a crime of no less magnitude than the abominable and revolting crime of unnatural familiarity with *boys*. . . . Whereupon the committee sent for Alger and to him specified the charges and evidence of his guilt which he neither denied or attempted to extenuate but received it with apparent calmness of an old offender—and hastily left town on the very next train for parts unknown. . . .

Alger's crime, the committee wrote, "is too revolting to think of in the most brutal of our race . . ."[34]

Alger's train from Brewster carried him to New York City, where he took a serious interest in aiding the youths at the Newsboys' Lodging House, and began to write their stories and his own name into the history of the American dream.

1873: Massachusetts versus James A. Snow; "Substantially Smith acquiesced"

On Sunday, August 20, 1871, James Snow committed sodomy with Willard A. Smith. On September 5, Smith took poison after apparently feeling remorse about his consensual participation in a homosexual act. Smith recovered and later testified against Snow. The prosecution of James Snow for sodomy is one of the earliest American legal cases involving the issue of consent. The alleged victim, Smith, admitted his participation in this and other "acts of a similar nature," but claimed that all "were against his will and his resistance." However, the district attorney prosecuting the accused Snow admitted "he believed that substantially Smith acquiesced," and was "a confederate or an accomplice." Smith's testimony thus legally required corroboration. The jury found Smith's testimony was corroborated, and so found Snow guilty. In historical perspective, the report of this case makes it clear that Snow was found guilty of an act between consenting persons, one of whom later denied he had consented. Although the testimony indicates that Smith, the alleged victim, was a "boy," the question of his age was not at issue. The major relevant testimony in this case is contained in the report of the Superior Court to which Snow appealed his lower court conviction.

Willard A. Smith testified "that on Sunday, August 20, 1871, between 12 and 1 o'clock, he was passing the building where the defendant [James A. Snow] had his rooms, and saw the defendant sitting at his window; that the defendant asked him to come up; that he went up, and the defendant locked the outside door; that then the defendant committed the act charged [sodomy]; that while in the act, the witness heard a loud rapping at the outside door, and the defendant went down and let somebody in; that he heard the defendant say he had been having a nap, and so locked the door; that the door from the defendant's room into the hall was open a little, and the witness looked out through the crack and saw the defendant and a Mrs. Morse come up stairs, and then saw Mrs. Morse go up the next flight; and that then the defendant came into his rooms again." He testified not only to the acts committed at the time charged in the indictment, but also to various other acts of a similar nature; and that all these acts were against his will and his resistance.

Mrs. Morse testified "that she occupied the third floor, and the defendant and his partner the second floor of the building. . . ."

Morse's testimony confirmed Smith's description of Snow's actions when Morse returned home.

One Bean, a physician, testified that on the evening of September 5, 1871, he was called to attend Smith, for having taken poison; . . . that on the same evening, while sitting in his office, the defendant called at about 11 o'clock, and asked him how Smith was, and if he would die; that the witness said it was uncertain; that the defendant then asked if Smith had told why he took it, or words to that effect; that the witness told him he had not; and that the defendant asked the witness the same question twice after this, once as he was sitting at his window a day or two afterwards, and once at an apothecary's shop, two or three days afterwards. . . .

One Emerson was allowed, against the defendant's objection, to testify that the defendant, on August 27, 1871, attempted to commit the same offence with him, and said that it would not hurt him, and that he had done it with other boys.

In his argument, the district attorney said that although Smith had testified that the acts were against his will and resistance, still he did not believe that there was such resistance as ought to have been made by Smith, and that notwithstanding any partial resistance, unwillingness or reluctance, he believed that substantially Smith acquiesced, and that in this view he agreed that he was in the situation of a confederate or an accomplice, and required corroboration.

After reviewing these statements made in the lower court, the Superior Court affirmed Snow's original conviction.[35]

1878: Montana Territory versus Mahaffey; The defendant "called him a boy prostitute"

In 1878, one Mahaffey, who had been found guilty by a lower court of "the infamous crime against nature," appealed his case to a higher Montana tribunal. The report of this appeal reviews the earlier testimony in the case.

The appellant [Mahaffey] has been convicted of the offense which is described in the statutes as "the infamous crime against nature either with man or beast." . . . The court below overruled the motion for a new trial, and we are required to review the testimony to determine the questions before us. The indictment alleges that the offense was committed "on or about the 9th day of November, A. D. 1877," at Deer Lodge, with B.*

B., a boy fourteen years of age, testified that the appellant committed the offense with his consent, at the Scott House, in Deer Lodge, on the night of November 9, 1877. Against the objection of the appellant, the witness then testified that the appellant had, on various occasions, committed this offense with him at the appellant's ranch, about seven miles from Deer Lodge before said date; and that the appellant called him a boy prostitute and threatened to put him in the penitentiary.

Against the objection of the appellant, L. P. Smith, a deputy sheriff, testified that he arrested the appellant and did not tell him what offense he was charged with; that on the way to the jail, the appellant stated he did not see what C.* wanted him

* The name of the witness is omitted in this report.—B. [Note in original.—J.K.]

arrested for; that witness said it was not C., but that he had been arrested on the complaint of B., and that he could judge what it was for; and that the appellant then said it would be one of the most interesting cases ever in court, and that B. was a boy prostitute.

C. testified that he was a brother of B.; that the appellant came to his house about a mile from Deer Lodge on the afternoon of November 9, 1877, and wanted B. to go to his ranch and work for him; that he objected because he wanted B. to go to school; that the appellant then wanted B. to go with him to Deer Lodge to get what the appellant owed him for work; and that B. went away with the appellant and did not return until the next day.

Frank Hyde testified that he was a clerk at said Scott House, November 9, 1877, and that the appellant and B. went to bed there in a room which he showed them, about eight o'clock.

The appellant testified in his own behalf that he went to C.'s house to hire B., and that he got him to come to Deer Lodge to get his pay; that, after paying him, they went to the Scott House and slept together, November 9, 1877; that they went to bed about eight o'clock, and that the appellant paid for the bed and had nothing to do with the boy as testified to by B.

The appellant contends that the court below erred in permitting B. to testify to the commission of the offense prior to November 9, 1877, on various occasions, on the ground that these acts constitute separate crimes, and that it was unnecessary to prove any intent except that which would be inferred by law from the act. . . . The rights of the appellant were protected by the court, and the jury were instructed that the appellant could not be convicted unless they found from the evidence that he committed the offense in Deer Lodge, on or about November 9, 1877. We think that the evidence was properly submitted to the jury.

The appellant [also] claims that the jury were not instructed correctly on the weight of the evidence of B. . . .

The last ground on which the appellant asks for a new trial is that the evidence of C., Smith and Hyde does not corroborate the testimony of the accomplice, B., within the meaning of the statute. . . . In the case at bar, the appellant, after failing in his attempt to hire B., induced him, for the ostensible purpose of paying his wages, to go to Deer Lodge, and remain at the hotel in the same bed during the night, when B. was only one mile from his home. The testimony of L. P. Smith may be treated as a corroboration of B. and an admission by the appellant. . . . The statement of the appellant to L. P. Smith that B. was a boy prostitute was applicable to the offense for the commission of which the appellant was on trial, and the jury were properly instructed respecting their duty in considering it. There is no error in the record.[36]

The appeals court affirmed the lower court's conviction of Mahaffey.

1880: United States Census;
The Defective, Dependent, and Delinquent Classes

The United States Department of the Interior, Census Office, *Report on the Defective, Dependent, and Delinquent Classes of the Population of the United States* includes the statistics collected at the tenth census, June 1, 1880.

A section on "The Prisoners of the United States, in 1880 . . ." lists those jailed for a "Crime against nature. (Synonym: sodomy, buggery, bestiality.)" A total of sixty-three prisoners are listed as being incarcerated for this crime. Nineteen of these are "Native white" and male; one is female. Eleven of these are listed as "Foreign born white" males. Thirty-two of these are "colored" males. The relative number of white and "colored" prisoners (thirty-one white, thirty-two "colored") is, of course, extremely disproportionate to the racial character of the general population. A listing by state of all those imprisoned for crimes against nature includes:

1 in Alabama,	2 in Massachusetts,	1 in Rhode Island,
3 in California,	1 in Michigan,	1 in South Carolina,
5 in Florida,	7 in Mississippi,	7 in Tennessee,
3 in Georgia,	1 in Missouri,	4 in Texas,
4 in Illinois,	1 in Montana,	2 in Virginia,
2 in Kentucky,	1 in Nebraska,	1 in Wisconsin
3 in Louisiana,	5 in New York,	
2 in Maryland,	6 in Pennsylvania,	

A list of those in prison for "Assault—with intent to commit [a] crime against nature" includes one "Native white" male, from Pennsylvania.

A list of "The Foreign-Born Prisoners of the United States" specifies eleven foreign-born out of a total of sixty-three in jail for a "Crime against nature," including:

2 from Germany,	3 from Ireland,	2 from Mexico
2 from England,	1 from Italy,	1 from Russia

A list of "Inmates of Reformatories of the United States in 1880" includes one "Native white" male incarcerated for a "Crime against nature." He was in the "Wisconsin Industrial School (for boys), Waukesha, Wis."[37]

1882: Anonymous;
A Homosexual Emigrant
"In consequence of the disgrace . . . I am obliged to reside in America"

Among the persecuted groups who emigrated to America were homosexuals. In the fall of 1882, a thirty-eight-year-old merchant, who had emigrated to the United States after a homosexual arrest and scandal in his native land, wrote "a long letter" to Dr. Krafft-Ebing, who published "the most important parts of it." A translation appeared in an American medical journal in 1888. Although the letter writer believes that homosexuality is a "disease," and is extremely self-pitying by current standards, his letter also emphatically protests his own "persecution" as a Gay person. Sending this letter to a prominent medical writer who conceived of homosexuality as an illness was itself an early, individual act of resistance against those who viewed it as "a horrible and unnatural crime." The emigrant's letter reads:

I have read your article in the *Zeitschrift für Psychiatrie*. By it I and thousands of others are rehabilitated in the eyes of every thinking and half-way fair-minded man, and I give you my heartiest thanks therefor. You will know how cases like mine are derided, execrated and persecuted. I well understand that science has taken hold of this matter so recently that in the eyes of one whose mind is sound and who is unversed in the nature of this disease, it appears as a horrible and unnatural crime. Ulrich[s] has not overestimated the prevalence of this disease. In my own city (13,000 inhabitants) I personally know of fourteen cases, and in a city of 60,000 people I know of eighty.

I will take the liberty of encroaching on your time by giving a short sketch of my life, and shall do so with all frankness. It will perhaps furnish you with data for your critical studies of this malady. You may make such use of these statements as you see fit so long as my name is suppressed. . . .

Until I was twenty-eight years old I had no suspicion that there were others constituted like myself. One evening in the castle garden at X——, where, as I subsequently found, those constituted like myself were accustomed to seek and find each other, I met a man who powerfully excited my sexual feelings, so much so that I had a seminal emission. With that I lost my better manhood and came often to the park and sought similar places in other cities.

You will readily conceive that with the knowledge thus acquired there came a sort of comfort—the satisfaction of association and the sense of no longer being alone and singular. The oppressive thought, that I was not as others were, left me. The love affairs which now followed gave my life a certain zest which I had never known before. But I was only hurrying to my fate. I had formed an intimate acquaintance with a young man. He was eccentric, romantic and frivolous in the extreme and without means. He obtained complete control over me and held me as if I were his legal wife. I was obliged to take him into business. Scenes of jealousy which are scarcely conceivable took place in my house. He repeatedly made attempts at suicide with poison and it was with difficulty that I saved his life. I suffered terribly by reason of his jealousy, tyranny, obstinacy and brutality. When jealous he would beat me and threaten to betray my secret to the authorities. I was kept in constant suspense lest he should do so. Again and again I was obliged to rid my house of this openly insane lover by making large pecuniary sacrifices. His passion for me and his shameless avarice drove him back to me. I was often in utter despair and yet could confide my troubles to no one. After he had cost me 10,000 francs, and a new attempt at extortion had failed, he denounced me to the police. I was arrested and charged with having sexual relations with my accuser, who was as guilty as myself! I was condemned to imprisonment. My social position was totally destroyed, my family brought to sorrow and shame, and the friends who had heretofore held me in high esteem now abandoned me with horror and disgust. That was a terrible time! And yet I had to say to myself 'You have sinned, yes, grievously sinned against the common ideas of morality, but not against nature.' A thousand times no! A part of the blame at least should fall upon the antiquated law which would confound with depraved criminals those who are forced by nature to follow the inclinations of a diseased and perverted instinct.

. . . I know of a case in Geneva where an admirable attachment between two men like myself has existed for seven years. If it were possible to have a pledge of such a love they might well make pretensions to marriage. . . . One thing is true. Our loves bear as fair and noble flowers, incite to as praiseworthy efforts as does the love of any man for the woman of his affections. There are the same sacrifices, the same joy in abnegation even to the laying down of life, the same pain, the same joy, sorrow, happiness, as with men of ordinary natures. . . .

In consequence of the disgrace which came upon me in my fatherland I am obliged to reside in America. Even now I am in constant anxiety lest what befell me at home should be discovered here and thus deprive me of the respect of my fellow-men.

May the time soon come when science shall educate the people so that they shall rightly judge our unfortunate class, but before that time can come there will be many victims.[38]

1890: United States Census;
Crime, Pauperism, and Benevolence

The U.S. Department of the Interior, Census Office, *Report on Crime, Pauperism, and Benevolence in the United States at the Eleventh Census, 1890*, lists offenses "Against public morals," among them "Crime against nature." No distinction is made between homosexuality and bestiality. The total crimes against nature number 224.

The figures for the "white" and "colored" populations are broken down separately. A total of 146 crimes against nature were by whites. Native-born whites committed 101 of these crimes. Fifty-one of these whites had native-born parents; seven had one foreign-born parent; thirty-two had parents both of whom were foreign; eleven offenders had "One or both parents [who were] unknown." Forty-five of these white offenders were themselves foreign born.

The "Total colored" crimes against nature equaled seventy-eight. Seventy-six of these were by "Negroes," two by Chinese. As in the 1880 census, the relative number of "white" and "colored" prisoners (146 white, 78 colored) is again disproportionate to the numbers of each group in the general population.

Two juvenile offenders were charged with crimes against nature; both were white; one had parents who were native; one had parents who were unknown.[39]

1892–1915: The Homosexual Underworld in American Cities

The following group of documents describe that troubled, underground city life which includes male homosexual transvestites and prostitutes, Lesbian prostitutes, allegedly orgiastic Black male homosexual transvestite "drag" balls, allegedly obscene Lesbian novels, male homosexual activity in parks and Turkish steam baths, police harassment and raids on Gay male bars, arrests, venereal disease, sexual exploitation, and suicide. This sordid and seamy (mostly male) homosexual underworld has not often been viewed as part of the whole sexual and criminalized underworld of "proper" heterosexual society, both mirroring and exaggerating its details. These documents generally originate with observers whose bias leads them to emphasize the grotesque, whose moral outrage prevents them from empathizing with the human being behind the caricature and from examining the very phenomena they report. They remain silent, for instance, about the male prostitute's customer. The possible survival of some Black "vadoux" (voodoo) customs in the "drag" ball is not explored, because of an hysterical, racist, and prudish judgment.

1892: Charles W. Gardener;
"The worst vice that N.Y. holds"

Detective Gardener, in his book *The Doctor and the Devil, or the Midnight Adventures of Dr. Parkhurst* (1894), describes an 1892 tour, with the crusading Reverend Dr. Charles H. Parkhurst, of New York City vice dens. The two were searching for evidence of collusion among the city's criminals, its politicians, and its police:

I had shown Dr. Parkhurst the depths of common vice . . . and I now proposed to show him something of the worst vice that N.Y. holds.

So I led the way to the "Golden Rule Pleasure Club." This dive was situated on West Third Street, in a four-story brick house. We entered the resort through the basement door, and as we did so a "buzzer," or automatic alarm, gave the proprietors of the house information that we were in the place. The proprietress, a woman known as "Scotch Ann," greeted us. She was quite a pretty woman, tall, black-haired and of graceful form.

"Good evening," she said smilingly. "Won't you come in."

The basement was fitted up into little rooms, by means of cheap partitions, which ran to the top of the ceiling from the floor. Each room contained a table and a couple of chairs, for the use of customers of the vile den. In each room sat a youth, whose face was painted, eye-brows blackened, and whose airs were those of a young girl. Each person talked in a high falsetto voice, and called the others by women's names.

* * *

I explained. The Doctor instantly turned on his heel and fled from the house at top speed.

"Why I wouldn't stay in that house," he gasped, "for all the money in the world."[40]

♀ 1892: Dr. Irving C. Rosse;
Homosexuality in Washington, D.C.

"Two male elephants . . . entwined their probosces together"

In a paper read at a meeting of the Medical Society of Virginia, at Allegheny Springs in September 1892, Dr. Rosse spoke on ". . . Perversion of the Genesic [procreative] Instinct." Rosse, a professor of nervous diseases at Georgetown University in Washington, D.C., warns of the wide "prevalence and spread of sexual crime," that is, sexual activity other than "normal [heterosexual] coitus." Dr. Rosse maintains that such "crimes of sexuality" are not confined to humans, and refers to "the biological beginnings of crime as observed in curious instances of criminality in animals." Since

we are warranted in saying that as many of the lower beings in the zoölogical scale show virtues having analogy to those of man, we must expect to find parallel vices. It is an error to suppose that aberration of the genesic instinct is confined to our species, time or race. . . . I have observed common instances of sexual perversion in dogs and turkeys. A short time since, at the Washington races, a celebrated stallion was the favorite on whom the largest bets were made. A friend of mine, having ascertained from the groom the day before the race that the horse had procured an ejaculation by flapping his penis against the abdomen, accordingly risked his pile on another horse, who, by the way, came in ahead. Only a few days ago, to escape a shower, I took refuge in the elephant house in the Washington Zoölogical Gardens, where are confined the two male elephants, "Dunk" and "Gold Dust." To my astonishment, they entwined their probosces together in a caressing way; each had simultaneous erection of the penis, and the act was finished by one animal opening and allowing the other to tickle the roof of his mouth with his proboscis, after the manner of the *oscula more Columbino*, mentioned, by the way, in some of the old theological writings, and prohibited by the rules of at least one Christian denomination.[41]

Dr. Rosse speaks of a case, known to the Washington police, of

a well-connected man with a very pallid complexion, who enticed messenger boys to a hotel, and after getting them under the influence of drink accomplished his fell purpose. A friend in the Department of Justice tells me of the trial in Philadelphia of a noted pederast who communicated syphilis to a dozen or more of his victims.

Rosse says that the observation of venereal disease symptoms,

even [in] the mouth, calls for the consideration of a hideous act that marks the last abjection of vice. So squeamish are some English-speaking people on this point that they have no terms to designate the "nameless crime" that moves in the dark. Many of the Continental writers, however, make no attempt to hide the matter under a symbolic veil, and deal with it in terms as naked and unequivocal as those used by the old historians, from whom hundreds of citations might be made. . . .[42]

Turning to the present, Rosse says that as an indication of the

state of immorality we have only to call to mind the unclean realism of Zola and Tolstoi, and the French lesbian novels, *Mademoiselle Giraud ma Femme*, by A. Belot, and *Mademoiselle de Maupin*, by Th. Gautier, whose point of departure is tribadism. . . . In our own country the surreptitious sale of such publications is carried to such an extent that agents of the Post Office Department yearly destroy tons of pornographic literature.[43]

Rosse continues:

A Washington physician, whom I see almost daily, tells me of a case of venereal disease of the buccal [oral] cavity in an old soldier whom he is treating. The patient with unblushing affrontery did not hesitate to say how it was contracted.

From a judge of the District police court I learned that frequent delinquents of this kind have been taken by the police in the very commission of the crime, and that owing to defective penal legislation on the subject he is obliged to try such cases as assaults or indecent exposure. The lieutenant in charge of my district, calling on me a few weeks ago for medical information on this point, informs me that men of this class give him far more trouble than the prostitutes. Only of late the chief of police tells me that his men have made, under the very shadow of the White House, eighteen arrests in Lafayette Square alone (a place by the way, frequented by Guiteau) in which the culprits were taken *in flagrante delicto*. Both white and black were represented among these moral hermaphrodites, but the majority of them were negros.[44]

But such men, says Rosse, do not hold a monopoly on "perversion,"

having had a neurotic patient whose conversation showed an extreme erotic turn of mind, I learned from her some particulars as to the existence and spread of saphism.

I know the case of a prostitute who from curiosity visited several women that make a specialty of the vice, and on submitting herself by way of experiment to the lingual and oral manœuvers of the performance, had a violent hystero-cataleptic attack from which she was a long time in recovering.

Through one of my patients of the opposite sex another case has come to my knowledge of a woman who practices the orgies of tribadism with other women after getting them under the influence of drink. . . .

. . . I take it for granted that what is true of Washington as regards sexual matters applies more or less to other American large cities.[45]

1893: Charles H. Hughes;
"An Organization of Colored Erotopaths"

In an 1893 note to a medical journal article on "erotopathia," or "morbid eroticism," Dr. Charles H. Hughes of St. Louis writes briefly but emotionally about Black male transvestites.

I am credibly informed that there is, in the city of Washington, D. C., an annual convocation of negro men called the drag dance, which is an orgie of lascivious debauchery beyond pen power of description. I am likewise informed that a similar organization was lately suppressed by the police of New York city.

In this sable performance of sexual perversion all of these men are lasciviously dressed in womanly attire, short sleeves, low-necked dresses and the usual ball-room decorations and ornaments of women, feathered and ribboned head-dresses, garters, frills, flowers, ruffles, etc., and deport themselves as women. Standing or seated on a pedestal, but accessible to all the rest, is the naked queen (a male), whose phallic member, decorated with a ribbon, is subject to the gaze and oscula-tions in turn, of all the members of this lecherous gang of sexual perverts and phallic fornicators.

Among those who annually assemble in this strange libidinous display are cooks, barbers, waiters and other employes of Washington families, some even higher in the social scale—some being employed as subordinates in the Government depart-ments.[46]

1894: John Berryman; Stephen Crane,
Flowers of Asphalt

John Berryman's biography of author Stephen Crane (1950) describes a street incident in New York City which led to the inception of a new Crane novel about male prostitution, to be called *Flowers of Asphalt*. According to Berryman, "One night in April or May of 1894," arts critic James Huneker met his friend Stephen Crane, and

they were on their way to the Everett House when a kid came up to them in Broadway, apparently begging. Huneker gave him a quarter but then as he tagged along saw that he was really soliciting. Crane, "damned innocent about everything except women," did not understand till they emerged into the glare of the hotel-front and could see the boy was painted, with big violet eyes like a Rossetti angel. Huneker thought his friend would vomit. Shortly, Crane became interested, took the boy in with them and fed him; his name was something like Coolan and he had, of course, a story; Crane quizzed him carefully. Told he was diseased and wanted to be treated, Crane rang up Irving Bacheller and borrowed fifty dollars to give him. He now began a novel about a boy prostitute. Huneker made him read [Joris-Karl Huysmans' novel] *A Rebours*, which he thought stilted. His book started in a railway station, with a country boy running off to New York—a scene that in Huneker's view Crane never surpassed. It was going to be called "Flowers of As-phalt" and was to be "longer than anything he had done." But Hamlin Garland, when Crane read him some of it, was horrified and begged him to stop. Whether he ever finished it Huneker didn't know. The manuscript has not been traced.[47]

1896: Colin A. Scott;
" 'The Fairies' of New York"

An article on "Sex and Art," by Colin A. Scott, published in *The American Journal of Psychology* in 1896, was written with the assistance of the famous psychologist G. Stanley Hall. Scott, a Fellow in Psychology at Clark University, writes about

the peculiar societies of inverts. Coffee-clatches, where the members dress themselves with aprons, etc., and knit, gossip and crochet; balls, where men adopt the ladies' evening dress are well known in Europe. "The Fairies" of New York are said to be a similar secret organization. The avocations which inverts follow are frequently feminine in their nature. They are fond of the actor's life, and particularly that of the comedian requiring the dressing in female attire, and the singing in imitation of a female voice, in which they often excel.[48]

1899: New York State Report;
Investigation of the City of New York
"They are called . . . Lady So and So and
the Duchess of Marlboro"

In 1899–1900, a New York State special legislative body, known informally as the Mazet Committee, composed of upstate politicians, mostly Republicans, was appointed "to Investigate the Public Offices and Departments of the City of New York," dominated by the Democratic bosses of Tammany Hall. The political conflict between the state committee and the city officials they were investigating is clear behind much of the testimony recorded in the committee's report (1900).

Mayor of New York City Robert A. Van Wyck, testifying on May 16, 1899, was asked by a committee member:

Q. Do you know that we now have male harlots thronging the streets, who have their peculiar places of resort, which can be found as easily as any saloon can be? Do you know that?

A. No, I do not.

Q. You never have heard of that?

A. No. I know there are whores in every big city in the world.

Q. But what do you think about the male department of that industry that has become so large in the city of New York in the last two years?

A. I know nothing about it. All I know about it is what occurred in London a few years ago. That is all I recollect about it.

Q. You never heard of it in the city of New York?

A. No.

Q. How is that?

A. They didn't indulge in that when I was a boy.

Q. What do you mean by that?

A. It was not going on then.

Q. What has that got to do with the condition of New York now—your knowledge of the condition of New York now?

A. My knowledge of the condition is as I observe it, as I pass through.

Q. What has the condition when you were a boy got to do with the condition now, while you are mayor of the city, for the last two years?

A. I think those boys do now what I did when I was a boy.

Q. You do?

A. Yes, sir; I don't think society is any worse than it was then.

Q. I did not think that you meant we should draw any inference from your probable course of life, and I am very sorry if you meant we should. I conceive this matter to be too serious, and on too high a plane of public morals to deal with in any such way as that.

A. Put a question. Ask a question and I will answer it.[49]

New York City Police Captain James K. Price, testifying before the state committee on May 31, 1899, was asked:

Q. Now, this Artistic club, 56 West Thirtieth street, kept by Samuel H. Bickard—did you close that up?

A. Yes.

Q. How did you succeed in doing that?

A. Pulled [raided] that two or three times.

Q. Did you get any convictions?

A. Yes.

Q. Who did you convict?

A. All the Nancys and fairies that were there.

Q. What do you mean by that—male prostitutes, male prostitutes?

A. Degenerates, yes, do you know what that is?

Q. That was such a place?

A. Yes.

Q. Whom did you get convicted?

A. Every one of them fined.

Q. Did you get Bickard convicted?

A. He is awaiting trial.

Q. Did you get him convicted?

A. No, he has not been tried yet.

Q. Did you get his manager convicted?

A. Yes.

Q. Who was that?

A. Fined the men that were there.

Q. You had those persons arrested, found in the place, fined for disorderly conduct?

A. Yes.

Q. Did you have anyone convicted for keeping a disorderly house?

A. The case has not been disposed of.

Q. Without convictions you have succeeded in closing three places there?

A. Oh, I closed a dozen. . . .

Q. So, Captain, it is possible for you to close a disorderly resort, even though the courts do not convict the proprietors of keeping them, isn't it?

A. I have closed thirty of them.

Q. Answer that question. It is possible, isn't it?

A. Yes, sir.

Q. Is there any place that you, as police officer, captain of your precinct, are unable to close?

A. Oh, yes; it requires evidence to close a place.

Q. You did not require evidence to close those three places?

A. Yes, sir; a crime committed in the presence of the officer and justifying immediate arrest, and then taken to court, the facts explained to the magistrate, the prisoner is fined, discourages them—drives them out in that way.[50]

Witness John R. Wood testified on June 1, 1899:

Last night I was at 392 Bowery. . . . that is a place where fancy gentlemen go; it is near Fifth street. It is . . . a place where male prostitutes resort. I was there last night in the performance of my duty, in company with Mr. Harris [another investigator]. There were such persons present. They were soliciting men at the tables—that is, men were soliciting men at the tables. I had no trouble in getting in; merely walked in. . . . I have been there before, about three times.

Q. (By Mr. O'Sullivan) And did you always observe the same conditions that you talk about?

A. Yes, sir; I did. . . . That is, I always observed these degenerate men there in large number, quite large numbers from twenty-five to fifty, and engaged in conversation with these degenerates together. They had promised to give a show, as they call it, and it seems that the thing fell through, or they were afraid to give it. And about 1:05 p.m., it looked very much like a put up job; some congressman or assemblyman was in there; he was pointed out to me some time ago—

Q. You mean some official; we will strike out congressman or assemblyman; some official whom you did not know by name?

A. Yes, sir; he whispered to the proprietor and the proprietor acted very mysterious after that; he seemed to try to hold us; we got suspicious and started to leave, and we left about five minutes to one, and as we stepped out of the place Captain Chapman walked in with a squad of men. I never saw Chapman there before. He ordered the place closed and said he wouldn't stand for any souvenir nights.

. . . I don't know whether this club has a certificate of incorporation. It is right back of the saloon. I don't know whether the place has a license or not. I don't know whether the saloon has a license. I did not make any inquiry. . . .

That is the place commonly called Paresis hall. . . .[51]

On the same day, Joel S. Harris testified:

I was with Mr. Wood last night at Paresis Hall, No. 392 Bowery. I observed the actions of the persons congregated there. I saw and heard immoral actions and propositions by degenerates there. Captain Chapman came in about five minutes to 1, as we stepped out. . . . We had been in the place about an hour or so; plenty of time for information to get from Paresis Hall to the stationhouse. Captain Chapman didn't say anything to us, but I overheard him say to the proprietor . . . that he would not stand for any dancing on souvenir night, and he wanted it shut up. I have been in that place before, recently, three or four times, and I have on each occasion noticed the same conduct as I have just testified to. That is a well-known resort for male prostitutes; a place having a reputation far and wide, to the best of my knowledge. I have heard of it constantly. I have never had any trouble in going in. You go in off the street with perfect ease. These men that conduct themselves there—well, they act effeminately; most of them are painted and powdered; they are called Princess this and Lady So and So and the Duchess of Marlboro, and get up and sing as women, and dance; ape the female character; call each other sisters and take people out for immoral purposes. I have had these propositions made to me, and made repeatedly. There is no difficulty in getting into that place.

Q. Mr. Hoffman—This place you refer to as Paresis Hall has a liquor license, has it not?

A. I'm sure I don't know; they sell liquor.

Q. Conducted in the front part of these premises?

A. Yes; and they serve liquors in the rear—in the back.[52]

Also on June 1, 1899, George P. Hammond, Jr., testified:

I know this place called Paresis Hall, and under your directions I have visited it a number of times. I have been in the place since April 1st to the present time fully half a dozen times. I knew of it before, as an officer of the City Vigilance League. I am in the produce business. When this committee began its sessions I took a vacation on the produce business and came in to help you. The character of the place is such that what we call male degenerates frequent the place, and it is a nightly occurrence that they solicit men for immoral purposes. They have one woman who goes there they call a hermaphrodite. These male degenerates solicit men at the tables, and I believe they get a commission on all drinks that are purchased there; they get checks. I have observed five or six of these degenerates frequent that place, possibly more; the last we were there we saw a greater number than we did previously. Those five or six are always to be found there; almost invariably you will find them there. They go from there across the street to a place called Little Bucks, opposite, and from there to Coney Island. I have never had any difficulty in getting in; not the least; I have been received with open arms. There are two ways of going in, one way up through the barroom, the other through a side entrance; any way at all that suits you can walk in. . . . They have a piano there, and these fairies or male degenerates, as you call them, they sing some songs.

After Hammond finished testifying, Mr. Hoffman of the committee concluded:

I judge there is a way to eradicate the kind of evils complained of by this witness at Paresis Hall. These places cannot exist unless they were accorded a Raines liquor license in the first instance, and the only way to eradicate that kind of evil is to have some restrictions in the excise department not to license this kind of places [sic].[53]

1905: Paul Näcke;
"The Homosexual Market in New York"

The traditional invisibility of homosexuals, their consequent isolation from their kind, and their difficulty in finding each other early resulted in the use of carefully worded newspaper advertisements as a means of contact. The following item by Paul Näcke appeared in German in the *Archiv für Kriminal-Anthropologie* (1906).

The Homosexual Market in New York. Some months ago Dr. Spitzka, of New York, sent me the following two ads from the metropolitan daily *The New York Herald*, of April 23, 1905, which implicitly refer to homosexual intercourse. These were *the only two* which he was able to find in a long span of time, I believe a year, although he had made a particular search for them. The offers themselves are as follows:

SIR.—Would you appreciate faithful, genteel companionship: refined, trustworthy gentleman. Address CONVERSATION,

270 Herald

FRIENDSHIP CLUB: CORRESPONDENCE EVERYWHERE: PARTICULARS FREE. BOX 24. CLEVELAND, OHIO.

In the ads themselves, as you can see, there is nothing extraordinary. They are even rather tamely worded. The remarkable and noteworthy element is rather that they are evidently so rare in New York and probably elsewhere in America as well, in contrast with our big cities, particularly Berlin and Munich. . . . Prudery cannot be the cause, as the ordinary advertising matter in the American papers, and very likely the *New York Herald* too, exhibits utter shamelessness. Or are we to conclude that over there it is so easy for the Urnings to find one another that advertising would be superfluous? In any case we should not be led to conclude the opposite, that in America's big cities homosexuality is less flourishing than in our country. It is probably even more flourishing, when we consider that many Urnings go to America because they have become involved in conflicts here, or fear that they will become. . . . Among the multitude of inferior individuals who cross the ocean year in and year out, there are probably more homosexuals than among the others, because there are probably more degenerate and inferior specimens of humanity among them than in the ranks of the heterosexuals, which, of course, in no way justifies the conclusion that homosexuality, in and of itself, is a specific form of degeneracy.[54]

1907: Charles H. Hughes;
"Homo Sexual Complexion Perverts in St. Louis"

In a "Note on a Feature of Sexual Psychopathy," published in 1907 in the medical journal *The Alienist and Neurologist*, which he edited, Dr. Hughes updates his report of 1893, here writing on the arrest of a group of Black male transvestites and white male homosexuals in St. Louis. It is difficult to say whether racism or

antihomosexual attitudes are more pronounced in Hughes's report; and his terminology and phrasing give one cause to doubt his own soundness of mind. Yet this
document hints at an aspect of an underground interracial, sexual subculture for
which there as yet is little documentation:

Male negroes masquerading in woman's garb and carousing and dancing with
white men is the latest St. Louis record of neurotic and psychopathic sexual perversion. Some of them drove to the levee dive and dance hall at which they were
arrested in their masters' auto cars. All were gowned as women at the miscegena-
tion dance and the negroes called each other feminine names. They were all arrested, taken before Judge Tracy and gave bond to appear for trial, at three
hundred dollars each, signed by a white man.

The detectives say that the levee resort at which these black perverts were
arrested, is a rendezvous for scores of west end butlers, cooks and chauffeurs.
Apartments in the house are handsomely furnished and white men are met there.
The names of these negro perverts, their feminine aliases and addresses appear in
the press notices of their arrest, but the names of the white degenerates consorting
with them are not given.

Social reverse complexion homosexual affinities are rarer than non reverse color
affinities, yet even white women sometimes prefer colored men to white men and
vice versa. Homosexuality may be found among blacks, though this phase of sexual
perversion is not so common or at least has not been so recorded, as between white
males or white females. . . .

A Moll, Krafft-Ebing, Havelock Ellis or Kiernan might find material in St. Louis
for further contributions to their studies of reverse sexual instinct. The contraire
sexual empfingdung [contrary sexual instinct] has had other illustrations here.
St. Louis has duplicated the woman stabber of Berlin since she set her mark at a
million inhabitants. These perverted creatures appear to be features of million
peopled cities and they come into the light, if the police are vigilant. The reverse
erotopath abounds among the nerve center degraded as well as the insistent and
persistent erotopath of cliteromania or satyriac imperative propulsion.

NOTE.—These St. Louis negro perverts gave feminine names that might belong to English
or American ladies of any city. The curious may find them and the names the blacks assumed
at the record office of the police courts.[55]

1914: Magnus Hirschfeld;
Homosexuality in Philadelphia, Boston,
Chicago, Denver, and New York

In his major work, *Homosexuality in Men and Women* (1914), Dr. Magnus
Hirschfeld, German sexologist and homosexual emancipation leader, describes several of the bleaker aspects of the underground homosexual life in American cities,
and includes a letter from a homosexual professor in Colorado. Hirschfeld's own
observations on American life are based upon a visit to the United States in
1893. They are here translated from the original German.

Homosexual life in the United States is somewhat more hidden than in the United Kingdom. During a visit to Philadelphia and Boston I noticed almost nothing of homosexuality, but visitors from those cities later assured me that there was "an awful lot going on" within private circles in these centers of Quakerism and Puritanism. . . .

Just a short time ago an admiral of the Pacific fleet was forced to tender his resignation because his homosexuality became publicly known. In general, however, homosexual scandals seem to occur less frequently in the United States than in the European states. On the other hand, American newspapers report with unusual frequency the arrests of men who dress in women's clothing and women who dress in men's clothing. These reports and events are often quite remarkable. For example, one man who simply could not stop dressing as a woman was [finally] forced to wear a sign on his waist with the legend: "I am a man."[56]

A large number of American transvestites are homosexual, but not all. In Chicago I was introduced to a Negro girl on Clark Street who turned out to be a male prostitute. I met two other transvestites, conversely, one from San Francisco and one from New York, who were heterosexual. Strongly sublimated homosexuality is also common in America; a good example is provided by the poet of comradely love, Walt Whitman. . . .

A Uranian [homosexual] scholar from the state of Colorado writes:

I know quite a number of homosexuals in Denver, personally or by hearsay. At this moment I can think of five musicians, three teachers, three art dealers, one minister, one judge, two actors, one florist, and one women's tailor. Parties are given by a young artist of exquisite taste and a noble turn of mind, and some of his homosexual friends appear at these in women's clothing. Prostitution is not common in Denver; male prostitutes can sometimes be met in the Capitol Gardens, but not a large number of them.

The Turkish baths which serve as meeting places in New York, Boston, Philadelphia, and Chicago offer us little. You seldom meet homosexuals in the baths here, but six of the nine masseurs who work in the baths of Denver are known to be tolerant and are probably themselves homosexuals.

Among the many Turkish baths in New York, one is frequently visited by homosexuals in the afternoon and one in the evening; baths are located on T—— Street in Boston and on P—— Street in Chicago. In Philadelphia there is one bath where about sixty homosexuals gather on Saturday night; the homosexual manager of the place supervises with proper consideration for his clientele. The Turkish baths of America are generally a very safe place for homosexuals. The entry price of one dollar is high enough to keep the ordinary male prostitute out. The people you meet have not come there to blackmail. Naturally, not all visitors at these baths are necessarily homosexual. Uranians from out of town are not at all reluctant to visit the baths, while people from the town have to be more careful. An acquaintance has written to me that knows of a Turkish bath in a small city in Ohio whose owner, a mulatto, is definitely homosexual.

In the vicinity of Denver there is a military fort with a force of a few hundred men. Last summer a soldier from there propositioned me on the street in Denver. I've heard that this happens quite frequently in San Francisco and Chicago. I recall meeting a soldier who was a prostitute long ago in San Antonio, Texas, and last summer I met a young sailor from Massachusetts. The latter was on leave and looking for homosexual intercourse out on the street late at night. In all of these cases it was difficult to tell whether the soldiers were really homosexual or just prostitutes, or whether they went with men for lack of anything better. It's never easy to draw the line, and things are so expensive nowadays that someone could easily be moved to earn a little pocket money in one way or the other.

Now I want to tell you something about the university at which I'm a professor. We have about 1,000 male students here, among whom the usual percentage of homosexuals is certainly to be found. I often notice [persons with] all the characteristics of homosexuals amongst the students. At the moment I know one about whom there can be no doubt. He's twenty-six, was born in Denver, and has lived here since he was eight. He is quite poor and has to live very economically; I've frequently taken the opportunity to get concert tickets for him and thus won his trust. He spends his leisure time decorating hats and designing women's clothes. He speaks enthusiastically about a few young men, but I'm convinced that he hasn't been involved with anyone. He's enraptured by music and fine perfumes. To date, I haven't dared to tell him about myself, because he's an extremely sensitive person. I'm absolutely sure about this case. Further, I know two law students who always stick together and who are teased for being like "man and wife." One of the two recently told me that he was together with an actor for one month last summer, and I know for a fact that the actor is homosexual.

Four years ago there was an engineering student here who was carrying on with boys in the YMCA building; he was arrested and taken to the police station, where he killed himself with a revolver. He was the son of a professor.

A former student of mine who left the university ten years ago—now he is a professor himself at one of the most respected universities in the Eastern states—revealed to me two years ago that he is a Uranian. Another homosexual student who finished three years ago is now a very talented staff member on a New York newspaper. The man with whom he had an affair [in Denver], and who admits to having already tried out every kind of homosexual activity, is now writing for a magazine in New York. He recently astonished his acquaintances by announcing his impending marriage. Another of our ex-students is one of the most celebrated actors in all of North America. As a boy he insisted upon being called by the girl's name "Sadie." In addition, I know one more homosexual here in our small town who cares for his aged mother and does all the domestic work. He is now forty-five years old, and earlier he is supposed to have worn a corset and thick rouge. I've *never* heard anyone say anything sensible about him. Whenever a troupe of actors gives a guest performance in the local theater, he likes to wait at the stagedoor; and I might add here that the actors are often "willing."

A few years ago a young woman with a resolute manner and a deep voice graduated from our university. I had long suspected her, and a woman friend recently made a remark which fully confirmed my suspicions. . . .

It scarcely needs to be mentioned that Americans frequently blame one or the other ethnic group for homosexuality. For example, a criminologist from the Southern states recently stated that male prostitution first spread into his area of the country with the immigration of the Italian "Vergazzi"; and one often hears Americans claim that the yellow-skinned population is strongly given to homosexuality. This may well be true, but there is no reason to imagine that homosexuality is any less widespread among the white and black populations.[57]

1915: Havelock Ellis;
Homosexuality in American Cities

In the 1915 edition of the famous volume, *Sexual Inversion*, Havelock Ellis writes:

As regards the prevalence of homosexuality in the United States, I may quote from a well-informed American correspondent:—

"The great prevalence of sexual inversion in American cities is shown by the wide knowledge of its existence. Ninety-nine normal men out of a hundred have been accosted on the streets by inverts, or have among their acquaintances men whom they know to be sexually inverted. Everyone has seen inverts and knows what they are. The public attitude toward them is generally a negative one—indifference, amusement, contempt.

"The world of sexual inverts is, indeed, a large one in any American city, and it is a community distinctly organized—words, customs, traditions of its own; and every city has its numerous meeting-places: certain churches where inverts congregate; certain cafes well known for the inverted character of their patrons; certain streets where, at night, every fifth man is an invert. The inverts have their own 'clubs,' with nightly meetings. These 'clubs' are, really, dance halls, attached to *saloons*, and presided over by the proprietor of the saloon, himself almost invariably an invert, as are all the waiters and musicians. The frequenters of these places are male sexual inverts (usually ranging from 17 to 30 years of age); sightseers find no difficulty in gaining entrance; truly, they are welcomed for the drinks they buy for the company—and other reasons. Singing and dancing turns by certain favorite performers are the features of these gatherings, with much gossip and drinking at the small tables ranged along the four walls of the room. The habitués of these places are, generally, inverts of the most pronounced type, *i.e.*, the completely feminine in voice and manners, with the characteristic hip motion in their walk; though I have never seen any approach to feminine dress there, doubtless the desire for it is not wanting and only police regulations relegate it to other occasions and places. You will rightly infer that the police know of these places and endure their existence for a consideration; it is not unusual for the inquiring stranger to be directed there by a policeman."[58]

Ellis adds a detail concerning city street life:

it is notable that of recent years there has been a fashion for a red tie to be adopted by inverts as their badge. This is especially marked among the "fairies" (as a *fellator* is there termed) in New York. "It is red," writes an American correspondent, himself inverted, "that has become almost a synonym for sexual inversion, not only in the minds of inverts themselves, but in the popular mind. To wear a red necktie on the street is to invite remarks from newsboys and others—remarks that have the practices of inverts for their theme. A friend told me once that when a group of street-boys caught sight of the red necktie he was wearing they sucked their fingers in imitation of *fellatio*. Male prostitutes who walk the streets of Philadelphia and New York almost invariably wear red neckties. It is the badge of all their tribe. The rooms of many of my inverted friends have red as the prevailing color in decorations. Among my classmates, at the medical school, few ever had the courage to wear a red tie; those who did never repeated the experiment."[59]

♀ 1892: F. L. SIM;
Alice Mitchell and the Murder of Freda Ward

On July 18, 1892, a young woman named Alice Mitchell was taken before the Shelby County Criminal Court in Memphis, Tennessee, in the hope of determining whether she was insane or of sound mind, and thus subject to stand trial for the violent murder of a young woman named Freda Ward, to whom Mitchell had been passionately attached. The details of Alice Mitchell's life and relations with Ward are described in a long report of her hearing, published soon afterward, in the *Memphis Medical Monthly*. At this hearing Alice Mitchell was judged to be insane, based on eyewitness accounts of her behavior and character traits, her own statements, and the "expert testimony" of a number of medical specialists. These "experts" agreed on a diagnosis of insanity and attributed the cause of her disordered mind to an inborn inheritance from her mother, who had a history of mental derangement.

The details of Mitchell's tragic romance with Ward leave no doubt that Alice Mitchell was a bewildered and lost young woman, her sense of reality confused, her emotional life beset by conflicting and passionate feelings. But the once-popular theory of constitutional insanity now seems an inadequate explanation of her problem. Mitchell's disturbance and violent behavior can today be seen as the result of a family experience, educational system, and society that conspired to frustrate her and drive her mad—by keeping her in ignorance of her own character and emotions, and in childlike ignorance of this society's own workings.

The following excerpt from the report by Dr. F. L. Sim, one of the "expert witnesses" at Mitchell's sanity hearing, gives the basic facts of the case as they were established in court.

Alice was a nervous, excitable child, and somewhat under size. As she grew she did not manifest interest in those childish amusements and toys that girls are fond of.

When only four or five years old she spent much time at a swing in the yard of the family in performing such feats upon it as skinning the cat, and hanging by an arm or leg. She was fond of climbing, and was expert at it.

She delighted in marbles and tops, in base ball and foot ball, and was a member of a children's base ball nine [team]. She spent much time with her brother Frank, who was next youngest, playing marbles and spinning tops. She preferred him and his sports to her sisters. He practiced with her at target shooting with a small rifle, to her great delight. She excelled this brother at tops, marbles, and feats of activity.

She was fond of horses, and from early childhood would go among the mules of her father and be around them when being fed. About six or seven years ago her father purchased a horse. She found great satisfaction in feeding and currying him. She often rode him about the lot bareback, as a boy would. She was expert in harnessing him to the buggy, in looking after the harness, and mending it when anything was amiss. To the family she seemed a regular tomboy.

She was willful and whimsical. She disliked sewing and needlework. Her mother could not get her to do such work. She undertook to teach her crocheting, but could not. She was unequal in the manifestation of her affections. To most persons, even her relatives, she seemed distant and indifferent. She was wholly without that fondness for boys that girls usually manifest.

She had no intimates or child sweethearts among the boys, and when approaching womanhood, after she was grown, she had no beaux and took no pleasure in the society of young men. She was sometimes rude, and always indifferent to young men. She was regarded as mentally wrong by young men toward whom she had thus acted.

Alice was a slow pupil at school. Efforts to teach her music and drawing were a failure. She would ask to have instructions repeated in a confused and absent way. She could not get her mind on the subject or remember what was said to her. The teachers were of opinion that she was badly balanced and not of sound mind. Since quitting school she has shown no taste for books or newspapers, and reads neither the one nor the other.

About the time her womanhood was established she was subject to very serious and protracted headaches. She had far more than the usual sickness at that period. She was subject to nervous spells, in which she would visibly tremble or shake. She is still at times subject to these attacks of extreme nervous excitement, but does not, now, and never did, wholly lose consciousness in them but upon one occasion.

For Freda Ward, a girl about her own age, she had an extraordinary fondness. Whenever she could do so she was with her. They lived neighbors, and spent as much of their time together as possible. The attachment seemed to be mutual, but was far stronger in Alice Mitchell than in Fred [Freda Ward].

They were very different in disposition. Fred was girl-like and took no pleasure in the boyish sports that Alice delighted in. Her instincts and amusements were feminine. She was tender and affectionate. Time strengthened the intimacy between them. They became lovers in the sense of that relation between persons of different sexes. May, a year ago, the Ward family moved from Memphis to Golddust, a small town on the Tennessee side of the Mississippi river, about eighty miles north of Memphis. The separation greatly distressed Alice, but an active correspondence by mail was at once opened, and in this way they modified the regret caused by the separation. In the summer after the removal of the Wards Alice visited her beloved Fred, and remained with her two or three weeks. They were continually together, and often seen embracing and clasped in each other's arms.

Alice got a promise that Fred should visit her in the fall or winter, and this promise was kept, Fred spending about two weeks with Alice in December, 1890.

During this visit Alice entertained the idea of taking her own life or that of Fred. She bought laudanum with that view. She considered the plan of giving it to Fred whilst sleeping, but in some way Fred was aroused and suspected that Alice had some design, either on her own life or that of Fred, and remained awake the greater part of the night. Alice showed her the bottle marked poison. The next day she went with Fred to the boat on her way home at Golddust, carrying the bottle of laudanum with her. She locked herself and Fred in a stateroom on the boat, and took the contents of the bottle with suicidal intent. She suffered greatly for many days for this rash act. The reason assigned by Alice was that Fred loved Harry Bilger and Ashley Roselle and she [Alice] meant to end her existence and troubles and leave Fred free to become the wife of her choice of the young man named. . . .

During this visit Alice manifested the most ardent attachment for Fred, and some days after Fred reached home she wrote Fred of her recovery, and then began again a regular correspondence, showing all the warmth of lover for lover.

In February, 1891, Alice proposed marriage. She repeated the offer in three separate letters. To each Fred replied, agreeing to become her wife. Alice wrote her upon the third promise that she would hold her to the engagement, and that she would kill her if she broke the promise.

Alice again visited Fred in June, 1891. She had saved from time to time small sums of money, amounting in the aggregate to about $15. With this sum she purchased a ring, and on her June visit formally tendered it to Fred as their engagement ring, and Fred accepted it as such.

They were often seen in each other's embraces, and the married sister of Fred, Mrs. Volkmar, remarked that they were disgusting in their demonstrations of love for each other.

Alice felt a sense of shame in allowing others to see her hug and kiss Fred. She did not think it proper for lovers to be openly hugging and kissing. Fred did not take that view, and rather reproached Alice for being ashamed of showing her love for her in that way.

On leaving, Alice got a pledge that Fred would pay her a visit the coming November. Their engagement was a secret then only known to themselves.

It was agreed that Alice should be known as Alvin J. Ward, so that Fred could still call her by the pet name, Allie, and Fred was to be known as Mrs. A. J. Ward. The particulars of formal marriage and elopement were agreed upon. Alice was to put on man's apparel, and have her hair trimmed by a barber like a man; was to get the license to marry, and Fred was to procure the Rev. Dr. Patterson of Memphis, and of whose church she was a member, to perform the marriage ceremony, and if he declined, they intended to get a justice of the peace to marry them. The ceremony performed, they intended to leave for St. Louis. Alice was to continue to wear man's apparel, and meant to try and have a mustache, if it would please Fred.

She was going out to work for Fred in men's clothes.

In the latter part of June, 1891, Ashley Roselle, before mentioned, began to pay court to Fred, who gave him one of her photographs. The watchful vigilance of Alice got track of this affair, and she remonstrated warmly with Fred, and charged her with deception and infidelity. Fred acknowledged she had done wrong, vowed unshaken fidelity to Alice, and promised never more to offend.

The scheme of marrying and eloping seemed almost ready for execution in the latter part of July. Fred was to take a St. Louis packet [boat] at Golddust and come to Memphis and notify Alice of her arrival, and they were then to marry and go at once by boat to St. Louis, as they had agreed to do. The boat Fred was to take was to reach Golddust at night between 10 and 2 o'clock.

By chance, Mrs. Volkmar, the married sister before referred to, with whom Fred was living, saw part of the correspondence of the girls, which disclosed the relations between them, and the plan to elope and marry. She was surprised and indignant. She communicated the fact to her husband, and he determined to watch Fred and prevent her from taking the boat for Memphis. He suspected a man was at the bottom of the affair, and watched with his Winchester rifle. No man appeared. When the boat whistled announcing her arrival, he went to the room of Fred. He found a light burning in her room, and she was dressed, had her valise packed, and was ready to take the boat. An exciting scene ensued. Mrs. Volkmar wrote to Mrs. Mitchell, the mother of Alice, and at the same time wrote Alice, returning the engagement ring and other love tokens, and declaring that all intercourse between the girls must at once cease. Mrs. Mitchell knew that Mrs. Volkmar was in feeble health, and thought that she had grossly exaggerated and misunderstood the matter. She told Alice of the letter received from Mrs. Volkmar. Alice listened in silence. Mrs. Mitchell destroyed the letter. She then knew nothing of Alice's secret.

The effect on Alice of the return of the engagement ring and the inhibition of all communication with Fred, was almost crushing. She wept, passed sleepless nights, lost her appetite, frequently declining even to come to the table.

She hid the returned tokens of love in the kitchen, in a cigar box, to which there was a lock and key. She would often go alone to this hiding place and gaze in an abstracted way upon these tokens of affection. She spent hours in the kitchen, alternately crying and laughing.

She told the cook that she was engaged to marry; said her father and mother were good to her; but her sisters were not kind. The cook supposed she was engaged to marry some man, and the sisters of Alice opposed the match. She had no notion that it was a woman she was engaged to marry. She thought they were not treating Alice right in the house, in some way, but did not know how. She thought Alice was not right in her mind. Alice showed her the engagement ring— would gaze upon it and pass from tears to laughter whilst doing so. The cook had a child about six years old, and Alice talked a great deal to this child—seemed to take a fancy to the child, in her distress. She said they would not lift her troubles off her.

In August and September the winter supply of coal for the family was being delivered, and she receipted five of the coal bills in the name of Fred Ward, and on being asked why she did so, replied that she was not conscious of doing so; that she was thinking of Fred, and used her name without knowing it. For weeks before the killing her eyes shone with a strange luster.

Alice was plump and round before the passion for Fred possessed her. After that she grew thin, and her face wore an anxious expression. She seemed absent and absorbed, and quite strange to her acquaintances.

That singularity of behavior which always characterized her, increased, until those who had long known her, concluded that she was mentally wrong.

November was the time when Fred was again to visit Memphis, according to her promise to Alice. On the first of November Alice clandestinely possessed herself of her father's razor. When she took it she was thinking of Fred. She feared they would take Fred from her. She could not bear the thought of losing her. Sooner than lose her, she would kill her. . . .

In January, 1892, Fred came to Memphis, but went to stay with Mrs. Kimbro, instead of Alice. She did not see or write to Alice, who had a burning desire to be with her, or receive some message from her. She tried to communicate with her by letter—wrote her two letters, and managed to get one of them into her hands during her stay at Mrs. Kimbro's. These letters told of her love in the most passionate terms. One was returned with the word "returned" written upon it in Fred's handwriting.

Alice sought opportunities to see Fred—to look upon her, to speak to her, but in vain. Fred's sister, or some one else, was on the lookout, and her desire was thus thwarted.

One day while upon the watch, she saw Fred go, unattended, into a photograph gallery. In a short time she came out, but did not observe or speak to Alice. She went from the photograph gallery to Mrs. Carroll's.

Alice thought of using the razor, which she had with her on the occasion, but found some difficulty in getting it out, and the feeling then to take the life of Fred with the razor passed off, and she returned to her home. At the time she thus thought of killing Fred, she loved her as much, or more, than ever. On January 18 Alice got the last letter she ever received from Fred. This letter told of Fred's continued love for Alice; but said she was not allowed to see her, or speak to her, and prayed the forgiveness of Alice.

Alice and Miss Lillian Johnson, an estimable neighbor girl, about the same age, were intimate, and loved each other, but as one girl loves another. She was aware of the ardent attachment of Alice for Fred, but did not at first suspect that it was different from the love of one girl for another.

On the morning of the homicide, Alice had the buggy horse shod and engaged Miss Johnson to drive with her that evening. Alice, Miss Johnson and the nephew of the latter, about 6 years old, occupied the buggy in the evening drive. Alice knew that Fred would probably take the boat that evening for home. . . . Without disclosing her purpose, she drove so as to meet Fred on her way to the boat. Josie Ward and Miss Purnell were with Fred. . . . She drove directly to the Customhouse, and all three got out of the buggy. In a few seconds Fred and her companions came up and turned north, in order to reach the way that led to the steamboat upon which Fred and her sister proposed to leave. Fred passed within less than two feet of Alice, who turned to Miss Johnson and said: "Oh, Lil; Fred winked at me." In a few seconds Alice said she must see Fred once more, and walked after Fred. She soon overtook her, and without a word cut her with a razor. Fred's sister undertook to interfere, but was slightly cut by Alice and forced to retire. Alice then turned upon Fred and again cut her, one of the wounds being mortal, cutting her throat almost from ear to ear. Fred fell to the earth and Alice ascended the steep walk to the buggy, in which she found Miss Johnson and her nephew. . . .

Persons who saw the prisoner as she ascended the hill from the scene of the homicide, describe her as almost in a run, looking wildly, with her hat off and her hair disheveled and streaming down behind her, and her face bloody. She moved with a quick, determined step to the buggy in which Lillian Johnson and her little nephew were seated, and seemed to take possession of it by violence—seizing the reins and grabbing the whip she lashed the horse and moved off at a dangerous speed. One of these persons followed her, fearing that she would overturn the buggy and injure the occupants. This person supposed from her appearance and manners that she was insane, and had violently taken possession of the buggy of some other person and was driving it in her mad fury in the most reckless manner. . . .

As they dashed along, she asked Miss Johnson if there was not blood on her face, and being told that there was, she requested Miss Johnson to take her handkerchief and wipe it off, but instantly checked her by saying, "No, let it remain; it is Fred's blood, and I love her so." Miss Johnson asked her what she had done. She replied, "Cut Fred." On reaching home, Alice drove in the back way, and on entering the house, asked for her mother, who was not in, and turning to her sister, said, "Do not excite my mother," but declined to say what had occurred. Presently her mother came, and she told her that she had cut Fred's throat. She appeared to be quite nervous. The blood was washed from her face, her cut fingers were tied up, and by that time, the chief of police arrived and told Mrs. Mitchell that he had come to arrest one of her daughters. She asked him not to take her away until her father could see her. He soon came, and Alice then went with the chief of police to the county jail. She appeared to be cool, and said she cut Fred because she loved her and because Fred did not speak to her. That night and the next morning she did not seem to realize that she had committed a criminal act. Nor does she yet realize it.

Alice intended to follow Fred on the boat and there kill her. Why she did so before she got on the boat she cannot tell. In her language, she more than loved Fred. She took her life because she had told her she would, and because it was her duty to do it. The best thing would have been the marriage, the next best thing was to kill Fred. That would make it sure that no one else could get her, and would keep her word to Fred. She saw no wrong in keeping her word and doing her duty, and now sees none.

For many nights before the killing, she was all the time dreaming of Fred. She says she now sees Fred, when awake and asleep, and can't understand that Fred is dead.

She shows no remorse nor regret for the bloody deed, but weeps when her love for Fred is referred to.

On the night of the homicide, on being asked if she and Fred had run off and married in St. Louis, what they would have done, she looked puzzled; said that she had never thought of that, and in turn inquired, what would they have done?

On the next morning she asked where Fred was. She showed no feeling or emotion when making this inquiry. Being told that her body was at Stanley & Hinton's, she turned to her mother, and with great feeling and with tears pouring from her eyes, begged her mother to take her to Fred and let her lie down with her.

She kisses passionately all the pictures and cuts of Fred she can lay hands on, and hunts the newspapers for them.

Alice J. Mitchell has been tenderly and carefully brought up by Christian parents. Her family is one of the best in Memphis, and Fred Ward's family is above exception.

Nothing coarse or immoral is known of Alice or Fred.[60]

♀ 1896: BERTRAND RUSSELL;
Helen Carey Thomas, Mary Gwinn, and Alfred Hodder

In the autumn of 1896, the English mathematician-philosopher Bertrand Russell and his wife, American-born Alys Smith, spent three months in the United States. They visited the late Walt Whitman's Camden, New Jersey, home, and saw members of Alys's family, including a cousin, the female president of Bryn Mawr

College, Helen Carey Thomas. Russell's *Autobiography* (1967) provides a brief but suggestive description of a troubled period in the relationship of Thomas and a female intimate Russell cites only as "Miss Gwinn." If there had been no conflict between Gwinn and Thomas, it is easy to imagine that Russell would not have recalled their relation at all; thus a great many homosexually relevant documents come to portray problematic episodes in the lives they record. Russell writes:

We went next to Bryn Mawr to stay with the President, Carey Thomas, sister of Bond Thomas. She was a lady who was treated almost with awe by all the family. She had immense energy, a belief in culture which she carried out with a business-man's efficiency, and a profound contempt for the male sex. The first time I met her, which was at Friday's Hill, Logan [Pearsall Smith, the father of Russell's wife] said to me before her arrival: "Prepare to meet thy Carey." This expressed the family attitude. I was never able myself, however, to take her quite seriously, because she was so easily shocked. She had the wholly admirable view that a person who intends to write on an academic subject should first read up the literature, so I gravely informed her that all the advances in non-Euclidean geometry had been made in ignorance of the previous literature, and even because of that ignorance. This caused her ever afterwards to regard me as a mere *farceur*. Various incidents, however, confirmed me in my view of her. For instance, once in Paris we took her to see *L'Aiglon*, and I found from her remarks that she did not know there had been a Revolution in France in 1830. I gave her a little sketch of French history, and a few days later she told me that her secretary desired a handbook of French history, and asked me to recommend one. However, at Bryn Mawr she was Zeus, and everybody trembled before her. She lived with a friend, Miss Gwinn, who was in most respects the opposite of her. Miss Gwinn had very little will-power, was soft and lazy, but had a genuine though narrow feeling for literature. They had been friends from early youth, and had gone together to Germany to get the Ph.D. degree, which, however, only Carey had succeeded in getting. At the time that we stayed with them, their friendship had become a little ragged. Miss Gwinn used to go home to her family for three days in every fortnight, and at the exact moment of her departure each fortnight, another lady, named Miss Garrett, used to arrive, to depart again at the exact moment of Miss Gwinn's return. Miss Gwinn, meantime, had fallen in love with a very brilliant young man, named Hodder, who was teaching at Bryn Mawr. This roused Carey to fury, and every night, as we were going to bed, we used to hear her angry voice scolding Miss Gwinn in the next room for hours together. Hodder had a wife and child, and was said to have affairs with the girls at the college. In spite of all these obstacles, however, Miss Gwinn finally married him. She insisted upon getting a very High Church clergyman to perform the ceremony, thereby making it clear that the wife whom he had had at Bryn Mawr was not his legal wife, since the clergyman in question refused to marry divorced persons. Hodder had given out that there had been a divorce, but Miss Gwinn's action showed that this had not been the case. He died soon after their marriage, worn out with riotous living. . . .[61]

Russell may be wrong about Hodder not being married to his first wife; another report says Hodder divorced the first Mrs. Hodder, quit teaching, and traveled to Europe with Mary Gwinn. There the two were married in 1904. Among others,

Hodder and Gwinn visited Gertrude Stein and her brother in Paris, where the Steins had taken up residence. Gertrude, who had just come through a triangular Lesbian affair of several years' duration, had long been fascinated by reports from Bryn Mawr graduates concerning Thomas, Gwinn, and Hodder. Stein was inspired to re-create the Thomas-Gwinn-Hodder affair in fictional form in one of her earliest short novels, *Fernhurst*, written late in 1904 or early 1905, but not published until 1971.[62]

♀ 1896: ALLAN M[c]LANE HAMILTON; "The Civil Responsibility of Sexual Perverts"

In an article published in the *American Journal of Insanity*, Dr. Hamilton, a "Consulting Physician to the Manhattan State Hospital," discussed the problem of establishing legal "responsibility," or soundness of mind, in cases concerning the disposal by male and female homosexuals of large sums of money or property. His paper is written for those doctors "called upon to give advice or testify" in cases involving the "medico-legal bearings" of Lesbian and male homosexual associations. Two cases are described in detail, both concerning families who questioned the sanity of homosexual relatives in disposing of their property. The trial of Henry B. Palmer is alleged to be "the first [legal case] in this country" involving the "civil rights" of a homosexual to control his own property. Hamilton displays extreme bias in his portrayal of the case involving Lesbianism, and unusual sympathy in that case concerning male homosexuality and blackmail. He seems to conceive of Lesbian associations as often involving a "feminine," passive woman, dominated and subjected to extortion by a manipulative, "masculine" woman. However, in the instance he describes, the supposed female victim is not at all passive in reaction to her family's and Hamilton's attempts to persuade her to drop her Lesbian liaison.

Discussing Lesbianism Hamilton refers to an important change in social attitudes toward women-loving women:

Until within a comparatively recent period the mere insinuation that there could be anything improper in the intimate relations of two women would have drawn upon the head of the maker of such a suggestion a degree of censure of the most pronounced and enduring character, but since the publication of the celebrated "*Mdlle. de Maupin*," which was written by Théophile Gautier about thirty years ago, and other romances from the pens of French and German writers, the eyes of observing persons have been opened to the fact that, as the result of a perverted sexual appetite, the relations of individuals may undergo an extraordinary change, so that one person may entertain for another all the ordinary feelings that he or she should feel for the opposite sex.[63]

Hamilton says that while he

does not for a moment dispute the existence of an all-absorbing friendship, . . . he realizes, as have others, that a great many of these too close attachments mean a transposition of sexual feeling, which leads to moral degradation, as well as impairment of individual rights, when a stronger will dominates a weaker.

Hamilton continues:

So far as I know no one has considered the medico-legal bearings of sexual perversion, except with relation to its criminal import.

In a rather extended investigation, which includes a knowledge of American *causes célèbres*, several of which have been personally seen, and as the result of consultations in disputed cases which have not found their way into court, the writer believes that in examples of both abnormal male and female attachments new issues arise.

He explains:

The circumstances under which dangerous intimacies occur vary greatly, and we are called upon to consider an active and passive agent, the former being usually a neurotic or degenerate, who is a sexual pervert, and whose life is pretty well given up to the gratification of his or her unnatural appetites.

Of the sexual female examples that have come under my notice the offender was usually of a masculine type, or if she presented none of the "characteristics" of the male, was a subject of pelvic disorders, with scanty menstruation, and was more or less hysterical or insane. The views of such a person were erratic, "advanced," and extreme, and she nearly always lacked the ordinary modesty and retirement of her sex. The passive agent was, as a rule, decidedly feminine, with little power of resistance, usually sentimental or unnecessarily prudish. Sometimes the subjects have been married women, with uncongenial husbands, and they nearly always had no desire for children, resenting the normal advance of the male. Again the unnatural attachment was casual, and in no way premeditated, the two women, for economical or other reasons, living together.

The mere infraction of moral laws, which such an alliance implies, is by no means the only evil that confronts us, for it can be readily understood that the weak victim can be made the tool of the designing companion, and extortion may be the end. Of course where the victim is under age, a variety of legal remedies present themselves, but if the woman be more than twenty-one the matter becomes more difficult, and we are then called upon to decide the question of responsibility, and to determine whether she is insane or not, and should be deprived of her civil rights. The difficulties that lie in the way of controlling the diversion of property may be very great while superficial appearances are apparently perfectly proper.

Several years ago I was consulted by the family of a rich young woman, who had, shortly before, come into possession of upward of $1,000,000. Her home life had been a quiet and religious one, and she was deeply attached to her mother and brothers, discussing with them her affairs, and under the brothers' direction investing her money, of which she had absolute control. About this time she was induced by a mutual friend to come on to New York and consult a woman doctor with regard to certain trivial uterine disorders, which resulted in her placing herself under the care of the latter. The doctor was a large-framed, masculine-looking woman of about forty, with short, black hair, a raucous, deep voice, and a manner of talking which was in marked contrast to her patient, who was gentle and refined. When it pleased her she did not hesitate to emphasize her conversation with oaths, and affected the carriage and manner of an energetic and coarse man. Her attire even was affected, and was in harmony with her other peculiarities. The patient's stay in the city in which the doctor lived was prolonged from month to month and finally various members of the family came from the East for the purpose, first, of investigating matters, and afterward of inducing the girl to go home, but without avail. Excuses, at first of a reasonable character, were followed by angry expostulation, and, after some time, the young woman went back to her home, while her medical adviser went to Europe for the summer. Her manner had greatly changed. She was dejected, preoccupied, and constantly talked of the woman doctor in a way to tire the patience of those about her; but in a few months she became elated by the receipt of several letters and, despite the persuasions of her mother, returned to New York and went to live with her medical adviser. About this time large drafts of money were made by the girl, coincidentally with the erection of a large and expensive house by the doctress, whom we will call Miss B., and I was then consulted by the family, and, after much difficulty, obtained an interview with the patient, Miss A., it being represented to her that her mental condition had been questioned. On this occasion she manifested a great deal of hatred to her family, which was unreasonable, and avowed her loyalty to her "good friends," and "defied" me to find her insane. No amount of reassurance and no appeal to her self-respect was of the least use, and she left me in an angry and obstinate mood. At this interview I was impressed with the peculiarity of manner and the intensity of feeling which might be exhibited by a woman who was defending her lover, and her defiant utterances were utterly unwarranted.

Finding I could not influence her in any way, and after ascertaining from the doctor that she was a well woman and did not need treatment, I communicated with her friends and enlisted the services of a female detective. The latter very diligently hunted up evidence, with the result that I learned that a veritable infatuation existed upon the part of Miss A., who went everywhere with Miss B., and who even, at times, occupied her bed. Other information, of a more convicting kind, was subsequently ascertained, and was verified by letters that burned with love and had been written by the older woman to the girl. No lover could have expressed himself more ardently to his mistress, and there was no doubt but what the stronger woman had not only poisoned the girl's morals, but had alienated her from her home and worked upon her for the purpose of getting her money, which she did.

In this case subsequent inquiry revealed the fact that this woman had debauched several young girls, one of whom eventually committed suicide. Of course, the office of the writer was a most difficult one, for none of the circumstances of the case at the time warranted the assumption of insanity, and at best criminal procedure would have been the only measure available. So far as the intellectual condition of the girl was concerned there was nothing in her conversation that would have convinced an ordinary jury that she was of unsound mind, and at that time her mental perversion was not of a recognized kind.

At best undue influence might have been urged, but the sums parted with, though large, were not extravagant in proportion to her income, and doubtless she would have explained her reason to the satisfaction of a sympathetic body of twelve men. It was with these facts in view that I felt it would be futile to take any steps to declare her a lunatic, and the only thing left was to take criminal proceedings against the other person who possessed such dangerous power. This her family felt loath to do, as the proceedings would lead to very great publicity and probably miscarry. . . .

The unexplained extravagances of a sexual pervert may raise the question of insanity and lead to an investigation as to his capacity. Such a case was that of Henry B. Palmer of New Brunswick, N.J., which I believe was the first in this country in which the question of this weakness arose in connection with the civil rights of a man, and the writer, who testified before the commission, attempted a differentiation between the various forms of sexual perversion and their relation to responsibility. Palmer, who was an elderly man, and whose brother took steps to have him declared a lunatic so that a committee of his estate and person might be appointed, came under my care a year or two ago. He was a prominent citizen of New Brunswick, where he occupied the position of president of a local insurance company and other offices of trust. His career had been a successful one, and at the time the proceedings were begun he was in possession of a large fortune.

The usual popular allegations of weak-mindedness, untidiness, and physical defects had been made by the petitioner, but the most serious charges were that the old man had not only lost large sums in foolish speculation, but had parted with much of his wealth in some way unknown, which he could not explain. I had been retained by the defendant, and, at my request, he presented himself for examination, and I was immediately impressed, so far as his appearance and conversation were concerned, with the fact that he was not insane, but the victim of avaricious relatives. There was nothing in his mental condition, dress, gait, or behavior that supported the theory of "senile dementia" that had been raised, so this diagnosis was quickly dismissed and there remained simply the charges of extravagance to be investigated. The chief of these was found to be nothing more than just such a form of speculation as nine persons out of ten occasionally indulge in. The other was more serious, for there appeared to be no doubt but that he had, within a period of twenty-five years, given one individual, who apparently had no earthly claim upon him, amounts from time to time aggregating $70,000. With some pressing he confessed that he had taken a young boy to the Centennial Exposition at Philadelphia in 1876, and occupied the same room and bed with him at an hotel.

What occurred it is needless to state, but his companion pursued the course of blackmail, which, as years went by, became more and more burdensome and excessive. Upon close questioning I learned that Palmer had never married, and had, from his earliest youth, manifested all the peculiarities of an *urning* [homosexual]. He had, as a boy, shunned the society of little girls and had maintained the most affectionate relations with his own sex, and it appeared that for all the years of his life he had the contrary sexual instinct, and upon only one occasion, when advanced in years, did it seriously render him liable to criminal prosecution. All this time he was a respected member of society and an officer of his church.

When I examined him he showed no indication of incapacity, and made wise suggestions as to investments and business affairs. His was clearly not a case of acquired or involutional insanity, but the possible loss of personal liberty and his belongings was so imminent, that I advised him to make a clean breast of his weakness rather than to run the risk of being considered irresponsible. In giving my testimony I . . . tried to make plain the distinction between sexual perversion of various kinds, dividing the weaknesses into three varieties, namely, those which were connected with . . . insanity, where loss of restraint exists . . . and where, of course, responsibility is lost; secondly, a form which is simply the ordinary result of depravity and libidinous curiosity and gratification in which responsibility is not lost; and a third form existed as an index of a defective organization, to which class I believe Palmer belonged. How far he was criminally responsible was a matter for the court and jury to decide. . . .

I am sorry to say that the distinctions I made did not meet with favor, and, probably more for the reputation of the town than anything else, the court held him to be "insane," believing that such a depth of depravity could not be anything else but a mark of insanity.[64]

♀ 1897: East Hampton *Star*;
Augusta Main
"She Dislikes Men and Dogs"

On December 31, 1897, a news item appeared in the East Hampton *Star* headed "She Dislikes Men and Dogs." Although this document of a woman in trouble with the law contains nothing explicitly about Lesbianism, it is one of those ambiguous items which, in lieu of more concrete evidence, can at least be termed "Lesbian-relevant," and is reprinted for its present charm, historical interest, and suggestiveness for further research.

A woman who loathes the sight of men and dogs, and hates them both cordially, is Miss Augusta Main, a spinster farmer near Berlin, N.Y. As she told a Justice, who held her to the grand jury in $1,000 bail for committing an assault on a male neighbor with intent to kill, she never sees men or dogs but what she aches to kill them.

When she discovers a man on her premises, she drops all work and makes them skedaddle. If, when ordered away, the man or men do not hurry, she pushes them along with a pitchfork or any other implement that happens to be handy. As a consequence, the men folks give her plenty of room.

Myron Beebe is the neighbor, whom she attempted to slay, and who swore out the warrant for her arrest. For a long time he has dared to cross her premises to get water from a well. It saved him a long walk, and he took the chances.

A few days ago, while Beebe was making the usual short cut to the well, Miss Main came out of her house with a big revolver, and without any parleying opened fire on the man. He ran for dear life, while the bullets whistled about his ears.

When he got home he found that out of the six shots fired two had perforated the overalls which he wore, while another had torn the rim of his hat. The other three bullets came within such close proximity that their whistle still rings in his ears.

Miss Main has, since she took the farm, performed all the work on the place without any male assistance, and does it well. She goes to market with a load of vegetables every week, and sells them herself. Every day she cleans out the stables, feeds the live stock and rubs down the horses. Only in harvest time does she seek outside help, and then she hires strapping young women.

All the tramps who come in the county know of her and give her a wide berth.[65]

♀ 1901: HAVELOCK ELLIS;
Suicide in Massachusetts

Ellis's Sexual Inversion *describes how the frustration of a Lesbian relationship by the families of the two women involved led to a suicide, reported in Massachusetts newspapers early in 1901.*

A girl of 21 had been tended during a period of nervous prostration, apparently of hysterical nature, by a friend and neighbor, 14 years her senior, married and having children. An intimate friendship grew up, equally ardent on both sides. The mother of the younger woman and the husband of the other took measures to put a stop to the intimacy, and the girl was sent away to a distant city; stolen interviews, however, still occurred. Finally, when the obstacles became insurmountable, the younger woman bought a revolver and deliberately shot herself in the temple, in presence of her mother, dying immediately. Though sometimes thought to act rather strangely, she was a great favorite with all, handsome, very athletic, fond of all out-door sports, an energetic religious worker, possessing a fine voice, and was an active member of many clubs and societies. The older woman belonged to an aristocratic family and was loved and respected by all.[66]

♀ 1913–29: Lesbianism in Prison

♀ 1913: Margaret Otis;
"A Perversion Not Commonly Noted"

One of the earliest reports of Lesbianism within a coercive, institutional setting—reform school—is by Margaret Otis and was published in the *Journal of Abnormal Psychology* in 1913. The specific "perversion" to which Otis refers is Lesbian relations between young white and black women. Otis's brief comments display a curious mixture of racism and puritanism, along with what in its day must have seemed an unusual, perhaps even radical, toleration. Her anti-Lesbian bias is tempered by the observation that "sometimes the love [of one young woman for another] is very real and seems almost ennobling." Behind the screen of Otis's judgments and fragmentary remarks there can vaguely be discerned the dynamics of a particular historical form of Lesbianism, occurring within a racist, antihomosexual, and coercive situation. From a modern, liberationist viewpoint, such Lesbian relations as Otis describes might be evaluated and interpreted as the expression of a legitimate need for affection among those placed within extremely alienating circumstances. Although economic class is not mentioned by Otis, the female re-form school population of which she speaks is obviously of working class origin, more specifically, what Marx called the lumpen proletariat. Otis's remarks thus provide a rare glimpse into one aspect of proletarian Lesbianism in the first quarter of twentieth-century America:

A form of perversion that is well known among workers in reform schools and institutions for delinquent girls, is that of love-making between the white and colored girls. This particular form of the homosexual relation has perhaps not been brought to the attention of scientists. The ordinary form that is found among girls even in high-class boarding-schools is well known, and this feature of school life is one of the many difficulties that presents itself to those in charge of educational affairs. The difference in color, in this case, takes the place of difference in sex, and ardent love-affairs arise between white and colored girls in schools where both races are housed together.

In one institution in particular the difficulty seemed so great and the disadvantage of the intimacy between the girls so apparent that segregation was resorted to. The colored girls were transferred to a separate cottage a short distance from the other buildings. The girls were kept apart both when at work and when at play. The girls were given to understand that it was a serious breach of rules for them to get together, and the white girls were absolutely forbidden to have anything to do with the colored. Yet this separation did not have wholly the desired effect. The motive of "the forbidden fruit" was added. The separation seemed to enhance the value of the loved one, and that she was to a degree inaccessible, added to her charms.

In this particular institution the love of "niggers" seemed to be one of the traditions of the place, many of the girls saying that they had never seen anything of the kind outside; but that on coming here, when they saw the other girls doing it, they started doing the same thing themselves, acting from their suggestion. A white girl on arriving would receive a lock of hair and a note from a colored girl asking her to be her love. The girl sending the note would be pointed out, and if her appearance was satisfactory, a note would be sent in reply and the love accepted. Many would enter into such an affair simply for fun and for lack of anything more interesting to take up their attention. With others it proved to be a serious fascination and of intensely sexual nature. This line from one girl's note shows the feeling of true love: "I do not love for the fun of loving, but because my heart makes me love." One case is on record of a girl, constantly involved in these love affairs with the colored, who afterwards, on leaving the institution, married a colored man. This, however, is unusual, for the girls rarely have anything to do with the colored race after leaving the school.

Opinions differ as to which one starts the affair. Sometimes the white girls write first, and sometimes the colored. "It might be either way," said one colored girl. One white girl, however, admitted that the colored girl she loved seemed the man, and thought it was so in the case of the others. Another white girl said that when a certain colored girl looked at her, she seemed almost to mesmerize her. "It made her feel crazy."

This habit of "nigger-loving" seems to be confined to a certain set of girls. These would congregate in one part of the dormitory to watch at the window for the colored girls to pass by on their way to work. Notes could be slipped out, kisses thrown and looks exchanged. Each of these girls was known to be a "nigger-lover." When questioned on the subject, some insist that they do it just for fun. One said that the girls would wave to the "niggers" just "to see the coons get excited."

The notes when captured show the expression of a passionate love of low order, many coarse expressions are used and the animal instinct is seen to be paramount. The ideal of loyalty is present. A girl is called fickle if she changes her love too often. "I don't like a deceitful girl," appears in one of the letters. That a girl should be true to her love is required by their peculiar moral code. "Fussing" with other girls is condemned. From one of the letters: "This morning when you were going to the nursery you threw a kiss to Mary Smith. If you care for her more than you do for me, why, don't hesitate to tell me. I don't love you because you said you loved me. I could have kept my love concealed if I cared to. I certainly will regret the day I ever wrote or sent my love to you if this downright deceitfulness does not stop."

The penalty for a girl who is fickle or who ceases to care for her lover seems to be a curse from the abandoned forlorn one. "It was not long ago that one of your friends sent me a message saying that you didn't love me, but you didn't want me to know that you didn't, for fear I would curse you. Well, you need have no fear. I never curse any one. I have been so careful over here of every little thing I did, for fear some one might carry something back to you, that I had been deceitful. No, indeed! I am not deceitful."

There is often a reaction from this emotional type of love. Girls formerly lovers abandon each other and hate takes the place of love. The mood will change and not even friendship remains. It is at this moment that the girl may be approached more easily in the way of influencing her to abandon her excessive emotional attitude. At this moment she may be brought to realize that such love is not lasting and does her harm rather than good.

Sometimes the love is very real and seems almost ennobling. On one occasion a girl, hearing that danger threatened her love in another cottage, was inconsolable, quite lost her head and called out: "Oh, my baby! my baby! What will become of my baby!" Her distress was so great that all fear of discovery was lost. She even called her name. The intense emotion dispelled all fear and anxiety for her love alone occupied the field of consciousness. Later, after suffering punishment for her fault, she wrote to a friend: "You can see by this that I am always thinking of you. Oh, sister dear, now this is between you and I. Lucy Jones asks me to give Baby up, for she tries to tell me that Baby does not love me. Don't you see what she is trying to do? To get my love back. Ah! sister darling, I might say I will give my Baby up, but ah, in my heart I love her and always shall." Again: "Ah! I shall never throw Baby down; I don't care what happens, for trouble does not change my mind one bit, and I hope it's not changing yours."

An interesting feature of these love episodes is found in the many superstitious practices, especially among the colored when they wish to win the love of a white girl. Curious love charms are made of locks of hair of their inamoratas. One practice is for a colored girl to bury a lock of hair of the white girl she fancies and this is sure to bring her love. These practices, some of so coarse a nature that they cannot be written down, seem to be part of the system, for system it must be called, so thoroughly ingrained it is in the school life.

When taken to task for their silliness, the girls say: "Well, we girls haven't much else to think about." True enough, they haven't much of the emotional nature that they crave, and it seems they must have the sensational and emotional in some form. One girl says: "When you have been in the habit of having a girl love, and she goes away, you have to get another; you just can't get along without thinking of one girl more than another." Sometimes, of course, the relation is a perfectly innocent girlish friendship, but even here jealousy enters in.

Some interested in this phase of the school life have asked: "Isn't it true that it is the defective girls who indulge in this low emotional love more than the others?" This is not found to be the case. Many sins are laid at the door of defectiveness, but mental defect does not explain everything. The reverse might rather be said to be the truth. Some of the girls indulging in this love for the colored have, perhaps, the most highly developed intellectual ability of any girls of the school.

One may ask how this phase of indulging the sexual nature is regarded by the girls themselves. The answer will be found in the fact that there are several distinct strata of moral standards in the school. There are some girls who consider themselves a little above the rest. Among these self-considered high-class girls the "nigger-lovers" are despised and condemned. They are held as not good enough to associate with. That water seeks its own level is true even among the delinquent girls themselves. Certain sets and cliques appear, and those who are "high up" scorn the "common kind."[67]

♀ 1919–20: Kate Richards O'Hare;
Prison Lesbianism

Kate O'Hare, a prison reformer, Socialist lecturer-organizer, and self-styled "Agitator," was indicted in 1917 under the U.S. Espionage Act for speaking against American participation in World War I. She was convicted and sentenced to five years in the Missouri State Penitentiary at Jefferson City. After appeals failed, O'Hare entered the penitentiary on April 15, 1919; another political prisoner in the penitentiary at the time was Emma Goldman. A Socialist amnesty campaign resulted in O'Hare's release on May 29, 1920. While still incarcerated, she published *Kate O'Hare's Prison Letters* (1919) and *In Prison* (1920), a detailed, eyewitness exposé of the horrifying treatment of female convicts. Her references to Lesbianism and masturbation, are, however, characterized by a traditional puritanism, and her account of an evil, Black female prison trusty fails to place this individual's authority and conduct within the larger prison power structure. Yet O'Hare's firsthand account remains a rare and chilling document of female prison life. *In Prison* conveys the general barbarity of conditions and the oppressive context of the prison Lesbianism discussed in the following excerpts.

"A thorough education in sex perversions," says O'Hare, "is part of the educational system of most prisons, and for the most part the underkeepers and the stool pigeons are very efficient teachers." She adds:

In the cellhouse the silence rule was the letter of the law, but it was enforced only spasmodically and at the whim and discretion of the negro stool pigeon who ruled the cellhouse twelve hours each day. . . . The prisoners who, by tips and gifts and sycophancy and willingness to submit to sex perversions, had a "stand in," could talk as much as they liked; but if for any reason a prisoner got in bad with the stool pigeon, she would be brutally punished for the violation of a rule ignored for the majority. . . .

It is a stark, ugly fact that homosexuality exists in every prison and must ever be one of the sinister facts of our penal system. In the Missouri State Penitentiary it is, next to the task, the dominating feature of prison life and a regular source of revenue to favoured stool pigeons. There seems to be considerable ground for the commonly accepted belief of the prison inmates that much of its graft and profits may percolate upward to the under officials. The negress trusty or stool pigeon, who had absolute control of the women's cell building and all its inmates from six in the evening until six in the morning, handled the details of pandering to the homosexual vices so rampant in the prison, and there was a regular scale of charges for permitting the inmates to indulge. The charge for the use of a pervert was usually fifty cents, and the charge for having the cell door left open at night by the stool pigeon was one dollar. In fact, homosexuality was not only permitted by this trusty, but indulgence was actively fostered by this coloured murderess, and, in the cases of young, helpless, and unprotected women actually demanded and enforced. In two or three instances at least I managed to have young and unperverted girls moved into cells near mine, where I could protect them from the demands made by the trusty that they submit to vicious practices.

Because this stool pigeon had sole charge of the cell house and of the lives of the women at night; because her word was always and unquestionably accepted without investigation by the matrons; because she, in fact, held the power of life and death over us, by being able to secure endless punishments in the blind cell, she could and did compel indulgence in this vice in order that its profits might be secured.[68]

♀ 1929: Charles A. Ford;
"Homosexual Practices of Institutionalized Females"

Ford, a member of the Ohio Bureau of Juvenile Research, details his investigation of Lesbianism among women in a "correctional" institution, most of whose inmates were imprisoned for "sexual indiscretions" (apparently a euphemism for heterosexual prostitution). Ford's article, published in the *Journal of Abnormal and Social Psychiatry* in 1929, conveys a fuller sense than Otis's pioneering report of those complex relations which developed among a particular group of women under the conditions of prison life. Especially striking is Ford's suggestion of various attempts at a protective inmate community, organized against those in authority, and efforts to resist the dehumanizing effects of prison life, a community including prisoner-sanctioned interracial Lesbian relations and written expressions of affection —composed with stolen pencils and paper. One may agree that Lesbianism and male homosexuality take on a particular character in prison without accepting Ford's theoretical distinction between a supposedly "temporary or pseudo inversion," resulting from the "artificial conditions" of prison, and an allegedly "pathological," true homosexuality. Ford's article is typical of many later works in assuming that homosexuality is the "problem," not the alienating society created by the prison situation.

To institutionalize individuals solves the problem of society temporarily, but this does not mean that once the individual is institutionalized he offers no problem. Even slight acquaintance with institutions shows a multiplicity of difficulties, one of the most universal of which is inmate homosexuality. . . . Because homosexuality is against the rules of the institution, it is carried on semi-secretly and no true statistics of its frequency can be collected. We cannot know, then, which type of institution has the greatest numerical problem, but in female institutions of the corrective type there are enough cases and enough ado about them to warrant some serious consideration of the problem. This statement is not meant to imply either a greater frequency or greater problem in female institutions but simply that the attitudes toward the problem justify its study.

Such studies are very few, however. In fact, but one that is directly concerned with this problem has been located, and in this Dr. Otis was concerned with but one phase of it, the colored and white girl relationships. Her study was conducted in one of the eastern states' institutions and describes conditions not unlike the ones that have come to the writer's attention in an entirely different location and fifteen years later. The colored relationships, the martyr feeling, the notes, the sexual significance, and the jealousies have all persisted. That the attitudes of the institutional heads and the same ineffectual means of meeting the situation have also persisted is both interesting and sad.

There has been considerable work done in the field of female homosexuality by such men as Ellis, Krafft-Ebing, and others. Their work in the main, was with different sorts of cases than the ones described in this paper. The condition they describe is truly pathological, usually superimposed upon a neurotic constitution and represents the sexual desires of a lifetime. The conditions are not the same for the institutionalized and they represent a sort of temporary or pseudo inversion. There are occasional references to this sort of thing in most of the books concerned with sexual pathology. . . . These references are not directly applicable, but are concerned with similar artificial conditions as in girls' schools or convents.

The following data were gathered in three main ways: (1) by observation of the inmates; (2) by contacts and interviews with the inmates before, during, or after their term, and (3) by interviewing the officers in charge of the institution. They are concerned largely, but not wholly, with one institution, a corrective one for female delinquents. Many of the inmates are retarded in mental development and some are actually feebleminded. As in most institutions of this type, the inmates are there mainly because of immorality, oftentimes coupled with other delinquencies as stealing and incorrigibility.

"Friend" is the term applied to those engaged in homosexuality. It is a generic term, and when a girl talks of her "friend" the only other question is concerned with the type of degree of homosexuality, which ranges from note passing with attendant imaginary homosexuality to mutual masturbation and cunnilinctus.

"Friends" are a sort of tradition in the school and have been a part of the order of things as long as it has been established. When a new girl arrives, she finds these "friendships" everywhere. She is approached by one or more of the girls in her cottage who ask which side she is on, the matrons' or the girls'. Upon her answer depends her future social plane. If she says she stands with the girls, she is tested in many small things, and then if she bears out her statement she becomes a candidate for a "friend". There is a sort of fraternity among the "friends" and those inmates who are not within the circle move on a different social plane and there is no voluntary community between them. Seeing this, it is not unusual that a new girl lines up with the "friends" and attains the popularity she craves. But entering the ranks is a voluntary matter and force is not brought to bear—if she chooses to remain out, she is let alone. If she chooses to stand with the girls, notes are circulated over the institution telling of the new girl and suggesting that someone make a "friend" of her.

A "friend", whether or not she is a new girl, is attained in a simple manner. Ordinarily, no long courtship is carried on, but there is simply a note written, telling that the "friendship" is wanted. The recipient, with the advice of others in her cottage, decides what she wants to do, and writes an answer if she accepts the "friendship". That is all there is to it, and the "friendship" is on. No attempt is made to limit one's self to one "friend"; in fact, it is part of the game to have more than one, if she can. Some girls have a "friend" in every cottage, including their own. Nor is the color line drawn. It is quite the thing for the white girls to have "colored friends" and only the "best" girls rate such favors. By "best" is meant those who lie best, stand up for other inmates best, and are most successful in breaking institutional regulations. Colored girls have not only "white friends" but colored as well. "Cottage friends" is the name of those who live in the same cottage.

The simplest type of "friend" association consists mainly in note passing and imaginary homosexual relationships. These notes are the slushy love note type of thing, filled with adolescent terms of endearment. They are passed from "friend" to "friend" by other inmates who happen by on errands. The relationship between the "friends" is usually husband and wife. That is, in the notes they pass one assumes the rôle of husband and the other of wife, and for the duration of that "friendship" that relationship holds, but the assumed rôle is not always the same for each person in other "friendships", either concurrent or subsequent.

Illustrative of style and content, the following notes are presented. They are uncorrected copies of actual notes passed between a colored girl and a white girl. The colored girl's note is presented first:

> You can take my tie
> You can take my coller
> But I'll jazze [copulate with] you
> 'Till you holler.

My dearest Wife Gloria:—

"I am writing to you because I have not written to you for so long and sweet heart you will have to forgive me but I love you just the same; that handchief that you sent me is to pertty to use and I am going to take it out with me when I go. Honey If you love me you will brake out your dam door and come an sleep with me and angle face if I could sleep with you I would not only hough and kiss you. But I will not take the time to write it for I guess you can read between lines. When I kiss you I thought I was in heaven and I was kissing one of the angles, up there if I were in cuba and you in spain the love I get for you will make a bool [bull?] dog break his chain, and I don't care what you use to be but I know what you are to day if you love me or I love you what has the world to say. You ask me no questions so why should I. I don't care what you use to be but I know what you are to day. I love you and you only.

x   o x o x o x o x o x o x o x o x o

from your love husben

> Ocean love to my wife Gloria Love.

The white girl then answered with this note:

> Land of Friends
> St. of Happiness
> Date—Hot Lips.

My dearest and Only husben Oscean:—

As I have time I will answer your seet love note that I get last night. Honey babe I sure do love you and you only and they had better lay off and I don't mean my be eather. You looked so sweet yesterday at the laundry. Sugar dady if I could sleep with you for one little night, I would show you how much I hontly and truly I love you. You are the only girl I have ever loved and the only one I ever will love if you go out before I do I will not have any friends for I am true blue to you and you had better be to me. Honey if you love me as much as I love you you will wate for me to night at the doorr. After the other girls have gone and I hope you will, for honey I sure do love you and you only and I want you to unstand it to. You are the first "Hill" friend I have ever had and the only one I entand to have for I love you, if you love me you will go to the Hospital for somethig for I go every morning, did you see me this morning in school. I saw you. Honey you are the sweetest thing I every lad my eys on. Will sweet heart, I will close for this time with all the love in my heart and all the kiss on my lips for you and you only. *C.*

> From your loving wife, Gloria Love to my
> Dearest husben Oscean Love.

One of the curiosities of these notes is the heading. Not all the notes carry such headings but many do. It is a perversion of the usual address, place, date, idea, as may be seen from the following samples taken from other notes:

You can take my collar,	Lovers' land,
You can take my tie,	Box of kiss,
But I love you until you die.	Date get you at last.
State Please be mine,	Please forgive me,
Date I love you,	Broken hearted,
Box Lonsome for you.	I want you back.

The notes are usually written in their rooms at night. The paper and pencils are stolen from the school rooms or library, or cut from the margins of books and magazines. Girls who are in the school steal the material by tucking it under their brassieres in such a way that it lays flat and escapes notice. Once in their cottage, they pass it out to other inmates. The notes are kept much as the proverbial lover treasures his letters. In this particular institution the window and door casings are not tight against the walls. These and similar spaces behind shelving become the depositories for both notes and supplies.

Not only are notes passed from "friend" to "friend" but also favors or presents. Ties, toiletries, handkerchiefs, and particularly brassieres, are the usual favors. The brassieres are made by the girls themselves and represent considerable work oftentimes. They are usually heavily embroidered, with love messages, nicknames, or initials. Such favors are often the means of detecting the pair, but even so, they pass about in a secret way.

With cottage "friends" the relationships are not so imaginary. Because they have access to actual physical contact, they resort to it rather than to notes and favors. Although cottage "friendships" do not imply a more perverted contact than loving, petting, kissing, etc., other practices as mutual masturbation and cunnilinctus do exist with this group. Here, too, we find the husband-wife relationships in existence. The role of husband is the more aggressive one. Generally speaking, such contacts are not made between noncottage "friends", but at times, when they are playing or working together, and the attendant is lax, it will happen. Among the girls the actual perversions are called by the initials of their slang names.

In all the relationships the sexual side is stressed. The girls think of themselves in the rôle of husband or wife or some other familial relationship. By this is meant that a particular pair will accept others into their fold as "children". These "children" enter into the "friend" fringe by writing notes to the other "children" and the "parents". Thus the "friendships" become very much involved and lead to the jealousies that can be expected.

Earlier it was pointed out that more than one "friend" was the usual goal. But though this is the goal, it is not carried on openly. When the "friend" finds she has a rival, it often leads to rather violent fights between the girls. These jealousies are even more real than the husband-wife jealousies of the everyday world and result in fist fights, hair pullings, trumped-up stories that put the rival in punishment, and every other conceivable type of trouble making activity. At times the rival does not present her best defense because punishment over a "friend" is another way of gaining favor with the girls. In general, greater oppression results in keener desires.

Oddly enough, "friends" are not always defended. For example, A and B are "friends". A is about to be placed out and receives a farewell note from B. Instead of treasuring this last note, she may put it in the matrons' hands as a magnificent gesture of her trustworthiness. On the other hand, A may send B a farewell note, in which case B may turn it in to the matron so that A will not be sent out. Sometimes the latter plan breaks the "friendship", but not always, and the chance is taken.

From the point of view of duration, it is interesting to note that noncottage "friendships" persist longer than cottage "friendships" and that the relationships not involving physical contact are more durable than those that do. Room partners are rarely, if ever, chosen as "friends", and if by chance cottage "friends" are unknowingly assigned to the same room the relationship ends almost at once. It seems rather clear from this that the element of danger must be operative for a continued "friendship", and it is equally clear that the "friendships" are not the type that will bear close association over a period of time.

Other means of communication than notes and favors are operative at times. These are such things as scratching the "friend's" initials or a silly love message on themselves so they will leave a scar, or allowing themselves to be bitten by the "friend". At times these methods have been a matter of serious concern to the authorities, but they come and go and applications of strong iodine solutions prevent many recurrences. Then, too, there is an intricate set of signs for conveying messages. The way the hair is worn, the color of tie or hair ribbon, a certain wave of the hand, or some peculiarity of gait, each has a particular meaning to the "friend".

Remembering that these things happen in an institution whose inmates are there primarily for sexual indiscretions, it does not seem unnatural that they should happen. Sex has consistently played a part in their lives; the fact that it was anti-social probably lent some zest to the situations. To some degree, they found these experiences pleasurable, and among others of the same kind they even find them glorified. Finding no heterosexual outlet for their sexual desires, it is most natural that they should turn their attention to the possible homosexual experiences. It is a sort of sublimation for a learned behavior pattern that has been thwarted. Supported by imaginative reproductions of previous pleasures, these "friendships", even of the nonphysical type, serve as a sublimation.

That these girls are not truly inverted is evidenced by the lack of fidelity, the ease with which the friendship is broken by close contact, and the fact that they do not persist in homosexuality after their release from the institution. Now and then actual neuropathic inverts may be found in the institution, but they are likely to be in even smaller percentage than in the rest of the world. This because homosexuals are not molested by the police so often for obvious reasons.

Throughout this discussion two main trends are seen to pervade the practice: first, sexual sublimation, and second, breaking rules. If this is as true as apparent, it would seem that the practice could be better controlled by affording socially acceptable sublimations and less attention to the efforts of repression. Treat it much as masturbation should be treated: neither forbidding nor encouraging it, but supplying the person with tiring, interesting activities and a maximum of social contacts. This would probably lead to an increase in its incidence temporarily, but eventually it could be expected to dwindle. The principles underlying the suggestion are the same as for any other reform, sublimation by positive measures rather than repression by negative ones.[69]

1915–16: GARDNER JACKSON;
Robert Frost, Stark Young, and Homophobia at Amherst

In 1915, a young man named Gardner Jackson entered Amherst College and joined a fraternity where he was for the first time confronted with heterosexual "orgies" and the homosexual advances of two members. He was also confronted by the interest of a popular homosexual English professor, Stark Young, as well as by the antihomosexual behavior of another teacher, poet Robert Frost, who urged Stark Young's dismissal. In 1953, Gardner Jackson recorded his reminiscences, which are now deposited in the Oral History Research Office of Columbia University. Interestingly, in these memoirs, it is the mixture of puritanism and jealousy motivating Robert Frost's antihomosexual attitudes and acts upon which Jackson focuses. Although dealing with the interest of a homosexual professor gave Jackson pause, it is Frost's bigotry that provokes Jackson's most critical comment. Frost's behavior constitutes a classic case of homophobia, a major form of trouble confronting Gay people.

Gardner Jackson first recalls his introduction to fraternity life at Amherst.

The fraternity was the strangest aggregation of human beings I've ever seen gathered together—really ill-fitting fellows one with another. In that fraternity life I had my first real indoctrination into the whole business of high, wide and handsome sex opportunities, which because of my bringing up, my God, horrified hell out of me. . . . The attempt was made to impress me into the joys of the use of a fraternity for strip poker games and all night [heterosexual] orgies, which I just never could engage in and just ran away from. . . .

The thing of the fraternity on the negative side that really seemed most bad to me was . . . a small delegation, as I remember, of eight or nine. They were not very high level fellows. There was one in particular who was a great problem to me. . . . The really disturbing aspect of him and one other fellow in the delegation was that they began quite early to manifest homosexual proclivities. That was *extremely* uncomfortable to me. I was the object of the approach of these two fellows. . . .[70]

Jackson reminisces:

. . . I had a hell of a freshman year. . . . I took English and English became a major piece of business for me, because of the two guys who were the two top fellows in the English department.

One of these was Robert P. Utter.

The other fellow was one Stark Young. Stark Young, for some reason, wanted me to be his protege. He made a real play for me both those two years, freshman and sophomore. It was a very upsetting and uncomfortable experience to me. I sound as if I were obsessed with this problem, but it, as in the fraternity, was a quite clear manifestation of homosexuality. He used to get Andy [Jackson's friend, Andrew R. Morehouse] and me down to his little home on Amity Street, as I remember, of an evening, with very dim lights, incense burning, and read us the off-color French, and whatnot, literature, trying to induce us into the joys of the abnormal business.[71]

In his sophomore year, Jackson took a Shakespeare course with Robert Frost, who also seems to have found this young man attractive:

I really can't explain why Robert Frost singled me out of the class to become his friend. My recollection is that he started by asking me to go on a walk with him one Saturday out across the Connecticut Valley. It had snowed and was very beautiful. We walked, I imagine, ten or twelve miles on that first walk. . . . he quite quickly . . . began to argue with me about going on in college. He thought that I oughtn't to, that it was a waste of my time, and that I ought to do what he said he had done, which was to interrupt his college course by going on the bum for a couple of years. I think he had a notion that I, in his judgment, had potentials as a writer.[72]

Jackson says that his relationship with Frost

became one involving rather intimate discussion about other members of the faculty and particularly about Stark Young, because he [Frost] seemed to find in Stark Young the exact opposite of himself and an opposite that he, in his expression, certainly seemed to loathe. He loathed him even too much. It was so much that it seemed to me to indicate an envy or a wishing that he might have some of the qualities or interests that Stark Young had. He seemed to me almost obsessed with a preoccupation to paw over Stark Young's eroticism and interest in erotic literature. . . . I found in Frost something of my own Puritan background, Puritan upbringing, and an interest in, and maybe an over-emphasized interest in, the stuff that was anti-Puritan. But of course his expression of real affection and warmth for me were obviously part of the relationship. It wasn't just a sheer intellectual relationship. I was very fond of him as a friend, and he seemed to be similarly fond of me as a guy whom he seemed to want to make his protege.

Jackson emphasizes Frost's

almost prurient interest in the non-moral, or maybe immoral, activities of the then literati. He didn't criticize their works, but rather the artists themselves, their habits, their way of life. . . .[73]

Robert Frost's biographer, Lawrance Thompson, discusses Gardner Jackson's reminiscences, explaining the conflict between Robert Frost and Stark Young (a brief commentary which the Permissions Manager of Holt, Rinehart and Winston would not allow to be quoted). Thompson reports Jackson's and other students' surprise at Robert Frost's malicious delight in spreading rumors about his fellow teachers. Stark Young, says Thompson, because of his popularity, was the focus of Frost's jealous dislike; Young's humor, teaching ability and success contrasted with Frost's inability to manage his own students. The naive Jackson, by mentioning Stark Young's homoerotic interests to Frost, gave Frost ammunition to use in his war against Young. Frost went so far as to ask Amherst President Meiklejohn to fire Young. But, Thompson notes, Meiklejohn thought Young too fine a teacher to fire simply because of his homoerotic proclivities.[74]

♀ 1925–27: CHRIS ALBERTSON;
Lesbianism in the Life of Bessie Smith

When you see two women walking hand in hand,
    Just look 'em over and try to understand:
They'll go to those parties—have the lights down low—
    Only those parties where women can go.
You think I'm lying—just ask Tack Ann—
    Took many a broad from many a man. . . .
                    "The Boy in the Boat" (1930)

I know women that don't like men
The way they do is a crying sin.
It's dirty but good, oh, yes, it's dirty but good
There ain't much difference, it's just dirty but good.
"It's Dirty But Good"[75] (1930)

A section in Chris Albertson's recent biography of Bessie Smith (1972) discusses the "wide range" of the famous Black blues singer's "sexual tastes." The narrative centers around Smith's violent conflict with her husband Jack Gee over the women in Smith's love life. Albertson's account provides a rare glimpse into the hectic affairs and husband-trouble of a Black, female, woman-loving blues singer in the mid-1920s.

For his biography of Bessie Smith, Albertson tape-recorded interviews with, among others, Ruby Walker, Smith's niece by marriage, who spent many years with her aunt as a performer in her shows and later as a close companion. Albertson's account of Bessie Smith's Lesbianism is evidently based on Ruby Walker's recollections. Albertson's biography is written with regard for accuracy of historical detail, and, in reference to conversations he quotes, Albertson says, "All dialogue . . . is taken verbatim from firsthand recollections; it may not give the actual words spoken, but I believe it captures the essence of what was said."

The Black blues songs quoted above indicate that Lesbianism was not an unmentionable subject on those Columbia recordings designed for sale to Black people and called "race records." The touring company organized by Bessie Smith included Boula Lee, a chorister with a sexual interest in other women. Male impersonator Gladys Fergusson is mentioned as an intimate of Bessie Smith's, and another famous blues singer, Bessie Smith's early teacher, Ma Rainey, is cited as a woman-loving woman. Porter Grainger, the Black composer of one of Bessie Smith's musicals, is mentioned as homosexual.[76]

Chris Albertson writes:

Bessie tried to keep Jack from discovering several aspects of her private life, such as the wide range of her sexual tastes. Fortunately Jack could not read; otherwise he might have seen a short item in a black gossip paper called the *Interstate Tattler*. Its publisher, Floyd Snelson, made other people's business his business. . . . His item on Bessie appeared in the paper's "Town Tattle" column on February 27, 1925, under the by-line "I. Telonyou":

Gladys, if you don't keep away from B., G. is going to do a little convincing that he is her husband. Aren't you capable of finding some unexplored land "all alone."

Fortunately for Snelson, Bessie, who was said to be chummy with male impersonator Gladys Ferguson at that time, neither saw nor heard about the item.

It is not known at what stage in her life Bessie began to embrace her own sex. Some have assumed that Ma Rainey, who was similarly inclined, initiated her, but this theory is supported by no more evidence than the improbable story of Bessie's "kidnapping." But by late 1926, when Lillian Simpson entered her life, Bessie's sexual relationships included women.

Like many young girls, Lillian, who had been a schoolmate of Ruby's, romanti-cized show business life. At sixteen her head was filled with hazy pictures of life on the road; her heart was set on becoming, at the least, a chorine. Ruby's tales of her touring experience impressed Lillian and she persuaded Ruby to teach her a few dance steps. Ruby then arranged an impromptu audition before Bessie in the Gee living room on 132nd Street. The last thing the show needed was another chorus girl, but Lillian's mother had once been Bessie's wardrobe mistress, so Bessie finally gave in, and even started teaching the young girl some additional steps.

And so Bessie headed south with Ruby and Lillian, joining her *Harlem Frolics* company in Ozark, Alabama, on the first of November. . . .

. . . Just before the troupe got ready to pull out of Ozark, a chorus girl told Bessie that while she was in New York, Jack had "messed around" with another chorus girl.

Without taking time to check out the story, Bessie jumped the girl, beat her up, and threw her off the railroad car, which was still parked on a dead track. . . . Then she stormed through the railroad car looking for Jack. . . .

Bessie didn't find Jack on the car . . . but she found his gun, and when she came out of their stateroom, Jack was standing over the sobbing girl, trying to find out what had happened.

A shot rang out. Bessie stood on the rear platform of the car, gun in hand.

"You no good two-timing bastard," she shouted, waving the gun in the air. "I couldn't even go to New York and record without you fuckin' around with these damn chorus bitches. Well, I'm gonna make you remember me today."

Jack started toward her. "Put that gun down, Bessie." Another shot sent him racing down the track. Bessie jumped off the platform and went after him, empty-ing the gun. "I've never seen Jack run so fast," recalls Ruby. "Everybody was scared to death that Bessie would kill him this time, but I think she missed him on purpose." A couple of hours later the troupe left Ozark without Jack.

Bessie had been on good behavior for several months, and now she was ready for some fun. Jack's departure after the alleged indiscretion provided both the opportunity and the excuse.

The troupe spent Christmas of 1926 on the road somewhere in Tennessee, where Bessie threw a small party for her gang. She went out and got eggs, milk, and liquor for eggnog, but after the girls had beaten the eggs and added sugar and liquor, Bessie had second thoughts about the milk—it seemed a shame to dilute that good corn liquor any further. The resulting concoction left no one sober.

As the party showed signs of ending, Bessie approached Ruby, cocked her head in Lillian's direction, and said, "I *like* that gal." Ruby assumed that she was referring to Lillian's dance routine, which had improved in the past month. "I'm glad you like her—she's doing good, ain't she?"

"No, I don't mean that," said her aunt. "I'll tell her myself, 'cause you don't know *nothin'*, child." Whereupon she walked over to Lillian, whispered something to her, and led her out of the room.

Ruby and Lillian shared a room, but when Ruby awoke the next day she saw that Lillian had not slept in her bed. No one in the troupe was shocked when Lillian and Bessie began sleeping together regularly. The one thing the members of the *Harlem Frolics* company were worried about was Jack's sudden, inevitable return.

Lillian herself seemed to adjust to her relationship with Bessie as quickly as she had adjusted to the other unorthodox aspects of her newly chosen profession. The day after her initiation, she confessed to Ruby what was going on, suggesting that Ruby didn't know what she was missing, and that she "try it" with Boula Lee, a chorus girl who was also the wife of the show's musical director, Bill Woods. Boula had made subtle passes at Ruby, but Bessie had warned her niece that she'd be sent home if she fooled around with any of the girls in the show.

Several days later, Bessie was on stage at the Frolic Theatre in Bessemer, Alabama, singing; the chorus was ready to go on. Ruby, first in line, stood in the wings not far from where Bessie was performing. Ruby had developed a boil under her left arm, and was holding her painful left arm in the air. Concentrating on her cue, she did not notice Dinah Scott [a male, comedian, and stage manager] sneaking up behind her. He grabbed her under the arms and Ruby let out a scream.

Bessie kept on singing, but she jerked her head in Ruby's direction and frowned: she never tolerated any noise from backstage during a performance. Helen, another chorine, ran forward with a tissue and put her arms around Ruby while she gently daubed at what was left of the boil.

Boula, looking on from the other side of the stage, misunderstood Helen's intentions. Shortly after the curtain came down, she stomped over to Ruby and asked her to step outside. "You ain't gonna mess around with them other bitches," she said, then lunged forward and scratched Ruby's face. Ruby fought back, and the two were deeply entangled when Bessie made a sudden appearance.

"I know Jack's gonna blame me for this," said Bessie, separating the two and knocking Boula clear across the small alley.

Jack was due to join the show that night, and when he showed up, Bessie was ready for him. Several members of the troupe were sitting in her room when Jack entered and looked around. "What y'all doin' up here drinkin'?"

"Nobody been drinkin' any liquor, nigger," said Bessie. "You're not in the police force, you're in show business, so don't come in here pushin' on people all the damn time."

During this exchange Ruby had been standing with her back to Jack. When Jack asked her to turn around, she explained—as her aunt had instructed her—that her face was scratched because she and some of the girls had fought over costumes. Bessie was adding a few details when Bill Woods, who had been standing quietly in the corner, blurted out, "It was one of them bulldykers who's after Ruby."

"What do you mean *one* of them?" Bessie shouted. "It was *your* wife!"

Jack grabbed Boula, carried her into the hall, threw her down the stairs, and ordered Woods to send her home. While Jack was out of the room, Bessie noticed the fear in Lillian's face. Turning to Ruby, she said, "Whatever you do, you better not tell on me and Lillian."

On January 10, 1927, Bessie's show began a week's engagement at the Booker Washington Theatre in St. Louis. Jack had left the troupe again, and Bessie and Lillian continued their affair. On their first day in St. Louis, Bessie entered the room shared by Ruby and Lillian. She walked up behind Lillian, leaned forward, and kissed her.

Embarrassed, Lillian looked at Ruby and jerked away. "Don't play around with me like that," she said.

Bessie grabbed her around the waist. "Is that how you feel?"

"Yes!" Lillian said. "That's *exactly* how I feel."

"The hell with you, bitch," said Bessie. "I got twelve women on this show and I can have one every night if I want it. Don't you feel so important, and don't you say another word to me while you're on this show, or I'll send you home bag and baggage."

For three days and nights Bessie ignored Lillian totally. On the fourth night Lillian did not show up at the theatre. The show went on without her, but as soon as the curtain fell Bessie started to worry. "She's just tryin' to pout," she told Ruby. Just then, Maud burst into the room. "I had left the theatre and gone into the hotel," she recalls. "When I passed Lillian's room, I saw an envelope sticking out from under the door. The door was locked, so I pulled the envelope out, opened it and saw that it was a suicide note. That's when I ran back to the theatre to get Bessie."

Without taking time to read the note, Bessie, with Ruby and Maud at her heels, ran next door to the hotel. When they reached Lillian's door, they smelled gas. Bessie tried to force the door, panicked, rushed downstairs, and got the proprietor. When he let them in, they found Lillian lying across the bed, unconscious. The proprietor had to break the windowpanes: Lillian had nailed the window shut. She was taken in an ambulance to the nearest hospital.

Bessie didn't sleep that night. The next morning she went to the hospital and got Lillian out. The episode apparently put an end to Lillian's inhibitions. "From that day on," says Ruby, "she didn't care where or when Bessie kissed her—she got real bold."

Bessie and company played the Roosevelt Theatre in Cincinnati during the week of January 17, and opened at the Grand in Chicago the following Monday. . . .

During their stay in Chicago Lillian first tried to leave the show. She had lost her inhibitions but not her fear; Jack, she knew, would find out about her and Bessie sooner or later, and she wanted to get out while the getting was good. Bessie persuaded her to stay.

But when they opened at the Koppin Theatre in Detroit on February 5, Lillian decided to leave once and for all. This time Bessie expressed no anger, made no pleas.

The affair with Lillian had kept Bessie relatively sober, but on the night following Lillian's departure, she cut loose. Detroit was a fine town for that. On previous trips, Bessie had befriended a woman* who ran a buffet flat. Buffet flats—sometimes referred to as good-time flats—were small, privately owned establishments featuring all sorts of illegal activities: gambling and erotic shows, as well as sex acts of every conceivable kind. These buffet flats were usually owned by women, who ran them with admirable efficiency, catering to the occasional thrill-seeker as well as to regular clients whose personal tastes they knew intimately. . . .

Each time Bessie appeared at the Koppin, her proprietress friend would send one or two cars to the stage door to transport Bessie and her party—usually a coterie of girls who knew how to keep their mouths shut—to the notorious establishment. The night after Lillian left, Bessie took five girls, including Ruby, with her. As they walked out the stage door she delivered a familiar threat: "If any of you tell Jack about this, you'll never work in my shows again."

---

* Immortalized by Bessie in "Soft Pedal Blues."

The house was packed with all kinds of people. Laughing pleasure-seekers, drinks in hand, formed human chains as they wandered up and down the linoleum-covered staircase, stopping in the various rooms along the way to take a peek at the shows. "It was nothing but faggots and bulldykers, a real open house. Everything went on in that house—tongue baths, you name it. They called them buffet flats because buffet means everything, everything that was in the life. Bessie was well known in that place."

Bessie's pleasure-seeking that night was limited to watching and drinking. That was usually the extent of her activity in such places, for she could ill afford to have word get back to Jack.

Although the flat's most popular attraction that season seemed to be a young man who made expert love to another man, Bessie was most intrigued by an obese lady who performed an amazing trick with a lighted cigarette, then repeated it in the old-fashioned way with a Coca-Cola bottle. . . .

After two hours or so, she gathered her girls together and took them back to Kate's theatrical boardinghouse, where the troupe was staying. . . .

As was their custom, especially on a closing night, they all changed into nightgowns and pajamas and paraded from room to room, drinking, eating some of Bessie's cooking, passing along the latest gossip.

On this night they all wound up in Bessie's room on the first floor. Marie, a young girl who did a ballet-tap dance number in the show, was wearing a pair of bright-red pajamas Bessie had bought her, and everybody laughed when she did a few comic steps in them. Bessie laughed loudest. "C'mon, Marie, show your stuff," she shouted.

. . . "We were drinking, clowning, and having ourselves a ball in Bessie's room, and, as usual, I was the first one to pass out—I just couldn't keep up with that crowd," recalls Ruby. Someone carried her to her room, which adjoined Bessie's, and a couple of hours passed before she was awakened by shouts and running footsteps outside her door. She jumped out of bed, dashed to the door, and opened it.

The first thing Ruby saw was Marie tearing down the corridor. Bessie, right on her heels, almost knocked Ruby over as she pushed into her room and locked the door behind her. All hell was breaking loose: Jack had made one of his surprise appearances and caught Marie in a compromising situation with Bessie.

Bessie was terrified as only Jack could make her. "If Jack knocks, you don't know where I'm at," she said to Ruby. They huddled together as Jack's heavy footsteps passed down the corridor. "Come out here, I'm going to kill you tonight, you bitch," he shouted.

There were further threats and pacing until Kate stepped out of her room and pleaded for calm.

"I think I know where she is," they heard Jack say in a softer tone, "but when she comes back, you tell her I'm lookin' for her." His voice trailed off as he stepped down the wooden stairway that led to the street.

Bessie waited a few seconds, then got Ruby to open the door and check the lay of the land. The other members of the troupe were now standing in their doorways or at the top of the staircase, waiting for Bessie to make her next move. She told them to gather whatever they could carry of their belongings, and head for the train depot. They all obliged, quickly and quietly—everybody was scared of Jack, and that night he was angrier than they had ever seen him.

No one took the time to dress. Carrying armloads of clothes and other personal effects, the troupe made its way through the cold February night to Bessie's railroad car. At Bessie's instructions no lights were turned on, and the dark car was hitched to the next outgoing train. Fortunately Jack didn't find them; an hour later the Empress, still in her pajamas, quietly slipped out of Detroit with her entourage.

The following chapter in Albertson's biography opens:

> *. . . There's two things got me puzzled, there's*
> *two things I don't understand;*
> *That's a mannish-acting woman, and a*
> *skipping, twistin' woman-acting man.*
> "Foolish Man Blues"

Bessie knew, of course, what she was singing about when she recorded those words in 1927. Most urban blacks—whether they indulged or not—accepted homosexuality as a fact of life. Jack probably did, too, but not when it was so close to home. Not that he was totally straitlaced—he did indulge in heterosexual promiscuity. He may have suspected Bessie's sexual interest in women before the incident with Marie, but that appears to have been his first actual confrontation with his wife's bisexuality. Clearly it was more than he was prepared to take.

Their getaway successful, Bessie and her company headed for Columbus, Ohio, where they were scheduled to open at the Pythian Theatre. Fortunately, most of the costumes and all the drops had been put on the train right after the last show in Detroit, but many of the troupe's personal effects had been left behind at Kate's in the hasty exit. "That's how I lost the only fur coat I ever had," Ruby recalls. "I had to leave it at Kate's—Bessie took us out of Detroit almost naked."

Following the first evening performance at the Pythian, some local admirers joined members of Bessie's troupe for a drink in her dressing room. . . . Any performer who had spent time with a Bessie Smith show was automatically on the alert for a sudden appearance of Jack, but this time he caught them all off guard. No one except Ruby even noticed him until he was halfway into the room. . . .

Jack charged into the crowded dressing room and knocked Bessie to the floor. "I'm not going to do any more to you now," he said, looking down at her, "but wait until the show is done tonight—you ain't a man, but you better be like one because we're gonna have it out." He would be waiting at the hotel, he said, and walked out.

Bessie wasn't ready to face Jack. "I'm in real trouble now," she told Ruby after clearing her room of performers and guests, "and I ain't about to mess with Jack as mad as he is. Fix my feathers, baby, and let's get this show over with and get out of town."[77]

♀ 1926–27: New York *Times*; The Reaction to *The Captive*
"The tyranny of her warped infatuation"

On September 30, 1926, J. Brooks Atkinson, in the *New York Times*, reviews *The Captive*, a tragedy translated from the French play by Edouard Bourdet, which had opened the previous night in New York City.

. . . As most theatre enthusiasts know by this time, "The Captive" writes the tragedy of a young woman, well-bred and of good family, who falls into a twisted relationship with another woman. For nearly half the play this loathsome possibility, never mentioned, scarcely hinted at, hangs over the drama like a black pall, a prescience of impending doom. A member of the Foreign Office, ordered to Rome, cannot understand why his oldest daughter refuses to accompany him. Thoroughly distraught, she puts him off with an evasion. Her old friend, Jacques Vierieu, she pleads, is in love with her, and may propose to her if properly manoeuvred. When her father departs Irène summons Jacques and tries to persuade him to play the part of fiancé, a part agreeable to him, but not on these false terms. For Irène refuses to confide in him, nor in any one else, the full truth of her frightful misery.

During the remaining two acts M. Bourdet directs his story expertly at high speed, facing the issue boldly and sounding the note of doom with increasing frequency. Fully conscious of his responsibilities, Jacques marries Irène immediately to save her from herself and to release her from the tyranny of her warped infatuation. For a year spent in travel they get on amicably and return to Paris, where they set up their home. But Irène does not escape for long; nor does Jacques. In self-defense he resumes a liaison with his former sweetheart. And just before the final curtain Irène succumbs. The sound of a closing door off-stage completes this sombre story.

Relentless in his presentation of this theme, M. Bourdet occasionally sets it off against the simple innocence of a little sister or the refreshing normality of Jacques and the charming Françoise Meillant. Without this illuminating relief "The Captive" might degenerate into commercial exploitation of a revolting theme. . . .[78]

On October 25, the *Times* indicates that the content of theatrical productions is becoming a subject of controversy in the political area.

MAKE SHOWS CLEAN, HINT FROM WALKER

Mayor Tells Catholic Actors Guild Some Producers Will Have to Change Ways.

READY TO TACKLE THEATRE

Opposed to Stage Censorship as "Un-American and Impossible of Performance."

That the City Administration may cross words with some of the theatrical producers unless the moral tone of several productions in town is elevated in the near future was intimated last night by Mayor Walker. . . .[79]

On October 29, the *Times* reports that three unidentified plays were under police investigation.[80]

On November 15, the *Times* reports the first test that year of the "play jury"; a body of twelve men and women who would meet that day

to decide whether "The Captive" is an objectionable and salacious play. "The Captive" deals frankly, although delicately, according to reviewers, with highly complicated and suggestive psychopathic relationships.

The play jury had been in operation the previous year, making judgments and advising the district attorney concerning material it found salacious in New York City theatrical performances. Organized groups of dramatists, producers, and actors had agreed that the "verdict of the jury shall in all cases be complied with." Some saw this informal play jury structure as a way of heading off state censorship by a legally appointed board. The district attorney had reportedly agreed to abide by the play jury's decisions. The jury's meeting on November 15 took place in the district attorney's office.[81]

The following day, November 16, the *Times* reports:

VOTE OF PLAY JURY FREES 'THE CAPTIVE'

Six Ballots Condemn the Play, Five Clear It, One Is Blank—Nine Needed to Convict.

THREE JURORS ARE WOMEN

Further Action Unlikely—Hornblow Sees Test of Whether Stage May Treat "Adult Subjects" Decently.

New York's play jury released "The Captive" yesterday from danger of suspension or expurgation after two hours of discussion. . . .

None of those present, either within or without the jury room, would comment on the procedure, except Mr. [Arthur] Hornblow [the play's translator], who said:

"This is a rather critical case for the theatre. It will test whether adult subjects may be treated hereafter in a decent way on the stage. The moving pictures have left the legitimate stage only the adult portion of the public, speaking from an intellectual standpoint.

"The type of persons who still go to the spoken drama are not the type who would be menaced by subjects of rather an advanced nature. . . ."[82]

On December 29, the *Times* reports:

MAYOR STARTS WAR ON IMMORAL PLAYS

Warns Producers Censorship Will Result Unless They Voluntarily Clean Stage.

THREAT BRINGS PROMISES

Theatrical Men Expected to Name Controller—Walker Told Public Wants 'Risque' Shows.

Mayor Walker, who recently imposed a 3 A.M. curfew on the night clubs, called the leading theatrical producers to the City Hall yesterday and warned them that censorship would result unless they voluntarily cleaned up the stage. The producers promised to cooperate with the Mayor. . . .

Many complaints have been received at the City Hall about the salacious dialogue and situations of certain plays and the nudity of chorus girls in certain musical shows now on Broadway. The last straw, it is understood, came when plans were announced for the production of a new play, said to be even more daring than one which has particularly aroused unfavorable comment because of the subject it deals with.[83]

The reference is to a forthcoming production of Mae West's play *The Drag*, which, like *The Captive*, dealt with an aspect of the homosexual subculture.
On January 21, 1927, the *Times* carries a letter from a concerned mother.

Suggestions for Play Censorship.

To the Editor of The New York Times:

As a mother of growing children there is one suggestion I would like to make to Mayor Walker on the subject of play censorship, and that is that all forms of sex perversion be banned as subjects for dramatic or musical comedy material.

Curiosity is one of the greatest of lures at the dangerous period of adolescence. I have been compelled to enlighten my children on subjects that they have heard discussed or seen depicted upon the stage that are dangerously suggestive and unnecessary. Nakedness and sex appeal along normal lines may discount modesty and outrage good taste, but perversion is a horror and social smallpox that should be treated in the segregation of the pest house laboratory.

ELSIE McCORMACK.

Jackson Heights, L. I., Jan. 18, 1927.[84]

On February 1, 1927, the *Times* reports:

Three committees, one composed of theatrical producers, another of actors and the third of playwrights, will meet tomorrow afternoon to ascertain how the stage may be purified so that the threatened drastic censorship of the theatre may be avoided. . . .

It is expected that tomorrow's meeting will discuss plans for presenting the case against censorship before the legislative committee at Albany, which is to hold a public hearing on a proposed censorship law. This law is modeled on the English plan and provides for the submission of manuscripts to a censor before production.

The entire movement is a direct result of Mayor Walker's warning to the producers that unless they voluntarily cleaned house stage censorship would follow. The producers will undoubtedly have certain proposals to submit to the Mayor when he returns from his trip to Havana, Cuba.

A "special" dispatch to the *Times* adds:

"Captive" Approved at Princeton

. . . .

The ninety Princeton seniors taking the course in the development of the drama under Dr. Donald Clive Stuart, asked to list all the plays they had seen during the term and to choose the one they liked best, giving their reasons, selected Edouard Bourdet's "The Captive." . . .

"The Captive" received fourteen votes for the best play, and it was seen by more students than any other. One man picked it because "it is a decent treatment of an indecent theme," another because "it fooled the play jury," but the principal reason for its popularity, according to the answers, is that it is a "beautifully made and beautifully presented play." Several men liked it because of the personal attractiveness of Helen Mencken.[85]

Another "special" dispatch to the *Times* is headed:

"The Drag" Opens at Bridgeport.

BRIDGEPORT, Conn. . . . "The Drag," a new play by Jane Mast [Mae West], author of "Sex," had its premier at the old Park Theatre here tonight after being barred from a Stamford theatre.

This is the play which is said to have caused the sudden action on the part of New York managers toward cleaning up the stage there. It is scheduled to open in New York soon.

The first night audience here included many visitors from New York. The play was ostensibly presented in the same spirit in which "Damaged Goods" was given to the theatre-going public. A physician was discovered at centre stage when the curtain rolled up on the first act. He was there with his moral when the final curtain fell. This presumably was intended to sterilize what went on.

The play purports to put across the message that certain persons are more to be pitied than censured. The Bridgeport police censor decided that there was a strong enough message in the play to warrant the local color used in lending force to the message.[86]

Two days later, on February 3, 1927, the *Times* reports:

STAGE WORKS OUT CENSORSHIP PLAN; CITY GETS IT TODAY

. . . . . .

After three hours of discussion at the offices of the Actors' Equity Association . . . representatives of the actors, producers and playwrights agreed yesterday on a tentative plan for regulating the theatre without censorship.

. . . If it is acceptable to the District Attorney and the city administration, it will be immediately worked out in detail and adopted, in the hope of averting the danger that the Legislature may establish an official censorship over the stage. . . .

The citizens' play jury plan is still nominally in effect, although since the last jury gave a favorable verdict on "The Captive" no effort has been made to invoke that tribunal.

The citizens' play juries functioned with unexpected liberality. . . . The failure of the jury to bring in more radical verdicts disappointed many members of the reform organizations which backed the play jury system. John S. Sumner, Secretary of the New York Society for the Suppression of Vice, and other sponsors withdrew their support and are now advocating censorship. . . .

William Morganstern, producer of "The Drag," said yesterday that he had his choice of any one of three theatres for that drama and that he expected to have it on Broadway at an early date, possibly next week.[87]

On February 9, a *Times* story suggested that a conference of police officials presaged raids on plays. And on February 10, the *Times*'s front-page main headline reads:

POLICE RAID THREE SHOWS, SEX, CAPTIVE AND VIRGIN MAN; HOLD ACTORS AND MANAGERS

ALL GO TO NIGHT COURT

Police Politely Serve the Warrants After the Final Curtains.

VICTIMS NOT UNWILLING

Submit Cordially to Arrests, Which Will Be Repeated Till Plays Are Purged.

41 ARE RELEASED IN BAIL

Two Shows Had Been Cleared by the Play Jury— Drive May Be Extended to Others.

Among those in *The Captive* cast arrested were its stars, Basil Rathbone and Helen Mencken. Mae West, the star of *Sex*, was also arrested, along with twenty cast members.[88]

The following day, February 11, a banner headline in the *Times* declares:

RAIDED SHOWS STAY OPEN; INJUNCTIONS STOP POLICE

. . . . . .

"The Captive," "Sex" and "The Virgin Man," the producers and casts of which were arrested Wednesday night, were performed last night under the protection of Supreme Court injunctions.

The management of "The Virgin Man" at the Princess Theatre had withdrawn advertising and sent out notices that the play would close Saturday night. After Wednesday night's raid, however, the management reconsidered the intention to close and announced that the show would continue open in the expectation of a long run. . . .

District Attorney Banton said yesterday that he would prosecute those implicated in the production of "The Captive" and "Sex" in spite of the fact that they had been acquitted by play juries. . . .

Varying reasons were advanced yesterday for the sudden police activity against shows which had been permitted to run without molestation for months. It was admitted that "Sex" was not worse than it was eleven months ago, and "The Captive" no worse than it was four months ago. Mr. Banton said that many complaints had come from many sources against the drama, showing that the public was thoroughly aroused. . . .[89]

On February 13, the *Times* reports:

RAIDED SHOWS PLAY TO CROWDED HOUSES

One [The Virgin Man], Expiring, Is Brought Back to Life
by Police Campaign—May Seek Bigger Theatre.

PRODUCER DROPS 'THE DRAG'

No Further Effort Will Be Made to
Present It, He Declares.[90]

On February 21, a *Times* headline reads:

CITY SPEEDS ACTION IN 'CAPTIVE' CASE

Impetus to State Censorship Seen if Play Wins—
Police Raiding Power at Stake.

INJUNCTIONS UP THURSDAY

Many Preachers Assail Sections of Theatre and
Press as Aids to Immorality.

. . . . . .

A speedy determination of the right of the police to raid attempted performances of "The Captive" will be sought by the city, according to Assistant Corporation Counsel Russell L. Tarbox, who said yesterday that a legal victory for "The Captive" would give the strongest possible impetus to the movement at Albany in favor of establishing a censorship of the stage by legislative enactment. . . .[91]

On February 26, a *Times* headline reads:

WALKER SATISFIED BY STAGE CLEAN-UP

Police to Take the Initiative Henceforth, He Says.

The report says that the mayor

believes that much good has been done by the suppression of "The Captive" and the suits brought against two other shows [*Sex* and *The Virgin Man*].[92]

On March 7, the *Times* reports John S. Sumner, head of the Society for the Suppression of Vice, advocated "an aggressive campaign for the establishment of legislative censorship." The report adds:

Maurice B. Blumenthal, who as Assistant District Attorney twenty-five years ago led the crusade which drove "Sappho" from the New York stage, discussed the censorship question in a statement yesterday. Describing the once scandalous staircase scene from "Sappho," which caused such moral indignation a quarter of a century ago, Mr. Blumenthal said:

"The decency of the show was challenged by many worthy citizens, and according to the standards of morality obtaining at that time the play was indecent. Our standards as to dress, conversation, conduct and morality generally have fluctuated, . . . but in the past twenty-five years they have been woefully lowered. . . ."

Speakers at a meeting of the Jewish Theatrical Guild referred to the theatrical presentation of "abnormality":

Censorship was characterized as "despotic" by Rabbi Nathan Krass, who said the only true censorship was that of the theatre-going public. "We don't want the stage converted into a dumping ground for the moral and spiritual garbage of the human race," he added, "and plays dealing with abnormality belong to the psychopathists and psychoanalysts. But unless the managers decide to discontinue vicious plays I fear the law will intervene."

Actor Wilton Lackaye is quoted as saying that "plays dealing with abnormality should not be available to invite the attendance of young girls. . . ."[93]

By this time the original production of *The Captive* had closed and Horace B. Liveright had negotiated to reopen it—if he could obtain a legal ruling to prevent police interference.

On March 9, the *Times* headline reads:

'CAPTIVE' IMMORAL, MAHONEY DECIDES

Justice Then Denies Injunction to Protect Liveright in Reproducing Play.

UPHOLDS LITERARY QUALITY

But Views Theme as Harmful to Some Persons in Audience Who Should Be Guarded.

DECISION TO BE APPEALED

Supreme Court Justice Jeremiah A. Mahoney ruled yesterday that "The Captive" was immoral and refused to grant an injunction preventing the District Attorney, the police and others from interfering with the effort of Horace B. Liveright to produce it. Mr. Liveright and his counsel, Arthur Garfield Hays, said that they would appeal immediately. . . .

Justice Mahoney gave the opinion that the drama had excellent literary quality and that it might not harm a mature and intelligent audience. On the other hand, he held that it might have dangerous effects on some persons in an indiscriminate, cosmopolitan audience. . . . On that ground, he held that the police and the District Attorney had acted correctly in seeking to stop "The Captive" and to prevent its revival.

The judge asked rhetorically if the obscenity statute did not look

to the protection, not of the mature and intelligent . . . but of the young and immature, the ignorant and sensually inclined?

The opinion referred to the affidavits of Police Commissioner McLaughlin that 70 per cent. of the audience on Saturday night, Feb. 5, were under 25 years of age. In a box near the police sat four boys not over 18 years. Women comprised 60 per cent. of the audience, and groups of unescorted girls in twos and threes sat together, the statements said.

"I can readily realize," continued Justice Mahoney, "that an audience of intelligent and mature minds could not possibly be swayed or influenced by any portrayal of a theme or characters, no matter how obscene, but the ordinary and average gatherings of human beings in a cosmopolitan city like this are not of such a nature and the law recognizes the fact that many people must be protected from their very selves.

"Taking into consideration the natural effect and tendency of this play, I readily have reached the conclusion that it does offend the statute against the obscene drama."[94]

On March 19, the *Times* reports that the case of *The Captive* had been appealed before the appellate division of the New York City court system on March 17.

Arthur Garfield Hays made the main argument in favor of "The Captive" as counsel for Horace B. Liveright, who bought the play after it had been raided by the police. Mr. Hays made his argument on the ground of free intellectual discussion of a problem in which, he contended, nothing immoral or lecherous took place.

Mr. Hays said that the statute under which action was taken against the play has to do with plays "which excite sexual or lecherous desire," and with plays which excite impure imagination.

"It is the contention of Mr. Liveright," he said, "that there is not a word, line or thought in the play that could or would excite lustful emotion; that, on the contrary, it is a literary masterpiece of high social value. The subject matter of 'The Captive' has been dealt with in some of the most famous classics of history. The matter is handled in a delicate, artistic, subtle and inoffensive manner. There is not an offensive or vulgar line in the play, nor is there any obscene or unrefined situation or action."

The same day's *Times* reports that the New York State legislature in Albany was presented with "the so-called theatrical 'padlock bill' proposed by District Attorney Banton of New York and other public prosecutors in the city . . ." The Republican measure backed by Banton was thought to have a good chance of passing.[95]

The following month, on April 6, 1927, the bill "to amend the penal law, in relation to immoral plays" became New York State law. This law declared that any person who "presents or participates in, any obscene, indecent, immoral or impure" production "which would tend to the corruption of the morals of youth or others" was guilty of a misdemeanor. The same was true of anyone presenting any work "depicting or dealing with, the subject of sex degeneracy, or sex perversion . . ." The owner of a building used for the performance of any such play was also guilty of a misdemeanor, and upon conviction could lose the required operating license.

This New York State statute outlawing the presentation of homosexuality on the state's stages remained on the books until a general recodification of the laws in 1967.[96]

1950–55: Witch-Hunt;
The United States Government
versus Homosexuals

A sampling of news stories from the years 1950 to 1955 conveys the mood created by the antihomosexual, anti-Communist witch-hunts occurring during that period and continuing for some time after. In the early 1950s, the fledgling homosexual emancipation organization, the Mattachine Society, was just getting started in Los Angeles, with a number of left-wing homosexuals prominent in the leadership. To understand the earliest years of the Mattachine movement it is essential to know about the simultaneous witch-hunting of "perverts" and "subversives" then taking place.

On March 1, 1950, the *New York Times* reports that John E. Peurifoy, in charge of the State Department security program, was asked by a Senate committee how many department employees had resigned while under investigation as security risks since the beginning of 1947. "Ninety-one persons in the shady category," replied Mr. Peurifoy. "Most of these were homosexuals."[97]

On March 9, the *Times* reports a Senate subcommittee inquiry into Senator Joseph McCarthy's charges that the United States government employed "red sympathizers." McCarthy was the first witness, and homosexuality as well as Communism was an issue. McCarthy had earlier declared in the Senate that a "flagrantly homosexual" State Department employee, discharged as a security risk in 1946, had had his job restored under "pressure" from a "high State Department official." McCarthy refused demands by Democrats that he state the name of the official. Later, the *Times* reports, McCarthy told reporters he did not know the name of the official, but asserted it was in the files and could be found by the subcommittee.[98]

On March 15, the *Times* reports McCarthy's testimony about another government employee:

A former State Department official, whose name he withheld, was reported in the Washington police files to be homosexual and had been allowed to resign from the State Department in 1948 only to find employment in a "most sensitive" place, the Central Intelligence Agency. Mr. McCarthy gave his name privately to the subcommittee. It was an "important" case, he asserted, because perverts were officially considered to be security risks because they were "subject to blackmail."[99]

On March 20 the *Times* reports that Representative John J. Rooney, Democrat of New York, had accused the Commerce Department of laxity in weeding out homosexuals and praised the State Department for vigilance in that regard.[100]

On April 19, a *Times* news story is headed:

PERVERTS CALLED GOVERNMENT PERIL

Gabrielson, G.O.P. Chief, Says They Are as Dangerous as Reds

. . . Guy George Gabrielson, Republican National Chairman, asserted today that "sexual perverts who have infiltrated our Government in recent years" were "perhaps as dangerous as the actual Communists."

He elevated what he called the "homosexual angle" to the national political level in his first news letter of 1950, addressed to about 7,000 party workers, under the heading: "This Is the News from Washington."

Giving National Committee support to the campaign of Senator Joseph R. McCarthy, Republican of Wisconsin, against the State Department, but without mentioning him by name, Mr. Gabrielson said: . . .

"Perhaps as dangerous as the actual Communists are the sexual perverts who have infiltrated our Government in recent years. The State Department has confessed that it has had to fire ninety-one of these. It is the talk of Washington and of the Washington correspondents corps.

"The country would be more aroused over this tragic angle of the situation if it were not for the difficulties of the newspapers and radio commentators in adequately presenting the facts, while respecting the decency of their American audiences."[101]

On April 25, the *Times* reports a Republican demand

that an inquiry to determine whether "disloyal" persons were employed, be expanded to encompass the subject of sexual perversion within the Government.[102]

On April 26, the *Times* reports:

Senator Kenneth S. Wherry of Nebraska, the Republican floor leader, told the Senate that he had just been advised by "the head of a Government agency" that a man accused by Senator McCarthy of being a pervert, though not a Communist, had resigned.

The *Times* continues:

The identity of this person was not disclosed. . . .

Senator Tydings had just stated that he had personally investigated the episode and was turning over "important matters" about it to his subcommittee.

Tydings then asked his Republican critics:

"Won't you stop this continued heckling about homosexuals and let us get on with the main work of finding Communists? . . ."[103]

On May 5, the *Times* reports that New York State's Republican Governor Dewey

accused the Democratic national administration of tolerating spies, traitors and sex offenders in the Government service.[104]

On May 20, a *Times* news story is based on the testimony of police Lieutenant Roy E. Blick:

INQUIRY BY SENATE ON PERVERTS ASKED

Hill and Wherry Study Hears There Are 3,500 Deviates in Government Agencies

. . . A Senate investigation of alleged homosexuals in the Executive Branch of the Government was recommended unanimously today by a Senate Appropriation subcommittee of ten members.

Perverts are described by intelligence officers as poor security risks because of their vulnerability to blackmail.

The inquiry was proposed on the basis of a private, preliminary study made by Senators Lister Hill, Democrat of Alabama, and Kenneth S. Wherry of Nebraska, the Republican floor leader, during which a Washington police vice officer said it was his "own judgment" that 3,500 perverts were employed in Government agencies.

The officer, Lieut. Roy E. Blick, testified, it was disclosed this afternoon in the publication of a partial transcript of his evidence that he thought 300 to 400 of these persons were in the State Department.

"A Quick Guess," He Says

This, he said at one point, was a "quick guess," in the sense that it was based upon his experience that arrested persons not connected with the State Department sometimes would say:

"Why don't you go get so-and-so and so-and-so? They all belong to the same clique."

"By doing that," Lieutenant Blick added "their names were put on the list and they were catalogued as such, as the suspect of being such."

The story reports that "Senators Hill and Wherry called many witnesses in closed hearings," and each filed separate and differing reports on the implications of their findings.

Both quoted a letter from Dr. R. H. Felix, Director of the National Institute of Mental Health, stating that the available data indicated that perhaps 4 per cent of the white male population of the country were "confirmed homosexuals."

Finds Deviates Everywhere

"While corresponding data for females are lacking," Dr. Felix added, "the prevalence is probably about the same." The letter continued:

"All available evidence indicates that homosexuality can be found in all parts of the country, both urban and rural, and in all walks of life. I have been unable to find any evidence whatsoever which indicates that homosexuality is more prevalent in the District of Columbia than in other sections of the country."

Senator Hill's report stressed Dr. Felix's statement that homosexuality was no more prevalent in Government than elsewhere, and he proposed that one of the subjects of the investigation be that of medical treatment and rehabilitation.

Senator Wherry, for his part, asserted that by Dr. Felix's "reasoning one could argue, but not very intelligently, that because there are an estimated 55,000 Communists in the United States the Federal Government should have a pro rata share, and that because there are a million criminals in the country none should complain if the Government has its share."[105]

On May 22, the *Times* reports that Senate Republican leader Wherry had

endorsed a move to hold secret hearings in the pending investigation of sex perversion among Federal employes.[106]

On June 15 the *Times* reports:

Pervert Inquiry Ordered

. . . A Senate subcommittee was ordered today to investigate police reports that about 3,500 sex perverts hold Federal jobs, some of them in the State Department.

The go-ahead was given by the Committee on Expenditures in the Executive Department to its "super" investigating subcommittee. Authority for the inquiry has been given by the Senate.

Heading the group will be Senator Clyde R. Hoey, Democrat of North Carolina. . . . He said that the new study would be "complete and thorough" and "the paramount objective is to protect the Government and the public interest."

The subcommittee intends to make "every effort to obtain all of the pertinent facts," but it will not "transgress individual rights" or "subject any individual to ridicule," he asserted. Mr. Hoey further promised that he would not "allow this investigation to become a public spectacle."

Senator Andrew F. Schoeppel, Republican of Kansas, was named to succeed Senator McCarthy on the panel. The latter has asserted that Communists, perverts and other security risks infest the State Department. He bowed out of the inquiry to avoid being in a position of judging his own accusations.

Senator Margaret Chase Smith, Republican of Maine, another regular member of the investigating group, did not ask to be disqualified and will serve. Other members of the panel are Senators John L. McClellan of Arkansas, James O. Eastland of Mississippi and Herbert R. O'Conor of Maryland, Democrats, and Karl E. Mundt, Republican of South Dakota.[107]

On June 17, the *Times* reports that among 130 State Department employees sent home from Germany as "questionable security risks" since the previous July, there were "two confessed homosexuals, . . . and others of dubious character or connections . . ."[108]

On July 13, the *Times* reports that the House of Representatives, by a vote of 327 to 14, had passed a bill

designed to permit department and agency heads to deal with persons who are bad security risks because they drink too much, talk too much, are perverts or have similar failings.[109]

In July, Max Lerner began a series of articles on homosexuality in his daily column in the New York *Post*. The first, dated July 11, entitled "The Tortured Problem . . . The Making of Homosexuals," focuses on various psychological theories of the causation and character of homosexuality, briefly raising, without answering it, "the question of why homosexuality gives our society so much concern."[110]

On July 17, Lerner's *Post* column, entitled "The Senator and the Purge," includes a revealing interview with antihomosexual crusader Senator Kenneth Wherry:

In a long interview, Senator Kenneth Wherry (R-Nebr.) talked to me about his crusade to harry every last "pervert" from the Federal government services. . . . Now in his second term, he has been a power in the Senate as Republican whip and now as floor leader. A man with a hearty manner in the traditional fashion of American politics, a bit pouchy, with glasses and graying hair, he looks like any small-town lawyer or businessman. Sometimes his answers to my questions became harangues so violent as to make me think he would explode, until I saw that they left him unshaken and friendly as ever. Despite years of hard work and political tension, life seems to have left no writing of any kind on his face. It is the face of a man for whom there are no social complexities, no psychological subtleties, few private tragedies.

I asked Senator Wherry whether the problem of homosexuals in the government was primarily a moral or a security issue. He answered that it was both, but security was uppermost in his mind. I asked whether he made a connection between homosexuals and Communists. "You can't hardly separate homosexuals from subversives," the Senator told me. "Mind you, I don't say every homosexual is a subversive, and I don't say every subversive is a homosexual. But a man of low morality is a menace in the government, whatever he is, and they are all tied up together."

"You don't mean to say, Senator," I asked, "that there are no homosexuals who might be Democrats or even Republicans?"

"I don't say that by any means," he answered. "But this whole thing is tied together."

I asked whether he would be content to get the homosexuals out of the "sensitive posts," leaving alone those that have nothing to do with military security. There might be "associations," he said, between men in the sensitive and the minor posts. "There should be no people of that type working in any position in the government."

I asked whether the Senator knew the Kinsey findings about the extent of homosexuality in the male population. He had heard of them. "In the light of these figures, Senator," I asked him, "are you aware of the task which the purge of all homosexuals from government jobs opens up?"

"Take this straight," he answered, pounding his desk for emphasis. "I don't agree with the figures. I've read them all, but I don't agree with them. But regardless of the figures, I'll take the full responsibility for cleaning all of them out of the government."

I asked on what he based his view that homosexuals represent an unusual security risk. I cited a group of American psychiatrists who hold that a heterosexual with promiscuous morals may also be a security risk, that some men might be reckless gamblers or confirmed alcoholics and get themselves entangled or blackmailed.

The Senator's answer was firm: "You can stretch the security risk further if you want to," he said, "but right now I want to start with the homosexuals. When we get through with them, then we'll see what comes next."

This brought me to the question of definitions. "You must have a clear idea, Senator," I said, "of what a homosexual is. It is a problem that has been troubling the psychiatrists and statisticians. Can you tell me what your idea is?"

"Quite simple," answered the Senator. "A homosexual is a diseased man, an abnormal man."

I persisted. "Do you mean one who has made a habit of homosexuality? Would you include someone who, perhaps in his teens, had some homosexual relations and has never had them since? Would you include those who are capable of both kinds of relation, some who may even be raising families?"

"You can handle it without requiring a definition," the Senator answered. "I'm convinced in my own mind that any homosexual is a bad risk."

"But how about those who get pushed out of their jobs when they are only in minor posts, when no security risk is involved, and when they are forced to resign for something they may have done years ago?"

"They resign voluntarily, don't they?" asked the Senator. "That's an admission of their guilt. That's all I need. My feeling is that there will be very few people hurt."

I cited a case in the State Department of a man who had once served in an American embassy and had allowed himself as a young man to be used by the ambassador. He is now in his forties, and his case is troubling the security officials.

"It might have happened," answered Senator Wherry, "but I'm not going to define what a homosexual is. I say not many will be hurt. The Army and Navy have used their rule of thumb on this. The military has done a good job."

"But not a complete job," I pointed out, "if we follow the Kinsey figures. They show that thirty per cent of the men between twenty and twenty-four—the age group most represented in the armed services—have had some homosexual experience. Would you have all of them purged?"

"I repeat," answered Senator Wherry, "we should weed out all of them— wherever they are on the government payroll." . . .

I raised a question about the encroachments on privacy. "Get this straight," answered Senator Wherry, "no one believes in freedom of speech more than I do. I don't like anyone snooping around. But I don't like Kinsey snooping around either."

I asked him what he meant by Kinsey's snooping around. He said, "That's how he got the figures, isn't it?" I said that the Kinsey interviews were voluntary and asked whether he had ever had a chance to study Kinsey's book or his methods.

"Well," he answered, "all I know is that Kinsey has never contacted me. Has he contacted you?"

I said I'd had a friendly talk with Dr. Kinsey, and I offered to get the Senator in touch with him.

"But look, Lerner," Senator Wherry continued, breaking the cobwebs of our discussion, "we're both Americans, aren't we? I say, let's get these fellows out of the government."

"We have to know what fellows we're talking about, Senator," I answered. "That's just what is bothering many of us. What homosexuals are bad risks? How do you treat the others? Can they be helped? Would you, Senator, bring doctors and psychiatrists into the picture and make them part of the machinery for dealing with this problem?"

"No," he answered, "I don't think doctors are needed. We can handle this by rule of thumb."[111]

The next day, July 18, Lerner's column, entitled "Lieutenant Blick of the Vice Squad," presents an amazing exposé.

In an age of experts Lieutenant Roy E. Blick, of the District of Columbia Police Department, rates as a very important man in Washington. He is head of the Vice Squad, one of whose tasks is to deal with homosexuals. "Go see Blick," I was repeatedly told as I tried to track down the security story about homosexuals. "He has the facts and figures." So I did.

Lieutenant Blick is a tough cop. When I came into his office he was in the midst of a phone conversation about homosexuals which would have been wonderful detail for a documentary except that no one would dare put it on the screen. Burly, graying, and just ungrammatical enough to match a Hollywood pattern for police lieutenants, Blick has been on the Vice Squad nineteen years, and he has a pride in his job. He has four detectives on his squad who do nothing but check on homosexuals.

He seemed worried about our interview. He didn't like being caught, he said, "between the Democrats and the Republicans." He was referring to his star-witness testimony before the Hill-Wherry subcommittee, in which he had given his classic estimate of five thousand homosexuals in Washington.

"I had no idea," Lieutenant Blick told me, "that I was getting into a political football." When I asked what made him think the homosexual inquiry was just politics, he said darkly, "Something I heard this morning," but wouldn't elaborate.

The committee summons to him had come as a surprise. I asked how it could have been, since Senator Wherry had talked privately with him before he had sprung him dramatically on the committee.

"Yes, the Senator came down here," he admitted, "and talked about these cases with me. But I didn't know what the committee wanted me for. I came there without a note. The figures I gave them were guesses, my own guesses, not official figures."

"We would all like to know," I said, "on what basis you reached your guesses."

Blick seemed to grow more restless at this point. He squirmed and twisted, thrust his hands up in a helpless gesture.

"We have these police records," he finally said. "You take the list. Well, every one of these fellows has friends. You multiply the list by a certain percentage—say three per cent or four per cent."

"Do you mean," I asked, "that your police list is only three or four per cent of the total, and you multiply it by twenty-five or thirty?"

A faltering "Yes."

"If your final estimate was five thousand, does that mean your police list was less than two hundred?"

"No," he answered doubtfully. Then he added, "I mean five per cent."

"You mean then that you multiplied your list by twenty?"

Again a "Yes," then a "No." Finally, "I multiply my list by five."

"You mean you started with a list of one thousand and multiplied by five to get five thousand?"

Blick shifted his gaze around the room. Again the upward thrust of the hands, as if to say "How did a good cop ever get into this sort of situation?" But he didn't answer my question.

I made a fresh start. "You have a list of the men you arrested?" He did.

"You also have a larger list, including men you never arrested?" After hesitation —yes, he had a larger list as well.

"Did the fellows you arrested give the names of others?"

"Yes," he answered, this time with eagerness, "every one of these fellows has five or six friends. Take Smith. We bring him in. We say to him, 'Who are your friends?' He says, 'I have none.' I say, 'Oh, come on, Smith. We know you fellows go around in gangs. We know you go to rug parties. Who are your friends?' Then he tells us—Jones, Robinson."

"So you put Jones and Robinson down on your list?" I asked.

"Yes, we put them down."

"And that's how you compiled your list?" Yes, it was.

"But you said a while ago that you took the count of the men you arrested, and multiplied by five."

"Yes, I did."

"Well, which do you do? Multiply by five, or add all the friends you find out about?"

"I do both."

"How much of each?"

Blick finally broke into a smile of relief. "Well, it's sixty-forty. Sixty per cent of it I put the friends down on the list, and forty per cent of it I multiply by five."

This adventure in higher mathematics had exhausted both of us. I thought back grimly to the reverent way Senators and security officers used Blick's estimate of five thousand homosexuals in Washington, with 3,750 in the government, and I reflected that this was how a statistic got to be born.

"Do you think five thousand are too many?" Blick asked me.

I thought of the Kinsey figures. "If you mean just any kind of homosexual, and use it loosely," I answered, "I suspect you are conservative."

He clutched eagerly at my answer. "That's what I keep saying," he went on, "I'm conservative in my figures. I'm conservative about everything, Mr. Lerner."

I asked how he got his figure for the number of homosexuals working for the government.

"Oh," he said, "I took the five thousand for Washington. And I figured that three out of four of them worked for the government."

We spent a long time talking about what types he counted as homosexuals for the purpose of his figures, but the problem of definition proved even more exhausting to both of us than that of statistics. Lieutenant Blick was a cop, not a logician or a mathematician. . . .

Lieutenant Blick glows at Senator Wherry's recommendation that the District Vice Squad be strengthened with a greater appropriation. He also wishes he had a Lesbian squad.[112]

On December 15, 1950, the Senate Committee on Expenditures in the Executive Departments issues an interim report on "Employment of Homosexuals and Other Sex Perverts in Government," a major document of the 1950s antihomosexual witch-hunt era.[113] On December 16, the *New York Times* headlines a page 3 story on the report.

FEDERAL VIGILANCE ON PERVERTS ASKED

Senate Group Says They Must Be Kept Out of Government Because of Security Risk

. . . A Senate investigating group labeled sexual perverts today as dangerous security risks and demanded strict and careful screening to keep them off the Government payroll. It said that many Federal agencies had not taken "adequate steps to get these people out of Government." . . .

Stressing the risk that the Government takes in employing a sex deviate or keeping one on the payroll, the subcommittee said:

"The lack of emotional stability which is found in most sex perverts, and the weakness of their moral fiber, makes them susceptible to the blandishments of foreign espionage agents."

Called 'Prey to Blackmailers'

The report also noted that perverts were "easy prey to the blackmailer." It said that Communist and Nazi agents had sought to get secret Government data from Federal employes "by threatening to expose their abnormal sex activities."

The subcommittee criticized the State Department particularly for "mishandling" ninety-one cases of homosexualism among its employes. It said that many of the employes were allowed to resign "for personal reasons," and that no steps were taken to bar them from other Government jobs. . . .

Tightening Laws Urged

The committee said that it was unable to determine accurately how many perverts now held Federal jobs. It added, however, that since Jan. 1, 1947, a total of 4,954 cases had been processed, including 4,380 in the military services and 574 on Federal civilian payrolls. . . .

In addition to strict enforcement of Civil Service rules about firing perverts, the subcommittee recommended tightening of the District of Columbia laws on sexual perversion, closer liaison between the Federal agencies and the police and a thorough inquiry by all divisions of the Government into all reasonable complaints of perverted sexual activity.[114]

On March 28, 1951, the *Times*, in a front-page story, reports:

. . . The State Department has dismissed a vice consul in Hong Kong for being an admitted homosexual and having accepted up to $10,000 in bribes to speed the issuance of visas. . . .

Three other members of the United States Consulate in Hong Kong were discharged at the same time for homosexuality. In conformity with the practice for such dismissals the State Department did not make their names public. It was stated, however, that they were not involved in the "visa irregularities."[115]

On April 28, 1951, the *Times* reports a statement by FBI chief J. Edgar Hoover:

Relative to what he described as "sex deviates in government service," Mr. Hoover said that since April 1, 1950, his agency had identified 406 in this category.[116]

On October 5, the *Times* reports:

The State Department disclosed today that four employes in Korea had resigned after having been accused of homosexual acts.[117]

On December 20, the *Times* reports a "lie detector" being employed by at least four government departments in loyalty investigations "to test men and women involved in 'sensitive' jobs related to national security."

In general the lie detector is used by the Federal agencies particularly to establish whether a person has been arrested, is a sexual pervert or associates with Communists or other subversive persons.[118]

Washington Confidential, a book published in 1951 by Jack Lait and Lee Mortimer, contains a chapter entitled "A Garden of Pansies," which well conveys some popular feelings and beliefs concerning homosexuals in that witch-hunt era:

The only way to get authoritative data on fairies is from other fairies. They recognize each other by a fifth sense immediately, and they are intensely gregarious. One cannot snoop at every desk and count people who appear queer. Some are deceptive to the uninitiated. But they all know one another and they have a grapevine of intercommunication as swift and sure as that in a girls' boarding school. Since they have no use for women in the main, and are uneasy with masculine men, they have a fierce urge, even beyond the call of the physical, for each other's society. They have their own hangouts, visit one another, and cling together in a tight union of interests and behavior.

Not all are ashamed of the trick that nature played on them. They have their leaders, unabashed, who are proud queens and who revel in their realm. . . .

No one knows how many lesbians there are, because the female—or is it male—of the pervert species is seldom spoken about and is much less obvious. Psychiatrists and sociologists who have made a study of the problem in Washington think there are at least twice as many Sapphic lovers as fairies. A large incidence of lesbianism is concomitant with the shortage of men, where women work together, live together, play together, so love together.

Some display themselves, strut around in fairy joints; all queers are in rapport with all others. You will see them also in some of the late bottle-clubs, on the make for the same girls the he-wolves are chasing.

The mannish women used to hang out at the Show Boat Bar, H and 13th, until the management drove them out. Now in David's Grill, formerly the Horseshoe, in back of the Mayflower Hotel, they outnumber the pansies who haunted the place. . . .

With more than 6,000 fairies in government offices, you may be concerned about the security of the country. Fairies are no more disloyal than the normal. But homosexuals are vulnerable, they can be blackmailed or influenced by sex more deeply than conventional citizens; they are far more intense about their love-life.[119]

The authors quote Congressman A. L. Miller of Nebraska, a physician, and "author of the District's new bill to regulate homos"; Miller told Lait and Mortimer of foreign agents being

given a course in homosexuality, then taught to infiltrate in perverted circles in other countries. Congressman Miller said: . . .

"The homosexual is often a man of considerable intellect and ability. It is found that the cycle of these individuals' homosexual desires follows the cycle closely patterned to the menstrual period of women. There may be three or four days in each month that the homosexual's instincts break down and drive the individual into abnormal fields of sexual practice. Under large doses of sedatives during this sensitive cycle, he may escape such acts.[120]

On January 14, 16, and 21, 1952, journalist Drew Pearson's private diary refers to unsubstantiated rumors, circulating among Congressmen, the FBI, and the White House, of Senator Joseph McCarthy's being involved in homosexual activity.[121]

On June 26, 1952, the *Times* reports that testimony before a closed Senate committee

showed that the State Department had discharged two employes last year on charges of homosexuality and that 117 others had quit when confronted with the charges. The State Department has a total of about 19,000 United States employes and hires about 9,000 foreigners to staff embassies.[122]

On August 31, the *Times* reports:

NAVY OUSTS SEX OFFENDER

Accused Officer Resigns—24 Sailors Also Being Dismissed

BOSTON . . .—A Navy spokesman said today an officer allegedly involved in homosexuality had been relieved of his ship command and had submitted his resignation from the service.

Lieut. Comdr. Bernard S. Solomon, First Naval District Public Information Officer, said that twenty-four enlisted men at the Newport, R. I., Naval Base also involved in the case were being discharged by administrative decree under conditions "other than honorable."[123]

On April 13, 1953, the *Times* reports

"Homosexual proclivities" have led to the dismissal of 425 State Department employes since 1947."[124]

In April 1953, ONE *Magazine*, an early homosexual emancipation periodical, published a letter from "Miss E. M." providing a rare personal account of one woman's experience of the United States government's antihomosexual witch-hunt, a story with its own ironic ending. "Miss E. M." writes:

I am particularly interested in the idea behind your magazine and the purpose of the Mattachine Foundation. My own experience offers ample evidence of the necessity of eliminating discrimination against the homosexual minority.

A couple of years ago, I was doing relief work in Germany. My work was with a private Relief Organization which functioned, as all such agencies must in occupied territory with the approval of the State Department. A year of my twenty month term of service lay behind me. I was full of pride which springs from the knowledge of a job well done, and I felt secure in the good relationship I had established with my fellow workers. All this was particularly gratifying, since for a period of years, my life had been full of turmoil and confusion known by all maladjusted homosexuals who have not recognized their plight.

I knew no others like myself, and had spent years involving others in emotional attachments which were essentially foreign to their nature. This frustrating and guilt ridden course led finally to a nervous collapse which was followed by a period of therapy as an out-patient of a psychiatric clinic.

Now, some five years later, life had begun to look like a happier proposition. I found myself increasingly attracted to men and was becoming confident that the future would find me able to establish a normal emotional attachment with a man which would eventually lead to marriage.

I shall never forget the pride I felt, that day in Germany when I was told I had been chosen to represent our Relief Unit at a conference in another city some 500 miles away. I was met at the station, after an overnight journey from Frankfurt by one of our workers. She escorted me to headquarters where I was to meet with our two top supervisors. As I sat down with them in the conference room I suddenly became aware of an uneasiness in their manner and a tension in the atmosphere. I felt with cold dread the discussion would not be concerned with German Refugees, but rather, in some unpleasant fashion, with me. My first thought was that someone in my family had died and this manner of breaking the news had been chosen to soften the blow. Little did I know, the numbing shock, the sickening embarrassment and the bitter hurt I was to endure instead.

I was told that my record from the Psychiatric Clinic had been brought to the attention of the State Department. Since my problems had been of a homosexual nature, the State Department demanded my immediate expulsion from Germany.

Reservation had been made for me on the plane that very night for the United States. My Chief Supervisors regretted that there was nothing further that they could do.

I was stunned and confused. The whole situation seemed like an evil dream. My plans for the future, my feelings of worthwhile accomplishment, and the work which had come to mean so much to me, were brought to an abrupt and cruel end.

During the flight across the Atlantic, I could do nothing but cry. I felt completely alone and found it impossible to accept the reality of the situation. I was met at La Guardia Field by two of our representatives and taken quickly to our headquarters in Washington. For two weeks in the Capital, I spoke with heads of our Personnel Department before I was told how the State Department had learned of my clinical record. I found out that the State Department had received their information from someone who had known me five years before and was now working in their Personnel Department. My own Organization had refused to act on hear-say. They had verified the fact that I had received treatment in the clinic. Since the State Department had threatened to inform Military Authorities in Germany my Organization had no other choice but to recall me.

I did everything I could to convince officials of my Organization of my dependability. The Staff Psychiatrist even vouched for me, but the Organization would not return me to foreign service, nor would they take issue with the State Department. They offered me a job in their local office, but I refused. Working with them in Washington would mean only one thing to me, that I had failed.

I could not let my family and friends know this had happened. Somehow I had to work things out in my own way. Having no particular plan in mind I left for New York City.

I had never known another homosexual, although I had spotted a few during my years at the University. Now that I was persecuted for having such inclinations I felt a close identification with others like myself. I remembered that in my own city there had been places where homosexuals congregated. I combed the streets in New York and finally one night found such a place. That night I met and talked with a kind of people I had never known, who spoke to me in a language I had never heard. Since this experience a whole new world has opened for me and I have learned to adjust to it.

While my expulsion from Germany has brought about major changes in my life, I have managed to make it a happy one, yet this injustice will always rankle. I shudder to think how this experience might have completely destroyed me.

Miss E. M.[125]

On March 13, 1954, the *Times* reports Senator Joseph R. McCarthy's charge that the Army had tried to stop his exposure of Communists in its ranks. McCarthy charged that Army officials had suggested he turn his attention to subversion and homosexuality in the Navy, Air Force, and the Defense Department. Army lawyer John G. Adams was said to have called McCarthy's office

to report he had collected "specific information for us about an Air Force base where there was a large number of homosexuals."[126]

On March 15, the *Times* reports that McCarthy's counsel, Roy Cohn, interviewed on television's "Meet the Press," had charged

that John Adams, Army counsel, actually had offered to map Air Force bases where there was a mess.[127]

On May 14, the *Times* reports the sixteenth day of the Army-McCarthy hearings. John G. Adams, Army counsel, testified, denying

that he had tried to divert the McCarthy committee from its Army investigations by holding out the "bait" of providing them with evidence of alleged homosexuals in the Air Force or the Navy.

Mr. Adams volunteered his own story of the map, first referred to by Roy Cohn. Adams said that Cohn and his aide Carr

had been telling him for some time that a big new Army investigation was about to break and he wondered whether the new inquiry might be concerned with reports that the Secretary of the Army had received "some very serious allegations with reference to homosexual behavior on the part of a group of Army officers at a large base in the South."

Adams

was particularly concerned that the McCarthy committee might have been tipped off about this report about the Army base by "a dissident employe," who had been trying to attract Congressional interest in the case.

Mr. Adams said he had drawn the map, with nine regions marked on it, and asked Mr. Cohn and Mr. Carr without success to indicate within which region their inquiry fell, offering to tell them if this was the same region where the Army was investigating the report of homosexual activity,

"I thought if they hit Area No. 4 and if No. 4 was the area which we were concerned about," he explained, "I would then know that the individual who was in Washington soliciting interest from among Congressional committees had given information to this committee, and I would know that it was necessary for us to put a number of additional people on the matter for the purpose of assembling facts, because an investigation might be ready, about to start."

He said the plan did not work, and he left the map there. . . .

Mr. Adams volunteered the statement that careful examination by Army officials "for a period of many weeks successfully put to rest any allegation that this homosexual ring did exist." He said this statement had been made to stop further newspaper speculation.[128]

On August 27, the *Times* reports that Representative John Phillips, Republican of California, had criticized the American Legion for putting itself "squarely on the side of homosexuals and subversives" in opposing a bill giving federal officials power to fire any employe "in the interests of the United States."[129]

On January 4, 1955, the *Times* details an Eisenhower Administration Civil Service Commission report of 8,008 "security risk" separations in the first sixteen months of its security program. A reported 5,912 individuals were dismissed or deemed suspect for reasons unrelated to disloyalty or subversion. The list included 655 cases involving "sex perversion."[130]

1955: HENRY HAY;
The House Un-American Activities Committee

In May 1954, a scandal-mongering periodical named *Confidential* carried an article on the Mattachine Foundation headed:

America, on Guard!
HOMOSEXUALS, INC.

A subhead read:

Don't sell the twisted twerps short! Once they met in secret. Today, they've organized as the "Mattachines," with a goal of a million members and a $6,000,000 bankroll!

Included in the story are some details of the anti-Communist hysteria which played a role in the group's early history:

Politics, rather than the problems of sex deviates seems at that time, to take up a major part of the night's business at each [Mattachine] meeting. When Harry Hay, one of the group's leaders, was mentioned in testimony before the House Un-American Activities Committee, the screams of protests hit a new high. And when the Society's steering committee hired attorney Michael Snider to set into motion the machinery necessary for incorporation under California law, there were wholesale resignations among the Pollyannas. [Snider, like Hay, was associated with left-wing causes; he had been called before HUAC and refused to testify under the Fifth Amendment.] Deciding that if the association wasn't Red it was definitely Pinko, hundreds of outraged queens spread their wings and flew as far away as possible.[131]

Henry (Harry) Hay, a founder of the original Mattachine Society, had been a member of the Communist party for eighteen years, from the mid-1930s until the early 1950s. In an interview with the present author Hay recalls that "during the Communist conspiracy trials of 1951–52 I had been quoted as a prominent Marxist teacher." In July 1955, one year after the appearance of the *Confidential* article, Hay was subpoenaed to appear before the House Un-American Activities Committee. Here, in an interview recorded on March 31, 1974, Hay recalls the story of his appearance before HUAC.

H.H.:   Because the story had come out in *Confidential* about my being mentioned in testimony before HUAC, I had to assume that HUAC knew about my activities in the Mattachine, as well as my activities in the Communist-run

California Labor School. I had to assume that when they called me to the stand they wouldn't ask me one sixty-four dollar question—"Are you now or have you ever been a member of the Communist party?"—they'd ask me two—the second about Mattachine. Consequently, I felt that I couldn't stand with the other fifty people who were being called before HUAC at the same time—people, all of whom I knew intimately or whom I had known in the past. I would be asked this second question about Mattachine, and these other people would feel as though they had been betrayed, that they were being marked by me. Out of respect for them—out of respect for myself, and my own past relationships, I couldn't do that to them.

Hay recalls that four or five lawyers were representing all the people who had been called before HUAC, and fund-raising parties were held to pay these attorneys.

H.H.:   I had to cut myself off from that and find my own attorney. This was the proper and honorable thing to do. I felt that people following these hearings—for example, people from the left in Ohio, who didn't know me or any of the other people—would all feel tarred by the same brush. I'm asked the question about Mattachine affiliation, and it covers all of them. Although this isn't the way I feel, this is the way they feel, and I have to give that some consideration.

Hay went to ask the advice of John McTernan, one of the lawyers representing major figures called before HUAC. The lawyer, says Hay,

was one of my very, very greatest friends, I had known him for years. I told him what the situation was, what I was afraid would be the questions. He looked at me very coldly and he said, "We're not going to condone queers, you know." So I said, "Thanks, John, thanks very much. Who do you suggest I go and see?" He said "Well, that's not my business. You find your own lawyer." And I've known this guy very, very well for an awfully long time! So that was it.

I knew who some of the other attorneys were. At this point I had six weeks to prepare for my HUAC appearance. I went to another lawyer, Vic Shapiro, and he said, "Yeah, I can understand John's position, but I also realize that you should be represented. I'm going to be called out of town—but maybe I can handle it. Let me see." Two weeks go by and he calls me up and he says he can't handle it. I've got about three weeks left. The rest of these people called by HUAC are being rehearsed all this time on how to handle themselves, you know? Vic says, "But you go and see Harriet So-and-so." I go and see Harriet, and she says no, she can't handle it, but go to see Rose somebody or other. I go and see Rose, and Rose says, "You know this is a tremendous thing, and I wish I could handle it, but I can't do it either, I've got too many other clients who've been called."

J.K.:   Was it really the Gay issue that was keeping these lawyers from helping you?

H.H.:   Sure. Of course. That was the issue; that was what I was going to see all these lawyers about. So they keep weaseling out, and weaseling out, and all of a sudden it's the end of the fifth week, and I've got one more week to prepare. And I go to see this little guy, Frank Pestana, a Portuguese, who was representing the Chicanos and Mexicans and Puerto Ricans and Portuguese in Los Angeles. Frank listened to my story and he said, "I'm busy to death, and I don't know how I'm going to get down there to the hearing, but of course I'll handle your case. This is one of the greatest studies in courage I've ever run into. Of course I'll help you." This is on a Friday afternoon. He said, "You get in here tomorrow morning at seven o'clock and I'll start your rehearsal."

It was a wonderful thing. I'm just about—I'm so close to tears I don't know what I'm going to do. I'm scared, I'm terrified at this point, you know? Well, anyway, he rehearsed me Saturday through Tuesday.

Hay's typed notes, preserved from the time of his HUAC appearance, include practice questions and rough answers concerning both Communist party and Mattachine membership. These notes indicate several ways Hay had prepared to answer any questions concerning his involvement in Mattachine:

Mr. Chairman, it appears to me that you are attempting to intrude upon areas of personal consciousness and conceptual opinions, an area in which the Supreme Court has ruled [you] have not the right to investigate. . . .

Hay would cite the Fifth Amendment as the basis for refusing to answer. If he was asked, "Are you now a homosexual, or have you ever been associated with a homophile organization?" Hay was planning to answer:

Mr. Chairman, . . . I'd be obliged if you'd refresh my memory by reading that section of the act under which this committee operates, which empowers you (reluctantly, of course,) to investigate the private perceptions, inclinations, and/or associations of citizens in regard to nonpolitical intimacies.

Under further questioning about whether he associated with homosexuals, Hay was prepared to add:

Mr. Chairman: many people—unthinkingly—might assume that actually your question could be easily answered with a simple "NO". But the facts are that there probably isn't a single person in this room who could say NO without perjuring himself. There are Armed Service Analyses that estimate GI prevalence at between 13%–15%. 13% would mean one man out of every eight. There are more than 8 men on your committee. Could you answer a simple NO to this question, and be upheld despite the stacked barrages of innuendos with which you yourselves harass your witnesses? Could the President? Could the Chief Justice of the Supreme Court? . . . . When it comes to the person's declaration of himself—now we have returned in history to the Star Chamber iniquities. . . . How does one prove that he is not what he is not—when the semi-official character of the customary publicity automatically incumbent upon [your] posing the question has already accustomed the public to accept that he may be such a one, regardless of what he may attempt [to say] to the contrary?

No, gentlemen. In answer to your question, I take pride in upholding my part in the duties and responsibilities required by the Fifth Amendment, by properly invoking it in this instance.

In regard to so-called nonincriminatory queries by the committee, Hay would answer:

> . . . In the light of my obligations as a citizen to uphold the Constitution, I maintain that ANY breach of my private consciousness is in itself a testimony against my civil right to defend the integrity of my convictions.[132]

Hay's recollection of his HUAC appearance continues:

H.H.   Wednesday I'm called to go down to the hearing. So I go down there, and it's pretty ghastly to listen to these stool pigeons lie about you. I listened to this for about four or five hours that day, and then more the next day. I was supposed to be called on Thursday, and I had to wait through Wednesday, Thursday, and Friday, listening to these bastards all week. I didn't testify until Saturday morning.

I was nervous when I got up there. What I did—and of course this was kind of dirty—I think this is real Gay consciousness, if you'll forgive me—I was gabby as all hell. I think they really thought they were going to get a bit of information. What happened was the attorney for the committee got a little confused with all my gab and asked me if I were a member of the party. I said no. That's when the shit hit the fan. This committee member—he wasn't a big man, but he was a very chunky sort of man—he got apoplectic-looking, and he stood up—he was holding on to the edge of his desk—and he stood up in such a way that he pushed this huge oak desk over on its face —*clunk*. He looked to me like the comandante from *Don Giovanni* rising up out of the floor. He was apoplectic. And he spits out, "When did you quit, out in the hall before you came in?" He was purple and swelling at the neck, out of his tight collar. That was when I let off my crack: "I'm not in the habit of confiding in stool pigeons or their buddies." Now "their buddies," of course, was the committee, and that could have put me in contempt. Everybody was asking everybody else, "What did he say??? Did you catch what he said???" They couldn't make me repeat it, and the poor little closet queen who was transcribing couldn't find it in the reams of paper ribbon jumbled up on the floor around him. My attorney had just about gone through the floor. He said, "My God, I can't get you out of this one. I just hope to God they don't find the transcript." The people in the court room were doubling up with laughter. Finally, one of the committee members said, "I think we know what the witness meant by his remarks, and I suggest that we dismiss him." And that was it. When I got down off the stand, I went over to the bailiff to sign myself out, and, you know, my fingers were locked together so I couldn't get them apart. He had to help me get my fingers loosened up. And then I couldn't hold the pen to sign the thing.

J.K.:   You must have been relieved when you left—they hadn't even mentioned your Gay organizing.

H.H.:   It turned out they didn't know about it. What I hadn't known was that the committee's information was more than five years old. But no, I wasn't relieved, I was prepared to handle the Gay question, and handle it well. I was sorry that they didn't ask. That's what I'd gone through this preparation for. I was going to take a Fifth Amendment position; I had a right to. But I was going to handle it on the basis that Gay is proud.[133]

1955: Anonymous; Witch-Hunt in Boise, Idaho;
An interview with a victim
"They lit a match to a bonfire"

On November 2, 1955, the *Idaho Daily Statesman* carried a front-page headline:

THREE BOISE MEN ADMIT SEX CHARGES

This was the start of a classic, local antihomosexual witch-hunt, which John Gerassi's careful, lengthy, detailed study has made one of the best-documented of such incidents. According to Gerassi's persuasive analysis, this witch-hunt originated in local ruling-class politics: "Idaho has long been ruled by a handful of rich Boise lawyers and businessmen," dubbed the "Boise gang"—a group interested primarily in economic power and profit. "It was this power elite," says Gerassi, "that, in 1955, went after the homosexuals." Some members of this elite "thought that they could use the scandal to rock City Hall, which was then in the hands of a fairly decent, reformist administration. . . . Other elite members aimed rather at the City Council, and specifically at a councilman whose son had been directly involved [in homosexual activity]. And still others were after one of their own elite members, the real 'Queen,' a man so wealthy that it was felt he was untouchable in any other way."[134]

On December 18, 1973, eighteen years after the event, the present author recorded an interview with one of the men sent to jail as a result of the Boise witch-hunt. The interviewer recalls: the subject, who chose to remain anonymous, spoke at great length and in detail, maintaining a cool tone throughout, a stratagem I interpreted as a means of protecting himself from getting too close to a deeply harrowing experience. As he spoke, I was struck by his resistant spirit, a quality no doubt connected with his ability to survive and maintain a sense of dignity in a situation designed to degrade him. On the other hand, I also noted his political naïveté in dealing with authorities conducting the witch-hunt. This misplaced sense of trust seems to have been typical in 1955 of Boise homosexuals, a group with no clear sense of their rights, who quite freely confessed their own homosexuality, and worse, that of others, to those who would later use this information against all of them—"confessions" traceable perhaps to a generalized sense of guilt about their homosexuality.

The subject at one point describes an official he believes to have been a repressed, perhaps unconscious, homosexual, who acted especially vindictively toward him. It is not often noted, but the evil in such cases is repression, not homosexuality.

The behavior of the Boise authorities in the name of morality is an obscenity not to be forgotten. Nor should the behavior of other straight Americans who cooperated with these officials, doing their jobs as usual. The authoritarian police-state tactics displayed in Boise, the utter disregard for the rights of homosexuals, is indicative of that deep hatred which still lies just below the surface in many American towns and cities, and which, without vigilance, could erupt violently again.

A victim of the Boise witch-hunt tells his story:

Boise is like most towns, they're run by a small group of people. They have a hold on it; they know what's going on; they keep it under control. The Catholic and Mormon churches are also powerful in Boise.

The motivation behind this? It started as a political thing. There were two men in Boise, a city councilman and a friend of his, an attorney. They were after a prominent city official. This official had a brother who was a notorious homosexual, a very wild, nelly, flitty thing. They felt if they could get this antihomosexual thing started they would get this official's brother into it, and therefore discredit the official. They hired a private detective to investigate the homosexual activity in Boise. This detective got the turmoil started, and then they dumped it in the lap of the city prosecuting attorney. I don't think anyone realized when they started what they were letting loose. It got so involved, so extensive.

Most of what this detective found involved people of very low income groups. One fellow ran a shoeshine parlor and had a lot of boys hanging around there. He was one they got right away. This broke in the paper. There was hysteria in Boise about young teen-age boys being seduced by older men; that's what they conveyed to the public. The city paper, the *Idaho Daily Statesman*, embellished on this. It kept emphasizing older men and young boys; it kept saying there was a sex ring of older men who were enticing these boys. There was no such thing; no such ring existed. The boys who were arrested in Boise all knew exactly what they were doing. Of the men arrested, very few knew any of the others. I knew one or two— had a nodding acquaintance with a couple of others. This thing got away from them right off the bat, the *Statesman* churned up so much turmoil. The public was immediately incensed; it was like they struck a match to a bonfire.

At some point they decided to bring in another investigator, a man who had done similar work for the federal government, the man John Gerassi calls Bill Goodman. He had been in Washington investigating homosexuality there—earlier, when they were having all the trouble. I read in the paper that they questioned a thousand to two thousand people in Boise. I know hundreds of Gay people left the city, schoolteachers, people in every walk of life—Gay people who had never gotten involved in anything, who were just afraid.

When I first read about this in the paper, I was upset and shocked. I never thought that any law-enforcement agency would go that far. Then, in a matter of days, they sent that shoeshine man to *life imprisonment*—he had served time once before, on a check charge, I believe. Because of this earlier charge they really threw the book at him. You could feel the public was really upset; they got so upset that the two United States senators had to come home from Washington to try to calm things down. They held public meetings in the high-school auditoriums. But this didn't calm things down at all. The people were hysterical; they were getting frantic.

I had very close straight friends who thought I should leave—they knew I was Gay—and they said, "This thing doesn't look like it's going to calm down; it looks like it's going to get worse." They said, "Why don't you get out of here?" The thing that really upset me the most was the shoeshine man being sentenced to life imprisonment. When I saw that, I thought, "Jesus Christ amighty, I better get the hell out of here—if they're going to start going that wild." I got out of Boise about the time the hysteria reached one of its peaks. I left for California.

I went to San Francisco and got a job. I didn't try to hide where I'd gone. I was writing to people, and talking to people from Boise, and keeping track of what was going on. It was in every paper on the Coast, you could see it on the front page wherever you went.

I hired an attorney, a woman attorney as a matter of fact, in case someone tried to come and arrest me. I knew my name had been mentioned several times in Boise. People kept saying, "Why don't you arrest *him* if you're arresting this guy, and this guy and this guy?" My attorney talked to the district attorney in Boise. She said she had heard my name had come up several times in this investigation. She wondered if they planned on arresting me, or having me in for questioning. He says "not at the present time," but if I were in the city they would like to question me, at my convenience. But they were not going to come down to California to get me for questioning.

I was working in San Francisco, although I hadn't officially picked up everything and moved there. I had a bag with some clothes in it, and was living at the YMCA, and was working as a food checker in a hotel. One day I was sitting there on my job, and in walked the sheriff from Boise, a San Francisco policeman, and one of the hotel managers. The manager was in hysterics. The sheriff said, "We don't have to take him right now; he can finish his shift." The manager said, "Oh, no, no, no. Get him out of here right now. We don't want him around!"

Obviously they must have had a lot of pressure put on them. Otherwise they would never have come all that way to get me. I tried to get hold of my attorney, but I couldn't. She was out of town for a week, on a case in some other place. The San Francisco policeman said, "I don't understand this; we wouldn't go over to Oakland to extradite somebody for a charge like this!" There was some sort of charge so they could bring me back to Boise for questioning. The court appointed me an attorney for this brief hearing, to see if I wanted to protest the extradition. I talked to my mother over the phone and she hired an attorney in Boise. I said, "Well, I'll come on home, and we'll just fight things from there." My father was very ill, and my mother wanted me to come home. She thought it would be easier for us to handle it there. So I asked the sheriff what time we would be leaving, and what time we'd arrive in Boise, so my lawyer could meet me. I'd known this sheriff all my life and his wife who was with him. The three of us rode back to Boise in the car together. There was no question of my being handcuffed or anything. It was just like three people on a trip.

Back in Boise the sheriff had instructions not to take me to his office or the police station where my mother and my lawyer were waiting for me. I was taken to this house where the guy Gerassi calls Bill Goodman was doing the questioning. I said that I wanted to call my attorney. I had never had any dealings with the police in my life up to this point. I'd never been arrested for anything, I don't think even a traffic ticket. You see my grandfather had been a deputy sheriff, and I had always trusted the police. I had always felt that when they told you something you could rely on it. I was to find out differently.

First they told me they understood I was the ringleader of this so-called teen-age sex ring, that I was the instigator of it. They were going to ask for life imprisonment for me. This was just to upset me and scare me and get me to talk. I wouldn't say much for quite some time.

They let me hear a tape. Years before, when I first came back from the Navy, I had had sex with this boy. He was the one on this tape, and ironically he was the son of one of the councilmen who started this whole thing. This boy was Gay. But on the tape he claimed I had held a gun on him and made him go down on me. I said, "That's not true. The whole thing's a lie." So they asked me to make a statement to clarify this. My mother had told me on the phone, "Whatever you do, don't sign anything." I didn't sign anything. I made a statement. I wrote out a statement telling exactly what had happened, but I didn't sign it. I still hadn't seen my lawyer. They told me that when they finished with me I could see my lawyer. They had me there about nine hours before they finally let me call my attorney. He had been looking all over the city for me. He knew I'd gotten into town, but he didn't know where they had taken me. The police told him I hadn't gotten there yet.

I told them what had happened with this boy. I'd taken a bunch of kids home after an outing. I had started home with this boy in my car, and he said, "Oh, I don't want to go home. I'll ride around with you, till you take the rest of the kids home." Then, when I'd finished, he said, "I don't want to go home yet; once I go home, my father won't let me out again." He said, "Let's just drive down by the river, and set and talk for a while." So we drove down there, and he immediately wanted to have sex. He was fourteen years old at the time according to Gerassi, but I don't think that's quite right. I think he was closer to sixteen. I may be wrong. I was in my late twenties. There was about a twelve-year difference between us. But the boy had been doing this for years; he knew exactly what he was doing. He told me he had sex with his cousin, one cousin especially, almost every day of the week. Of course the cousin loved it. And so did he. Every chance he'd get he'd stay over to his cousin's place all night, or his cousin'd come over to his place. He knew damn well what he was doing. He was an expert by that time. The boy went down on me, and I went down on him, and later I took him home. This happened at least three or four years prior to the hysteria in Boise. So I corrected the kid's taped statement. The authorities had originally found out about this boy and me through a letter one of the Gays arrested had written out of jail.

The authorities also asked me about some fellows from the air base who I had been running around with. I said there was nothing sexual involved; we were simply friends. Later, these two friends came to visit me to find out if I had been questioned about them, because they had been questioned about me. I told them that I had said nothing. Although we had had sex, I denied it.

So anyway, they took me to the county jail and fingerprinted me. Then my grandmother came down and bailed me out. Finally, they charged me with this incident with the councilman's son—this "infamous crime against nature." They also said that two other fellows who had been arrested had reported my having sex with them, but the boy was the only one they were going to charge me with. If I would go to court on this particular incident, they wouldn't charge me with the other two. The parents of the boy were absolutely livid. They went to the judge and asked that I be sentenced for life, to string me up by the neck. Well, I was able to prove beyond a shadow of a doubt that the boy was homosexual. Not only had he had sex with me, but numerous other people, including all his male cousins.

He'd carried on with them for a number of years. That was verified by the parents eventually.

I think a lot of the Gays arrested fell into the same trap I did. They weren't hysterical to the point they listed everybody they knew, but the authorities would say, "Well, Joe Jones said he had sex with you." And the Gay would answer, "No, it wasn't him, it was So-and-so." And they would sort of pull the information out of them, without them sitting down and writing out the names. "Bill Goodman" was a very cool, calm, collected man who knew what he was doing. He never pressured you, or threatened you. He had a way of sort of soft-pedaling every-thing, just sort of conversational in tone and attitude, saying, "Well, this person said such and such." I just sort of fell into his trap. He'd done this so much, his method of getting information from people was very slick, very clever. The only person he really had a problem with was this attorney who finally beat the case, because he knew what "Goodman" was trying to do. This attorney had experience with the law and the way investigators work, and he wouldn't say anything. Others talked when they didn't have to.

I had my case postponed a couple of times because of my father's illness. My father was operated on in January 1956, just three or four weeks after I was brought back to Idaho. They found he had cancer. The doctor who operated on him took his entire stomach out and his pancreas and his spleen. He lasted from January until May. He just sort of withered away; there was nothing you could do about it. It was just a matter of time. The doctor felt that by giving him time he could straighten out his affairs. When I got home, most of the time I spent taking care of him. My mother would feed him through a tube, and I would give him morphine shots to keep him going until it was over. All this coming at once, it was a pretty bad situation. I'm surprised that my mother stood up through it all.

After my father died, my grandfather had a stroke. Possibly part of this was due to my situation, and possibly because my father had died at such an early age. My grandfather was upset because he was in his seventies at the time, and felt it was wrong for a younger man to go when he should have gone instead. My grandfather was that kind of person. Finally he went into a coma for several days, until he finally passed away in August.

In September I had a hearing. We went down to the prosecuting attorney's office—myself, my mother, and my lawyer. The prosecuting attorney and his assistant were there. The assistant was Gay, I think. You know, "It takes one to know one." The district attorney wanted me to change my plea to guilty. I had pled not guilty up to this point to "infamous crimes against nature" with this boy. If I would change my plea to guilty they would try to get whatever they could for me—because I had cooperated and hadn't put them through the financial expense of having a trial.

The D.A. says he understood the whole situation, that the boy was just as Gay as I was. He asked me if I had anything to say. My main comment was to ask why a few people should be singled out for something thousands had been doing. This was my objection. He says, "All I can say is you were too dumb not to keep your mouth shut. You should have been smarter. When you were called in by Goodman you should not have said one word, and fought it." I said, "That just shows you what I was taught as a child—to always trust a policeman—that that was bull. I'm finding out that you can't trust anybody."

The assistant prosecutor says, "Well, you must say we've done some good, because there's not a homosexual left in this city now." And my mother says, "Well, you missed one." He looks at her with a kind of puzzled expression on his face. And my mother says, "You'd better look in the mirror when you get home." Well, he hit the ceiling. I think it was at that point that he decided he was going to get me in prison, one way or another. Neither my mother nor myself are known for keeping our mouths shut. I'm very outspoken at times, as you've probably gathered. I guess I get it from her as a family trait. I'm sure she meant to make her point, and she did.

We went on; the assistant prosecutor had been insisting all along that I should take a year in prison, and then they'd parole me. I said, "I don't know why I should spend any time at all in prison. I haven't done anything." He said, "You've committed a crime against society. Society rebels against this sort of behavior, and you have to pay the penalty for it. You have to be made to realize that you've committed a crime." I said, "But I don't think I've committed any crime. As far as I'm concerned, it was a natural act to me—although it may not be to you."

By the time my actual hearing came around, we had decided to change my plea to guilty. The parents of the boy agreed to go to the judge and ask for leniency in my case, because they found out their own son was homosexual and that he had instigated the whole thing, not me. All this other business of them claiming I was in charge of a teen-age sex ring was a bunch of bullshit. They had no basis for any other charges. By this time things had calmed down, and they wanted this out of the way. So they agreed to ask for probation in my case, or whatever the judge would agree to. They would recommend leniency if I would plead guilty.

My attorney told me, "Now when you go in to see the judge, be sure to act like you're ashamed, like you're sorry. It's very important to play as dejected and down as you can." I said, "That's going to be very difficult for me." He says, "I know, but you can do it, you've got to do it." So they presented their case, we presented my character witnesses, and then the judge asked me to take the stand, and I went briefly over my past. They asked me particularly about when I first had sex with a man. I told them generally about my development as a homosexual. He asked a lot of questions, the judge did. Then I told him about my Gay career in the Navy. And he asked, "Didn't they send you to a psychiatrist?" I said, "Well, yes, but the psychiatrist was Gay, and all he did was have an affair with me instead of psychoanalyzing me."

The hearing was progressing rather well, I thought. Then the judge said, "Are you sorry now that you have committed such a crime?" Well, I just tried to say it as simply as I could, without any emphasis one way or another, that I did not feel that I had committed a crime, that I had performed an act which was perfectly natural to me, and obviously perfectly natural to the other party. I felt I was being persecuted. "Be that as it may," the judge says, "I realize your attitude toward the thing, but I'm set here to judge you because society says you have committed a crime, and I have to carry out my end of it."

We finished up the hearing and the judge said to my attorney, "Do you wish to have the sentencing today?" I think this is the point we made a very bad mistake. I think if we'd gone ahead with the sentencing at that time I'd have gotten only a probation, and I could have gotten out of the state right then. But I felt, and my attorney felt, that we needed my psychiatrist's report. The psychiatrist that I had been sent to was the state psychiatrist. I had seen him during the months I was waiting for these hearings.

We waited a week before we took the sentence. I had a lot of people go to the judge and ask that I be given consideration. I also know there were a number of people who went to the judge and condemned me, some of them very viciously. When I came up for sentencing the judge said, "I have never had a case where I've had so many outside interests want to talk to me." He said, "It was very difficult for me to come to a decision about this." He finally sentenced me, I think it was to seven years—anyway he suspended that sentence and gave me three years' probation, providing I spent the first six months in the county jail.

I went into the county jail. A friend of my family's was sheriff, so when I went in I was immediately made a trusty. I wasn't locked up all the time; I was made a cook. By then the assistant prosecutor, the one my mother had had words with, had become prosecuting attorney. He went immediately to the sheriff and told him to take me off trusty. I was to be put back in a cell by myself where I was to spend the entire six months. The sheriff told him, "I'm running this jail, and I'll run it the way I want to run it. You're not telling me how to run this jail! I'm keeping him a trusty, and if you don't like it, screw you!"

There were two deputies working there, one of them a childhood friend of my mother and father. My parents had gone to school with him and his sister. He and another guy were the main deputies. Behind the sheriff's back they conspired with the prosecuting attorney to entrap me, so they could arrest me again. The sheriff didn't know anything about this. Looking back on it I don't know why I didn't realize what was going on, except I still had this idea I hadn't done anything wrong. By this time I should have gotten it through my thick head that they were out to get me. In fact, the prosecuting attorney had come up to the kitchen where I worked and threatened me. "One way or the other," he says, "I'm going to have you in state prison."

First they sent up a deputy sheriff, a young guy who couldn't have been over twenty-one or twenty-two years old. There was a shower right off the kitchen. There was no reason on earth for him to take a shower up there. But every day, twice a day, he would take a shower there, when he'd come on duty and go off duty. He'd always leave the door open and parade around with nothing on, to see if I'd make a pass at him. Now it was really funny, because he was not the type of person I would have picked to make a pass at, but they didn't know this.

Then they went up to the cells, a couple of floors up where the prisoners were, and went around and called the fellows down. They'd say, "Look, you've got an eighteen-month sentence coming up. Now all you have to do is to let this guy make a pass at you and then turn state's evidence, and we'll get you off with a lighter sentence; we'll let you go." Several of these guys later told me about this, how they'd been propositioned. They questioned at least a dozen guys upstairs, young guys that they thought I'd go for, and who they thought would play ball with them.

Finally, they put a young kid down in my cell. He was one of three or four kids arrested for stealing gasoline, who were going to be charged. This one kid was about eighteen; he was the oldest of the bunch. When I would go around with the food at night, I realized later, they'd watch to see who I'd talk to, who I liked. They transferred this kid down to the kitchen to wash dishes. Since he was only eighteen at the time, this was theoretically against the rules; they could not have prisoners under twenty-one associating with prisoners over twenty-one, but they did it anyway. There was also another fellow who had been in prison before; he was in again for a manslaughter charge and was going to get a year in the county jail. They obviously set this up with him—told him they'd let him out if he'd pull this thing off. They put the three of us together in the trusty tank. There was an election, and a new sheriff came in, and they started setting the thing up immediately.

One night I was in bed with this kid. We'd had sex several times before. He was having a good time. Right while I was in the middle of going down on him there was this flash of light. I thought the third trusty had gotten up to take a leak and had hit the light bulb. A couple of seconds elapsed. Then this third trusty says, "All right, you goddamn cocksucker, get out of that bed." He turned on the light. He had a stool in his hand, and he was going to hit me with it if I started toward him. In the other hand he had a flashbulb camera. He'd taken our picture. He banged on the door, saying "I've got it. Come and get it!" The deputy immediately took the camera and let him out. It wasn't but a matter of minutes, but what they were there. They took the boy and brought him upstairs to the regular lockup.

They took me downstairs at three or four in the morning, and charged me and mugged me and booked me all over again. They rode my ass constantly about what a degraded, filthy, vile, horrible individual I was, about how they couldn't wait to get me locked up for the rest of my life. They put me in solitary confinement. They wouldn't let me out of there. They took my shoelaces away from me; they were afraid I was going to kill myself. That was the furthest thing from my mind, although I will admit I was shook, but I'm not the type of person to want to kill myself.

A couple of days later on visiting day, my mother and Mike, my lawyer, came to see me. The authorities told them they were sorry, but they couldn't visit me. The deputy took them into an office, and he says, "We arrested him in his cell for having sex with a trusty." He turned to my mother and he says to her, "You'll thank me for this later on. I've finally taken this burden from your shoulders. We're going to put him away for the rest of his life, away from society where he belongs." My mother hauled off and knocked him clear across the room. Mike, my lawyer, told me. The deputy was going to have her arrested for assault and battery. Mike said, "If you do, you're going to get another one from me."

They finally let my mother and Mike up to see me, and of course they were both furious. They said, "Why couldn't you have waited until you got out of here?" I said, "Well, my God, after being in here four or five months, what would you expect me to do?" They said, "Didn't you know they were going to try to trap you?" I said, "No, it never entered my mind." Mike said, "Well, my God, it should have. I warned you." I says, "You didn't warn me about them trying to trap me." He says, "I thought you might have sense enough to realize they might try it." I said, "No, I figured the whole thing was over with. All I was doing was getting out." Mike said, "Well, you're not out now."

I'd had just a month to do when this happened. My six months would have been up. The prosecuting attorney—he was very slick about this whole incident, he never charged me, never prosecuted. All he did was show the picture to the judge, and say, "I want his probation revoked. I want him sentenced on the original charge." The judge said, "I want to know what a camera was doing in that cell." It turned out it was the prosecuting attorney's own camera. The prosecuting attorney said, "That has nothing to do with this case, your honor. All we're asking is that you sentence him on the original charge." The judge says, "I'm aware of what you're asking me, but this is the fishiest thing I've come in contact with for quite some time." When it came out in the paper that I had been rearrested in jail, everybody knew it was a frame to get me into state prison. The prosecuting attorney said to me when we were coming out of court, "Well, I got you. Now you're going to serve that year and many more."

The judge sentenced me to seven years in the penitentiary. I heaved a big sigh of relief when I heard that, 'cause, God, I was petrified. Without Mike telling me, I kept my mouth shut that day. I thought the judge was going to sentence me to life or thirty or forty years. Even a prison guard said to me, "This is the biggest bunch of bullshit I've heard of in my life." He apologized for having to handcuff me to take me up there to prison.

I think the worst night I ever spent during this whole thing was the first in state prison. I had no idea what to expect. I came in late in the day and slept in what they call "fish row." That was a miserable night; I didn't sleep a wink. The next day they start you through orientation. First they give you an old shirt, and an old pair of pants, ten sizes too big for you. For two or three days you only have these clothes that are too big for you, and you have to hold them up. You can't let them go, or they'll fall down to the ground. This was just to humiliate you, to make you feel bad. Finally they give you your own clothes, and you get a cell assigned to you.

The warden and the assistant warden said, "God, we don't want you Boise guys in here. It's creating absolute turmoil up here." He says, "We're afraid to put you out on the yard. We're afraid there's going to be a riot, or some kind of killing or knifing over one of you guys." He says, "We've got to protect you because otherwise the city would be up in arms." So to protect us they locked us up in solitary cells, in what they called One House. That was the place they put all the people who had been arrested for sexual perversion of some kind, either child-molesting —a father who'd fucked his daughter or fucked his son—or somebody that had been caught inside the prison having sex. We couldn't get out of our cell, except once in the morning for breakfast, once in the afternoon for dinner. That was it. They did take us out in the middle of the day sometimes, when the weather was good, and let us exercise for an hour. But they wouldn't let anyone near us. They had a guard by us all the time, so we couldn't get near anyone and no one could get near us. So it was really double jeopardy, because they lock you up inside a place you're incarcerated in to begin with.

They kept us locked up for six months. For six months I went through every book in the library, I knitted doilies, I went through four bookkeeping courses. I was by myself in a cell maybe a yard wide and a yard deep. No toilets. We had a shit pail with disinfectant in it. We constructed our own toilet seats for our little pails, which we took out and emptied twice a day, then filled up with disinfectant again. They loved us so much they put the entire TB ward on the deck right below us, because it didn't make any difference if the homosexuals and sexual perverts got TB.

The captain of the yard was an old friend of my family's. I'd known him all my life. The first thing he said to me was, "Now just go out there and find yourself a jock and settle down, so we won't have any trouble with you." I said, "How am I going to settle down with somebody when I'm locked up in my cell twenty-four hours a day?" He said, "Well, don't worry about that right now."

About the third or fourth day I was there, I was going through the chow line. You have three minutes to eat. I still eat awfully fast; I never got out of the habit. For all the time I was in there I had to eat fast, get in and get out. You eat with a man sitting up on a little roost with a machine gun, watching you while you eat. You can't speak and you can't look around. You just have to look at your plate, and eat and get out. As I was going through the chow line I saw this gorgeous guy handing out silverware. You wore anything—they didn't pay attention to how you dressed—and he was wearing a shirt that was completely open, with the sleeves torn out. He had been a prizefighter. He was a beauty, about six feet three or four. I looked at him, and he looked at me. I went on and sit down. He could walk around, so he took a bench and he sit up at the front. He set up there with his legs apart and just looked at me all the time I was eating. When I got outside, he was waiting there. He said, "You got any magazines?" "No," I said. "OK," he said. And off he went. His name was Larry. Later he brought me a big stack of magazines and shoved them in my cell and walked away without saying a word. Before the month was out, Larry and I found a way to become lovers.

You couldn't play the field in there; you got one fellow and you stayed with him until that broke up, and then you could go to someone else. But once you got with someone you were supposed to stay with him. As it happened, this first fellow I tied up with was let out. Then I went to another one. Then he went into solitary confinement. I went from him to one more.

I was in for eighteen months, six of that in a solitary cell. Ordinarily, when they're ready to let you out, you go through a parole board. But they didn't do that with us. They evidently wanted to keep it quiet about when we were getting out. There was always pressure from people in Boise who didn't want us to get out. It was never published in the paper when we were released. They would just call each one of us out individually and tell us that we were leaving in the next couple of days. And then we were gone. Families, and the people with some money who could afford a lawyer, kept pressuring to get us out. My mother and my lawyer would come to see me every week, one or the other of them, or both, and they'd keep pressuring the warden.

When we got out, we were all required to leave the state and not return until after our one year probation was up. I left for good. One man who was sentenced to life, who actually did nine years, he got out and then finally went back to Boise. By that time it was forgotten about. A lot of the others couldn't go back and face their friends, they were so ashamed at being arrested. And their friends or their employers hadn't stood behind them.

There was one friend of mine, one friend in particular, who was so ashamed, so upset and degraded by this thing, that when he was finally released on probation— he didn't actually serve any time—he went at once to San Francisco. He literally drank himself to death in a few weeks because he was so ashamed. It was a direct result of having been arrested and having been exposed.

This whole thing was horrible. I don't think there was any reason for it, only some people's personal gain, either power or some vindictiveness against others. I don't think it was conducted fairly. The people who went to jail took the brunt of it for several thousand. We were just the unfortunate ones.

It's not something I like to think about much. I try to put it out of my mind, I try to think about other things. Occasionally I'll be with a group of people and someone will mention the Boise incident, relating it to something that's happening today, and I'll just set there and smile.

♀ 1960: Fannie Mae Clackum versus the United States; "She was never informed of any charges against her"

One of the relatively few American legal cases involving charges of Lesbianism was heard by the United States Court of Claims. On January 20, 1960, Judge Madden delivered the court's opinion in the case of Fannie Mae Clackum versus the United States. The facts in Clackum's case against the United States Air Force are stated in Madden's decision; her case was argued and decided on the basis of the sufficiency of the evidence to prove Lesbianism. It is notable that the United States government's behavior toward Clackum involved such outrageous violation of individual rights that even Judge Madden was provoked to ask rhetorically: "What's going on here?" Madden's decision states:

The plaintiff was separated from the United States Air Force on January 22, 1952, with a discharge "under conditions other than honorable." She asserts that the purported discharge was invalid, and sues for her pay from the date of the purported discharge. The following "Statement of Facts Alleged", contained in the following four paragraphs, is copied from the Government's brief.

On February 2, 1951, plaintiff was a reservist in the United States Air Force (WAF—Women in the Air Force) and was ordered to active duty as an airman. She was stationed thereafter at Barksdale Air Force Base, Louisiana, in the grade of corporal, with duty in Headquarters and Headquarters Squadron, 301st Air Base Group.

On April 18, 1951, plaintiff, among others, was called before her commanding officer and a representative of the O.S.I. (Office of Special Intelligence) and interrogated on matters of homosexuality concerning which plaintiff alleges she had no knowledge. Thereafter, until January 1952, plaintiff was repeatedly interviewed by an officer of the O.S.I. concerning homosexual activities and informed that she was under investigation. She was never informed of any charges against her by the Air Force, although in October 1951 she was informed that some action was contemplated against her. Also in October 1951 plaintiff was called before her commanding officer and was given an opportunity to resign. . . . Upon being offered the opportunity to resign, plaintiff refused to resign and demanded in writing that she be tried by court-martial. The purpose of this demand was to require the Air Force to confront her with the basis of the accusations against her and to afford her an opportunity to present evidence in her own behalf.

Although charges were preferred against plaintiff under the Uniform Code of Military Justice, the charges were not referred for investigation under the provisions of the Code, they were not brought to her attention, and she had no knowledge of them until after her discharge. After plaintiff was given an opportunity to resign and refused, she was given a psychiatric examination but was not informed of the report of the psychiatrist. No sworn evidence against plaintiff was taken or received by the O.S.I. or by the Air Force, and prior to her discharge plaintiff was not confronted with the nature of the evidence against her. Plaintiff was demoted to the grade of private on January 22, 1952 and on that same day was discharged from the service under conditions other than honorable. . . .

Plaintiff brought suit in this Court on June 8, 1956. By agreement of the parties, the Court suspended proceedings in this Court to permit plaintiff to file an application before the Air Force Board for the Correction of Military Records on the ground that plaintiff had failed to exhaust her administrative remedies. An application was filed and was denied by the Air Force Board for the Correction of Military Records. The suspension of proceedings in this Court was then removed.

Some of the effects upon a soldier of a discharge "under conditions other than honorable" are briefly stated in Air Force Regulations . . . dated January 12, 1951, . . . which says that the person so discharged may be deprived of many rights as a veteran under both Federal and State legislation, and may expect to encounter substantial prejudice in civilian life. . . .

One's reaction to the foregoing narrative is "What's going on here?"

A woman soldier is interrogated about homosexual matters and is orally told that some action is contemplated against her. She is called before her commanding officer and is offered an opportunity to resign. She indignantly denies the implied charges involved in the situation and demands in writing that she be tried by a court-martial so that she can learn what the charges are, face her accusers, and present evidence in her own behalf. Although charges were preferred against her, they were not referred for investigation as the statutes governing courts-martial require, and neither the charges nor the evidence upon which they were based were ever made known to the soldier until after her discharge. She was summarily given a discharge "under conditions other than honorable", her reputation as a decent woman was officially destroyed, her rights to her accrued pay and accrued leave, and to the numerous and valuable benefits conferred by the nation and many of the states upon former soldiers were forfeited.

Air Force Regulations . . . related to the handling of homosexual charges against enlisted personnel. They provided for a resignation agreeing to accept an undesirable discharge with all its damaging consequences. If the soldier refused to so resign, the regulations provided that a trial by general court-martial would be considered. If the evidence in the case indicated that conviction by a general court-martial was unlikely, then the Secretary of the Air Force was, by the regulations, authorized to "direct discharge and administratively determine whether an undesirable, general, or honorable type of discharge certificate will be furnished."

A dishonorable discharge is, for a soldier, one of the most severe penalties which may be imposed by a court-martial. Elaborate provisions for review of court-martial sentences within the military hierarchy, and potentially by the Court of

Military Appeals, are included in our military laws. Yet the Air Force regulations discussed above provide that if the evidence at hand is so unsubstantial that a conviction by a court-martial would be unlikely, the executive officers of the Air Force may themselves convict the soldier and impose the penalty. It is as if a prosecuting attorney were authorized, in a case where he concluded that he didn't have enough evidence to obtain a conviction in court, to himself impose the fine or imprisonment which he thought the accused person deserved.

The Government defends this remarkable arrangement, and its operation in the instant case, on the ground that it is necessary in the interest of an efficient military establishment for our national defense. We see nothing in this argument. The plaintiff being a member of the Air Force Reserve, on active duty, the Air Force had the undoubted right to discharge her whenever it pleased, for any reason or for no reason, and by do soing preserve the Air Force from even the slightest suspicion of harboring undesirable characters. But it is unthinkable that it should have the raw power, without respect for even the most elementary notions of due process of law, to load her down with penalties. It is late in the day to argue that everything that the executives of the armed forces do in connection with the discharge of soldiers is beyond the reach of judicial scrutiny. . . .

After her discharge, the plaintiff appealed to the Air Force Discharge Review Board. Such an appeal is provided for in the Air Force Regulations. Her appeal and that of another female non-commissioned officer were heard together. They were represented by counsel. They had access to a brief which had been written by an investigator, and which summarized conversations which he had had with various persons. The plaintiff and the other appellant testified at length, directing their testimony to the incidents mentioned in the conversations summarized in the investigator's brief. Their testimony was, of course, entirely favorable to themselves. Some members of the Board asked some questions of the appellants. None of the answers to these questions tended to show that the appellants were guilty. Testimonials of good character from Air Force superiors, civilian employers, clergymen and other acquaintances were placed in evidence.

No witnesses other than the two appellants testified. None of the persons mentioned in the investigator's brief as having made statements derogatory to the appellants were called to testify.

The appellants' counsel made an able argument on their behalf. Among other things, he pointed out the absurdity of the following oracular item in the investigator's brief:

> Psychiatric evaluation of appl. (appellant) 21 Nov. 51 reflected a diagnosis of sexual deviate manifested by homosexuality latent.,

in view of the plaintiff's uncontradicted testimony that the only psychiatric interview to which she was subjected lasted from 20 to 30 minutes.

The hearing was closed and the Discharge Review Board made the following [findings]

> After consideration of the evidence of record, including the 201 file in the case, the Board finds:
> a. That the discharge of the applicants under the provisions of AFR 35–66

(discharge of homosexuals) was in accord with the regulations in force at the time.

b. That the character of the discharges was amply supported by the evidence of record.

c. That no additional evidence of sufficient weight and credibility as to warrant reversal of the prior action in these cases has been adduced before the Air Force Discharge Review Board.

Conclusions

The Board recommends that no change be made in the type of discharge certificates presently in effect.

The "evidence of record" upon which the Board based its finding of guilt was obviously not the evidence received at the hearing. All of the evidence received at the hearing tended to prove the plaintiff's innocence. The "evidence of record" was a dossier of affidavits of persons, some of whom were not even mentioned in the investigator's brief which was made available to the plaintiff at the time of her hearing before the Discharge Review Board, although the statements made in their affidavits, if believed, were extremely damaging to the plaintiff. None of the affidavits was seen by the plaintiff or her counsel until July 24, 1959, long after the plaintiff's case was pending in this court.

The "evidence of record" also contained the confidential reports of the Office of Special Investigations which were forwarded to the Air Force Personnel Counsel and the Secretary of the Air Force, and which have never been made available to the plaintiff or her counsel.

The so-called "hearing" before the Air Force Discharge Board was not a hearing at all, in the usual sense of that word. It was a meaningless formality, to comply with the regulations. The "evidence" upon which the case was going to be decided, and obviously was decided, was not present at the hearing, unless the undisclosed dossier which contained it was in the drawer of the table at which the Board sat. The appellant and her counsel were futilely tilting at shadows. However vulnerable the secret evidence may have been, there was no possible way to attack it.

The plaintiff was, after the proceeding before the Discharge Review Board, as before, a soldier dishonorably discharged, officially branded by her Government as an indecent woman, deprived of valuable rights and benefits which are given to other ex-soldiers. And all this without any semblance of an opportunity to know what the evidence against her was, or to face her accusers in a trial or hearing.

As we have said, the plaintiff is suing for her pay as a soldier, on the theory that her purported discharge was illegal and invalid. The Government says that even if the discharge actually issued was invalid, the Air Force could have validly discharged her at the time it invalidly did so, and therefore she is not entitled to be paid. There are, of course, many situations in which, if a party had acted somewhat differently, he would not have violated the legal rights of the other person and would not be liable for damages.

In the instant case, the dishonorable nature of the discharge was its very essence, the most important thing about it. We feel no urge to dissect the discharge and discard its essence, retaining only its effect of getting the plaintiff out of the Air Force and off its payroll, thus leaving her to suffer, without compensation, all the other penalties which the discharge imposed upon her.

Our conclusion is that the purported discharge of the plaintiff was invalid, and did not effect the plaintiff's separation from the Air Force.[135]

The government's motion to dismiss Clackum's petition was denied.

1965–69: SARA HARRIS;
The Puritan Jungle
A homosexual "is better off dead"

For her book *The Puritan Jungle; America's Sexual Underground* (1969), journalist Sara Harris recorded interviews from 1965 to 1969 with "lesbians, [male] homosexuals, hustlers, vice cops, alcoholics, sadists, masochists, transvestites, wife swappers, and the wives they swap," as well as others directly involved in the sexual underworld of that antisexual society under investigation. Harris talked with John Sorenson, a former head of the Miami vice squad, and Duane Barker, another ex-vice squad chief and aide to the Florida legislative committee that issued a notorious antihomosexual report in 1964. Harris's interviews with Sorenson and Barker are classic studies of two extreme antihomosexuals; these interviews provide insight into the situation of Gay people in trouble, from the viewpoint of two representatives of "law and order."

John Sorenson of Miami, Florida, is a leader of his community, a Baptist church deacon and former head of the Miami vice squad. His convictions regarding the sexual leanings and patterns of a large minority in America, its homosexuals, are on the one hand complex and on the other—backed as they are by his God and Bible—terrifyingly simple.

"I would rather see any of my children dead than homosexual. . . . And for the reason I feel there is no cure and because of the complete degeneracy of these people. They appear on the surface to be respectable, but they're the lowest forms of people. . . ."

Sorenson continues:

"It says in the Old Testament that: 'If a man lieth with another man as he lieth with woman he *should be put to death.' It's an abomination*. . . . And also in the New Testament it says that 'these persons will never see the Kingdom of God'— homosexuals.

"There is hope, though, there's a little hope for the homosexual in the New Testament. . . . in First Corinthians, Paul starts out by saying that 'drunkards and thieves and homosexuals and warmongers and so forth—these will never see the Kingdom of Heaven.' But then he goes into the eleventh verse and says, 'But there are some of you, ye can be saved. Ye can be sanctified to the blood of the Lord

Jesus Christ.' In other words, they *may* be cured by the Grace of God. . . . But it's such a slim chance that, if I had the choice—my children are all Christians—I would say 'take them now before they become homosexuals because if they become homosexuals, they wouldn't have a chance to enter the Kingdom of God unless by some miracle the Lord forgave them and overlooked what they were. Or unless they came to the Lord—which is so rare. It's so rare for a homosexual to say, 'Lord, I'm sorry. Take me out of this life.' It happens once in a while, once in a blue moon."

I ask Mr. Sorenson if I have understood him correctly. Is he saying that because a homosexual cannot be acceptable to God, he is better off dead?

"Correct."

"And you would have him so?"

"Yes."

Moralizing about homosexuality Sorenson says:

"I think the sin of homosexuality is worse than the sin of murder. But, see here," and his voice lowers in intensity, "we're getting into a point of hate and this we want to avoid. We're going to lose whatever sense we have about the thing. We can't hate them. The point is to love them. Now, how do you do this? How do you love a homosexual? You love him this way. You put him in prison."

Seeing my incredulity, he says: "You put the homosexual in prison out of love not hate, because if he's ever going to have a chance it's going to be by taking him away from making other people like he is. Because this is the worst thing he can do. Being a homosexual is bad enough, but the fact that he might make someone else that way—this is the most horrible thing he can do. So you're really doing him a favor by taking him out of circulation. If you could put him in a hospital—if you had laws that would do that—but you don't. You don't have laws."

Harris asks Sorenson

how long he would keep a homosexual in prison if the law were in his hands.

"As long as I felt there was a danger of him getting out and infecting children," he says without hesitation. "Now, you take a young homosexual, say, at thirty, thirty-five. This person here is death on children. . . . He is the most dangerous person. I'd keep him in prison for twenty years till he was fifty-five. You wouldn't have as much of a problem then. The kids wouldn't bother with him in the first place. He wouldn't have the attraction."

"How about homosexuals who have relationships only with each other? Two consenting male adults who have relationships, in private, with one another. You feel there *are* such homosexuals, don't you?"

"Oh, certainly, there are such. And I think it's just as much an abomination. . . . there are so many people that say, 'Well, if two men wanted to walk into another room and do something by themselves, I couldn't care less.' Well, this is not my philosophy at all. I could care because those two have got to come out of that room again and they may be schoolteachers teaching my children and I don't want any sick person teaching my children and yet there are sick people in our schools right now teaching our children. And they are mentally ill. Anybody will tell you they're mentally ill. And yet here they are teaching our children reading, writing, arithmetic, science and so forth. And their philosophies and their morals spill over."

Sorenson tells Harris:

"We've got to remember the Bible, the Old Testament. In it, the thief wasn't killed, nobody was killed (and that would include the hustler) except the homosexual. God looked on him as somebody terrible you'd better wipe out before he destroys the whole world."

I pursue the point, asking that if he were responsible for writing the law regarding homosexuals, would he demand the death penalty.

"If homosexuality could be a reason for the death penalty, you would see almost a stop to this whole thing," Mr. Sorenson says with conviction.[136]

Harris continues:

John Sorenson introduced me to Duane Barker, the man who handles all facets of investigative work for Dade County schoolteachers. He scrutinizes them all for narcotics addiction, drunkenness, absence without leave from schools they have taught in formerly, and, of course, homosexuality. He, too, was once head of the morals squad. He also served, for one year, in 1963, with the Florida legislative committee, called by most people, the Johns' Committee in "honor" of its presiding senator, Charley E. Johns, which was set up to investigate such matters as communism, fascism—and homosexuality—among people in focal positions. The Johns' Committee was called to account by most Florida newspapers for its methods of obtaining information, as well as by the Florida section of the American Civil Liberties Union, liberal churchmen and their congregations.

Duane Barker was detailed to pry out the Florida homosexuals in powerful positions, a task he executed all too faithfully—as many heterosexuals, from the director of the American Civil Liberties Union to numerous newspapermen, can testify. Among other accomplishments, he composed a brochure intended "to investigate and report on the extent of infiltration into agencies supported by state funds by practicing homosexuals . . ." Although formally named *Homosexuality and Citizenship in Florida*, the report was more popularly called "The Purple Pamphlet," a cognomen acquired, no doubt, from its mournful purple cover.[137] Much of its philosophy echoed that espoused by John Sorenson; but what is of interest is that it has been banned in Florida and also in many other states as hardcore pornography. The reason: there are two photos, one of two males embracing passionately in the nude, and the other of a young man, nude except for a black "posing strap." . . . "The Purple Pamphlet" is available only in those shops which sell pornography, and then only under-the-counter, unless the dealer believes you are an officer in plainclothes—in which case, it is not available at all. It defines homosexuality as "the greatest abomination." Although worded more temperately than some of Mr. Sorenson's speeches, its findings were hailed and upheld by state assemblymen and senators—until public pressure forced them to abandon the report.

Speaking of homosexuality, Barker told Harris:

"I guess I shouldn't be so worried about the damn thing. But our kids—listen, you've got to worry about them. Right?" His eyes now take on more intensity, his tone becomes more measured, less spontaneous. "I'll tell you when I first became interested in the whole problem. The reason I got involved with the fags, to begin with, is because I was a juvenile officer in Dade County at a time when a juvenile officer in Brown County, a good-looking young fellow you'd never suspect, turned out to be homo. Well, I was shocked to think these people—a person like that— could get into police work. And with juveniles, too. But let me tell you, since I've gotten to know them, I think they can do anything. They're the best dupes in the world. They have the best grapevine in the world. I've heard that Mr. J. Edgar Hoover made a comment that if he had the grapevine in the FBI that the gay world has, he could fire half his agents and still get twice as much work done. And, believe me, I know what he means. From my own personal experience.

"I was in Tampa some years ago when I was working with the Johns' Committee, and I was talking with a homosexual informant and he was reading to me out of this diary he had—his own diary. And in one place in the diary, he described a massive arrest that took place in one of our major cities in the U.S., seventy-five or eighty men arrested, transvestites, homosexuals and so forth. They were up in a dance hall the police raided. They had a large meat loaf on the table shaped like a human penis and they were eating this meat loaf when the police came in.

"Well, my informant had written up everything about the raid in his diary, including the names of the major people arrested and what they were charged with, everything. And the most interesting thing about the whole business is the fellow I'm talking about wasn't even there at the time. He was in Paris. And by checking back and getting other people to help, just for the sake of curiosity, just because he wanted to know, practically every homo, every queer in Paris knew about the raid in a matter of hours, three and a half, to be exact."

Later in Harris's interview with Barker, she reports:

He draws a deep breath and says, "If only our area wasn't so attractive to fags. When I say 'attractive,' I'm talking about all the hedges we've got, the greenery. Now this may sound like a small thing but it isn't to homos, who want privacy. Any house in which you find homos living, you'll also find a lot of shrubs, hedges, trees, a dog in the driveway. Anything they can put up to keep people going by from getting tag [license plate] numbers from the cars they have in their driveways when they're having parties. And they're always having parties."

When I ask why people's license tag numbers should be taken merely because they are attending a party at someone's house, he seems not to hear.

As Barker continues talking with Harris, she relates:

Suddenly he gets caught up by the heat of his emotion. "These people who get all shook up, nervous and angry about the gay people and civil rights. 'Let them be out in the open,' they say, and there won't be any problems. That's as much as they know about the whole thing. 'No stigma!' they say. 'No blackmail!' Fiddlesticks.

"Approval of consensual acts between adults! My God, how can they be so stupid? Don't they know that all their ideas can lead to is perversion of our children? Don't they *care* what happens to the children of this country, to the young people? Don't they *care* whether they're protected or not? *Don't they even love America's kids?*"[138]

♀ 1966–67: Louisiana versus Mary Young and Dawn DeBlanc; "Unnatural carnal copulation"

In 1966, Mary Young and Dawn DeBlanc were charged "with having committed a crime against nature" under the law of Louisiana, and became the principals in one of the few Lesbian-related, precedent-setting legal decisions in American history. They were tried before a jury of five, in the Criminal Court, Orleans Parish, before Judge Frank J. Shea. A legal document describes events leading to their arrest:

During cross-examination a police officer testified that he talked to one of the accused (Dawn DeBlanc) over the telephone to arrange a meeting with her and other women at a motel for sexual relations and to settle a price for prostitution, and that during this conversation she mentioned that sometimes they "gave a show".

During the trial, Young and DeBlanc's lawyer unsuccessfully objected to the admission as evidence:

(1) of photographs of appellants in the nude made in the motel room where the crime was committed and where they were arrested and (2) of certain comic books found at that time in the purse of one of them and said in brief to be obscene.

The photographs had been taken after the defendants' arrest.
Reporting on the case, Judge Shea said

that in his general charge he instructed the jury on the law defining "crime against nature" and explained that any actual joining or connection of a genital organ of one person and the mouth of another constituted this crime; and he states that in his opinion he sufficiently informed the jury of what acts must have been performed to constitute the offense charged.

Judge Shea refused the defense's request that the jury be given special instructions concerning the law on entrapment. The judge claimed that the question of entrapment had been covered adequately in his general charge to the jury.
The judge also denied the defense's motion for a new trial based on their allegation "that there was no evidence of the commission of the offense": "unnatural carnal copulation."

The record discloses that officers who were in the motel room and witnessed the acts which formed the basis of the charge testified that there was oral copulation by and between both of the accused, and these witnesses described in detail the acts showing the unnatural carnal copulation.

Mary Young and Dawn DeBlanc were convicted and sentenced to thirty months in the parish prison. They appealed their case to the Louisiana Supreme Court, which heard their plea on November 7, 1966. This court ruled, in part:

The statute, of course, requires proof of an "unnatural carnal copulation". As pointed out by this court, . . . this phrase simply means "any and all carnal copulation or sexual joining and coition that is devious and abnormal because it is contrary to the natural traits and/or instincts intended by nature, and therefore does not conform to the order ordained by nature".

On January 16, 1967, the Louisiana Supreme Court affirmed the convictions of Young and DeBlanc, setting the precedent that:

Oral copulation by and between two women constituted "unnatural carnal copulation" within statute proscribing such conduct.[139]

II

TREATMENT
1884-1974

Introduction

The following chronological survey of documents relating to the medical treatment of homosexuals in America demonstrates that Lesbians and Gay men have long been subjected to a varied, often horrifying list of "cures" at the hands of psychiatric-psychological professionals, treatments usually aimed at asexualization or heterosexual reorientation. This treatment has almost invariably involved a negative value judgment concerning the inherent character of homosexuality. The treatment of Lesbians and Gay men by psychiatrists and psychologists constitutes one of the more lethal forms of homosexual oppression.

Among the treatments are surgical measures: castration, hysterectomy, and vasectomy. In the 1800s, surgical removal of the ovaries and of the clitoris are discussed as a "cure" for various forms of female "erotomania," including, it seems, Lesbianism. Lobotomy was performed as late as 1951. A variety of drug therapies have been employed, including the administration of hormones, LSD, sexual stimulants, and sexual depressants. Hypnosis, used on Gay people in America as early as 1899, was still being used to treat such "deviant behavior" in 1967. Other documented "cures" are shock treatment, both electric and chemical; aversion therapy, employing nausea-inducing drugs, electric shock, and/or negative verbal suggestion; and a type of behavior therapy called "sensitization," intended to increase heterosexual arousal, making ingenious use of pornographic photos. Often homosexuals have been the subjects of Freudian psychoanalysis and other varieties of individual and group psychotherapy. Some practitioners (a Catholic one is quoted) have treated homosexuals by urging an effort of the will directed toward the goal of sexual abstinence. Primal therapists, vegetotherapists, and the leaders of each new psychological fad have had their say about treating homosexuals. Even musical analysis has reportedly assisted a doctor in such a "cure." Astrologers, Scientologists, Aesthetic Realists, and other quack philosophers have followed the medical profession's lead with their own suggestions for treatment.[1]

Such negative treatment history is made more obscene by the early existence and discussion of an alternative—a form of treatment aimed at helping homosexuals feel good about—and give active, unsublimated expression to—their sexual-affectional attractions. This dissenting tradition is exemplified in the following survey by the "adjustment therapy" advocated by the homosexual emancipation pioneers Magnus Hirschfeld and E. I. Prime Stevenson, and that described by A. A. Brill.

This survey of treatment history is based largely upon doctors' reports of their own work, upon the relevant writings of early homosexual emancipationists, and upon a taped interview with a homosexual victim of shock treatment. Most of these documents are excerpted from medical journals (ironically, now one of the richest sources for Gay history research). These journal articles, even more than medical books, reveal doctors communicating with each other on a privileged, "insider" basis. Here they discuss the results of their latest "experiments"; they counsel each other against undue "pessimism" concerning "cures"; they caution each other that the display of "too much sympathy" for homosexual patients inhibits their desire to become heterosexual. Occasionally a doctor urges law reform, particularly that type which would increase the authority of the psychiatric-psychological establishment in matters concerning homosexuality.

The treatment of homosexuality by medical practitioners is of relatively recent origin, and is closely tied to the conceptualization of homosexuality as a medical-psychological phenomenon, a "mental illness." This conceptualization is itself a fairly recent invention: European discussion of homosexuality as a medical phenomenon dates to the early 1800s. Before that time, ecclesiastical authorities conceived of homosexuality as essentially a theological-moral phenomenon, a sin. Next, legislative bodies declared it a legal matter, a crime. The historical change in the conception of homosexuality from sin to crime to sickness is intimately associated with the rise to power of a class of petit bourgeois medical professionals, a group of individual medical entrepreneurs, whose stock in trade is their alleged "expert" understanding of homosexuality, a special-interest group whose facade of scientific objectivity covers their own emotional, economic, and career investments in their status as such authorities. At its time of origin, the medical practitioners' concept of homosexuality as a sickness may have been a liberal and humane advance over the conception and punishment of homosexuality as a crime. In 1976, psychiatrists and psychologists are among the major ideologues of homosexual oppression.

Research is now starting to trace the exact historical process by which these medical businessmen (for they are mostly males) acquired the power to define the character of homosexuals—and to trace that political movement by which Gay people are beginning to redefine themselves, struggling for power over that society which affects their lives. Today, Gay liberationists are challenging the long-accepted, medically derived notion that homosexuality is essentially a psychological phenomenon—any more than it is a political, economic, or historical one. They are disputing that view by which the complex human phenomena of homosexual behavior, emotion, life-style, culture, and history are reduced to mere psychology. Neither homosexuality nor heterosexuality, they argue, is encompassed by the psychological. Calling for the reconceptualization of homosexuality in broad, humanistic, and social terms, Gay people are today beginning the work of reconceptualizing themselves.

In the following documents, purely theoretical passages are generally deleted, for they tend to obscure the actual character of that treatment upon which this section focuses. These documents indirectly suggest the physical pain and mental anguish which treatment by medical practitioners has inflicted through the years upon countless anonymous

Lesbians and Gay men, whom it was ostensibly designed to "help." A few of the treatment histories included describe severely disturbed, obsessive and compulsive individuals. Most of these reports contain (inadvertent) hints of those antihomosexual attitudes which helped drive these people mad; some reports indicate quite clearly that treatment itself drove these lost souls deeper into insanity.

The medical treatment literature documents a history of horrors, one of which has been the way Gay people themselves were made the agents of their own violation and destruction. Treatment has been perpetrated, sometimes, upon acquiescent victims. The very act of entering treatment for one's homosexuality involved a negative evaluation of one's own, often basic, feelings. There is clearly a link between socially induced feelings of guilt and worthlessness, and the self-punishing behavior of some homosexuals reported in these documents. Numbers of these histories concern guilt-ridden, self-hating homosexuals, who have so internalized society's condemnation that they seek out cruel forms of treatment as punishment; they play what can only be termed a masochistic game, in which the doctor is assigned, and accepts, a truly sadistic (as well as remunerative) role. There is surely a link between self-punishment as an internally motivated individual act and punishment as an external legal sanction, between castration as an early form of legal punishment (as proposed by Thomas Jefferson, and enacted into law in Pennsylvania) and castration as an early form of medical treatment.

A connection between the legal and medical establishments is also evident when doctors prominent in the business of treating homosexuals are simultaneously employed by the penal system. Justice is literally on their side when these agents of the medico-legal establishment seek to "rehabilitate" homosexuals who have come into active conflict with the law. This law derives from religious concepts, and Judeo-Christian morality is frequently found in these medical texts, propagated in secularized, pseudoscientific terms, even though such strictures supposedly have no place in a society theoretically based on separation of church and state.

The question of doctors' responsibility is not answered satisfactorily by reference to patients' alleged voluntary and informed consent to treatment and their desire to "go straight." For despite the current popularity of a simplistic libertarian ideology, we are not always in touch with, and do not always know, our own deepest feelings and best interests. In ways Gay people themselves have not fully realized, we do not yet always know our own minds, we are not always immediately able to affirm our own deepest desires. In this respect the present author's own history is like that of many:

> I entered analysis, voluntarily I thought, with the idea that my "problem" was my homosexuality, and my goal a heterosexual "cure," although even then I was wise enough to know I never wanted to be "adjusted" to a society which was itself desperately in need of radical change. Paradoxically, my experience in therapy turned out to be an extremely good one, helping me to know and affirm positive parts of myself, among them my homosexuality. By accident I had found a therapist who helped people to find and be themselves, who did *not* view my "problem" as I did myself. But it was only with the development of the Gay liberation movement, and my own involvement in it, that it came to me, in a rather brief and mind-spinning few months, that I, too, was a member of an oppressed group. Only then, after perhaps ten years of therapy, and only as a result of this organized movement of Gay people, did I understand that I had earlier been socially pressured into feeling myself a psychological freak, in need of treatment. In entering therapy, my goal had, in truth, not been voluntarily chosen at all.

Therapists who do not help their homosexual patients to fully explore the possibility of homosexuality as a legitimate option have not helped to expand those individuals' freedom.

The treatment documents demonstrate that the conflict between Gay people and the psychiatric-psychological profession is of long standing; it did not begin with the recent Gay liberation movement. Dr. Edmund Bergler's lecture (not excerpted) before the New York Psychoanalytic Society in 1942 provides evidence of those antihomosexual views which have led many Gay people to despise psychiatrists and psychologists—a conflict of whose origin Bergler is blithely unaware. Bergler's report indicates no sensitivity on his part to the fact that the "ill-repute enjoyed by our therapy among homosexuals" might be due to those therapists' negative evaluation of homosexuals as "sick" (Bergler's term). Bergler has no awareness that recurring conflicts with his homosexual patients (reported by himself) just might have something to do with his own attitudes toward "perverts" and "perversion" (his terms). His characterization of homosexuals as "injustice" collectors, who provoke trouble upon themselves to justify self-pity, must have struck some homosexuals as a provocative way of blaming the victim—even before the rise of the Gay liberation movement. The great irritation Gay liberationists will no doubt feel while reading Bergler's account today is simply a more conscious, less ambivalent form of that same dislike experienced (according to his own report) by many of Bergler's patients. Even in pre-Gay liberation days some homosexuals must have resented, however ambivalently, Bergler's positive evaluation of their pain—based on his belief that a certain high level of guilt indicated a good prognosis for heterosexual reorientation. In Bergler's report, it is indeed odd to find a man supposedly concerned with the alleviation of mental suffering so positively gleeful about the guilt feelings of homosexuals. If, as Bergler points out, many Gay people in treatment with him displayed masochistic tendencies, then he was undoubtedly the sadist in those partnerships. Bergler's provocative comments do raise serious questions about masochism as a form of socially conditioned Gay self-oppression, and about the often sadistic treatment of Gay people by psychiatrists and psychologists.[2]

Bergler's antihomosexual views are typical of many other doctors, few of whom show any sign of seriously questioning their own motives, feelings, and fundamental assumptions in treating homosexuals. Their basic system of values has remained quite simple and unchanged through the years. America's psychological establishment has quite simplemindedly propagated the absolute virtues of heterosexuality, marriage, monogamy, parenthood, and the most traditional, narrow definitions of femininity, masculinity, and of male and female roles. The doctors' reports are characterized by a complacent, middle-class sensibility, a smug philistinism. This moralizing is most evident in the earliest documents quoted—those from the end of the nineteenth century and the start of the twentieth. At that time, doctors un-self-consciously invoked morality—God, country, family—in describing their treatment of homosexuals. More recent documents usually replace such overt moralizing with quieter, often unspoken, hidden evaluations, expressive of a technocratic consciousness focused on getting a job done, a new heterosexual created. Doctors have increasingly turned to technical language and jargon to disguise and suppress their own emotions and underlying values. Although secularization has transformed the rhetoric, mystification remains.

The focus here is on treatment—actual medical practice—rather than on either of the two other major areas of medical discourse on homosexuality: its alleged nature, its supposed cause. These character assessments and etiological discussions have often been of a highly abstract, theoretical, and speculative character, disassociated from any social reality. The literature on treatment, on the other hand, conveys what was actually done to, and even experienced by, Lesbians and Gay men. The diverse theories of the alleged character and cause of homosexuality, and their relation to particular forms of treatment, do need to be studied in social-historical perspective—an important task for the future. Here, the doctors' causative theories may often be inferred from the type of treatment they prescribe. Aversion therapy, for instance, rests upon the tenets of behavioral psychology holding that homosexuality is a learned response, capable of being unlearned. This concept is only distantly related to the more complex notion of those psychoanalysts who regard sexual orientation as the outcome of early experience, especially within the family, by which social norms and role models come to influence the undefined psyche of a child. Opposed to both these views are various physiological theories of causation, now generally regarded as outmoded, according to which homosexuality is either treatable by biological means, such as hormones, or is an unalterable, hereditary trait. It is now becoming clear that the causation of homosexuality cannot be understood apart from the causation of sexual orientation of every variety (including heterosexuality, bestiality, and object fetishism)—if the subject is to be studied at all. Past interest in the subject was almost always motivated and obscured by either pro- or antihomosexual views: the cause of homosexuality is inborn, it was argued, therefore homosexuals should be free of legal harassment or medical treatment; or homosexuality is a "bad thing," which understanding might make alterable. Contemporary Gay liberationists emphasize that study of the cause and cure of heterosexuals' seemingly obsessive antihomosexuality should have higher priority.

Except for their vested interest in incomprehension, it should not be too difficult for even the most obtuse psychiatrists to understand that to characterize homosexuals as products of arrested emotional development, or to propagate any such all-encompassing negative judgment, is to perpetuate an oppression that has caused Gay people much mental anguish. By the suffering they have caused, the damage they have done, psychiatric-psychological professionals have revealed their own moral character. There is a special obscenity about bigotry in the guise of "help," antihomosexual pronouncements in the name of "mental health," or similar prejudice from religious authorities in the name of morality. The early Puritans were at least open about their hate; homosexuals were "abominations," to be punished by death. Simple. Clear. Contemporary puritans are less candid. Today, Gay liberationists are doing what they can to delegitimize those "experts" who have done their best to delegitimize them. The psychiatric-psychological profession's collective responsibility for causing homosexuals years of pain invalidates its claim to speak as a humane and moral authority on the subject of homosexuals' "mental health." It might begin to rehabilitate itself by publicly recognizing its own role in Gay oppression and by using its very real power to call for the immediate, universal repeal of all laws criminalizing sexual activity between consenting persons, as well as for civil rights legislation to protect individuals discriminated against on the basis of sexual or affectional orientation.

Not all the medical treatment literature conveys quite so much in quite so little space as the following British report, dating to 1964, of aversion treatment, summarized succinctly by Weinberg and Bell:

Aversion therapy was conducted with a male homosexual who had a heart condition. The particular form of aversion therapy involved creation of nausea, by means of an emetic, accompanied by talking about his homosexuality. The second part of the therapy involved recovery from the nausea and talking about pleasant ideas and heterosexual fantasies, which was sometimes aided by lysergic acid. In this case, the patient died as a result of a heart attack brought on by the use of the emetic.[3]

♀ 1884: DR. JAMES G. KIERNAN;
Anaphrodisiac Measures
"Cold sitz baths [and] a course of intellectual training"

In an article on "Sexual Perversion," published in the *Detroit Lancet*, Dr. Kiernan of Chicago, a professor of legal psychiatry, surveys the American, German, and other early writings on homosexuality. Kiernan believes homosexuality "occurs nearly as frequently in females," differing from K. H. Ulrichs who, he says, regards homosexuality as found only in males. Kiernan says "the most curious" American report of homosexuality is that involving two females—the case of "Joe" (or Lucy Ann Lobdell), and her female lover (described in Part III, "Passing Women"). Kiernan also cites the history of one of his own patients,

a twenty-two-year-old girl who had a neurotic ancestry on the paternal side. Her face and cranium are asymmetrical. The patient has always liked to play boys' games and to dress in male attire. She has felt herself at certain times sexually attracted by some of her female friends with whom she indulged in mutual masturbation; these feelings come at regular periods, and are then powerfully excited by the sight of the female genitals. The patient in the interval manifests only repugnance to attentions from men. She has been struck with the fact that while her lascivious dreams and thoughts are excited by females, those of females with whom she has conversed, are excited by males. She, therefore, looks upon these feelings as of a morbid nature. At times she is troubled by imperative conceptions, such as that if she turns her head around she will break her neck; to avoid this ideal danger she at times carries her head in a very constrained position.

Treatment

To remove this condition is out of the question, and Dr. Wise has recommended that these patients be sent to asylums. Krafft-Ebing and Kirn proposed that these patients should be excepted from legal penalties and allowed to follow their inclinations when harmless and not violating public decency. The case last cited I have treated as if it were a case of nymphomania and aided the patient's will by using [an]aphrodisiac measures, such as cold sitz baths, etc., at the same time instituting a course of intellectual training. So far the patient has been by these means able to keep the feeling under control.[4]

Ten years after the preceding article was published, Dr. Kiernan, in another medical journal essay, describes the subsequent history of his female patient—a history indicating how a Lesbian might become invisible in an apparently heterosexual marriage.

For a long time the patient was enabled to keep the feeling [for women] under control and it was for some years quiescent. The patient later formed a friendship with a woman of like literary and musical tastes. This friendship became a perverted love and the two were almost inseparable. To secure the companionship of her friend the patient was induced to marry the friend's brother. The union was not congenial to the patient except that it secured the companionship of her friend. Sexual intercourse excited perverse images in which the husband (who resembled the sister) appeared as another sister. Under these images the patient endured and even enjoyed sexual intercourse and conceived a languid liking for her husband, who was much attached to her and his sister and chivalrous in his kindness to them. These relations lasted some years, the esteem and liking of the wife for the husband increasing, but paling before the devoted, deep, though perverted affection for the sister. The sister died from an acute attack of pneumonia, devotedly nursed by both wife and husband. The marriage had been unfruitful, but less than a year after the sister's death, a daughter was born who much resembled her. The wife's esteem passed through love of the sister, to intense maternal love of the daughter, as resembling the sister; through this to normal love of the husband as the father and brother. The congenital tendency to females is now entirely kept in check by this love.

The denouement in this case and the mental phenomena indicate to one that there is entirely too much sympathy wasted on these patients, since sympathy to them is as poisonous as to the hysteric whose mental state is very similar.

Insistence on the morbidity of the pervert ideas and prohibition of sexual literature as in the sexual neurasthenic [individual suffering from nervous exhaustion allegedly of sexual origin] together with allied psychical therapy and anaphrodisiac methods cannot but benefit. These patients, like the hysteric, will not "will" to be cured while they are subjects of sympathy.[5]

♀ 1893: DR. F. E. DANIEL; Castration
"It might be well enough to . . . asexualize all criminals"

Dr. Daniel of Austin, Texas, first presented a paper on eugenic castration at an international medico-legal congress held in New York in 1893. Originally entitled "Should Insane Criminals or Sexual Perverts Be Allowed to Procreate?" this paper was reprinted in three different medical journals, the last in 1912.

Daniel asserts that sexual "perversion," alcoholism, insanity, and criminal tendencies are transmitted by heredity; they appear with alarming frequency among "the lower classes, particularly negroes." Among the sexual perversions, Daniel includes rape, masturbation, sodomy, and pederasty. These perversions, he says, have not been adequately studied:

There is an innate repugnance to going deeply into investigation in a field where . . . we are sure to find so much revealed that is shocking to every sense of decency, disgusting and revolting. And I know of no attempt anywhere being made to either cure sexual perversion in males (except as to general treatment for insanity in asylums), or to suppress its expression in unnatural gratification; our laws are defective, and do not deal intelligently with the subject. Certainly I know of nothing being done to arrest its descent to coming generations.

Daniel declares the urgent need for study of "perversions" and argues that justice is not served by punishing sexual criminals by death.

The aim of jurisprudence should be, in addition to the repression of crime, a removal of the causes that lead to it, and reform, rather than the extermination of the vicious. It should comprehend both therapeusis and prophylaxis in the widest sense; thus, drunkenness should be cured, and intemperance prevented. . . . So with the sexual sins; the offender should be rendered incapable of a repetition of the offense, and the propagation of his kind should be inhibited in the interest of civilization and the well-being of future generations.

These ends are not fulfilled by hanging, electrocution, or burning at the stake. . . .

In lieu thereof, and as a solution to the most difficult problem in sociology which confronts the learned professions today, and as a measure calculated to fulfill all the ends and aims of criminal jurisprudence, castration is proposed. I say "castration" and not "asexualization," because that [?] applies as well to women; and in sexual perversion the woman is usually passive; she can not commit a rape, at all events (though she can practice sexual abominations that shock morals, wreck health, and worse, can transmit her defects to posterity). In light of the Alice Mitchell case [see Part I], it might be well enough to adopt Dr. Orpheus Evert's suggestion, and asexualize all criminals of whatever class. . . .

In light then of the very evident doubt as to the sanity of those who commit sexual crimes, and, therefore, of their responsibility; and particularly as it is impossible in the present state of our knowledge to draw a line and say where, in mental alienation, unsoundness to the extent of irresponsibility for acts exists, I would substitute castration as a penalty for all sexual crimes or misdemeanors, including confirmed masturbation.

Daniel cites contemporary research which indicates that hysteria and "hystero-epilepsy" in women can be cured by removal of the ovaries. He adds:

In light of these facts, I think we are warranted in at least making the experiment on a scale large enough to test the operation as a therapeutic measure; we know the operation would be prophylactic and protective, both to society and to posterity.

It has occurred to the profession to test Baftey's ideas of the curative effect of the removal of the ovaries, for disturbance in the female similar to those in males now under consideration; and the experiment was being made on a large scale in the Pennsylvania hospital by Dr. Joseph Price and others (*Jour. Am. Med. Assn.*, Jan. and Feb., 1893), when such an outcry was raised that it had to be discontinued before any definite results could be formulated. The board of charities, through their "legal member," put a stop to it, on the ground that it is unlawful to unsex a woman without her consent; and being presumably insane, these women could not give their consent. Thus, great regard was had for the *posterity* of these afflicted creatures.[6]

Daniel continues:

It does seem that the scheme of our government, and the tendency of our civilization is to foster the criminal and mentally defective classes. . . . Is it not a remarkable civilization that will break a criminal's neck, but will respect his testicles?

Daniel urges that legislators consult medical experts when drafting criminal statutes.

Touching the legality of castrating a patient as a therapeutic measure, I had a conversation recently with Governor J. S. Hogg of this State. He was for four years Attorney General of Texas, and is distinguished for his great legal ability. He assured me that there is not a doubt of the legal right on the part of a superintendent of an insane asylum to castrate a patient for mental trouble if, in his judgment, it be necessary or advisable. He would have the same right to castrate a patient as he would have to bleed him in the arm, or to amputate a limb, or do any other operation. . . .

While we can not hope ever to institute a Sanitary Utopia in our day and generation, it would seem within the legitimate scope and sphere of Preventive Medicine, aided by the enactment and enforcement of suitable laws, to eliminate much that is defective in human genesis, and to improve our race mentally, morally and physically; to bring to bear in the breeding of people the principles recognized and utilized by every intelligent stock raiser in the improvement of his cattle; and in my humble judgment the substitution of castration, as advocated above, for the useless and cruel execution of criminals, is the first step in the reformation. I predict that in twenty years the beneficial results of castration for crimes committed in obedience to a perverted (diseased) sexual impulse will be established and appreciated.

Rape, sodomy, bestiality, pederasty and habitual masturbation should be made crimes or misdemeanors, punishable by forfeiture of all rights, including that of procreation; in short, by castration, or castration *plus* other penalties, according to the gravity of the offense.[7]

1895: MARC-ANDRÉ RAFFALOVICH; Abstinence
"Every man has not the right to lay claim to the sexual satisfaction of his desires"

Raffalovich's "observations and recommendations" concerning homosexuality first appeared in a French medical journal; the same year they were translated and published in the American *Journal of Comparative Neurology.* Born into a wealthy

Russian-Jewish family which later emigrated to Paris, Raffalovich's interest in Roman Catholicism is indicated here by his argument for the repression of both hetero- and homosexual activity. Raffalovich opens with a criticism of the medical treatment held to be progressive in Europe at the time. His remarks are also a thinly veiled polemic against Oscar Wilde:

We can hardly cure the inverts. Hypnotism is not satisfactory and marriage is the worst of remedies, sacrificing the peace and health of the children to the improbable cure of the father and his doubtful restoration. There are already too many inverts and perverts who are married and who are fathers and hypocrites for marriage to save the honor of a homosexual. . . .

The physicians who try to cure inverts have not sufficiently noted the dangers to which they expose their patients. . . . I do not think much of permanent cures of the sexual sense. Every imperfect cure may make of an invert a pervert; and if the invert is dangerous and contagious, the pervert is much more so. . . . Let the medical healer remember this before undertaking a congenital invert. Rather than to add the vices of the normal man to the abnormality which he has, the superior invert (it is he alone who would have a strong desire to change his condition; the inferior inverts find adequate satisfaction all too easily) should try—under proper direction—to lift himself above himself and his vice. The tendencies of our time, particularly the prevalent contempt for religion, make chastity more difficult for every one, and the invert suffers more from this than others. . . . If chastity were a virtue in better favor I should commend it to the physicians as a more effective remedy than to send the invert to a "puella" [prostitute] to prepare him for marriage and paternity.

"The invert," says Raffalovich,

has not the courage to go to the limit and to aspire to chastity; he invents arguments in favor of his own propensities. If he were the superior being that he imagines himself and if he had any religion, he would shake off the bonds of the flesh and make himself useful to humanity. . . .

The day when the invert ceases to call for the indulgence of society, he will begin to justify himself in the eyes of truly superior men. Because heterosexuality is not suppressed [the invert argues] homosexuality ought to be equally favored. Strange logic, if the repression of heterosexuality is one of the problems of the future, as I believe it to be. . . .

Krafft-Ebing is the representative of those who claim justice for the invert, and I ask nothing better; but it ought to be emphasized that his demand has as its basis the theory that every man has a right to sexual satisfaction. If one grants the right to heterosexuals, I do not see how it can be refused to the inverts; especially as the refusal to them in no respect changes the condition of things. But in my opinion every man has not the right to lay claim to the sexual satisfaction of his desires.[8]

♀ 1895: DR. HAVELOCK ELLIS; Abstinence
"A wholesome . . . course of physical and mental hygiene"

The English sexologist Havelock Ellis first published several of his pioneering essays on homosexuality in American medical journals. In the *Alienist and Neurologist* published in St. Louis, Ellis writes on "Sexual Inversion in Women" (1895). Ellis's critique of his medical colleagues' attempts to change the sexual-affectional orientation of homosexuals is associated with his advocacy of sexual abstinence as a treatment goal. Here Ellis speaks of treating those nervous disorders —exhaustion, hysteria, and epilepsy—which he says sometimes accompany congenital Lesbianism:

In the treatment of sexual inversion it is to these associated nervous disorders that our attention may best be devoted. In the absence of such symptoms the sexual invert will not as a rule appear before the physician. And this may be as well, for in such cases by mistaken assurances of permanent cure, and by encouraging marriage, it is easily possible to bring about very disastrous results, to the patient, to her husband and to the probably neurotic offspring. The physician would do well in such cases to cherish a certain judicious scepticism concerning his own powers. It is sometimes not difficult by "suggestion" or actual hypnotism (as practiced by Schrenck-Notzing) to persuade the patient that she is cured. In this way she may be plunged into a position that is falser and more miserable, more degrading to herself and dangerous to others, than her original position. It is too often forgotten that, as Raffalovich has pointed out, to the congenitally inverted person the normal instinct is just as unnatural and vicious as homosexuality is to the normal man or woman; so that in a truly congenital case "cure" may simply mean perversion, involving the general demoralization that usually accompanies perversion. The best ideal to hold out in such cases—even although the ideal may not be perfectly reached—is not the ideal of normal love but the ideal of sexual abstinence in so far as indulgence may be doing injury to others. Very great and permanent benefit may be imparted by treating the associated neurotic conditions and general impairment of health. By a wholesome and prolonged course of physical and mental hygiene the patient may be enabled to overcome the morbid fears and suspicions which have sometimes been fostered by excessive sympathy and coddling, and the mind may thus indirectly be brought into a tonic condition of self-control. The inversion will not thus be removed but it may be rendered comparatively harmless, both to the patient herself and to those who surround her. If the physician is not satisfied with this result he will need all the tact and judgement and caution he possesses to avoid disaster.[9]

1896–97: DRS. HAVELOCK ELLIS AND
E. S. TALBOT; Castration
"I think it was that operation . . . that caused my insanity"

A detailed case history involving the effects of castration was sent to Havelock Ellis by Dr. E. S. Talbot of Chicago. In 1896, Ellis published an initial report in the British *Journal of Mental Science*.

On the 28th March, 1894, at noon, in the open street in Chicago, Guy T. Olmstead fired a revolver at a letter-carrier named William L. Clifford. He came up from behind and deliberately fired four shots, the first entering Clifford's loins, the other three penetrating the back of his head, so that the man fell and was supposed to be fatally wounded. Olmstead made little attempt to escape, as a crowd rushed up with the usual cry of "Lynch him!" but waved his revolver exclaiming, "I'll never be taken alive," and when a police officer disarmed him, "Don't take my gun; let me finish what I have to do." This was evidently an allusion, as will be seen later on, to an intention to destroy himself. He eagerly entered the police-van, however, to escape the threatening mob.

Olmstead, who was 30 years of age, was born near Danville, Ill., in which city he lived for many years. . . .

Guy Olmstead began to show signs of sexual perversity at the age of 12. He was seduced (we are led to believe) by a man who occupied the same bedroom. Olmstead's early history is not clear from the data to hand. It appears that he began his career as a school teacher in Connecticut, and that he there married the daughter of a prosperous farmer; but shortly after he "fell in love" with her male cousin, whom he describes as a very handsome young man. This led to a separation from his wife and he went West.

He was never considered perfectly sane, and in October, 1886, we find him in the Kankakee Insane Asylum. . . . His illness was reported as of three years' duration, and caused by general ill health; heredity doubtful, habits good, occupation that of a school teacher. His condition was diagnosed as paranoia. On admission he was irritable, alternately excited and depressed. . . .

Olmstead's history is defective for some years after he left Kankakee. In October, 1892, we hear of him as a letter-carrier in Chicago. During the following summer he developed a passion for William Clifford, a fellow letter-carrier about his own age, also previously a school teacher, and regarded as one of the most reliable and efficient men in the service. For a time Clifford seems to have shared this passion, or to have submitted to it, but he quickly ended the relationship and urged his friend to undergo medical treatment, offering to pay expenses himself. Olmstead continued to write letters of the most passionate description to Clifford, and followed him about constantly until the latter's life was made miserable. In December, 1893, Clifford placed the letters in the postmaster's hands, and Olmstead was requested to resign at once. Olmstead complained to the Civil Service Commission at Washington that he had been dismissed without cause, and also applied for reinstatement, but without success.

In the meanwhile, apparently on the advice of friends, he went into hospital, and in the middle of February, 1894, his testicles were removed. No report from the hospital is to hand.

The effect of removing the testicles was far from beneficial, and he began to suffer from hysterical melancholia. A little later he went into hospital again. On March 19th he wrote to Dr. Talbot from the Mercy Hospital, Chicago: "I returned to Chicago last Wednesday night, but felt so miserable I concluded to enter a hospital again, and so came to Mercy, which is very good as hospitals go. But I might as well go to Hades as far as any hope of my getting well is concerned. I am utterly incorrigible, utterly incurable, and utterly impossible. At home I thought for a time that I was cured, but I was mistaken, and after seeing Clifford last Thursday I have grown worse than ever so far as my passion for him is concerned. Heaven only knows how hard I have tried to make a decent creature out of myself, but my vileness is uncontrollable, and I might as well give up and die. I wonder if the doctors knew that after emasculation it was possible for a man to have erections, commit masturbation, and have the same passion as before. I am ashamed of myself; I hate myself; but I can't help it. I am without medicine, a big, fat, stupid creature, without health or strength, and I am disgusted with myself. I have no right to live, and I guess people have done right in abusing and condemning me. I know now that this disease was born in me, and will leave me only when my breath leaves me. And this is all the harder to bear when I think I might have been a gentleman but for this horror, which has made me attempt suicide, caused me to be incarcerated in an insane asylum three years, and resulted in my being locked up in a cell in an almshouse in Connecticut for three weeks. I have friends among nice people, play the piano, love music, books, and everything that is beautiful and elevating; yet they can't elevate me, because this load of inborn vileness drags me down and prevents my perfect enjoyment of anything. Doctors are the only ones who understand and know my helplessness before this monster. I think and worry till my brain whirls, and I can scarce refrain from crying out my troubles." This letter was written a few days before the crime was committed.

When conveyed to the police-station Olmstead completely broke down and wept bitterly, crying: "Oh! Will, Will, come to me! Why don't you kill me and let me go to him!" (At this time he supposed he had killed Clifford.) A letter was found on him, as follows: "Mercy, March 27th. To Him Who Cares to Read. Fearing that my motives in killing Clifford and myself may be misunderstood, I write this to explain the cause of this homicide and suicide. Last summer Clifford and I began a friendship which developed into love." He then recited the details of the friendship, and continued: "After playing a Liszt rhapsody for Clifford over and over, he said that when our time to die came he hoped we would die together, listening to such glorious music as that. Our time has now come to die, but death will not be accompanied by music. Clifford's love has, alas! turned to deadly hatred. For some reason Clifford suddenly ended our relations and friendship." In his cell he behaved in a wildly excited manner, and made several attempts at suicide, so that he had to be closely watched. A few weeks later he wrote to Dr. Talbot:—"Cook County Gaol, April 23,—I feel as though I had neglected you in not writing you in all this time, though you may not care to hear from me, as I have never done anything but trespass on your kindness. But please do me the justice of thinking that I never expected all this trouble, as I thought Will and I would be in our graves and at peace long before this. But my plans failed miserably. Poor Will was not dead, and I was grabbed before I could shoot myself. I think Will really shot himself, and feel certain others will think so too when the whole story comes out in court. I can't understand the surprise and indignation my act seemed to engender, as it was perfectly right and natural that Will and I should die together, and nobody else's business. Do you know I believe that poor boy will yet kill himself, for last November when I in my grief and anger told his relations about our marriage he was so frightened, hurt, and angry that he wanted us both to kill ourselves. I acquiesced gladly in his proposal to commit suicide, but he backed out in a day or two. I am glad now that Will is alive, and am glad that I am alive, even with the prospect of years of imprisonment before me, but which I will cheerfully endure for his sake. And yet for the last ten months his influence has so completely controlled me, both body and soul, that if I have done right he should have the credit for my good deeds, and if I have done wrong he should be blamed for the mischief, as I have not been myself at all, but a part of him, and happy to merge my individuality into his."

Olmstead was tried privately in July. No new points were brought out. He was sentenced to the Criminal Insane Asylum. Shortly afterwards, while still in the prison at Chicago, he wrote to Dr. Talbot: "As you have been interested in my case from a scientific point of view there is a little something more I might tell you about myself, but which I have withheld because I was ashamed to admit certain facts and features of my deplorable weakness. Among the few sexual perverts I have known I have noticed that all are in the habit of often closing the mouth with the lower lip protruding beyond the upper." (Usually due to arrested development of upper jaw.) "I noticed the peculiarity in Mr. Clifford before we became intimate, and I have often caught myself at the trick. Before the operation my testicles would swell and become sore and hurt me, and have seemed to do so since, just as a man will sometimes complain that his amputated leg hurts him. Then, too, my breasts would swell, and about the nipples would become hard and sore and red. Since the operation there has never been a day that I have been free from sharp, shooting pains down the abdomen to the scrotum, being worse at the base of the penis. Now that my fate is decided I will say that really my passion for Mr. Clifford is on the wane, but I don't know whether the improvement is permanent or not. I have absolutely no passion for other men, and have begun to hope now that I can yet outlive my desire for Clifford, or at least control it. I have not yet told of this improvement in my condition, because I wished people to still think I was insane, so that I would be sure to escape being sent to the penitentiary. I know I was insane at the time I tried to kill both Clifford and myself, and feel that I don't deserve such a dreadful punishment as being sent to a States prison. However, I think it was that operation and my subsequent illness that caused my insanity rather than passion for Clifford. I should very much like to know if you really consider sexual perversion an insanity."

In the 1897 edition of *Sexual Inversion*, Havelock Ellis adds several later details of Olmstead's history.

When discharged from the Criminal Insane Asylum, Olmstead returned to Chicago and demanded his testicles from the City Postmaster, whom he accused of being in a systematized conspiracy against him. He asserted that the Postmaster was one of the chief agents in a plot against him, dating from before the castration. He was then sent to the Cook Insane Hospital. It seems probable that a condition of paranoia is now firmly established.

Talbot and Ellis conclude their original 1896 report:

The removal of the testicles, the apparently depressing effect of the operation, and the speedy occurrence of the crime after it, should suggest caution to the surgical psychiatrists who advocate the castration of inverts and sexual perverts generally. Such persons are frequently of unstable mental balance, so that the mutilation produces a depressing effect, while it does not remove the perverted tendency.[10]

1899–1909: DR. H. C. SHARP; Vasectomy "The patient becomes of a more sunny disposition"

In a paper titled "The Sterilization of Degenerates," read before the American Prison Association in Chicago in 1909, Dr. H. C. Sharp, physician at the Indiana Reformatory, discusses his treatment program first instituted in 1899. This program originated in that eugenics movement which sought to end the procreation of lower working-class and social-deviant groups of many kinds:

There is no longer any questioning of the fact that the degenerate class is increasing out of all proportion to the increase of the general population. . . . [This class of degenerates includes] most of the insane, the epileptic, the imbecile, the idiotic, the sexual perverts; many of the confirmed inebriates, prostitutes, tramps and criminals, as well as the habitual paupers found in our county poor asylums; also many of the children in our orphan homes. . . .

The medical profession has done much in the way of developing preventive medicine, but few and feeble have been its efforts in searching out and applying remedies to check the growth of degeneracy in our country. For this condition to go unchecked eventually means a weakening of our nation.

Castration is [one] means that has been suggested for the purpose of preventing procreation in the unfit. A superintendent of the Kansas Feeble Minded Institution thus operated upon forty-eight boys in that institution about the year 1898. . . . [Castration] is, as I have repeatedly stated, of much gravity and causes entirely too much mental and nervous disturbance to ever become popular or justifiable as a medical measure, but there is one operation that I heartily endorse as an additional punishment in certain offenses. . . . Since October, 1899, I have been performing an operation known as vasectomy. . . . This operation is indeed very simple and easy to perform. I do it without administering an anesthetic either general or local. It requires about three minutes time to perform the operation and the subject returns to work immediately, suffers no returns, and is in no way impaired for his pursuit of life, liberty, and happiness, but is effectively sterilized. I have been doing this operation for nine full years. I have two-hundred and thirty-six cases that have afforded splendid opportunity for post operative observation and I have never seen any unfavorable symptoms. . . . there is no disturbed mental or nervous condition following, but, on the contrary, the patient becomes of a more sunny disposition, brighter of intellect, ceases excessive masturbation, and advises his fellows to submit to the operation for their own good.[11]

1899: DR. JOHN D. QUACKENBOS; Hypnosis
"It becomes my Christian manhood to act only as the vice-regent of the Almighty"

Hypnosis was first applied to the treatment of homosexuality by Baron Albert von Schrenck-Notzing, a German physician and occultist, whose book *Therapeutic Suggestion in Psychopathia Sexualis* appeared in an American edition in English in 1895. Hypnosis as a treatment for homosexuals was advocated in America as early as 1893, when Dr. Henry Hulst of Michigan suggested it as an alternative to the castration advocated by Dr. F. E. Daniel. An early, detailed American report on the use of hynosis in the treatment of "sexual perversion" was presented by Dr. John D. Quackenbos of Columbia University at an 1899 meeting of the New Hampshire Medical Society. Earlier that winter, Quackenbos had begun quietly testing the use of hypnosis in "removing criminal impulses and substituting conscience-sensitiveness for moral anaesthesia." When the *New York Times* reported on his test on April 30, 1899, Quackenbos's work received wide publicity.

Quackenbos first describes his own feelings after inducing a hypnotic trance:

The responsibility of the moments that follow is awful, beyond any power of mine to picture to you. I stand in a closer relation to that sleeping mind than father or mother, teacher or preacher, husband or wife, can ever attain; and it becomes my Christian manhood to act only as the vice-regent of the Almighty in the use I make of this great power and sacred opportunity. Would I dare to soil a soul so completely at my mercy with a single untoward thought? . . .

Quackenbos notes that the success of "hypno-science" depends largely upon the patient's desire to be cured, and then he turns to examples:

The cases I have successfully treated by hypnotism may be classified under the following heads.

> Excessive cigarette smoking.
> Hopeless dishonesty.
> Kleptomania.
> Sexual perversions.
> Dangerous delusions.
> Wilfullness, disobedience, and untruthfulness in children.

I will present from my case book typical illustrations of each vice or moral defect, with an outline of the treatment pursued and the results. . . .

The sexual perversions that have been modified or removed by hypnotic treatment are nymphomania, masturbation, gross impurity, unnatural passion for persons of the same sex. . . . A gentleman of twenty-five, occupying a position of trust in the office of one of our great life insurance companies, came to me, and wept with mortification as he recounted the story of his abnormal attachment to handsome young men. Women possessed no attractions for him, but there were certain youths whom he loved to sit beside, place his arms around, and thus induce a pleasurable sexual excitement. As he described it, nature had given him a woman's brain. This young man was hypnotized on the ninth of May, but did not pass into the stage of profound lethargy. The line of suggestion was in the direction of his no longer having the abnormal feeling, of resistance, of acquiring a natural desire for the opposite sex properly directed and controlled. The consequences of indulging the unnatural lust were then pictured as moral, mental, and financial ruin, and the results of a happy marriage were depicted as involving the greatest human happiness. A noticeable effect of the first treatment was exaltation of the will power and an acquired ability to resist. Nobody having unnatural attractions crossed the patient's path between the first and second hypnotisms, and he felt no longer drawn toward a fellow clerk who had previously caused him a great deal of trouble. After the second treatment he was enabled to throw off the influence with comparative ease. The object of the treatment to come will be to eradicate it entirely.[12]

1904: ANONYMOUS; Pudic Nerve Section
"I am if anything, worse than before"

At the request of an unnamed, thirty-nine-year-old "homosexualist," an anonymous doctor performed an operation intended to eliminate "reverse sexual instinct feelings and impulses." An autobiographical case history of this "gentleman degenerate" (the patient's own name for himself) appears in the *Alienist and Neurologist*, a St. Louis, Missouri, medical journal, edited by Dr. Charles H. Hughes. The doctor reports:

In this case an operation was performed on the filaments of the pudic nerve supplying the testes, but the morbid inclination still persists, notwithstanding the operation and a course of chologogues, antiseptic intestinal treatment and full bromism [sedation].

This man is a competent accountant and a cultured gentleman, much distressed still by his persisting malady and has [now] asked to be castrated and talks earnestly of suicide as a not far distant resort in the event of failing of relief. This case appears to be in the head and not in the genitals.

Having endeavored after this operation to convince this unfortunate man that the trouble was now in his brain and mind alone and that he should do as other men have to do and do do, keep his passionate impulses in abeyance to the higher purposes of his nature and the nobler ambitions of life, he answered as follows:

"What you claim can be accomplished through efforts on my part is impossible —of course you will dispute this. Were our positions reversed for a month, you could understand. If the difficulty is with the head, all I have to say is that it has centered there with such vigor and tenacity that it would appear to me that the elimination of the trouble in one center has been doubly concentrated in another. The head of my firm has heard about my weakness and certain insinuations have been spread broadcast, resulting in my displacement from my position. I will be upon the streets next week—to go where—the Lord only knows.

"I can not change this unfortunate condition—for if I could it would be an awful stigma upon me if I did not. You are certainly a grand man—in your profession—yet there must be something about my brain construction that even is beyond you. Let me ask you—would extreme methods (you know my meaning) amount to anything? If so I will go into a charity hospital and have it done. Do something, I must. I have told you the truth. It means that or worse." . . .

The sufferings of this unfortunate are real. The training of the inhibitory centers of the cortex over the lower centers of the brain and cord have evidently been sadly neglected in this man's youth. . . .

In a letter six months subsequent to the [first pudic nerve] operation he writes as follows: "I am if anything, worse than before, as I now follow in the street those who attract me."[13]

♀ 1908: EDWARD I. PRIME STEVENSON
(Xavier Mayne, pseud.); Adjustment therapy
"A psychiater can best give sympathy, enlightenment, moral encouragements to self-respect"

In his pioneering American defense of homosexuality, The Intersexes (1908?), Stevenson, writing as the pseudonymous Xavier Mayne, offers a pro-homosexual alternative to the generally prevailing antihomosexual treatments. Stevenson asks rhetorically whether

Uranian [homosexual] mankind is "curable"? The word presupposes something too much. . . . Can we "cure" Nature? Can we make the leopard change his spots?

We . . . meet here a series of fundamental errors of not only the popular notion, but of even the scientific mind, time and again; viz, that the Uranian suffers from a nervous disease; that his status is indisputably "pathological;" . . . and that in consequence of being intersexual he is morally vicious, degenerate, and criminal. . . . We see how statute-books visit on him the penalty of his "contrary" intersexual condition, with truculent severity. But this all is acting toward a man much as if the man were to be punished because he has a leg or arm shorter than his next-door neighbour, or prefers vegetable diet to fleshmeats. Of "moral cure" often there should be no question, because no need. Complete, inborn, intersexual uranianism cannot be "cured". The shame of a gross blunder falls to the psychiater who promises a "cure" of what is not a disease. Too many a doctor, otherwise intelligent and honest, advises marriage as a "remedy"; or experimentally commits his patient to courses of useless "normal" sexuality. In vain does the real, innate Uranian seek to feel as to woman the absorbingly aesthetic, the intellectual, the sexual drawing awakened in him by a male. . . . Complete, natural similisexualism [homosexuality] is no real abnormality, no disease. It is unchangeably intersexualistic Nature. Undoubtedly a well-gratified, skilful, virile psychiater should strive to "cure" an imperfect, fanciful and superficial similisexualism. . . . But to the inbred Uranian coming to a physician for help, a psychiater can best give sympathy, enlightenment, moral encouragements to self-respect, counsels against anything obviously degenerative to soul or body, in such mystic, disturbing, tyrannic instincts. The intersexual type must be stimulated toward an elevated intellectual and ideal plane, in his sexualism. He must be helped to make the most of himself before God and man. He must be warned from cowardly wishes for death; urged to carry his burden bravely. . . . Ignorantly unjust sentiments of society against legitimate satisfaction of similisexual instincts, the want of equable laws for man, woman and intersex, will slowly be bettered. Meantime must the man who is homosexual be taught that he is not more criminal or monstrous than the "normalist." Common-sense, science and humanity together demand this sort of medical-psychiatric sentiment; and in time social ideas and laws, the world around, will endorse such logical, humane acceptances.

The fact is much in evidence that the best type of Uranian often does not wish nor seek a "Cure" when once enlightened as to himself, and is clear about his moral position. Such intersexuals in a large proportion have no desire to change psychology or lot, unless perhaps such wishes come in hours of bitterness, under social persecution and injustice, or when some unhappy passion overflows. But often not even then would the Uranian be other than he is! He suffers. For his own sake, and for the sake of others he wishes that their lot were better. But there is likely to be firm in his soul the conviction that the impulse in him is pure, is perhaps the truest and highest sort of love; that in the Scriptural phrase, it is a "thing of God." Races, laws, society long may persist in repudiating or punishing it. But the world will progress slowly to wider sexual insights. Coming generations will redeem a present-day and ignorant intolerance of similisexual impulses, when united to sound ethical concepts, to superiour intelligences and to respectable lives.

Later, turning briefly to the subject of Lesbianism, Stevenson adds:

In accepting marriage 'curatively' or otherwise, a large proportion of the feminine Intersex are in situations closely like those of Uranians. The Uraniad faces a physical and psychic predicament that often is profoundly pathetic. She cannot avoid it as easily as can the Uranian. Often she must begin it with interrupting her feminosexual relationships; which rupture by itself makes life a tragedy for her— that frequently brings it to a dark climax. Feminosexual friendships are shattered, or must be changed radically in quality, as the man appears on the scene. . . . The wife must learn submission to the hated masculine embraces. . . . Neuropathic experiences can claim a vast part in her married existence. Woman is shut out from much that distracts and helps a masculine similisexual. Not only are fewer her chances of escaping anything she dreads; her opportunities of continuing uraniadistic intimacies are less favourable. One can say that the real Uraniad often is even more the *victim* of marriage than the masculine intersex. Many Uraniads have not the temperaments to bear up, to philosophize, to endure the nuptial tie, to be consoled—transformed.[14]

1913: DR. A. A. BRILL; Psychoanalysis
"Most of these patients recover, though they are content to remain homosexual"

Dr. Brill, chief of the psychiatry clinic at Columbia University, studied psycho-analysis under Sigmund Freud in Vienna and conducted joint consultations with Dr. Magnus Hirschfeld in Berlin. In 1913, Brill summed up ten years of clinical experience with homosexuals in a paper read before the annual meeting of the American Medical Association.

Of the abnormal sexual manifestations that one encounters none, perhaps, is so enigmatical and to the average person so abhorrent as homosexuality. I have discussed this subject with many broad-minded, intelligent professional men and laymen and have been surprised to hear how utterly disgusted they become at the very mention of the name and how little they understand the whole problem. Yet I must confess that only a few years ago I entertained similar feelings and opinions regarding this subject. . . . Since then I have devoted a great deal of time to the study of this complicated phenomenon, and it is therefore no wonder that my ideas have undergone a marked change. *Tout comprendre c'est tout pardonner* [To understand everything is to forgive everything], I have met and studied a large number of homosexuals and have been convinced that a great injustice is done to a large class of human beings, most of whom are far from being the degenerates they are commonly believed to be.

Brill reviewed the studies of homosexuality conducted by Freud, Hirschfeld, and other German physicians who agree that homosexuality is compatible with mental and physical health:

My own findings concur with these views. Most of the inverts I know belong to our highest types both mentally and physically and show absolutely no hereditary taints. Without entering into a detailed discussion of this question I will say that I am convinced that homosexuality as such is entirely independent of any defective heredity or other degenerative trends. . . .

It is interesting to note how the inverts themselves view their inversion. Some take it as a matter of course and demand the same rights as the normal. They are perfectly contented with their lot, and seldom consult a physician. "I would not for the world have anybody interfere with my personality; I just wish to consult you about a *modus vivendi* for myself," writes a young inverted clergyman on asking me for an appointment. Some, however, struggle against it and consider it a morbid manifestation. It is only the latter who can be helped by treatment.

There may be some congenital inverts, but of the forty-nine cases that I have analyzed I always discovered one or more early affective sexual impressions which favored the development of homosexuality.

Brill points out that to begin uncovering these childhood impressions often requires weeks of psychoanalysis. On the average, Brill notes, he spends an hour with the patient six times a week for six months. Even recognizing homosexuality may take some time:

Strange as it may seem, the diagnosis of homosexuality is not always an easy matter. . . . There is naturally no difficulty when one is confronted with an absolute invert who acknowledges his inversion. There are, however, a number of inverts who are really ignorant of their inversion. Eleven out of my forty-nine patients did not realize that they were homosexual, although nearly all of them had had homosexual experiences some time in their lives. They sought treatment for psychosexual impotence or for some neurosis. I have also seen patients who were treated for a long time for psychosexual impotence by prostatic massage, etc., who were all the time aware of their inversion. They kept silent because the treatment gave them pleasure or because they were ashamed or afraid to tell the doctor the true state of affairs. For many reasons the average doctor is not especially affable to a homosexual patient, and many a sensitive invert has had cause to regret his confidence in the doctor. . . .

As we are dealing with a psychic manifestation, the hope for a cure of homosexuality lies in psychotherapy. I can never comprehend why physicians invariably resort to bladder washing and rectal massage when they are consulted by homosexuals, unless it be to kill the homosexual cells in the prostate so that their place may be taken by heterosexual cells, as one physician expressed himself when one of my patients asked him how massage of the prostate would cure his inversion. It is an unfortunate fact that such ridiculous ideas are often heard in the discussion of psychosexual disturbances. Only a few months ago a patient told me that he was told by two physicians that his hope for a cure lay in castration.

When hypnosis came into vogue a great many workers in this field utilized it in the treatment of homosexuality. It was soon found that it failed to come up to expectation. . . . In the treatment of my cases I use exclusively psychonalysis. Freud, Sadger and others, have used this method for a number of years, and the results obtained are very gratifying.

Brill's paper concludes with three case studies illustrating Freudian concepts of the origins of homosexuality. Each of these patients, he states, was "cured" by psychoanalysis, though they apparently remained homosexual.

Brill's paper before the American Medical Association was followed by comments. Dr. d'Orsay Hecht of Chicago felt Brill's analysis revealed antihomosexual attitudes. Hecht was

impressed with the effort of Dr. Brill to correct homosexuality by decrying it. But if in the eye of the specialist homosexuality is but a contravention, socially speaking, and if it has just as much right to a hearing from the point of view of a sexual act as has heterosexuality, I really cannot see why the homosexual should care to be delivered from his homosexuality, except that he feels disgraced by it. Then again, a large number of homosexuals are in no way abhorrent of themselves in respect to their natures; they seem to be perfectly happy and perfectly well adjusted, probably in a restricted sense, and these patients probably are not worth while treating as Dr. Brill treats them. If we accept homosexuality as a condition which has as much right to exist as heterosexuality, why should we address ourselves to the duty of treating it?

I am wondering, too, whether or not the antisocial attitude toward the homosexual individual is, so far as the law is concerned, out of all proportion to the offense as it is conceived by the medical man. It is a fact that in Great Britain, for instance, the attitude on the part of the British law toward the offense of sodomy as a social crime is tremendously severe.

Dr. Ross Moore of Los Angeles adds:

One point that occurred to me as Dr. Brill was reading, and which was not particularly clear to me, was this: In the early part of his paper he spoke about a number of patients coming to him for some psychosis or for impotence, who did not know before they came to him that they were homosexual, and I wondered whether Dr. Brill, or any of us in carrying on such work as Dr. Brill has carried on in his cases, might not be in danger of doing society an injury as society sees the matter, or the patient an injury, by suggesting to him the possibility of homosexual conditions—whether or not it is a cure to make the man understand that he is homosexual.

A final question is raised by Dr. Albert E. Sterne of Indianapolis:

It is hard for me again to realize, not only from the paper that Dr. Brill has given us, but also in personal conversations with him, how he can feel satisfied, and how he can convince others, that these individuals are absolutely cured. He simply takes the statement of the patient that he no longer indulges in the practice that he had earlier acknowledged. That may be convincing to Dr. Brill, but it is pretty difficult at a distance to be convinced.

Dr. Brill explains his conception of "cure":

Most of these patients recover, though they are content to remain homosexual. . . .

With reference to the question of determining that a person is homosexual:

A patient came to me who was said to have nothing the matter with his sexual life, but who had convulsions. I had seen him not more than three times when I said to him. "You are homosexual," and I explained what I meant. He told me that while at college he never indulged in sexual acts, and that for this reason he used to wrestle, during which he would have ejaculation, and he selected his partners. Unquestionably from the beginning of his existence he was homosexual, although he was able to have sexual intercourse with his wife, but he was compelled to marry when quite young; he was "prodded into it," as he said. He came

to me to be treated for neurosis, but the neurosis was simply the result of homosexual lack of gratification.[15]

1914: DR. MAGNUS HIRSCHFELD;
Adjustment Therapy
"Homosexuality alone does not stop one from
becoming an able human being"

The founder and head of the first homosexual emancipation organization in
Germany, Dr. Hirschfeld was a physician and sexologist. He was attacked vehemently by Wilhelm Stekel and others who rejected his idea that homosexuality is an
inborn variation, therefore unchangeable, therefore unjustly criminalized. Hirschfeld visited the United States in 1893 (when he was twenty-five) and again in 1930;
a few of his important works were translated into English. But his influence was felt
more strongly in Europe than America. His ideas did have some influence on Americans, however. Both A. A. Brill and Edward I. Prime Stevenson (excerpted previously)
accepted his basic concept: homosexuality is not a sickness; self-acceptance will
often alleviate homosexuals' symptoms of mental disturbance. Hirschfeld describes
an American homosexual physician who benefited from his therapy. In his monu-
mental *Homosexuality in Men and Women* (1914) Hirschfeld presents his conception
of "adjustment" or "adaptation therapy" for homosexuals. The existence, at an early
date, of a therapy accepting homosexuality as an unequivocally viable and valuable
orientation, a therapy aimed at helping homosexuals "adapt" to their sexual-affectional orientation in a hostile society, makes particularly obscene and inexcusable
the dominant tendency of psychiatric-psychological professionals—to try to reorient
homosexuals to heterosexuality.

Hirschfeld describes his concept of the doctor's role when treating a "true" ("congenital") homosexual:

Our first concern is to set the homosexual man or woman at ease. We shall explain that homosexuality is an innate drive, incurred through no fault of the patient,
and is not a misfortune in and of itself, but rather becomes so as a result of the unjust evaluation which it comes up against, causing morally fine homosexuals (and
we do not only include the abstinent) to "suffer more wrong than they commit." We
shall further explain that the misfortune of being homosexual is often exaggerated,
for many in no way perceive it as such, and that homosexuality alone does not stop
one from becoming an able human being and a socially useful citizen, even though
now this is accomplished with considerable difficulty. We shall demonstrate this
through historical examples, and then discuss the wide extent of homosexuality in
the past and present, in order to free the patient who feels extremely isolated from
the torturing experience of loneliness. . . .

The depressing attempts at sexual relations with the opposite sex should be
given up, as should the idea of marriage, which, apart from its lack of consideration
for the partner, can only worsen one's own situation. Medicines possibly being em-

ployed for the purpose of increasing potency should no longer be taken. Bromide sedatives and above all morphine should without exception be discontinued. . . .

In order to have the patient clearly informed about his condition (especially important for those whose melancholy often brings thoughts of suicide) it is therapeutic to suggest to him two valuable activities: the reading of worthwhile books; contacts with homosexuals of high intellectual calibre. Of worthwhile readings I will mention the dialogues of Plato, Alexander von Gleichen-Russwurm's *Friendship; A Psychological Exploration*, [Edward] Carpenter's fine works, the *Yearbook for Sexual Intermediate Types* (containing many biographical articles), the diaries of [August] von Platen, and Elisàr Kupffer's *Chivalric Affection and Comrade Love in Western Literature*. . . .

In a similar way, it is very valuable to have the patient meet mentally and intellectually balanced homosexuals, who have come to accept themselves. Of course, one must be careful, because it can happen that the wish to meet "spiritually superior" people can be used only as a pretext to look for sexual release. . . .

One must repeat to the patient that, even today, Plato's division is valid—the division between sublimated and physical activities. One needs both, not only the physical side, to find any sort of happiness. . . .

The most complex problem to be discussed with the homosexual is that of active sexual satisfaction. If we could take into consideration only medical-hygienic questions, if we could proceed unhampered by prejudices and certain laws (whose bases we consider irrelevant), we would try and establish a minimum and a maximum of such activity for the patient in question. . . . But for the physician things are not that easy. It has even been suggested—and some legal experts have confirmed this— that a physician who advises a patient to have homosexual intercourse would be liable to prosecution. A few medical experts, concerned about the well-being of their patients, conscious of their responsibilities, have advised sexual activity, despite everything, particularly in cases where the suppression of all sexual desire has caused grave neurotic disturbances. These doctors knew that only through sexual activity could the patient reach a state of relaxation, that this activity worked almost like a remedy made just for such disturbances, the only medicine that would be beneficial.

I recall an American doctor—and I could add many similar instances—who suffered from such severe headaches that he had lost all joy in living. He couldn't sleep, could hardly work, and consulted one specialist after another. The day that he decided to admit to himself his homosexual inclinations, and began to act on them (where previously he had expended much energy on forcing himself to repress his desires) all his ailments disappeared at once. One didn't recognize this person, previously always despondent, irritable, taciturn, who had radiated defeat. Now he radiated well-being, he could sleep, his headaches were gone, and he could work better than ever. . . .

The duty of the physician towards a homosexual is by no means exhausted with this therapy, which might be called the adaptation or adjustment technique. Again and again we encounter particular problems of great importance to the patient; decisions have to be made which presuppose, not only a knowledge of homosexuality in general, but of the special conditions of the individual patient. Let me give just a few examples. One patient wants to know whether it wouldn't be best for him to emigrate to a country where he could live his life-style freely (there are enough countries where this would be possible); another patient wants to know whether he wouldn't make things easier if he would tell his relatives all about himself, especially if he would tell his parents—he may even ask the physician to do this. A third patient has accepted his homosexual inclinations—he doesn't need help in this respect—but he has fallen for one particular person, and this person is totally indifferent; another patient, a public employee, let us say, or member of the armed forces, needs advice urgently: should he change jobs, or retire prematurely so that he will get his pension? He is sure that one day he will not be able to stay abstinent and this would endanger everything. And many who have committed the error of getting married now want to consult with the physician as to how to arrange things with the spouse. . . .

When homosexuals have asked my advice, I have always maintained the following: regular, intensive work, whether manual or intellectual, is the most important condition for their well-being. There are several reasons for this. First, any useful activity fills the existence of a person, it is an aim in itself; then it makes him forget his problems; further, he can prove his usefulness to himself and his family. And work is an anchor; if anything detrimental should happen, it gives one the inner strength needed, the belief in one's importance.

I consider it a big step forward that, more often than in earlier times, homosexuals tell their relatives about themselves, either directly or through the physician. Lesbians, generally, are more reluctant to do so. Even if mother and the siblings suffer, even if father is scared, it is far better to be open. . . .

We have already discussed the disturbances stemming from abstinence. These are not different from those we encounter in heterosexual men and women who have suppressed their libidos ruthlessly. One shouldn't underestimate these symptoms because they are only "a case of nerves" and are not lethal. It is enervating enough to be constantly plagued by headaches, to suffer from insomnia, to be unable to do good work, to be constantly depressed and in need of sex. Those who can always find sexual satisfaction should not underestimate the complaints of those homosexuals who are denied this. It is a bit too easy to dismiss such lamentations, as was done recently by a famous legal expert: "The homosexuals should spare us their constant squawking." . . .

If we summarize what we have found about the treatment of male and female homosexuality, we must conclude that genuine homosexuality cannot be "cured," either through surgery, medication, or any psychotherapy. . . . Even if the physician cannot treat homosexuality per se, he can treat the homosexual patient. Above all, he'll discover that the adaptation therapy which we have detailed will be of considerable help.[16]

1914: DR. CHARLES H. HUGHES; Castration
"The second operation . . . excised the testes entire"

A report of an unsuccessful pudic nerve operation to eliminate homosexuality appeared in 1904 in a medical journal edited by Dr. Hughes. Here Hughes provides a case study of a "cure" effected by castration.

Four years ago, a gentleman of ordinary moral, intellectual and physical parts and psychic impulsions, save for the affliction which distinguished him, voluntarily came into our professional care. He was, by occupation, a professional book-keeper of ability and recognized as an expert in his line in the adjusting of accounts of business firms and estates.

He had ordinarily a fair degree of control of his abnormal passionate propensity, especially under judicious and extremely heroic bromide management, fruit and vegetable, (meat prohibited diet, oysters and fish excluded), predigested food, malted cereals, etc., and ptomaine elimination, i.e., two complete evacuations under salol, protoiodid of mercury or podophyllin and other laxatives, substituting or alternating. His bowels were kept free of ptomaines and flatus so that the least possible amount of irritation might proceed from them to genitals or brain. Tonic electrizations from spine to genitalia and tranquilizing brain electro seances were likewise employed.

But the patient got tired of being under treatment, he being an intelligent reading man, and solicited a radical operation of which he had learned and solicited the more certainly effective surgical operation. He had been much mortified in his relation with certain employers to whom, through his morbidly erotic inclinations and perverse unguarded displays, the higher inhibitions of his cerebrum having inopportunely failed him at times, to his great chagrin and mortification and with loss of several valuable positions.

It was pitiful to see and hear this unfortunately and unhappily dowered gentleman of otherwise good and proper instincts confess his painful, and to the world in general abhorrent, unnatural propensity to erotopathic evil. . . .

This gentleman was about 28 or 30 years old. In his youth he had reciprocal homo-sexual associates but he assured me that their mutual affection was mostly platonic. He was not given to lascivious bestiality. His peculiar sexual perversion distressed him much because of the damage it did to his business interests and the consciousness that he was abnormal and unnatural and so regarded by some of his associates, who knew him well.

He detailed more instances of his sexual perversion than it would be worth while to enumerate. He displayed his failing by following those about, whom he loved and seeking to be much and too continuously in their company and in inopportune, erotic handpressing, kissing and embracing, when not strongly and overmasteringly self-guarded. He, on one occasion, lost a very valuable position by a sudden, inopportune and ecstatic embrace of his superior at a most improper and inopportune time, even if the party had been a female and he a normal and accepted lover.

He was erotically pure in heart and by nature abhorred all lasciviousness. He was inclined to be exceedingly affectionate in his demeanor toward me so that I had to be particularly matter of fact and brief in my interviews with him when he would come for prescriptions, treatment or counsel, especially for the constant current galvanism of head to the lumbo-genital area, which I soon discovered it was wise therapeutics to discontinue. . . .

Hoping to stop erections and thereby to probably make a salutary psychic impression without positive asexualization, for he was (except for his sexual perversion) a splendid man who might become, if normal, the father of splendid children, this unfortunate man was operated on. The first operation, taken with the consent, but not with the counsel of a neurologist, was an excision of the dorsales penis nerve. This procedure did not arrest the pervert erotism nor obliterate it.

Vasectomy would have done better. The obliteration of other branches of the internal pubic nerve would have done better.

But the second operation a year or so after excised the testes entire.

The sequellae of this last surgical procedure were peculiar. It gave the gentleman tranquility and satisfaction. After the operation he lost his erotic inclinations towards his own sex but showed a social inclination towards asexualized ladies, one of his imperative and special requests of me, being that I might find and introduce to him a lady who had been oophorectomised for a similar *contraire sexuel empfindung* [*sic*—contrary sexual feeling]. . . .

The specially notable feature in the character of this case and the one which particularly justifies its addition to the considerably large number of similar cases now on record in the literature of psychic perversion, is the display of pronounced normal Platonic regard for the sex to whom he was rather averse than otherwise, while under the dominion of his perverted homo-sexual passion, before the surgical procedure had accomplished asexualization.

There is no other case precisely like this to my knowledge in the records of sexual psychopathy.[17]

♀ 1920: DR. SIGMUND FREUD; Psychoanalysis
"Really she was a feminist, . . . and rebelled against the lot of woman in general"

In "The Psychogenesis of a Case of Female Homosexuality," which appeared in German and was translated into English in 1920, Dr. Freud presents his only detailed case study of the psychoanalytic treatment of a Lesbian. In this influential paper Freud includes a general and "pessimistic" statement on the prospects for "curing" (eliminating) homosexual attraction.

The removal of genital inversion, or homosexuality, is in my experience never an easy matter. I have rather found that success is possible only under specially favourable circumstances, and even then that it essentially consists in being able to open to the restricted homosexuals the way to the opposite sex, till then barred, thus restoring their full bisexual functions. After that it lay with themselves to choose whether they wished to abandon the other way, banned by society, and in individual cases they have done so. One must remember that in normal sexuality also there is a limitation in the choice of object; in general to undertake to convert a fully developed homosexual into a heterosexual is not much more promising than to do the reverse, only that for good practical reasons the latter is never attempted.

In actual numbers the successes achieved by psycho-analytic treatment of the manifold forms of homosexuality are not specially striking. As a rule the homosexual is not able to give up his pleasure-object, and one cannot convince him that if he changed to the other object he would find again the pleasure he has renounced. If he comes at all to be treated it is mostly through the pressure of external motives, such as the social disadvantages and dangers attaching to his choice of object, and such components of the instinct for self-preservation prove to be too weak in the struggle against the sexual impulses. One then soon discovers his secret plan, namely, to obtain from the striking failure of his attempt the feeling of satisfaction that he has done everything possible against his abnormality, to which he can now resign himself with an easy conscience. The case is somewhat different when consideration for beloved parents and relatives has been the motive for his attempt to be cured. Then there really are libidinous tendencies present which may develop energies opposed to the homosexual choice of object, though their strength is rarely sufficient. It is only where the homosexual fixation has not yet become strong enough, or where there are considerable rudiments and remains of the heterosexual choice of object, *i. e.* in a still oscillating or in a definitely bisexual organisation, that one may make a more favourable prognosis for the psycho-analytic therapy.[18]

Freud provides the following background information on his patient.

A beautiful and clever girl of eighteen, belonging to a family of good standing, had aroused displeasure and concern on the part of her parents by the tender passion with which she pursued a certain lady, about ten years older than herself. The parents asserted that this lady, in spite of her distinguished name, was no better than a cocotte. It was said to be a well-known fact that she lived with a married woman-friend, having intimate relations with her, while at the same time she carried on promiscuously with a number of men. The girl did not contradict these evil reports, but she continued to be none the less enamoured of the lady in question, although she herself was by no means lacking in a sense of decency and propriety. No prohibitions and no supervision hindered the girl from seizing every one of the rare opportunities of being together with her beloved friend, of ascertaining all her habits, of waiting for her for hours outside her door or at a tram halt, of sending her gifts of flowers, and so on. It was evident that this one interest had swallowed up all others. The girl did not concern herself with any further educational studies, placed no value on social functions or girlish pleasures. . . .

One day it happened, as, indeed, was sooner or later inevitable in the circumstances, that the father met his daughter in the company of the lady. He passed them by with an angry glance which boded no good. Immediately after the girl rushed off and flung herself over a neighbouring wall on to the railway line. She paid for this undoubtedly serious attempt at suicide with a long stay in bed, though fortunately little permanent damage was done. After her recovery she found it easier to get her own way than before. The parents did not dare to oppose her so vigorously, and the lady, who up till then had coldly declined her advances, was moved by such an unmistakable proof of serious passion and began to treat her in a more friendly manner.

Freud also provides information on the patient's parents.

When [the father] first came to know of his daughter's homosexual tendencies he boiled over with anger and tried to suppress them by threats; at that time he perhaps hesitated between different, though equally painful, views, whether to regard her as vicious, as degenerate, or as mentally afflicted. . . . There was something about his daughter's homosexuality that aroused the deepest bitterness in him, and he was determined to combat it with all the means in his power; the depreciation of psycho-analysis so widespread in Vienna did not prevent him from turning to it for help. If this way failed he still had in reserve the strongest countermeasure; a speedy marriage was to awaken the natural instincts of the girl and stifle her unnatural tendencies.

. . . The mother . . . did not take her daughter's passion so tragically as did the father, nor was she so incensed at it. She had even for a long time enjoyed her daughter's confidence concerning the love affair, and her opposition to it seemed to have been aroused mainly by the harmful openness with which the girl publicly displayed her feelings.[19]

Freud discusses the character of his patient's same-sex relationships:

With none of the objects of her passion had the patient enjoyed anything beyond a few kisses and embraces; her genital chastity, if one may use such a phrase, had remained intact. As for the demi-mondaine who had aroused the girl's most recent, and by far her strongest, emotions, she [the demi-mondaine] had always treated her coldly and had never allowed any greater favour than the kissing of her hand. Probably the girl was making a virtue of necessity when she kept insisting on the purity of her love and her physical repulsion against the idea of sexual intercourse. But perhaps she was not altogether wrong when she boasted of her wonderful beloved that, although of noble birth and forced into her present position only by adverse family circumstances, she had preserved, even in such a situation, a great deal of dignity. For the lady used to recommend the girl, every time they met, to withdraw her affection from herself and from women in general, and she had persistently rejected the girl's advances up to the time of the attempted suicide.

A second point, which I next tried to clear up, concerned the girl's own motives on which the psycho-analytic treatment might be based. She did not try to deceive me by saying that she felt any urgent need to be freed of her homosexuality. On the contrary, she said she could not conceive of any other way of being in love, but she added that for her parents' sake she would honestly help in the therapeutic endeavour, for it pained her very much to be the cause of so much grief to them.[20]

> Freud's analysis of the patient's adolescence focuses upon her alleged Oedipus complex. He speculates that her strong affection, as a young teen-ager, for a small boy implied an unconscious desire to have a male child by her father. When her mother later actually gave birth to a son, the daughter, allegedly "exasperated and embittered," turned away from men altogether; "she foreswore her womanhood, and sought another goal for her libido."[21] "She changed into a man," says Freud, "and took her mother in place of her father as her love-object."[22] Freud concludes that "the analysis revealed beyond all shadow of doubt that the beloved lady was a substitute for—the mother."[23] Freud adds:

The analysis showed, further, that the girl had suffered from childhood from a strongly-marked "masculine complex." A spirited and pugnacious girl, not at all prepared to be second to her slightly older brother, she had, after inspecting his genital organs, developed a pronounced envy of the penis, and the thoughts derived from this envy still continued to fill her mind. Really she was a feminist, she felt it to be unjust that girls should not enjoy the same freedom as boys, and rebelled against the lot of woman in general.[24]

Freud describes the course of treatment and his decision to terminate the case.

The analysis went forward almost without any signs of resistance, the patient actively participating intellectually, though absolutely tranquil emotionally. Once when I expounded to her a specially important part of the theory, one touching her nearly, she replied in an inimitable tone, "Oh, how interesting," as though she were a *grande dame* being taken over a museum and glancing through her lorgnon at objects to which she was completely indifferent. The impression one had of her analysis was not unlike that of an hypnotic treatment, where the resistance has in the same way withdrawn to a certain limit beyond which it then proves to be unconquerable. . . .

. . . In reality she transferred to me the deep antipathy to men which had dominated her ever since the disappointment she had experienced through her father. Bitterness against men is as a rule easy to gratify with the doctor; it need not evoke any violent emotional manifestations, it simply expresses itself in rendering futile all his endeavours and in clinging to the neurosis. I know from experience how difficult it is to get the patient to understand just this mute kind of symptom and to make her aware of this latent, and often excessively strong, hostility without endangering the treatment. So I broke it off as soon as I recognized the girl's attitude to her father, and gave the advice that, if it was thought worth while to continue the therapeutic efforts, they should be carried out by a woman doctor.[25]

Freud concludes with a statement on treating homosexuals, in which distinctions between sexual orientation, "masculine" and "feminine" role-playing, and physical gender are hopelessly confused.

Psycho-analysis has a common basis with biology, in that it presupposes an original bisexuality of human beings (as of animals). But psycho-analysis cannot elucidate the intrinsic nature of what in conventional or in biological phraseology is termed "masculine" and "feminine": it simply takes over the two concepts and makes them the foundation of its work. When we attempt to reduce them further, we find masculinity vanishing into activity and femininity into passivity, and that does not tell us enough. In what has gone before I have tried to explain how far we may reasonably expect, or how far experience has already proved, that the elucidations yielded by analysis furnish us with the means for altering inversion. When one compares the extent to which we can influence it with the remarkable transformations that [Eugen] Steinach has effected in some cases by his [gonad transplant] operations, it does not make a very imposing impression. Still it would be premature or a harmful exaggeration were we at this stage to indulge in hopes of a "therapy" of inversion that could be generally used. The cases of male homosexuality in which Steinach has been successful fulfilled the condition, which is not always present, of a very patent somatic "hermaphrodism." Any analogous treatment of female homosexuality is at present quite obscure.[26]

1930: DR. WILHELM STEKEL; Psychoanalysis
"Successful treatment . . . depends upon the desire of the patient to get rid of his inversion"

Dr. Stekel of Vienna presented his views on the treatment of homosexuality in the American *Psychoanalytic Review*. Stekel is far more optimistic than Freud concerning the conversion of homosexuals, via psychoanalysis, into heterosexuals. Arguing strongly against Hirschfeld, Stekel maintains that "all persons are bisexual"; the homosexual's repressed heterosexuality can be brought to the surface in two or three months of successful psychoanalysis. The only reason that many homosexuals fail to be "cured," he argues, is because they "lack faith" in the psychoanalyst; they flee from his picture of homosexuality as an "illness":

We must understand that the psychoanalysis which projects the true picture meets with the keenest resistance of the patient. It is very difficult to induce an invert to undergo treatment but more difficult to keep him. If he remains, the success is fairly certain, providing too many errors are not made in the technique of psychic treatment. The procedures are as follows: The homosexual visits the physician having heard his ailment is curable. He mentions that he would be very content in his existing state if it was not subject to punishment. He is doubtful as to the possibilities of a cure—since childhood he had these inclinations—he has tried to have feminine relations, at which attempts he was either impotent or derived no pleasure. He agrees to treatment—and despite all caution does not return after a few days. . . .

The prognosis for successful treatment of a homosexual depends upon the desire of the patient to get rid of his inversion. Patients who come to the analyst of their own volition, who do not stress their happiness or are not proud of their inversion—such patients suffer because of their affliction and can be greatly helped.

Dr. Stekel summarizes:

Tersely expressed: This disease in question is not a congenital condition but a psychic state which can be handled by treatment correctly applied. This belief is substantiated by the fact that in the last year four of my homosexual patients have married and are extremely happy. These were the only ones I analyzed to the end.[27]

♀ 1932: DR. HELENE DEUTSCH; Psychoanalysis
"She had become a vivid, radiant person"

An article by Dr. Helene Deutsch, "On Female Homosexuality," first appeared in English translation in the American *Psychoanalytic Quarterly* for 1932. Dr. Deutsch, a student and colleague of Freud, in this classic report, discusses the treatment of a woman she psychoanalyzed in 1920.

Although the patient was aware of her sexual inversion, she did not indulge in homosexual practices; she knew that her erotic potentialities and fantasies were directed towards members of her own sex, and she would unequivocally become sexually excited when she embraced and kissed certain women. . . . The women were not in any instance of a masculine type, and she herself was blond and feminine. She felt no hostility towards men, had a number of male friends, and accepted their favors and courtship without protestation. She had married a man of outspoken masculine appearance, and had several children by him to whom she gave a maternal, even if not excessively warm, response. . . .

The patient came into analysis on account of neurotic difficulties. She had suffered for years from depressions and feelings of anxiety with a particular ideational content: she could not find the courage to assume the fitting authoritative attitude towards women in her employ. As a matter of fact, she expected a great deal of her servants and was upset when they failed to meet her demands, but she was quite unable to give them orders, much less to reprimand them. . . .

In recent years, her depressions had become more and more frequent and were intimately associated with the danger of suicide. The patient had already made a number of unsuccessful suicidal attempts; the last one had brought her to the verge of death. . . .

After about eight months' analysis childhood memories began to appear. . . . The memories went back to the time between the patient's fourth and sixth years when she was masturbating to an alarming extent—at least from the mother's point of view. It was impossible to decide whether this masturbation really exceeded the normal amount, nor could we determine the content of the fantasies which, presumably, had accompanied the masturbation. But it is a fact, according to the patient's statement, that the mother resorted to the following method of checking the patient's masturbation: she bound the patient's hands and feet, strapped them to the crib, and said, as she stood looking on, "Now play if you can!" This aroused two reactions in the little girl. One was ungovernable rage against her mother, which was prevented by the fetters from discharge in motor activity. The other was intense sexual excitement, which she tried to satisfy by rubbing her buttocks against the bedding, regardless of her mother's presence, or perhaps to vent her spite on her mother.

The most dreadful thing in this scene, for her, was the fact that her father, summoned by the mother, was a passive witness and did not offer to help his little girl despite his tender affection for her.

The patient stopped masturbating after this childhood scene, and with this renunciation for a long while repressed her sexuality. At the same time, she repressed her hatred for her mother, to which she had in reality never given full expression. . . .

From this time on, all sexual excitement was bound up with the maternal prohibition and with the most intense aggressive impulses toward the mother. . . . It is, therefore, comprehensible that the patient should reply to the direct question, why she had never yielded to a homosexual attachment, with the answer that she was afraid of becoming subjugated to the sexual partner. She was, indeed, afraid of being masochistically attached to her mother. . . .

After the above-mentioned part of the analysis had been worked through (after eight months) the father made his first real appearance as a topic of analytic material, and at the same time all of the impulses belonging to the œdipus complex were revived, starting with the chief, unremitting, reproach against the father that he had been too inactive to love his daughter. . . .

I hoped that the patient's libidinal future would shape up more satisfactorily with a revival of the father relationship, especially when this relationship had been retouched and corrected. I referred her to an analyst of the fatherly type. Unfortunately, the transference did not advance beyond respect and sympathy, and the analysis was interrupted after a short time. About a year later I met the patient and saw that she had become a vivid, radiant person. She told me that her depressions had entirely disappeared. The wish to die which had been almost continuously present and her nostalgia had apparently receded completely. At last she had found happiness in a particularly congenial and uninhibited sexual relationship with a woman. The patient, who was intelligent and conversant with analysis, informed me that their homosexual relationship was quite consciously acted out as if it were a mother-child situation, in which sometimes one, sometimes the other played the mother—a play with a double cast, so to speak. Moreover, the satisfactions sought in this homosexual love play involved chiefly the mouth and the external genitalia. No "male-female" contrast appeared in this relationship; the essential contrast was that of activity and passivity. The impression gained was that the feeling of happiness lay in the possibility of being able to play *both* rôles.

The result of her analysis was evident. . . . It was evident that the overcoming of her hostility toward the analyst [Deutsch] had brought with it the overcoming of her anxiety and, consequently, a positive libidinal relationship to women could appear in place of the anxiety and hostility which had caused the neurotic symptoms—only, of course, after the mother-substitute object had paid off the infantile grievances by granting her sexual satisfactions. The analytic treatment had not brought about the further and more favorable solution of the mother attachment, that is, a renunciation of her homosexuality and an inclination towards men.[28]

Dr. Deutsch's grandson, Nicholas Deutsch, who is active in the Gay liberation movement in Boston, in 1974 related to the present author an anecdote referring to the foregoing case history, or one similarly concluded.

This is a story my grandmother told me; she had just begun practicing on her own, under Freud's supervision, in Vienna, and she took on a patient who was a Lesbian. My grandmother was disturbed because, although the analysis finally concluded successfully—the woman could deal with various problems in her life— she was still a Lesbian. My grandmother was rather worried about what Freud would say about this turn of events. When she next saw Freud the first thing he said was, "Congratulations on your great success with Miss X." My grandmother, startled, said, "But she's still a Lesbian." To which Freud replied, "What does it matter as long as she's happy?"[29]

♀ 1933: DR. LA FOREST POTTER;

Psychonanalysis and Hormone Medication
"Some we would probably kill. Others we would cure"

In his book *Strange Loves: A Study in Sexual Abnormalities*, Dr. Potter of New York City, author of numerous works for the general public, focuses on the subject of homosexuality—probably an attempt to cash in on the interest generated by the U.S. publication of Radclyffe Hall's *The Well of Loneliness* (1929) and Blair Niles's *Strange Brother* (1930). Potter, whose book is cited in the Kinsey report on women as a source on Lesbianism, believes homosexuality to be caused by psychological and hormonal disturbances.

Claiming that "many people fail to recognize homosexuality when they see it," Potter relates a story told to him by two patients, a mother and a daughter. A friend in the West had sent eighteen-year-old Mabel to visit them in New York. Young Mabel soon took to kissing and embracing the mother, who woke up one night to find her "attempting to have sexual relations with her." The daughter was called.

The girl then confessed before the two women that she was a lesbian and had fallen deeply in love with Mrs. M———. The women were horrified at first. But then they realized that this child was more to be pitied than scolded. They looked at her compassionately.

"Don't throw me out," the girl begged. "Everyone has thrown me out. Nobody has ever yet tried to help me."

"But do you want to be helped?" questioned the mother.

"God knows I do," she exclaimed. "Those who are the same as I only drag me down. And the nice people like you cast me out. I don't know what to do. The only happiness I've ever known has been with you. And now I've lost that, too."

And so these ladies had their first contact with abnormal sexual life. They brought the girl to me for treatment and stood by her. I explained the whole case to them, so that they would understand.

"Can she be cured?"

"Yes," I answered, "if she wants to be."

But she did not want to be cured, as experience proved, and as I strongly suspected, the moment I elicited her psycho-analytic reactions.

And so, shortly afterwards, she drifted away. When last I heard of her she had settled down into a lesbian relationship with one of the most notorious tribades in New York.

All of which emphasizes what I have before stated—that no homosexual *can be cured*, or even relieved of his or her abnormality, *who will not whole-heartedly cooperate towards this end*.[30]

Potter mentions his successful treatment of another Lesbian

whose psychology was subsequently modified by argument, and whose libido was brought back to normal by stimulation of the ovaries and thyroid, and by the internal administration of ovarian substance and corpus luteum [both hormones]. . . .

So it merely requires that the *right* instruction, the *right* environment, the *right* opportunities be afforded, and thousands of women and girls, who now follow lesbian practices might once more become normal individuals. They might even become happy wives and mothers, if only their mental condition could be corrected by therapeutic or normal suggestion, and their endocrine system toned up by administration of such extracts as would enhance their feminine characteristics and reactions.

In brief, the lesbian, in her attitude of hopelessness and her protestations of incurability, is self-deluded. She is making a gesture, which creates in her inverted mind some similitude of the heroic, the martyred, the harried power of nature—an attitude which, in an enormous number of cases, is totally unwarranted.

For there is much that medical science and psychology has to offer these women, if only they will accept this help. . . .

Medical men are often asked the question "Cannot these abnormals be reclaimed by marriage? Is it not possible to bring to these people a realization of their degeneracy, and instil into them a clearer concept of the fineness and fullness of life?"

To this question I must reply that, where the condition is *acquired*, not *hereditary*; where the *will to be normal* is overpoweringly strong; where there exists the fullest co-operation; marriage may help marvelously in restoring normal mental and psychical equilibrium. . . .[31]

Concerning the treatment of male homosexuals, Dr. Potter describes his work with a young musician obsessed and frightened by his attraction to other males.

I made a physical examination of the boy and found that he needed certain endocrine stimulation and other adjunct treatment. This I prescribed for him. Then I proceeded to tell him what I thought of his mental processes.

I told him that many of the greatest people in the world had had an excessive sexual urge. That this force they fought, or felt was overpowering them, was the greatest creative force on earth. That all men and women who accomplished anything at all, were super-sexed people. . . .

I told the young man that he could take this passion, this great capacity for love, and transmute it from a sex urge into a living creative power. . . .

I told him that, instead of being ashamed of this passion, he should be proud of it. That he should control it, and pour it out in his work, so that men would recognize the power of his creation when they heard his music. . . .

This young man came to me for several months. At the expiration of this time I told him that he was cured. It is interesting to note that the boy had progressed so rapidly in his work during these months that he had won a scholarship in one of our most important schools for musical education. And today all the suffering of his soul he pours out through his violin. I understand that he is fast becoming recognized as one of the leading American musicians, with a great future predicted for him.

He is quite normal now. He has poise such as few men have, although he is strangely quiet, and extremely modest. However, one can feel the force of his spirit when he talks of music. For music is his life: his passion.

I feel that he is now cured so far as his abnormality is concerned. And that sometime, when the spark strikes the powder of his inflammable nature he may develop a sincere and potent heterosexual love.

Until this time he may find satisfaction in his freedom from abnormal sexual craving and in what he has been able to achieve musically, by reason of sublimating his inverted desire.[32]

Turning to "The Tragedy of Oscar Wilde," Potter adds:

It is a great pity, in a way, that Wilde happened to have been born thirty or forty years too soon. Were he alive today, and were he willing to co-operate toward the relief or the removal of his endocrine unbalance, it is more than likely that a great deal might have been done for this erratic genius.

We could have subjected the overactive thymus to X-ray radiation, atrophied the gland and suppressed the overactivity of its function—which was one of the principal causes of Wilde's lack of sexual normality.

Then we could have built up the masculine characteristics, by means of proper combinations of post-pituitary, adrenal and testicular extracts.

We could also have given Wilde the benefit of an informed psychologic and psycho-analytic concept—the proper understanding of which might have worked wonders in his brilliant brain.[33]

Dr. Potter's book ends with a plea for further research and deeper understanding, leading to sweeping "reforms" in the treatment of "abnormals" of all types:

Some we would probably kill. Others we would cure. Still others we might treat with a sense of justice now denied them. And many thousands, now living only in the shadows of normality, might be brought safely back from the no-man's land of their present existence.

All of which would go far in helping to build hope, happiness, kindness, love, tolerance, and understanding, in millions of human beings who are only waiting for the light that shall disclose these blessings to them.[34]

1935: DR. LOUIS W. MAX;
Aversion Therapy (Electric)
"Low shock intensities had little effect"

At a meeting of the American Psychological Association on September 6, 1935, Dr. Louis W. Max of New York University reported on "Breaking Up a Homosexual Fixation by the Conditioned Reaction Technique," the first documented use of aversion therapy on a homosexual. A summary of his presentation states:

A homosexual neurosis in a young man was found upon analysis to be partially fetishistic, the homosexual behavior usually following upon the fetishistic stimulus. An attempt was made to disconnect the emotional aura from this stimulus by means of electric shock, applied in conjunction with the presentation of the stimulus under laboratory conditions. Low shock intensities had little effect but intensities considerably higher than those usually employed on human subjects in other studies, definitely diminished the emotional value of the stimulus for days after each experimental period. Though the subject reported some backsliding, the "desensitizing" effect over a three month period was cumulative. Four months after cessation of the experiment he wrote, "That terrible neurosis has lost its battle, not completely but 95% of the way." Advantages and limitations of this technique are discussed. . . .[35]

♀ 1940: DR. NEWDIGATE M. OWENSBY;
Pharmacologic Shock
"Metrazol was administered until fifteen shocks were produced"

In 1937, Dr. Owensby of Atlanta, Georgia, began treating male and female homosexuals by convulsive shock inducted with Metrazol, a chemical stimulant. In 1940, he explains the motive for his research before the annual meeting of the Southern Psychiatric Association.

The prevalence of homosexuality is increasing with an unparalleled rapidity, according to the police, jail officials, court attachés and others who have occasion to contact such individuals. . . . Since homosexuality is no respecter of race, creed, sex or social milieu it has become a matter of serious concern in the bringing up of a child of either sex and unless comprehensive measures are employed to inform parents of its dangers, a disintegration of our present code of morality is threatened.

Whatever else may have been responsible for the increase in homosexuality certainly the attitude of the public in assuming it to be an atavistic form of degeneracy, beyond the power of man to correct, has played a dominant rôle. This attitude has been responsible for the enactment of laws imposing such an extreme penalty that a person so afflicted placed his liberty, and in some states his life, in jeopardy if he sought treatment for the correction of his dyslogistic disorder. Because of widespread prejudice, the homosexual has been forced to develop such defense, compensatory or escape measures necessary to assist him in making life more tolerable, but I am of the opinion that many of them are willing and anxious to make any sacrifice, or accept any hardship they may be called upon to endure, to become sexually normal people with a home and a wife and children that they cherish.

Concerning treatment, Dr. Owensby received responses from homosexuals which he finds striking.

Paradoxical as it may be, every male homosexual I have talked with made the unequivocal statement that he had no desire to change his sexual habits and that those who did were motivated by an attempt to escape the penalty exacted by society for homosexual practices.[36]

In a preliminary report published in the *Journal of Nervous and Mental Diseases* for 1940, Dr. Owensby presents several treatment histories.

Case 1.—A white male of 19 years had been arrested and sentenced to prison because of moral turpitude (homosexuality). He was paroled for treatment and promised a pardon if his perversion was corrected. The family history was not enlightening. Homosexual experiences began during his fourteenth year and continued thereafter. Feminine mannerisms were evident. Metrazol was administered until fifteen shocks were produced. All homosexual desires had disappeared after the ninth shock, but treatment was continued until all feminine mannerisms had been removed. Normal sex relations were established and eighteen months later there had been no return of homosexual tendencies. He was granted a pardon.

Case 2.—A white male aged thirty-four years. Had been a homosexual since his fifteenth year. He was frank enough to admit that the only reason for seeking treatment was fear of exposure and subsequent disgrace. All homosexual desires disappeared after seven grand mal attacks were induced by Metrazol. He was married four months later. At the expiration of ten months he stated there had been no recurrence of homosexual desires or practices.

Case 3.—A white male aged forty-four years. Had been a homosexual since early youth. Most of his past life had been spent in penal institutions because of the opportunities to indulge his perversion. He seemed proud of the fact that he was a "man-woman." Was constantly inebriated when out of prison. Metrazol was administered until ten grand mal attacks had occurred. He appeared to be regenerated after the ninth seizure. His common law wife states that, with the exception of an occasional overindulgence in alcohol, he has been a normal, hard working man for the past six months.

Case 4.—A white male aged twenty-five years. Has been a homosexual since his fifteenth year. His mother was a neurotic. A sister had a manic-depressive attack. A brother was an alcoholic. The patient was seclusive and spent most of his free time in his room. Would take an occasional trip to another city in order to satiate his homosexual desires. Was reluctant to discuss his perversion. Six grand mal attacks were induced by Metrazol. Normal sex relations became established shortly thereafter and at the expiration of three months the patient claimed to be sexually healthy.

Case 5.—A white male aged twenty-six years. Married. Had indulged in active homosexuality since his seventeenth year. Appeared to be an ambulatory schizophrenic. His marriage had been arranged by a doting mother. Had never been self supporting. An obvious personality change followed the sixth induced grand mal attack. Whereas he had formerly been indifferent to his family and friends, he began to show interest and affection for them. He secured a position after returning home and became self supporting. Six months after receiving the Metrazol treatment, he reported that he had continued to be free from all homosexual desires.

Case 6.—A white female aged twenty-four years. Name and address given were admittedly fictitious. Said to have been a lesbian since puberty. Promiscuous. Preferred the active role. Inclined to boast of her conquests. Inebriate for past four years. Ten grand mal seizures were induced by Metrazol. Became infatuated with an intern after the treatment had been discontinued and frequently complained of nocturnal emissions [?]. Remained institutionalized for six weeks after the last treatment and appeared to be healthy in every way. No subsequent reports.[37]

A second Lesbian treated by Dr. Owensby, in a brief testimonial, endorses the effect of Metrazol.

"I am now 29 years old and recently the pharmacologic shock treatment was called to my attention as a possible cure. Although I had no confidence in its ability, or anything else, for that matter, to cure homosexuality, I was more than eager to give it a fair try. I have taken the prescribed treatments and, frankly, I am amazed with the results. I no longer have the slightest desire for a woman—in fact, the very thought of being intimate with a woman is the most disgusting thing I can think of. Whenever I now feel the biological urge, it is a man I want to be with and at long last I have a chance to have a complete and happy life, the kind of a life I have always wanted but heretofore failed to have."[38]

Dr. Owensby's apparent success in "correcting" homosexuality has not been duplicated. Reporting in the *Journal of Nervous and Mental Disease* for 1949, Dr. George N. Thompson concluded on the basis of six case studies that Metrazol-induced shock has no effect on sexual orientation.[39]

1941: DRS. SAUL ROSENZWEIG and
R. G. HOSKINS; Hormone Medication
"An empirical test of the influence of sex hormones"

Drs. Rosenzweig and Hoskins of Worcester, Massachusetts (a psychologist and an endocrinologist, respectively) published one of the earliest detailed American reports on the use of sex hormones to treat homosexuality. The doctors thank various pharmaceutical firms for supplying the hormone products for their experiments: E. R. Squibb & Sons; the Schering Corporation; Ayerst, McKenna & Harrison; and the Eli Lilly Corporation. The obscenity of such an experimental "test," in this case using possibly cancer-causing substances on a Black subject, needs only to be pointed out. The doctors report in the journal *Psychosomatic Medicine* on their test:

The availability of a remarkably typical male homosexual patient led us to make an empirical test of the influence of sex hormones upon attitudes and behavior in his case. The clarity of the results, although negative, may justify a brief report of the case.

The patient, A. D., a male negro of 46, entered the Northampton State Hospital in 1921 and 4 years later was transferred to the Worcester State Hospital with a diagnosis of "constitutional psychopathic personality without psychosis." He had completed the seventh grade of grammar school at the age of 12 and shortly thereafter joined a travelling stock company as a chorus boy. The company was managed by a man whom the patient describes as having been "like a father to me." "I ate with him and slept with him. He was a beautiful man." The patient remained with this company for about a year. Later he worked for two years in a laundry but from time to time took part in amateur performances in which he danced and sang. At the age of 24 a diagnosis of appendicitis led to an operation. Upon discharge from the hospital he learned that his manager-friend had died. This event apparently represented a great blow to him. Shortly afterward he began to show the symptoms which led ultimately to his commitment to hospital. These consisted mainly of seclusiveness, shyness, pronounced effeminacy, and excessive preoccupation with drawing, painting, designing of women's clothes and similar "artistic" activities. His speech became disjointed and unresponsive and for two years he refrained from leaving his home. He talked of wearing women's clothes and often went to bed with presumably imaginary ailments.

Upon admission to the Worcester State Hospital he showed no pronounced psychotic symptoms. In the diagnostic summary he was described as follows:

> He is a short, stocky negro who, except for his large masculine genitals, is in every respect a woman. He shows an exaggerated female gait and speech and all the mannerisms of a clinging-vine type of female, spends hours at his toilette, and says he is fond of being well-groomed. With men he is coy, silly, and affected. With the other sex he talks as one woman to another. He daily asks for cathartics and is overinterested in the needs of his lower intestinal tract. He knows he is considered effeminate, but says that that is the way God made him. He further excuses his peculiarities on the ground that he is an artistic genius and therefore entitled to a few eccentricities. He fully expects to become one of the famous members of his race, which, he says, is the most beautiful of all races. He avoids all references to his sex life but under repeated questioning admits having played a passive rôle in homosexual acts. . . . In brief, we have a negro of passive homosexual type with feminoid make-up, without evidence of psychosis. Mental deficiency, if present, is of a high grade or borderline degree.

During the intervening fifteen years the patient has changed little. . . . A highly characteristic feature is his preoccupation with the movement of his bowels, the significance of which is obvious in terms of psychoanalytic doctrines. He admits that he enjoys violent movements of the bowels and that is the reason why he likes epsom salts. It was assumed that changes in this interest might serve as one indicator of shifts in the strength of his libido.

Sex-hormone medication began with this patient on October 16, 1939, and continued with several variations and intermissions until the middle of April, 1940.

From October 16 to November 20, 1939 he was given orally the potent synthetic estrogen, Stilboestrol (Squibb), in dosage of 5 mgm. three times a week.

On December 6 he received an implant of a 150-milligram tablet of Testosterone (Schering), which was embedded in the subcutaneous tissues beneath the inferior angle of the left scapula.

On December 20, 1939 to February 7, 1940, intramuscular injections were given of a gonadotropic preparation derived from pregnant-mare serum (Anteron-Schering). The dosage was 1 cc. or 250 units twice weekly. . . .

An attempt was then made to enhance the responsivity to sex hormones by the use of desiccated thyroid (Armour). This was begun on February 1 at 1 grain daily and continued throughout the remainder of the study.

On February 9, Pituitary Gonadotropic—Pranturon (Schering)—was substituted for the pregnant-mare preparation, also in dosage of 1 cc. twice weekly. At the same time Testosterone Propionate by intramuscular injection was begun in dosage of 50 mgm. twice a week. Both were continued until February 29.

On March 9 another estrogenic preparation was begun, Ayerst, McKenna and Harrison's Emmenin being used in dosage of 1 teaspoonful three times daily. This was discontinued on March 21.

Finally, from April 6 to 12 another estrogen, Estriol (Lilly), was given in the large dosage, 0.24 mgm. three times a day.

As is well known, Stilboestrol has a tendency to produce nausea and even vomiting. The patient experienced a certain amount of nausea but not enough to warrant discontinuing the medication. This effect aside, none of the drugs of the entire series gave rise to any detectable change of behavior or attitude. In particular, no change whatever could be detected in his preoccupation with defecation.

The dosage of the various preparations was purely arbitrary but was of the order that frequently has been found to be clinically effective in suitable cases. While optimal amounts of some of the preparations may not have been used, it is believed that enough was given to change significantly the estrogen and the androgen titres as well as the ratios between the two. In the case of Estriol, at least, the dosage was definitely high. Had the personal psychodynamics of the patient been primarily dependent upon hormonal factors it seems highly probable that at least minor shifts of preoccupation and attitude would have been detectable with changes of medication.

As one possibility, it follows that in such cases, in which the homosexuality is of long standing—thirty-five years in this instance—and in which the personality structure has been altered at an early date the autogenous hormonal factors are no longer of significant potency. Neither is the personality-structure amenable to alteration by endocrine medication.

Summary

In a male patient presenting marked homosexuality of thirty-five years' standing a variety of estrogenic, androgenic, and gonadotropic preparations were administered.

No influence upon the behavior or the personality of the patient could be detected.[40]

1944: DRS. S. J. GLASS and
ROSWELL H. JOHNSON; Hormone Medication
"An actual intensification of the homosexual drive"

In the *Journal of Clinical Endocrinology*, Drs. Glass and Johnson of Los Angeles report on two years of experiments (on eleven individuals) designed to establish the effect of "organotherapy" (hormone medication) in the "clinical management" of male homosexuals. The Schering Corporation and Ayerst, McKenna & Harrison are thanked for "kindly" supplying free pharmaceutical products. The doctors conclude:

Treatment led to the following results. Insofar as homosexuality is concerned, organotherapy failed to influence the psychosexual behavior in eight of the subjects but seemed to benefit the other three. . . .

Among the eight who failed to respond favorably [four] subjects . . . complained of an actual intensification of the homosexual drive so that further treatment was withheld or abandoned by them. In view of the antecedent hopes of the subjects, any influence that suggestion might have had in their cases would presumably have been in the direction of alleviation rather than accentuation of their homosexuality. . . .

The organotherapy of homosexuality has not reached a stage where one may simply administer androgens and gonadotropins to all cases with confidence of success. The fact is that sometimes instead of helping one gets a worsening of the condition.[41]

1944: DR. SAMUEL LIEBMAN; Electroshock
"My vision of the world on fire"

In an article entitled "Homosexuality, Transvestism, and Psychosis," Dr. Samuel Liebman presents a classic case study of the effect of electroshock on a homosexual. As in the reports of Daniel (1893) and of Rosenzweig and Hoskins (1941), earlier excerpted, antihomosexual attitudes and racism are linked; here the experimental subject is a Black male homosexual transvestite.

This 23-year-old colored male was admitted to the Norwich State [mental] Hospital on November 15, 1941, at which time he was dressed in a very effeminate manner. His hair was oiled and covered with a hairnet, incorporated in which were two carnations and a number of beads as a corsage placed over his forehead. His eyebrows were tweezed and arched. He had mascara on his eyelids. His cheeks and lips were rouged and there was powder on his face. His finger nails were manicured and lacquered. He wore bracelets on his wrists, rings on his fingers, beads and a crucifix about his neck. He was garbed as follows: male sport clothing under which was a blue silk blouse and, as part of his undergarments, he wore a woman's silk chemise and shirt.

His general manner was effeminate. He spoke with a high pitched voice and showed effeminate mannerisms in walking, in the carrying of his hands, etc. He spoke rather freely of his homosexuality, of being a female impersonator and stated: "I am a homosexual. Are there any others in this ward?"

Physical examination at this time revealed our patient to be in excellent nutritional state but having a rather effeminate physical make-up. No pathological physical or neurological findings were noted except for some peculiar serration of his teeth. . . .

The patient was generally quite overactive, overtalkative and restless. He constantly annoyed the personnel, requesting his hair curlers, rouge, lipstick and other items of feminine apparel, stating that he liked to wear them as they made him feel better. He took exercises to "maintain the figure" and was observed singing, dancing about the ward and making overt homosexual advances to other patients. The patient, himself, was clean, neat and meticulous in his personal appearance but continually demanded attention, making noise to attract it if necessary. Because of his complete disregard for other patients' feelings, it was essential that he sleep in a room by himself.

On November 23, he became excited, threw a chair over his head, broke a flower pot, and because of his excitement, it was necessary to send him to the disturbed ward. On the disturbed ward, he maintained a superior attitude toward the other patients but made overt sexual advances to many of them. He spoke continuously about his wealth and activities and stated that he was not colored; that he was part Indian, Cuban, etc. He quieted down in a short time and on December 2, was returned to the admission building. There, he remained excited and overactive but to a lesser degree than previously noted.

Following a spinal puncture, the patient got up, walked about a bit singing and chanting the Lord's prayer and other religious hymns. He constantly requested the examiner and various other members of the ward personnel to order his gowns, furs, clothing and other items of feminine apparel from various department stores.

The patient answered all questions put to him readily, but soon became quite rambling in his speech, going from topic to topic in great detail and showing a tendency to a flight of ideas although there was no marked distractibility in his conversation. At intervals, his speech became somewhat incoherent and irrelevant. . . .

The patient wrote voluminously. Part of these writings included: "Dreams—my vision of the world on fire," "The story of my life," etc. Many letters were also written, addressed to his friends, his "prospective husband," his family, etc.[42]

Dr. Liebman provides a resume of the patient's background.

There is nothing of note in his early childhood and early development except that he is said to have always been a nice boy, was obedient, cheerful, pleasant and never seemed nervous.

While in grammar grades, the patient was effeminate, "a sissy," gestured with his hands and had a "pussy-foot walk." He was always neat, never a behavior problem and was better than the average Negro scholar. He read poems, and never played rough games.

When the patient graduated from high school in June, 1937, he was thirtieth in a class of 36. The principal remembers our patient as being effeminate and as taking offense in a feminine way. Because of his color he was more or less of a social outcast and his actions were such that he did not fit into the group very well. He had a defensive, persecuted sort of attitude which bordered on perpetual sullenness, but he seemed to have an inflated opinion of himself. He attempted to attend activities which the other colored boys did not. He always dressed well but wore "very obnoxious perfume." The patient enjoyed being in the spotlight and tried to attract attention. . . .

In grammar school, the patient seemed to be fond of both boys and girls and they seemed to get along quite well. As he grew older, however, the color line became more marked and the patient seemed to withdraw and had no close friends. . . .

His present illness is said to have started about the middle of August, 1941. He was working for a respectable widow whose elderly father was paralyzed, taking care of the father. Patient is said to have managed this invalid better than any nurse they previously had. At first he did not drink, kept himself unusually clean and generally had a "nice expression" on his face. He seemed anxious to do everything the right way, and, in fact, was apt to be offended if anyone thought he was not doing things the best way.

Early in August, 1941, the patient began going around with other colored people in the local community and it was at this time that he started to drink. He became a bit excitable, irritable, would "carry on about water for his bath, about having more time off," etc. His voice became high pitched and he seemed more sensitive. On August 18, he was arrested for "getting into a brawl with a white man of poor character" in a tavern. He was given ten days in jail. Following the expiration of his jail sentence, the patient attempted to return to work but his employer was a bit suspicious of him because he had used two names, talked in an "outlandish fashion" about buying a car, having a chauffeur and a cook. He began to smoke at this time. The general tenor of his behavior increased. He then began running around in buses between several of the cities about Hartford "making a general spectacle of himself." He went into beauty parlors for permanent waves, walked the floors in department stores as though he belonged there, and when he appeared in court for the evasion of bus fare, he wore curlers in his hair and presented a generally feminine make-up.

In court, the patient stated that he had an engagement at eleven o'clock to buy a Packard and get a chauffeur, that he impersonated females on the stage, and had an appointment to sing in Hollywood that night. He continued, stating that he belonged to a nudist camp but refused to stay there because they "played leap frog."

On November 15, 1941, the patient was admitted to the Norwich State Hospital.

On December 19, 1941, he was placed on electroshock therapy and received a total of 8 treatments, resulting in 8 convulsions. On December 29th the patient stated: "What on earth ever made me act like I did before I came here? No wonder they locked me up, I must have been crazy. Imagine me in Fox's trying on furs and evening gowns! How am I ever going to face those people again?" He remained pleasant and somewhat hyperactive but was eager to co-operate. The following day, December 30th, he remarked again: "I wonder why I acted like that. I know I'm a homosexual. Some of the best people in H. are, but that is no reason for me to make a fool out of myself, getting permanents, wearing jewelry, etc."

Following a treatment on December 31, the patient seemed somewhat confused, depressed, apprehensive and suspicious, asking, "Will I be all right? Is my brother all right?" The next day he was rather preoccupied, seemed somewhat suspicious of the other patients, kept watching them intently and was unable to work. He said: "All these people are interested in me. They are clever and can read my mind."

On January 2, the patient said: "I was poisoned at noon and am going to die a horrible death tonight." He remained distrustful of the other patients, not sure of just what he should say or how he should behave. He was somewhat depressed and expressed vague suicidal ideas. The last treatment was given January 5, 1942. The patient continued to improve, became more alert, took an active interest in his environment, saying: "I feel much better." He became interested in ward activities and got along so well that he was given ground privileges and permitted to walk around the institution property.

When interviewed on February 18, the patient

spoke more freely about his sexual experiences and told of his overt passive and active homosexuality. He denied heterosexual experiences. He was correctly oriented and his memory was good. The main picture was that of an apathetically depressed individual who was quite preoccupied with feelings of guilt and bizarre, vague, delusional and hallucinatory experiences which he could not understand. His memory was not impaired. Orientation was good and sensorial faculties showed no great change. . . .[43]

Summary

This case is that of a definitely hereditarily tainted individual who was reared in a foster home completely removed from his siblings. In this peculiar home situation, he became overtly homosexual, transvestitic and psychotic. With electroshock therapy, the patient recovered from his psychosis and transvestism although he remained overtly homosexual.

Since the above was written I have been informed that the patient was returned to the hospital on November 21, 1942, because of difficulties with the police (theft, breach of peace, and resisting an officer). He was overactive, euphoric, overtly homosexual and somewhat troublesome on the ward. On December 4, he was started on electroshock (convulsive doses) and received 13 treatments. He showed symptomatic improvement, was considered not psychotic, and was discharged on March 12, 1943 to the police.[44]

1945: THOMAS V. MOORE;
Psychoanalysis or Abstinence
"A human being comes into the world to use his powers
. . . in the service of God and the social order"

A lengthy review of American and European research on the "pathogenesis" and psychiatric treatment of "homosexual disorders" was made by Thomas V. Moore of the Catholic University of America. Because he believes homosexuality to be a sickness and a sin, Moore opposes the repeal of sodomy statutes.

Various movements have been started in a number of nations to do away with penal laws against homosexuality. Before one lends support to such a movement, he should consider something more than the problem whether or not the homosexual is a sick man or a criminal. Homosexuality is to a very large extent an acquired abnormality and propagates itself as a morally contagious disease. It tends to build up a society with even a kind of language of its own, and certainly with practices foreign to those of normal society. It tends to bring about more and more unfruitful unions that withdraw men and women from normal family life, the development of homes, and the procreation of children. The growth of a homosexual society in any country is a menace, more or less serious, to the welfare of the state. . . . Granted that some homosexuality may have a biological factor, it is still a matter of importance to control the spread of homosexuality due to psychological causes. Furthermore, it is not evident that homosexuals in whom there is perhaps a biological trend to homosexuality cannot with some effort make a normal heterosexual adjustment. Laws that would countenance the supposed biological rights of homosexuals would therefore rest on false foundations. Laws that would recognize the homosexual as a mental patient and send him to a mental hospital rather than to jail, however, would be a step forward in the handling of this problem.[45]

Turning to the subject of psychotherapy, Moore states:

The fundamental step in treatment is to awaken in the patient a desire to become a normal man and lead a normal life. I have found that in order to do this one has to make the patient realize that his homosexuality is not inexorably determined by the laws of heredity or his own physical constitution. Homosexuals often have the idea that they can no more be cured by psychotherapy than a woman could be changed into a man. Furthermore, they refuse to attempt to change themselves and, like almost all the world, resist being changed by anyone else. Some years ago when it seemed that glandular therapy might be a hopeful method of treatment, I suggested it to a male homosexual. He absolutely refused to consider it, because, he said, "I don't want to be any different from what I am." He had come, not to be cured of his homosexuality, but merely to be made more comfortable in his own mind about continuing it. But it would be malpractice for a psychiatrist to help the patient to remain in his pathological condition and feel more comfortable in its perpetuation. So at the outset of treatment it is well to have an understanding about its objective. A psychiatrist can help the patient to change himself; he cannot impose a transformation of personality.

The treatment of homosexuals must be directed by true guiding principles. If we examine the matter objectively, trying to rise above the clouds of passion and desire, we will admit that a human being comes into the world to use his powers and functions in the service of God and the social order. . . .

Sex pleasure is associated with genital function in married life that children may be sought and brought into the world and trained to do the work that lies before them in the social order. . . .

. . . it is a moral duty for a homosexual who is unwilling to make a nonsexual adjustment in life to attempt to lay aside all homosexual contacts and activity and look forward to the appearance of a heterosexual urge, to eventual marriage and a happy family life.

One should realize that for various reasons this task will be one of widely varying difficulty for different individuals. But one should also know that there is nothing in the literature which enables us to say that for any particular individual it is an impossible task. It is a task, however, which many homosexuals will be unwilling to attempt. If, however, one has a proper sense of moral obligations, he will realize that it is his duty to attempt it or resign himself to a nonsexual adjustment in life. Many such nonsexual adjustments are possible. I have in mind a botanist who never married, but whose love of nature, particularly of the plant world, gave him a very happy life unmarred by unhappy sexual episodes. . . .

Let us suppose that a homosexual expresses a willingness to get rid of his homosexuality and hopes for an eventual heterosexual adjustment. What is the first step? The dropping of all homosexual contacts. The homosexual will be likely to tell you about a perfectly innocent attachment to an individual of the same sex with whom nothing wrong has ever occurred and with whom he is perfectly certain that nothing wrong ever will occur. In spite of the innocence of the friendship, if he or she hopes for an eventual heterosexual adjustment, all homosexual outlets must be closed, and particularly one must sacrifice any tender personal attachments to a member of the same sex. As long as the heart is personally devoted to one individual, it can never become absorbed in another. Thus the starting point must be the cutting off of all homosexual contacts and tender personal attachments to members of the same sex. . . .[46]

1948: DRS. JOSEPH W. FRIEDLANDER and RALPH S. BANAY; Lobotomy
"The lobotomy was seized on by him . . . as the ultimate of spankings"

In 1942, Drs. R. S. Banay and L. Davidoff of New York report in the *Journal of Criminal Psychopathology* on the "Apparent Recovery of a Sex Psychopath after Lobotomy."[47] Within a few years, Dr. Banay was obliged to revise his positive postoperative evaluation. In 1948 Banay collaborated with Dr. J. W. Friedlander of

Chicago on a follow-up study of the same patient entitled "Psychosis Following Lobotomy in a Case of Sexual Psychopathy".

The later case study opens with an account of the patient's background.

J. S. was born in 1887 in a New England town of 15,000, where he lived with his parents until he was 42 (1929). He was enuretic [wet his bed] until the age of 15. In general he was a "good" child but occasionally displayed temper tantrums to his mother, whom he "worshiped." He considered his childhood happy.

He completed two years of high school and a year of secretarial school at the age of 18. He did well in all subjects except mathematics. In school he was never punished for any delinquency. While he had many friends, he characterized himself as "shy and retiring" and "a stutterer." He attended the school dances but never learned to dance. Bookishly inclined, he fancied himself a dentist or a doctor, but made no actual step toward becoming either. . . .

Drafted in July 1918, he served six months in the Army, with two promotions. There was no history of court-martial, hospitalization or overseas duty. He smoked but did not drink, gamble or use narcotics. At home he attended the Methodist Church regularly with his mother, but after her death he was converted to Catholicism through a homosexual friend whom he met in a park. Prior to the age of 52 he had never been arrested.

Work History.—Commuting 10 miles (16 kilometers) to Boston during the first five years of his secretarial career (1906–1911), J. S. worked under five different employers. He denied being fired, attributing these changes to his "nervousness." For eighteen years (until 1929), he earned $35 a week as secretary to the superintendent of schools in his home town. Forced to leave town because of his homosexuality, he went to New York City. During the next five years he earned $43 a week as a stenographer for a bankers' association but lost his job because a new employer preferred women stenographers. During the following year and a half (1934–1936) he had no steady employment and required "relief" for six weeks. Until he was sentenced to prison, three years later, he worked for several WPA projects as a stenographer at $25 a week.

Psychosexual History.—J. S. played with dolls until he was 7, delighted to dress as a girl at 8, and periodically slept with his mother until he was 10 years of age. When he was 12, she caught him in mutual sex play with another boy. Indignantly dismissing the other boy, she began spanking her son, whose trousers were already down. His penis remained erect. Thereafter, he managed to make known to her various acts, notably stealing and masturbation, to which she consistently responded with spanking. Further incentive to his provocative behavior was provided by his father, who gave him money for each whipping. When J. S. was 14, the spankings invariably induced ejaculation. Two years later, his mother caught him in passive anal intercourse with a friend. The flagellation that followed was the last such act committed by her. Meanwhile, J. S. had learned to beat himself, using "the same strap mother used," and later induced friends to spank him. This led to homosexual acts, anal and later oral, preferably in the receptive role, without his sacrificing the dominance of his original masochism. . . .

While he considered himself "temperamental," he had no neurotic complaints other than constipation and insomnia until he was about 30 years old. He then began to have headaches, relieved only by sexual gratification, preferably with small boys. At 52, when he was arrested for such gratification, he was sentenced to prison rather than to a psychiatric institution because his abnormal behavior was diagnosed as a sexual psychopathy. After more than a year in prison, he was referred to one of us (R. S. B.) in an agitated state. A year of psychotherapy brought no relief. Lobotomy was recommended because his history justified his fears, his symptoms included tension, depression, obsession and compulsion and he was considered otherwise incorrigible. Following the method of Freeman and Watts, Dr. Leo Davidoff performed the operation with use of local anesthesia on Nov. 22,1941.

> When the right side of the ventricle was reached, the needle was reinserted slightly more to the anterior. On each side then, the needle was swept downward toward the orbital plate and upward toward the vertex. Afterwards a narrow peri-orbital elevator was inserted on each side and the incision repeated in order to make sure that the pathways were cut.

In the immediate postoperative period, J. S. was confused, disoriented, incontinent and euphoric; he masturbated, fingered his rectum and sucked the feces-laden finger. All these symptoms disappeared by the third postoperative week.

Mental Status.—In October 1940, J. S. was referred to one of us (R. S. B.) because of his extreme nervous tension. He appeared timorous, meek and abjectly apologetic. He stuttered and trembled; his hands perspired, and his voice quavered. At times he strenuously closed his eyes as if to blot out the present exigency. He was filled with self pity. Overwhelmed with fear of committing future sexual assaults on children, he was obsessed with the idea that on release from prison he might commit an act punishable by death. When not in panic, he was preoccupied with masochistic homosexual fantasies, masturbating compulsively two or three times daily. He complained of headaches, insomnia and a sense of weakness but had no delusions, hallucinations or defect in sensorium. Intelligence was bright normal, or even superior. The educational supervisor of the prison, to whom J. S. was assigned as secretary, characterized him as a capable, fast and conscientious worker, handicapped only by his agitated state. His judgment was not impaired, and his insight was fairly good. In prison, at any rate, he was painfully aware of his abnormalities and begged for help, accepting the lobotomy eagerly. . . .

For a year after operation, J. S. remained in prison, under the observation of one of us (R. S. B.). On his discharge, in November 1942, he reported weekly to the parole board until his parole period expired, in May 1944. In prison, he had been befriended by a Pentecostal minister who had made professional visits to Sing Sing Prison, and who once casually invited J. S. to his new home in Chicago. Finding the minister, J. S. then stayed in Chicago.

When J. S. was discovered in the hospital at Hines, his recent memory was so poor that none of his statements concerning his postoperative career could be relied on. The information that constitutes the postoperative data came from independent sources. . . .

When J. S. came to Chicago, in June 1944, his friend the minister found him a room and employed him to type and file letters. In October, the minister secured him a job as a "secretary" in a laundry. The proprietor, an official of the Christian Industrial League, conducted services in his laundry for the benefit of his employees. Shortly after hiring him, he recognized that J. S. was confused, unreliable and unable to work. Although he maintained a charitable interest in him and paid the hospital bill when J. S. broke his arm, he would not rehire him. From March to November 1945, J. S. did odd jobs—typing and passing out handbills from door to door. His performance as a handbiller was characterized by his employer, who continued to give him small gifts long after he fired him, as "undependable in every way. Absolutely didn't know what he was doing." In November the minister obtained work for J. S. in a funeral home at $15 a week and lodging. He was required to answer the phone, type and be present at each funeral. Because he would leave his job and was cheerfully incompetent when available, he was fired two weeks later. This was his last known job. Shortly thereafter, he received an inheritance of $1,000 from an aunt.

What happened to the patient and to the $1,000 between December 1945 and February 1946, when he was next heard from, is unknown. J. S. complacently explained that he lost the money when a "drunk" pushed him from a bridge into the Chicago River. From February until September he lived in the Christian Industrial Shelter. Here he was provided with food, room, and $1 a week for laundry and pleasure. He then moved to the Loop Gospel Mission, a similar organization, but was asked to leave six weeks later because he "made mistakes in his clothes [incontinence] and was too lazy to work around the dormitory." He lived next in a rooming house, where he was discovered in squalor, half starved, bedbug-bitten and exuding a profound stench. Obviously incontinent of bladder and bowel, J. S. was separated from his clothes only with the help of soap, water and scissors. The infection of his foot was then noted, and he was brought to the hospital at Hines.

Psychosexual History.—The parole report gave J. S. a clean slate with respect to deviate sexuality. On six occasions J. S. told the parole officer that he was completely free of abnormal desires, and in the final interview he declared himself "physically and mentally free to live a good, clean life."

The diary he wrote in 1943 overlaps the period during which he was on parole. . . . The following dates are given, with their complete entries:

> March 14: Fair—mild. Sick with a cold. Home all day. To Prospect Park in
>   evening. Met man.
> July 13: Fair—hot. Left 4 p. m. Met boy in park tonight.
> August 8: Fair—hot. Went to Church in a. m. To Ft. Green Park in after-
>   noon—sailor. Hard day *No food.*
> August 25: Fair—warm. To Central Park tonight. 2 sailors.
> October 12: Fair—milder. Holiday. Went to Staten Island. Found a number
>   there.

Besides the diary, the trunk contained clippings from newspapers and magazines, which, from the condition of the paper, appeared to be of recent origin. Seven of these were pictures of boys: 3 of boys smiling; 1 of a boy lying on the ground crying; another of a boy in swimming trunks, and 1 of a boy taking a bath. The last was a sketch of two boys fighting, one on his back and the other on top, lunging a blow. Three cartoons showed a man being whipped. In another cartoon, a woman held a whip in one hand and, in the other, a leash with three small boys attached. Finally, there was a picture of a rattlesnake coiled to strike.

In addition, there were thirty-two scraps of paper bearing the handwriting of J. S., three in green ink and the rest in pencil. Although undated, none of the papers appeared to be old or yellow, and the pencil writing was sharp and distinct. Stamped on one, but penciled out, were the name and Chicago address of the patient's minister friend. The notes were all obscene, with 61 references to a variety of sexual practices, including even coitus. In the order of frequency, the perversions were: masochism (spanking), 21 references; anal intercourse, 12 references; heterosexual relations, 9 references; fellatio, 8 references; voyeurism, 5 references; anilingus, 4 references, and masturbation, 2 references. The two mildest and briefest notes are reproduced in full:

1. Please *FEEL OF MY BARE ASS AND COCK*. I have *no drawers on*. $.25 if you will *PULL* MY *COCK* HARD $.25.
2. Sammy, if we could be *all alone* somewhere and no one would know anything about it if I stripped off *bare* naked, and laid down on the floor or bed would you *spank* my nice soft ass just as *hard* as you could with your belt and *rubber hose*. I haven't had a *spanking* for a long time and how I want one. Perhaps you might know of some place. Would pay you $1.00.

When confronted with these notes, in an attempt to learn why he wrote them, J. S. yielded no reliable information. Because of his suggestibility, he "admitted" alternately that the boys named in the notes were real or imaginary. Although it is probable that he continued to practice perversions in Chicago, the evidence suggests that such episodes were well hidden. Thus, the laundry employer and the heads of the Shelter and Mission were not aware of his homosexuality. At the hospital at Hines, furthermore, there was no record of any homosexual activity. Yet he had firsthand knowledge of the parks and described several homosexual attachments in Chicago, one of which is known to have had a basis in reality. This concerned a boy of 17, who worked at the laundry with J. S. and whose unsavory character led the laundry owner to fire him. J. S. was known to be inexplicably attached to this boy and was heard inviting him to his room. The two often left work together.

Medical History.—After the immediate postoperative confusional state, J. S. emerged amazingly tranquil and apparently free of his erotic fantasies, but still courteous, meek and apparently intellectually intact. The only deficit noted was a reduced energy output. The parole record contained few references to his health or mental status. In December 1942, the parole officer reported, "His memory is very poor . . . ; he gets lost very easily and cannot seem to remember directions." Ten days later, on losing a job, J. S. explained, "My head was getting in bad condition." Later, he again complained of his memory, blaming the operation. . . .

In the interval between his two Chicago hospitalizations, J. S. was known to complain of headaches; his mental condition can readily be inferred from the postoperative work history. On admission to the hospital at Hines, on Dec. 20, 1946, he presented a swollen and tender left ankle and foot. Placed in the surgical ward with a diagnosis of "severe cellulitis of the left foot and lower leg," he was given penicillin. Two weeks later the infection cleared and he was walking. Because he was confused, irrational and enuretic, a psychiatric consultation was requested. The consultant noted impairment of memory, circumstantiality, poor orientation for time, confabulation and childishness. With a tentative diagnosis of psychosis with cerebral arteriosclerosis or presenile psychosis, the patient was transferred to the psychiatric ward on Jan. 6, 1947. . . .

. . . he enjoyed nearly all the tests and offered no resistance to the cystoscopic examination or to the pneumoencephalographic study, from which he suffered only a mild headache of a few hours' duration. He smoked almost incessantly but not more than a third of a cigaret at a time. He wrote brief letters daily to the same few people. In nearly all letters he followed the statement that he felt fine with an urgent appeal for 15, 25 or 50 cents, or, in the case of a relative, for $1.00.

More often than not, he was mildly euphoric, exhibiting joy when offered an orange or a piece of candy. Next to eating, he was happiest singing and playing operatic arias, old waltzes and hymns on the piano before an audience. In general, he performed creditably, even though he never remembered the words and sometimes fumbled at the keyboard, lapses which he concealed by humming and improvising finales. His euphoria, however, occasionally gave way to anxiety. When electroshock was being given in the next room, he sometimes walked about, murmuring, "Oh, this is terrible; this is terrible!" On other occasions, he would complain bitterly, "There is nothing to do. I get so bored." . . .

. . . When told to write out his thoughts, sexual and asexual, as well as the events of the day, he wrote, "No sexual thoughts" repeatedly. For variety, he added: "No sexual trouble," "no trouble sexually," "no unusual thoughts" or "no unnecessary sexual thoughts." For an unknown length of time, his mother and Christ had been telling him "to be of good cheer"; sometimes they ordered him to stop masturbating. Often he saw as well as heard them. Once he showed a flash of insight: "But they're dead. Christ is dead, and mother is dead." Perplexed, he finally broke into a smile, saying, "But their spirit lives on." . . .

His vocabulary indicated a better than average intelligence which had deteriorated. His judgment was childish; he was concerned only with his day to day existence. Insight, likewise, was absent. While willing to grant that dates sometimes confused him, he considered his mind sound and his hallucinations "a gift of God." Whenever he was asked about the lobotomy, he typically replied, "It was a perfect success—no desire for the homosexual."[48]

In a lengthy "Comment" on the case history, Drs. Banay and Friedlander offer a brief psychoanalytic interpretation of the patient's preoperative symptoms, focusing especially on his masochism. They conclude with the remark:

The lobotomy was seized on by him as an appeasement to his superego, and conceivably as the ultimate of spankings.

Drs. Friedlander and Banay then take up their "primary concern":

It is imperative that we determine whether the post-operative changes in the patient were actually due to lobotomy.

The doctors discuss, and reject, the possibility that the patient's symptoms were caused by disease. They then turn to current research on the effects of lobotomy, and conclude with a terse summary of their findings:

Our patient showed rapid improvement after the immediate postoperative period, stabilization for a year and then progressive decline. Lobotomized in November 1941, he was first recognized as psychotic in March 1945 and demented in January 1947. Since there is no evidence for any complicating factor, and we can explain all our findings in terms of the effects of the operation itself, we conclude that the lobotomy produced the dementia.[49]

1953: DRS. J. SRNEC and K. FREUND;
Aversion Therapy (Emetic)
"For the provocation of nausea and vomiting emetine was made use of"

In 1953, the *International Journal of Sexology* presented an influential report on the "experimental treatment" of male homosexuality conducted in Czechoslovakia by Drs. J. Srnec and Kurt Freund. This was the first article on conditioned-reflex therapy since that of Dr. Louis Max in 1935 (excerpted earlier). The Czech doctors pioneered in the use of visual aids (slides) and emetics (nausea-inducing drugs). They were also the first to suggest treatment to induce aversion toward homosexuality and to produce heterosexual arousal—techniques later widely adopted in the United States. The doctors report:

The experimental procedure consists of two phases. First, the patient is given coffee or tea with emetine, much like in the treatment of alcoholism. Ten minutes later a subcutaneous injection is given of a mixture of emetine, apomorphine, pilocarpine and ephidrine. . . . He is then shown films and slides of men dressed up, further sportsmen in bathing suits and men in the nude. Approximately 5–10 minutes after the beginning of the session he feels unwell and begins to vomit as a result of the administered drugs. The procedure lasts half to three quarters of an hour. The patient had been instructed earlier to visualise the persons on the screen as partners of homosexual rapproachement. For the provocation of nausea and vomiting emetine was made use of only a few times, at most 6 times in one course. . . .

In the second phase films are shown in which women appear in situations that would rouse sexual appetite in normal men. The films are shown in the evening before bedtime after the patient received an injection of 50 mgs. testosterone the same morning. This procedure is repeated between 5 to 10 times, either on successive days or at longer intervals, depending on the patient's condition. . . .

Of the 25 persons who went through the entire procedure 10 achieved predominant heterosexuality at practically full sexual activity. Three of them adapted in such a way that their homosexual manifestations receded almost entirely with insufficient heterosexual activity; in the remaining 12 the condition remained practically the same as it was before. Four of the 10 patients who had turned predominantly heterosexual relapsed, 2 of these underwent a second course and regained predominant heterosexuality. The third attended one more session and never turned up again. The fourth has stayed relapsed and has so far shown no interest in repeating the treatment. One of the incompletely adapted patients relapsed and refuses to repeat the treatment. In 4 out of the 12 who showed no change at the completion of the procedure there had been an improvement at the beginning of the treatment but later on relapsed. It is very likely that the chosen procedure has a therapeutic effect and provides in some cases of this deviation a means for their adaptation. . . .

It may be hoped, however, that more effective methods will one day take the place of the procedure described which may then be relegated to an auxiliary role.[50]

1953: DR. KARL M. BOWMAN and BERNICE ENGLE; Castration

"Therapeutic castration . . . seems to be a valid subject for research"

Dr. Bowman and Ms. Engle, director and research assistant, respectively, at the Langley Porter Clinic (San Francisco), collaborated on a number of reports on homosexuality during the 1950s and '60s. Dr. Bowman was earlier director of Bellevue Hospital's division of psychiatry and a professor of psychiatry at the University of California Medical School; he also acted as consultant to the Surgeon General of the United States Army (long associated with research at the Langley Porter Clinic). In 1952, Dr. Bowman urged that a long-term study of the "anatomical, physiological, endocrine, psychological and psychiatric . . . effects of castration in sex deviates" be conducted at the Langley Porter Clinic. His proposal was detailed in a report on "Sexual Deviation Research," prepared for a Judiciary Subcommittee of the California State Assembly. This report suggests that homosexual offenders committed under California's sex psychopath laws be subjected to studies of the effect of sex hormone administration upon brain metabolism.[51]

In "The Problem of Homosexuality" (1953), an article intended for a broad readership and published in the *Journal of Social Hygiene*, Bowman and Engle fail to distinguish between homosexual acts based on mutual consent and those involving coercion. They summarize the generally ineffective attempts to treat homosexuality with electro- and pharmacological shock. They then discuss the more positive potential suggested by

Castration here and abroad

Surgical methods have also been applied to treatment of homosexuality. Several European countries, notably Denmark, have used castration as therapy for sexual criminals, including homosexuals who attacked young males. According to reports, the rather extensive experience in countries like Denmark, other Scandinavian countries, Switzerland and Holland has resulted in fairly strong though not uncritical support. Danish therapists have found a distinct reduction of desire, so that castrates have been able to avoid further sexual crimes.

One or two reports in this country advocate the treatment, but the medical attitude is, in general, adverse. However, there has been no really serious investigation here of the actual results of castration nor of its therapeutic aspects. Therapeutic castration therefore seems to be a valid subject for research, under carefully controlled scientific study.

The authors add:

A long-term study of the effects of lobotomy upon various sexual activities is in progress, but results have not yet been reported.[52]

1953: DR. ERNEST HARMS;
Group Psychotherapy and Abstinence
"A first 'Homo-Anonymous' was started"

In an article entitled "Homo-Anonymous," for the journal *Diseases of the Nervous System*, Dr. Harms of New York City describes the successful application to homosexuals of a "therapeutic principle" established by Alcoholics Anonymous. This method of group self-help was first suggested by one of Dr. Harms's patients.

During the years that I have been working in the psychotherapeutic field, I have encountered a number of cases of sex deviation among men. Until three years ago I held the same sceptical attitude about radical aid to these people as is held by other psychotherapists. At about that time a 30 year old musician came to me with his male friend who was professionally active in the fine arts. Both were refined personalities who lived together on a deviate level.

As the musician expressed it:

"the more brutal forms" of this deviation did not satisfy him . . . and he was living a "haunted life," "divorced from himself" with "rare human satisfactions" which he occasionally found with some young artist and finally with the friend with whom he lived at the time that I met him. He was full of conflicts and rationalizations of his problem. He felt he would like to "overcome" his condition if this was humanly possible. He had read a great deal of the literature concerning his problem which had "in its entirety left him with a feeling of bad taste." There was, he felt, "nothing objectionable in relationships between men as long as they remained on a non-physical level." He referred to Platonic concepts and ideas of other patterns of masculine friendships which excluded women. Here he questioned whether or not psychotherapy might not be applied to sublimate physical homosexuality into some kind of Platonic friendship between such men. He mentioned Alcoholics Anonymous and asked whether or not a similar movement might not be possible. . . .

I was astounded by the idea which had never in any form entered my working or thinking. There was no reason not to attempt it. . . . We had a weekly one hour session to which they brought all their questions and which in the end amounted to a kind of dual analysis. . . . After eight sessions they announced that they felt "completely established in their safe relationship" which did not include physical deviation.

At this point the musician asked me whether there might be a possibility of helping other men by forming friendships under these same conditions and he offered to meet with others if I would collaborate. I agreed and brought a young man who had a similar pattern of deviation. At first we arranged a connection with the musician and later all three met in a weekly joint session. A first "Homo-Anonymous" was started. (I selected this name over the objection of our musician friend and I do not doubt that a less obvious title will be of greater service when it develops into a definite working field.) . . . I hear occasionally about this group and that it is working successfully. . . .

I . . . am not certain how large such groups might be, since four was the largest we reached. There are also problems of secrecy which must be clarified, because of the legal and social implications of this work.

I have discussed this problem with professional colleagues and have found little enthusiasm for making similar attempts, for reasons which I cannot discuss here. I am publishing this short communication in this journal which addresses itself to the practitioner, in the hope that some among them may be willing to test further the value of this idea.[53]

♀ 1954: DR. FRANK S. CAPRIO; Psychoanalysis "Many [Lesbians] become quite disturbed at the thought that psychiatrists regard them as 'sick individuals' "

Dr. Caprio's *Female Homosexuality* appeared in 1954, at the time of a virulent antihomosexual witch-hunt in Washington, D.C., where Caprio happened to make his home. *Female Homosexuality* was the first American medical book dealing extensively with Lesbianism to be published since Chideckel's *Female Sex Perversion* (1935) and Henry's *Sex Variants II* (1941); by default, Caprio became an "expert" on the subject.

The intellectual level of Caprio's work is indicated by his quoting, in total seriousness, "case histories" drawn from the pages of two magazines: *My Confession* (September 1953) and *Life Romances* (August 1953). The latter contains a case study entitled "Poignant Confessions of a Lesbian," allegedly from the files of "Dr. J. L. T.," a psychiatrist. In her book on attitudes toward Lesbianism, Dolores Klaich points out that this case is taken directly from Krafft-Ebing's *Psychopathia Sexualis*.[54]

A few quotes from Caprio adequately convey his ideas. In a section on "Prevention, Treatment, and Prognosis" of Lesbianism, Caprio writes that in his experience

lesbians who seek psychiatric treatment are, for the most part, conscientious in wanting to control their compulsive needs for homosexual gratifications. While every psychoanalyst has instances where lesbians continue to engage in homosexual practices during and after treatment, the majority of them report with pride that psychoanalysis has enabled them to make an adequate heterosexual adjustment. Many patients of mine, who were formerly lesbians, have communicated long after treatment was terminated, informing me that they are happily married and are convinced that they will never return to a homosexual way of life.

The policy of self-acceptance and resignation recommended by some therapists is an unwise one as there are many inverts who do not wish to accept the status of being a homosexual. Such advice gives the person a feeling of futility, as though homosexuality was inborn and psychotherapy would only prove fruitless.

Recommending marriage, per se, as a possible solution is also bad advice. In many instances inverts who do marry very often lead a bisexual existence unknown to their mates.

Since lesbianism is a *symptom* and not a pathological entity, moderate psychoanalytic treatment concentrates on changing the basic character structure (the personality pattern) and thus eliminates the mental block that stands between the patient and a heterosexual adjustment. . . .

The psychotherapist must be kind and yet firm, sympathetic and understanding. He must not preach to his patient and attack inversion from a purely moral point of view. Neither should he scold or frighten his patient with the consequences that are apt to develop if she refuses to disassociate herself from a lesbian friend. . . .

. . . The lesbian must be reëducated and given a healthier understanding of her total personality. In this respect I favor Stekel's approach—the active method of shortening the period of analysis and taking a more active role in helping the patient understand herself and arrive at her own conclusions relative to the psychodynamics of her inversion. . . .

As we might expect, many inverts do not wish to be changed. They prefer to think that their affliction is a congenital one so that they can use this as an excuse for not assuming the responsibilities associated with marriage and family life. . . . Many desire to live a life of dissipation and are indifferent to the penalties exacted upon them by society. They are unwilling to give up contact with homosexual circles.

Others, of course, because of their struggle with this problem seek help. Many of them are sincere and put forth a genuine effort to respond to treatment. It is claimed that a willingness to be cured is halfway to health. This particularly applies to lesbians.

The prognosis therefore is a favorable one wherever there exists this genuine wish to be helped.

Dr. Caprio closes his book with a few summary paragraphs, among them:

The vast majority of lesbians are emotionally unstable and neurotic. Many of them become quite disturbed at the thought that psychiatrists regard them as "sick individuals" in need of treatment. . . .[55]

1957: DR. SAMUEL B. HADDEN;
Group Psychotherapy
"It is obvious that the homosexual . . . hates psychiatrists"

Dr. Samuel B. Hadden has been one of the more prolific American writers on homosexuality, particularly on its treatment in groups. A review of his numerous articles reveals that his first one, "Attitudes Toward and Approaches to the Problem of Homosexuality" (1957), already contains every idea found in his later writings. Although Haaden's more recent articles display a superficial tolerance, his ideas, restated relentlessly, have remained basically unchanged through the years. In this, his first article, Hadden opposes homosexual law reform and advocates group (as opposed to individual) therapy, with participants all of whom are homosexual.

To many physicians homosexuals are a revolting group of individuals, labeled by them as perverted social outcasts. Others regard homosexuals as pitiable abnormals, the result of glandular imbalance, pathetic freaks of nature. More and more the psychiatrist is coming to regard homosexuals as basically neurotic persons with compulsive trends. . . .

In an examination of attitudes toward the homosexual, it might be well to inspect the homosexual's attitude toward himself. From recent literature released by homosexual sympathizers it is obvious that the homosexual, like many an alcoholic, hates psychiatrists but, unlike the alcoholic, he rejects the idea of being considered sick or neurotic. He bitterly resents his acts being labeled as criminal, and would prefer being regarded as a special kind of individual, extraordinarily endowed, and one who should be free from the restraining laws of the community. . . .

. . . it is not usual for homosexuals to seek treatment of their own volition; more frequently they come under therapy after being arrested, at which time part of the sentence imposed is that they shall seek psychiatric assistance or be sent to jail. Proof that they are seeing a psychiatrist regularly is all that is necessary. More than once I have been called upon by an officer of the court to give a note to the effect that I have been seeing certain homosexuals who were simply fulfilling the letter of the court's requirement, with no real motivation for treatment. Many times the homosexual is similarly forced into treatment when the nature of his sexual maladjustment becomes known to members of his family. Otherwise the psychiatrist is likely to see the homosexual only when he becomes anxious because he is being blackmailed, or when he finds he is less able to attract adults and is turning to younger and younger boys. They are most pathetic when the growing sense of isolation from the main stream of society overwhelms them, and sometimes suicide seems the only solution. . . .

There is no question that the treatment of homosexuality leaves much to be desired. To accept it as a hopeless condition, however, will not contribute to the solution of the problem or add to the state of happiness of future generations of homosexuals, even though laws are modified to their wishes. . . .

Long ago I concluded that most of those afflicted with this problem were basically neurotic, so I eventually began to include them in psychotherapeutic groups.

Soon it became clear to me that the average homosexual felt so socially stig-matized that it was very difficult for him to present his problem for discussion before peers who were heterosexually adjusted. Only after he had gained consider-able insight and ego strength and was confident of group acceptance could he reveal this phase of his neurotic maladaptation. As homosexual acts of childhood and adolescence were under discussion by the group it was then brought out, but the anxiety it produced in the group caused the homosexual to feel completely rejected and to drop out of the sessions.

From a limited experience in treating an exclusively homosexual group one of the beneficial effects observed is the speed with which the group breaks down the rationalization of its component members. It becomes quite apparent that the smug rationalizations are a faulty protection against the intense anxiety which exists about their abnormality. In such groups, discussion of the particularly brutal crimes committed by homosexuals, the high suicide rate, the loneliness and the ostracism that these individuals must eventually face are soon brought to the fore, and discussion along these lines quickly demonstrates that even those who have avowed that they wish to be nothing more than insatiable homosexuals soon have their rationalizations shattered, and then seek to change to a normal pattern of behavior.

From this treatment experience I am convinced that homosexuality can be favorably influenced by a group psychotherapeutic approach. The group can ef-fectually destroy the rationalizations of its members who would like to defend their belief that they really want to be homosexuals rather than face the fact that they need not be, and can bring realization that they must seek assistance in the working through of the conflicts which have effected their psychosexual arrest.

Before concluding I want to return to a further discussion of the public attitude and our policy concerning the homosexual. Sentences to prison should be reserved for those who have become publicly offensive and dangerous, but even these in-dividuals should be placed under intensive treatment during their confinement. Those who have been arrested for lesser infractions of the code might be given a suspended sentence conditioned upon psychiatric treatment, with their sincerity regarding treatment being assured by some type of court supervision. . . .

As a research project I should like to see a large number of males who have been convicted of homosexual offenses brought into group psychotherapy. Rather than establish a clinic at the taxpayers' expense, I believe that homosexual offend-ers should be held responsible for the maintenance of such a research project. I feel that they should carry the full burden of cost for treatment designed to reintegrate them into the main stream of society as self-respecting and respected citizens. The alcoholic, through the psychiatrically sound program of Alcoholics Anonymous, has contributed much to the solution and understanding of alco-holism at little cost to the public. I am sure that the homosexual who conscien-tiously seeks help will not plead for special legislation to make it easier for him to continue his maladjusted pattern of sexual behavior when once it is demonstrated to him that he can regain a position in society through effective psychotherapy.[56]

♀ 1959: DR. RICHARD C. ROBERTIELLO; Psychoanalysis
"She could picture being married to him very easily. . . .
Now she was looking forward to having a baby"

In his book *Voyage from Lesbos* (1959), Dr. Robertiello details the psycho-analysis of a Lesbian patient, "Connie"—an analysis whose sexist assumptions about women's proper role now seem transparent in the light of recent feminist critiques.

According to Robertiello, analysis revealed that Connie's fear of incest with her father had blocked her heterosexual development. Through dream analysis and free association, she became aware of her unconscious incestuous wishes; she then decided to discontinue analysis. The story continues from this point.

Connie had just about completed four years of analysis. While she was better in many ways, her basic problems were still unsolved. I hoped that this was indeed no more than an especially strong resistance and that, for her sake, Connie would return to complete her analysis.

. . . I didn't hear a word from Connie for five and a half months. Then one day she called my office. She sounded happy over the phone. She said there had been some promising developments and she wanted to see me. I was delighted and gave her an appointment for the next day.

Connie looked radiant when she came in; there was no trace of that old depressed look. She told me that things had begun to fall into place for her during the past few weeks after attending a party at the apartment of a neighbor. Everyone there was heterosexual. She got a little high and one of the married men managed to get her outside and proceeded to "neck" with her. Right after this, Connie said, she "started putting the insight to use." . . .

At the next session Connie said that one of the men she met at the resort [visited earlier] had called her for a date. . . . She described a dream: "I dreamt about this married man at my office. We were attending a wedding and I was attracted to him. I felt very mellow. He put his hand on my fanny. I got annoyed and told him not to do that. I would have preferred him to kiss me. . . . I felt his touching me in the dream was a disrespectful gesture. I guess, when I think of men, I think of their not caring for me as a person, but just using me as a body. Other girls find men just to go to bed with, but I just can't do that. I want to be emotionally involved with a man, to get married. . . ."

Connie was bringing up some of her old problems—her attraction to married men, her anticipation of exploitation by men and her rivalry with women. Nevertheless, she had them well enough under control so that she could avoid calling on the homosexual defense. . . .

Connie had a few dates with Dave, a man she had met at the weekend resort. . . .

Connie started the next session by telling me about her weekend: "I went away for the weekend with Dave. We slept together. This morning I got up as hostile as could be at him, but I don't feel that way now. It was a pleasant weekend. I enjoyed it. I feel generally good, but with a few doubts. He's not the kind of guy you could easily fall in love with. I wonder if he isn't just interested in conquests for their own sake and this is another one. I think I should see him, but see others, too. I've been attracted to a lot of other men besides him. I told him I want to get married eventually. He talks about other women sometimes and how much he likes his freedom. I guess I was angry this morning because I felt exploited, and then I feel guilty about how much money he spent on me. Maybe I feel I'm exploiting him, too. I'm not sure whether sex with him is exploitation or an expression of affection. I didn't enjoy the actual sex act as much as the rest of it. I thought he was a little on the rough side. I had no great anxiety, though, and I wasn't too shy about his walking around in the nude. I wasn't too shy about being exposed myself either."

I told Connie that it was important for her to realize that if she anticipated exploitation she would be more likely to get it. If a man sees that a woman doesn't trust him and, therefore, cannot love or respect him, he may then decide to exploit her since he feels no mutual love relationship is possible with her. . . .

At the next session Connie reported a rather amusing dream. "I gave this gay girl some food in the same bowl I feed my cat. There was still some cat food left in it. I thought it was a rather evil dream." Connie went on, "The first thing I think about in the morning is Dave. I really feel in love. It's always a nice warm feeling. I wait for his calls. I've been thinking about marriage, but, even if it doesn't come off, I won't go to pieces. I don't think there are many men around like Dave. He has a lot of insight into what I'm thinking and he tries to please me. It seems impossible that I'm falling in love so fast. Do any of your patients make a pass at you? People say you always fall in love with your analyst before you fall for anybody else. It always bothered me that I didn't know what to call you. I felt our relationship was rather stilted—more than I wanted it to be. You always call me Miss M———. I'd rather have you call me by my first name. I feel I want to be more buddy-buddy." . . .

The next session Connie said, "Things are stormy. They're not going well. . . . But despite the fact that things aren't going too well, I don't feel too depressed or despondent. . . . If things don't work out with Dave, I'll find somebody else."

I felt that this was an important session because it showed that, even if Connie had a setback with one man, she wouldn't revert to homosexuality and that she felt confident about finding another man. I felt much more secure about the stability of her change after this session.

During the same session Connie told me she had this dream during the period she was arguing with Dave: "I saw a sheep that was masculine and looked like a wolf. It was dressed up in men's clothing. It was burning from the inside out— really horrible. It must have been in terrible pain." Connie saw that she was expressing anger at Dave when she saw him as "a wolf in sheep's clothing."

She said that the argument with Dave had ended after the dream and that she felt much better. He was speaking very encouragingly about marrying her. Meanwhile, Connie noticed that many men seemed attracted to her. She expressed how grateful she was to me and to analysis for the fact that everything was working out so well. She said she was finally beginning to realize how it felt to be well-adjusted. The only thing that really bothered her was her trouble sleeping. I told her she had to expect some manifestations of anxiety for a while since she was in the process of making such a big change. She said that she actually felt very secure about Dave now. She felt sure she loved him and that he loved her and she could picture being married to him very easily. The feeling that he was exploiting her was waning.

She said she was trying to help this other "gay" girl who was in the process of becoming "straight." For the first time she could say that she was actually happy, Connie told me. She felt less guilty about her parents and more objective about them. No longer did she feel compelled to visit them; she felt she was weaning herself from them. Now she was looking forward to having a baby.[57]

1959: DRS. A. B. SMITH and A. BASSIN;
Group Psychotherapy
"A more conforming sexual adjustment"

In 1959, a report on group treatment of male homosexuals appeared in the *Journal of Social Therapy*. Here psychology and law enforcement are fully meshed. The report's authors are psychologists Alexander B. Smith of the Kings County Court and Alexander Bassin of Yeshiva University; both were also affiliated with the Brooklyn BARO Civic Center Clinic, devoted to the psychological treatment of criminals—"sexual psychopaths"—including homosexuals. (The BARO Clinic was organized in 1953 by a "group of public-spirited citizens under the direct supervision of Dr. Ralph S. Banay," whose 1948 report on lobotomy appears earlier in this section.)

Smith and Bassin report in detail on a group of homosexuals formed in 1957 at the initiative of a twenty-two-year-old referral from the Court of Special Sessions. The three other group members were a thirty-two-year-old married Black referred by the Court of Special Sessions, an eighteen-year-old victim of police entrapment referred by the Youth Counsel Bureau, and a twenty-two-year-old "guilt-ridden" self-referral. The two psychologists clearly make "conformity" their standard for improvement and their treatment goal.

At the BARO Clinic we have observed that the attitudes of homosexuals who have undergone group therapy have changed with respect to social conformity: one of the group members has undertaken marriage, another has started to have heterosexual intercourse exclusively, a third has come to accept his problem more realistically. . . .

Smith and Bassin report that after two years of therapy the initiator of the group married. The Black husband showed "better acceptance of the difference between male and female sex roles." The self-referral showed "greater acceptance of the masculine role." Apparently the youngest member of the group continued to reject heterosexuality, but is said to have displayed "better adjustment." The authors conclude:

We may explain these changes on the basis that the homosexual offender has become a member of a primary group composed of patients who have passed with him through the trauma of arrest and conviction, and are now engaged within the therapy group of defining a more conforming sexual adjustment which is stimulated, first, by the role prescription of the treatment setting and, secondly, by the accepting, permissive, "client-centered" approach of the group therapist. . . .

As treatment progresses, the homosexual offender apparently becomes increasingly motivated to assume a more conforming sexual role as his ego defenses relax and he finds it possible to communicate about his attitude toward sexual intercourse, his feeling of status frustration, his concepts of society and his other problems which are similar to those of the larger population. At the end, if treatment progresses according to course, he may acquire the same satisfying kinds of role patterns of law-abiding behavior he formerly was able to obtain only from homosexual intercourse.[58]

1959: DRS. MOSES ZLOTOW and ALBERT PAGANINI; Lobotomy

"The patients . . . had become serious management problems for the hospital"

In the *Psychiatric Quarterly*, Drs. Zlotow and Paganini present the first large-scale follow-up study of the effects of lobotomy on sexual behavior. Their report was based upon observation and comparison of the pre- and postoperative "erotic manifestations" of one hundred lobotomized males, selected at random from the patients at Pilgrim State Hospital, New York.

The doctors briefly explain the grounds upon which patients were routinely lobotomized, and then summarize their findings.

The indications for lobotomy in all of these patients were almost the same: that is, the patients were long-term schizophrenics who had become serious management problems for the hospital because of aggressive, assaultive, destructive and extremely unpredictable behavior. The control of this behavior was accomplished in a majority of the patients by lobotomy, but it was subsequently noted that— usually in from two to five years following operation—the patient's behavior again became a problem in management. Instead of the assaultiveness and aggressiveness, a problem in overt sexual behavior began to appear.[59]

Oddly, the case reports that follow do not detail much "aggressive, assaultive, destructive" behavior, the main justification for the lobotomies. Homosexual and autoerotic activity appear, in these reports, to constitute the "management problem" for which lobotomy was performed. Among the authors' "representative case studies" is the following:

E. R. (Homosexual before operation; no homosexuality immediately post-operatively but subsequent development of homosexuality in the past two years)

This patient was admitted to Manhattan State Hospital in 1931 at the age of 21 and was diagnosed as a case of dementia praecox, paranoid. According to the history, the father stated that he believed the patient masturbated, although he never observed him doing so. The patient had joined the coast guard at the age of

16, started to drink heavily, and always drank in the company of men. Before his hospital admission, he had been dating girls but his history revealed homosexual practices since he was 16 or 17. Apparently the patient consorted with men in Greenwich Village with whom he practised both active and passive fellatio. The patient admitted that he had become a "fairy" and had spent most of his time in the Village.

He began to hear voices calling him a fairy and he had guilt feelings about his homosexual affairs; he became impotent and, subsequently, was more anxious about this problem. At Manhattan State Hospital, the patient apparently adjusted fairly well, was not obviously involved in any sexual deviations and was released on convalescent status. During his convalescent care period, the patient took a job for about three months, then began to feel that people were looking at him because they knew that he was a "fairy." He attempted to have sexual relations with a girl and became disturbed when he was impotent.

In 1933, E. R. was admitted to Pilgrim State Hospital. Subsequently, it was noted that he participated in passive fellatio on the ward. He developed and expressed open ideas of hostility toward his mother. He explained this by stating that someone gave him a theory or explanation about what makes homosexuals. He said, "If your mother has many intercourses with men, you will become a homosexual." The patient slept poorly, ate poorly; roamed about the dormitory.

In August 1951, he had a prefrontal lobotomy. Immediately following the operation, and for approximately two years afterward, the patient showed considerable improvement in behavior. He became quiet and well-behaved, but was still hallucinatory. He was somewhat disinterested in his surroundings and apathetic, and it was not until the end of 1953 that he became involved in active autoerotic and homoerotic manifestations. In the beginning of 1954, he again became disturbed in his behavior and for the next two years this patient masturbated excessively, and participated in all types of homoerotic and autoerotic manifestations —kissing, fondling other patients, engaging in active and passive fellatio. He became assaultive and disturbed, presumably because of his sexual deviations. He now has to be closely supervised; is actively hallucinating, hearing female voices and refusing to divulge their content. This patient has shown an increase in his sexual manifestations after operation.

A second patient with a different diagnosis, also lobotomized as a "management problem":

C. G. (*Sexual manifestations disappeared after lobotomy*)

This man was admitted to Pilgrim State Hospital in 1940 at the age of 19. He was subsequently diagnosed as dementia praecox, hebephrenic type. According to the history, the patient was single; never mixed with the opposite sex, was shy, and would not talk to girls. He became rather hostile toward his mother and was attached to his father. No sexual irregularities were noted by the family, but the patient admitted freely that he masturbated privately. After admission, the patient was occasionally seen to participate in kissing and fondling on the ward. Occasionally he was observed performing active fellatio and masturbating actively. He was lobotomized in July 1951. After lobotomy, no sexual deviations were reported except that, on interview, the patient admitted occasional masturbatory practices but denied any other sexual activities.

A third case:

G. A. (*No sexual deviations before; sexual manifestations afterward*)

G. A. was first hospitalized in 1941 at the age of 22. He was described as having been withdrawn and as never engaging in any heterosexual relations. Due to his assaultive tendencies, a prefrontal lobotomy was performed in 1947 at the Neurological Institute in New York, following which he showed some improvement in his behavior. However, he was subsequently admitted to Pilgrim State Hospital in 1948, at which time he was described as emotionally dilapidated, silly and unable to carry on a logical conversation. He was restless and markedly disturbed. In 1950, it was noted that he kept his hands inside his clothes, played with his genital organs and showed homoerotic tendencies, annoying other patients during the night. At present, he is described as being the worst management problem in a continued treatment building. He is severely regressed and displays his genitals openly. This patient requires constant supervision because of his sexual approaches to other patients, activities that frequently end in altercations and assaultive behavior on the ward.

Drs. Zlotow and Paganini summarize their conclusions:

1. Sixty patients of a total of 100 show autoerotic or homoerotic manifestations five years after lobotomy. Two-thirds of the patients who show these manifestations after lobotomy have shown them before lobotomy. The remaining one-third do not constitute a real increase in such activity, but an apparent one, caused by masking of this behavior by the aggressive behavior of the patient before lobotomy and by lack of adequate observation. Therefore, the writers feel that there are no *new* homoerotic or autoerotic manifestations brought out by lobotomy.

2. Lobotomy, in the majority of cases, does not change the pattern of sexual behavior which existed prior to operation.

3. The preoperative sexual pattern was masked in some patients, giving rise to the belief that lobotomy increases the autoerotic and homoerotic manifestations, but this belief was not borne out by the writers' data.

4. It is the writers' conviction that release of sexual inhibitions is not a predominant factor in the increase or decrease of postoperative homoerotic and autoerotic manifestations in hospitalized patients.[60]

1963: DR. MICHAEL M. MILLER;
Aversion Therapy (Hypnotic)
"Suggestions of filth . . . were implanted in their subconscious"

In the *Journal of the National Medical Association* (an organization of Black physicians), Dr. Michael M. Miller of Howard University reintroduced the suggestion that hypnosis may be of use in treating the "homosexual neurosis."

For many years there has existed a widespread tendency to disparage the use of hypnosis in the treatment of male homosexuality and homosexuality in general. Clinical experience has amply demonstrated that psycho-analytic treatment of homosexuality is relatively ineffective and prolonged. . . .

The author's decision to experiment with hypnosis in attempting to create aversion reactions was based on a number of considerations. . . . It appeared likely that the aversion and disgust reaction could be prolonged and intensified if a conditioned reflex reaction could be established in the subconscious mind of the patient and, furthermore, that in order for this aversion to occur and be fixated it must be established beyond the reach of conscious resistances and ego defenses. . . .

Clinical experience has revealed that those who turn to homosexuality have been preconditioned by a faulty rearing process which has caused them to reject their natural sexual roles.

It seemed to Miller that hypnotherapy might correct such "faulty emotional conditioning." Indeed, says Miller,

by means of hypnotic suggestion and conditioning, the author has been able . . . to create deep aversions in the male homosexual to the male body. . . .

This procedure, preliminary investigation of which began in 1959, has thus far been attempted on four male patients ranging in age from 26 to 38. . . . Three of the four patients reported can be termed bisexuals, in that they manifested some conscious and unconscious heterosexual desires. The fourth patient had never revealed any sexual interest in females prior to treatment. . . .

In the course of his experiments, Miller

found many male homosexuals and in particular the effeminate, passive type to possess a rather high degree of sensitivity to specific sensations of smell, taste and touch. Like females, they are particularly sensitive to body odors and use deodorants and perfumes extensively. Further, that they tend to be fastidious, and they are often averse to a lack of cleanliness and personal hygiene on the part of their sexual partners and often compulsive about their own cleanliness. A majority of the patients selected had already experienced specific traumatic disgust reactions with certain male partners. Under hypnosis, it was possible to exploit such sensitivities and aversions by regressing these individuals back to the time of their most disturbing disgust reactions and by means of revivification to cause them affectively to relive, potentiate, and establish such unpleasant reactions.

Posthypnotic suggestion was given to the effect that these same "disgust reactions" would recur whenever they were in intimate contact with a male body. These patients after a number of conditioning sessions under hypnosis became highly sensitive to close contact with males, perceiving them as foul smelling, filthy, disgusting and distinctly unpleasant.

The most revolting odors were found to be those of urine, feces, stale perspiration and bad breath. One of the cases seen very recently by the author and not reported in this paper revealed considerable revulsion to the odor and taste of semen and tended to associate it with the odor of Clorox. Suggestions of filth associated with the male genitalia of their partners were implanted in their subconscious and reinforced periodically during the hypnotic trance. It was further suggested to the patients that because they were particular about their own personal hygiene, they were especially revolted by the uncleanliness of other males. This was to prevent any excessive sensitivity or disturbance about their own cleanliness. . . .

Discussing the psychological dynamics behind the use of hypnotherapy, Miller says:

The basic consideration here is that early homosexual erotic experiences are associated with pleasure and that the invert desires to relive these early pleasures. Thus, if the pleasurable associations can be converted or diverted to disgust reactions, and these responses sufficiently established by hypnotic suggestion, the individual might conceivably be repulsed rather than attracted. . . .

Dr. Miller presents a sample case study:

This patient was found to be sensitive to the odors of stale sweat, urine and feces. Hypnotic suggestion was employed to potentiate these disgust and nauseous feelings and to strongly associate these with the male body. On the other hand he was given strong suggestions regarding the attractiveness and loveliness of the female body. He promptly broke off all homosexual activity, complaining of increased tension, headaches and insomnia. At this time, Librium, 10 mg. t.i.d. and Doriden, 0.5 gm. were given for relaxation and rest. His tension was fairly well controlled with the above medication.

For several weeks he complained of a marked loss of sexual feeling. He began to have dreams of burly men pursuing him and trying to hurt him. This was interpreted as evidence of his repressing homosexual desires. After two months of treatment, the patient expressed a slight amount of sexual interest in a woman of 40 whom he had known for many years and with whom he felt relatively secure and comfortable. Positive suggestions [were] then given under hypnosis to increase his sexual desire for her and to give this desire active expression. He has now reached the point where he enjoys petting with her and has for the first time caressed a female breast. He last reported a fantasy of having normal sexual relations with her.

Miller adds:

Reconditioning a male homosexual's physical reactions to other males obviously does not alter his basic attraction to and love for men nor his anxieties about and hostility toward women. Physical aversion to men, however, makes possible a withdrawal from the seeking of neurotic sexual gratification and enhances the likelihood that the patient may attempt to make sexual contact with females, especially if attraction to the latter is enhanced by hypnotic suggestion. . . .

Dr. Miller also mentions a Lesbian patient:

There is every indication that similar results can be attained with female homosexuals. Thus far the author has had only one case and this patient has done splendidly. She is now enjoying a gratifying normal heterosexual relationship and strongly desires marriage and children.[61]

♀ 1967: DR. HARVEY E. KAYE, and others;
Psychoanalysis
"Ten definitely did not want their homosexuality cured"

Modeled closely on Irving Bieber's collaborative study of male homosexuals (1962), a major study of Lesbians undergoing psychoanalysis was made by a group of eight psychiatrists and psychologists headed by Dr. Harvey E. Kaye of New York City. In a paper first presented in 1967 to the Society of Medical Psychoanalysts in New York, these writers note:

Homosexuality in women has been a strikingly neglected clinical entity, when contrasted with the very considerable attention given to male homosexuality. Indeed, a survey of the literature reveals little in the area of comparison or control studies with nonhomosexuals. . . .

Feeling a deep void in basic knowledge and research in this area, a Research Committee on Female Homosexuality was established by the Society of Medical Psychoanalysts. The committee undertook the task of acquiring basic clinical data within the psychoanalytic framework, leaving the more highly inferential theoretical constructs to wait upon the acquisition of more concrete factual information. We are presenting our preliminary findings in this paper.

We initially polled the more than 150 psychoanalysts in the society to ascertain the number of female homosexuals who were in analysis at that time. At least 50 cases were in treatment, far less than the number of male homosexuals who had been in treatment at the time of a similar male homosexual study with the same group of analysts. It would be interesting to speculate on why there are so many less [*sic*] female homosexuals in treatment than male homosexuals, or why, as is our impression, the women manifest a greater tendency to leave treatment prematurely; but this is not within the scope of this presentation. . . .

A comparison study was made of a group of 24 female homosexual patients in psychoanalysis with a group of 24 female nonhomosexual patients. The questionnaire method was utilized, with the patients' analysts filling out the questionnaires.

Our goal was geared toward the establishment of basic clinical data in this area, keeping highly inferential theoretical considerations at a minimum. Within the limitations of the methodological and statistical factors inherent in such a study, the following is a summation of our findings and conclusions.

Homosexuality in women, rather than being a conscious volitional preference, is a massive adaptational response to a crippling inhibition of normal heterosexual development. . . .

Along this vein, we have found a developmental constellation of traits or activities in which the girl shies away from the female role. We believe, furthermore, that these may constitute early prodromata [symptoms] of a potential homosexual adaptation, which should alert parents and family physicians. These are: (a) a tendency toward seeking physical fights in childhood and early adolescence; (b) a tendency to dislike and play less with dolls; (c) a trend toward excessive play with guns; (d) preference to playing boys' rather than girls' games, and a tendency not to play house; (e) a tendency to see themselves as tomboys; and (f) development of strong crushes on women during puberty and adolescence.[62]

On the subject of treatment, the writers state:

The primary reasons for our H[omosexual] group entering analysis were depression and anxiety. Only seven stated that they wanted their homosexuality cured, while ten definitely did not want their homosexuality cured; two were undecided. We had no answer to this question in five questionnaires. With this as background, let us examine the analysts' evaluation of results of treatment.

At the start of treatment, fifteen women had been exclusively or predominantly homosexual. At the end of treatment, "the fifteen cases in the homosexual range were reduced to eight,"

approximating a 50% shift toward the heterosexual end of the spectrum. Furthermore, of the nine patients who were exclusively homosexual at the beginning of their analyses, only four were still exclusively homosexual either at the termination of treatment or at the time during their treatment when their analysts filled out their questionnaire. Obviously, a follow-up study is called for at some future time. At any rate, this indicates a substantial positive treatment potential in homosexual women, a potential which should not be lost sight of in evaluating the treatability of female homosexuals who present themselves for therapy. Apparently at least 50% of them can be significantly helped by psychoanalytic treatment.[63]

1967: JOSEPH R. CAUTELA;
Aversion Therapy ("Covert Sensitization")
"The patient [imagines] pictures of homosexuals and vomits on them"

In an article for *Psychological Reports*, Joseph R. Cautela of Boston College describes a new variant of aversion therapy used to treat homosexuality and other "maladaptive approach responses" such as alcoholism and delinquent behavior; the treatment is called "Covert Sensitization." The term "covert" is used because the patient is subjected only to verbal suggestion, not to any "overt" stimuli such as photos, films, emetics, shock. "Sensitization" refers to the creation in the patient of "an avoidance response to the undesirable stimulus."

The therapist's task, according to Cautela, is first to determine for a given patient the situations and "sexual characteristics" that are arousing. These are then organized into a hierarchy of arousing situations and characteristics whose attractiveness the therapist systematically tries to destroy. For example, if a male homosexual finds the naked body of X sexually stimulating, the therapist may give him the following instructions:

I want you to imagine that you are in a room with X. He is completely naked. As you approach him you notice he has sores and scabs all over his body, with some kind of fluid oozing from them. A terrible foul stench comes from his body. The odor is so strong it makes you sick. You can feel food particles coming up your throat. You can't help yourself and you vomit all over the place, all over the floor, on your hands and clothes. And now that even makes you sicker and you vomit again and again all over everything. You turn away and then you start to feel better. You try to get out of the room, but the door seems to be locked. The smell is still strong, but you try desperately to get out. You kick at the door frantically until it finally opens and you run out into the nice clean air. It smells wonderful. You go home and shower and you feel so clean.

One essentially builds up a hierarchy of the desirable sexual objects and the available contacts of likely sexual stimulation. Covert sensitization is applied to all items in the hierarchy, with the most desirable sexual object usually being treated first.

Scenes are also [verbally] presented in which the patient sees pictures of homosexuals and vomits on them. Homework similar to that given in the treatment of the other disorders is given in this case as well. The homosexual patient is also told that if he sees someone and becomes sexually attracted to him or whenever he starts to have a sexual fantasy about an undesirable sexual object, he is immediately to imagine that the object is full of sores and scabs and he vomits on the object.

Examples.—this method has been only recently applied to homosexuals. I have treated two cases; one case has been treated at Temple Medical School.

One of my cases was a delinquent in a training school. According to his reports and those of the staff and of other boys in the training school, he has not engaged in homosexual behavior since the termination of covert sensitization treatment and has now been released from the training school.

My second case was a member of the Armed Forces. This individual's behavior was primarily vicarious. All his sexual fantasies, with and without masturbation, were homosexual in nature. This behavior has been reduced to about four temptations a week which last about a second. This case is still in the process of treatment.

In the Temple Medical School case, it has been four months since the last therapeutic session, and the patient has not engaged in any homosexual behavior to date, according to his own reports and those of his wife. He is continuing with the homework.

All in all, the preliminary results are promising, although much work still remains to be done in this area.[64]

♀ 1970: IVAN TOBY RUTNER;

Aversion Therapy and Desensitization

"She had tried very hard to live the life of a heterosexual but had received no cooperation from the opposite sex"

Behaviorist treatment of a Lesbian is described in *Psychological Reports* in 1970. The study was carried out by Ivan Toby Rutner at the Behavioral Research unit at Jacksonville State Hospital in Illinois. Rutner's "double-barrel approach" combines covert sensitization, intended to increase anxiety toward homosexuality, and desensitization, intended to reduce anxiety toward heterosexuality. The patient and the procedures are described as follows.

Kate was a 20-yr.-old practicing homosexual who voluntarily admitted herself to a state mental hospital. She reported that she had hospitalized herself in an attempt to overcome her homosexuality and to lead a "normal life." Kate had engaged in homosexual behavior for approximately 4 yr. For the last two of these years she resided in a "gay" neighborhood and considered herself a member in good standing of that sub-culture. In addition to her homosexual behavior, Kate was quite concerned with the total repulsion she felt toward men. The only heterosexual behavior she had ever experienced was with her father and brothers who had sexually attacked her repeatedly since the age of nine. Upon admission to the hospital, Kate was placed on a locked female ward which housed several other homosexuals. Once on the ward, she experienced strong sexual desires toward these women and on several occasions participated in the on-going, non-scheduled nightly ward activities.

Procedure

Kate was instructed to record the daily frequency of her homosexual desires for a three-day period. From this report, a baseline indicating covert behavior was obtained. She was instructed to continue this recording throughout the course of treatment.

STEP I

After instruction in progressive relaxation, . . . a treatment of covert sensitization . . . was begun. Kate was told to relax and to visualize herself, as vividly as possible, starting to kiss and fondle her "friend." At this time, it was suggested to her that she was getting extremely nauseous and sick to her stomach. When she signaled that she felt nauseous she was told to imagine herself turning away from her "friend" and leaving the scene, at which time it was suggested to her that she was beginning to feel calm and relaxed. She was instructed to signal when she felt calm and relaxed. This procedure was repeated several times alternating nausea and relaxation trials. Kate was then instructed to repeat the process without the therapist's aid. When she was capable of achieving nausea and relaxation without assistance, she was dismissed and told to practice this procedure five times a day throughout the course of treatment.

STEP II

Kate was seen again 1 wk. after being instructed in covert sensitization. At this time an attempt was made to desensitize her to men. A hierarchy of anxiety-producing situations was constructed and the desensitization process was begun. . . . Kate underwent two desensitization sessions on consecutive days. In the first session, Kate progressed through six items of the 11-item hierarchy. The session was terminated when Kate could tolerate, without anxiety, visualizing a scene in which she was kissed lightly on the cheek by a man. The second session consisted of successfully mastering the five remaining items in the hierarchy. This session was terminated when Kate could tolerate, without anxiety, visualizing a scene in which she was being kissed and hugged passionately by a man.

STEP III

Immediately following the completion of the hierarchy, the covert sensitization instructions were modified. The new instructions called for: kissing and hugging her "girlfriend" to result in nausea, kissing and hugging a man to result in relaxation. Kate was instructed to continue practicing covert sensitization five times a day.

Over a period of one month, the frequency of Kate's homosexual desires dropped from thirty per day to zero. She was then released from the hospital.

In a follow-up approximately 2 mo. later, Kate reported that she had not engaged in any homosexual behavior since leaving the hospital and that she was diligently searching for a man. Unfortunately, this "new behavior" was not maintained. In a subsequent interview held approximately 2 mo. after the first follow-up, Kate reported that she had given up and had rejoined the homosexual community. She claimed that she had tried very hard to live the life of a heterosexual but had received no cooperation from the opposite sex. While this development might be disappointing, it should not have been totally unexpected. For a behavior to be maintained, it must be reinforced. If no reinforcement is made available, behavior will undergo extinction. This appears to be what happened to Kate's "new" heterosexual behavior. Since it was not reinforced, it extinguished and was replaced by the "older" maladaptive behavior which was reinforced and was thus maintained. This regression was probably due not to the inadequacy of the treatment procedures but rather to the therapist's failure to arrange reinforcement contingencies in the environment to maintain the "new" behavior.[65]

1974: ANONYMOUS; Electroshock
"The agony of the years after"

On November 13, 1964, a young man, who will here remain anonymous, was involuntarily committed by his parents to a private mental hospital in a Southern state. There he was given what one of his doctors termed "a course of electro-convulsive treatment"—electric shock. After hospitalization of two and a half months, the patient was discharged to his parents. In an interview with the present writer on April 29, 1974, the subject indicated that his parents' desire to "cure" his homosexuality was the reason for his confinement and shock treatment.[66] This is verified by a number of incidents recalled by the subject, as well as by a recent correspondence with his parents concerning their reason for committing him.

Anon.: I was born in 1940, and I lived in one Southern state for my first eighteen years, till I graduated from high school. Then I went to art school in a neighboring state, stayed two and a half years there and quit. Then I went to a nearby city and stayed about three years. During that time I visited my parents off and on, and they even came to visit me. At the end of one particular visit, they asked why I didn't go to a psychiatrist. I said I didn't think there was any reason to. I didn't think they were serious. They never came out and asked about my Gay life. That was a taboo subject with them. They said they just thought I might need psychological help. Even when I was sixteen they had taken me to a psychologist to have tests; they didn't want me to go to art school unless the doctor thought I was worth it.

In 1962, I was twenty-two. 1962 is the first commitment. I was living in this state near my parents and I'd gotten a job. I understood later that they came to that state to arrange this commitment.

In the United States, it's not hard for your nearest relatives to commit you, especially if they can pay for it.[67] And this was very cheap. This was a state hospital, so it was only $37.50 a week.

The policemen came for me at work. They said, "We're not allowed to explain anything. You have to come with us." That was it. I realized what was happening when they drove me through the hospital gates and I saw the sign: —— STATE HOSPITAL. I said to myself, "Well, they did it. I guess my parents are more concerned than I realized—for my well-being."

What made them commit me was a postcard I had gotten from an older friend. My mother asked, "What man writes to another man, 'There are many pretty boys on board ship but I don't touch a one'? Now what does he mean by that?" My mother brought it up to the psychiatrist when she committed me the first time.

I stayed in that state hospital and I just got bored. There were 2,700 patients, and I saw a doctor twice. They did ask about my ideas about sexuality. I had this German female doctor. I told her what I thought— that sex expressions could not be limited to one sex, and peoples' sex expression could be what they wished; I said a homosexual or a heterosexual act, it doesn't matter. She said, "Don't you think that's abnormal?" I said, "No." They let it go at that. I stayed there until I got tired of it. After seven weeks I decided I would leave. I walked away.

J.K.: Didn't they come after you?

Anon.: I went to live in a city about sixty miles away. I kept clear of anyone my parents might contact, anyone I'd known before. I called my parents after six months.

J.K.: Your parents hadn't tried to track you down?

Anon.: I don't know. They didn't say anything about it.

Almost two years went by. I did odd jobs and things. In 1964, I came to New York and stayed five months doing temporary work, typing mostly. Then my former art teacher, who was retiring, offered me her class—back in my hometown. I had never tried teaching, so I said OK. I went back there in September of 1964, and I started giving art lessons. On November 13, my parents committed me again.

J.K.: When you went back home, weren't you afraid that your parents might commit you again?

Anon.: I didn't have any fear of that; I should have. It came as a total surprise when they committed me again, just like the first time. I thought my parents had gotten over feeling that I was sick.

This was a much more sophisticated hospital. It was like a resort. During the time I had shock treatment it cost $350 a week.

J.K.: How did you get committed that time?

Anon.: I don't remember the actual details, but I do have copies of the letters I wrote from the hospital. In one I said, "The same thing happened that happened before." So it must have been the same procedure: they just went to the police and signed the papers.

J.K.: Was it specifically because you were Gay?

Anon: I didn't know until I was out. I actually asked afterward. I was visiting my sister-in-law, and I asked her, "Why did they commit me? Did they really think I needed help?" She said, "Oh, you know; it was all over the Gay bit. That's all they were concerned about. They don't think you should be Gay." My brother, her husband, was the third signature on my commitment that time. He knew I was Gay. I'd met him at a Gay party once. He said to me, "What are you doing here?" I said, "What are you doing here?" He said, "I won't write home if you don't." He was already married at the time. Maybe he was guilty about some Gay activity. I had no feeling of guilt. After my commitment my brother said, "If I'd known what they were going to do, I would never have signed the paper. But I thought it was the best thing to do at the time. Our parents were so concerned."

J.K.: Do you remember what state of mind you were in the month before you were committed in November 1964?

Anon.: I've gone back to my notes and letters from that time thinking maybe I was totally flipped out. But I wasn't. I found notes and letters I wrote the day of my commitment that indicate I knew what I was doing. There were a few depressing times. There were arguments with my parents about why I was continuing relationships with people who they considered abnormal. I wrote a note to myself the day before my commitment about an argument we'd had. It was about writing to my friends who were obviously homosexual. I must have told my mother it was none of her business.

J.K.: Your parents were reading your mail?

Anon.: They read a few things.

J.K.: Do you think your parents feel guilty now about committing you, and about the shock treatment?

Anon.: A person who has become a close friend of theirs is a psychologist, and he asked them, "Why did you ever commit him for that?" My mother answered, "We just didn't know." Now she says they shouldn't have done it. I realize that they did what they thought was right at the time. They felt responsible, the typical attitude of intelligent parents. If they weren't so intelligent I think it wouldn't have happened. They didn't know that shock treatment was so bad. My mother said, "We didn't know what we were doing. The doctors convinced us to do it. We never would have done it if we knew the result."

J.K.: What was it like in the institution that time? Were there other Gay people there?

Anon.: I think so, but then you really never knew. Everyone was undergoing the same kind of shock treament, both males and females.

They give you sodium pentothal beforehand, but I do remember being taken to one particular shock treatment. You're in your pajamas, and you just lie down on a table. Then you don't remember any more because they give you a shock. The shock itself erases anything you were experiencing before, any memory of it. I had seventeen shock treatments—I did have awareness enough to ask one of the nurses how many times I had had it, and she said, "I'll look it up." She said seventeen.

J.K.: When you come out of the shock treatment, what is it like?

Anon.: I remember being shaved with an electric razor and thinking, "Isn't that strange? I can't move." I thought, "Why is he shaving me, and where am I, and why can't I do it myself, and why can't I stand up, and why can't I move my arms?" Then I probably lost consciousness again. You're not aware of much.

I do remember after my own shock treatment listening to other people having shock treatment. I don't think that should be allowed. I was in the next ward. You hear that horrible scream. There's one loud scream—

"Ahhhhh!!!"—very loud, each time they give you a shock, as the lungs are being evacuated. You hear what sounds like hundreds of people having shock treatment. They always did it in the morning, it went on all morning, three hours of those loud, single screams, one person at a time.

I do remember being very affectionate in the hospital during the time I had shock treatment. I thought I knew everyone. I would hug anyone.

J.K.: That seems to be the opposite of what was intended.

Anon.: Right, it was like making out with everyone, it didn't make any difference, male or female. I was going around feeling very close to everyone. They didn't respond with any affection. But I would do it anyway.

In the hospital I made copies of all my letters. I had a feeling at that time that I wouldn't remember, or that they wouldn't send them. I found out later that they hadn't sent some of them. John, who had been my lover in New York, told me later that he got no mail from me. He said he kept writing letters to someone who didn't answer. Another person, a friend, did get my letters. There's a gap in my letters in December '64. I always say I had shock treatment for Christmas that year. But I don't know if I actually had one on December 25.

The two doctors I had just weren't very hip people. One was a more aware, advanced person, a younger man. He was a very intelligent and much more involved person than the other. I remember what he said— these were his very words, I remember this very well. He said, "I don't see any reason why you should have been here. I've read through your files, I've read your whole case history, and you should never have been here." He said, "There's nothing wrong with being Gay. That's up to you. There's certainly no reason for you to stay." He had just come to the hospital, he was new. The very morning he said that, my other doctor had said some-thing quite different. I don't know how many times I had discussed with him my ideas of sexuality, but finally he screamed out, "Then you're *sick* and I will not see you again! This is your last interview."

The same day, the new doctor said I could go home. I told him, "I'm in no state to go home." At that time I was so disoriented I didn't want to leave. He said, "Well, you can get out. I could let you go today if you want." I thought, "Is he just saying this? Maybe this is just another game." I became wary of their games. You don't trust anyone at that point. At the same time I wanted them to release me. When you're confined, you do have this sense that you want freedom more than anything. I said, "I'll go in a few days." I said I'd have to call my parents to come and get me. So we made all the arrangements and I left.

I was still in no state to be at home. My mother would ask me, "Well, what do you want to do?" She still felt very concerned. She said, "Your mail and Christmas gifts are in there from all your friends in New York." I said, "What friends in New York? I was never in New York." She gave me this look and said, "Don't talk like that! You know you were in New York. You were there for five months. How can you be so silly?" You're very sensitive at that point and you think, "My God, what's happened to me?" You don't remember anything.

Then another time we got to discussing homosexuality. I said I still felt it didn't make any difference which sex I had a feeling for if I liked someone. She screamed, "$6,200 for nothing! You haven't changed a bit." She said, "It was a total waste of time and money. The psychiatrists, they're stupid people, they don't know what they're doing."

I had group therapy with my parents after the shock treament. The psychologist who didn't agree with my ideas of sexuality conducted this group, with the parents and outpatients, fifteen to eighteen people, once a week. In the group I was the only Gay one. At one session they brought up the Gay issue. We always went to the main problems we were supposed to be there for. I said it was not a problem for me. They said, "Don't you think you're abnormal, thinking you can have feelings for males as well as females?" I said, "No. I think you could be subnormal for not being able to have those feelings." The doctor says, "I'm afraid we got him too late." That was his explanation. Right in front of me he says, "He should have had therapy earlier and it would have been different." I remember the doctor saying he had had a homosexual in group therapy, "and now he's married."

After that particular session, on the way home, this horrible fight erupted in the car. My mother started hitting me. She hit me first so I figured I'd hit her back. I kicked her in the face, from the back seat of the car. Usually shock treatment makes you docile, and at the time I was taking these heavy tranquilizers, too. My father was upset. He wouldn't get involved in the screaming and yelling. He just kept out of it and said we should calm down. I don't think he ever felt as responsible as my mother did for my homosexuality. She really thought she'd created a monster.

I only went to about six sessions of group therapy, and then I came back to New York. I wanted to see who this person was who was writing to me, and to see all these other people I was supposed to know. I was fascinated to find out about an experience I was supposed to have had which I had absolutely no memory of. When I had come home from the hospital, I had read all of these letters from total strangers. I had no memory of them. One person was obviously my lover; he wrote me these wonderful letters. I thought, "I have to see who he is." He planned to meet me when I finally decided to go back to New York. I thought, "How will I recognize him?" Well, he recognized me, of course. When I met the other people I had known, I didn't remember them at all. But I pretended I did. I went along with everything. I became a very good actor then, by acting like I had a memory, which I didn't. I had absolutely none. It was extremely difficult.

I told my lover after about three months. I said, "I didn't remember you when I came back." It upset him so much that I didn't tell anyone else after that. He said, "How did you do what you did?" He meant—make love. I said, "I just did it. I must have done it before, so I did it." Sometimes people would see me and say, "Hi! Where have you been? I haven't seen you for years." That's a weird experience when you have no recollection of them at all. You act like you remember them because you don't want to offend them. I did explain a few times, but the explanation was so long it just wasn't worth it, and people got so upset hearing it that they didn't want to talk.

I had the most extreme depressions after shock treatment—for the next three years. During these periods of depression it just seemed so hopeless, like I didn't have the strength to go on. Yet I'd resolved I'd never commit suicide. The depressions came from realizing that I didn't have my full faculties and from not knowing how long my memory would take to come back. I'd think: "It's going on and on and on; it's been five years, six years, eight years." You think it will never end. The depressions resulted from an accumulation of things, from it seeming such a struggle to concentrate. To accomplish any little thing seemed such an effort. I became almost immobile.

Other times I'd be very spacy, very up. After the shock treatment the doctor told me, "You're supposed to take these heavy tranquilizers for at least two years." After I was home for a while I took a drink my parents offered me, and I realized I was drooling. I couldn't even hold my mouth shut. I said, "I'm not taking these pills. This is dangerous." I threw the pills out. Maybe I wouldn't have spaced if I had taken the tranquilizers. I figured I'd rather space than not be able to function.

After shock treatment, it's like you've gotten stoned, like you're spacing. For the first eight years after shock treatment, I never knew if I would be able to connect my thoughts. I'd be walking down the street in New York and would have these flashes—and there would be nothing. I'd suddenly not know where I was. I'd think, "My God, I have to find out where I am. Why doesn't anything look familiar?" I would be typing at work and suddenly not be able to remember what city I was in. I'd think, "I have to remember!" A lot of times I'd forget my name and address. That might last for an hour and a half. But that's a long time when your mind is really going. The feeling was panic. But then I always said to myself, "Sit down and it'll come back." I always had awareness enough to think, "It's going to be temporary." When I left the hospital the doctor had said, "You'll have times when you won't know where you are—you'll feel disoriented, but it'll be temporary." I was told that much.

The fear of loss of memory is one of the worst experiences I had after shock treatment, the fear that I might at any point experience this amnesia. That amnesia happened maybe a thousand times. And you never know how long it will last, and you'll just forget where you are, for a few seconds, or minutes, or an hour. It could happen anywhere. You don't remember what you were doing or saying. And you don't want to show that you're upset, that you don't know where you are. Those memory lapses are over now, mostly. I noticed a definite change in January, 1972. Almost suddenly my thoughts connected. It was a wonderful feeling.

On the street a couple of years ago a woman said, "Sir!" and she reached out and grabbed my hand. She said, "Would you just stand by me for a few minutes? I want to get my bearings, I just want someone to be here. I don't know where I am. Will you tell me where I am?" I told her and she said, "Oh, thank you." I asked her later if she'd had shock treatment. She said, "Yes." I asked, "How long were you in the hospital?" She said, "Oh, I don't remember—a long time, many months. I just got out of the hospital, and I don't want to go back." She said, "My son thinks I shouldn't have left." She calmed down, then she remembered what she had to do. I had coffee with her and talked to her for about twenty minutes. I was on my lunch hour.

I think the people who prescribe shock treatment don't know what it can do to you—for years afterward. They know what the temporary result is. The doctor emphasized that there would be a memory loss. He said the treatment "rearranges your memory bank"—I think that's the terminology he used. But it doesn't rearrange it. For a while it removes it.

The main thing about shock is not the treatment itself, it's the agony of the years after—always having this sense that you will forget exactly where you are. That's bad, you know?

III

PASSING WOMEN
1782-1920

♀ Introduction

The women whose lives are documented here worked and dressed and lived in what were customarily the occupations and styles of males. Most actually passed as men; the evidence suggests they were also attracted to and had sexual and emotional relations with other women. They both passed as men and passed beyond the restricted traditional roles of women.

Since the old ways of viewing such women are confused and clouded by outmoded, limiting preconceptions, labels, and stereotypes, the reports of these lives should be read carefully and closely, with an open mind and a fresh eye for meaningful detail. The stereotyping of the Lesbian as a tough, aggressive "butch" and the general stereotyping of "feminine" and "masculine" roles have recently been prime targets for Lesbian liberationists and feminists. Examination of these passing women's lives exposes the historically relative character of "masculinity" and "femininity," helping to reveal the person behind the stereotype, the human actor behind the role, as well as the socially conditioned character of role and stereotype. Such stereotyping will only disappear when the social situation of women and men has been equalized, the traditional sexual division of labor and power revolutionized.

Despite their masculine masquerade, the females considered here can be understood not as imitation men, but as real women, women who refused to accept the traditional, socially assigned fate of their sex, women whose particular revolt took the form of passing as men. A basic feminine protest is a recurring theme in all these lives, appearing sometimes as a conscious, explicit feminism, other times as an inchoate, individual frustration, an only partly verbalized discontent, a yearning to break through the narrow bounds of the traditional female role—sometimes as a most pragmatic female survival tactic.

In a most radical way, the women whose lives are recounted here rejected their socially assigned passive role; they affirmed themselves as self-determined, active, assertive, powerful—in the way they knew, the guise of men. These passing women can only be understood within the framework of a feminist analysis.

Such an analysis immediately points to a basic contradiction at the heart of this early form of female revolt. While these women rejected the traditional feminine role, they embraced the traditional masculine one. Their society had defined power, initiative, and assertion as "masculine," and their act of "passing" implicitly confirmed this social definition. They found no legitimate alternative mode of life completely outside the customary "masculine-feminine" duality. The contradiction between their female gender and "masculine" pose often condemned them to a sense of false identity.

In personal terms, this inauthenticity might mean a life of fantasy, mental confusion and loss of reality possibly leading to madness. Their passing implied an inability to totally accept their own feelings and aspirations as those of women, which their physiological configuration always necessarily reminded them they were. In their hearts and consciences these women knew they were, at least in part, imitations, fakes, frauds. They knew their activity, especially any sexual activity with other women, was, if not legally, then morally condemned. Posing as men might not always help them personally overcome this negative social evaluation and the guilt it could evoke. Appearing to the world as men, they could not but sometimes appear to themselves as immoral impostors. They might convince the world they were men, but they had also to convince themselves of their legitimacy. The pressures engendered by their double identity might sometimes prove overwhelming, and be resolved by self-destructive means.

In a most dramatic way, these documents reveal with what absolute intellectual certainty and passionate emotional rigidity certain kinds of work, behavior, and costume were once considered either "masculine" or "feminine." Certain occupations or activities which in present-day America have become sex-neutral were earlier felt to be "male" or "female" in the same essential sense in which a vagina is female, a penis male, with a correspondingly strong negative response to any questioning of this sex typing.

The lives of these women throw into social-historical perspective that "masculinity" and "femininity" customarily assumed as "natural." By locating such sex-role assumptions in a particular social and temporal context, by placing them in historical perspective, the study of these lives can help free us from our own still-prevalent preconceptions. For however much the development of labor-equalizing and highly industrialized means of production are at present breaking down the traditional sexual division of labor, the old, sexually polarized world view still commonly holds sway over our minds.

The categorization of these women as Lesbian transvestites tends to narrow understanding rather than expand it. The terms *transvestism* and *cross-dressing*, focusing as they do on clothing, divert our attention from other equally important factors in these women's lives. While females or males taking the clothes and roles of the "opposite" sex have long been described, the terms *transvestism* and *cross-dressing* are fairly recent historical inventions. German sexologist Magnus Hirschfeld published a book, *Die Transvestiten*, in 1910, and English homosexual emancipation theorist Edward Carpenter, writing in an American journal, used the term *cross-dressing* in 1911. In 1913 and 1920, the terms *D'Eonism, aesthetic,* and *sexo-aesthetic inversion* were used by Havelock Ellis to categorize the same phenomena, but were either too clumsy or esoteric to become popular.[1]

While the adoption of the *costume* of the "opposite" sex is certainly important in these passing women's lives, their adoption of the occupation, vocabulary, tone of voice, gesture, walk, sports, and aspirations of the "other" sex are equally significant. To appreciate the full complexity of these lives, the concept of transvestism or cross-dressing needs to be supplemented by such concepts as *cross-working* and *cross-speaking*. If such terms seem odd, it is because they emphasize what is ordinarily taken for granted as given and eternal—the historically and socially determined sexual division of labor and sex polarization of American society.

A number of documents here raise most complex questions about the sexual nature, psychical or physical, of the individuals involved. One report, for instance, definitely indicates, and others suggest, the existence of some physical abnormality. Such suggestions, however, cannot be taken at face value; they seem inextricably linked to prevailing notions of homosexuality as a congenital phenomenon, often displaying physical "stigmata." Even the actual presence of some physical anomaly, although certainly important, does not by itself determine individuals' gender identification or the object and character of their sexual attraction, and only raises new questions. The testimony of the individual concerned cannot be taken as *de facto* evidence of even such an objective characteristic as physical gender. Lucy Ann Lobdell, in the 1880s, claims to have "peculiar organs that make me more like a man than a woman," but an examining doctor reports he cannot "discover any abnormality of the genitals, except for an enlarged clitoris . . ." What constitutes an "enlarged clitoris" is not defined, and other references indicate the existence of a popular medical mythology linking Lesbianism and clitoris size. Lobdell's own statement can be interpreted as arising from a desire to justify and explain her Lesbian sexual relations.

The exploration of these passing women's lives requires giving up the common labeling and limiting categorizations for a multifaceted descriptive study of each individual. Too often, academics act as if to name something is to know it; the order-loving mind may well be calmed by such pigeonholing, but the reality of these women's lives will remain elusive.

In trying to understand the character and meaning of these lives, we must note that the distinction between biologically determined *gender* and socially defined "masculinity" and "femininity" is basic. The concept of *gender identity* may also be useful, although difficult to apply, as it refers to both physical gender and socially conditioned psychological identification, and may, if carelessly used, convey all the traditional, politically loaded assumptions about "masculinity" and "femininity." It is also useful to distinguish analytically between *sexual attraction*, whatever its object, character, or origin, and the desire to *dress, pass,* and *work* as the "opposite" sex.

The lives here are discussed and documented in a variety of sources: Lobdell's and Sheridan's autobiographies; biographies; Brown's college memoirs; Walker's medical treatise; a working-class newspaper of the 1860s; a Wisconsin newspaper of the 1890s; the *New York Times* of the early twentieth century; a medical journal essay; doctors' reports; insane asylum records; and early books defending homosexuality.

Many of these lives involve extraordinary adventure, rebellion, courage, and struggle, either detailed or hinted at by writers whose antique attitudes and language often impart what now seems a certain quaint charm to their reports. But to view these passing women as amusing curiosities, eccentrics or exotics, or, alternatively, as pitiable freaks, is not only to condescend and denigrate, it is also to close oneself to a sense of actual lives lived, of immense difficulties encountered, of joy and pain experienced—of individual human beings who, however different they may be from the majority, share a common humanity.

The women whose stories are reported here include a Revolutionary War soldier, a hunter, an innkeeper, three Civil War soldiers, a student, an alleged thief, three doctors, a boilermaker's apprentice and union official, a Tammany Hall politician and bail bondsman, a sailor, an adventurer, a watercolor artist, a railroad cook, a confidential secretary to a foreign diplomat, a farmer, a typesetter, a society gentleman, a bellboy and later factory worker. They are working class and professional, middle and upper class. Although these women sometimes took on the less attractive and ignoble qualities of men, their unconventional and difficult lives seem to express a positive strength, vivacity, and incredible daring—a spirit of resistance to women's oppression, the very contradictions of which help raise them above the ordinary, lending them a certain heroic grandeur. These were certainly extraordinary women.

♀ 1782–97: HERMAN MANN;
Deborah Sampson
"Animal love, on her part, was out of the question"

Deborah Sampson was born in Plymton, near Plymouth, Massachusetts, on December 17, 1760. She was of Pilgrim stock, her mother a descendant of Governor William Bradford, her father a descendant of Miles Standish and of John Alden. After abandoning his family, Sampson's father reportedly died in a shipwreck, and her mother could not alone support her six children. Deborah became a servant in a family of Middleborough, Massachusetts; she received some education and grew to be a strong, aspiring, and able woman. When her term of servitude expired in 1779, Sampson taught for six months at a local school.

On September 3, 1782, the twenty-two-year-old Sampson was excommunicated from the First Baptist Church of Middleborough. Church records say that it "withdrew fellowship" from Deborah Sampson because she

was accused of dressing in men's clothes, and . . . was strongly suspected of being guilty, and for some time before behaved very loose and unchristian like, and at last left our parts in a sudden manner, and it is not known where she is gone. . . .[2]

Four months earlier, on May 20, 1782, Sampson, disguised as a male, had enlisted in the Continental forces under the name of Robert Shurtleff. She was mustered into service at Worcester as a member of the fourth Massachusetts Regiment, fought in several battles, and was wounded in one near Tarrytown, New York. When she was hospitalized with a fever in Philadelphia, her true sex was discovered. She was honorably discharged by General Henry Knox at West Point on October 25, 1783, after serving one and a half years in the Revolutionary army. In 1785, back in Massachusetts, Sampson married a farmer, Benjamin Gannett; she gave birth to three children: Earl, Mary, and Patience.

In 1797, Herman Mann anonymously published in Dedham, Massachusetts, a book entitled *The Female Review*, a semifictionalized biography of Deborah Sampson's life and adventures in male disguise as a soldier in the American Revolutionary army.[3] Several suggestive and curious passages in this work refer to Sampson's romantic, though allegedly chaste liaisons with other women, while posing as a male. Quite apart from any accuracy these tales may have, their very existence in a book subscribed to by respectable New Englanders in the late 1700s is of interest. Sampson's cross-dressing and the nominally "pure," heterosexual character of her romances no doubt made these stories seem acceptable at the time.

Because Mann's writing is often almost unintelligible, at times florid to the point of absurdity, his account of Sampson's three romantic attachments will simply be summarized. Once during the Revolution, Sampson is accused by a captured British sergeant of alienating the affection of "his girl," whom Sampson allegedly caused to "pay attention to her." Sampson's more extended and detailed romance with a rich and beautiful young woman from Baltimore is said to be intensely felt by both women. In the process of explicitly denying any erotic aspect to this romance, Mann manages to detail enough of what did *not* happen to lend his volume a certain sexually suggestive character; it must have been a spicy book for its day.

In a third episode, Sampson, discharged from the army but still wearing male disguise, returns to her uncle's house in Stoughton, Massachusetts, where she assumes the name of Ephraim Sampson (a younger brother), hiding her true identity. Here, her free conduct with women causes her biographer to comment:

But her correspondence with her sister sex!—Surely it must have been that of sentiment, taste, purity; as animal love, on her part, was out of the question. But I beg excuse, if I happen not to specify every particular of this agreeable round of acquaintance. It may suffice, merely, to say, her uncle being a compassionate man, often reprehended her for her freedom with the girls of his villa; and them he plumply called fools, (a much harsher name than I can give them) for their violent presumption with the young *Continental*. Sighing, he would say—their unreserved imprudence would soon detect itself—a multitude of illegitimates![4]

Later, toward the close of his book, Sampson's biographer adds:

But to mention the intercourse of our Heroine with her sex, would, like others more dangerous, require an apology I know not how to make. It must be supposed, she acted more from necessity, than a voluntary impulse of passion; and no doubt, succeeded beyond her expectations, or desires. Harmless thing! . . . An inoffensive companion in love! . . . Had she been capacitated and inclined to prey, like a vulture, on the innocence of her sex; vice might have hurried vice, and taste have created appetition. Thus, she would have been less entitled to the clemency of the public. For individual crimes bring on public nuisances and calamities: And debauchery is one of the first. But incapacity, which seldom begets desire, must render her, in this respect, unimpeachable.

Remember, Females, I am your advocate; and, like you, would pay my devoirs to the Goddess of love. Admit that you conceived an attachment for a *female soldier*. What is the harm? She acted in the department of that sex, whose embraces you naturally seek. From a like circumstance, we are liable to the same impulse.

Finally, Mann denies the gossip "that Mrs. [Deborah Sampson] Gannett refuses her husband the rites of the marriage bed."[5]

After the original publication of Mann's biographical narrative in 1797, he then prepared a romanticized "Address" about her adventures, which Deborah Sampson Gannett first presented at a public lecture in Boston in 1802, then toured to various New England and New York towns.

For her Revolutionary War services, Deborah Sampson Gannett received a pension from the state of Massachusetts and later, on the petition of Paul Revere, another pension from the United States government. After she died in 1827, the United States Congress passed an "Act for the relief of the heirs of Deborah Gannett, a soldier of the Revolution, deceased."[6]

♀ 1829–91?: LUCY ANN LOBDELL,
DR. P. M. WISE, and others;
Lucy Ann Lobdell
"I can not submit to see all the bondage with which woman is oppressed"

The life of Lucy Ann Lobdell is detailed from birth to death in several documents. Her inclusion here will be understood as her story progresses. The discovery of Lobdell's rare, extraordinary autobiographical Narrative of her early life, published in 1855, permits her to introduce herself.[7]

On December 2, 1829, a daughter, Lucy Ann, was born to Sarah and James Lobdell of Westerlo, in Albany County, New York. Their first offspring, a daughter, had died at the age of about two years, and Lucy Ann, their second-born, became, as she said of herself, later, "their pet—almost a spoiled child." In her Narrative, Lucy Ann Lobdell describes herself as an adventurous child, who at an early age often wandered into the woods alone and got lost, until the call of her distressed mother indicated the way home. Her mother finally tied "a bell on the little truant," the better to keep track of her whereabouts.[8]

Lucy Ann Lobdell recalls that she was in her tenth or twelfth year (1839–41) when she

had the charge of some hundred chickens, turkeys, and geese, that I used to raise and sell, and then I had half the money I made in that business and in tending the dairy. . . . In consequence of my keeping poultry, I learned to shoot the hawk, the weasel, the mink, and even down to the rat. . . .[9]

This activity early encouraged the young girl's independent and assertive spirit.

In 1843, the fourteen-year-old Lobdell, then in school,

possessed a temperament which made me foremost in mischief as well as in study. My delight in each was about equal. . . . I would frequently contrive, during the hours of study, to read from another book, which I would conceal from the teacher's eye, and still have my lesson more perfect than half the scholars who were more studious, but less vivacious.[10]

Lobdell soon found herself enjoying the constant company of a William Smith until her

father began to look after and into my love affairs, as he termed them; at the same time he said I must discard Mr. Smith at once.

Both Lucy Ann and William felt that Lobdell had "no right to control," and, finding that they were in love, the two young people

concluded to see no more of each other for present, for we had decided to open a correspondence.

This secret correspondence continued until Lobdell's sisters, Mary and Sarah, discovered William's "dozen or more 'love' letters,"

and all our sorrows and complaints became known. My sisters deeply sympathized with and pitied me, which roused my pride; and the result was, I got sick of the idea of loving Mr. Smith.

When Smith proposed to her, Lobdell wrote back, rather evasively, that she "was not my own mistress yet," and too young to decide to marry. Lobdell also describes the mutual attraction between herself and a Mr. St. John, which ended tragically when St. John died of consumption.[11]

In the 1840s, when Lobdell was still in her teens, she met and kept company with George Washington Slater for five or six months. Finally, she told Slater that she was

obliged to discard him, as father was not willing that I should have anything more to say to him whatever.

As Lucy Ann Lobdell describes it, Slater immediately became "as pale as death," and his

sorrowful eyes bent upon mine with a pity which I mistook for love . . .

Slater wildly declared his love and left in great agitation, Lobdell promising to see him one more time. When the next visit occurred, Slater was just as agitated as before, and Lucy Ann watched him go "reeling away," wondering if he could bear his pain without expiring. Lobdell continues:

Night came, and at nine o'clock, I retired to my bedroom, but not to sleep, for the God that made me gave me a tender heart, and nerved me with a daring spirit; I therefore waited till all was quiet, and then arose and dressed myself in my brother's clothes, stole out of my bedroom-window, and went to the stable, and took one of father's horses, and away I rode to learn what had become of Mr. Slater. I at length learned his whereabouts, without being discovered, for I saw someone was up in a room about five miles from my home. I at once alighted, and looked in at a window, and saw Mr. Slater and someone standing beside his bed that appeared to be a doctor. I then left and ran to where I had tied my horse, and jumped upon his back with a lighter heart than I had when I dismounted, for I felt that some kind hand would aid and take care of him. When I got within half a mile of home, it commenced raining very hard, and I got as wet as I could be. . . .

The next day, says Lobdell,

when I appeared before my mirror, I learned how much an adventure added health and beauty to the cheek.[12]

> Despite her father's strong opposition, she continued to see Slater, out of pity, it seems, for his distressed state and lonely, "outcast" position in the world. Fearing that she was forming too close an acquaintance with Slater, one which she might later regret, Lobdell "therefore made up [her] mind to leave home" and the district school she was attending, and go to a school then in Coxsackie, Greene County, New York, where she stayed with an aunt.

I had the money I had made in raising calves and poultry to pay for my schooling, and all the expenses I incurred in going to school.

Eventually, says Lobdell,

Father wrote and said if I wanted to live at Coxsackie he would sell out and come and buy there, if I wanted him to. I wrote him a letter and told him I was not going to stay there, and I at the same time told him of lands that were selling very cheap in Delaware and Sullivan Counties. . . .[13]

> In a short time Lobdell was again living with her family in Delaware County.
> Slater now appeared on the scene again. Lobdell told her father that she "had no joy" in Slater "for my early love was no more." But because Slater was "a good workman, and an innocent boy," Lobdell agreed to marry him, if he could get her father's consent. Although her father wished her to wait, and Lucy Ann Lobdell agreed, Slater insisted on an early marriage, and this took place with the agreement of both of Lobdell's parents. When it came to paying the five-dollar marriage fee, Slater told Lucy Ann Lobdell he hadn't the cash, but "that he had some considerable money coming to him" for work done at Westerlo. Lobdell replied that her brother would attend to the matter of the money. "I told brother, as I handed him some cash, to settle the marriage fee. . . ."[14]
> When a Methodist meeting was held in the neighborhood, the newly married Lucy Ann and George Slater attended, and after several more meetings

Slater, myself, and twenty or more others, experienced and professed religion.
As the ministers had visited our house very frequently I had become quite a curious person for them to talk with, as my sentiments varied from theirs with regard to their belief very much.

> Lucy Ann's assertiveness and intimate discourse with the preachers seems to have antagonized the less intellectual Slater, apparently making him jealous. A Dr. Hale, married to a cousin of Lucy Ann's, also objected vehemently to her speaking up to

the preachers, and castigated her sharply for it. He later apologized, and Lucy Ann rather grudgingly

told him I could forgive him if my heavenly Father could. But whether God had forgiven him or not is not in my power to say. But in a short time the news came to me that Doctor Hale was crazy, and soon after he was sent to the asylum at Utica. He appears to be quite rational at different times, but he is there now at the asylum, a poor crazy being.[15]

Lucy Ann taught for a time at the district school, and then moved with Slater into a home of their own nearby. Slater now became jealous of Lucy Ann's friendship with a more intellectual male boarder, and even, it seems, of her ability to play the violin. She disliked Slater's vulgarity, and that of his card-playing friends. The overt antagonism between George Slater and Lucy Ann continued to grow, and Slater began publicly to accuse his wife of paying attention to other men, saying he was sorry he had paid five dollars to marry her, and that he would pay five or ten dollars to be unmarried. Afraid of Slater's anger, which he had displayed on several occasions, Lucy Ann decided not to live with him any longer, and moved back with her parents. In the fall of 1852, Slater moved out of the neighborhood, leaving the twenty-three-year-old Lucy Ann pregnant.[16]

Lucy Ann relates that after Slater went away,

I used often to go hunting to drive care and sorrow away; for when I was upon the mountain's brow, chasing the wild deer, it was exciting for me; and as times were hard, and provisions high, I was often asked by father, who had become decrepit, if I could not go and shoot him some venison, as he was obliged to stop hunting. I used to feel sorry to see my poor father so lame, and hear him ask me to shoot him some deer. I at length put on a hunting-suit I had prepared, and away I started in pursuit of some meat.[17]

Although she later became adept at hunting, Lucy Ann relates, with humor, one farcical first attempt to shoot a deer.

The rifle went off, and so did the deer. I began to think that I should have to coax the deer to me the next time, and hold the rifle against him in order to kill him.

Another time, what she thought was a panther started around a tree toward her:

As soon as I got a fair sight at his heart, I fired, and O horror! such a noise as I heard in an instant caused my hair to stand erect, I believe, for I felt a cold sensation crawl over me that seemed to freeze the blood in my veins. The moment I fired, the animal turned and jumped, and ran out of sight; I reloaded my rifle, and ran after him.[18]

In 1853 and 1854, an account of Lucy Ann by Mr. Talmadge, a traveling peddler, was, she says, given much publicity in the newspapers, bringing many hunters into the area and many requests for her to play her violin. Lucy Ann gives one version of Talmadge's account.

"I must relate an adventure that I met with a few days since. As I was trudging along one afternoon, in the town of Freemont, one of the border towns of Sullivan county, I was overtaken by what I, at first, supposed was a young man, with a rifle on his shoulder. Being well pleased with the idea of having company through the woods, I turned round and said, 'Good afternoon, sir.' 'Good afternoon,' replied my new acquaintance, but in a tone of voice that sounded rather peculiar. My suspicions were at once aroused, and to satisfy myself, I made some inquiries in regard to hunting, which were readily answered by the young lady whom I had thus encountered. She said that she had been out ever since daylight; had followed a buck nearly all day, and had got but one shot and wounded him; but as there was little snow, she could not get him, and was going to try him the next day, hoping that she could get another shot, and was quite certain that she could kill him. Although I can not give a very clear idea of her appearance, I will try to describe her dress. The only article of female apparel visible was a close-fitting hood upon her head, such as is often worn by deer hunters; next, an india-rubber over-coat. Her nether limbs were encased in a pair of snug-fitting corduroy pants, and a pair of Indian moccasins were upon her feet. She had a good looking rifle upon her shoulder, and a brace of double-barrelled pistols in the side-pockets of her coat, while a most formidable hunting-knife hung suspended by her side. Wishing to witness her skill with her hunting instruments, I commenced bantering her in regard to shooting. She smiled, and said that she was as good a shot as was in the woods, and to convince me, took out her hunting-knife, and cut a ring, about four inches in diameter, on a tree, with a small spot in the centre; then stepping back thirty yards, and drawing up one of her pistols, put both balls inside the ring. She then, at eighteen rods from the tree, fired a ball from her rifle into the very centre. We shortly came to her father's house, and I gladly accepted of an invitation to stop there over night.

"The maiden-hunter instead of setting down to rest as most hunters do when they get home, remarked that she had got the chores to do. So, out she went, and fed, watered, and stabled a pair of young horses, a yoke of oxen, and three cows. She then went to the saw-mill, and brought a slab on her shoulder, that I should not liked to have carried, and with an axe and saw, she soon worked it up into stove-wood. Her next business was to change her dress, and get tea, which she did in a manner which would have been creditable to a more scientific cook. After tea, she finished up the usual house-work, and then sat down and commenced plying her needle in the most lady-like manner. I ascertained that her mother was quite feeble, and her father confined to the house with the rheumatism. The whole family were intelligent, well-educated, and communicative. They had moved from Schoharie county into the woods about three years before; and the father was taken lame the first winter after their arrival, and has not been able to do anything since, and Lucy Ann, as her mother called her, has taken charge of, ploughed, planted, and harvested the farm; learned to chop wood, drive the team, and do all the necessary work.

"Game being plenty, she had learned how to use her father's rifle, and spent some of her leisure time in hunting. She had not killed a deer yet, but expressed her determination to kill one, at least, before New-Year's. She boasted of having shot any quantity of squirrels, partridges, and other small game. After chatting some time, she brought a violin from a closet, and played fifteen or twenty tunes, and also sang a few songs, accompanying herself on the violin, in a style that showed she was far from being destitute of musical skill. After spending a pleasant evening, we retired. The next morning she was up at four o'clock, and before sunrise, had the breakfast out of the way, and her work out of doors and in the house done; and when I left, a few minutes after sunrise, she had got on her hunting-suit, and was loading her rifle for another chase after the deer."[19]

Meanwhile, George Slater continued to publicize slanderous reports of Lucy Ann's "sprees" with other men. When he returned and wished to live together again, Lucy Ann told him she could care for herself and her baby daughter, Helen, without him. About this same time (1854), she began once more to use her maiden name, and in October she decided to leave her child and her parents' home to seek a living elsewhere. She explains the reasons for this decision.

First, my father was lame, and in consequence, I had worked in-doors and out; and as hard times were crowding upon us, I made up my mind to dress in men's attire to seek labor, as I was used to men's work. And as I might work harder at house-work, and get only a dollar per week, and I was capable of doing men's work, and getting men's wages, I resolved to try, after hearing that Mr. Slater was coming, to get work away among strangers.

I accordingly got up one morning, and it seemed as if I must go that day. I did not dare to tell our folks my calculations, for I knew that they would say I was crazy, and tie me up, perhaps. So I went up stairs, saying I was going to dress, and go a hunting as I was accustomed to. I hurried and put on a suit of clothes, and then my hunting-suit outside. When I came down stairs, mother came toward me, and was going to take hold of me to see what made me look so thickly dressed. I saw her move, and stepped out doors saying that I must hurry, as it was getting late. I drove the cow up before I left, and then hurried up the mountain. I could not even kiss my little Helen, nor tell her how her mother was going to seek employment to get a little spot to live, and earn something for her as she grew up. So, I stole away with a heavy heart, for I knew that I was going among strangers, who did not know my circumstances, or see my heart, so broken, and know its struggles. As I was walking down to the Hankins Depot, I met one of our nearest neighbors. He called to me, and asked me where I was going. I made no reply, but walked on; and I had got but a few yards, when I heard him say, "There goes the female hunter." I kept on walking in the meantime a pretty good pace, and then I stepped a little one side in the bushes to change my hunting attire. I in a few minutes saw some one pass the road who appeared to be in search of me. After the lapse of a short time, I walked out of the woods in a different direction, and went to Miss Hawkins's, and she kept me over night. I arose in the morning at four o'clock, and walked to the Callicoon Depot, and bought a ticket for Narrowsburgh.[20]

Adding that she intends to write another book on her adventures in male attire, Lucy Ann Lobdell, in a last explicitly feminist appeal, further explains

the reasons for my adoption of man's apparel. The first reason, then, is this: I have no home of my own; but it is true that I have a father's house, and could be permitted to stay there, and, at the same time, I should be obliged to toil from morning till night, and then I could demand but a dollar a week; and how much, I ask, would this do to support a child and myself. I tell you, ladies and gentlemen, woman has taken upon herself the curse that was laid on father Adam and mother Eve; for by the sweat of her brow does she eat her bread, and in sorrow does she bring forth children. Again, woman is the weaker vessel, and she toils from morning till night, and then the way her sorrows cease is this—her children are to be attended to; she must dress and undress them for bed; after their little voices are hushed, she must sit up and look after the preparations for breakfast, and, probably, nine, ten, eleven, or twelve o'clock comes round before she can go to rest. Again, she must be up at early dawn to get breakfast, and whilst the breakfast is cooking, she must wash and dress some half a dozen children. After finishing up the usual morning's house-work, such as washing dishes, making beds, and filing the kitchen-floor, then comes the dinner as usual. Then comes the husband—the puddings have been burned a trifle when mother was busy at something else; then come complaints in regard to the pudding. Well, mother was busy with Bridget or Patrick, settling some quarrel or blows, and now mother has made father a little out of taste with the dinner. And this is the way the world is jogging along.

And, now, I ask, if a man can do a woman's work any quicker or better than a woman herself; or could he collect his thoughts sufficiently to say his prayers with a clear idea? No; if he was confused and housed up with the children all day, he would not hesitate to take the burden off his children's shoulders, and allow woman's wages to be on an equality with those of the man. Is there one, indeed, who can look upon that little daughter, and feel that she soon will grow up to toil for the unequal sum allotted to compensate her toil. I feel that I can not submit to see all the bondage with which woman is oppressed, and listen to the voice of fashion, and repose upon the bosom of death. I can not be reconciled to die, and feel my poor babe will be obliged to toil and feel the wrongs that are unjustly heaped upon her. I am a mother; I love my offspring even better than words can tell. I can not bear to die and leave that little one to struggle in every way to live as I have to do. . . .[21]

. . . Help, one and all, to aid woman, the weaker vessel. If she is willing to toil, give her wages equal with that of man. And as in sorrow she bears her own curse, (nay, indeed, she helps to bear a man's burden also,) secure to her her rights, or permit her to wear the pants, and breathe the pure air of heaven, and you stay and be convinced at home with the children how pleasant a task it is to act the part that woman must act. I suppose that you will laugh at the idea of such a manner of convincing; but I suppose it will not do to convince the man of feeling, who can see and pity, and lend a helping hand to release the afflicted, the child of your bosom, the choice of your heart, young man.[22]

> Finally, in a few last theologically oriented paragraphs, Lucy Ann Lobdell mentions the sorrows she has felt and wounds she has suffered during the course of her adventures:

though some do call me a strange sort of being, I thank God, in whom I believe, and in whom I trust, and who is my defence, and I can praise Him, that He has given me a heart, that He will mould and fashion after His holy will; and as nothing is more calculated to make a heaven on earth than the love of God, I can say, that my affliction has taught me a thousand truths of His loving kindness; for whomsoever the Lord loveth, He chasteneth, and scourgeth every son and daughter of Adam. . . . If you love God, and keep His commandments, you will get to heaven in spite of professed preachers, or churches, or the devil and all his dominies; and though your name may be cast out as evil, you can rejoice, knowing that if you but endure to the end you will be saved. Amen!

Your humble servant,

L. A. LOBDELL.[23]

In 1855, in New York, there was "Published for the Authoress" the *Narrative of Lucy Ann Lobdell, the Female Hunter of Delaware and Sullivan Counties, New York*, an autobiography of forty-seven pages. Part personal history, part self-explanation and justification, part self-advertisement, part self-defense against Slater's public attack, part explicit feminist appeal, and small part religious invocation, Lucy Ann's is an extraordinary account.

Twenty-eight years later, in 1883, there appeared in a St. Louis medical journal, *The Alienist and Neurologist*, one of the earliest American reports of Lesbianism.

CASE OF SEXUAL PERVERSION.

By P. M. Wise, M. D., Willard, N. Y.,
Assistant Physician of The Willard Asylum for the Insane.

The case of sexual perversion herewith reported, has been under the writer's observation for the past two years and since the development of positive insanity. The early history of her abnormal sexual tendency is incomplete, but from a variety of sources, enough information has been gleaned to afford a brief history of a remarkable life and of a rare form of mental disease.

CASE.—Lucy Ann Slater, *alias*, Rev. Joseph Lobdell, was admitted to the Willard Asylum, October 12th, 1880; aged 56, widow, without occupation and a declared vagrant. Her voice was coarse and her features were masculine. She was dressed in male attire throughout and declared herself to be a man, giving her name as Joseph Lobdell, a Methodist minister; said she was married and had a wife living. She appeared in good physical health; when admitted, she was in a state of turbulent excitement, but was not confused and gave responsive answers to questions. Her excitement was of an erotic nature and her sexual inclination was perverted. In passing to the ward, she embraced the female attendant in a lewd manner and came near overpowering her before she received assistance. Her conduct on the ward was characterized by the same lascivious conduct, and she made efforts at various times to have sexual intercourse with her associates. Several weeks after her admission she became quiet and depressed, but would talk freely about herself and her condition. She gave her correct name at this time and her own history, which was sufficiently corroborated by other evidence to prove that her recollection of early life was not distorted by her later psychosis.

It appeared she was the daughter of a lumberman living in the mountainous region of Delaware Co., N.Y., that she inherited an insane history from her mother's antecedents. She was peculiar in girlhood, in that she preferred masculine sports and labor; had an aversion to attentions from young men and sought the society of her own sex. It was after the earnest solicitation of her parents and friends that she consented to marry, in her twentieth year, a man for whom, she has repeatedly stated, she had no affection and from whom she never derived a moment's pleasure, although she endeavored to be a dutiful wife. Within two years she was deserted by her husband and shortly after gave birth to a female child, now living. Thenceforward, she followed her inclination to indulge in masculine vocations most freely; donned male attire, spending much of the time in the woods with the rifle, and became so expert in its use that she was renowned throughout the county as the "Female Hunter of Long Eddy." She continued to follow the life of trapper and hunter and spent several years in Northern Minnesota among the Indians. Upon her return to her native county she published a book giving an account of her life and a narrative of her woods experience that is said to have been well written, although in quaint style. Unfortunately the reporter has been unable to procure a copy of this book as it is now very scarce. She states, however, that she did not refer to sexual causes to explain her conduct and mode of life at that time, although she considered herself a man in all that the name implies. During the few years following her return from the West, she met with many reverses, and in ill health she received shelter and care in the alms-house. There she became attached to a young woman of good education, who had been left by her husband in a destitute condition and was receiving charitable aid.[24] The attachment appeared to be mutual and, strange as it may seem, led to their leaving their temporary home to commence life in the woods in the relation of husband and wife. The unsexed woman assumed the name of Joseph Lobdell and the pair lived in this relation for the subsequent decade; "Joe," as she was familiarly known, followed her masculine vocation of hunting and trapping and thus supplying themselves with the necessaries of life.

An incident occurred in 1876 to interrupt the quiet monotony of this Lesbian love. "Joe" and her assumed wife made a visit to a neighboring village, ten miles distant, where "he" was recognized, was arrested as a vagrant and lodged in jail.

On the authority of a local correspondent, I learn that there is now among the records of the Wayne Co. (Pa.) Court, a document that was drawn up by the "wife" after she found "Joe" in jail. "It is a petition for the release of her 'husband, Joseph Israel Lobdell' from prison, because of 'his' failing health. The pen used by the writer was a stick whittled to a point and split; the ink was pokeberry juice. The chirography is faultless and the language used is a model of clear, correct English." The petition had the desired effect and "Joe" was released from jail. For the following three years they lived together quietly and without noticeable incident, when "Joe" had a maniacal attack that resulted in her committal to the asylum before-mentioned.

The statement of the patient in the interval of quiet that followed soon after her admission to the asylum, was quite clear and coherent and she evidently had a vivid recollection of her late "married life." From this statement it appears that she made frequent attempts at sexual intercourse with her companion and believed them successful; that she believed herself to possess virility and the coaptation of a male; that she had not experienced connubial content with her husband, but with her late companion nuptial satisfaction was complete. In nearly her own words; "I may be a woman in one sense, but I have peculiar organs that make me more a man than a woman." I have been unable to discover any abnormality of the genitals, except an enlarged clitoris covered by a large relaxed præputium. She says she has the power to erect this organ in the same way a turtle protrudes its head—her own comparison. She disclaims onanistic practices. Cessation of menstrual function occurred early in womanhood, the date having passed from her recollection. During the two years she has been under observation in the Willard Asylum she has had repeated paroxysmal attacks of erotomania and exhilaration, without periodicity, followed by corresponding periods of mental and physical depression. Dementia has been progressive and she is fast losing her memory and capacity for coherent discourse.

Referring to other early European reports of "congenital" female and male homosexuality, Dr. Wise says that Krafft-Ebing

discusses fully the relation of society to these sufferers and suggests they should be excepted from legal enactments for the punishment of unnatural lewdness; thus allowing them to follow their inclinations, so far as they are harmless, to an extent not reaching public and flagrant offense.

It would be more charitable and just if society would protect them from the ridicule and aspersion they must always suffer, if their responsibility is legally admitted, by recognizing them as the victims of a distressing monodelusional form of insanity. It is reasonable to consider true sexual perversion as always a pathological condition and a peculiar manifestation of insanity.

The subject possesses little forensic interest, especially in this country, and the case herewith reported is offered as a clinical curiosity in psychiatric medicine.[25]

With that summation does Dr. Wise close his 1883 report of the remarkable Lucy Ann Lobdell.

Recent historical research in the archives of what is now called the Willard Psychiatric Center (Willard, New York) has revealed the existence of the original medical records of Lucy Ann Slater.

The records include four items: two certificates of insanity, each signed by a doctor; a judge's admission order; and the doctors' logbook with two large pages of entries concerning Lucy Ann Slater. Both certificates of insanity, in almost identical words, list the doctors' reasons for Lucy Ann Slater's commitment. One reads:

1st She is uncontrollable indecent & immoral & insists on wearing male attire calling herself a huntress

2nd She threatens the lives of her companions.

3rd She does herself violence.[26]

The doctors' logbook, covering ten years, begins:

Lucy Ann Slater   Hancock———   Delaware Co.
                         Admitted, Oct. 12th 1880.

Age 56—Single Widow—N.Y.—Vagrant—Has had good common education. No religion—Said to be hereditary on maternal side—Insanity commenced over twenty years ago. The early history of her insanity is unknown. It is said she has worn male attire for twenty years. She claims to be a man at times. At other times she says she wears it because it is more convenient for hunting purposes—Has never been in an asylum, but has been in the county alms house at different times, and is now transferred from there.—She has usually been considered harmless & wandered about the country without molestation, but latterly she has made some threats of violence— . . .

When admitted she was in good bodily health, conversation was incoherent & actions silly. She was dressed throughout in male attire, and said she intended to continue to wear it.

Dementia

The record states that Lucy Ann Slater was "brought from the county alms house" by its keeper, and the superintendent of the poor, on his order and by the medical certification of two doctors. A following entry, partially obscured, indicates that she "has been very much disturbed" at times, and that her physical health is poor, characterized by lung irritation and "severe hemorrhoids. Remains in bed." The logbook continues:

Feb. 23rd 1881. Hall # 2. Dorm. Condition has improved, and for the past two months she has been quite composed. Frequently wet and dirty at night. Occasionally destructive.

Jan. 7th 1882. Has had several periods of disturbance since the above. When she is excited she calls herself Jos. & when composed Lucy. Bodily health fair.

Aug. 3rd 1882. Is gradually becoming more demented, and erotic tendencies weakening. Her perversion of sexual inclination continues. She says she lived with Maria Perry for twelve years and wanted to marry her but Maria would not consent. She attempted to have sexual intercourse with her. At present she is incoherent & foolish—

Oct. 25th 1882. She has been disturbed for about a week. Her sexual perversion is not usually well marked; Bodily strength fair

Nov. 7th [18]83. Has been fairly quiet through the summer, and altogether more comfortable. Has had less sexual perversion. Dementia increasing. Practices masturbation and the practice is increasing. No menses.

Feb. 19—1885. When quiet talks quite well and is inactive. Excitement lasts for shorter periods and quiet lasts longer. Was slightly excited a short time since. When disturbed is wet and dirty at night, violent, talkative and noisy and inclined to cohabit with other patients, restless and sleepless, tears bedding. She is now quiet and good natured. Physical health good.

June 5—1885. Has passed through an excited period twice since last entry but neither of them were very marked. Transferred today to *D. B. 4.* Has slept in dormitory but on account of erotic tendencies needs a single room at times.

March 24th 1886. 2 D. B. 4—Since transfer has been usually quiet orderly, & pleasant, and bodily health good. Yesterday she had an attack of facial paralysis of the left side with loss of sensation & partial loss of motion in the affected side. Not much constitutional disturbance & refuses to go to bed.

April 6th 1887. Has apparently recovered from the above attack & is about the [illegible] as usual. Though at times complains of headaches.

Ap. 2nd 1888. Has been excited & restless & untidy a part of the year.

May 1st 1889. No change.

March 19—[18]90. Continues in good bodily health. Has improved somewhat & says "she has gotten over her old ideas." Has been quiet and orderly for some months past.

Thus ends the last logbook entry; Lucy Ann Lobdell apparently died a short time later.[27] The key to understanding Lobdell's difficulties and later decline into madness seems to lie in the conflict of this assertive, intelligent, proud female with that behavior her society declared proper and improper for women. As a feminist, Lobdell early pushed against these social restraints and limiting definitions, a woman finally trapped and doomed by her inability to work her way free of them.

In Lobdell's life there is a complex connection between feminist protest, transvestism, Lesbianism, and her theologically based association of sin, guilt, punishment, physical illness, and mental derangement. Lobdell's description of Dr. Hale connects his wrongheaded castigation of her (for debating the local preachers) and Hale's subsequent transformation into a "poor crazy being" incarcerated in an asylum, a fate which oddly foreshadows Lobdell's own later state.[28]

In another section (not quoted because of its peripheral relevance), Lobdell also suggests that the troubles and physical illness (cancer) of a Peter Smith are punishment for "sin."[29] Other passages in her *Narrative* suggest the connection in her mind between sinning and suffering. It is not difficult to imagine the moral pressures upon an unconventional woman like Lobdell, and her own susceptibility to guilt over Lesbianism. Her religious training no doubt made her aware of the passage in the Bible (Romans 1:26) condemning female homosexuality as a "vile affection." Lobdell's own eventual madness may be understood as the final stage in a complex personal-historical chain leading from aspiration, to assertion, to transvestism, to Lesbianism, to overt persecution (her being jailed upon the discovery of her sex), to guilt, to derangement.

♀ 1863: *Fincher's Trades' Review*;
"A Curious Married Couple"
"Thirty-four years of pretended matrimony"

In 1863, *Fincher's Trades' Review* (subtitled *An Advocate of the Rights of the Producing Classes* and published in Philadelphia) carries the first of several reports of transvestite women, some of whom are clearly indicated to have had close, meaningful relations with other females. *Fincher's* appealed especially to those white, Protestant, semiskilled workers of British origin then emigrating to America and becoming active in this country's growing trade-union movement. The English settings of two of these stories were, no doubt, of special interest to *Fincher's* readers. Reports of these English women are included here for their indications of American attitudes of the 1860s toward female intimacy and female cross-dressing.

The seeming innocence of these reports, their authors' apparent failure to recognize, even unconsciously, any sexual "irregularities" in these stories of, for instance, two women living together for thirty-four years as "man and wife," suggests a consciousness very different from the sexualized awareness so prevalent in present-day America. Lack of sexual innuendo in these old reports does not, of course, rule out the existence of overt sexual relations between the women described.

On July 25, 1863, *Fincher's* carries a feature story about Englishwoman Mary East and her "wife" of 34 years, a classic couple in the literature of female transvestism.

A Curious Married Couple

In 1731, a girl named Mary East was engaged to be married to a young man for whom she entertained the strongest affection; but upon his taking to evil courses, or, to tell the whole truth, being hanged for highway robbery, she determined to run no risk of any such disappointment from the opposite sex in future. A female friend of hers having suffered in some similar manner, and being of the like mind with herself, they agreed to pass for the rest of their days as man and wife, in some place where they were not known. The question of which should be the husband was decided by lot in favor of Mary East, who accordingly assumed the masculine habit, and under the name of James How, took a small public house at Epping for himself and consort. Here, and subsequently at other inns, they lived together in good repute with their neighbors for eighteen years—during which neither experienced the least pang of marital jealousy—and realized a considerable sum of money. The supposed James How served all the parish offices without discovery, and was several times a foreman of juries. While occupying the *White Horse* at Poplar, however, his secret was discovered by a woman who had known him in his youth; and from that time the happy couple became the victims of her extortion. First five, then ten, then one hundred pounds were demanded as the price of her silence, and even these bribes were found to be insufficient. At last, however, the persecutor pushed matters too far, and killed the goose that laid such golden eggs. James brought the whole matter before a magistrate, and attired, awkwardly enough, in the proper garments of her sex, herself witnessed against the offender, who was imprisoned for a considerable term. Exposure, however, of course followed upon the trial, and the *White Horse* had to be disposed of, and the landlord and landlady to retire from public life into retirement. After thirty-four years of pretended matrimony, Mrs. How died; the disconsolate widower survived long afterwards, but never again took to himself another spouse. Neither husband nor wife had ever been seen to dress a joint of meat; nor did they give entertainment to their friends like other couples; neither, although in excellent circumstances, (having acquired between three and four thousand pounds), did they keep man-servant or maid-servant, but Mary East served the customers and went on errands, while her wife attended solely to the affairs of the house.[30]

In the next few months, *Fincher's* carries four features about American females who, dressed as men, had served as soldiers in the Civil War; the stories, however, mention nothing suggesting particularly close relations with other women.[31]

♀ 1863: PHILIP H. SHERIDAN;
Two Amazons in the Union Army
"An intimacy had sprung up"

The *Personal Memoirs of Philip H. Sheridan* (1888), Union army general, refers to a pair of female transvestite Civil War soldiers between whom "an intimacy had sprung up."

As Sheridan recalls, foraging expeditions sent out to bring back food for his Union troops fighting in the South usually encountered heavy enemy fire. After one of these expeditions returned successfully, says Sheridan,

the colonel in command, Colonel Conrad, of the Fifteenth Missouri, informed me that he got through without much difficulty; in fact, that everything had gone all right and been eminently satisfactory, except that in returning he had been mortified greatly by the conduct of *the two females belonging to the detachment and division train at my headquarters.* These women, he said, had given much annoyance by getting drunk, and to some extent demoralizing his men. To say that I was astonished at his statement would be a mild way of putting it, and had I not known him to be a most upright man and of sound sense, I should have doubted not only his veracity, but his sanity. Inquiring who they were and for further details, I was informed that there certainly were in the command two females, that in some mysterious manner had attached themselves to the service as soldiers; that one, an East Tennessee woman, was a teamster in the division wagon-train and the other a private soldier in a cavalry company temporarily attached to my headquarters for escort duty. While out on the foraging expedition these Amazons had secured a supply of "apple-jack" by some means, got very drunk, and on the return had fallen into Stone River and been nearly drowned. After they had been fished from the water, in the process of resuscitation their sex was disclosed, though up to this time it appeared to be known only to each other. The story was straight and the circumstance clear, so, convinced of Conrad's continued sanity, I directed the provost-marshal to bring in arrest to my headquarters the two disturbers of Conrad's peace of mind. After some little search the East Tennessee woman was found in camp, somewhat the worse for the experiences of the day before, but awaiting her fate contentedly smoking a cob-pipe. She was brought to me, and put in duress under charge of the division surgeon until her companion could be secured. To the doctor she related that the year before she had "refugeed" from East Tennessee, and on arriving in Louisville assumed men's apparel and sought and obtained employment as a teamster in the quartermaster's department. Her features were very large, and so coarse and masculine was her general appearance that she would readily have passed as a man, and in her case the deception was no doubt easily practiced. Next day the "she dragoon" was caught, and proved to be a rather prepossessing young woman, and though necessarily bronzed and hardened by exposure, I doubt if, even with these marks of campaigning, she could have deceived as readily as did her companion. How the two got acquainted I never learned, and though they had joined the army independently of each other, yet an intimacy had sprung up between them long before the mishaps of the foraging expedition. They both were forwarded to army headquarters, and, when provided with clothing suited to their sex, sent back to Nashville, and thence beyond our lines to Louisville.[32]

♀   1867: *Medical Times and Gazette*;
"Aberrations of the Sexual Instinct"
"It is an aberration of the sexual instinct in any girl to aim at occupations which are incompatible with the duties of matrimony"

In 1867, an anonymous essay in the London *Medical Times and Gazette*, no doubt by a doctor, presents a classic defense and summary of traditional attitudes toward women. The article constantly refers to life in the United States, and the article was probably read by and influenced American physicians. Although not referring explicitly to the passing women who are the subject of the present section, this essay is included as providing important background material for the understanding of the social pressures on such individuals. This article well illustrates how any unconventional woman, whose behavior deviated from social norms, might have been condemned as a "sexual aberration."

The essay condemns as an aberration every form of "sensual gratification without any union of the sexes," that is, not directly related to procreation, including the sinful "voluntary mental indulgence" on "sexual ideas." It emphasizes "the dangers of unchaste thought, even without unchaste act." It specifically condemns "those dark crimes which as the law says, are not to be named by Christian men . . ."[33]

The essay calls all forms of birth control a sexual aberration, specifically citing New England as an area in which the limiting of family size is in practice. It quotes from the book *New America* by Hepworth Dixon, an English author who traveled in the United States, that a "conspiracy" exists among "young, fashionable American women" not to have children—in order to retain their beauty and remain attractive to men. This early family planning is said to be

greatly aided in America by that other sexual aberration, which seeks to put the sexes on an equality and identity so far as possible,

educating women beyond what is necessary to the "feminine" sphere of activity, making them overly intellectual.[34]

The report points approvingly to the theological-political foundation of all those "commonplace" institutions associated with private property, which a male often takes for granted:

What a matter of course it seems for a man to speak of *my* wife, *my* children, *my* love, *my* bankers' book, *my* mutton, *my* wine, *my* profession or business, *my* last will! Such privileges, however, really rest on our religious and political systems.[35]

The essay then lists and denounces "a miscellaneous set of sexual aberrations" fostered by "every sexual and social heresy now rampant in America, . . ." a reference to religious and utopian groups. The Shakers are condemned for fostering celibacy (because they consider marriage and carnal relations sinful). "Free lovers" are denounced for openly advocating sexual exchanges outside of marriage. "Spiritualists," believing in "the perfect equality of the sexes on earth," are condemned for advocating "free love." "Bible Communists" or "Perfectionists," who "have all things in common," are denounced for believing it "a duty to eat, drink, and love to their heart's content—wives and children to be common—as all other property." The Perfectionists' marriage system is criticized for making every male and female the husband or wife of all others, with "no 'exclusive attachments.' " Young Perfectionists are allegedly supposed "to associate in love first with those older than themselves." Finally, the Mormons are condemned for believing it a duty to enjoy life, for practicing polygamy, and for destroying women's power in the home, thus making them the slaves and toys of men.[36]

The article continues:

Having now gone the round of the grosser aberrations of the sexual instinct, let us come to *Androgynism*, or the intrusion of one sex into the other's province. The funniest example of the intrusion of men into woman's field is afforded by the Chinese in the United States, who in California and the West do the work of women by preference—wash clothes, nurse babies, and do housework; but there is some excuse, for women are scarce. There were 730,000 more men than women in the United States in 1860. . . .[37]

Relating "Androgynism" and the growth of feminism, the author declares that woman is now becoming the "aggressor."

She demands absolutely equal rights with man; his pantaloons (*fem.* pantalettes) and latch-key. She demands admission to all offices and dignities, and that she shall have the privilege of doing all that man does. Woman in America, says Hepworth Dixon, is thrown "into a thousand restless agitations about her rights and powers, into debating woman's place in creation, woman's mission in the family; into public hysteria, into table-rapping, into anti-wedlock societies, into theories about natural marriage, free-love, and artistic maternity; into anti-offspring resolution, into sectarian polygamy, into free trade of the affections, into community of wives." These moral phenomena have their starting-point in America, where they are ascribed by Dixon to the scarcity of women; consequently to their power and self-consciousness of importance. . . .[38]

According to this report, the problems women are protesting arise partly from their "inevitable" biologic sex and physiological childbearing function. This admittedly requires "sacrifice of time, of health (at least temporarily), and comfort" and a mental focus on "nutritive functions" rather than sensitivity and intellectuality.

So long as woman is the childbearer, she must be the weaker vessel, the stay-at-home partner; the management of house-hold and children falls to her lot; but she has some compensation—she feels the comfort of a protector, and rejoices in her weakness. "I don't want equal rights; I like to be taken care of," was the sensible observation of a New York bride to Mr. Dixon.[39]

> The author also admits that certain evils are heaped upon women "by the selfishness and cruelty of man." Mainly, it seems, this is manifested by the inferior education of women which makes them incapable of employment—even in "domestic service." The essay affirms the need for improving women's education,

and multiplying lucrative employment for them within the sphere of their own sex; but we think they make a mistake in undertaking duties which are better fulfilled by men. It is an aberration of the sexual instinct to any girl to aim at occupations which are incompatible with the duties of maternity, and an equal aberration to smother those maidenly instincts which should lead her not to intrude into the occupations which custom has associated with the male sex. There is no intrinsic sin in riding astride a horse, or in wearing boots and breeches, but there is harm in violating those decent rules by which the conduct of either sex is regulated. We say it in all kindness, that for a girl to present herself at a public Medical examination is as great an aberration of sexual instinct, as it would be if a young man were to leave the dissecting room and apprentice himself to Madame Elise or Mademoiselle Coutuiere. For, after all, women cannot get rid of their sex. What is their real glory, their very life-purpose? To be mothers . . .

> American Bayard Taylor, in his novel *Hannah Thurston*, is said to emphasize the virtues of matrimony, motherhood, and female dependence on men, presenting

a singular picture of modern American life and manners, and makes one feel that all America is not poisoned by communism and women's rights.[40]

> Finally, the author hopes to have "shown how indissolubly the relations of the sexes are connected with religious and public polity; and we may add that any attempt to disturb either is fraught with danger to the whole social fabric." In a most astonishing way this essay associates politics, religion, feminism, utopianism, private property, monogamy, the sexual division of labor, "masculinity" and "femininity," abortion, birth control, and homosexuality. This reactionary propaganda of 1867 paradoxically suggests a concept of sexual politics connected in modern America with advanced radical thought.

♀ 1879–82: ELLEN COIT BROWN;
         "Scandal" at Cornell University
         "A woman dressed up in a man's suit"

> Ellen Coit Brown entered Cornell University in 1879, earned her B.S. in 1882, and wrote about her college days some time before her death in 1957. In recalling the character of the relations between the sexes in her college days, Brown says she "cannot remember one instance of philandering or sweethearting among us. Those

young people did not slip off into the woods in couples. . . . We were on trial and we knew it, on trial before the world and before our own public, and discretion sat upon us, men and women alike." In a tantalizingly brief, though suggestive, account, Ellen Coit Brown recalls an event which shook the staid Cornell campus, illustrating the shock that female cross-dressing could provoke.

We had only one scandal while I was there, but it was terrific. At a concert in town one evening a handsome girl student was observed to have with her as an escort a young gentleman not immediately identifiable, rather small and slight in appearance. Before the evening was over some snoop-minded person had realized that the escort was really a woman dressed up in a man's suit. Next day, the story was all over town. The university expelled the handsome girl, but not the mouse-like companion who was her intimate—I suppose the university felt that this was too utterly utter and they *must* take note of it. When I came up to the campus the next morning and joined a friend ahead of me on the path, she told me, very soberly what had happened. She felt the tragedy, as we all did.

For several days the women of Cornell went about in a mood of chastened gloom, feeling and acknowledging disgrace. No one will ever know from me the name of that handsome girl—and I suppose everybody else is dead; but I want to add that later on she beat on the closed doors of the university so persistently that they let her in again. She graduated successfully and lived a long and exemplary life, thereafter, employing her brilliant talent in fruitful ways suitable to the virtuous, and to Cornell women. Her mouselike companion who wore the man's suit never appeared at college again but faded into anonymity.[41]

♀ 1894: The *Badger State Banner*;
ANNA MORRIS/FRANK BLUNT and
GERTRUDE FIELD
Field "fell upon the neck of the prisoner and wept for half an hour"

The *Badger State Banner*, published in Black River Falls, Wisconsin, carried the following news on January 18, 1894:

ANNA MORRIS GIVEN ONE YEAR

Anna Morris, alias Frank Blunt, the woman who has tried to be a man for the last fifteen years, was sentenced to the penitentiary for one year by Judge Gilson at Fond du Lac. She was arrested several months ago in Milwaukee charged with stealing $175 in Fond du Lac. It was then discovered that the prisoner was a woman, although she had worn masculine attire nearly all her life. A jury convicted her of larceny and a motion for a new trial was overruled. After the sentence had been passed Gertrude Field, a woman who claimed to have married the prisoner in Eau Claire, fell upon the neck of the prisoner and wept for half an hour. This woman has furnished all the money for Blunt's defense, and now proposes to carry the case to the Supreme Court.[42]

♀ 1901: The *Weekly Scotsman*, the *New York Times*,
        and others; Murray Hall
        She played "pinochle and was sweet on women"

In 1901, the death in New York City of Murray Hall attracted wide attention in the press when it was revealed that this political organizer who had voted in elections had been a woman living in male disguise. Contemporary newspaper accounts leave many questions unanswered, but the reports of Hall's two "marriages" and her being "sweet on women" suggest Lesbianism.

Havelock Ellis, whose source is the *Weekly Scotsman*, February 9, 1901, confirms that Hall's real name was Mary Anderson, and claims (in contradiction to other reports) that she was born in Govan, Scotland: "Early left an orphan, on the death of her only brother, she put on his clothes and went to Edinburgh, working as a man. Her secret was discovered during an illness, and she finally went to America. . . ."[43] Although Murray Hall's life is described in these old newspaper accounts in words that now seem quaint, the difficulties of such a life must have been great.

The *New York Times* of January 19, 1901, reports:

MURRAY HALL FOOLED MANY SHREWD MEN

How for Years She Masqueraded in Male Attire.

HAD MARRIED TWO WOMEN

Was a Prominent Tammany Politician and Always Voted—Senator Martin Astonished.

Murray H. Hall, the woman who masqueraded as a man for more than a quarter of a century . . . was known to hundreds of people in the Thirteenth Senatorial District, where she figured quite prominently as a politician. In a limited circle she even had a reputation as a "man about town," a bon vivant, and all-around "good fellow."

She was a member of the General Committee of Tammany Hall, a member of the Iroquois Club, a personal friend of State Senator "Barney" Martin and other officials, and one of the most active Tammany workers in the district.

She registered and voted at primaries and general elections for many years, and exercised considerable political influence with Tammany Hall, often securing appointments for friends who have proved their fealty to the organization—never exciting the remotest suspicion as to her real sex.

She played poker at the clubs with city and State officials and politicians who flatter themselves on their cleverness and perspicacity, drank whisky and wine and

Left: "Murray Hall voting at a New York election—Hall was locally well known as a politician for thirty years, and only her death revealed the fact that she was a woman"—caption from illustration in *Munzey's Magazine* (New York, 1901). *Right:* From *Jahrbuch für sexuelle Zwischenstufen* (*Yearbook for Sexual Intermediate Types* [Leipzig, 1901]), the periodical of the Scientific-Humanitarian Committee, a German homosexual emancipation organization.[44]

smoked the regulation "big black cigar" with the apparent relish and gusto of the real man-about-town.

Furthermore, Murray Hall is known to have been married twice, but the woman to whom she stood before the world in the attitude of a husband kept her secret as guardedly as she did.

The discovery of "Murray Hall's" true sex was not made until she was cold in death and beyond the chance of suffering humiliation from exposure. She had been suffering from a cancer in the left breast for several years, as Dr. William C. Gallagher of 302 West Twelfth Street, who attended her in her final illness, discovered; but she abjured medical advice for fear of disclosing her sex, and treated herself. When she felt that life was at a low ebb she sent for Dr. Gallagher, the awful fear of exposure being supplanted by the dread of death. He made an examination and found that the cancer had eaten its way almost to the heart, and that it was a matter of only a few days, when death must ensue.

He kept this information from the patient, fearing the shock might hasten death. He deceived himself, for "Murray Hall" knew as well as Dr. Gallagher that the end was near. In years gone by, from time to time, "Murray Hall" had purchased volume after volume of works on surgery and medicine until she possessed a good medical library. Those books were studied, and the knowledge gleaned, no doubt, served to a good purpose in avoiding detection.

C. S. Pratt, a bookseller, is quoted as saying:

". . . I knew Hall well, having had many dealings with him, and believed him to be either a native of Ireland or a person of Irish extraction. He was well read and had no use for light literature. What he wanted and what I always sold him was some work on science. He would always ask to examine the book at home, and if it struck his fancy he would pay any price I fixed without quibble. He seemed to me to be a modest little man, but occasionally he showed an irascible temper. He would never talk about himself and shunned garrulous and inquisitive companions. In fact, when I met him on the street he was either accompanied by his black and tan dog or some woman or women, strangers to me, who I supposed were clients.

"During the seven years I knew him I never once suspected that he was anything else than what he appeared to be. While he was somewhat effeminate in appearance and talked in a falsetto voice, still his conduct and actions were distinctively masculine. This revelation is a stunner to me and, I guess, to everybody else who knew him."

"I wouldn't believe it if Dr. Gallagher, whom I know to be a man of undoubted veracity, hadn't said so," said Senator Bernard F. Martin. "Well, truly, it's most wonderful. Why, I knew him well. He was a member of the Tammany district organization, a hard worker for his party, and always had a good argument to put up for any candidate he favored. He used to come to the Iroquois Club to see me and pay his dues, and occasionally he would crack a joke with some of the boys. He was a modest little fellow, but had a peppery temper and could say some cutting things when anyone displeased him. Suspect he was a woman? Never. He dressed like a man and talked like a very sensible one. The only thing I ever thought eccentric about him was his clothing. Now that they say he's a woman, I can see through that. You see, he also wore a coat a size or two too large, but of good material. That was to conceal his form. He had a bushy head of black hair, which he wore long and parted on the left side. His face was always smooth, just as if he had just come from the barber's."

Joseph Young, one of Senator Martin's aides, who knew Hall, is quoted as exclaiming:

"A woman? Why, he'd line up to the bar and take his whisky like any veteran, and didn't make faces over it, either. If he was a woman he ought to have been born a man, for he lived and looked like one."

In reference to Hall's career as a "professional bondsman," the *Times* reports of her:

The singular character often befriended unfortunates for a consideration, and was doing a profitable business until, on one occasion, he qualified in a sum that aroused the Court's suspicion.

On investigating the bondsman's alleged wealth it was discovered that Hall had only about $5,000 in real estate, which consisted of five lots in West Chester willed to him by his "wife," "and a few thousand dollars in bank."

Hall was arrested after attending a meeting at the Iroquois Club one night and locked up in the Macdougal Street Station, but didn't stay long.

On the way to the station the policeman who had the prisoner in charge accepted an invitation to step into Skelly's saloon, at Tenth Street and Greenwich Avenue. They had several drinks, for which Hall paid. In the meantime Skelly had sent out for several politicians, who accompanied the officer and his prisoner to the station house. Skelly furnished a bond and Hall was released.

The party returned to Skelly's and had more drinks. Then Hall and several friends went to the Grapevine, Eleventh Street and Sixth Avenue, then to Teddy Ackerman's, across from Jefferson Market, drinking wine in both places until they reached a high state of enthusiasm.

Assaulted a Policeman.

Hall was coaxed outside, refused to go home, and started in to whip Policeman O'Connor, who tried to arrest him, and succeeded in putting a storm cloud draping under the officer's eye before he was handcuffed. Hall was finally returned to the station house two hours from the time of the first arrest, locked up, and kept over night. Next day his political friends "squared it," and he was released.

Hall's acquaintances, including Senator Martin, say that he appeared to be about fifty years of age. The death certificate places the age at seventy years.

John Bremer, proprietor of the Fifteenth Ward Hotel, Ninth Street and Sixth Avenue, knew Hall well, and had some business dealings with him. "He was a shrewd, bright man, in my estimation," said Mr. Bremer, "and I wouldn't believe he was a woman if it wasn't for Dr. Gallagher's statement.

"He used to send people from his intelligence office to room here for a day or two, and often came himself to see somebody stopping here. He'd drink anything from beer up, but I never saw him smoke, though they say he did, and chew, too."

"Yes, 'n play poker or pinochle and was sweet on women," broke in a lawyer who lives at the hotel. "I've known him for a number of years. He could drink his weight in beer and stand up under it.

"Why, I saw him play poker with a party of the Jefferson Market clique one night, and he played the game like a veteran. And for nerve, well, I can't believe that he was a woman, that's all. . . . He had a cigar in his mouth that night, but I don't believe he lit it.

"So he's a woman, eh? Well, I've read of such characters in fiction, but, if it's true, Hall's case beats anything in fact or fiction I can recall."

Mrs. Meyer's Story

Mrs. Johanna Meyers, who keeps a newsstand and cigar store at 109 West Tenth Street, knew Hall for many years.

"He used to come in here and buy papers and books, but never tobacco," she said yesterday. "His wife used to come in, too. She was a large, good-looking woman, almost twice her husband's weight. She did most of the business in the intelligence office up to the time of her death. She never intimated to me that her husband was a woman, neither did Hall himself nor their adopted daughter, Minnie.

"Last week Wednesday Mr. Hall sent a servant around here with a message that he was very sick and for me to call without fail between 2 and 3 o'clock next afternoon. My husband was very bad from the grip at the time, and I didn't get a chance to go. He didn't send for me again. He thought a great deal of me and used to come in and sit down and read for hours.

"On my last birthday he gave me a large cake for a present. Not once did I ever suspect from word or action that he was masquerading and was really a woman. I believe that he meant to confide in me and tell me his secret when he sent for me. If I had only suspected I certainly would have gone to see him. His adopted daughter, Minnie, was here this morning.

"The poor girl is terribly shocked over the disclosure. She said she had always believed her foster father was a man, and never heard her foster mother say anything that would lead her to suspect otherwise."

Minnie Hall, the adopted child, is the sole heir. She is twenty-two years old, and Lawyer Thomas Moran, who drew the will, says she is the only beneficiary named. The estate, he said, will not exceed $10,000 or $12,000.

Where Murray Hall came from, or who she really was, no one seems to know, not even the adopted daughter. It was about twenty-five years ago that "he" first came to public notice in New York. About that time he opened an employment bureau in Sixth Avenue, near Twenty-third Street. He had with him a woman known as his wife.

After about three years the wife made complaints to neighbors that her husband was making her life miserable: that he flirted with clients and paid altogether too much attention to other women. This woman suddenly disappeared. Whither she went, when or how, no one knows. The husband never spoke of her after her disappearance, and no one cared enough to make inquiries.

About fifteen years ago Hall moved to a building between Seventeenth and Eighteenth Streets, where he soon after introduced the woman who was known as Mrs. Hall as his second wife. The couple seemed to get along peaceably until seven years ago, when they moved to 145 Sixth Avenue. Then, neighbors say, they quarrelled, Mrs. Hall declaring her husband was too attentive to other women. That was the first known of Minnie Hall, the adopted daughter.

Who the child was or where she came from is as much a mystery as the early history of Murray Hall. How a woman could for so many years impersonate a man without detection, deceiving even her physician and some of the cleverest men and women in New York with whom she frequently came in contact, though the secret must have been known to at least two others—the wives—is a mystery quite as inexplicable as the character that accomplished the feat.[45]

The next day, January 20, 1901, the New York *Tribune* reports that Hall's funeral had taken place, adding:

Yesterday morning the crepe on the door at No. 145 Sixth Avenue was taken down and the doors of the intelligence office were thrown open. Neither the adopted daughter of the dead woman nor any of the servants in the place would talk about the funeral. They said it was strictly a private family affair. Where the woman was buried, who the mourners were and the other details of the funeral were not forthcoming.[46]

On January 29, 1901, the New York *Tribune* reports:

MURRAY HALL INQUEST CLOSED.

The Coroner's Jury Officially Declares That Hall Was a Woman

At the Criminal Courts Building yesterday afternoon the story of Murray Hall . . . was told before Coroner Zucca and a jury. The legal determination of the sex of this woman is important, as involving the disposition of an estate of about $5,000 under the will of Murray Hall.

Miss Imelda Hall, the adopted daughter, was the first witness. She said she always supposed Murray Hall was a man. She was not a legally adopted daughter, she said.

"How long had Murray Hall suffered from this cancer?"

"Six years."

"Had she a doctor?"

"Yes. Dr. Gallagher had been visiting her for about a year."

A letter written by Murray Hall to the District Attorney was read at this point, complaining of having been sandbagged by William Reno some years ago. When asked about this, the witness said, "Yes, he once complained of it."

"Wouldn't you better say she?" asked the Coroner.

"No, I will never say she."

Dr. W. C. Gallagher said he had known Murray Hall about a year, and that cancer of the breast was a disease peculiar to women. When asked if he did not know that she was a woman when he first attended her, he declined to answer. He said positively that she was a female. He thought the cancer might have been caused by the sandbagging alleged in the letter to the District Attorney, but he was not sure.

The jury decided that Murray Hall was a female and had died from natural causes.[47]

And on March 20, 1901, the New York *Tribune* concludes:

MURRAY HALL'S WILL FILED.

Woman Who Masqueraded as a Man Leaves Directions for Headstone for "Wife's" Grave.

The will of Murray H. Hall, . . . was filed for probate yesterday afternoon. . . .

The document bequeaths all of the property, real and personal, to Imelda A. Hall, and directs that on the death of the testatrix Imelda A. Hall shall cause to be erected a suitable headstone over the grave of Cecilia F. L. Hall, the wife of Murray Hall. Imelda A. Hall is appointed executrix.[48]

♀ 1901: MARIAN WEST;
"A curious phase of the problem of sex"
"Women who have passed as men"

In 1901, following the Murray Hall revelations, Marian West authored an article in *Munzey's Magazine*, published in New York. Titled "Women Who Have Passed As Men," it is subtitled "A Curious Phase of the Problem of Sex—Historical Instances of Women Who Have Fought Their Way Through the World In Masculine Disguise." Although the majority of historical examples cited are not American, West's article is interesting as an indication of her attitude toward female transvestism.

Speaking of the recently deceased Murray Hall, West says:

As to Hall's motives for the deception, one can only conjecture that she preferred the freedom of a man as well as masculine opportunities, and quickly took what she wanted.[49]

West's article goes on to describe other historical examples of transvestite women: first, British army surgeon Dr. James Barry, who died on July 15, 1865. Although West in 1901 does not specify this, overt Lesbianism is suggested by her comment:

Barry always made herself agreeable to women, but snubbed men unmercifully. More than once she got herself into difficulties by the compromising attentions which she paid to married women. At mess she would tell outrageous stories of her own exploits as a Don Juan.

Marian West then discusses the social reasons for a decline in women's attempts to dress, work, and live as men.

Notwithstanding these and other known instances, women seem to have become less adventurous with every generation. Those of the present day do a great many things that were undreamed of by their grandmothers, but dressing up in men's clothes and going out into the world to seek their fortunes is not one of them. There are obstacles to such an enterprise nowadays which once did not exist, such as the telegraph, which prevents many a person who desires temporary seclusion from getting it. . . .

Today, moreover, many active careers are open to women, and in these they can work off the superfluous life and energy that makes an uneventful domestic life unendurable, and that used to effervesce and spill over for lack of a proper outlet.

Another reason lies in the fact that we have so much more refinement, so much less openness of speech, among us that a decent woman—and some of our adventuresses have been decent women—would find it hard to accustom herself to mingle on equal terms with men.[50]

West next cites the example of Hannah Snell who, being deserted by her husband for another woman, dressed herself as a male and set out in the world to find and take vengeance on her unfaithful spouse. In 1745, she joined the British army, and later the British marines. There is the hint of overt Lesbianism in West's recounting that Snell's

lack of a manly beard was certainly a real trial to her, for the sailors, contemptuous, would "damn her in their familiar way, and stigmatize her with the disagreeable title of Miss Molly Gray." She met this odious title with "a smile and an oath," but resented it so bitterly that she resolved to live it down at any cost. In consequence, when the ship put in at Lisbon, she flung herself head first into a series of adventures whose nature was anything but doubtful. The result was all she could have wished. As her loyal historian tells us, "Our heroine, by thus affecting a gaiety of heart that was not sincere, and by acting such parts as in secret gave her the utmost disgust, gave a new turn to her character, and her title to manhood was no more suspected."

West does not comment on the complex irony of a female dressed as a male resenting being called the contemporary equivalent of "fag" and proving her "manhood" (actually her Lesbianism) by pursuing erotic relations with other women.

Lesbianism seems indicated in West's comments that Snell, hearing that her unfaithful husband had been executed,

arrived at Portsmouth a hilarious widow, who bunked and drank jovially with her sailor companions, made outrageous advances to a widow of less guile, then slipped off to London to avoid being led to the altar.

West relates that Snell, in an "unquotable scene," eventually revealed her true sex to her sailor companions. Snell then capitalized on the ensuing publicity by going on the stage. She is said to have refused an offer of marriage from one of her former male companions, and to be

planning to spend the rest of her days, still in her masculine attire, having lately purchased "a new suit of decent men's apparel as an incontestable proof of her aversion to the present fashionable hoop."[51]

The autobiography of an Irish woman, Christian Davis, born in 1667, West says, presents that woman's story without "the whitewash brush" and, adds West suggestively, "Davis comes out of her adventures none too well, from a modern standpoint. . . ." Davis's husband having been forcibly "impressed" into military service, this woman is said to have "disposed of her children in various ways," put on her husband's clothes, and set out in search of him, experiencing a year of high adventure. The second winter, West quotes Davis as saying:

"I was in Gorkham, where my grief for my husband being drowned in the hopes of finding him, I indulged in the natural gaiety of my temper, and lived very merrily." One of her diversions she found in laying siege to the heart of a good and sweet young girl, and winning it with ease. A duel and a wound followed, and presently Mrs. Davis drifted back to Dublin again, to find her family wanting "neither health nor the necessaries of life. I found means to converse with them, but I was so much altered by my dress, and the fatigues I had undergone, that not one of them knew me, which I was not sorry for. . . . I resolved to remain incog[nito]."[52]

The rest of Davis's interesting story, in West's account, seems thoroughly heterosexual.

♀ 1901: The *New York Times*;
Caroline/Charles Winslow Hall and
Giuseppina Boriani
" 'All artists are more or less eccentric' "

On October 1, 1901, another apparently male individual, Charles Winslow Hall, became seriously ill and died on the ocean liner which was bringing *her* home to America. Hall's illness and death resulted in the revelation of her true sex. Reports of the "husband-wife" relationship of Hall and Giuseppina Boriani today suggest the likelihood of sexual relations between the partners, although the *New York Times* write-ups of this incident do not hint at any link between the female couple and "unmentionable vice."

Notable here is the incipient feminism in Caroline Hall's reported dissatisfaction with the "lack of opportunities in the world" for women as the motive for her transvestism. The *New York Times* report reads:

BOSTON WOMAN POSED AS MAN WITH A WIFE

Sex of Liner's Passenger Revealed Through Fatal Sickness.

HAD LIVED TEN YEARS IN ITALY

An Artist and Had Won Prizes in Shooting Contests— Said to Be Daughter of Col. Hall, U.S.A., Retired.

The strange story of a woman who preferred to pass for a man was revealed by the death of Miss Caroline Hall of Boston, a cabin passenger on the steamship Citta di Torino, which arrived from Naples and other Mediterranean ports on Sunday. On the passenger list Miss Hall appeared as "Mr. Charles Winslow Hall," and with her on the ship was Mrs. Hall, whom she spoke of as "my wife." It was not until "Mr." Hall was stricken with a mortal illness that the ship's surgeon made the discovery that the supposed man was a woman.

There was nothing about "Mr." Hall that would have led any one to suspect her sex. She smoked cigars—big strong ones—and drank brandy. She was taken ill during the first part of the voyage and was forced to remain in her cabin until death claimed her early yesterday morning, a few hours after the vessel came into port. During her illness the supposed wife waited on her and continued to speak of her as her husband.

The dead woman was thirty-nine years old and is said to have been the only daughter of a Col. Hall, a retired army officer living in Boston, who is reputed[ly] wealthy. She was of slender build, medium height, and with a short crop of light hair, cut pompadour. She dressed well and carried herself with the air of a man. Her voice and gestures were masculine.

"Mr. and Mrs. Charles W. Hall" boarded the di Torino when that vessel was at Genoa, on Sept. 9. The vessel carried seventy-five cabin passengers. About one day after the vessel sailed "Mr." Hall was taken ill and forced to retire to her cabin. Her companion remained with the sick woman, who grew steadily worse, and Surgeons Giulio Angrisain and Nicola Rann had to be called in. They found the patient very low with consumption, and in making an examination Dr. Angrisain was astounded to find that "Mr." Hall was a woman.

She confessed her sex and begged the ship's surgeons not to make it public. She was informed that it was necessary to tell the Captain, and the doctors did so, though the sick woman earnestly requested them not to. None of the passengers, however, was aware that the sick "man" was a woman. "Mrs." Hall attended her companion until the end, and the latter continued to call her "wife."

"Mr." Hall is described by those who became acquainted with "him" on the voyage as being something of a "jolly fellow," who frequented the smoking saloon, talked sports and drank plenty of brandy.

The Coroner's office was notified of the death and a Coroner's physician last night visited the ship, and the body was removed to Swinburne Island, where an autopsy was performed. In the meantime "Mrs." Hall had telegraphed to her companion's father in Boston.

Early last evening the following telegram was received on board the vessel:

Boston Highlands, Sept. 30, 12:30 P.M.

Miss Caroline Hall. Will be at steamship at 7 o'clock.

ALBERT J. (or G.) Hall.

Albert Hall is said to be cousin of the dead woman.

About 6 o'clock, it was learned, a cab drove up to the steampship pier and a man, who said he came from Boston, inquired very earnestly if "Caroline Hall" was aboard. He was sure she had been a passenger, and if she was not on the ship, he wanted to know what hotel she had gone to. Obtaining no satisfaction, the man went away, not saying what his name was.

All day long in the saloon of the Torino "Mrs." Hall remained near the dead, waiting for the latter's relatives to come for the body. She is an Italian woman of about thirty-five years of age, dark-eyed and with a rather good-looking face, surmounted by a mass of wavy dark hair. She cannot speak English and did not seem willing to tell all of the strange story. After much difficulty the following details were gathered about Caroline Hall and the strange relationship which existed between "Mr. and Mrs. Hall."

The dead woman had resided abroad for over ten years. Most of her time was spent in Italy, and three years ago she met Giuseppina Boriani at Milan. The two women became fast friends. About this time Caroline began to assert her belief that women were not afforded as many opportunities in the world as men. She was an artist, and in addition was an excellent rifle shot. It was easier for men to get about, she asserted, and after brooding for some time over the disadvantages of being a woman she decided to adopt male attire, and her friend humored her whim.

For over two years she traveled about as "Mr. Hall," and under that name entered several shooting contests and won prizes. Then again she went about the country painting and working at art and found that it was much easier going about alone when every one believed she was a man. Just when the Boriani woman began to assume the role of "Mrs. Hall" is not clear.

Some time ago Miss Hall decided to return to Boston and see her father. He is eighty years old, and she thought that she might not see him alive unless she went at once. Her friend she asked to accompany her, and in order that she might better carry out her assumed role, Miss Boriani was entered on the ship's manifest as "Mrs. Hall." Miss Hall would have made the trip to Boston as "Mr. Hall" had not death overtaken her and revealed her secret.[53]

The *Times* of October 2 continues the story, giving additional information, and leaving one wondering about the sad fate of Hall's "wife," Giuseppina Boriani.

"MR." HALL'S FATHER.

Woman Who Masqueraded as a Man Was a Daughter of J. R. Hall, a Boston Architect.

. . . A well-known Boston architect, J. R. Hall, is the father of Miss Caroline Hall, the artist, who died at sea while disguised as a man, and whose body is now in New York. Mr. Hall is not, however, a retired army officer. He has designed several important buildings here, including one of the theatres.

An aunt of the dead woman, at whose home the father lives, he being an invalid, admitted the identity to-day and said that the news had proved a great shock to Mr. Hall. In response to a question, the aunt, Miss Hall, said:

"All artists are more or less eccentric. I, at least, never knew of the eccentricity to which you refer."

The Veloce Line, to which the Citta di Torino belongs, received a message yesterday afternoon from a Mr. Hall of Boston, who said he would take charge of the body of the dead woman.

The steamship officials said they did not know what Miss Boriani, Caroline Hall's companion, would do, but they could say that she would not be a passenger on the Citta di Torino when it left this port.[54]

♀ 1902: DRS. ROBERT SHUFELDT, MARY WALKER,
and others; Dr. Mary Walker
"The most distinguished sexual invert in the United States"

Despite the 1902 medical journal article referring to "Dr. M——— W———, of Washington" as "the most distinguished sexual invert in the United States," and the fact that Dr. Mary Walker dressed in customarily male apparel, the exact nature of her own sexual proclivities remains a mystery.[55] Walker was a militant and outspoken feminist, with a program for women's emancipation including "dress reform" as one of its major propositions. Walker was certainly a transvestite, although this did not involve any attempt at "passing," distinguishing her from the other women considered here. She is included because her history suggests connections between passing women, female transvestism, the dress-reform branch of the feminist movement, and Lesbianism.

Mary Edwards Walker was born on November 26, 1832, near Oswego, New York. Her parents were farmers, her father a self-taught medical student. The names of two older sisters, Luna and Aurora Borealis, suggest a certain originality on the part of her parents. After attending the local common school, Mary Walker continued her education at the Falley Seminary in Fulton, New York, taught briefly, then entered Syracuse Medical College, graduating in 1855. She practiced medicine for several months in Columbus, Ohio, then returned to Rome, New York, and married a fellow medical student, Albert Miller, though she never took his name. The two practiced medicine together in Rome for a few years.

As an active youngster, Walker had disliked the restrictiveness of female clothing. When the feminist dress-reform movement, associated with the name of Amelia Bloomer, arose in the early 1850s, Walker quickly adopted the new pants outfit, and became an active writer-participant.

Walker separated from her husband in 1859 due to his unfaithfulness, and to possible sexual incompatibility, and after several unsuccessful attempts finally obtained a New York divorce in 1869.

During a brief attendance at Bowen Collegiate Institute in Hopkinton, Iowa, Walker was suspended when she refused to resign from the all-male debating society.

When the Civil War began in 1861, Walker traveled to Washington and tried unsuccessfully to be appointed a surgeon in the Union army, meanwhile volunteering her services in a city hospital and helping to organize an association to assist women visiting male relatives stationed in the capital. In 1862, after earning a degree from the New York Hageio-Therapeutic College, Walker went south, volunteering her services in Union army tent hospitals. Despite the strong opposition of a male medical director and a group of enlisted men, in 1863 Walker was officially appointed an assistant surgeon in the Union army, and she adopted the same uniform as her fellow officers.

Captured by the Confederates in April 1864, Walker was imprisoned until she was exchanged for a Confederate prisoner. She briefly supervised a hospital for women prisoners in Kentucky, and headed an orphanage in Tennessee, where her personality is said to have antagonized those around her. She was ordered back to

Mary Walker
(Wendell, Albany; New York Public Library)

Washington in 1865 and soon left the federal service. Later, in 1865, she was awarded a congressional Medal of Honor for meritorious service.

During the Civil War years Walker began to receive rather wide attention in the press, and her fame spread. After the war, in 1866, she was elected president of the small National Dress Reform Association, and made a successful speaking tour of England. In 1867, she returned to Washington and lived for a few years with an energetic young female teacher and aspiring attorney, Belva Lockwood, the two working together in the women's suffrage movement. Walker became increasingly isolated from the majority of suffragists when her argument that the federal Constitution already gave women the vote caused her to oppose a proposed female suffrage law. Walker was further alienated from the suffragists when she began to dress regularly not only in pants, but also in a jacket, shirt, stiff collar, bow tie, and top hat.

Walker's first book, *Hit*, was published in New York in 1871. This autobiographical, philosophical work is dedicated

TO

MY PARENTS;

And also

TO THE

PRACTICAL DRESS REFORMERS,

The truest friends of humanity, who have done more for the universal elevation of woman in the past dozen years, than all others combined. You, who have *lived* the precepts and principles that others have only *talked*—who have been so consistent in your ideas of the equality of the sexes, by dressing in a manner to fit you for the duties of a noble and useful life.

And also

TO MY

PROFESSIONAL SISTERS,

Of whatever School or Pathy, and all women who are laboring for the public good in any capacity.

And lastly,

TO THAT

GREAT SISTERHOOD

Which embraces women with their thousand unwritten trials and sorrows, that God has not given to men the power to comprehend, I dedicate this work, in hope that it will contribute to right your wrongs, lighten your burdens and increase your self-respect and self-reliance, and place in your hands that power which shall emancipate you from the bondage of all that is oppressive.[56]

In *Hit*, Walker's constant, central, and deeply felt concern is for the "oppression" of women, her chapter headings suggesting the range of her discussion: "Love and Marriage," "Dress Reform," "Tobacco," "Temperance," "Woman's Franchise,"

"Divorce," "Labor," "Religion." She objects to women being treated as "dolls" by men, and to females losing their own last names in marriage; she suggests that "Mrs." be accompanied by the term "Misterer" to indicate a man's married status. Walker believes strongly in the sacredness of marriage, but *not* in "contracts." She is in favor of divorce when two people have ceased to love each other. She argues for equal pay and job opportunities for women, and recommends that sons should learn housekeeping as well as daughters. She is against slavery, and she condemns the "unequal distribution of capital" because it adversely affects all working people, especially working women. "Away in the distant future," says Walker, "the people of the day will charge the great land-owners, and stock-owners, and *great every-bodies*, with selfishness unparalleled. . . ."[57]

In Walker's second book, *Unmasked, or The Science of Immorality. To Gentlemen. By a Woman Physician and Surgeon*, published in Philadelphia in 1878, her deep concern for the plight of women is even more emphatically expressed. This is a popular medical and sex manual, a feminist lecture and warning, directed at men, intended to affect for the better their treatment of women. It is easy to mock the book's strange mixture of mythological medical folklore, sexual superstition, and practical medical advice, its combination of a traditional puritanism with what must have struck its readers as a titillating sexual explicitness. But its eccentricities are probably no greater than many other sex and medical manuals of its day, while its underlying, deep-felt concern for women and its angry feminism distinguish it from other works of this genre. This book contains probably the most important indications of Walker's sexual views and clues as to her own erotic life.

As presented in *Unmasked*, Walker's puritanism and feminism seem intimately linked. The solution, for instance, to the double standard of sexual morality for men and women, is for men to be continent, not for women to be freer. Walker's first concern is always what she considers the good of women; her puritanism and other views follow. Her puritanism can also be understood in the context of the actual and, no doubt, often brutal sexual treatment of women by men which she observed, or of which she was told. Also, paradoxically, while Walker's views are puritanically conservative, her sexual explicitness is, for its day, radically blunt.

Arguing that "the ordinary costume of women" diseases both husband and wife leading to morbid sexual acts, Walker, in 1879, explicitly discusses and emphatically condemns heterosexual anal intercourse because of the pain she says it inevitably causes women. In another section, Walker also condemns a different exploitative form of anal sexuality, Turkish pederasty. Walker also comments on, and condemns, heterosexual oral acts:

Of all the iniquities of the social evil we have yet to relate the following as the most heinous possible:

The idea has been disseminated that the "eating of semen by women and the sipping of the exundations of women by men, will promote health, prolong life, and promote beauty."

This consummation of the basest of degradations is practiced not only by the fast [dissolute] but by husbands and their wives.

The public money might better be expended in teaching the monstrousness and results of baseness so vile that adjectives cannot be found sufficiently expressive to reach the case, instead of arresting for disseminating obscene matter.

Such degradation not only debases so that the whole expression of face is soon so hateful that one is repelled at a glance, but the brain is so injured that an incurable phase of insanity results.

What is thrown off by men and women have a certain mission and effect, and is then not only of no more use, but is a positive injury if retained. Nature makes no mistakes, and her laws cannot be infringed without penalties.

In a subsection of her chapter on "Social Evil," Walker discusses "Masturbation," condemning its harmful effects on both women and men:

The world was shocked when [the phrenologists] Fowler & Wells sent forth the truths to the world regarding the practice of masturbation being so great among the young.

Many people were quite angry because of the sweeping assertions made by these doctors, but close observation proved that all was true. The great injury to body and mind from this cause cannot be computed. The wrecks in insane asylums all over the country, the loss of general health, the inability to be stable, and a long category of evil results are now clearly to be discerned. All of which result from the utter ignorance of the subject. Tobacco, intoxicating drinks, pepper, and the heating and dragging of the mother's clothing all effect the boy in utero so that an effort for relief is made by masturbation. . . .

After puberty it frequently occurs that no amount of sexual variety or excess will prevent men from masturbation. This is sometimes practiced in the beds of their wives. . . .

Not only are the boys addicted to this practice, . . . but one has only to visit the teachers of schools of every grade and age, where girls are sent, to be convinced to what an extent the wrongs of parents are visited upon daughters as well as sons.

No one can practice this vice without the sure marks of the same being left in the face.

In a certain country the making of rubber male organs for the purpose of facilitating girls in masturbation is a lucrative business. . . .

This kind of masturbation, like all other ways of secret vice, sooner or later leads to sexual relations.

The effects of this vice on men are numerous. The most usual are consumption, insanity, softening of the brain and disease of the cuticle, and while all these are the effect on women, there is also an elongation of the clitoris, and a formation of warty excrescences on the vulva. Men or women who are addicted to this vice, cannot become parents of either a superior mental or physical type of humanity, because of loss of power. Such a person cannot be a desirable husband or wife, because of the loss of magnetic power.

Nothing so destroys the ability to think deeply, logically, gradually and connectedly as does orgasm even in the natural way if frequent, but especially is this true when produced in other ways.

Despite Walker's condemnation of masturbation, she speaks against an incredibly sadistic mechanical antimasturbation device marketed in 1870. Walker is also justifiably indignant about the rape of a Native American woman. In a remarkably modern-sounding statement she advocates *woman always having supreme control of her person*, as regards invasion by men . . .[58]

Walker emphasizes that sex organs are for procreation only, and that sexual activity and impulses should be strictly controlled. This emphasis on procreation as the only legitimate motive for sex would seem to rule out any conscious sanctioning of Lesbian activity, the tenor of Walker's argument suggesting that she herself probably directed her energy into nonsexual channels. Walker's life and feminist works certainly indicate that she cared deeply for women, but any specifically sexual attraction was probably sublimated.

In 1887, at age fifty-five, Mary Walker began the first of several midwestern tours in a "dime museum sideshow." After 1890, she returned to the town where she was born and became involved in several legal entanglements with relatives and neighbors. A plan to open a training school for young women was never realized. In 1917, a federal review board declared her Civil War citation as undeserved and officially withdrew it, though she defiantly continued to wear her Medal of Honor. The same year, Walker telegrammed Kaiser Wilhelm, offering her farm site for a peace conference, an act which received much publicity.

Poor and alone, Mary Walker died on February 21, 1919, and was buried in the little Oswego town cemetery in her black frock coat.

♀ 1902: The *Alienist and Neurologist*; "Marriages Between Women" "George" Greene and "William" C. Howard

An anonymous report in a St. Louis medical journal, the *Alienist and Neurologist* (1902), cites the discovery of two "cases of marriages between women." One member of each couple dressed and passed through the world as a male, her true sex undiscovered until her death.

Two recent cases of marriages between women have been disclosed by the death of the alleged "husband" ("George" Greene, a well-known citizen of Ettrick, Va.), who died at the age of 75. The wife called in assistance to prepare the body, when deceased was discovered to be a woman. "'He" had been born in England, but came to the United States when a child. "He" early exhibited proclivities for male attire to which the family soon became accustomed. "He" worked for several years as a man and married (at the age of 40) a widow. The couple maintained their relationship without discovery until Greene's death, at the age of 75.

"William" C. Howard died in Canandaigua, New York, at the age of 50. The refusal of the "widow" and "children" to permit an undertaker to prepare the body for burial led to a coroner's inquest, which disclosed the fact that "William" was a woman. "William" had early manifested male proclivities. "His" family had been unable to induce "him" to adopt female attire. When a girl on "his" father's farm "he" donned male attire and took up masculine occupation, taking care of horses and cattle and doing chores. The family ceased to remonstrate with her, at length growing accustomed to her male attire and often joking about the attentions she paid her own sex. She escorted girls to parties and spent money on them freely. Finally she "married" a woman named Dwyer and later adopted two children. The couple took a farm near Canandaigua and settled down quietly.

There was nothing especially feminine in either Greene or Howard; while Howard's ancestral family knew the real condition of things, they do not seem to have looked upon the relationship as at all abnormal. This would appear to indicate that the relatives of inverts have a certain tolerance for homosexuality. The influence of training at the indifferent periods in the development of homosexuality is suggested by the Howard case. The donning of male attire for convenient purposes may have stimulated a potential inversion previously latent.[59]

♀ 1903: EDWARD I. PRIME STEVENSON
(Xavier Mayne, pseud.); Harry Gorman
A "curious confraternity—or sorosis"

American, Edward Irenaeus Prime Stevenson, in his 1908 defense of homosexuality, *The Intersexes*, written under the pseudonym Xavier Mayne, describes the case of "Harry Gorman," who is called an instance of "Viraginous [manlike] and Concealed Uraniadism; Coarse Type . . ." Influenced by earlier German writers, Mayne calls Lesbians "Uraniads" and male homosexuals "Uranians." Although Mayne suggests some physical hermaphroditism may have characterized Gorman's Lesbian "Associates," no evidence is cited, and this interpretation seems connected less with fact than the prevailing theory, derived from Magnus Hirschfeld and others, that homosexuality—and "masculinity" and "femininity"—are physiological in origin. Most interesting in this report is the reference to a group of working-class, female, Lesbian transvestite railroad operatives, who "often met together and made themselves a little merry. . . ."

A noteworthy example of extreme masculinism, coincident with the merely feminine physique as being otherwise almost lost, came to notice in a hospital in Buffalo, in the United States, in 1903. A certain "Harry Gorman", an employé of the New York Central Railway, a robust, athletic, heavily built "man-cook" of about forty, was discovered to be a woman, so far as sexual organization committed one to the conclusion. Nothing else in Gorman could bear out such a sexual classification. For more than twenty years she had concealed her sex, with perfect ease. All the atmosphere of femininity was not only unsympathetic but impossible to her. She did heavy work, drank liquors moderately, and not as an alcoholic, smoked strong cigars, frequented saloons and dance-houses every night, and was untrammelled by any feminine conditions of existence. She swore that "nothing would hire" her to wear women's habiliments. When in the hospital (on account of a broken limb) a clergyman, with pressing views of decorum—if less psychologic sense—came to visit the patient. The visitor wished to argue a relapse toward female apparel and demeanour. "Harry Gorman" refused to grant the well-meaning gentleman any more interviews. She had voted as a man in several elections—of course illegally. More than this. "Harry Gorman" (the real name was not published in notices of the case) declared that she knew of "at least ten other women", who dressed as men, appeared wholly manlike, and were never suspected of being otherwise, also employed in the same railway-company; some of these being porters, train-agents, switchmen and so on. They often met together and made themselves not a little merry over the success of their transference from one class of humanity to another. The medical examination of Gorman in anatomical detail, is not at the writer's hand: nor did "Harry Gorman" communicate anything as to the similisexual [homosexual] intercourse between the members of this curious confraternity—or sorosis. But that most of the group were similisexual is to be inferred, probably with some organic abnormalities, in one case or another.[60]

♀ 1906: DRS. HAVELOCK ELLIS and
      EUGENE DE SAVITSCH; Nicholas de Raylan
      She "drank, smoked and was well known to chorus
      girls"

Two short summaries of the life and death of "Nicholai [or "Nicholas"] de Raylan" each add details about this Lesbian transvestite. The first account is by Havelock Ellis.

In Chicago in 1906 much attention was attracted to the case of "Nicholai de Raylan," confidential secretary to the Russian Consul, who at death (of tuberculosis) at the age of 33 was found to be a woman. She was born in Russia and was in many respects very feminine, small and slight in build, but was regarded as a man, and even as very "manly," by both men and women who knew her intimately. She was always very neat in dress, fastidious in regard to shirts and ties, and wore a long-waisted coat to disguise the lines of her figure. She was married twice in America, being divorced by the first wife, after a union lasting ten years, on the ground of cruelty and misconduct with chorus girls. The second wife, a chorus girl who had been previously married and had a child, was devoted to her "husband." Both wives were firmly convinced that their husband was a man and ridiculed the idea that "he" could be a woman. I am informed that De Raylan wore a very elaborately constructed artificial penis. In her will she made careful arrangements to prevent detection of sex after death, but these were frustrated, as she died in a hospital.[61]

In 1958, Dr. Eugene de Savitsch, in a book on homosexuality and "transsexualism," still speaks of homosexuals as those whose

body may be essentially that of the male but the sexual impulse predominantly that of the female, and vice versa.

A startling example of that kind has been reported . . . in the case of a woman who led the life of a man. The individual, known under the name of Nicholas de Raylan and former secretary of Baron von Schlippenbach, the Russian Consul in Chicago, declared himself to be the son of a Russian admiral. He had been twice married, but at his death on December 18th, 1906, in Phoenix, Arizona, was declared to be a woman. Investigation resolved the mystery into the following tangled contradictions: Declaration of the hospital physicians at Phoenix, Arizona, that de Raylan was a woman; declaration of his first wife, and of his second wife, that he was a man; records of the Superior Court, which show that the first Mrs. de Raylan was given a divorce on the ground of infidelity; records of the War Department, which show that he enlisted as a soldier during the Spanish-American War; testimony of friends and neighbours that he led a gay life, drank, smoked and was well known to chorus girls.

He was well educated, and was evidently a graduate of one of the Russian universities.

For two years he suffered from tuberculosis and went to Phoenix where he hoped to recover his health. No news was received of him until telegrams were sent out announcing his death, coupled with the declaration that he was a woman who had lived all her life as a man, married, fought as a soldier and worked in the office of the Russian Consul. De Raylan's first wife, who secured a divorce for infidelity, said the trouble was his fondness for chorus girls. His second wife, a member of the chorus, wept on learning of de Raylan's death, declaring that talk of his being a woman was nonsense. The post-mortem examination showed a female with an imperforate hymen, undoubtedly a virgin, with uterus, tubes, ovaries and vagina present and in the normal position. An imitation penis and testicles made of chamois skin and stuffed with down were suspended in the right place by means of a band around the waist.

One of the most incredible parts of the story is the Spanish-American War episode. We can only presume that the examination of recruits was a bit more sketchy then than it is nowadays. It is still more incredible that the individual was apparently a well-integrated personality who led a useful life until the last two years, when tuberculosis put an end to his unique career.

It was suggested by the experts that there might have been some glandular deficiency, but this was very difficult to establish because the autopsy technique in Phoenix, Arizona, in 1906, was probably not much more thorough than was the examination of recruits. The essential facts, however, are there, confirmed by the legal and medical authorities.[62]

♀   1908?: EDWARD I. PRIME STEVENSON
(Xavier Mayne, pseud.);
Anna Mattersteig/Johann Bürger and
Martha Gammater
"She 'felt herself wholly like a man' "

Anna Mattersteig's claim, in Stevenson's report of about 1908, that she " 'felt herself wholly like a man' " suggests that Mattersteig may have actually thought herself to be of the male gender, what today is commonly labeled a transsexual identification. The term *transsexual*, however, is so loaded with traditional assumptions connecting gender and "masculinity" and "femininity" as to render it of the most controversial and doubtful character. The solution to the problem of confused gender can be of the gravest practical import to those who, seeking help, fall into the hands of those doctors claiming to be "experts" on the subject, and offering only surgical (or technological) treatment. Here, it must suffice to say that to label Anna Mattersteig transsexual does nothing to explain the complex interrelations between her presumable sexual activity with another woman, her male identification, and her cross-dressing and passing. According to Stevenson:

A pertinent case occurred lately in the city of St. Louis, in the United States of North America. Through the statement of a local physician, a type-setter in the town was taken into custody, when employed in the office of a local journal, on a charge of abduction and as being a woman, though known as "Johann Bürger". The facts soon were clear. Anna Mattersteig was her real name. She was thirty years old. She was living matrimonially with another young woman, Martha Gammater, the daughter of a Leipzig jeweller, and had so lived before they came from Germany. Then, but apparently not earlier, Martha Gammater had discovered that she was the partner of a woman, not of a veritable man. The shock had made the wife insane. At the time of the arrest, she was in an asylum. Anna Mattersteig appeared in court in full male attire, and looked like a fine-appearing man. She disclaimed any intention of contravening the law, in respect of her impersonation and of the abduction (for such it had been) of her companion. She declared that she had assumed the role simply because she "felt herself wholly like a man" and was sure that only by a mistake of Nature had she come into the world at all otherwise. She "would suffer any penalty" rather than wear women's apparel.[63]

In reference to Martha Gammater, it would be elucidating to know if it was the alleged shock in discovering her husband was a woman or the shock of exposure and outraged public opinion that drove Gammater insane. It would also be interesting to know more about Mattersteig's prosecution for "abduction"—what this so-called abduction entailed, and who brought her before the courts. The apparent illegality of Mattersteig's transvestite "impersonation" is the first time such a juridical issue has been mentioned; a study of the laws concerning female transvestism and impersonation would also be of interest.

♀ 1909: DR. HAVELOCK ELLIS; Bill
" 'She drank, she swore, she courted girls' "

A quaint and, indeed, somewhat fanciful-sounding tale of what seems to have been Lesbian transvestism is recounted by Havelock Ellis. This report's charm arises partly from the contrast between the attitudes of 1909 and 1976 toward women engaging in such activities as drinking, swearing, fishing, and camping. Such behavior, found so utterly peculiar for a woman in 1909, is now quite ordinary; the present quality of this story is thus intimately tied to the historical change in the situation of women. The story of "Bill" also brings out that farcical potential in the situation created by tranvestite disguise, that doubling which has for so long been an element in theatrical comedy, humor arising from the transposition to one sex of that activity customarily assigned to the other. This example shows how particular activities in a sex-polarized society become sex-linked in an apparently essential way; viewing this behavior in historical perspective makes clear the social relativity of its "masculine" or "feminine" character.

In St. Louis, in 1909, the case was brought forward of a young woman of 22, who had posed as a man for nine years. Her masculine career began at the age of 13 after the Galveston flood which swept away all her family. She was saved and left Texas dressed as a boy. She worked in livery stables, in a plough factory, and as a bill-poster. At one time she was the adopted son of the family in which she lived and had no difficulty in deceiving her sisters by adoption as to her sex. On coming to St. Louis in 1902 she made chairs and baskets at the American Rattan Works, associating with fellow-workmen on a footing of masculine equality. One day a workman noticed the extreme smallness and dexterity of her hands. "Gee, Bill, you should have been a girl." "How do you know I'm not?" she retorted. In such ways her ready wit and good humor always disarmed suspicion as to her sex. She shunned no difficulties in her work or in her sports, we are told, and never avoided the severest tests. "She drank, she swore, she courted girls, she worked as hard as her fellows, she fished and camped; she told stories with the best of them, and she did not flinch when the talk grew strong. She even chewed tobacco." Girls began to fall in love with the good-looking boy at an early period, and she frequently boasted of her feminine conquests; with one girl who worshipped her there was a question of marriage. On account of lack of education she was restricted to manual labor, and she often chose hard work. At one time she became a boiler-maker's apprentice, wielding a hammer and driving in hot rivets. Here she was very popular and became local secretary of the International Brotherhood of Boiler-makers. In physical development she was now somewhat of an athlete. "She could outrun any of her friends on a sprint; she could kick higher, play baseball, and throw the ball overhand like a man, and she was fond of football. As a wrestler she could throw most of the club members." The physician who examined her for an insurance policy remarked: "You are a fine specimen of physical manhood, young fellow. Take good care of yourself." Finally, in a moment of weakness, she admitted her sex and returned to the garments of womanhood.[64]

♀ 1914: CORA ANDERSON;

Cora Anderson/Ralph Kerwinieo

"Is it any wonder that I determined to become a member of this privileged sex . . ?"

In 1914, the *Day Book* of Chicago, an "Adless Daily Newspaper" given to tabloid-style, splashy headlines, rather lurid features, short news items, advice columns, cartoons, and jokes, carried signed stories, datelined Milwaukee, Wisconsin, about Cora Anderson who had reportedly lived for thirteen years as Ralph Kerwinieo. How much credence can be given to these reports' veracity will depend on evidence discovered in other sources. Even as they stand the *Day Book* articles document attitudes toward female cross-dressing and close female–female relations.

According to the *Day Book*, Cora Anderson had been brought before Judge Page in Milwaukee and charged with "disorderly conduct" after Marie White, her long-time companion, had revealed her secret. Six months earlier, Anderson had left the home she shared with White, and on March 24, 1914, had actually married (before Justice of the Peace Edward J. Burke) the young Dorothy Klenowski. The two had

"Cora Anderson as Ralph Kerwinieo."   "Cora Anderson in Real Life."

Marie White and Dorothy Klenowski
"THE TWO WOMEN WHO WERE WIVES OF
MAN-WOMAN"

"Cora Anderson, from a photograph taken
when she was acting the man."

(Photos and captions from *The Day Book*, 1914.)

met at a dance hall. The story is given special interest by the fact that Anderson is said to have "a dark skin" and claimed to be an American Indian. South America is the birthplace listed on her recently discovered marriage certificate. Dorothy Klenowski is described as blond, and the marriage may have been interracial, as well as unisexual. After a hearing, Anderson was reportedly set free and commanded to wear women's clothes.

According to the *Day Book*, in 1901 Anderson and Marie White, who are said to have studied to be nurses at the Provident Hospital in Chicago, "found out how hard it was for a woman (especially a woman with a dark skin) to make an honest living, and decided to double up and form a home." They began their masquerade as Mr. and Mrs. Kirwinieo in Cleveland, Ohio, where "Ralph" worked as a bellboy at the Hollenden Hotel, then at the same job in Milwaukee, at the Plankington. Later "Ralph" obtained work with a manufacturer named Cutler. The stories emphasize that Anderson was guilty of no "immoral" conduct, and that her marriage to Klenowski was never consummated.[65] The need to specify such erotic detail indicates that by 1914 female transvestism was associated in the public mind with Lesbianism. Despite the denial of sexual relations, one may justifiably wonder if Cora Anderson's associations with women were actually as nonerotic as claimed. Interestingly throughout all the stories occur comments on the oppressed position of women in America of 1914. The last two *Day Book* stories allegedly present Cora Anderson's own written "impressions of the world and its male population." Anderson begins:

This world is made by man—for man alone.
I, who have lived as a man among men, realize it.
I, who have talked with men as a man, know it.
And whatever man may say about "the hand that rocks the cradle rules the world," they know that nothing rules men but their desires and there is no ruler in this world but sex. . . .
When I started out as a nurse I did so with the highest ideals. . . . But I found that steady work in my profession—like every woman's work in the world—depended upon the giving of myself. . . .
Two-thirds of the physicians I met made a nurse's virtue the price of their influence in getting her steady work.
Is it any wonder that I determined to become a member of this privileged sex, if possible?
This disguise also helped me to protect my chum as well as myself. She could stay in the home, and, believe me, as long as society, with its double code and double standards of morals, is as it is now, the only place for a woman is in the home.[66]

In her last "confession" Anderson adds:

Down deep in their hearts men interpret that old prophesy about inheriting the earth and the fullness thereof as for themselves alone. . . .
Women don't tell the things I am writing even to each other, but every young woman who is brought in contact with many men . . . knows that I speak the truth.

And, at that, man is not so much to blame as our wrong conditions, which I am glad to say are slowly getting better. In the future centuries it is probable that woman will be the owner of her own body and the custodian of her own soul. But until that time you can expect that the statutes of the [concerning] women will be all wrong. The well-cared-for woman is a parasite, and the woman who must work is a slave.

The woman's minimum wage will help, but it will not—cannot—effect a complete cure.

A girl or woman needs more money to live decently than a man. . . . Respectability is always costly. Her clothes cost MUCH more. I had a good illustration of this when I was compelled to buy a woman's hat when I was told by the court I must dress in woman's clothes.

The hat, a very modest black one trimmed with jet, cost $5, and it can only be worn for about six months, and then I'll probably have to hand out another five for something new.

The derby I was wearing when the police were told I was a woman cost me $3 and I had worn it two years.

With the present wage conditions there are thousands of young women who are living in a state of semi-starvation and they are always surrounded by the most terrible temptation.

Oh, I know that some of [the] greatest reformers insist that a girl's virtue is not affected by under-nourishment, disease and nervous collapse; but if these well housed, well fed, well dressed people were put in a dirty, ugly room, if their clothes did not protect them from the cold, if their stomachs were never filled, would not even the staunchest lose some of her self-respect when looking forward to an old age? It is only a matter of wonder to me that so many girls keep clean and decent through it all.

There should be a woman's minimum [wage] law in every state, but that is not all that is necessary to protect a woman and keep her fit for her highest office—motherhood. . . .

Some people in reading these articles may think I am very bitter against the men. This is not so. I am only bitter against conditions—conditions that have grown up in this man-made world. You cannot blame anyone who makes anything for making it to suit the maker. Power is always ruthless.

Every man, whether he is on a desert island or on the great white way, in his secret heart, echoes Robinson Crusoe's boast when he looks upon the world: "I am lord of all I survey. . . ."

Up to date, notwithstanding all our "reforms," our "votes for women," our "women in the industrial field," our "growing class of women with big brains and great hearts," it is still a man-made world—made by men for men. . . .

Do you blame me for wanting to be a man—free to live life as a man in a man-made world?

Do you blame me for hating to again resume a woman's clothes and just belong?[67]

♀ 1918–20: DR. J. ALLEN GILBERT;
"Homosexuality and Its Treatment"
"Society . . . is responsible for her existence as she is"

In the last Lesbian life in this series, the spare, unemotional language of Portland, Oregon, psychiatrist J. Allen Gilbert enhances the power of a report which reads with the interest of fiction. Here, in vivid detail, is the account of "H" (whom research has identified as Alberta Lucille Hart), said to have been born on October 4, 1892. She spent her youth in Albany, Oregon, graduating from Albany College in 1912, then attended Stanford University and medical school. Although Dr. Gilbert does not distinguish between his own writing and his subject's, he indicates that his article is based on a chronological "auto-biography" written by "H" herself. Gilbert's report begins:

The patient who served as the subject of the following history applied to me for psycho-analytic examination and treatment for a phobia which had been troubling her ever since childhood. For manifest reasons, her name is withheld, but will be designated as "H." Age, 26. Unusually high grade of intelligence, alert, ambitious and, all in all, decidedly of the higher grade of humanity, when judged by the customary standards.

The psychoanalysis, with reference to her phobia, was unusually successful in disclosing the underlying cause. H had no idea of revealing her homo-sexuality when she came for treatment for the phobia. Psychoanalysis revealed only too plainly that her phobia was really an old association which indelibly associated her phobia with a step-father, who was distasteful to an extreme.

The psychoanalysis revealed other side lights which were a thorough surprise to both H and myself. She proved to be a splendid subject for both the hypnoid and word-association method. A very few tests with each made it perfectly plain that there was some sexual affair at the bottom of her difficulties. I decided to put my suspicions at her rather bluntly and observe the effect. Consequently, I said, "Even our short investigation up to this point seems to indicate that the whole trouble is connected in some way with sex."

As chance would have it, she was not eyeing me at the time that I said it, though she usually looks one squarely in the eye during conversation. At the mention of the last word, "sex," like a flash her eyes met mine; there was a momentary hesitation with a quick reassertion of self-control; and, very adroitly the conversation was changed and carried along until she could leave without abruptness, and she closed the consultation.

Judging from her manner of leaving, I feared that I had offended her and suspected that there would be no further interviews on the subject. However, after the expiration of about two weeks, she came to the office again. She entered the consultation room with manifest uneasiness, and, as she started to talk, her eyes wandered here and there as if in search of something on which to rest. Hesitation and embarrassment were manifest. Finally, she met the issue squarely. She explained that since she last saw me she had had quite a struggle to bring herself to disclose a fact which was not known, except to a very few intimate friends, as will be seen from the following history. She made up her mind that this was her chance to meet the difficulty and correct it, if possible; at least, to do the best for the condition that could be done. She then recited in somewhat disconnected and fragmentary form the following facts, which she later wrote out as an autobiography in chronological order at my request. . . .[68]

Personal History.—H was born Oct. 4, 1892. Healthy infant of 10 pounds. Good health during infancy except for an attack (probably broncho-pneumonia) at 15 months, which resulted in complete recovery. After death of father in August, 1892, removed with mother to the farm home of maternal grandparents.

Very active child as soon as she was able to walk. Played with and teased small dog a great deal as a baby—would love the dog at one time, and later run after him with a stove poker to torment him. Not afraid of strangers after age 1½ years. Always would go to men before women. When away from home insisted on being with father rather than mother. First public appearance at 4 years, no fear at all. From first showed much initiative. When in house imitated whatever mother did, outside always played "horse and wagon." When mother would talk to her about father being dead and how they were left alone, she would always say that she would grow to be a man and take care of mother. Also insisted on sitting on the right side of the buggy when driving with mother, giving as a reason that she was the "man" of the family. Up to the age of four seemed to like dolls; these dolls were all girl dolls except one rag doll; always played hospital with them for patients or at taking them somewhere. Never played very much with dolls after this except in hospital game. Learned alphabet by herself from building blocks before age of 3. Between three and four, got so she could read Sunday School papers. Slept with mother till her second marriage. Even when very young, she always wanted pockets on her clothes [apparently a "masculine" desire]. About 5 or 6 years began to like women and "make up with" them sooner than men. Mother says she never noticed anything unusual about child except her activity and inclination to boys' games, up to age of 6 or 7. H's first clear memory is of standing at window looking across road while grandmother curled her hair. She always remembers a large volume of bible stories with lurid illustrations of which she was fond. Vague correlated memories of the trip to P—at age of 4—trip on train, large stores, street cars, new blue suit with gold braid, etc. Hazy memories of large dog, Bruce, of whom H was very fond, also of trips to barn and animals seen there. Very much interested in horses. Some time before age of 5, had some firecrackers which child enjoyed very much.

Mother married second time when child was 4½ years old. H disliked this man, and has unorganized memories of his courting her mother and of her own resentment at losing her mother's company. Remembers preparations for wedding, the ceremony, and the supper afterwards. Went to live in a small town with mother and stepfather. Lived beside a small canal and played with a boy of the same age who lived across canal. In a fit of anger one day, H threw a kitten down stairs and killed it. Disliked stepfather, would play rough noisy games with him, but absolutely refused to allow him to dress or undress her. Vague memories of going with parents to various social functions. Vivid memory of Xmas celebration with tree at

"H," or Alberta Lucille Hart, the subject of Gilbert's history,
at Albany College, Oregon, 1911.

LUCILLE HART. The remainder of the Junior class are justly proud of their "agitator." She is very active in the Student Body affairs and is a famous debator. We hesitate to mention it, but we fear that her dreams of blessed spinsterhood will be *only* dreams. She "appreciates" tennis and all athletic sports, but her use of English is "fierce;" this is the source of daily trial and concern to Miss Irvine's soul. In the words of ———— "With all her faults, we love her still."

(Photos and caption above from the Albany College yearbook, 1911.)

church, a Santa Claus, and presents. Also saw her first corpse at a funeral, but got no impression of horror.

When H was 5 years old, her maternal grandmother suffered a nervous breakdown, and Mr. and Mrs. B. with the child moved back to farm to care for her. They lived there until H was 10 years old. During early part of this period H showed some jealousy as before for stepfather; as child grew older, other interests crowded it more into the background. Severely ill for 3 or 4 months at age of 7 with whooping cough—recovery good and general health better afterward. Child taken regularly to church and Sunday school and became rather ultra-religious. Slept in same room with mother and stepfather, and used to wonder what they were doing when the love demonstrations became too audible. Grandmother's inordinate fear of chimney fires caused a dread of them in H's mind also—she used to pray to avoid them. H was not allowed to attend the country school but studied irregularly at home. Very dull in arithmetic and spelling, but loved to read. Spanish-American war stimulated child's interest in history and geography. Intensely interested in Civil War; for several years by aid of wooden guns, it was the favorite game. Grandfather read single tax, politics and current events to child who was much interested in Presidential campaign of 1896, and in its issues. Child had no fairy stories or literature of that type. H read a great deal, *e.g.,* Sunday-school magazines, novels, biographies, travels, adventure stories. She dramatized the books read and acted them out as far as possible. Volume of H. M. Stanley's African travels was a favorite; the pictures of naked savages and the stories of hunts and battles were enjoyed especially. Began to wonder about sexual matters. Read the "family Doctor Book" and looked up many words in dictionary. Read "Pilgrim's Progress" about this time; this resulted in the child's becoming afraid of the dark for the first time; she concealed this fear so well that the family never suspected it.

Was a very active child. Did a boy's work about the farm, milked the cows, learned to ride and drive horses. Very fond of grandfather, whom she followed everywhere. Liked to listen to the men who came to the place, discussing politics, agriculture, etc. Always played at barn or in tool house unless confined to the house by stormy weather, when "store" or "hospital" was the favorite game. Never played house or at being the mother of dolls. At the age of 7 H refused to play with dolls with small girl visitor unless as head and father of the family. Spent all money earned for pocket-knives which she lost rapidly. Often recited in public and won several prizes; enjoyed these appearances greatly. H was an obstinate independent child who resented anything that smacked of "bossing." Undemonstrative and shy about showing feelings—although very affectionate underneath. Family had a large number of cats. H was fond of these animals but had a streak of cruelty which made her often beat them. Forced by isolation to play almost wholly alone. Developed self-reliance, *e.g.,* having chopped a finger off with a double bitted ax, H dressed wound herself and said nothing about it to the family.

Always regarded herself as a boy, and thought she would be a boy if only the family would cut her hair and let her wear trousers, which she earnestly besought them to do. Always liked to wear boys' clothes and felt most natural in them— often wore overalls in summer. Had a marked aversion to undressing downstairs before the family; those present being mainly women. Enjoyed hearing maids talk of their admirers and social pleasures. Remembers distinctly the pleasure derived from reading love scenes in novels, which, later, she would always dramatize with self in rôle of hero opposite the girl then admired. Much given to day dreaming, which always concerned love affairs with herself in the masculine part and the achievement by herself of fame and fortune. Indifferent to her own clothes but enjoyed looking at shirts and collars, etc. Made collars and cuffs out of pasteboard which she wore in the effort to look as much like a man as possible. Being married as a man was a favorite imagination—visualized herself as kissing and making love to these women of her dreams. Exact nature of the sex act was not yet clear in her mind, all information thus far having been derived from reading, stolen glimpses of forms of men and women, and observation of animals about the farm. Was desperately "in love" with each of a series of maids employed about the house; wrote long effusions to them which she usually tore up, but which she now and then gave to the object of her affections. H would have been glad to kiss these girls and come in physical contact with them, but was always afraid to do so.

Dislike for stepfather persisted. His teasing child with a pop-gun and the association of him with her first hearing the report of a shot-gun produced a phobia for that sort of a noise which still persists at the age of 26. (This phobia was her reason for first consulting me. Psychoanalysis revealed its underlying cause with unusual promptness and success.) However, H was still fond of adventurous stories and listened eagerly to those told by men returned from eastern Oregon and the Klondike, wishing that she too might do those things.

Possessed a very disagreeable temper and when in a rage would throw herself upon the floor, hold her breath, froth at the mouth, kick, etc. This temper persisted with little attempt at control until H was in her 'teens.

From 10–12, H lived on a fruit farm with mother and stepfather. No illness of note. Still noisy and active. Picked prunes, milked, cared for horses, rode bicycle, played in very high and dangerous swing, etc. Hated all sorts of housework and would never do any unless compelled. Fond of farm animals, never afraid of them. Only went into town on rare occasions; preferred the farm. Still religiously inclined. Often seriously thoughtful when alone, and never lonely although alone a good deal. Careless about appearance; comfort and convenience came first. Dislike for stepfather still marked; very fond of mother, although undemonstrative.

Still read a great deal—travel, adventure and love stories. Especially fond of "Tom Brown's Schooldays" and "Tom Brown at Oxford." Still dramatized all she read; especially the love scenes. Not studious in school. Always fond of teachers. Inclined to idealize women teachers and visualize love scenes with them. Liked to talk to them and wait on them but never told them of her erotic feelings or made any attempt at physical contact. Crude drawing of intercourse circulated at school amused H greatly, though it horrified the girls. No interest in boys like other girls had. Was leader and champion of girls *vs.* boys when disagreements arose; almost choked to death one especially obnoxious lad in such a fight. Liked to play "Black Man" and "Crack the Whip," etc. Was noted for being rough in play. Was not afraid of the dark now and used to be sent home as escort with a maid who lived at some little distance from H's home. Greatly admired two rather fast young college men who visited at the home, and tried to ape them in manner and actions; attempted to make a cigarette of leaves and paper and smoke them. Liked older people better than children, men more than women. Still followed men about over the farm and helped with work of the farm.

Had a girl chum of same age who lived across the road, with whom she played almost all the time—but toward whom she never had any sexual inclination. By age 12 had a fairly complete knowledge of sexual reproduction. Conducted personal anatomical research by aid of chum, and studied "comparative anatomy" on available animals. Cut peep holes in the back wall of the boys' toilet at school to further the discoveries. Still slept in the same room as mother and stepfather—began to understand what went on. Periods of erotic excitement began and soon became frequent and noteworthy. Erotic day dreams about other girls of her own acquaintance with whom she fancied herself in love—herself always in the rôle of the male. Also had these dreams concerning purely imaginary women. Never spoke of these day dreams to anyone. Never made any attempt at physical contact with any of these girls, although the mental picture of it caused intense excitement. H's romancings always stopped short at marriage and did not go on to a home and children. By age of 12 was familiar with physical appearance of both sexes. When H heard mother and stepfather having intercourse at night, she vaguely resented such treatment of her mother and yet experienced an intangible, pleasant excitement at the thought of the relation so near at hand.

Two women dominated this period. (1) Nell P., who was about 16 at the time, fair, blue-eyed, very attractive, with beautiful auburn hair. The attraction for her persisted for several years even through infatuations for others. H visualized many love scenes with her, always ending in marriage. When Nell P. once spent some weeks in H's home, she delighted to wait on her and be near her. H would have liked to touch her and kiss her but was afraid. (2) H admired Olga P., her teacher, a little later during this period. She was about 21 or 22, tall, and dark. H often dreamed of being a boy-pupil of Miss P. and about 18 or 20 years old, so that in any time of physical indisposition of Miss P., H could relieve her or take her to the Doctor or, finding her with a sprained ankle, carry her home a la "Tom Brown at Oxford." Dreamed over many love scenes with this girl.

Family moved to town so that H could have better school advantages. Entered seventh grade. H was "green as a gourd," thin, poorly dressed, and unattractive. Seat-mate was tall, dark, good-looking and very scornful of H. D. B., who was small, slight and dark, was kind to H on this first day of school and so won her heart. Town children annoyed H by making fun of her clothes and calling her the living skeleton. Consequently, H shrank into her shell and began to have some interest in her work and study at home. She rapidly became the best pupil in her class. An elderly woman, Mrs. C., who lived in the same block was kind to H, would talk to her and hear her troubles. H used to read a great deal in Mrs. C's Encyclopoedia Britannica. This association lasted with H till she was 18 years old. A "gang" of girls played on a vacant hill near H's home and H wished greatly to join them but was not permitted to do so. Took a long walk with her mother on Sunday afternoons. The religious routine for the years from 12–18 included two church services. Sunday school and Christian Endeavor Society every Sunday, with family worship once or twice daily besides. H gradually came to know the girls of the neighborhood a little and play with them somewhat. Joined in outdoor games whenever possible, often sneaking away from home to do so. Some spasmodic interest in collecting butter-flies, bugs, beetles. Purchased a piccolo with her own earnings with which she made day and night hideous. Schoolmates ridiculed sun-bonnet that H was forced by her mother to wear until H wore fascinator or felt hat all summer rather than the despised bonnet. Mother tried to coddle her and dressed her too warmly—consequently she took cold easily. Always active and lively. Menstruation began at $12\frac{1}{2}$ years—irregular at first, but not painful. Thyroid enlargement came on about twelve years and persisted till 16 when it disappeared—never any symptoms except swelling. Upon entering the eighth grade, H met a teacher who had a profound influence over her till after she graduated from high school. Miss B. was small and dark with piercing black eyes. H admired her for her ability and respected her greatly but had no sexual inclination for her at all. Passed into high school with the highest grades in her class.

By this time H was deeply infatuated with D. B., who had affected her sexually from the first. However, H did not suspect the nature of the affection. She liked to be with D. B. as much as possible and was always quick in her defense either physically or verbally. H would spend hours alone with D. B. whenever it was possible, ensuing in such a state of nervous excitement that violent exercise came as a relief. Always wanted to love her and kiss her, but never dared to do so. Never embraced D. B. or spent a night with her in all the years they were together. At this time H began also to build air castles of life with D. B. as husband and wife. In these dreams H was a doctor and they had a beautiful home. H loved to visualize a whole evening in this home—e.g., return from the office, dinner with D. B., long evening spent at home love-making or out driving, followed by retiring together and intercourse. These dreams always left H in great excitement. She enjoyed visualizing the sexual act with herself always in the active rôle, and every possible variation of place and posture. Without instruction from any one, she began to masturbate at the climax of these dreams. H even derived savage pleasure from the thought of indignities offered D. B. by herself, e.g., inspection of H of her perineum, forcing her to urinate, etc., in her presence. But she was always overcome by love and pity afterward and in her dream would apologize to D. B. For some unknown reason, H's mother objected to her association with D. B. and so much of their companionship had to be clandestine in real life. This objection was transformed in H's dream life into an active persecution of D. B. as H's wife—against which H valiantly defended her. She thought D. B. the most attractive girl in the world and was plunged into despair when a small quarrel deprived her of D. B.'s company. In vacations H spent as many afternoons and evenings with D. B. as possible, reading to her, talking, or kodaking. Wrote stories and novelettes to read to D. B. in the hope of hearing her praises.

In high school H soon came into prominence. Took great interest in all student activities and had a great deal of responsibility in them. Was student body officer, executive committeeman, manager of H. S. paper, on debating team, etc. Wrote for school paper and in various essay contests with considerable success. The teacher, Miss B. was H's guide and adviser in these undertakings. H admired certain boys very much but never thought of them in a love relation. She played ball on evenings and Saturdays with the boys of the neighborhood until 18 years of age. Began to take interest in physical culture and to take cold baths and systematic exercise. This resulted in rapid physical improvement and increased strength.

H formed definite habit at this stage of dreaming aloud to herself after retiring concerning the romances that occupied her mind; these dreams were accompanied by definite erotic excitement. At 15, she became infatuated with a married woman living across the street who was about 25 years old, tall, fair, and attractive (Mrs. S.). She had just lost her six-year-old daughter and liked to talk to H of the child, religion, etc. For more than a year H spent as much time with her as possible, and wrote a "novel" with Mrs. S. as heroine opposite herself as hero. Never touched Mrs. S. or kissed her or had any physical intimacy whatever. A certain peculiar perfume used by Mrs. S. always appealed to H. H visualized a portion of the novel she wrote in her day dreams in bed every night; marked voluptuous excitement accompanied these dreams, also masturbation at times. After about a year, Mrs. S. moved away and H did not see her again for 10 years, although she always remembered her with fondness.

All this time, D. B., although somewhat in abeyance, retained her hold on H's affections and now reigned again supreme. Always kept up her school work and retained her prominence in school life. Cared but little for social pleasures and never went to parties where boys were present because she did not "get on" socially with them, did not like them, could not talk "small talk" like other girls, and knew the boys did not like her. Was but little interested in clothes and permitted her mother to select them, wearing whatever was provided. Showed absolutely no interest in household matters and absolutely refused to cook and sew. Intensely interested in athletics, especially football, in which she became an expert as to rules and records. Was an omnivorous reader of history, politics, current events, and novels. Enjoyed public speaking and debating greatly. When D. B. was forced to stay out of school by illness, H painfully made a written translation of a large part of Cæsar for her.

At 17 years, for some months H dreamed of courting and marrying a young teacher in the high school, Mrs. P. The most intimate details of love-life and home-life were visualized with intense erotic excitement. At times during all these episodes H would return to the old dreams of D. B. There was always the warmest affection between them which resulted in much time spent together and many gifts from H. At 17 H spent an afternoon alone with Nell P., now married, who was then pregnant for the first time. She found that the girl had all the old attraction for her but rather resented the fact of her pregnancy and the pain it would entail her.

An injury at age of 14 had resulted in dysmenorrhoea which was treated and relieved about this time. Amount of flow began to decrease slightly and gradually. Health good, abundant energy, never tired, masturbation never carried to excess. Began to show more interest in clothes but had marked preference for tailored things and clothes and ties.

D. B. still foremost in dream life. H spent much time with her and had for her a very real devotion. Was extremely jealous of boys and men who showed D. B. attentions. H went to a few parties during her last year in high school but was not very popular except as a clown for purposes of entertainment. Took great pleasure in showering gifts upon D. B., who was very poor. H was generous and extravagant in money matters. D. B. once told H that she would have married her had she been a man. Still H never embraced D. B. or spent a night with her or masturbated in her presence.

About this time, H met a distant cousin, Henry, who was attentive to her for some months. Enjoyed being with him and even did a certain amount of "spooning" though she did not enjoy the latter.

Twice during this period H met attractive girls with whom she was thrown for a few weeks and to whom she was definitely attracted. Separation occurred in both cases, however, and after a few months H thought but little of them.

During this period, H began to have some control over her temper so that paroxysms of earlier years gradually ceased. Family would not give her an allowance so she had only what money she could pick up herself. Began working in spare time and vacations for a photographer; developed a violent interest in this work and became quite successful as a scenic photographer, in which line she continued till the age of 22. When scarce of cash, would steal what was necessary from mother's or grandfather's pocketbooks; never liked this and was glad to quit it so soon as possible. Also took music lessons on the mandolin for four years and became moderately good performer. Was graduated from H. S. in June, 1908, with second rank in class.

H entered local college in 1908. Knew no one there and so studied and worked hard all the first year, going out but little until spring. Took usual college course. Discovered a decided liking for physics, economics, philosophy and allied subjects. Took second place in local oratorical contest. Came into father's estate in spring and went wild over the joy of spending money. Became popular because of the money-spending. H was aware all year of an attraction to a classmate, E. C., but had not had an opportunity to know her well. Acquaintance followed an accident in the spring. E. C. was short, dark, brown-eyed, attractive though not very pretty, and very popular with both boys and girls. During the last five weeks of this year, H was with her almost constantly, although nothing more than ordinary love-making and kisses passed between them. At the same time H was going about somewhat with E. C.'s brother, though she cared nothing for him. H worked all summer at photography except for a few weeks spent at E. C.'s home in the mountains. While they were apart, H wrote E. C. violent, daily love-letters. During H's second year in college the intimacy ripened and she spent much money on gifts for E. C., mainly candy, flowers and jewelry. Also took her driving or auto-mobiling several times weekly. They attended a great many public functions together. H never went to dances or to parties where she would have to be much with men. H spent at least one night a week with E. C. Their relationship progressed to more intimacy—there was much kissing and love-making, and also some actual sexual experiences, during which H had E. C. manipulate her. Mutual masturbation was resorted to at times. There was no thought of shame on either side. E. C. seemed devoid of passion but very anxious to give H pleasure. H possessed more sexual knowledge than the average woman, but knew nothing of psychopathy and did not realize that her own condition was abnormal; it always seemed perfectly right to her. H always played the rôle of lover toward E. C. During the first night they spent together (at the close of H's freshman year) neither slept at all; H made violent love to E. C. with constant kisses and caresses but no actual sexual advances; E. C. seemed half-stunned and did not respond very warmly but neither did she resist. After the eight weeks' separation during vacation H was wildly excited at seeing E. C. and could hardly wait for the privacy of a bedroom before embracing her; she spent the night thus, which only served to increase her passion. However, H did not masturbate in E. C.'s presence. During the second year, when they practiced mutual manipulation, H derived great pleasure from this contact with E. C., though the latter seemed to care very little for the manipulation of her own person. H also liked to caress and fondle E. C.'s body but this never seemed to gratify her greatly. It gradually came about that E. C. did most of the active manipulating till a certain stage of excitement was reached by H and involuntary spasmodic movements began on her part. H really loved E. C. very tenderly and very passionately. Saw her first light opera with E. C., which produced pronounced though inhibited sexual excitement.

H was a better student than E. C. and delighted to aid her in her work. She also furnished her money to live on and cared for her in every possible way. H was active in all student activities; leader of Women's Debating team, first associate on college team, college representative in State Oratorical contest, manager of College Annual, etc. Active in Y. W. C. A. also, although she had a private conviction that the Christian religion was a fraud. Was a leader in many strenuous college pranks. Active in sports, *e.g.*, tramping, tennis, hunting. In vacations did commercial photography in the mountains, camping and traveling with a pack-horse. Became more fastidious personally and in her dress, but still delighted in strictly tailored clothes. Now began to wear shirts, collars and ties—also to wear suits almost wholly, keeping the coat on when indoors. Also began to take week-end trips to a neighboring city where—always with E. C. in tow—she "took in" theaters, comic operas, vaudeville, cafes, etc.

During this time H had no other affairs. D. B. had become a stenographer and gradually they drifted apart, although still warm friends when they met. There was one young woman on the faculty for whom H entertained a sort of idealizing passion which never came to light in any way. For her other friends, H had a genuine unsentimental affection. Her relations with the men of the college were frank, friendly and unsentimental. H's family opposed the social life of the school, so that much "sneaking out" and deception were necessary for H. Clashes with mother were frequent as she resented H's growing independence and tried to dictate to her as a child. H never made her mother a confidante, and during this period began to have an actual physical aversion to her and regard her as an enemy.

In 1910 H decided to enter —— University. Since E. C.'s parents could not afford the expense, H took her with her at her own expense, since the separation would have been unbearable.

H entered premedical department at —— University; also took up work in economics and philosophy. Was active in Social Service Club, Physiology Club and Philosophy Club. Leader of Women's Glee and Mandolin Clubs and founded first Women's Debating Club. Was officer in women's dormitory. Refused Greek letter election because E. C. was not bidden by the same sorority. Did a lot of outside reading in economics, philosophy and psychology. Did considerable investigation of social service work in S——. Worked hard and received very high grades in studies. H became intimate with a small group of girls who represented almost every type and line of work; liked them all very much but had no love affairs with any of them. Devoted to E. C.—rarely went anywhere without her. E. C. went now and then to dances with men; H was jealous but still wanted her to have a good time and so permitted it. H enjoyed caring for E. C., paid her bills, bought her clothes, and showered her with gifts and luxuries. Went to the city almost every week-end, usually taking E. C. along. Became very fond of the theater, operas and concerts. Met people in S—— who frequented cafes, and with them began to go to late suppers, cabarets, and drink and smoke. Often went down in the tenderloin, dance-hall district. There H met a dancing girl who had not yet become a professional prostitute; this girl was big-hearted, young and attractive; she and H became quite intimate for a few months; H used to visit her in her apartment. There was a definite sexual attraction on H's part, also some experiences in tribadism. H also met a married woman about 8 years her senior who was small, dark, witty—a cripple from childhood; the warmest friendship sprang up between them, which still persists 7 years later; there never has been any trace of sexuality in it. First rift now came between E. C. and H. E. C. insisted upon H having a completely feminine wardrobe for formal occasions, to which H submitted with rather poor grace. Still insisted on extremely tailored things for all other times. Also E. C. did not approve of H's smoking, drinking and going to fast cafes. However, H persisted in doing these things, attempting to placate E. C. afterwards by handsome gifts. E. C. did not approve of H's extreme democracy and disregard of convention, e.g., scolded her severely when she carried lumber and materials for some shelves in their room out from the saw-mill and through the campus to the Hall. Consequently, the passion of this partnership subsided somewhat; until ordinary lovemaking and kissing constituted almost all of their relationship. The summer between these two years was uneventful for H, being spent partly in scenic photography and partly visiting the family. Last year in college much like the former one. Status remained almost unchanged between E. C. and H, except that H now met with financial reverses which worried her greatly. Seemed impossible for the "firm" to get along with less than $300–350 per month. H concealed the true situation from E. C. and went on living as lavishly as ever to her [sic]. The personal relationship was now well regulated; there was always kissing and loving and once or twice weekly sexual relationship, during which E. C. would manipulate H and give her orgasm and definite relief. It is doubtful whether E. C. ever had an orgasm.

When graduated, H was deeply in debt and greatly embarrassed financially. Abandoned plans for medical education temporarily. Spent the summer at commercial photography.

At the end of this period H was a strong, well-built young person of great vitality. She had done considerable rowing, motoring, and swimming, and had become an adept in camping in the open. Very fond of music and the theater. Showed rather a talent for comic "stunts" such as are used in glee clubs. Addicted to late hours, theaters, midnight suppers and revelry; drank and smoked freely also. Relations with men were still of friendly, frank, unsentimental type; liked to work with men but socially cared only for women.

Intercourse with man undertaken by H at 21 years out of pure curiosity. Man was normal and potent. H states that there was some slight physical pleasure but that the mental disgust was so great as to render the whole affair so obnoxious that she left unceremoniously at 3 A.M. This disgust was due, H considers, to the fact that she cared nothing for the man and that sexual relations without love have always seemed vulgar and loathesome to her.

In September, 1912, H obtained position as agent for library of Children's books with which she had fair success and at which she worked until February, 1913. H met W. H. about September 20, at which time she was greatly worried over her financial troubles and treatment by E. C. E. C. upbraided her severely for getting into debt, for drinking, smoking, and being unconventional, etc. This had led to marked coolness between them. An attempt by H at suicide was accidentally discovered and frustrated. H was at once attracted by W. H., who was 12 years older than she. W. H. was small, very fair, with soft brown eyes; she was very intelligent and well educated, came of a prominent Southern family, had been reared in wealth, and had traveled abroad extensively. The attraction was mutual. They spent as much time together as possible during the fall. W. H. had always been very popular with men and was engaged when she met H. This was soon broken off, however. Tacit lovemaking began in a few weeks. They made several trips during the fall to P—— where they went to shows and cafes, drank and celebrated generally. Finally, in December, 1912, while spending the night with W. H., quite without premeditation and hardly realizing what she did, H proposed that they plan to live together permanently and have a home; to this W. H. assented at once. H was stunned and miserable when daylight came to discover to what she had committed herself, as she felt bound in honor to E. C. However, she could see no way of escape from her dilemma. W. H. was intensely jealous of E. C. and now set about separating E. C. and H, which she accomplished during the winter and spring. H now wrote only occasionally to E. C. and these not love-letters. W. H. was also very jealous of H because she and her friends were younger than herself. H and W. H. spent much time together—together practically every night after February, when H secured work in town where W. H. was located. The sexual nature of the relation was recognized by both. The method used was tribadism and that in excess. However, this only seemed to have a good effect on H, who had boundless energy and strength and gained steadily in weight. W. H. assumed management of H's salary, so that H was able to pay many old bills. First, H was in a real-estate office, and then was accountant and general utility man in a wholesale and retail meat business. In her spare time she did typewriting, polished floors, waxed furniture, painted woodwork, built furniture and window-boxes, etc. With economy, gradually got most of the debts paid, but had no estate left for professional education. During spring, W. H. had guest I. C., an attractive red-haired girl who was a remarkable pianist. H thought her very sweet and attractive. During the summer, H spent every week-end with W. H. Also spent one week at E. C.'s home only to find all the old attraction gone. Had a furious reckoning with W. H. for this visit. H and W. H. spent about two weeks at shore in September, during which time they became reconciled and returned to former status. H borrowed some money through W. H. and entered medical school in the fall of 1913. Plan then was to establish a permanent home together after H was started on her profession. H found in this relationship that bodily contact and rhythmical motion sufficed for her own complete pleasure. W. H. enjoyed the sexual relation as much as did H. A night rarely passed without gratification. H's attitude was entirely masculine. Each felt that the inability to have a family of their own was the only drawback, so they planned to adopt a boy and a girl. There was an engagement ring to signalize the contract. Spent almost all their time together in lovemaking. H always attended to all business matters when they were together and both considered her position as absolutely masculine. Often the mere sight of W. H. or her belongings would produce intense excitement in H, who always ardently welcomed contact with W. H. Sometimes she would allow W. H. to assume initiative in lovemaking, but this always resulted in such intense excitement for H that she would seize W. H. and go on to the orgasm without waiting. W. H.'s attraction for H was almost purely sexual.

H was the only woman in her class and had a rather severe initiation. Much interested in work, studied hard, seldom went out. Forced to practice rigid economy. Lived with a woman several years older than she in an apartment; they were good friends but there never was a trace of sexuality in the friendship. At first was very lonely for W. H. and went to see her every two weeks. Then I. C. began to be very kind to H and they saw a good deal of each other. H always thought of I. C. as inferior mentally, but companionable and lovable. Liked to go to the theater with her and lounge before the open fire in the evenings in I. C.'s home while she played. H took to spending almost every Saturday evening and Sunday with I. C.; this lasted all winter and spring. Between them there was lovemaking and kissing, which I. C. seemed to enjoy greatly. This caused sexual excitement in H but there was never any actual relationship between them. H took the masculine rôle here so completely that I. C. often said going about with her was exactly like going with a man. H assumed the small gallantries and courtesies of men. H often dreamed after retiring of courting and marrying I. C.; also visualized actual intercourse with her as a male; this was accompanied by sexual excitement and masturbation. W. H. was extremely jealous of I. C.; wrote much about her to H; they had many "scenes" over it. H now began to resent W. H.'s holding her so strictly to account and distrusting her in general; her ardor for W. H. had now cooled markedly, except when in actual physical contact, when sexual excitement would always occur.

E. C. was in the same city as H in May, 1914. H had not written to her all winter, but when they met there was a complete confession of everything on H's part and a reconciliation. In the next month, W. H. and H completely broke off their relations; W. H. felt very bitter over this. H spent most of the summer working in the mountains, was with E. C. a good deal; everything seemed to have settled back to the old level between them with moderate sexual indulgence.

In spring of 1914, a male fellow-student made advances to H in a laboratory in the college. This was a complete surprise to H, who was very angry and departed hastily. Further advances were always repelled though sometimes pressed with considerable violence by [the] man. H is a friend of this man, likes many things about him, finds him mentally congenial, but is always disgusted when he attempts contact or familiarity. The man is bestial and outspoken in his passion. H is a friend of his wife and disapproves thoroughly of his neglect of his family. H does not believe that any relation between them now would be possible.

During second year in medical school, there was complete reunion between E. C. and H. The former was working in another locality, but H wrote ardent daily letters and visited her at Xmas. H saw a good deal of I. C. too, but there was nothing more serious than "spooning." In the spring of 1915 I. C. left the city; H has not seen her since and does not correspond with her. During the year H met also E. H. C., who was a tall, fair, stylish girl with plenty of energy and life and a decided fondness for men. They became warm friends and were closely associated for several months. There were a number of men who used to come to their apartment for "dutch feeds" and "beer parties"; these were always jolly, unsentimental affairs totally devoid of any illicit happenings. There was then no trace of the sexual that H was conscious of in her friendship for E. H. C. But, in September, 1915, H visited E. H. C. in her home and found herself extremely jealous of a young man who was paying marked attention to E. H. C. Since then H has felt a strong attraction to E. H. C. but has always inhibited it so there has never been more than a goodnight kiss between them. There exists between them a genuine friendship outside a sexual basis. On one occasion when they were discussing which of them should do a certain errand, E. H. C. said, "Oh, you go do it, you're more like a man than I am, anyhow."

H spent a part of the summer with E. C. and began to realize that they had drifted so far apart that she would never be able to feel for E. C. the same passionate love as formerly. However, she thought it best to go on in the same relation with her if possible. The sexual part of the relation had been largely superseded. To H's consternation, when she spent Thanksgiving and Xmas with E. C. she found her society dull and boresome and very little attraction left. Companionship was impossible because they had different ideals and viewpoints and standards. Many things about E. C. that had once been attractive H now thought childish and silly.

During the following school year, there were only two transient flirtations—one with a girl whom H treated professionally and another with a waitress. During May a visit with E. C. brought H almost to the verge of distraction; she could no longer care for the girl and yet E. C. loved her and begged for the old love in return. They parted after a week's visit in uncertainty. E. C. heartily disapproved of H's manner of dressing, her freedom with men, her disregard for conventionality, her drinking, swearing and smoking. During the ensuing summer H wrote to E. C. only a few times and these were not love letters.

In May, 1916, H met Mrs. D. at a boarding house where she had moved. Mrs. D. was a beautiful young woman, who was unhappily married. She had one child, a boy 2½ years old. Her husband had gone to another city to locate, and she was to join him later. H felt at once a very strong attraction for Mrs. D. but avoided her, fearing to get entangled with her. Forced to spend a night with her by circumstances, H succumbed to temptation and made violent love to the lady who—much to H's surprise—responded warmly. Afterward Mrs. D. confessed to attraction to H as soon as they met. One evening, before anything had passed between them H sat beside her on the couch with her hand on Mrs. D.'s ankle. H was at the time feeling an intense sympathy for her. Mrs. D. later said that she purposely remained on the couch for a long time so as not to disturb this contact, finding it enjoyable. After one week's ardent lovemaking—during which no sexual relations were established, although both were sexually excited—H left for a distant city for a summer's work. While there she wrote daily ardent love letters to Mrs. D., and received almost daily ones in return, in which the expressions of love were more restrained though unmistakable. While in this city H heard many lectures by Emma Goldman and became much interested in anarchism. In the fall, when H saw Mrs. D. again, she was more madly than ever in love. They spent four days together in the country early in the fall that were packed full of most ardent, tender love. Even yet, however, there had been no intercourse between them, though both became highly excited. During the autumn, they were much together, H's infatuation increasing all the while. An elderly wealthy man who had divorced his wife also became interested in Mrs. D. The most intense jealousy existed between H and this Mr. R. Mrs. D. at H's instigation set about securing a divorce now, and this was accomplished at Xmas. During October and November actual sexual relations were established between them; these occurrences were infrequent, about once in two weeks, and accompanied by the most passionate excitement and orgasms in each. They were prefaced by all the arts of lovemaking that H knew—kisses, caresses, fondling of the body, titillation, etc. The modus operandi was the traditional one between the sexes except that the hand was substituted for the membrum virile. During this excitement, Mrs. D. would call H "Dear boy" unconsciously. Mrs. D. professed to find complete gratification and much more enjoyment than with her husband. H proposed going to an eastern city together, where she could establish herself in practice and Mrs. D. could engage in some business until they were on their feet; after that she proposed to support Mrs. D. and her child and let her live her own life if she would see H several evenings a week and spend a night with her now and then; H did not ask to be allowed to live with Mrs. D. However, Mrs. D. decided she could not do this and "threw H overboard" shortly after receiving her divorce. It is noteworthy that B., Mrs. D.'s child, was very fond of H but that he was also jealous of her relations with his mother and noted the caresses and kisses that passed between them when he was about. During the spring Mrs. D. left the city and H saw her only once after their break until May, 1917. In the meantime Mrs. D. had become engaged to the elderly man, Mr. R., whom she wanted for his money.

H had been frantic all fall with the fear of losing Mrs D., neglected her work to be with her, spent all her money on taking her about to all functions possible. She also began to drink rather heavily. In January, after there was no hope of Mrs. D.'s doing as she wished, she began to drink more heavily than ever and became sunken in the depths of despair. She considered suicide very seriously, brooded incessantly over Mrs. D.'s faithlessness, neglected her work, came very near running away from everything to parts unknown. Vowed never to love another woman. Spent all her time in incessant activity; went about to all the shows, etc., and was never alone when she could help it. Moved into a residential hotel to be near some friends of hers. At this hotel, saw a very attractive young woman in whom she knew she could get interested; consequently, fearing another heartbreak, she avoided this girl sedulously. In May Mrs. D. returned to the city. H saw her a few times; by this time she had acquired enough self-control not to go off her head during the interviews. The physical charm of the woman was as potent as ever, but H found that she could not respect Mrs. D., who was planning to marry a man whom she did not love, for his money. Mrs. D. also confessed that she loved H very sincerely but did not have the "nerve" to face the criticism that would follow the union; she said her friends and associates had already ridiculed her severely on H's account. However, each time H saw her there was mutual lovemaking and, upon one occasion, sexual relations. When they parted in June, Mrs. D. wept and said her heart was broken. H has not seen her since.

H was graduated from medical school in June with the highest honors in her class. She at once took up hospital work. . . .

H had known for some time that she was "not like other girls," but her condition seemed so natural to herself and she was so strong and healthy that she gave the matter but little thought. However, her mode of dressing—men's coats, collars, ties, tailored hats, English shoes, etc.—made her conspicuous and the object of so much criticism and conjecture as to make her very uncomfortable. When her skirt was hidden in any way, she was often mistaken for a man.

During her second year in medical school, H found out through perusal of various professional books her true condition. At first she was plunged into self-condemnation and misery, but very soon came to take a saner view and face her problem as best she could. In the spring of 1917 she consulted a physician-psychiatrist who tried psychotherapy to no avail.

Side-lights

From early youth H has had the habit of saying such things as "The other fellows and I," "What could a fellow do?"

H has always enjoyed managing things, buying tickets, checking baggage, paying bills, tipping servants, carrying packages, opening doors, etc., for women she is with.

Ability to Pass for a Man

1. H was in the habit of wearing men's clothes to masquerade parties, etc., when in college. Always looked well and natural in them. Was once almost ejected from a girls' party when masking in a wig and dress-suit.

2. In the course of her photographic work in mountains H always wore men's clothes, and would often pass with many people for a boy. Had an actual fist fight with one old man who thought her a boy.

3. Wore men's clothes on a long motor trip in 1916. Was mistaken by many for a young man until the long hair came into evidence.

4. Mistaken for a man in Y. W. C. A. gymnasium and hastily ejected before error was discovered.

5. Photographs taken of her in her usual clothes in 1917 have been taken for those of a man by numerous people who did not know her. Her friends have commented on the masculinity of the pictures also.

6. A close friend in 1917 remarked to H on her boyishness of voice and action, saying that the combination of an adult mind with such youthfulness was most unusual in a woman 26 years old. The same lady resented H's way of looking at her extremely low-necked waist and said she would leave the table if H did not stop it.

7. H, upon seeing a crowd of men standing on a corner on a very windy day laughing at the women who were trying to cross the street, resented their amusement and yet had an impulse to do the same thing.

8. Waitress at H's hotel in 1917 said that she would fall in love with H if only she were a man.

9. H made a pleasure trip in 1917 with a young woman friend; she registered at the desk of a hotel as "Miss —— —— and Dr. H." There was considerable difficulty in persuading this functionary that everything was all right.

10. Many kodak pictures of H have been exhibited as those of a man without being questioned.

Treatment

As is well known, such a history renders the prognosis rather gloomy, so far as correction of the difficulty is concerned. However, we decided not to evade the

issue but avail ourselves of whatever means we could command. Suggestive therapeutics in the hypnoid state proved unavailing. Complete hypnosis was also resorted to without satisfactory results. It was impossible to induce the deeper stages
of hypnosis.

A number of things militated against the efficiency of suggestive therapeutics,
chief of which was her own mental attitude with reference to the female sex as a
whole. At the start, she entered with a will into the correction of the difficulty, if
such were possible. One day, when she came to the office, she said she had been
thinking the affair all over and would like to ask several questions before continuing treatment further. The main query in her mind was as to whether correction of
the difficulty as psychologically pathological would deprive her of her masculine
ambitions and tastes with a consequent substitution of the characteristics common
to the female. She had an utter loathing of the female type of mind. It can readily
be seen that no predictions could be offered or promises made to such a query.
Failing to get any definite assurance as to what would constitute success in the
treatment we were undertaking, her enthusiasm waned and she absolutely refused
to run any chances of losing her general masculine psychological characteristics in
exchange for any benefit that might be derived from a proper orientation of herself
as a female sociological unit in the social world of sex. It can be readily seen that it
was not only impossible to make any definite predictions as to what suggestive
therapeutics might accomplish, but the circumstances of the case threw one into a
somewhat confused state of mind when he tried to figure out just what results were
desirable and to justify the application of suggestive therapeutics in such a psychological muddle. I am free to confess that the case presented the most difficult
problems of any that ever entered my office. What to do for the girl or what to
advise her to do offered a riddle, the solution of which is still unsettled to a large
degree. With apologies for the treason to the underlying principles of psychotherapy involved in the mental attitude with which I undertook the treatment, "just as
I expected," suggestion was a failure.

After treatment, aimed at the pathological condition as such, proved itself unavailing, she came with the request that I help her prepare definitely and permanently for the rôle of the male in conformity with her real nature all these years.
This suggestion fairly bristled with difficulties.

Physical examination revealed predominance of the female type with deviations
sufficiently marked to attract attention. The whole tendency of dress was toward
male attire, retaining, however, the skirt as the trade mark of femininity. She was
repeatedly taken for a man when the skirt was hidden from view. Male hose
supporters, male socks, pajamas for night dress, tailored suits which would afford
numerous pockets, male type of hat, and even the cane were adopted, not as
artificial concessions to mere personal idiosyncrasy, but as natural components of
her normal make-up. The hips, while relatively larger than would conform to the
strictly male type, still fell short of the average female contour. The breasts, when
in standing position, presented nothing to suggest deviation from the female type,
except, possibly, an unusual flabbiness. However, on lying down, they flattened out
and practically disappeared. Palpation revealed complete absence of any glandular
tissue in the upper halves of the breasts. Patient says they are undergoing atrophy.
Vaginal examination revealed practically normal conditions in the pelvis. However, digital examination caused an unusual amount of pain and the process produced disgust as well as pain and distress. The clitoris was abnormally large and

patient stated that, at times of sexual excitement, it presents turgescence and throbbing to the point of distress. Menstruation was always painful and has been gradually decreasing in duration. Now lasts from two to three days.

After long consideration, she came to the office with her mind made up to adopt male attire in conformity with her true nature and try to face life under conditions that might make life bearable. Suicide had been repeatedly considered as an avenue of escape from her dilemma. Preliminary to the adoption of male attire she came to me with the request that I remove her uterus with two definite ends in view, viz: (1) to relieve her of the dysmenorrhoea and the inconvenience of dealing with the flow in male attire, and (2) to sterilize her. Inasmuch as pregnancy was a very remote possibility sterilization assumed less importance than the other item, though both ends were obtainable by the same process. Between the two operations of oöphorectomy and hysterectomy there is but one choice, for reasons too well known. She realized and urged the advisability of sterilization of herself as well as of any individual, afflicted as she was. Sensible to the extreme, she accepted her condition as one of abnormal inversion and was ready to face the affair on its merits. After long hesitancy and deliberation on my part, the only rational course seemed to be the adoption of the procedure, which was accordingly carried out. Hysterectomy was performed,[69] her hair was cut, a complete male outfit was secured and having previously identified herself with the red cross, she made her exit as a female and started as a male with a new hold on life and ambitions worthy of her high degree of intellectuality. Having an "M.D." degree she applied for and was appointed to a position in a hospital where she "made good" in every way until she was recognized by a former associate under the operation of that fanciful law of chance which threw one of her former intimate associates across her track. Then the hounding process began, which our modern social organization can carry on to such perfection and refinement against her own members.

Destructive criticism is always easy. Let him who finds in himself a tendency to criticize offer some constructive method of dealing with the problem on hand. He will not want for difficulties. The patient and I have done our best with it.

Addenda

The above history has been withheld to date in order to give opportunity for any further developments that might be essential to the completeness of the picture as a whole. The case has now settled down into what may be looked upon as a permanent adjustment to existing social conditions, so far as that is possible. Her natural male instincts carried her into associations with the female sex and positive attractions were unavoidable. Women of normal sex life felt themselves attracted by her because of her aggressive male characteristics. One, to whom she is now married, fell in love with her because of her psychological characteristics.

Legal aspects of the affair were taken up with the most competent legal advice obtainable. Being in time of war, the chance of the draft came up as a strong possibility. This was arranged to meet the requirements of the law and precautions were taken to afford relief in case of embarrassing complications. The illegal aspects of male attire in public were also met by legal authority and the final step of marriage was taken in order to complete the picture of normal life, so far as such is possible under the conditions detailed above. This feature of the affair was the most doubtful of the whole program and it received my protest, though I must confess that my protest was indefensible except on grounds of a prejudice and a habit of thinking begotten of long years of conformity to social dogmata, most of which are indefensible. At any rate, it was done—possibly for the best. There are certainly numerous and rational arguments in defense of the procedure.

In the interest of brevity, let it be stated that she is now married to a normal woman of high degree of mentality and decided physical attractions. All parties to the deal were fully cognizant of all the facts involved before entering into the contract and they now have a home apparently happy and peaceful based upon psychological attractions with such ministration to the physical as existing conditions can render possible.

She is now practicing her profession in a neighboring state in male garb, making good as a man and known only as a man. In fact, from a sociological and psychological standpoint she is a man.

If society will but let her alone, she will fill her niche in the world and leave it better for her bravery in meeting the issue on the merits of the case as best she knew. Instead of criticism and hounding, she needs and deserves the respect and sympathy of society, which is responsible for her existence as she is.[70]

While a detail or two have apparently been altered to disguise the identity of "H," the basic authenticity of this narrative is assured by recent investigation, based on the information supplied in Dr. Gilbert's article. Research has established that "H" was Lucille Hart, a junior at Albany College in Oregon, and an editor of the college yearbook of 1911, which includes several photos of her, a brief description (reproduced), and lists her as a debater in a local oratorical contest. Alberta Lucille Hart, from Albany, Oregon, is listed in the Stanford University register for 1911–12; she is registered in a physiology class, and at a dormitory. In 1916 she is listed as a summer-school student from Portland in "Actinography [a branch of biochemistry dealing with muscle contraction] Clinical Medicine," at the Stanford School of Medicine. Stanford records confirm that Alberta Lucille Hart's birthday was October 4, the same month and day as that of "H"; the year listed is not, however, 1892, the year of "H's" birth, as given by Dr. Gilbert. Despite this last discrepancy, the evidence clearly establishes the identity of "H" beyond all reasonable doubt.[71]

Dr. Gilbert's account raises many issues. First, despite the confusion of Dr. Gilbert and "H" herself about her sexual nature, "H" is clearly a Lesbian, a woman-loving woman. Dr. Gilbert's final statement that "H" is now married to a "normal" woman would be laughable if one did not know the difficult preceding history. The marriage involves two women, one of whom has had a hysterectomy and passes for a male—two women living and loving together, two Lesbians.

Despite Gilbert's comment about an "abnormally" large clitoris (the same value judgment made about Lucy Ann Lobdell in the early 1880s), Gilbert's physical examination is not reported to have revealed other than a perfectly formed, if not "average" female. It is also clear from Gilbert's report that "H" does not identify herself as of the male gender. She does not wish to possess a male body; she wants to play "the role of a male," not be male. It is not the male's penis she covets, but the male's socially given power. Her decision as a young girl to be the "man" in the family expressed her wish to care for and take care of her own mother, another

EDITORIAL STAFF
Eva Cushman, Frances Chase, Buena V. Bicknell, Lucille Hart,
George Ihida, Grover C. Birtchet
(From the Albany College yearbook, 1911.)

woman. In order to do this she "regarded herself as a boy"—but only in the sense of "wanting pockets on her clothes" (a poignant sign of "masculinity" mentioned twice by Dr. Gilbert), in wearing short hair and trousers, in playing boys' games, in reading adventure stories and fantasizing herself as the romantic, dashing hero, in hating housework and "small talk," in being inquisitive about the world, an active, "obstinate, independent child," in having "masculine ambitions," in loving and wanting to be loved by another female.

Clearly, too, "H" could only perceive her own situation in the world in heterosexual terms, according to the traditional heterosexual model of male-female husband-wife relations. She found no alternative, no way of transcending this socially dominant model.

According to her report, "H" had "no thought of shame" about her first active Lesbian relations. Shame came later, she says; it was learned—from such sources as medical textbooks in which she read about her "true condition." It is noteworthy that this shame only came to her as an adult; so prevalent and widely accepted today is the idea that all important feelings are acquired and set in childhood. It is noteworthy, too, that if her analysis with Dr. Gilbert did not itself create her feeling of shame about Lesbianism, it clearly intensified it. This story represents one more example of the pernicious treatment of Gay people by the medical profession. "H" entered therapy to cure a specific, minor phobia; she ended by having a hysterectomy.

It is precisely the late-created shame "H" felt, and her analysis itself, that motivated her request to be sterilized. Since there was obviously no liklihood of "H" becoming pregnant, her desire to be sterilized clearly expresses her need to neutralize guilt about Lesbianism, to legitimize for herself her socially unsanctioned relations. Despite her active Lesbian career, "H" apparently still needed to come to terms with feelings about the impropriety of two women having sex. Although her hysterectomy was in a sense voluntary, the social pressures to which she was subjected suggest that in another and just as true sense it was socially coerced. Notable also is the complicity here of an even rather benign, sympathetic, undogmatic psychiatrist in his patient's own strange move to be sterilized—a move that may be characterized as *justification by punishment*, a psychic ploy Gay people have sometimes in the past adopted to legitimize themselves. There is a macabre irony in this not unkind doctor's falling readily into the sadistic role offered him by his patient.

The story of "H" illustrates only too well one extreme to which an intelligent, aspiring Lesbian in early twentieth-century America might be driven by her own and her doctor's acceptance of society's condemnation of women-loving women.[72]

IV

NATIVE AMERICANS/ GAY AMERICANS 1528-1976

Introduction

These documents on male and female homosexuality among American Indians present 448 years of testimony from a wide variety of observers: military men, missionaries, explorers, trappers, traders, settlers, and later medical doctors, anthropologists, and homosexual emancipationists; in a few rare instances the voices of Gay Indians are heard. The sources quoted tell as much, and often more, about the commentator's sentiments about Native homosexuality than they do about its actual historical forms. The commentator is briefly characterized in the introduction to each document, to suggest what particular group interest may lie behind each observation. Documents are presented here chronologically, according to the date of the event referred to, or, alternatively, if such date was unknown, according to the time during which the writer traveled or lived among the people observed, or according to the document's date of composition or publication. The intention of this arrangement is to suggest a sense of the sequence and change in types of commentators and commentary, to set both in historical perspective. This arrangement separates material referring to the same tribe and geographic location in favor of a general historical overview of the topic. This chronological presentation has the effect of focusing as much on the observer as on the subject of observation, a historical perspective which, for example, locates anthropologists as simply one among the groups in the sequence of outside observers of Native American life. In this perspective the particular value judgments of anthropologists emerge almost as clearly as the more overt judgments of those early observers who made no pretense to objectivity.

Documents not originally in English are translated, but, when possible, the foreign word referring to homosexuality is included. The materials gathered here are limited arbitrarily to those referring to tribes living in the area that became the mainland United States. A variety of American Indian homosexualities are documented. That most commonly described involves reversal of the customary sex roles—cross-dressing, cross-working, cross-speaking—as well as homosexual activity. This Native American homosexual is the often-mentioned "berdache," originally the French name for these Indians. The Native words for such people varied with different tribal languages. The focus of many of the following documents exclusively upon the berdache phenomenon may well have less to do with its incidence than with the fascination of heterosexual white observers and their lack of knowledge of less immediately obvious types of Native homosexuality. If, for example, uninformed anthropologists today made field trips to New York's Greenwich Village, among the native Gay population they would surely first notice the most obvious "queens." Those outsiders who observed Native American customs may well have been guilty of exactly this error of perception. Suspicions as to this skewing of accounts is aroused by the failure, in virtually every report of a berdache, to discuss the homosexuality of the berdache's non-cross-dressing sexual partners. Tribal attitudes toward and the character of this nonberdache partner are passed over in silence.

Although many of the earliest accounts quoted refer only to cross-dressing, later, more informed and detailed observations suggest that homosexuality was often another aspect of the phenomenon in question. A few of these early reports suggest that a male berdache was available sexually to women as well as men, although details are not pursued; some references may describe a heterosexual or bisexual transvestite; some berdaches were probably exclusively homosexual. Other documents associate the berdache with a lack of heterosexual potency. Some reports connect cross-dressing and sex role reversal with alleged physical anomalies, although these reports are often confused: early observers repeatedly use the term *hermaphrodite* to refer to an individual who would today be identified as a homosexual transvestite; later documents indicate that physical malformations were not actually indicated. Interestingly, the physical characteristics, occupations, and activities of the "effeminate" male homosexual of Native societies do not correspond with the stereotype of the "effeminate" male in white, Anglo-Saxon society; the Native male berdache is often described as big, husky, strong, a fast runner, and a fighter. These documents concerning the Native berdache do raise interesting questions about the relation between sex role reversal (especially cross-dressing and cross-working) and homosexuality.

Some documents here hint at the existence of homosexual relations between two apparently "normal" males. These reports refer to "special friendships" and a "blood brotherhood"—especially intimate relations between two males, often of a lifelong character, and often described so as to emphasize their sensual, deeply emotional aspect. Other documents suggest the existence of homosexual relations between adults and youths. A number of reports suggest that homosexuals often performed religious and ceremonial functions among their people; the exact character and meaning of these roles is often not detailed. Tribal attitudes toward various types of homosexuals apparently varied, although these documents suggest that, before the inroads of Christianity, homosexuals generally occupied an institutionalized, important, and often respected position within many Native groups.

The fact that relatively few documents refer to Native American Lesbianism seems no true indication of the prevalence of Lesbianism in Indian society but is more likely an index of what whites were ready or willing to hear about, investigate, and discuss. A new interest and research in Native Lesbianism will probably uncover additional sources. That such sources may exist is suggested by early references to Lesbianism among South American natives. Larco Hoyle's survey of a large collection of the erotic Peruvian pottery (dating to A.D. 100–1200) that survived the systematic destruction by missionaries shows that 1 percent depicts Lesbian relations. Francisco Guerra's research into the sexual life of South and Central American natives uncovered other early references to Lesbianism. Guerra quotes Bishop Las Casas (1542) on the punishment for Lesbianism among the Aztecs:

> If one woman committed sin with another they died strangled in the same way [as those brothers who committed incest with their sisters].

A Mexican confessionary written in 1565 by a Franciscan friar refers to Lesbianism, as well as sodomy between men. Another confessionary, written in 1599, also refers to Lesbianism. Gregorio Garcia, writing in 1604, says

> it was the law that those who committed the nefarious sin should die. The Indians of New Spain kept this law, without missing one point, and they executed it with great severity; they had the same penalty with the woman who laid down with another, because it was also against nature.

A confessionary of 1634, and one of 1697, ask about Lesbian relations. A work on Mexican native history (1698) says that the laws of pre-Conquest Mexicans declared that "the man who dressed like a woman, or the woman who dressed like a man were hanged. . . ."[1] Documents mentioning the existence of Lesbianism among Native Americans appear to increase in more recent years as sexual relations between women became a more mentionable subject in heterosexual white society.

Most of the documents here suggest that Native societies were highly polarized along sexual lines; a strict sexual division of labor seems to have been common, although not universal. The same documents also suggest the generally subordinate position of women in Native cultures. Knowledge of the relative status and condition of women and men and the tribal division of labor and roles is essential for understanding the character of homosexuality among Native Americans. In studying these documents, the extent of white, Christian influence on Native cultures is also an important question to keep in mind, as are questions concerning the structure and character of Native families and the nature of mores, especially those relating to all aspects of sexuality. Those wishing to understand any particular form of Native homosexuality in depth will find it necessary to study the original sources of the documents excerpted.

Since the end of the nineteenth century, pioneering researchers have attempted to bring together information and documentary accounts and to sum up what is known about homosexuality among Native Americans. Hubert Howe Bancroft's five volumes on *The Native Races of the Pacific States of North America* (1875) is an amazing early collection of footnoted documentary sources which does not shy away from the explicit discussion of sodomy. Edward Westermarck's two-volume historical analysis of *The Origin and Development of Moral Ideas* (1908) contains a chapter on "Homosexual Love" with numerous primary references to Native American homosexuality. One product of the early German homosexual emancipation movement was Ferdinand Karsch-Haack's research and writing on homosexuality among native peoples, collected in 1911 in *Das gleichgeschlechtliche Leben der Naturvölker* [The same-sex life of primitive peoples], still the major collection of source materials on the subject. Also in 1911, pioneering English homosexual emancipationist Edward Carpenter began to write on homosexuality among native peoples, later collecting these articles in his *Intermediate Types Among Primitive Folk; A Study in Social Evolution* (1914).

In 1935, W. W. Hill published "The Status of the Hermaphrodite and Transvestite in Navaho Culture," an early American anthropological journal article attempting to sum up information about homosexuality within one tribe. In 1940, well-known anthropologist A. L. Kroeber, in a psychology journal essay, declared in a footnote that "the time is ready for a synthetic work" on homosexuality and transvestism in Native American culture. No major comprehensive work has yet appeared. In 1950, Don W. Dragoo, a graduate student in anthropology at Indiana University prepared a paper on "Transvestites in North American Tribes." In 1951, Clellan S. Ford and Frank A. Beach published their often-quoted, influential book, *Patterns of Sexual Behavior*, with an important chapter summarizing the information on and attitudes toward "Homosexual Behavior" in seventy-six societies, including a number of American Indian tribes. In 1965, anthropologist Marvin K. Opler summarized and discussed earlier work on "Anthropological and Cross-Cultural Aspects of Homosexuality." The following year, anthropologist David Sonenschein wrote on "Homosexuality as a Subject of Anthropological Inquiry," an important "plea for research," and a discussion of methodologies. In 1968, anthropologist Sue-Ellen Jacobs published "Berdache: A Brief Review of the Literature." In 1971, a few references to homosexuality among Natives of what is now the United States were included in Dr. Francisco Guerra's documentary anthology, *The Pre-Columbian Mind; A Study into the Aberrant Nature of Sexual Drives, Drugs Affecting Behavior, and the Attitudes Towards Life and Death.* . . . In 1975, Donald A. Forgey discussed "The Institution of the Berdache Among the North American Plains Indians." Forgey comments in passing that "a thorough, comprehensive investigation" of the berdache among Native Americans is still lacking. The present historical survey attempts to show that documentary materials for a large-scale study do exist.

The intention here is simply to present in one place and in historical order some of the major and varied types of historical source materials referring to Native American homosexuality. Years of additional research, study, and analysis will be required to come to a clear, reliable understanding of these documents, to realize their hidden meanings and implications, to more fully understand the place of homosexuality in Native American life and history.

The existence of homosexuality among the people who originally inhabited the United States will no doubt hold a certain special fascination for those Lesbians and Gay men who are today beginning to repossess the national and world history of their people—part of their struggle for social change and to win control over their own lives. One fact that emerges clearly here is that the Christianization of Native Americans and the colonial appropriation of the continent by white, Western "civilization" included the attempt by the conquerors to eliminate various traditional forms of Indian homosexuality—as part of their attempt to destroy that Native culture which might fuel resistance—a form of cultural genocide involving both Native Americans and Gay people. Today, the recovery of the history of Native American homosexuality is a task in which both Gay and Native peoples have a common interest.

1528–36: ALVAR NÚÑEZ CABEZA DE VACA;
"I saw a devilish thing"

Spanish explorer Cabeza de Vaca's report of his five-year captivity among the Indians of Florida, from 1528 to 1533, states:

During the time that I was thus among these people I saw a devilish thing, and it is that I saw one man married to another, and these are impotent, effeminate men [*amarionados*] and they go about dressed as women, and do women's tasks, and shoot with a bow, and carry great burdens, . . . and they are huskier than the other men, and taller. . . .[2]

1540: HERNANDO DE ALARCÓN;
"Men in womens apparell"

The earliest Gay-related data for any part of California is found in Captain Alarcón's brief observation, dating to 1540, of the natives of that area.

There were among these Indians three or foure men in womens apparell.[3]

1562–67: RENÉ GOULAINE DE LAUDONNIÈRE;
"Many hermaphrodites"

Captain Laudonnière's account of four French expeditions into Florida during the years 1562–67 observes:

There are in all this country many hermaphrodites, which take all the greatest paine and beare the victuals when they goe to warre.[4]

1564: JACQUES LE MOYNE DE MORGUES;
"Hermaphrodites"

In 1564, Le Moyne traveled to Florida as an artist with the French expedition commanded by Laudonnière. About twenty years later, in London, Le Moyne wrote a travel memoir accompanied by sketches. These pictures and descriptions are now known only by the engravings and translations made of them by Theodore de Bry, first published in 1591.

"Employments of the hermaphrodites."

Le Moyne's text reads:

Hermaphrodites, partaking of the nature of each sex, are quite common in these parts, and are considered odious by the Indians themselves, who, however, employ them, as they are strong, instead of beasts of burden. When a chief goes out to war, the hermaphrodites carry the provisions. When any Indian is dead of wounds or disease, two hermaphrodites take a couple of stout poles, fasten cross-pieces on them, and attach to these a mat woven of reeds. On this they place the deceased. . . . Then [the hermaphrodites] take thongs of hide, three or four fingers broad, fasten the ends to the ends of the poles, and put the middle over their heads, which are remarkably hard; and in this manner they carry the deceased to the place of burial. Persons having contagious diseases are also carried to places appointed for the purpose, on the shoulders of the hermaphrodites, who supply [those ill] with food, and take care of them, until they get quite well again.[5]

♀ 1593–1613: FRANCISCO DE PAREJA;
Confessional

The Spanish-born Pareja went to Florida as a Franciscan missionary to the Indians in 1595. He served at San Juan del Puerto (the area of modern Jacksonville) until 1616. Pareja was by report a man of great sanctity and incredible zeal, with expert knowledge of Timucuan, the language of the Timucua natives, who

286

lived on the Atlantic coast in the area between modern Georgia and Florida. Pareja's *Confessionario* (Confessional) details those questions a priest should ask his penitents, translating these questions from Spanish to Timucuan. As the editors of Pareja's *Confessionario* say, he probably asked about that behavior he had observed, or had good cause to think existed; his questions suggest that among the Timucuans "both female and male homosexuality occurred, with some special emphasis on boyish pederasty."

Pareja's work also contains an early reference to Native American Lesbianism. Under questions "For Married and Single Women" Pareja includes: "*Mujer con mujer, has tenido acto, como si fuera hombre?*" Literally translated this reads: "Woman with woman, have you acted as if you were a man?" Pareja's recent editors translate this as: "By chance, have you had intercourse as if you were a man?"

Pareja's questions continue:

For Sodomites

Have you had intercourse with another man?
Or have you gone around trying out or making fun in order to do that?

For Boys That Are in the Custom of Doing This

Has someone been investigating you from behind?
Did you consummate the act?[6]

1673–77: JACQUES MARQUETTE;
"They pass for Manitous . . . or persons of Consequence"

Jesuit Father Marquette's account of his first voyage down the Mississippi in 1673–77 declares:

I know not through what superstition some Ilinois, as well as some Nadouessi, while still young, assume the garb of women, and retain it throughout their lives. There is some mystery in this, For they never marry and glory in demeaning themselves to do everything that the women do. They go to war, however, but can use only clubs, and not bows and arrows, which are the weapons proper to men. They are present at all the juggleries, and at the solemn dances in honor of the Calumet; at these they sing, but must not dance. They are summoned to the Councils, and nothing can be decided without their advice. Finally, through their profession of leading an Extraordinary life, they pass for Manitous,—That is to say, for Spirits,—or persons of Consequence.[7]

1702: PIERRE LIETTE;
"The sin of sodomy prevails"

The "Memoir of Pierre Liette on the Illinois Country," written in 1702 at the end of a four-year sojourn at Chicago, reports of the Miamis:

The sin of sodomy prevails more among them than in any other nation, although there are four women to one man. It is true that the women, although debauched, retain some moderation, which prevents the young men from satisfying their passions as much as they would like. There are men who are bred for this purpose from their childhood. When they are seen frequently picking up the spade, the spindle, the axe, but making no use of the bow and arrows, as all the other small boys do, they are girt with a piece of leather or cloth which envelops them from the belt to the knees, a thing all the women wear. Their hair is allowed to grow and is fastened behind the head. They also wear a little skin like a shoulder strap passing under the arm on one side and tied over the shoulder on the other. They are tattooed on their cheeks like the women and also on the breast and the arms, and they imitate their accent, which is different from that of the men. They omit nothing that can make them like the women. There are men sufficiently embruted to have dealings with them on the same footing. The women and girls who prostitute themselves to these wretches are dissolute creatures.[8]

1711–17: JOSEPH FRANÇOIS LAFITAU;
"Men Who Dress as Women" and "Special Friendships"

Lafitau's *Customs of the American Savages, Compared with the Customs of Ancient Times,* is based on his own experience as a Jesuit missionary in French Canada (1711–17), and on his readings in the literature which had appeared previously on native peoples of both hemispheres, as well as on comparative material drawn from ancient Greek and Latin sources. Unlike many other merely descriptive chronicles, Lafitau's important work includes analysis, interpretation, and historical comparisons.

In a section on "Men Who Dress as Women" among the Native peoples of the Americas, Lafitau writes:

If there were women with manly courage who prided themselves upon the profession of warrior, which seems to become men alone, there were also men cowardly enough to live as women. Among the Illinois, among the Sioux, in Louisiana, in Florida, and in Yucatan, there are young men who adopt the garb of women, and keep it all their lives. They believe they are honored by debasing themselves to all of women's occupations; they never marry, they participate in all religious ceremonies, and this profession of an extraordinary life causes them to be regarded as people of a higher order, and above the common man. Would these not be the same peoples as the Asiatic adorers of Cybele, or the Orientals of whom Julius Fermicus speaks, who consecrated priests dressed as women to the Goddess of Phrygia or to Venus Urania, who had an effeminate appearance, painted their faces, and hid their true sex under garments borrowed from the sex whom they wished to counterfeit?

The view of these men dressed as women surprised the Europeans who first encountered them in America; as they did not at first guess the motives for this species of metamorphosis they were convinced that these were people in whom the two sexes were confounded. To be sure our old Relations called them no other than hermaphrodites. Although the religious spirit which made them embrace this state causes them to be regarded as extraordinary human beings, they have never-the-less really fallen, among the savages themselves, into the contempt into which the priests of Venus Urania and Cybele were held of old. Whether they effectively attracted this contempt upon themselves by subjecting themselves to shameful passions, or because the ignorance of Europeans as to the causes of their condition caused shameful suspicions to fall upon them, these suspicions so entered into their [the Europeans'] minds that they imagined the most disadvantageous things that could be imagined. This imagination so kindled the zeal of Vasco Núñez de Balboa, the Spanish captain who first discovered the South Sea, that he put a large number of them to death by setting wild dogs upon them, which those of his nation had used to destroy a large part of the Indians.[9]

In another section of the same work Lafitau writes on *Des Amitiés particulières,* or "special friendships," among the Natives of America. This section includes a long comparison with homosexuality among the Greeks; the excerpt here focuses on Lafitau's references to the Native Americans.

The *Athenrosera*, or special friendships among young men, which are instituted in almost the same manner from one end of America to the other, are one of the most interesting sides of their customs, since they entail a most curious chapter of Antiquity, and serve to reveal to us what was practiced in that regard, particularly in the Republic of the Cretans and in that of the Spartans. . . .

These bonds of friendship, among the Savages of North America, admit no suspicion of apparent vice, albeit there is, or may be, much real vice. They are highly ancient in their origin, highly marked in the constancy of their practice, consecrated, if I dare say as much, in the union which they create, whose bonds are as close as those of blood and nature, and cannot be dissolved, unless one of the two makes himself unworthy of the union by acts of cowardice that would dishonor his friend, and is compelled to renounce his alliance, as several Mission-aries have told me that they have seen examples. The parents are the first to encourage them and to respect their rights. . . .

These friendships are bought by presents which the friend makes to whomever he wishes to have as a friend; they are maintained by mutual tokens of benevo-lence; they become Companions in hunting, in war, and in fortune; they have a right to food and lodging in each other's cabin. The most affectionate compliment that the friend can make to his friend is to give him the name of Friend: last of all, these friendships age with them, and they are oftentimes so well cemented that a heroism is encountered such as that between Orestes and Pylades. . . .

I have also read in one of our Relations° that among some prisoners who had been brought to Onnontagué, there were two so powerfully united in friendship that when one had been condemned to the stake, and the other spared, the one who had been spared was so grieved that his companion had not been pardoned as well that he could not hide his sorrow, and his threats and lamentations compelled those who had adopted him to deliver him to execution: both of them were then put to death, and the Missionary who tells the story observes that he was quite happy to administer Baptism to them, and to see them die in a condition of great piety, by which the Iroquois were no less charmed than they had been by the zeal of the Missionary himself.

In one of our Missions, the Missionaries suppressed attachments of this kind on account of the abuses which they feared would result from them. . . .[10]

1721: PIERRE FRANÇOIS XAVIER DE CHARLEVOIX;
"Effeminacy and lewdness"

Charlevoix's *Journal of a Voyage to North-America.* . . . contains a letter this Jesuit explorer and historian wrote in July 1721 concerning the tribes of the Seven Nations, especially the Iroquois, the Illinois, and others of the Louisiana area.

It must be confessed that effeminacy and lewdness were carried to the greatest excess in those parts; men were seen to wear the dress of women without a blush, and to debase themselves so as to perform those occupations which are most peculiar to the sex, from whence followed a corruption of morals past all expression; it was pretended that this custom came from I know not what principle of religion; but this religion had like many others taken its birth in the depravation of the heart, or if the custom I speak of had its beginning in the spirit, it has ended in the flesh; these effeminate persons [*Efféminés*] never marry, and abandon themselves to the most infamous passions, for which cause they are held in the most sovereign contempt.[11]

c. 1750: GEORG HEINRICH LOSKIEL;
"Unnatural sins"

Loskiel's *History of the Mission of the United Brethren among the Indians in North America*, published in German in 1789 and in English in 1794, is based upon detailed reports by two missionaries of the Moravian Church (a German Protestant denomination) who arrived in the American colonies in 1742 and 1750. These missionaries were active among the Indians of Pennsylvania, New York, and North Carolina. In terms that, in German, refer clearly to homosexuality, Loskiel reports:

In relations between the sexes, the Indians are modest and decent. Publicly, at least, one seldom observes lascivious, immoral, or indecent behavior among them. It cannot be denied that in this respect they are far superior to the majority of peoples. But this does not mean that they are free of lewdness [*Unzucht*], and unnatural sins [*unnatürliche Sünden*] are not uncommon among them.[12]

1751–62: JEAN BERNARD BOSSU;
"Most of them are addicted to sodomy"

Bossu's work in French, translated as *Travels in the Interior of North America, 1751–1762*, speaks of sodomy and "perversion" among the Choctaws.

The people of this nation are generally of a brutal and coarse nature. You can talk to them as much as you want about the mysteries of our religion; they always reply that all of that is beyond their comprehension. They are morally quite perverted, and most of them are addicted to sodomy. These corrupt men, who have long hair and wear short skirts like women, are held in great contempt.[13]

1775–76: PEDRO FONT;
"Sodomites, dedicated to nefarious practices"

The diary of Jesuit Father Font, written during his second journey to California, with the expedition of Juan Bautista de Anza, 1775–76, says of the California natives:

Among the women I saw some men dressed like women, with whom they go about regularly, never joining the men. The commander called them *amaricados*, perhaps because the Yumas call effeminate men *maricas*. I asked who these men were, and they replied that they were not men like the rest, and for this reason they went around covered this way. From this I inferred they must be hermaphrodites, but from what I learned later I understood that they were sodomites, dedicated to nefarious practices. From all the foregoing I conclude that in this matter of incontinence there will be much to do when the Holy Faith and the Christian religion are established among them.[14]

1777: FRANCISCO PALÓU;
"The abominable vice will be eliminated"

Palóu's biography of Junípero Serra and of the nine Franciscan missions founded in California was published in Mexico, where Palóu himself was a missionary. In a chapter on the "Founding of the Santa Clara Mission" (in 1777), Palóu relates a discovery that took place in the mission at St. Antonio, California.

Two laymen arrived at the house of a convert, one of them in the usual clothing, but the other dressed like a woman and called by them a *Joya* [Jewel] (since that is the name they are given in their native tongue). Once the priests had been alerted, the head of the Mission went to the house with a sentry and a soldier. The couple was caught in the act of committing the nefarious sin. They were duly punished for this crime, but not with the severity it properly deserved. When they were rebuked for such an enormous crime, the layman answered that the *Joya* was his wife! They were not seen again in the Mission or its surroundings after this reprimand. Nor did these disreputable people appear in the other missions, although many *Joyas* can be seen in the area of Canal de Santa Barbara; around there, almost every village has two or three [of them]. But we place our trust in God and expect that these accursed people will disappear with the growth of the missions. The abominable vice will be eliminated to the extent that the Catholic faith and all the other virtues are firmly implanted there, for the glory of God and the benefit of those poor ignorants.[15]

1801: ALEXANDER HENRY and
DAVID THOMPSON;
"His father . . . cannot persuade him to act like a man"

The manuscript journals of Henry and Thompson describe their *Exploration and Adventure among the Indians on the Red, Saskatcheuan, Missouri, and Columbia Rivers.* An entry of January 2, 1801, is titled by its 1897 editor "Swiftness of the One-Eyed Sodomist."

Berdash, a son of Sucrie [Sucre, Sweet, or Wiscoup], arrived from the Assiniboine, where he had been with a young man to carry tobacco concerning the war. This person is a curious compound between a man and a woman. He is a man both as to members and courage, but pretends to be womanish, and dresses as such. His walk and mode of sitting, his manners, occupations, and language are those of a woman. His father, who is a great chief amongst the Saulteurs, cannot persuade him to act like a man. About a month ago, in a drinking match, he got into a quarrel and had one of his eyes knocked out with a club. He is very troublesome when drunk. He is very fleet, and a few years ago was reckoned the best runner among the Saulteurs. . . .[16]

1804–10: NICHOLAS BIDDLE;
"Men Dressed in Squars Clothes"

The *Original Journals of the Lewis and Clark Expeditions* . . . contains diary notes by Nicholas Biddle which report of the Mandan Indians that on Saturday, December 22, 1804,

a number of Squars & men Dressed in Squars Clothes Came with Corn to Sell to the men for little things. . . .[17]

Notes by Biddle, dating to April 1810, among the letters and documents of the Lewis and Clark expedition, report:

Among Minitarees if a boy shows any symptoms of effeminacy or girlish inclinations he is put among the girls, dressed in their way, brought up with them, & sometimes married to men. They submit as women to all the duties of a wife. I have seen them—the French call them Birdashes.[18]

♀ c. 1811: CLAUDE E. SCHAEFFER;
The Kutenai Female Berdache

A rare, detailed history of a female berdache among the Kutenai Indians of western Montana and neighboring parts of Idaho and British Columbia describes her variously as a courier, guide, prophet, warrior, and peace mediator. Modern Kutenai verbal tradition refers to her birth and childhood. The earliest written reference to the Kutenai berdache dates to June 1811 and is found in Gabriel Franchere's account of events at Fort Astoria, in the Oregon area, where this woman appeared, dressed as a male and accompanied by a "wife." In 1966, Claude E. Schaeffer published a lengthy history of the Kutenai female berdache, based on all available written sources, and on traditional Kutenai oral legend collected among this tribe between 1935 and 1965. The following abridged version of Schaeffer's work focuses on that material of major interest for the study of Lesbianism.[19] Schaeffer writes:

There was general agreement among my informants that the Kutenai berdache was born and raised in the Lower Kutenai country. . . .

. . . Informants denied that she was an intersexed individual, word of which would have been impossible to conceal from her people. Her baby name, according to Mary White Pete, was *qúqunok ṗatke*, 'one standing (lodge) pole woman'. As a young woman she was said to have been quite large and heavy boned. She wished to marry at this time, but because of her unusual size none of the young men were attracted to her.

The Kutenai girl reached maturity at the time employees of the North West Company were first entering the Kutenai country from the east. Eneas Abraham [a Native informant] said that a party of fur traders arrived in the Lower Kutenai region, and upon their departure she accompanied them. . . .

We are fortunate in having information about the marriage of the Kutenai woman from David Thompson [who in 1811 refers to her as] . . .

> the Woman who three years ago was the wife of Boisverd, a Canadian, and my servant; her conduct was then so loose that I had to request him to send her away to her friends. . . .[20]

From the above it would seem that the Kutenai woman had married Thompson's servant, a Canadian named Boisverd in 1808. . . .

After more than a year's absence Madame Boisverd returned to her own people. She had a strange tale to relate. According to her story, her husband had operated upon her and thereby transformed her into a man. She told her relatives, 'I'm a man now. We Indians did not believe the white people possessed such power from the supernaturals. I can tell you that they do, greater power than we have. They changed my sex while I was with them. No Indian is able to do that.' Thereafter she changed her name to *Kaúxuma núpika*, 'Gone to the spirits'. And whenever she encountered anyone she performed a little dance as an indication of her sexual transformation. Soon she began to claim great spiritual power. Her people were unable to understand these strange happenings and some believed she was bereft of her senses.

Following Madame Boisverd's return, she began to assume the habits and pursuits of the opposite sex. Men's shirts, leggings and breech cloths were now substituted for the women's dresses she had previously worn. She seems to have had little or no difficulty adapting herself to the new garments, since she evaded detection in such garb at Fort Astoria for an entire month. She also began to carry a gun as well as bow and arrow. Now she wished to marry a person of her own sex and is said to have approached several young unmarried women in succession, all of whom refused her. . . .

The rumor now got around that in revenge Madame Boisverd wished to bring about the death of those girls who refused her through use of her recently-acquired supernatural power. As a result people came to fear and avoid her. So she was obliged to seek the company of divorcees and widows.

Finally Madame Boisverd found one woman from the area along the Kootenay River, southeast of modern Nelson, B. C., who had been abandoned by her husband and was willing to live with her. The two were now to be seen constantly together. The curious attempted to learn things from the consort but the latter only laughed at their efforts. A rumor ran through the community that Madame Boisverd had fashioned an artificial phallus of leather for use in marital intimacy but the godemiche, these inquisitive individuals surmised, failed to deceive her 'wife'. Soon the news circulated about the camp that Madame Boisverd was becoming jealous of her companion. The former accused her friend of having an affair openly with a man and began to beat her.

About this time or shortly after—it is difficult to know the exact order in which some of these events take place—the Kutenai berdache, as we may now speak of her, started to gamble with a group of men at Duck Creek and lost by wager her bow, quiver of arrows, and bark canoe. Her 'wife' became angry at this loss of property and . . . left her 'husband' and returned to her own people. Thereafter, the Kutenai berdache is said to have changed wives frequently.

The berdache, in keeping with her newly assumed status, now began to manifest an interest in raiding and warfare. . . . Her assumption of a warrior's role . . . represents a considerable achievement, greater perhaps than that of women warriors among the Plains tribes. . . . The masculine ideal among the Kutenai, certainly the Lower Kutenai, was . . . the skilled hunter, capable of providing game and fish for his family in a forested region of rather limited resources. . . .

The reports of modern Kutenai disagree as to the details of the berdache's first war excursion [which failed to come upon any enemy horses and decided to return home.]

Upon coming to a stream, the raiders would [undress and] wade across together but the berdache always hung back so as to cross alone. . . . Her brother, puzzled by this behavior, determined to learn the truth about her.

At the next stream, a shallow one, he decided to ford and then return to observe his sister. . . . he turned and ran back, coming upon his sister in the middle of the stream. She was nude, and he verified his suspicion that her sex had not been changed. She, in turn, saw him and crouched down in the water, pretending that her foot was caught between two rocks. She realized that her brother was aware of her true condition. . . .

. . . Starting out next morning, the raiders reached present Elmira on Lake Pend d'Oreille. . . . All tried to cheer the leader, who was down-hearted over an unsuccessful trip. He replied, that of course they would not be permitted to give the Victory Song upon reaching camp, but that anyone who wished could select a new name. None of the men accepted the offer. The berdache spoke up, however. . . . she had selected a new name for herself. Explaining that her injury had forced her to sit down in the stream and that her brother had witnessed it, she declared that now she wished to be called Sitting-in-the-water-Grizzly (*qánqon kámek klaúla*). The warriors cheered her. Not approving of her action, her brother remarked to his friends that he would call her *Qánqon*, a derisive term taken from her self-conferred name. Stating that he would never use her new name, a meaningless term for her, he threatened to expose her.

[The berdache] now took a new female companion from the present Creston area for her wife. It was not long before she again evinced jealousy of her consort's behavior. One night the two began to quarrel inside their mat lodge. The berdache began to beat her wife. Nearby was located the dwelling of her brother. Hearing their loud voices, he came out and began to call, 'Qánqon! Qánqon! Qánqon!' The quarrel ceased at once. The brother continued, 'You are hurting your woman friend. You have hurt other friends in the same way. You know that I saw you standing naked in the stream, where you tried to conceal your sex. That's why I never call you by your new name but only *Qánqon*.' Thus the brother carried out his threat in the hearing of the entire camp. People thereafter spoke of her as *Qánqon*. . . .

The earliest documentary reference to the Kutenai woman appears in Gabriel Franchere's account . . . of events at Fort Astoria. It was June, 1811. . . .

> On the 15th some natives from up the river Columbia, brought us two strange Indians, a man and a woman. . . .[21]

Alexander Ross's comment on the same event runs as follows:

> Among the many visitors who every now and then presented themselves, were two strange Indians, in the character of man and wife, from the vicinity of the Rocky Mountains. . . .
>
> The husband, named Ko-come-ne-pe-ca, was a very shrewd and intelligent Indian, who addressed us in the Algonquin and gave us much information respecting the interior of the country. . . .[22]

. . . *Qánqon* maintained her disguise at Astoria until David Thompson arrived a month later. . . .

For July 15, the day of David Thompson's arrival at Astoria, Franchere . . . writes:

> He [Thompson] recognized the two Indians, who had brought the letter addressed to Mr. J. Stuart, and told us that they were two women, one of whom had dressed herself up as a man, to travel with more security. . . .[23]

[On July 22, a party including David Thompson and the two Indians departed down the river for the interior.]

In her journey downstream, it will be noted that *Qánqon* predicted the imminent end of the Indians and their land in a devastating plague and through the agency of two enormous supernaturals. Thompson . . . continues:

> Having proceeded half a mile up a Rapid, we came to four men who were waiting for us . . . the four men addressed me, saying, when you passed going down to the sea, we were all strong in life, and your return to us finds us strong to live, but what is this we hear, casting their eyes with a stern look on her [the "man woman"], is it true that the white men . . . have brought with them the Small Pox to destroy us; and two men of enormous size, who are on their way to us, overturning the Ground, and burying all the Villages and Lodges underneath it; is this true, and are we all soon to die. I told them not [to] be alarmed, for the white Men who had arrived had not brought the Small Pox, and the Natives were strong to live, and every evening were dancing and singing. . . . At all which they appeared much pleased, and thanked me for the good words I had told them; but I saw plainly that if the man woman had not been sitting behind us they would have plunged a dagger in her. . . .[24]

Thompson . . . [on] August 2nd, had this final entry:

> It is with some regret we proceed past several parties of the Natives, they are all glad to smoke with us, and eager to learn the news; . . . the story of the Woman that carried a Bow and Arrows and had a Wife, was to them a romance to which they paid great attention and my interpreter took pleasure in relating it. . . .[25]

Upon his arrival at the Okanagon, [Alexander] Ross [a member of the expedition] . . . concludes his remarks with the following statement. It will be noted that [in Ross's version] *Qánqon*'s predictions to the Indians deal not with death and destruction but with a great outpouring of gifts to be made them by the White people.

> In the account of our voyage I have been silent as to the two strangers who cast up at Astoria, and accompanied us from thence; but have noticed already, that instead of being man and wife, as they at first gave us to understand, they were in fact both women—and bold adventurous amazons they were. In accompanying us, they sometimes shot ahead, and at other times loitered behind, as suited their plans. The stories they gave out among the nonsuspecting and credulous natives as they passed, were well calculated to astonish as well as to attract attention. Brought up, as they had been, near the whites—who rove, trap, and trade in the wilderness—they were capable of practicing all the arts of well-instructed cheats; and to effect their purpose the better, they showed the Indians an old letter, which they made a handle of, and told them that they had been sent by the great white chief, with a message to apprize the natives in general that gifts, consisting of goods and implements of all kinds, were forthwith to be poured in upon them; that the great white chief knew their wants, and was just about to supply them with everything their hearts could desire; that the whites had hitherto cheated the Indians, by selling goods in place of making presents to them, as directed by the great white chief. . . .
>
> These stories, so agreeable to the Indian ear, were circulated far and wide; and not only received as truths, but procured so much celebrity for the two cheats, that they were the objects of attraction at every village and camp on the way; nor could we, for a long time, account for the cordial reception they met with from the natives, who loaded them for their good tidings with the most valuable articles they possessed—horses, robes, leather, and higuas; so that, on our arrival at Oakinacken, they had no less than twenty-six horses, many of them loaded with the fruits of their false reports.[26]

Up the Okanagon River the two Kutenai Indians with their richly-laden pack train of 26 horses guide David Stuart, and two men to the Shuswap region. . . . We lose sight of them at the Thompson River. . . .

[John Franklin relates that the Kutenai berdache, whom he says the Natives called "Manlike Woman," acquired the reputation of having supernatural powers and making prophecies subversive to the ruling class of white traders. She reportedly predicted to the Indians]

> that there would soon be a complete change in the face of the country; fertility and plenty would succeed to the present sterility; and that the present race of white inhabitants, unless they became subservient to the Indians, would be removed and their place be filled by other traders, who would supply their wants in every possible manner. The poor deluded wretches, imagining that they would hasten this happy change by destroying their present traders, of whose submission there was no prospect, threatened to extirpate them. . . .[27]

. . . for the next 14 years we have no word of the Kutenai berdache in the historical literature, while traditional sources are silent about her as well. In 1825, however a Kutenai woman wearing men's clothing is mentioned in the journal of

John Work, Hudson's Bay Company trader at Flathead Post. Bundosh, as she is known here, has been satisfactorily established as the same Kutenai woman mentioned earlier by the Astorians and by David Thompson. . . .[28] The entries referring to her follow:

> Monday 12—The Kootenay chief with about a dozen of his men arrived. . . . A woman who goes in mens clothes and is a leading character among them was also tipsy with ¾ of a glass of mixed liquor and became noisy. . . .
> Tuesday 13 . . . A present was also given to Bundosh, a woman who assumes a masculine character and is of some note among them, she acted as interpreter for us, she speaks F. Head well. . . .[29]

It was probably during these years that another largely masculine activity—shamanism—was evidenced by *Qánqon*, one known to us only through the accounts of modern Kutenai. Chief Paul claimed that she had treated and cured his father, Chief David, of illness. . . .

A period of 12 years elapses before our next historical reference to the Kutenai berdache. It is contained in the journal of W. H. Gray, the missionary, who was journeying to the states in 1837, travelling with Francis Ermatinger, the Hudson's Bay Company trader to the Flathead. A party of Flathead was virtually surrounded by Blackfoot and Bowdash, as she is known here, had gone back and forth trying to mediate between them. On her last trip she deceives the Blackfoot while the Flathead, as she knew, were making their escape to Fort Hall and the fur rendevous.

[Gray's journal reports:]

> June 13th . . . We have been told that the Black Feet have killed the Kootenie woman, or Bowdash, as she is called. She has hitherto been permitted to go from all the camps, without molestation, to carry any message given her to either camp.[30]

The modern Kutenai are unaware of *Qánqon*'s role as intermediary in Flathead-Blackfoot peace negotiations, although Eneas Abraham stated that 'she got mixed up with two groups fighting one another.' Instead they assign the cause of her death to a Blackfoot Indian ambush. . . . [Francis Simon, a Native informant, relates:]

> It had taken several shots to seriously wound her. Then while she was held in a seated position by several warriors, others slashed her chest and abdomen with their knives. Immediately afterwards the cuts thus made were said to have healed themselves. This occurred several times but she gave no more war cries. One of the warriors then opened up her chest to get at her heart and cut off the lower portion. This last wound she was unable to heal. It was thus *Qánqon* died. No wild animals or birds disturbed her body, which is said to have gradually decayed.

1819–20: EDWIN JAMES and T. SAY;
"Sodomy is . . . not uncommonly committed"

In his *Account of an Expedition from Pittsburgh to the Rocky Mountains in the Years 1819 and '20 . . .* Edwin James quotes a member of the expedition, T. Say, "who had spent some time among the Konzas," near Omaha, on the Platte and Konzas Rivers.

"Sodomy is a crime not uncommonly committed; many of the subjects of it are publicly known, and do not appear to be despised, or to excite disgust; one of them was pointed out to us; he had submitted himself to it, in consequence of a vow he had made to his mystic medicine, which obliged him to change his dress for that of a squaw, to do their work, and to permit his hair to grow."

Later James himself adds of the Omahas:

Among their vices may be enumerated sodomy, onanism, & various other unclean and disgusting practices. What is related of the Illinois by Hennepin,* may, with equal truth, be applied to the Omawhaws. But to the honour of humanity, it may be remarked that those abominable traits of character are not generally conspicuous among them.[31]

1823: WILLIAM H. KEATING;
"Numerous stories of hermaphrodites"

Keating's *Narrative of an Expedition to the Source of St. Péter's River . . . in the Year 1823, . . . under the Command of Stephen H. Long . . .* reports the religious beliefs of a Native named Wennebea.

He believed the sun to be the residence of a male Deity, who looks placidly upon the earth. . . . The moon, on the contrary, he held to be inhabited by an adverse female Deity, whose delight is to cross man in all his pursuits. If during sleep, this Deity should present herself to them in their dreams, the Indians consider it as enjoined upon them by duty, to become *cinaedi*; they ever after assume the female garb. It is not impossible that this may have been the source of the numerous stories of hermaphrodites, related by all the old writers on America.[32]

1826: THOMAS A. McKENNEY;
"What they call a *man-woman*"

In a letter of August 4, 1826, published in his *Sketches of a Tour to The Lakes, of the Character and Customs of the Chippeway Indians, . . .* McKenney writes:

My Dear * * *

I had hoped to have seen one of these anomalies, which are sometimes found among the Chippeways, and I believe among other tribes in the West. It is what they call a *man-woman*. I have it from undoubted authority, that such do exist. This singular being, either from a dream, or from an impression derived from some other source, considers that he is bound to impose upon himself, as the only means of appeasing his manito, all the exterior of a woman; and undergo all the drudgery which the men exact from the squaws. So completely do they succeed, and even to the *voice*, as to make it impossible to distinguish them from the women. They contract their walk; turn in their toes, perform all the menial offices of the lodge; wear, of course, petticoats, and breast coverings, and even go through the ceremony of marriage! Nothing can induce these men-women to put off these imitative garbs, and assume again the pursuits and manly exercises of the chiefs. It is like taking the black veil. Once committed thus far, they are considered as beyond redemption, (unless their vow shall be limited, as is sometimes the case; as for example, until they take an enemy alive) and live, and die, confirmed in the belief that they are acting the part which the dream, or some other impression, pointed out to them as indispensable.[33]

c. 1828: ISAAC McCOY;
"His presence was so disgusting"

McCoy, author of a *History of the Baptist Indian Missions*, visited the Osage in about 1828, and writes:

Among some of the uncultivated tribes to the north, there are instances, though rare, of men assuming the office of women. They put on women's apparel, and mingle with them, and affect the manner and appearance of females as much as possible, and continue this folly during life. While I was at the Osage villages, one of these wretches was pointed out to me. He appeared to be about twenty-five years of age, was tall, lean, and of a ghost-like appearance. His presence was so disgusting, and the circumstances of the case so unpleasant, that I spoke not a word to him, and made few inquiries about him. He was said to be in a declining state of health, and certainly his death would not have been lamented.[34]

1830: JOHN TANNER;
"One of those who make themselves women"

As a boy, in about 1790, Tanner was captured by Indians in Kentucky. Adopting Native customs, he lived most of his life in the Northern woods. He was for some years employed as an interpreter at Sault Ste. Marie; in 1836, he shot and killed James L. Schoolcraft and fled to the wilderness, where he died about 1847. In 1830, Tanner published an autobiographical narrative which was widely read.

Some time in the course of this winter, there came to our lodge one of the sons of the celebrated Ojibbeway chief, called Wesh-ko-bug, (the sweet,) who lived at Leech Lake. This man was one of those who make themselves women, and are called women by the Indians. There are several of this sort among most, if not all the Indian tribes; they are commonly called A-go-kwa, a word which is expressive of their condition. This creature, called Ozaw-wen-dib, (the yellow head,) was now near fifty years old, and had lived with many husbands. I do not know whether she had seen me, or only heard of me, but she soon let me know she had come a long distance to see me, and with the hope of living with me. She often offered herself to me, but not being discouraged with one refusal, she repeated her disgusting advances until I was almost driven from the lodge. Old Net-no-kwa was perfectly well acquainted with her character and only laughed at the embarrass-ment and shame which I evinced whenever she addressed me. She seemed rather to countenance and encourage the Yellow Head in remaining at our lodge. The latter was expert in the various employments of the women, to which all her time was given. At length, despairing of success in her addresses to me, or being too much pinched by hunger, which was commonly felt in our lodge, she disappeared, and was absent three or four days. I began to hope I should be no more troubled with her, when she came back loaded with dry meat. She stated that she had found the band of Wa-ge-to-tah-gun, and that that chief had sent by her an invitation for us to join him. . . . I was glad enough of this invitation, and started immediately. At the first encampment, as I was doing something by the fire, I heard the A-go-kwa at no great distance in the woods, whistling to call me. Approaching the place, I found she had her eyes on game of some kind, and presently I discovered a moose. I shot him twice in succession, and twice he fell at the report of the gun; but it is probable I shot too high, for at last he escaped. The old woman reproved me severely for this, telling me she feared I should never be a good hunter. But before night the next day, we arrived at Wa-ge-to-te's lodge, where we ate as much as we wished. Here also, I found myself relieved from the persecutions of the A-go-kwa, which had become intolerable. Wa-ge-tote, who had two wives, married her. This introduction of a new inmate into the family of Wa-ge-tote, occasioned some laughter, and produced some ludicrous incidents, but was attended with less un-easiness and quarreling than would have been the bringing in of a new wife of the female sex.[35]

1832–39: GEORGE CATLIN;
"Dance to the Berdashe"

Artist George Catlin's *Letters and Notes on the Customs and Conditions of the North American Indians*, written during his eight years of travel among the Native Americans (1832–39), contains engravings from Catlin's original paintings, ac-companied by his comments on the scenes depicted. Of the Sioux, Sacs, and Foxes' "Dance to the Berdashe" Catlin writes:

Dance to the Berdashe . . . is a very funny and amusing scene, which happens once a year or oftener, as they choose, when a feast is given to the "Berdashe," as

George Catlin, "Dance to the Berdashe."

he is called in French, (or *I-coo-coo-a*, in their own language), who is a man dressed in woman's clothes, as he is known to be all his life, and for extraordinary privileges which he is known to possess, he is driven to the most servile and degrading duties, which he is not allowed to escape; and he being the only one of the tribe submitting to this disgraceful degradation, is looked upon as *medicine* and sacred, and a feast is given to him annually; and initiatory to it, a dance by those few young men of the tribe who can, as in the sketch, dance forward and publicly make their boast (without the denial of the Berdashe), that Ahg-whi-ee-choos-cum-me hi-anh-dwax-cumme-ke on-daig-nun-ehow ixt. Che-ne-a'hkt ah-pex-ian I-coo-coo-a wi-an-gurotst whow-itcht-ne-axt-ar-rah, ne-axt-gun-he h'dow-k's dow-on-daig-o-ewhicht non-go-was-see.

Such, and such only, are allowed to enter the dance and partake of the feast, and as there are but a precious few in the tribe who have legitimately gained this singular privilege, or willing to make a public confession of it, it will be seen that the society consists of quite a limited number of "odd fellows."

This is one of the most unaccountable and disgusting customs, that I have ever met in the Indian country, and so far as I have been able to learn, belongs only to the Sioux and Sacs and Foxes—perhaps it is practiced by other tribes, but I did not meet with it; and for further account of it I am constrained to refer the reader to the country where it is practiced, and where I should wish that it might be extinguished before it be more fully recorded.[36]

♀   1841: PIERRE-JEAN DE SMET;

"A woman . . . who once dreamed that she was a man"

The Jesuit Father de Smet's "Personal Observations Made during Many Thousand Miles of Travel" among the "Wild Tribes of the North American Indians," in 1841, discusses the Natives' beliefs in regard to dreams.

302

Among the Crows I saw a warrior who, in consequence of a dream, had put on women's clothing and subjected himself to all the labors and duties of that condition, so humiliating to an Indian. On the other hand there is a woman among the Snakes who once dreamed that she was a man and killed animals in the chase. Upon waking, she assumed her husband's garments, took his gun and went out to test the virtue of her dream; she killed a deer. Since that time she has not left off man's costume; she goes on the hunts and on the war-path; by some fearless actions she has obtained the title of "brave" and the privilege of admittance to the council of the chiefs. Nothing less than another dream could make her return to her gown.[37]

1846: FRANCIS PARKMAN;
"Romantic . . . friendships"

Parkman's famous narrative of his 1846 journey on the Oregon Trail refers to a "romantic" friendship between two male Sioux, Rabbit and Hail-Storm, one of the rare allusions to male–male intimacy not involving cross-dressing; Parkman's own descriptions of Hail-Storm stress his sensual beauty.

Parkman first sees Hail-Storm among a group of "mountain men" in the home of a white man, about seven miles from Fort Laramie.

The most striking figure of the group was a naked Indian boy of sixteen, with a handsome face, and light, active proportions, who sat in an easy posture in the corner near the door. Not one of his limbs moved the breadth of a hair. . . .

Later Parkman and Reynal, a Native companion, have just returned from an unsuccessful antelope hunt, when they spy

the Hail-Storm, his light, graceful figure reclining on the ground in an easy attitude, while with his friend the Rabbit, who sat by his side, he was making an abundant meal from a wooden bowl of *wasna*, which the squaw had placed between them. Near him lay the fresh skin of a female elk, which he had just killed among the mountains, only a mile or two from the camp. No doubt the boy's heart was elated with triumph, but he betrayed no sign of it. He even seemed totally unconscious of our approach, and his handsome face had all the tranquillity of Indian self-control,—a self-control which prevents the exhibition of emotion without restraining the emotion itself. It was about two months since I had known the Hail-Storm, and within that time his character had remarkably developed. When I first saw him he was just emerging from the habits and feelings of the boy into the ambition of the hunter and warrior. He had lately killed his first deer, and this had excited his aspirations for distinction. Since that time he had been continually in search of game, and no young hunter in the village had been so active or so fortunate as he. All this success had produced a marked change in his character. As I first remembered him he always shunned the society of the young squaws, and was extremely bashful and sheepish in their presence; but now, in the confidence of his new reputation he began to assume the air and arts of a man of gallantry. He wore his red blanket dashingly over his left shoulder, painted his cheeks every day with vermilion, and hung pendants of shells in his ears. If I observed aright, he met with very good success in his new pursuits. . . .

Parkman adds:

Neither should the Hail-Storm's friend the Rabbit, be passed by without notice. The Hail-Storm and he were inseparable; they ate, slept, and hunted together, and shared with one another almost all that they possessed. If there be anything that deserves to be called romantic in the Indian character, it is to be sought for in friendships such as this, which are common among many of the prairie tribes.[38]

♀ c. 1850–c. 1895: GEORGE DEVEREUX; "The Case of Sahaykwisā"

Dr. Devereux, a Freudian-oriented psychiatrist who has written on homosexuality for many years, in 1937 first published his long study, "Institutionalized Homosexuality of the Mohave Indians." One of the best-known articles on Native American homosexuality, Devereux's essay includes the history of a remarkable woman named Sahaykwisā. Devereux's revised version of Sahaykwisā's story, published in 1961, is excerpted here.

The Case of Sahaykwisā

This case was reported by Hivsū Tupōma, additional data having been obtained from Tcatc:

Sahaykwisā (that is, Masahay Matkwisā—girl's shadow or soul), a fullblood Mohave woman of the Nyoltc gens, was born around the middle of the nineteenth century and was killed toward the end of that century, at the approximate age of forty-five. She was a Lesbian transvestite, formally referred to as a hwamē, which suggests that she may actually have undergone the initiation rite for female transvestites. Even her personal name appears to have been of the masculine type, since Mohave men often select names referring to women—usually in a derogatory manner—just as some women select names which are a slur on men.

Sahaykwisā was apparently not a hermaphrodite, since all informants agreed that she was feminine in appearance and had large breasts. On the other hand she allegedly never menstruated in her life. How credible this last statement may be is hard to decide in retrospect. Since Sahaykwisā professed to be a man, she would certainly not have discussed her menses with anyone. On the other hand, given the fact that the Mohave had no menstrual pads at that time, had she menstruated people could have noticed traces of her menses on her skirts and thighs, although they may have chosen to ignore these telltale stains which were incompatible with her socially accepted "masculinity."

Her dress, too, was described in somewhat puzzling terms. She is said to have worn short skirts "like a man." Taken literally, this statement is self-contradictory, since Mohave men originally wore breechcloths. Perhaps the informant simply meant to suggest that, unlike most of her female contemporaries, Sahaykwisā did not wear a Mother Hubbard. Moreover, since she occasionally prostituted herself to whites, it seems necessary to assume that her attire—though unconventional in terms of Mohave standards prevailing at that time—was a predominantly feminine one. Finally, all informants stressed that she was "rich enough to wear real shoes," and not just Mohave sandals, because she occasionally prostituted herself to whites, though part of her relative prosperity was due to her being an industrious farmer and hunter, as well as a practicing shaman specializing in the treatment of venereal diseases. Since such specialists are, by definition, lucky in love, it is likely that her striking ability to find wives was only partly due to her well-observed reputation of being a good provider. The principal reason for her marked success in obtaining wives was probably the belief that, being a specialist in venereal diseases, she was necessarily lucky in love.

In addition to functioning as a healer, Sahaykwisā also began to practice witchcraft in her middle twenties, but was not accused of being a witch until some five years later.

The first of Sahaykwisā's wives to be mentioned by the chief informant was a very pretty girl, whom many men tried to lure away from her "husband" by ridiculing the Lesbian. Thus, one suitor said: "Why do you want a hwame for a husband? A hwamē has no penis; she only pokes you with her finger." Sahaykwisā's wife was, however, not impressed by this argument, and replied: "That is all right for me, if I wish to remain with her," whereupon her suitor gave up and left her alone. However, shortly thereafter another suitor appeared on the scene and also tried to persuade her to leave her "husband," saying: "She has no penis; she is just like you are. If you remain with her, no 'other' man will want you afterwards." Finally, even though Sahaykwisā was an excellent provider, who cultivated her fields well and did all the work a husband is supposed to do, her wife liked the second suitor well enough to elope with him. After her wife left her, Sahaykwisā began to attend dances and flirted with girls who were present, which caused a man, who noticed this, to say sneeringly: "Why don't you leave those women alone? You can't do anything with them anyway!" Behind her back people even called her Hithpan Kudhāpe, which means split vulvae, and refers to one of the postures female homosexuals assume during coitus. However, since this is a bad insult, no one dared to call her Hithpan Kudhāpe to her face.

Before Sahaykwisā could induce another girl to marry her, her former wife, who had eloped with a man, decided to return to her. "Despite his boasts, she found him less satisfying than Sahaykwisā had been." The male husband let her go and did nothing further about it.

After regaining her wife, Sahaykwisā often took her to dances. At such gatherings the hwamē sat with the men and, boasting in a typically masculine manner, described to them the pudenda of "his" wife. However, while Sahaykwisā was busy boasting, people teased her wife, saying: "Your husband has neither a penis nor testes." One man even exclaimed: "I'll be damned if I don't criticize both you and your 'husband!' He too is a woman and has just what you have! But don't tell your husband I said so, because your husband will be angry with me." However, the girl was getting so tired of being teased that she ended up by complaining of all these sneers to Sahaykwisā, who became so angry that she told her wife to leave. The girl replied: "If you tell me to go, I shall go," and left Sahaykwisā forthwith.

After a while Sahaykwisā found herself another wife, who also had to endure a great deal of teasing and ridicule. In addition, people also jeered both at Sahaykwisā's former wife and at her new husband, who, be it noted, was not the man she had married after first running away from Sahaykwisā. People would tell this man: "Just poke her with your finger, that is what she likes; use your finger, that is what she is accustomed to. Don't waste your penis on her!" To make matters worse, Sahaykwisā's former wife took it upon herself to tease the hwamē's current wife: "Well do I know what you are getting. She pokes her finger into your vagina. Mine still hurts because her fingernails scratched me." Sahaykwisā's current wife resented all this teasing and complained to her "husband" who, this time, instead of getting angry, haughtily replied: "Never mind what my former wife tells you! She wants to come back to me—that is all!" Sahaykwisā's wife insisted that this was not true, but the hwamē retorted: "I know better," and let it go at that.

Eventually Sahaykwisā and her current wife met the former wife and the latter's husband at a dance. When the former wife once more heaped ridicule on Sahaykwisā's current wife, the latter felt that she had stood more than enough and decided to have it out with the former wife. At first the two women only hurled insults at each other, but when the men who were present began to egg them on, they actually began to fight. As for Sahaykwisā and the former wife's current husband, they remained seated, and maintained the dignified bearing befitting men when women are fighting over them. The rest of the crowd behaved, however, in a quite undignified manner and began to jeer at the transvestite: "The hwamē is proud now! She thinks that maybe she has a penis!" Finally a practical joker pushed the fighting women on top of Sahaykwisā, so that all three rolled around in the dust. Soon after this incident Sahaykwisā's current wife also decided that she could not bear the insults any longer and deserted the hwamē.

The desertion of her second wife disappointed Sahaykwisā a great deal and made her so resentful that she painted her face black, the way a warrior on the warpath, or a man going to fight his wife's seducer does, picked up her bow and arrows and went away (apparently giving people the impression that she was going to fight her eloping wife's paramour). We think, however, that she must already have had some other girl in mind, since, instead of going to the home of the eloped wife, she went to another camp, where she was very badly received. The married woman she wished to visit jeered at her and insultingly spoke to her the way one woman speaks to another woman: "She thinks maybe that the bow and arrows suit her. She thinks she is a man." These remarks did not appear to ruffle Sahaykwisā. She calmly replied, "Yes, I can shoot game for you," and then left. We think she must have felt encouraged, because we say that if a girl or woman insults her suitor, he can be pretty certain of winning her in the end. A few days later Sahaykwisā visited this woman once more and asked her to grind corn for her, which is precisely what a bride is supposed to do the moment she reaches her new husband's camp. Surprisingly enough, the woman complied and ground corn for the hwamē. The news of this spread like wildfire all over the reservation, and people said, "I bet she will get herself another wife. What can be the matter with all these women who fall for a hwamē?" The third time Sahaykwisā visited this camp, the woman left her husband and eloped with the hwamē. The husband, a thirty-five-year-old man named Haq'au, did nothing about it at that time: "He could not very well fight with a transvestite."

Actually, Sahaykwisā's ability to obtain one wife after another surprised no one; she was a venereal-disease specialist and was therefore automatically expected to be lucky in love. Moreover, she was a good provider, who earned a living not only by practicing shamanism but also by farming and hunting and, according to some, also by prostituting herself occasionally to whites. In brief, she earned enough to give her successive wives quantities of beads and pretty clothes.

Yet, in the end, Sahaykwisā's third wife also deserted her and returned to Haq'au, who took her back, though not without some hesitation, "since she had lowered herself by becoming the wife of a hwamē," and perhaps also because people warned him that Sahaykwisā—who, by this time, was a recognized healer and a practitioner of witchcraft—might bewitch him. "She will get even with you," people said, but Haq'au took back his former wife all the same.

When Sahaykwisā heard that her wife had gone back to Haq'au she once more picked up her bow and arrows and went from her house, which was on the southern outskirts of Needles, California, to Haq'au's camp, which was on the northern edge of that town. She did not actually go to Haq'au's house, but stood at a certain distance from it, looking at the camp. She did this several times, "thinking of how she could bewitch this woman." People who noticed what she was doing warned Haq'au, but he was not afraid, and jestingly replied: "Let her come! The next time she comes, I will show her what a real penis can do." The next time Sahaykwisā approached his camp, he waylaid her in the bushes which surrounded his camp, tore off her clothes, and assaulted her. Then he left her in the bushes and returned to his camp. As for Sahaykwisā, she picked herself up and left the scene without saying a word to anyone.

After this occurrence Sahaykwisā ceased to court women. Of course, by that time she had already bewitched quite a few women, put their captive souls in a place of her own, and cohabited with these souls in dream. Moreover, after being raped she became a regular drunkard and developed a craving for men. Not seldom, when she was blind drunk, some men would drag her to some hidden spot and farm her out to various men—some of them whites—at so much per intercourse. Of course, by this time she was on the downgrade and, like any wanton kamalōy, was considered fair game.

It was at this time that Sahaykwisā fell in love with an elderly man named Tcuhum, who, like herself, was of the Nyoltc gens. Tcuhum refused to cohabit with her, however, telling her, "You are a man." The spited and angry Sahaykwisā thereupon bewitched him, in order to have intercourse at least with his ghost in dream. Yet, despite his refusal to cohabit with her, Tcuhum died without revealing to anyone that she had bewitched him, which led people to believe that he must have wanted to become her victim—that is, because, in a way, he loved her.

After Tcuhum's death Sahaykwisā started an affair with Tcuhum's son Suhurāye, of the Hyoltc gens, who was at that time about forty or forty-five years of age. At the same time she also had an affair with Suhurāye's friend Ilykutcemidhō, of the Ootc gens, who was about fifty years old. These three traveled together to a certain place, some thirty miles north of Needles, where all three intended to work for a living. However, by this time, Sahaykwisā longed so much for the company of those whom she had bewitched that she began to look for a chance to be killed, so as to be able to join her retinue of ghosts forever. Hence, during that trip—that is, either while traveling north, or else after reaching her destination—she became drunk once more and openly told her lovers that she had bewitched Tcuhum and boasted of it until the two baited men picked her up and threw her into the Colorado River, where she drowned.

I (Hivsū Tupōma) was living at that time in Needles and, some two weeks after Sahaykwisā's murder, I heard that people had noticed some buzzards circling over a sandbank. When they investigated, they found Sahaykwisā's partly decomposed body, which had run aground there. I and some others then picked up the corpse and carried it back to the Mohave settlement, where it was cremated in the usual manner. At first people thought that she had jumped into the river while drunk, . . . but later learned that she had been murdered. They did nothing about it, because witches *should* be killed and *wish* to be killed. It is said that, except for Tcuhum, who, though of her own gens, was not really related to her, Sahaykwisā had not bewitched any one of her relatives.

"What happened to Sahaykwisā's former wives?" Devereux asks his informant. The answer is "One of them, a woman named Nyoltc, of Sahaykwisā's own gens, is still alive." "Could I see her?" Devereux asks.

You should not even try to talk to her about her life with Sahaykwisā—she is still quite touchy about that episode and does not like to be reminded of it.[39]

♀ 1855–56: EDWIN T. DENIG;
"Biography of Woman Chief"

Denig's "Biography of Woman Chief," written in 1855–56, is one of the rare documents of female role reversal, excluding cross-dressing but including taking to herself four wives. The Crow "Woman Chief" is the most famous female war leader in the history of the upper Missouri tribes.

Perhaps the only instance known of a woman attaining the rank of chief among any of the tribes whose histories we attempt has happened among the Crows. It has ever been the custom with these wandering people to regard females in an inferior light in every way. They have no voice in council, or anything to say at assemblies formed by men for camp regulations. Even the privilege of intimate conversation with their husbands is denied them when men are present. They have their own sphere of action in their domestic department, from which they are never allowed to depart, being considered by their husbands more as a part of their property than as companions.

This being the case, they seldom accompany parties to war. Those who do are of the lowest possible description of character, belong to the public generally, have no home or protection. Sometimes females of this stamp are taken along to make and mend shoes, dry meat, cook, etc., but they are never allowed to take part in battle. Even if they were, their inexperience in the use of weapons would soon cause their death. For such as these there is no opportunity to distinguish themselves. They must be content with the station of servant and that of the very lowest kind of drudgery.

The case we are about to relate is that of a Gros Ventre of the Prairie woman taken prisoner by the Crows when about 10 years of age. From a personal acquaintance of 12 years with this woman we can lay her true history before the reader.

Shortly after her capture the warrior to whom she belonged perceived a disposition in her to assume masculine habits and employments. As in the case of the Berdêche who, being male inclined to female pursuits, so this child, reversing the position, desired to acquire manly accomplishments. Partly to humor her, and partly for his own convenience, her foster father encouraged the inclination. She was in time placed to guard horses, furnished with bow and arrows, employing her idle time in shooting at the birds around and learning to ride fearlessly. When further advanced in years she carried a gun, learned to shoot, and when yet a young woman was equal if not superior to any of the men in hunting both on horseback and on foot.

During her whole life no change took place in her dress, being clad like the rest of the females with the exception of hunting arms and accouterments. It also happened that she was taller and stronger than most women—her pursuits no doubt tending to develop strength of nerve and muscle. Long before she had ventured on the warpath she could rival any of the young men in all their amusements and occupations, was a capital shot with the rifle, and would spend most of her time in killing deer and bighorn, which she butchered and carried home on her back when hunting on foot. At other times she joined in the surround on horse, could kill four or five buffalo at a race, cut up the animals without assistance, and bring the meat and hides home.

Although tolerably good looking she did not, it seems, strike the fancy of the young men, and her protector having been killed in battle, she assumed the charge of his lodge and family, performing the double duty of father and mother to his children.

In the course of time it happened that the Blackfeet made a charge on a few lodges of Crows encamped near the trading fort in their country—our heroine being with the lodges. . . . Several men were killed and the rest took refuge within the fort. . . . The [Blackfeet] made a stand beyond the reach of guns and by signs exhibited a desire to speak to someone in the fort. Neither Whites nor Crows could be found to venture out. But this woman, understanding their language, saddled her horse and set forth to meet them. Everyone sought to detain her, but she would not be persuaded. The fort gates were opened and she went on her dangerous errand. . . . Several Blackfeet came to meet her, rejoicing in the occasion of securing an easy prize. When within pistol shot, she called on them to stop, but they paid no attention to her words. One of the enemies then fired at her and the rest charged. She immediately shot down one with her gun, and shot arrows into two more without receiving a wound. The remaining two then rode back to the main body, who came at full speed to murder the woman. They fired showers of balls and pursued her as near to the fort as they could with safety approach. But she escaped unharmed and entered the gates amid the shouts and praises of the Whites and her own people.

This daring act stamped her character as a brave. It was sung by the rest of the camp, and in time was made known to the whole nation. About a year after, she collected a number of young men and headed her first war excursion against the Blackfeet. Fortune again favored her. She approached their camp in the night, stole 70 horses and drove them with great speed toward her home. But the enemies followed, overtook them, and a sharp skirmish ensued, which resulted in the Crows getting off with most of the animals and two Blackfeet scalps. One of the two Blackfeet the woman chieftain killed and scalped with her own hand. The other, although shot down by one of her followers, she was the first to strike and take from him his gun while he was yet alive 'tho severely wounded. It may reasonably be supposed that coups such as these aided to raise her fame as a warrior, and according to their own usages, from the fact of striking first the bodies of two enemies, she could no more be prevented from having a voice in their deliberations. Other expeditions of a still more hazardous nature were undertaken and successfully carried through by this singular and resolute woman. In every battle around their own camp or those of their enemies some gallant act distinguished her. Old men began to believe she bore a charmed life which, with her daring feats, elevated her to a point of honor and respect not often reached by male warriors, certainly never before conferred upon a female of the Crow Nation. The Indians seemed to be proud of her, sung forth her praise in songs composed by them after each of her brave deeds. When council was held and all the chiefs and warriors assembled, she took her place among the former, ranking third person in the band of 160 lodges. On stated occasions, when the ceremony of striking a post and publicly repeating daring acts was performed, she took precedence of many a brave man whose career had not been so fortunate.

In the meantime she continued her masculine course of life, hunting and war. Heretofore her attention had been but little attracted to personal gain in the way of barter. Whatever hides she brought home from the hunt were given to her friends, 'tho the meat was cured and dried by herself and the children under her charge. When horses were wanting she drew upon her enemies for a supply and had been heretofore uniformly successful. She had numbers of animals in her possession, with which she could at any time command other necessaries.

But with Indians it is the same as with civilized persons. The richer they become the more desirous they are to acquiring more. As yet no offer of marriage had been made her by anyone. Her habits did not suit their taste. Perhaps they thought she would be rather difficult to manage as a wife. Whatever the reason was, they certainly rather feared than loved her as a conjugal companion, and she continued to lead a single life. With the view of turning her hides to some account by dressing them and fitting them for trading purposes, she took to *herself a wife*. Ranking as a warrior and hunter, she could not be brought to think of female work. It was derogatory to her standing, unsuited to her taste. She therefore went through the usual formula of Indian marriage to obtain an authority over the woman thus bought. Strange country this, where males assume the dress and perform the duties of females, while women turn men and mate with their own sex!

Finding that employing hands advanced her affairs in the lodge, in a few years her establishment was further increased by taking three more wives. This plurality of women added also to her standing and dignity as a chief; for after success at war, riches either in horses or women mark the distinction of rank with all the Prairie tribes. Nothing more was now in her power to gain. She had fame, standing, honor, riches, and as much influence over the band as anyone except two or three leading chiefs. To either of their offices she could in no wise expect to succeed; for to be a leader required having strong family connection, extensive kindredship, and a popularity of a different description from that allotted to partisans. This being the case she wisely concluded to maintain her present great name instead of interfering with the claims of others to public notice. For 20 years she conducted herself well in all things appertaining to war and a hunter's life.

In the summer of 1854 she determined to visit in a friendly way the Gros Ventres of the Prairie. . . . [In 1851 the Gros Ventres and Blackfeet had] evinced a willingness to abstain from war excursions, and sent friendly messages to the Crows and Assiniboines containing invitations to visit them. The Assiniboines did so, were well received, hospitably entertained by the Gros Ventres, and dismissed with horses as presents. . . . With the view of ascertaining how far their hostile spirit had been quelled, and perhaps of gaining a goodly number of horses, this Woman Chief undertook a visit there, presuming that, as she was in fact one of their nation, could speak their language, and a general peace was desired, she could associate with them without being harmed. Many old and experienced fur traders endeavored to dissuade her from this journey, as her feats against them [the Gros Ventres] were too notorious to be easily overlooked. But contrary to the advice of her friends she proceeded.

When near the camp, however, she encountered a large party of the Gros Ventres of the Prairie who had been to Fort Union and were returning home. These she boldly met, spoke to, and smoked with. But on their discovering who she was, they took the advantage while traveling with her to their camp to shoot her down together with the four Crows who had so far borne her company.

This closed the earthly career of this singular woman and effectually placed a bar to any hopes of peace between the Crows and her murderers. Neither has there since appeared another of her sex who preferred the warrior's life to that of domestic duties.[40]

1876: H. CLAY TRUMBULL;
" 'Brothers by adoption' "

In his book on *Friendship the Master-Passion Or The Nature And History Of Friendship, And Its Place As A Force In The World*, first published in 1892, H. Clay Trumbull describes an event of 1876 which illustrates the "warm friendship" existing between two Native "brothers by adoption."

An officer of the United States army, who has given much study to the customs of the North American Indians, tells of the warm friendship sometimes existing between men of the same tribe, or even between two men of hostile tribes, under the name of "brothers by adoption." Speaking of the Arapahoe warriors in this connection, he says: "They really seem to 'fall in love' with men; and I have known this affectionate interest to live for years, surviving lapse of time and separation." An illustration of the heroism inspired by such a friendship is given by this officer, as coming under his own observation. Three Bears and Feather-on-the-Head were attached friends, and were together as scouts in the United States service. In the early gray of a cold morning in the late autumn of 1876, the government force to which these scouts were attached made a surprise attack on an Indian village in a cañon of the Big Horn Mountains. The horse ridden by Three Bears becoming unmanageable dashed ahead of the attacking party, carrying his rider into the very heart of the village, where all were now aroused for the defense of their homes and lives. Seeing his friend's desperate peril, Feather-on-the-Head urged forward his pony, in order to save his friend or to die with him. Throwing himself from side to side of his pony to avoid the thick-flying shots of the enemy as he dashed on, Feather-on-the-Head reached the center of the village just as the horse of Three Bears had fallen under him. Sweeping past the spot where his imperiled friend stood, at the full speed of his pony, Feather-on-the-Head caught up Three Bears and mounted him behind himself. Then together the two hero-friends flew unharmed through the shower of bullets out of that valley of death, and regained their place with their command in safety. Who will say that this act of Indian heroism through friendship is undeserving of mention alongside of the heroic exploits in the legends of Greece and Rome and the Norseland?[41]

1889: A. B. HOLDER;
"A Peculiar Sexual Perversion"

An article by a physician, Dr. A. B. Holder of Memphis, Tennessee, titled "The Bote. Description of A Peculiar Sexual Perversion Found Among North American Indians," appeared in the *New York Medical Journal* in 1889.

The word bō-tĕ′ I have chosen as being the most familiar to me and not likely to convey a wrong impression, since I shall be the first, perhaps, to translate into English and define it. It is the word used by the Absaroke Indians of Montana, and literally means "not man, not woman." . . .

The practice of the bote among civilized races is not unknown to specialists, but no name suited to ears polite, even though professional, has been given it. The practice is to produce the sexual orgasm by taking the male organ of the active party in the lips of the bote, the bote probably experiencing the orgasm at the same time. Of the latter supposition I have not been able to satisfy myself, but I can in no other way account for the infatuation of the act.

Of all the many varieties of sexual perversion, this, it seems to me, is the most debased that could be conceived of.

In the Crow or Absaroke tribe, of which I have had medical charge for two years, there are at present five bote, . . . and about this number has flourished for years past.

While in reports of physicians and others concerning various Indian tribes I find no mention of this class, and while in personal replies from physicians in charge of more than twenty agencies I have been able to get little positive evidence concerning them, yet I feel assured that the bote is to be found in nearly all tribes of Indians, of the Northwest at least. . . .

One of the bote accredited to the Absaroke tribe is a Sioux, and I can assert, on perfectly reliable testimony, that among the Lower Gros Ventres there is a larger number of them than in the Absaroke tribe. A bote, a description of whom will be introduced presently, told me that the tribes of his acquaintance living in the Northwest had bote as follows: Flatheads, four; Nez Percés, two; Gros Ventres, six. Sioux, five; Shoshonis, one. There seems a species of fellowship among them, and I have no reason to doubt the correctness of his statement.

The bote wears the "squaw" dress and leggins, parts the hair in the middle and braids it like a woman's, possesses or affects the voice and manner of a woman, and constantly associates with that sex as being of it. The voice, features, and form, however, never so far lose masculine qualities as to make it at all difficult to distinguish the bote from a woman. One of them does "squaw" work, such as sweeping, scouring, dish-washing, etc., with such skill and good nature that he frequently finds employment among the white residents.

Usually the feminine dress and manner are assumed in childhood, but the art to which they subsequently devote themselves does not generally become a practice till toward puberty. One little fellow while in the Agency Boarding School was found frequently surreptitiously wearing female attire. He was punished, but finally escaped from school and became a bote, which vocation he has since followed. . . .

In the manner of making the mujerado [allegedly a physically effeminized male homosexual] and his importance in the traditional rites of the people among whom he is found, Dr. Hammond gives him a position of greater dignity than I can assign the bote, whose making I adjudge the work of his own perverted lust, and whose tolerance I attribute not to any respect in which he is held, but to the debased standard of the people among whom he lives.

There is, moreover, a difference in the method of the practice of their vocation. Pederasty is by no means unknown among the tribes of Indians where the bote is found, but the bote is less than any other a pederast. With him it is the oral and not the rectal cavity into which he admits the male organ. . . .

That the bote is a study of practical as well as scientific value to the surgeon is evident to one whose practice has brought him in contact with examples in the white race, not only of the mujerado but of his more disgusting cousin, the bote. With the former every specialist is familiar. . . . Of the latter, a striking example was the case of an officer in the United States army, who was recently caught *in flagrante delicto*, the other party being an enlisted man, and allowed to resign from a Western post. He confessed the practice of the habit for years, showing that there is no bottom to the pit into which the sexual passion, perverted and debased, may sink a creature once he has become its slave.[42]

1896–97: MATILDA COXE STEVENSON;
"A death which caused universal regret"

Anthropologist Matilda Coxe Stevenson, in a report on "The Zuñi Indians . . ." based on fieldwork dating to 1896–97, discusses examples of male transvestites, their adoption of the roles and work customary for women, and the tribal reactions to this. In two last brief, tantalizing sentences, Stevenson hints that homosexual relations comprise "a side to the lives of these men which must remain untold."

The custom of youths donning female attire at puberty, which exists to some extent among the pueblos of New Mexico and Arizona, has given rise to conflicting statements. An assertion made, not only by the writer after her first visit to Zuñi, but also by others, was that these persons were hermaphrodites. One is led into this error by the Indians, who, when referring to men dressed as women, say "She is a man," which is certainly misleading to one not familiar with Indian thought. . . . After more intimate acquaintance with the pueblos the writer is able to give the facts as they are. Men who adopt female attire do so of their own volition, having from childhood hung about the house and usually preferring to do the work of women. On reaching puberty their decision is final. If they are to continue woman's work they must adopt woman's dress; and though the women of the family joke the fellow, they are inclined to look upon him with favor, since it means that he will remain a member of the household and do almost double the work of a woman, who necessarily ceases at times from her labors at the mill and other duties to bear children and to look after the little ones; but the ko'thlama [a man who has permanently adopted female attire] is ever ready for service, and is expected to perform the hardest labors of the female department. The men of the family, however, not only discourage men from unsexing themselves in this way, but ridicule them. There have been but five such persons in Zuñi since the writer's acquaintance with these people; and until about ten years ago there had been but two, these being the finest potters and weavers in the tribe. One was the most intelligent person in the pueblo, especially versed in their ancient lore. He was conspicuous in ceremonials, always taking the part of the captive Kor'kokshi in the dramatization of the Kïa'nakwe. His strong character made his word law among both the men and the women with whom he associated. Though his wrath was dreaded by men as well as by women, he was beloved by all the children, to whom he was ever kind. Losing his parents in infancy, he was adopted by an aunt on his father's side, and the loving gratitude he exhibited for his aunt and her grief at his death afforded a lesson that might well be learned by the more enlightened. Such was his better side. He was said to be the father of several children, but the writer knew of but one child of whom he was regarded as certainly being the father. The other ko'thlama, who was one of the richest men of the village, allied himself to a man during one of the visits of the writer to Zuñi, and to the time of her departure from Zuñi in 1897 this couple were living together, and they were two of the hardest workers in the pueblo and among the most prosperous. The third and fourth assumed woman's attire during the absence of the writer. The fifth, a grandson on the maternal side of Nai'uchi, elder brother Bow priest, donned the dress during the visit of the writer to Zuñi in 1896. The mother and grandmother were quite willing that the boy should continue in the work in which he seemed interested, but the grandfather, who was much disgusted, endeavored to shame him out of his determination to follow woman's work. He did not, however, attempt any authority in the matter, and on the boy's reaching manhood the trousers were replaced by woman's attire. There is a side to the lives of these men which must remain untold. They never marry women, and it is understood that they seldom have any relations with them.[43]

Later, Matilda Coxe Stevenson movingly describes, in a classic statement, the death of her friend We'wha, a Zuñi male transvestite, whose true gender had been unknown to her, and apparently unknown to President Cleveland and other politicians whom We'wha had visited during a six-month stay in Washington.

A death which caused universal regret and distress in Zuñi was that of We'wha, undoubtedly the most remarkable member of the tribe. This person was a man wearing woman's dress, and so carefully was his sex concealed that for years the writer believed him to be a woman. Some declared him to be an hermaphrodite, but the writer gave no credence to the story, and continued to regard We'wha as a woman; and as he was always referred to by the tribe as "she"—it being their custom to speak of men who don woman's dress as if they were women—and as the writer could never think of her faithful and devoted friend in any other light, she will continue to use the feminine gender when referring to We'wha. She was perhaps the tallest person in Zuñi: certainly the strongest, both mentally and physically. Her skin was much like that of the Chinese in color, many of the Zuñis having this complexion. During six months' stay in Washington she became several shades lighter. She had a good memory, not only for the lore of her people, but for all that she heard of the outside world. She spoke only a few words of English before coming to Washington, but acquired the language with remarkable rapidity, and was soon able to join in conversation. She possessed an indomitable will and an insatiable thirst for knowledge. Her likes and dislikes were intense. She would risk anything to serve those she loved, but toward those who crossed her path she was vindictive. Though severe she was considered just. At an early age she lost her parents and was adopted by a sister of her father. She belonged to the Badger clan, her foster mother belonging to the Dogwood clan. Owing to her bright mind and excellent memory, she was called upon by her own clan and also by the clans of her foster mother and father when a long prayer had to be repeated or a grace was to be offered over a feast. In fact she was the chief personage on many occasions. On account of her physical strength all the household work requiring great exertion was left for her, and while she most willingly took the harder work from others of the family, she would not permit idleness; all had to labor or receive an upbraiding from We'wha, and nothing was more dreaded than a scolding from her.

In the fall of 1896 a Sha'läko god was entertained at her home. Although at this time We'wha was suffering from valvular heart disease, she did most of the work, including the laying of a stone floor in the large room where the ceremonial was to occur. She labored early and late so hard that when the time came for holding the ceremony she was unable to be present. From this time she was listless and remained alone as much as possible, though she made no complaint of illness. When a week or more had passed after the close of the great autumn ceremonial of the Sha'läko, and the many guests had departed, the writer dropped in at sunset to the spacious room in the house of We'wha's foster father, the late José Palle. We'wha was found crouching on the ledge by the fireplace. That a great change had come over her was at once apparent. Death evidently was rapidly approaching. She had done her last work. Only a few days before this strong-minded, generous-hearted creature had labored to make ready for the reception of her gods; now she was preparing to go to her beloved Ko'thluwala'wa. When the writer asked, "Why do you not lie down?" We'wha replied: "I can not breathe if I lie down: I think my heart break." The writer at once sent to her camp for a comfortable chair, and fixed it at a suitable angle for the invalid, who was most grateful for the attention. There was little to be done for the sufferer. She knew that she was soon to die and begged the writer not to leave her.

From the moment her family realized that We'wha was in a serious condition they remained with her, ever ready to be of assistance. The family consisted of the aged foster mother, a foster brother, two foster sisters with their husbands and children, and an own brother with his wife and children. The writer never before observed such attention as every member of the family showed her. The little children ceased their play and stood in silence close to their mothers, occasionally toddling across the floor to beg We'wha to speak. She smiled upon them and whispered. "I can not talk." The foster brother was as devoted as the one related by blood.

During two days the family hoped against hope. Nai'uchi, the great theurgist, came three times and pretended to draw from the region of the heart bits of mutton, declared to have been "shot" there by a witch who was angry with We'wha for not giving her a quarter of mutton when she asked for it. We'wha appeared relieved when the theurgist left. She knew that she was dying and appeared to desire quiet. After Nai'uchi's last visit, the foster brother, with streaming eyes, prepared te'likinawe (prayer plumes) for the dying, the theurgist having said that her moments on earth were few. We'wha asked the writer to come close and in a feeble voice she said, in English: "Mother, I am going to the other world. I will tell the gods of you and Captain Stevenson. I will tell them of Captain Carlisle, the great seed priest, and his wife, whom I love. They are my friends.* Tell them good-by. Tell all my friends in Washington good-by. Tell President Cleveland, my friend, good-by. Mother, love all my people; protect them; they are your children; you are their mother." These sentences were spoken with many breaks. The family seemed somewhat grieved that We'wha's last words should be given to the writer, but she understood that the thoughts of the dying were with and for her own people. A good-by was said to the others, and she asked for more light.

It is the custom for a member of the family to hold the prayer plumes near the mouth of the dying and repeat the prayer, but this practice was not observed in We'wha's case. She requested the writer to raise the back of the chair, and when this was done she asked if her prayer plumes had been made. Her foster brother answered "Yes," whereupon she requested him to bring them. The family suppressed their sobs that the dying might not be made sad. The brother offered to hold the plumes and say the prayers, but We'wha feebly extended her hand for them, and clasping the prayer plumes between her hands made a great effort to speak. She said but a few words and then sank back in her chair. Again the brother offered to hold the plumes and pray, but once more she refused. Her face was radiant in the belief that she was going to her gods. She leaned forward with the plumes tightly clasped, and as the setting sun lighted up the western windows, darkness and desolation entered the hearts of the mourners, for We'wha was dead.

* At the time of We'wha's visit to Washington Hon. John G. Carlisle was Speaker of the House of Representatives. The speaker and Mrs. Carlisle were very kind to We'wha, and upon her return to Zuñi she found a great sack of seed which had been sent by the Speaker.

Blankets were spread upon the floor and the brothers gently laid the lifeless form upon them. After the body was bathed and rubbed with meal, a pair of white cotton trousers were drawn over the legs, the first male attire she had worn since she had adopted woman's dress years ago. The rest of her dress was female. The body was dressed in the finest clothing; six shawls of foreign manufacture, gifts from Washington friends, besides her native blanket wraps, and a white Hopi blanket bordered in red and blue, were wrapped around her. The hair was done up with the greatest care. Three silver necklaces, with turquoise earrings attached and numerous bangles, constituted the jewels.

We'wha's death was regarded as a calamity, and the remains lay in state for an hour or more, during which time not only members of the clans to which she was allied, but the rain priests and theurgists and many others, including children, viewed them. When the blanket was finally closed, a fresh outburst of grief was heard, and then all endeavored to suppress their sobs, for the aged foster mother had fallen unconscious to the floor. The two brothers carried the remains unattended to the grave. The sisters made food offerings to the fire. The foster brother on his return prepared prayer plumes for each member of the immediate family, and also the writer. The little procession, including the foster mother, who had recovered sufficiently to accompany the others, then made its way to the west of the village and on the river bank deposited the clothing, mask, and prayer plumes in the manner heretofore described. Upon the return to the house the foster mother had the rest of We'wha's possessions brought together that they might be destroyed. All her cherished gifts from Washington friends, including many photographs, were brought out; all must be destroyed. This work was performed by the mother, who wept continually. All was sacrificed but pictures of Mr and Mrs Carlisle, Mr Stevenson, and the writer. These were left in their frames on the wall. With another outburst of grief the old woman declared they must remain, saying: "We'wha will have so much with her. I can not part with these. I must keep the faces of those who loved We'wha and whom she loved best. I must keep them to look upon."[44]

♀ 1901–02: WILLIAM JONES;
"Two Maidens Who Played the Harlot with Each Other"

In a rare report concerning Lesbianism among Native Americans, in a study of "Fox Texts," based on information obtained in 1901–02, William Jones, includes a section of "Parables," the sixth of which is titled "Two Maidens Who Played the Harlot with Each Other." This is summarized in a note as "an account of how two young women had sexual intercourse with each other, and how, as a result of the unnatural union, one gave birth to an unnatural offspring"—a legend possibly suggesting heterosexual male and/or Christian influence.

It is said that once on a time long ago there were two young women who were friends together. It is told that there were also two youths who tried to woo the two maidens, but they were not able even so much as to talk with one another. After awhile the youths began to suspect something wrong with them. It is reported that this took place in the summer.

So it is said that once during the summer, the two maidens started away to peel off bark. The youths followed after, staying just far enough behind to keep within sight of them. The girls went a long way off, and over there is where they stripped off bark. While (the girls) were peeling the bark (the youths) all that time kept themselves hidden from them.

After awhile (the youths) no longer heard the sound of (the maidens) at work. Whereupon they began to creep up to where they were. When they drew nigh, behold, the maidens were then in the act of taking off their clothes! The first to disrobe flung herself down on the ground and lay there. 'Pray, what are these (girls) going to do?' was the feeling in the hearts of (the youths). And to their amazement the girls began to lie with each other!

Thereupon one of the youths whistled, and both together ran up to where (the girls) were. One that was lying on top instantly fell over backwards. Her clitoris was standing out and had a queer shape, it was like a turtle's penis.

Thereupon (the maidens) began to plead with (the youths): 'Oh, don't tell on us!' they said to them. 'Truly it is not of our own free desire that we have done this thing. We have done it under the influence of some unknown being.'

It is said that afterwards one of the maidens became big with child. In the course of time, strange to relate, she gave birth, and the child was like a soft-shell turtle![45]

1902: S. C. SIMMS;
"An Indian agent endeavored to compel these people . . . to wear men's clothing"

Research dating to 1902 is the basis for a note by S. C. Simms on "Crow Indian Hermaphrodites" in the 1903 American Anthropologist.

During a visit last year to the Crow reservation, in the interest of the Field Columbian Museum, I was informed that there were three hermaphrodites in the Crow tribe, one living at Pryor, one in the Big Horn district, and one in Black Lodge district. These persons are usually spoken of as "she," and as having the largest and best appointed tipis; they are also generally considered to be experts with the needle and the most efficient cooks in the tribe, and they are highly regarded for their many charitable acts.

On one occasion, while making a canvass of the tipis of the Pryor district, I came upon an individual who, I was told, was "half man and half woman." Shortly afterward the person came out dressed in woman's attire, consisting of a loose calico frock fitted in at the waist with a profusely beaded strap, and a pair of moccasins. This person was almost gigantic in stature, but was decidedly effeminate in voice and manner.

I was told that, when very young, these persons manifested a decided preference for things pertaining to female duties, yet were compelled by their parents to wear boys' attire; as soon as they passed out of the jurisdiction of their parents, however, they invariably donned women's clothes.

A few years ago an Indian agent endeavored to compel these people, under threat of punishment, to wear men's clothing, but his efforts were unsuccessful.[46]

1907–12: ROBERT HENRY LOWIE;
"One surviving berdache"

In a discussion of the *Social Life of the Crow Indians*, based on research dating to 1907–12, Lowie records:

At present there is but one surviving berdache, who lives in the Bighorn District. I saw him once at Lodge Grass. He is probably over fifty years of age, stands 5 ft. 7 inches, and is of a large build. According to several informants, former agents have repeatedly tried to make him don male clothes, but the other Indians themselves protested against this, saying that it was against his nature. Henry Russell [a resident of the Crow Reservation, and Lowie's interpreter] told me that this berdache once fought valiantly in an encounter with the Sioux. He has the reputation of being very accomplished in feminine crafts.

It is impossible to detect a berdache at birth, but as he grows up his weak voice distinguishes him from other boys. Berdaches naturally associate with girls and pretend to have sweethearts among the men.[47]

1908: EDWARD WESTERMARCK;
"Homosexual Love"

The year 1908 saw the publication of one of the major early documented historical surveys in English on worldwide manifestations of homosexuality—Edward Westermarck's chapter on "Homosexual Love" in his two-volume book on *The Origin and Development of Moral Ideas*.[48] The Finnish scholar, a professor at the University of London, was one of the earliest writers to study the varieties of same-sex relations, including a summary and listing of early references to male homosexuality among the Native peoples of what is now the United States, and a brief comment on Lesbianism.

Westermarck lived for many years in Tangier, studying Moroccan culture at first hand. According to anthropologist Omer C. Stewart, Westermarck's autobiographical *Memories of My Life*

allow for the conclusion that he himself enjoyed homosexual attraction for various males, and he describes living and traveling with male companions. Furthermore there is a tradition passed on orally in professional anthropology that Westermarck was a practicing homosexual.[49]

If so, Westermarck's work represents one of the early English-language attempts by a homosexual to study, present, and repossess the history of his own people.

♀ 1909: ROBERT HENRY LOWIE;
"She eloped with her sister-in-law"

Lowie's essay on *The Assiniboine*, published by the American Museum of Natural History in 1909, reports an Assiniboine legend involving Lesbianism, which this anthropologist had noted during a study of the tribe's mythology.

"A man was walking with his wife and sister. The woman wished to have intercourse with the girl. While her husband was hunting, she eloped with her sister-in-law. The man did not know where they could have gone. He looked for them in the camp, and finally concluded that they had been killed. He grieved very much over their death. In midwinter, he once went out hunting. Remembering the two women, he began to cry. He thought they must have perished from the cold. He ascended a hill. Here he heard a noise. He had no gun or knife, nevertheless he walked towards the sound. His wife and sister being dead he also wished to die. Towards sunset he reached the place where he had heard the noise, and caught sight of a human head. He recognized his sister, and immediately guessed that his wife was also there. Stepping nearer, he saw smoke rising from among the bushes and heard a child crying by the fireplace. He could hear the women talking. His wife was playing with the infant. He knew that she must have married his sister. He saw his sister nursing the child. Approaching he asked, 'Which of you has seduced the other?' His sister answered. 'Your wife persuaded me to elope with her.' The infant was continually crying. It looked like a football; it had no bones in its body, because a woman had begotten it. The man killed the child, then he bade the women go home. When they were near the camp, he told his sister to walk ahead. Then he killed his wicked wife with his knife. His sister ran to camp and told a man she met that her brother was slaying his wife, begging him to save her. But before the stranger arrived, the husband had killed his wife and severed her limbs from the body. He did not kill his sister. Though the slain woman had many relatives, none cared to avenge her death."[50]

1911: EDWARD CARPENTER;
Intermediate Types Among Primitive Folk

Edward Carpenter and John Addington Symonds were the two pioneering figures in the early English homosexual emancipation movement. Citing the research on homosexuality among "primitive" peoples published in Germany in Magnus Hirschfeld's *Jahrbuch für sexuelle Zwischenstufen* [Yearbook for sexual intermediate types], especially the anthropological work of Ferdinand Karsch-Haack, as well as the English-language compilations of documents by Westermarck and Bancroft,

Carpenter was himself among the first to take up the discussion of Native homosexuality—as part of his campaign to demonstrate the contributions, functions, and high status of male and female homosexuals in various "primitive" societies.

In July 1911, Professor G. Stanley Hall's *American Journal of Religious Psychology and Education* published Carpenter's essay on homosexuality among Native peoples, later reprinted as four chapters on "The Intermediate Sex in the Service of Religion" in Carpenter's book *Intermediate Types Among Primitive Folk: A Study in Social Evolution* (1914).[51] Carpenter's sources on male homosexuality among the Native peoples of what is now the United States include Catlin, Lafitau, W. A. Hammond, Maximilian, John T. Irving, W. H. Keating, Charlevoix, and A. B. Holder.

♀ 1911: FERDINAND KARSCH-HAACK;
The Same-Sex Life of Primitive Peoples

A professor of zoology at the University of Berlin, Ferdinand Karsch-Haack (1853–1936) was an early member of the Scientific-Humanitarian Committee, the German homosexual emancipation organization headed by Dr. Magnus Hirschfeld. Although Karsch-Haack accepted the congenital theory of homosexuality advanced by his contemporaries, he reacted against the preponderance of medical studies, arguing that it was less important to understand homosexuality's etiology than its varied manifestations. This interest motivated his survey of "primitive" societies, which in turn led him to the conclusion that homosexuality is a universal and fundamentally natural phenomenon. Karsch-Haack planned a five-volume series on the ethnology of homosexuality which remained uncompleted. His *Das gleichgeschlechtliche Leben der Naturvölker* [The same-sex life of primitive peoples] did, however, appear in 1911.[52] Over five hundred pages in length, it presents a comprehensive compilation of primary source materials on male homosexuality among the North and South American Indians, Australian aborigines, Malayans and Melanesians, Eskimos and other Arctic peoples, and Black Africans. A short, though important, section on Lesbianism is included. To the present day, Karsch-Haack's study remains the major source book on native homosexuality.

♀ 1914: DOUGLAS C. McMURTRIE;
"A Legend of Lesbian Love among the North American Indians"

In a medical journal article, Dr. D. C. McMurtrie, an American physician who wrote extensively on homosexuality, discusses Robert H. Lowie's and William Jones's earlier reports of legends of Native American Lesbianism (both previously quoted). Here only the introduction and conclusions of McMurtrie's essay are excerpted.

Lesbian love, the sexually inverted phenomenon of love relations between women, is found to exist among all peoples regarding whom complete and accurate data concerning the *vita sexualis* is available. It is noteworthy, however, that, in comparison with information regarding the homosexual relation between men, the material on the analogous manifestation between women is extremely scanty.

There are several reasons why this should be the case. In the first place homosexuality among men is of far greater extent than homosexuality among women, the former category comprising not only the subjects of true sexual inversion but also a large group of pederasts. Among homosexual women—speaking in general terms only and not going into the scientific *minutiae*,—there is no class corresponding to the pederasts, and the superficial total is thus reduced.

Further, male homosexuality has been a subject of popular information, through the widespread knowledge regarding "Greek love." That such a relation as Lesbian love exists is unknown to the majority of even the most intelligent people.

One other factor is of moment. The women among all peoples generally live together in fairly close proximity, and intimacy between a pair would not be a subject of as extensive observation or comment as a similar liaison between two men.

For these reasons, among others, I do not consider it safe to conclude that paucity of data necessarily indicates extreme rarity of the incidence of the phenomenon. Any material bearing on the subject is, however, of particular interest.

The Indian legends cited in Lowie's 1909 report and in Jones's study, based on information gathered in 1901–02, both reflect negative attitudes toward Lesbianism. In reference to these legends McMurtrie concludes:

The tales cited are, of course, legends only, units in the tribal mythology. Legends among primitive people, however, usually have their genesis in some actual occurrence, exaggerated and distorted though it may be in the course of its hereditary transmission. It is also true that legendary tales reflect the attitude which public opinion takes, or would take, regarding the occurrences related. We thus see indicated the opprobrium attaching to inverted love relationships between women. The eventuation of the tales is probably due to the primitive conception that all sexual relations yield offspring. From this was deduced the idea that unnatural intercourse should yield unnatural offspring.

Without attempting any further interpretation or evaluation of these fragments of primitive lore, they are here presented by reason of their psychological and anthropological interest.[53]

♀ 1930: LESLIE SPIER;
"Transvestites or berdaches"

In his work on "Klamath Ethnography," for the 1930 *University of California Publications in American Archaeology and Ethnology*, Spier writes a section on "Transvestites," including comments on male homosexuality and non-cross-dressing Lesbians.

Transvestites or berdaches (tw!ǐnnǎ'ĕk) are found among the Klamath as in all probability among all other North American tribes. These are men and women who for reasons that remain obscure take on the dress and habits of the opposite sex. Their number is small. Five men who lived as women were cited by an informant, two women who lived as men, and others are known. One of the former was from the Dalles. This is a very minor fraction in a population numbering upward of two thousand. Kroeber has assumed that such individuals are invariably psychologically abnormal, homosexual; I am not sure. . . . At any rate their abnormality is socially canalized: they are permitted to live as they desire despite the distaste of the normal Klamath for the practice, and the scorn and taunting to which he subjects them.

It is to the point to note that the men who turned women adopted woman's dress, pursuits, personal habits, and speech, and in one case at least married. Neither of the two women affected male garb; one married and made some pretense of men's habits, the other is rather simply a case of an irregular sex life.

Spier's female histories follow:

A woman named Co'pak lived like a man although she retained women's dress. She married a woman who lived with her a long time and finally died. She observed the usual mourning, wearing a bark belt as a man does at this time to prevent the back from growing bowed. She tried to talk like a man and invariably referred to herself as one.

Another women still living has had relations with both women and men. She never adopted men's garb but told them that she was a man. She is today a common prostitute, an abnormal, irascible person. Those she lived with were all older women, not young girls. This practice is known as sawa'lǐnǎa, to live as partners. They say of such: they have lots of partners, friends (snewǎ'ĕts doma' sawa' lǐnǎa'sgǐtkt). Other Klamath of any standing have always avoided her and her women partners. She was never married to a man.[54]

♀ 1931: C. DARYLL FORDE;
"Casual secret homosexuality among both women and men"

In his "Ethnology of the Yuma Indians" for the 1931 *University of California Publications in American Archaeology and Ethnology*, Forde reports on "Transvestites," including references to "female inverts," and "Casual secret homosexuality among both women and men."

Both male and female inverts are recognized; the females are known as kwe'rhame, the males as elxa'. Elxa' are more numerous. Such persons are considered to have suffered a change of spirit as a result of dreams which occur generally at the time of puberty. Such dreams frequently include the receiving of messages from plants, particularly the arrowweed, which is believed to be liable to change of sex itself. An elxa´ known to one informant [had a dream implying] his future occupation with women's work.

> When he came out of the dream he put his hand to his mouth and laughed four times. He laughed with a woman's voice and his mind was changed from male into female. Other young people noticed this and began to feel towards him as to a woman.

As a rule parents are ashamed of such children, but there is no attempt to force them or suppress the tendency. In some cases the "transformation" is publicly recognized, friends are invited, and in the case of an elxa´ food is prepared by him. It is, in any case, customary for an elxa´ to undertake women's work, fetching water and grinding corn.

An elxa´ later goes to live with a man; such a pair often remains together permanently. It is considered unwise to interfere with them for the elxa´ has more power than the ordinary man and is thought to have a peaceful influence on the tribe.

Female inverts (kwe´rhame) are rarer, but they too realize their character through a dream at puberty. The characteristic dream is of men's weapons. As a small child the kwe´rhame plays with boys' toys. Such women never menstruate; their secondary sexual characteristics are undeveloped or in some instances are male. Parents object more strongly to kwe´rhame than to elxa´ and attempt to bully them into feminine ways.

Casual secret homosexuality among both women and men is well known. The latter is probably more common. This is not considered objectionable but such persons would resent being called elxa´ or kwe´rhame.[55]

♀ 1931: EDWARD WINSLOW GIFFORD; Kamia "origin story"

Gifford's study of *The Kamia of Imperial Valley*, published in the *Bureau of American Ethnology Bulletin* in 1931, describes a tribal "origin story":

The Kamia ancestors camped on the eastern side of Salton Sea, from which place they later scattered. . . . The dispersal of the people from their camping place at Salton Sea was due to fear created by the appearance from the north of a female transvestite (Warharmi) and two male twins called Madkwahomai. These were the introducers of Kamia culture. . . . the transvestite and the twins . . . were the bearers of the seeds of cultivated plants.[56]

♀ 1933: EDWARD WINSLOW GIFFORD;
"Female transvestites"

Gifford's study of "The Cocopa," for the 1933 *University of California Publications in American Archaeology and Ethnology*, reports on both male and female "transvestites." About the latter Gifford writes:

Female transvestites (war'hameh). Male proclivities indicated by desire to play with boys, make bows and arrows, hunt birds and rabbits. Young man might love such girl, but she cared nothing for him; wished only to become man. Hair dressed like man's, nose pierced. Such females not menstruate or develop large breasts. Like men in muscular build, but external sexual organs of women. Attempted sexual intercourse with women, married, established households like men. Fought in battle like men.[57]

1943: WILLARD WILLIAMS HILL;
"Transvestites among the whites"

Hill's anthropological study of Navaho humor includes a section on "Humor Based on the Unfamiliar Actions of Foreigners." Hill reports that the clothing of white people is a subject for comment:

Once during a ceremonial which was attended by an unusual number of tourists, one of the older [Navaho] men remarked, "There must be a great many more transvestites among the whites than among the Navaho because so many white women wear trousers."[58]

1947: DOROTHEA LEIGHTON and
CLYDE KLUCKHOHN;
"Hermaphrodites or homosexuals"

In their 1947 book, *Children of the People: The Navaho Individual and His Development*, physician Leighton and anthropologist Kluckhohn write:

In the old days a few men (some of them probably hermaphrodites or homosexuals) donned women's clothing and took up women's occupations. Some such persons are still known, but all of them are middle-aged or older. It may be that the bachelors in their thirties who live in various communities today are individuals of these two types who fear the ridicule of white persons and so do not change clothing.[59]

1951: CLELLAN S. FORD and FRANK A. BEACH;
"Homosexual Behavior"

Ford and Beach's *Patterns of Sexual Behavior*, published in 1951, devotes one chapter to male and female homosexual activity. The authors collected information on homosexuality in seventy-six societies and found that male homosexual activities were regarded favorably in forty-nine (sixty-four percent). Among these favorably inclined cultures are the following American Indian groups: Creek, Crow, Hopi, Mandan, Maricopa, Menomini, Natchez, Navaho, Omaha, Oto, Papago, Ponca, Quinault, Seminole, Tubatulabal, Yuma, Yurok, and Zuñi. In addition, the Chiricahua, Crow, Ojibwa, and Yuma were found to approve female homosexual relations. Against this, only four Indian tribes were found to disapprove of male homosexual relations: the Chiricahua (which, as mentioned, approve Lesbian relations), Ojibwa (which likewise approve Lesbianism), Klamath, and Pima.[60] Ford and Beach's book was quickly taken up by the American homosexual emancipation movement, which used its cross-cultural research and conclusions to place the antihomosexuality of contemporary Western society in a socially and historically relative perspective.

1959: W. DORR LEGG;
"The Berdache and Theories of Sexual Inversion"

In 1959, W. Dorr Legg discusses the berdache and homosexuality in the *ONE Institute Quarterly*, a publication of a California "homophile" organization involved in homosexual emancipation research and education. Legg's brief study indicates the American homosexual rights movements' early interest in Native American homosexuality, and in the usefulness of such cross-cultural and historical information in questioning some of the traditional anthropomorphic, atemporal, and oppressive theories of homosexuality.

Legg discusses that theory which suggests that homosexual behavior originates in the reversal (or "inversion") of the "natural" sex roles of males and females. Although he does not question the very idea of "natural" sex roles, Legg does point out that when such roles are actually specified they turn out to refer to that behavior which is the most commonly associated with a particular sex in a particular society. He also points out that what is perceived as "natural" in one society may not conform at all to what is considered "natural" in another. He argues that cross-cultural and historical considerations suggest that very little behavior considered "masculine" or "feminine" in Western society is actually "natural" in any biological sense, but is actually culturally conditioned.

Citing several early documents referring to Native American homosexuality and transvestism, Legg concludes that such reports do suggest connections between sex role reversal ("inversion") and same-gender erotic attraction. But Legg is one of the few to point out that Native American homosexuality also includes the much less commonly discussed phenomenon of same-gender sexual behavior unconnected with sex role reversal, such as cross-dressing. Legg asks, what is the sexual orientation of the tribal leader who marries and has sexual relations with the berdache? What is the sexual character of those Native American youths whom George Catlin describes as participants in an orgiastic dance to the berdache, those youths whom Catlin calls a society of "odd fellows"? Legg's essay raises useful questions still to be answered.[61]

♀ 1964: J. J. HONIGMANN;
"Both male and female homosexuality"

In his 1964 book, *The Kaska Indians: An Ethnographic Reconstruction,* Honigmann writes on Native Lesbianism:

Female homosexuals simulated copulation by "getting on top of each other." Such women were often transvestites, but no male transvestites could be recalled. Sometimes if a couple had too many female children and desired a son to hunt for them in later years, they selected a daughter to be "like a man." When she was about five years old the parents tied the dried ovaries of a bear to her inner belt. She wore this amulet for the rest of her life in order to avoid conception. The girl was raised as a boy. She dressed in masculine attire and performed male allocated tasks, often developing great strength and usually becoming an outstanding hunter. She screamed and broke the bow and arrows of any boy who made sexual advances to her. "She knows that if he gets her then her luck with game will be broken." Apparently such a girl entered homosexual relationships.

Among the Dease River Kaska it is reported:

Berdaches were unknown but the informant agreed that both male and female homosexuality sometimes occurred. Homosexual men engaged in sodomy, oral contacts being carefully avoided. Two women achieved orgasm through clitoral friction.[62]

1964: BOB WALTRIP;
Elmer Gage

An extremely rare interview with a homosexual Native American appeared in *ONE Magazine* in 1965. It is based on a recording made on December 26, 1964, by Bob Waltrip; the subject is Elmer Gage, a thirty-five-year-old, six-foot Mohave, who lived on the Colorado River Reservation.

For unknown numbers of years the Mohave Indians have lived along the lower part of the Colorado River farming the rich bottomlands and managing to make a living from the river itself. Presently, their reservation lies along the river from

Needles, California south to Yuma, Arizona. The U.S. Bureau of Indian Affairs helps them in managing their lives, granting them land allotments which they can either farm or lease to the number of large produce companies that raise lettuce and melons along the river. Most of the Mohaves choose to lease out their land and attempt to live on the income this offers.

Elmer Gage is such an Indian. He lives on the Colorado River Indian Reservation along with his 83 year old aunt, whom he calls his grandmother. Both he and his aunt lease their land, and are able to live—not comfortably, perhaps—in a two-room house, secluded in a maze of brush and trees. In his small town, Elmer is almost universally known as a homosexual. The white townspeople consider him something of a village idiot. The Indian boys tease each other about sleeping with him, yet their teasing is somehow not ridicule of him. Among the Indians he is accepted with equanimity, and their laughter is as much at themselves as at him. His fellow tribesmen treat him as if he were an unattractive woman. They often talk about making love to him (in a crowd which includes him), yet it is understood that they don't really mean it. Men being men, however, more than a few of them actually do share his bed when they're sure none of the others will catch them at it.

Elmer supplements his land-lease income by making Indian artifacts which he sells to tourists through local variety stores, and through the Tribal Council—an organization of Indians who work together for their mutual benefit. In an era when most Indian art pieces have a "made in Japan" stamp on the back, Elmer is faced with bitter competition. It takes him hours to make a beaded belt, which he must sell at a ridiculously low price in order to sell it at all. Since he works slowly and with extreme care, it would be safe to assume that he is paid not more than fifty cents an hour for his labor. The injustice of this is immediately apparent when one considers that Elmer is recognized as being one of the last remaining makers of genuine Mohave Indian artifacts.

Mr. Gage is a thirty-five year old man, standing about six feet tall, with a happy, well-fed air about him. Though delicate of bearing, he has prodigious physical strength—the fruit of long hours of hard farm labor. He has the evenness of temper and the quick wit that is peculiar to Mohaves.

He and a few others are Bird Dancers. Bird dancing (a charming dance with one man and three or four women which imitates the actions of birds) is a social dance that is performed for celebrations and various other gatherings. He has danced before statesmen, movie stars, and foreign dignitaries, yet his success has been relatively small. In plain, unpleasant truth, no one cares any more.

Elmer's "grandmother" is a magnificent old woman, who wears the ceremonial tattoo of the Mohaves, which has been abandoned for many years. This tattoo consists of five thin blue parallel lines running from the lower lip to the bottom of the chin. Her face is arresting in its unique beauty. Her hands move with a fascinating grace as she performs such mundane tasks as cooking and sewing. While talking, her elegant, expressive hands are continually in motion, punctuating phrases and adding a singular symmetry to her speech. Although her eyes are growing dim, she can still weave and sew, and is one of the very few Mohaves remaining who knows the reason behind many of the tribal ceremonies and stories.

The following interview was recorded the day after Christmas, 1964. We three sat around the table in the Gage home while a half-coyote puppy frisked on the floor and "Constantine and the Cross" raged across the television screen. We ate *pinal*, which is a sort of stone-ground wheat cereal made by the Maricopa Indians —close relatives of the Mohaves.

Q: Elmer, how long have you been making art objects for sale to tourists, and what kind of things do you make?

E: Gee, I started a long time ago during school. About 1947. Selling things to the tribe. I make necklaces, bola ties (maybe I'll make you one for Christmas), beaded belts, complete cradle boards, Mohave ceremonial dolls. Also pottery. I make ceremonial costumes, like for the Bird Dancers. My own costumes. Beaded earrings. Headdresses. All kinds of stuff.

Q: You mentioned ceremonial dolls. What exactly are they?

E: The Mohaves have a ceremony where they try to bring the dead back., They make a doll and dress him in the dead man's clothes. They have a ceremony where they dance these dolls. Of course the dolls I make for tourists are just little ones—copies. But I can also make the real ones. The life-sized ones.

Q: Where did you learn to make all these things?

Grandma: I taught him how to do these things when he was young. He was interested. Like the cradle boards for babies. You have to know they're different. For boys we have a narrow board to put them on, and for the girls it's a little more wider, like this (motioning with her hands). They always are happier when a boy baby's born. (Laughing.) I don't know why. But Elmer learned all these things— how to make things. And when something's going on he goes there and watches. That's how he learns.

Q: Can any of the other Mohaves make the things Elmer makes?

Grandma: Um-hum. Some of them could if they wanted to.

Q: Do they?

E: No. It seems like I'm the only one that's keeping these traditions alive.

Q: And after you're gone these things will just die?

E: Yes.

Q: Doesn't anybody care? Any of the Mohaves?

E: No. Young people don't take any interest in these things. They just stand around the Oasis. (A local tavern.)

Q: It seems a shame that they don't take more interest.

E: (Shrugging) They're just getting modern. What can you do?

A pause here, while the television movie ended.

Q: Grandma, how did you get your tattoo, and what does it mean?

Grandma: (laughing) The Mohaves—which is pronounced Hahm-ah-*kah*-va in Indian language—say that you can't go to the happy hunting ground unless you have this tattoo. If you're not wearing one when you die they say you'll go into a kangaroo rat's hole and he'll lock you up there and you'll just stay there. There was a man in Needles, California when I was twenty-five and he wanted to tattoo me. He kept on pestering me and I finally let him, though I didn't want to. It *hurt*. That was in 1906, when I was young. I was already a baptised Episcopalian, but I thought it wouldn't hurt to make sure. (a pause) Oh, they just say that about the rat's hole and everything. They don't know. Just like heaven and hell. They don't really know.

(We ate some more pinal for awhile, and then Grandma retired, leaving Elmer and myself alone.)

Q: Does your grandmother know you're gay?

E: I don't know. She still talks about me getting married. But I tell her I have to stay with her and take care of her. I went into the service—the Army—in 1951, and left her by herself. But she couldn't take care of herself so I had to get a discharge and come back here to take care of her. She's so old. I hate to think of when she'll die.

Q: Do you think being gay has proven a disadvantage in any way?

E: I guess so. I can't say. We all have bad things in our life. I can't say if it's a disadvantage being gay because I've been this way so long. Who knows? It's a disadvantage being a lot of things. It's a disadvantage not having money . . . a lot of things.

Q: Do you ever feel inferior because of your homosexuality?

E: All of us feel inferior for one reason or another.

Q: How do you feel about the people here? They seem to treat you rather cavalierly. How do you react to this kind of treatment?

E: You mean, how do I like being made fun of? I don't like it much. When they start to talk about me I just go along with it. I'm not crazy about it. But, for the most part, we all get along. They don't mean any harm by it.

Q: How did you learn about sex?

E: From other boys my age. Of course, it took me awhile to get it all straight in my mind. But we played around a lot and I enjoyed it. Now most of these kids are married and have children of their own.

Q: Do you regret not having children?

E: I don't know. I don't think so. They're kind of frightening, the little ones. They're always falling on their heads and everything. I probably wouldn't know how to raise a kid if I had one. I'd probably be a nervous wreck.

Q: What was the extent of your education?

E: Up to the tenth grade, then I got out.

Q: Why?

E: They said I was old enough to get out and work. I wanted to go on, but the social worker wouldn't help me. Grandma had a stroke and couldn't work in the cotton any more, so I quit school and took care of her.

Q: Tell me something about your private life, if you would. Do you have a steady lover?

E: No. I never have had. But I've been in love.

Q: Wth a straight guy?

E: Yes.

Q: It's pretty awful, isn't it?

E: Yes, it's pretty awful.

Q: Do you find it a hindrance to be living in a small town rather than a city?

E: Yes, as far as having fun goes. But I feel kind of obligated here. I feel like I'm kind of responsible for it in some way. It's as if I were needed here—not only by Grandma but by other people too. I would feel kind of guilty leaving it, but at the same time I want to get away and have a life of my own. I want to go to California—maybe L.A.—but I can't because of Grandma. This is her house, and her hospital is near by. So we have to stay here.

Q: Do you think you'll eventually find a steady lover and "settle down" as the saying goes?

E: Well, I'm pretty well settled down already. Only without the lover. I hope I'll find somebody. I want to find somebody. But I'm not really sure that I will. I'm not sure of anything. They say the most adventuresome hunt in the world is the hunt for a lover. I'll admit that it's taking me a damn long time to bring him to bay. But I still hope.

It's hard to find anyone here because everyone knows everyone else's business. But some of the boys run around with me. We have a good time. Oh, I don't mean like sex all the time. I mean we have a good time like friends—singing Mohave songs and dancing Bird and stuff like that.

But it gets lonely living here with only Grandma. And I'm not getting any younger. I get depressed sometimes, thinking that life is passing me by. I wish there was something I could do to kind of break out of the rut. But I don't know what it is.

Q: Then you don't have any plans for the future?

E: I have *dreams* for the future. But it doesn't do much good to actually plan. I found that out a long time ago. I could *plan* to inherit a million dollars and marry a handsome movie star. But it wouldn't do much good, that kind of planning. The only things I plan are things like fixing the leak in the roof and making myself a new shirt. I guess everybody else is pretty much the same way.

Q: I guess they are at that. Do you consider yourself an average American?

E: Of course. There's nothing special about me. Oh, deep down inside we all think we're special, but we're not, actually. You know, most people don't know what Indians are like. They've seen so many television westerns they think we all still ride horses and run around half naked with headdresses and everything. The only time I dress in the traditional dress is for things like state fairs and lecture tours and things like that. It's all like a show. This picture of me (see inset) is just a kind of publicity picture. The Bird Dancers go on tours once in awhile, dancing for audiences, and everyone thinks all Mohaves dress in bright costumes and hop around like birds. I was at a gas station in town one day and this guy from Pennsylvania pulled in and we started talking. He asked if this was really an Indian reservation, and I told him it was. Then he asked me if there were any wild Indians around. He didn't even know I was an Indian. I told him that all the Indians around here were tame as kittens.

Q: Do you regret it when people don't recognize you as an Indian?

E: Yes. I hate to see the Indian pass from the scene. Most Easterners mistake me for a Mexican. One time when I was on a visit to Disneyland this tourist came up to me and started talking Spanish. Now I speak English and I speak the Mohave language, but I can't understand Spanish, so I told him I wasn't a Mexican but a Mohave. He said "What's that?"

The Indian is gradually being absorbed into the white culture. Mixed marriages and things like that. Before too long there will be no more pure-blooded Indians left.

Q: I guess that's true. Well, you've told us a lot about yourself, but I'm running out of questions. Do you have any closing words for our readers?

E: God no. I don't know anything. Except that I would like to say that the American Indian is pretty much like the American anyone else. Indians dress like everyone else. They live in the same kinds of houses and work at the same jobs and drive the same kinds of cars. As for me, being gay has its disadvantages. But I don't think I would like to change. I guess I'm just on my own personal little warpath—not against whites but against heterosexuals who think everyone should be like them. I'm not always happy, but I'm always me. And they can like it or lump it. Life's too short to spend your time being something you don't want to be. Like the old saying, "To thine own self be true." I'm true to myself and my own nature. I think that's all anyone has a right to ask of me.[63]

♀ 1975–76: DEAN GENGLE;
Gay American Indians (G.A.I.)
"We do want to get other groups started"

A brief news story reports the formation in July 1975, in San Francisco, of the first Gay American Indian liberation organization.

While native Americans are organizing to reclaim their culture, gay Indians are organizing, too.

Barbara Cameron and Randy Burns are co-leaders of the newly-formed Gay American Indians group in San Francisco. Barbara works at the American Indian Center in the city.

Randy is a student at San Francisco State and a member of the Student Council of American Natives.

Together, they are attempting to return to the bases of Gay Indian pride.

"When I first came to San Francisco, I didn't know anyone, gay, Indian, or anything," Randy said. "I remember reading an article in *Fag Rag* about the place gay people had in the Indian culture before the invasion of the white man's values and education.

"I was like a lot of Indian people who came to the city. During the '40s and '50s, the Bureau of Indian Affairs relocated many Indians to the cities. A lot of them were gay Indians who had 'lost' the respect of their tribes. They came to the cities and turned suicidal, alcoholic and stereotypically cross-dressed."

Barbara Cameron
(Photo: Crawford Barton.)

"My grandparents were forced to attend an eastern boarding school and had Christianity beat into them," Barbara added. "I thought, you know, that I was the only lesbian Indian in the world. Then I met my lover. I was really alienated. I felt trapped between my Indian culture and the society. That's the position of most gay Indians because it's the position of Indians as a whole. I really align myself with Indians first and gay people second."

"So in July of '75, Barbara and I and some others—about 10 of us—decided to start GAI," Randy said.

They had little trouble organizing, but there were some objections to their distributing fliers, announcing the group's formation, at the American Indian Center.

"The former director of the center asked me if I wasn't worried about offending some people when I put up our fliers," Randy said. "I ignored the question, and went ahead with putting them up."

From that beginning in July, the group has grown to about 30 members.

"We were first and foremost a group for *each other*," Barbara said. "Bringing together gay Indians is our most important current task. We have no grandiose plans beyond that."

"It has really brought together old and young Indians in a new way," Randy said. "We are really trying to break down stereotypes in both directions. In the Indian community, we are trying to realign ourselves with the trampled traditions of our people. Gay people were respected parts of the tribes. Some were artists and medicine people. So we supply speakers from the group to appear at Indian gatherings. Sometimes we are booed or jeered, but it doesn't last long.

"In the gay community, we're trying to break down the image of the Indian as a macho militant that gay white people have."

"We also participate in demonstrations and political action for Indian concerns," Barbara adds. "We cooperate with third world groups. We also have a weekly radio show on KPOO here in the city."

Randy is Piute. Barbara is Lakota (Sioux). There are about 20 tribes represented in the group. It is predominantly male, but that imbalance is offset by having dual male/female leadership.

"The heavy male trip does bother me somewhat," Barbara admitted. "But we do what we can to consciously combat sexism in the group. We are trying to reach more lesbian Indians. It will take a long time. For now, it's important that Indians know that there *are* gay Indians, both sexes."

How do they feel about the Bicentennial?

"Angry," Barbara stated flatly. "It's ridiculous. What should Indians celebrate? Two-hundred years of broken promises, land theft, genocide and rape? It is one thing to talk about 'celebration' and another to look at the little Vietnam the government has going in South Dakota. We're going to be demonstrating in Philadelphia in '76. There are plans for demonstrations at Mount Rushmore. Gay Indians will be there."

How does it stand, historically and personally, between gay people and Indians?

Barbara summarizes: . . . Probably the most together tribe in the country, the ones who have best retained the old ways and traditions, are the Pueblos. Gay people are still accorded positions of respect in the tribe. Some are healers, medicine people. . . .

What are the plans for the immediate future?

"Like we said, we don't have any grand plans," Randy said. "We do want to get other groups started. We'll likely begin in New York City, then try to branch out to New Mexico, Minneapolis, places where some of us have personal contacts.

"We hope to get a forum going in *Akwesasne Notes*, the national newspaper of the American Indian Movement. We need to get our own newsletter going, too. Mostly, though, our work will continue to be among ourselves: mutual support, socializing, and help."

Their optimism is refreshing. It is new, born of a growing awareness that America isn't what it could be. They are using "white man's medicine": the media, communications, and politics. If they do succeed in reasserting the wisdom of native American tribes concerning gay people, all of us will benefit.[64]

V

RESISTANCE
1859-1972

Introduction

The persecutor desires the victims to remain ignorant of their oppression. But even less does the oppressor want these victims to imagine the possibility of resistance. The victims' awareness of oppression may, by itself, lead only to fatalistic resignation before what seems an overwhelming force. Knowledge of resistance suggests that even under conditions of extreme persecution there exists the possibility of struggle. Knowledge of past and forgotten rebellion, large or small, successful or unsuccessful, is nourishment for the hungry spirits of the dispossessed; it provides food for present survival and energy for renewed struggle. It is exemplary.

American Gay history includes a long and little-known tradition of resistance. This resistance has taken varied forms, from the isolated acts of lone individuals, from the writing of letters, poems, essays, book-length treatises defending homosexuality, or novels presenting homosexuals as human beings—to the consciously "political" organizing of a group united for action against antihomosexual bigots and institutionalized persecution. In its more individualistic forms, this resistance may today not always be immediately recognizable as such. From the perspective of a Gay liberation or Lesbian-feminist consciousness, some acts and writings which in their own time constituted resistance may now appear to be reactionary and oppressive. An early novel appealing to the sympathy of heterosexuals may have been a daring act in its day, while to a contemporary Gay liberationist it appears useless and even repugnant. Thus, it is important to study each act of resistance in the context of its time.

In this section, Walt Whitman's direct and profound influence on the two leading English pioneers of homosexual emancipation, John Addington Symonds and Edward Carpenter, is for the first time set in the perspective of American and English Gay liberation history. This chronological survey presents some of those homosexually relevant writings of Whitman which inspired Symonds and Carpenter, their letters of response, and Whitman's comments on the two Englishmen, as recorded by Horace Traubel. Also cited are Symonds's and Carpenter's own major homosexual emancipation writings, and Symonds's successful attempt to enlist in his crusade for homosexual liberation two Americans, Thomas Sergeant Perry and a professor named Peirce(?), of Cambridge, Massachusetts. The reaction of American novelist Henry James to Symonds's emancipationist efforts is also recorded. These documents begin to suggest some of the complex interconnections among the English-speaking homosexual emancipation pioneers of the late nineteenth and early twentieth centuries, throughout which Whitman's influence can now be traced as an original and motivating force. These documents establish the existence of an international homosexual resistance in which the American poet played a primary, initiating role.

This section also includes four groups of documents relating to the development of an organized homosexual emancipation movement in the United States. If the words of the pseudonymous Earl Lind can be trusted, the *Cercle Hermaphroditos* was formed in about 1895 by "androgynes" ("feminine"-identified male homosexuals) "for defense against the world's bitter persecution." Although in Lind's description the group appears to have been a casual social gathering, the *Cercle* may be considered an early precursor of later homosexual emancipation organizations.

The first well-documented emancipation organization of American homosexuals is the Chicago Society for Human Rights, founded by Henry Gerber and chartered by the state of Illinois in 1924. The society, named after the *Bund für Menschenrecht*, demonstrates the early influence in America of the organized German homosexual emancipation movement. Documents on the Chicago society include Gerber's published descriptions of its founding and history, as well as the group's official charter, discovered in the research for the present book and here reprinted for the first time. Also included are several newly discovered writings by Gerber on homosexuality, originally published in 1934 in a short-lived mimeographed literary periodical.

In an interview with the present author, Henry Hay for the first time describes his conception, in August 1948, of a homosexual rights organization which, a few years later, became the first Mattachine Society. Here, in the words and from the viewpoint of its founder, is the history of the original Mattachine, a story that, because of Hay's radical political associations, has not before been told.

The first organized and successful Lesbian liberation organization in the United States, the Daughters of Bilitis (DOB), was founded by Del Martin and Phyllis Lyon in 1955. In 1958, with the encouragement of Martin and Lyon, Barbara Gittings founded the original New York chapter of DOB. In an interview, Gittings describes this group's early years. In following years Gittings would become one of the editors in chief of the DOB magazine, *The Ladder*, published continuously from 1956 until 1972—this publication itself being one of the single most important manifestations of the organized American Lesbian resistance movement.

The American resistance to Lesbian oppression as traced in this section also includes such diverse phenomena as "Miss S's" defense of her "divine gift of loving," published in 1897 in Symonds's and Ellis's *Sexual Inversion*; Emma Goldman's public lectures in 1915 defending homosexuality, including her description of these lectures' positive effect on one particular Lesbian; F. W. Stella Browne's argument, published in the United States in 1923, against the repression of active Lesbian relations; Radclyffe Hall's appeal for sympathy from the American public, via the 1929 publication of *The Well of Loneliness*; Ella Thompson's legal appeal to the Georgia Supreme Court, whose decision of 1939 established that two females could not be prosecuted under the state's sodomy law; Alma Routsong's fictional recreation in the 1960s of the love berween two American women of the early nineteenth century—her expression in the novel *Patience and Sarah* of a developing Lesbian-feminist consciousness.

The documents gathered here demonstrate the existence of an American tradition of resistance to homosexual oppression, a history going back far beyond the Stonewall Rebellion of June 1969, when Lesbians and Gay men in New York actively fought police harassment, the event marking the birth of the recent Gay liberation movement.

1859–1924: WALT WHITMAN, JOHN ADDINGTON SYMONDS, ♀ EDWARD CARPENTER; "In paths untrodden"

WALT WHITMAN

Although Whitman scholars have customarily deemphasized the celebratory character of his poems of male—male love and dismissed his sexual politics as totally deluded, in the perspective of homosexual emancipation history, Whitman emerges as a founding father. Besides his importance as a poet, the evidence demonstrates Whitman's direct and powerful influence on the work of the two major, early English political philosophers of homosexual liberation, John Addington Symonds and Edward Carpenter—evidence presented in parallel chronological surveys. Whitman's place within Gay history, especially as an influence on the early homosexual emancipation movement, has not been carefully explored. When the many biographical and analytical works on the American poet are finally surveyed in this historical perspective and in detail, their truly scandalous suppression or bigoted interpretation of Whitman's homosexuality will emerge with startling clarity and force. Until then, the following survey of some major documents is intended to suggest the initiatory, pivotal role of Whitman, despite his own evasions and even outright disavowal, as a pioneer in the history of the homosexual resistance.

Happily for the history of Gay liberation, Walt Whitman precisely dates his resolution "To celebrate the need of comrades": an "afternoon" in September 1859. The poem recording this resolution first appears in the 1860 edition of *Leaves of Grass*, as number 1 in the new "Calamus" section, whose theme is male—male love:

IN paths untrodden,
In the growth by margins of pond-waters,
Escaped from the life that exhibits itself,
From all the standards hitherto published—from the pleasures,
     profits, conformities,
Which too long I was offering to feed to my Soul;
Clear to me now, standards not yet published—clear to me that
     my Soul,
That the Soul of the man I speak for, feeds, rejoices only in
     comrades;
Here, by myself, away from the clank of the world,
Tallying and talked to here by tongues aromatic,
No longer abashed—for in this secluded spot I can respond as I
     would not dare elsewhere,
Strong upon me the life that does not exhibit itself, yet contains all
     the rest,
Resolved to sing no songs to-day but those of manly attachment,
Projecting them along that substantial life,
Bequeathing, hence, types of athletic love,
Afternoon, this delicious Ninth Month, in my forty-first year,
I proceed, for all who are, or have been, young men,
To tell the secret of my nights and days,
To celebrate the need of comrades.[1]

Poem number 4 of the same edition unequivocally identifies the symbolic meaning of calamus, a grass- or rushlike plant growing around the edges of ponds.
"Henceforth," says Whitman, this calamus plant shall "be the token of comrades,"
because at such a pond "I last saw him that tenderly loves me—and returns again,
never to separate from me."[2] In the first edition of *Leaves of Grass* (1855),
Whitman also refers to calamus or "sweet-flag" (another common name for the
same plant), using it explicitly as a phallic symbol.[3] The "Calamus" poems are thus
unambiguously identified with the love of males for males, and this love is explicitly
erotic. The poems themselves emphasize the physical, as well as emotional, expression of male intimacy. Whitman's "Calamus" poems evoke a great variety of those
deep feelings connected with love—in particular, the love of males for males,
expressed in the most physical of terms. These feelings range from the deepest
despair to the most positive, passionate love.

In the first verse of the 1860 edition of *Leaves of Grass*, "Proto-Leaf," Whitman
states his poetic program: among his subjects he will write of "sexual organs and
acts!"—describing them "with courageous clear voice," proving them "illustrious."
He immediately adds that he "will sing the song of companionship"—he will show
what alone will unify the states—those states which "are to found their own ideal of
manly love, indicating it in me." He continues:

I will therefore let flame from me the burning fires that were
     threatening to consume me,
I will lift what has too long kept down those smouldering fires,
I will give them complete abandonment,

I will write the evangel-poem of comrades and of love,
(For who but I should understand love, with all its sorrow and
    joy?
And who but I should be the poet of comrades?)[4]

In his verse, Whitman begins to formulate, in poetic terms, a conception of sexual politics. "Calamus" poem number 5 emphasizes the social, unifying function of male comradeship.

STATES!
Were you looking to be held together by the lawyers?
By an agreement on a paper? Or by arms?

Away!
I arrive, bringing these, beyond all the forces of courts and arms,
These! to hold you together as firmly as the earth itself is held
    together.

.   .   .   .

There shall from me be a new friendship—It shall be called after
    my name,
It shall circulate through The States, indifferent of place,
It shall twist and intertwist them through and around each other—
    Compact shall they be, showing new signs,
Affection shall solve every one of the problems of freedom,
Those who love each other shall be invincible. . . .

.   .   .   .

It shall be customary in all directions, in the houses and streets,
    to see manly affection,
The departing brother or friend shall salute the remaining brother
    or friend with a kiss.

There shall be innovations,
There shall be countless linked hands.

.   .   .   .

These shall be masters of the world under a new power,
They shall laugh to scorn the attacks of all the remainder of the
    world.

.   .   .   .

These shall tie and band stronger than hoops of iron,
I, extatic, O partners! O lands! henceforth with the
    love of lovers tie you.[5]

In poem 35 Whitman says:

I believe the main purport of These States is to found a
    superb friendship, exalté, previously unknown,
Because I perceive it waits, and has been always waiting,
    latent in all men.[6]

"I wish to infuse myself among you," says Whitman, "till I see it common for you to walk hand in hand."[7]

Although Whitman's sexual politics, as expressed in these poems of 1860, was later somewhat elaborated in prose, his views always retained a certain vagueness. Nevertheless, Whitman's writings are remarkable for suggesting, at an early date, intimate connections between homosexual emancipation and the full development of democracy, including a general sexual and human liberation. While some of Whitman's verses belong among the world's most beautiful love lyrics, his clear, spare, passionate, poems of male–male love also contain the seeds of a sexual politics whose far-reaching implications are only becoming clear with the recent development of the women's and Gay liberation movements and related theoretical analyses.

JOHN ADDINGTON SYMONDS

John Addington Symonds, born in 1840, the son of a well-to-do physician, would become a historian of Renaissance Italy and classical Greece, a literary scholar, critic, essayist, poet, translator, and biographer, as well as one of the two major English pioneers of homosexual emancipation.

In 1858, the eighteen-year-old Symonds first saw and fell in love with the fifteen-year-old Willie Dyer—one April Sunday—in church on his Easter holidays. To this meeting, and the relationship that followed, Symonds later dated his "birth" (what might now be called his "coming out"), the conscious realization of his homosexuality. In 1864, Symonds married Janet Catharine North, and the first of their three daughters arrived the following year. Also in 1865, the twenty-five-year-old Symonds first heard Walt Whitman's poems read aloud to him by a friend. Symonds was immediately overwhelmed and fascinated by the poet's bold expression of male–male love, and he began a lifelong inquiry into the character and writings of that American, especially into the precise meaning and intent of his "Calamus" series.[8]

On April 8, 1867, Symonds writes a close friend and confidant, Henry Graham Dakyns, that he is going to see Moncure D. Conway, American Unitarian clergyman and militant abolitionist, then traveling in Europe. Conway had published an article on Whitman in an English periodical, and Symonds says:

I shall not omit to ask him questions about the substance of Calamus—as adroitly as I can with a view to hearing what nidus [nest] for it there is actually in America.[9]

On April 15, Symonds reports that he and Conway had liked each other immediately; Conway had given Symonds an edition of Whitman's poetry—sent by Whitman "to some worthy proselyte." But Conway, says Symonds, remained evasive:

I c[oul]d not get him to say anything explicit about Calamus. This, I think means that Calamus is really very important & that Conway refuses to talk it over with a stranger. He cannot be oblivious of its plainer meanings.[10]

Symonds was determined to question Conway more closely if he ever saw him again. Symonds's efforts to obtain proof of Whitman's exact meaning would continue for a quarter of a century.

In 1871, Whitman published an essay, "Democratic Vistas," expanding in prose on the social implications of male–male love, developing his idea of sexual politics. Leaping speculatively ahead in time, Whitman optimistically suggests that even before the bicentennial arrives in 1976, "much that is now undream'd of, we might then see established. . . ."

Intense and loving comradeship, the personal and passionate attachment of man to man—which, hard to define, underlies the lessons and ideals of the profound saviours of every land and age, and which seems to promise, when thoroughly develop'd, cultivated and recognized in manners and literature, the most substantial hope and safety of the future of these States, will then be fully express'd.

In a note Whitman adds:

It is to the development, identification, and general prevalence of that fervid comradeship, (the adhesive love [between males], at least rivaling the amative love hitherto possessing imaginative literature, if not going beyond it,) that I look for the counterbalance and offset of our materialistic and vulgar American democracy, and for the spiritualization thereof. Many will say it is a dream, and will not follow my inferences: but I confidently expect a time when there will be seen, running like a half-hid warp through all the myriad audible and visible worldly interests of America, threads of manly friendship, fond and loving, pure and sweet, strong and life-long, carried to degrees hitherto unknown—not only giving tone to individual character, and making it unprecedently emotional, muscular, heroic, and refined, but having the deepest relations to general politics. I say democracy infers such loving comradeship, as its most inevitable twin or counterpart, without which it will be incomplete, in vain, and incapable of perpetuating itself.[11]

That same year on October 7, 1871, Symonds writes his first letter to Whitman enclosing his poem titled "Love and Death," on heroism inspired by an intimate friendship between males—expressing in an indirect way his burning interest in the meaning of "Calamus":

My dear Sir.

When a man has ventured to dedicate his work to another without authority or permission, I think that he is bound to make confession of the liberty he has taken. This must be my excuse for sending to you the crude poem in wh[ich] you may perchance detect some echo, faint & feeble, of your Calamus.—As I have put pen to paper I cannot refrain from saying that since the time when I first took up Leaves of Grass in a friend's rooms* at Trinity College Cambridge six years ago till now, your poems have been my constant companions. . . . I have found in them pure air and health—the free breath of the world—when often cramped by

* This note sign is discussed within footnote 12.

illness and the cares of life. What one man can do by communicating to those he loves the treasure he has found, I have done among my friends.

I say this in order that I may, as simply as may be, tell you how much I owe to you. He who makes the words of a man his spiritual food for years is greatly that man's debtor.[12]

Five months later on February 7, 1872, after receiving Whitman's reply praising the poem "Love and Death," Symonds writes his second letter to the poet, again trying in his circumspect manner to elicit some comment connecting the "Calamus" theme with homosexuality—simultaneously expressing fear that his inquiries might offend, despite Whitman's praise.

I was beginning to dread that I had struck some quite wrong chord—that perhaps I had seemed to you to have arrogantly confounded your own fine thought & pure feeling with the baser metal of my own nature. What you say has reassured me and has solaced me nearly as much as if I had seen the face and touched the hand of you—my Master!

For many years I have been attempting to express in verse some of the forms of what in a note to Democratic Vistas (as also in a blade of Calamus) you call "adhesiveness." I have traced passionate friendship through Greece, Rome, the medieval & the modern world, & I have now a large body of poems written but not published. . . .

It was while engaged upon this work (years ago now) that I first read Leaves of Grass. The man who spoke to me from that Book impressed me in every way most profoundly and unalterably; but especially did I then learn confidently to believe that the Comradeship, which I conceived as on a par with the Sexual feeling for depth & strength & purity & capability of all good, was real—not a delusion of distorted passions, a dream of the Past, a scholar's fancy—but a strong & vital bond of man to man.

Yet even then how hard I found it—brought up in English feudalism educated at an aristocratic public School (Harrow) and an over refined University (Oxford)—to winnow from my own emotions and from my conception of the ideal friend, all husks of affections and aberrations and to be a simple human being. *You* cannot tell quite how hard this was, & how you helped me.

I have pored for continuous hours over the pages of Calamus (as I used to pore over the pages of Plato), longing to hear you speak, *burning* for a revelation of your more developed meaning, panting to ask—is this what you would indicate?—Are then the free men of your lands really so pure & loving & noble & generous & sincere? Most of all did I desire to hear from your own lips—or from your pen—some story of athletic friendship from which to learn the truth. Yet I dared not to address you or dreamed that the thoughts of a student could abide the inevitable shafts of your searching intuition.

Shall I ever be permitted to question you & learn from you?

What the love of man for man has been in the Past I think I know. What it is here now, I know also—alas! What you say it can & shall be I dimly discern in your Poems. But this hardly satisfies me—so desirous am I of learning what you teach. Some day, perhaps—in some form, I know not what, but in your own chosen form—you will tell me more about the Love of Friends! Till then I wait. Meanwhile you have told me more than anyone beside.—

I have been led to write too much about myself, presuming on what you said, that you should like to know me better.——[13]

A few weeks later, on February 25, 1872, having received an encouraging token from Whitman (a newspaper containing a new poem by the American), Symonds writes again. Once more Symonds's main subject is male–male intimacy, though he forgoes any mention of "Calamus." Symonds this time encloses his poem "Callicrates," which he describes as "a study of Greek friendship" concerning "the most beautiful man among the Spartans."[14]

The following year, 1873, while deep in his study of Greek history and culture, Symonds wrote *A Problem in Greek Ethics*, a classic, early defense of homosexuality, which he did not dare publish, even privately, until ten years later. In this essay, Symonds presents his analysis of that historic form of Greek love involving an older and younger male in an affectionate, sexual, and pedagogical relation—a relation revealing homosexuality (Symonds feels) in its most positive, ideal light, and as a normal part of Greek society.[15]

On January 29, 1877, Symonds writes again to Whitman:

To me as a man your poems—yourself in your poems—has been a constant teacher and loved companion. . . . I wait the time when I shall be able here in England to raise my voice with more authority than I yet have in bidding men to know you: for I feel that you have for us here in the old country a message no less valuable to us than to your own people.[16]

In the period between 1878 and 1890, Symonds led an active homosexual life, attempting to establish ongoing relationships at different times with Christian Buol and Angelo Fusato, as well as making advances to numbers of other men.[17] In 1883, Symonds finally published a small, ten-copy edition of his homosexual defense, *A Problem in Greek Ethics*, written a decade earlier. He privately circulated it among a select group of friends, asking them for their opinions, as well as to be discreet in discussing it.

That Symonds's homosexual emancipation efforts had some early influence in the United States is documented by his correspondence with Thomas Sergeant Perry, an American educator, literary historian, editor, and friend of Henry James. On March 27, 1888, Symonds writes to Perry, with whom he had already been corresponding for some years. With some trepidation, Symonds had earlier sent Perry his homosexual defense. Symonds evidently received an encouraging reply from the American, and now apologizes

for suddenly interrupting our correspondence, just at the point when you were taking so much interest for me in the essay I sent you on Greek Morals, & when you were clearly expecting further communications.

Perry suggested that Symonds read M. H. F. Meier's German encyclopedia entry on "Paederastie" (1837). Symonds replies that if Meier's article

is as complete as you report (and of this I can have no doubt), the necessary work has been already done. Information is accessible to scholars. And I think I shall be wise to keep my own essay in obscurity. I shall not, however, let it lie by, particularly after what you have said upon the subject. On the contrary, I will go through the whole matter again, whenever I can get at Meyer's article . . . & at some other books wh[ich] bear upon the topic. . . . I can then [form] a judgment whether my essay possesses any independent value.[18]

On March 28, 1888, Horace Traubel began to visit Whitman almost daily and to write down their conversations—a process Traubel kept up for four years, compiling a series of detailed notes which now comprise five printed volumes, and additional, as yet unpublished manuscripts. These volumes reprint many of Symonds's and Edward Carpenter's letters to Whitman, and record his comments about both Englishmen. Following the chronological sequence of Whitman's references to Symonds and Carpenter it becomes clear that Whitman was long perfectly conscious of both men's interest in his "Calamus" theme and homosexuality.

On April 27, 1888, Traubel reports Whitman discussing Symonds's second letter, (of February 7, 1872, see page 342) which had inquired about the "Calamus" poems:

Talked an hour or more about Symonds. W. very frank, very affectionate. "Symonds is a royal good fellow. . . . But he has a few doubts yet to be quieted— not doubts of me, doubts rather of himself. One of these doubts is about Calamus. What does Calamus mean? What do the poems come to in the round-up? That is worrying him a good deal—their involvement, as he suspects, is the passional relations of men with men—the thing he reads so much of in the literatures of southern Europe and sees something of in his own experience. He is always driving at me about that: is that what Calamus means?—because of me or in spite of me, is that what it means? I have said no, but no does not satisfy him. But read this letter—read the whole of it: it is very shrewd, very cute, in deadliest earnest: it drives me hard—almost compels me—it is urgent, persistent: he sort of stands in the road and says: 'I won't move till you answer my question.' You see, this is an old letter—sixteen years old—and he is still asking the question: he refers to it in one of his latest notes. He is surely a wonderful man—a rare, cleaned-up man—a white-souled, heroic character. Look at the fight he has so far kept up with his body [Symonds had tuberculosis]—yes, and so far won: it is marvellous to me, even. I have had my own troubles—I have seen other men with troubles, too— worse than mine and not so bad as mine—but Symonds is the noblest of us all. . . . You will be writing something about Calamus some day," said W., "and this letter, and what I say, may help to clear your ideas. Calamus needs clear ideas: it may be easily, innocently distorted from its natural, its motive, body of doctrine."

Symonds's letter to Whitman about "Calamus" is read, and this conversation follows:

Said W.: "Well, what do you think of that? Do you think that could be answered?" [Traubel replied:] "I don't see why you call that letter driving you hard. It's quiet enough—it only asks questions, and asks the questions mildly enough." [Whitman replied:] "I suppose you are right—'drive' is not exactly the word: yet you know how I hate to be catechised. Symonds is right, no doubt, to ask the questions: I am just as much right if I do not answer them: just as much right if I do answer them. I often say to myself about Calamus—perhaps it means more or less than what I thought myself—means different: perhaps I don't know what it all means—perhaps never did know. My first instinct about all that Symonds writes is violently reactionary—is strong and brutal for no, no, no. Then the thought intervenes that I maybe do not know all my own meanings: I say to myself: 'You, too, go away, come back, study your own book—an alien or stranger, study your own book, see what it amounts to.' Sometime or other I will have to write him definitively about Calamus—give him my word for it what I meant or mean it to mean."[19]

On May 24, 1888, Whitman gave Traubel an apologetic letter from Symonds dated June 13, 1875, in which the Englishman expressed anxiety about being "importunate or ill-advised" in sending his poem, "Callicrates," and for asking questions about "Calamus." Traubel reports that Whitman calls this

"a beautiful letter—beautiful . . . You will see that he harps on the Calamus poems again—always harping on 'my daughter.' I don't see why it should but his recurrence to that subject irritates me a little. This letter was written thirteen years ago. . . . Symonds is still asking the same question. I suppose you might say—why don't you shut him up by answering him? There is no logical answer to that, I suppose: but I may ask in my turn: 'What right has he to ask questions anyway?' " W. laughed a bit. "Anyway, the question comes back at me almost every time he writes. He is courteous enough about it—that is the reason I do not resent him. I suppose the whole thing will end in an answer, some day. It always makes me a little testy to be catechized about the Leaves—I prefer to have the book answer for itself." I took the Symonds letter and read it. . . .

I said to W.: "That's a humble letter enough: I don't see anything in that to get excited about. He don't ask you to answer the old question. In fact, he rather apologizes for having asked it." W. fired up. "Who is excited? As to that question, he does ask it again and again: asks it, asks it, asks it." I laughed at his vehemence: "Well, suppose he does. It does no harm. Besides, you've got nothing to hide. I think your silence might lead him to suppose there was a nigger in your wood pile." "Oh nonsense! But for thirty years my enemies and friends have been asking me questions about the Leaves: I'm tired of not answering questions." It was very funny to see his face when he gave a humorous twist to the fling in his last phrase. Then he relaxed and added: "Anyway, I love Symonds. Who could fail to love a man who could write such a letter? I suppose he will yet have to be answered, damn 'im!"[20]

On September 7, 1888, Whitman gave Traubel Symonds's very first letter (dated October 7, 1871, see page 341) telling his friend:

"A Symonds letter is a red day for my calendar. . . . I am always strangely moved by a letter from Symonds: it makes the day, it makes many days, sacred."

Whitman says of Symonds's many letters over the years:

"they are all of the same character—warm (not too warm), a bit inquisitive, ingratiating."[21]

On March 3, 1889, Symonds writes to his close friend and confidant, Horatio Forbes Brown:

I have chosen this particular moment to begin a new literary work of the utmost importance—my "Autobiography."[22]

Thirty years earlier, in 1863, Symonds had first conceived of writing his sexual and affectional "confessions."[23]

On March 27, Symonds writes to his confidant Henry Dakyns that, inspired by reading the autobiographies of Cellini and Gozzi, whose lives he was researching,

I have begun scribbling my own reminiscences. This is a foolish thing to do, because I do not think they will ever be fit to publish. . . .

I do not know therefore what will come of this undertaking. Very likely I shall lay it aside, though the fragment is already considerable in bulk & curious in matter—& I feel it a pity . . . not to employ my skill upon such a rich mine of psychological curiosities as I am conscious of possessing.

. . . I believe I shall go forward, & leave my executors to deal with what will assuredly be the most considerable product of my pen.

You see I have "never spoken out." And it is a great temptation to speak out, when I have been living for two whole years in lonely intimacy with men who spoke out so magnificently as Cellini and Gozzi did.[24]

On December 6, 1889, Symonds writes to his daughter Margaret, his confidant, concerning a new work on contemporary homosexuality.

I have just completed the painful book I told you I was writing. . . . If I were to publish it now, it would create a great sensation. Society would ring with it. But the time is not ripe for the launching of "A Problem in Modern Ethics" on the world. The Ms lies on my table for retouches, & then will go to slumber in a box of precious writings, my best work, my least presentable, until its Day of Doom.

I am glad to have got through the fierce tension of this piece of production, even though I am left with a gnawing pain in my stomach—stomach or heart, I know not which. . . .[25]

On December 9, 1889, Symonds writes Whitman a kind of love letter, profusely thanking the American for the deep and positive influence of his writings. If ever they should meet, adds Symonds, even in an afterlife, he will pursue Whitman with certain questions:

I shall ask you about things which have perplexed me here—to which I think you alone could have given me an acceptable answer. All such matters will probably sink into their proper place in the infinite perspective; and when we meet, a comrade's hand-touch and a kiss will satisfy me, and a look into your eyes.

Symonds adds that, upon reading the new edition of Whitman's "complete" works, a copy of which the poet had sent him,

I miss—and I have missed for many years in new editions—the poem which first

thrilled me like a trumpet-call to you. It was called: "Long I thought that knowledge alone would suffice me". Why have you so consistently omitted this in the
canon of your works?

Upon me, your disciple, it made a decisive impact. "I put down the book, filled
with the bitterest envy." And I rose up, to follow you. I miss the words now.—

I am old now, and you are older in years, though everlastingly young, in ways
not given to all men to be so. So perhaps I ought not ask why you omitted that
poem from "Calamus," and what you meant by it. It means for me so infinitely
much. I cannot say how much.[26]

> The poem Symonds missed appeared only in the 1860 edition of *Leaves of Grass*, as
> "Calamus" number 8. This is the love lyric in which Whitman resolves (for what
> turned out to be just that moment) to give up the search for knowledge and his role
> as poet-prophet of America to "go with him I love,/It is enough for us that we are
> together. . . ."[27]
>
> On May 6, 1890, Symonds writes to Havelock Ellis, thanking him for a copy of
> his recently published book, *The New Spirit*, which includes a chapter on Whitman
> as a modern-day prophet of love, the first work to emphasize the central importance
> of Whitman's poetry of love and sex. But Ellis's explication was not explicit enough
> for Symonds, who writes to him:

I wish you had said more about "Calamus": or, if you have formed an opinion,
that you would tell me what you think. In many ways Whitman clearly regards his
doctrine of Comradeship as what he might call "spinal". Yet he nowhere makes it
clear whether he means to advocate anything approaching its Greek form, or
whether he regards that as simply monstrous. I have tried but have not succeeded
in drawing an explicit utterance upon the subject from him. But I felt that until my
mind is made up on this important aspect of his prophecy, I am unable to judge
him in relation to the gravest ethical and social problems.

I have ventured to touch on this point to you because I see, from the note to p.
108 [*New Spirit*], that you have already considered it—and, as it seems to me,
have both arrived at the conclusion that Whitman *is* hinting at Greek feeling, and
also that his encouragement of "manly love" would necessarily and scientifically
imply a corresponding degradation of women.

I am inclined to think that Whitman in comradeship includes any passionate
form of emotion, leaving its mode of expression to the persons concerned. It is
also obvious that he does not anticipate a consequent loss of respect for women.
And are we justified in taking for granted that if modern society could elevate
manly love into a new chivalry, this would prejudice what the world has gained by
the chivalrous ideal of woman?

His own deepest utterances on the subject are, I think, in "Primeval my love for
the woman I love" and "O earth my likeness."

I should much like to hear your views upon the matter; because, as I said
before, I cannot estimate Whitman in his most important relations without being
more sure than I am of the ground he takes up in Calamus: nor can I so forecast
the future as to feel certain what would happen to the world if those instincts of
manly love which are certainly prevalent in human nature, and which once at least
were idealized in Greece, came to be moralized and raised to a chivalrous intensity.

In one word, does Whitman imagine that there is lurking in manly love the stuff of a new spiritual energy, the liberation of which would prove of benefit to society? And if so, is he willing to accept, condone or ignore the physical aspects of the passion?[28]

> In the summer of 1890, Symonds makes one more effort to obtain from Whitman a statement clarifying the exact relationship between his "Calamus" poems and homosexuality.[29] Symonds had, by this time, been writing Whitman for nineteen years, again and again questioning him about the meaning of his poems and male–male love. Symonds's interest was now not only personal, not mere curiosity; he hoped to enlist Whitman as an explicit ally in the cause of homosexual liberation. On August 3, 1890, Symonds questions Whitman more directly than ever before, clearly seeking a clarification for use in the public dissemination of Whitman's philosophy. After some preliminaries, Symonds says:

I want next to ask you a question about a very important portion of your teaching, which has puzzled a great many of your disciples and admirers. To tell the truth, I have always felt unable to deal, as I wish to do, comprehensively with your philosophy of life, because I do not even yet understand the whole drift of "Calamus." If you have read Mr Havelock Ellis' "New Spirit," which contains a study of your work in thought and speculation, you may have noticed on p: 108 that he expresses some perplexity about the doctrine of "manly love," and again on p: 121 he uses this phrase "the intimate and physical love of comrades and lovers."

This reference to Havelock Ellis helps me to explain what it is I want to ask you. In your conception of Comradeship, do you contemplate the possible intrusion of those semi-sexual emotions and actions which no doubt do occur between men? I do not ask, whether you approve of them, or regard them as a necessary part of the relation? But I should much like to know whether *you are prepared to leave them to the inclinations and the conscience of the individuals concerned?*

For my own part, after mature deliberation, I hold that the present laws of France and Italy are right upon this topic of morality. They place the personal relations of adults of both sexes upon the same foundation: that is to say, they protect minors, punish violence, and guard against outrages of public decency. Within these limitations, they leave individuals to do what they think fit. But, as you know, these principles are in open contradiction with the principles of English (and I believe American) legislation.

It has not infrequently occurred to me among my English friends to hear your "Calamus" objected to, as praising and propagating a passionate affection between men, which (in the language of the objectors) has "a very dangerous side," and might "bring people into criminality."

Now: it is of the utmost importance to me as your disciple, and as one who wants sooner or later to diffuse a further knowledge of your life-philosophy by criticism; it is most important to me to know what you really think about all this.

I agree with the objectors I have mentioned that, human nature being what it is, and some men having a strong natural bias toward persons of their own sex, the enthusiasm of "Calamus" is calculated to encourage ardent and *physical* intimacies.

But I do not agree with them in thinking that such a result would be absolutely prejudicial to Social interests, while I am certain that you are right in expecting a new Chivalry (if I may so speak) from one of the main and hitherto imperfectly developed factors of the human emotional nature. This, I take it, is the spiritual outcome of your doctrine in Calamus.

And, as I have said, I prefer the line adopted by French and Italian legislature[s] to that of the English penal code.

Finally, what I earnestly desire to know is whether you are content to leave the ethical problems regarding the private behavior of comrades toward each other, to the persons' own sense of what is right and fit—or whether, on the other hand, you have never contemplated while uttering the Gospel of Comradeship, the possibility of any such delicate difficulties occurring.

Will you enlighten me on this? If I am not allowed to hear from yourself or from some one who will communicate your views, I fear I shall never be able to utter what I want to tell the world about your teaching, with the confidence and the thorough sense of not misinterpreting you in one way or the other which are inseparable from truly sympathetic and powerful exposition. . . .

It is perhaps strange that a man within 2 months of completing his 50th year should care at all about this ethical bearing of Calamus. Of course I do not care much about it, except that ignorance on the subject prevents me from forming a complete view of your life-philosophy.[30]

Whitman carefully composed a draft of his reply to Symonds, opening offhandedly and ingenuously with minor matters. He then feigns surprise that Symonds again asks the question he has dwelt on so many times before, and finally and emphatically denies any homosexual content in his poetry. It is noteworthy that Whitman remains perfectly friendly to Symonds in this letter and afterward; Whitman's answer has often been characterized as hostile. One writer typically and mistakenly says, "The anger fairly burns from his scalding reply."[31] The original of Whitman's letter is not extant, but his entire penciled draft is published with his correspondence. This draft, dated August 19, 1890, whose final version was probably somewhat altered, reads:

Y'rs of Aug: 3d just rec'd & glad to hear f'm you as always . . . Ab't the questions on Calamus pieces &c: they quite daze me. L of G. is only to be rightly construed by and within its own atmosphere and essential character—all of its pages & pieces so coming strictly under *that*—that the calamus part has even allow'd* the possibility of such construction as mention'd is terrible—I am fain to hope the pages themselves are not to be even mention'd† for such gratuitous and quite at the time entirely undream'd & unreck'd possibility of morbid inferences —wh' are disavow'd by me & seem damnable. Then one great difference between you and me, temperament & theory, is *restraint*—I know that while I have a horror of ranting & bawling I at certain moments let the spirit impulse, (?demon) rage its utmost, its wildest, damnedest—(I feel to do so in my L of G. & I do so).

---

* WW originally wrote "open'd."
† He substituted "even mention'd" for "blamed."

I end the matter by saying I wholly stand by L of G. as it is, long as all parts & pages are construed as I said by their own ensemble, spirit & atmosphere.

I live here 72 y'rs old & completely paralyzed—brain & right arm ab't same as ever—digestion, sleep, appetite, &c: fair—sight & hearing half-and-half—spirits fair—locomotive power (legs) almost utterly gone—am propell'd outdoors nearly every day—get down to the river side here, the Delaware, an hour at sunset—The writing and rounding of L of G. has been to me the reason-for-being, & life comfort. My life, young manhood, mid-age, times South, &c: have all been jolly, bodily, and probably open to criticism—

Tho' always unmarried I have had six children—two are dead—One living southern grandchild, fine boy, who writes to me occasionally. Circumstances connected with their benefit and fortune have separated me from intimate relations.

I see I have written with haste & too great effusion—but let it stand.[32]

Five days after answering Symonds, on August 24, 1890, Whitman writes to his Canadian psychiatrist friend Dr. Maurice Bucke, who had criticized Symonds on another matter:

—you are a little more severe on Symonds than I sh'd be—he has just sent me a singular letter, wh' I have answe'd (tho't at first I w'd not answer at all, but did). . . .

Whitman adds:

(sometimes I wonder whether J A S don't come under St Paul's famous category). . . .

The reference is to St. Paul's condemnation of homosexuals.[33]
Symonds replies to Whitman on September 5, 1890:

My dear Master

I am sincerely obliged to you for your letter of August 19. It is a great relief to me to know so clearly and precisely what you feel about the question I raised. Your phrases "gratuitous and quite at the time undreamed and unrecked possibility of morbid inferences—which are disavowed by me and seem damnable," set the matter as straight as can be, base the doctrine of Calamus upon a foundation of granite.

I am not surprised; for this indeed is what I understood to be your meaning, since I have studied Leaves of Grass in the right way—interpreting each part by reference to the whole and in the spirit of the whole. The result of this study was that the "adhesiveness" of comradeship had no interblending with the "amativeness" of sexual love.

Yet you must not think that the "morbid inferences," which to you "seem damnable," are quite "gratuitous" or outside the range of possibility. Frankly speaking, the emotional language of Calamus is such as hitherto has not been used in the modern world about the relation between friends. For a student of ancient literature it presents a singular analogue to the early Greek enthusiasm of comradeship in arms—as that appeared among the Dorian tribes, and made a chivalry for prehistoric Hellas. And you know what singular anomalies were connected with this lofty sentiment in the historic period of Greek development.

Again, you cannot be ignorant that a certain percentage (small but appreciable) of male beings are always born into the world, whose sexual instincts are what the Germans call "inverted." During the last 25 years much attention, in France, Germany, Austria and Italy, has been directed to the psychology and pathology of these abnormal persons. In 1889 the Penal Code of Italy was altered by the erasion of their eccentricities from the list of crimes.

Looking then to the lessons of the past in ancient Greece, where a heroic chivalry of comradeship grew intertwined with moral abominations (I speak as a modern man), and also to the Contemporary problem offered by the class of persons I have mentioned—who will certainly have somehow to be dealt with in the light of science, since the eyes of science have been drawn towards them: looking, I say, to both these things, it became of the utmost importance to know for certain what you thought about those "morbid inferences." For you have announced clearly that a great spiritual factor lies latent in Comradeship, ready to leap forth and to take a prominent part in the energy of the human race. It is, I repeat, essential that the interpreters of your prophecy should be able to speak authoritatively and decisively about their Master's *Stimmung* [disposition of mind], his radical instinct with regard to the emotional and moral quality of the comradeship he announces.

I am sorry to have annoyed you with this discussion. But you will see, I hope now, that it was not wholly unnecessary or unprofitable.

With the explanation you have placed in my hands, and which you give me liberty to use, I can speak with no uncertain voice, and with no dread lest the enemy should blaspheme.

The conclusion reached is, to my mind, in every way satisfactory. I am so profoundly convinced that you are right in all you say about the great good which is to be expected from Comradeship as you conceive it, and as alone it can be a salutary human bond, that the power of repudiating those "morbid inferences" authoritatively—should they ever be made seriously or uttered openly, either by your detractors or by the partizans of some vicious crankiness—sets me quite at ease as to my own course.

I will tell my bookseller in London to send you a copy of the "Contemporary" in which there is an essay by me on the "Dantesque and Platonic Ideals of Love." You will see something there about the Dorian Chivalry of Comradeship to wh[ich] I have alluded in this letter. It seems to me, I confess, still doubtful whether (human nature being what it is) we can expect wholly to eliminate some sensual alloy from any emotions which are raised to a very high pitch of passionate intensity. But the moralizing of the emotions must be left to social feeling and opinion in general, and ultimately to the individual conscience.[34]

Thus ends the long correspondence between Symonds and Whitman.

On October 12, 1890, Symonds writes to Ernest Rhys, quoting Whitman's disavowal of "morbid" and "damnable" inferences, commenting:

That is clear enough; & I am extremely glad to have this statement—though I confess to being surprised at the vehemence of the language.[35]

On January 12, 1891, Symonds writes to Dr. John Johnston, another English disciple of Whitman who had visited the poet in America. Johnston had written to Symonds, sending him some photographs of Whitman. Symonds says:

It is, indeed, extremely good of you to do so much for a stranger. I take it as a sign that our Master Walt has the power of bringing folk together by a common kinship of kind feeling.—I suppose this is the meaning of "Calamus", the essence of the doctrine of Comradeship. . . .

I wonder what more than this "Calamus" contains, whether the luminous ideal of a new chivalry based on brotherhood and manly affection will ever be realized.[36]

> On January 16, 1891, Symonds writes to confidant Henry Dakyns about *A Problem in Modern Ethics*, an essay, he warns Dakyns, "not intended for all eyes."

I have had a great deal of experience, both personal & through the communications of friends, relating to the subject of that essay lately. It is a strange chapter in human psychology, and the issues are not, I think, as yet to be forecast or apprehended. I feel that, as Whitman says, there is "something exalté previously unknown" ready to leap forth in the due time of the Spirit—which spirit will possibly have to work with man for yet 5 millions of years (more not impossibly) upon the planet.

I wish I could tell you some of the strange things—sweet & dear & terrible & grim—which I have learned in the course of my experiments & explorations.[37]

> On January 23, 1891, Symonds writes to Dakyns:

I am glad to hear you have got my Essay. If you would do me a kindness, please scribble over its blank pages etc, something of your thoughts, & send the printed thing back to me. If you like, I will return it to you. But, as you know, it is only sent forth to stimulate discussion. I thought that the best way to do this would be to give it the form of a Ms in print, wh[ich] I have done.

Enough of that. Though I must say that I am eager about the subject from its social & juristic aspects.

You know how vitally it has in the past interested me as a man, & how I am therefore in duty bound to work for an elucidation of the legal problem.[38]

> On February 21, 1891, Symonds writes a deep-felt letter to Whitman's American disciple Horace Traubel, saying in part:

I exchanged some words by letter with Walt lately about his "Calamus." I do not think he quite understood what I was driving at. But that does not signify. I wish you would tell me what you & your friends feel to be the central point in this most vital doctrine of comradeship. Out here in Europe I see signs of an awakening of enthusiastic relations between men, which tend to assume a passionate character. I am not alarmed by this, but I think it ought to be studied.[39]

> On February 23, 1891, Symonds writes to author Edmund Gosse, to whom he had sent a copy of *A Problem in Modern Ethics*, mentioning T. S. Perry of Boston as sympathetic to homosexual law reform:

What I should dearly desire, apropos of "the Problem," is just what you express, namely that we might come together, & have a good talk about it. . . .

As you observe, the great thing, with regard to "The Problem," is to reach the opinion of sensible people who have no sympathy with the peculiar bias. I have sent the essay to two such men: T. S. Perry of Boston, quite one of the most learned & clearest-headed men in the USA; & to my old friend John Beddoe, . . . eminent as an ethnologist. Both reply emphatically that they agree with my conclusions & suggestions on the legal point, but that they do not think it possible for the vulgar to accept them.

In regard to the legalization of homosexuality Symonds adds:

The way of thinking among the proletariate, honest artizans, peasants, etc, in Italy & Switzerland—where alone I have fraternized with the people—is all in favour of free trade.

Gradually, then, I collect from various sources the impression that if our penal code could be freed from those laws *without discussion*, the majority of unprejudiced people would accept the change with perfect equanimity. It is also curious how much the persons I have interrogated knew about it, & how much they accept it as a fact of human nature. What everybody dreads is a public raking up of the question; & as the vast numerical majority has no personal interest in it, things remain as they are.[40]

On May 20, 1891, Symonds writes to Henry Dakyns, mentioning a radical defense of homosexuality sent from the United States:

I have received a great abundance of interesting & valuable communications in consequence of sending out a few copies of that "Problem in Modern Ethics." People have handed it about. I am quite surprised to see how frankly ardently & sympathetically a large number of highly respectable persons feel toward a subject which in society they would only mention as unmentionable.

The result of this correspondence is that I sorely need to revise, enlarge, & make a new edition of my essay; & I am almost minded to print it in a PUBLISHED vol: together with my older essay on Greek Morals & some supplementary papers.

The oddest information sent me has come from 1) America, in the shape of sharply-defined acute partisanship for Urningthum, 2) London, in the shape of about twelve Ms confessions of English Urnings, & two extraordinary narratives made by professed Hypnotists of "cures(?)" effected in cases of inveterate sexual inversion.[41]

The "acute partisanship" for homosexuals was displayed by a Professor "Pierce (?)," an American mathematician of Cambridge, Massachusetts, who probably sent Symonds the defense later published as "A Letter from Professor X" (reprinted in this section).[42]

On June 22, 1891, Symonds writes to Edmund Gosse about his "fierce" new American "ally." Symonds says he has

composed an appendix to my "Problem," combining several new considerations brought home to me by the correspondence wh[ich] that sparely circulated essay has educed. I found a fierce & Quixotic ally, who goes far beyond my expectations in hopes of regenerating opinion on these topics, in a Prof: Pierce (?) of Cambridge Mass. He ought to be in Europe now. . . . If he crosses your path in London, look after him, & mention me. I hear he professes Mathematics.[43]

Edmund Gosse passed his copy of *A Problem in Modern Ethics* along to novelist Henry James, who thus became another of the few Americans to read Symonds's pioneering defense soon after its publication. James had met Symonds once, briefly, early in 1877. In 1882, upon publication of James's essay on Venice, James had sent Symonds a copy of this essay in appreciation for Symonds's own writings on Italy. Early in James's friendship with Gosse, James had been told about Symonds's problematic marriage. A month after James's one letter to Symonds, James's notebook entry of March 26, 1884, outlines his short story, "The Author of Beltraffio," a chilling and fascinating work which James, either consciously or unconsciously, based on his perception of Symonds and his wife. James also knew that his old friend from Newport, Rhode Island, Thomas Sergeant Perry, corresponded with Symonds on the subject of homosexuality.

After Gosse showed James *A Problem in Modern Ethics*, James wrote back, thanking him for "bringing me those marvelous outpourings." James adds:

J.A.S. is truly, I gather, a candid and consistent creature, and the exhibition is infinitely remarkable. It's, on the whole, I think, a queer place to plant the standard of duty, but he does it with extraordinary gallantry. If he has, or gathers, a band of the emulous, we may look for some capital sport. But I don't wonder that some of his friends and relations are haunted with a vague malaise. I think one ought to wish him more *humour*—it is really *the* saving salt. But the great reformers never have it—and he is the Gladstone of the affair.

As his own note of humor, James signed his letter "yours—if I may safely say so!—ever H.J."[44]

In July 1891, Symonds writes to Havelock Ellis:

I have privately printed two essays, which deal with the psychological problem [of homosexuality] in ancient Greece and modern Europe. . . . The real point now is legislative. France and Italy stand in glaring contrast to England and Germany. And the medical and forensic authorities who are taking it up, seem quite ignorant both of history and fact. Their pathological hypothesis will certainly not stand the test of accumulated experience.

The subject of homosexuality, says Symonds,

ought to be scientifically, historically, impartially investigated, instead of being left to Labby's inexpansible legislation.

"Labby" was Henry du Pré Labouchere, member of the House of Commons, who in 1885 had sponsored a law making the punishment for homosexuality two years at hard labor.[45]

On December 29, 1891, Symonds writes his confidant Horatio Forbes Brown, concerning the sexually explicit autobiography which he, Symonds, has

so passionately, unconventionally set down on paper. Yet I think it a very singular book—perhaps unique, in the disclosure of a type of man who has not yet been classified. I am anxious therefore that this document should not perish. . . . I want to save it from destruction after my death, and yet to preserve its publication for a period when it will not be injurious to my family. I do not just now know how to meet the difficulty. . . . You will inherit my MSS if you survive me. But you take them freely, to deal with them as you like, under my will. . . .[46]

On February 27, 1892, Symonds thanks the American Horace Traubel for his letters concerning Whitman's precarious health. Later the same night, Symonds continues:

You do not know, & I can never tell any one, what Whitman has been to me. Brought up in the purple of aristocratic school and university, provided with more money than is good for a young man, early married to a woman of noble name & illustrious connections, I might have been a mere English gentleman, had not I read Leaves of Grass in time.

I am not sure whether I have not abused the privilege of reading in that book. It revolutionized my previous conceptions, & made me another man. Revolution is always a bad thing. And so, bred as I have described myself, it is possible that I have not attained to that real & pure nobility of nature in dealing with my fellow-men which Whitman teaches & exemplifies.

I only know that he made me a free man: he helped me to work at my chosen trade, literature, for better or for worse, as I was made to do it: but he also made me love my brethren, & seek them out with more perhaps of passion than he would himself approve.

Working upon a nature so prepared, as mine was, the strong agent of Whitman's spirit could hardly fail to produce a fermentation.

He says himself: I shall do harm as well as good.

To clinch all, he has only done for me good; & the harm which may have come to me, from intemperate use of his precepts, is the fault of my previous environment or of my own feeble self.

If I have seemed to be cold, here & there, about Whitman, it is not because I am not penetrated with his doctrine; but because I know by experience how powerfully that doctrine works, & how it may be misused & misunderstood.

Symonds adds:

If Whitman is able to hear a word from an old friend, whisper in his ear that so long as I live I shall endeavour to help on his work, & to the best of my poor ability shall try to do this in his spirit.[47]

On March 26, 1892, Walt Whitman died, after a long illness. His inspiration, however, remained a living force in the continuing homosexual emancipation work of Symonds, later of Edward Carpenter.

On June 13, 1892, Symonds writes a friend who was sharing rooms with Havelock Ellis, to ask Ellis

if he would take a book from me on "Sexual Inversion" for his Science Series?

Symonds adds:

the historical study of Greece is absolutely essential to the psychological treatment of the subject now. It is being fearfully mishandled by pathologists and psychiatrical professors, who know nothing whatsoever about its real nature. . . .[48]

A week later on June 20, 1892, Symonds writes to Ellis, glad to hear he is disposed to consider collaboration on a book about homosexuality:

This, I feel, is one of the psychological and physiological questions which demand an open treatment at last. The legal and social persecution of abnormal natures requires revision. . . .

. . . The so-called scientific "psychiatrists" are ludicrously in error, by diagnosing as necessarily morbid what was the leading emotion of the best and noblest men in Hellas. . . . The theory of morbidity is more humane, but it is not less false, than that of sin or vice.

If they are to collaborate, says Symonds,

we should have to agree together about the *legal* aspects of the subject. I should not like to promulgate any book, which did not show the absurdity and injustice of the English law. The French and Italian Penal Codes are practically right, though their application is sometimes unfair. (Do not imagine that I want to be aggressive or polemical.)

I am almost certain that this matter will very soon attract a great deal of attention; and that it is a field in which pioneers may not only do excellent service to humanity, but also win the laurels of investigators and truth-seekers.

If you do not feel able to collaborate with me, I shall probably proceed to some form of solitary publication, and I should certainly give my name to anything I produced.[49]

On July 7, 1892, Symonds writes to Ellis:

With regard to "abnormal" and "morbid." I think sex-inverts can only be called "abnormal" in so far as they are in a minority, i.e. form exceptions to the large rule of sex. I doubt, from what I have observed in the matter, that sexual inversion is ever and by itself morbid. It may often of course co-exist with morbidity. . . . One great difficulty is to estimate how much it is a matter of habit: that is to say, to what extent the sexual instinct is indifferent, and liable to be swayed one side or another by custom and surrounding. What I know about the Greeks and Persians (I know little about Eskimos) and what I observe in Italy, leads me to attach very great influence to custom and example: but the more one ascribes to such causes, the less can one talk on morbidity.[50]

On July 8, 1892, in an intimate letter to his beloved daughter Margaret, Symonds, who had tuberculosis, reveals that he is haunted by thoughts of death and unfinished work:

Before I go hence & see the lovely earth no longer, I want to do so much still. I want to . . . publish my work on Sexual Aberrations, & to get my Autobiography finished.[51]

In January 1892, Symonds had written the first of a series of letters to Edward Carpenter. Whitman, and a sense of each other's interest in homosexuality, linked the two men. On December 29, 1892, Symonds writes to Carpenter:

I am so glad that H. Ellis has told you about our project. I never saw him. But I like his way of corresponding on this subject. And I need somebody of medical importance to collaborate with. Alone, I could make but little effect—the effect of an eccentric.

We are agreed enough upon fundamental points. The only difference is that he is too much inclined to stick to the neuropathical theory of explanation. But I am whittling that away to a minimum. And I don't think it politic to break off from the traditional line of analysis, which has been going rapidly forward in Europe for the last 20 years upon the psychiatric theory. Each new book reduces the conception of neurotic disease.

I mean to introduce a new feature into the discussion, by giving a complete account of homosexual love in ancient Greece. . . .

It is a pity that we cannot write freely on the topic. But when we meet, I will communicate to you facts which prove beyond all doubt to my mind that the most beneficent results, as regards health and nervous energy, accrue from the sexual relation between men: also, that when they are carried on with true affection, through a period of years, both comrades become united in a way which would be otherwise quite inexplicable.

The fact appears to me proved. The explanation of it I cannot give, & I do not expect it to be given yet. Sex has been unaccountably neglected. Its physiological & psychological relations even in the connection between man & woman are not understood. We have no theory which is worth anything upon the differentiation of the sexes, to begin with. In fact, a science of what is the central function of human beings remains to be sought.

This, I take it, is very much due to physiologists, assuming that sexual instincts follow the build of the sexual organs; & that when they do not, the phenomenon is criminal or morbid. In fact, it is due to science at this point being still clogged with religious & legal presuppositions. . . .

My hope has always been that eventually a new chivalry, i.e., a second elevated form of human love, will emerge & take its place for the service of mankind by the side of that other which was wrought out in the Middle Ages.

It will be complementary, by no means prejudicial to the elder & more commonly acceptable. It will engage a different type of individual in different spheres of energy—aims answering to those of monastic labour in common or of military self-devotion to duty taking here the place of domestic cares & procreative utility.

How far away the dream seems! And yet I see in human nature stuff neglected, ever-present—parish [pariah?] and outcast now—from which I am as certain as that I live, such a chivalry could arise.

Whitman, in Calamus, seemed to strike the key-note. And though he repudiated (in a very notable letter to myself) the deductions which have logically to be drawn from Calamus, his work will remain infinitely helpful.[52]

On January 21, 1893, Symonds writes again to Carpenter, saying in part:

I will copy out for you Whitman's very singular letter to me about Calamus, when I have time. I feel sure he would not have written it, when he first published Calamus. I think he was afraid of being used to lend his influence to "Sods" [sodomites]. Did not quite trust me perhaps. In his Symposium Speeches,° he called me "terribly suspicious" . . .

The blending of Social Strata in masculine love seems to me one of its most pronounced, & socially hopeful, features. Where it appears, it abolishes class distinctions, & opens by a single operation the cataract-blinded eye to their futilities. In removing the film of prejudice & education, it acts like the oculist & knife. If it could be acknowledged & extended, it would do very much to further the advent of the right sort of Socialism.†[53]

On February 13, 1893, Symonds describes to Carpenter Whitman's reaction on being questioned directly about homosexuality:

I wrote in the Summer of 1890 to Whitman, asking him what his real feeling about masculine love was, & saying that I knew people in England who had a strong sexual bias in such passions, felt themselves supported & encouraged by Calamus. . . .

Whitman's retort is quoted, and Symonds continues:

That is all that is to the point. He rambles on about his being less "restrained" by temperament & theory than I (J.A.S.) am—"I at certain moments let the spirit impulse (female) rage its utmost wildest damnedest (I feel I do so sometimes in L. of G. & I do so)."[54]

After completing his autobiography, John Addington Symonds died in Rome in April 1893. When Henry James heard the news, he privately paid tribute to that "poor, much-loved, much-doing, passionately out-giving man."[55]

♀ EDWARD CARPENTER

Edward Carpenter was, with Symonds, one of the two major English homosexual emancipation pioneers, a calling inspired in part by the works of Whitman. Another iconoclast American, Henry David Thoreau, also influenced Carpenter to turn against commercialism and toward the English socialist movement led by William Morris. Carpenter became a socialist organizer and lecturer, as well as an exponent of Oriental philosophy, prison reform, and an early, outspoken advocate of the women's and homosexual emancipation movements of his time.

Edward Carpenter's "passionate sense of love" for males first found overt expression when he was twenty, in 1864, his freshman year at Cambridge divinity school. At that time he discovered others like himself and made, he says, a few special friends "with whom he occasionally had sexual relations."[56] Four years later, in 1868, Carpenter first read Whitman's poems, in the little garden outside his rooms at Trinity Hall, Cambridge. In 1873, Carpenter's "recoil" from the clerical life "was strengthened by a new enthusiasm for Greek sculpture" seen on a trip to Italy, and also by several "inspiring friendships." In the summer of 1874, he renounced his Holy Orders and took a job lecturing in the industrial towns of northern England.[57] The same year, on July 12, 1874, Carpenter wrote his first letter to Walt Whitman, reporting the American poet's profound influence on many individuals in England, relating this to the developing self-consciousness of women and of the working class, and thanking Whitman for legitimizing for him "the love of men:"

My dear friend . . .

My chief reason for writing (so I put it to myself) is that I can't help wishing you should know that there are many here in England to whom your writings have been as the waking up to a new day. . . . I know that you do care that those thoughts you weary not to proclaim should be seized upon by others over the world and become the central point of their lives. . . . When I say "many" of course I do not mean a multitude (I wish I did) but many individuals—each, himself (or herself, for they are mostly women—fluid, courageous and tender) the centre of a new influence. All that you have said, the thoughts that you have given us, are vital—they will grow—that is certain.

In Whitman's writings, Carpenter discerns a new spirit under "the old forms, . . . reshaping the foundations before it alters the superstructure . . ." For "English respectability" there is almost no hope, says Carpenter. Money and materialism rule:

Yet the women will save us. I wish I could tell you what is being done by them—everywhere—in private and in public. The artisans too are shaping themselves. While Society is capering and grimacing over their heads they are slowly coming to know their minds; and exactly as they come to know their minds they come to the sense of power to fulfil them. . . .

You hardly know, I think, in America (where the life, though as yet material, is so intense) what the relief is here to turn from the languid inanity of the well-fed to the clean hard lines of the workman's face. Yesterday there came (to mend my door) a young workman with the old divine light in his eyes—even *I* call it old though I am not thirty—and perhaps, more than all, he has made me write to you.

Because you have, as it were, given me a ground for the love of men I thank you continually in my heart. (—And others thank you though they do not say so.) For you have made men to be not ashamed of the noblest instinct of their nature. Women are beautiful; but, to some, there is that which passes the love of women.

It is enough to live wherever the divine beauty of love may flash on men; but indeed its real and enduring light seems infinitely far from us in this our day. Between the splendid dawn of Greek civilization and the high universal noon of Democracy there is a strange horror of darkness on us. We look face to face upon each other, but we do not know. At the last, it is enough to know that the longed-for realization is possible—will be, has been, *is* even now somewhere—even though we find it not. . . . Slowly—I think—the fetters are falling from men's feet, the cramps and crazes of the old superstitions are relaxing, the idiotic ignorance of class contempt is dissipating. If men shall learn to accept one another simply and without complaint, if they shall cease to regard themselves because the emptiness of vanity is filled up with love, and yet shall honor the free, immeasurable gift of their own personality, delight in it and bask in it without false shames and affectations—then your work will be accomplished: and men for the first time will know of what happiness they are capable.

. . . It is a pleasure to me to write to you, for there are many things which I find it hard to say to any one here. And for my sake you must not mind reading what I have written.[58]

> On January 3, 1876, Carpenter writes once more to Whitman, asking "Will it ever be that human love . . . will cease to be a mere name?" Picking up on Whitman's poetically expressed desire to "infuse myself among you till I see it common for you to walk hand in hand," Carpenter says:

Dear friend, you have so infused yourself that it is daily more and more possible for men to walk hand in hand over the whole earth. As you have given your life, so will others after you—freely, with amplest reward transcending all suffering—for the end that you have dreamed. . . . What have we dreamed? a union which even now binds us closer than all thought high up above all individual gain or loss—an individual self which stands out free and distinct, . . . love disclosing each ever more and more. See, you have made the earth sacred for me.

Meanwhile, they say that your writings are "immoral": and you have to defend yourself against people who will misunderstand your defence as they misunderstood your original words. Need I say that I do not agree with them in the least? I believe on the contrary that you have been the first to enunciate the law of purity and health which sooner or later must assert itself. After ages perhaps man will return *consciously* to the innocent joyous delight in his own natural powers and instincts which characterized the earlier civilizations. I do not understand what it is to be "shocked" by these things: it seems to me childish. But in the meantime it is certain that people do not understand. In some way or other our modern civilization has become narrowed and one-sided. People's minds are dwarfed: one portion of their nature grows up in the dark (and ceases to be healthy). Men have lost the freedom (free masonry) of Nature and are plagued with insane doubts of their Duty. For a time I suppose men must grow up in swaddling bands of morality, and a certain instinct makes them cling to them till they have grown to be greater than, and the masters of, morality. But I think indeed the time has come for people to learn to unwrap these bands, and that from this time there will be a world-wide growth in the direction you have pointed out. So while I regret sometimes that there are things in your writings which make it difficult, sometimes impossible, to commend them to some who might otherwise profit by them, yet I feel it is best that they should be there. Their presence delays the understanding and acceptation of your message, but your message would not be complete without it, and slowly, gradually, increasingly, without end, its grandeur will dawn upon men.

I feel that my work is to carry on what you have begun. You have opened the way: my only desire is to go onward with it. Though it is out of all question to suppose that one generation or ten generations will make much difference in men's minds in the direction of the ideal state, still—to contemplate that ideal and to live slowly translating it into real life and action is quite certainly the only good—and is sufficient. I do not think of anything that I have done except as preparation. . . .[59]

In April 1877, Edward Carpenter left England on his first trip to the United States. On May 2, Carpenter knocked at the door of 431 Stevens Street, Camden, New Jersey. There, in the home of Walt Whitman's brother, Carpenter met the poet face to face. Carpenter's account of this and subsequent meetings, published in 1897, is rather uninspired; the more interesting aspects of their discourse perhaps went unrecorded. A few days later, Carpenter joined Whitman in the country, where he had gone to stay with the Stafford family, whose printer son, Harry, was one of the American poet's great loves. Carpenter seems also to have been quite taken by him.

In May 1880, Edward Carpenter went to live near Sheffield with a working-class friend, Albert Fearnehough—and Fearnehough's wife. Here Carpenter started work on a book of poetry modeled after Whitman's, entitled *Toward Democracy*, first published in 1883. In 1884, Carpenter made his second trip across the ocean, and on June 7 again visited Whitman. On the morning of June 30, Carpenter paid his last visit to the poet's small house at 328 Mickle Street in Camden, New Jersey, and reports:

We had a long and intimate conversation. He was very friendly and affectionate, and sat by the open window . . . while he talked about "Leaves of Grass." "What lies behind 'Leaves of Grass' is something that few, very few, only one here and there, perhaps oftenest women, are at all in a position to seize. It lies behind almost every line; but concealed, studiedly concealed; some passages left purposely obscure. There is something in my nature *furtive* like an old hen! You see a hen wandering up and down a hedgerow, looking apparently quite unconcerned, but presently she finds a concealed spot, and furtively lays an egg, and comes away as though nothing had happened! That is how I felt in writing 'Leaves of Grass.' . . . I think there are truths which it is necessary to envelop or wrap up."[60]

On October 23, 1885, Carpenter, back in England, writes a "practical" letter to Whitman, announcing his plans to bring out a second edition of *Toward Democracy*. This was the first edition to include a few poems of overt homosexual inspiration, described by one contemporary reviewer as "not wholesome to read." Carpenter's letter to Whitman adds:

I send you a photo I had taken a little time ago with a young fellow who is an old friend of mine—in Sheffield—it is not very good of me, though very fair of 'tother one.[61]

On May 15, 1888, Whitman, going through his papers, handed Traubel Carpenter's first letter thanking Whitman for giving Carpenter "a ground for the love of men" (letter of July 12, 1874, see page 359). Whitman said of this letter:

"It is beautiful, like a confession. . . . I seem to get very near to his heart and he to mine in that letter: it has a place in our personal history—an important place. Carpenter was never more thoroughly Carpenter than just there, in that tender mood of self-examination. . . . Carpenter is a thoroughly wholesome man—alive, clean, from head to foot."[62]

A few days later on May 21, 1888, Whitman gave Traubel another letter from Carpenter, commenting:

"The best of Carpenter is in his humanity: he manages to stay with people: he was a university man, yet managed to save himself in time."

So many university men, said Whitman,

"rather sympathize with the struggles of the people—but they are for the most part way off—remote: they only see the battle from afar. Carpenter manages to stay in the midst of it."[63]

On December 6, 1888, Traubel says Whitman was writing a letter to Carpenter, from whom, earlier that day, a visitor had arrived with an introduction. Whitman mistakenly told Traubel that Carpenter had visited the United States three or four times—apparently Carpenter had made a strong impression. Whitman continued:

"Carpenter is a youngish man . . . : Italian in appearance: radical of the radicals: come-outer: one of the social fellows in England who get constitutions by the ears—stir up thought, progress. . . . I question at times: isn't there too much of this? too much crying, screaming, for progress? Should n't the brakes be put down?" But he "always rejected" his "suspicions." He came "around inevitably to" his "optimism." . . .

W. said Carpenter had "come of wealthy parents." "The father died: . . . Edward came in for his share of the patrimony: quite a showable share it was, too." C. had been "much attached" to a young man whose "great ambition had been to get a farm of his own to work, to live upon: Edward encouraged him. When he came into his money Edward invested in land: the friend was married: the three lived together. . . . What would "come out of Carpenter's life" was "yet to be developed."

Whitman added:

"These vivid young fellows—what are they going to lead us to? The world abounds with 'em: earnest, astute, clarified, wanting to act, seeking progress, progress, progress—the fever of the age!" Then he laughed. "After all" was he "not as radical as the most radical of 'em?"[64]

On December 29, 1888, Whitman gave Traubel another Carpenter letter (of January 3, 1876, see page 360), part of which was suspiciously missing:

The signature was cut out. Consequently some of the writing on the other side of the sheet is gone. . . . [Whitman] called it "one of Carpenter's early fine letters"—

adding: "He was never nobler than then, in that period of interrogating enthusiasm."

Carpenter's letter began with a reference to one of Whitman's more explicitly homoerotic "Calamus" poems, and went on to speculate about a future world of love. Whitman comments:

"Edward was beautiful then—is so now: one of the torch-bearers, as they say: an exemplar of a loftier England: he is not generally known, not wholly a welcome presence, in conventional England: the age is still, while ripe for some things, not ripe for him, for his sort, for us, for the human protest: not ripe though ripening. O Horace, there's a hell of a lot to be done yet: don't you see? a hell of a lot: you fellows coming along now will have your hands full: we're passing a big job on to you."[65]

In 1894, the year after John Addington Symonds's death, Edward Carpenter began to publish through the Manchester Labour Press, a socialist printing plant, a series of three pamphlets: *Sex-Love; Woman;* and *Marriage.* In January 1895, Carpenter's fourth pamphlet, *Homogenic Love and Its Place in a Free Society,* was published "for private circulation only" by the same Labour Press. *Homogenic Love* is a classic, early defense of homosexuality, "homogenic" being Carpenter's alternative to "homosexual"—a term he objected to because of its half-Greek, half-Latin derivation. In this essay, Carpenter suggests that the "special function" of same-sex unions is the "social and heroic work" of generating philosophical concepts and ideals which help to transform human lives and society.

Using Whitman's sexual politics as a point of reference, Carpenter further suggests a connection between feminism and Lesbianism—especially in the United States:

It is noticeable . . . that the movement among women for their own liberation and emancipation, which is taking place all over the civilized world, has been accompanied by a marked development of the homogenic passion among the female sex. It may be said that a certain strain in the relations between the opposite sexes which has come about owing to a growing consciousness among women that they have been oppressed and unfairly treated by men, and a growing unwillingness to ally themselves unequally in marriage—that this strain has caused womankind to draw more closely together and to cement alliances of their own. . . . such comrade-alliances—and of a quite passionate kind—are becoming increasingly common, and especially perhaps among the more cultured classes of women, who are working out the great cause of their sex's liberation; nor is it difficult to see the importance of such alliances in such a campaign. In the United States where the battle of Women's independence has been fought, more vehemently perhaps than here, the tendency mentioned is even more strongly marked.[66]

Carpenter's public work as a leader of a movement for homosexual freedom had begun. It was gaining momentum when the conviction of Oscar Wilde in April 1895, caused a reactionary panic, which held back the homosexual emancipation movement in England for some time.

In July and August of 1897, Carpenter published, in a London journal called *The*

Reformer, a long essay on homosexuality titled "An Unknown People." In the same year, Carpenter's anonymous sexual history, written by himself, appeared as "Case VI" in *Sexual Inversion* by Havelock Ellis and John Addington Symonds. The Ellis-Symonds book was first published in Berlin, in German, in 1896, then in London, revised and in English, in 1897. The first English edition included Symonds and Ellis's names as coauthors on the title page, but the Symonds family and executor Horatio Brown, fearing scandal, succeeded in buying up and destroying almost all existing copies. A second edition of 1897 removed Symonds's name as coauthor of the text, as did all subsequent editions. Brown also prohibited the publication of Symonds's sexually explicit autobiography until 1976.[67]

In 1898, George Merrill moved in with Edward Carpenter, and the two lived together as lovers for thirty years, until Merrill's death in 1928. In 1902, Carpenter edited and first issued *Iolaus: An Anthology of Friendship,* one of the first collections of homosexually relevant documents of male–male intimacy. Carpenter's *Days with Walt Whitman* (1906) is surprisingly silent on the subject of homosexuality. But in the same year, an expanded fifth edition of Carpenter's previously published *Love's Coming of Age* for the first time included a chapter on homosexuality—the essay, "An Unknown People," now revised and retitled "The Intermediate Sex." In 1910, Carpenter first published an essay on important connections between homosexuality and religion in early civilizations (reprinted in 1911 in G. Stanley Hall's *American Journal of Religious Psychology and Education*). In 1914, this article became part of Carpenter's book, *Intermediate Types among Primitive Folk,* a survey of anthropological research into homosexuality among native peoples and in classical Greece and medieval Japan. In 1916, Carpenter published *My Days and Dreams,* "autobiographical notes" explicit about his homosexuality, though they deemphasize its personal and political import.

In 1922, Carpenter read a paper on Whitman before the British Society for the Study of Sex Psychology, "the only official organization" formed by English male homosexuals in the early part of the twentieth century. Two years later the society published Carpenter's paper as the pamphlet *Some Friends of Walt Whitman: A Study in Sex Psychology.* Here Carpenter is more explicit about Whitman than he was ever before in print. Whitman's "Calamus" poems, says Carpenter,

illustrate and give expression to what we would now call the homo sexual passion —which passion, although at that time ignored and unacknowledged by the world, was burning fiercely within him and pressing for deliverance.[68]

Carpenter criticizes Symonds for asking Whitman if he accepted the fact that his poems might stimulate physical relations among men. Whitman, says Carpenter,

could hardly with truthfulness deny any knowledge or contemplation of such inferences; but if on the other hand he took what we might call the reasonable line, and said that, while not *advocating* abnormal relations in any way, he of course made allowance for possibilities in that direction and the occasional development of such relations, why, he knew that the moment he said such a thing he would have the whole American Press at his heels, snarling and slandering, and distorting his words in every possible way. Things are pretty bad here in this country; but in the States (in such matters) they are ten times worse. Symonds ought to have known and allowed for this, but apparently did not do so.[69]

Carpenter said that Symonds's question to Whitman, and Whitman's answer, "has given a handle to the reactionary folk and a push in the direction of Comstock and his crew." (The American Anthony Comstock and his followers in the Society for the Suppression of Vice, formed in the 1870s, were crusaders against obscene literature, abortion, and paintings of the nude.) Carpenter continues:

We must remember, too, how different, the atmosphere on all these matters was then [1891] (especially in the U.S.A.) from what it is now [1924] in the centres of modern culture, and in places like Oxford and Cambridge and London, where you can nowadays talk as freely as you like, and where sex variations and even abnormalities are almost a stock subject of conversation.

Personally, having known Whitman fairly intimately, I do not lay great stress on that letter. Whitman was in his real disposition the most candid, but also the most cautious of men. An attempt was made on this occasion to drive him into some sort of confession of his real nature; and it may be that that very effort aroused all his resistance and caused him to hedge more than ever.

Carpenter emphasizes:

There is no doubt in my mind that Walt Whitman was before all a lover of the Male. His thoughts turned towards Men first and foremost, and it is no good disguising that fact. A thousand passages in his poems might be quoted in support of that contention. . . .[70]

Carpenter discusses Whitman as a prophet of a developing homosexual emancipation movement of general social import:

In the case of Whitman—united as he was by most intimate ties to one or more men-friends, we see already the emergence of a new organic inspiration and a new power of life. His poems radiate this power in all directions. Thousands of people date from their first reading of them *a new era in their lives.* . . . Thousands date from the reading of them a new inspiration and an extraordinary access of vitality carrying their activities and energies into new channels. How *far* this process may go we hardly yet know, but that it is one of the factors of future evolution we hardly doubt. I mean that the loves of men towards each other—and similarly the loves of women for each other—may become factors of future human evolution just as necessary and well-recognised as the ordinary loves which lead to the . . . propagation of the race. If so, we may safely say that we see here in operation a great power which is already playing its part in moulding the world, and one which we are morally bound not to deny and disown, and not to run away from, at the risk of denying our humanity and committing the sin, so execrated in the New Testament, of blasphemy against the Holy Ghost.[71]

c. 1895: EARL LIND
(Ralph Werther/Jennie June, pseuds.);
The *Cercle Hermaphroditos*
To "unite for defense against the world's bitter persecution"

Two autobiographical works by the pseudonymous Earl Lind (who also called himself Ralph Werther/Jennie June) propose arguments for the legal and social acceptance of homosexuals. Lind's *Autobiography of an Androgyne* (1918) and *The Female Impersonators* (1922) present the life history of this "feminine"-identified and eccentric male homosexual born in 1874.[72] These rare accounts also convey a sense of the social attitudes toward homosexuals, and of one aspect of the underground Gay life in New York City at the turn of the century.

Lind argues that homosexuality, as a congenital condition, carries no moral guilt, cannot be spread by example, and harms no one; therefore legal and social penalties should be abolished. However, his own shame and guilt often led him to consider suicide and into various forms of self-punishment, including the decision to have himself castrated at age twenty-eight. His extravagant "feminine" role-playing was based upon an acceptance and extreme exaggeration of the most traditional concept of "femininity." What Kate Millett has said of the homosexual characters of Jean Genet may be applied to Earl Lind: "Because of the perfection with which they ape the 'masculine' and 'feminine' of heterosexual society, [Genet's] homosexual characters represent the best contemporary insight into its constitution and beliefs." Millett adds: Genet's homosexuals "have unerringly penetrated to the essence of what heterosexual society imagines to be the character of 'masculine' and 'feminine,' and which it mistakes for the nature of male and female, thereby preserving the traditional relation of the sexes."[73]

Although it is difficult to know exactly where Earl Lind's accounts pass from fact to fiction, his comment on "Paresis Hall" as a homosexual "resort" in New York City in the late 1800s is documented by another reliable source.[74] Lind's account of "the Hall" includes a description of a group which may be, if not apocryphal, the earliest American prototype of a homosexual emancipation organization, the *Cercle Hermaphroditos*, formed by "androgynes" ("feminine"-identified male homosexuals) to "unite for defense against the world's bitter persecution":

Evenings at Paresis Hall.

During the last decade of the nineteenth century, the headquarters for avocational female-impersonators [male homosexual transvestites] of the upper and middle classes was "Paresis Hall," on Fourth Avenue several blocks south of Fourteenth Street. In front was a modest bar-room; behind, a small beer-garden. The two floors above were divided into small rooms for rent. . . .

Paresis Hall bore almost the worst reputation of any resort of New York's Underworld. Preachers in New York pulpits of the decade would thunder Philippics against the "Hall," referring to it in bated breath as "Sodom!" They were laboring under a fundamental misapprehension. But even while I was an habitué, the church and the press carried on such a war against the resort that the "not-care-a-damn" politicians who ruled little old New York had finally to stage a spectacular raid. After this, the resort, though continuing in business (because of political influence), turned the cold shoulder on androgynes and tolerated the presence of none in feminine garb.

But there existed little justification for the police's "jumping on" the "Hall" as a sop to puritan sentiment. Culturally and ethically, its distinctive clientele ranked high. Their only offence—but such a grave one as to cause sexually full-fledged Pharisees to lift up their own rotten hands in holy horror—was, as indicated, female-impersonation during their evenings at the resort. A psychological and not an ethical phenomenon! For ethically the "Hall's" distinctive clientele were congenital goody-goodies, incapable (by disposition) of ever inflicting the least detriment on a single soul. . . . But the "Hall's" distinctive clientele were bitterly hated, and finally scattered by the police, merely because of their congenital bisexuality [in modern terminology, "homosexuality"]. The sexually full-fledged were crying for blood (of innocents), as did the "unco' good" [those professedly strict in matters of morals] in the days of witch-burning. Bisexuals must be crushed—right or wrong! The subject does not permit investigation! . . .

. . . The full-fledged had innumerable opportunities for the satisfaction of their instincts. Androgynes had only "the Hall' with the exception of three or four slum resorts frequented by only the lowest class of bisexuals who had never known anything better than slum life.

Why deprive cultured androgynes of their solitary rendezvous in the New York metropolitan district and give *carte blanche* to the thousands of similar heterosexual resorts?

Paresis Hall was as innocuous as any sex resort. Its existence really brought not the least detriment to any one or to the social body as a whole. More than that: It was a necessary safety-valve to the social body. It is not in the power of every adult to settle down for life in the monogamous and monandrous love-nest ordained for all by our leaders of thought. . . .

While in this book I use the resort's popular name, androgyne habitués always abhorred it, saying simply "the Hall." The full nickname arose in part because the numerous full-fledged male visitors—it was one of the "sights" for out-of-towners who hired a guide to take them through New York's Underworld—thought the bisexuals, who were its main feature, must be insane in stooping to female-impersonation. They understood "paresis" to be the general medical term for "insanity." The name also in part arose because in those days even the medical profession were obsessed with the superstition that a virile man's association with an androgyne induced paresis in the former, it not yet having been discovered that this type of insanity is a rare aftermath of syphilis. . . .

On one of my earliest visits to Paresis Hall—about January, 1895—I seated myself alone at one of the tables. I had only recently learned that it was the androgyne headquarters—or "fairie" as it was called at the time. Since Nature had consigned me to that class, I was anxious to meet as many examples as possible. As I took my seat, I did not recognize a single acquaintance among the several score young bloods, soubrettes, and androgynes chatting and drinking in the beer-garden.

In a few minutes, three short, smooth-faced young men approached and introduced themselves as Roland Reeves, Manon Lescaut, and Prince Pansy—aliases, because few refined androgynes would be so rash as to betray their legal name in the Underworld. Not alone from their names, but also from their loud apparel, the timbre of their voices, their frail physique, and their feminesque mannerisms, I discerned they were androgynes. . . .

Roland was chief speaker. The essence of his remarks was something like the following: "Mr. Werther—or Jennie June, as doubtless you prefer to be addressed—I have seen you at the Hotel Comfort, but you were always engaged. A score of us have formed a little club, the CERCLE HERMAPHRODITOS. For we need to unite for defense against the world's bitter persecution of bisexuals. We care to admit only extreme types—such as like to doll themselves up in feminine finery. We sympathize with, but do not care to be intimate with, the mild types, some of whom you see here to-night even wearing a disgusting beard! Of course they do not wear it out of liking. They merely consider it a lesser evil than the horrible razor or excruciating wax-mask.

"We ourselves are in the detested trousers because having only just arrived. We keep our feminine wardrobe in lockers upstairs so that our every-day circles can not suspect us of female-impersonation. For they have such an irrational horror of it!"

On the basis of different visits to an upper room permanently rented by the CERCLE HERMAPHRODITOS, I am going to build up a typical hour's conversation in order to disclose into what channels the thoughts of ultra-androgynes run when half-a-score find themselves together. The reason for its unnatural ring is that I omit the nine-tenths that were prattle, retaining only the cream that I consider of scientific value.

It was about eight o'clock on an evening of April, 1895. Some of the hermaphroditoi were still in male apparel; some changing to feminine evening dress and busy with padding and the powder-puff; some in their completed evening toilette ready to descend to the beer-garden below to await a young-blood friend.[75]

> One of the "hermaphroditoi" remarks how common it is for "rather mannish women [to] fall in love with us Mollie Coddles." An androgyne named Angelo-Phyllis is reminded of the murder of a young heiress, a "gynander" (in modern terminology, a "Lesbian"). Lind notes that this "anecdote deals with only one of a number of similar occurrences in New York. Gynanders, as well as androgynes, are doomed to suffer murder at the hands of hare-brained prudes because of the false teaching of the leaders of thought." Phyllis recalls the story:

"Perhaps you read in the papers two years ago how a New York young woman disappeared, and the utmost efforts of the police were not rewarded with the least trace. She was of that mannish type. . . .

"I myself have no doubt of the fate of the poor girl. When the papers were full of rumors and hypotheses about her, I repeatedly wrote my theory to her father. When he ignored my letters, I gave the police my theory. They likewise thought it absurd and refused to investigate along the lines I suggested.

"When some mannish women find it impossible to marry an effeminate man, they adopt some petite cry-baby woman as their soul-mate. The papers stated that the last trace of Mollie Dale was her carrying away from O'Neil's several purchases. The latter immediately struck me as such alone as a gallant would buy to present his lady-love. When I told the police, they said: 'Absurd! Who ever heard of one woman being in love with another!'

"On leaving O'Neil's, Mollie Dale absolutely dropped out of sight for all time. It was as if the earth had suddenly yawned for her body and closed again so rapidly as to be unseen by the people nearby. . . .

"My theory, hermaphroditoi, is that Mollie went right from O'Neil's to her cry-baby chum's. Probably within walking distance, because every soul in New York was asked through the newspapers over and over again if they had met on any public conveyance the morning of Mollie's dropping out of sight a young lady of her description, so detailed as to give even the pattern of her shoes, besides her much published photographs. Her disappearance was at the time the seven-days wonder of New York and every one was discussing it.

"The rule with men-women—as with us women-men—is never to breathe to any one of their every-day circle a word about their sweethearts because of the misunderstanding and horror evidenced by people ignorant of psychology. As a rule the soul-mates of us better-class bisexuals belong to a much lower social stratum. Very likely Mollie's lived in one of the thousands of tumbledown tenements within walking distance of O'Neil's.

"According to my theory, hermaphroditoi—and I have seen a hundred times more of life than the average man, and possess some sense notwithstanding people not knowing me well set me down as only a high-grade idiot because of my outward frivolousness and an unfortunate infantile carriage—the cry-baby's husband or father had only just learned of what he, as well as ninety-nine out of every hundred men, mistakenly regarded as the horribly corrupting influence of the poor martyr Mollie on the hare-brained cry-baby. Ignorant that men-women are victims of birth and that their so-called 'depravity' brings not the least harm to any one, and insanely angry with Mollie into the bargain, he that very morning bludgeoned her in his apartment. And he happened to succeed in disposing of the corpse.

"I thought of Mollie when last week the papers told about an unrecognizable female body, bent double, having been found in a trunk filled with salt that for two years had rested unclaimed in the trunk-room of the third-class Hotel X—just the type that a tenement-dweller would select to harbor such a trunk. The murderer was evidently a meat-packer, familiar with the processes of salting down.

In such strange ways a continuous string of both men-women and women-men are being struck down in New York for no other reason than loathing for those born bisexual. And public opinion forbids the publication of the facts of bisexuality, which, if generally known, would put an end to these mysterious murders of innocents."

A little later, another member of the *Hermaphroditos* makes his appearance.

"Here's Plum. Plumkin, you look as if you had lost your last friend!"
The 23-year Mollie Coddle sobbed: "Everything looks dark. Two days ago I was fired. I have hardly slept a wink since. I have hope for the future only in the

grave. Some bigot denounced me to the boss. He called me into his private office. As this had never happened before, I guessed the reason. . . ."

Plum outlined his conference. I have listened to several similar confessions. The following is a composite.

Plum: "I confess to being a woman-man and throw myself upon your mercy."

Fairsea: "That confession is sufficient, and proves you an undesirable person to have around!"

Plum: "It will be hard to find a new job, since I have been with you for five years and must depend on your recommendation."

Fairsea: "Knowing your nature, Plum, I could not recommend you *even to shovel coal into a furnace!*"

Plum: "But you have steadily advanced me for five years! Why should to-day's discovery make any difference in your opinion of my business ability?"

Fairsea with a sneer: "An invert ought to leave brain work for others! He ought to exhaust himself on a farm from sunrise to sunset so that the psychic movings would be next to non-existent. He should pass his life in the back woods; not in a city. He has no right in the front ranks of civilization where his abnormality is so out of place!"

Plum: "You mean that he should commit intellectual and social suicide in obedience to the æsthetic sense of Pharisees?"

Fairsea: "Certainly! The innate feelings and the conscience, as well as the Bible, teach that the invert has no rights! I myself have only deep-rooted contempt for him! Every fibre in my body, every cell in my tissues, cries out in loud protest against him! He is the lowest of the low! I dare say that at the bottom of your heart, Plum, you are thoroughly ashamed of the confession you made a moment ago?"

Plum: "By no means. I have learned to look upon bisexuality as a scientist and a philosopher. But you have just shown yourself to be still groping in the Dark Ages.

"No, Mr. Fairsea, I can hardly bring myself to be ashamed of the handiwork of God. A bisexual has no more reason than a full-fledged man or woman to be ashamed of his God-given sexuality.

"You appear, Mr. Fairsea, to be unable to get my point of view. All in my anatomy and psyche that you gloat in calling depraved and contemptible I have been used to since my early teens. If your views have any justification in science or ethics, I am unable to see it. Although it almost breaks my heart to be made an outcast and penniless by yourself, I prefer that lot, knowing I am in the right, than to be in the wrong even if sitting, as yourself, in the chair of president of the X—— Company.

"How do you define 'depraved', Mr. Fairsea? If in such a way as to exclude Socrates, Plato, Michael Angelo, and Raphael, then you exclude me also."

Fairsea: "But the phenomenon works against the multiplication of the human race. Nature, with this in view, instilled in all but the scum of mankind this utter disgust for the invert. To the end of the continued existence of the race, he must be condemned to a life of unsatisfied longing. For this reason he should be imprisoned for life, not for only ten or twenty years as the statutes now provide!

"We strictly segregate diphtheria and scarlet fever, Plum. Why should we not similarly quarantine against inversion?"

Plum: ". . . THE BISEXUALS' BEING AT LIBERTY OCCASIONS NOT THE LEAST DETRI-MENT TO ANY INDIVIDUAL, NOR TO THE RACE AS A WHOLE. . . . the segregation of bisexuals would affect for a lifetime tens of thousands of our most useful members of society. It would occasion, among these already accursed by Nature, additional intense mental suffering, despair, and suicide. . . .

"And as to race suicide, Mr. Fairsea. . . .

". . . Hasn't the human race survived the best decades of classic Greece? While the Greeks are acknowledged by all modern historians to have attained the highest development of mind and body ever known, they at the same time gave to the women-men who happened to be born among them—as among all races of all ages—an honorable place. And by far more place, both in their personal and social life, than in the case of any other nation of the ancient or modern world."

Fairsea: "But I had hoped that the human race had evolved above this phe-nomenon! I hate to believe it of the human race! Because the phenomenon lowers humanity down to the lowest levels of animal life! I—"

Plum: "So does eating!"

Fairsea: "I detest it! My disgust is innermost and deepseated! To begin now to show any mercy to the invert, after having for two thousand years confined him in dungeons, burned him at the stake, and buried him alive, would be a backward step in the evolution of the race!

"Plum, the invert is not fit to live with the rest of mankind! He should be shunned as the lepers of biblical times! If generously allowed outside prison walls, the law should at least ordain that the word 'UNCLEAN' be branded in his forehead, and should compel him to cry: 'UNCLEAN! UNCLEAN!' as he walks the streets, lest his very brushing against decent people contaminate them!"

Plum: "All that is only bigotry and bias! Nearly every man's conduct is still governed by bias!"

Fairsea: "I even acknowledge that it is bias! For bias is justifiable in matters of sex! . . . You say that medical writers have declared inverts *irresponsible!* That declaration proves that they know nothing about them! You say inverts are as-saulted and blackmailed! They deserve to be! It would be wrong for any one at all to show any leniency! Their existence ought to be made so intolerable as to drive them to lead their sexual life along the lines followed by all other men! Your case, Plum, fills me with such disgust that I could not rest knowing you were around the office!"

Roland brought the conversation to a close: "Mankind are so steeped in ego-tism! Whatever they are not personally inclined to is always horribly immoral! Whatever they are instinctively inclined to is always supremely right!"[76]

♀ 1897: "DR. K."; "A Note on Sexual Inversion" in Women
"Current views of homosexuality are . . . cruelly unjust"

The first two English editions of Havelock Ellis and John Addington Symonds's *Sexual Inversion* contain "A Note on Sexual Inversion" in women by "Dr. K.," who Ellis describes as "an American woman physician, who kindly assisted me in obtaining cases. . . ." Although from a modern liberationist viewpoint Dr. K.'s statements contain much that is extremely oppressive, in 1897 they constituted a liberal Lesbian defense. A footnote quotes Dr. K. to the effect that homosexuality,

wherever found, indicates a psychic condition which can be properly governed but cannot be eradicated.

She suggests that nervous "affectations" sometimes result from homosexuality, or from

the vices which sometimes accompany it. But such effects are not an inevitable result. Of the eight cases which I have reported to you, seven are perfectly sound, physically, and four are remarkable for their intellectual qualities. . . . In all such cases I would recommend that the moral sense be trained and fostered, and the persons allowed to keep their individuality, being taught to remember always that they are different from others, and that they must not infringe upon the happiness or rights of others, rather sacrificing their own feelings or happiness when necessary. It is good discipline for them, and will serve in the long run to bring them more favour and affection than any other course. This quality or idiosyncrasy is not essentially evil, but, if rightly used, may prove a blessing to others and a power for good in the life of the individual, nor does it reflect any discredit upon its possessor.[77]

In her "Note," Dr. K. records the general impressions to which her study of "sexual inversion" in women have given rise.

A number of cases of inversion in women have come under my observation. In some of these cases there is a hereditary neurasthenic or psychopathic tendency, but it must be borne in mind that there are few people in modern life, perhaps none, who could be pronounced absolutely free from such a *Belastung* [burden].

The persons whom I have questioned acknowledge their feelings to be unusual, and perhaps morbid, but they unite in declaring them to be absolutely ineradicable. One invert thus describes the needs of her nature: "A desire for a deep spiritual communion with a friend who has the same tastes, aspirations, and interests. Embraces and endearment, and a perfect faith in the other's purity of heart. These are the necessary conditions." I may also quote the following passage from a letter written by a young inverted woman to her friend: "Remember, dear, I am not asking you to love me as I love you, neither do I wish to make you remarkable in any way. I shrink from everything of the kind as much as anyone. I am simply exercising my right in loving you as I do—with a love which I know has God's sanction and blessing. The world has not learned friendship's blessing yet, but I know, for I have learned it through my misfortune, that it is possible for human souls to be made strong and beautiful by the spiritualising effect of love, the kind of love that I have given you. During all the years that I have known you my one desire has been to make my influence over you tend upward. I love you for the strength and purity and beauty of your character, and my only reason for telling you about my peculiar nature is to make you understand, if possible, that my affection for you is earnest and sincere. I cannot bear to have you treat it lightly, or to be considered weak and sentimental. Be brave and honest with me. You have known me now for seven years; you know that this inversion does not affect my moral sense, yet you have not written to me since I told you of it, and I cannot understand your silence. It is so unlike you."

While the feeling, doubtless, has a sexual basis, it is in many cases not recognised, and the love, though intense, is purely spiritual in character, and is placed upon a high plane. Moreover, this moral attitude is not attained as the result of conscious effort on the part of these persons; it seems rather to be a natural tendency. This may be explained in several ways. There may be a congenitally feeble [sexual] instinct, or it may be that the instinct, through having been gratified only in an emotional or spiritual way, has been entirely subordinated to the higher feelings.

The cases which I have investigated have no unfavourable physical or mental symptoms. On the contrary, their health is as sound as their morals. They are, as a rule, persons of a highly wrought nervous organisation, and of unusual mental power. Inquiries of this character must be carried on with the utmost caution. There is an inevitable tendency to form conclusions before the subject is adequately mastered, and facts are almost invariably looked at from the standpoint of some theory which so colours and distorts them, that weak corroborative evidence is apt to be invested with undue strength and strong adverse evidence carelessly to be dismissed as weak. Most of the cases heretofore investigated are of persons belonging to the criminal or quasi-criminal classes, and conclusions drawn from these cases are necessarily tainted with this imperfection. Homosexual phenomena are in such instances difficult to disentangle from other phenomena—the stigmata of criminality—which may be of great significance, or of little or no significance whatever, in the solution of the problem of homosexuality.

Furthermore, the testimony of the homosexual, or of those who describe themselves as homosexual, is doubtless in many cases not entitled to full credence. Every person is impelled by a law of his nature to justify his conduct in his own eyes, and in the eyes of others. This is, of course, especially true where any habit or feeling exists which is condemned by the prevailing opinion of mankind. Under this influence one who admits himself to be homosexual is apt, on the one hand, to magnify any evidence tending to show a congenital element which necessarily excludes the idea of personal responsibility, and, on the other hand, largely to ignore or to understate evidence of exactly opposite significance, which, perhaps, exists in equal abundance.

. . . it is clear to me that homosexual investigations are attended with great difficulties. In studying the cases which have fallen under my observation, I have tried to keep these difficulties always in view. My own cases have not been sufficiently numerous to justify broad conclusions, but they have thoroughly convinced me that the current views with regard to homosexuality are grossly erroneous and cruelly unjust.

One thing has been made perfectly clear: whether congenital or acquired, *homosexuality is not in itself a mark of mental deficiency or of moral degradation.* All feelings are capable of abuse, and the homosexual feelings, like the ordinary sexual feelings, have beyond question led to degraded practices; but I have had the fortune to have found a number of cases of inversion where the persons have been distinguished for unusual strength and purity of character, and for far more than the average intelligence and energy. To denounce such persons as degraded is the height of cruelty—a cruelty which must necessarily produce an acute sense of injustice and feelings of bitter resentment.[78]

♀   1897: "Miss S."; "This divine gift of loving"

The first Engligh edition of Havelock Ellis and John Addington Symonds's *Sexual Inversion* (1897) contains the short history of an American Lesbian, including a statement by her concerning "inversion."

Miss S., age 38, living in a city of the United States of America, a business woman of fine intelligence, prominent in professional and literary circles. Her general health is good, but she belongs to a family in which there is a marked neuropathic element. She is of rather phlegmatic temperament, well poised, always perfectly calm and self-possessed, rather retiring in disposition, with gentle, dignified bearing.

She says she cannot care for men, but that all her life has been "glorified and made beautiful by friendship with women," whom she loves as a man loves women. Her character is, however, well disciplined, and her friends are not aware of the nature of her affections. She tries not to give all her love to one person, and endeavors (as she herself expresses it) to use this "gift of loving" as a stepping-stone to high mental and spiritual attainments. She is described by one who has known her for several years as "having a high nature, and instincts unerringly toward high things."[79]

The 1901 edition of *Sexual Inversion* contains an additional statement, clearly by the same American Lesbian, on what is called "the moral position of inverts"; in the context of its time this statement constitutes an early Lesbian defense.

"Inverts should have the courage and independence to be themselves, and to demand an investigation. If one strives to live honorably, and considers the greatest good to the greatest number, it is not a crime nor a disgrace to be an invert. I do not need the law to defend me, neither do I desire to have any concessions made for me, nor do I ask my friends to sacrifice their ideals for me. I too have ideals which I shall always hold. All that I desire—and I claim it as my right—is the freedom to exercise this divine gift of loving, which is not a menace to society nor a disgrace to me. Let it once be understood that the average invert is not a moral degenerate nor a mental degenerate, but simply a man or a woman who is less highly specialized, less completely differentiated, than other men and women, and I believe the prejudice against them will disappear, and if they live uprightly they will surely win the esteem and consideration of all thoughtful people. I know what it means to an invert—who feels himself set apart from the rest of mankind —to find one human heart who trusts him and understands him, and I know how almost impossible this is, and will be, until the world is made aware of these facts."[80]

1897: "Professor X."; Homosexual love is "a natural, pure and sound passion"

The first English edition of *Sexual Inversion* (1897) also contains a "Letter from Professor X.," a scientist and "American of eminence." His statement, described as "representing the farthest point to which the defense of sexual inversion has gone, . . ." disappeared from the book after the edition of 1901. The professor defends homosexuality as one pole of a "normal," "natural" bisexuality. Havelock Ellis writes:

Professor X., in a letter to Symonds (who described him as "an American of eminence, who holds a scientific professorship in one of the first universities of the world"), has carried to the furthest extent the theory of the sexual indifference of the genital impulse, and the consequently normal nature of homosexuality. He writes: "I have considered and enquired into this question for many years; and it has long been my settled conviction that no breach of morality is involved in homosexual love; that, like every other passion, it tends, when duly understood and controlled by spiritual feeling, to the physical and moral health of the individual and the race, and that it is only its brutal perversions which are immoral. I have known many persons more or less the subjects of this passion, and I have found them a particularly high-minded, upright, refined, and (I must add) pure-minded class of men. In view of what everybody knows of the vile influence on society of the intersexual [heterosexual] passion, as it actually exists in the world, making men and women sensual, low-minded, false, every way unprincipled and grossly selfish, and this especially in those nations which self-righteously reject homosexual love, it seems a travesty of morality to invest the one with divine attributes and denounce the other as infamous and unnatural.

"There is an error in the view that feminine love is that which is directed to a man, and masculine love that which is directed to a woman. That doctrine involves a begging of the whole question. It is a fatal concession to vulgar prejudice, and a contradiction to all you have so firmly adduced from Greek manners, and, indeed, I may say, to all the *natural* evolution of our race. Passion is in itself a blind thing. It is a furious pushing out, not with calculation or comprehension of its object, but to anything which strikes the imagination as fitted to its need. It is not characterised or differentiated by the nature of its object, but by its own nature. Its instinct is to a certain form of action or submission. But how that instinct is determined is largely accidental. Sexual passion is drawn by certain qualities which appeal to it. It may see them, or think that it sees them, in a man or a woman. But it is in either case the same person. The controlling influence is a certain spiritual attraction, and that may lie in either. The two directions are equally natural to unperverted man, and the *abnormal* form of love is that which has lost the power of excitability in either the one or the other of these directions. It is *unisexual* love (a love for one sexuality) which is a perversion. The normal men love both.

"It is true enough that in primitive society all passion must have been wholly or mainly animal, and spiritual progress must have been conditioned on subduing it. But there is no reason why this subjugation should have consisted in extirpating, or trying to extirpate, one of the two main forms of sexual passion, and cultivating the other. The actual reasons were, I take it, two: (1) to reserve all sexual energy for the increase of the race; (2) to get the utmost merely fleshly pleasure out of the exercise of passion. Whether either of these reasons adds to the spiritual elevation of love may be doubted. Certainly not the second, which is now the moving influence in the matter. It is true enough that all passion needs to be unceasingly watched, because the worst evils for mankind lie hidden in its undisciplined indulgence. But this is quite as true of intersexual as of homosexual love. I clearly believe that the Greek morality on this subject was far higher than ours, and truer to the spiritual nature of man; that our civilisation suffers for want of the pure and noble sentiment which they thought so useful to the state; and that we ought to think and speak of homosexual love, not as 'inverted' or 'abnormal,' as a sort of colour-blindness of the genital sense, as a lamentable mark of inferior development, or as an unhappy fault, a 'masculine body with a feminine soul,' but as being in itself a natural, pure and sound passion, as worthy of the reverence of all fine natures as the honourable devotion of husband and wife, or the ardour of bride and groom."

I present this statement of Prof. X.'s as representing the furthest point to which the defence of sexual inversion has gone, or, indeed, could go, unless anyone were bold enough to assert that homosexuality is the only normal impulse, and heterosexual love a perversion. . . .[81]

♀ 1900–23: EMMA GOLDMAN;
The Unjust Treatment of Homosexuals
"No daring is required to protest against a great injustice"

Emma Goldman, anarchist activist and organizer, lecturer and agitator, feminist, spokesperson for the new drama, advocate of birth control and free speech, was in Paris in 1900. Writer Oskar Panizza asked her to spend an evening with himself, Dr. Eugene Schmidt, and Oscar Wilde. In her excitement to meet both Wilde and Panizza whom she admired, Goldman accepted the invitation, forgetting she had a previous important committee meeting. The evening with Panizza and Wilde never came about. A few days later, Dr. Schmidt called on the disappointed Goldman, and the two went for a walk. As Goldman describes it in her autobiography, she had some years earlier publicly defended Wilde in the United States:

During our walk in the Luxembourg I told the doctor of the indignation I had felt at the conviction of Oscar Wilde. I had pleaded his case against the miserable hypocrites who had sent him to his doom. "You!" the doctor exclaimed in astonishment, "why, you must have been a mere youngster then. How did you dare come out in public for Oscar Wilde in puritan America?" "Nonsense!" I replied; "no daring is required to protest against a great injustice." The doctor smiled dubiously. "Injustice?" he repeated; "it wasn't exactly that from the legal point of view, though it may have been from the psychological." The rest of the afternoon we were engaged in a battle royal about inversion, perversion, and the question of sex variation. He had given much thought to the matter, but he was not free in his approach, and I suspected that he was somewhat scandalized that I, a young woman, should speak without reservations on such tabooed subjects.[82]

In the early decades of the twentieth century, Goldman became well known as a magnetic speaker on controversial topics; the subjects of her lectures frequently brought about police violence and mob attempts to silence her. When she lectured on homosexuality, however, censorship apparently came from another source—her own anarchist comrades.

Here, Goldman writes in her autobiography of her speaking tour of 1915.

My tour this year met with no police interference until we reached Portland, Oregon, although the subjects I treated were anything but tame: anti-war topics, the fight for Caplan and Schmidt, freedom in love, birth-control, and the problem most tabooed in polite society, homosexuality. Nor did [Anthony] Comstock and his purists try to suppress me, although I openly discussed methods of contraception before various audiences.

Censorship came from some of my own comrades because I was treating such "unnatural" themes as homosexuality. Anarchism was already enough misunderstood, and anarchists considered depraved; it was inadvisable to add to the misconceptions by taking up perverted sex-forms, they argued. Believing in freedom of opinion, even if it went against me, I minded the censors in my own ranks as little as I did those in the enemy's camp. In fact, censorship from comrades had the same effect on me as police persecution; it made me surer of myself, more determined to plead for every victim, be it one of social wrong or of moral prejudice.

The men and women who used to come to see me after my lectures on homosexuality, and who confided to me their anguish and their isolation, were often of finer grain than those who had cast them out. Most of them had reached an adequate understanding of their differentiation only after years of struggle to stifle what they had considered a disease and a shameful affliction. One young woman confessed to me that in the twenty-five years of her life she had never known a day when the nearness of a man, her own father and brothers even, did not make her ill. The more she had tried to respond to sexual approach, the more repugnant men became to her. She had hated herself, she said, because she could not love her father and her brothers as she loved her mother. She suffered excruciating remorse, but her revulsion only increased. At the age of eighteen she had accepted an offer of marriage in the hope that a long engagement might help her grow accustomed to a man and cure her of her "disease." It turned out a ghastly failure and nearly drove her insane. She could not face marriage and she dared not confide in her fiancé or friends. She had never met anyone, she told me, who suffered from a similar affliction, nor had she ever read books dealing with the subject. My lecture had set her free; I had given her back her self-respect.

This woman was only one of the many who sought me out. Their pitiful stories made the social ostracism of the invert seem more dreadful than I had ever realized before. To me anarchism was not a mere theory for a distant future; it was a living influence to free us from inhibitions, internal no less than external, and from the destructive barriers that separate man from man.[83]

In 1923, a major article by Emma Goldman appeared in the *Yearbook for Sexual Intermediate Types*, issued by the Scientific-Humanitarian Committee, Germany's leading homosexual rights organization. Here, in translation, the committee's head, Dr. Magnus Hirschfeld, introduces Goldman to the *Yearbook's* readers:

I received the following essay from the American freedom fighter Emma Goldman, friend and intellectual ally of Prince Peter Kropotkin and of Louise

Michel. In her periodical, *Mother Earth*, and in countless speeches given over several decades across the breadth of the United States, Goldman has campaigned boldly and steadfastly for individual rights, and especially for those deprived of their rights. Thus it came about that she was the first and only woman, indeed the first and only American, to take up the defense of homosexual love before the general public. During the World War, she used all of her resources to condemn armed violence and was therefore thrown into prison when America entered the war. After two years' imprisonment in Jefferson City, Missouri (and anyone who knows "free" America will realize what two years at hard labor means there), she was deported. Since this had never before happened to an American woman, it aroused enormous interest and won the sympathy of many who had previously been indifferent or opposed to Goldman.[84]

Hirschfeld's preface closes with "the wish that Goldman may soon be permitted to return to her home and activities in America from the exile in which so many have been languishing since the chaos of the World War."

Goldman's article was a response to an earlier piece by Karl von Levetzow alleging the Lesbianism of Louise Michel, a charismatic French anarchist who died in 1905. Goldman's essay is cast in the form of a letter dated Berlin, March 1923: it constitutes a pro-homosexual but critical and sophisticated discussion of that form of defense which tried to establish the same-sex orientation of worthy, talented, or famous historical figures—as a response to the popular, totally negative portrayal of homosexuals.

Dear Dr. Hirschfeld:

I have been acquainted with your great works on sexual psychology for a number of years now. I have always deeply admired your courageous intervention on behalf of the rights of people who are by their natural disposition unable to express their sexual feelings in what is customarily called the "normal" way. Now that I have had the pleasure of making your personal acquaintance and observing your efforts at first hand, I feel more strongly than ever the impress of your personality and the spirit which has guided you in your difficult undertaking. Your willingness to place your periodical at my disposal, giving me the opportunity to present a critical evaluation of the essay by Herr von Levetzow on the alleged homosexuality of Louise Michel, is proof—if such proof were ever required—that you are a man with a deep sense of justice and interested only in the truth. Permit me to express my sincere appreciation both for this gesture and for your brave and courageous stand in the service of enlightenment and humaneness in opposition to ignorance and hypocrisy.

Above all, I feel obliged to preface my response to the statements of the above-mentioned author with a few brief comments. In challenging what I regard as erroneous presuppositions on the part of Herr von Levetzow, I am in no way motivated by any prejudice against homosexuality itself or any antipathy towards homosexuals in general. Had Louise Michel ever manifested any type of sexual feelings in all those relationships with people whom she loved and who were devoted to her, I would certainly be the last to seek to cleanse her of this "stigma." It is a tragedy, I feel, that people of a different sexual type are caught in a world which shows so little understanding for homosexuals, is so crassly indifferent to the various gradations and variations of gender and their great significance in life. Far be it for me to seek to evaluate these people as inferior, less moral, or incapable of higher feelings and actions. I am the last person to whom it would occur to "protect" Louise Michel, my great teacher and comrade, from the charge of homosexuality. Louise Michel's service to humanity and her great work of social liberation are such that they can be neither enlarged nor reduced, whatever her sexual habits were.

Years ago, before I knew anything about sexual psychology and when my sole acquaintance with homosexuals was limited to a few women I had met in prison (where I was held because of my political convictions), I spoke up in no uncertain terms on behalf of Oscar Wilde. As an anarchist, my place has always been on the side of the persecuted. The entire persecution and sentencing of Wilde struck me as *an act of cruel injustice and repulsive hypocrisy* on the part of the society which condemned this man. And this alone was the reason which prompted me to stand up for him.

Later I came to Europe, where I became acquainted with the works of Havelock Ellis, Krafft-Ebing, Carpenter, and some others, which first made me fully aware of the crime which had been perpetrated upon Oscar Wilde and his kind. From then on I defended in the spoken and written word those whose entire nature is different in regard to sexual feelings and needs. It was primarily your works, dear Doctor, which helped me to illuminate the extremely complex problems of sexual psychology and to mold the entire position of my audience in a more humane way toward these questions.

From all of this, your readers may recognize that any prejudice or antipathy towards homosexuals is totally foreign to me. On the contrary! Among my male and female friends, there are a few who are of either a completely Uranian or a bisexual disposition. I have found these individuals far above average in terms of intelligence, ability, sensitivity, and personal charm. I empathize deeply with them, for I know that their sufferings are of a larger and more complex sort than those of ordinary people. But there exists among very many homosexuals a predominant intellectual outlook which I must seriously challenge. I am speaking here of the practice of claiming every possible prominent personality as one of their own, attributing their own feelings and character traits to these people.

To be sure, this is not a homosexual peculiarity but instead a psychological characteristic of *all* those who are publicly held in disdain. Such people are always inclined to cite the most prominent individuals of all ages in support of their cause. *Misery seeks company.* One notes, for example, that Jews are almost inclined to attribute Jewish origins, or at least Jewish character traits, to all the significant men and women in the world. A similar practice is to be found among the Irish; the people of India will always tell us that theirs is the greatest civilization, etc., etc. We encounter the same phenomenon among political outcasts. Socialists like to claim men like Walt Whitman and Oscar Wilde as advocates of the theories of Karl Marx, while anarchists see kindred spirits in Nietzsche, Wagner, Ibsen, and others. Many-sidedness has always been a sign of true greatness, no doubt; but I have always felt it rather importunate to claim great creative personalities for my ideas *so long as they themselves have not expressed their agreement with them.*

If one were to believe the assurances and claims of many homosexuals, one would be forced to the conclusion that no truly great person is or ever was to be found outside the circle of persons of a different sexual type. Social ostracism and persecution inevitably spawn sectarianism; but this outlook, narrow in its perspective, often renders people unjust in their praise of others. Without wishing to offend Herr von Levetzow in any way, I must say that he seems to be strongly influenced by the sectarian spirit of many homosexuals, perhaps unconsciously so. Beyond that, he has an antiquated conception of the essence of womanhood. He sees in woman a being meant by nature solely to delight man with her attractiveness, bear his children, and otherwise figure as a domestic and general household slave. Any woman who fails to meet these shopworn requirements of womanhood is promptly taken as a Uranian by this writer. In light of the accomplishments of women to date in every sector of human intellectual life and in efforts for social change, this traditional male conception of womanhood scarcely deserves regard any longer. I nonetheless feel compelled to pursue the outmoded views of this writer concerning Louise Michel to some extent, if only to show the reader what nonsensical conclusions can be reached if one proceeds from nonsensical presuppositions.

Goldman next presents a summary of the evidence which led von Levetzow to "diagnose" Michel as a Lesbian: as a child, she was an avid reader and was keenly interested in the natural sciences; her behavior was generally tomboyish, and she paid little attention to her appearance. As an adult, she placed little value on physical attractiveness and displayed courage and stamina unusual for a woman. Men, Levetzow claimed, played a minor role in her life; and she loved music (especially Wagner) and sculpture. Goldman heatedly rejects the idea that these traits are typical of female homosexuals, and also points to several deep relationships that Michel had with men. She willingly concedes, however, that Michel's deepest relationships were with women.

Modern woman is no longer satisfied to be the beloved of a man; she looks for understanding, comradeship; she wants to be treated as a human being and not simply as an object for sexual gratification. And since man in many cases cannot offer her this, she turns to her sisters.

Goldman states that her only desire is to see Michel

portrayed as she actually was: as an extraordinary woman, a significant thinker, and a profound soul. She represented *a new type of womanhood* which is nonetheless as old as the race, and she had a soul which was permeated by an all-encompassing and all-understanding love for humanity. In short, Louise Michel was a complete woman, free of all the prejudices and traditions which for centuries held women in chains and degraded them to household slaves and objects of sexual lust. The new woman celebrated her resurrection in the figure of Louise, the woman capable of heroic deeds but one who remains a woman in her passion and in her love.[85]

1906–07: The German Homosexual Emancipation Movement and the United States

Starting in 1897, with the founding of the Scientific-Humanitarian Committee in Berlin by Dr. Magnus Hirschfeld and others, a German homosexual emancipation movement was under way. The committee's goals were to abolish the German law against male homosexuality, to change the public's generally negative opinion of homosexuals, and to interest homosexuals themselves in the struggle for their rights. The committee campaigned for law reform, published emancipation literature and the *Yearbook for Sexual Intermediate Types* (1899–1923), held public forums, and sent speakers on lecture tours.

1906: Otto Spengler;
"People just faint when the subject is broached"

In May 1906, Otto Spengler, one of the Scientific-Humanitarian Committee's directors, "gave a warmly applauded lecture on sexual intermediates before the German Scientific Society in New York." In the monthly newsletter of the Scientific-Humanitarian Committee, Spengler describes the discussion following his presentation:

The debate was very lively. Representatives of all the professions were in the audience—ministers, lawyers, doctors. This was probably the first such speech given in New York, and I managed to make some headway with my limited resources. You can deduce the inflexibility of the people from this incident: after the topic had been illuminated from all sides, a lawyer stood up and maintained . . . that homosexuals belong in prison. This shows plainly what educational efforts are still required here, where such educated people are so stupid. I have entered into correspondence with Dr. William Lee Howard, who told me that he will soon be publishing an English-language work on the subject in question. Then, I hope, there will be more understanding here. Now, people just faint when the subject is broached.[86]

1907: Dr. Georg Merzbach;
"We have won a great battle"

In March 1907, the Scientific-Humanitarian Committee's Dr. Georg Merzbach, then making a lecture tour of the United States, spoke on homosexuality problems before the New York Society of Medical Jurisprudence. Dr. Merzbach writes Magnus Hirschfeld in Germany about this lecture:

My dear colleague Hirschfeld:
Yesterday evening I gave my first English lecture on our area of specialization,

and I can tell you at the outset that it made a truly sensational impression upon a select audience which, considering the circumstances in this country, was extraordinarily large. . . .

Merzbach continues:

The pictures and explanations I presented were received with tumultuous applause —an unusual thing, given the coolness of American scholars. A number of very distinguished doctors and legal scholars participated in the [almost two-hour] discussion, while Professor Beck, the surgeon, stood at my side as an interpreter to prevent misunderstandings in the heat of the exchange. . . . Naturally, rather naive questions were posed in the discussion, as well as some which were quite intelligent. I will mention a few: "Can homosexuality be eradicated by castration? What indications of homosexual tendencies does the animal kingdom provide? The names of historic or famous homosexuals, and the evidence thereof? Doesn't homosexuality lead ultimately to paranoia or other psychoses? Can homosexuals have children? Oscar Wilde, Shakespeare, Hamlet?" Some people spoke out forcefully against the penalization of homosexual acts so long as they are not punishable . . . on other grounds (coercion, etc.). The entire thing made such an overwhelming impression that Professor Beck, who had arranged the lecture, told me that he had never witnessed such success in presenting a scientific topic. . . . I had expected, and colleagues had predicted, a courteous but cool reception because of the subject matter; and now we have had this singular success in the very country where bigotry and prudishness are truly at home. Three ministers whom I had invited also attended the lecture and gave it their undivided attention. I can tell you, in the words of the dying messenger from Marathon who shouted to the Athenians: . . . "We have won a great battle."[87]

1907: Anonymous; A Letter from Boston
"Here . . . we really need this kind of activity"

In 1907, the German *Monthly Reports of the Scientific-Humanitarian Committee* prints a letter from Boston, Massachusetts, supporting the committee's efforts to combat bigotry against homosexuals and discussing the situation in the United States. The American correspondent writes:

I'm always delighted to hear about even the smallest success you have in vanquishing deep-rooted prejudices. And here in the United States we really need this kind of activity. In the face of Anglo-American hypocrisy, however, there is at present no chance that any man of science would have enough wisdom and courage to remove the veil which covers homosexuality in this country. And how many homosexuals I've come to know! Boston, this good old Puritan city, has them by the hundreds. The largest percentage, in my experience, comes from the Yankees of Massachusetts and Maine, or from New Hampshire. French Canadians are also well represented.

Here, as in Germany, homosexuality extends throughout all classes, from the slums of the North End to the highly fashionable Back Bay. Reliable homosexuals have told me names that reach into the highest circles of Boston, New York, and Washington, D.C., names which have left me speechless with astonishment. I have also noticed that bisexuality must be rather widespread. But I'll admit that I'm rather skeptical when homosexual friends say that they're far more attracted by the female sex. I'm often amused by someone assuring me of his bisexuality and later meeting him where there are no women.

There is astonishing ignorance among the Uranians I've come to know about their own true nature. This is probably a result of absolute silence and intolerance, which have never advanced real morality at any time or place. But with the growth of the population and the increase of intellectuals, the time is coming when America will finally be forced to confront the riddle of homosexuality.[88]

♀ 1923: F. W. STELLA BROWNE;
"Studies in Feminine Inversion"
"Truth and . . . human dignity are incompatible with
things as they are"

The publication in the United States of this paper, first read to the British Society for the Study of Sex Psychology, is evidence of the influence of that sexual emancipation discussion group upon a small audience of thoughtful Americans. Browne's paper appeared in the New York *Journal of Sexology and Psychology* in 1923. The British Society for the Study of Sex Psychology, founded in 1914, is called by historian Timothy d'Arch Smith "the only official organization" of English homosexuals in the early part of the twentieth century. Among the pamphlets published by the society were Edward Carpenter's forthright statement on Whitman's homosexuality, *Some Friends of Walt Whitman: A Study in Sex-Psychology* (1924), and F. W. Stella Browne's *Sexual Variety & Variability Among Women and their Bearing upon Social Reconstruction* (1915). Margaret Sanger, the pioneering American birth control advocate, and Dr. William Robinson, an American sexologist and reformer, are said to have been in communication with the British society, and an American branch is said to have been planned.[89]

Browne's "Studies in Feminine Inversion," although including much that is extremely negative by current standards, was doubtless perceived in its own time as a fairly advanced Lesbian defense: Browne places the burden of the Lesbian's problems on a repressive society and argues for the positive effect of physically expressed female-female affection. Here, Browne's case studies have been deleted; the focus is on her "comments and conclusions." Browne begins by explaining to her audience that her presentation is based on

only very fragmentary data, and suggestions on a peculiarly obscure subject. They have, however, this validity, that they are the result of close and careful observation, conducted so far as I am consciously aware, without any prejudice, though they would probably be much more illuminating had they been recorded by an observer who was herself entirely or predominantly homo-sexual.[90]

After presenting her case histories, Browne says:

This problem of feminine inversion is very pressing and immediate, taking into consideration the fact that in the near future, for at least a generation, the circumstances of women's lives and work will tend, even more than at present, to favour the frigid [sexually repressed] and next to the frigid, the inverted types. Even at present, the social and affectional side of the invert's nature has often fuller opportunity of satisfaction than the heterosexual woman's, but often at the cost of adequate and definite physical expression. And how decisive for vigor, sanity and serenity of body and mind, for efficiency, for happiness, for the mastery of life, and the understanding of one's fellow-creatures—just this definite physical expression is! The lack of it, "normal" and "abnormal," is at the root of most of what is most trivial and unsatisfactory in women's intellectual output, as well as of their besetting vice of cruelty. How can anyone be finely or greatly creative, if one's supreme moral law is a negation! Not to *live*, not to *do*, not even to try to understand.

In the (Lesbian) cases which I have called A. and B., sexual experience along the lines of their own psychic idiosyncrasy would have revealed to them definitely where they stood, and as both are well above the average in intelligence, would have been a key to many mysteries of human conduct which are now judged with dainty shrinking from incomprehensible folly and perversity.

I am sure that much of the towering spiritual arrogance which is found, e.g., in many high places in the Suffrage movement, and among the unco' guid generally, is really unconscious inversion.

I think it is perhaps not wholly uncalled-for, to underline very strongly my opinion that the homo-sexual impulse *is not in any way superior* to the normal; it has a fully equal right to existence and expression, it is no worse, no lower; *but no better*.

By all means let the invert—let all of us—have as many and varied "channels of sublimation" as possible; and far more than are at present available. But, to be honest, are we not too much inclined to make "sublimation" an excuse for refusing to tackle fundamentals? The tragedy of the repressed invert is apt to be not only one of emotional frustration, but complete dislocation of mental values.

Moreover, our present social arrangements, founded as they are on the repression and degradation of the normal erotic impulse, artificially stimulate inversion and have thus forfeited all right to condemn it. There is a huge, persistent, indirect pressure on women of strong passions and fine brains to find an emotional outlet with other women. A woman who is unwilling to accept either marriage—under present laws—or prostitution, and at the same time refuses to limit her sexual life to auto-erotic manifestations, will find she has to struggle against the whole social order for what is nevertheless her most precious personal right. The right sort of woman faces the struggle and counts the cost well worth while; but it is impossible to avoid seeing that she risks the most painful experiences, and spends an incalculable amount of time and energy on things that should be matters of course. Under these conditions, some women who *are not innately or predominantly homosexual* do form more or less explicitly erotic relations with other women, yet these are makeshifts and essentially substitutes, which cannot replace the vital contact, mental and bodily, with congenial men.

No one who has observed the repressed inverted impulse flaring into sex-antagonism, or masked as the devotion of daughter or cousin, or the solicitude of teacher or nurse, or perverted into the cheap, malignant cant of conventional moral indignation, can deny its force. Let us recognise this force, as frankly as we recognise and reverence the love between men and women. When Paris was devouring and disputing over Willy and Colette Willy's wonderful Claudine stories, another gifted woman-writer, who had also touched on the subject of inversion, defended not only the artistic conception and treatment of the stories (they need no defence, and remain one of the joys and achievements of modern French writing), but also their ethical content: Mme. Rachilde wrote *"une amoureuse d'amour n'est pas une vicieuse"* [a woman in love with love is not depraved].

After all: every strong passion, every deep affection, has its own endless possibilities, of pain, change, loss, incompatibility, satiety, jealousy, incompleteness: why add wholly extraneous difficulties and burdens? Harmony may be incompatible with freedom; we do not yet know, for few of us know either. But both truth and the most essential human dignity are incompatible with things as they are.[91]

1924–25: The Chicago Society for Human Rights; "To combat the public prejudices"

On December 10, 1924, the state of Illinois issued a charter to a nonprofit corporation named the Society for Human Rights, located in Chicago. This society is the earliest documented homosexual emancipation organization in the United States, as is evidenced by the group's charter, unearthed in the research for this book.

According to this charter, the object of the society's formation is

to promote and to protect the interests of people who by reasons of mental and physical abnormalties are abused and hindered in the legal pursuit of happiness which is guaranteed them by the Declaration of Independence, and to combat the public prejudices against them by dissemination of facts according to modern science among intellectuals of mature age. The Society stands only for law and order; it is in harmony with any and all general laws insofar as they protect the rights of others, and does in no manner recommend any acts in violation of present laws nor advocate any matter inimical to the public welfare.

The management of the society is vested in a board of seven, listed in the charter as:

Rev. John T. Graves, President
Al Meininger, Vice-President

Certificate Number _8018_

STATE OF ILLINOIS

OFFICE OF
THE SECRETARY OF STATE

To all to whom these Presents Shall Come, Greeting:

Whereas, a CERTIFICATE, duly signed and acknowledged, has been filed in the Office of the Secretary of State on the 10th day of December A.D. 1924 for the organization of the _____

SOCIETY FOR HUMAN RIGHTS, CHICAGO, ILLINOIS

under and in accordance with the provisions of "AN ACT CONCERNING CORPORATIONS" approved April 18, 1872 and in force July 1, 1872 and all acts amendatory thereof, a copy of which certificate is hereto attached:

Now Therefore, I, LOUIS L. EMMERSON, Secretary of State of the State of Illinois, by virtue of the powers and duties vested in me by law, do hereby certify that the said

SOCIETY FOR HUMAN RIGHTS, CHICAGO, ILLINOIS

is a legally organized Corporation under the laws of this State.

In Testimony Whereof, I hereto set my hand and cause to be affixed the Great Seal of the State of Illinois. Done at the City of Springfield this 10th day of December A.D. 19 24 and of the Independence of the United States the one hundred and 49th.

SEAL

LOUIS L. EMMERSON

SECRETARY OF STATE.

Charter: Society for Human Rights, Inc., 1924.

386

THIS STATEMENT MUST BE FILED IN DUPLICATE.

STATE OF ILLINOIS, } ss.

‾‾‾‾‾Cook‾‾‾‾‾ County.

FEE $10

To LOUIS L. EMMERSON, Secretary of State:

We, the undersigned‾‾‾‾‾ **Rev. John T. Graves,**

‾‾‾‾‾ **Henry Gerber,**

‾‾‾‾‾ **Al Meininger**

PAID
DEC 10 1924
$ 10⁰⁰ ▨▨
F.T.

citizens of the United States, propose to form a corporation under an Act of the General Assembly of the State of Illinois, entitled, "An Act concerning Corporations," approved April 18, 1872, and all acts amendatory thereof; and for the purpose of such organizations we hereby state as follows, to-wit:

1. The name of such corporation is‾‾‾‾‾

Society for Human Rights, Chicago, Illinois,   *OK*

(Incorporated not for Profit)

2. The object for which it is formed is **to promote and to protect the interests of people who by reasons of mental and physical abnormalties are abused and hindered in the legal pursuit of happiness which is guaranteed them by the Declaration of Independence, and to combat the public prejudices against them by dissemination of facts according to modern science among intellectuals of mature age. The Society stands only for law and order; it is in harmony with any and all general laws insofar as they protec̶t̶ i̶n̶f̶r̶i̶n̶g̶e̶ the rights of others, and does in no manner recommend any acts in violation of present laws nor advocate any matter inimical to the public welfare.------**

3. The management of the aforesaid **Society** shall be vested in a board of ‾‾‾‾‾ **seven** ‾‾‾‾‾ Directors.

4. The following persons are hereby selected as the Directors to control and manage said corporation for the first year of its corporate existence, viz.:

NAME	NUMBER	STREET	CITY	STATE
Rev. John T. Graves, President	1151	Milton Ave.	Chicago,	Illinois
Al Meininger, Vice-President	1044	North Franklin St.,	Chicago,	Ill
Henry Gerber, Secretary	1710	Crilly Court,	Chicago,	Illinois
Ellsworth Booher, Treasurer	1151	Milton Avenue,	Chicago,	Illinois.
Fred Pangburn, Trustee	1838	East 101st St.	Cleveland,	Ohio.
John Sather, 5855 Trustee	5855	University Ave.,	Chicago,	Illinois
Henry Teacutter, Trustee	1710	Crilly Court,	Chicago,	Illinois

5. The location is in the city of‾‾‾‾‾ **Chicago** ‾‾‾‾‾in the county of‾‾‾‾‾ **Cook**

in the State of Illinois, and the post office address of its business office is at No.‾‾‾‾‾ **1710**

‾‾‾‾‾ **Crilly Court** ‾‾‾‾‾ Street in the said city of‾‾‾‾‾ **Chicago**

SIGNED,

Rev. John T. Graves

Al Meininger

Henry Gerber

(005)

ss.

387

Henry Gerber, Secretary
Ellsworth Booher, Treasurer
Fred Panngburn, Trustee
John Sather, Trustee
Henry Teacutter, Trustee

The charter is signed by Rev. John T. Graves, Al Meininger, and Henry Gerber.[92]

In 1953, twenty-nine years after the society's founding, a short, anonymous letter from Henry Gerber, published in ONE, the then new homosexual emancipation monthly magazine, briefly described the fate of the early organization.[93]

In 1962, ONE published a more detailed account of the historic Chicago society, written by Henry Gerber, this time under his own name:

Just 37 years ago, in 1925, a few of my friends and myself were dragged off to jail in Chicago causing our own efforts to ameliorate the plight of homosexuals to come to an early end.

From 1920 to 1923, I had served with the Army of Occupation in Germany after World War I. In Coblenz on the Rhine I had subscribed to German homophile magazines and made several trips to Berlin. . . . I had always bitterly felt the injustice with which my own American society accused the homosexual of "immoral acts." I hated this society which allowed the majority, frequently corrupt itself, to persecute those who deviated from the established norms in sexual matters.

What could be done about it, I thought. Unlike Germany, where the homosexual was partially organized and where sex legislation was uniform for the whole country, the United States was in a condition of chaos and misunderstanding concerning its sex laws, and no one was trying to unravel the tangle and bring relief to the abused. . . .

I realized at once that homosexuals themselves needed nearly as much attention as the laws pertaining to their acts. How could one go about such a difficult task [that of homosexual emancipation]? The prospect of going to jail did not bother me. I had a vague idea that I wanted to help solve the problem. I had not yet read the opinion of Clarence Darrow that "no other offence has ever been visited with such severe penalties as seeking to help the oppressed." All my friends to whom I spoke about my plans advised against my doing anything so rash and futile. I thought to myself that if I succeeded I might become known to history as deliverer of the downtrodden, even as Lincoln. But I am not sure my thoughts were entirely upon fame. If I succeeded in freeing the homosexual, I too would benefit.

What was needed was a Society, I concluded. My boss, whom I had pleased by translating a work of philosophy from the German, helped me write a Declaration of Purpose for our new Society for Human Rights, the same name used by the homosexuals of Germany for their work.[94] The first difficulty was in rounding up enough members and contributors so the work could go forward. The average homosexual, I found, was ignorant concerning himself. Others were fearful. Still others were frantic or depraved. Some were blasé.

Many homosexuals told me that their search for forbidden fruit was the real spice of life. With this argument they rejected our aims. We wondered how we could accomplish anything with such resistance from our own people.

The outline of our plan was as follows:

1. We would cause the homosexuals to join our Society and gradually reach as large a number as possible.

2. We would engage in a series of lectures pointing out the attitude of society in relation to their own behavior and especially urging against the seduction of adolescents.

3. Through a publication named *Friendship and Freedom* we would keep the homophile world in touch with the progress of our efforts. The publication was to refrain from advocating sexual acts and would serve merely as a forum for discussion.[95]

4. Through self-discipline, homophiles would win the confidence and assistance of legal authorities and legislators in understanding the problem; that these authorities should be educated on the futility and folly of long prison terms for those committing homosexual acts, etc.

The beginning of all movements is necessarily small. I was able to gather together a half dozen of my friends and the Society for Human Rights became an actuality. Through a lawyer our program was submitted to the Secretary of State at Springfield, and we were furnished with a State Charter. No one seemed to have bothered to investigate our purpose.

As secretary of the new organization I wrote to many prominent persons soliciting their support. Most of them failed to understand our purpose. The big, fatal, fearful obstacle seemed always to be the almost willful misunderstanding and ignorance on the part of the general public concerning the nature of homosexuality. What people generally thought about when I mentioned the word had nothing to do with reality. . . .

Nevertheless, we made a good start, even though at my own expense, and the first step was under way. The State Charter had only cost $10.00. I then set about putting out the first issue of *Friendship and Freedom* and worked hard on the second issue. It soon became apparent that my friends were illiterate and penniless. I had to both write and finance. Two issues, alas, were all we could publish. The most difficult task was to get men of good reputation to back up the Society. I needed noted medical authorities to endorse us. But they usually refused to endanger their reputations.

The only support I got was from poor people: John, a preacher who earned his room and board by preaching brotherly love to small groups of Negroes; Al, an indigent laundry queen; and Ralph whose job with the railroad was in jeopardy when his nature became known. These were the national officers of the Society for Human Rights, Inc. I realized this start was dead wrong, but after all, movements always start small and only by organizing first and correcting mistakes later could we expect to go on at all. The Society was bound to become a success, we felt, considering the modest but honest plan of operation. It would probably take long years to develop into anything worth while. Yet I was will to slave and suffer and risk losing my job and savings and even my liberty for the ideal.

One of our greatest handicaps was the knowledge that homosexuals don't organize. Being thoroughly cowed, they seldom get together. Most feel that as long as some homosexual sex acts are against the law, they should not let their names be on any homosexual organization's mailing list any more than notorious bandits would join a thieves' union. Today [1962] there are at least a half dozen homophile organizations working openly for the group, but still the number of dues-

A copy of *Friendship and Freedom*, the "paper" published by the Chicago Society for Human Rights, appears prominently in this photo of a collection of early, mostly German, homosexual emancipation periodicals, verifying both the existence of the American periodical and suggesting the authenticity of Gerber's account. No copies of *Friendship and Freedom* are now known to be extant.[96]

paying members is very small when we know that there are several million homosexuals in the U.S.

The Society, says Gerber, "decided to concentrate our efforts on the State of Illinois," and to focus on reform of those laws criminalizing homosexual acts.

We had agreed to make our organization a purely homophile Society, and we had argued and decided to exclude the much larger circle of bisexuals for the time being. Neither I nor John, our elected president, had been conscious of the fact that our vice-president, Al, was that type. In fact, we later found out that he had a wife and two small children. . . .

One Sunday morning about 2 a.m., I returned from a visit downtown. After I had gone to my room, someone knocked at the door. Thinking it might be the landlady, I opened up. Two men entered the room. They identified themselves as a city detective and a newspaper reporter from the *Examiner*. The detective asked me where the boy was. What boy? He told me he had orders from his precinct captain to bring me to the police station. He took my typewriter, my notary public diploma, and all the literature of the Society and also personal diaries as well as my bookkeeping accounts. At no time did he show a warrant for my arrest. At the police station I was locked up in a cell but no charges were made against me. In the morning I was given permission to call my boss who, for my work's sake, fixed my status as "absent on leave."

With a few other persons, unknown to me, I was taken to the Chicago Avenue Police Court where I also found John the preacher and Al the laundry queen and a young man who happened to be in Al's room at the time of arrest. No one knew what had happened. A friendly cop at the station showed me a copy of the *Examiner*. There right on the front page I found this incredible story:

Strange Sex Cult Exposed[97]

The article mentioned Al who had brought his male friends home and had, in full view of his wife and children, practiced "strange sex acts" with them. Al's wife had at last called a social worker who reported these "strange doings" to the police. A raid of the flat, the report continued, had turned up John, a preacher, and Henry, a postal employee, and all were put under arrest. Among the effects in Al's flat they found a pamphlet of this "strange sex cult" which "*urged men to leave their wives and children.*"

What an outright untruth; what a perversion of facts! John was alone in his room when arrested, and I was too. We were not with Al; nor did we know of his being married and having children.

There had been no warrants obtained for our arrests. The police, I suppose, had hoped or expected to find us in bed. They could not imagine homosexuals in any other way. My property was taken without excuse. This, in the United States *anno domini* 1925 with the Constitution to protect the people from unreasonable arrest and search. Shades of the Holy Inquisition.

So, that was it! Al had confessed his sins but assured us that the reports of the detective and reporter were distorted. On Monday, the day after our arrest, in the Chicago Avenue Police Court, the detective triumphantly produced a powder puff which he claimed he found in my room. That was the sole evidence of my crime. It was admitted as evidence of my effeminacy. I have never in my life used rouge or powder. The young social worker, a hatchet-faced female, read from my diary, out of context: "I love Karl." The detective and the judge shuddered over such depravity. To the already prejudiced court we were obviously guilty. We were guilty just by being homosexual. This was the court's conception of our "strange cult."

The judge spoke little to us and adjourned court with the remark he thought ours was a violation of the Federal law against sending obscene matter through the mails. Nothing in our first issue of *Friendship and Freedom* could be considered "obscene" of course.

At this first trial the court dismissed us to the Cook County Jail. Our second trial was to be on Thursday. They separated John from Al and me. In our cell Al broke out crying and felt deeply crushed for having gotten us into the mess. George, who had been arrested with Al, did not lose any time while a guest of the Chicago police. Among the prisoners was a young Jew who asked me if I wanted a lawyer. He recommended a friend of his, a "shyster" lawyer who practiced around criminal courts. I made a request to see him and he appeared the next morning. He seemed to be a smart fellow who probably knew how to fix the State Attorney and judges. He had the reputation of making a good living taking doubtful cases. He also handled the bail bond racket and probably made additional money each month from this shady practice.

The lawyer told me at once that our situation looked serious. But he said he could get me out on bail. He would charge $200.00 for each trial. I accepted his services, although I know that it would have been cheaper to merely accept the maximum fine of $200.00.

We were in a tough spot. . . . The following Thursday the four of us were taken before the same judge. This time two post office inspectors were also present. Before the judge appeared in court, one of the inspectors promised that he would see to it that we got heavy prison sentences for infecting God's own country.

As the trial began, our attorney demanded that we be set free since no stitch of evidence existed to hold us. The judge became angry and ordered our attorney to shut up or be cited for contempt. The post office inspectors said that the federal commissioner would take the case under advisement from the obscenity angle. The second trial was then adjourned until Monday. The lawyer made one last request that we be released on bail. The judge hemmed and hawed but set bail at $1,000.00 for each of us. The lawyer made all the arrangements and collected his fees.

Being a free man once more, I went down to the post office to report for work. But I was told that I had been suspended—more of the dirty work of the post office inspectors. Next I called upon the managing editor of the *Examiner*. I confronted him with the article in the paper. He told me he would look into the matter and make corrections, but nothing was ever done. I had no means to sue the paper, and that was the end of that.

Meanwhile a friend of mine succeeded in getting me a better lawyer—the one who had made our request for a charter. He agreed to take my case, also for $200.00 a trial. Calling the shyster, I told him of my inability to pay for another trial. . . .

. . . I knew before hand that our case would be dismissed since my new lawyer advised me that everything had been "arranged" satisfactorily.

The day of the third trial we met a new judge. The detective who had made the arrests was there, the prosecuting attorney, the two post office inspectors, and even my first lawyer who found he had become interested in the case. The judge, who had reviewed our earlier trials, immediately reprimanded the prosecution. He said "It is an outrage to arrest persons without a warrant. I order the case dismissed." Al who had pleaded guilty to disorderly conduct received a fine of $10.00 and costs. The social worker was not present at this trial. Our lawyer told the judge in the presence of the baffled post office inspectors that he knew for sure that the Commissioner would take no action as far as the alleged obscenity of mailed literature was concerned. The judge also ordered the detective to return my property to me. I got my typewriter, but my diaries had been turned over to the postal inspectors and I never saw them again. I had never put down in my diaries anything that could be used against me, fortunately. . . .

. . . The experience generally convinced me that we were up against a solid wall of ignorance, hypocrisy, meanness and corruption. The wall had won. The parting jibe of the detective had been, "What was the idea of the Society for Human Rights anyway? Was it to give you birds the legal right to rape every boy on the street?" . . .

The lawyer advised me he could get my post office job back. But I had no more money for fees and took no action. After a few weeks a letter from Washington arrived advising me that I had been officially dismissed from the Post Office Department for "conduct unbecoming a postal worker." That definitely meant the end of the Society for Human Rights.[98]

In June 1932, a periodical titled *The Modern Thinker* published an essay, "In Defense of Homosexuality," by "Parisex," a pen name of Henry Gerber. An introduction to the essay explains that it "is one of the numerous replies" attacking "The Riddle of Homosexuality" by W. Beran Wolfe, M.D., which had appeared in the April issue.[99]

In his rejoinder, Gerber congratulates Dr. Wolfe for urging that laws against homosexuality be struck down, but notes that oppression by church and state are historical antecedents to the more insidious persecution by modern psychoanalysts. He charges psychoanalysts with constructing a new set of myths and taboos which rival the Sodom legend in their pernicious effects on homosexuals. He challenges the categorization of homosexuality as a neurotic symptom, and the popular notion of a "cure." Gerber rejects Wolfe's attribution of insecurity, antisocial behavior, and criminal tendencies to homosexuals. He argues that those homosexuals who are disturbed have been made so by societal oppression.

Wolfe is attacked for relying upon the concepts of Freud, Jung, and Adler; in rebuttal, Gerber approvingly cites Havelock Ellis and Magnus Hirschfeld. This leads Gerber to discuss the "nature versus nurture" debate on the origins of homosexuality. Gerber refuses to align himself with either position, conceding that both inborn and social reasons may influence sexual object choice. Gerber further objects to Wolfe's single-minded focus upon sexual acts, and suggests that psychology should deal equally with purely affectional ties between members of the same gender. He argues that the institution of marriage, and even monogamy, is disintegrating under the impact of modern conditions, and, citing Edward Carpenter, Gerber envisions a future society which will fully accept the unique contributions of its homosexual members.

Gerber concludes:

After all, it is highly futile for Dr. Wolfe to worry about neurotic homosexuals when the world itself, led and ruled by the strong heterosexual "normal" men is in such chaotic condition, and knows not where to turn.

It is quite possible that if called upon, the homosexuals of this country would put up the money to send Dr. Wolfe to Washington to examine these great big "normal" men, who guide the destinies of millions, to find their "neurosis" and to cure it.[100]

In 1934, Gerber is listed as circulation manager of a mimeographed literary magazine entitled *Chanticleer*, and twelve articles by him are included under his own name. Three are devoted entirely to homosexuality, the others contain passing references.[101]

The February 1934 issue of *Chanticleer* includes Gerber's review of "Recent Homosexual Literature," and his critical comments on the novels *The Well of Loneliness, Twilight Men*, and *Strange Brother* as "anti-homosexual propaganda." Gerber's introduction accuses a coalition of capitalists, clerics, and politicians of defending monogamy and suppressing sexual freedom of all kinds:

The 100% patriots are vociferously proclaiming that this is a Free Country; however, when asked if Love is free, or if they are for Free Love, they conveniently avoid the issue by retreating with sundry maledictions and such epithets as "Bolshevic, Libertine, Swine." In my last article, in the initial issue of "Chanticleer", I pointed out that politicians and priests clamor for bigger and better morons. They are in fact responsible for sex suppression in America. Capitalism, loyally supported by the churches, has established a Public Policy that the Sacred Institution of Monogamy must be enforced; and such a fiat is the deathknell to all sexual freedom. Monogamy is the ideal of this state and all deviations from this ideal are strictly suppressed, including free love in all of its forms, birth control, and homosexuality. For these forms of sexual freedom, if free to practice, would defeat the sacred institution of monogamy. In Russia, where the government is no longer capitalistic and is not bound to religious sex superstitions, sex is free. One may gratify one's sexual appetite as one may see fit, just as one may choose what to eat for supper. Sex only becomes a social concern there when children are born, in which case both parents are held mutually responsible.

Homosexuality has until recently been strictly taboo and no "decent" author or publisher considered it fit to mention in print. However, in the last decade, several medical works have appeared about homosexuality and recently a few books of homosexual fiction have dared to show themselves among the flood of heterosexual books.

Gerber disposes of *The Well of Loneliness* (he is quoted in the following history), and then goes on:

TWILIGHT MEN, by Andre Tellier, deals with a young Frenchman, who comes to America, is introduced into homosexual society in New York, becomes a drug addict for no obvious reason, finally kills his father and commits suicide. It is again excellent anti-homosexual propaganda, although the plot is too silly to convince anyone who has known homosexual people at all.

STRANGE BROTHER, by Blair Niles, is the story of a sensitive young man. The author causes him to go through as many mental sufferings as she can, then puts a pistol in his hand and lets him shoot himself and end the book. Again an ideal anti-homosexual propaganda, but no more logical than the book mentioned before.[102]

The September 1934 *Chanticleer* contains Gerber's comments on "Hitlerism and Homosexuality," in which he discusses the reaction to the then recent murders by

Hitler of Ernst Roehm, SA chief, and other SA officers, June 29 to July 1, 1934. In this essay, Gerber mistakenly credits Roehm with leading a group in opposition to Hitler's tyranny.

Gerber writes, in part:

A few weeks ago Herr Adolf Hitler in part justified the bloody murder of his intimate friends with the accusation that his Chief of Staff of Nazi storm troops and his clique had been guilty of the most revolting (to normal healthy people) sexual aberrations. It seems strange that Hitler should have found that out so late. After having been intimately associated with Roehm all his life, he must have been well acquainted with Roehm's inclinations. But such a little slip of memory does not bother the great corporal.

A short time ago an American journalist pointed out in the liberal "Nation" that the whole Hitler movement was based on the homosexual Greek attachments of men for each other, and the same Jewish author stated that it was another of the Hitler contradictions that the "Leader" should have acquiesced in the burning of the books of Dr. Magnus Hirschfeld, who had dedicated his life to the liberation of the enslaved homosexuals in all lands. Thus we get a glimpse of the insanity of the whole movement: A Jewish doctor working for the interests of homosexuals is persecuted by a heterosexual mob, led by homosexuals.

Of course, our American journalists who reap large profits from the publication of all the filthy details of heterosexual and homosexual perverts, especially among the "Pillars of Society" in Hollywood and New York alike, managed to get one of their reporters into the bedroom of Herr Roehm just before Hitler arrived to call his erstwhile bosom friend to face the muzzle of his own gun, and even such a conservative and "decent" paper as the New York Times (I was told) reported that while no evidence could be found in Roehm's boudoir, his chief of police was found in bed with a fair young man. The newspapers of America were strangely compromised by this Hitler story. Should they praise the murderer Hitler for suppressing homosexuals, or should they give credit to Roehm and his homosexual camorra [society] for being the only men in Germany virile enough to attempt to wipe out the unspeakable Hitler? The newspapers condemned both and saved their faces.

Changing the subject, Gerber discusses the legal oppression of homosexuals.

Have you ever honestly asked yourself why homosexuals should be persecuted or punished by law? Of course, you know that in France, Spain, Belgium, Russia, Czecho-Slovakia, Mexico, South America, and even in our own Philippine Islands, homosexuals are not persecuted or punished unless they commit anti-social acts. . . .

. . . Wonder no one thought of blaming our depression on homosexuality. If Hoover had only thought of it, he would have been reelected, for when it comes to persecute homosexuals, no lies and defamations are too stupid not to be believed. . . .

No one has yet brought forth a plausible reason why homosexuals should be wiped out, except the age-old reasoning which is also applied to atheism and communism, that it is contrary to the welfare of the state (the profit and exploitation system of the capitalists). That is the real and only reason, and the churches have conveniently joined the chorus and labeled homosexuals "unnatural," "abnormal," and what not. With the waning of capitalism and organized religion, the opposition of the governments to homosexuals will also wane, as has been seen by the example of Russia and Czecho-Slovakia. You cannot, therefore blame homosexuals, if they throw in their support with the communists and atheists.

As a matter of fact, when the German Reichstag Committee, chosen to revise the German Penal Code, voted, the socialists and communists outvoted the nationalist and clerical party, and brought about the repeal of the notorious paragraph 175 which punished homosexuals for their acts (but not female homosexuals), in 1927 [1929 is correct].

Roehm and his valiant men have been defeated, but the homosexuals will go on fighting to rid the world of tyranny.[103]

The December 1934 *Chanticleer* includes Gerber's "More Nonsense About Homosexuals," a review of the book *Strange Loves* by La Forest Potter, M.D.

. . . I think the history of psychology is . . . damning evidence of man's credulity and outright stupidity. The volume under review by Dr. La Forest Potter, who boasts of being a "late member of the New York County Medical Society, Massachusetts Medical Society," etc., etc. . . . proves to me two significant facts: 1) that the medical authorities in America, of which Dr. Potter is a shining example, are about 100 years behind the times, and 2) that most psychologists in this country are mere yes-men who blindly and obediently follow the current authorized moral code without any regard to common sense or the results of modern scientific research. . . .

While the title of the book would indicate that the author had in view *all* phenomena of sex which seem strange to him and to the ignorant public alike, Dr. Potter deals mainly with homosexuality. . . . such a title is a profitable device for the sale of books, for the morons are always looking for something new and "strange" in sex matters. In other words, the book of Dr. Potter is just another instance of the morbid sex racket, a lurid description of sex abnormalities under the moral guise of condemnation of the queer sinners dealing in such "strange" loves in order to get the filthy details by the post office censors of "obscene" literature. Krafft-Ebing was perhaps the first author to start this racket and the volume in review is evidence of the sad fact that the end of it is not yet.

In the accepted fashion of Krafft-Ebing's pot-boiler, Dr. Potter goes through the various artificial classification of homosexuals. He has Chapters on the Riddle of Homosexuality, . . . a chapter on the history of . . . the various unsuccessful attempts of "scientists" to solve the "riddle," . . . special chapters on Lesbians (female homosexuals), in which the author makes the sensational statement that "there isn't a man on earth who has a Chinaman's chance against a Lesbian, once she has thoroughly seduced a woman to her wiles" (any doctor having knowledge of gynecology ought to know the reason to be due to the fact that males are very deficient in the fine art of satisfying a woman's sexual needs), [etc.]. . . .

. . . Dr. Potter views the psychoanalytical method of dealing with homosexuals and cites cases in which homosexuals have been "cured" by psychoanalysts. . . .

But the author does evidently not think so much of this "cure" of homosexuals, for he cautiously warns that homosexuals can be cured only if they want to be cured. The only way to cure a [male] homosexual of his foible is to make him love women, a very simple process indeed, but Dr. Potter does not seem to realize that heterosexual men can be cured exactly in the same fashion from their love for women, by getting them to like men. By the same method, Pop-eye, the sailor cures children who do not like spinach by making them believe that spinach is really good for them and that every normal citizen must eat it.[104]

♀ 1929: The American Reaction to *The Well of Loneliness*; "On behalf of a misunderstood and misjudgd minority"

The Lesbian contribution to the homosexual resistance has often taken the form of fiction. Radclyffe Hall's *The Well of Loneliness*, first published in England in 1928, may be seen in a political light as an attempt, characteristic of its time, to win sympathy from heterosexuals, to change their negative attitudes toward and social persecution of Lesbians. The story of the American publication and defense of this famous English Lesbian novel is part of the history of the homosexual emancipation movement in the United States, and of reaction to it.

Radclyffe Hall's decision to write a novel that would "speak on behalf of a misunderstood and misjudged minority" is recalled by Una Troubridge, Hall's lover of many years. Troubridge's biography of Hall (or "John" as she was known among her intimates) describes the scene.

It was after the success of *Adam's Breed* [1926] that John came to me one day with unusual gravity and asked for my decision in a serious matter: she had long wanted to write a book on sexual inversion, a novel that would be accessible to the general public who did not have access to technical treatises. At one time she had thought of making it a 'period' book, built around an actual personality of the early nineteenth century. But her instinct had told her that in any case she must postpone such a book until her name was made; until her unusual theme would get a hearing as being the work of an established writer.

It was her absolute conviction that such a book could only be written by a sexual invert, who alone could be qualified by personal knowledge and experience to speak on behalf of a misunderstood and misjudged minority.

It was with this conviction that she came to me, telling me that in her view the time was ripe, and that although the publication of such a book might mean the shipwreck of her whole career, she was fully prepared to make any sacrifice except—the sacrifice of my peace of mind.

She pointed out that in view of our union and of all the years that we had shared a home, what affected her must also affect me and that I would be included in any condemnation. Therefore she placed the decision in my hands and would write or refrain as I should decide.

I am glad to remember that my reply was made without so much as an instant's hesitation: I told her to write what was in her heart, that so far as any effect upon myself was concerned, I was sick to death of ambiguities, and only wished to be known for what I was and to dwell with her in the palace of truth.

Then and there she set to work on *The Well of Loneliness*.[105]

On August 30, 1928, the *New York Times* reports:

TO PRINT BANNED BOOK HERE

Alfred Knopf Gets American Rights to "Well of Loneliness."

LONDON, Aug. 29.—"The Well of Loneliness," the book on sex matters suppressed by its publishers here . . . is to be published in America. . . .

. . . Its publishers assert it treats skillfully a seriously growing psychological problem, but the Home Secretary apparently thought otherwise. His action in requesting its suppression has been interpreted as meaning that a book censorship has been established in England.

The situation is complicated by the fact that Compton Mackenzie, . . . has just published "Extraordinary Women," which treats satirically the same problem which Miss Radclyffe Hall treated seriously. Critics here are now asking why one book was suppressed and the other allowed.[106]

On October 6, 1928, in a dispatch from Great Britain, the *New York Times* reports:

George Bernard Shaw and H. G. Wells have added the weight of their authority to protest against the attack on the freedom of literature which was made when the original ban was imposed [in England]. . . . "I read it, and read it again," said Shaw today, "and I repeat that it ought not to have been withdrawn. It speaks of things people ought to know about. . . ."

Miss Radclyffe Hall herself described the seizure of the books as an outrage against literature and an attack on personal freedom.[107]

On December 15, 1929, Covici-Friede of New York published *The Well of Loneliness* after Alfred Knopf had apparently received legal advice on the possibility of prosecution and changed his mind about bringing out the book.[108]

On January 12, 1929, the *New York Times* reports:

POLICE SEIZE NOVEL BY RADCLYFFE HALL

Detectives of Inspector Bolan's staff seized yesterday afternoon more than 800 copies of Radclyffe Hall's novel, "The Well of Loneliness," and served summonses on D. S. Friede of the Covici-Friede Publishing Corporation. . . . The summons was issued . . . on complaint of John S. Sumner, secretary of the Society for the Suppression of Vice, that the book violated . . . the Penal Code relating to the circulation of indecent literature.

Mr. Sumner said last night that his action was taken as a result of complaints received by the society.

Calling Hall's book "a study of a woman's fight for social adjustment despite abnormality," the *Times* reports:

P. Covici and D. S. Friede, the publishers in America, brought out the book on Dec. 15 [1928]. Since then more than 20,000 copies have been sold and the book ranks near the top of the "best sellers." They characterized the seizure and court action as "absurd." . . .

The publishers announced that they would fight the court action "as far as it can be carried."[109]

On January 23, 1929, the *Times* reports:

PUBLISHER IS ARRAIGNED.

Court to Read "Well of Loneliness" Before Deciding Friede's Case.

Two copies of "The Well of Loneliness," by Radclyffe Hall, English novelist, were given to Magistrate Bushel in the West Side court yesterday for reading. . . .[110]

On February 1, 1929, the *Times* reports:

Despite the fact that it has been defeated at several previous sessions of the Legislature, the clean books bill, designed to prevent the sale and distribution of obscene literature, was introduced today.[111]

On February 22, 1929, the *Times* reports:

NOVEL 'LONELINESS' IS RULED OBSCENE

Magistrate Holds Publishers of Radclyffe Hall Book for Trial on Charge.

SAYS IT AIMS TO DEPRAVE

Admits Literary Merit of Work Is Not Disputed— Covici Promises Fight "to the Bitter End."

Magistrate Hyman Bushel in the Tombs Court ruled yesterday that the book "The Well of Loneliness" . . . is obscene and was printed and distributed in this city in violation of the penal law.[112]

Bushel's ruling sent *The Well of Loneliness* on to be tried for obscenity in the Court of Special Sessions.
On April 20, 1929, the *Times* reports:

Justices Salomon, Healy and McInerney in Special Sessions declared yesterday that the book "The Well of Loneliness," . . . although dealing with "a delicate social problem," was not published and sold in this city in violation of the law against objectionable literature.

The court thereupon discharged Donald Friede, president of the Covici-Friede Corporation, American publishers of the book. . . .

Only the day before Friede was convicted by a jury in Boston of violating the Massachusetts statute against objectionable literature for his distribution there of Theodore Dreiser's book, "An American Tragedy."

The final court found that *The Well of Loneliness* was not obscene.[113]

In 1964, lawyer Morris Ernst, who had defended the American publisher of *The Well of Loneliness* thirty-five years earlier, describes and sums up the case, placing it in historical and legal perspective. Ernst reprints the whole of Bushel's original finding that *The Well of Loneliness*, because it was too positive a portrayal of "inversion," was obscene—a decision interesting to read today, when Hall's book appears to many Lesbians and Gay men as horribly apologetic. Ernst writes:

The censorious seldom, if ever, had placed a taboo upon an entire subject matter or theme, a whole area of thought. Usually, the attack had been against a specific technique used in presenting the theme, such as four-letter words of Anglo-Saxon origin or specific sexual descriptions. Until after the middle of the 1920's, no court opinion had been addressed directly to the question of banning the literary expression of an entire area of human knowledge or human behavior.

Then, in both drama and the novel, the question was raised: Should the public be denied the right to read a book or see a play on the subject of female homosexuality?

Curiously enough, the test of the subject arose first on the stage. In our culture the theater has been substantially unmolested by the censors except in just the period we are now discussing, the 1920's and 1930's. Social scientists may tell us the basis of this immunity. Perhaps it is the high price of tickets, conveying an exemption that in literature is traditionally assured to expensive editions . . . The fact that children were less likely to be exposed may have distracted the leers of the "Comstocks" to more fertile fields of attack. . . .

Even at the peak of Comstock's power, he had not been able to force upon theatrical producers the yoke in which he held book publishers. In 1905 he had made the attempt. His target was George Bernard Shaw's new play, *Mrs. Warren's Profession*, which scandalized many people because it dealt with prostitution. . . . Comstock announced that if anyone staged the play by "the Irish smut-dealer," he would prosecute. He did, too, but a three-man court ruled by a vote of 2 to 1 that *Mrs. Warren's Profession* did not fall within the scope of the New York State Obscenity Law.

However, female homosexuality was another matter. Lesbian-oriented plays such as Edouard Bourdet's *The Captive* in 1927 were closed down, and the resulting furor led the New York Legislature—since New York City is the center of the thespian arts—to pass a law against the performance of any drama that dealt with sexual perversion.

The law, interestingly, was directed not only against the offending play but also against the theater in which it was performed. The theater owner could lose his license and the theater be closed.

Two years later, in 1929, the courts were called upon to consider whether the same objections applied to a novel, specifically, *The Well of Loneliness*, by Radclyffe Hall. This was a work of "restraint and literary merit," to use the words of the most horrified of the judges who presided over its fate. The prosecutor objected not to any identified episode of lesbian lovemaking but to its mere idea. In that era all discussions of sexual relations other than those between male and female were illegal in the eyes of the State. There had been a few novels touching on the love of man and man, or woman and woman. But no law had been made as to the lines of permissibility or impermissibility. Nevertheless, in *The Well of Loneliness* case the cultural taboo frightened many editors of our mass media. One of our most distinguished publishers [Knopf] had actually set up *The Well of Loneliness* in type. He was then advised by an able attorney to desist from publication because the book was, or at least might be held to be, obscene and illegal.

Donald Friede, of Covici, Friede, a couragous publisher, took over the publishing rights and dared the legal conventions. When brought into the Magistrate's Court in New York City, he not only defended his imprimatur but defended it stoutly and, what is still more important, without the least trace of apology. Unlike many other publishers before and after him, he acted as if he really believed what the Constitution guaranteed—freedom of the printed word. The case came to court without any dispute as to facts such as "Was the book published?" "Was it sold?" "Who sold it?" and all the other details that are really irrelevant in most battles over freedom for the mind of man.

The judge who first heard the case addressed himself to it in terms of that familiar text of Lord Chief Justice Cockburn in 1868: Would the book corrupt those into whose hands it was likely to fall?

Psychiatrists of esteem differed widely as to its possible influence or effect. Leaders of that profession were afraid to testify, some going so far as to indicate that the book might conceivably corrupt our culture, some suggesting that it might turn our nation into an "Isle of Lesbos." Others with great sobriety of thought replied with questions: Do we favor forcing this problem or issue or situation into dirty, secret underground avenues for future discussion? If there be a problem, since sexual relations between men and women are deemed to be preferable, do we still believe that man has his best chance of finding a wise solution by open debate in the marketplace of thought, or by suppression of all writings on the subject? Do we sweep the entire problem under the bed?

When the case came before Judge Hyman Bushel sitting without a jury in the Magistrate's Court of New York City, he wrote a lengthy opinion. For those who have not read the book itself and who may be interested in techniques of testing for the obscene, Judge Bushel's view is set forth at length to show what he read *in* and *out* of the volume. He does point out that there are no unclean words, that the book is well written and carefully constructed as a piece of fiction. He decides, however, that the book should be banned because the "depraved" relationships are idealized and extolled and, what bothers him most, because lesbian love and lesbian lovers are not held up to shame. We assume that the good judge might have concluded that the book was legal if Radclyffe Hall, the author, had had the characters apologetic for what they did to life and what life did to them.

This opinion should be read with care. The judge was offended, shocked, and discouraged. He will not object if we add that he was not a man who had lived in an ivory tower. He was married and he had grown up in the hurly-burly of a big city. But we must be gentle with him, for in 1929 few women in our land had ever heard the word "lesbian." If the mass media of that era referred at all to such a way of life, it was only by indirection or with euphemisms. It was understandable that Judge Bushel might conclude that the volume was offensive, according to his own likes.

People v. Friede
City Magistrate's Court of New York City (1929)

BUSHEL, City Magistrate. Friede and another person are charged with having violated the New York Penal Law by their possession and sale of a book entitled "The Well of Loneliness." Evidence proving possession and sale of the book by Friede had been introduced and is not controverted by him.

This court in a prosecution of this character is not the trier of the fact. Its judicial province is limited to a determination of the question as to whether as matter of law it can be said that the book which forms the basis of the charge in question is not violative of the statute. The evidence before me, however, is the same as that which would be presented to the tribunal vested with the power of deciding the facts as well as the law.

An "Unnatural" Crew

The book here involved is a novel dealing wih the childhood and early womanhood of a female invert. In broad outline the story shows how these unnatural tendencies manifested themselves from early childhood; the queer attraction of the child to the maid in the household, her affairs with one Angela Crossby, a normally sexed, but unhappily married, woman, causing further dissension between the latter and her husband, her jealousy of another man who later debauched this married woman, and her despair, in being supplanted by him in Angela's affections, are vividly portrayed. The book culminates with an extended elaboration upon her intimate relations with a normal young girl, who becomes a helpless subject of her perverted influence and passion, and pictures the struggle for this girl's affections between this invert and a man from whose normal advances she herself had previously recoiled, because of her own perverted nature. Her sex experiences are set forth in some detail and also her visits to various resorts frequented by male and female inverts.

Literary Merit—Yes

The author has treated these incidents not without some restraint; nor is it disputed that the book has literary merit. To quote the people's brief: "It is a well-written, carefully constructed piece of fiction, and contains no unclean words." Yet the narrative does not veer from its central theme, and the emotional and literary setting in which they are found give the incidents described therein great force and poignancy. The unnatural and depraved relationships portrayed are sought to be idealized and extolled. The characters in the book who indulge in these vices are described in attractive terms, and it is maintained throughout that they be accepted on the same plane as persons normally constituted, and that their perverse and inverted love is as worthy as the affection between normal beings and should be considered just as sacred by society.

Moral Value—No

The book can have no moral value, since it seeks to justify the right of a pervert to prey upon normal members of a community, and to uphold such relationship as noble and lofty. Although it pleads for tolerance on the part of society of those possessed of and inflicted with perverted traits and tendencies, it does not argue for repression or moderation of insidious impulses. An idea of the moral tone which the book assumes may be gained from the attitude taken by its principal character towards her mother, pictured as a hard, cruel, and pitiless woman, because of the abhorrence she displays to unnatural lust, and to whom, because of that reaction, the former says: "But what I will never forgive is your daring to try and make me ashamed of my love. I'm not ashamed of it; there's no shame in me."

The theme of the novel is not only antisocial and offensive to public morals and decency, but the method in which it is developed, in its highly emotional way attracting and focusing attention upon perverted ideas and unnatural vices, and seeking to justify and idealize them, is strongly calculated to corrupt and debase those members of the community who would be susceptible to its immoral influence.

Justice Cockburn Rides Again

Although the book in evidence is prefaced by a laudatory commentary by Havelock Ellis, yet it is he who, in his scientific treatise on the subject, states: "We are bound to protect the helpless members of society against the invert." The court is charged with that precise duty here. The test of an obscene book laid down in *Regina* v. *Hicklin*, is "whether the tendency of the matter charged as obscenity is to deprave or corrupt those whose minds are open to such immoral influences, and who might come into contact with it." Although not sole and exclusive, this test is one which has been frequently applied. It may be accepted as a basis for judicial decision here.

Its application and soundness are assailed by learned counsel for Friede, who argue that it seeks to gauge the mental and moral capacity of the community by that of its dullest-witted and most fallible members. This contention overlooks the fact that those who are subject to perverted influences, and in whom that abnormality may be called into activity, and who might be aroused to lustful and lecherous practices are not limited to the young and immature, the moron, the mentally weak, or the intellectually impoverished, but may be found among those of mature age and of high intellectual development and professional attainment.

Men may differ in their conceptions as to the propriety of placing any restrictions upon a literary work or absolute freedom of expression and interchange of ideas. This conflict between liberty and restraint is not new to the law. However, the Legislature has spoken on that subject in the enactment of the law in question. Even if the courts were not (as a matter of fact they are) in accord with the public policy it declares, they would not be free to disregard it, because it may be founded upon conceptions of morality with which they disagree. Moreover, the Legislature has not sought to set up a literary censorship, or attempted to confine thought and discussion in a strait jacket of inflexible legal definition, but has imposed upon the courts the duty of protecting the weaker members of society from corrupt, depraving, and lecherous influences, although exerted through the guise and medium of literature, drama or art. The public policy so declared was reaffirmed by the Legislature by its recent amendment to the Penal Law, making it a misdemeanor to prepare, advertise, or present any drama, play, etc., dealing with the subject of sex degeneracy or sex perversion.

Defendants' counsel urge that the book is to be judged by the mores of the day. The community, through this recent legislation, has evinced a public policy even more hostile to the presentation and circulation of matter treating of sexual depravity. The argument, therefore, that the mores have so changed as to fully justify the distribution of a book exalting sex perversion is without force. . . .

The defendants' brief refers the court to eminent men of letters, critics, artists, and publishers who have praised "The Well of Loneliness." Were the issue before the court the book's value from a literary standpoint, the opinions of those mentioned might, of course, carry great weight. However, the book's literary merits are not challenged, and the court may not conjecture as to the loss that its condemnation may entail to our general literature, when it is plainly subversive of public morals and public decency, which the statute is designed to safeguard. Moreover, it has been held that the opinions of experts are inadmissible.

I am convinced that "The Well of Loneliness" tends to debauch public morals, that its subject-matter is offensive to public decency, and that it is calculated to deprave and corrupt minds open to its immoral influences and who might come in contact with it, and applying the rules and recognized standards of interpretation as laid down by our courts, I refuse to hold as matter of law that the book in question is not violative of the statute. Accordingly, and under the stipulation entered into in this case, that the testimony taken upon the summons shall be the testimony taken upon the complaint, if one is ordered, I hereby order a complaint against these defendants.

Friede carried on the fight. On April 19, 1929, a three-man appellate court, after reading the opinion of the lower court and after reading the book, unanimously came to a contrary opinion and held that the book was not obscene in a very brief decision. The difference of opinions of the lower and appellate jurists in this case shows how subjective the legal test for obscenity was at that time—and still is. The judicial mind reviewing this particular book came out 3 to 1 in its final verdict, with no facts in dispute—the same book, the same words, the same basic theme. . . .

The reversal of Donald Friede's conviction in *The Well of Loneliness* case was the victory of three judges over their lower brother—a timely imposition of perhaps more sophisticated taste and jurisprudence in order to free an important book.

The great significance of *The Well of Loneliness* case is that since the book was allowed open circulation no theme, as a theme, has been banned by our courts. The censors have had to find other reasons for suppressing the written word—and of course they have not run out of pretexts.[114]

In 1934, five years after the American publication of *The Well of Loneliness*, Henry Gerber, the founder of the first documented homosexual emancipation organization in the United States (see earlier section), reviews Radclyffe Hall's novel in an obscure mimeographed periodical. Gerber finds that Hall's negative portrayal of Lesbianism makes *The Well* "ideal anti-homosexual propaganda," just the opposite of Judge Bushel's opinion that the novel's positive image of Lesbianism makes the book pro-homosexual and immoral. Gerber writes:

That the appearance of *The Well of Loneliness* should have brought about a storm of protest and subsequent suppression of the book in England, was to be foreseen, for England is perhaps the most hypocritical country in matters of sex. The same book appeared soon afterwards, published by an enterprising New York firm, which successfully convinced the American guardians of morality that inasmuch as this book is really a strong indictment of homosexuality, it is as anti-homosexual propaganda, really a "moral" book. The volume by Miss Radclyffe Hall will perhaps go down in literary history as the classical homosexual novel. It is frankly the autobiography of a Lesbian. She is brought up as a boy and develops into a thorough homosexual. (This theory of acquired homosexuality, of course, is extremely silly. If it were true, in a family of six children brought up in an exactly alike environment, all six would have to become homosexual. This never happens and proves that there must be at least a predisposition to homosexuality—probably endocrinally—in the individual developing this trait.) By reason of falling into two vital errors in her conduct of life, the heroine goes through highly morbid spasms of self-pity. She tries to win the sympathy of ostracising socalled "normal" society, and falls in love with a heterosexual girl, who is snatched from her arms by a male competitor in love. Had she joined her own circle, which is large in every metropolitan city and ostracised in turn the self-righteous society who despised her, not for personal reasons, but for the sheer stupidity of traditional thinking and acting, and had she chosen a homosexual girl as her partner, there would have been no morbid story; it would not have been such ideal anti-homosexual propaganda, and the publisher would have rejected the manuscript, well aware of the fact that he could be sent to jail for saying anything in favor of homosexuals.[115]

♀ 1939: Ella Thompson versus J. C. Aldredge, Sheriff; "Sodomy . . . cannot be accomplished between two women"

On January 12, 1939, the Georgia Supreme Court issued its decision in the proceeding by plaintiff Ella Thompson against Sheriff J. C. Aldredge to review an earlier adverse judgment against her in the Superior Court of Fulton County. The tantalizingly brief report of Thompson's appeal records one of the rare Lesbian-related legal cases in American history. Ella Thompson's appeal represents a courageous and unusual act of resistance against an attempt at the legal prosecution of sexual activity between two women.

Ella Thompson had been convicted in lower court on "an indictment charging her with sodomy, both participants in the act being alleged to be females." Thompson appealed, her lawyers asking that the indictment be discharged on the grounds that she "is being illegally restrained of her liberty, in that the indictment on which she was convicted was null and void."

With all the judges concurring, Justice Grice of the Georgia Supreme Court ruled:

This record presents the question whether the crime of sodomy, as defined by our law, can be accomplished between two women. By Code . . . sodomy is defined as "the carnal knowledge and connection against the order of nature, by man with man, or in the same unnatural manner with woman." Wharton, in his Criminal Law . . . lays down the rule that "the crime of sodomy proper can not be accomplished between two women, though the crime of bestiality may be." We have no reason to believe that our law-makers in defining the crime of sodomy intended to give it any different meaning. Indeed the language of the Code above quoted seems to us to deliberately exclude the idea that this particular crime may be accomplished by two women, although it may be committed by two men, or a man and a woman. That the act here alleged to have been committed is just as loathsome when participated in by two women does not justify us in reading into the definition of the crime something which the lawmakers omitted.

The petitioner's conviction was a nullity and she is entitled to be discharged.

Judgment reversed.

The legal precedent was established in Georgia that

The crime of sodomy as defined by statute cannot be accomplished between two women.[116]

1948–53: HENRY HAY;
Founding the Mattachine Society
"A call to me . . . more important than life"

The man who conceived and was a principal figure in the founding of the first Mattachine Society, Henry Hay, here for the first time details the early history of that homosexual emancipation organization. Because of Hay's eighteen-year Communist party membership and activity, his role as a founding father of the American homosexual liberation movement has not before been told. In an interview recorded by the present author on March 31, 1974, and in a long correspondence referring to original documents of the period, Henry Hay recounted his version of the conception and founding of the Los Angeles Mattachine.

Hay was born on April 7, 1912, at Worthing, in Sussex, England. His father managed gold mines in West Africa, then worked for the Anaconda Copper Company in Chile. His parents returned with their children to their native America in 1917; Hay grew up in Los Angeles, graduating with honors from Los Angeles High School in the summer of 1929. He studied in a Los Angeles lawyer's office for a year, witnessing the stock market crash of October, which wiped out his father and many others. In February 1930, at age seventeen, Hay reports

Henry Hay, 1938.

I enticed an "older" gentleman (he must have been at least 33) to "bring me out" by finagling his picking me up in Los Angeles's notorious Pershing Square. Poor guy—he was appalled to discover, subsequently, that I was both a virgin and jail-bait! Champ Simmons didn't really turn me on, but he was a very decent human being; he was gentle and kind and taught me a great deal.

A link of a kind perhaps peculiar to Gay male history connects the abortive Chicago Society for Human Rights (1924–25) and Henry Hay, the founder of the Mattachine Society. Hay says that

Champ, the guy I seduced into picking me up and bringing me out into the Gay world, had himself been brought out by a guy who was a member of that Chicago group. So I first heard about that group only a few years after its sad end.[117] My impression was that the society was primarily a social thing. But just the idea of Gay people getting together at all, in more than a daisy chain, was an eye-opener of an idea. Champ passed it on to me as if it were too dangerous; the failure of the Chicago group should be a direct warning to anybody trying to do anything like that again.

J.K.:   Do you think your knowledge of that 1920s' organizing attempt played any role in your later conceiving and starting a Gay organization?

H.H.:   Only indirectly. It was one of the things that sank into my memory. In my own life, in the following year, in the fall of 1930, I went to Stanford University. In the fall of 1931, I decided, on the basis of not a great deal of information and not too much experience, that I didn't want to live the life of a lie, so I declared myself on campus to all the people that I knew: to the eating club I belonged to, to the fraternities who were rushing me—

J.K.:   You declared yourself as Gay?

H.H.:   Yes. I said I would understand perfectly if they all felt they had to stay away for their own security and position—and most of the people I knew did stay away, but the people I loved best said, "Okay, what else is new?"

I first conceived of a Gay group in August 1948, in Los Angeles. What happened was this: I went to a beer bust at the University of Southern California, run by some Gay guys I knew. Half the people there were students—one or two were theology students, some legal students—and we got to talking about the Henry Wallace presidential campaign. Wallace was running on the Progressive party ticket. I came up with the idea that we should start a group called "Bachelors for Wallace." With the help of a couple of quarts of beer, we worked up quite a case for what the Bachelors for Wallace would do, what we would ask for—constitutional amendments, etc. It sounded like a great idea.

J.K.:   This was to be an openly Gay group?

H.H.:   Yes. We didn't have the words in those years, but that was what we were going to be. I went home and was all excited and sat up all night, writing out the original prospectus for the group. The next day I called up the guy who had given the party and asked for the addresses and telephone numbers of all the people there. I called up all these guys and said, "Look, we can get this whole thing going." They said, "What thing?" I found out that the only one who remembered anything except his hangover was me. Well, I thought it was too good an idea to drop, so I started putting it in some kind of order. I said, "Let's see, to get started I'll get in touch with all the other homosexuals I can." They said, "You're mad! You're out of your mind! We can't do anything like this!" Then I said, "Wait a minute. Supposing we got some really influential people, like ministers and sympathetic sociologists, and psychologists to condone it, to sponsor it. Then what?" "Well," they said, "well—yes, it's possible. Get 'em, and we'll think about it."

So I went around to a couple of ministers I knew—Unitarians—and some sociologists from UCLA, and a couple of psychologists who were around the progressive movement who were sort of open-minded. One minister, one sociologist, and one psychologist said, "That's not bad; that might be a very useful new idea. You get one of these groups started, and we'll come and visit it. If it's going in the right direction, we'll consider offering our names." This went on for quite a while.

J.K.:   Can you say why you conceived of a Gay organization at the time you did?

H.H.:   The anti-Communist witch-hunts were very much in operation; the House Un-American Activities Committee had investigated Communist "subversion" in Hollywood. The purge of homosexuals from the State Department took place. The country, it seemed to me, was beginning to move toward fascism and McCarthyism; the Jews wouldn't be used as a scapegoat this time—the painful example of Germany was still too clear to us. The Black organizations were already pretty successfully looking out for their interests. It was obvious McCarthy was setting up the pattern for a new scapegoat, and it was going to be us—Gays. We had to organize, we had to move, we had to get started.

I was going back and forth, back and forth, trying to get homosexuals interested and to get the sponsors to lend their names—I was caught in the middle, because one group wouldn't move without the other. What I needed was some other person's point of view, and I wasn't getting that. Then, in July 1950, I met "X." He was on the fringe of the old left, but he wasn't a practicing member of anything. He was a refugee from Auschwitz; he and his family had come through some horrible experiences, and he was rather badly hurt as a child. He thought the group was a great idea, but he had a number of other people he wanted to go to. That's why I rewrote the prospectus.

Hay's original prospectus for a Gay organization was written in August 1948; he prepared a second version in 1949; a third version was written in July 1950, soon after Hay met "X," his first "recruit." Hay's third prospectus is a six-page, dittoed document headed:

Preliminary Concepts . . . copyrighted by Eann MacDonald
July 7th, 1950

Eann MacDonald was Hay's pseudonym. The group's name follows, underlined in red:

International Bachelors Fraternal Orders for Peace and Social Dignity
sometimes referred to as Bachelors Anonymous[118]

The group is described as "a service and welfare organization devoted to the protection and improvement of Society's Androgynous Minority." The reasons for the group's formation are listed as follows:

encroaching American Fascism . . . seeks to bend unorganized and unpopular minorities into isolated fragments. . . .

. . . the Androgynous Minority was . . . stampeded into serving as hoodlums, stool pigeons . . . hangmen, before it was ruthlessly exterminated [a reference to the Nazi extermination of homosexuals];

. . . government indictment of Androgynous Civil Servants . . . [legally establishes] GUILT BY ASSOCIATION;

. . . under the Government's announced plans for eventual 100% war production all commerce . . . would be conducted under government contract . . . making it impossible for Androgynes to secure employment;

. . Guilt of Androgynity BY ASSOCIATION, equally with Guilt of Communist sympathy, . . . can be employed as a threat against . . . every man and woman in our country . . . to insure thought control and political regimentation;

. . . in order to earn for ourselves any place in the sun, we must . . . work collectively on the side of peace, . . . in the spirit . . . of the United Nations Charter, for the full-class citizenship participation of Minorities everywhere, including ourselves;

WE, THE ANDROGYNES OF THE WORLD, HAVE FORMED THIS RE-
SPONSIBLE CORPORATE BODY TO DEMONSTRATE BY OUR EFFORTS
THAT OUR PHYSIOLOGICAL AND PSYCHOLOGICAL HANDICAPS NEED
BE NO DETERRENT IN INTEGRATING 10% OF THE WORLD'S POPULA-
TION TOWARDS THE CONSTRUCTIVE SOCIAL PROGRESS OF MAN-
KIND.

The group's service function is compared to Alcoholics Anonymous; among its
aims are adjustment of members to the "enlightened . . . ethics of the standard
community"; "to understand ourselves and then demonstrate this knowledge to the
community"; "to regulate the social conduct of our minority" (promiscuity, "violation of public decency," etc.); "to dispel the fears and antagonisms of the community . . ."; "to present to the community a . . . social analysis upon which . . .
progressive sexual legislation" can be based; to make "common cause with other
minorities in contributing to the reform of judicial, police, and penal practices . . .";
and to provide "a collective outlet for political, cultural, and social expression to
some 10% of the world's population."

The prospectus goes on for four more pages to detail the group's proposed work
for law reform, against "police brutality" and blackmail, for "self-determination of
nations and national minorities," and to provide legal services and bail money,
study groups, forums, cultural and recreational activities, group discussions, therapeutic groups, and first-aid squads. Participants are to remain anonymous; membership is to be nondiscriminatory as to race and political affiliation, and a complex
membership classification system is outlined. Groups are to be "mainly geographical." "Supplementary subsidiaries" are envisioned, such as "International Spinsters'
Orders," and "Well-Wishers Auxiliaries." The group's decision-making process was
not spelled out; a small governing committee would make policy and run the
organization.

J.K.: How did your original 1948 prospectus differ from that 1950 version?

H.H.: At first I had not been so concerned with planting the organization underground. The goals and ideology never changed particularly; I felt that what
we had to do was to find out who we were, and that what we were for would
follow. I realized that we had been very contributive in various ways over
the millennia, and I felt we could return to being contributive again. Then
we could be respected for our differences not for our samenesses to heterosexuals. Our organization would renegotiate the place of our minority into
the majority. To a large extent that's what the whole movement was about.
I was thinking of an amendment to the United States Constitution.

J.K.: What kind of actions and tactics were envisioned?

H.H.: I didn't know at that time. We would have to move with what the times
would allow. The 1948 prospectus outlined the basic idea. The 1949 version
described how we would set up the guilds, how we would keep them underground and separated so that no one group could ever know who all the
other members were and their anonymity would be secured. The 1950
prospectus is basically like the 1949 one.

J.K.: Where did your idea of this type of secret organization originate?

H.H.: In July 1950, I was still a well-sought-after teacher of Marxist principles,
both in the Communist party and the California Labor School. I was teach-

ing a course in music history at the Labor School, and was dealing with the Guild System and the Freemasonry movement, particularly at the time of Maria Theresa, when to be a member of the Freemasonry was to court the death sentence. Both Mozart and Haydn had been Freemasons, courting punishment. This is also the way the Communist party had moved as a political organization in 1930–37, when it had been truly underground. I thought of the Freemason movement and the type of Communist underground organization that had existed in the 1930s, which I had known and been part of. So I began to work up the structure specified in the prospectus of 1950. The whole organizational setup was based on what I had learned from the old left and, interestingly, was not too different from that structure employed by Algeria in its successful liberation struggle with France in the sixties. At this time, incidentally, I was married and had two children, but I felt I had to move back into my own Gay part of the world again. I felt I should bring the best from the heterosexual side to contribute to my side of the fence—to bring all I had learned in terms of organizational principles in moving back to my own.

The Korean War had broken out just ten days before my meeting "X," in July 1950. At that time, all over the country there was a movement, sponsored by progressives to get as many signatures as possible for the Stockholm Peace Petition against the war. From August through October 1950, "X" and I undertook to get five hundred of these petitions signed on the Gay beach in Los Angeles, in Santa Monica. And we got them, too, by God! We went down to the Gay beach and got them *filled*! And the Korean War was going full blast! We also used this petition activity as a way of talking about our prospectus. We'd go up to them on the beach—of course, this is an entirely different period, you understand, so when people went to the Gay beach then they'd talk about everything else except being Gay. We would tell them what we knew about the war, about the story of North Korea attacking South Korea being a fake. Then we'd get into the Gay purges in U.S. government agencies of the year before and what a fraud that was. Then we'd ask, "Isn't it high time we all got together to do something about it?" Everybody agreed, but nobody could think of anything to do without committing themselves. But at least they signed the petition, and some of the guys gave us their names and addresses—in case we ever got a Gay organization going. They were some of the people we eventually contacted for our discussion groups.

Despite the success of this initial action, "X" and I worked from August to October 1950, but basically we were getting nowhere. Finally, in November 1950 I said, "There's a guy in my Labor School class, Bob Hull, and he has a friend; I think they might be interested." I didn't know for sure if they were Gay or not. I thought these guys were Gay, but whether they would want to reveal themselves to me I didn't know. So I swallow hard, and clench my fists, and on Thursday night at the class I hand out a prospectus in an envelope to Hull. On the following Saturday afternoon he calls up and asks whether he could come over. He sounds kind of distant. Well, Bob Hull, Chuck Rowland, and Dale Jennings come flying into my yard waving the prospectus, saying, "We could have written this ourselves—when do we begin?" So we sat down and we began.

The first thing we did was set up a semipublic-type discussion group, so you didn't have to reveal yourself if you didn't want to. Only certain persons would be invited at first, but later they'd be invited to ask some friends.

J.K.: These were to be discussions of Gayness?

H.H.: Yes.

Three surviving discussion group reports from a slightly later date (September–October 1951) describe the group's consensus, as recorded by the chairman. The subject of two discussions is "Sense of Value," the third is "Social Directions of the Homosexual."[119] The chairman for this last group is Henry Hay, and his report contains a variety of conclusions, among them:

Sexual energy not used by homosexuals for procreation, as it is by heterosexuals, "should be channelized elsewhere where its end can be creativity."

"Homosexuals are 'lone wolves' through fear" of heterosexual society; they "understandably retreat more within themselves."

"A homosexual has no one to whom he must account, and in the end . . . he must decide everything for himself."

"Those in greatest need are sometimes the most reluctant to help each other or themselves, tending to think of personal experiences as things apart from the mutual effort towards betterment."

"Some glad day there shall be a body of knowledge which would . . . show that homosexuals . . . have much in common."

Society's attack on homosexuals would lessen if society realized homosexuals' "potential ability to offer a worth-while contribution."

In April 1951, the "Missions and Purposes" of the Mattachine Society, a California corporation, were written; they were ratified on July 20. The first stated purpose is "TO UNIFY" those homosexuals "isolated from their own kind," to provide a principle from which "all of our people can . . . derive a feeling of 'belonging.'" The second principle is "TO EDUCATE" homosexuals and heterosexuals. In reference to education, the society is said to be developing an "ethical homosexual culture . . . paralleling the emerging cultures of our fellow-minorities— the Negro, Mexican, and Jewish Peoples." The third purpose is "TO LEAD"; the "more . . . socially conscious homosexuals [are to] provide leadership to the whole mass of social deviates." An additional "imperative" need is for "political action" against "discriminatory and oppressive legislation." The society is said to assist "our people who are victimized daily as a result of our oppression," and who constitute "one of the largest minorities in America today."[120]

H.H.: We didn't start calling ourselves the Mattachine Society until the spring of 1951.

J.K.: What was the origin of the name "Mattachine"?

H.H.: One of the cultural developments I had discussed and illustrated in my Labor School class on "Historical Materialist Development of Music" was the function of the medieval-Renaissance French *Sociétés Joyeux*. One was known as the *Société Mattachine*. These societies, lifelong secret fraternities of unmarried townsmen who never performed in public unmasked, were dedicated to going out into the countryside and conducting dances and

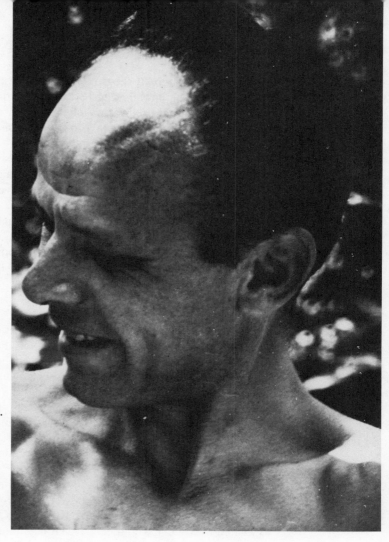

Henry Hay, May 1951.

rituals during the Feast of Fools, at the Vernal Equinox. Sometimes these dance rituals, or masques, were peasant protests against oppression—with the maskers, in the people's name, receiving the brunt of a given lord's vicious retaliation. So we took the name Mattachine because we felt that we 1950s Gays were also a masked people, unknown and anonymous, who might become engaged in morale building and helping ourselves and others, through struggle, to move toward *total* redress and change.

About the fall of 1951 I decided that organizing the Mattachine was a call to me deeper than the innermost reaches of spirit, a vision-quest more important than life. I went to the Communist party and discussed this "total call" upon me, recommending to them my expulsion. They rejected "expulsion," and, in honor of my eighteen years as a member and ten years as a teacher and cultural innovator dropped me as "a security risk but as a lifelong friend of the people."

At the start of our organizing, "X" and others felt that if we made bad mistakes and ruined the thing it might be many, many years before the attempt to organize Gay people would be tried again. So we had to do it right, if possible. That's why we operated by unanimity and were very slow moving. We talked about the prospectus of the foundation, made our contacts with a fighting lawyer, who had defended one of us in court on a Gay charge, applied for a preliminary charter for a nonprofit corporation, and began (as of late November 1950) to have our discussion groups.

J.K.: Did any women come to the early meetings?

H.H.: The meetings were mostly male. A few women came and protested that they were not included, and after that more women came.

J.K.: What about the "two mothers" and a "sister" I've read were involved in the original Mattachine?

H.H.: When my wife decided that we had to go through a divorce because of my activity in the new society—which she felt was inimical as far as the children were concerned—I told my mother about it. About then we were beginning to think in terms of a foundation, and I asked my mother, "Would you act as one of the directors?" She said, "Yes."

J.K.: What kind of a woman was your mother that in the early 1950s she would be that positive about Gays?

H.H.: She wasn't. That isn't the point at all. She was a very well-developed Edwardian lady, and anything that her older son did was bound to be good. I don't think the sexual part of it ever crossed her mind.[121] Homosexuality meant that I was in love with men, not with women. She had nothing more than an understanding of "homophile"—don't you see? The sex part of it never occurred to her. When she met the men and women of our original organizing committee, they were all very sweet, nice people; as far as she was concerned, that was it.

J.K.: Who was the Romayne Cox reportedly associated with the original Mattachine?

H.H.: "X" was number two. Bob Hull, Chuck Rowland, and Dale Jennings were three, four, and five. Then came Konrad Stevens and James Gruber, a couple. Stevens's sister was named Romayne Cox. And Stevens's mother was named Mrs. D. T. Campbell, Helen Campbell—they're the women you asked about. Stevens's mother knew he was Gay, and knew about his pair-relationship with Jim. Stevens's sister thought they were both fine people, and he had a good relationship with her children. So their support was natural.

J.K.: What kind of role did these women play in the organization?

H.H.: I think both Helen Campbell and Romayne attended a couple of discussion groups; one discussion was held at their house. It was kind of constrained as far as the fellows were concerned, but it passed off OK. The address of the foundation was my mother's home. She was at all the foundation meetings, but she never attended a discussion group. All the guys loved her; she was a sweet, warm sort of lady of the manor; she had that presence, which made the Mattachine people feel that they were something fine, special.

In the spring of 1952, Dale Jennings, one of the original Mattachine members, was arrested by the Los Angeles vice squad on the charge of soliciting an officer to commit a homosexual act. Jennings denied the charge, but, as he later said:

Even if I had done all the things which the prosecution claimed . . . I would have been guilty of no unusual act, only an illegal one in this society.[122]

The Mattachine Foundation took over Jennings's defense; Jennings publicly admitted his homosexuality but claimed himself innocent of the specific charges. The Mattachine Society of Los Angeles Citizens' Committee to Outlaw Entrapment issued leaflets, one headed "Now Is the Time to Fight," and another "Anonymous Call to Arms," proclaiming:

Now Is the Time to Reveal . . . the Full Threat to the Entire Community of the Special Police Brutality Against the Homosexual Minority.[123]

"THE ISSUE," said the committee, "IS CIVIL RIGHTS." The public was invited to be present when the case of *Los Angeles* versus *William Dale Jennings* was called to trial on May 19, 1952. A $2\frac{1}{4}$-page, single-spaced letter to media representatives invited their attendance.[124] Hay recalls that not one of them came.

In *ONE Magazine*, soon after the event, Jennings described his hearing:

The trial was a surprise. The attorney, engaged by the Mattachine Foundation, made a brilliant opening statement to the jury. . . .

His client was admittedly homosexual, the lawyer said, but

the only true pervert in the court room was the arresting officer. He asked . . . that the jury feel no prejudice merely because I'd been arrested; these two officers weren't necessarily guilty of the charges of beating another prisoner merely because they were so accused; it would take a trial to do that and theirs was coming the next day. The jury deliberated for forty hours and asked to be dismissed when one of their number said he'd hold out for guilty till hell froze over. The rest voted straight acquittal. Later the city moved for dismissal of the case and it was granted. . . .

Actually I have had very little to do with this victory. Yes, I gave my name and publicly declared myself to be a homosexual, but the moment I was arrested my name was no longer "good" and this incident will stand on record for all to see for the rest of my life. In a situation where to be accused is to be guilty, a person's good name is worthless and meaningless. Further, without the interest of the Citizens' Committee to Outlaw Entrapment and their support which gathered funds from all over the country, I would have been forced to resort to the mild enthusiasm of the Public Defender. Chances are I'd have been found guilty and now be either still gathering funds to pay the fine or writing this in jail.

Yet I am not abjectly grateful. All of the hundreds who helped push this case to a successful conclusion, were not interested in me personally. They were being intelligently practical and helping establish a precedent that will perhaps help themselves if the time comes. In this sense, a bond of brotherhood is not mere blind generosity. It is unification for self-protection. Were all homosexuals and bisexuals to unite militantly, unjust laws and corruption would crumble in short order and we, as a nation, could go on to meet the really important problems which face us. Were heterosexuals to realize that these violations of our rights threaten theirs equally, a vast reform might even come within our lifetime. This is no more a dream than trying to win a case after admitting homosexuality.[125]

In July 1952, the Citizens' Committee to Outlaw Entrapment issued a leaflet headed:

Victory!

"You didn't see it in the papers, but it . . . did happen in L.A." For the "first time in California history an admitted homosexual was freed on a vag-lewd [vagrancy-lewdness] charge." The victory was "the result of organized work," the contributions of time, effort, and money by "people who believe in justice for . . . the homosexual." The victory publicized and brought new recruits into the Mattachine Society.[126]

Rumors of "subversive" Communist influence among the Mattachine leadership were already circulating. George Shibley, the lawyer who had won Dale Jennings's case, was said to have left-wing connections (he was later called before the House Un-American Activities Committee). Henry Hay reports that he himself was "fingered and quoted as a prominent Marxist teacher" when a Congressional committee investigated Communist activity in Los Angeles in March 1952. In February 1952, a Mattachine "Official Statement of Policy on Political Questions . . ." emphasized that the organization took no stand on political matters, except those related to "sexual deviation." The group "has never been, is not now and must never be identified with any 'ism'."[127]

In the fall of 1952, Mattachine questionnaires were sent to candidates in the upcoming Los Angeles City election. Board of Education candidates were asked if they supported "a non-partisan psycho-medical presentation of homosexuality" in required senior high school hygiene courses. They were also asked if they favored a guidance program for young people beginning "to manifest subconscious aspects of social variance." Finally, candidates were asked if they favored high-school counselors' being trained to guide "young people manifesting such problems." The questionnaire sent to city council candidates asked their positions on Los Angeles vice squad behavior and on entrapment.[128]

On March 12, 1953, Paul Coates, a columnist for the *Los Angeles Mirror*, reported that "a strange new pressure group" claiming "to represent the homosexual voters of Los Angeles is vigorously shopping for campaign promises." Coates mentioned that the Mattachine articles of incorporation

were drawn up by an attorney named Fred M. Snider, who was an unfriendly witness at the Un-American Activities Committee hearings. Snider is the legal adviser for Mattachine, Inc.

Coates's column ends: "It is not inconceivable" that homosexuals, "scorned" by the community,

might band together for their own protection. Eventually they might swing tremendous political power.

A well-trained subversive could move in and forge that power into a dangerous political weapon.

To damn this organization, before its aims and directions are more clearly established, would be vicious and irresponsible.

Maybe the people who founded it are sincere.

It will be interesting to see.[129]

Henry Hay reports the Mattachine reaction to the Coates column.

H.H: We all thought it was pretty good, and so we ran off twenty thousand copies to send out to our mailing list and to be distributed city- and statewide. Wow! *Whammo!* We'd forgotten what the detail about Fred Snider's being unfriendly to the House Un-American Activities Committee would do to the middle-class Gays in Mattachine. We had been getting in this status-quo crowd; the discussion groups had been growing by leaps and bounds. When Paul Coates's article appeared, all the status-quo types in the discussion groups were *up in arms*; they had to get control of that damn Mattachine Foundation, which was tarnishing their image, giving them a bad name. This is when the real dissension began between the founders and the middle-class crowd.

J.K.: Can you describe the history of the 1953 split between the Mattachine founders and their opponents?[130]

H.H.: What the opposition wanted was an open, democratic organization. In order to be such an organization, all the idealism that we held while we were a private organization would have to go. In 1953, Joe McCarthy was still around, and we would have to become respectable. "All we want to do is to have a little law changed, and otherwise we are exactly the same as everybody else, except in bed." That position—"we're exactly the same"—characterized the whole Mattachine Society from 1953 to 1969.

In 1953 we had a convention. It was to meet at the little First Universalist Church at Ninth and Crenshaw in Los Angeles. The minister, Wallace Maxey, was on the foundation's board. On the second weekend in April 1953, on April 11, the convention was called—and five hundred people showed up. Now, mind you, this was 1953, and five hundred Gay people show up in one place, as representatives of Gay organizations each delegate presumably representing up to ten people.[131] Can you imagine what that was like? This is the first time it's ever happened in the history of the United States. There we were, and you looked up and all of a sudden the room became vast—well, you know, *was there anybody in Los Angeles who wasn't Gay?* We'd never seen so many people. And in each other's presence you can't shut 'em up. This isn't the period when you hugged much yet—but nevertheless there was an awful lot of hugging going on during those two days.

That Saturday, April 11, 1953, Hay addressed the convention. His speech was published the following month in ONE Magazine, anonymously, under the title, "Are You Now or Have You Ever Been a Homosexual?" It was designed to answer charges of Communist influence over the Mattachine Society. In this long, wide-ranging talk Hay reiterates that the Mattachine Foundation "chooses to consider itself strictly non-partisan and non-political in its objective and in its operations." Its goal is to stir up debate about the place of homosexuals in American society:

But in the very raising of the need for such debate, The Mattachine Foundation deliberately put itself squarely in opposition to a dominant section of the status quo, and elects to become a victim of the myriad implications and slanders derivative of that opposition.[132]

Hay recalls the then recent homosexual purges of United States government agencies, based on the principle that the susceptibility of homosexuals to blackmail by a foreign power makes them security risks. "It is notable," says Hay,

that not one single political or pressure group among the liberals, let alone the left wing, lifted either voice or finger to protest the monstrous social and civil injustice and sweeping slander of this dictum. The complete hostility with which the [homosexual] Minority was surrounded by this indictment was a clear barometer of the outright antipathy unitedly maintained by every color of political opinion. It is significant to note that no alarm was raised then . . . or since . . . and no purge directed, at married [male] heterosexuals with a weakness for bulging busts, blonde secretaries, or National Hop-Week Queens.[133]

The government purges, and later those of state and private employers, had included not only those who were themselves allegedly homosexual, but also their friends, says Hay. As he points out, any group that

sets itself up as a vehicle by [which] the articulate homosexual minority can at least be heard . . . in effect sets itself up in opposition to a majority opinion held equally by the right wing, the liberals, and the left. The Foundation has known from the beginning that it could expect support *only* from those non-prejudiced people who could recognize the enormous potential of the Minority even in the face of the social struggle that would be required. It should be stated here that the Left was the first political grouping to deny any social potential to the Minority by going on public record with the opinion that the perverts (note the term) were socially degenerate and to be avoided as one avoids the scum of the earth. The Foundation idea was conceived only when the Right, in the substance of the State Department actions, followed suit some ten years later.[134]

Hay defends the refusal of the Mattachine's lawyer, Fred M. Snider, to testify before the House Un-American Activities Committee, based on his Fifth Amendment right not to be forced to testify against himself. Hay continues:

The Foundation, in a modest way, constitutes itself a guardian of the homosexual minority's right to keep its own counsel and social conscience. To do this, the Foundation must deliberately oppose the present status quo policy of our National Administration concerning homosexuals. . . . In order to guarantee that it will be able to do this, the Foundation must keep itself clear as a body to be able to invoke the safeguards of the 1st, 5th, 9th, and 10th amendments. . . .

In taking such a stand as a body, and by simultaneously re-affirming its basic principle of aligning itself with, and participating in, *no* partisan political action whatsoever at any time, the Foundation is declaring that it hereby reserves the right to advance suggestions, to criticise, and to evaluate at any and at all times the status quo between the begrudging community majority and the contending coalition of the homosexual minority. . . . The Foundation is acutely aware that such a declared role invalidates it completely as a fountain-head of leadership. But, in truth, it must be recorded that the Foundation never conceived of its contribution as more than that of a modest fountain-head of inspiration and encouragement.[135]

Hay closes by affirming the Mattachine leaders' determination to protect the anonymity of members by refusing to testify before governmental investigating agencies—even if this refusal should lose the Mattachine the support of prominent professional people. "It would be pleasant," Hay continues,

if the social and legal recommendations of the Foundation could be found impeccable both to the tastes of the most conservative community as well as to the best interests of the homosexual minority. But since there must be a choice . . . the securities and protections of the homosexual minorities must come first.[136]

On Sunday, the second day of the Mattachine convention, Hay recalls,

about ten o'clock in the morning, the other members of the original board showed up at my house. Bob Hull reported that a congressional investigating committee was coming out West to look into nonprofit foundations which were feeding the left, part of the whole Red-baiting campaign. We realized that we couldn't bear investigation. We original Mattachine founders and our lawyer would all show up as either having been "fellow travelers" or actual Communist party members. None of us were party members any longer, but some had been. We couldn't answer that "Have you ever been?" question without taking the Fifth Amendment against self-incrimination. Bob Hull said to me, "Look, we can't hold this thing. That speech you made yesterday, that was a disaster." The middle-class groups were all for pulling out, the whole society seemed to be falling apart—it looked like the *Titanic* going down.

At that moment I suddenly realized for the first time that *we weren't unanimous any more*. Our original dream was gone. I thought, "We'll have to dissolve anyway, because of this investigating committee. What we'll do is I'll make an announcement to the convention that the original board has decided to dissolve itself—and we will give the convention the Mattachine name." They were already having committee meetings to find new names. So at the convention that afternoon I made the announcement that the foundation, for reasons important to itself, had decided to dissolve.

J.K.: You decided to pull out because of the Red-baiting, because of the investigation coming up?

H.H.: That was one reason. Also, several of the guys on the steering committee were saying, "The convention's running in this direction, and we have to run with it." They were being opportunistic. It was more important to them to run with the crowd than oppose it.

J.K.: Do you think you may have withdrawn at the wrong time, that you should have stayed and fought?

H.H.: I didn't feel I had the forces to withstand the investigation, the Red-baiting. I was pretty sure we couldn't—that we would go under.

J.K.: What were the basic ideological differences between the original Mattachine and the group after 1953?

H.H.: The original society was based upon this feeling of idealism, a great transcendent dream of what being Gay was all about. I had proposed from the very beginning that it would be Mattachine's job to find out who we Gays were (and had been over the millennia) and what we were for, and, on such bases, to find ways to make our contributions to our parent hetero society. It would be upon such contributions that we would renegotiate the relationships of Gays to the hetero majority. But such bargaining was always to be between Gays and straights as *groups*, never as individual Gays making deals behind the scenes. The Mattachine after 1953 was primarily concerned with legal change, with being seen as respectable—rather than self-respecting. They wanted to be dignified by professional "authorities" and prestigious people, rather than by the more compelling dignity of group worth.

The meeting that ended Henry Hay's principal involvement in the emancipation organization he had conceived and founded was a major event at the start of Jim Kepner's long activity in the homosexual movement. Although just one of those involved in homosexual emancipation, Kepner is mentioned here to emphasize the continuity within this movement—that an ending for one man was a beginning for another. Kepner's account, in a letter to the present author, of the 1953 Mattachine convention differs somewhat from Hay's; the exact details and implications of this historic turning point in the American Gay liberation movement will no doubt be modified and amplified by others who were present, and by future researchers. Jim Kepner sums up his recollections of the Mattachine convention of 1953:

Starting with boundless optimism, we bogged down hopelessly in organizational details. The antagonisms between the conservatives and the founders were bubbling to the fore. Still, I don't think the optimism was quite shattered. In spite of the loss of a good many people, the needless and endless fights on constitutional amendments, the whole thing remained an exhilarating experience. At least those of us who knew that new organizations are not easy to build from the ground up retained the feeling that we at last had a viable homophile movement that was organized, however badly, and that we were on our way. That was really big news, setbacks notwithstanding, and we were determined to make good on the setbacks.[137]

♀ 1958: BARBARA GITTINGS;
Founding the New York Daughters of Bilitis
"It was a long, hard journey"

Barbara Gittings was born in 1932 in Vienna, where her father was a member of the United States diplomatic service; she, a brother, and a sister attended Catholic schools in Montreal, Canada. Her family returned permanently to the United States at the start of World War II. During her first year at Northwestern University, Gittings's close but nonsexual friendship with another female student caused rumors of Lesbianism. Although untrue of this particular relationship, the charge provoked Gittings's first serious exploration of her sexual orientation. Turning mainly to books, Gittings began her own intensive investigation, trying to find out about homosexuality—about herself.

In 1956, on vacation, Gittings went to San Francisco and sat in on a meeting of the year-old Lesbian organization the Daughters of Bilitis (DOB). In 1958, Gittings was active in founding the first East Coast chapter of DOB in New York City, and was elected its first president, serving three years until 1961. Gittings edited the Lesbian periodical *The Ladder* from 1963 until the summer of 1966, then joined Frank Kameny and the Mattachine Society of Washington, D.C., in fighting the United States government's policy of firing homosexuals in its employ. In the fall of 1971, Gittings appeared on television with six other Lesbians to present a forceful Gay liberation viewpoint on the nationally syndicated David Susskind show. More recently, Gittings has headed the Task Force on Gay Liberation of the American Library Association.[138]

In an interview taped on July 19, 1974, Barbara Gittings spoke with the present author about her development as a Lesbian, and about the founding and early history of the New York Daughters of Bilitis.[139]

J.K.: Will you tell about the impact of first realizing in college that you were a Lesbian?

B.G.: Putting the label on myself was a big step forward, even though I had a negative attitude about that label. I went to a psychiatrist in Chicago and told her about myself, and she said, "Yes, you are a homosexual." And then she offered to "cure" me. I didn't have the money for that, so I didn't go back to her. Some people say, "She shouldn't have given you a label." I disagree. I think she did me an enormous service, because once I said, "Yes, that's me, that's what I am," I was able to work with it. I had been living throughout my high school years and first few months of college with this hazy feeling: "I don't quite know what's happening to me." It was a fog of confusion. Now I had something clear-cut I could come to grips with. So I stopped going to classes, I started going to the library to find out what it meant to be homosexual. I was very aggressive about finding that literature on homosexuality. I went through the stacks, I went through reference books, I went to medical dictionaries, I went to ordinary dictionaries, I went to encyclopedias, I went to textbooks, the chapters on "abnormal psychology," sections called "sexual deviations" and "sexual perversions." That kind of labeling affects your image before you get to the material. But it didn't bother me too much because I was so anxious to read about myself. The overall impression I got was: I must be the kind of person they're talking about, because I am homosexual, and they're describing homosexuals, but I don't recognize much of myself in this.

At one extreme I remember a scientific study in which a group of male heterosexuals and a group of male homosexuals were compared for micrometric measurements of their bodies—the diameter of the cranium, the circumference of the neck, the length of the nose, the length of the earlobe, the circumference at the hips—to see if there were significant differences between the two groups. The fact that it was about male homosexuals really didn't bother me that much. Most of the material was on male homosexuals. But I couldn't see that there were significant body differences, so this kind of study puzzled me. And then at the other extreme there'd be pop-level material which said "the homosexual's favorite color is green." That upset me, because my favorite color was blue. I actually thought I ought to change my color preference, in order to fit in. I did believe for a while that there were group characteristics that applied to all homosexuals. But then I began to say, "Well, no, there must be different kinds of homosexuals. They can't all be that much alike."

What really changed my image and gave me a much more positive feeling about homosexuality—even though I still thought it was a misfortune that needed to be changed—were the novels. In some of the so-called scientific materials I read, there were references to fiction titles, and I began to seek these out. As I remember, *The Well of Loneliness* was the first book I latched on to. It was widely mentioned in the documentary literature and was also more available than others. That really hit home, because even though there were differences between myself and the heroine, I still identified with her emotional state, with her feelings. The book has an unhappy ending, of course. It was distressing to me, I suppose, that at the end she deliberately sends away her lover, in order to allow the younger woman the chance of "normal happiness." It seemed to me that she had sacrificed needlessly.

I was living at home at the time. I had flunked out of college and gone back home in disgrace. I had taken a clerical job, and I was spending my spare time in the public library and going to secondhand bookstores. My father went into my room one day, found my copy of *The Well of Loneliness*, and wrote me a letter about it. We were living in the same house, and he couldn't bring himself to talk to me about it. He sent me a letter telling me this was an immoral book, that I had no business owning it, and that I should dispose of it. Not by giving it away, where someone else would be contaminated by it; I had to dispose of it by burning. Well, I simply hid it better and told him that I had disposed of it. This incident reinforced my sense of taboo about the subject matter.

Then I began to find other books. I remember specifically *Extraordinary Women* by Compton Mackenzie, *Dusty Answer* by Rosamond Lehmann, and an earlier novel by Radclyffe Hall, which was not explicitly Lesbian but which did have a covert Lesbian theme, and was strongly feminist, although I didn't see it as such at the time—a book called *The Unlit Lamp*. I searched these out, I made some effort to get them, and they, in turn, led me to other titles. The fiction made a big difference, because here were human beings that were fleshed out in a dimension that simply wasn't available in the scientific materials, which were always examining us from a clinical point of view in which we were diseased case histories. I appreciated the novels, because even though most of them had unhappy endings, they did picture us as diverse people who had our happinesses.

J.K.: Was there no one you could talk to about the subject?

B.G.: No, I didn't know anyone to talk to. So I went looking in the bars. I didn't have much success talking to people in the bars, especialy about the literature. These were women's bars in New York City. I had great difficulty in finding women who had read the same books I had. It was important to me to meet other Lesbians as Lesbians, but I still needed more than that. I needed to find Lesbians who shared my interests. Once when I went to a bar in New York City I had with me Colette's very first novel, from the Philadelphia Free Library, one of the Claudine series, *Claudine à l'école*, and it hap-

From Sidonie G. Colette's *Claudine à l'école* (1905?).[140]

pened to have illustrations. There was an illustration of Claudine's two female schoolteachers who were having an affair—one sitting on the lap of the other, embracing very ardently. I was fascinated by the novel, and fascinated by the picture, a line drawing. It seemed to me very bold to have a picture like that in a book published early in the twentieth century for the general public. I was in this bar and trying to talk to somebody—and I showed her this book, and this drawing, trying to make her understand why this is such a remarkable illustration, and she says, "Oh, at home I've got a lot sexier pictures than that." I didn't understand what she meant; now I do!

There weren't people I could talk to about the kind of literature I was interested in. A few people had read *The Well of Loneliness*. Fewer still read any of the others, novels like those of Gale Wilhelm which I found, and which, I recall, had happy endings—for a change. The literature was very important to me. The nonfiction literature gave me a bad picture of myself, a picture I had to work against. The fiction, despite stereotypes, despite unhappiness, despite bad characters, was much more positive.

J.K.: Would you say that you were looking in those books for a sense of Lesbian community?

B.G.: Oh, very much so, although I wouldn't have put it in those words. That's something I think now, but at the time I would have said, "I'm looking for my people." Then I was so glad to find that my people existed, that there was literature about them, and a literature that portrayed them as human beings. There was definitely a sense of community, and of history, conveyed by the novels; I really appreciated them enormously—and I started collect-

423

ing. I used to go to the secondhand bookstores and search out the titles, starting with the list in Donald Webster Cory's *The Homosexual in America*, which really was remarkable. I even wrote to the publisher, and found that Cory lived in New York City. I had two or three meetings with him to discuss the literature. I was keenly interested in seeing what more there was. I must admit I hadn't done any analysis of his book. I was simply interested in compiling a large list of literature, finding out what was available, getting to see it for myself. Cory also told me about the existence of ONE, Inc., and the Mattachine Society out in Los Angeles and San Francisco. In the summer of 1956, I made a trip out there—I guess I made it for that reason. I went to the offices of ONE in Los Angeles, and they told me about the Mattachine Society in San Francisco and about a relatively new organization called the Daughters of Bilitis, which was then scarcely a year old. So I contacted the Mattachine Society when I arrived in San Francisco, and they put me in touch with Daughters of Bilitis who, fortuitously, were having a meeting that very evening—and I went. That was my first contact with Daughters of Bilitis.

They had just started putting out *The Ladder*, and they were into their first or second issue. They were discussing it at that meeting. That was the first time I had sat down with a dozen or fifteen Lesbians outside of a bar situation. It was very appealing to me, it was something I had been looking for, the chance to be with people of my own kind in a setting other than the bars.

J.K.: What was it like—that setting?

B.G.: Somebody's living room in San Francisco. It was a pleasant atmosphere; there were refreshments. There were about fifteen women discussing the business of putting out a periodical. I had to do a good deal of listening to try to understand. Even then I was pretty assertive, because I sounded off about the name of the organization. Having just heard about it, and having just been invited by these nice people, I said the name was too complicated, too long, too difficult to pronounce, too difficult to spell, and what the hell, Bilitis was a bisexual fictional character anyway, not even a real person, not even truly a homosexual. What were they doing with a name like that? It wasn't very nice of me, but they seemed to take it with reasonably good spirits. They must have already been accustomed to having upstart Lesbians coming up out of nowhere and coming to their meetings. So I wasn't anything special. Del Martin and Phyllis Lyon were very much the leaders. They definitely ran the show. They had strong ideas, and they saw to it that they were carried out.

J.K.: What happened between 1956 and '58?

B.G.: I probably kept in some kind of touch; perhaps I kept in mail contact with Del and Phyllis. I think I may have subscribed to *The Ladder*.

J.K.: According to my information, there was a Mattachine convention in New York City in 1958. On Sunday, September 7, there was a meeting called "for all women in the New York area who are interested in forming a chapter of the DOB."[141] Do you remember that first meeting at all?

B.G.: A vague recollection, yes. It was on Sixth Avenue, a small loft building where the Mattachine had offices. I think only about eight or ten of us met. A no-

The *Ladder's* publication provoked two anonymous letters from Black writer Lorraine Hansberry, which convey one New York woman's response, in 1957, to a specifically Lesbian periodical. Hansberry writes:

I'm glad as heck that you exist. You are obviously serious people and I feel that women, without wishing to foster any strict *separatist* notions, homo or hetero, indeed have a need for their own publications and organizations. Our problems, our experiences as women are profoundly unique as compared to the other half of the human race. Women, like other oppressed groups of one kind or another, have particularly had to pay a price for the intellectual impoverishment that the second class status imposed on us for centuries created and sustained. Thus, I feel that THE LADDER is a fine, elementary step in a rewarding direction.

Hansberry ends the same letter by asking:

Considering Mattachine, Bilitis, ONE, all seem to be cropping up on the West Coast rather than here where a vigorous and active gay set almost bump one another off the streets—what is it in the air out there? Pioneers still? Or a tougher circumstance which inspires battle?[142]

In another anonymous letter, Hansberry connects antihomosexuality and anti-feminism.

I think it is about time that equipped women began to take on some of the ethical questions which a male-dominated culture has produced and dissect and analyze them quite to pieces in a serious fashion. It is time that 'half the human race' had something to say about the nature of its existence. Otherwise—without revised basic thinking—the woman intellectual is likely to find herself trying to draw conclusions—moral conclusions—based on acceptance of a social moral superstructure which has never admitted to the equality of women and is therefore immoral itself. As per marriage, as per sexual practices, as per the rearing of children, etc. In this kind of work there may be women to emerge who will be able to formulate a new and possible concept that homosexual persecution and condemnation has at its roots not only social ignorance, but a philosophically active anti-feminist dogma. But that is but a kernel of a speculative embryonic idea improperly introduced here.[143]

tice had been sent out to DOB's mailing list contacts in the New York area, and I suppose to women who were on the Mattachine mailing list.

J.K.: Do you remember anything about the kind of women who did show up? What had brought them there?

B.G.: Our motives were pretty hazy. We didn't have any clear sense of what we were going to do. It just seemed enough that Lesbians were getting together. Just sheer survival of the group was important at first. Even though we had San Francisco DOB's four-part statement of purpose when we started the New York chapter, the discussions were awfully vague and groping. We kept seeking for ways of making the meetings interesting, without having clearly said to ourselves, "What exactly are we meeting for?" We continued in a rather chaotic condition for a very long time. Most of the time it was just "Well, of course we should continue; when will the next meeting be?" It was taken for granted that it was desirable to continue.

DOB had its four-part statement of purpose printed inside the front cover of *The Ladder*, and that, supposedly, provided guidelines for us. The Daughters of Bilitis was defined as "A Women's Organization for the Purpose of Promoting the Integration of the Homosexual into Society. . . ." The word Lesbian was not used once. Four purposes were listed:

1. Education of the variant . . . to enable her to understand herself and make her adjustment to society . . . this to be accomplished by establishing . . . a library . . . on the sex deviant theme; by sponsoring public discussions . . . to be conducted by leading members of the legal, psychiatric, religious and other professions; by advocating a mode of behavior and dress acceptable to society.

2. Education of the public . . . leading to an eventual breakdown of erroneous taboos and prejudices. . . .

3. Participation in research projects by duly authorized and responsible psychologists, sociologists, and other such experts directed towards further knowledge of the homosexual.

4. Investigation of the penal code as it pertains to the homosexual, proposal of changes, . . . and promotion of these changes through the due process of law in the state legislatures.[144]

"Education of the variant", not even the word *"Lesbian!"* "Adjustment" became a major controversy phrase later on. The idea of having Gay people speak was totally foreign to us at the time.

It never occurred to us in those early days that we could speak for ourselves, that we had the expert knowledge on ourselves. We were the ones explored, but we thought we needed the intervention of experts to do the exploring. Homosexuality had traditionally been the domain of people in law, religion, and the behavioral sciences.

J.K.: In reviewing *The Ladder* from the early sixties I was struck by the fact that you even invited "experts" to speak who totally put down Gays.

B.G.: At first we were so grateful just to have people—anybody—pay attention to us that we listened to and accepted everything they said, no matter how bad it was. That is how different the consciousness at the time was. But, I must emphasize, it was essential for us to go through this before we could arrive at what we now consider our much more sensible attitudes. You don't just spring full blown into an advanced consciousness. You do it step by step. Well, this was the important first step. We invited people who were willing to come to our meetings; obviously, it turned out to be those who had a vested interest in having us as penitents, clients, or patients.

J.K.: It was enough that someone was interested in you.

B.G.: You'll hear the same thing from other people who have been around the movement a long time. It's hard for you who came in later to understand. Just to be mentioned, no matter what they said, was important at first. It broke the taboo of silence about homosexuality—anything that helped break the silence, no matter how backward; how silly or foolish it may look to us today, was important. The first publications, the first discussion groups and lectures and panels—these carried a lot of weight with us. When somebody with professional credentials came to address your meetings, that legitimized the existence of your organization. And then when you went out and approached other people, you could say that Dr. So and So or the Rev. So and So had addressed you; that made you less pariahlike to these other people whom you needed.

J.K.: When did that change? Only after the Stonewall resistance in 1969 when Gay people fought back against police harassment?

B.G.: Oh no, the changes, all these consciousness changes were definitely fomenting in the sixties, well before Stonewall. The one thing that Stonewall represents, in my view, is a sudden burgeoning of grass-roots activity. It doesn't represent a distinctly changed consciousness in the movement. The militancy—the "we are the experts, not these non-Gays"—all that developed well before Stonewall, thanks largely to Frank Kameny; he was the first one who articulated a complete, coherent philosophy for the Gay movement.

J.K.: When did he begin to have an impact?

B.G.: In 1961, after he lost his case, by a decision of the Supreme Court, to get his federal job back, he said, "All right, I've gone as far as I can go as an individual. I need other people to help me push." And so he founded the Washington, D.C., Mattachine Society in late 1961. It is amazing to us now—but again we have to remember that we are wise in hindsight—when he articulated the idea that homosexuality was not a sickness, and had Washington Mattachine, and later New York Mattachine, adopt this view, that was a controversial thing to do in the movement. When Kameny said that in the absence of scientific evidence to the contrary, we are not sick—homosexuality is not a sickness—many movement people disputed him, saying, "We have to leave that up to the experts." DOB's own research director, Florence Conrad, a woman who lived on the West Coast, opposed Kameny and engaged in a written debate with him which I published in *The Ladder*. She strongly opposed Kameny's idea; she felt we did not have the credentials or the right to stand up and say this for ourselves. That's how far we've come in ten years. Now we even have the American Psychiatric Association running scared.

Point number one of DOB's purpose was "education" of the Lesbian. I began to chafe at that later on and to feel that this was not a valid purpose. It had too much the ring of "We're going to teach you to be a nice little girl so that you can fit into society." I objected to this toward the middle of the sixties. But I didn't think very critically in those very first years. All I had then was a joiner's temperament. This was the group that hit closest to home, so I joined. I also had a feeling that something ought to be done, but our perception of the "problem" was very hazy at that time.

J.K.: What was the "problem" as you perceived it in those early days?

B.G.: My personal problem, mainly, was one of self-image. I have traveled a long, long way since the days when I thought it was a misfortune to be homosexual, that I should do everything possible to change.

J.K.: So it was to feel better about yourself that you got involved in DOB?

B.G.: I don't know that I did it with that clear an idea. It was more a desire to ameliorate the bad conditions of life for Gay people, to make the inevitable more bearable—certainly not to insist on a full and equal place in society. In the early years of the movement, in the fifties, the purpose of our organizing was to find out more about the nature and cause of homosexuality, to get this information out to the general public, to soften their dislike and hostility, to try to persuade them to grant us some privileges. By the late '6os, we began to see that discussing the cause and the nature of homosexuality would not help us. We began to insist on our rights, to spell them out clearly, to go to court to get them, to demand what was ours. The whole consciousness changed; in the early days, it was much more nebulous.

J.K.: In those days, I've gathered, the idea was that anti-Gay prejudice, the difficult situation Gays were in, was based on some sort of misunderstanding: if straight people would only understand us and see we were just like them, we would be accepted. Education was the answer, because the problems we had were based on miseducation.

B.G.: That's right. We felt that if only we knew more about what kind of people we were, and could get this information out, the public would say, "Oh, well, they're not such bad characters after all."

J.K.: *The Ladder*, November 1958, says New York DOB is sharing space with Mattachine, Barbara Gittings is president, Jody Shotwell is secretary, Mary Dorn is treasurer; there were two meetings a month. Can you describe those meetings? What was their mood? How many people showed up?

B.G.: Oh, it varied, from ten to twelve, to as many as thirty-five or forty. I realize now that these women were showing up in order to meet others. It was that simple. Up until the mid-sixties, every single one of the Gay organizations flatly denied it acted as any kind of agency for social introductions. The reason for this was simply to avoid flak from the outside society that we might be in the business of "procuring," arranging for "immoral contacts."

J.K.: I think that's important. It seems to me that one of the main impetuses behind the Gay movement is Gay people's desire to meet other Gays, to break out of our isolation.

B.G.: Now, of course, it's easy for us to look back and say how silly we were to deny that. But it wasn't silly at the time. We had some heavy discussions over the possibilities of criticism deriving from any suggestion that we were acting as places for social meetings. While we did have social events, we always called them fund-raisers. Nowadays, with hindsight, we sometimes get a little bit arrogant, because we look back and say, "Oh, how could people have been so silly?" It wasn't silly. In the context of the time.

I remember one letter from a parent—she had gotten hold of a mailing her daughter had received, and she wrote a vile letter of condemnation with the word *pervert* spelled "prevert." Well, by that time, we were feeling a little bit more graceful about ourselves, and were able to laugh over the word "prevert." Still, there was reason to think we could get into more trouble than we could cope with. That kind of feeling carried over for a very long time. When DOB had its third national convention in 'sixty-four in

New York City, Donald Webster Cory was one of the speakers. That was the time he gave his swan song to the Gay movement. In his speech he chided us for not saying openly that it was a legitimate purpose of our organizations to provide a social place. After all, he said, under what better auspices can homosexuals meet each other? He was prophetic on that issue of socializing. Because only a few years later everyone was saying, "Well, of course, what better place for Gay people to meet each other but in places sponsored and run by Gay people?"

J.K.: You people seem to have been very concerned with what the straight society thought of you.

B.G.: Oh, very much so. Appearance and behavior were very important. We needed the acceptance of society, we thought. So we geared ourselves to getting it. There was an incident at an early Daughters of Bilitis national convention (in Los Angeles, I think), where a woman who had been living pretty much as a transvestite most of her life was persuaded, for the purposes of attending that convention, to don female garb, to deck herself out in as "feminine" a manner as she could, given that female clothes were totally alien to her. Everybody rejoiced over this as though some great victory had been accomplished—the "feminizing" of this woman. Today we would be horrified at anyone who thought this kind of evangelism had a legitimate purpose. Yet at the time, I remember, I joined in the rejoicing. At the same time there was some kind of mental reservation in me; I felt there was something grotesque about this woman's trying to look "normal" for the purposes of appearances at this convention. The resulting appearance simply wasn't that persuasive—and what was it really for, since we were essentially among ourselves? We always had the idea we were totally exposed to the world, but when you came right down to it, we were really mostly exposed to ourselves and those few non-Gay speakers whom we invited. During the first years of New York DOB's existence there was another debate about a woman who lived as a transvestite, who was accepted even at her place of work as a woman who chose to live and dress as a young man. But in DOB there was discussion over her appearance, whether it was acceptable. It was a controversy that probably wouldn't even arise today, or would arise in a different form.

J.K.: Can you talk about the activities that went on in the early days of New York DOB—coffee sessions, business meetings, lectures, dinners, forums?

B.G.: Practically all took place in New York City; occasionally we went across the river to someone's living room in New Jersey. We were always rather hard put for places to meet. Especially when the Mattachine Society was out of offices for a while. Both groups were living out of a postal box.

The year after our organization began, in 1959, we started to put out a New York DOB newsletter. I did the newsletter myself. We sent these out to our mailing list of about 150 or so, hoping that women would find something of interest and would come along.

J.K.: What was it like editing that newsletter?

B.G.: There wasn't much to edit. It was a matter of putting together the words that would announce our events. I was working at an architectural firm, and sometimes I was supposed to stay overtime for company business. Sometimes I would use that time after hours to cut the stencils for the DOB newsletter, using a stylus and the light tables, and I'd do the drawings and run it off on the company's mimeograph machines, preferably on colored paper, and type up all the envelopes, and stuff all the envelopes, and send the damn things out. It was an awful lot of work.

J.K.: Were you afraid of getting caught?

B.G.: Yes, I was. And I was caught. It might have been around 'fifty-nine or 'sixty. One of my mailings got into the hands of my bosses. Unfortunately, I had used a company envelope with a sticker over the name, with another return address, either mine or DOB's. Somebody received it—I assume someone other than the Gay person who was supposed to receive it—and had gone to the trouble of tearing or soaking off the sticker, had uncovered the company name, and had written a letter to the company complaining about this stuff being sent out. And so I was called in. My immediate boss, a woman, got stuck with dealing with me.

J.K.: Did she ask you what the organization was?

B.G.: I explained it to her with my heart zipping about ten miles away from me in all directions. I was very scared. I didn't know what was going to happen. Was I going to be fired? Was I going to get a severe talking to? I explained the purposes of the organization, and I did not deny I was using company time and company materials. All she said was that she knew something about the subject of Lesbianism because she had been in the armed service. She was not saying that she was Gay, merely that she was acquainted with the existence of Lesbianism.

J.K.: Did she let you get away with it?

B.G.: I don't remember exactly what she said, but I wasn't fired. I was simply told to be more careful about this sort of thing.

J.K.: The New York Mattachine Society existed and was open to women. Why was a separate women's organization started?

B.G.: The reason wasn't the sort of thing you get today, when people say, "Men are male chauvinist pigs; we have to have a separatist organization so women can gain strength from each other." Today we would give you reasons we couldn't give you then. Somehow it was a more comfortable setting to be among ourselves. Yet there were times when we cooperated with the Mattachine Society in jointly sponsoring particular events, like panel discussions. I remember one on religion. Why the need for a separate group? One had been started; women seemed to enjoy being together.

One important motivating principle for the whole movement was overcoming invisibility—not that we spelled it out quite that plainly at the time. For people who are invisible, overcoming invisibility is a major step in improvement of self-image, in coming to grips with who you are. Think of all the isolated Gay people for whom the sheer existence of groups of their own, that they could turn to, was an enormous improvement over the old situation where they felt totally cut off. They might still be isolated, geographically, but as long as they knew that a thousand miles away there was a group, as long as they could occasionally get some kind of publication, it was so much better than simply living in their own little cocoon.

J.K.: Early issues of *The Ladder* carry letters from all over the United States, from little towns. The women who write say how important it is just to have the knowledge that the DOB exists, that the magazine exists.

In September 1959, there was a Mattachine convention in Denver; Del Martin spoke about DOB and Lesbians in the movement. She said that DOB was "often accused of competing with Mattachine," a charge she denied. Del Martin continued:

> At every one of these conventions I attend, year after year, I find I must defend the Daughters of Bilitis as a separate and distinct women's organization. First of all, what do you men know about Lesbians? In all of your programs and your "[Mattachine] Review," you speak of the male homosexual and follow this with—oh, yes, and incidentally there are some female homosexuals, too, and because they are homosexual all this should apply to them as well. *ONE* [*Magazine*] has done little better. For years they have relegated the Lesbian interest to the column called "Feminine Viewpoint." So it would appear to me that quite obviously neither organization has recognized the fact that Lesbians are *women* and that this twentieth century is the era of emancipation of women. Lesbians are not satisfied to be auxiliary members or second-class homosexuals. So if you people do wish to put DOB out of business, you are going to have to learn something about the Lesbian, and today I'd like to give your first lesson.[145]

I was surprised to find such a militant feminist statement in 1959. A short time later, at the first DOB national convention in 1960, Del Martin described DOB as being open to "any woman, heterosexual or homosexual, over 21 who desired . . . the integration of the homosexual into society through education, both of the variant and of the public . . . as to their responsibilities." That also expresses the feeling of the time?

B.G.: Yes, we have to be good boys and girls in order to earn our place in society. Of course, that viewpoint is anathema to us today. We have a right to be here, and we have a right to have our place in society—as long as we don't violate other people's rights. All the early organizations claimed they were open to both Gays and straights, although ninety-nine out of a hundred members were homosexual. We always insisted that straight people too were members, so you weren't "tainted" necessarily by belonging to the organization.

J.K.: The early *Ladder*s indicate there was tremendous fear of joining, about having one's name associated with DOB.

B.G.: Most people used pseudonyms at the time. It was common in the movement, with few exceptions. Del Martin was one of the exceptions. I always used my own name. I never made a conscious decision to do that, it's just that I never felt sufficient pressure to use a pseudonym.

J.K.: What about your family? Were you afraid they would hear?

B.G.: No, it never occurred to me; it was unlikely. How would they hear about it? There wasn't that much publicity. In fact, we couldn't even get publicity. One of the first problems we had was that the *Village Voice* wouldn't take ads. DOB and the other organizations were refused ads completely. Eventually, that door was broken down by Randy Wicker, by sheer persistence; and finally the *Voice* accepted ads for "homophile" meetings.

J.K.: In May 1960, at the first national DOB convention, Dr. Frank Beach was on a panel entitled "Why the Lesbian?"—commenting on statements by four women. One Lesbian's statement reportedly "eluded" Beach "completely." This woman is said to have declared "she didn't believe in any of the standard 'causes' for Lesbianism, . . . that she was more inclined to believe that women were just plain sick of being dominated by men and were seeking their own souls!"[146] Interesting such a statement was made then.

B.G.: I would probably have been annoyed by such a response at the time. I would have felt the person was not treating the question seriously, that indeed there was some kind of cause that we should look for.

J.K.: What about the feminist aspect of the statement?

B.G.: I wouldn't have bought that at the time, and I don't buy it now. Lesbianism has nothing to do with being tired of being dominated by men. I find that theory objectionable. I would have found it objectionable at that time because I thought the respondent was being arrogant, not treating the question seriously, that we had an obligation to supply properly thought-out answers. I would have thought she was thumbing her nose at the speaker. Today I find it objectionable for an entirely different reason. I object to any theory that makes us reactors instead of initiators, that says women become Lesbians as a reaction to being dominated by men. That's not why you become Lesbian. If women were in no way dominated by men, they'd still become Lesbians.

J.K.: Did you go to any of those early national DOB conventions?

B.G.: The first I remember going to was the one in Los Angeles, in 'sixty-two. It featured Evelyn Hooker. We had the usual lineup of outside experts.

J.K.: The president of DOB was interviewed by Paul Coates on television in Los Angeles.

B.G.: That was among the first television appearances in the movement. Naturally we were excited. There were very, very few people in our movement who could afford to be seen on camera. The invitations to appear were a breakthrough, a breaking of the silence.

J.K.: Can you describe some of the major differences between the early years of DOB and the Gay liberation movement in 1974? What progress has been made, what needs to be done?

B.G.: Well, we've made enormous progress. One of the most significant changes in the movement has been to stop focusing on ourselves, to realize that the problem is not with us but with them out there, with the outside world. That came about roughly in the mid-sixties. Unfortunately, I see some tendency to reverse this, to devote a lot of energy to consciousness-raising. I really don't understand why this is so necessary for Gay people today—they shouldn't have to go through a whole reeducation trip. Gay people growing up now, with the benefit of positive literature, which I didn't have, and with the benefit of several hundred organizations around the country, which I didn't have, shouldn't need to spend a year raising their consciousness.

J.K.: I'm surprised you say that, because you've emphasized how important it was for you to change your image of yourself.

B.G.: Oh, yes, but I did that by working with other people. The talk was incidental to what we were trying to do. I find it hard to understand people for whom talk is the goal. If a group of people sit down to prepare posters for a demonstration, a hell of a lot of consciousness-raising goes on while you're figuring what to put on the posters. This advances you a lot further and a lot faster than six months of sitting around with other people trying to figure out why you are and who you are. Writing a hard-hitting leaflet, or a good, short article for the local paper—doing something, to me, is consciousness-raising in and of itself.

Then there's the whole civil rights matter, which we take so much for granted today. We were not nearly as willing to insist on a whole variety of civil rights as a matter of course back in the fifties as we are today.

Now we have several thousand people in the movement instead of a few dozen as at the beginning. It used to be that everyone in the movement literally knew every other person active in the movement. I suppose, for some people, the pleasures of being in a little club disappeared when the movement grew. But I think this is a great improvement, because not only are many more people coming in to do the work, but many more kinds of work can be taken up. The existence of Gay professional organizations is something that we wouldn't have dreamed of ten years ago.

Despite the progress, the vast majority of Gay people are still living masked and closeted lives, and do have to be concerned with what the straight world thinks. In my view, the purpose of Gay liberation is to change this. I feel the purpose of the movement is to get all those closet doors opened. It should be possible for Gay people to live their lives, feeling good about themselves, without having to worry about what anyone is going to think about them, and without having special problems of self-image. This is what I look forward to. Those of us who are lucky enough to be able to be out and active in Gay liberation have a special responsibility to those who cannot afford to come out yet. What we're saying to them is: "Hang in there, people, because those of us who are out are oiling the closet hinges just as fast as we can."

Having gone through many years of unhappiness, uncertainty, and negative feelings about myself, I want to see to it that younger Gay people don't have to go through the same thing. Those years of worrying and wondering were, in a way, productive for me. I'm assertive and I kept grappling with it until I finally evolved a positive view of my Gayness. But it was a long, hard journey, which might have broken someone else. People shouldn't have to go through that.

♀ 1962–72: ALMA ROUTSONG;
Writing and Publishing *Patience and Sarah*
"I felt I had found my people"

According to Alma Routsong, author (under the pen name Isabel Miller) of the Lesbian novel *Patience and Sarah*, her book was not written with any conscious political aim. Yet her work clearly captures and expresses, in fictional form, that Lesbian-feminist consciousness developing in America in the 1960s. Although its author's intention was simply to write the love story of two women, her work is important in that Lesbian literary-political tradition—the Lesbian defense in fictional form. As such, the writing of *Patience and Sarah* constituted an act of Lesbian resistance. The following interview makes clear how Routsong's experience as a woman and Lesbian was central in shaping the consciousness expressed in her book—and in inspiring its conception, writing, and publication.

Alma Routsong's novel, which she first published herself under the title *A Place for Us* (1967), relates the story of Patience White and Sarah Dowling, detailing the development of their love against the background of a hostile, puritanical, New England farm community in 1816. The two women alternately narrate their own story, as each experiences it. Their words have a naive simplicity, belying the sophisticated wisdom of their thought. The language of the novel is the perfect verbal equivalent of those "primitive" paintings of which, in the book, Patience White is the creator. The novel has a lovely unity of style and content, but quite apart from its literary quality (always a matter of subjective judgment), *Patience and Sarah*—inspired as it was by two women who actually lived and farmed together in Greene County, New York, about 1820—suggests how knowledge of American Lesbian history may serve the culture of a people in search of its past.

Although reliable generalizations are elusive at this early stage of research, it appears that fiction by Lesbians has played a special role in the resistance to that oppression denying Lesbians existence altogether, or presenting only the most negative image of women-loving women. The Gay male and Lesbian resistance differ in that the Lesbian defense more often took the form of literature (the novel, short story, or poetry). Thus while Radclyffe Hall's and Alma Routsong's novels vary totally in viewpoint, they both may be seen as contributions to a literary-political genre—the Lesbian fiction-defense. Given the special import of Lesbian literature, it is no accident that the major early work in Lesbian studies is Jeannette H. Foster's *Sex Variant Women in Literature* (1956). First published privately by Foster, this bibliographical-historical survey was itself a pioneering, invaluable contribution to the American Lesbian resistance. Other bibliographies of Lesbian-relevant literature by Marion Zimmer Bradley and Barbara Grier (Gene Damon, pseud.) point to an early appreciation among Lesbians of the importance of fictional sources for the study of women-loving women.[147]

On January 20, 1975, Alma Routsong spoke with the present author about the genesis of *Patience and Sarah*.

J.K.: Can you describe how you came to write this novel?

A.R.: My lover and I were touring New York State and were visiting the folk art museum at Cooperstown. I was wandering through it, not really concentrating on anything, when my lover said: "Psst, psst!" and called me back, pointing to this picture of a mermaid by Mary Ann Willson. There was a card beside it that said Miss Willson and her "farmerette" companion lived and worked together in Greenville Town, Greene County, New York, circa 1820. Then we went into the next room—a small library—and found a book by Lipman and Winchester, called *Primitive Painters in America*, with a short piece about Mary Ann Willson.[148] It said that she and Miss Brundidge had a "romantic attachment." I was absolutely taken by it. I didn't want to travel any more. I didn't want to see Harriet Tubman's bed. I wanted to go home and research Willson and Brundidge, find out all about them, and write a book about them. I spent about a year going to the library,

Mary Ann Willson, *Mermaid* (c. 1820).

trying to find out about them. I looked up all the Willsons and all the Brundidges in the Forty-second Street geneological library. It's a great library, but it didn't have anything about them.

J.K.: Did you also research that time period?

A.R.: I read everything I could find. It was very frustrating. I tried to read some of the fiction from the time, too—James Fenimore Cooper. God, he was awful!

J.K.: Did you read any personal narratives of women?

A.R.: I couldn't find any that included erotic relations with other women. When I was keeping a diary, before I came out, I didn't say anything about that subject either. I was afraid.

J.K.: To even write about Lesbian feelings in your personal diary?

A.R.: Yes. When I finally found a woman to have an affair with—my first love affair—I couldn't resist writing about her, but I always burned what I wrote. So I'm not surprised if other women didn't keep very good records. Romaine Brooks's diary doesn't have any erotic detail at all, and her relationships are never specified.

Before *Patience and Sarah*, I had started several books about myself and my friends, but I became overwhelmed with guilt and couldn't finish them. This historic situation I could project into; it was ideal for the hangup I had about not tattling. Once I accepted that the book would have to be fictional, it went along fairly well.

It was really wonderful to be writing Gay love scenes, and about Gay people. I loved it. In the book, Patience and Sarah stop in New York City on their way up the Hudson. They stay in a boarding house for the first night. In my own experience, when my lover and I left town together, we were so exhausted the first night that we didn't make love. So I thought Patience and Sarah shouldn't make love; it wouldn't be realistic. But part of me said, "Yes, they do make love." Another part said, "Well, they might be overheard." Then I realized: new lovers aren't noisy. So I wrote a love scene.

I felt that I was really using myself in my work for the first time—not disguising, which I had always done before, trying to find heterosexual equivalents.

J.K.: Will you describe the publishing history of *Patience and Sarah*?

A.R.: I finished the manuscript in 1967. I really knew it was good, and I thought that anyone would be happy to publish it. I sent it to my former agent, who was then an editor at Doubleday, and she sent it back to me in a week. I began to get a clue that it was going to be a little more difficult to get published than I had thought. I sent the manuscript to five or six publishers, and they all kept it a long time; I got good readings from top editors, and they rejected it. I don't think they had any moral objections to the subject. They just didn't think the book would sell. It was just a matter of business.

My lover supported me while I was researching and writing the book. She really believed in me, and I'm still moved by that. We're not together any more, but I firmly believe that without her—not only the economics part, but just the fact that she never lost faith in the novel as a valuable thing to be doing—I wouldn't have been able to write it. Even when it became clear that the book wasn't going to get published, at least probably not in my lifetime, I still believed in it. I thought maybe the time just hadn't come, and that my heirs would have to publish it. A writer can put a manuscript away for five hundred years if necessary. Anyway, I got a job and gave up trying to peddle the book.

J.K.: You had been peddling it yourself?

A.B.: Yes. My agent at the time wouldn't handle it. I think the novel's very threatening to straight women, and closet Gay women. If they say they like it, people will think they're Gay.

Then my mother died, and I went home for her funeral. My brother had owed me five hundred dollars for twenty years. I thought he was never going to pay me, and I was never going to mention it to him. In our family, one doesn't mention money—I think that's one reason we don't have any. On the day of my mother's funeral, my brother gave me a check. It was an awkward amount, not enough to change my life with. So I just put it in the bank. A few months later I was on the Staten Island ferry, and it came to me in a marvelous blinding flash that I could publish my book with that money. I also had a little income tax refund. It cost me $850 to have a thousand copies offset. My lover and I designed and drew the cover. I typed the text and took the job to a printer who specialized in small runs. It was really fun.

We thought we could advertise and sell by mail. But we learned a sad thing: a Lesbian won't put her name on a piece of paper and mail it to a stranger. We put an ad in the *New York Review of Books*. We got one order—from a man. That ad cost $50, and we got $2.25 out of it. That obviously wasn't the right approach so I wrote a letter to the New York Daughters of Bilitis and asked them if I could come and talk to them about the book. After I contacted DOB, Kay Tobin called up and wanted to know about the book. She said, "When does the man come in?" I said, "There isn't any man." She said, "There's always a man in Lesbian books who takes the lover away." I said, "Not in this one."

J.K.: What made you think of going to DOB?

A.R.: It was the only Lesbian organization I'd ever heard of. Ann Aldrich had mentioned it and made fun of it in her book *We Walk Alone*. Anyway, I went to DOB and gave a little talk, and that night they bought twenty-five copies. I began to see where the market was. I left fifteen more copies with them, and when I went back the next week, they had sold them and they gave me the money. It was intoxicating. It was marvelous. I felt I had found my people. I felt they were the ones I had written the book for, and that it was getting to them. It was much more gratifying to me than any of my other books. Even though I had published it myself, and I was obviously a failure from the world's point of view, the fact that my people were reading my book and loving it, meant more to me than anything else that has ever happened in my life.

I also wrote to Gene Damon, the editor of *The Ladder*, and she told her friends to read the book. People she had recommended me to were willing to send me their names. She vouched that I wasn't an FBI fink, or whatever. I think it's hard now to imagine how terrified people were about ordering that book. Then some of the Gay bookshops and feminist bookshops began ordering it. By the time it went out of print we were getting orders from universities for women's studies courses.

J.K.: You sold out a thousand copies?

A.R.: Yes, at $2.25 a copy. That was a little high for a paperback then, but our unit cost was high. We didn't make any money on it. What happened next was that I went up to a feminist conference at Barnard College in the spring of 1971. Kate Millett spoke, and women were milling around at the edge of the stage afterward. I went up with my shopping bag full of books, and a woman bought one from me. I don't know who she was, except that she was a friend of Charlotte Sheedy, who was then a free-lance manuscript scout. And that evening Charlotte Sheedy said to this woman who had bought my book, "Oh, if only I could find a good Lesbian novel. I think the time has come." And the woman said, "I bought one today up at Barnard." Charlotte Sheedy took the book to Dial without telling me. Dial rejected it. Then she took it to McGraw-Hill, and McGraw-Hill took it. She was right; the time had come. The hardback came out in 1972, and Fawcett brought out a paperback in 1973. In the fall I quit my job. I got a fair amount of money—nothing fantastic, but enough to live on for about two and a half years. I have just lately had to go back to work again. So that's basically the publishing history. The book did fairly well commercially.

J.K.: I don't suppose it got any reviews when you published it yourself?

A.R.: No, just in a couple of Gay papers—and they were negative.

J.K.: Negative?

A.R.: Haven't you noticed how hard it is to please Gay people? One bad review was in the newspaper *Gay*. A woman reviewer, Sorel David, thought the feminist consciousness was unrealistically high for that stage in history. She just wasn't caught up by the book. It didn't move her.

J.K.: And the other bad review in the Gay press?

A.R.: It was in the *Advocate*. I didn't read it. When the McGraw-Hill edition came out, the Johnson City, Texas, paper gave me a great review! The same in all kinds of places you wouldn't expect, like Sacramento and Grand Rapids. The *New York Times* also reviewed it favorably and the *Village Voice*. I didn't get any other particularly positive reaction from the East Coast. But all of what we consider middle American backward places gave me really enthusiastic reviews. I think men gave it the best reviews. They didn't have to worry—nobody was going to think *they* were Lesbians!

J.K.: Can you talk a little more about the Lesbian reaction to *Patience and Sarah*?

A.R.: One of the first letters I got was from a woman who didn't sign her name. She said her lover was married, and that her lover's marriage and her own anger had destroyed them. She thanked me for reminding her what it was supposed to be about. That moved me very much. Even though she hadn't had the experience in the book, she knew that's what she had tried for. And I've been surprised, since Patience and Sarah are a monogamous couple, that a lot of commune people like it. There's supposed to be a Lesbian commune out in Portland, Oregon, that carries it around like a talisman. You wouldn't think they would identify with it, but they do. I got a letter from a married woman in the Midwest. She was longing, and lost, and forlorn, and was glad there was something to read about two women in love. She reminded me of myself. I used to read those Lesbian paperbacks—every one I could get.

J.K.: The Lesbian-feminist consciousness in your book seems very personally felt. How did you come to have that feeling and those ideas by 1967?

A.R.: I was a self-taught feminist. I hadn't been in the movement at all, and I didn't realize that these were commonplace ideas. I had learned them in my gut, through my life, and I was rather surprised that a lot of other women had been learning them at the same time. But we hadn't begun talking to each other yet.

J.K.: Had you read of the feminist literature that was beginning to come out?

A.R.: No. I don't think I even read *The Feminine Mystique* until after writing *Patience and Sarah*. When I did read Friedan's book, I wrote her a fan letter. I wouldn't read her book when it first came out because I thought it was *in favor* of the feminine mystique! I didn't want to hear any more bullshit about how women are supposed to do this or that.

J.K.: What experience of yours had made you a feminist?

A.R.: Marriage! I was married to a man for fifteen years, and had children, and lived the straight life to the hilt—I really lived the straight life. At first it didn't cross my mind that I might be considered an inferior creature. But when I began to realize that there was a certain kind of condescension toward me because I was a woman, I got madder and madder and madder. It was slow. I don't claim to be any great genius as a feminist; it took me a long time to catch on. A lot of things puzzled me. Maybe it's unrealistic that it doesn't take Patience and Sarah that long to catch on.

J.K.: Your book suggests a strong connection between Lesbianism and feminism. When did you first see that?

A.R.: They were unconsciously linked in my mind. I really didn't see a linkup until the movement, until later, after writing the book. I put the book together without being awfully conscious of a missionary motive. That's true, for instance, of the scene where Patience is teaching Sarah how to act like a lady, how not to hear anything, not to see anything, not to respond to anything, not to put her hands in her pockets, not to cross her legs, not to stride— these million little (or huge, really) socially required inhibitions.

J.K.: Did you experience something like that—being taught how to be a lady?

A.R.: Yes, but I didn't learn. Also I was in the Navy. When you're a woman wearing a Navy uniform, you are assumed *not* to be a lady, and all kinds of men think they have a right to make comments on your body, and announce whether they would like to fuck you. By putting on a Navy uniform, you have made a certain kind of statement about yourself in their minds. That made me indignant. I didn't see any reason why I shouldn't be able to walk along the street without that kind of harassment. Even if men considered it a compliment, it was still harassment. I wasn't free to move.

J.K.: Will you say more about being married, and discovering at a certain point that you were a Lesbian—is that what happened?

A.R.: No, I had an inkling that I was a Lesbian before I got married—I kept falling in love with my women friends. I had tried to act on it but hadn't had any success. I had gruffly and grouchily announced that I was attracted —and been turned down. I became convinced that being Gay meant constant rejection, pain, and frustration. I considered it a disaster. I don't think I thought there was anything wrong with it, in itself, but it was not a good adaptation to the world. So this guy fell in love with me, and he was really a fine person, and I thought what a golden opportunity to become part of life—not to be this constant outsider. Not being an outsider made me happy for about four years. It was great to fit in and be more or less content, doing all the things everybody else did. When I finally woke up sexually, I could no longer be contented in a heterosexual relationship. It just wasn't a complete enough experience. It wasn't emotionally fulfilling. By then I had children, and I had all these commitments—mortgages, and cars—and I had written a novel, which was considered a sort of textbook of happy heterosexuality. So I thought I had an image to maintain. That became absolutely meaningless to me later on, but for a while it seemed important.

J.K.: You published *Patience and Sarah* under the pen name "Isabel Miller." Did you use this pseudonym because of the Lesbian content?

A.R.: I used it because it was *not* the name I had used before. It happens that people who read *Patience and Sarah* immediately think they want to read my other books. Practically all my mail asks "Please tell me the name of your other books." These books are not Gay. And they're not me any more. I'm not interested in them. They're out of print. By using a new name I wanted to start a new thing. Also, my children were very young then, and I didn't want to embarrass them. I picked this pen name because Miller was my mother's maiden name and Isabel is an anagram of Lesbia.

J.K.: I'd like to know more about the personal origins of the consciousness that comes through in *Patience and Sarah*. You must have had some really profound experience rebelling against the traditional female role.

A.R.: Yes. I remember not being allowed to drive my father's car. In Michigan, you could get a driver's license when you were fourteen, and I just took it for granted that when I became fourteen I would get a driver's license, as my brother had. I got to be fourteen and I couldn't have a driver's license. I couldn't believe it. I fought and yelled and screamed. I brought it up all the time; I didn't drop it. But my father wouldn't let me drive. I didn't learn to drive until I was nineteen and had left home. That still makes me indignant. It took me years to realize it was because I was a girl. By myself I pieced together all sorts of things like that as oppressions.

I remember thinking I could be friends with men—this was after I was married. But there's a social pressure for a woman not to have men friends. I was not interested in these men sexually, and I really resented the misunderstanding of my friendships. I don't know if that's a feminist issue or not. But the assumption that if you're a woman you can't have any relationships with men that aren't sexual is irritating, to say the least. All kinds of things pile up.

I went to a shrink when I was about thirty to see if he could cure me of being Gay. I hadn't yet had any Gay experience, but I longed for it, and this was interfering with my adjustment to marriage and motherhood. I thought, not that it was a bad thing, but that it was inconvenient for me to have these useless longings. I thought that if only I could be rid of them I could do what I was supposed to do more happily. I remember telling this shrink that I felt deprived as a writer; I felt that I had a talent not initially inferior to Mark Twain's, but I couldn't go up and down the Mississippi and couldn't do the things he had done to expand his life experiences and wisdom. I resented the limitations placed on my knowledge because I was a woman. I put that in *Patience and Sarah*. Once the parson finds out that the "Sam" he's been traveling with is Sarah, a female, he stops teaching her. She can see him asking himself, before everything he says, "Is this fitting or useful for a woman to know?" As a young woman I wanted to know about all kinds of things, and men in those days were very careful about what they let women know—not intellectual things, but about real life, how things really happen. I didn't feel rid of that disadvantage till I got into a woman's consciousness-raising group and realized that I was learning more about real human nature than I would ever find out on a Mississippi riverboat.

J.K.: Can you say more about your idea of the relationship between Lesbianism and feminism? It seems such an important part of *Patience and Sarah*.

A.R.: I feel that there's something about the male ego—I hope this may be changing. If you're a woman and going into a relationship with a man, you've got to flatter him in a certain way by your own inferiority. That makes development of yourself difficult. While you love men, and need their love, need their approval, there are certain adaptations you have to make that are crippling to you. I was horrified to read that men are turned on by the peculiar unnaturalness of the walk of a woman in high heels. It excites them, it makes her butt move in a certain way, and it makes her helpless—she can't run—he feels so solid beside her. There are all kinds of ways that women who love men cripple themselves like that.

I was attracted to a man a few years ago. I was appalled because my immediate thought was, "I've got to lose weight!" There were things I would have to do to make myself more attractive to him. Fortunately, I recovered immediately. But I was surprised at the working of my mind, and what you do if you want a man—it's very different from what you do if you want a woman.

I thought my husband and I lived pretty much as equals, even though I was home with the children and he went out to work. My lover was angry that I didn't hate him, and she was determined to trap him into making a statement that would turn me off him. She was a good manipulator, and she managed to do it. She trapped him into saying that if he married again he did not want an intellectual woman: "A man likes to be one jump ahead of a woman." When I realized he had resented my not being one jump behind him our whole life together, it turned me off. So many good things that had happened between us were invalidated because he minded my not being inferior to him. It was a struggle for him to put up with our equality—that came as a shock to me. I have not gotten over it. Yes, Lesbianism and feminism are tied together.

I've been hurt by women much more than by men. But even when I have a broken heart and am wiped out, there's something in me saying, "Well, at least it's over a woman—at least she's worth it. At least I'm not feeding the male ego—that God damn beast."

J.K.: Has your consciousness changed appreciably since writing *Patience and Sarah*? Is there anything you would say differently if you were writing the book in 1975?

A.R.: One of the things some people complain about in the novel is what seems to be role-playing: Sarah dressing like a man. I think that was necessary; I wouldn't change that. Sarah needs to have had the experience that enables her to chop down trees when she and Patience finally get out on their farm alone. One of the jokes in the book is that although Sarah dresses like a man she's not butch, she's not male-identified. Men's clothes are not male identification; they're *freedom*. Sarah's basic feeling comes out when she's with the parson, traveling as a boy; she gets into all these fights and she doesn't always lose, but she still doesn't like it. She realizes for the first time not only that she is a woman, but that she values womanliness more than manliness. She doesn't want to be in the kind of constant struggle and fighting and competition that men are in. The idea of Sarah going out into the world as a young man—well, actually, it's a great archetypal idea. It's in Shakespeare. I think it's a recurrent fantasy of little girls.

J.K.: On what did you base the character of the parson?

A.R.: Well, I'd read about Parson Weems, who made up the cherry tree story about George Washington. He'd been unfrocked for making people laugh at prayer, and had written a book advocating some kind of birth control, which made him an outcast. I liked him, and I used him as a start for Parson Peel. I also projected a lot of myself into the parson; I'm more Parson Peel than I am anyone else in the book.

J.K.: In what ways?

A.R.: He always wants to know how people manage to live. Do they pray or sing or have a friend, or hope for heaven? How do they keep going? No matter how many times he hears the same story, he's always interested. He goes off with a load of dirty laundry over his shoulder, and comes back with the laundry woman's life story. He sleeps late in the morning and writes at night.

He sings hymns. He's bisexual, which I sort of am, although I don't act on it because I've had to make a choice. If I have to choose, I choose women. I put a lot of myself into the parson. I made him elegant as a joke—I'm not elegant—I don't have a ruffled shirt, and two rows of buttons on my waistcoat.

Since I wrote *Patience and Sarah*, my idea of strict monogamy has changed a lot. I still think monogamy was necessary for their time and situation. They had no Gay community at all. But I wouldn't be interested now in writing about monogamy. I think the problem today is to develop a kind of support community, to not be so exclusive, to help each other when we need it, to be there for each other.

I've also become more cynical since writing *Patience and Sarah*. A lot of women who had been hurt much more than I found the novel naive; I agree now, in a certain way. I think the book's true, but it's also naive. I've been around quite a lot since I wrote it, and I know better how difficult most relationships are. I didn't make Patience and Sarah's relationship difficult enough—I hinted at the difficulty, but I didn't make it as difficult as most really are.

J.K.:   It seems to me that *Patience and Sarah* expresses a Lesbian and feminist consciousness characteristic of the particular time you were writing it. In artistic form it makes a statement much like the one other Lesbians were making in more directly political ways. Your book seems to fit into a Lesbian literary-political tradition. Although its viewpoint is entirely different, *The Well of Loneliness* is in the same tradition; it was a political act as well as an artistic one.

A.R.:   I think Radclyffe Hall was antihomosexual, though. I first read *The Well of Loneliness* when I was about seventeen. I was working in the library in my home town, and a woman came in who I now realize must have been a Lesbian. She wanted to know if we had *The Well of Loneliness*. I somehow sensed that was a book I should know about. We didn't have it. But I went out baby-sitting that night, and it was in that house, and I read it. I was very excited. The love scenes really turned me on. But I didn't like the characters. I didn't like the arrogance of the heroine, Stephen. I remember being offended, since it was obviously very autobiographical, at how Hall kept emphasizing what a terrific writer Stephen was. And that famous last section where she makes this piteous plea for the world to understand. I just didn't like it. Hall should have fit it in better. Hall has Stephen give up Mary so Mary can be saved by marrying Martin. At the end Stephen's in this wipe-out of grief; she might better have thought, "Maybe someday we won't have to feel that our love is such a bad thing that we have to send our lovers off." That last plea for pity just doesn't come out of the Stephen situation. It's just so rhetorical.

J.K.:   I do see *Patience and Sarah* as a political as well as an artistic statement.

A.R.:   The novel may incidentally be a political statement, but that wasn't what I had in mind. I was trying to motivate my characters—creating them was an artistic problem.

J.K.:   How do you feel about yourself as a writer in relation to the liberation movements of Lesbians and Gay men?

A.R.:   I don't want to write about anything else. I feel that, even though I've been rather unproductive, I really am a writer, and I really am a good writer. One of the things Gay people need is to have our artists pay attention to us, use us as their topic. It's disappointing when Gay people with big talent don't want to give it to us.

J.K.:   I think that Gay people have a lot to tell about surviving under difficult conditions. I hope that in your future writings you'll tell about that.

A.R.:   I want to.[149]

VI

LOVE
1779-1932

Introduction

The subject is intimate, deep-felt, often passionate relations between persons of the same sex—love.

This same-sex love is documented in a variety of sources: the published letters of Alexander Hamilton to John Laurens; the diaries of Ralph Waldo Emerson concerning Martin Gay; Emerson's reminiscences of Margaret Fuller; travelers' accounts of male homosexuality in Melville's South Seas; the monographic analysis by Taylor and Lasch of the friendship between Sarah Edgarton and Luella Case; the male homosexual pastoral escape, Charles Warren Stoddard's contribution to a literary genre; the autobiographical *Intimate Memories* of Mabel Ganson Dodge Luhan; the previously unpublished manuscript letters of Almeda Sperry to Emma Goldman; the fictional portrayal of Lesbian lovers by Helen R. Hull.[1]

These sources record and express a great variety of intimate same-sex relations: the bold, though mannered, seductive teasing in Hamilton's love letters to Laurens; the uneasy intensity of Emerson's illicitly conceived fascination with Martin Gay; the passionate teen-age "crush" of Margaret Fuller; the repressed and distorted male—male attractions often portrayed by Melville; the erotically tinged fantasies of Sarah Edgarton about Luella Case; the paternalistic feeling of Stoddard's narrator for a South Sea native; the unself-consciously erotic attractions of Mabel Luhan; the strong, "unabashed" love of Almeda Sperry for Emma Goldman; the idealized, romantic love of Alexander Berkman for Johnny Davis; the matter-of-fact love of Margaret and Amy in

Hull's novel *The Labyrinth*; the "superior" love-sex relation of "Mary Casal" and "Juno"; the deep feeling of the heterosexually identified Dorothy Thompson for the sophisticated Christa Winsloe.

If it be objected that there is nothing particularly "homosexual" about some of these documents, the answer is that the consideration of male–female relations has not been restricted to its narrowly erotic aspects; there is every reason why the historical study of same-sex relations should not be. In the past, Gay people were limited and reduced to their sexuality—even to its most negative manifestations. *Homosexual* has been the term by which Gay people were simultaneously categorized, summarized, and reduced to the less-than-human—denied their humanity on the basis of their sexuality. Gay liberationists emphatically affirm the real and potentially positive character of that sexuality, yet at the same time they assert that their humanity is not fully encompassed by it—they are Gay human beings.

The study of Gay history, if it is not to be limited by the old, narrow definition of "homosexual," should not confine itself to studying only the overt or even sublimated erotic, but should take in the full range, variety, and subtlety of same-sex relations. These relations should not be analyzed in isolation, as has been done, for instance, in almost all past psychological studies of the causes of homosexuality. To the extent that same-sex relations partake of, are intimately influenced by, and affect the character of relations between the sexes, these also should be studied. In this undertaking it is doubtful if it will prove useful or enlightening to try to "fit" past relations into one pole or the other of the traditional hetero–homo dichotomy. The term *homosexual*, with its emphasis on same-sex genital contact directed toward orgasm, is particularly inadequate as a means of encompassing and understanding the historical variety of same-sex relations. Categorizing human relations as homosexual or heterosexual should be replaced by research aimed at revealing the multiple aspects of the particular relations under study. Characterization, not categorization, is the order of the day.

The documents here present same-sex intimacy within a variety of social institutions, movements, and occupations: the American Revolutionary army is the setting of Hamilton's love for Laurens; college the setting of Emerson's infatuation with Martin Gay; a small town is the locale of Thoreau's love for Edmund Sewall; a geographic area, New England, the setting of Emerson's, Margaret Fuller's, Thoreau's, and other passionate same-sex relations; sailor life is the occupational setting of Melville's portrayals of male–male attractions; a religious movement, Unitarianism, the setting of Sarah Edgarton's and Luella Case's loving correspondence; the South Seas is the exotic, pagan setting of Stoddard's homosexual pastoral; an upper-middle-class home the setting of Luhan's youthful attraction to her nursemaid; a political-philosophical movement, anarchism, is the context of Sperry's love for Emma Goldman; jail the setting of Alexander Berkman's love for Johnny Davis; female professional life is the setting of Margaret and Amy's liaison in Hull's *The Labyrinth*; a big city the setting of the love of "Mary Casal" for "Juno"; and heterosexual marriage is the institutional context of Dorothy Thompson's attraction to Christa Winsloe. The American women's rights movement is the setting of a number of passionate same-sex relations between feminists.[2]

All these same-sex relationships occur within particular temporal and social situations. The traditional concept of "situational homosexuality" or "pseudohomosexuality," implying the existence of some nonsituational, "true" homosexuality, is misleading. All homosexuality (and heterosexuality) is situational—situated within a specific time, society, and class—and takes on a particular character in that context. "Situational homosexuality" as it occurs in prison, for instance, often mirrors in extreme form the most exploitative aspects of the larger society. Generalizations about homosexuality based on the prison situation or, as has been common, on the situation of homosexuals in psychotherapy, illegitimately jumps from a specifically situated form of homosexuality to the allegedly universal. Whatever continuity there is in the character of homosexuality from one specific context to another arises from the long and continued existence of a violently antihomosexual society. All the same-sex relations documented here existed under the pressures of this society; they cannot be understood apart from this negative historical context.

The idea of homosexuality per se, an ahistorical, unchanging entity, divorced from any specific context, is antihomosexual in effect. By associating homosexuality with some particular, problematic aspect of same-sex relations found within an antihomosexual society, and by generalizing these, homosexuality and homosexuals are blamed for the difficulties created by a hostile environment. Such generalizing is one way of keeping homosexuals in their place—allowing them, perhaps, the possibility of "adjusting" to a "bad thing," or changing their orientation—but denying them the possibility of self-affirmation as Gay people.

These documents reflect heterosexual moralists' sharp distinction between homosexual feelings and activity. This value judgment is often presented as a description of reality. By declaring homosexuality unmentionable, Judeo-Christian society tried to discourage even the thought of it; declaring such feelings a sin, it without doubt succeeded in suppressing some homosexual activity. Quite apart from this reality, and the needs of factual description, the philosophers of heterosexuality traditionally insist on an emphatic moral distinction between homosexual activity and feeling: it is not quite so bad to feel it as to do it. Homosexual activity has an earthy, pungent, sweaty reality which heterosexual morality has wished to etherealize into some sort of disembodied "pure" emotion. Heterosexual morality has clouded the understanding of homosexual reality.

A historic, classic example of this conceptual separation of feeling from action occurred in 1955. In that year, Father Edward Lucitt, head of the Catholic Holy Name Society of Camden, New Jersey, led a protest against the naming of a new Delaware River bridge after Walt Whitman, whom he called a "homoerotic." Father Lucitt based his statement on Gay Wilson Allen's then recently published biography of Whitman. The *New York Times* interviewed Allen who, the paper reports, said

> he had no intention of implying Whitman was a homosexual.
> "I used the term 'homoerotic' rather than 'homosexual' because the latter suggests sex perversion," Dr. Allen declared. "There is absolutely no evidence that Whitman engaged in any perverted practice."

Allen said that Whitman's writings showed "a strong affection for man," hence were "homoerotic." He added: "Many saints show the same feeling."[3] Aside from the historical question of the character and evidence of Whitman's sexual life (which Allen suppressed or deemphasized), there is clearly a moral evaluation implicit in this use of the term homoerotic. The same judgment—that it is less bad to feel homosexual attraction than to act on it—lies behind many allegedly descriptive statements about such diverse individuals as Sappho, Gertrude Stein, and Hart Crane.

As late as 1971, Patricia Meyerowitz, a supposed authority on Gertrude Stein, writes concerning Stein's thirty-nine-year intimacy with Alice B. Toklas:

there is a great divide between emotional attachments and active sexual relationships. That is to say, they do not automatically coexist. Simply stated, Alice and Gertrude made a home for themselves with an emotional attachment as the bond that kept them together. But lesbianism—never.[4]

In his 1969 biography of Hart Crane, John Unterecker describes Crane's love affair with Emil Opffer as "that open, generous affection we call Platonic love," an

enormously heightened friendship characterized by mutual understanding and devotion. "There was nothing dirty in it," Opffer told me, just as thirty-six years before Crane had told Waldo Frank that the relationship was founded not so much on sex as on "a purity of joy."[5]

Opffer, with his ambiguous "there was nothing dirty in it" (to be sure!), seemingly collaborated with Crane's biographer in euphemizing what was apparently a sexual love affair. Whitman certainly collaborated with his biographers by his own indirections, inventions, and outright denial; Stein and Toklas, with their Victorian reticence, did the same. The job of biographers, one would think, is to cut through such evasions; heterosexual morality, however, seems to interfere with such work. The fact is that traditional biographers, whatever the reality of their subjects' lives, have not wanted them to be homosexually active; these biographers' wishes have been mother to their obfuscation. When one reads over and over again that such and such a relation only existed in the realm of feeling, one confirms one's impression that the demands of morality are overruling the demands of objective research and clear, factual description. Surely someone before the later twentieth century actually slept with someone else of the same sex![6] The above examples represent a recurring analytic pattern—the deactivation of the homosexual—an intellectual process by which traditional, antihomosexual academics have defused a potentially explosive object.

A sharp, either/or distinction between erotic and nonerotic relations is another common polarity by which puritan morality has mystified intimate same-sex relations. Even the participants in such relations have perceived them from the standpoint of this morality. The radical opposition of the sexual and nonsexual often finds expression within the following documents, clouding the reality they reflect. This opposition sometimes takes the form of a radical distinction between sensual and nonsensual love, sometimes between erotic love and nonerotic friendship. Sometimes an allegedly nonerotic love-friendship is opposed to love involving carnal relations.

In the 1830s and '40s, Margaret Fuller writes in her journal that "a woman may be in love with a woman, a man with a man," and refers to her own personal and "passionate" experience. This same-sex love, says Fuller, is similar to love between the sexes, "only it is purely intellectual and spiritual, unprofaned by any mixture of the lower instincts." A paradox implicit in Fuller's statement also appears in other documents: on the moral scale of puritanical values, because it is allegedly nonsexual, same-sex intimacy is judged superior to relations between the sexes, which commonly involve the "lower instincts." Antisexual puritanism may thus result in heterosexual relations being judged inferior to (allegedly "pure") same-sex intimacies. This negative valuation of heterosexual relations is developed in several documents.

The idea of a nonsexual love-friendship is implicit in the words of the puritanical New England minister Thomas Wentworth Higginson to a young interviewer about William Hurlbut: "I never loved but one male friend with a passion." A paradox emerging here is that the secure belief in the idea of a nonsexual "passion" made possible the unself-conscious, unembarrassed expression of same-sex attraction, clearly including a sensual component. The existence of only a heterosexual model for conceptualizing sexual feelings insured that such feelings were perceived as having nothing to do with the tabooed same-sex love. Higginson writes his mother that the "slender, graceful, dark," black-eyed, "raven"-haired Hurlbut is "like some fascinating girl." Higginson is free to rapturously detail Hurlbut's physical beauty, and the strength of his own fascination, with no sense that he is confessing anything improper. Higginson's widow in 1914 innocently speaks of the letters engendered by her late husband's "romantic friendship" with Hurlbut as being "more like those between man and woman than between two men."[7]

The distinction between sexual and nonsexual relations lies behind the 1867 pronouncements on *The Friendships of Women* by William R. Alger, another New England minister. In defending Sappho from unmentionable "foul aspersions" cast upon her name, Alger says Greek modes of literary expression and thought did not distinguish between "sensual and sentimental love," although Greek behavior and feelings apparently did. Sappho's "passionate but pure sentiments" for other women are said to have remained "uncorrupt."[8]

Susan B. Anthony in 1868 perceived her feelings for her "friend" Anna Dickinson as "mother yearnings," in 1895 as "motherly love," and "elderly sister's love,"—familial feelings supposedly free of sensuality; at the same time, Anthony invited Dickinson to share her double bed, urged her "not to *marry* a man," and recalled a previous visit when she had "snuggled the wee child in my long arms."[9]

Henry David Thoreau, while believing many puritanical ideas about sensuality and being obsessed with the problem of intimacy with other males, was seemingly one of the few to question the traditional love/friendship distinction. In the fall of 1839 he writes in his journal:

> Commonly we degrade Love and Friendship by presenting them under the aspect of a trivial dualism.

Although Thoreau does not develop the thought, and his exact meaning is not clear, his comment seems to question the idea of nonsexual platonic love and point to the fact that friendship divorced from sensuality may be trivialized, that erotic relations divorced from friendliness may be degraded.

A number of the documents quoted here indicate the presence of an erotic element in puritan reality denied by puritan morality. The absolute distinction between erotic and nonerotic relations is a product of obscurantist puritan ideology rather than an accurate reflection of puritan society. The clear-cut separation of sensual and "spiritual" relations has probably more often existed in the ethereal clouds of moral discourse than in the earthly realm of human intercourse. We should be wary of taking the good puritans at their own word, by their own self-conception. Puritan morality did not always, or even often, describe accurately the emotional and erotic lives of puritans.

There is no intention here to imply that all close relations are "really" sexual, or that all intimate same-sex friendships are homosexual. Those now commonly heard ideas are silly, superficial vulgarizations of Freudianism. The perception associated with Freud, that a broadly defined sexuality was often present in relations earlier considered sacred and asexual (those between parents and children, children and children, students and teachers, for instance) cut through the distinction between sexual and nonsexual relations, so that today this puritanical idea seems naive. Since Freud, Thomas Wentworth Higginson's idea of a purely spiritual, nonerotic "passion" appears contradictory—passion seems inherently a matter of feeling, of the senses, of sensuality, of the erotic. Now, the contemporary American consciousness may even be oversexed. And yet, if our tendency is to err in seeing manifestations of the erotic under as well as in every bed, historians have long erred in the opposite direction, ignoring the existence and meaning of even the most blatantly sexual. Investigation is only now beginning into that important erotic and affectional history which puritan morality has denied, as it has denied the historic existence of Gay people.

Until recently, the relationship between wife and husband within heterosexual marriage has been the only model for human intimacy that sanctions erotic relations. In recent years, the increasing legitimacy of heterosexual liaisons outside of marriage, and the surfacing of homosexual partnerships, has resulted in more common and casual acceptance of that relation characterized by the term *lovers*. Not surprisingly, in the present texts, "friend" and "friendship" recur as the terms characterizing same-sex intimacies. Historically, "friendship" has been the only legitimate model for same-sex relations, other than those characterized by familial ties (mother and daughter, father and son, sister and sister, brother and brother). The international literature on "friendship," from which some of the present American selections are chosen, provides important historical materials for the study of the changing social forms of same-sex intimacy.

For example, the popular work of the New England minister William Rounseville Alger on *The Friendships of Women* (1867) contains two especially relevant chapters, one on "Friendships of Women with Women," the other on "Pairs of Female Friends." Although most of Alger's examples are European, Margaret Fuller's passionate same-sex relations are discussed. In addition, Alger's comments on the intimacies of Eleanor Butler and Sarah Ponsonby (the "Ladies of Llangollen"), on Brentano and Günderode, and on Sappho are of special interest. Another work by an American minister, Henry Clay Trumbull, *Friendship the Master-Passion Or The Nature And History Of Friendship, And Its Place As A Force In The World* (1892), is of interest, but even more prim than Alger's in speaking of passionate same-sex relations, though Trumbull does discuss such same-sex relations in the Bible, among the ancient Greeks and among American Indians. His omissions are perhaps more suggestive; there is no mention of Sappho, Walt Whitman, or Thoreau (although Emerson's maddeningly abstract and tame discourses on love and friendship are cited).

At the turn of the century, the European literature on same-sex "friendship" verged on the explicitly homosexual. In 1900 in Berlin, a writer on homoerotic themes, Elisàr von Kupffer, published an anthology whose title translates as *Chivalric Affection and Comrade Love [Freundesliebe] in World Literature*—the first of a series of collections of homosexual literature; with an "ethical-political introduction," von Kupffer's work was hailed by contemporary German homosexual emancipationists as a turning point in the emergence of their movement. In 1902, the pioneer English homosexual emancipationist Edward Carpenter published the first edition of his *Ioläus: An Anthology of Friendship*, a collection of historical materials relating to same-sex intimacy from "Pagan" to "Modern Times." In 1911, Alexander von Gleichen-Russwurm's work published in Germany, titled *Friendship: A Psychological Exploration*, constituted an early defense of homosexuality—criticized by Magnus Hirschfeld because it emphasized the emotional to the exclusion of the erotic. The German word *Freund* has long been used in the sense of lover, *Freundschaft* denoting an erotic-affectional relation, either hetero- or homosexual. In 1961 in England, Anderson and Sutherland edited *Eros: An Anthology* of *Friendship*, a collection of historic literary works on those intimate relations between males "strong enough to be called love," a survey of homoerotic world literature.[10]

To introduce other kinds of evidence on the relevance of "friendship" to Gay history: Lafitau's reference in 1724 to *les amitiés particulières* (special friendships) among Native American males, is only the first-known of such comments about "romantic friendships" between Indian men. Homoerotic friendships between American women are touched on in "The Female World of Love and Ritual: Relations between Women in Nineteenth-Century America," a recent, feminist-inspired historical monograph by Carroll Smith-Rosenberg.[11] The present discussion and documentation of same-sex friendship-love continues in an old tradition.

A number of the present documents of loving involve problems of historical interpretation because it is difficult to know at a later date what feelings and behavior are implied by an earlier era's manner of speech. For example, the loving letters of Alexander Hamilton to John Laurens present the dilemma of interpreting to what extent his epistolary language is a mere formal, literary convention and to what extent it is an honest expression of emotion, referring to some deep-felt, perhaps physical relation. To what extent does Hamilton's language reveal the nature of this relation? Hamilton biographer, J. C. Miller, is obviously embarrassed by, and at a loss to explain, what he mockingly calls his subject's "touching declaration" to Laurens, "I love you." Since a biographer like Miller fails to further elucidate the contemporary meaning of Hamilton's loving words, the nonspecialist cannot be faulted for failing to establish their exact meaning. Hamilton's letters must, of course, be seen in the social context of their time; what today sounds like rather blatant declarations of homosexual love may have had quite different connotations in 1779—or they may not. But even if Hamilton's terms of endearment are interpreted as reflecting no correspondingly strong emotional attraction or physical relation—if they are emotionally empty rhetorical flourishes—the very permissibility of such formal terms suggests more lenient social attitudes toward male-male intimacy. That even such formal expressions of love between men have today become "suspect" in heterosexual society is indicative of a profound alienation. Anti-homosexual bigotry may ironically take its toll on heterosexuals and homosexuals alike.

Hamilton's urging his friend Laurens to "put on the toga" and come with him to Washington is only one of the many classical allusions in the following texts. The model for Hamilton's relationship with Laurens, and for Hamilton's attitude toward women, appears to be Greek. References to both male and female same-sex intimacy among the ancient Greeks and Romans, especially references to historical and mythological same-sex couples, recur throughout these documents. These classical references are relevant to homosexual history and bear further investigation. It would be useful, for example, to have a historically reliable, chronological survey of those references to Sappho dealing, however gingerly, with Lesbianism. Such a survey would, for instance, help to clarify the implications of young Willa Cather's rhapsodic newspaper commentary on Sappho, dating to 1895. Trustworthy information about the same-sex lovers of Greek mythology would help to identify the homosexually relevant references in Thoreau's journals.

The fact that the study of the classics was an established part of American higher education in the eighteenth and nineteenth centuries created the odd situation that that puritanical society was often in closer touch than our own with the pre-Christian world in which certain forms of homosexuality were openly discussed. To be sure, the homosexuality of ancient Greece was not "taught," but the student of classical literature and history was likely, in one way or another, to pick up knowledge of the ancient world's different attitude toward same-sex intimacy. It may even prove possible to establish that classical allusions were, historically, one of the semisecret languages used by American homosexuals to speak of those same-sex relations otherwise unnameable among Christians. Future research will no doubt reveal the homosexually relevant content of many classical allusions in the documents that follow.

The history of same-sex loving traced in the following texts is but one aspect of the changing social forms of love and hate, the social history of emotion, the sociology of sensibility—the study of the quality of human lives at a particular time, in a particular society. This study is of interest because to many of us today the possibilities and limitations of human intimacy within our own lives and society have become profound and pressing personal and political questions. Those of us dispossessed of all but our ability to work—and dispossessed also of heaven—know we have only our short time here, only our feeling for ourselves and others. For the life of us we need to know more about the possible forms of intimacy between women and women, between men and men, between the sexes, and among all the dispossessed. We need to know how slavery, feudalism, capitalism, socialism, and communism have or can affect not only material consumption but also the quality of our lives. For we have learned, even in the best of times, that the spirit may be hungry, the self impoverished, the affections poor—love may have died. Looking outward with clear eyes we can see that capitalist society, in making competition, property, and profit primary and absolute virtues, has also institutionalized possessiveness, greed, jealousy, envy, anxiety, fear, and hate. If we want to learn what kind of society and social change might make friendliness the rule instead of the exception, the study of the history of human intimacy may help us define, and struggle to create, that radically new and revolutionary political economy of love.

1779–83: ALEXANDER HAMILTON to JOHN LAURENS; "I wish, my dear Laurens . . . [to] convince you that I love you"

Born in the British West Indies in 1757, Alexander Hamilton was forced to go to work at the age of twelve because of his father's business failures. In 1772, generous relatives sent young Hamilton to college in New York, but he soon dropped his studies to join the growing American colonial liberation movement as a talented pamphleteer. In 1776, Hamilton commanded an artillery company and fought with George Washington in several battles; the next year Hamilton became one of the general's valued aides, was promoted to lieutenant-colonel, and worked hard to systematize the American war effort. After a quarrel with Washington in 1781, Hamilton headed an infantry regiment in Lafayette's corps. From 1782 to 1783, Hamilton served a term in the Continental Congress, then began a law practice in New York.

John Laurens, born in 1754 into a prominent family of Charleston, South Carolina, was sent to school in England and Switzerland. Laurens married in October

1776, and three months later returned to America to take part in the Revolution. He joined George Washington's staff as a volunteer aide, fought and was wounded in several battles, and was commissioned a lieutenant-colonel by Congress. In December 1778, Laurens, angry at certain "constant personal abuse" of his general, fought a duel to defend Washington's honor. Elected to the South Carolina assembly in 1779, Laurens withdrew from this political post to fight against a British invasion. When Charleston capitulated to the British in 1780, Laurens was held as a prisoner of war until his exchange for a British officer held by the Americans. That year, at age twenty-six, Laurens was sent by Congress to France on a successful mission to obtain much-needed money and supplies. Returning to America, he rejoined the Revolutionary army, taking an active part in several battles.

The letters reprinted here begin in 1779, when Hamilton was twenty-two and Laurens was twenty-five. Both young revolutionaries were part of that close male circle surrounding General Washington—his "family," as the general called them. Speaking of the intimate friendships formed among these aristocratic young gentlemen "of good family and breeding" who served as Washington's immediate military aides, Hamilton's biographer John C. Miller declares in 1959:

> The friendships thus formed in the army were compared by the young men themselves to that of Damon and Pythias, and they expressed their devotion in the high-flown literary language of the day. In their letters it is not uncommon to find them addressing each other in terms certain to provoke a riot in even the best-regulated present-day barracks or mess hall. For example, John Laurens, one of Washington's aides, saw nothing strange in writing to his friend Richard Meade in this strain: "Adieu: I embrace you tenderly. . . . My friendship for you will burn with that pure flame which has kindled you your virtues." Laurens addressed Hamilton as "My Dear" and his letters abound in flowery protestations of undying affection, to which Hamilton responded with the touching declaration: "I love you."
>
> Hamilton and Laurens belonged to a generation of military men that prided itself not upon the hard-boiled avoidance of sentiment but upon the cultivation of the finer feelings. Theirs was the language of the heart, noble, exalted and sentimental. For Hamilton and Laurens were not merely soldiers doing a job; they were classical scholars whose thoughts and actions were colored by the grandeur of antiquity. They lived—and often died—by the code of the heroes of Plutarch.[12]

The American Revolution was in progress; John Laurens had left camp for South Carolina, hoping to be authorized by that colony's assembly to organize battalions of Black slaves to fight the British. In April, 1779, Hamilton writes to him:

Cold in my professions, warm in [my] friendships, I wish, my Dear Laurens, it m[ight] be in my power, by action rather than words, [to] convince you that I love you. I shall only tell you that 'till you bade us Adieu, I hardly knew the value you had taught my heart to set upon you. Indeed, my friend, it was not well done. You know the opinion I entertain of mankind, and how much it is my desire to preserve myself free from particular attachments, and to keep my happiness independent on the caprice of others. You sh[ould] not have taken advantage of my sensibility to ste[al] into my affections without my consent. But as you have done it and as we are generally indulgent to those we love, I shall not scruple to pardon the fraud you have committed, on condition that for my sake, if not for your own, you will always continue to merit the partiality, which you have so artfully instilled into [me].[13]

Forwarding several letters which had arrived from Laurens's wife, Hamilton continues:

And Now my Dear as we are upon the subject of wife, I empower and command you to get me one in Carolina. Such a wife as I want will, I know, be difficult to be found, but if you succeed, it will be the stronger proof of your zeal and dexterity. Take her description—She must be young, handsome (I lay most stress upon a good shape) sensible (a little learning will do), well bred, . . . chaste and tender (I am an enthusiast in my notions of fidelity and fondness). . . . But as to fortune, the larger stock of that the better. . . . Though I run no risk of going to Purgatory for my avarice; yet as money is an essential ingredient to happiness in this world—as I have not much of my own and as I am very little calculated to get more either by my address or industry; it must needs be, that my wife, if I get one, bring at least a sufficiency to administer to her own extravagances. N[ota] B[ene] You will be pleased to recollect in your negotiations that I have no invincible antipathy to the *maidenly beauties* & that I am willing to take the *trouble* of them upon myself.

If you should not readily meet with a lady that you think answers my description you can only advertise in the public papers and doub[t]less you will hear of many . . . who will be glad to become candidates for such a prize as I am. To excite their emulation, it will be necessary for you to give an account of the lover—his *size*, make, quality of mind and *body*, achievements, expectations, fortune, &c. In drawing my picture, you will no doubt be civil to your friend; mind you do justice to the length of my nose and don't forget, that I [——].

Here approximately five words are illegible due to mutilation of the original manuscript. Hamilton continues:

After reviewing what I have written, I am ready to ask myself what could have put it into my head to hazard this Jeu *de follie*. Do I want a wife? No—I have plagues enough without desiring to add to the number that *greatest of all*; and if I were silly enough to do it, I should take care how I employ a proxy. Did I mean to show my wit? If I did, I am sure I have missed my aim. Did I only intend to [frisk]? In this I have succeeded, but I have done more. I have gratified my feelings, by lengthening out the only kind of intercourse* now in my power with my friend. Adieu

Yours.
A Hamilton[14]

Laurens was still in South Carolina five months later on September 11, 1779. On that date, Hamilton writes to him:

* See comment in note 14.

454

I acknowledge but one letter from you, since you left us, of the 14th of July which just arrived in time to appease a violent conflict between my friendship and my pride. I have written you five or six letters since you left Philadelphia and I should have written you more had you made proper return. But like a jealous lover, when I thought you slighted my caresses, my affection was alarmed and my vanity piqued. I had almost resolved to lavish no more of them upon you and to reject you as an inconstant and an ungrateful ———.

A space is here left blank in the manuscript, a word left unwritten by Hamilton, who continues:

But you have now disarmed my resentment and by a single mark of attention made up the quarrel. You must at least allow me a large stock of good nature.[15]

Laurens was with the American army in South Carolina when British forces arrived off that colony's coast and began the attack on Charleston which ended with that city's capture. Laurens was taken prisoner on May 12, 1780, and on a parole restricting him to the state of Pennsylvania arrived in Philadelphia. On June 30, 1780, Hamilton writes to Laurens:

I have talked to the General about your exchange; but the rigid rules of impartiality oppose our wishes. I am the only one in the family who think you can be exchanged with any propriety, on the score of your relation to the Commander in Chief. We all love you sincerely; but I have more of the infirmities of human nature, than the others, and suspect my self of being byassed by my partiality for you.

Hamilton reveals that he is now engaged to be married.

Have you not heard that I am on the point of becoming a benedict? I confess my sins. I am guilty. Next fall completes my doom. I give up my liberty to Miss Schuyler. She is a good hearted girl who I am sure will never play the termagant; though not a genius she has good sense enough to be agreeable, and though not a beauty, she has fine black eyes—is rather handsome and has every other requisite of the exterior to make a lover happy. And believe me, I am lover in earnest, though I do not speak of the perfections of my Mistress in the enthusiasm of Chivalry.

Is it true that you are confined to Pensylvania? Cannot you pay us a visit? If you can, hasten to give us a pleasure which we shall relish with the sensibility of the sincerest friendship.

Adieu God bless you. . . .

A Hamilton

The lads all sympathize with you and send you the assurances of their love.[16]

On September 16, 1780, Hamilton writes to Laurens, still under arrest and confined to Pennsylvania:

That you can speak only of your private affairs shall be no excuse for your not writing frequently. Remember that you write to your friends, and that friends have the same interests, pains, pleasures, sympathies; and that all men love egotism.

In spite of Schuylers black eyes, I have still a part for the public and another for you; so your impatience to have me married is misplaced; a strange cure by the way, as if after matrimony I was to be less devoted than I am now. Let me tell you, that I intend to restore the empire of Hymen and that Cupid is to be his prime Minister. I wish you were at liberty to *transgress* the bounds of Pensylvania. I would invite you after the fall to Albany to be witness to the *final consummation*. My Mistress is a good girl, and already loves you because I have told her you are a clever fellow and my friend; but mind, she loves you *a l'americaine* not *a la françoise*.

Adieu, be happy, and let friendship between us be more than a name

A Hamilton

The General & all the lads send you their love[17]

Two years passed. Laurens fought in the battle at Yorktown, then returned to South Carolina and took part in the continuing skirmishes with British troops. In a letter to Laurens dated August 15, 1782, Hamilton describes being delegated to Congress, assuring Laurens, "We have good reason to flatter ourselves peace on our own terms is upon the carpet." Hamilton continues:

Peace made, My Dear friend, a new scene opens. The object then will be to make our independence a blessing. To do this we must secure our *union* on solid foundations; an herculean task and to effect which mountains of prejudice must be levelled!

It requires all the virtue and all the abilities of the country. Quit your sword my friend, put on the *toga*, come to Congress. We know each others sentiments, our views are the same: we have fought side by side to make America free, let us hand in hand struggle to make her happy. . . .

Yrs for ever

A Hamilton[18]

On August 27, 1782, in a minor shoot-out with a British foraging party, John Laurens was killed; it is doubtful if Hamilton's last letter reached him.

1820–34: RALPH WALDO EMERSON and MARTIN GAY;
"Why do you look after me? I cannot help looking out as you pass"

Essayist, poet, philosopher, and lecturer Ralph Waldo Emerson was born in Boston in 1803, entered Harvard at the age of fourteen, and graduated four years later in 1821. The earliest extant volume of Emerson's journal begins in 1820, during his senior year at Harvard, when he was seventeen, and records Emerson's growing fascination with a fellow student, Martin Gay.

Martin Gay, from Hingam, Massachusetts, entered Harvard in 1819 and continued to enthral Emerson for a number of years. Gay received an M.D. degree in 1826 and went on to become a well-known doctor, chemist, member of the Boston Society of Natural History, and Fellow of the American Academy of Arts and Sciences. He was said to possess a "delicate regard for the feelings of others" and to be a lover of "the beautiful in nature and art," cultivating his aesthetic interests at home and on travels in Europe.

Emerson's brief, intense, apparently secret attraction to Gay is especially interesting because of Emerson's later influence on Margaret Fuller, Henry David Thoreau, and Walt Whitman, three others with passionate same-sex attachments. Emerson's evident concern about the morality of his own attraction certainly affected his relations with, and evaluations of, the lives and writings of Thoreau, Whitman, and Fuller.

In Emerson's first journal referring to Martin Gay the word "GAY" is written in capitals across part of the page. The editors of these published journals state that in the text the name "Gay" has been crossed out, apparently by Emerson, who repeatedly went back and carefully deleted or disguised most journal references to him. This entry, like several others, also contains, according to the editors, "unrecoverable cancelled matter"—evidently deleted by Emerson himself.

[August 8, 1820]

—There is a strange face in the Freshman class whom I should like to know very much. He has a great deal of character in his features & should be a fast friend or a bitter [unrecoverable cancelled matter] enemy. His name is Gay[.] I shall endeavor to become acquainted with him & wish if possible that I mght be able to recall at a future period the singular sensations which his presence produced at this.—[19]

Two months later, the new fall term started and Emerson and Gay apparently were eyeing each other. Emerson writes, say his editors, presumably about Gay:

Oct. 24th [1820]

I begin to believe in the Indian doctrine of eye-fascination. The cold blue eye of has so intimately connected him with my thoughts & visions that a dozen times a day & as often . . . by night I find myself wholly wrapped up in conjectures of his character & inclinations. . . . We have had already two or three long profound stares at each other. Be it wise or weak or superstitious I must know him.[20]

A week later, Emerson's "opinion" of Gay goes up and down with each new report of his behavior. The last week in October 1820, Gay and two other sophomores took an "active part" in a now obscure student "rebellion"; Gay and the others were suspended (evidently temporarily), and a freshman was "admonished." The hand sign that appears in the entry below, and in the original journal, points to a sketch by Emerson, identified as Gay, pasted on the page over the verses.

Nov. 1. [1820]

My opinion of ☞ was strangely lowered by hearing that he was "proverbially idle." This was redeemed by learning that he was a "superior man." This week, a little eventful in college, has brought a share of its accidents to him.

Martin Gay, by Emerson.

October

Perhaps thy lot in life is higher
Than the fates assign to me
While they fulfil thy large desire
And bid my hopes as visions flee
But grant me still in joy or sorrow
In grief or hope to claim thy heart
And I will then defy the morrow
Whilst I fulfil a loyal part.[21]

Five months later, in the summer of 1821, Emerson again refers to an unnamed "friend," presumably, according to the editors, Gay. When writing this entry, Emerson left a blank space for the friend's name, then later went back and filled in the space with meaningless letters and pseudoletters, intended, suggest the journal's editors, to confuse prying eyes. Part of this entry was canceled by Emerson and has been reconstructed by its editors. The note at the very end refers to Emerson's plans to burn his diary called the "Wide World."

[April 1, 1821]

Well, I am sorry to have learned that my friend is dissolute; or rather the anecdote which I accidentally heard of him shews . . . him more like his neighbours than I should wish him to be. . . . I shall have to throw him up, after all, as a cheat of fancy. Before I ever saw him, I wished my *friend* to be different from any individual I had seen. I invested him with a solemn cast of mind, full of poetic feeling, & an idolater of friendship, & possessing a vein of rich sober thought. When I saw   's pale but expressive face & large eye, I instantly invested him with the complete character which fancy had formed and though entirely unacquainted with him was pleased to observe the notice which he appeared to take of me [?]. For a year I have entertained towards him the same feelings & should be sorry to lose him altogether before we have ever exchanged above a dozen words.

N[ota] B[ene] By the way this book is of an inferiour character & contains so much doubtful matter that I believe I shall have to burn the second number of the Wide World immediately upon its completion.[22]

A month after the preceding entry, Emerson's journal records his more active pursuit of actual contact with his unnamed "friend," presumably, according to the editors, Martin Gay. The entry contains many cancellations, some "unrecoverable." A pen-and-ink sketch by Emerson of a man's head and shoulders profile is at the right center of the page, and the text of the May 10th entry flows around it.

May 2, 1821

I am more puzzled than ever with 's conduct. He came out to meet me yesterday and I observing him, just before we met turned another corner and most strangely avoided him. This morning I went out to meet him in a different direction and stopped to speak with a lounger in order to be directly in 's way, but [unrecoverable matter] turned into the first gate and went towards Stoughton. All this baby play persists without any apparent design, and as soberly as if both were intent on some tremendous affair. With a most serious expectation of burning this book I am committing to it more of what I may by and by think childish sentiment than I should care to venture on vagabond sheets which Somebody else may light upon. (Mr Somebody, will it please your impertinence to be conscience-struck!)

May 10th Huzza for my Magician! he engages me finely. I am as interested in the tale and as anxious to know the end as any other reader could be. By the by this tale of mine might be told, with powerful effect by a man of good voice and natural eloquence.[23]

The "Magician," say the journal's editors, probably refers to Emerson's story about a witch, Uilsa, and her son, Vahn the Magician, fragments of which are found in Emerson's notebooks.

Sometime, probably in 1821 or 1822, Emerson in his journal poignantly questioned an unnamed friend, presumably, according to his editors, Martin Gay:

Why do you look after me? I cannot help looking out as you pass [.][24]

A notebook, possibly of 1821, includes a few lines of verse which Emerson's editors suggest contain a disguised reference to Martin Gay. They are headed: "From Frodmer's Drama 'The Friends.' " There is no dramatist named Frodmer; the title, verse, and theme of "Friendship" are Emerson's. The lines that follow parallel others Emerson wrote to or about Martin Gay; "Malcolm" is no doubt a substitute for "Martin." Lines one to four of the verse are heavily canceled and have been reconstructed. In the middle of the verse, between the lines, is much practice calligraphy. A drawing of a figure wearing an elaborate headdress appears in the right margin of the original journal.

From Frodmer's Drama "The Friends"

Malcolm, I love thee more than women love
And pure and warm and equal is[?] the feeling
Which binds us and our destinies forever
But there are seasons in the change of times
When strong excitement kindles up the light
Of ancient memories[25]

After graduating from Harvard, Emerson recalls, in a journal entry of February

26, 1822, his lack of success and the daily mortification of his college career. But later, after revisiting the Harvard campus, he "felt a crowd of pleasant thoughts," and listed numbers of enjoyable experiences. The entry ends: "I met   [.]" Emerson still thought, finally, of that unnamed individual who had made such an impression, and whom the journal editors suggest was Martin Gay.[26]

Two days after the preceding entry, on February 28, 1822, Emerson finds that his "pleasant social feelings" of the last few days have prevented his writing satisfactorily intellectual journals—"the mind has not possessed sufficiently the cold frigid tone which is indispensable to become so oracular." A passage in Latin follows, which the journal's editors translate as:

"Although the praise and honor of my thoughts has not been as great as before, yet it acquires a greater joy and pleasure, since I believed I felt the beginnings of love. I saw a [male] friend, though an old one, unknown; I saw another [female] known and to be known; both, perhaps, if it pleases God, will make a part of life, a part of me. I regret telling important matters with the words that a beginner is accustomed to use."[27]

The editors suggest the "[male] friend" may have been Martin Gay.

On May 7, 1822, apparently after encountering Martin Gay, and twelve months after the journal entry in which he spoke of pursuing his unnamed male friend, Emerson finds himself returning "to the identical thoughts & temperament which I had a year ago." Emerson's (perhaps unconscious) play on the word gay ("gay banners," gay "deciever" [sic]) suggests a curious association in his mind between this term, his "queer acquaintance with Gay," and male–male love:

Now I'm a hopeless Schoolmaster just entering upon years of trade to which no distinct limit is placed; toiling through this miserable employment even without the poor satisfaction . . . of discharging it well, for the good suspect me, & the geese dislike me. Then again look at this: there was pride in being a collegian, & a poet, & somewhat romantic in my queer acquaintance with [Gay;] and poverty presented nothing mortifying in the meeting of two young men whom their common relation & character as scholars equalised. But when one becomes a droning schoolmaster, and the other is advancing his footing in good company & fashionable friends, the cast of countenance . . . on meeting is somewhat altered. Hope, it is true, still hangs out, though at further distance, her gay banners; but I have found her a cheat once, twice, many times, and shall I trust the deciever again?

On November 29, 1822, Emerson confides to his journal that the "ardour of my college friendship for [Gay] is nearly extinct." He muses that his agreeable excitement over Gay was "a curious incident in the history of so cold a being [as himself], and well worth a second thought." He adds that "To this day, our glance at meeting, is not that of indifferent persons. . . ."[28]

Twelve years later, Emerson considers in his journal the purpose of education; he refers to the self-questioning and psychological "self-discord" of young males—and wonders about Shakespeare's sonnets addressed to "beautiful young men."

April 30 [1834].

There are more purposes in Education than to keep the man at work. Self-questioning is one; a very important end. The disturbance, the self-discord which young men feel is a most important crisis, indispensable to a free, improvable race creature. Give me the eye to see a navy in an acorn.

If I could write like the wonderful bard whose sonnets I read this afternoon, I would leave all, and sing songs to the human race. . . . how remarkable every way are Shakspear's sonnets. Those addressed to a beautiful young man seem to show some singular friendship amounting almost to a passion which probably excited his youthful imagination. They are invaluable for the hints they contain respecting his unknown self.[29]

♀ 1823–50: MARGARET FULLER;
"A woman may be in love with a woman"

Writer, educator, feminist, transcendentalist, and rebel, Margaret Fuller was born at Cambridgeport, Massachusetts, in 1810. Fuller's life included several complex, deeply emotional relations with other females—as a youngster of thirteen with an unnamed Englishwoman, later with a teacher; her adult relations included close friendships with English feminist Harriet Martineau and New Englanders Caroline Sturgis and Elizabeth Peabody. Among Fuller's published works is a translation from the German of a book about Karoline von Günderode and her passionate relations with Bettina Brentano von Arnim.[30]

Fuller's birth had been a disappointment to her father, Timothy Fuller, who, wanting a son, decided to give his daughter the education then reserved for males. As soon as she began to speak, Margaret Fuller was trained in English and Latin grammar; at the age of seven she was reading in the original the literature of Greece and Rome. Her unusual learning made Fuller intellectually mature beyond her age, but took its toll in much physical and mental anguish, as she later recounted. In 1823, as a lonely child of thirteen, cut off from her peers, one day in church Fuller first noticed and fell in love with a visiting Englishwoman. Margaret Fuller writes of her "First Friend."

As my eye one day was ranging about with its accustomed coldness . . . it was arrested by a face most fair, and well-known, as it seemed at first glance—for surely I had met her before, and waited for her long. But soon I saw that she was a new apparition foreign to that scene, if not to me. Her dress—the arrangement of her hair, . . .—the intelligent and full picture of her eye, whose reserve was in its self-possession, not in timidity—all combined to make up a whole impression, which, though too young to understand, I was well prepared to feel. . . .

. . . Then, the first sight, the first knowledge of such a person was intoxication.

She was an English lady, who, by a singular chance, was cast upon this region for a few months. Elegant and captivating, her every look and gesture was tuned to a different pitch from anything I had ever known. She was in various ways "accomplished," as it is called, though to what degree I cannot now judge. She painted in oils;—I had never before seen any one use the brush, and days would not have been too long for me to watch the pictures growing beneath her hand. She played the harp: and its tones are still to me the heralds of the promised land I saw before me then. She rose, she looked, she spoke; and the gentle swaying motion she made all through life has gladdened memory, as the stream does the woods and meadows.

As she was often at the house of one of our neighbours, and afterwards at our own, my thoughts were fixed on her with all the force of my nature. It was my first real interest in my kind, and it engrossed me wholly. I had seen her,—I should see her,—and my mind lay steeped in the visions that flowed from this source. . . .

Should the first love be blighted, they say, the mind loses its sense of eternity. . . . I thank Heaven that this first feeling was permitted its free flow. The years that lay between the woman and the girl only brought her beauty into perspective, . . . and made her presence to me a gate of Paradise. . . . over a whole region of new life I ruled proprietor of the soil in my own right.

Her mind was sufficiently unoccupied to delight in my warm devotion. She could not know what it was to me, but the light cast by the flame through so delicate a vase cheered and charmed her. All who saw admired her in their way; but she would lightly turn her head from their hard or oppressive looks, and fix a glance of full-eyed sweetness on the child, who, from a distance, watched all her looks and motions. She did not say much to me—not much to any one; she spoke in her whole being rather than by chosen words. Indeed, her proper speech was dance or song, and what was less expressive did not greatly interest her. But she saw much, having in its perfection the woman's delicate sense for sympathies and attractions. We walked in the fields, alone. Though others were present, her eyes were gliding over all the field. . . . Like a guardian spirit she led me through the fields and groves, and every tree, every bird greeted me, and said, what I felt, "She is the first angel of your life."

One time I had been passing the afternoon with her. She had been playing to me on the harp, and I sat listening in happiness almost unbearable. Some guests were announced. She went into another room to receive them, and I took up her book. It was Guy Mannering, then lately published, and the first of Scott's novels I had ever seen. I opened where her mark lay, and read merely with the feeling of continuing our mutual existence by passing my eyes over the same page where hers had been. It was the description of the rocks on the sea-coast where the little Harry Bertram was lost. . . . I was the little Harry Bertram, and had lost her,—all I had to lose,—and sought her vainly in long dark caves that had no end, plashing through the water; while the crags beetled above, threatening to fall and crush the poor child. Absorbed in the painful vision, tears rolled down my cheeks. Just then she entered with light step, and full-beaming eye. When she saw me thus, a soft cloud stole over her face, and clothed every feature with a lovelier tenderness than I had seen there before. She did not question, but fixed on me inquiring looks of beautiful love. I laid my head against her shoulder and wept,—dimly feeling that I must lose her and all,—all who spoke to me of the same things,—that the cold wave must rush over me. She waited till my tears were spent, then rising, took from a little box a bunch of golden amaranths or everlasting flowers, and gave them to me. They were very fragrant. "They came," she said, "from Madeira." These flowers stayed with me seventeen years. "Madeira" seemed to me the fortunate isle, apart in the blue ocean from all of ill or dread. Whenever I saw a sail passing in the distance,—if it bore itself with fulness of beautiful certainty,—I felt that it was going to Madeira. . . .

I can tell little else of this time,—indeed, I remember little, except the state of feeling in which I lived. For I *lived*, and when this is the case, there is little to tell in the form of thought. We meet—at least those who are true to their instincts meet—a succession of persons through our lives, all of whom have some peculiar errand to us. There is an outer circle, whose existence we perceive, but with whom we stand in no real relation. . . . Another circle, within this, are dear and near to us. . . .

But yet a nearer group there are, beings born under the same star, and bound with us in a common destiny. These are not mere acquaintances, mere friends, but, when we meet, are sharers of our very existence. There is no separation; the same thought is given at the same moment to both,—indeed, it is born of the meeting, and would not otherwise have been called into existence at all. These not only know themselves more, but *are* more for having met, and regions of their being, which would else have laid sealed in cold obstruction, burst into leaf and bloom and song. . . .

To this inmost circle of relations but few are admitted, because some prejudice or lack of courage has prevented the many from listening to their instincts the first time they manifested themselves. If the voice is once disregarded, it becomes fainter each time, till, at last, it is wholly silenced, and the man lives in this world a stranger to its real life, deluded like the maniac who fancies he has attained his throne, while in reality he is on a bed of musty straw. Yet, if the voice finds a listener and servant the first time of speaking, it is encouraged to more and more clearness. Thus it was with me,—from no merit of mine, but because I had the good fortune to be free enough to yield to my impressions. Common ties had not bound me; there were no traditionary notions in my mind; I believe in nothing merely because others believed in it; I had taken no feelings on trust. Thus my mind was open to their sway.

This woman came to me, a star from the east, a morning star, and I worshipped her. She too was elevated by that worship, and her fairest self called out. To the mind she brought assurance that there was a region congenial with its tendencies and tastes, a region of elegant culture and intercourse, whose object, fulfilled or not, was to gratify the sense of beauty, not the mere utilities of life. In our relation she was lifted to the top of her being. She had known many celebrities, had roused to passionate desire many hearts, and became afterwards a wife; but I do not believe she ever more truly realized her best self than towards the lonely child whose heaven she was, whose eye she met, and whose possibilities she predicted.[31]

When her English friend returned across the sea, Fuller says her home seemed suffocating and dull.

At age fourteen, Fuller was sent to a girl's school in Groton, Massachusetts, where she stayed for two years. In the late 1820s, back in Cambridge, she won a reputation in intellectual circles as a brilliant conversationalist. From 1833 to 1836, Fuller lived with her family in Groton, doing much of the housekeeping and caring for the younger children. In 1836, Bronson Alcott hired Fuller to teach languages at his progressive school; there she and another teacher, Elizabeth Peabody, became devoted friends. From 1837 to 1839, Fuller held a less demanding job as a teacher in Providence, Rhode Island. During the second winter in Providence, she translated and published a book about Goethe, and in the summer of 1839 wrote her first criticism. Fuller moved back to the Boston area the same year, and began to hold her famous conversations with groups of interested women.

A letter of 1839 from Fuller to a female friend describes Fuller's feelings about herself as a woman and discusses her relation with this correspondent, a female with whom she had been close in her Cambridge days. "From a very early age," Fuller writes her friend, "I have felt that I was not born to the common womanly lot." She lived her life alone; she "was always to return to myself, to be my own priest, pupil, parent, child, husband, and wife." Her destiny, Fuller felt, was to be a "thinker," a "poetic priestess," so she "did not look on any of the persons, brought into relation with me, with common womanly eyes." Fuller tells her friend:

I also lived with you more truly and freely than with any other person. We were truly friends, but it was not friends as men are friends to one another, or as brother and sister. There was, also, that pleasure, which may, perhaps, be termed conjugal, of finding oneself in an alien nature. Is there any tinge of love in this? Possibly! At least, in comparing it with my relation to ——, I find *that* was strictly fraternal. I valued him for himself. I did not care for an influence over him, and was perfectly willing to have one or fifty rivals in his heart. . . .

. . . With your letter, vanished a last regret. You did not act or think unworthily. It is enough. As to the cessation of our confidential intercourse, circumstances must have accomplished that long ago; my only grief was that you should do it with your own free will, and for reasons that I thought unworthy. I long to honour you, to be honoured by you. Now we will have free and noble thoughts of one another, and all that is best of our friendship shall remain.[32]

Also in 1839, in the context of critical comments on literature, Fuller writes:

If I were a man, and wished a wife, as many do, merely as an ornament or silken toy, I would take —— as soon as any I know. Her fantastic, impassioned, and mutable nature would yield an inexhaustible amusement. She is capable of the most romantic actions;—wild as the falcon, and voluptuous as the tuberose,—yet she has not in her the elements of romance, like a deeper and less susceptible nature. . . .[33]

In 1840, Fuller, Emerson, and others joined to produce *The Dial*, a quarterly journal of transcendentalism, which was issued for four years. Fuller was the editor for the first year and later remained a major contributor. Fuller also took part in planning an ideal transcendental community, but when Brook Farm actually began operation in 1841, she chose not to live there. A trip through the Midwest in 1843 widened Fuller's sense of the world, and in 1844 her first original book was published—*Summer on the Lakes*. In December she went to New York City to become literary critic for Horace Greeley's *Tribune*. In 1845, Fuller's *Woman in the Nineteenth Century* was published, becoming an influential feminist classic. The year 1846 saw the publication of her *Papers on Literature and Art*, an important collection of critical essays. In New York, Fuller researched and wrote a series of reports on prisons and other public institutions. On August 1, 1846, as a foreign correspondent for the *Tribune*, Fuller sailed for Europe, finding that her fame had preceded her. She reached Rome in August 1847 and became increasingly involved in the developing Italian national liberation movement. She met and became the lover of Giovanni Angelo, the Marquis d'Ossoli, a young Roman nobleman and rebel with whom she conceived a child, then finally married. Fuller took active part in the Italian revolution of 1849, and after the republic was overthrown, began a history of the rebellion. In May 1850, the Ossolis sailed for America, and on July

19, a few hours out of New York, in a storm off the coast of Fire Island, their ship was wrecked and the Ossolis were drowned.

In 1851–52, the *Memoirs of Margaret Fuller Ossoli* were published, edited by Emerson, W. H. Channing, and J. F. Clarke; these are the two volumes from which the selections here have been taken. These two volumes, as Fuller biographer Mason Wade points out, were subjected to "the bowdlerizing activities" of the three editors, who also partially destroyed the value of Fuller's original manuscripts "by the unpardonable liberties" they took with them, apparently actually physically destroying whole sections of text.[34] In light of what remains, it would be interesting to know more about the sort of material eliminated.

In volume one of the *Memoirs*, Emerson wrote a section on Margaret Fuller's temperament. "I think," says Emerson, that in Fuller's case "there was something abnormal in those obscure habits and necessities which we denote by the word Temperament." Emerson speaks of a "barrier" which kept Fuller at a distance from him; he speaks of Fuller's strength, which made her always have "so much to say of her *fate*." He speaks of her "jubilation" and her "pain."

She had read that a man of letters must lose many days, to work well in one. Much more must a Sappho or a sibyle.

Emerson speaks of Fuller's "energy," "passion," and vulnerability, but emphasizes the degree to which, for him, she remained "inscrutable." He adds:

She had a feeling that she ought to have been a man, and said of herself, "A man's ambition with a woman's heart, is an evil lot." In some verses which she wrote "To the Moon," occur these lines:—

> "But if I steadfast gaze upon thy face,
>   A human secret, like my own, I trace;
>   For, through the woman's smile looks the male eye."

And she found something of true portraiture in a disagreeable novel of Balzac's, *"Le Livre Mystique,"* in which an equivocal figure exerts alternately a masculine and a feminine influence on the characters of the plot. . . .

I think most of her friends will remember to have felt, at one time or another, some uneasiness, as if this athletic soul craved a larger atmosphere than it found; as if she were ill-timed and mismated, and felt in herself a tide of life, which compared with the slow circulation of others as a torrent with a rill. She found no full expression of it but in music. Beethoven's Symphony was the only right thing the city of the Puritans had for her.[35]

In volume two of the *Memoirs*, Emerson writes a section on Margaret Fuller and "Friendship."

It is certain that Margaret, though unattractive in person, and assuming in manners, so that the girls complained that "she put upon them," or, with her burly masculine existence, quite reduced them to satellites, yet inspired an enthusiastic attachment. I hear from one witness, as early as 1829, that "all the girls raved about Margaret Fuller," and the same powerful magnetism wrought, as she went on, from year to year, on all ingenuous natures. The loveliest and the highest endowed women were eager to lay their beauty, their grace, the hospitalities of sumptuous homes, and their costly gifts, at her feet. When I expressed, one day, many years afterwards, to a lady who knew her well, some surprise at the homage paid her by men in Italy, —offers of marriage having there been made her by distinguished parties,—she replied: "There is nothing extraordinary in it. Had she been a man, any one of those fine girls of sixteen, who surrounded her here, would have married her: they were all in love with her, she understood them so well." . . .

I am to add, that she gave herself to her friendships with an entireness not possible to any but a woman, with a depth possible to few women. Her friendships, as a girl with girls, as a woman with women, were not unmingled with passion, and had passages of romantic sacrifice and of ecstatic fusion, which I have heard with the ear, but could not trust my profane pen to report. There were, also, the ebbs and recoils from the other party,—the mortal unequal to converse with an immortal, —ingratitude, which was more truly incapacity, the collapse of overstrained affections and powers. At all events, it is clear that Margaret, later, grew more strict, and values herself with her friends on having the tie now "redeemed from all search after Eros."[36]

> Immediately following the last selection, Emerson presents an undated fragment from Margaret Fuller's journal, edited, expurgated, and asexualized without acknowledgment. In his 1940 biography of Fuller, Mason Wade presents part of this journal in what is presumably its original, accurate version. The first, third, and last paragraphs below are from Emerson's version, the rest from Wade.

At Mr. G.'s we looked over prints, the whole evening, in peace. Nothing fixed my attention so much as a large engraving of Madame Récamier in her boudoir. I have so often thought over the intimacy between her and Madame de Staël.

It is so true that a woman may be in love with a woman, and a man with a man. It is pleasant to be sure of it, because it is undoubtedly the same love that we shall feel when we are angels, when we ascend to the only fit place for the Mignons, where *sie fragen nicht nach Mann und Weib* [literally: "they do not ask about man or woman"]. It is regulated by the same laws as that of love between persons of different sexes, only it is purely intellectual and spiritual, unprofaned by any mixture of lower instincts, undisturbed by any need of consulting temporal interests; its law is the desire of the spirit to realize a whole, which makes it seek in another being that which it finds not in itself. Thus the beautiful seek the strong, the mute seek the eloquent; the butterfly settles on the dark flower. Why did Socrates love Alcibiades? Why did Kaiser so love Schneider? How natural is the love of Wallenstein for Max, that of Madame de Staël for Récamier, mine for ——! I loved —— for a time with as much passion as I was then strong enough to feel. Her face was always gleaming before me; her voice was still echoing in my ear. All poetic thoughts clustered around the dear image.

This love was a key which unlocked for me many a treasure which I still possess; it was the carbuncle which cast light into many of the darkest caverns of human nature. She loved me, too, though not so much, because her nature was "less high, less grave, less large, less deep." But she loved more tenderly, less passionately.

She loved me, for I well remember her suffering when she first could feel my faults and knew one part of the exquisite veil rent away—how she wished to stay apart and weep the whole day.

I do not love her now with passion, but I still feel towards her as I can to no other woman. I thought of all this as I looked at Madame Récamier.[37]

1837–91: HERMAN MELVILLE;
"This infinite fraternity of feeling"

Through the years, a number of literary analysts have pointed to "homosexual" elements in the creative work and life of Herman Melville. The fact is that Melville's writings do include numerous scenes of striking relevance to the study of American male–male intimacy. This chronological survey of Melville's writings points to some of the most important textual evidence of deep-felt, male–male love relations. The focus here is on Melville's writings themselves, considered as documents of their time and as products of the personality, experience, and creative ability of one individual. Some external and biographical information is introduced to shed additional light on Melville's life and work.

To consider Melville's creative writing as historical document does not, of course, mean that one may assume its autobiographical accuracy. But if the congruence between Melville's personal history and fictional portrayals cannot be taken for granted, neither should they be ignored; such parallels call for further study. Whatever specific autobiographical significance it may have, Melville's frequent and suggestive treatment of intimate male–male relations reveals his lifelong concern with the quality of profound, often erotically tinged male–male attractions.

In 1837, at the age of seventeen, Herman Melville left his mother and seven siblings and shipped out of New York City as a cabin boy on the *Highlander* bound for Liverpool—the start of his career as a sailor. Melville's novel *Redburn* (1849) is partly based on incidents of its author's maiden voyage. Richard Chase and Somerset Maugham, in speaking of *Redburn*, point to homosexual elements in the characters of both the evil, tyrannical Jackson, and the more sympathetically portrayed Harry Bolton.[38]

In January 1841, Melville shipped out of Fairhaven, Massachusetts, aboard the whaler *Acushnet*, headed for the South Seas—his second voyage. After eighteen months, Melville could no longer stand the hard life on the whaler, and in July 1842 he jumped ship in the Marquesas Islands with his friend Richard Tobias Greene. After a trek through the jungle, Melville found himself detained by the Taipis natives, with whom he lived for about a month; he later made use of this experience (with numerous borrowings and inventions) in his first novel, *Typee* (1846). After escaping from the Taipis, Melville succeeded in reaching and sailing off on an Australian whaler. He then worked for a time in Tahiti, studying the island life, later making use of his impressions in the novel *Omoo* (1847).

Of all the Polynesian Islands, the Marquesas and Tahiti, where Melville lived, are the very ones upon which the existence and toleration of homosexuality is openly discussed and documented in numerous early reports—sources known and referred to by Melville. In *Omoo*, Melville, in fact, specifically mentions in passing the "unnatural crimes" of the Tahitian prince Pomaree II, well known for his homosexuality (a homosexual reference, incidentally, missed by Newton Arvin in his Melville study).[39]

Melville's first novel, *Typee* (1846), based on his experience in and readings on the Marquesas, contains no unambiguous reference to homosexuality, but a striking portrait of Marnoo, a "Polynesian Apollo," painted in loving physical detail, is relevant to the study of male–male attraction.

The stranger could not have been more than twenty-five years of age, and was a little above the ordinary height; had he been a single hair's breadth taller, the matchless symmetry of his form would have been destroyed. His unclad limbs were beautifully formed; whilst the elegant outline of his figure, together with his beardless cheeks, might have entitled him to the distinction of standing for the statue of the Polynesian Apollo; and indeed the oval of his countenance and the regularity of every feature reminded me of an antique bust. But the marble repose of art was supplied by a warmth and liveliness of expression only to be seen in the South Sea Islander under the most favorable developments of nature. The hair of Marnoo was a rich curling brown, and twined about his temples and neck in little close curling ringlets, which danced up and down continually when he was animated in conversation. His cheek was of a feminine softness, and his face was free from the least blemish of tattooing, although the rest of his body was drawn all over with fanciful figures, which—unlike the unconnected sketching usual among these natives—appeared to have been executed in conformity with some general design. . . .

Struck by his demeanor, and the peculiarity of his appearance, so unlike that of the shaven-crowned and face-tattooed natives in general, I involuntarily rose as he entered the house, and proffered him a seat on the mats beside me. But without deigning to notice the civility, or even the more incontrovertible fact of my existence, the stranger passed on, utterly regardless of me, and flung himself upon the further end of the long couch that traversed the sole apartment of Marheyo's habitation.

Had the belle of the season, in the pride of her beauty and power, been cut in a place of public resort by some supercilious exquisite, she could not have felt greater indignation than I did at this unexpected slight.[40]

> When the narrator finally talks to "this all attractive personage," he learns that Marnoo possesses "taboo" status, allowing him to travel safely among otherwise hostile tribes. The narrator recalls that an individual receives "taboo" protection because of his special friendship with a member of another tribe.
>
> The novel *Omoo* (1847), based on Melville's experience of and reading about Tahiti, includes a chapter on "Friendships in Polynesia." The sailor narrator has just referred to the "troops of 'tayos' or friends, eager to form an alliance after the national custom, and do our slightest bidding":

The really curious way in which all the Polynesians are in the habit of making bosom friends at the shortest possible notice, is deserving of remark. Although, among a people like the Tahitians, vitiated as they are by sophisticating influences, this custom has in most cases degenerated into a mere mercenary relation, it nevertheless had its origin in a fine, and in some instances, heroic sentiment, formerly entertained by their fathers.

In the annals of the island are examples of extravagant friendships, unsurpassed by the story of Damon and Pythias: in truth, much more wonderful; for, notwithstanding the devotion—even of life in some cases—to which they led, they were frequently entertained at first sight for some stranger from another island.

The narrator describes a friendship with Poky, a native of a small island not far from Tahiti, where his vessel briefly docks:

Of course, among the simple-hearted natives, we had a friend all round. Mine was Poky, a handsome youth, who never could do enough for me. . . .

Though there was no end to Poky's attentions, not a syllable did he ever breathe of reward; but sometimes he looked very knowing. At last the day came for sailing, and with it, also, his canoe, loaded down to the gunwale with a sea stock of fruits. Giving him all I could spare from my chest, I went on deck to take my place at the windlass.

As the narrator's ship finally sails away, his last view is of this native:

Long as I could see him at all, there was Poky, standing alone and motionless in the bow of his canoe.[41]

Thus ends part one of Melville's Omoo.

Part two opens with a chapter entitled "We Take unto Ourselves Friends." Here the narrator depicts his less idyllic relation with a Tahitian named Kooloo.

Among others, Kooloo was a candidate for my friendship; and being a comely youth, quite a buck in his way, I accepted his overtures. By this, I escaped the importunities of the rest; for be it known, that, though little inclined to jealousy in love matters, the Tahitian will hear of no rivals in his friendship. . . .

The way this "tayo" of mine expressed his regard, was by assuring me over and over again, that the love he bore me was "nuee, nuee, nuee," or infinitesimally extensive. . . .

In the course of a few days, the sailors, like the doctor and myself, were cajoled out of every thing, and our "tayos," all round, began to cool off quite sensibly. So remiss did they become in their attentions, that we could no longer rely upon their bringing us the daily supply of food, which all of them had faithfully promised.

As for Kooloo, after sponging me well, he one morning played the part of a retrograde lover; informing me, that his affections had undergone a change; he had fallen in love at first sight with a smart sailor, who had just stepped ashore quite flush from a lucky whaling-cruise.

It was a touching interview, and with it, our connection dissolved. . . .[42]

In August 1843, Melville enlisted as a seaman on the frigate United States, later using this experience in writing White Jacket, or The World in a Man-of-War (1850). In chapter 89, "The Social State in a Man-of-War," Melville cites literary references to incest in allusion to shipboard homosexuality. Speaking of the "evils" associated with naval life and the close confinement of sailors, Melville says:

Like pears closely packed, the crowded crew mutually decay through close contact, and every plague-spot is contagious. Still more, from this same close confinement—so far as it affects the common sailors—arise other evils, so direful that they will hardly bear even so much as an allusion. What too many seamen are when ashore is very well known; but what some of them become when completely cut off from shore indulgences can hardly be imagined by landsmen. The sins for which the cities of the plain were overthrown still linger in some of these wooden-walled Gomorrahs of the deep. More than once complaints were made at the mast in the Neversink, from which the deck officer would turn away with loathing, refuse to hear them, and command the complainant out of his sight. There are evils in men-of-war, which, like the suppressed domestic drama of Horace Walpole, will neither bear representing, nor reading, and will hardly bear thinking of. The landsman who has neither read Walpole's *Mysterious Mother*, nor Sophocles's *Œdipus Tyrannus*, nor the Roman story of Count Cenci, dramatized by Shelley, let that landsman guardedly remain in his ignorance of even worse horrors than these, and forever abstain from seeking to draw aside this veil.[43]

It would be surprising if Melville did not experience some contact with homosexuality in the all-male environment of a sailing vessel. Although early documentation of same-sex relations aboard United States ships is scarce, known reports happen to date from the time of Melville's first years as a sailor. In 1839, the school ship *Columbus* is said by sailor Jacob Hazen to have been

a den where . . . every kind of sinful vice . . . are the continual order of the day; . . . where crimes abound of even so deep and black a dye that it fires the cheek with shame to name them.

The journal of sailor F. P. Torrey records that in January 1841 two men were discharged without trial from the ship *Ohio*, apparently for a homosexual offense. A United States government report for the years 1846–47 records at least five floggings for homosexual crimes on this nation's vessels; and an 1848 report lists one clearly homosexual offense.[44] Homosexuality on the high seas was probably much more common than these figures indicate; Melville's comments in *White Jacket* indicate that not all reported cases were prosecuted.

In 1847, Melville married Elizabeth Shaw and settled in New York City. The first book published after his wedding, *Mardi* (1849), celebrates bachelorhood, equates marriage with suicide, and pictures a close emotional relation between two males, Taji and Jari.[45]

After an 1849 trip to England and France, Melville moved with his family to Pittsfield, Massachusetts, forming an intimate friendship with Nathaniel Hawthorne, who lived nearby. Robert K. Martin has recently pointed out that Melville's anonymous review, in 1850, of Hawthorne's *Mosses from an Old Manse* reveals and expresses Melville's love for Hawthorne in extraordinarily erotic language: "A man of a deep and noble nature had seized me in this seclusion. . . . The soft ravishments of the man spun me round about in a web of dreams. . . . But already I feel that Hawthorne had dropped germinous seeds into my soul. He expands and deepens down, the more I contemplate him; and further and further, shoots his strong New-England roots into the hot soil in my Southern soul."[46] In 1851, Melville completed and published *Moby-Dick*, a work containing several classic, unusually evocative passages concerning male–male intimacy. In chapter 3 the hero, Ishmael, arrives late at night at the Spouter Inn in the seaport of New Bedford, Massachusetts.

I sought the landlord, and telling him I desired to be accommodated with a room, received for answer that his house was full—not a bed unoccupied. "But avast," he added, tapping his forehead, "you haint no objections to sharing a harpooneer's blanket, have ye? I s'pose you are goin' a whalin', so you'd better get used to that sort of thing."

I told him that I never liked to sleep two in a bed; that if I should ever do so, it would depend upon who the harpooneer might be, and that if he (the landlord) really had no other place for me, and the harpooneer was not decidedly objectionable, why rather than wander further about a strange town on so bitter a night, I would put up with the half of any decent man's blanket.[47]

> Ishmael has dinner and time passes, but the harpooner still has not returned, so Ishmael makes a plan concerning his sleeping arrangements.

No man prefers to sleep two in a bed. In fact, you would a good deal rather not sleep with your own brother. I don't know how it is, but people like to be private when they are sleeping. And when it comes to sleeping with an unknown stranger, in a strange inn, a strange town, and that stranger a harpooneer, then your objections indefinitely multiply. Nor was there any earthly reason why I as a sailor should sleep two in a bed, more than anybody else; for sailors no more sleep two in a bed at sea, than bachelor Kings do ashore. To be sure they all sleep together in one apartment, but you have your own hammock, and cover yourself with your own blanket, and sleep in your own skin.

The more I pondered over this harpooneer, the more I abominated the thought of sleeping with him. It was fair to presume that being a harpooneer, his linen or woollen, as the case might be, would not be of the tidiest, certainly none of the finest. I began to twitch all over. Besides, it was getting late, and any decent harpooneer ought to be home and going bed-wards. Suppose now, he should tumble in upon me at midnight—how could I tell from what vile hole he had been coming?

"Landlord! I've changed my mind about that harpooneer.—I shan't sleep with him. I'll try the bench here."[48]

> Finding he cannot sleep because of the cold drafts of air whirling about his makeshift bed, Ishmael decides to wait up for the harpooner, who by midnight has still not returned. Questioning the landlord further about the harpooner, Ishmael is told that he is out "peddling his head." Not understanding, Ishmael exasperatedly demands an explanation from the landlord.

"About this harpooneer, whom I have not yet seen, you persist in telling me the most mystifying and exasperating stories, tending to beget in me an uncomfortable feeling towards the man whom you design for my bedfellow—a sort of connexion, landlord, which is an intimate and confidential one in the highest degree. I now demand of you to speak out and tell me who and what this harpooneer is, and whether I shall be in all respects safe to spend the night with him. And in the first place, you will be so good as to unsay that story about selling his head, which if true I take to be good evidence that this harpooneer is stark mad, and I've no idea of sleeping with a madman; and you, sir, *you* I mean, landlord, *you*, sir, by trying to induce me to do so knowingly, would thereby render yourself liable to a criminal prosecution."[49]

The landlord relates that the harpooner has just arrived from the South Seas and is trying to sell a curio from that region, an embalmed and shrunken head. When Ishmael protests that this harpooner sounds dangerous, the landlord retorts simply, "He pays reg'lar," again urging Ishmael to accept the offered bed.

"But come, it's getting dreadful late, you had better be turning flukes—it's a nice bed: Sal and me slept in that ere bed the night we were spliced. There's plenty room for two to kick about in that bed; it's an almighty big bed that."[50]

Ishmael finally accepts the originally offered sleeping arrangement, strips, tumbles into bed, and falls asleep. He is awakened by the return of the harpooner, a fearsome-looking, tattooed South Seas Islander. After a great commotion when Ishmael and the native, Queequeg, discover each other, the hero finally resolves to accept his bedpartner, turns in for the night, and finds that he "never slept better in my life."

The next chapter begins:

Upon waking next morning about daylight, I found Queequeg's arm thrown over me in the most loving and affectionate manner. You had almost thought I had been his wife.

Ishmael has difficulty realizing it is Queequeg's tattooed arm that covers him.

It was only by the sense of weight and pressure that I could tell that Queequeg was hugging me.[51]

Ishmael feels strange at

waking up and seeing Queequeg's pagan arm thrown round me. But at length all the past night's events soberly recurred, one by one, in fixed reality, and then I lay only alive to the comical predicament. For though I tried to move his arm— unlock his bridegroom clasp—yet, sleeping as he was, he still hugged me tightly, as though naught but death should part us twain. I now strove to rouse him— "Queequeg!"—but his only answer was a snore.

Ishmael next discovers Queequeg's tomahawk in the bed.

A pretty pickle, truly, thought I; abed here in a strange house in the broad day, with a cannibal and a tomahawk! "Queequeg!—in the name of goodness, Queequeg, wake!" At length, by dint of much wriggling, and loud and incessant expostulations upon the unbecomingness of his hugging a fellow male in that matrimonial sort of style, I succeeded in extracting a grunt; and presently, he drew back his arm, shook himself all over like a Newfoundland dog just from the water, and sat up in bed, stiff as a pike-staff, looking at me.[52]

The events of the following day are reported in chapter 10, "A Bosom Friend." Ishmael observes Queequeg more closely as the two warm themselves by a fire, alone in the Spouter Inn, while a storm rages outside. Ishmael is struck by Queequeg's seeming

entirely at his ease; preserving the utmost severity; content with his own companionship; always equal to himself.[53]

Observing Queequeg, Ishmael begins

to be sensible of strange feelings. I felt a melting in me. No more my splintered heart and maddened hand were turned against the wolfish world. This soothing savage had redeemed it. There he sat, his very indifference speaking a nature in which there lurked no civilized hypocrisies and bland deceits. Wild he was; a very sight of sights to see; yet I began to feel myself mysteriously drawn towards him. And those same things that would have repelled most others, they were the very magnets that thus drew me. I'll try a pagan friend, thought I, since Christian kindness has proved but hollow courtesy. I drew my bench near him, and made some friendly signs and hints, doing my best to talk with him meanwhile. At first he little noticed these advances; but presently, upon my referring to his last night's hospitalities, he made out to ask me whether we were again to be bedfellows. I told him yes; whereat I thought he looked pleased, perhaps a little complimented.[54]

Ishmael and Queequeg continue to talk together, feeling a growing sense of fellowship. Ishmael then

proposed a social smoke; and [Queequeg], producing his pouch and tomahawk . . . , quietly offered me a puff. And then we sat exchanging puffs from that wild pipe of his, and keeping it regularly passing between us.

If there yet lurked any ice of indifference towards me in the Pagan's breast, this pleasant, genial smoke we had, soon thawed it out, and left us cronies. He seemed to take to me quite as naturally and unbiddenly as I to him; and when our smoke was over, he pressed his forehead against mine, clasped me round the waist, and said that henceforth we were married; meaning, in his country's phrase, that we were bosom friends; he would gladly die for me, if need should be. In a countryman, this sudden flame of friendship would have seemed far too premature, a thing to be much distrusted; but in this simple savage those old rules would not apply.

After supper, and another social chat and smoke, we went to our room together. He made me a present of his embalmed head; took out his enormous tobacco wallet, and groping under the tobacco, drew out some thirty dollars in silver; then spreading them on the table, and mechanically dividing them into two equal portions, pushed one of them towards me, and said it was mine. I was going to remonstrate; but he silenced me by pouring them into my trowsers' pockets. I let them stay.

As a "good Christian," Ishmael has doubts if he may "unite" with this pagan in his nightly religious ceremony, but conquering these qualms he finally joins Queequeg in his ritual.

That done, we undressed and went to bed, at peace with our own consciences and all the world. But we did not go to sleep without some little chat.

How it is I know not; but there is no place like a bed for confidential disclosures between friends. Man and wife, they say, there open the very bottom of their souls to each other; and some old couples often lie and chat over old times till nearly morning. Thus, then, in our hearts' honeymoon, lay I and Queequeg—a cosy, loving pair.

The next chapter adds:

We had lain thus in bed, chatting and napping at short intervals, and Queequeg now and then affectionately throwing his brown tattooed legs over mine, and then drawing them back; so entirely sociable and free and easy were we; when, at last, by reason of our confabulations, what little nappishness remained in us altogether departed, and we felt like getting up again, though daybreak was yet some way down the future.[55]

> "A Squeeze of the Hand," chapter 94 of *Moby-Dick*, is no doubt one of the most erotically suggestive scenes of male–male intimacy in American literature. A whale has been killed, brought to the side of Ishmael's ship, and the "cutting and hoisting operations" have begun, "even to the baling of the Heidelberg Tun or Case"—the upper part of the whale's head, forming a great vat of spermaceti, an oily substance used in making ointments, etc. Narrator Ishmael relates that while some sailors aboard the *Pequod* were employed with this baling,

others were employed in dragging away the larger tubs, so soon as filled with the sperm; and when the proper time arrived, this same sperm was carefully manipulated ere going to the try-works, of which anon.

It had cooled and crystallized to such a degree, that when, with several others, I sat down before a large Constantine's bath of it, I found it strangely concreted into lumps, here and there rolling about in the liquid part. It was our business to squeeze these lumps back into fluid. A sweet and unctuous duty! No wonder that in old times this sperm was such a favorite cosmetic. Such a clearer! such a sweetener! such a softener! such a delicious mollifier! After having my hands in it for only a few minutes, my fingers felt like eels, and began, as it were, to serpentine and spiralize.

As I sat there at my ease, cross-legged on the deck; after the bitter exertion at the windlass; under a blue tranquil sky; the ship under indolent sail, and gliding so serenely along; as I bathed my hands among those soft, gentle globules of infiltrated tissues, woven almost within the hour; as they richly broke to my fingers, and discharged all their opulence, like fully ripe grapes their wine; as I snuffed up that uncontaminated aroma,—literally and truly, like the smell of spring violets; I declare to you, that for the time I lived as in a musky meadow; I forgot all about our horrible oath; in that inexpressible sperm, I washed my hands and my heart of it; I almost began to credit the old Paracelsan superstition that sperm is of rare virtue in allaying the heat of anger: while bathing in that bath, I felt divinely free from all ill-will, or petulance, or malice, of any sort whatsoever.

Squeeze! squeeze! squeeze! all the morning long; I squeezed that sperm till I myself almost melted into it; I squeezed that sperm till a strange sort of insanity came over me; and I found myself unwittingly squeezing my co-laborers' hands in it, mistaking their hands for the gentle globules. Such an abounding, affectionate, friendly, loving feeling did this avocation beget; that at last I was continually squeezing their hands, and looking up into their eyes sentimentally; as much as to say,—Oh! my dear fellow beings, why should we longer cherish any social acerbities, or know the slightest ill-humor or envy! Come; let us squeeze hands all round; nay, let us all squeeze ourselves into each other; let us squeeze ourselves universally into the very milk and sperm of kindness.

Would that I could keep squeezing that sperm for ever! For now, since by many prolonged, repeated experiences, I have perceived that in all cases man must eventually lower, or at least shift, his conceit of attainable felicity; not placing it anywhere in the intellect or the fancy; but in the wife, the heart, the bed, the table, the saddle, the fire-side, the country; now that I have perceived all this, I am ready to squeeze case eternally. In visions of the night, I saw long rows of angels in paradise, each with his hands in a jar of spermaceti.[56]

Melville dedicated *Moby-Dick* to Nathaniel Hawthorne and sent his friend a copy; Hawthorne replied with a letter of praise. Melville's answer describes his feelings upon receiving Hawthorne's "joy giving and exhultation breeding letter."

I felt pantheistic then—your heart beat in my ribs and mine in yours, and both in God's. A sense of unspeakable security is in me this moment, on account of your having understood the book. I have written a wicked book, and feel spotless as the lamb. Ineffable socialties are in me. I would sit down and dine with you and all the gods in old Rome's Pantheon. It is a strange feeling—no hopefulness is in it, no despair. Content—that is it; and irresponsibility; but without licentious inclination. I speak now of my profoundest sense of being, not of an incidental feeling.

Whence come you, Hawthorne? By what right do you drink from my flagon of life? And when I put it to my lips—lo, they are yours and not mine. I feel that the Godhead is broken up like the bread at the Supper, and that we are the pieces. Hence this infinite fraternity of feeling.

Turning the page and changing moods, Melville continues:

My dear Hawthorne, the atmospheric skepticisms steal into me now, and make me doubtful of my sanity in writing you thus. But, believe me, I am not mad . . . ! But truth is ever incoherent, and when the big hearts strike together, the concussion is a little stunning. . . . Ah! it's a long stage, and no inn in sight, and night coming, and the body cold. But with you for a passenger, I am content and can be happy. I shall leave the world, I feel, with more satisfaction for having come to know you. Knowing you persuades me more than the Bible of our immortality.[57]

Melville signed only his first name, the one occasion in his letters, except those to his family, in which he did so.

In *White Jacket*, Melville had cited literary references of incest in allusion to "even worse horrors"—shipboard homosexuality. But while homosexuality might only be alluded to, Melville could defy puritanical reactions by publishing a romance (for a female audience) in which incest is the explicit theme. In *Pierre or The Ambiguities* (1852), the words *incest* and *incestuous* at one point appear four times in four consecutive sentences—Melville thus insuring that readers understood his theme. The novel suggests incestuous closeness in Pierre's relations with his mother; his fiancée, Lucy Tartan, is referred to as "little sister"; the mysterious Isabel, who attracts and finally marries Pierre, may be his half-sister. Moreover, hints of homosexual incest color Pierre's early relationship with his cousin, Glen Stanly. As the narrator describes it:

In their boyhood and earlier adolescence, Pierre and Glen had cherished a much more than cousinly attachment. At the age of ten, they had furnished an example of the truth, that the friendship of fine-hearted, generous boys, nurtured amid the romance-engendering comforts and elegancies of life, sometimes transcends the bounds of mere boyishness, and revels for a while in the empyrean of a love which only comes short, by one degree, of the sweetest sentiment entertained between the sexes. Nor is this boy-love without the occasional fillips and spicinesses, which at times, by an apparent abatement, enhance the permanent delights of those more advanced lovers who love beneath the cestus of Venus. Jealousies are felt. The sight of another lad too much consorting with the boy's beloved object, shall fill him with emotions akin to those of Othello's; a fancied slight, or lessening of the every-day indications of warm feelings, shall prompt him to bitter upbraidings and reproaches; or shall plunge him into evil moods, for which grim solitude only is congenial.

Nor are the letters of Aphroditean devotees more charged with headlong vows and protestations, more cross-written and crammed with discursive sentimentalities, more undeviating in their semi-weekliness, or dayliness, as the case may be, than are the love-friendship missives of boys. Among those bundles of papers which Pierre, in an ill hour, so frantically destroyed in the chamber of the inn, were two large packages of letters, densely written, and in many cases inscribed crosswise throughout with red ink upon black; so that the love in those letters was two layers deep, and one pen and one pigment were insufficient to paint it. The first package contained the letters of Glen to Pierre, the other those of Pierre to Glen, which, just prior to Glen's departure for Europe, Pierre had obtained from him, in order to re-read them in his absence, and so fortify himself the more in his affection, by reviving reference to the young, ardent hours of its earliest manifestations.[58]

> Pierre has long fantasized that, "prior to his own special devotion to Lucy, the splendid Glen had not been entirely insensible to her surprising charms." Two males, first in love with each other, later conforming to society's heterosexual norm to the extent of falling in love with the same woman: a classic paradigm of sorts, suggestive of those relations complicating the life of Henry David Thoreau; a situation that, in Melville's Gothic melodrama, ends in grand tragedy. That Pierre's story has more than casual autobiographical significance is indicated by the remarkable fact that when Melville's son Stanwix was born, while he was working intensely on *Pierre*, on the birth certificate Melville wrote his own name and that of his mother (not his wife) as parents of the new child.[59]
>
> In 1856–57, Melville made a tour of Palestine, Italy, and England, visited Hawthorne in Liverpool, and brought back to America a reproduction of Guido Reni's picture of *Beatrice Cenci*, lover-slayer of her father, as well as a lifelong memory of a sculpture of Antinoüs, the adolescent lover of the Roman Emperor Hadrian. Melville described this sculpture as "head like moss-rose with curls and buds—rest all simplicity." Melville returned to America with (in Leslie Fiedler's words) "an icon of incest justified and of homosexuality glorified."[60]
>
> After his return from Europe, Melville did not see Hawthorne again; the two had become estranged. Soon after Hawthorne's death on May 19, 1864, Melville wrote the first stanza of "Monody," a poetic lament for their lost and soured intimacy.

To have known him, to have loved him
After loneness long;
And then to be estranged in life,
And neither in the wrong;
And now for death to set his seal—
Ease me, a little ease, my song![61]

Written about 1871, Melville's "After the Pleasure Party" is a poem whose difficult allusions to Platonic sexual myth, Sapphic legend, and homosexuality have been analyzed in a provocative essay by Walter Sutton.[62] The poem tells of a "pleasure party"—an outing at an Italian villa—at which "Urania," after years of study and sexual sublimation, is suddenly struck with passionate love for a young man who is busy eyeing other, younger females. The aging Urania is a "plain old bramble"; her love is unrequited. But she is now disillusioned with her previous ascetic life; she is torn by new feelings: jealous of those whom her beloved finds attractive, shame at her doting love, and despair at the idea that her yearning will never be fulfilled. Rejecting Christianity and celibacy, she turns to art to raise herself above "the sexual feud." Melville warns at the end that this solution is futile, for (he seems to say) when love is frustrated it turns to anger, and this anger turns against the self.

According to Sutton, in this poem Melville

> employs the apparently feminine central character, Urania, as an indirect means of expressing a feeling toward the male companion of the poem which is actually homosexual in nature.

"Indications of bisexuality in Melville's work," says Sutton,

> long noted by critics, are now recognized as evidence of a basic conflict in the author's personality. Melville's most recent biographer, Newton Arvin, refers to this conflict as "the central fact behind his work."

While Sutton suggests that the poem's themes of concealed homosexuality and sexual repression have biographical significance, he stresses "the probably impossible feat of relating the poem to a specific incident in Melville's life." He emphasizes that the difficulty of this and other of Melville's works arises from "the necessity of [his] dealing indirectly . . . with subjects which were socially unacceptable." Sutton states that this poem's subject is not merely the effect of frustrated love on character, but the specific effect of "frustrated bisexual love," especially on the creative work of an artist.[63]

In his long poem *Clarel*, published in (1876), Melville, who had earlier, in the usual fashion, equated homosexuality with the sins of Sodom and Gomorrah, now has the character "Mortmain" argue quite differently. The evil citizens who brought destruction on the biblical cities of the plain, he says, were

> Guilty of sins scarce scored as crimes
> In any statute known, or code—
> Nor now, nor in the former times:
> Things hard to prove: decorum's wile,
> Malice discreet, judicious guile. . . .
> And hate which under life's fair hue
> Prowls like the shark in sunned Pacific blue.
> ". . . 'Twas not all carnal harlotry,
> But sins refined, crimes of the spirit. . . .[64]

Melville's *Clarel* also includes an intimate scene between the title character and "Vine," a figure based on Nathaniel Hawthorne. While on a pilgrimage through

Palestine, Clarel one day sees the "pure," "virginal," unworldly Vine alone in a glade and joins him. Although "prior advances" by Clarel had gone "unreturned" by Vine, Clarel still "yearned" then for "communion true / and close," fervently wishing Vine would "let go each alien theme" of his speech and "Give me thyself!" But Vine rambles on, not suspecting "Clarel's thrill / Of personal longing. . . ." Vine talks theology while Clarel tries to follow, his "divided mind" and "heart's desire" interfering with his comprehension. Clarel thinks how pleasant such talk would be if it followed "confidings that should wed / Our souls in one; —Ah, call me *brother!*" Clarel's "passionate mood" is "so feminine," and his long "hungering unfed" caused him to reject any relation except that which will fulfill his desperate desire for intimacy.

Clarel lets fall "some inklings" of his mood, which provoke in Vine "a change— / A shadow." Vine's darkening face is taken by Clarel as a rebuke. Clarel wonders if Vine's reaction means that his fond "dream of love" of "man toward man—the soul's caress—" is impossible of realization? This inference stings Clarel until, "glancing up, unwarned," he sees "the serious softness" of Vine's eyes fixed upon him, then sees these eyes shyly withdraw. "Enslaver," Clarel silently accuses Vine, would you "fool me / With bitter-sweet, sly sorcery . . . ?" Then, answering himself, Clarel denies the legitimacy of his feelings for Vine, labeling them "sick."[65] The mood is broken, the moment for intimacy has passed. Clarel's yearning for Vine remains unfulfilled, as did, apparently, Melville's for Hawthorne.

Melville's story-poem "John Marr" (1888) vividly evokes the feelings of a lonely, aging sailor who "passionately yearns" for the now-lost fraternity once known to him at sea. This "kinless man," says Melville, "had affections which once placed, not readily could be dislodged or resigned to a substitute object." John Marr's present neighbors are "staid," "ascetic," "narrowly religious," and unfamiliar with "the companionship afloat of the sailors." In his isolation, Marr dreams of his old shipmates, and he imagines they dream of him.

> I yearn as ye. But rafts that strain,
> Parted, shall they lock again?
> Twined we were, entwined, then riven,
> Ever to new embracements driven,
> Shifting gulf-weed of the main! . . .
>
> Nor less, as now, in eve's decline,
> Your shadowy fellowship is mine.
> Ye float around me, form and feature:—
> Tattooings, ear-rings, love-locks curled;
> Barbarians of man's simpler nature,
> Unworldly servers of the world.
> Yea, present all, and dear to me,
> Though shades, or scouring China's seas. . . .
>
> . . . But to clasp, retain;
> To see you at the halyards main—
> To hear your chorus once again![66]

In 1891, three months before his death, Melville completed *Billy Budd, Sailor,*

"Dedicated to Jack Chase/ Englishman/ Wherever that great heart may now be." Melville had served with Chase forty-eight years earlier on the frigate *United States*, and Chase's name had appeared in 1850 as that of the "Handsome Sailor" of *White Jacket*.

Billy Budd is replete with themes and passages relevant to male–male intimacy; the whole story may be seen as a study of types of male love—explicit, implicit, conscious, unconscious, open, and suppressed—against the background of a puritanical society.

The first paragraph in *Billy Budd* introduces the archetype Melville calls the "Handsome Sailor": that extraordinary, striking male whose regal presence combines strength, beauty, and virtue, and who is the object of adoration from his fellows. Billy Budd is such a Handsome Sailor.

The captain of the merchant ship from which Billy is "impressed" into service in His Majesty's navy bemoans the loss of his "best man," Billy Budd.

"Before I shipped that young fellow, my forecastle was a rat-pit of quarrels. . . . But Billy came; and it was like a Catholic priest striking peace in an Irish shindy. . . . a virtue went out of him, sugaring the sour ones. They took to him like hornets to treacle."

Except for one called Red Whiskers, all the sailors loved Billy. " 'Out of envy, perhaps,' " Red Whiskers tried to pick a fight with the Handsome Sailor. After Billy gave him " 'a terrible drubbing,' " even he also came to love the Handsome Sailor:

"But they all love him. Some of 'em do his washing, darn his old trousers for him; the carpenter is at odd times making a pretty little chest of drawers for him. Anybody will do anything for Billy Budd. . . . Ay, Lieutenant, you are going to take away the jewel of 'em; you are going to take away my peacemaker!"

"And," adds Melville, "with that the good soul had really ado in checking a rising sob."[67]

"As the Handsome Sailor," Billy's position aboard his new ship, the *Bellipotent*,

was something analogous to that of a rustic beauty transplanted from the provinces and brought into competition with the highborn dames of the court. But this change of circumstances he scarce noted. As little did he observe that something about him provoked an ambiguous smile in one or two harder faces among the bluejackets. Nor less unaware was he of the peculiar favorable effect his person and demeanor had upon the more intelligent gentlemen of the quarter-deck.[68]

The narrator describes the complex love-hate for Billy that develops in the heart of the ship's master-of-arms, John Claggart. Smiling at Billy, calling him a "sweet and pleasant young fellow," joking equivocally about his handsomeness while simultaneously being "down" on Billy and secretly conspiring to injure him, Claggart is as antagonistic to Billy Budd as he is attracted. Melville indicates it was Billy's "significant personal beauty" that "had first moved" Claggart against him. That Claggart's is no simple homosexual attraction Melville also makes clear; evil, such as his, partakes "nothing of the sordid or sensual"—"Claggart's was no vulgar form of passion." Claggart envies Billy, and for more than his beauty; he envies

Billy's lack of malice, his innocence of that hate which possesses Claggart's own spirit.[69] This attraction-repulsion is detailed in a suggestive passage.

When Claggart's unobserved glance happened to light on belted Billy rolling along the upper gun deck in the leisure of the second dogwatch, exchanging passing broadsides of fun with other young promenaders in the crowd, that glance would follow the cheerful sea Hyperion with a settled meditative and melancholy expression, his eyes strangely suffused with incipient feverish tears. Then would Claggart look like the man of sorrows. Yes, and sometimes the melancholy expression would have in it a touch of soft yearning, as if Claggart could even have loved Billy but for fate and ban. But this was an evanescence, and quickly repented of, as it were, by an immitigable look, pinching and shriveling the visage into the momentary semblance of a wrinked walnut.

Upon "any abrupt unforseen encounter with Billy" says the narrator, "a red light would flash forth" from Claggart's eye

like a spark from an anvil. . . . That quick, fierce light was a strange one, darted from orbs which in repose were of a color nearest approaching a deeper violet, the softest of shades.[70]

While Melville suggests that Claggart's malice is "a depravity of nature," innate to him, this malice seems clearly the result of a suppressed and distorted attraction; his temperament is a product not of homosexuality but of puritanical repression. The captain of the *Bellipotent*, Edward Fairfax Vere, also notices Billy Budd.

Now the Handsome Sailor as a signal figure among the crew had naturally enough attracted the captain's attention from the first. Though in general not very demonstrative to his officers, he had congratulated Lieutenant Ratcliffe upon his good fortune in lighting on such a fine specimen of the *genus homo*, who in the nude might have posed for a statue of young Adam before the Fall.[71]

A love relationship of a kind arises between Captain Vere and Billy. After Billy had inadvertently killed Claggart and been condemned to death, Vere goes to Billy's compartment to inform him privately of the sentence. What happens during that interview Melville does not describe. He hints however that

Captain Vere in end may have developed the passion sometimes latent under an exterior stoical or indifferent. He was old enough to have been Billy's father. The austere devotee of military duty, letting himself melt back into what remains primeval in our formalized humanity, may in end have caught Billy to his heart, even as Abraham may have caught young Isaac. . . . But there is no telling the sacrament . . . wherever . . . two of great Nature's nobler order embrace.[72]

Billy Budd may be read as a story of love between men—of love blighted and love affirmed, even though at the moment of death. It was in thus affirming the goodness of male–male love that Melville brought his own life's work to a close.

1838–57: HENRY DAVID THOREAU;
"I have glimpses of a serene friendship-land"

Henry David Thoreau, born in 1817 in Concord, Massachusetts, lived most of his life in that town. Thoreau entered Harvard in 1833, at age sixteen, and in 1837 began to keep a journal which he continued until his death. These journals include numerous entries on Thoreau's close, complex, and often problematic relations with other men: his older brother, John; the young Edmund Sewall; his mentor and fellow Concordian, Ralph Waldo Emerson; the poet William Ellery Channing; and Harrison G. O. Blake of Worcester. Among other males to whom Thoreau refers are Alex Therien, a group of anonymous railroad workers, and Walt Whitman. In these journals, and in his poetry and essays, Thoreau often explores and tries to sum up the meaning and quality of his intimate interactions with men—that special love-friendship which is a recurrent theme of his writing. The following selections focus on this theme of same-sex intimacy, an experience shaped by the pressure of a repressive New England puritanism.[73]

Thoreau writes his journals to seek some universal meaning in his particular experience; the entries do not attempt to record the details of his everyday life but to generalize and speculate about its significance. Thoreau's abstraction from the particular to the universal has the effect of coding and mystifying his journals, concealing the specific character of that experience which originally gave rise to them; this experience must frequently be reconstructed by reference to the external events of Thoreau's life, documented in other sources. Here, also, certain speculative interpretations must necessarily be made to elucidate otherwise ambiguous passages.

Thoreau's earliest writings suggest that his young manhood included some intense experience of loving. No female sweetheart is known, and it would not have been unusual if Thoreau had found one special friend among his Harvard schoolmates— as did Emerson, Higginson, and Henry Ward Beecher in their college days.[74] During the summer of 1837, Thoreau did live for a time with a Harvard friend, the classical scholar Charles Stearns Wheeler, in a little hut near Flint's Pond, Lincoln, New Hampshire.[75] Although the object of his affection has not been identified, the twenty-one-year-old Thoreau rhapsodized in a poem written in the following spring about the joy and importance of loving.

Friendship

April 8 [1838].

> I think awhile of Love, and, while I think,
>   Love is to me a world,
>   Sole meat and sweetest drink,
>   And close connecting link
>   'Tween heaven and earth.

. . . .

I fain would ask my friend how it can be,
But, when the time arrives,
Then Love is more lovely
Than anything to me,
And so I'm dumb.

For, if the truth were known, Love cannot speak,
But only thinks and does;
Though surely out 't will leak
Without the help of Greek,
Or any tongue.

Thoreau stresses what "power there is in love":

When under kindred shape, like loves and hates
And a kindred nature,
Proclaim us to be mates,
Exposed to equal fates
Eternally; . . .

While one and one make two,
And two are one.

In the two closing and most deeply felt stanzas, Thoreau describes the two lovers.

Two sturdy oaks I mean, which side by side
Withstand the winter's storm,
And, spite of wind and tide,
Grow up the meadow's pride,
For both are strong.

Above they barely touch, but, undermined
Down to their deepest source,
Admiring you shall find
Their roots are intertwined
Insep'rably.[76]

This poem presents a number of themes which recur in Thoreau's writings. Love-friendship, a typical Thoreauvian-transcendental equation, is of immense importance, being a kind of nourishment for the soul. The "friend" whose advice he seeks is of ambiguous gender, an ambiguity characteristic of Thoreau's style. However, the "kindred shapes" of the two "mates" suggests two males, as does the "two sturdy oaks" metaphor. The "Greek" reference may well be an allusion to that classical male–male love of which Thoreau later explicitly writes. The Greek reference is also possibly a pun referring to the interests of Thoreau's friend, Charles Stearns Wheeler, a classical scholar. This love "cannot speak," a phrasing which curiously anticipates Alfred Douglas's famous "love that dare not speak its name." This is a secret love—above ground the narrator and his lover barely seem to touch, but underground their roots are "intertwined insep'rably." This intertwining, the romantic "two are one" concept, suggests that merging, symbiotic love which re-appears in Thoreau's life and writings.

On June 17, 1839, eleven-year-old Edmund Sewall of Scituate visited Concord for a week. After five days of sailing and hiking with Edmund, the twenty-two-year-old Thoreau fell in love with him, writing in his journal:

Rencounter

June 22. Saturday. I have within the last few days come into contact with a pure, uncompromising spirit, that is somewhere wandering in the atmosphere, but settles not positively anywhere. . . . Such [spirits] it is impossible not to love; still is their loveliness, as it were, independent of them, so that you seem not to lose it when they are absent, for when they are near it is like an invisible presence which attends you.[77]

Two days later, after Edmund's departure, Thoreau writes a love poem.

Sympathy

June 24 [1839].

Lately, alas, I knew a gentle boy,
Whose features all were cast in Virtue's mould,
As one she had designed for Beauty's toy,
But after manned him for her own stronghold.

. . . .

So was I taken unawares by this,
I quite forgot my homage to confess;
Yet now am forced to know, though hard it is,
I might have loved him, had I loved him less.

Each moment, as we nearer drew to each,
A stern respect withheld us farther yet,
So that we seemed beyond each other's reach,
And less acquainted than when first we met.

We two were one while we did sympathize,
So could we not the simplest bargain drive;
And what avails it now that we are wise,
If absence doth this doubleness contrive?

Eternity may not the chance repeat,
But I must tread my single way alone,
In sad remembrance that we once did meet,
And know that bliss irrevocably gone.

. . . .

If I but love that virtue which he is,
Though it be scented in the morning air,
Still shall we be truest acquaintances,
Nor mortals know a sympathy more rare.[78]

Despite this poem's unambiguous masculine pronoun and the undisputed fact of Edmund's recent visit, "Sympathy" was long said by Thoreau's friends and biographers to refer to Edmund's sister Ellen, who visited Concord the following month. This heterosexualizing is now discounted. It is interesting to note that Edmund's parents knew of and even delighted in Thoreau's poetic elegy to their son. Ironically, the sexually innocent nineteenth-century consciousness made possible an expression and acceptance of male–male love which twentieth-century homophobic America would consider suspect.

The seventeen-year-old Ellen Sewall arrived in Concord for a two-week stay on July 20, 1839.[79] Henry Thoreau and his older brother, John, both liked Ellen and had met her on numerous previous occasions. Henry Thoreau's alleged romantic feelings for Ellen Sewall would become a legend; his love for Edmund Sewall would remain undiscussed.

Toward the end of July, Thoreau writes in his journal:

July 25 [1839]. There is no remedy for love but to love more.[80]

The line echoes and answers that line in the poem about Edmund Sewall: "I might have loved him, had I loved him less." Thoreau, it seems, now thought the remedy for his attraction to Edmund was "loving more." This "more" is ambiguous; Thoreau may have been thinking of loving Edmund "more," or of loving Ellen as well as her brother, or of loving others—or of all these possibilities.

Ellen Sewall returned home on August 3, 1839. John Thoreau, apparently intent on wooing, sent her a gift. During the first half of September, the Thoreau brothers made a thirteen-day trip on the Concord and Merrimack rivers; that fall when they returned, John Thoreau went immediately to visit Ellen Sewall. Her five-year-old brother George was entertained by John's stories but kept calling him "Henry," a significant confusion of identities others would also later make.[81] That same fall, while John Thoreau was wooing Ellen, Henry Thoreau was writing in his journal quite unambiguously and sensuously about young males:

[Nov. 5, 1839]
These young buds of manhood in the streets are like buttercups in the meadows, —surrendered to nature as they.

Nov. 7. I was not aware till to-day of a rising and risen generation. Children appear to me as raw as the fresh fungi on a fence rail. By what degrees of consanguinity is this succulent and rank-growing slip of manhood related to me?[82]

Later that same fall, Thoreau wrote about "true friendship" between men—many lines of which echo his poem about Edmund.

Friendship

Fall of 1839. Then first I conceive of a true friendship, when some rare specimen of manhood presents itself. It seems the mission of such to commend virtue to mankind, not by any imperfect preaching of her word, but by their own carriage and conduct. We may then worship moral beauty without the formality of a religion.

They are some fresher wind that blows, some new fragrance that breathes. They make the landscape and the sky for us.

The rules of other intercourse are all inapplicable to this. . . .

I am only introduced once again to myself.

Conversation, contact, familiarity are the steps to it and instruments of it, but it is most perfect when these are done, and distance and time oppose no barrier. . . .

Commonly we degrade Love and Friendship by presenting them under the aspect of a trivial dualism. . . .

But alas! to be actually separated from that parcel of heaven we call our friend, with the suspicion that we shall no more meet in nature, is source enough for all the elegies that ever were written. But the true remedy will be to recover our friend again piecemeal, wherever we can find a feature, as Æetes gathered up the members of his son, which Medea had strewn in her path.

The more complete our sympathy, the more our senses are struck dumb, and we are repressed by a delicate respect, so that to indifferent eyes we are least his friend, because no vulgar symbols pass between us. On after thought, perhaps, we come to fear that we have been the losers by such seeming indifference, but in truth that which withholds us is the bond between us.[83]

> At Christmas 1839, Henry and John Thoreau joined their aunt Prudence Ward for a visit to the Sewalls in Scituate. Upon returning home, Henry Thoreau sent Mr. Sewall a book of poems, and John Thoreau sent gifts to Ellen, Edmund, and George. Henry Thoreau then sent Ellen some of his own poems—for which Ellen in her next letter forgot to thank him.[84] At that time, however, Henry Thoreau's mind was on other things—specifically that famous Greek "community" of male "friends."

Friends

Jan. 26 [1840]. They are like air bubbles on water, hastening to flow together.

History tells of Orestes and Pylades, Damon and Pythias, but why should not we put to shame those old reserved worthies by a community of such?

Constantly, as it were through a remote skylight, I have glimpses of a serene friendship-land, and know the better why brooks murmur and violets grow. . . .

This conjunction of souls, like waves which meet and break, subsides also backward over things, and gives all a fresh aspect.

I would live henceforth with some gentle soul such a life as may be conceived, double for variety, single for harmony,—two, only that we might admire at our oneness,—one, because indivisible. Such community to be a pledge of holy living. How could aught unworthy be admitted into our society?[85]

A few days later, he continues:

Jan. 29. [1840]. A friend in history looks like some premature soul. The nearest approach to a community of love in these days is like the distant breaking of waves on the seashore. An ocean there must be, for it washes our beach.

This alone do all men sail for, trade for, plow for, preach for, fight for.[86]

The following month, Thoreau continues to think of "romantic" attractions between friends, and of biblical and Greek love of several varieties.

Feb. 18 [1840]. All romance is grounded on friendship. What is this rural, this pastoral, this poetical life but its invention? Does not the moon shine for Endymion? Smooth pastures and mild airs are for some Corydon and Phyllis. Paradise belongs to Adam and Eve. Plato's republic is governed by Platonic love.[87]

The following month, Edmund Sewall was enrolled by his parents in the school run by John and Henry Thoreau and came to live with the Thoreau family in Concord. That month, Thoreau writes rather cryptically in his journal:

March 20 [1840]. . . .
Love never degrades its votaries, but lifts them up to higher walks of being. They *over-look* one another. . . .
We will have no vulgar Cupid for a go-between, to make us the playthings of each other, but rather cultivate an irreconcilable hatred instead of this.[88]

Three months later, Ellen Sewall again visited Concord, and Thoreau took her for a boat ride, recording in his journal:

June 19 [1840]. The other day I rowed in my boat a free, even lovely young lady, and, as I plied the oars, she sat in the stern, and there was nothing but she between me and the sky. So might all our lives be picturesque if they were free enough, but mean relations and prejudices intervene to shut out the sky, and we never see a man as simple and distinct as the man-weathercock on a steeple.[89]

Although this entry has been cited as evidence of Thoreau's romance with Ellen Sewall, it is open to quite a different interpretation. Thoreau's feeling of freedom with Ellen seems to have evoked in him the wish that all his social intercourse might remain as unclouded by "mean relations and prejudices"—very possibly a reference to his problematic feelings for Edmund.

Eight days later, Thoreau was again writing about an intense, complex relationship with a venerated male friend.

[June 27, 1840]. . . .
Our friend's is as holy a shrine as any God's, to be approached with sacred love and awe. Veneration is the measure of Love. . . .

In no presence are we so susceptible to shame. Our hour is a sabbath, our abode a temple, our gifts peace offerings, our conversation a communion, our silence a prayer.[90]

Two days after this, Thoreau complains of his lack of success in relating to even one (male) friend.

June 29 [1840]. Of all phenomena, my own race are the most mysterious and undiscoverable. For how many years have I striven to meet one, even on common manly ground, and have not succeeded![91]

In July 1840, John Thoreau proposed to Ellen Sewall and she rejected him.[92] In the fall of 1840, if Henry Thoreau was feeling romantic about Ellen (as his biographers allege), his *Journal* entries do *not* show it. He was, on the contrary, thinking specifically of his "love" for an unambiguously male "friend."

Saturday   Oct. 17th 1840.

In the presence of my friend I am ashamed of my fingers and toes. I have no feature so fair as my love for him. There is a more than maiden modesty between us. I find myself more simple and sincere than in my most private moment to myself. I am literally true *with a witness*.

We would sooner blot out the sun than disturb friendship.[93]

The following two days, Henry Thoreau writes cryptically about a "secret" kept hidden behind closed doors—closeted. In elliptical language, Thoreau speaks of his intense, complex relation with a male.

Sunday   Oct. 18th 1840. . . .

I cannot make a disclosure—you should see my secret.—Let me open my doors never so wide, still within and behind them, where it is unopened, does the sun rise and set—and day and night alternate.—No fruit will ripen on the common.

Monday   Oct. 19th 1840.

My friend dwells in the distant horizon as rich as an eastern city there. There he sails all lonely under the edge of the sky, but thoughts go out silently from me and belay him, till at length he rides in my roadsted. But never does he fairly come to anchor in my harbor. Perhaps I afford no good anchorage. He seems to move in a burnished atmosphere, while I peer in upon him from surrounding spaces of Cimmerian darkness. His house is incandescent to my eye, while I have no house, but only a neighborhood to his.

Tuesday   Oct. 20th 1840.

My friend is the apology for my life. In him are the spaces which my orbit traverses.[94]

In early November 1840, Henry Thoreau reportedly wrote to Ellen Sewall asking her to marry him; his letter has been destroyed, but it is suggested that his journal entry of November 1 contains a partial rough draft.

Nov. 1st 1840.

The day is won by the blushes of the dawn.

I thought that the sun of our love should have risen as noiselessly as the sun out of the sea, and we sailors have found ourselves steering between the tropics as if the broad day had lasted forever.[95]

Two days before Ellen wrote her reply rejecting Thoreau's proposal, a poem in Thoreau's journal shows he was "conscience stricken" and disturbed. Continuing the day-love metaphor of the November 1 entry, Thoreau's poem of November 7 concludes:

> I did not think so bright a day
> Would issue in so dark a night,
> I did not think such sober play
> Would leave me in so sad a plight,
> And I should be most sorely spent
> When first I was most innocent.
>
> I thought by loving all beside
> To prove to you my love was wide,
> And by the rites I soared above
> To show you my peculiar love.[96]

Although Thoreau's disturbance has been interpreted as arising from an anticipated rejection to his proposal to Ellen, it may well have quite different origins. Possibly, Thoreau had earlier decided the "remedy" for loving Edmund was to love his sister. He had therefore proposed to Ellen, hoping by that act to "prove" that he did not love Edmund alone. Not surprisingly, this convoluted and confused psychic strategem failed; Thoreau's proposal to Ellen did not make his love "wider," and Thoreau came to regret the proposal itself. He did not feel that love for Ellen he thought the act of proposing might evoke in him. Ellen Sewall solved Thoreau's difficulty by rejecting his proposal.

Two months later, Thoreau recovered some of his serenity and felt other attractions of a definitely bisexual character.

Jan. 1st 1840.

All men and women woo me. There is a fragrance in their breath.[97]

And a month later he is again musing quite happily about a male.

[Feb. 9, 1841.]

My life at this moment is like a summer morning when birds are singing. . . . My friend thinks I *keep* silence, who am only choked with letting it out so fast. Does he forget that new mines of secrecy are constantly opening in me?[98]

Two weeks later he writes:

Feb. 22 [1841]. Love is the tenderest mood of that which is tough—and the toughest mood of that which is tender. It may be roughly handled as the nettle, or gently as the violet. It has its holidays, but is not made for them. . . .

Friends will be much apart; they will respect more each other's privacy than their communion. . . .

We have to go into retirement religiously, and enhance our meeting by rarity and a degree of unfamiliarity. Would you know why I see thee so seldom, my friend? In solitude I have been making up a packet for thee.[99]

He concludes a few days later:

[Feb. 26, 1841.]

If my world is not sufficient without thee, my friend, I will wait till it is and then call thee. You shall come to a palace, not to an almshouse.[100]

Three days later, Thoreau writes about himself, emphasizing the importance of that love which is the basis of his sense of self. His seeing himself in the lichens growing on rocks is psychologically suggestive: these plants consist of fungi in symbiotic union with algae. Thoreau's love involves a symbiotic merging with his loved ones.

[Dec. 15, 1841]

I seem to see somewhat more of my own kith and kin in the lichens on the rocks than in any books. It does seem as if mine were a peculiarly wild nature, which so yearns toward all wildness. I know of no redeeming qualities in me but a sincere love for some things, and when I am reproved I have to fall back on to this ground. This is my argument in reserve for all cases. My love is invulnerable. Meet me on that ground, and you will find me strong. When I am condemned, and condemn myself utterly, I think straightway, "But I rely on my love for some things." Therein I am whole and entire. Therein I am God-propped.[101]

Less than a month later, on January 11, 1842, John Thoreau died a painful death from tetanus—in his brother's arms. On January 22, Henry Thoreau appeared to be seriously ill with all the symptoms of his brother's disease; in a few days, however, he began gradually to recover, although he remained weak and depressed for months. For several years thereafter, Henry is said to have had "tragic dreams" on the anniversary of John's death. For the rest of his life he reacted with extreme emotion to any mention of his brother's death.[102] Henry's sympathetic illness appears to have paralleled his sympathetic love, first for Edmund Sewall, then for Ellen Sewall, the object of his brother's affection. In retrospect, Henry's love for Ellen seems just as unreal as his illness. These symbiotic attachments point to a complex web of human relations and feelings in which Henry's incestuous, homosexual love and rivalry with his brother were a key element. Puritanical repression led to a confused tangle of human passions.

In the spring of 1845, Thoreau began, in an impossible-to-read, virtually coded handwriting, a curious and confused essay on sexual relations, evidence that this subject was much, and quite consciously, on his mind.[103]

A few months after composing his sex essay, on Independence Day, 1845, shortly before his twenty-ninth birthday, Thoreau moved to his famous cabin at Walden

Pond, not far from Concord. Just ten days later, Thoreau describes meeting five railroad workers, one of whom makes a special impression. Later that same day, Thoreau has his first meeting with the colorful Alex Therien. The passage about Therien appears first:

[July 14, 1845] . . .
Who should come to my lodge just now but a true Homeric boor, one of those Paphlagonian men? Alek Therien, he called himself; a Canadian now, a wood-chopper, a post-maker; makes fifty posts—holes them, *i.e.*—in a day; and who made his last supper on a woodchuck which his dog caught. And he too has heard of Homer. . . . And now I must read to him, while he holds the book, Achilles' reproof of Patroclus on his sad countenance.

"Why are you in tears, Patroclus, like a young child (girl)?" etc. etc. . . .

He has a neat bundle of white oak bark under his arm for a sick man, gathered this Sunday morning. "I suppose there's no harm in going after such a thing to-day." The simple man. May the gods send him many woodchucks.

And earlier to-day came five Lestrigones, railroad men who take care of the road, some of them at least. They still represent the bodies of men, transmitting arms and legs and bowels downward from those remote days to more remote. They have some got a rude wisdom withal, thanks to their dear experience. And one with them, a handsome younger man, a sailor-like, Greek-like man, says: "Sir, I like your notions. I think I shall live so myself. Only I should like a wilder country, where there is more game. I have been among the Indians near Appalachicola. I have lived with them. I like your kind of life. Good day. I wish you success and happiness."[104]

In 1852, for several months, Thoreau's *Journals* refer to the subject of sex.[105] Journal entries beginning on March 4 refer to a friend, generally agreed to have been William Ellery Channing, who irked Thoreau by relating sexual jokes.[106] Although there is a definite note of puritanism in Thoreau's comments, especially on first reading, his comments also suggest an opposite and contradictory feeling—a reaction against those involuted puritans who, because of their own fundamental disgust at sex, reduced it by joking to the level of their own originally negative perception. The April 12, 1852, entry reads:

I lose my respect for the man who can make the mystery of sex the subject of a coarse jest, yet, when you speak earnestly and seriously on the subject, is silent. I feel that this is to be truly irreligious. . . . What were life without some religion of this kind? Can I walk with one who by his jests and by his habitual tone reduces the life of men and women to a level with that of cats and dogs? The man who uses such a vulgar jest describes his relation to his dearest friend. Impure as I am, I could protest and worship purity.[107]

Two months later, Thoreau comments on the physical beauty of the naked bodies of boys whom, at a distance, he has watched swimming.

[June 12, 1852.]
Boys are bathing at Hubbard's Bend, playing with a boat (I at the willows). The color of their bodies in the sun at a distance is pleasing, the not often seen

flesh-color. I hear the sound of their sport borne over the water. As yet we have not man in nature. What a singular fact for an angel visitant to this earth to carry back in his note-book, that men were forbidden to expose their bodies under the severest penalties! A pale pink, which the sun would soon tan. White men! There are no white men to contrast with the red and the black; they are of such colors as the weaver gives them. I wonder that the dog knows his master when he goes in to bathe and does not stay by his clothes.[108]

> On October 16, 1856, Thoreau was shocked to discover a fungus of unmistakably male and erotic shape. He took it home, observed and described it in detail, even drew a sketch of it—all the while clucking his tongue over what he felt to be nature's pornographic creation. When Thoreau's journal was published in 1906, its editors suppressed this particular sketch (see page 492). On October 16 Thoreau writes of finding

a rare and remarkable fungus, such as I have heard of but never seen before. The whole height six and three quarters inches. . . . It may be divided into three parts, pileus, stem, and base,—or scrotum, for it is a perfect phallus. One of those fungi named *impudicus*, I think. In all respects a most disgusting object, yet very suggestive. . . . It was as offensive to the eye as to the scent, the cap rapidly melting and defiling what it touched with a fetid, olivaceous, semiliquid matter. In an hour or two the plant scented the whole house wherever placed, so that it could not be endured. I was afraid to sleep in my chamber where it had lain until the room had been well ventilated. It smelled like a dead rat in the ceiling, in all the ceilings of the house. Pray, what was Nature thinking of when she made this? She almost puts herself on a level with those who draw in privies.[109]

> In November, 1856, just one month after his unsettling encounter with the phallic fungus, Thoreau, who was in the New York area, first encountered in the flesh that poet-singer of the phallus, Walt Whitman. Accompanied by Bronson Alcott and Sarah Tyndale, Thoreau made a morning visit to Whitman's Brooklyn home. There in the poet's bedroom, to which Whitman led his visitors, amidst a great confusion of bedclothes, books, and a chamber pot, with unframed pictures of Hercules, Bacchus, and a satyr looking on, Thoreau met the bard whose *Leaves of Grass* (1855) he had already read. Alcott's journal reports that Thoreau and Whitman were both reserved, looking "like beasts, each wondering what the other might do, whether to snap or run." Each seemed to be thinking about his opposite: "Well, you're almost as great as I am!"[110]
>
> A few days after this encounter, on November 19, 1856, Thoreau wrote to his friend H. G. O. Blake about Whitman. Both he and Alcott, says Thoreau,

were much interested and provoked. He is apparently the greatest democrat the world has seen. Kings and aristocracy go by the board at once, as they have long deserved to. A remarkably strong though coarse nature, of a sweet disposition, and much prized by his friends. . . . I am still somewhat in a quandary about him,— feel that he is essentially strange to me, at any rate; but I am surprised by the sight of him. He is very broad, but, as I have said, not fine. He said that I misapprehended him. I am not quite sure that I do.[111]

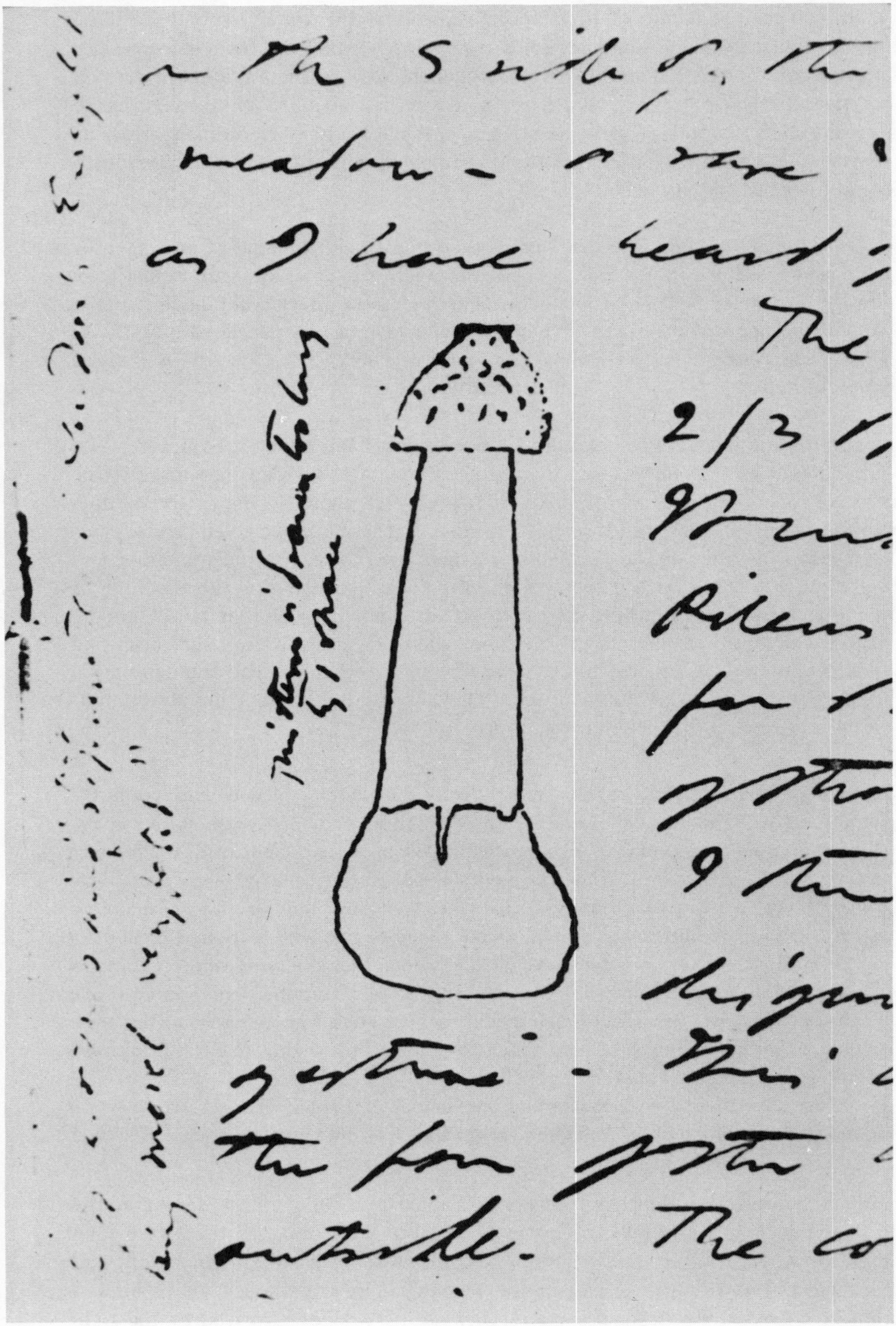

If Thoreau felt Whitman to be "essentially strange," it was certainly a sad failure of communication: the two had much in common. That they could not speak intimately and openly is poignant evidence of that very repression which each in his own way opposed.

Twelve days later, back in Concord, Thoreau confides to his diary about a current love affair.

[Dec. 1, 1856]. . . .
I love and could embrace the shrub oak with its scanty garment of leaves rising above the snow, lowly whispering to me. . . . Rigid as iron, clean as the atmosphere, hardy as virtue, innocent and sweet as a maiden is the shrub oak. In proportion as I know and love it, I am natural and sound as a partridge. I felt a positive yearning toward one bush this afternoon. There was a match found for me at last. I fell in love with a shrub oak.[112]

A few days later, Thoreau again writes Blake about Whitman, troubled by the poet's affirmation of sensuality.

Dec. 7 [1856]
That Walt Whitman, of whom I wrote to you, is the most interesting fact to me at present. I have just read his 2nd edition (which he gave me) and it has done me more good than any reading for a long time. . . . There are 2 or 3 pieces in the book which are disagreeable to say the least, simply sensual. He does not celebrate love at all. It is as if the beasts spoke. I think that men have not been ashamed of themselves without reason. No doubt, there have always been dens where such deeds were unblushingly recited, and it is no merit to compete with their inhabitants. But even on this side, he has spoken more truth than any American or modern that I know. I have found his poem exhilirating encouraging. As for its sensuality,—& it may turn out to be less sensual than it appeared—I do not so much wish that those parts were not written, as that men & women were so pure that they could read them without harm, that is, without understanding them. One woman told me that no woman could read it as if a man could read what a woman could not. Of course Walt Whitman can communicate to us no experience, and if we are shocked, whose experience is it that we are reminded of? . . .

We ought to rejoice greatly in him. He occasionally suggests something a little more than human. You cant confound him with the other inhabitants of Brooklyn or New York. . . . How they must shudder when they read him! He is awefully [*sic*] good.

Leaves of Grass, says Thoreau, "is a great primitive poem,—an alarum or trumpet-note ringing through the American camp." He adds:

I did not get far in conversation with him,—two more being present,—and among the few things which I chanced to say, I remember that one was, in answer to him as representing America, that I did not think much of America or of politics, and so on, which may have been somewhat of a damper to him.

Thoreau concludes that Whitman "is a great fellow."[113]

Two months later, Thoreau is still thinking about sensuality, justifying his own now ascetic life:

[Feb. 7, 1857.]

Chastity is perpetual acquaintance with the All. . . . You think that I am impoverishing myself by withdrawing from men, but in my solitude I have woven for myself a silken web or *chrysalis*, and, nymph-like, shall ere long burst forth a more perfect creature, fitted for a higher society.[114]

♀ 1839–46: SARAH EDGARTON and
LUELLA J. B. CASE;
"You are kissing away the venom of some angry hornet from my lips"

The correspondence of Sarah Edgarton and Luella Case began in 1839, when Case was contacted by Edgarton for a contribution to the Universalist Church annual publication, *The Rose of Sharon*, which she edited. The letters between Edgarton in Shirely, Massachusetts, and Case in Lowell quickly transcended the two women's literary and religious concerns, documenting an ardent, loving friendship, filled with vague yearnings for an even greater intimacy. The Edgarton–Case correspondence was researched and analyzed by William R. Taylor and Christopher Lasch in an essay from which the women's letters have been excerpted and arranged chronologically.[115]

Sarah Edgarton, the daughter of a manufacturer and the tenth of fifteen children, was educated at home, as was the custom of the day. Born in 1819, she was twenty when this correspondence begins. Luella Case was several years older than Edgarton and married to Eliphalet Case, who had earlier abandoned a career as a Methodist revivalist preacher for his wife's more rationalistic, humanitarian Universalism. He finally left preaching altogether for a career in journalism and various business speculations which eventually ruined him. Both Luella Case and Sarah Edgarton were active in the Universalist Church and were aspiring writers; neither was satisfied with the traditional female role of wife and mother.

In an early letter of Case to Edgarton, the subject is ideal (female) friendship. On October 18, 1839, Case writes that for her "an association with cultivated minds of differing orders of intellect" combined with "a friendly feeling" is "something to be prized above all else." She apparently did not consider the possibility of establishing such an association with her husband. Case writes Edgarton:

Life is short, and kindred spirits are few, the chances of their meeting are fewer still, and poor human nature has so many jarring strings, that, after all, friendship is something more to be worshipped as an ideal good, than a real, and possible thing, something that *may be*, rather than something that *is*.[116]

Three months later, on January 8, 1840, Sarah Edgarton shared with Luella Case her many "falterings and doubts" about her writing. She did not want to be great, she wanted to do good, she said. Detailing her dream of their working together on *The Rose*, Edgarton asked Case to become her assistant editor.

Will you accept? How I would like it and how light would be the labor thus shared! Come to me when the flowers and birds are come, and we will dwell with them in greenwood bowers—and our papers and books shall be with us and we will read and talk, and form plans and be the happiest editorial wood-nymphs that ever watched over the flowers and *our* flower, the dear little "Rose", shall be the sweetest and purest that ever blest a dryad's care, and we will—Oh, dear, why should I sketch so bright a picture? Can it ever be a copy from nature—a scene from history—*our* history, my beloved friend? Would, indeed, that it might be, but life is for the most part made up of darker views, and *perhaps* higher pursuits. Nevertheless, I cannot but often dream of hours like these—they seem so soft, and sweet, and unalloyed—so like a fairy life, in which, invisible dwellers in Nature's holy sanctuaries, we should quietly work unseen blessings for the race of man, and bless ourselves in our deeds. You see how *self* predominates in these dreams, how I would draw you from all your domestic ties, and make you a very girl with myself. I am very foolish, I know—a perfect *natural*, for in my baby-days I had the same wild fantasies floating in my brain, and the same dreamy desires for gipsy freedom. I would be one of Diana's maids of honor, and if it be true that she condescended to kiss Endymion, who knows but she would allow me to love some shepherd—pastoral or divine? Pardon me, I will cease.[117]

Case's reply of February 2, 1840, encourages her friend's literary efforts, and says that were it not for her domestic commitments,

so much should I like your vocation, and its duties, with all your prospects of success, that . . . I should forthwith take in good earnest your jesting hint about being assistant "editor", and jump on board your barque, content to let the wind that would fill your sails, carry along my humble self, down the unreturning current.

Case adds, in the language of phrenology, the popular pseudoscience of personality:

A nice couple of voyagers we would make, with my *destructiveness*, of which I have plenty, and to spare, to offset your *benevolence*, and *adhesiveness*, of which you might lend me occasionally from your superabundance. We would brush away all the noisy mosquitoes with our handkerchiefs, and, if now and then, a wasp exhibited his disposition to break the peace of our commonwealth, we would give him such a blow as would teach him better manners for the future.[118]

Edgarton writes back:

If we could live and work together, if you would guide the "barque," and let me merely dip the oars; if you would suffer me to brush away the musquitoes [*sic*] that vex your ears, while you are kissing away the venom of some angry hornet from my lips, why, then, I should be ever very happy, let what evils would assail us. But can we ever be voyagers thus together?[119]

On February 23, 1840, Case humbly justifies her own inclusion in such an editorial partnership by reminding herself that it requires more than genius to "reform the age." Case also admits she writes not only to do good, but "for a more selfish reason, 'pour me amuser' [to please me]."[120]

On August 7, 1840, Case writes to Edgarton of her acquaintance with "a most delightful, fascinating woman," a Mrs. Sawyer of Boston, with whom she "fell quite in love"—"or my admiration would take that name, were I a gentleman." Case says of Sawyer: "She is as graceful and interesting as her own beautiful German translations."

On April 26, 1841, Case writes of another woman, twenty years older than herself, now deceased, whose friendship she had most cherished in her girlhood.

She was gentle, and refined, and spiritual in every impulse, and though . . . believing a sterner faith than she knew mine to be, I cannot recall one word, or look, that does not fall softly, and pleasantly on my recollection. To her society, I owe much of the cultivation of those tastes, and the power of living within myself that after experience has found so valuable.[121]

A few months later, in July 1841, Case again writes praising "a sweet flower"—a woman Edgarton would be sure to admire

for her beauty, and for the true womanly character of her mind—so pure, and so full of all the holy, domestic affections.[122]

On December 15, 1842, Case writes of falling "half in love" with a woman, Sheba Smith, whom she has not met, but whose novel, *Western Captive,* she has read. Case imagines that Smith "must have a beautiful soul."[123]

In 1844, Sarah Edgarton became engaged, at age twenty-five, to a divinity student of twenty, A. D. Mayo. On March 26, 1844, Case responds to Edgarton's announcement of marriage plans in a less than ecstatic manner.

And so you are engaged, are you Sarah? Well, I am much flattered by your confidence in the matter, and thus far, though *sorely tempted,* have told no individual being of it, not even my liege lord himself. . . .

From your description, I like your lover very much, and do not wonder you have been taken "captive, hand and heart" . . . I like the name of your intended— like all you say of him, but I wish he were a little *older,* dear Sarah. Do not mistake me—I am not foolish enough to think a year or two of seniority on the lady's part can have any influence on married happiness, but young gentlemen of twenty rarely have the character fixed, and are sometimes addicted to inconstancy, especially if of an ideal and loving temperament. But there may be traits of the heart and mind that can over-balance the temptations of youth.

She adds:

Your last letter gratified me very much, and so far from being disposed "to laugh at your childishness," I was much interested in the minutiae of your description, and half inclined to fall in love with him myself. Dont be frightened. Falling-in-love-days are all over with me *now,* besides, I have plenty else to do. . . . It would be a beautiful and blessed thing if we could keep the freshness, and glory of our youthful feelings all along our journey to the grave—even to its verge—but it may not be. Life has its autumn as well as its spring, and we look to *immortality* alone for the unsealing of the frozen fountains and the awaking of the perished flowers.[124]

Edgarton's marriage brought her friendship with Case to an abrupt end. Only a few brief surviving letters were written after Edgarton's announced engagement. Two years later, in 1846, Case left her husband and moved back to her girlhood home, Kingston, New Hampshire, where she spent the last ten years of her life. In 1848, Sarah Edgarton died at age twenty-nine.[125]

In 1963, William R. Taylor and Christopher Lasch analyzed the friendship of Edgarton and Case against the background of the family and female–female relations in New England (1839–46). The authors emphasize that as female writers Edgarton and Case represent a group of American women who, in the 1830s and '40s, being discontented with the traditional female role, aspired to a literary life. Taylor and Lasch "doubt that the restlessness of [these] American women was nothing more than the slave's determination to be free," discounting the existence of women's oppression as sufficient explanation for the dissatisfaction and literary aspirations of such women.[126]

Taylor and Lasch write that the impulse that drove even rather "ordinary" women such as Edgarton and Case into writing was

an ideal of the literary life—an ideal of pure friendship between women, based on a shared sensitivity.

What Edgarton and Case sought in literature was

companionship, and their most eloquent flights—expressed in the amorous language which was the characteristic style of feminine friendship in the nineteenth century—were addressed not to the muse but to each other.

Edgarton and Case's correspondence make it clear, say Taylor and Lasch,

that the work of "reforming the world" was not at bottom what concerned these women. The importance of reform . . . lay rather in the fact that it furnished the setting for a friendship which had very little to do with reform—a friendship founded, in fact, on a very different ideal, the dream of "gipsy freedom."[127]

Comparing the intimacy of Edgarton and Case to that portrayed by Henry James in *The Bostonians* (1885), Taylor and Lasch argue that to attach the label "Lesbian" to such a relation, as some critics have done,

does violence to its subtlety and complexity, if only because such labels—at least as they are ordinarily used—carry with them the suggestion of perversity and abnormality, the suggestion that when one uses them one is describing a "case". . . . Our point . . . is that in such a society as nineteenth century America the kind of behavior we are concerned with here may have been normal rather than perverse.[128]

While Taylor and Lasch's analysis is persuasive, two important qualifications may be made. They are mistaken if their denial of "perversity and abnormality" is taken as a denial of any erotic component in the "normal" female friendships they are analyzing. Sensuality, for instance, becomes overt in Edgarton's fantasy about her friend "kissing away the venom of some angry [male!] hornet from my lips," but it exists just under the surface in much of their correspondence. To be sure, the nineteenth-century ideal of female friendship included no conscious sexuality, but the deep, loving feelings engendered in such passionate attachments certainly did include an important erotic element.

Taylor and Lasch are also mistaken, it seems, in so radically separating the oppression of women, their rebellion against the traditional female role, and the desire for intimate intercourse with other women; all three factors are linked in a most important and mutually reinforcing way. Taylor and Lasch discount a feminist reaction to women's oppression as a source of the female impulse toward sisterhood; they suggest that the social conditions fostering close female attachments have less to do with the oppression of women than with the fact that church and family no longer provided women with affectionate, understanding contacts. The dispersal and migration of the population, they argue, had caused a breakdown of the tightly knit family, which had earlier provided women with "a community of sympathy and understanding." Therefore Edgarton and Case

turned to the sorority as their model of the ideal society—the sisterhood of sensibility.

For the same reasons, Taylor and Lasch suggest that

men, in the same period, turned to the Masons or immigrants to their national and fraternal orders—as an alternative to emotional anarchy.[129]

But why, ask Taylor and Lasch, did the ideal of sorority or fraternity come to exclude members of the opposite sex?

The answer seems to lie in the myth of the purity of women, so deeply cherished by the nineteenth century.

The myth of the sanctity of women, of motherhood and of the home, was an attempt to hold together not only the family, but a whole society "on the verge of chaos." But, say Taylor and Lasch, the cult of women and the Home contained contradictions that tended to undermine the very things they were supposed to safeguard. Implicit in the myth was a repudiation not only of heterosexuality but of domesticity itself. It was her purity, contrasted with coarseness of men, that made woman the head of the Home (though not of the family) and the guardian of public morality. But that same purity made intercourse between men and women at last almost literally impossible and drove women to retreat almost exclusively into the society of their own sex, to abandon the very Home which it was their appointed mission to preserve.[130]

1862–63: WALT WHITMAN;
New York–Brooklyn–Washington diary

Among the as yet unpublished Whitman manuscripts in the Library of Congress are two notebook diaries of 1862–63 in which the poet lists the names of men he met while traveling about New York City, Brooklyn, and Washington, D.C. In four cases, Whitman adds that he "slept with" the males named. By itself the phrase "slept with" is ambiguous. But even if it is interpreted in its most limited, least controversial sense, the poet's practice of meeting, taking home, and simply bedding down for the night with male strangers is curious behavior—and certainly of special interest to the historical study of male–male relations and to homosexual history in particular. In the context of all the other evidence of Whitman's homoerotic feelings and associations, the most reasonable interpretation is that his "slept with" is a euphemism for sexual relations. These diaries provide evidence of a previously obscured aspect of Whitman's relations with men; they throw new light on the origins of those homoerotic lyrics which are among the world's greatest love poetry and those writings which deeply influenced the early English homosexual emancipation pioneers. Because Whitman's poetry of male–male intimacy and his love letters to Peter Doyle are more readily available, his little-known diaries will represent him here.

It is relevant to inquire why, among the voluminous detailed published works about Whitman, only the introduction to one minor collection of his erotic poetry so much as mentions the existence of these revealing and suggestive diary entries.[131] Although he examined these diaries, Gay Wilson Allen, in his major biography of Whitman, emphasizes that "only a few details of Whitman's life during the fall of 1862 have survived."[132] While this is the period covered by the diaries in question, Whitman's sleeping with male pickups is not mentioned by Allen. Although the debate about Whitman's sexual orientation and about its implications for his writings has been quietly under way since the late 1800s, this intimate diary evidence has never been placed before the public. Perhaps future research will establish whether the failure to mention the content of these diaries has been a matter of conscious suppression or unconscious repression.

In analyzing and establishing the exact meaning of these entries, the very fact that Whitman records his "sleeping with" a male indicates that it had some special, more than casual significance he wishes to recall. On October 11, 1862, when

Whitman met David Wilson near Middaugh Street in Brooklyn—and "slept with" him—he had not simply offered a homeless young man a place to stay for the night. Wilson had his own place; Whitman notes that Wilson lives on Hampden Street.

These diaries also contain other homosexually suggestive details. Whitman describes Daniel Spencer as "somewhat feminine." Frederick Goodall is "in dry goods"; the dry goods salesman or "counter-jumper" of 1860 was looked down upon as effeminate.[133] Also, although it may have been more common in the 1860s than today for persons of the same gender to sleep together for practical reasons, the ordinariness of such arrangements does not mean that their sexual possibilities were not often acted upon. The early literature on masturbation, in fact, warns against the "dangers" of two girls or two boys sleeping in one bed; a resulting form of homosexuality, characteristic of the time, was perceived as, and labeled, "mutual masturbation."[134]

In the summer of 1862, when these diary entries begin, the forty-three-year-old Whitman was living with his family on Portland Avenue in Brooklyn. The relevant entries of 1862 refer to Brooklyn or New York.[135]

Dan'l Spencer (Spencer, pere, 214 44th st. & 59 William somewhat feminine—5th av (44) May 29th)—told me he had never been in a fight and did not drink at all gone in 2d NY Lt Artillery deserted, returned to it   slept with me Sept. 3d[.][136]

+Theodore M Carr—Deserted Capt. Dawson's Co. C Monitors Co. C Col Conks 139th Reg. N.Y. Vol—met Fort Greene forenoon Aug. 28—and came to the house with me—is from Greenville Greene County 15 miles from Coxsacki left Sept. 11th '62[.][137]

Peter Calhoun, Oct. 10 '62 aged 23, born in Rome, N.Y. worked on canal 3 years—his affair with the woman in Brooklyn and N.Y.—my ride with him a trip or more at night—40 5th av has one brother younger, larger, works on the river—Pete told me of his taking the $100 from home—also of David Helpers care of him when he had the bad disorder[.]

David Wilson night of Oct. 11, '62 walking up from Middagh—slept with me—works in a blacksmith shop in Navy Yard—lives in Hampden st.—walks together Sunday afternoon & night—is about 19[.][138]

Horace Ostrander Oct. 22 '62 24 4th av. from Otsego co. 60 miles west of Albany was in the hospital to see Chas. Green about 28 y'rs of age—about 1855 went on voyage to Liverpool—his experiences as a green hand (Nov. 22 4th av.) slept with him Dec. 4 '62. Frederick Goodall, English, in the dry goods (was the man that told me I was at a "social" in 27th st.)[139]

Jerry Taylor [Oct. 9, 1863; Washington, D.C.], N.J. of 2d dist. reg't slept with me last night[.][140]

1867–1909: CHARLES WARREN STODDARD;
"South Sea Idyl"
"I must get among people who are not afraid of their instincts"

Charles Warren Stoddard was born in Rochester, New York, in 1843. His father was a manufacturer and later a broker who, in 1855, moved with his family to San Francisco. In 1857, Charles Stoddard returned East to attend an academy in Western New York, then rejoined his family in California. He worked in a bookstore, had his first poem published anonymously in 1861, and began to contribute verse regularly to the *Golden Era*, a periodical which also published Samuel Clemens and Bret Harte. In the fall of 1864, Stoddard, in poor health, traveled for the first time to the Hawaiian islands. Returning to San Francisco, Stoddard continued to write and in 1867 saw his poems published in a volume edited by Bret Harte. That same year he is said to have converted to Catholicism. Also that year, on February 8, the twenty-four-year-old Stoddard sent his first letter to Walt Whitman, beseeching him for an autograph.[141]

From Honolulu, Hawaii, Stoddard wrote to Whitman for the second time on March 2, 1869. Years later, Whitman and his friend-secretary Horace Traubel, going through Whitman's papers, came upon Stoddard's letter:

To Walt Whitman.

May I quote you a couplet from your Leaves of Grass? "Stranger! if you, passing, meet me, and desire to speak to me, why should you not speak to me? And why should I not speak to you?"

I am the stranger who, passing, desires to speak to you. Once before I have done so offering you a few feeble verses. I don't wonder you did not reply to them. Now my voice is stronger. I ask—why will you not speak to me?

So fortunate as to be travelling in these very interesting Islands I have done wonders in my intercourse with these natives. For the first time I act as my nature prompts me. It would not answer in America, as a general principle,—not even in California, where men are tolerably bold. This is my mode of life.

At dusk I reach some village—a few grass huts by the sea or in some valley. The native villagers gather about me, for strangers are not common in these parts. I observe them closely. Superb looking, many of them. Fine heads, glorious eyes that question, observe and then trust or distrust with an infallible instinct. Proud, defiant lips, a matchless physique, grace and freedom in every motion.

I mark one, a lad of eighteen or twenty years, who is regarding me. I call him to me, ask his name, giving mine in return. He speaks it over and over, manipulating my body unconsciously, as it were, with bountiful and unconstrained love. I go to his grass house, eat with him his simple food, sleep with him upon his mats, and at night sometimes waken to find him watching me with earnest, patient looks, his arm over my breast and around me. In the morning he hates to have me go. I hate as much to leave him. Over and over I think of him as I travel: he doubtless recalls me sometimes, perhaps wishes me back with him. We were known to one another perhaps twelve hours. Yet I cannot forget him. Everything that pertains to him now interests me.

You will easily imagine, my dear sir, how delightful I find this life. I read your Poems with a new spirit, to understand them as few may be able to. And I wish more than ever that I might possess a few lines from your pen. I want your personal magnetism to quicken mine. How else shall I have it? Do write me a few lines for they will be of immense value to me.

I wish it were possible to get your photograph. The small lithograph I have of you is not wholly satisfactory. But I would not ask so much of you. Only a page with your name and mine as you write it. Is this too much?

My address is San Francisco, Calif., Box 1005, P. O. I shall immediately return there. In all places I am the same to you.

Chas. Warren Stoddard.

Traubel adds:

W. had written a reply to S.—very short, only a few words. I read this also to W. The two letters had been pinned together. W. said: "He is right: occidental people, for the most part, would not only not understand but would likewise condemn the sort of thing about which Stoddard centers his letter." I read what W. said in reply:[142]

Washington, / June 12, 1869.

Charles W. Stoddard, Dear Sir:

Your letters have reached me. I cordially accept your appreciation, & reciprocate your friendship. I do not write many letters, but like to meet people. Those tender & primitive personal relations away off there in the Pacific Islands, as described by you, touched me deeply.

In answer to your request, I send you my picture—it was taken three months since. I also send a newspaper.

Farewell, my friend, I sincerely thank you, & hope some day to meet you.

Walt Whitman[143]

Traubel reports:

W. said: "It's wonderful how true it is that a man can't go anywhere without taking himself along and without finding love meeting him more than half way. It gives you a new intimation of the providences to become the subject of such an ingratiating hospitality: it makes the big world littler—it knits all the fragments together: it makes the little world bigger—it expands the arc of comradery."[144]

In September 1869, Stoddard's "A South Sea Idyl" was published in San Francisco in *The Overland Monthly*, edited by Bret Harte. In 1962, a Whitman scholar referred to the "thinly veiled homosexual overtones" of the "Idyl," whose narrator describes his relations with a sixteen-year-old native named Kana-ana.[145] In the context of Stoddard's letters to Whitman, the homosexuality of the "Idyl" seems scarcely veiled at all.

At the start of his "Idyl," Stoddard introduces the Doctor, a moralistic, puritanical white man whose disapproving countenance always looks "savage"—and the narrator, who, in contrast to the Doctor recommends to the reader:

It is best to be careful how you begin to moralize too early: you deprive yourself of a great deal of fun in that way. If you want to do any thing particularly, I should advise you to do it, and then be sufficiently sorry to make it all square.[146]

This narrator tells his story, set in an unspecified South Seas locale:

I'm not so sure that I was wrong, after all. Fate, or the Doctor, or something else, brought me first to this loveliest of valleys, so shut out from every thing but itself, that there were no temptations which might not be satisfied. Well! here, as I was looking about at the singular loveliness of the place—you know this was my first glimpse of it . . . right in the midst of all this, before I had been ten minutes in the valley, I saw a straw hat, bound with wreaths of fern and *maile;* under it a snow-white garment, rather short all around, low in the neck, and with no sleeves whatever.

There was no sex to that garment; it was the spontaneous offspring of a scant material and a large necessity. I'd seen plenty of that sort of thing, but never upon a model like this, so entirely tropical—almost Oriental. As this singular phenomenon made directly for me, and having come within reach, there stopped and stayed, I asked its name, using one of my seven stock phrases for the purpose; I found it was called Kana-ana. Down it went into my note-book; for I knew I was to have an experience with this young scion of a race of chiefs. Sure enough, I have had it. He continued to regard me steadily, without embarrassment. He seated himself before me; I felt myself at the mercy of one whose calm analysis was questioning every motive of my soul. This sage inquirer was, perhaps, sixteen years old. His eye was so earnest and so honest, I could return his look. I saw a round, full, rather girlish face; lips ripe and expressive—not quite so sensual as those of most of his race; not a bad nose, by any means; eyes perfectly glorious— regular almonds—with the mythical lashes "that sweep," etc., etc. The smile which presently transfigured his face was of that nature that flatters you into submission against your will.

Having weighed me in his balance—and you may be sure his instincts didn't cheat him (they don't do that sort of thing)—he placed his two hands on my two knees, and declared, "I was his best friend, as he was mine; I must come at once to his house, and there live always with him." What could I do but go? He pointed me to his lodge, across the river, saying, "There was his home, and mine."[147]

After this first brief, romantic meeting with Kana-ana, the narrator leaves with the Doctor for a week, but secretly promises to stop with the young islander on his return trip.

How many times I thought of him through the week! I was always wondering if he still thought of me. I had found those natives to be impulsive, demonstrative, and, I feared, inconstant. Yet why should he forget me, having so little to remember in his idle life, while I could still think of him, and put aside a hundred pleasant memories for his sake? . . .

That was rather a slow week for me, but it ended finally; and just at sunset, on the day appointed, the Doctor and I found ourselves back on the edge of the valley. . . . I let the Doctor ride ahead of me . . . and it was quite in the twilight when I heard the approach of a swift horseman. I turned, and at that moment there was a collision of two constitutions that were just fitted for one another; and all the doubts and apprehensions of the week just over were indignantly dismissed, for Kana-ana and I were one and inseparable, which was perfectly satisfactory to both parties!

The plot, which had been thickening all the week, culminated then, much to the disgust of the Doctor, who had kept his watchful eye upon me all these days—to my advantage, as he supposed. There was no disguising our project any longer, so I out with it as mildly as possible. "There was a dear fellow here," I said, "who loved me, and wanted me to live with him; all his people wanted me to stop, also: his mother and his grandmother had specially desired it. They didn't care for money; they had much love for me, and therefore implored me to stay a little. Then the valley was most beautiful; I was tired; after our hard riding, I needed rest: his mother and his grandmother assured me that I needed rest. Now, why not let me rest here awhile?"

The Doctor looked very grave. I knew that he misunderstood me—placed a wrong interpretation upon my motives; the worse for him, I say. He tried to talk me over to the paths of virtue and propriety; but I wouldn't be talked over. Then the final blast was blown: war was declared at once. The Doctor never spoke again, but to abuse me; and off he rode in high dudgeon, and the sun kept going down on his wrath. Thereupon I renounced all the follies of this world, actually hating civilization—feeling entirely above the formalities of society. I resolved on the spot to be a barbarian, and, perhaps, dwell forever and ever in this secluded spot. . . . So Kana-ana brought up his horse, got me on to it in some way or other, and mounted behind me to pilot the animal and sustain me in my first bareback act. Over the sand we went, and through the river to his hut, where I was taken in, fed and petted in every possible way, and finally put to bed, where Kana-ana monopolized me, growling in true savage fashion if any one came near me. I didn't sleep much, after all. I think I must have been excited. I thought how strangely I was situated: alone in a wilderness, among barbarians; my bosom friend, who was hugging me like a young bear, not able to speak one syllable of English, and I very shaky on a few bad phrases in his tongue. We two lay upon an enormous old-fashioned bed with high posts. . . . The bed, well stocked with pillows, or cushions, of various sizes, covered with bright-colored chintz, was hung about with numerous shawls, so that I might be dreadfully modest behind them. It was quite a grand affair, gotten up expressly for my benefit. The rest of the house—all in one room, as usual—was covered with mats, on which various recumbent forms and several individual snores betrayed the proximity of Kana-ana's relatives. How queer the whole atmosphere of the place was! . . .

. . . Kana-ana was still asleep, but he never let loose his hold on me, as though he feared his pale-faced friend would fade away from him. He lay close by me. His sleek figure, supple and graceful in repose, was the embodiment of free, untrammeled youth. You who are brought up under cover, know nothing of its luxuriousness. . . .

The narrator drops off to sleep again. When he awakens, he finds that his "companion-in-arms" has already

resumed his single garment—said garment and all others he considered superfluous after dark—and had prepared for me, with his own hands, a breakfast. If it is a question how long a man may withstand the seductions of nature, and the consolations and conveniences of the state of nature, I have solved it in one case; for I was as natural as possible in about three days. . . .

I wonder what it was that finally made me restless and eager to see new faces? Perhaps my unhappy disposition, that urged me thither, and then lured me back to the pride of life and the glory of the world. Certain I am that Kana-ana never wearied me with his attentions, though they were incessant. Day and night he was by me. When he was silent, I knew he was conceiving some surprise in the shape of a new fruit, or a new view to beguile me. I was, indeed, beguiled; I was growing to like the little heathen altogether too well. What should I do when I was at last compelled to return out of my seclusion, and find no soul so faithful and loving in all the earth beside? Day by day, this thought grew upon me, and with it I realized the necessity of a speedy departure.

But the narrator continues to enjoy the pleasures of his idle life with Kana-ana.

We had fitful spells of conversation upon some trivial theme, after long intervals of intense silence. We began to develop symptoms of imbecility. There was laughter at the least occurrence, though quite barren of humor; also, eating and drinking to pass the time; bathing to make one's self cool, after the heat and drowsiness of the day. So life flowed out in an unruffled current, and so the prodigal lived riotously and wasted his substance. . . .

[Kana-ana] would mesmerize me into a most refreshing sleep with a prolonged and pleasing manipulation. It was a reminiscence of the baths of Stamboul not to be withstood. Out of the sleep I would presently be wakened by Kana-ana's performance upon a rude sort of harp, that gave out a weird and eccentric music. The mouth being applied to the instrument, words were pronounced in a guttural voice, while the fingers twanged the strings in measure. It was a flow of monotones, shaped into legends and lyrics. I liked it amazingly; all the better, perhaps, that it was as good as Greek to me, for I understood it as little as I understood the strange and persuasive silence of that beloved place, which seemed slowly, but surely weaving a spell of enchantment about me. I resolved to desert peremptorily, and managed to hire a canoe and a couple of natives, to cross the channel with me. There were other reasons for this prompt action.

Hour by hour I was beginning to realize one of the inevitable results of Time. My boots were giving out, . . . and their soles had about left them. . . . Yet, regularly each morning, my pieces of boot were carefully oiled, then rubbed, or petted, or coaxed into some sort of a polish, which was a labor of love. Oh, Kana-ana! how could you wring my soul with those touching offices of friendship!—those kindnesses unfailing, unsurpassed!

Having resolved to sail early in the morning, . . . all that day—my last with Kana-ana—I breathed about me silent benedictions and farewells. I could not begin to do enough for Kana-ana, who was, more than ever, devoted to me. He almost seemed to mistrust our sudden separation, for he clung to me with a sort of subdued desperation. That was the day he took from his head his hat—a very neat one, plaited by his mother—insisting that I should wear it, (mine was quite in tatters) while he went bare-headed in the sun. That hat hangs in my room now, the only tangible relic of my prodigal days. My plan was to steal off at dawn, while he slept—to awaken my native crew, and escape to sea before my absence was detected. I dared not trust a parting with him, before the eyes of the valley. Well, I managed to wake and rouse my sailor boys. To tell the truth, I didn't sleep a wink that night. We launched the canoe, entered, put off, and had safely mounted the second big roller just as it broke under us with terrific power, when I heard a shrill cry above the roar of the waters. I knew the voice and its import. There was Kana-ana rushing madly toward us; he had discovered all, and couldn't even wait for that white garment, but ran after us like one gone daft, and plunged into the cold sea, calling my name, over and over, as he fought the breakers. I urged the natives forward. I knew if he overtook us, I should never be able to escape again. We fairly flew over the water. I saw him rise and fall with the swell, looking like a seal, for it was his second nature, this surf-swimming. I believe in my heart I wished the paddles would break or the canoe split on the reef, though all the time I was urging the rascals forward; and they, like stupids, took me at my word. . . . We lost sight of the little sea-god, Kana-ana, shaking the spray from his forehead like a por-poise; and this was all in all. I didn't care for any thing else after that, or any body else, either. I went straight home and got civilized again, or partly so, at least. I've never seen the Doctor since, and never want to. He had no business to take me there, or leave me there. I couldn't make up my mind to stay; yet, I'm always dying to go back again.

So I grew tired over my husks: I arose and went unto my father. I wanted to finish up the Prodigal business: I ran and fell upon his neck and kissed him, and said unto him: "Father, *if* I have sinned against Heaven and in thy sight, I'm afraid I don't care much. Don't kill any thing: I don't want any calf. Take back the ring, I don't deserve it; for I'd give more this minute to see that dear, little, velvet-skinned, coffee-colored Kana-ana, than any thing else in the wide world— because he hates business, and so do I. He's a regular brick, father, molded of the purest clay, and baked in God's sunshine. He's about half sunshine himself; and, above all others, and more than any one else ever can, he loved your Prodigal."[148]

On April 2, 1870, Stoddard again wrote Whitman, later sending him a copy of his "Idyl." Years afterward, Traubel reports Whitman handed him Stoddard's letter, saying:

"It's a rather beautiful letter: startling, too, I should say: not offensively so, however: but read it first.["]

SAN FRANCISCO, CAL.,
2d April, 1870.

To Walt Whitman. In the name of CALAMUS listen to me! before me hangs your beautiful photograph, twice precious, since it is your gift to me. Near at hand lies your beloved volume and with it the Notes of Mr. Burroughs.

May I not thank you for your picture and your letter? May I not tell you over and over that where I go you go with me, in poem and picture and the little volume of notes also, for I read and reread trying to see you in the flesh as I so long to see you!

I wrote you last from the Sandwich Islands. I shall before long be even further from you than ever, for I think of sailing towards Tahiti in about five weeks. I know there is but one hope for me. I must get in amongst people who are not afraid of instincts and who scorn hypocracy. I am numbed with the frigid manners of the Christians; barbarism has given me the fullest joy of my life and I long to return to it and be satisfied. May I not send you a proze *idyl* wherein I confess how dear it is to me? There is much truth in it and I am praying that you may like it a little. If I could only know that it has pleased you I should bless my stars fervently.

I have been in vain trying to buy from our Library a copy of your Leaves, edition of 1855. I think it your first and I have somewhere read that you set the type for it yourself. Is it true? Do you think I could obtain a copy of it by addressing some Eastern publisher or bookseller?

You say you "don't write many letters." O, if you would only reply to this within the month! I could then go into the South Seas feeling sure of your friendship and I should try to live the real life there for your sake as well as for my own. Forgive me if I have worried you: I will be silent and thoughtful in future, but in any case know, dear friend, that I am grateful for your indulgence.
Affectionately yours,

CHARLES WARREN STODDARD.

"I have had other letters from him," said W.: "when they turn up you shall have them: he is your kind of a man some ways: I would like to have you meet him some day: he is still alive—somewhere: he did go off I believe as he threatens in the létter: he is of a simple direct naïve nature—never seemed to fit in very well with things here: many of the finest spirits don't—seem to be born for another planet—seem to have got here by mistake: they are not too bad—no: they are too good: they take their stand on a plane higher than the average practice. You would think they would be respected for that, but they are not: they are almost universally agreed to be fools—they are derided rather than reverenced."[149]

A few weeks after receiving Stoddard's April 2 letter, and undoubtedly after giving his answer some thought, on April 23, 1870, Whitman replied to Stoddard. The letter suggests Whitman was perfectly aware of Stoddard's active homosexuality and supportive of it—a statement quite the opposite of Whitman's later, better-known denial and condemnation of homosexuality in a letter to John Addington Symonds.

Washington / April 23, 1870

Dear Charles Stoddard,

I received some days since your affectionate letter, & presently came your beautiful & soothing South Sea Idyll which I read at once.

. . . I have just re-read the sweet story all over, & find it indeed soothing & nourishing after its kind, like the atmosphere. As to you, I do not of course object to your emotional & adhesive nature, & the outlet thereof, but warmly approve them—but do you know (perhaps you do,) how the hard, pungent, gritty, worldly experiences & qualities in American practical life, also serve? how they prevent extravagant sentimentalism? & how they are not without their own great value & even joy?

It arises in my mind, as I write, to say something of that kind to you—

I am not a little comforted when I learn that the young men dwell in thought upon me & my utterances—as you do—& I frankly send you my love—& I hope we shall one day meet—

—I wish to hear from you always,

Walt Whitman[150]

In 1873, Stoddard's "A South Sea Idyl" was reprinted with two new parts and a new title, "Chumming With a Savage," in a volume whose English edition was called *Summer Cruising in the South Seas.* In the new sections, the narrator describes bringing his South Seas native friend to America in an unsuccessful experiment. The youth finally returns to his island, now unhappily unable to readjust and miserable without his comrade, pining away until he drowns in the sea, accidentally or intentionally. It would be interesting to know whether these additions to the "Idyl" had any basis in Stoddard's experience.

The same year, 1873, Stoddard went to Europe as a traveling correspondent for the San Francisco *Chronicle,* serving for a short time in London as secretary to Mark Twain, whom he had known in California.[151]

Stoddard lived in England and Italy for three years, toured Egypt and Palestine in 1876–77, then returned to San Francisco. After two years he moved to Hawaii, living there from 1881 to 1884, writing the story of his conversion to Catholicism (published in 1885 as *A Troubled Heart and How It Was Comforted at Last*). Stoddard was professor of English at Notre Dame University in Indiana from 1885 to 1886, then a lecturer in English literature at Catholic University, Washington, D.C., from which he was forced to resign in 1902. Stoddard tried to support himself by writing, but his health failed, and he went to live with friends in Cambridge, Massachusetts. Returning to San Francisco in 1905, he soon moved to Monterey, California, where he died in 1909. The year before Stoddard's death, the American Edward I. Prime Stevenson ("Xavier Mayne") quoted extensively from "A South Sea Idyl" in his pioneering popular defense of homosexuality, *The Intersexes.*[152] It is not known if Stoddard ever saw a copy of Mayne's work.

1868–1948: Male–Male Intimacy in the American West

A few brief documents suggest a different image of male–male relations in the American West than has traditionally been portrayed. The accompanying unidentified and undated photograph of males dancing together includes a young couple in what appears to be a western setting.[153]

1868–78: Don Rickey, Jr.;
"Mrs. Nash" of Custer's Seventh Cavalry

In a study of the American West, in a section on "Crime, Vice, and Punishment," Don Rickey, Jr. cites

the well-documented account of a "Mrs. Nash," who held the post of company laundress in the Seventh Cavalry. Always heavily veiled, this person remained with the regiment, married to a succession of soldier-husbands, from 1868 to 1878. She did not leave the service when her "husbands" were discharged, and in 1878 was cohabiting with a corporal at Fort Meade, Dakota Territory. The corporal accompanied his unit on an extended campaign in the summer of 1878, and "Mrs. Nash" died during his absence. When some of the garrison ladies went to lay her out, the shocking truth was revealed. "Mrs. Nash" was a man! The corporal's comrades ridiculed him unmercifully, and unable to bear their scorn, he committed suicide with his revolver. Here is evidence of a series of homosexual liaisons, embracing a period of ten years, which must have been known to many of the rank and file.

The documents concerning "Mrs. Nash" show that homosexuality "existed to some extent among the enlisted men serving in the frontier West."[154]

1891: A. Castaigne; "A Miners' Ball"

An engraving dated 1891 portrays an all-male scene.[155]

The following brief description of a miners' party, although of a later date, perfectly evokes the engraving below. *Tex* (1922), a western novel by the popular Clarence Mulford, author of the Hopalong Cassidy series, describes the male–male partnership of "Sinful" and "Hank."

A roar of laughter came from the celebrating miners and all eyes turned their way. Sinful and Hank were dancing to the music of a jew's-harp and the time set by stamping, hob-nailed boots. They parted, bowed, joined again, parted, curtsied and went on, hand in hand, turning and ducking, backing and filing, the dust flying and the perspiration streaming down.[156]

1919: Badger Clark;
"The Lost Pardner"

A collection of Western poetry by Badger Clark, entitled *Sun and Saddle Leather*, was published in three editions between 1915 and 1919. Badger Clark was brought up in the West. As a boy he lived in Deadwood, South Dakota; as an adult he settled on a small ranch in Arizona where he wrote most of his Western poems. *Sun and Saddle Leather* concludes with a suggestive verse, "The Lost Pardner."

I ride alone and hate the boys I meet.
    Today, some way, their laughin' hurts me so.
.   .   .   .
I hate the steady sun that glares, and glares!
    The bird songs make me sore.
I seem the only thing on earth that cares
    'Cause Al ain't here no more!

And him so strong, and yet so quick he died,
    And after year on year
When we had always trailed it side by side,
    He went—and left me here!

We loved each other in the way men do
    And never spoke about it, Al and me,
But we both *knowed*, and knowin' it so true
    Was more than any woman's kiss could be.
.   .   .   .
What is there out beyond the last divide?
    Seems like that country must be cold and dim.
He'd miss this sunny range he used to ride,
    And he'd miss me, the same as I do him.

It's no use thinkin'—all I'd think or say
    Could never make it clear.
Out that dim trail that only leads one way
    He's gone—and left me here!

The range is empty and the trails are blind,
    And I don't seem but half myself today.
I wait to hear him ridin' up behind
    And feel his knee rub mine the good old way.[157]

1948: Alfred C. Kinsey and others;
Male Homosexuality in Rural Areas

The Kinsey report on *Sexual Behavior in the Human Male* (1948) discusses the relation between rural–urban background and the frequency of homosexual activity. The report suggests that none of the "city-bred homosexual institutions" (bars, restaurants, baths) are

known in rural areas, and this may well account for a somewhat lower rate of the homosexual among farm boys.

On the other hand, the highest frequencies of the homosexual which we have ever secured anywhere have been in particular rural communities in some of the more remote sections of the country. The boy on the isolated farm has few companions except his brothers, the boys on an adjacent farm or two, visiting male cousins, and the somewhat older farm hand. . . . the moral codes of the rural community may impose considerable limitations upon the association of boys and girls under other circumstances. Moreover, farm activities call for masculine capacities, and associations with girls are rated sissy by most of the boys in such a community.

All these factors "are conducive to a considerable amount of homosexuality among the teen-age males" in the most isolated of the western rural areas of America; there is much less "in the smaller farm country of the Eastern United States."

Beyond this, there is a fair amount of sexual contact among the older males in Western rural areas. It is a type of homosexuality which was probably common among pioneers and outdoor men in general. Today it is found among ranchmen, cattle men, prospectors, lumbermen, and farming groups in general—among groups that are virile, physically active. These are men who have faced the rigors of nature in the wild. They live on realities and on a minimum of theory. Such a background breeds the attitude that sex is sex, irrespective of the nature of the partner with whom the relation is had. . . . Such a group of hard-riding, hard-hitting, assertive males would not tolerate the affectations of some city groups that are involved in the homosexual; but this, as far as they can see, has little to do with the question of having sexual relations with other men. This type of rural homosexuality contradicts the theory that homosexuality in itself is an urban product.[158]

Summing up the rural–urban comparison, the reports states:

Homosexual activities occur less frequently among rural groups and more frequently among those who live in towns or cities. . . . this is a product not only of the greater opportunity which the city may provide for certain types of homosexual contacts, but also of the generally lower rate of total [sexual] outlet among males raised on the farm. . . . in certain of the most remote rural areas there is considerable homosexual activity among . . . miners, hunters, and others engaged in out-of-door occupations. The homosexual activity rarely conflicts with their heterosexual relations, and is quite without the argot, physical manifestations, and other affectations so often found in urban groups. There is a minimum of personal disturbance or social conflict over such activity. It is the type of homosexual experience which the explorer and pioneer may have had in their histories.[159]

♀ 1879–1900: MABEL GANSON DODGE LUHAN and VIOLET SHILLITO;
Intimate Memories

Mabel Ganson was born into a wealthy family in Buffalo, New York, in 1879. Ganson's long life as author and patron of the arts included marriage to four husbands and several well-publicized heterosexual affairs. Mabel Dodge Luhan (as she called herself, after her first and fourth husbands) published in 1932 volume one of her four-part autobiography, collectively titled *Intimate Memories*. An important source on American literary and artistic circles in the early part of the twentieth century, Luhan's memoirs also present a frank, forthright description of her deep feelings for, and intimate relations with, other young women during her youth.

During the early years of the twentieth century, Mabel Dodge Luhan's famous salons attracted many of the pioneering artists and social rebels of her day. Her home at 23 Fifth Avenue became a center of Greenwich Village artistic and intellectual life before World War I. There Margaret Sanger spoke about birth control, John Reed and Walter Lippmann discussed socialism, and the listeners at different times included Max Eastman, Carl van Vechten, Lincoln Steffens, and Gertrude Stein. In 1913, Luhan became the moving spirit behind the influential show of post-Impressionist painting held in New York's Sixty-ninth Regiment Armory. In the early 1920s, Luhan was involved in a much-discussed and losing struggle with Frieda Lawrence to influence the creative direction of D. H. Lawrence's writing. Luhan is also known as a patron of the artists' colony at Taos, New Mexico.

The first volume of Luhan's *Intimate Memories*, subtitled *Background*, is "Dedicated to Buffalo, New York / 1879–1900." In chapter two, "The Breast," Luhan describes her fascination as a youngster with a Swedish housekeeper named Elsa.

If the long quiet hours in the nursery were dull with Mary Ann for my sole companion, anyway they were better than the times when I was left there alone. For often she would say: "Now you be good till I come back. I have to go and iron," or some other excuse like that, and off she would go for a gossip with the other "girls." I found this out very soon by summoning the courage to follow her on tiptoe down the back stairs, and there she would be in the cozy kitchen with a cup of hot tea in one hand and on her pale, thin face a shadow of faint animation hardly ever to be seen in our room.

There was always some play going on among the girls down there. And once they had a visitor, a fat gay female who roistered and teased them and chuckled and nagged until they retaliated with some daring rejoinder, when, to my inexpressible amazement, I saw her rip open the front of her dress and drag her great breast out from the shelving corset that supported it. With a quick pressure she directed a stream of pale milk right across the room on to the three squawking servant girls, who hid their faces from this shower. Such a novelty as this became a matter of conjecture to me that lasted for . . . who knows how long? I couldn't get the picture out of my mind. Continually I saw again the fine stream of grayish milk striking across the room, and I longed to see it again in actuality. That it came like that out of a woman allured my imagination and was fascinating to think about because it stirred something hidden inside me and gave me new feelings.

Some time later I tried to make it happen again. My mother was away visiting Grandma Cook in New York. I do not remember Mary Ann's being about any more at this time, but we had for a "second girl" a big fair Swedish girl named Elsa. I was attracted by her; she seemed to me to have so much life in her. I begged her to sleep with me. I told her I was afraid at night with my mother gone from the room next to mine, so she sat with me until she thought I slept and later she came and got into my big bed: the bed where Mary Ann had slept beside me for years. But I had not gone to sleep. I had been waiting for her; I had no plan, no thought, of what I wanted—I just wanted.

I waited, quiet, until I knew she was asleep and then I drew nearer to her. She lay on her back and in the darkness I felt her soft breath coming from her open mouth. I felt, rather than saw, how stupid she looked, but I liked her so: I liked her stupid, fair, gentle presence that was yet so throbbing and full of life. With a great firmness, I leaned over her and seized her big warm breast in both hands. It was a large, ballooning, billowing breast, firm and resilient and with a stout, springing nipple. I leaned to it and fondled it. I felt my blood enliven me all over and I longed to approach the whole of my body to her bosom, to cover her completely by my entire surface and have the bounding breast touch me at every point. I rolled it ecstatically from side to side and slathered it with my dripping lips. As my sudden new, delicious pleasure increased, I grew rougher. I longed now to hurt it and wring something from it. I wanted to pound it and burst it. Suddenly I remembered that other breast seen long ago in the kitchen, and I wanted to force from this one the same steely stream of milk that I felt within it, resisting me. However Elsa slept through all this is more than I know, but she never became conscious. I and that breast were alone in the night and that was what I wanted. I worked it back and forward; I approached my body to it in every way I could think of doing to see how it would feel. I held it, pushed it up hard and taut between my two small cold feet, and finally I had enough and, relinquishing it, I fell asleep. Of the awakening the next day I remember nothing, only that night, that first battle and thunder of the flesh, I remember as though it were yesterday.[160]

In 1893, the fourteen-year-old Mabel Ganson became enamored with a young woman named Margaret Strane, described in chapter five, "Intimations."

Margaret Strane came to live across the street with her Aunt Amelia. She was a silent, rather haughty-looking girl of about sixteen. I knew her when I was about fourteen years old. She wasn't pretty, but she had heavy-looking blue eyes and there was an attraction about her of a dark nature, so that always after I had been with her, after one of our low-voiced, secret times, I felt uncomfortable. I felt dissipated and unstrung and miserable. . . .

Margaret appeared there in the silent house and she was a silent girl. When I came upon her somewhere in a dark corner of the somber rooms, she rose, and together we made our way to some place yet more silent, more secret, where we would be undisturbed. And then without preamble I would reach out to her and run my hands over her small breasts that budded out provocative through the thin summer muslin. "Let me see them," I would whisper, and still in silence she would open her dress and let me come nearer. She watched me with a coldness, a contemplative coldness, that had something strange about it. I was filled with wonder and delight but she had no feeling in her—only cold curiosity.

Her small breasts were like two strangers to her whom she did not know, but I knew them—I experienced their mystery and allure and the magnetism that came from them almost visibly. They filled me with a delicious, thrilly feeling that I did not feel for Margaret Strane, that cold girl. Her breasts seemed to draw love from me, but she—never. I cared nothing for her at all. I do not know what went on in her, but something in my passion for her two flowers pleased her, I suppose, since she was always willing to give them to me. I loved them and tried to forget her. I caressed them and put my lips to them and feelings coursed through my nerves, but Margaret Strane remained unmoved—watching.

There was something queer and something wrong about it or I would never have felt so sad as I did when I left her. As soon as I was alone, I went down into the profound depression of girlhood. But I forgot it soon and returned to her again and again. When I remember Margaret, everything about her is forgotten except— and they are so vivid still—her two white flowery breasts with their young pointed nipples leaning towards me.[161]

In the 1890s, the teen-age Mabel Ganson attended Miss Graham's private school in New York City, met Mary Shillito, and first heard of Mary's legendary sister Violet.

Miss Graham's School

Mary Shillito was something new. She had been brought up in Paris with her sister Violet, her father representing there one side of a great firm of Cincinnati merchants. Mary had a completely foreign air. She lapsed into French all the time, and indeed her parents had brought the girls to New York *to learn English*. How strange that seemed to me! They had separated the two girls, who had never been away from each other, and Violet was up at Miss Ely's School on Riverside Drive.

When Mary Shillito arrived at Miss Graham's, says Luhan,

somewhat later than I did, after school had opened, I approached her, full of curiosity. And because the other girls instantly sized her up as a half-wit and were ready to make her the butt of their jokes about "foreigners" and "Frenchies," she was in a panic in no time, her fingers at her lips with that horrid habit she had of nibbling at her nails, looking like a rabbit driven into a corner. I went up to her and drew her into my room, not with any intention to save or protect her but because I wanted to sample her, to savor her quality—to reach through her to the places where she had been, and to the life she had known.

It was all of Violet that she told me. "Veeolette," she called her. Veeolette was extraordinary—that fact emerged immediately. When Mary talked of her sister she was *all there*, more than most people, really. She conveyed to me by some magic in herself the magical, the transcendent power of Veeolette. She, by words forgotten now, part English and part French, and more than by words by some direct communication of unspeakable things, made known to me that Veeolette was an ineffable being, perhaps the only being on this earth so powerful, so profound, so spiritual. *"Une grande belle âme. Elle sait tout* [A great beautiful soul. She knows all]," Mary said.

"And your father and mother, what are they like?" I asked, absolutely enthralled, my own soul expanding at once to receive Veeolette, whom I felt I must know as soon as possible.

"Un cochon et une vache [A pig and a cow]," replied Mary, succinctly, with a curious vividly wicked flash in her eyes. *"Les pauvres!* [Poor things!] They don't know what they have in their house! They do not know my sister. To them she shows an obedient child. She knows that they are not of her quality, that they can never *understand."*

Mary said this word with a burden of immense secrecy in it, a depth of meaning in her lowered voice, accompanying it with a look to me of confidential meaning that she thought I would understand but the significance of which I did not get at all, beyond its importance and the esoteric roll of widened eyes.

I did not care to reveal to her that I was less comprehending than she thought me, but I did long to know more. I tried, with as much adroitness as I could, to get her to tell me really what Veeolette was like anyway.

"Elle contient un grand mystère [She contains a great mystery]," Mary told me. *"Personne au monde ne pourrait la toucher si elle ne le veut. Elle a une telle force d'âme* [No one in the world could touch her if she was unwilling, she has such power of soul]. If you look in her eyes you see something there," continued Mary.

"But what does she look like?" I persisted. "Is she pretty?" For pretty was what all the girls craved to be. Pretty, with large "soulful eyes," curly hair, and spotless skins.

"Veeolette pretty!" exclaimed Mary, shocked. *"Jamais! Elle est belle—elle est étrange—elle a des yeux* [Never! She is beautiful—she is unusual—she has such eyes]—I cannot tell what it is in them! But she is not pretty. Oh, no!"

Sometimes Mary would meet her sister on Saturdays and they would go together to a concert or a lecture at the desire of the parents, who knew they must let them meet sometimes, for Mary suffered so at the separation. She would return after one of these outings vivid and renewed by the contact, and full of secret confidences about Veeolette.

"Elle déteste cette école [She hates that school]. She says it is more stupid than she *concevait* [had thought] it would be. The girls are *crétins* [idiots] and the teachers *dégénerées* [degenerates]. She find it *tellement facile* [so easy] to fool them all. *Elle a une telle force. Indomptable, vous savez!* [She has such power. Invincible, you know!] When she wants to leave the school—at night when all are sleeping she go where she like in New York. *La semaine passée* [last week] she heard the end of Beethoven's Fifth Symphony—*pas comme à Munich, naturellement* [not the same as in Munich, of course]—she say they play Beethoven here as though it were *acte de conscience* [act of conscience], not like in Europe where it is *un acte de foi!* [act of faith!] She get back at Ely (Mary pronounced it Aylee) and into her bed and nobody know."

"But how?" I asked amazed, for this was just the kind of adventurous life I would have loved myself—though the risks in my case would have been for something else besides Beethoven, so differently had our tastes been formed. Too barren my own life seemed; so rich, so varied the European girlhood. I determined on the instant to know Beethoven. It meant so much to Veeolette; it should be the same for me. I always had something very strongly "arrivist" in me. I *would* arrive. By hook or crook, I would go everywhere into the invisible worlds. I would know everything, feel everything, be everything. "How did she unlock doors and things?" I queried.

"*Je ne sais pas. Violette a une grande facilité pour toute chose. Elle sait faire ce qu'elle désire faire* [I do not know. Violette has a great facility for everything. She knows how to do anything she wants to do]. Locked doors! *Ce n'est rien pour ma sœur! Elle sait passer partout—dans la petite vie extérieure comme dans la grande vie intérieure* [That's nothing for my sister! She knows how to go anywhere—in the small outer life as in the great inner life]."

This was the first time I heard *"la grande vie intérieure"* mentioned, but it became a familiar phrase to me—part of the code of our subtle, occult, secret feminine existence.

I longed for Veeolette more than I ever had for any one in my life. I sent her messages by Mary and she brought me answering ones from her sister: messages that she would deliver to me with that rolling widening of the eyes, emphasizing the secret meaning with an infinitely knowing expression—almost of malice—in its depths.

"Veeolette says, '*Attendez, l'heure viendra. Faut pas forcer les pouvoirs spiritueles: laissez faire* [Wait. The hour will come. One must not force the spiritual powers: one must let them alone].' She says she knows you well already, that she love you but that you need patience—*la restrainte. Tu seras enrichie par le temps perdu: de plus, que le temps n'est jamais perdu* [restraint. You will be enriched by the lost time; and furthermore, that time never really is lost]." These deep, wise sibylline utterances of Veeolette's about me plunged me into an ecstasy of *feeling*. The little serpents within me coiled and uncoiled. Her words, brought by Mary, with an air of mystery and of secret knowledge that the two shared, outshining anything else in the world for pure marvel, threw a veil of exquisite illusion about me. The world grew fairylike and strange. The colors of life shimmered and fluctuated as never before. Veeolette had, by her presence in the world, the effect of a color organ on the blank screen that my life seemed to me nearly always. She emanated from her hidden seclusion, up there at Miss Ely's School on Riverside Drive, a powerful stream of magic.

Never was such a glamorous being as Veeolette, both before I ever saw her and afterwards.[162]

It was in Paris that Mabel Ganson first met "Veeolette."

Paris and Veeolette

. . . Mary took me up two floors in a small lift that she ran by pressing buttons, and when we came to the solemn, dark door of her apartment she was trembling a little, for we had all thought a great deal of that moment and here it was. Veeolette and I would soon be face to face. The first moments are blurred, but after a while we were all in their small suite of rooms, talking and laughing. . . .

Violet Shillito did not burst on me all at once: she came into me gradually, opening slowly to my preceptions like a flower that reveals its beauty slowly bit by bit as one looks deeper into it. At the first glance she seemed all brown and dusky, ruddy tones—a red-brown girl of medium height and with a flat, slender body that swayed backwards a little. Her hair was soft and dark and done in a knot on the top of her head. Her eyes were red-brown and slanted up a little at the corners, while her mouth was drawn over her teeth, which projected ever so little, in a willful way that would keep the lips closed, while Mary with the same defect let her lips gape open to the undisciplined teeth that pushed their way outwards or left her under lip to support their large white surfaces. Violet's nose was the most sensitive feature she had, after her small eyes that smiled a compassionate understanding of everything in life. Her nose was small and high-bridged and delicately pointed out into the world as though she constantly apprehended the unseen with some kind of invisible antennæ that groped and sensed the things about her. Her nostrils were close and fine and constantly trembled with delicate nervousness. Violet seemed to receive her impressions with that sensitive pointed nose of hers. It wasn't a silly, unbridled nose like those of certain English women, with their ridiculous Peter Newell stupidity. It was a short, high organ of intelligence—aristocratic and discriminating, and a little sensual.

Violet was vivid and glowing. She did not fluctuate with a rising and falling fire as Mary did. She was one of those who burned forever with "a hard, gemlike flame." Her hands were delicious. Very full of character—rather short with round padded fingers and very soft and white. As they lay at ease in her lap, or as they were in use, they were so full of intelligent, involuntary life and expression of their own that it almost seemed they watched one and listened to one and, along with Violet herself, felt love and pity and pardon.

For that was what Violet did. She completely understood and understanding, she forgave. I have never known any man or woman with such wisdom and such love as she had. She knew everything intuitively and at the same time she had a very unusual intelligence—teaching herself Italian for her pleasure in order to read Dante in the original when she was sixteen, learning to read Greek in order to read Plato and the dramatists. She was studying higher mathematics at the Sorbonne the first year I knew her, "for the beauty."

The first glimpse we had of each other, I looked at her and knew her, and impulsively felt I would love her best of all the world forever, for I saw her genius and I felt her singular power. And she looked at me and loved me too for whatever she saw in me, and knew me better, too, better than I knew myself—knew that I would love her and leave her behind without a breath of compassion when it came my time to proceed on my way; knew that I would take her and, without pity or imagination, drop her; knew all this, but more than this—knew that that was my destiny, that I could not help myself, that some inner law would always lead me.

I did not seem less significant or less lovable to her because I was not the forever kind. She took to me as I did to her and our hearts bounded to each other. . . .

Violet played Chopin for me. She had a little grand piano there in the small salon and she used to play late in the afternoons before dark, or evenings by candlelight, when I had gone there to dine.

Then, when the limit of romantic love and sadness had been sounded, she would play Beethoven and cut deeper channels for feeling and beauty to flow in—the acceptance of life and resignation to its betrayals. Mary's tears flowed when Violet played Beethoven. Nothing had ever deepened me or opened such wide gates as Violet and what she gave me. A whole new world of personalities and experiences in the books and music in her little salon. . . . The great lack was humor. The principal motive was pain in all these lives I touched. The words in *Amiel's Journal* that I first found there also sound the weariness of the vision they all celebrated: *"Que vivre est difficile, oh, mon cœur fatigué!"* [How difficult it is to be alive, oh, my weary heart!] This was the note of the *fin de siècle* [end of the century]—of more than that, of the end of the great era that had lasted for hundreds of years. Since those days I have seen coming into the world something new, something braver than resignation or sorrow nobly borne. Sorrow has had its day, and weariness too. The world has had a rebirth and a new set of values has taken the place of the old ones. I think that Violet knew she would not go on into the new life and that I perhaps might. She was old —— old —— when I knew her. She seemed to have imaginatively lived all lives and sounded every depth. She was like the Mona Lisa, a photograph of whom hung near the piano, and to whom she led me that first day, saying: *"Vois-tu? Elle est un grand réservoir. Elle sait tout, elle contient tout. Et elle aime tout de même. Pour elle le monde et les hommes sont des enfants, a Côté de sa sagesse* [Do you see? She is a great reservoir. She knows all, she contains all. And she loves all equally. For her, the world and people are children beside her great wisdom]."

She was weary —— weary —— weary; the old, exquisite pattern growing dim —— civilization coming to pieces —— and Violet knowing it —— because she had reached the last phase, which is consciousness of the relative state and where, if one belongs to the old order, the wave at its crest sights the shore and falls back into dissolution. Violet was, of all the people I have ever known of the old world (and by the old world I mean the thought, the feeling, and the knowing of the past) the highest evolved, the one who had reached the farthest. She held all the past within her, and she felt the end was near at hand: she spoke often of the debacle that was upon the heels of the world, upon her own heels—of everything going under. She could not do anything about life. She could scarcely live in actions at all: all her living was of the intuition—a culture that she and her psychic ancestors had created and cultivated, carrying its increasing weight through endless generations, and that I and my kind would take over and perhaps painlessly, without effort, carry over into the new life in which she would have no part, her work being ended. . . .[163]

Luhan describes a visit to the Shillitos' country house in France.

I saw Violet against the dark immovable mass of the château as she walked towards us, knee-deep in the grasses already yellowing, for it was July. She had on a soft blue batiste dress open at the neck, and a coarse straw hat trimmed with black velvet bows and a wreath of poppies and wheat. Her arms were bare to the elbow and there was such an expression of something in their soft pink curves, in her substantial wrists and padded, intelligent hands. I could not think what it was they expressed so fluently, but it was something vital and feminine and even matronly. Mary's hands and arms, for instance, had none of this look. They were fluttering and trembling all the time; they had great sensibility and nervousness, and of course were feminine too; but they were more an artist's hands, while, come to think of it, Violet's hands looked like a mother's hands, like the large, capable, tender hands of the Madonnas.

Violet had come across the fields to meet the cart. She stood in the long grass and smiled at me with her deep, intentional, loving smile. Any one to whom Violet has given that look will never forget it. The words "look" or "smile" describe adequately enough the gestures with which people convey themselves outwardly to the world. But what happened between Violet and the one to whom she felt she could give her spirit was so vital and electric and intense that her buried ardor leaping to her eyes seemed to flash past the barrier of her flesh and enter one in a swift possession, and go running into one's secret channels like a permeating, sweet elixir. No, the word "look" cannot tell about it—it made one understand the Immaculate Conception.

Thus Violet, by the bestowal of her love upon me, entered my cosmos, bringing with her all the subtleties and beauties of the ages that were embodied in her. This is the vital transmission of truth and culture forever; by these channels alone the "river of light" flows on in the race. Truth is not to be found sealed in the pages of books; it has to be given by one to another in an embrace of the spirit.

I looked at Violet as she waited in the tall grasses, with the dark masses of the château behind her. And I thought that she looked as though she had come out of the round turrets to meet us, leaving her tapestry frame when she saw us on the road. She was always like that; she belonged to all ages, she was like a synthesis of the past. . . . Once in a great while Nature creates a marvelous human being, but very rarely. Most people go through their lives without ever coming across one of these efflorescent souls and never even know what they have missed. After all these years, Violet's great significance lives in me yet and I realize my good fortune. I have never seen a man or a woman who came anywhere near her in development. As Mary said to me at Miss Graham's: *"Elle sait tout* [she knows all]*."*

I got out and walked with her to the little house where they were living. . . . I remember only the room in which I spent the night with Violet, Mary sleeping next to us in a small adjoining dressing-room.

The picture comes back to me clearly: Violet and Mary and I standing on the old stone floor that had a few strips of rush matting on it, standing in our little flannel peignoirs, brushing our hair, while two candles on the muslin-covered dresser threw great shadows of us over the whitewashed walls. The smell of it comes as actually as the sight—for Violet was rubbing a thick white cream on her face and hands and as I sniffed its lovely perfume she told me to take some and try it and I took the little white jar. It was Crême Simon. I have used it ever since and it always makes me think of Violet and the Château de Pierrefonds.

When we blew out our candles and lay down together in the bed, the moon slanted in a long beam of white through the oblong of window high up on the wall. . . .

Violet and I lay in the quiet stone room, and I let it all drift into myself, all the past of that place.

I turned in my dreams to Violet where she lay beside me, a long, stiff effigy in the white light from the moon shining on the wall. I saw her smile gleaming still and sweet and subtle. She knew me and could read my imaginings as though they unfurled before me in scrolls of thought from behind my brow.

"What?" I asked her tenderly, more to let her know by the tone of my voice that I loved her than that she should tell me what I knew already. I reached out my hand and laid it shyly upon her left breast, cupping it with my palm. Instantly it was attuned to a music of the finest vibration. From between her young breast and the sensitive palm of my hand there arose all about us, it seemed, a high, sweet singing. This response we made to each other at the contact of our flesh ran from hand and breast along the shining passages of our blood until in every cell we felt each other's presence. This was to awaken from sleep and sing like morning stars. We lay in silence that yet was full of shrill, sweet sound, and all that stone room became vital with the overflow of our increased life, for we passed it out of us in rapid, singing waves—an emanation more fine and powerful than that from radium.

We needed no more than to be in touch like that with each other, just hand and breast, to make our way into a new world together. *"Je t'aime* [I love you]," murmured Violet, and I answered, *"Et je t'aime* [And I love you]."

I looked at her again across the dim light and I saw her smile once more—a different smile. She looked happy, rueful, merry, and a little resigned.

"Je ne savais pas que je sois sensuelle [I didn't know that I was sensual]," she whispered, *"mais il paraît que je le suis* [but it seems that I am]."

"Et pourquoi pas? [And why not?]" I asked, for it seemed to me if that was what was meant by *sensualité* it was exquisite and commendable and should be cultivated. It was a more delicious life I felt in me than I had ever felt before. I thought it was a superior kind of living too. I looked at Violet questioningly. Since she had that music in her, surely she, so cognizant of fine values, would appreciate it as I did. But she didn't answer. She gave a tiny little sigh and continued to smile, but a deeper, a different meaning had come into it now. Something incredibly antique and compassionate, like an unaging goddess fresh and unfaded, yet of the most ancient days, seemed to gaze at me from under her drooping lids. I saw again in her the Kwannon look—Kwannon, the goddess of mercy who knows the meaning of everything and still smiles her small smile, the merciful goddess who has reached the end of her long evolution and who forfeits Nirvana to come back to earth and help men complete their destiny.

Just in flashes like that, we were not together. She was, in her intuitions and her wisdom, infinitely removed from me. The most lonely creatures in the world are at these times—uncompanioned. I felt my own childhood comforted and assuaged when I saw that look on her face. I felt some one there ahead of me in the invisible distance, some one who would be there before me and wait, no matter how slowly I came on behind her, and who would show me the way. As a child I had felt no one in front of me—an unopened space with no paths in it had encircled me; my parents had seemed like dim, dull figures far, far behind. I could not make them a part of my journey. I had to set off alone by myself and I was always alone. But now I knew there was some one on beyond me, that she, not I, knew loneliness.

Craven, I tasted the comfort of this and it was stronger than any sympathy I had for that girl who had taken my place of isolation in the life of the spirit.

Violet did not draw away from me. Our natural harmony sang on through that night and the next, when we came together again. But into her eyes that compassionate look that was like a mother's who knows more than the child can understand and so is mute, that sweet, rueful, loving smile was on her face now all the time we were together, and it was called there by that glad life of our blood, which for want of a better term I must call music—but that she had named to me by the term *sensualité*.[164]

♀ 1895: WILLA CATHER; Sappho
"Her lyre . . . responded only to a song of love"

In her newspaper column for the Lincoln, Nebraska, *Journal* of January 13, 1895, twenty-two-year-old Willa Cather writes of "Three Women Poets," Christina Rossetti, Elizabeth Barrett Browning, and last, and more briefly, Sappho. The column, occasioned by the death of Rossetti, is one of the most significant comments on poetry made by Cather during her years in Lincoln. Interestingly, besides her remarks on the love poetry of Sappho, Cather focuses on Rossetti's "Goblin Market" (1862), a work whose homoeroticism is analyzed by Jeannette Foster in her study of Lesbian-relevant themes in literature. Cather's deep-felt, singing words on Sappho describe her as the poet par excellence of love. Cather does not specify a particular variety of love, nor does she name any particular translations, and it is not clear to what extent she knew Sappho as the poet of women-loving women. In Cather's time and earlier, Sappho's life and works were often heterosexualized. For example, J. Herman Merivale's 1833 translation of Sappho's plea to Aphrodite makes Sappho's beloved a male, whereas the original clearly identifies her as a woman. It does seem likely that Cather had some knowledge of Sappho's association with the poetry of female homosexual love. The concluding paragraph of Cather's 1895 article speaks of Sappho.

There is one woman poet whom all the world calls great, though of her work there remains now only a few disconnected fragments and that one wonderful hymn to Aphrodite. Small things upon which to rest so great a fame, but they tell so much. If of all the lost riches we could have one master restored to us, one of all the philosophers and poets, the choice of the world would be for the lost nine books of Sappho. Those broken fragments have burned themselves into the consciousness of the world like fire. All great poets have wondered at them, all inferior poets have imitated them. Twenty centuries have not cooled the passion in them. Sappho wrote only of one theme, sang it, laughed it, sighed it, wept it, sobbed it. Save for her knowledge of human love she was unlearned, save for her perception of beauty she was blind, save for the fullness of her passions she was empty-handed. She was probably not a student of prosody, yet she invented the most wonderfully emotional meter in literature, the sapphic meter with its three full, resonant lines, and then that short, sharp one that comes in like a gasp when feeling flows too swift for speech. She could not sing of Atrides [the Atridae?], nor of Cadmus, nor of the labors of Hercules, for her lyre, like Anacreon's, responded only to a song of love.[165]

♀ 1912: ALMEDA SPERRY to EMMA GOLDMAN;
"I am a savage, Emma, a wild, wild savage"

A collection of previously unpublished love letters to Emma Goldman, anarchist leader, vividly conveys the emotions and varied life experience of Almeda Sperry, their complex author. The letters detail and evoke Sperry's tender-brutal relationship with her husband Fred; her bitter-funny cash relationship with Carnegie Steel Company boss "Newt"; her loving relationship with Florence, a graphically described woman friend; her own poor working-class childhood—and her passionate affair of the heart with Emma Goldman.[166]

Little is now known about Almeda Sperry; the Boston University library which holds her letters furnishes no biographical information. What is known of Sperry comes from an examination of her letters by the present author, and by Alix Kates Shulman, who discovered them while researching the life of Emma Goldman.

Sperry's letters indicate that she was born on July 13, 1879, and so was thirty-three when she wrote, in 1912, from New Kensington, Pennsylvania, where she was then living. Sperry told Goldman that she worked to get the streets paved, to have lectures on sex delivered to students at a nearby school, and to establish a socialist reading room. By 1912, she had become an anarchist, had been involved in union organizing, and occasionally wrote for radical newspapers. As a child, her parents beat her to force her to go to church, which made her hate that institution and all religious hypocrisy. At the time of these letters she had a drinking problem, and she called herself an alcoholic. She was full of contradictions, some of which, along with poverty, may have led to the physical ills of which she often complains. She had been a prostitute at the age of twenty-one, and continued occasionally to sell herself "for mercenary reasons"—an act which she calls "most horrible" and "appalling." At the same time she was pained by her friend Florence's "vulgar" language and tried to reform her; her husband Fred's "lacivious" taunts, she says, "lacerate" her "soul." She was an eloquent and angry feminist, seeing men as sex-obsessed poseurs; at the same time she was emotionally tied to her husband Fred.

Sperry was not afraid to express her passionate love for Emma Goldman, and seems to have suffered little or no guilt over her clearly erotic fantasies about her friend. It is difficult to know exactly what occurred between Sperry and Goldman, but there is no doubt about the character and intensity of Sperry's feelings, so strongly and unambiguously expressed. The letters indicate that Goldman returned Sperry's affection, though with less passion and desperate need than Sperry felt. In one undated, and atypically puritanical statement, Sperry tells Goldman:

Never mind about not feeling as I do. I find restraint to be purifying. Realization is hell for it is satisfying and degenerating.

In another undated letter Sperry writes to Goldman:

God how I dream of you! You say that you would like to have me near you always if you were a man, or if you felt as I do. Dearest, I would not if I could. I would soon die. . . . the thought of distance adds to my terrible pain—so pleasurable. I want no *calm* friendships. The thoughts of annihilation used to appeal to me. Today they do not. . . .

> The letters do suggest that Goldman in her personal relations with Sperry had come close to that tabooed homosexual activity which she early and publicly defended in lectures, to the chagrin of even her unconventional anarchist comrades. The writings of Goldman, Alexander Berkman, and Almeda Sperry suggest that at least some American anarchists were, at an early date, more than usually tolerant and open-minded about homosexuality.[167]
>
> Sperry's letters to Goldman refer unself-consciously to Sperry's sexual attraction to both women and men; some letters simultaneously express sexual longing for Goldman and for a specific male. Both Sperry and Goldman attempted to live out in their own lives the kind of nonpossessive, nonmonogamous relations that their anarchist ideals led them to uphold in theory. This was difficult for Sperry: these letters show her struggling with intense jealousy—at Goldman's devotion to the anarchist cause, which Sperry experienced as a personal rival for Goldman's time and affections.
>
> In these letters, Sperry writes with a directness, simplicity, and depth of feeling which at times transforms these documents into a kind of prose poetry, allowing us to enter readily into the intimate life of this vitally alive, struggling woman. If in reading these private letters we sometimes feel intruders, we should remember that Emma Goldman saved this correspondence, at some point returned it to Sperry, who herself preserved it. In one undated letter, Sperry tells Goldman:

I have shown you the secret places of my soul thinking if I did so without any reservation that it would help the cause along. I would not care if you told my story to the public or even use my name from the platform.

> Sperry, one would think, would approve the present use of her letters, even quite enjoy it.
>
> Writing in 1912, Sperry imbued her letters with a spirited, personal, deeply felt socialist-anarchist-feminist consciousness, which gives this correspondence a lively, contemporary sound. As Sperry said of herself, "I aint dead *yet* and I aint done for, either."
>
> A question from Emma Goldman about past love relations with men evokes from Sperry this deep-felt reply:

March 4th '12

My own Dear—my cherry-blossom—my moon-beam shimmering on a dark pool at night—my mountain, so calm, so serene—my drop of dew hidden in the heart of a wild rose: I do not know whether I have loved deeply and passionately or not; if you mean have I ever loved a man I will frankly say that I never *saw* a man. I have seen bipeds who pose as men but never saw a *man*. No, I have never deeply loved any man. I seem to exact too much. The men are lying pups and all they are after is sex.

Writing of a woman friend, Sperry says:

you know she has auburn hair and I made a verse about it—it goes,

> "Into thy glowing mass
> I thrust
> The thin line
> Of my crimson lips
> Thrilling
> With lust."

The rest I don't remember. . . . You know that isn't poetry—it is just the way I felt.

The following month, on April 2, Sperry, in a depressed mood, writes Goldman that "something seems to have broken in me, I do not care for anything any more. One thing though, I love you." A few weeks later on April 20, feeling better, Sperry vividly describes another friend, Florence, bringing to life in words another woman as "unconventional" as herself.

Apr. 20th [1912]

In the daytime I loaf a good deal in Florence ———'s office — there all the radicals drop in from time to time. . . .

Florence . . . is a girl of nineteen who is as mature looking as a woman of 45. She is a mixture of French and Irish and is the most unconventional creature I have ever met; she is fat but it is a hard fat; she has dark looking eyes and dark hair and soft, caressing hands, well shaped but with spatulate nails. She thinks that when a woman marries each kid should be by a different man. She has the prettiest mouth I ever saw. . . . we made a bargain—I'm to stop drinking and she will stop using crude language—very vulgar language. . . . Florence means to marry for money only—she is unscrupulous and selfish with those she don't like. She literally oozes sex and tells me that there are only two men she has ever met often who have not asked her for intercourse. She tells me that she shakes with desire for intercourse but is afraid of 'getting in' wrong—that is, having a baby. I am not telling you this for gossip I'm only describing Florence. I said to her, "Insidious poison, how did I ever become acquainted with you?" and she said, "I flirted with you."

Florence isn't a Christian either; she used to get a beating every Sunday when she lived at home—they beat her to make her go to church. She wants someone to place a bomb under every church in Kensington so she can light them.

She likes perfumed cigarettes only wont smoke for fear of ruining her voice—she likes drink but says [of herself], "I don't like to hold Florence's head the next morning." She would like to masturbate only she said she read a doctor book once and it scared the devil out of her. I certainly have fun with Florence—we say whatever comes into our heads. I say things to her I don't say to you for I'm always afraid of losing you. . . .

Well, I'll smoke a few more cigarettes and dream of you before I turn in. I like to think of you from the first glimpse I ever had of you. Tonight I approach you with reverence.

Three months later on July 28, in a letter addressed "Dearest," Sperry writes to Goldman:

The reason that I have been reticent with you lately was because I have been ashamed of myself and did not want to tell you what I was doing; you see, I went on that trip with Newton. Newton is a Carnegie steel man whom I have known since panic times. Fred and I were living in Braddock at the time and the larder was pretty empty—in fact I helped clean out a flat for a peck of potatoes and some onions and some cabbage and I also did several ironings. Then I said to myself, "Anybody who works like this is a damned fool." So I got a friend of mine to introduce me to Newt, who had nothing to do during the panic but walk the streets and spend his money as his salary was going on all the time; he is pretty well heeled at that. So I've had Newt ever since the panic times and when he asked me to take a trip with him this summer I hated to kill the goose that lays the golden eggs for God knows that Fred don't make enuf to keep me in cigarettes and magazines. So I went on the trip and I never had a more miserable time in all my life as one can find out more about a person by living under the same roof with them a day than they can find out by seeing them every day for a year. I must say that I am more disgusted with men than I ever was and if I ever give Fred up it will have to be a 'cookoo' that gets me the next time. I never saw a man that works for the United States Steel trust that was in the least successful either as a major or as a minor boss that wasn't a god-damned hog; they can eat more and hold more booze than any one that I ever saw. Newt is a stout man with a bay window belly. I have seen him with three and four different meats in front of him at the table— no wonder he gets gout; he is a Christian too, by the powers, and thinks that his relations with me are a sin. I have always let him believe that I was a Christian, too, until lately and one day I couldn't stand it any more and I said, "See here! I'm damned if I don't tell you just what I believe in;" he looked in amazement for he never heard me swear before—and then I gave him a tirade on my beliefs of all sorts. Do you think that he got disgusted? No, he grinned and got an erection of the penis; he is like all the rest of the Christians—he has as much real christianity in him as my big toe has. And he has an ox-like brain that is exasperating; all he knows how to do is to horse hell out of the men to increase the tonnage of the mills. I never was so god damned mad at myself in all my life—when we'd get in a coach he would make me sit facing him all the time—so he would be sure of having me, I s'pose and he always tries to make me smear my face with cream and powder. I'll bet that he wont want me to go on a vacation with him again in a hurry for I chased him all over the map. I darn near killed myself doing so but he was some tired, too. I wish that I had been feeling well—he'd be up in his heaven tuning his harp by now—he'd have died of appoplexy [sic].

How will the 26th of August suit you for me to come to see you—that is, if you would like to meet me after telling you all this? I don't care—I'll be darned if I go hungry for anybody. . . .

Write to me, dear, I need it. Let me know when it is your pleasure to have me come to see you. I want to *touch* you—I want to see whether you really have substance or whether you are merely one of my dreams.

Lovingly A

On August 8, replying to a letter from Goldman, Sperry again discusses her own love and sex relations with men.

I have absolutely no reciprocation as far as passion is concerned for a man who pays me for sex. So bent is such a man for self-gratification that he seldom bothers to find out whether the woman responds or not and if he does want response he can easily be "bluffed." Nearly all men try to buy love—if they don't do it by marrying they do it otherwise and that is why I have such a contempt for men. Love should be worship but love seems to be with most people—ejaculation. I fear I never will love any man. I've seen too much and I am no fool.

Referring to the possibility of leaving her husband, Sperry thinks she

shall have him somewhere in the background always. Habit is even stronger than love and it is nice to sleep with someone so that when a person wakes up in the middle of the night why one can touch the other person and not feel so alone. And then, too, in the winter time—when the wind howls. My word! If I were alone then, I'd ask the nearest male who had any kind of health to sleep with me, just for the sake of his animal warmth. My word! I have no civilization whatever, have I? But as far as violence is concerned, violence don't hold me to anyone. It is the sweet part of Fred that holds me—and the fact that we have been thru strikes, panics and hunger and sickness together. The time he went to cut my throat I kicked him in the abdomen and he forgot about wanting to slit my neck. You can ask my mother if she ever got a whimper out of me when she beat me. A loving glance, a pressure of the hand, a smile and I was her willing slave but a beating or a hit alongside the head and she was the one to fear then—not I. The inner part of me is untamed—it's never been licked. . . .

I am a savage, Emma, a wild, wild savage. And they can't tame me with their puling conventions, their stinking houses nor their damned religion. And it is the untamed part of me that loves you because you don't want to put leading strings on it. If you did I would tell you that you are a liar and your book is a lie.

And it is the wild part of me that would be unabashed in showing its love for you in front of a multitude or in a crowded room. My eyes would sparkle with love—they would follow you about and love to gaze upon you always and every part of my body would be replete with satisfaction of its expression of love.

God! God! God! God!

A

On August 24, Sperry responds to a letter from Goldman.

Dearest:

It is so very, very sweet of you to address me with endearing terms. I assure you that no one in the world appreciates such expressions of endearment more than myself, especially when they emanate from such a tower of strength as yourself. I suppose that the reason that you are such a tower of strength is that you are thoroly purged from all superstition. I note where you say that love should not mean worship as that smacks too much of slavishness for you. I discuss that matter because I naturally wanted to find just what your definition of the term meant.

In a letter of uncertain date, Sperry refers to Goldman's hope that they may spend some time together in the country.

Dear . . . I, too, wish that I could spend a week with you in the country. I am with you in spirit, at any rate. Just before you sink into slumber, dear heart, I rest in your arms. I browse amongst the roots of your hair—I kiss your body with biting kisses—I inhale the sweet, pungent odor of you and you plead with me for relief.

After spending a week in the country with Goldman, Sperry again speaks of her deep feelings for her friend.

Sept. 23rd [1912]

Dearest: I have been flitting about from one thing to another today, in vain endeavor to quell my terrible longing for you. But my work is done and now that I have sat down to think, I am instantly seized with a fire that races over my body in recurrent waves. My last thots at night are of you. I dream of you during my slumbers and that hellish alarm clock is losing some of its terrors for me for my first waking thots are of you.

Dear, that day you were so kind to me and afterwards took me in your arms, your beautiful throat, that I kissed with a reverent tenderness, reminded me somehow of the threat of that bird I shot—you remember my telling you of that.

Do you know, sweet cherry-blossom, that my week with you has filled me with such an energy, such an eagerness to become worthy of your friendship, that I feel that I must either use my intensity towards living up to my best self or ending it all quickly in one last, grand debauch. . . .

. . . How I wish I [was] with you on the farm! You are so sweet in the mornings—your eyes are like violets and you seem to forget, for a time, the sorrows of the world. And your bosom—ah, your sweet bosom, unconfined.

Lovingly,
Almeda

On October 11, 1912, Sperry writes to Goldman:

Of course I have an ache for you but it is a sad ache, not a passionate ache. I do not believe in allowing passion to rule one's head for then it is not love but lust[.]

On top of a typed letter, hand-dated October 21, Sperry scrawls in pencil:

Don't you ever show this to anybody.

The typed letter begins:

Do you know, dear, that sometimes I feel quite cruel towards you? When I do not hear from you I wish I were a giant with thirty league boots, I would stride to where you are, grab you up with my big paws and dump you down into the middle of this community and whenever you would try to escape I would push you back into it again just to let dispair [*sic*] creep into your heart. I would like to strike you in the mouth. I think, "She is at the tail end of a blind alley anyhow. To hell with other people—damn the swine! they do not understand any part of her and she is giving, giving, giving herself to them. She will die in extreme poverty, if she does not die in harness. . . ." And then I think, "Can it be possible that I feel vulgar jealousy? Well, this is the first time." And then—I kiss your feet and ask for forgiveness.

> In the same letter, in a hand-written section dated the next day, October 22, Sperry continues a feverish dialogue with herself about her mixed feelings for Goldman.

And then sometimes I think, "Perhaps she is just studying me—all my personalities for the good of her cause—studying this peculiar product of our civilization. Her cause is first. But if I were really assured of this fact I would carve her heart out. Mark how the blood spurts! But by carving her heart out, Almeda, you would only acknowledge your weakness and you do love to kiss her hands, Almeda, and lay your head on her wonderful bosom. So get strong, Almeda, get strong—as she is and such unbidden thoughts will not come into your head. And haven't you had proof that the human side responds to you? But her cause—her cause comes first! But doesn't it in you, Almeda? Think! What else is worth while living for? Lower your head in shame.

> Sperry's jealousy and anger at Goldman apparently continued to grow and find expression. At some point, in a reconciliation attempt, Goldman sent Sperry a rose, which Sperry immediately sent back, then waited in agony during the next weeks, fearing that her rejection of Goldman had finally been successful. On December 12, Sperry wrote Goldman asking her not to forsake her. Still not hearing from Goldman, on December 20 Sperry wrote again, apologizing for her "crime" against Goldman, expressing gratitude to her friend, and declaring, "I have rooted jealousy out of me, Emma, *rooted* it!" On December 23, Sperry received a Christmas card from Goldman, who, it seems, continued to accept her friend—jealousy, anger, love, and all. Sperry immediately replied:

Dec. 23rd 1912

Dearest: I have just received your card and am filled with a great peace. I am a little remorseful for wanting to hear from you so badly. . . . I will never again have anger for you nor ever feel impatient again for I have lived a thousand years in the last two weeks.

Tell me, Emma, why is it that when a person knows he has been as bad as he can be—why is it that he picks out the one he loves the most to hurt? And why did I have to show you the savage part of me and want to even beat you? I hope you got your fill of the 'primitive.'

I am so glad you looked into my eyes that day. It is a good thing that one-half of me is decent. I wish I had had a mother like you. You are my mother. Fred said that day I sent the rose back—you know I woke up screaming—[Fred said:] "O, will you *never* be anything else but a child? If I know *Em*, she won't pay any attention to it." Then I went to sleep again for Fred always knows. . . .

Ah your dear eyes! There are many things I cannot do now since you looked at me that way. I reckon I must love you more than I ever loved anybody because I used to do everything I felt like doing without stopping to consider others. You are the first person who ever "got my goat." I reckon its because I believe in you. If I didn't I'd kill you.

Almeda

In a letter addressed to "Honey bug," written on the following day, Christmas Eve (and continued on Christmas), a calmer Sperry tells Goldman:

I am so sorry you have a cold. You must wear spats on rainy or slushy days. I was thinking about that the day I touched your ankle at the Colonial. Low cut shoes are foolish on a rainy day—ones skirts get wet at the bottom and make ones ankles wet. . . .

. . . I shall have all those things you wish for me in the coming year if you keep on loving me—you sweet dear. If you were here I would kiss your hands—not from servility—I am servile to no one—but because they are such sweet little ducks of hands. I would do more than that—I am famished to rest my head on your bosom.

Lovingly, A

1912: ALEXANDER BERKMAN;
Prison Memoirs of an Anarchist
"The springs of affection well up within me"

Alexander Berkman, born in Kovno, Russia, on November 18, 1870, was already imbued with strong libertarian impulses when he emigrated to America. In 1888, he was active in the New York anarchist movement and helped organize the first memorial to workers killed in the earlier Haymarket tragedy. Berkman had planned to return to Russia to carry on the anarchist struggle when, in May 1892, the workers at the Carnegie Steel Company plant at Homestead, Pennsylvania, went on strike. On July 6, when strikebreakers hired by the company confronted striking workers, seven persons were killed in the "Homestead massacre." On July 12, when the state militia took over in Homestead, the strike seemed broken.

Influenced by the writings of anarchist leader Johann Most, Berkman, together with Emma Goldman, decided the political situation called for the assassination of Henry Clay Frick, general manager of the Homestead steel mills. On July 23, 1892, the twenty-one-year-old Alexander Berkman shot and stabbed Frick, but did not succeed in killing him. For this assault, Berkman served fifteen years in the Western Penitentiary of Pennsylvania and was released in 1906.

Upon his release, Berkman joined Emma Goldman in editing the anarchist periodical *Mother Earth*; in 1912 he published *Prison Memoirs of an Anarchist*, a rich autobiographical account of his confinement. Berkman again became active in working-class organizing, and later began publishing *The Blast*, an anarchist periodical, in San Francisco. In 1916, Berkman, Goldman, and others opposed United States entry into World War I, organizing working-class groups to that end; they were arrested for their antiwar activities and Berkman was sentenced to two years in the Atlanta penitentiary.

In prison, Berkman spent most of his time in solitary confinement for protesting the brutal treatment of other inmates. When he was released in September 1919, the United States government began deportation proceedings, and in 1920 Berkman was put on a ship bound for the Soviet Union, whose October Revolution both he and Emma Goldman had publicly supported. Berkman remained in Russia for two years; his two books, *The Kronstadt Rebellion* and *The Bolshevik Myth* convey his disillusionment with Soviet communism.

The rest of Berkman's life was devoted to helping political prisoners in Soviet jails and to writing *Now and After, the ABC of Communist Anarchism*. In 1936, at age sixty-six, failing health caused Berkman to take his own life.

Berkman's *Prison Memoirs* contain several passages concerning homosexuality in Pennsylvania's Western Penitentiary. In his introduction to a 1970 reprint of Berkman's *Memoirs*, Paul Goodman comments, "His telling of the sexual scenes is especially notable." Among all those who have written about prison homosexuality, says Goodman,

> Berkman alone unsophisticatedly goes to the essence, the longing, being in love, and love, that would inevitably occur. His embarrassed conversations are quite wonderful; I do not know any novels of sixty years ago to equal them. He does not mention any scenes of sexual brutality, however, though this also would be the nature of the case where men are not free. Being in prison is one of the conditions that most need fellow-feeling, but it is one of the worst conditions for it.[168]

In the first scene, set in the prison stocking shop, Berkman describes a colorful fellow inmate named Red, who introduces him to the subject of homosexuality. Internal evidence dates this event to 1892, Berkman's first year of imprisonment. Red speaks:

"Permit me to introduce to you, sir, a gentleman who has sounded the sharps and flats of life, and faced the most intricate network, sir, of iron bars between York and Frisco. . . .

"They'se goin' to move me down on your row, now that I'm in this 'ere [prison hosiery] shop. Dunno how long I shall choose to remain, sir, in this magnificent hosiery establishment, but I see there's a vacant cell next yours, an' I'm goin' to try an' land there. Are you next, me bye? I'm goin' to learn you to be wise, sonny. I shall, so to speak, assume benevolent guardianship over you; over you and your morals, yes, sir, for you're my kid now, see?"

"How, your kid?"

"How? My kid, of course. That's just what I mean. Any objections, sir, as the learned gentlemen of the law say in the honorable courts of the blind goddess. You betcher life she's blind, blind as an owl on a sunny midsummer day. . . ."

"Hold on, Red. You are romancing. You started to tell me about being your 'kid'. Now explain, what do you mean by it?"

"Really, you—" He holds the unturned stocking suspended over the post, gazing at me with half-closed, cynical eyes, in which doubt struggles with wonder. In his astonishment he has forgotten his wonted caution, and I warn him of the officer's watchful eye.

"Really, Alex; well, now, damme, I've seen something of this 'ere round globe, some mighty strange sights, too, and there ain't many things to surprise *me*, lemme tell you. But *you* do, Alex; yes, me lad, you do. . . . I never got such a stunner as you just gave me. Why, man, it's a body-blow, a reg'lar knockout to my knowledge of the world, sir, to my settled estimate of the world's supercilious righteousness. Well, damme, if I'd ever believe it. Say, how old are you, Alex?"

"I'm over twenty-two, Red. But what has all this to do with the question I asked you?"

"Everythin', me bye, everythin'. You're twenty-two and don't know what a kid is! Well, if it don't beat raw eggs, I don't know what does. Green? Well, sir, it would be hard to find an adequate analogy to your inconsistent immaturity of mind; aye, sir, I may well say, of soul, except to compare it with the virtuous condition of green corn in the early summer moon. You know what 'moon' is, don't you?" he asks, abruptly, with an evident effort to suppress a smile. . . .

"I suppose I do."

"I'll bet you my corn dodger you don't. . . .

". . . In plain English, sir, I shall endeavor to generate within your postliminious comprehension a discriminate conception of the subject at issue, sir, by divesting my lingo of the least shadow of imperspicuity or ambiguity. Moonology, my Marktwainian Innocent, is the truly Christian science of loving your neighbor, provided he be a nice little boy. Understand now?"

"How can you love a boy?"

"Are you really so dumb? You are not a ref[orm school] boy, I can see that."

"Red, if you'd drop your stilted language and talk plainly, I'd understand better."

". . . You love a boy as you love the poet-sung heifer, see? Ever read Billy Shakespeare? Know the place, 'He's neither man nor woman; he's punk.' Well, Billy knew. A punk's a boy that'll ———"

"What!"

"Yes, sir. Give himself to a man. Now we'se talkin' plain. Savvy now, Innocent Abroad?"

"I don't believe what you are telling me, Red."

"You don't be-lie-ve? What th' devil—damn me soul t' hell, what d' you mean, you don't b'lieve? . . ."

"No, Red, I meant it quite seriously. You're spinning ghost stories, or whatever you call it. I don't believe in this kid love."

"An' why don't you believe it?"

"Why—er—well, I don't think it possible."

"*What* isn't possible?"

"You know what I mean. I don't think there can be such intimacy between those of the same sex."

"Ho, ho! *That's* your point? Why, Alex, you're more of a damfool than the casual observer, sir, would be apt to postulate. You don't believe it possible, you don't, eh? Well, you jest gimme half a chance, and I'll show you."

"Red, don't you talk to me like that," I burst out, angrily. "If you—"

"Aisy, aisy, me bye," he interrupts, good-naturedly. "Don't get on your high horse. No harm meant, Alex. You're a good boy, but you jest rattle me with your crazy talk. Why, you're bugs to say it's impossible. Man alive, the dump's chuckful of punks. It's done in every prison, an' on th' road, everywhere. Lord, if I had a plunk for every time I got th' best of a kid, I'd rival Rockefeller, sir; I would, me bye."

"You actually confess to such terrible practices? You're disgusting. But I don't really believe it, Red."

"Confess hell! I confess nothin'. Terrible, disgusting! You talk like a man up a tree, you holy sky-pilot."

"Are there no women on the road?"

"Pshaw! Who cares for a heifer when you can get a kid? Women are no good. I wouldn't look at 'em when I can have my prushun.* Oh, it is quite evident, sir, you have not delved into the esoteric mysteries of moonology, nor tasted the mellifluous fruit on the forbidden tree of—"

"Oh, quit!"

"Well, you'll know better before *your* time's up, me virtuous sonny."[169]

In the next sequence, datable to early 1897, Berkman has been placed in an underground cell for misbehavior.

The hours drag on. The monotony is broken by the keepers bringing another prisoner to the dungeon. I hear his violent sobbing from the depth of the cavern.

"Who is there?" I hail him. I call repeatedly, without receiving an answer. Perhaps the new arrival is afraid of listening guards.

"Ho, man!" I sing out, "the screws have gone. Who are you? This is Aleck, Aleck Berkman."

"Is that you, Aleck? This is Johnny." There is a familiar ring about the young voice, broken by piteous moans. But I fail to identify it.

"What Johnny?"

"Johnny Davis—you know—stocking shop. I've just—killed a man."

In bewilderment I listen to the story, told with bursts of weeping. Johnny had returned to the shop; he thought he would try again: he wanted to earn his "good" time. Things went well for a while, till "Dutch" Adams became shop runner. . . . Davis would have nothing to do with him. But "Dutch" persisted, pestering him all the time; and then—

"Well, you know, Aleck," the boy seems diffident, "he lied about me like hell: he told the fellows he *used* me. Christ, my mother might hear about it! I couldn't stand it, Aleck; honest to God, I couldn't. I—I killed the lying cur, an' now—now I'll—I'll swing for it," he sobs as if his heart would break.

A touch of tenderness for the poor boy is in my voice, as I strive to condole with him and utter the hope that it may not be so bad, after all. Perhaps Adams will not die. He is a powerful man, big and strong; he may survive.

Johnny eagerly clutches at the straw. He grows more cheerful. . . . Perhaps the Board will even clear him, he suggests. But suddenly seized with fear, he weeps and moans again.

* A boy serving his apprenticeship with a full-fledged tramp [note in original].

When more men are cast into the underground cells, they bring news from above. Johnny Davis interrupts their talk

to inquire anxiously about "Dutch" Adams, and I share his joy at hearing that the man's wound is not serious. He was cut about the shoulders, but was able to walk unassisted to the hospital. Johnny overflows with quiet happiness; the others dance and sing. I recite a poem from Nekrassov; the boys don't understand a word, but the sorrow-laden tones appeal to them, and they request more Russian "pieces." . . .

Late in the evening the young prisoners are relieved. But Johnny remains, and his apprehensions reawaken. Repeatedly during the night he rouses me from my drowsy torpor to be reassured that he is not in danger of the gallows, and that he will not be tried for his assault. I allay his fears by dwelling on the Warden's aversion to giving publicity to the sex practices in the prison, and remind the boy of the Captain's official denial of their existence. These things happen almost every week, yet no one has ever been taken to court from Riverside on such charges.

Johnny grows more tranquil, and we converse about his family history, talking in a frank, confidential manner. With a glow of pleasure, I become aware of the note of tenderness in his voice. Presently he surprises me by asking:

"Friend Aleck, what do they call you in Russian?"

He prefers the fond "Sashenka," enunciating the strange word with quaint endearment, then diffidently confesses dislike for his own name, and relates the story he had recently read of a poor castaway Cuban youth; Felipe was his name, and he was just like himself.

"Shall I call you Felipe?" I offered.

"Yes, please do, Aleck, dear; no, Sashenka."

The springs of affection well up within me, as I lie huddled on the stone floor, cold and hungry. With closed eyes, I picture the boy before me, with his delicate face, and sensitive, girlish lips.

"Good night, dear Sashenka," he calls.

"Good night, little Felipe."

In the morning . . . Johnny begs the Deputy Warden to tell him how much longer he will remain in the dungeon, but Greaves curtly commands silence, applying a vile epithet to the boy.

"Deputy," I call, boiling over with indignation, "he asked you a respectful question. I'd give him a decent answer."

"You mind your own business, you hear?" he retorts.

But I persist in defending my young friend, and berate the Deputy for his language. He hastens away in a towering passion. . . .

Johnny is distressed at being the innocent cause of the trouble. . . . But the hours pass without the Deputy returning, and our fears are allayed. The boy rejoices on my account, and brims over with appreciation of my intercession.

The incident cements our intimacy; our first diffidence disappears, and we become openly tender and affectionate. The conversation lags: we feel weak and worn. But every little while we hail each other with words of encouragement. [The insane] Smithy incessantly paces the cell; the gnawing of the river rats reaches our ears; the silence is frequently pierced by the wild yells of the insane man, startling us with dread foreboding. The quiet grows unbearable, and Johnny calls again:

"What are you doing, Sashenka?"

"Oh, nothing. Just thinking, Felipe."

"Am I in your thoughts, dear?"

"Yes, kiddie, you are."

"Sasha, dear, I've been thinking, too."

"What, Felipe?"

"You are the only one I care for. I haven't a friend in the whole place."

"Do you care much for me, Felipe?"

"Will you promise not to laugh at me, Sashenka?"

"I wouldn't laugh at you."

"Cross your hand over your heart. Got it, Sasha?"

"Yes."

"Well, I'll tell you. I was thinking—how shall I tell you? I was thinking, Sashenka—if you were here with me—I would like to kiss you."

An unaccountable sense of joy glows in my heart, and I muse in silence.

"What's the matter, Sashenka? Why don't you say something? Are you angry with me?"

"No, Felipe, you foolish little boy."

"You are laughing at me."

"No, dear; I feel just as you do."

"Really?"

"Yes."

"Oh, I am so glad, Sashenka."

In the evening the guards descend to relieve Johnny; he is to be transferred to the basket [cell], they inform him. On the way past my cell, he whispers: "Hope I'll see you soon, Sashenka." . . .

I feel more lonesome at the boy's departure. The silence grows more oppressive, the hours of darkness heavier.[170]

> Time passes. Berkman is moved by the plight of those driven insane by intolerable prison conditions and placed in "crank row," called "the graveyard of the living dead."

The sight of the terrible misery almost gives a touch of consolation to my grief over Johnny Davis. My young friend had grown ill in the foul basket. He begged to be taken to the hospital; but his condition did not warrant it, the physician said. Moreover, he was "in punishment." Poor boy, how he must have suffered! They found him dead on the floor of his cell.[171]

> In a chapter titled "Passing the Love of Woman," dating to about 1902, Berkman describes his conversations about homosexuality with "Doctor George," a fellow prisoner who has served many years for his alleged complicity in a bank robbery in which a cashier was killed. The doctor's background is Catholic, Berkman reports, and a great-grandfather was a signer of the Declaration of Independence. Doctor George is described as a Jeffersonian democrat, a liberal intellectual, an antiimperialist, whose experience of prison has made him question the justice of the entire American legal system, the very idea of punishment, the efficacy of any legal remedy for social ills.
>
> Berkman says of Doctor George:

My friend is very bitter against the prison element variously known as "the girls," "Sallies," and "punks," who for gain traffic in sexual gratification. But he takes a broad view of the moral aspect of homosexuality; his denunciation is against the commerce in carnal desires. As a medical man, and a student, he is deeply interested in the manifestations of suppressed sex. He speaks with profound sympathy of the brilliant English man-of-letters [Oscar Wilde], whom the world of cant and stupidity has driven to prison and to death because his sex life did not conform to the accepted standards. . . .

. . . In detail, my friend traces the various phases of his psychic development since his imprisonment, and I warm toward him with a sense of intense humanity, as he reveals the intimate emotions of his being. A general medical practitioner, he had not come in personal contact with cases of homosexuality. He had heard of pederasty; but like the majority of his colleagues, he had neither understanding for nor sympathy with the sex practices he considered abnormal and vicious. In prison he was horrified at the perversion that frequently came under his observation. For two years the very thought of such matters filled him with disgust; he even refused to speak to the men and boys known to be homosexual, unconditionally condemning them—"with my prejudices rather than my reason," he remarks. But the forces of suppression were at work.[172]

> The doctor discusses prison masturbation ("self-abuse"), which he feels, if practiced no more often than heterosexual coition, is not harmful—but which "dangerously" grows on one in prison. Berkman continues:

For a moment George pauses. The veins of his forehead protrude, as if he is undergoing a severe mental struggle. Presently he says: "Aleck, I'm going to speak very frankly to you. I'm much interested in the subject. I'll give you my intimate experiences, and I want you to be just as frank with me. I think it's one of the most important things, and I want to learn all I can about it. Very little is known about it, and much less understood."

"About what, George?"

"About homosexuality. I have spoken of the second phase of onanism. With a strong effort I overcame it. Not entirely, of course. But I have succeeded in regulating the practice, indulging in it at certain intervals. But as the months and years passed, my emotions manifested themselves. It was like a psychic awakening. The desire to love something was strong upon me. Once I caught a little mouse in my cell, and tamed it a bit. It would eat out of my hand, and come around at meal times, and by and by it would stay all evening to play with me. I learned to love it. Honestly, Aleck, I cried when it died. And then, for a long time, I felt as if there was a void in my heart. I wanted something to love. It just swept me with a wild craving for affection. Somehow the thought of woman gradually faded from my mind. When I saw my wife, it was just like a dear friend. But I didn't feel toward her sexually. One day, as I was passing in the hall, I noticed a young boy. He had been in only a short time, and he was rosy-cheeked, with a smooth little face and sweet lips—he reminded me of a girl I used to court before I married. After that I frequently surprised myself thinking of the lad. I felt no desire toward him, except just to know him and get friendly. I became acquainted with him, and when he heard I was a medical man, he would often call to consult me about the stomach trouble he suffered. The doctor here persisted in giving the poor kid salts and physics all the time. Well, Aleck, I could hardly believe it myself, but I grew so fond of the boy, I was miserable when a day passed without my seeing him. I would take big chances to get near him. I was rangeman then, and he was assistant on a top tier. We often had opportunities to talk. I got him interested in literature, and advised him what to read, for he didn't know what to do with his time. He had a fine character, that boy, and he was bright and intelligent. At first it was only a liking for him, but it increased all the time, till I couldn't think of any woman. But don't misunderstand me, Aleck; it wasn't that I wanted a 'kid.' I swear to you, the other youths had no attraction for me whatever; but this boy—his name was Floyd—he became so dear to me, why, I used to give him everything I could get. I had a friendly guard, and he'd bring me fruit and things. Sometimes I'd just die to eat it, but I always gave it to Floyd. And, Aleck—you remember when I was down in the dungeon six days? Well, it was for the sake of that boy. He did something, and I took the blame on myself. And the last time—they kept me nine days chained up—I hit a fellow for abusing Floyd: he was small and couldn't defend himself. I did not realize it at the time, Aleck, but I know now that I was simply in love with the boy; wildly, madly in love. It came very gradually. For two years I loved him without the least taint of sex desire. It was the purest affection I ever felt in my life. It was all-absorbing, and I would have sacrificed my life for him if he had asked it. But by degrees the psychic stage began to manifest all the expressions of love between the opposite sexes. I remember the first time he kissed me. It was early in the morning; only the rangemen were out, and I stole up to his cell to give him a delicacy. He put both hands between the bars, and pressed his lips to mine. Aleck, I tell you, never in my life had I experienced such bliss as at that moment. It's five years ago, but it thrills me every time I think of it. It came suddenly; I didn't expect it. It was entirely spontaneous: our eyes met, and it seemed as if something drew us together. He told me he was very fond of me. From then on we became lovers. I used to neglect my work, and risk great danger to get a chance to kiss and embrace him. I grew terribly jealous, too, though I had no cause. I passed through every phase of a passionate love. With this difference, though—I felt a touch of the old disgust at the thought of actual sex contact. That I didn't do. It seemed to me a desecration of the boy, and of my love for him. But after a while that feeling also wore off, and I desired sexual relation with him. He said he loved me enough to do even that for me, though he had never done it before. He hadn't been in any reformatory, you know. And yet, somehow I couldn't bring myself to do it; I loved the lad too much for it. Perhaps you will smile, Aleck, but it was real, true love. When Floyd was unexpectedly transferred to the other block, I felt that I would be the happiest man if I could only touch his hand again, or get one more kiss. You—you're laughing?" he asks abruptly, a touch of anxiety in his voice.

"No, George. I am grateful for your confidence. I think it is a wonderful thing; and, George—I had felt the same horror and disgust at these things, as you did. But now I think quite differently about them."

"Really, Aleck? I'm glad you say so. Often I was troubled—is it viciousness or what, I wondered; but I could never talk to any one about it. They take everything here in such a filthy sense. Yet I knew in my heart that it was a true, honest emotion."

"George, I think it a very beautiful emotion. Just as beautiful as love for a woman. I had a friend here; his name was Russell; perhaps you remember him. I felt no physical passion toward him, but I think I loved him with all my heart. His death was a most terrible shock to me. It almost drove me insane."

Silently George holds out his hand.[173]

♀ 1923: HELEN R. HULL; *The Labyrinth*
" 'I know a little thing or two about love' "

Author Helen Rose Hull was born in Albion, Michigan; both of her parents were teachers. The family library was an early source of Hull's interest in literature, and her grandfather for many years edited and published a newspaper in Constantine, Michigan. Hull reports that books and printing were so much a part of her early years that she cannot remember when she did not intend to write. Her first short stories were published in 1915, her first novel in 1922.

According to Jeannette Foster, several of Hull's works contain Lesbian-relevant themes. "As early as 1918," says Foster, "the *Century Magazine* published Hull's short story 'The Fire,' which treats

a small-town girl's love for the middle-aged spinster who gave her not only art lessons but her first contact with a mellow and cultured personality. . . . The innocent friendship is broken off by the girl's jealous mother on the ground that "it's not healthy or natural for a girl to be hanging around an old maid."

Hull's first novel, *Quest* (1922), says Foster, tells the story of Jean, who,

falls in love at twelve with a [female] high-school teacher, and simultaneously forms a feverish alliance with a classmate [also female] considerably older and less naïve who adores the same woman.

It is the classmate

who draws the mother's fire here, and she terminates the connection with a touch of melodrama which leaves her daughter wary of variant [Lesbian] emotion, in the same way that the family situation [tension between her parents] has affected her with regard to heterosexual love. Jean's subsequent relations with men are inhibited, and her two or three very warm friendships with girls and women during college and her early years of teaching never approach the intensity of her first love.[174]

Catherine, the central character of Hull's novel *The Labyrinth* (1923), feels herself lost within confines of the traditional female role of wife-mother-lover-housekeeper; she is searching for a way out. In contrast, Catherine's younger sister, Margaret, a minor figure in the novel, a successful and socially conscious business-woman, seems well on the way to putting aside her "infantile traits"—by leaving her mother's house—and establishing a loving home with her tenderly adored Amy.

Although the word Lesbian is never used about Margaret and Amy's love, its character is made perfectly clear. Hull goes so far as to emphasize Margaret's green dress, green hat, green coat, green eyes, and green identification card, a color symbolism, no doubt intended as an "in" clue to Margaret's sexual orientation— green being one of those colors traditionally associated with homosexuality.[175] Despite Margaret's gay coloring, and what (to a reader) are revealing references to her love life, her well-educated sister Catherine and Catherine's psychologist husband are apparently quite unaware of her orientation.

Because the Lesbian characters in Hull's book are minor ones, such a work may not receive much attention as a document of Lesbian American history. Yet *The Labyrinth* presents a rare picture of an aspiring, professionally employed Lesbian couple in the early 1920s. Hull's portrait of this couple is remarkable for its positive, matter-of-fact treatment, and for connecting this Lesbianism with an emphatic, though decidedly middle-class, feminism. Throughout the story, Margaret's antagonism to her sister's psychologist husband, Charles, is based on his assumption of traditional male privilege and ideas about his wife's proper place; Margaret mockingly calls him "the King." Margaret's feminism, by current standards horribly snobbish and antiworking-class, is probably an accurate representation of the views held by a certain small class of more privileged American women in the 1920s.

Although fictional sources present special difficulties and ambiguities when analyzed as social document, selections from Hull's *The Labyrinth* are included here to suggest the importance of such material for future research, especially for the historical study of women-loving women.

In the first selection from *The Labyrinth*, the central character, Catherine, who has recently returned to work as a statistician with a private bureau of social welfare, meets her sister, Margaret, for lunch. Earlier references have established that Margaret lives with her mother and has spent her summer vacation "with that friend of hers." The sisters' traditionalist mother has referred to Margaret as one of those "modern women" who wants "to set up housekeeping with her friend." Margaret, has also, says her mother, "been thinking, too, I am afraid."[176] This sequence introduces Margaret to the reader; the narration is from Catherine's viewpoint.

Margaret was waiting at the elevator entrance, a vivid figure in the milling groups of befurbished stenographers and shoddier older women. She came toward Catherine, and their hands clung for a moment. How young she is, and invincible, thought Catherine, as they waited for the elevator to empty its load. Margaret had Catherine's slimness and erect height; her bright hair curled under the brim of her soft green hat; there was something inimitably swagger about the lines of her sage-green wool dress and loose coat, with flashes of orange in embroidery and lining. In place of the sensitive poise of Catherine's eyes and mouth, Margaret had a downright steadiness, an untroubled intensity.

"How's it feel to be a wage-earner?" She hugged Catherine's arm as they backed out of the pushing crowd into a corner of the car. "You look elegant!"

"Scracely that." Catherine smiled at her. "Now you do! Did you design that color scheme?"

"I matched my best points, eyes and high lights of hair." Margaret grinned. Her eyes were green in the shadow. "Ever lunched here? I thought you might find it convenient. Lots of my girls come here."

They emerged at the entrance of a large room full of the clatter of dishes and tongues.

"I'll take you in on my card to-day. If you like it, you can get one." Margaret ushered Catherine into the tail of the line which filed slowly ahead of them. . . . [Margaret] extended her green card. "A guest, please." . . .

They found a table under a rear window, where they could unload their dishes of soup and salad around the glass vase with its dusty crêpe-paper rose. . . .

Margaret hitched her chair closer to Catherine.

"Now tell me all about it." She tore the oiled paper from the package of crackers; her hand had the likeness to Catherine's, and the difference, which her face suggested. Fingers deft and agile, but shorter, firmer, competent rather than graceful. "Mother says you've hired a wet-nurse and abandoned your family. I didn't think you had it in you!"

"I know. You thought I was old and shelved."

"Just a tinge of mid-Victorian habit, old dear."

"You young things need to open your eyes."

"I have opened 'em. See me stare!" . . .

"Your old job?" proceeded Margaret.

"A new study—teaching conditions in some middle-western states. I am to organize the work."

Margaret's questions were direct, inclusive. She did have a clear mind. Her business training has rubbed off all the blurry sentiment she used to have, thought Catherine.

"And you can manage the family as well?"

"This woman Henrietta sent me is fine. It's a rush in the morning, baths and breakfast. Flora [a "maid"] can't come in until eight, and I have to get away by half past eight. No dawdling."

"And the King doesn't mind?"

Catherine flushed. Margaret had dubbed Charles the King years ago, but the nickname had an irritating flavor. "He's almost enthusiastic this week," she said. "Now tell me about yourself. What's this about your leaving Mother?"

". . . I'm house-hunting." Margaret laughed. . . .

"But I thought you were so comfortable——"

"Too soft. You don't know—" Margaret was serious. "I can't be babied all my life. All sorts of infantile traits sticking to me. You got away."

"Mother said you'd been reading a foreigner named Freud."

"Well!" Margaret was vigorously defensive. "What of it?"

Catherine dug her fork into the triangle of cake.

"I thought Freud was going out. Glands are the latest."

"I bet Charles said that." Margaret grinned impishly as she saw her thrust strike home. "Well, tell him I'm still on Freud. Anyway, I want to try this. Amy and I want to live together. When you wanted to live with Charles, you went and did it, didn't you?"

"I'm not criticizing you, Marge. Go ahead! Don't bristle so, or I'll suspect you feel guilty."

"I do." Margaret had a funny little smile which recognized herself as ludicrous. "That's just the vestige of my conflict."

Catherine asks Margaret:

"How's the job?"

"All right. I spent the morning hunting for a girl. She's been rousing my suspicions for a time. Going to have an infant soon. That's the third case in two months." . . . "But I've got a woman who'll take her in. She can do housework for a month or so before she'll have to go to the lying-in home."

Catherine watched her curiously. There was something amazing about the calm, matter-of-fact attitude Margaret held.

"Do you hunt for the father?"

"Oh, the girl won't tell. Maybe she doesn't know."

"If I had your job, I'd waste away from anger and rage and hopelessness about the world."

"No use." Margaret shrugged. "Wish I could smoke here. Too pious. No." She turned her face toward her sister, her eyes and mouth dispassionate. "Patch up what can be patched, and scrap the rest. I'm sick of feelings."

Catherine was silent. Margaret, as the only woman in a responsible position in a chain of small manufacturing plants, occasionally dropped threads which suggested fabrics too dreadful to unravel.

"Time's up." Margaret rose. "Directors' meeting this afternoon, and I want to bully that bunch of stiff-necked males into accepting a few of the suggestions I've made. I have a fine scheme." She laughed. "I make a list pages long, full of things, well, not exactly preposterous. Women would see them all. But they sound preposterous. And buried somewhere I have the one thing I'm hammering on just then. Sometimes I get it, out of their dismay at the length of the list."

"Here, I may as well go along." Catherine slid out of the chair.

"Will you be home Sunday?" Margaret stopped at the corner. Catherine had a fresh impression of her invincible quality, there in the sunlight with the passing crowds.

"Charles is in Washington. Come in and see the children."

"The King's away, eh?" Margaret waved her hand in farewell. "I'll drop in."[177]

An intervening scene establishes that Margaret and Amy are now living together. In a visit with her sister, speaking about children, Margaret says, " 'Maybe I'll want some, some day. . . . Now I've got Amy—and love enough to keep from growing stale. . . .' " Parting, Margaret tells her sister, with a "grimace," that she wants to see how Charles likes her "new arrangement" with Amy.[178]

In the next selection, Catherine and Margaret are again lunching together, when Margaret asks her sister how she's spending the money she's now earning. The sequence indicates Margaret's (and apparently Hull's) strong, though elitist, feminism, characterized by contempt for allegedly less intelligent working women.

"You draw a decent salary." Margaret pulled the collar of her heavy raccoon coat up against a snow-laden draft from the opened door. "What do you spend it for? You haven't bought a single dud. Why, you don't slip off your coat because the lining is patched. Does Charles make you give him your salary envelope?"

Catherine was silent. . . .

"Well?" Margaret poured. "I'm curious."

"Only a rich man can afford a self-supporting wife," said Catherine lightly. "I was figuring it up last night. I've got to make at least a hundred a week."

"What for?" insisted Margaret.

"Everything. There's not a bill that isn't larger, in spite of anything that I can do. Food, laundry, clothes. You have no idea how much I was worth! As a labor device, I mean."

"Um." Margaret glinted over her mouthful of cake. "I always thought the invention of wives was a clever stunt."

"They can save money, anyway. I tried doing some of the things evenings, ironing and mending, but I can't."

"I should hope not!"

"Well, then, I have to pay for them. Charles can't. It wouldn't be fair."

"You look as if you were doing housework all night, anyway." Margaret's eyes gleamed with hostility. "Why can't the King take his share? You're as thin as a bean pole."

"Wait till you get your own husband, you! Then you can talk."

"Husband!" Margaret hooted. "Me? I'm fixed for life right now."

"They have their good points." Catherine rose, drawing on her gloves. Margaret paid the bill and tipped with the nonchalance of an unattached male.

"That's all right." Margaret thrust her hands deep into her pockets and followed her sister. She turned her nose up to sniff at the sharp wind, eddying fine snow flakes down the side street. "I know lots of women who prefer to set up an establishment with another woman. Then you go fifty-fifty on everything. Work and feeling and all the rest, and no King waiting around for his humble servant." . . .

They walked swiftly down the Avenue; Catherine felt drab, almost haggard, worn down, by the side of Margaret's swinging, bright figure.

"How's your job?" she asked. "You haven't said a word about it."

"Grand." Margaret's smile had reminiscent malice. "You know, I've persuaded them to order new work benches for the main shop. I told you how devilish they were? Wrong height? Well, I cornered Hubbard last week. It was funny! I told him I'd found a terrible leak in his efficiency system. He's hipped on scientific efficiency. I tethered him and led him to a bench." She giggled. "I had him sitting there cutting tin before he knew where he was, and I kept him till he had a twinge of the awful cramp my girls have had. Result, new benches."

"You won't have half so much fun when you accomplish everything you want to, will you?"

"That's a hundred years from now, with me in the cool tombs." They stepped into the shelter of the elevator entrance to the Bureau. "I'm working now on some kind of promotion system. Of course, most of the girls are morons or straight f.m.'s, but there are a few who are better."

"What are 'f.m.'s'?"

"Feeble-mindeds. Like to do the same thing, simple thing, day after day. It takes intelligence to need something ahead." She grinned at Catherine. "They make excellent wives," she added. "Now if you didn't have brains, you'd be happy as an oyster in your little nest."

The splutter of motors protesting at the cold, the scurry of people, heads down into the wind, gray buildings pointing rigidly into a gray, low sky—Catherine caught all that as background for Margaret, fitting background. Margaret was like the city, young, hard, flashing.

"Of course, f.m.'s make rotten mothers," she was finishing. "In spite of the ease with which, as they say, they get into trouble."

"You know," Catherine's smile echoed the faint malice in her sister's as they stood aside for a puffing, red-nosed little man who bustled in for shelter—"I think you take your maternal instinct out on your job. Creating—"

"Maternal instinct! Holy snakes!" Margaret yanked her gloves out of her pockets and drew them on in scornful jerks. "You certainly have a sentimental imagination at times."

"That's why you don't need children," insisted Catherine. "Just as Henrietta Gilbert [a friend] takes it out on other people's children."

"You make me sick! Drivel!" Margaret glowered, gave her soft green hat a quick poke, and stepped out of the lobby. "Good-by! You'll lose your job, maundering so!"

"Good-by. Nice lunch." Catherine laughed as she hurried for the waiting elevator.[179]

In the next selection Margaret, for the first time, brings Amy to meet Catherine and Charles.

The bell in the hall sounded.

"Company to-night!" Catherine drooped. "I'm worn to a frazzle."

It was Margaret; her gay, "Hello, King Charles!" floated reassuringly to Catherine, dabbing powder hastily on her nose, brushing back her hair from her forehead.

"I brought my partner in to meet you two. Amy, this is the King, and my sister, Catherine—Amy Spurgeon."

Margaret, clear, sparkling, watching them with her humorous grin, as if she had staged a vaudeville act. Amy Spurgeon, slight, dark, her lean, high-cheekboned face sallow and taciturn over the collar of her squirrel coat, a flange of stiff hair black under the soft brim of her gray fur hat. Catherine nibbled at her in swift glances as they sat down in the living room. Margaret had talked about her. "Amy has to have a passion for something." She looked it, with the criss-crosses of fine lines at the corners of her black eyes, and the deep straight lines from nostrils past her mouth. Militant suffragist, pacifist—"She had a passion for the Hindus last winter. Now she has one for me. I can't be a cause, exactly, but she finds plenty of causes on the side." She looks like an Indian, decided Catherine, a temperamental, rather worn and fiery Indian.

Margaret and Charles were sparring; they couldn't even telephone each other without crossing points. . . .

Catherine tells the group about Flora, her "maid," whom family-trouble is keeping from work, and whom Catherine had visited at home that day.

"You shouldn't have gone into a nigger tenement alone!" said Charles.

"Why not?" demanded Amy. "Aren't negroes people?" . . . Catherine smiled at Charles. "But it wasn't dangerous. Only unpleasant."

"Poor Flora." Margaret was grave. "I didn't know she had any children." . . .

"Well"—Charles drew at his pipe and paused, impressively—"you can see what happens to a family when the mother isn't at home."

"Listen to the King!" Margaret flared indignantly. "What about the man? Living on her, and—" . . .

Charles had a dangerous little twitch under one eye.

Catherine worries who will care for her own household, with Flora gone:

"I can't," said Catherine, "haul in a stranger from an agency to leave here all day."

"Well, then," Margaret was briskly matter of fact, "there's just one thing to do. Give up this foolish notion of a career, and step into Flora's empty place."

Charles made a little leap at that idea, and then sank away from it, with a faint suggestion in his mouth of a disappointed fish watching a baited hook yanked out of reach.

"Or," went on Margaret gravely, "Charles can stay at home. So much of your work could be done here anyway, Charles. One eye on the stew and the other on some learned tome."

"Why not?" Amy's tense question knocked the drollery out of the picture. "Why wouldn't that be possible? After all, Mrs. Hammond, you have spent years doing that very thing."

"The King would burn the stew, of course." Margaret rose, sending a light curtsey toward Charles. "Come along, Amy. If we're to walk home. . . ."

When Catherine returned from the door, her eyes crinkled at the sight of Charles sunk behind the pages of his evening paper.

"Poor old thing!" she said. "Did they rumple his fur the wrong way?"

He crashed the sheets down on his knee, and lifted his face, the tips of his ears red.

"Whatever does Margaret want to lug that thing around with her for."

"I guess she's all right." Catherine was at the window, looking at the pale glowing bowl of the city sky before she drew the shade. "Devoted to Margaret."

"Ugh! I'd like that devoted to me!"

"Don't worry!" Catherine drew the shade, and turned laughing. "She won't be. She seems violently anti-man."

"Wasn't she one of the females they had to feed through the nose down there at Washington?"

"That's rather to her credit, isn't it?"

"She's that fanatic type, all right. All emotion, unbalanced, no brain. Now Margaret has some intelligence. But she's being influenced by this woman. I can see a difference in her. To think that she chose herself to leave your mother for that!"

"I think few people influence Margaret." Catherine moved quietly about the room, picking up books left by Spencer, a toy of Letty's, Marian's doll. "She's hard headed, you know."

"Well," said Charles with great finality, "she won't ever capture any man while she has that female attached to her. Great mistake for a nice girl like Margaret to tie herself up with that woman. She seems the real paranoia type."[180]

In an intervening sequence, Charles assures Catherine and Margaret's mother that Margaret will find living with Amy inconvenient, adding, " 'These violent crazes for—for freedom—or people—or causes—wear themselves out.' "[181] Catherine realizes that Charles is also referring to her own quest for a new life.

In the following selection, Catherine meets Margaret and Amy in Amy's private luncheon club.

She looked about the room, large and low, with separate nodules of women. Margaret's bright head shot up from the group near the fireplace, and Margaret swung across the room toward her, slim and erect in her green dress. Amy strolled after her; she had removed her squirrel turban, but her dark hair still made a stiff flange about her thin face.

"This is fine! We've saved a table—" and Catherine, following them into the dining room, edging between the little tables, found herself drawn into the pattern of sound.

"I'm sorry I am late." She slipped her coat over the chair. "The President was talking to me"—she had to release some of the tiny, humming insects—"about my trip west." She told them about that trip. It stepped forward out of dream regions into reality as she talked, as they put in questions, sympathetic, approving questions.

"What does the King say?" Margaret smiled at her.

"Oh, he doesn't *say* much." Catherine laughed. Why, she could joke about him! She felt a hard brilliance carry her along, as if—she sent little glances about the room, at the women near her—something homogeneous about them—unlike the girls at the St. Francis, still more unlike the woman who lunched at the Acadia, or at Huylers—something sufficient, individual—"What kind of a club is this, anyway?"

"We wanted a place downtown here where we could have good food. All the lugs are in the kitchen. Wonderful cook!" Amy leaned across the table, her eyes afire. She could be intense over food, too, then! "A place where one might bring a guest. City Club too crowded, too expensive, too—too too! for independent women. There were eleven of us, originally. We called it the "Little Leaven," you know. Now there are several hundred. All sorts. Writers, artists, editors. That's a birth control organizer, and the woman with her is an actress. Anybody interesting comes to town, we haul her in to speak in the evening. Men always have comfortable clubs. This is for us."

"Good food, certainly."

"I thought if you were interested, I'd put you up. For membership. The dues aren't high, and now you are downtown, you might like to run in. Always someone here to lunch with, someone of your own kind."

Catherine smiled. Part of her was amused, but part of her shone, as if Amy's intensity, admitting her to the leaven, polished that hard brilliance—

"I'd like it!" she declared. "Lunching has been irksome."

She watched the women again. They seemed less homogeneous, more individual, as she looked.

"Well, I've been thinking about you." Amy was directed at her with astonishing concentration. "Since I met you. What you need is more backing. You feel too much alone."

Catherine felt Margaret's uneasiness, akin to her own faint shrinking from the access of personal probing.

"You need, as I told Margaret the other night, to touch all these other women who have stepped out of their grooves. It's wonderful, what that does for you. It's solidarity feeling, workers go after it in their unions, and women so much lack it. You think you are making a solitary struggle, and you're only part of all this—" Her sudden gesture sent her empty tumbler spinning to the edge of the table. Margaret's quick hand caught it.

"Don't begin an oration, Amy," she said.

"It's true." Catherine was bewildered to find tears in her eyes, and a rush of affection toward Amy—she might be fanatic, but a spark from her overfanned fires could warm you! "Are any of these celebrities married?" she asked, with apparent irrelevance.

"Oh—" Amy shrugged. "I think they have husbands, some of them. Hard to tell. That woman there has just got her divorce, I know."

She had a moment with Margaret later, standing near the fireplace, while Amy rushed off to greet a newcomer.

"She's a funny old dear, isn't she?" Margaret was nonchalant.

"I like her," said Catherine.

Margaret looked up in frank pleasure.

"I hoped you would. She's really fine, if you get her." Her eyes, traveling across to the small figure in the fur coat, one arm raised in emphasis, were tender. "You'd roar if you heard her comments on Charles. She has a certain cosmic attitude toward all men, lumps them. I'm thrilled, Cathy, at your trip. And your salary! You show some pick-up on this job."

"Will you take me shopping for decent clothes?" Catherine regarded her sister wistfully. "I'm going to dress the old thing up for once."

"Will I! I've always wanted to."

The following section continues:

During the next weeks Catherine lunched frequently at Amy's club. "You were quite right," she told her one day. "I needed perspective. This place and these women make the whole business of my working seem matter of course. As if I'd be a fool not to. That's a more comforting feeling than my old one, that I might be only an egoistic pig."

"That's the trouble with ordinary married women," declared Amy. "They are all shut up in separate cages, until they don't have an idea what is happening outside."

"Marriage isn't a cage, exactly."

"You just aren't entirely out, yet."

"At least there is comfort in finding that other women want the same thing I want, and get it."

But marriage wasn't a cage, she thought, later. She found herself not so much imprisoned as bewildered. It's more like a labyrinth. There are ways out, if you can find them. Out, not of marriage itself, but out of the thing people have made of it—for women.[182]

When the last selection from *The Labyrinth* opens, Catherine has earlier suffered several family crises, the failure of her psychologist husband's clinic, his subsequent depression, and her small son Spencer's accident. Spencer's head injury, while she is away on a business trip, provokes in Catherine extreme guilt and indecision about continuing her professional career. As the scene begins, her husband, Charles, has just taken the two healthy children out for a Sunday afternoon walk when Margaret rings the bell.

Margaret pounced at her, shook her gently, hugged her, marched her back to the living room.

"Fine! Everyone else is out. Now I can bully you." She dragged off her gloves. "You look as if you needed it, too," she said. She leaned forward abruptly and touched Catherine's hand. "Spencer! Oh, it has been awful, I know," and surprisingly her eyes grew brilliant with tears. "But he's honestly not hurt, is he? . . . Spencer's not the sort I want changed by any knock on his head."

"No." Catherine shivered. "They all say there is absolutely no danger."

"Well." Margaret was silent a moment.

She had to say that, to be rid of it, thought Catherine.

"But I know what you've been up to." Margaret's tears were gone. "Wallowing in sentimental regrets. Listening to mother suggests that you must surely see your duty now. And the King, too! Just when I was so proud of you, and using you for an example of what a woman really could do, could amount to, and everything." She laughed. "Don't be a renegade, Cathy."

"Pity to spoil your example, huh?"

"Exactly. Have you seen your boss since you came back? I thought not. Cathy, go and see him. Dress up and go down to your office. Drag yourself out of your home, sweet home, long enough to remember how you felt. If you'll promise that, I won't say another word. Psychological and moral effect, that's all."

"I don't want to see him until I make up my mind."

"It isn't your mind you are making up. It's"—Margaret waved her hand—"it's your sentiment tank. Oh, I know. I have a soft heart, myself, Catherine."

"There's another thing." Margaret had turned her upside down, as she had feared, and she was hunting feverishly in the scattered contents of her scrapbag self. "Charles." Reticence obscured her. "He's been disappointed about that clinic. He does need—"

"Anybody," declared Margaret with quick violence, "anybody needs somebody else loving 'em, smoothing 'em down, setting 'em up, brushing off the dust. I know! But you can do that anyway. That just goes on—"

"I wonder. You're a hard-boiled spinster, Margaret. What do you know about it?"

"I know a little thing or two about love. You do it all the time, through and around whatever else you are doing. Not from nine to five exclusively." She settled back, a grimace on her lips, as the door rattled open and Letty's piping was heard. "Didn't stay long, did he? You promise me you'll go down to the Bureau. Quick! Or I'll fight with the King like a—"

"Yes, I'll go down." Catherine laughed. "I'd have to anyway."

And Margaret, smiling at her, ran out to meet Spencer.[183]

♀ 1930: "MARY CASAL" and "JUNO";

"A union between two women could be of a higher type . . . than any other"

The autobiography of the pseudonymous "Mary Casal," published in Chicago in 1930, presents the extraordinarily frank sexual and affectional life history of an American Lesbian. Born in 1864 and growing up in rural New England, Casal's book presents a rarely heard early Lesbian voice detailing her own history—from just after the Civil War through the first part of the twentieth century. Her portrayal of the sexual life of her time and place has nothing in common with the asexualized image passed down to us by traditional writers and historians.

Casal's family was poor; her father had become a farmer after his earlier professional career as a singer ended with the failure of his tenor voice. Her father and a sister are presented as affectionate, her mother as loving—underneath a frighteningly stern, strict, puritanical exterior. The last of nine children, Casal was painfully aware as a young girl of the tears her mother still shed for three offspring dead before Casal's birth. Her early "protective" feeling for her mother seems to have later been generalized into "sympathy," especially for other women.

As young as age three or four (1867–68), Casal liked playing with boys, liked boys' work, sports, and comfortable clothes, wanted a boy's knife, and a boy's "large handkerchief." She hated dolls and housework, early developing what she calls "masculine tastes." The discovery that she was not built sexually like her male playmates distressed her. Although she says she early wanted to be a boy, her actual desire is clearly to *act* in what was customarily and rigidly defined as the "male role."[184]

At age eight or nine (1872–73), Casal recalls rebuffing the sexual advances of a "hired man." She details the later repeated and successful attempts of an older male family "friend" to have sexual intercourse with her. She reports numerous other sexual advances by males, young and old, relatives, neighbors, family friends, acquaintances. She describes her fear and confusion as a young girl about how to deal with these repeated molestations. Her argument for greater freedom of sexual discussion among parents, educators, and children is based on her own negative childhood experiences.[185]

Casal's history includes a series of emotional involvements with other females, accompanied by varied forms of active sexual expression. Her first feeling of "love" for another girl, although unrequited, included physical attraction; it began in grammar school and lasted for many years. Her next love for a "girl friend" began when she was about twelve (1876), and continued during two summer vacations, accompanied by kisses, nights spent together "in loving embrace," many verbal declarations of affection, and letters written during winter separations. Her third love was for a female high school teacher whose embraces and kisses, Casal says, she enjoyed "hugely."[186]

Finishing high school at age fifteen (1879), Casal went on to graduate from a midwestern coeducational university where a brother-in-law was a professor. There she fell in love with the university president's daughter, who "seemed quite happy" to receive her kisses. Casal was also attracted to another musically talented college "girl friend," but unsuccessfully competed with her amorous brother-in-law for this young woman's affection. The sexual advances of another young woman were met by Casal with disinterest, as she says she liked to woo, not be wooed. During her second year in college Casal felt a great attraction to Flo, a professor's wife, who physically responded to the extent of "little kisses and big kisses" given when Casal stayed overnight at her friend's home. Although the relationship with Flo apparently did not develop further sexually, it was for Casal a deep and happy love.[187]

After finishing college, Casal taught briefly in a "little New England school" near her family's home. Disturbed by her sexual attraction to women, and wanting to have children, as well as to prove herself "normal," at age twenty (1884) Casal married an old family friend whom she did not love. This marriage, a disaster, finally ended in divorce. During the period of her marriage, Casal twice became pregnant, once by her friend Flo's husband, to whose advances she submitted specifically with the aim of having a child. Both babies died at birth, and her desire for motherhood was not realized.[188]

Casal describes moving from one occupation to another at about five- or six-year intervals, successful at each undertaking, but feeling a strong need for change. She invents a toy, patents it, markets it herself, and becomes a successful business-woman. At this time, her earlier emotional involvements with women culminate in her meeting and taking up life with her great love, a woman she calls "Juno." Next Casal runs a small, successful private school in the large studio apartment she shares with Juno on Washington Square. Later she is the secretary in an art gallery where she daily enjoys the view of four of Corot's most famous paintings. She is successful as a commercial artist—a designer of "Christmas cards, favors, place cards, and the like." Living in the country for a time with Juno, Casal farms and gardens, enjoying the activity and contact with the earth. Both Casal and Juno work for some years as assistants to a rich, female philanthropist. While traveling in Europe, Casal sells an article for "several hundred dollars" to a New York magazine, and in Paris she works for a religious organization. Late in her career, Casal heads a large "fresh air and convalescent home" for youngsters about forty miles from New York City, said to be run "for the people connected with the East Side mission" belonging to "one of the richest churches" in the city. There Casal tries out her own ideas of sex education.[189]

Retiring from public life after her love affair with Juno has ended, Casal moved from the eastern United States to the opposite side of the continent and writes her intimate life story, published when she was sixty-six. As the last member of her large family still alive, Casal explains that she can detail her early life without embarrassment to any relations. She does not reveal her own identity, however— probably to protect those of her acquaintances still living. Casal's book is, in part, an early and rare American example of a political-literary genre, the homosexual (in this case, Lesbian) defense. Casal pointedly upholds her "higher type" of sexual-emotional relation as "normal" for her—and as "normal" as its equivalent hetero-sexual counterpart. A moving section describes how she and Juno think they are the only emotionally and sexually involved women in the world until they meet a fascinating and worldly older woman (whom she calls "Phil"—short for Philoso-pher), from whom they learn they are not alone.[190]

Many of the childhood experiences Casal describes and protests appear today as the tribulations of a young girl in a male-dominated society, for example sexual advances by males which she felt had to be endured, even submitted to. Casal is quite traditional in her concept of "masculinity" and "femininity," speaking of what she experiences as her "dual" "masculine" and "feminine" nature. Her "feminine" self desires to bear and raise children, and feels "protective," motherly affection for others, particularly women. What she calls her "masculine" side is sexually attracted to females, dislikes traditionally "feminine" occupations, activities, and chatter, and desires to intervene assertively in the world. In college, Casal says, she did not join the sororities that sought her membership, and the national organizations for women never appealed to her. She has, however, "affiliated with men's organizations, when women were eligible," and has "enjoyed working with men in business."[191] Although Casal is no feminist, her primary personal and emotional concern is for women. Her desire to give pleasure and affection to other women so predominates that not until her relation with Juno does she allow herself to receive reciprocal pleasure in sex. That even this strong, independent woman was a victim of the traditional male-oriented ideology is a poignant reminder of its power.

Casal's autobiography is also written with the explicit aim of breaking that prudish conspiracy of silence about sex which she found so damaging as a young girl. She strongly opposes the corporal punishment that often followed adults' discovery of children's sexual investigations. She is for "reasoning" with children about sex, for encouraging them to speak and ask questions. She emphasizes the "tortures of unsatisfied sexual desire," especially for women, citing the example of a sister of a relative who went mad from sexual repression; she speaks of other women suffering the same fate.[192] While Casal argues for freer sexual expression, it is a terrifying comment on the sexual mystification of her day that she herself believes in and propagates a whole series of oppressive sexual shibboleths.

Casal's plea for free sexual expression is totally contradicted by her argument for greater control and sublimation of sexual impulses. She thinks that masturbation leads to physical disease and constitutes a "peril"—an idea she takes pains to pass along to the youngsters under her care. She seems to feel that the death of her first child was connected with her "indulgence" in physical lovemaking with a woman the night before its birth. She seems to believe in, and be worried about, the possibility of inherited homosexuality, passed from mother to child. And she is totally traditional in her condemnation of Gay males as promiscuous child-molesters. Casal actually argues for the separation of love and sex, taking the philosophical stance that sex is necessarily selfish, while love is altruistic.[193] In a way she never anticipated, the import of her own argument for sexual enlightenment is emphasized by the awful irony of her own puritanism.

In the selection quoted here, Casal describes her meeting and great early love affair with Juno. Although this section describes a period of great happiness, she later details a period of intense sorrow when this love affair disintegrates. Casal is not defensive about her suffering, however, accepting both her joy and pain as part of a life rich in experience and deeply felt.

Here, the possibility of selling thousands of the toys she has invented brings Casal to New York City, where she seeks a room in a hotel for "women only," run by a religious organization.

When I entered the office to engage a room I found a "fat (un)fair and forty" female smugly sitting at the desk. She turned to me with a typical "Christian" expression on her face, which could not hide the uncompromising, cruel mouth. . . . One could readily see that she could turn a young girl into the streets of that great city, late at night, and a stranger, because she was not of the faith which would entitle her to a bed and safe refuge. I learned later this had been done many times in this Christian hotel!

. . . As I stood waiting for the fat one to wait on someone before me, I saw beyond her, over in the rather hidden corner of the office, a youngish girl sitting on a low stool with her head bowed and over her face the most beautiful hands I had ever seen. She was weeping in suppressed sobs. The tears seemed to be coming from the soul rather than from the eyes.

When asked what the fat one could do for me, I wanted to say "Please comfort that girl." But of course that wouldn't do in such a holy place, so I told her I would like a room. It was in July, and it hardly surprised me to find my room very warm. I had plenty to think about. I had answered with fidelity all the questions asked me, and had been given a room. I looked about me and was greatly amused by the expensively printed warnings hanging on the walls. I read the wonderful words of Christ also printed and framed, and hung as a comfort to the hearts of the selected, who were of the "right" faith. A plea for charity! I fell to wondering about the young woman in tears. What comfort could be found on or in the fat bosom, when the hard mouth showed how hollow it was, where instead there should have been charity for all.

Those beautiful hands were before me far into the night. The excessive heat in that stuffy room also contributed toward keeping me awake. I thought little of my discomfort, however, as my heart ached for that girl, whose very hands showed she was out of her sphere. I wondered.

One was allowed to engage a room for only one day at a time but, in spite of the heat, I was determined to try one more night, all on account of the sobs of a stranger.

In the morning, I went to the office to see whether my moral status still measured up to the required standard and—there at the desk—sat the girl with the beautiful hands. The tears had been dried and she looked up at me with eyes shining with love and human kindness.

Here was one who could not turn away a girl on account of her religion, were she not bound by rules so stern she could not evade them. And even in such a case I was sure she would suggest some way of protecting her.

Turning to me she asked sweetly what she could do for me, instead of "what did I want." I said I wished to engage my room for the following night. When she found which room I had occupied, she turned to me in astonishment and said: "You are the first woman occupying that room in the summer who has not entered a violent protest in the morning about the heat! I will see that you have a better one tonight."

My business kept me out until quite late in the afternoon. In acknowledgment of her courtesy in regard to the room, and remembering her anguish when I first saw her, I brought her a bunch of lovely violets when I returned.

She was just going "off duty" when I went to the office. As she had given me a better room and had had my things moved, she said she would show me where it was, as she was going to that floor. She was greatly pleased with the flowers, and her lovely eyes thanked me more than words. I found my room was directly across the hall from hers.

Something told me that here was the girl of my dreams. I wasn't looking for her; she just came into my life, and I knew. But how to convince her that she was to be my mate was the question.

There must be no crude awakening. I knew at once that she was not in her natural environment; that she had been gently reared, but that, through some calamity, she was here making a brave and successful fight.

While I naturally hated the whole atmosphere of that whited sepulcher, I did not hate this one human being connected with the conduct of its business, so I stayed on, engaging my room day by day and never asking to have it changed. Let us call my new friend Juno. We met frequently in the hall, in going to and from our rooms. I had found out her schedule quite by accident, and found I was making my business engagements fit into ones which seemed now of more vital importance to me. John Drew [a famous actor] was about to open a new play, and I bought two tickets for the night when I knew Juno was to be free. When I told her, at one of our chance meetings in the corridor between our rooms, that I had the tickets, and asked her to take pity on me, as I had no one with whom to go, she hesitated. She said she had always observed a custom of the house never to accept an invitation to go out with a guest. But she also said she longed to go and, after a little urging, she consented.

She wore a charming, simple little gown which just suited her. I say "little" simply as a term of endearment, for Juno was taller than I, and had a magnificently proportioned figure. I dressed in my only change from the day suit, in a handsome black tailored suit with a black hat and white silk shirt. I called a hansom when we were away from the hotel, for fear of hurting the feelings of the dames who did not smile on this growing friendship.

I remember little of the play. By this time, I was madly in love with Juno and longed to put my arms about her and tell her of it. It all seemed so natural and right to me, I inwardly rebelled, of course, against convention which said "it isn't done." Patience was my watchward for success, as I knew more certainly each minute that we were made for each other and that in time she would know it too.

On the way home, we stopped at a very conservative hotel, where it was permissible and wholly respectable for two ladies to have supper without a male escort. We had a delightful supper and talk, and lingered long, as there had been no "time limit" for her that evening. She told me much about her life before she took the position in which I found her. As I had surmised, she had been brought up in very different surroundings, an orphan. All her brothers and sisters had been married, she was engaged to be herself, and was deeply in love with the man. It developed, however, that there were reasons why she could not marry this man, and she had decided to find solace in hard work. She had also decided that she would never marry.

After this first evening, which she said she had enjoyed more than anything she had done since she had left her home, we had many little chats and walks together. I referred one day to the tears she was shedding the first time I ever saw her hands.

She laughingly said she remembered that evening so well. She had heard my voice when I was going through the awful questioning and longed to look up, even through her tears, but she did not dare to with those eyes so red. However, she did go to the register as soon as I had gone upstairs and found out my name. Perhaps she, too, had that feeling that we were to mean more to each other. She then told me why she was so silly that night. This was her first experience in earning her living, as the rich relative who had brought the children up in the most luxurious surroundings had cut them off without a penny when he found that they were contemplating marriage. The occasion of the tears was that some well meaning woman had left the change of twenty-five cents on the desk and told Juno to keep it for herself! She thought there could be no greater disgrace in life than to have to receive a "tip" from a common woman. She had no time to refuse it, and she dared not throw it after her—a woman with so little discrimination.

Now my way was clear. I felt that if I could win her love, I might bring to her even greater happiness than she had anticipated with the man whom she thought she loved. Furthermore, I would not in any way be interfering with any future marriage plans.

It was apparent that she thought I was different from any woman she had ever known, and that she was both interested in and attracted by me. We had many long walks together and went often to art galleries and to the theater. Our tastes were much alike, and this comradeship was the foundation upon which I was working.

My sexual passions were not aroused by my contact with her. I longed to caress her and give some sign of my love, but I could not do so as yet.

The elderly dames, after the pattern of the one whom I had found in charge of the hotel when I arrived, while they were always polite to me and I feel liked me, were alert in their warnings to Juno about forming a friendship which might interfere with her work. Juno was the only young person on the "staff." They were terrified that I might take her away, for they, as well as everyone else with whom she came in contact, loved her sincerely.

Juno was entirely out of her element in the place, yet she was doing her work with a degree of enthusiasm sufficient to sap her vitality quickly. The dames had no knowledge of me other than they gained by the questions they asked when I applied for admission to the hotel. They told Juno that, notwithstanding the fact that I was a charming woman, she should be a little careful about succumbing to my charms. In after years we often laughed at these precautions against losing her taken by the dames.

Our friendship grew. She would often drop into my room on her way to bed, after an evening on duty. I would leave my door slightly ajar so she could see that I was lying on the bed and reading.

My personal appearance? If someone else were writing about that I believe they would say: She had a wonderful complexion and smooth skin, soft brown hair which curled in little ringlets about the forehead and neck (it is now snowy white, wavy in front and cut in a "boyish bob"), which were white and with correct lines; not too fat (as I am now), artistic hands, also pronounced as capable ones; a figure true to form, of about "size forty" at that time; graceful in all movements; a voice soft and well modulated; speaking good English, enunciating her words easily but clearly, and so on.

One evening I had loosened my necktie and the collar of my light blue shirt—a color then quite in vogue—and was impatiently waiting for my girl to be through with her work and to peep in to say good night and give me the sweet little kiss, as we had progressed to that stage by this time. Very proper little kisses, however.

My feelings for her at this time were not of an amorous nature. My heart was calling for her as a mate. We were so in sympathy on every subject we touched. We loved the same things in music, literature, and art. The music we heard together stirred her as it did me, with a depth of emotion we hardly understood. I occasionally got glimpses of her passionate and hungry nature and longed to open the gates of pent-up emotion.

During this rapturous period of wooing, I was occupied in a sort of a desultory way with the large contract for my toy, but I must confess my heart was somewhere else. There were orders enough ahead to keep the home forces busy, so I could wait, as indeed it was in a measure necessary for me to do, in dealing with so large a concern, with all its complicated machinery.

My other two friends claimed a part of my time, but my heart and thoughts were so wholly taken up with what I knew to be *the one* whom I had sought all my life, that I allowed no opportunity for a possible resumption of former intimacies with either.

I was patiently waiting for the right time to declare my love—until a beautiful foundation of sympathy and companionship could be firmly established, as any wise and normal lover should do.

Hundreds of little ways came to my mind, day by day, in which to nourish the perfect flower that waxed stronger, and grew and grew.

The time and opportunity came at last, when I was sure that she not only loved me but was also "in love" with me (but did not realize it), for me to tell her as gently as possible how deeply I was in love with her and what I hoped would be the culmination of this great love—that we could really belong to each other with a more intense love than she had ever dreamed possible. Of course, she was mystified. My kiss that night was more intense than ever before, and her lips willingly yielded to mine . . .

She was truly worried. She said she loved me madly, but not as she had ever supposed she could love a woman—even more than she had loved the man whom she was engaged to marry. She wondered whether I really were a woman. I assured her that I was, and a wholly normal one, telling her of my two children, and so forth.

I talked about our possible marriage. Why not? I had thought the thing out and I argued that a union of hearts and souls constituted a real union, call it marriage if need be. My experience had shown me that to most men, and very likely to some women, marriage merely meant a legitimized permission to cohabit for the relief of sexual desire.

To me it seemed that a union between two women could be of a higher type, and creative of a more secure happiness and good than any other. At this time I was convinced that I was the only woman who had ever thought of matters in this way. I am sure my thoughts were far from anything but the highest type of love in all its beauty.

We decided it would be best for both of us to think things over quietly, before we finally decided to bind ourselves to each other in solemn compact.

Having at last concluded the deal upon which I had been working, I found it necessary to go to a city about twelve hours distant by rail. Of course we were to write often. Juno's decision would naturally have its influence upon my future field of action, as she knew. I arranged for flowers and fruits to be sent to her regularly during my absence, and was quite the accepted "lover."

She had much to consider, too, in making any change such as we had pictured. It would become necessary for her to change or at least to re-arrange her work, so that we could live together. We had planned to have our own apartment, each to go on with some work through the day, but to have our evenings and nights at home to ourselves.

The parting was hard, for we were very dear to each other and had been together for quite a while, enjoying every minute of our companionship.

I waited twenty-four hours after arriving before I wrote to her. That had given me time to reassure myself, and she too had been able to think things over. The letter I wrote must have carried to her some idea of the love I felt for her and probably gave her a vivid picture of what our life would be, if lived as one. The following afternoon after I had made a very good deal with a large firm in that city, and so kept the home fires burning, I received a telegram from her: "Come, every bit of me wants you," signed with an initial.

I canceled business engagements for the next day and hustled about to find that, by taking a night boat (a mode of travel I had always hated), I could reach the city early in the morning of a day I knew Juno was to be free. I wired her to be at our quiet and conservative hotel at a certain hour in the morning, and to wait if I were late.

How it rained all night! I knew, for I walked the covered deck until nearly morning. It was still pouring when, after a short sleep, I resumed my impatient marathon with renewed vigor.

The next chapter continues:

The boat docked and the rain fell in torrents. I called a cab and gave the driver directions to go to a wholesale florist, anywhere he could find one on the way uptown. It took some persuasion to get the big bunch of violets from the wholesaler, but I did so, and sped away to my love. The wonderful violets alone would have told the story of my love for her, for they personified everything beautiful.

When I arrived, Juno was waiting for me in the parlor of our hotel, eager, and with a most ardent welcome. After the necessary formalities, we were shown to our room. When we were alone our arms were about each other and our lips met in the first kiss that was a pledge of a great and beautiful love. She loved the violets and, in our enthusiasm, it was rather hard to come to earth and make some plans.

She had arranged for a free day. That was an important point gained. Then, being both very normal beings, we felt that we must have the breakfast to which we were accustomed. A delicious one was ordered, and we sat and loved and talked and thought. She wondered.

After the removal of the breakfast dishes, we began to talk of our love. I tried to make her see that for me it was not a passing fancy and that I believed it was a serious matter to her. We discussed all phases of marriage, and I gave her my views, based on my own experience. She, of course, felt that there could never be a man in her life again. So we decided that a union such as ours was to be could be made as holy and complete as the most conventional marriages, if not more so.

I suggested that we read the marriage ceremony together as a sort of benediction to our union. We had built up a firm foundation for our lives in the love we held for each other. Our coming together was not for animal satisfaction. There was a real sympathy of ideas and ideals and, as a by-product, as it were, was to come the physical relief of sex desire. As I always carried my prayer book with me, we very solemnly read the service, and meant every word of it. . . .

We both believed that I was the only one in the world who desired the love of a woman. The time for mere conversation was over. I found willing response to my caresses.

She, too, wanted to show her love, as I had mine. At last I had reached the heights of physical love.

Poets have written and sung of "that day of love" or "that night of love" in words and tones which could not express the bliss of it, so why should I try to do so?

We lingered and loved and rested, and felt there could be no end to the desires which arose. It was the expression of about twenty-five years of suppression of emotion in both of us. In a sane moment, we dressed and took a long drive and had lunch at a favorite restaurant in the Park, and then returned to our room early in the afternoon. We had to make plans now for the future. . . .[194]

♀ 1932–33: DOROTHY THOMPSON and
CHRISTA WINSLOE;
"This incredible feeling of sisterhood"

The remarkably frank diary of Dorothy Thompson reveals a heterosexually identified woman in the process of living through and attempting to understand and "justify" her strong erotic feelings for another woman.

Dorothy Thompson was a newspaper and magazine writer, radio commentator, lecturer, and political analyst who became a celebrity in the 1930s when she was expelled from Nazi Germany by Hitler, angered over an interview that Thompson had published. By 1932, Thompson had been an organizer for the Woman Suffrage Party (1914–17), a European correspondent for several U.S. newspapers, and had authored two books, *The New Russia* (1928), and *I Saw Hitler* (1932). She had been married and divorced from Josef Bard, and was at the time of this diary married to novelist Sinclair Lewis.

Thompson's marriage to Lewis was already in the process of collapse when they decided to spend the winter together in a villa at Semmering, in the hills above Vienna—an attempt to recapture their early love. In December 1932, Thompson and Lewis held a ten-day Christmas and New Year party attended by a houseful of friends, among them the Baron and Baroness Hatvany—the Baroness better known as Christa Winsloe, author of the novel and film *Mädchen in Uniform*. This was the story of schoolgirl Manuela's love for a female teacher—one of the first films with a Lesbian theme to be shown in the United States. The German-born Christa Winsloe was also a sculptor and storyteller, whose sophisticated European charm and culture had interested Thompson when the two women first met in the 1920s.[195] Now Thompson's conscious and strong erotic attraction for Winsloe provoked her to record and analyze these feelings in her diary.

This intimate journal reveals Thompson's struggle to characterize and come to terms with her Lesbian feelings. Thompson is torn by what she experiences as contradictory emotions: on the one hand she is attracted to men and experiences her Lesbianism as a sickening "perversion," "weak," and "ridiculous." On the other hand, her Lesbian attraction includes intense and positive feelings of intimacy, tenderness, protectiveness, peace, warmth, and "sisterhood." Thompson struggles to affirm these positive feelings—specifically against the Freudian denigration of them as "neurotic" and "immature." Thompson was also probably struggling against her husband's negative view of Lesbianism; Sinclair Lewis's most recent novel, *Ann Vickers*, published just a few months earlier, concerns a career woman, feminist, and reformer driven to suicide by her liaison with a possessive, cruel Lesbian.[196]

In the opening section of her diary, Thompson recalls two earlier and similar attractions to women. One, referred to as "G.," has been identified as Gertrude Franchot Tone, a leader in the women's suffrage movement in the area near Niagara Falls, a left-wing socialist, daughter of a state senator, wife of Dr. Frank Tone, a conservative Republican corporation president, mother of Ned and Franchot Tone, the actor. The other female lover, "F." (not identified), was a "sapphic" lover of Thompson's in Berlin.[197] Thompson's diary also refers to "C.," Christa Winsloe, Christa's friend Jill, Christa's husband "Laci," Thompson's own husband "Hal" (Sinclair Lewis), their young son Michael (or "Mikey"), her first husband Josef (Bard), and her former male lover, "E."

The following diary entries focus on Thompson's erotic feelings for women and men; a few passages of peripheral interest have been deleted. Thompson never destroyed this journal, although she occasionally (though not uniformly) penciled out the last six letters of "Christa." Thompson willed this diary along with her other papers to the Syracuse University library, obviously wishing to pass on to posterity this intimate fragment of herself. In the present text, the name Christa has been restored where it originally appeared.[198]

In January 1964, a review in the Lesbian magazine *The Ladder* by Gene Damon and Lee Stuart discussed Vincent Sheean's then just published biography of Dorothy Thompson which first revealed and reprinted her intimate diary. Damon and Stuart feel that Thompson's journal is "painful to read—a little too intimate," and conclude that it "should have been published . . . about 50 years from now," though it is admittedly an "important contribution to the field of variant [Lesbian-relevant] biography."[199] In 1976, perhaps, Thompson's diary will seem less painfully intimate, more the fascinating record of an intelligent woman's struggle for self-affirmation.

Dec. 28 [1932].

So it has happened to me again, after all these years. It has only really, happened to me once before: with G. (Then I was twenty and G. was 37, and I see her still quite vividly. She wore a black broadcloth tailored suit with white frills and a *jabot* and big hat. She was very handsome, full-figured, and womanly, and I wanted to be close to her, to be like her. I took my fortnight's free vacation and went all the way to Northern Canada to be with her—she was at Gerryowen [the summer "camp" of Gertrude Tone's relatives]—just in order to, while exploring in a canoe, say: "Why, it's you—so near." Just to be near her. I fell in love with W. before it wore off, or went away, and all the time my feeling for G. was in the background. Sometimes I think I love her better than anyone, and there's a queer tenderness between us still).

I don't count F. Then, so many other elements entered. (Are there similar elements counting now?) But one was curiosity and that plays no rôle now. I behaved awfully badly with F. In the end I hated (and feared) her. Just the same I still remember when she pulled my cheek down to hers that afternoon in Berlin (Schiffbauerdamm 28) and her soft scented mouth—

Only I should like to have left it there. I should have left it there. The rest seemed such a perversion, a perversion of a love for a man. One loves men differently, and the culmination of love for a man, with me, is very simple. Those forms of sapphic love were like making love to—being made love to by—an impotent man. One sickens.

There's something weak in it and, even, ridiculous. To love a woman is somehow ridiculous. *Mir auch passt es nicht. Ich bin doch heterosexuel.* [It doesn't suit me, either. I am heterosexual.] Even according to the very simple Freudian definition which determines the matter by the location of the orgiastic sensation. Like Marguerite in Faust, the *womb* throbs—not something else, more surface. All this petting is nothing without the deep thrust to the heart of one.

Well, then, how account for this which has happened again. The soft, quite natural kiss on my throat, the quite unconscious (seemingly) even open kiss on my breast, as she stood below me on the stairs—there were a dozen people around—"Good-bye," she said, *"Liebes* [dear one]." Anyone might have done that, said that—Martha, or Frances. But when I walked into the room at Wohlbebeng and she stood there, still in her hat and jacket; it was seven in the morning and I wore green pajamas. "Hello," I said and went to shake hands. It was six years since I had seen her. But instead we kissed. I thought she looked much older: much too heavy, and tired. What was the sudden indescribable charm in that too-soft face, and the heavy-lidded eyes. (The upper lid is very arched, the lower straight). Anyhow immediately I felt the strange, soft feeling—curious—of being at home, and at rest: an enveloping warmth and sweetness, like a drowsy bath. Only to be near her; to touch her when I went by. She has a quite simple, unconscious way of kissing the inside of one's arm—I say "She has a way" and she only did it once. "Don't go away," I wanted to say. "Don't go."

Her name suddenly had a magic quality. C. I wanted to say it. To use it. I talked about her to others, to hear her name. Like holding an amulet in your hand, that was what saying her name is like. I love this woman. There it stands, and makes the word love applied to any other woman in the world ridiculous.

Jealousy! It is absurd! I could laugh at myself . . . except that I couldn't! Jealous of Jill. Not a sign. Jill is beautiful, young, somehow glamorous, and unhappy. It's the last that attracts my dear. They went away together. The door of Jill's room stood open and the door of C's—wide, open and empty. I went for a walk with E. [a former (male) lover] and in the woods he turned suddenly and put both hands on my cheeks and we clung together. His mouth tasted deliciously of love, like the smell of semen, and I could have lain down with him right there in the woods then and there as I could have done for five years, except that we agreed we wouldn't—the old leap of the heart and womb were there, and we walked along, greatly shaken, but even then the sweet wistfulness, the heart's reaching towards warmth—that remained—and as we walked my heart said her name over and over, and said: she went with Jill.

There's me. The me I know & the world knows which says all this is ridiculous & exaggerated. What's she to Jill or Jill to her—Jill's in love with her Pole, after all. But so am I with E. and happily married too, and yet wanting that curious tenderness, that pervading warm tenderness—there are no words for it, only her name said over & over expresses it. Come back, Christa! Come back! I have the feeling that something will happen to me in connection with this, and that it will make me unhappy.

Jan. 2 [1933]

I have got to go on writing about this in an attempt to justify it. There's a critic in me these days—a creature created by experience, who takes me firmly by the hand, pushes aside the curtain and insists upon my looking forward, down the road. (The critic says, to be sure, Don't write in a diary, particularly with your careless habits. You ought to have a locked book like the Queen of Rumania & wear the key on a bangle: only I would lose the bangle). But I must try at last to understand myself, because if at forty one has no wisdom—in two years I'll be forty—then what has one?

We went to Budapest and there she [Christa] was on the platform, in a black fur coat—lamb, with a high collar of sable and a brown tilted hat. She looked exquisite—beautiful and worldly, as I remember her.

The curious thing is how vividly I remember things about her, after all these years. Once at Lainz, in summer, there was a teaparty, which dragged on. She was going somewhere to dinner later and wore a white dress—some thin stuff, embroidered all over with small white beads. Consciously, I only thought: she looks beautiful. This never happened to me, then. But years afterward I bought a dress like that, because she had worn one. Another day we walked through the villa—it was an ugly house, with big bare rooms full of bad furniture and the usual imperial taste. When we went through her bedroom, the bed had been opened for the night, and the bidet pulled out. I was somehow shocked at the insouciant and quite unveiled presence. But I remark it now only because I remember it after nearly ten years. I wondered what sort of life she led. She had the animals which she loved and modelled in the garden. I could see her in tweeds, always walking alone. She seemed to me always lonely, repressed, and volcanic. Even then I wondered at her relation with [her husband] Laci. I don't usually speculate about people—what they do in bed. I have inhibitions—and I hate that people should speculate about me—still many questions crossed my mind about Laci. I think he never understood her at all, but was fascinated by her—and still is. I hated his children and wondered why Laci who seemed not greatly to care for them inflicted them on her. L., after all, was my friend, and surely in those days I bored Christa; I belonged to the political side of the dinner table. The émigrés chattered and she listened to them polite and remote. I listened otherwise—professionally. But though all my connections were with L.—he was my friend—all my sympathies were with C. but, I thought, we shall never be friends. It's a different world.

We rode on the train together to Berlin and she told me she would get a divorce. Laci was going to marry B., who was twenty, young and "unverdorben [unspoiled]" flattering to a man going on toward fifty. I thought: Laci is a fool: one doesn't throw away a wife like this woman, so distinguished and so sensitive. But Jews return to Jews, particularly Jewish men to Jewish women. Suddenly, yesterday, in the midst of dinner, Laci said to me: "Now, as I hear C's voice I remember that when our love was young and I would go to her, she would say, 'Beloved, it is so good you are here—I have missed you and needed you—come close to me, darling.' She would say it," said Laci, imitating her admirably, "All in the same tone of voice, soft, running the words along evenly, as though she were saying 'I hear it is raining in Vienna and the opera program has been changed.' I tried to make love to her in the same tone, but I could not. I would try to say erotic things, flattering things, tender things all in the same voice, but always I had to raise it."

That was like J.: "Aren't you *ever* excited—" when I was perishing of excitement. Stupid. But L. must have been stupid to her, otherwise. He was so bungling, yesterday, and made me bungling. Together we hurt her. It was about the money. I had asked Lyon to help her get out what she wanted and he said he would, but when L. told her so, triumphantly, she was wounded, and I saw that the fool had no idea of what was really going on in her mind. She expects from L. tenderness and protection. That she still has a claim to, she thinks, after the years. With what tenderness she always treated him! "L. wants a divorce, so I must give it to him. I feel very badly about it." I remember how she said it. How she worked for him when he was in prison. What she wants L. to say is: "C, what do you want to do, and I will help you do it. Don't worry ever about money if I have any." Give *her* a chance to be generous. She wants to act nobly and not haggle. The tone was all wrong.

Anyway, she walked away, and my heart was like lead. I could hardly speak during dinner. Literally I *ached* with chagrin & self-hatred. Immediately afterward she was kind and warm, and she put her arms about me, and the rest of the day was heavenly.

I put the incident down here as a record of my own sensibility to this woman. What in God's name does one call this sensibility if it be not love? This extraordinary heightening of all ones impressions; this intensification of sensitiveness; this complete identification of feeling? It was so when I read her book and suddenly felt that I *must* translate it, because in its essence I might have written it myself. *I* was Manuela, as she is Manuela, and everything that has happened to her has in essence, and other circumstances, happened to me. This incredible feeling of sisterhood.

In the end I translate all my emotional states into replicas of an earlier, family relation. My love for Josef [Thompson's first husband] broke because with him I could not do so. He remained a strange & sweetly assaulting male—and no "blood relation of mine." The overwhelming sweetness and understanding in my relation with Hal [Sinclair Lewis] is that he is close to me as my brother. "My sister, my darling!" Our son is of *our* blood, as near and known to me as my own hands and heart. I was afraid to have Josef's child—afraid that its eyes would be black and its hair thick and curling, and its ways not my ways. A little stranger. Michael has always been there. I played with my son in my own nursery.

(But [playwright Robinson] Jeffers made Orestes say: "I have fallen in love outward!" Oh, I have tried and I have failed! Only if I renounced this pounding of the blood, this periodic delirium, could I know what Jeffers means. To be in love with no one, but with the world. But that's an illness, too. From now on I shall "affirm myself," and let the Freudians make the best of it. Affirm myself, and try, in the light of my own peculiar experience, to be wise).

At Hatvan [Hungary], when the crisis about the money was over, the day was magical. The place suits Christa. I wanted (ungrateful guest) to take it away from the Hatvanys all together and give it to Christa. If I'd been God, I would have. . . . Christa belongs to land, animals, a wide house, unpretentious hospitality. I'd like her to be terribly rich because it would hurt her a bit but would do her good—and everyone else.

. . . We walked in the garden and then ate lunch. (But in the garden the contretemps with Laci occurred and lunch choked me). Afterward we went to the vineyard, the stables, and the wine cellar, and Christa went with me in the car. C. and Irene. The rest in a carriage.

(Oh, you baby! Oh, you love-struck adolescent! What a moment, during which it was decided who was to ride with whom! Believe me I laugh at myself. I am perfectly conscious that I am absurd. But do you think the self-mockery and the clear, rational consciousness helps one bit that curious, sweet, faint feeling. It does *not!*) . . .

C. began to look tired. But she had begun to look tired in the morning when L. and I talked of money to her.

I told her I should like to translate her book. She looked pleased—or was she? But I would do it very, very well. I know that. And would somewhat (perhaps) satisfy my intense need to do something for Christa. So I didn't mind even if I seemed *zudringlich* [pushy], because I *know* I would do it more carefully and lovingly than most, and care and love are needed to make a good translation. It's a very feminine book, too. And I know what it's all about, innerly, and that, too, is necessary in the translator, because the book is subtly and delicately written.

So then we had supper & left & went home.

We kissed each other & she called me "liebling" [darling] and said: "I will write to you & telephone, and you shall not get rid of me." And I felt full of beatitude.

I put all this down to look at it: The result: There is not the *slightest* indication that the extraordinarily intense erotic feeling I have for this woman is in any way reciprocated. I *feel*, of course, that it is—but the wish is so easily father to the thought. And if it isn't, I stand to make a damned bore of myself to a woman from whom, in the last analysis, I want only a warm friendship, and the opportunity to go on loving her no more articularly [sic] than heretofore.—

Thompson left Christa in Budapest, then returned to the villa in Semmering:

Suddenly I was glad, glad, glad to be home with the party over. Hal was in his room. When I came in he was glad. I could see he was awfully glad. I stood a long time in his arms, loving his familiar feel and smell, rubbing my face on his face. What are you going to do? he said, and I said: First of all take a bath. So he said: Stop in on your way down. I stopped in in a dressing gown and nothing else and he said: Come to my bed. So I did and it was awfully good. Especially good, with me just too tired to expect it to be and suddenly it was there and very wonderful. Afterward—quite a while afterward—he said: Darling, I didn't do anything. Did you? And I hadn't. And I didn't. It would be nice to have a new child as the end-of-the-party. So I slept all afternoon.

I write all this out to be clear. Obviously there are two quite different feelings. I don't love Hal any less. Rather more.

Mikey [Thompson's young son] came into my room at about six. "Mammy wead," he said, and climbed with his books into my bed. I kissed the back of his neck and he smelled delicious, like a kitten. "Mammy's pet," he said and grinned delightfully. I think he will be a terribly attractive male.

I have been very, very happy. And all the time, every moment, I have thought of Christa.

> At the time of this diary Thompson is feeling erotically attracted to Christa, wondering if her attraction is reciprocated; during the next difficult years the two women grew more intimate. Having no desire to return to Hungary or her native, now Nazi-occupied Munich, Christa was persuaded by Thompson to come to the United States, where by 1934 the two were known among at least some of their friends as a "couple." Finally, disappointed at the prospect of making a living in the United States as a writer, Christa returned to Europe in 1935, making her home in southern France. When the Nazis occupied the area in November 1942, Thompson heard no more of Christa Winsloe until after the war, when she learned that an "ordinary criminal," posing as a member of the French underground, had murdered her friend on June 10, 1944.[200]

ACKNOWLEDGMENTS

Many people's work is contained within these pages.

Phyllis B. Katz, my mother, read the manuscript and gave valuable suggestions based on many years of editorial experience. Her generous financial support and help with numerous unpleasant, but necessary, tasks add up to a large contribution to this volume, one which I take special pleasure in acknowledging.

Stephen W. Foster's inspired research assistance led to the discovery of numbers of important documents; his specific contributions are gratefully acknowledged in many of the notes in the back of this volume.

James D. Steakley's vast knowledge of the history and literature of the early German homosexual emancipation movement led to the discovery of a number of documents referring to the United States; his translations of these, his aid in selecting material to be reprinted, and his help in preparing introductions, contributed immeasurably to the creation of this history, and to my own pleasure in preparing it.

J. Michael Siegelaub contributed his expert advice on the complex logistics of organizing the many and varied tasks connected with my work on this book; his affectionate, sensitive, and continuing support helped bring this project to a successful conclusion.

Jim Kepner is to be thanked for his numerous, informative, multipaged, single-spaced letters concerning (especially) the early history of the Mattachine Society, and for his encouragement.

Barbara Gittings, Henry Hay, Alma Routsong, and two anonymous Gay males are to be thanked for allowing me to record and use interviews with them. Hay is also to be thanked for his many, multipaged, single-spaced letters concerning the founding of the Mattachine Society.

Support and assistance of different kinds were given by Carol Alpert, Ellen Alpert, Louis Crompton, John D'Emilio, Ed Drucker of Elysian Fields Booksellers, Jeffrey Escoffier, Herbert Freudenberger, Richard Hall, Becky Johnston, Carol Joyce, Robert Joyce, Jr., Jacqueline Hunt Katz, William Loren Katz, Dennis Lampkowski, Ted Rauch, David Roggensack, Robert Roth, Albert Wolsky, and Constance Zoff. The late Howard Brown is remembered for his interest and assistance. The consciousness-raising group with whom I have met weekly since the summer of 1975 provided continuing encouragement. In addition to the formal dedication, this book is written in loving memory of my father, Bernard Katz, who taught me to be outraged at social injustice, and about the need for united action toward radical social change.

The following individuals or institutions also contributed to the making of this book:

ACKNOWLEDGMENTS

Dan Allen
Elizabeth Amada
Richard Amory
Roger Austen
Robb Baker
Rosalyn Baxandall
Eric Bentley
Robert Benton
Drew Betterton
Neil Big
E. Carrington Boggan
Vern L. Bullough
Joseph Cady
Dan Caldano
Robert Carter
William Chalson
Annie Chamberlain
Janet Cooper
Nicholas Deutsch
Martin Duberman
Andrew Dvosin
Wayne Dynes
James Elliot
Michael Folsom
James Foshee
Ron Gold
Meredith Grey
Edward F. Grier

Foster Gunnison
Bert Hansen
Craig Hanson
Walter Harding
Chris Hinrichs
Stephen Holtzman
Richard Howard
Institute for Sex Research, Inc.
Christopher Isherwood
Karla Jay
Warren Johansson
Gregory Kane
Sidney Kaplan
Mimi Keifer
Maurice Kenny
Morris Kight
Seymour Kleinberg
Jean Kramer
John Kyper
John Lauritsen
Michael J. Lavery
W. Dorr Legg
Lee Lehman
Reed Lenti
Charles Lockwood
Doris Lunden
Keith McKinney
Nan Bauer Maglin

Toby Marotta
Robert A. Martin
Robert K. Martin
Carole Turbin Miller
Wilbur Miller
Richard George Murray
New York Mattachine Society
ONE, Inc.
Nick Patricca
Richard Plant
Nath Rockell
Craig Rodwell
Baird Searles
Martha Shelley
Dan Sherbo
Alix Kates Shulman
Carroll Smith-Rosenberg
Julia Stanley
Edward Strug
Peter Tamony
David Thorstad
Rich Wandel
Antony Ward
Steve Weinstock
Edmund White
George Whitmore
Randy Wicker

I wish to thank several people at Thomas Y. Crowell Company for their generous and warmhearted assistance—Nick Ellison and Arlene Reisberg—and also Ellen Tabak for copy editing, and Charles Choset and Teri Ashley for proofreading a difficult manuscript.

The responsibility for this book's contents is, of course, my own.

J. K.

COPYRIGHT ACKNOWLEDGMENTS

The publisher acknowledges permission to reprint excerpts from the following:

Bessie by Chris Albertson, copyright © 1972 by Chris Albertson, reprinted by permission of Stein and Day Publishers.

Female Homosexuality by Frank S. Caprio, copyright © 1954 by Frank S. Caprio, reprinted by permission of Citadel Press, Inc.

"Covert Sensitization" by Joseph R. Cautela, *Psychological Reports*, vol. 20, no. 2 (1967), copyright © 1967 by Southern Universities Press, reprinted by permission of *Psychological Reports* and the author.

"On Female Homosexuality" by Helene Deutsch, trans. by Edith B. Jackson, *Psychoanalytic Quarterly*, vol. 1 (Oct. 1932), copyright © 1932 by the Psychoanalytic Quarterly, Inc., reprinted by permission of the *Psychoanalytic Quarterly* and the author.

Drawing of Martin Gay by Ralph Waldo Emerson, in *Journals of Ralph Waldo Emerson*, copyright © 1909 by Edward Waldo Emerson, 1937 by Raymond Emerson, reprinted by permission of Houghton Mifflin Co.

The Journals and Miscellaneous Notebooks of Ralph Waldo Emerson edited by William H. Gilman and others, copyright © 1960 by the President and Fellows of Harvard College, reprinted by permission of Harvard University Press.

Censorship; The Search for the Obscene by Morris L. Ernst and Alan U. Schwartz, copyright © 1964 by Joan E. Goldstein and Alan U. Schwartz, reprinted by permission of the copyright holders.

"Reclaiming the Old New World. Gay was Good with Native Americans" by Dean Gengle, *The Advocate* (Jan. 28, 1976), copyright © 1976 by Liberation Publications, Inc., reprinted by permission.

The Papers of Alexander Hamilton edited by Harold C. Syrett, assoc. ed., and Jacob E. Cooke, vols. 2 and 3 copyright © 1962 by Columbia University Press, reprinted by permission.

The Puritan Jungle by Sara Harris, copyright © 1969 by Sara Harris, reprinted by permission of G. P. Putnam's Sons.

"Homo-Anonymous" by Ernest Harms, *Diseases of the Nervous System*, vol. 14, no. 10 (1953), reprinted by permission of Physicians Postgraduate Press.

"The Kaska Indians: An Ethnographic Reconstruction" by J. J. Honigmann, copyright © 1964 by Human Relations Area Files, Inc., reprinted by permission.

The American Idea of Success by Richard M. Huber, copyright © 1971 by Richard M. Huber, reprinted by permission of McGraw-Hill Book Co.

The Labyrinth by Helen R. Hull, copyright © 1923 by Macmillan Publishing Co., reprinted by permission of the estate of Helen R. Hull.

The Reminiscences of Gardner Jackson (1959), in the Oral History Collection of Columbia University, copyright © 1972 by the Trustees of Columbia University in the City of New York, reprinted by permission of the Oral History Research Collection.

"Homosexuality in Women" by Harvey E. Kaye and others, *Archives of General Psychiatry*, vol. 17 (Nov. 1967), copyright © 1967 by the American Medical Association, reprinted by permission.

Sexual Behavior in the Human Male by Alfred C. Kinsey, Wardel B. Pomeroy, Clyde E. Martin, copyright © 1948 by W. B. Saunders Co., reprinted by permission of the Institute for Sex Research, Inc.

Washington Confidential by Jack Lait and Lee Mortimer, copyright © 1951 by Crown Publishers, Inc., reprinted by permission.

"Two 'Kindred Spirits': Sorority and Family in New England, 1836–1846" by William R. Taylor and Christopher Lasch, reprinted in *The World of Nations: Reflections on History, Politics and Culture* by Christopher Lasch, copyright © 1972 by Christopher Lasch, reprinted by permission of Alfred A. Knopf, Inc.

The Unfinished Country: A Book of American Symbols by Max Lerner, copyright © 1959 by Max Lerner, reprinted by permission of Simon & Schuster, Inc.

"Homosexuality and its Treatment" by J. Allen Gilbert, *Journal of Nervous and Mental Disease*, vol. 52, no. 4 (Oct. 1920), copyright © 1920 by Smith Ely Jelliffe, reprinted by permission of The Smith Ely Jelliffe Trust.

"Homosexuality, Transvestism, and Psychosis: A Study of a Case Treated with Electroshock" by Samuel Liebman, *Journal of Nervous and Mental Disease* vol. 99, no. 6 (1944), copyright © 1944 by Smith Ely Jelliffe, reprinted by permission of The Smith Ely Jelliffe Trust.

Intimate Memories, vol. 1, *Background* by Mabel

ACKNOWLEDGMENTS

Dodge Luhan, copyright © 1933 by Harcourt, Brace and Co., Inc., reprinted by permission of J. Evans.

"Breaking Up a Homosexual Fixation by the Conditioned Reaction Technique: A Case Study" by Louis William Max, *Psychological Bulletin*, vol. 32 (1935), copyright © 1935 by the American Psychological Association, reprinted by permission.

Alexander Hamilton: A Portrait in Paradox by John Chester Miller, copyright © 1959 by Harper and Row Publishers, Inc., reprinted by permission.

"Hypnotic-Aversion Treatment of Homosexuality" by Michael M. Miller, *Journal of the National Medical Association*, vol. 55, no. 5 (1963), copyright © 1963 by the National Medical Association, Inc., reprinted by permission.

Consciousness in Concord; the Text of Thoreau's Hitherto "Lost Journal," 1840–41, Together with Notes and Commentary by Perry Miller, copyright © 1958 by Perry Miller, reprinted by permission of Houghton Mifflin Company.

"The Pathogenesis and Treatment of Homosexual Disorders: A Digest of Some Pertinent Evidence" by Thomas V. Moore, *Journal of Personality*, vol. 14 (1945), copyright © 1945 by Duke University Press, reprinted by permission.

The Oregon Trail by Francis Parkman, edited by E. N. Feltskog, copyright © 1969 by the Regents of the University of Wisconsin, reprinted by permission.

"To Be Accused Is To Be Guilty: 2. The Ever-Present Past" by "Miss" E. M., *ONE Magazine*, vol. 1, no. 4 (April 1953), copyright © 1953 by ONE Inc., reprinted by permission.

Forty Miles a Day on Beans and Hay: The Enlisted Soldier Fighting the Indian Wars by Don Rickey, Jr., copyright © 1963 by the University of Oklahoma Press, reprinted by permission.

Moreau de Saint Méry's American Journey, copyright © 1947 by Kenneth Roberts and Anna M. Roberts, reprinted by permission of Doubleday & Co., Inc.

"A Note on the Ineffectualness of Sex Hormone Medication in a Case of Pronounced Homosexuality" by Saul Rosenzweig and R. G. Hoskins, *Psychosomatic Medicine*, vol. 3, no. 1 (1941), copyright © 1941 by American Elsevier Publishing Co., Inc., reprinted by permission.

Voyage from Lesbos: The Psychoanalysis of a Female Homosexual by Richard C. Robertiello, M.D., copyright © by Richard C. Robertiello, reprinted by permission of Citadel Press, Inc.

"A Double-Barrel Approach to Modification of Homosexual Behavior" by Ivan Toby Rutner, *Psychological Reports*, vol. 26, no. 2 (1970), copyright © 1970 by Psychological Reports, reprinted by permission.

"The Kutenai Female Berdache: Courier, Guide, Prophetess, and Warrior" by Claude E. Schaeffer, *Ethnohistory*, vol. 12, no. 3 (1965), reprinted by permission of the American Society for Ethnohistory.

"Group Therapy with Homosexuals" by Alexander P. Smith and Alexander Bassin, *Journal of Social Therapy*, vol. 5, no. 3 (1959), copyright © 1959 by Journal of Social Therapy, reprinted by permission.

"Klamath Ethnography" by Leslie Spier, *University of California Publications in American Archaeology and Ethnology*, vol. 30, no. 1 (1930), copyright © 1930 by the Regents of the University of California, reprinted by permission of the University of California Press.

The Letters of John Addington Symonds ed. by Herbert M. Schueller and Robert L. Peters, copyright © 1967–69 by the editors, reprinted by permission of the Wayne State University Press.

Zespedes in East Florida, 1784–1790 by Helen Hornbeck Tanner, copyright © 1963 by Helen Hornbeck Tanner, reprinted by permission of the University of Miami Press.

Dorothy Thompson Diary [1932] in the George Arents Research Library, Syracuse University, reprinted by permission of Morgan Guaranty Trust Co. as executor of the estate of Dorothy Thompson Kopf.

Drawing by Henry David Thoreau with manuscript Journal of Oct. 16, 1856, reproduced by permission of The Pierpont Morgan Library, N.Y.C.

The Life of Radclyffe Hall by Una, Lady Troubridge, copyright © 1961 by Una Vincenzo, Lady Troubridge, reprinted by permission of Citadel Press, Inc.

Margaret Fuller: Whetstone of Genius by Mason Wade, copyright © 1940 by Hugh Mason Wade, reprinted by permission of The Viking Press, Inc.

"Merimaid" (painting) by Mary Ann Willson, reproduced by permission of the New York State Historical Association, Cooperstown, N.Y.

"Elmer Gage: American Indian" by Bob Waltrip, *ONE Magazine* (March 1965), copyright © 1965 by ONE, Inc., reprinted by permission.

"Autoerotic and Homoerotic Manifestations in Hospitalized Male Postlobotomy Patients" by Moses Zlotlow and Albert E. Paganini, *Psychiatric Quarterly*, vol. 33, no. 3 (1959), copyright © 1959 by Human Sciences Press, reprinted by permission.

Photograph of Barbara Cameron by Crawford Barton, reproduced by permission of Barbara Cameron and Crawford Barton.

Almeda Sperry manuscript letters to Emma Goldman in the Emma Goldman Collection, Mugar Memorial Library, Boston University, reprinted by permission of Mugar Memorial Library, Special Collections.

The New York Times, 1926–27, 1928–29, 1950–54, copyright © 1926/27/28/29/50/51/52/53/54 by The New York Times Company, reprinted by permission.

"Is Homosexuality Curable?" by Wilhelm Stekel, trans. by Bertrand S. Frohman, *Psychoanalytic Review*, vol. 17, no. 4 (Oct. 1930), copyright © 1930 by the National Psychological Association for Psychoanalysis, reprinted by permission of the editors and publisher.

"The Limitations and Complications of Organotherapy in Male Homosexuality" by S. J. Glass and Roswell H. Johnson, *Journal of Clinical Endocrinology*, vol. 4, no. 11 (1944), copyright © 1944 by J. B. Lippincott Co., reprinted by permission.

A NOTE ON THE NOTES
AND BIBLIOGRAPHIES

Notes to the introductions preceding each of the six parts of this book detail only those sources not mentioned later in the text.

The notes identify sources quoted in the main text; they also include additional information and sources in roughly chronological order. The alphabetical bibliographies following each section of notes cite all sources quoted in the main text, and some titles selected from those mentioned in the notes. The bibliographies also include some sources not mentioned in the text or notes. Following most bibliographic citations the particular page(s) of interest are included in parentheses.

For reasons beyond the author's control, it has not always been possible to provide uniform or complete data for each source citation or for each informational note. It has been judged more important to occasionally provide partially complete source references than to omit these citations altogether.

Transcripts of the taped interviews printed in this book were edited for reading clarity, then sent to the interviewees and re-edited according to their suggestions.

A number of important, out-of-print works cited here have been reprinted by Arno Press in a series edited by the present author, entitled "Homosexuality: Lesbians and Gay Men in Society, History, and Literature"; a 23-page catalog is available from Arno Press.

Abbreviations used in the notes: NAW refers to Edward T. James, Janet Wilson James, Paul S. Boyer, eds. *Notable American Women, 1607–1950* (Cambridge, Mass.: Harvard University Press, 1972), 3 vols. DAB refers to Allen Johnson, ed., *Dictionary of American Biography* (New York: Scribner's, 1927–36).

The notes and main text are indexed; for cross-references, check the index.

NOTES

Introduction

1. In Germany, as early as 1863, socialist leader Ferdinand Lassalle defended a homosexual comrade in the radical labor movement. In 1895, socialist leader Eduard Bernstein defended Oscar Wilde and homosexuality in the official journal of the then Marxist Social Democratic Party. In 1898, another prominent socialist leader, August Bebel, publicly supported homosexual emancipation. Later, Social Democrats and Communists actively supported homosexual law reform. In the Soviet Union, the Bolshevik government decriminalized homosexual acts in 1917. (The Stalinist regime recriminal-

ized homosexual acts in 1934.) See John Lauritsen and David Thorstad, *The Early Homosexual Rights Movement (1864–1935)* (N.Y.: Times Change Press, 1974), p. 13–14, 32–33, 36–37, 52, 56–61, 62–69. See also James D. Steakley, *The Homosexual Emancipation Movement in Germany* (N.Y.: Arno, 1975).

NOTES

I. Trouble: 1566–1966

1. E[dmund] B. O'Callaghan, ed., *Calendar of Historical Manuscripts in the Office of the Secretary of State, Albany, N.Y.* (Albany: Weed, Parsons, 1865; photo reprint as *Calendar of Dutch Historical Manuscripts*, Ridgewood, N.J.: Gregg Press, 1968), p. 213, 251–52.

2. Bartolome Barrientos, "Vida y Hechos de Pero [*sic*] Menendez de Auiles . . ." in Genaro García, ed. *Dos Antiguas Relaciones de la Florida publicalas por primera vez . . .* (Mexico City: J. Aguilar, 1902), p. 111.

3. Gonzalo Solís de Merás, *Pedro Menendez de Aviles; Adelantado; Governor and Captain-General of Florida . . .* trans. by Jeannette Conner (Deland, Fla.: Florida State Historical Society, 1923), p. 180–81. Additional sources on the French Lutheran interpreter, the murder victim, whose name was Guillaume, are in the following: Barrientos p. 105, 110–11; Charles E. Bennett, *Laudonnière and Fort Caroline* (Gainesville, Fla.: University of Florida, 1964), p. 107–08; [Andres González de Barcia Carballido y Zúñiga] *Barcia's Chronological History of the Continent of Florida . . . from 1512 . . . until the Year 1722*, trans. Anthony Kerrigan (reprint, Westport, Conn.: Greenwood Press, 1951), p. 113, 118. I wish to thank Stephen W. Foster for informing me of these documents.

4. H. R. McIlwaine, ed., *Minutes of the Council and General Court of Colonial Virginia, 1622–1632, 1670–1676 . . .* (Richmond: Colonial Press, 1924). I wish to thank John D'Emilio for informing me of this and the following document.

5. Edmund S. Morgan, "The First American Boom: Virginia 1618 to 1630," *William and Mary Quarterly*, vol. 28, no. 2 (April 1971); p. 193.

6. McIlwaine, p. 34. In this and the following texts from the Virginia Council Minutes, punctuation, abbreviations, and old English spellings have been edited, spelled out in full, modernized, and regularized for clarity in reading; quotation marks have been added; nothing of substance is changed. The old English "Richard Williams als Cornush" has been translated as "Richard Williams also Cornish" following the definition of "als" in the OED.

7. McIlwaine, p. 42. A passage on p. 47 adds: "It is ordered that William Cowse shall come up from Hog Island and here in Court to make choice of his master with whom he is willing to dwell with, either with Captain Weste or with Captain Hamer, with whom he hath already agreed." The manner of settling the state's fee for disposing of Richard Cornish is also discussed.

8. McIlwaine, p. 78.

9. McIlwaine, p. 81.

10. McIlwaine, p. 83. These *Minutes* add: "It is ordered that a warrant be sent for Richard Evans and Arthur Avelinge his man, to appear here at James City on Monday next . . ." (See note 11).

11. *Minutes*, p. 85. These *Minutes* add: "Arthur Avelinge by the oath he hath formerly taken deposeth that William Barker read the warrant to him, where he by name was commanded to appear at James City and that after Robert Saben called the said deponent to come up with him according to the warrant, but he being Richard Evans servant, his said master answered he would see the warrant before he should come up.

"It is ordered that Richard Evans for his offence in disobeying the Governor's command shall lie neck and heels 3 hours in the market place, and shall pay 100 weight of tobacco towards the building of the new bridges at Elizabeth City, and be put out of his place, except upon his good behavior Captain Tucker shall approve him hereafter."

12. McIlwaine, p. 93.

13. "Francis Higgeson's Journal . . ." in *The Founding of Massachusetts*, ed. Stuart Mitchell (Boston: Massachusetts Historical Society, 1930), p. 71. The old English "u" in the text has been changed to a "v." The information on hanging appears in Edwin Powers, *Crime and Punishment in Early Massachusetts: 1620–1692* (Boston: Beacon, 1966), p. 43.

In 1629, the inquisitive neighbors of Thomas Hall of the Virginia Colony made several physical attacks upon Hall in order to ascertain his true gender. Hall claimed to be a hermaphrodite, but the evidence indicates he was a perfectly formed male, who had, however, been brought up as a female. The evidence also suggests that Hall was heterosexual in orientation. This document is relevant to the phenomena of sex-role reversal, the factors determining it, and the social attitudes toward it. The *Minutes of the Council and General Court of Colonial Virginia* record that on March 25, 1629, Governor John Pott examined three witnesses in this curious case, including Hall him/herself. The court ordered it, publicly proclaimed that Hall was "a man and a woman," and he was required to "go clothed in man's apparell," only his head covered like a woman, "with an apron before him," and was placed on good behavior (McIlwaine p. 194–95).

In 1641, a young servent named Hackett was executed in the Massachusetts Bay Colony for bestiality. See John Winthrop, *History of New England from 1630 to 1649*, ed. James Savage, 2 vols. (Boston: Little, Brown, 1853), vol. 2, p. 58–59; also see Powers p. 442, 624 note 92. The punishment for homosexuality in the colonies must be understood in relation to the contemporary punishments for other, especially sexual, crimes.

Vern L. Bullough's *Sexual Variance in Society and History* (N.Y.: Wiley, 1976), a documented, international survey, was published too late for comment here. It contains references to important documents of homosexual history, including a colonial American Lesbian reference (p. 519–22).

14. William R. Staples, ed., *The Colonial Laws of Massachusetts Reprinted from the Edition of 1672 . . . Together with the Body of Liberties of 1641* (Boston: Rockwell and Churchill, 1890), p. 35n. I wish to thank Louis Crompton for informing me of this document, which is to appear with others in Crompton's pioneering article "Homosexuals and the Death Penalty in Colonial America," the *Journal of Homosexuality*, vol. 1, no. 4 (1976), the first major piece of historical research on homosexuality and American law.

15. William Bradford. *Of Plymouth Plantation*, ed. Samuel Eliot Morison (N.Y.: Knopf, 1952), p. 316.

16. Bradford, p. 316–17, 321–22.

17. Bradford, p. 404–05.

18. Bradford, p. 407.

19. Bradford, p. 408–12; rape case p. 320 note 6. John Winthrop discusses the details of the rape case (vol. 2, p. 54–57). I wish to thank Louis Crompton for help with this research.

20. Bradford, p. 321. Bradford's Plymouth Colony figures prominently in a brief, striking, but undocumented comment by Geoffrey May in his book on *Social Control of Sex Expression*: "The strict precautions taken by the Puritans against social intercourse between the unattached of the opposite sexes led to two foreseeable consequences. The one was an exaggerated amount of homosexual expression. Though historians do not comment upon the fact, the early records of Plymouth Colony show that of the prosecutions for all sex offenses, between one-fifth and one-fourth were for various homosexual

practices. When one considers the comparative difficulty of discovering sexual intimacy between members of the same sex, this proportion of court actions is a large one. In Massachusetts Bay, except for the few cases of actual sodomy, the records are not so revealing. But numerous are the records of 'defiling,' of 'uncleanness,' of 'unclean practices,' and the like, which may well have been a euphemistic expression of varieties of homosexuality" (Geoffrey May, *Social Control of Sex Expression* [N.Y.: Morrow, 1931], p. 247).

21. Winthrop, vol. 2, p. 324. A reference to the execution of Plaine is in Bernard Christian Steiner, *A History of the Planatation of Menunkatuck and of the Original Town of Guilford, Connecticut* . . . (Baltimore, 1897), p. 47. I wish to thank Robert Carter for the Latin translation.

22. O'Callaghan, p. 103. It would be interesting to know what Dutch word appears for "faggots" in the original manuscript. This translation, published in 1865, is the earliest-known American usage of the word "faggot" (for kindling) in a situation involving homosexuality. *The Calendar* also includes a reference to attempted "sodomy" by N. G. Hillebrant or Hillebtantsen in 1658 (p. 201, 319), and to the alleged homosexual rape by J. Q. van der Linde (or Linden) in 1660 (p. 213, 251–52). Van der Linde was sentenced to be "tied in a sack and cast into the river and drowned until dead;" the victim was to be "privately whipped, and sent to some other place. . . ."

23. J. Hammond Trumbull, *The True-Blue Laws of Connecticut and New-Haven* (Hartford: American Pub. Co., 1879), p. 201. I wish to thank Louis Crompton for informing me of this document, which appears in his article "Homosexuals and the Death Penalty in Colonial America."

Edward Hyde, Lord Cornbury, the transvestite governor of New York and New Jersey (1702–08), an utterly corrupt and despised colonial official, appears to have been entirely heterosexual! The first document I know of suggesting Hyde's homosexuality dates to the 1880s. Contemporary documents (as far as I know) refer only to his cross-dressing, corruption, and several children. A subject for research; see Lewis Morris to the Secretary of State, Feb. 9, 1707, in E. B. O'Callaghan, ed., *Documents Relative to the Colonial History of the State of New York* (Albany: Weed, Parsons, 1855), vol. 5, p. 33, 38, etc.; William Smith, *The History of the Late Province of New-York . . . to . . . 1762* (N.Y.: New-York Historical Society, 1829), vol. 1, p. 194; "A Governor in Petticoats," *The Historical Magazine* (Morrisania, N.Y.: Dawson), 2nd ser., vol. 2 (1867), p. 169; J. Romeyn Brodhead, "Lord Cornbury," *The Historical Magazine* (Morrisania, N.Y.) new ser., vol. 3, no. 1 (Jan. 1868), p. 71–72; Philip Henry Stanhope, *History of England; Comprising the Reign of Queen Anne . . .* 3rd ed. (London, 1853), vol. 1, p. 79; E. C. Spitzka, "A Historical Case of Sexual Perversion," *Chicago Medical Review*, Aug. 20, 1881, p. 378–79; James Grant Wilson, ed., *The Memorial History of the City of New-York, from its First Settlement to the Year 1892* (N.Y.: New York History Co., 1892), vol. 2, p. 86–88; Charles Worthen Spencer, "The Cornbury Legend," *N.Y. State Historical Association Proceedings* (Albany), vol. 13 (1914), p. 309–20; Arthur D. Pierce, "A Governor in Skirts," *New Jersey Historical Society Proceedings*, vol. 83, no. 1 (Jan. 1965), p. 1–9. A large portrait of Hyde, in a bright blue, low-necked dress and white gloves, is sometimes on exhibit at the New-York Historical Society; it is quite a sight.

In 1775, the British Colonial Secretary, Lord George Germain, is said to have had or aspired to a homosexual relation with the American Benjamin Thompson; see Mitchell A. Wilson, *American Science and Invention, A Pictorial History* (N.Y.: Simon and Schuster, 1954), p. 26; Alan Chester Valentine, *Lord George Germain* (Oxford: Clarendon Press, 1962), p. 472–75.

24. Thomas Jefferson, *The Papers of Thomas Jefferson*, ed. Julian P. Boyd (Princeton, N.J.: Princeton University, 1950–), vol. 2, p. 325.

25. Jefferson, p. 497. The note continues (the source references need deciphering): "12.Co.37. says 'note that Sodomy is with mankind.' But Finch's L.B.3.c.24. 'Sodomitry is a carnal copulation against nature, to wit, of man or woman in the same sex, or of either of them with beasts.' 12.Co.36. says 'it appears by the antient authorities of the law that this was felony.' Yet the 25.H.8. declares it felony, as if supposed not to be so. Britton c.9. says that Sodomites are to be burnt. F.N.B.269.b. Fleta.L.1.c.37. says 'pecorantes et Sodomitae in terra vivi confodiantur.' The Mirror makes it treason. Bestiality can never make any progress; it cannot therefore be injurious to society in any great degree, which is the true measure of criminality in foro civili, and will ever be properly and severely punished by universal derision. It may therefore be omitted. It was antiently punished with death as it has been latterly. L1.Aelfrid.31. and 25H.8.c.6. See Beccaria §.31. Montesq."

26. George Washington, *The Writings of George Washington . . .* ed. by John C. Fitzpatrick (Washington, D.C.: U.S. Govt. Ptg. Of., 1934), vol. 11, p. 83–84.

27. Helen Hornbeck Tanner, *Zéspedes in East Florida, 1784–1790*, Hispanic-American Institute, University of Miami Hispanic-American Studies, no. 19 (Coral Gables, Fla.: University of Miami, 1963), p. 167–68. I wish to thank Stephen W. Foster for informing me of this document.

28. Médéric-Louis-Elie Moreau de St. Méry, *St. Méry's American Journey*, trans. and ed. Kenneth Roberts and Anna M. Roberts (Garden City, N.Y.: Doubleday, 1947), p. 284, 286.

29. Thomas Harris and Reverdy Johnson, *Reports of Cases Argued and Determined in the Court of Appeals of Maryland, In 1810, 1811, 1812, 1813, 1814, & 1815* (Annapolis, Md.: Jonas Green, 1826), vol. 3, p. 154.

Publications in law use a citation style different from that used in other fields. In legal references the above citation would appear as Davis *v.* State, 3 Har. & J. 154. The fledgling Gay history researcher should not be deterred by the apparent difficulty in understanding legal citations, obtaining access, and finding materials in law libraries. A brief guide to legal citations and research is in Kate L. Turabian, *A Manual for Writers . . .* 4th ed. (Chicago: University of Chicago, 1973), p. 112–117. I wish to thank Robert Roth for help with this research.

The various indexes to American legal cases list cases dealing with homosexuality under the general category "Sodomy" (along with cases dealing with bestiality and, occasionally, cases involving heterosexual anal or oral acts). "Sodomy" cases are also cross-referenced with "Divorce" and "Libel and Slander" cases. See, for instance, the *Century Edition of the American Digest; A Complete Digest of All Reported American Cases from the Earliest Times to 1896*, vol. 44 ["Sodomy"] (St. Paul, Minn.: West, 1903); *American Digest System 1906 Decennial Edition of the American Digest; A Complete Digest of All Reported Cases from 1897 to 1906*, vol. 18 ["Sodomy"] (St. Paul, Minn.: West, 1910); *American Digest System 1926; Third Decennial Edition of the American Digest; A Complete Digest of All Reported from 1916 to 1926*, vol. 24 ["Sodomy"] (St. Paul, Minn.: West, 1929). This index continues up to the *Seventh Decennial Digest* of all decisions of the state and federal courts between 1956 and 1966. From 1967 until the present (Jan. 1976), *West's General Digest* lists "sodomy" cases year by year. For a listing of early "sodomy" cases also see *The American and English Encyclopedia of Law*, eds. D. S. Garland and L. P. McGehee, supervisor, J. Cockcroft, 2nd ed., vol. 25 ["Sodomy"] (Northport, L.I., N.Y.: Edward Thompson, 1903). *The Cyclopedia of Law and Procedure*, eds. W. Mack and H. P. Nash (N.Y.: American Law Book Co., 1903) also contains a section on "Sodomy" and a listing of cases. *The Index to Legal Periodicals* lists cases dealing with homosexuality under varied headings, such as "Sex Crimes."

Research in the above sources produced the following list of American legal cases involving homosexuality up to 1900. ("Sodomy" cases involving bestiality are here eliminated.) Only the legal citations are given:

New York, 1861: Lambertson v. People (Supm. Ct. Gen. T.) 5 Park. Crim. (N.Y.) 200 (Lambertson guilty of anal intercourse with Peter Cohen).

Mass., 1873: Commonwealth v. Snow; 111 Mass. 411 (document quoted in main text).

Louisiana, 1876: State v. Grusso; 28 La. Ann. 952.

Montana, 1878: Territory v. Mahaffey; 3 Mont. 112 (document quoted in main text).

Calif., 1881: People v. Williams; 59 Cal. 397.

Texas, 1883: Ex parte Bergen; 14 Tex. App. 52.

Texas, 1889: Medis v. State; 27 Tex. App. 194; 11 S.W. 112; 11 Am. St. Rep. 192.

Virginia, 1890: Houston v. Com.; 87 Va. 257; 12 S. E. 385 (homosexuality?).

Conn., 1891: Mascolo v. Montesanto; 61 Conn. 50; 23 Atl. 714; 29 Am. St. Rep. 170.

Texas, 1893: Prindle v. State; 31 Tex. Cr. R. 551; 21 S. W. 360; 37 Am. St. Rep. 833 (homosexuality?).

Washington, 1893: State v. Place; 5 Wash. 773 (homosexuality?).

Calif., 1894: People v. Moore; 103 Cal. 508; 37 Pac. 510.

Georgia, 1894: Hodges v. State; 94 Ga. 593; 19 S. E. 758.

Mass., 1894: Commonwealth v. Dill; 160 Mass. 536; 36 N.E. 472 (homosexuality?).

Calif., 1895: People v. Hickey; 41 Pac. 1027; 109 Cal. 275.

Illinois, 1897: Honselman v. People; 168 Ill. 174; 48 N.E. 304.

Missouri, 1897: State v. Smith; (Sup.) 137 Mo. 25; 38 S.W. 717.

Calif., 1897: People v. Boyle; 48 P. 800; 116 Cal. 658 (homosexuality?).

Calif., 1897: People v. Wilson; 51 P. 639; 119 Cal. 384.

Texas, 1898: Darling v. State; 47 S. W. 1005 (homosexuality?).

Florida, 1899: Simmons v. State; 41 Fla. 316; 25 So. 881 (homosexuality?).

Washington, 1899: State v. Romans; 57 P. 819; 21 Wash. 284.

Further homosexual "sodomy" cases are reported up to the present day.

30. Harris and Johnson, p. 154–55.

31. Harris and Johnson, p. 155–58.

32. Louis Dwight, [Sodomy among juvenile delinquents] (Boston: April 25, 1826), 2 p. Cataloged under above title in the Union Theological Seminary Library. I wish to thank Warren Johansson for informing me of this document, and for providing the following footnote: "The word *Kinshon*, which appears in Dwight's text in the meaning which *punk* had a century later, merits a commentary.

"It is evidently identical with the word recorded by the OED and by Farmer and Henley as *kinchin* 'a boy trained as a thief's accomplice.' The first quotation for the term is from 1561, so that it has a long history in English thieves' argot.

"The etymon of the word is German *Kindchen* 'little child,' which however belongs to the literary language and has no special function in criminal slang.

"In the meaning in which it is used in the text of 1826, it does not seem to be recorded in any of the existing dictionaries of American English or American slang."

Allusions to male homosexuality in San Quentin prison dating back to 1858 are found in Kenneth Lamott, *Chronicles of San Quentin; the Biography of a Prison* (N.Y.: McKay, 1961). In 1858, it was recommended that all boys under eighteen be kept in county jails rather than being sent to San Quentin (p. 17). In 1860, a San Quentin doctor refers to prisoners' diseases caused by "libidinous indiscretions" (p. 12). A description of a strike of San Quentin prisoners on May 27, 1897, mentions "Kid's Alley" (p. 144). In 1925, every Sunday morning a "Jocker's Ball," including male–male dancing, was held at San Quentin (p. 200, 268; the source is an article by E. B. Block in

Sunset, July 1926). The 1944 segregation of homosexuals in San Quentin is cited (p. 249).

33. 1st Patrol District, "In the Matter of Complaint against Edward McCosker Policeman [1846]," (19p., no pagination) New York City, Municipal Archives and Records Service, Collection: City Clerk—Filed Papers, Location: 3198. Description: . . . Complaints against Policemen, 1845–1846. I wish to thank Wilbur Miller for informing me of this document. All the following quotations are from the above. In these quotations, spelling has been made uniform, punctuation and quotation marks have been added, the original documents have been edited for clarity in reading; nothing of substance is changed.

34. Records of the Unitarian Church, Brewster, Mass., 1866, quoted in Richard M. Huber, *The American Idea of Success* (N.Y.: McGraw-Hill, 1971), p. 45–46, 469 note 5. "Friar Anselmo," a poem by Alger on the theme of good deeds as a form of repentance, begins to suggest one motivation of his social work. The poem was originally published in the *New York Weekly,* Aug. 5, 1872 (see the otherwise superficial *Horatio's Boys; The Life and Works of Horatio Alger, Jr.* by Edwin P. Hoyt [Radnor, Pa.: Chilton, 1974], p. 62–63, 254. Clues to a subtle understanding of the "Prince and the Pauper" theme in the pederastic form of male homosexuality (and, by analogy, of Alger) may be found in Timothy d'Arch Smith's wonderfully researched *Love in Earnest; Some Notes on the Lives and Writings of English "Uranian" Poets from 1889 to 1930* (London: Routledge & Kegan Paul, 1970). Smith's work is a gold mine of documented information on many aspects of Gay male history.

35. Albert G. Browne, Jr., and John C. Gray, Jr., reporters, *Massachusetts Reports 111; Cases Argued and Determined in the Supreme Judicial Court of Massachusetts; November 1872–March 1873* (Boston: Houghton, Mifflin, 1884), p. 411–13. Legal citation: Commonwealth *v.* Snow, 111 Mass. 411.

36. Henry N. Blake and Cornelius Hedges, *Reports of Cases Argued and Determined in the Supreme Court of Montana Territory from the August Term, 1877, to January Term, 1880, Inclusive* (San Francisco: Bancroft-Whitney, 1911), vol. 3, p. 114–15. Legal citation: Territory *v.* Mahaffey, 3 Mont. 112.

37. U.S. Dept. of the Interior, Census Office, *Report of the Defective, Dependent, and Delinquent Classes of the Population of the United States, As Returned at the Tenth Census (June 1, 1880),* by Frederick Howard Wines, Special Agent (Washington, D.C.: U.S. Govt. Ptg. Ofc. 1888), p. 506–07, 508–09, 516–17, 562–63. I wish to thank Louis Crompton for informing me of this document.

An outbreak of gonorrhea in 1883–84 in a boys' reformatory is discussed by R. Winslow, "Report of an Epidemic of Gonorrhoea Contracted from Rectal Coition," *Medical News* (Phila.), vol. 49 (1886), p. 180–82.

Michale Davitt's *Leaves from a Prison Diary* . . . published in New York (Ford's National Library, vol. 1, no. 2, [1886]) is said to discuss homosexuality.

In 1884, in Stuttgart, two young homosexual "Yankees" are said to have gotten themselves in trouble in King Charles's court. This court, says E. I. Prime Stevenson "in the earlier eighties of the last century, was the scene, of a complicated political and homosexual drama, reminding one of the dilemmas of King Edward II of England; in the ascendency, notoriously homosexual, gained over King Charles by two American favourites, neither of them much passed his teens, both of humble origins. They fairly exploited the enamoured king—for their common benefit—instead of being rivals (a truly Yankee stroke of cynical practicality) until they were expelled the city, by a ministerial coalition against them; ending thus the famous 'Jackson-Woodcock Affair' of 1884" (Xavier Mayne, pseud., *The Intersexes; A History of Similisexualism as a Problem in Social Life* [Naples?]: Privately printed [by R. Rispoli, 1908?]; photo reprint, N.Y.: Arno, 1975, p. 239).

38. [Richard] von Kraff[t]-Ebing, "Perversion of the Sexual Instinct—Report of Cases," trans. H. M. Jewett, *Alienist and Neurologist* (St. Louis, Mo.), vol. 9, no. 4 (Oct. 1888), p. 567–70.

39. U.S. Dept. of the Interior, Census Office, *Report on Crime, Pauperism, and Benevolence in the United States at the Eleventh Census: 1890, Part 1, Analysis,* (by) *Frederick H. Wines, Special Agent* (Washington, D.C.: U.S. Govt. Ptg. Ofc., 1896), p. 18–20. I wish to thank Louis Crompton for informing me of this document.

40. Charles W. Gardner, *The Doctor and The Devil, or Midnight Adventures of Dr. Parkhurst* (N.Y.: Gardner, 1894; reprint, N.Y.: Vanguard, 1931), p. 57. I wish to thank Wilbur Miller for informing me of this document.

An early newspaper reference to what sounds like either homosexuality or heterosexual prostitution appears in the New York *Herald*, June 29, 1846, p. 1: A "young man who considers himself somewhat respectable in this community, keeping store in Warren street," is reported to have been "detected" by a citizen "in one of those revolting and disgraceful acts which are nightly practiced on the Battery and in the vicinity of the City Mall." The offender had tried to bribe his discoverer, and here the trouble began, the paper reports. Perhaps additional research would clarify the nature of the disturbance. I wish to thank Charles Lockwood for this reference.

A homosexual German visitor to the U.S. in about 1871–72 reports that homosexuality is "more ordinary" here than in his own country, and that he was always "able to indulge his passions more openly, with less fear of punishment." He discovered in the U.S. that he was "always immediately recognized as a member of the [homosexual] confraternity" (J. L. Caspar and Carl Liman, *Handbuch der Gerichtlichen Medicin* [Berlin: Hirschwald, 1889], vol. 1, p. 173; partially translated by John Addington Symonds in *A Problem in Modern Ethics* [London: (no publisher) 1896], p. 116 n.)

A promising title for further research is *Sodom in Union Square, or Revelations of the Doings in Fourteenth Street. By an Ex-Police Captain.* N.Y.: 1879; 36 p.

Edward Van Every's *The Sins of New York as "Exposed" by the Police Gazette* indicates that a story by columnist "Paul Prowler" reports his observations of a homosexual New York bar, "Armory Hall," run by one Billy McGlory and apparently dating to the 1880s (N.Y.: Stokes, 1931), p. 215, 217. In Van Every' words: "The waiter girls who served the drinks were reinforced by a number of simpering males who were painted to resemble women and togged up in feminine raiment, and who in falsetto voices exchanged disgusting badinage among themselves and with the patrons. This type of pervert was then something new. . . ." Van Every says "it remained for Billy McGlory first to advertise such moral deformity." Van Every cites no exact source, and a Library of Congress search of the *Gazette* from Dec. 1879 through Feb. 1880 failed to locate this interesting column. Van Every also cites relevant *Gazette* references to Oscar Wilde's American tour of 1882 (p. 202–03); Dr. Mary Walker is mentioned (p. 136–37).

Wilde's American tour and his second visit of 1882–83 is a subject for research. See *The Letters of Oscar Wilde*, ed., Rubert Hart-Davis (N.Y.: Harcourt, Brace & World, 1962); Rupert Croft-Cooke, *The Unrecorded Life of Oscar Wilde* (N.Y.: McKay, 1972). Croft-Cooke maintains that Wilde was actively homosexual by the time he came to America (p. 32, 34). Lloyd Lewis and Henry Justin Smith's *Oscar Wilde Discovers America* (N.Y.: Harcourt, Brace, 1936) reports that in N.Y. in 1882 Wilde was called a "Charlotte-Ann." An early slang dictionary lists the third "common" meaning of "Mary-Ann" as "a sodomite" (John S. Farmer [and W. E. Henley], *Slang and Its Analogues Past and Present* [orig. pub. 1890–1904], vol. 4, p. 12; photo reprint, N.Y.: Arno, 1970).

41. Irving C. Rosse, "Sexual Hypochondriasis and Perversion of the Genesic Instinct," *Journal of Nervous and Mental Disease* (N.Y.), whole ser. vol. 19, new ser., vol. 17, no. 11 (Nov. 1892), p. 799.

42. Rosse, p. 803. Rosse also cites a New York *Herald* report (n.d.) of a New York homosexual bar, the Slide, being closed by the police.

43. Rosse, p. 805. The two classic French Lesbian novels Rosse mentions were first published in English translation, in the U.S., in the 1890s: Theophile Gautier, *Mademoiselle de Maupin; A Romance of Love and Passion; Illustrated . . . from designs by Toudouze* (Chicago: Laird & Lee, 1890); other eds.: N.Y.: 1897; London, 1930 [trans., revised, and amended by Alvah C. Bessie]; see Foster p. 64–66, 76, 82; Adolphe Belot, *Mademoiselle Giraud, My Wife* (Chicago: Laird & Lee, 1891); see Foster, p. 81–83, 97, 114, 220, 331, 363, 376. Honoré de Balzac's *Cousin Betty* (Boston: Dana Estes, 1901), trans. by James Waring; see Foster p. 63–64, 218, 362. See note 63 below. (Jeannette H. Foster, *Sex Variant Women in Literature*, [N.Y.: Vantage, 1956]).

44. Rosse, p. 806.

45. Rosse, p. 807.

46. [Charles H. Hughes], "Postscript to Paper on 'Erotopathia,'—An Organization of Colored Erotopaths," *Alienist and Neurologist* (St. Louis, Mo.), vol. 14, no. 4 (Oct. 1893), p. 731–32. Dr. Hughes's paper titled "Erotopathia.—Morbid Eroticism" is in the same issue of the *Alienist and Neurologist*, p. 531–78. References to an "androgynous" band of Blacks being raided by the police in Washington, D.C. and to a New Orleans "vadoux" society are in Rosse p. 802, 805–07. Rosse is apparently Hughes's source.

47. John Berryman, *Stephen Crane* (N.Y.: Sloan, 1950), p. 86. Berryman's notes include a complicated explanation of his source. The hero of Huysmans's *A Rebours* ("Against the Grain," 1884) was modeled on the homosexual Count Robert de Montesquiou, who is also said to have served as a model for characters created by Oscar Wilde and Marcel Proust (see Philippe Julian, *Prince of Aesthetes: Count Robert de Montesquiou, 1855–1921* [N.Y.: Viking, 1968]; and Barbara Grier [Gene Damon, pseud.], "Lesbiana," *The Ladder*, vol. 12, no. 9 [July 1968], p. 8–9).

A photo of a "Male Sexual Pervert" (in drag) and comments on male homosexuals and "Lesbians" in American cities are included in Allan McLane Hamilton's essay on "Insanity in its Medico-Legal Bearings," in *A System of Legal Medicine*, eds. A. M. Hamilton and Lawrence Godkin, 3 vols. (N.Y.: Treat, 1894–97), vol. 2, p. 49–50.

Valuable, detailed descriptions of "Paresis Hall," other homosexual bars, and Gay life in New York in the late nineteenth century are found in two volumes by Earl Lind, pseud., *Autobiography of an Androgyne*, ed. with introduction by Alfred W. Herzog (N.Y.: Medico-Legal Journal, 1918) and *The Female Impersonators . . .* ed. with an introduction by Alfred W. Herzog (N.Y.: Medico-Legal Journal, 1922; both photo reprint, N.Y.: Arno, 1975).

Soldier prostitution in San Francisco in 1898 is cited by Stevenson (*Intersexes*, p. 221–22).

48. Colin Scott, "Sex and Art," the *American Journal of Psychology* (Worcester, Mass.), vol. 7, no. 2 (Jan. 1896), p. 216.

49. New York State, *Report of the Special Committee of the* [N.Y.S.] *Assembly Appointed to Investigate the Public Offices and Departments of the City of New York . . . transmitted to the Legislature January 15, 1900*, 5 vols., (Albany: James B. Lyon, 1900), vol. 1, p. 940–41. I wish to thank Wilbur Miller for informing me of this document, and Stephen W. Foster for additional information. The politics of the Mazet Committee are discussed in Gerald Astor, *The New York Cops; An Informal History* (N.Y.: Scribner, 1971), p. 88–91. The London scandal "of a few years ago" may be the Cleveland Street affair (1889–90) or, more probably, the Oscar Wilde case (1895). For Cleveland Street, see Herbert M. Schueller and Robert L. Peters, eds., *The Letters of John Addington Symonds*, 3 vols. (Detroit: Wayne State University, 1969), note 4, p. 556.

50. N.Y. State, *Report*, vol. 5, p. 1382–83.

51. N.Y. State, *Report*, vol. 5, p. 1394–95.

52. N.Y. State, *Report*, vol. 5, p. 1429–30. Spelling in original text corrected.

53. N.Y. State, *Report*, vol. 5, p. 1431–32.

54. Paul Näcke, "Der homosexuelle Markt in New-York," *Archiv für Kriminal-Anthropologie und Kriminalistik* (Leinz), vol. 22 (1906), p. 277. I wish to thank Warren Johansson for translating this document.

55. Charles H. Hughes, "Homo Sexual Complexion Perverts in St. Louis. Note on a Feature of Sexual Psychopathy," *Alienist and Neurologist* (St. Louis, Mo.), vol. 28, no. 4 (Nov. 1907), p. 487–88.

Stevenson's *Intersexes* (1908?) cites numerous examples of homosexual life in American cities (see espec. p. 423, 426, 430, 431, 434, [male prostitutes in cars on Riverside Drive, N.Y.C.] 436, [N.Y.C. baths] 440.) Adele Spitzeder, founder of the "Daschauer Bank" and "passionately" Lesbian, is said by Stevenson to have toured America with an all-female orchestra—after serving a prison term (p. 527–28).

A Chicago Vice Commission report of 1911 refers to homosexuality (*The Social Evil in Chicago; A Study of Existing Conditions with Recommendations* . . . [Chicago: Gunthorp-Warren, 1911], p. 39, 56, 126, 139, 240, 247, 290–91, 295–98, 305, 348).

56. A note refers to Hirschfeld's *Die Transvestiten; eine Untersuchung über den erotischen Verkleidungstrieb mit umfangreichem casuistischen und historischen Material* ("Transvestites: Research into the Erotic Disguise-urge, with Exhaustive Causuistics and Historical Material";) (Leipzig: Max Spohr, 1910), p. 362.

57. Magnus Hirschfeld, *Die Homosexualität des Mannes und des Weibes* (Berlin: Louis Marcus, 1914), p. 550–54. I wish to thank James Steakley for informing me of this document and translating it. A brief autobiographical sketch of Hirschfeld is in *Encyclopedia Sexualis*, ed. Victor Robinson (N.Y.: Dingwall-Rock, 1936) p. 317–21; photo reprint in *A Homosexual Emancipation Miscellany; c. 1835–1952* (N.Y.: Arno, 1975).

58. Havelock Ellis, *Studies in the Psychology of Sex*, 4 vols. (N.Y.: Random House, 1936), vol. 2, part 2, *Sexual Inversion*, "3rd ed.," 1915, p. 350–51.

59. Ellis (1936), p. 299–300. Homosexuality in Greenwich Village, N.Y.C., 1920–30, is commented on by Caroline Ware (*Greenwich Village; 1920–1930* [N.Y.: Harper Colophon, 1935], p. 96, 237, 253).

60. [F. L. Sim,] "Forensic Psychiatry. Alice Mitchell Adjudged Insane," *Memphis* (Tenn.) *Medical Monthly*, vol. 12, no. 8 (Aug. 1892), p. 379–89. Dr. Sim was the editor of the *Monthly* and this article appears in the "Editorial Department." Other sources on the Alice Mitchell case: T. G. Comstock, "Alice Mitchell of Memphis; a Case of Sexual Perversion or 'Urning' (a Paranoiac)," *Medical Times; the Journal of the American Medical Profession* (N.Y.), vol. 20 (1892), p. 170–73; Arthur Macdonald, "Observation de sexualité pathologique feminine," *Archives d'anthropologie criminelle*, May 1895; Richard von Krafft-Ebing, *Psychopathia Sexualis*, trans. of 10th German ed. by F. J. Rebman (N.Y.: Rebman, 1904), p. 550; Frank S. Caprio, *Female Homosexuality; A Psychodynamic Study of Lesbianism*, foreword, Karl M. Bowman (N.Y.: Evergreen Black Cat, Grove Press, 1962), p. 175–76; O. D. Cauldwell, "Lesbian Love Murder," *Sexology*, July 1950. Caprio says: "The case apparently made a lasting impression on the legal profession for in the Sept. 7, 1930, issue of the *Commercial Appeal*, Paul Coppock wrote: 'Freda Ward's killing and the trial of Alice Mitchell still live in the history of famous cases taught young lawyers and in the world's anthologies of sex psychology and sex pathology.' " Caprio cites Cauldwell to the effect that Mitchell committed suicide in the mental institution by jumping into a water tank.

In a medical journal article of 1892, Rosse mentions another case of "morbid love between two young women, one of whom murders the other . . . Such a case was tried on the Eastern Shore of Maryland a few years ago" (p. 808).

In 1893, Dr. Edward C. Mann refers to an outbreak of Lesbianism: "In one instance I have known of this morbid sexual love for a person of the same sex, starting probably, with some one girl, of a faulty nervous organization, in a young ladies' seminary,— almost assumed the form of an epidemic (genesis erethism),—and several young ladies were brought up before the faculty, and were told that summary dismissal would follow if this were not at once dropped. The terrible mischief which was thus arrested, and doubtless originated with an insane girl, in this case evidently assumed an hysterical tendency in others not insane, but who might have easily become so if they were neuropathically endowed, as they doubtless were" ("The Trial of Josephine Mallison Smith," *Alienist and Neurologist*, vol. 14, no. 3 [July 1893], p. 474).

The American reaction to the trials of Oscar Wilde is a subject for research. I have found few American references to Wilde's trouble. In March 1895, Wilde brought libel charges against the Marquess of Queensberry who had earlier charged the writer with posing as a sodomite; Queensberry was acquitted. In April 1895, Wilde was tried on a sodomy charge; the trial ended in a hung jury. In May, at a second trial, Wilde was found guilty and sentenced to two years in prison. Willa Cather alludes to Wilde's trouble and condemns him in the Lincoln, Nebraska, *Journal*, May 19, 1895 ("The Aesthetic Movement: 'fatal and dangerous' "); Cather is more sympathetic in her column of Sept. 28, 1895 ("Oscar Wilde: Hélas"; both reprinted in *The World and the Parish: Willa Cather's Articles and Reviews, 1893–1902*, selected and ed. with a commentary by William M. Curtain [Lincoln: University of Nebraska, 1970], p. 153–54, 263–66). Emma Goldman says she publicly defended Wilde in her speaking engagements before the American public (*Living My Life*, 2 vols. [N.Y.: Dover, 1971], vol. 1, p. 269. Quoted in part V). Bertrand Russell recalls that on a visit to the U.S. in 1896 no one seemed to know about Wilde's trouble (*The Autobiography of Bertrand Russell*, 3 vols., vol. 1, *1872–1914* [Boston: Little, Brown, 1967], p. 205–07). On April 26, 1895, Henry James answers his brother William's queries about the Wilde trial, which had started that day, calling Wilde's fall "hideously tragic." James wrote to Edmund Gosse that Wilde's trial was "hideous," and to Paul Bourget that Wilde's sentence was "cruel." In Nov. 1895, James refused to sign a petition for Wilde circulated by the American poet Stuart Merrill. But James did approach a Member of Parliament about easing Wilde's prison conditions (Leon Edel, *Henry James; The Treacherous Years* [Phila.: Lippincott; 1969], p. 122, 128–30).

61. Russell, vol. 1, p. 205–07. For important additional details see Edith Finch, *Carey Thomas of Bryn Mawr* (N.Y.: Harper, 1947); and Lennox Strong, "American Women; Carey Thomas . . ." *The Ladder*, vol. 12, no. 3 (Feb.–March 1968), p. 9–15. Also see Elaine Kendall, *Peculiar Institutions; an Informal History of the Seven Sister Colleges* (N.Y. Putnam, 1976) on the Sapphic preferences of Thomas and other founders of the major American women's colleges.

62. Gertrude Stein, *Fernhurst, Q.E.D., and Other Early Writings* with "A Note on the Texts" by Donald Gallup and introduction by Leon Katz (N.Y.: Liveright, 1973), paper, p. xxxi–xxxvii. The information cited is from Katz's introduction.

63. Gautier's *Mlle. de Maupin* was first published in French in 1835, the same year as Balzac's *The Girl with the Golden Eyes*, another Lesbian novel. See note 43 above.

64. Allan M[c]Lane Hamilton, "The Civil Responsibility of Sexual Perverts," *American Journal of Insanity* (Chicago), vol. 52, no. 4 (April 1896), p. 503–09. Hamilton is described here as "Consulting Physician to the Manhattan State Hospital, Member of the New York Neurological Society . . ."

65. "She Dislikes Men and Dogs," *East Long Island* [*N.Y.*] *Star*, Dec. 31, 1897, from the *Chicago Chronicle*, n.d., reprinted in the *East Hampton* [*N.Y.*] *Star*, "The Way It Was—Seventy-Five Years Ago—1897," Dec. 28, 1972. I wish to thank Carol Joyce and Robert Joyce, Jr., for informing me of this document.

In 1900, in the American South, a homosexual English artist is said to have been "assassinated" by the outraged brother of the artist's young male lover; the murderer was acquitted (Stevenson, *Intersexes*, p. 501–02).

66. Havelock Ellis, *Studies in the Psychology of Sex; Sexual Inversion* (Phila.: Davis, 1901), p. 120–21.

In early Nov. 1907, reports Stevenson, there occurred in a suburb of New York City an attempted murder and a suicide involving a butler and the son of a prominent family (*Intersexes*, p. 176, 500–01). Stevenson also reports an American homosexual being blackmailed in Berlin, and the blackmailer's arrest (*Intersexes*, p. 466; the source is Hirschfeld's *Jahrbuch für sexuelle Zwischenstufen*). Blackmail in America is mentioned in passing by Stevenson (p. 469); the attempted blackmail of an American army officer in Naples is also mentioned (p. 472). Stevenson cites the criminal trial in Berlin of "Frau K.," a Lesbian who had been "the associate in letters and science" of many eminent German, Italian, and American writers on sociology, criminology, and psychiatric medicine (p. 529).

67. Margaret Otis, "A Perversion Not Commonly Noted," *Journal of Abnormal Psychology* (Boston), vol. 8, no. 2 (June–July 1913), p. 113–16.

An early reference to Lesbianism among incarcerated insane women was reportedly made by Dr. James G. Kiernan (*Journal of Nervous and Mental Disease*, 1888), who is said to have found "tribadism" to be "relatively frequent among the female insane in the overcrowded (five patients to two beds) female wards of the Cook County [Illinois] Insane Hospital" (Hughes, "Erotopathia," p. 575).

68. Kate [Douglas] Richards O'Hare, *In Prison, by . . . Sometime Federal Prisoner Number 21669* (N.Y.: Knopf, 1923), p. 96–97, 111–13.

69. Charles A. Ford, "Homosexual Practices of Institutionalized Females," *Journal of Abnormal and Social Psychiatry*, vol. 23 (Jan.–March 1929), p. 442–48. Ford is further identified as an MA.

Although there is a large literature on homosexuality among male prisoners, there is a much smaller literature on prison Lesbianism. See the major bibliographies on homosexuality.

Early references to male homosexuality in prison are: Douglas C. McMurtrie, "Notes on Homosexuality: An Attempt at Seduction; An Example of Acquired Homosexuality in Prison; A Commentary on the Prevalence of Inversion in Germany," *Vermont Medical Monthly*, vol. 19 (1913), p. 66–68; Douglas C. McMurtrie, "Notes on Pederastic Practices in Prison," *Chicago Medical Recorder*, vol. 36 (Jan. 1914), p. 15–17; H. R. Hoffman, "Sex Perversion and Crime," *Archives of Neurology and Psychiatry* (Chicago), vol. 3, no. 2 (Feb. 1920), p. 210; Samuel Kahn, "A Study of Homosexuals and Their Education in New York Correction Hospitals," M. A. thesis, N.Y. University, School of Education, 1923, 149 p. A story, "An Allegation in Lavender," by Gene Fowler is said to impute the homosexuality of a prominent penologist (in *The Great Mouthpiece . . .* N.Y.: Grosset, 1931.) Louis Berg's *Revelations of a Prison Doctor* includes a chapter titled "Men Like Women" (N.Y.: Minton, Balch, 1934). Samuel Kahn's *Mentality and Homosexuality* (Boston: Meador, 1937) discusses prisoner homosexuality. Many additional references to male homosexuality in prison may be found in the major bibliographies on homosexuality.

70. Gardner Jackson, "The Reminiscences of Gardner Jackson," recorded summer 1953, Oral History Collection of Columbia University (1959), typewritten transcript, p. 59, 61.

71. Jackson, p. 66–67.

72. Jackson, p. 70.

73. Jackson, p. 72–74.

74. Lawrance Thompson, *Robert Frost, The Years of Triumph, 1915–1938* (N.Y.: Holt, Rinehart and Winston, 1970), p. 104–06, 553 note 17.

In the spring of 1919, Franklin D. Roosevelt, as Acting Secretary of the U.S. Navy, established a vice squad to investigate homosexuality at the Naval Training Station at Newport, R.I. (documented by Frank Burt Freidel in *Franklin D. Roosevelt*, 2 vols. [Boston: Little, Brown, 1952–54], vol. 1 *The Apprenticeship*, p. 41, 46–47, 96–97, 280–81, 287). Roosevelt later claimed he had not known, in Freidel's words, "that the investigators, while acting as decoys to trap perverts, had several times engaged in sodomy." When FDR learned of this in Sept. 1919, he is said to have immediately ordered the squad to stop its work. Later, a navy court of inquiry began an investigation of the investigators, taking six thousand pages of testimony (comprising fifteen volumes), and finding Roosevelt's actions "unfortunate and ill-advised." The Newport case became a public scandal when Roosevelt's political opponents accused him of condoning the vice squad's committing sodomy to trap homosexuals. In the summer of 1921, a subcommittee of the Senate Naval Affairs Committee (two Republicans, one Democrat) released to the press their majority report on "Alleged Immoral Conditions at Newport," denouncing FDR's "most deplorable, disgraceful, and unnatural proceeding." The *New York Times* (July 20, 1921) called this report's details "unprintable." See reprint: U.S. Senate 67th Congress, 1st Sess. Committee on Naval Affairs, "Alleged Immoral Conditions at Newport (R.I.) Naval Training Station. Report . . ." (Washington, D.C.: U.S. Govt. Ptg. Ofc., 1921; photo reprint N.Y.: Arno, 1975, in *Government Versus Homosexuals*). Also see Elliot Roosevelt, ed., *F.D.R., His Personal Letters*, 3 vols. (N.Y.: Duell, Sloan and Pearce, 1947–50), vol. 2, p. 517, 519–22.

A monthly magazine, *Broadway Brevities and Society Gossip*, from Jan.–Dec. 1924 ran a twelve-part series on homosexuality in the U.S., including many photos, lists of bars, and outraged letters. The issue of Jan. 1925 includes additional material. I wish to thank James D. Steakley for this information, based on his research in the German homosexual periodicals of the 1920s.

75. "It's Dirty But Good" and "The Boy in the Boat" are quoted by Peter Tamony, "Dike: A Lesbian" (San Francisco: mimeographed, May 1972), p. 12, 14. I wish to thank Peter Tamony for sending me this etymological study. See *The Boy in the Boat*, Paramount Recording 14010-B (Master L 561); reissue of Paramount 13024, recorded c. Oct. 1930, Grafton, Wis.; George Hannah, vocal, M. L. Lewis, piano. See also side A, "Freakish Blues."

76. Chris Albertson, *Bessie* (N.Y.: Stein and Day, 1974), paperback, p. 13, 140.

Tony Jackson, the popular Black singer-pianist-composer (of "Pretty Baby") was homosexual. According to Jelly Roll Morton, "Tony [Jackson] happened to be one of those gentlemens that a lot of people call them lady or sissy, . . . and that was the cause of him going to Chicago about 1906. He liked the freedom there" (Alan Lomax, *Mister Jelly Roll; The Fortunes of Jelly Roll Morton* . . . [N.Y.: Universal Library, Grosset and Dunlap, 1950], p. 45; Lomax quotes from *Jelly Roll Morton*, Library of Congress Recordings, vol. 7, side 1, band 1 [interview with Morton recorded May–June 1938]).

77. Albertson, p. 116–26.

78. J. Brooks Atkinson, "The Play . . . Tragedy from the French," *New York Times*, Sept. 30, 1926, p. 23, col. 1.

79. *New York Times*, Oct. 25, 1926, p. 34, col. 1.

80. *New York Times*, Oct. 29, 1926, p. 12, col. 2.

81. *New York Times*, Nov. 15, 1926, p. 23, col. 7.

82. *New York Times*, Nov. 16, 1926, p. 11, col. 2.

83. *New York Times*, Dec. 29, 1926, p. 1, col. 5.

84. *New York Times*, Jan. 21, 1927, p. 14, col. 6.

85. *New York Times*, Feb. 1, 1927, p. 1, col. 5.

86. *New York Times*, Feb. 1, 1927, p. 3, col. 1.

87. *New York Times*, Feb. 3, 1927, p. 1, col. 6.

88. *New York Times*, Feb. 9, 1927, p. 1, col. 8.

89. *New York Times*, Feb. 11, 1927, p. 1, col. 1.

90. *New York Times*, Feb. 13, 1927, p. 1, col. 4.

91. *New York Times*, Feb. 21, 1927, p. 19, col. 1.

92. *New York Times*, Feb. 26, 1927, p. 15, col.2.

93. *New York Times*, March 7, 1927, p. 11, cols. 1, 3. *Sappho*, a play by Alphonse Daudet and Adolph Bêlot, appears to have been first performed in the U.S. in 1895, and revived in 1900 when it caused a great scandal (see clippings and material in the Theater Collection of the New York Public Library at Lincoln Center). Also see Alphonse R. Favreua, "The Reception of Daudet's Sapho in the United States" (Michigan Academy of Science, Arts, and Letters. Papers, vol. 30 [1945], p. 581–88).

94. *New York Times*, March 9, 1927, p. 27, col. 1.

95. *New York Times*, March 19, 1927, p. 3, col. 1.

96. *Laws of the State of New York* (Albany: J. B. Lyon, 1927), p. 1731–32. This law appears to have been amended in Sept. 1931 to exclude actors and musicians. This statute remained in effect until the revision in 1967 of the entire penal code of New York State. I wish to thank E. Carrington Boggan and Robert Roth for help with this research.

An incredible homosexual witch-hunt dating to the late 1930s, in one of the smaller cities of the U.S., is reported by an anonymous "reliable source" in Arno Karlen's *Sexuality and Homosexuality; A New View* (N.Y.: Norton, 1971), p. 313. The arrest and confession of an eminent married man led to the arrest of some thirty others. The judge sentenced all to six months on the road gang or an alternative of surgical emasculation. He claimed that in the last five years many men had chosen the operation and that the results were perfect. This alternative was not accepted. The suicide of a local doctor ended this antihomosexual crusade.

On April 23, 1941, William C. Bullitt brought to President Franklin D. Roosevelt reports of alleged homosexual acts committed by Roosevelt's Under Secretary of State, Sumner Welles. Welles had long been a close friend of both FDR and Eleanor Roosevelt. The President told Bullitt he already "had a full report" on Welles, and was sure his future action would be more careful. Bullitt urged FDR to dismiss Welles for his "past crimes" and reported that Secretary of State Cordell Hull "considered Welles worse than a murderer." FDR indicated that he would retain Welles, and the interview ended in extreme acrimony.

In Aug., 1943, FDR, informed that Bullitt had been spreading tales of Welles's homosexuality—and that Drew Pearson and Robert Allen were about to publish rumors —was forced to request Welles's resignation. After this, FDR, in a fury, ended his close association with Bullitt. A tactfully edited version of Bullitt's long memorandum of his 1941 interview with FDR and a discussion of the case are in *For the President, Personal and Secret: Correspondence between Franklin D. Roosevelt and William C. Bullitt*, ed. Orville H. Bullitt (Boston: Houghton Mifflin, 1972), p. 512–18. Bullitt's original memorandum detailing Welles's "crime" is in the private collection of a Bullitt family member (Orville H. Bullitt to J.K., May 17, 1974).

On March 14, 1942, naval intelligence police raided a homosexual brothel on Pacific Street, Brooklyn, near the navy yard. Gustave Beekman, the brothel's manager, was arrested; he was told that by cooperating with the federal investigating agencies he could lighten his sentence. His cooperation led to the arrest of several foreign agents. On May 1 the New York *Post* carried the first news story of the incident and named the chairman of the Senate Naval Affairs Committee as a regular patron of the brothel. This was

David I. Walsh, Democrat of Massachusetts. On May 20, in the U.S. Senate, Alben Barkley of Kentucky read excerpts from an FBI report on the case which denied that Senator Walsh had ever visited the brothel. The case was closed. As his reward, Gustave Beekman was double-crossed by federal agents and the judge. He was arraigned on a common sodomy charge and received the maximum sentence—twenty years! He entered Sing Sing on Oct. 5, 1942, and was released on April 1, 1963, at the age of seventy-eight (C. A. Tripp, *The Homosexual Matrix* [N.Y.: McGraw-Hill, 1975], p. 224–27, citing New York *Post*, May 1, 1942, May 5, May 6; *New York Times*, May 20, May 21, Oct. 6, 1942). Also see "The Walsh Case," *Nation*, May 30, 1942; "The Case of Senator Walsh," *Time*, June 1, 1942; "Scandal Scotched," *Newsweek*, June 1, 1942.

Between Jan. 1, 1947, and Oct. 31, 1950, it is reported that "4,954 cases involving a charge of homosexuality or other types of sex perversion had been handled" by the armed services or civilian agencies of the federal government. "The bulk of these (4,380) were in the Armed Services, while only 574 were in civilian service" (Committee on Cooperation with Governmental [Federal] Agencies of the Group for the Advancement of Psychiatry, "Report on Homosexuality with Particular Emphasis on This Problem in Governmental Agencies," Report No. 30 [Topeka, Kan.: Jan. 1955], p. 5).

97. *New York Times*, March 1, 1950, p. 2, col. 8.

98. *New York Times*, March 9, 1950, p. 5, col. 4.

99. *New York Times*, March 15, 1950, p. 3, col. 15.

100. *New York Times*, March 20, 1950, p. 5, col. 1.

101. *New York Times*, April 19, 1950, p. 25, col. 3.

102. *New York Times*, April 25, 1950, p. 5, col. 1.

103. *New York Times*, April 26, 1950, p. 3, col. 2.

104. *New York Times*, May 5, 1950, p. 15, col. 3.

105. *New York Times*, May 20, 1950, p. 8, col. 2.

106. *New York Times*, May 22, 1950, p. 8, col. 6.

107. *New York Times*, June 15, 1950, p. 6, col. 4.

108. *New York Times*, June 17, 1950, p. 6, col. 3.

109. *New York Times*, July 13, 1950, p. 1, col. 2, p. 12, col. 5.

110. Lerner's *New York Post* article dated July 11, 1950, is reprinted in the volume of his collected writings titled *The Unfinished Country; A Book of American Symbols* (N.Y.: Simon and Schuster, 1959), p. 311–13. His following articles are quoted from this same edition. I wish to thank Stephen W. Foster for informing me of these documents.

111. Lerner, p. 313–16.

112. Lerner, p. 316–19.

113. U.S. Congress, Senate, Committee on Expenditures in the Executive Departments, *Employment of Homosexuals and Other Sex Perverts in Government; Interim Report Submitted to the Committee on Expenditures in the Executive Departments by Its Subcommittee on Investigations Pursuant to S. Res. 280*, 81st Cong., 2nd Sess., 15 Dec. 1950, Sen. Doc. 241. Photo reprint in *Government Versus Homosexuals* (N.Y.: Arno, 1975).

114. *New York Times*, Dec. 16, 1950, p. 3 col. 4.

115. *New York Times*, March 28, 1951, p. 1, col. 6.

116. *New York Times*, April 28, 1951, p. 7, col. 3.

117. *New York Times*, Oct. 5, 1951, p. 2, col. 4.

118. *New York Times*, Dec. 20, 1951, p. 20, col. 4.

119. Jack Lait and Lee Mortimer, *Washington Confidential* (N.Y.: Crown, 1951), p. 90, 94.

120. Lait and Mortimer, p. 91, 96.

121. Drew Pearson, *Diaries, 1949–1959,* ed. Tyler Abell (N.Y.: Holt, Rinehart and Winston, 1974), p. 188–89, 190, 192. I wish to thank Stephen W. Foster for informing me of this document, which I was not permitted to reprint.

122. *New York Times,* June 26, 1952, p. 4, col. 4.

123. *New York Times,* Aug. 31, 1952, p. 32, col. 6.

124. *New York Times,* April 13, 1953, p. 20, col. 2.

125. ("Miss") E. M., "To Be Accused Is To Be Guilty: 2. The Ever-Present Past," *ONE* (Los Angeles), vol. 1, no. 4 (April 1953), p. 3–4.

126. *New York Times,* March 13, 1954, p. 7, col. 2.

127. *New York Times,* March 15, 1954, p. 16, col. 4.

128. *New York Times,* May 14, 1954, p. 1, col. 1, p. 13, col. 3.

129. *New York Times,* Aug. 27, 1954, p. 7, col. 1.

130. *New York Times,* Jan. 4, 1955, p. 14, col. 4.

131. Kenneth Frank, "America, on Guard: Homosexuals, Inc.," *Confidential,* vol. 2, no. 2 (May 1954), p. 18. I wish to thank Warren Johansson for locating and providing me with a copy of this document. Hay recalls that an earlier story on Mattachine had appeared in *Confidential* in the spring of 1952. Hay says this first article had reported that he himself had appeared before HUAC, which was untrue. Hay also says the 1954 *Confidential* story is in error concerning "the protests when the Steering Committee hired Michael (Fred) Snider. Snider had first been hired in March 1951, before we had even finalized the name Mattachine" (H.H. to J.K., n.d.; postmarked Feb. 9, 1976).

132. Henry Hay, ten typescript documents: (1–3) "On Associations" numbers "I–III"; (4) "Do you want to leave these hearings?"; (5) "On Recollections"; (6) "On Whether Certain 'Stooling' Is True"; (7) "(in answer to any queries concerning persons, associations, or opinions)"; (8) "A Tactic to Nullify the $64.00 Question?"; (9) "More standard tactics"; (10) "(in answer to so-called non-incriminatory queries)"; in the collection of Hay. I wish to thank Henry Hay for providing me with carbons and photocopies of these documents.

133. The official transcript of Hay's testimony before HUAC, according to Hay, omits some of his testimony, and so differs from his recollections. See "Testimony of Harry Hay, Accompanied by Counsel, Frank Pestana," in U.S. Congress, Un-American Activities Committee, House, *Hearings,* 84th Cong., 1st Sess., vol. 1, 1955. *Investigation of Communist Activities in Los Angeles, California area, hearings, 84th Congress, 1st Session, June 27-July 2, 1955,* 4 parts, part 4, p. 1872–75. Informer Stephen A. Wereb's testimony concerning Hay, p. 1790–91.

134. John Gerassi, *The Boys of Boise; Furor, Vice and Folly in an American City,* (N.Y.: Collier, 1968), paperback reprint, p. 20–22.

135. Margaret H. Pierce, reporter, *Cases Decided in the United States Court of Claims . . .* (Washington, D.C.: U.S. Gov. Ptg. Ofc., 1962), p. 405–10. Legal citation: [Fannie Mae] Clackum *v.* the United States, 148 Ct. of Claims 404 (1960).

On the night of Sept. 2, 1960, in Northampton, Mass., Professor of English Newton Arvin and a fellow instructor in the classics department at Smith College were arrested in their homes on charges of possessing obscene photographs and literature (what would now probably appear to be positively tame pornography). Arvin was also charged with "being a lewd and lascivious person in speech and behavior." He was identified in the press as the author of books on Hawthorne, Whitman, and Melville. The arrests were made after an investigation by the State Police Bureau of Pornography, the local police, and a postal inspector (suggesting the involvement of the federal government). This was the start of a classic, tragic, and obscene antihomosexual witch-hunt whose history is still to be researched and written (hopefully, while some of those who witnessed it and were its victims might still be interviewed). The headlines of the local papers suggest the train of events: "2 Smith Educators Deny Immoral Picture Charges," *Springfield Union,* Sept. 3, 1960; "Morals Probe Brings About More Arrests," same, Sept. 6; "New Raid Is Made

In Morals Case," same, Sept. 7; "Four More Deny Guilt in Morals Probe," same, Sept. 7; "Trio In Smith Morals Probe Given Leave," same, Sept. 9; " 'Smut Ring' Stories Said Not Correct," same, Sept. 10; "Court Denies Dorius on All but a Single Motion," Sept. 19, *Springfield Daily News*; "Prose and Pix," *Newsweek*, Sept. 19; "Smith Will Take Action in Scandal, *Springfield Union*, Sept. 21; " 'Hamp Morals Cases Result in Fines, Jail," same, Sept. 21; "Smith Teacher Is Convicted On Morals Charge," same, Oct. 14; "Prof. Arvin Retired By College," Oct. 27, *Springfield Daily News*; "Steps Are Taken In Morals Appeals," same, Nov. 2; "Smith Professor's Cases Appealed," Nov. 6, *Springfield Union*; "Smith Prof. Accused in Morals Case," April 15, 1961, *Springfield Daily News;* "Smith Vice Case Ruling Overturned," same, March 1, 1962; "Newton Arvin Dies in 'Hamp," *Springfield Union*, March 23, 1963. Antihomosexual hysteria in Washington at the same date as the Northampton events suggests the larger political context in which it must be understood (see *New York Times* Sept. 7, 1960, p. 1, col. 7; Sept. 8, p. 16, cols. 5, 8; Sept. 12, p. 7, col. 1; Sept. 16, p. 5, col. 4; Sept. 17, p. 8, col. 4). I wish to thank Sidney Kaplan for help with this research.

136. Sara Harris, *The Puritan Jungle; America's Sexual Underground* (N.Y.: Putnam, 1969), p. 165–69, 171–72. I wish to thank Stephen W. Foster for informing me of this document.

137. The "Purple Pamphlet" is officially titled "Homosexuality and Citizenship in Florida; A Report of the Florida Legislative Investigative Committee," Tallahassee, Fla., Jan. 1964; photo reprint in *Government Versus Homosexuals* (N.Y.: Arno, 1975).

138. Harris, p. 175–79, 184–86.

139. *Southern Reporter; Second Series; Volume 193 So. 2nd; Cases Argued and Determined in the Courts of . . . Louisiana . . .* (St. Paul, Minn.: West, 1967), p. 243–45. Legal citation: State *v.* Young [, Mary, and DeBlanc, Dawn,] La., 193 So. 2d 243.

Bibliography

I. TROUBLE: 1566–1966

Albertson, Chris. *Bessie*. N.Y.: Stein and Day paperback, 1974. (P. 14, 116–26, 140.)

Berryman, John. *Stephen Crane*. N.Y.: Sloan, 1950. (P. 86.)

Blake, Henry N., and Hedges, Cornelius. *Reports of Cases Argued and Determined in the Supreme Court of Montana Territory from the August Term, 1877, to January Term, 1880, Inclusive*. San Francisco: Bancroft-Whitney, 1911. (Vol. 3, p. 112–18; Territory v. Mahaffey, 3 Mont. 112.)

[Boise, Idaho. Witch-Hunt in.]

"Three Boise Men Admit Sex Charges," *Idaho Daily Statesman*, Nov. 2, 1955, p. 1.

"Crush the Monster" (editorial), *Idaho Daily Statesman*, Nov. 3, 1955.

"This Mess Must Be Removed" (editorial), *Idaho Daily Statesman*, Nov. 18, 1955. See Gerassi, John.

Anonymous. Interviewed by Jonathan Katz, N.Y.C., Dec. 18, 1973.

Bourdet, Edouard. *The Captive*. A play trans. from *La Prisonnière*. Adapted by Arthur Hornblow, Jr. Produced by the Charles Frohman Co. at the Empire Theatre, N.Y.C., Sept. 29, 1926.

A list of all the relevant news items of the period of *The Captive's* production can be found in the *New York Times Index* under "Theatre-Censorship-NYC." An annotated, chronological list of most important *New York Times* news items follows:

Sept. 30, 1926, p. 23, col. 1. Atkinson, J. Brooks. Review of *The Captive*.

Oct. 10, 1926, sec. 8, p. 1, col. 1. Atkinson, J. Brooks. "Trenchant Tragedy" (review).

Oct. 25, 1926, p. 34, col 1. Mayor Walker predicts interference in theater if no change is made.

Oct. 29, 1926, p. 12, col. 2. Three plays under investigation; names withheld.

Nov. 15, 1926, p. 23, col. 7. Play jury will deliberate on *The Captive*; review of organization.

Nov. 16, 1926, p. 11, col. 2. *Captive* released by play jury.

Dec. 29, 1926, p. 1, col. 5. Mayor Walker warns producers that, unless they voluntarily clean up stage, censorship will result; managers may name director.

Dec. 30, 1926, p. 22, col. 1. District Attorney Banton defends play jury against implied criticism by Mayor Walker.

Jan. 21, 1927, p. 14, col. 6. McCormack, Elsie, letter, suggestions for play censorship, wants ban on "sex perversion" themes.

Feb. 1, 1927, p. 1, col. 5. *Captive* voted best play by fourteen Princeton students; *The Drag*, opens in Bridgeport, Conn.

Feb. 3, 1927, p. 1, col. 5. Banton abolishes play jury; will prosecute indecent plays under criminal law.

Feb. 9, 1927, p. 1, col. 4. Conference of police officials presages play raids.

Feb. 10, 1927, p. 1, col. 8. Police raid *Sex*, *Captive*, and *Virgin Man*, forty-one actors and managers, including Helen Menken and Mae West, arrested and released on bail.

Feb. 11, 1927, p. 1, col. 1. Raided shows stay open under protection of Supreme Court injunction; Banton wants jail sentences for authors and managers.

Feb. 12, 1927, p. 1, col. 6. Police have blanket order for arrests in any theaters.

Feb. 13, 1927, p. 1, col. 4. Raided shows play to crowded houses.

Feb. 17, 1927, p. 1, col. 6. *Captive* withdrawn by Gilbert Miller and Frohman Co.; court charges dropped; H. B. Liveright plans to produce it.

Feb. 17, 1927, p. 20, col. 5. Mayor Walker, in Miami, backs police action, but thinks stage will do own housecleaning.

Feb. 19, 1927, p. 32, col. 2. Liveright will not produce *Captive* until it is cleared by courts.

Feb. 20, 1927, p. 1, col. 2. Liveright asks writ to reopen *Captive*.

Feb. 21, 1927, p. 19, col. 1. Speedy action against *The Captive* sought by city.

Feb. 22, 1927, p. 9, cols. 3–5. Banton receives notice of injunction against interference with new production of *The Captive*; issues statement on *The Captive*.

Feb. 25, 1927, p. 24, col. 2. Justice Mahoney considers application for injunction to protect Liveright in attempt to revive *Captive*.

Feb. 26, 1927, p. 15, col. 2. Mayor Walker expresses satisfaction with stage clean-up; Liveright cancels sailing to carry on *Captive* fight. Cardinal Hayes says law should prevent production of immoral plays; A. D. Flower proposes Shakespeare as stage cure.

March 2, 1927, p. 27, col. 3. Plea for injunction restraining District Attorney from interference with revival of *The Captive*.

March 7, 1927, p. 11, cols. 1, 3. Abnormal plays scored by W. Lackaye.

March 9, 1927, p. 27, col. 1. Justice Mahoney rules *Captive* immoral; but says censorship authority rests with jury rather than bench; denies injunction to protect Liveright in producing *Captive*; A. G. Hays, defense counsel, will appeal.

March 14, 1927, p. 2, col. 2. Mayor Walker promises police action to revoke licenses of offensive shows.

March 15, 1927, p. 1, col. 7. District Attornies Banton and Dodd advocate legislative measure giving License Commissioner power to revoke theater licenses and District Attorney power to padlock after conviction is obtained.

March 18, 1927, p. 1, col. 8. Banton aids Republican leaders to draft new bill enforcing penal law against immoral plays; scope of present law extended.

March 19, 1927, p. 3, col. 1. Banton measure goes to Legislature; A. G. Hays argues for *The Captive*. Senator B. R. Wales introduces Banton's measure.

March 24, 1927, p. 3, col. 4. Senate passes Wales Bill.

March 26, 1927, p. 6, col. 5. Wales Bill passed in Assembly.

April 4, 1927, p. 8, col. 4. Wales padlock bill awaits Governor's approval; no public hearing asked.

April 8, 1927, p. 1, cols. 5, 6. Gov. Smith signs Wales Bill; Banton says it applies to cabarets and night clubs as well as theaters.

Browne, Albert G., Jr., and Gray, John C., Jr. *Massachusetts Reports 111; Cases Argued and Determined in the Supreme Judicial Court of Massachusetts; November 1872-March 1873.* Boston: Houghton, Mifflin, 1884. (P. 411–17: Commonwealth *v.* Snow, 111 Mass. 411.)

Captive, The. See Bourdet, Edouard.

Clackum[, Fannie Mae,] *v.* The United States. Pierce, Margaret H., reporter. *Cases Decided in the United States Court of Claims* (Jan. 1–31, 1960). Vol. 148. Washington, D.C.: U.S. Govt. Ptg. Ofc., 1962. (P. 404–10.) Legal citation: Clackum *v.* the United States, 148 Ct. of Claims 404 (1960).

Commonwealth *v.* Snow. See Browne, Albert G., Jr.

Comstock, T. G. "Alice Mitchell of Memphis; A Case of Sexual Perversion or 'Urning' (a Paranoiac)," *Medical Times; the Journal of the American Medical Association* (N.Y.) Vol. 20 (1892): p. 170–73.

Crompton, Louis. "Homosexuals and the Death Penalty in Colonial America," *The Journal of Homosexuality.* Vol. 1, no. 4 (1976).

Davis *v.* State. See Harris, Thomas, and Johnson, Reverdy.

Dwight, Louis. [Sodomy among juvenile delinquents.] Boston, April 25, 1826. 2 p. Printed broadside signed by Dwight, cataloged under above title in the Union Theological Seminary Library, N.Y.C.

Ellis, Havelock. *Studies in the Psychology of Sex; Sexual Inversion.* "2nd ed." Phila.: F. A. Davis, 1901. (P. 120–21.)

———. *Studies in the Psychology of Sex.* 4 vols. N.Y.: Random House, 1936. Vol. 2, part 2. *Sexual Inversion* ("3rd ed.," 1915). (P. 299–301, 350–51.)

Ford, Charles A. "Homosexual Practices of Institutionalized Females." *Journal of Abnormal and Social Psychology.* Vol. 23 (Jan.–March 1929): p. 442–48.

Frank, Kenneth. "America, on Guard: Homosexuals, Inc.; Don't sell the twisted twerps short! Once they met in secret. Today, they've organized as the 'Mattachines' with a goal of a million members and a $6,000,000 bankroll!" *Confidential.* Vol. 2, no. 2 (May 1954): p. 18–19.

Gardner, Charles W. *The Doctor and the Devil, or Midnight Adventures of Dr. Parkhurst.* N.Y.: Gardner and Co., 1894; reprint: N.Y.: Vanguard, 1931. (P. 57.)

Gerassi, John. *The Boys of Boise; Furor, Vice and Folly in an American City.* N.Y.: Collier paperback, 1968. (P. 20–22.)

Hamilton, Allan M[c]Lane. "The Civil Responsibility of Sexual Perverts." *American Journal of Insanity* (Chicago). Vol. 52, no. 4 (April 1896): p. 503–11. (P. 503–09.)

Harris, Sara. *The Puritan Jungle; America's Sexual Underground.* N.Y.: Putnam, 1969 (P. 165–69, 171–72, 75–79, 184–86.)

Harris, Thomas, and Johnson, Reverdy. *Reports of Cases Argued and Determined in the Court of Appeals of Maryland, In 1810, 1811, 1812, 1813, 1814, & 1815.* Annapolis, Md.: Jonas Green, 1826. (Vol. 3, p. 154.) Davis *v.* State, 3 Har. & J., 154.

Hay, Henry. Interview tape-recorded by Jonathan Katz, March 31, 1974. In the collection of Jonathan Katz.

———. Ten typescript documents: (1–3) "On Associations" nos. "I-III"; (4) "Do you want to leave these hearings?"; (5) "On Recollections"; (6) "On Whether Certain 'Stooling' Is True"; (7) "(in answer to any queries concerning persons, associations, or opinions)"; (8) "A Tactic to Nullify the $64.00 Question?"; (9) "More standard tactics"; (10) "(in answer to so-called nonincriminating queries)." Collection of Henry Hay; carbons and photocopies in collection of Jonathan Katz.

———. "Testimony of Harry Hay, Accompanied by Counsel, Frank Pestana," July 2, 1955, in U.S. Congress Un-American Activities Committee, House, *Hearings,* 84th Cong., 1st Sess., vol. 1, 1955. *Investigation of Communist Activities in Los Angeles, California Area, Hearings, 84th Congress, 1st Session, June 27–July 2, 1955.* 4 parts. (Part 4, p. 1872–75. Also see p. 1790–91.)

Higgeson, Francis. "Francis Higgeson's Journal . . ." In *The Founding of Massachusetts.* Edited by Stuart Mitchell. Boston: Mass. Historical Society, 1930. (P. 71.)

Hirschfeld, Magnus. *Die Homosexualität des Mannes und des Weibes* ("Homosexuality in Men and Women"). Berlin: Louis Marcus, 1914. (P. 550–54.)

———. *Die Transvestiten; eine Untersuchung über den erotischen Verkleidungstrieb mit umfangreichem casuistischen und historischen Material* ("Transvestites: Research into the Erotic Disguise-urge, with Exhaustive Casuistics and Historical Materials"); Leipzig: Max Spohr, 1910. (P. 362.)

Hughes, C[harles] H. "Erotopathia.—Morbid Eroticism," *Alienist and Neurologist* (St. Louis,

Mo.). Vol. 14, no. 4 (Oct. 1893). p. 531–78. Also in *Transactions of the Pan-American Medical Congress*, 1893. Washington, D.C.: 1895, part 2: p. 1830–52.

———. "Homo Sexual Complexion Perverts in St. Louis. Note on a Feature of Sexual Psychopathy." *Alienist and Neurologist* (St. Louis, Mo.). Vol. 28, no. 4 (Nov. 1907): p. 487–88.

———. "Postscript to Paper on 'Erotopathia.'—An Organization of Colored Erotopaths." *Alienist and Neurologist* (St. Louis, Mo.). Vol. 14, no. 4 (Oct. 1893): p. 731–32.

Huber, Richard M. *The American Idea of Success*. N.Y.: McGraw-Hill, 1971. (P. 45–46, 469 note 5.)

Jackson, Gardner. "The Reminiscences of Gardner Jackson." Recorded summer 1953. Oral History Research Office, Columbia University, 1959. Transcript. (P. 59, 61, 66–67, 70, 72–74.)

Jefferson, Thomas. *The Papers of Thomas Jefferson*. Ed. by Julian P. Boyd. Assoc. eds. Lyman H. Butterworth and Mina R. Ryan. Princeton, N.J.: Princeton University Press, 1950–. (Vol. 2, p. 325, 497.)

Kraff[t]-Ebing, [Richard] von. "Perversion of the Sexual Instinct—Report of Cases." Trans. H. M. Jewett. *Alienist and Neurologist* (St. Louis, Mo.). Vol. 9, no. 4 (Oct. 1888): p. 565–81. (P. 567–70.)

———. *Psychopathia Sexualis, With special Reference to Antipathetic Sexual Instinct; A Medico-Forensic Study*. Trans. of 10th German ed. by F. J. Rebman. N.Y.: Rebman, 1904.

Laws of the State of New York Passed at the One Hundred and Fiftieth Session of the Legislature [Jan. 5–March 25, 1927] . . . Vols. I–II. Albany, J. B. Lyon, 1927.

Lerner, Max. *The Unfinished Country; A Book of American Symbols*. N.Y.: Simon and Schuster, 1959. (Includes: "The Tortured Problem . . . The Making of Homosexuals," dated July 11, 1950: p. 311–13; "The Senator and the Purge," dated July 17, 1950: p. 313–16; "Lieutenant Blick of the Vice Squad," dated July 18, 1950: p. 316–19.)

McCosker, Edward. See New York City.

McIlwaine, H. R., ed. *Minutes of the Council and General Court of Colonial Virginia, 1622–1632, 1670–1676* . . . Richmond: Colonial Press, 1924. (P. 34, 42, 78, 81, 83, 85, 93.)

M., E. ("Miss"). "To Be Accused Is To Be Guilty: 2. The Ever-Present Past." *ONE* (Los Angeles). Vol. 1, no. 4 (April 1953): p. 3–4.

Moreau de St. Méry, Médéric-Louis-Elie. *St. Méry's American Journey*. Trans. and ed. by Kenneth and Anna M. Roberts. Garden City, N.Y.: Doubleday, 1947. (P. 284, 286.)

Morgan, Edmund S. "The First American Boom: Virginia 1618 to 1630," *William and Mary Quarterly*. 3rd ser. Vol. 28, no. 2 (April 1971): p. 169–198. (P. 193, 194.)

Näcke, Paul. "Der homosexuelle Markt in New-York." *Archiv für Kriminal-Anthropologie und Kriminalistik* (Leinz). Vol. 22 (1906): p. 277.

New York City. "1st Patrol District. In the Matter of Complaint against Edward McCosker Policeman [1846]." 19 p., no pagination. Municipal Archives and Records Service. Collection: City Clerk—Filed Papers. Location: 3198. Description: . . . Complaints against Policemen, 1845–46.

New York State. *Report of the Special Committee of the [N.Y. State] Assembly Appointed to Investigate the Public Offices and Departments of the City of New York . . . transmitted to the Legislature January 15, 1900.* ("Mazet Committee.") 5 vols. Albany: James B. Lyon, State Printer, 1900. (Vol. 1, p. 940–41; vol. 5, p. 1382–83, 1394–95, 1429–30, 1431–32.)

O'Callaghan, E[dmund] O., ed. *Calendar of Historical Manuscripts in the Office of the Secretary of State, Albany, N.Y.* Albany: Weed, Parsons, 1865. Photo reprint (with title as *Calendar of Dutch Historical Manuscripts*), Ridgewood, N.J.: Gregg Press, 1969. (P. 103, 201, 211, 213, 251–52, 319.)

Otis, Margaret. "A Perversion Not Commonly Noted," *Journal of Abnormal Psychology* (Boston). Vol. 8, no. 2 (June–July 1913): p. 113–16.

Powers, Edwin. *Crime and Punishment in Early Massachusetts: 1620–1692*. Boston: Beacon, 1966. (P. 43, 300–01, 307, 309, 312, 442, 573, 607, 608, 609, 624.)

Rosse, Irving C. "Sexual Hypochondriasis and Perversion of the Genesic Instinct." *Journal of Nervous and Mental Disease* (N.Y.). Whole ser. vol. 19, new ser. vol. 17, no. 11 (Nov. 1892): p. 795–811. Also in *Virginia Medical Monthly* (Richmond). Vol. 19 (1892): p. 633–49.

Russell, Bertrand. *The Autobiography of Bertrand Russell*. 3 vols. Vol. 1, *1872–1914*. Boston: Little, Brown, 1967. (P. 205–07.)

Scott, Colin. "Sex and Art," *The American Journal of Psychology* (Worcester, Mass.). Vol. 7, no. 2 (Jan. 1896): p. 153–226. (P. 216.)

[Sim, F. L.] "Forensic Psychiatry. Alice Mitchell Adjudged Insane," *Memphis* [Tenn.] *Medical Monthly.* Vol. 12, no. 8 (Aug. 1892): p. 377–428.

"She Dislikes Men and Dogs," *East Long Island* [N.Y.] *Star*, Dec. 31, 1897. From the *Chicago Chronicle*, n.d. Reprinted as "The Way It Was . . . Seventy Five Years Ago, 1897" in the *East Hampton* [N.Y.] *Star*, Dec. 28, 1972.

Solís de Merás, Gonzalo. *Pedro Menendez de Aviles; Adelantado; Governor and Captain-General of Florida* . . . Trans. Jeannette Conner. Deland, Fla.: Florida State Historical Society, 1923. (P. 180–81.)

Southern Reporter; Second Series; Volume 193 So. 2nd; Cases Argued and Determined in the Courts of Alabama, Florida, Louisiana, Mississippi. St. Paul, Minn.: West, 1967. (P. 243–45.) Legal citation: State *v.* Young, 193 So. 2d 243.

Staples, William R., ed. *The Colonial Laws of Massachusetts Reprinted from the Edition of 1672 . . . Together with the Body of Liberties of 1641.* Boston: Rockwell and Churchill, 1890. (P. 35 n.)

State *v.* Young[, Mary, and DeBlanc, Dawn,]. See: *Southern Reporter*.

Stevenson, Edward I. Prime (Xavier Mayne, pseud.). *The Intersexes; A History of Simili-sexualism as a Problem in Social Life.* [Naples?]: Privately printed [by R. Rispoli, 1908?] Photo reprint, N.Y.: Arno, 1975.

Tamony, Peter. "Dike: A Lesbian." San Francisco: mimeographed, May 1972. 15 p. (P. 12, 14.)

Tanner, Helen Hornbeck. "Zéspedes in East Florida, 1784–1790." Hispanic-American Institute. *University of Miami Hispanic-American Studies, No. 19.* Coral Gables, Fla.: University of Miami, 1963. (P. 167–68.)

Territory *v.* Mahaffey. See Blake, Henry N., and Hedges, Cornelius.

Thompson, Lawrance. *Robert Frost, The Years of Triumph, 1915–1938.* 2 vols. N.Y.: Holt, Rinehart and Winston, 1970. (Vol. 2, p. 104–06, 553 note 17.)

Trumbull, J. Hammond. *The True-Blue Laws of Connecticut and New-Haven.* Hartford: American Publishing Co., 1879. (P. 201.)

U.S. Congress, Senate Committee on Expenditures in the Executive Departments. *Employment of Homosexuals and Other Sex Perverts in Government; Interim Report Submitted to the Committee on Expenditures in the Executive Departments by Its Subcommittee on Investigations Pursuant to S. Res. 280.* 81st Con., 2nd sess., 15 Dec. 1950. Sen. Doc. 241. 26 p. Photo reprint in *Government Versus Homosexuals.* N.Y.: Arno, 1975.

U.S. Dept. of the Interior, Census Office. *Report of the Defective, Dependent, and Delinquent Classes of the Population of the United States, As Returned at the Tenth Census (June 1, 1880), by Frederick Howard Wines, Special Agent.* Washington, D.C.: U.S. Govt. Ptg. Ofc., 1888. (P. 506–09, 516–17, 562–63.)

U.S. Dept. of the Interior, Census Office. *Report on Crime, Pauperism, and Benevolence in the United States at the Eleventh Census: 1890.* Part 1, Analysis. [By] Frederick H. Wines, Special Agent. Washington, D.C.: U.S. Govt. Ptg. Ofc., 1896. (P. 18–20, 139.)

Washington, George. *The Writings of George Washington* . . . Ed. John C. Fitzpatrick. 39 vols. Washington, D.C.: U.S. Govt. Ptg. Ofc., 1934. (Vol. 11, p. 83–84.)

Witch-Hunts: 1950–54. A list of all relevant news items of this period of antihomosexual witch-hunts can be found by checking each year of the *New York Times Index* under "Homosexuality" and noting the cross-references.

A chronological list of the most important *New York Times* news items of this period follows. Other important sources are bracketed:

March 1, 1950, p. 2, col. 8. Dismissals on grounds of homosexuality.

March 9, 1950, p. 1, cols, 2, 3. McCarthy on homosexual dismissal.

March 12, 1950, p. 36, col. 3. McCarthy on informant.

March 15, 1950, p. 1, cols. 6, 8. McCarthy on homosexual in CIA.

March 20, 1950, p. 5, col. 1. Commerce Dept. accused of laxity on homosexuals.

April 1, 1950, p. 2, col. 3. House rejects bill to bar employment of homosexuals.

April 19, 1950, p. 25, col. 3. Republican leader calls sexual perversion "perhaps as dangerous as Communists."

April 25, 1950, p. 5, col. 1. Republicans seek probe expansion to include sexual perversion issue.

April 26, 1950, p. 1, col. 4. Senator Wherry cites resignation of homosexual; Jenner assails stress on homosexuals.

May 5, 1950, p. 15, col. 3. Gov. Dewey says Truman administration tolerates sex offenders.

May 20, 1950, p. 8, col. 2. Senate subcommittee urges Senate probe of homosexuals in Govt. agencies as poor security risks. Senators Hill and Wherry quote Washington Police Lt. Blick that 3,500 perverts are employed by Govt.

May 21, 1950, p. 43, col. 1. Senator Hoey says inquiry should be secret.

May 22, 1950, p. 8, col. 6. On committee to make probe.

May 25, 1950, p. 19, col. 1. Senate committee approves probe resolution.

[*Newsweek*, vol. 35, p. 18 (May 29, 1950), "New Shocker."]

[*Time*, vol. 55, (May 29, 1950), p. 16. "Tyranny or Blasphemy."]

June 8, 1950, p. 8, col. 5. Probe authorized.

June 15, 1950, p. 6, col. 4. Subcommittee headed by Senator Hoey ordered to proceed.

June 17, 1950, p. 6, col. 3. Homosexuals among 130 U.S. Govt. employes sent home from Germany as security risks.

[*Science Newsletter*, vol. 58 (July 1, 1950), p. 5. "Sexual Pervert Probe."]

[Lerner, Max, July 11, 17, 18, 1950 N.Y. *Post* columns. See Lerner, Max.]

[Major, Ralph H. "New Moral Menace to Our Youth," *Coronet*, Sept. 1950.]

[Senate subcommittee report, Dec. 15, 1950. See U.S. Congress.]

Dec. 16, 1950, p. 3, col. 4. Senate subcommittee report; perverts seen as dangerous security risks.

March 28, 1951, p. 1, col. 6. Dismissal of homosexuals in U.S. consulate in Hong Kong.

April 28, 1951, p. 7, col. 3. FBI reports 406 cases of sexual perversion uncovered since April 1950.

Oct. 5, 1951, p. 2, col. 4. Four State Dept. employes in Korea resign on charges of homosexuality.

Oct. 24, 1951, p. 26, col. 5. E. M. Kates scores treating victims of homosexuality as criminals.

Dec. 20, 1951, p. 1, col. 2. Lie detector used by some Govt. agencies to establish if job applicants or employes are sexual perverts.

[Lait and Mortimer, *Washington Confidential*, 1951. See Lait, Jack, and Mortimer, Lee.]

March 26, 1952, p. 25, col. 6. Deputy Under Sec. of State reports ouster of 126 homosexuals since Jan. 1951.

June 26, 1952, p. 4, col. 4. Resignation of 117, and 2 ousters on perversion charges.

Aug. 31, 1952, p. 32, col. 6. Officers and 24 enlisted men allegedly involved in homosexuality leave service.

Feb. 7, 1953, p. 6, col. 4. McCarthy on homosexuals in the State Dept.

March 14, 1953, p. 32, col. 1. Sixteen Govt. employes ousted as sexual deviates since Jan. 20.

April 13, 1953, p. 20, col. 2. House Committee reports 425 employes ousted on moral grounds since 1947.

April 21, 1953, p. 32, col. 1. McCleod reports 19 ousted since March 3 on homosexual charges.

[M., E. ("Miss"), April 1953. See M., E.]

July 3, 1953, p. 6, col. 4. McCleod reports 107 ousted in 1953 for homosexuality or security reasons.

July 25, 1953, p. 6, col. 1. H. Boisvert says he was ousted because he reported to superiors in Dept. on "subversives and sex deviates;" charge denied.

["Miami Junks the Constitution," *ONE* (Los Angeles), vol. 2, no. 1 (Jan. 1954), p. 16–21. First of a number of articles on a local witch-hunt.]

Feb. 18, 1954, p. 14, col. 5. Govt. agencies to classify security cases into those whose files contain data on sex perversion, etc.

March 2, 1954, p. 13, col. 3. Civil Service Comm. reports separations as security risks; 31 with information indicating perversion.

March 3, 1954, p. 13, col. 2. Security separations.

March 13, 1954, p. 1, col. 8. McCarthy charges that Army offered to trade data on homosexuals in Air Force if he stopped Army probe of subversives.

March 15, 1954, p. 1, col. 8, p. 16, cols. 4, 5. Cohn amplifies charge that Army offered data on sexual perversion in Air Force; McCarthy claims to have secret witness who can back charges against Army.

April 29, 1954, p. 16, cols. 2, 3. Army official says he got no data on homosexuals in Air Force.

May 14, 1954, p. 1, col. 1. Army lawyer Adams says map of U.S. he drew for Cohn was to find out if McCarthy planned probe of homosexuality at Southern Army base which Army was then investigating and later found groundless.

Aug. 27, 1954, p. 7, col. 1. Rep. Teague scores Rep. Phillips for having said American Legion was on "side of homosexuals and subversives" in opposing 1953 bill.

Aug. 28, 1954, p. 15, col. 4. Nat'l. Commander of American Legion demands Phillips apology.

Aug. 28, 1954, p. 1, col. 6; sec. 4, p. 2, col. 4. Appeals court reverses conviction of J. D. Provo; finds U.S. had no right to examine him on collateral issue of homosexuality.

Aug. 30, 1954, p. 19, col. 1. American Legion committee denounces Phillips.

Oct. 12, 1954, p. 1, col. 1. Civil Service Commission reports that 5,183 ousted May 28, 1953–June 30, 1954, included sex perverts, etc.

Winthrop, John. *The History of New England from 1630 to 1649.* Ed. James Savage. 2 vols. Boston: Little, Brown, 1853. (Vol. 2, p. 58–59, 324.)

NOTES

II. Treatment: 1884–1974

I wish to thank James D. Steakley for his help in compiling this part, and for writing a first draft of the general introduction and introductions to the documents. Responsibility for the final versions is my own.

1. The various treatment types mentioned are all documented in the following section and notes. Documentation of hysterectomy Part 3, "Passing Women," p. 276, 606n. 69. Primal therapy, Vegetotherapy, musical analysis, astrology, Scientology, and Aesthetic Realism are documented by Ralph Blair, *Etiology and Treatment Literature on Homosexuality*, The Otherwise Monograph Series, no. 5 (National Task Force on Student Personnel Services and Homosexuality, 1972), p. 36–37; also see Blair "Part II: Treatment," for a good, documented discussion and summary of the subject of treatment.

Some of the early medical documents suggesting surgical measures for masturbation, satyriasis, etc., are cited by Vern L. Bullough and Martha Voght in "Homosexuality and the 'Secret Sin' in Pre-Freudian America," *Journal of the History of Medicine and Allied Sciences*, vol. 28, no. 2 (April 1973), p. 143–55; and G. J. Barker-Benfield, *The Horrors of the Half-Known Life; Male Attitudes Toward Women and Sexuality in Nineteenth-Century America* (N.Y.: Harper & Row, 1976), on sexual surgery, p. 82–83, 88–90, 91 ff., 97, 104, 120–32, 286–87, 292–93. Also see note 5 below.

One of the strangest treatment documents meriting further research is an extract from an address in 1866 by Dr. W. D. Buck, President of the New Hampshire State Medical Society: "A distinguished surgeon in New York city, twenty-five years ago [1841], said, when [Guillaume] Dupuytren's operation for relaxation of the *sphincter ani* was in vogue, every young man who came from Paris found every other individual's anus too large, and proceeded to pucker it up. The result was that New York anuses looked like gimlet-holes in a piece of pork." The apparent homosexual implications of this may be misleading. Buck goes on to say that the uterus, also, is being subjected to "surgical operations, and is now-a-days subject to all sorts of barbarity from surgeons anxious for notoriety." His statement is aimed at primitive abortion and birth control measures ("A Raid on the Uterus," *New York Medical Journal*, vol. 5 [Aug. 1866], p. 464). A brief biography of Dupuytren is in John Talbott, *A Biographical History of Medicine* (N.Y.: Grune & Stratton, 1970), p. 342–44. I wish to thank Stephen W. Foster and Dennis Lampkowski for help with this research.

2. Edmund Bergler, "Eight Prerequisites for the Psychoanalytic Treatment of Homosexuality," *Psychoanalytic Review* (N.Y.), vol. 31 (1944); see especially p. 255, 260, 266, 268–69, 277–79, 281–86. Also see Bergler's "Suppositions about the Mechanism of Criminosis," *Journal of Criminal Psychopathology*, vol. 5 (1943), p. 215–46 (especially case 4, p. 235). Permission to reprint excerpts from Bergler's papers was denied.

3. Martin S. Weinberg and Alan P. Bell, *Homosexuality; An Annotated Bibliography* (N.Y.: Harper and Row, 1972), p. 287. The source of the case cited is "Fatal Emetine Poisoning from Aversion Treatment," Re W. T. (Westminster Inquest, Feb. 7, 1964), *Medico-Legal Journal*, vol. 32, no. 2 (1964), p. 95. The Weinberg and Bell bibliography contains a large, useful, alphabetical, annotated listing of books and articles dating from 1940 to 1968 on the treatment of homosexuals. The index provides a guide to types of treatment, and the introduction lists the various indexes and guides used in the compilation. Documents on various treatment forms through 1969 are listed and indexed in William Parker, *Homosexuality; A Selective Bibliography of Over 3,000 Items* (Metuchen, N.J.: Scarecrow Press, 1971). The Institute for Sex Research provides mimeographed bibliographies on "Homosexuality—Aversion and Behavior Therapy" (Nov. 1972) and "Homosexuality Therapy: Pre-1940" (May 1974).

4. James G. Kiernan, "Insanity. Lecture XXVI.—Perversion," *Detroit Lancet*, vol. 7, no. 11 (May 1884), p. 483–84.

5. James G. Kiernan, "Psychical Treatment of Congenital Sexual Inversion," *Review of Insanity and Nervous Disease* (Milwaukee, Wis.), vol. 4, no. 4 (June 1894), p. 295.

In 1889, the *Medical and Surgical Reporter* of Philadelphia published a lecture on "Sexual Perversion, Satyriasis and Nymphomania" which Dr. G. Frank Lydston had delivered at the Chicago College of Physicians and Surgeons. Although he discusses male and female homosexuality, Lydston makes no specific recommendation for treatment. But since he links homosexuality with satyriasis and nymphomania, there is an unspoken suggestion that it should be similarly treated; for the two "perversions" of which he speaks Lydston suggests "removal of irritation of the sexual apparatus," "anaphrodisiac remedies," "attempts to restrain sexual excesses, or to break the habit of masturbation." But if the "disease" is organic, it is probably incurable and requires more radical treatment: "In women, extirpation of the ovaries, or the procedure of Mr. Baker Brown—clitoridectomy—may be performed. Howe recommends the application of the actual cautery to the back of the neck. Basing this treatment upon the theory that the disease takes its origin in over-excitation of the nerve fibres of the cerebellum or some of the ganglia in the neighborhood, he also suggests blisters and setons to answer the same purpose. Dry cupping to the nucha is also serviceable. Means to restore the general health are always indicated. In the severe cases of the maniacal form of excessive sexual desire the asylum is usually our only recourse" (G. Frank Lydston, "Sexual Perversion, Satyriasis and Nymphomania," *Medical and Surgical Reporter* [Phila.], vol. 61, no. 11 [Sept. 14, 1889], p. 285).

6. See "Removal of the Ovaries as a Therapeutic Measure in Public Institutions for the Insane," *Journal of the American Medical Association* (Chicago), Feb. 4, 1893, p. 135–37. Dr. Price mentioned: p. 136–37. Also see "Domestic Correspondence," same, Feb. 18, 1893, p. 182–83.

7. F. E. Daniel, "Castration of Sexual Perverts," *Texas Medical Journal* (Austin), Aug. 1893, p. 255–71; reprint; *Texas Medical Journal* (Austin), vol. 27, no. 10 (April 1912) p. 371–72, 376–81. A note (p. 369) adds: "Under the title, 'Should Insane Criminals or Sexual Perverts be Permitted to Procreate?' this paper was read at the Joint Session of the World's Columbian Auxiliary Congress—Section of Medical Jurisprudence—and the International Medico-Legal Congress, August 16th, 1893, and also before the American Medico-Legal Society, New York, October 11th, 1893, and pub-

lished in the 'Medico-Legal Journal' for December, and in the 'Psychological Bulletin,' New York." Dr. Daniel is identified in the 1912 reprint as the editor of the *Texas Medical Journal*.

Material on treatment of homosexuality is in R. von Krafft-Ebing's *Psychopathia Sexualis, with Special Reference to Contrary Sexual Instinct. A Medico-Legal Study.* Authorized trans. of the 7th enlarged and rev. German ed. by Charles Gilbert Chaddock (Phila.: F. A. Davis, 1893).

8. Marc André Raffalovich, "Uranism, Congenital Sexual Inversion. Observations and Recommendations . . ." trans. C. Judson Herrick, *Journal of Comparative Neurology* (Granville, Ohio), vol. 5 (March 1895), p. 33–34, 36–37, 42, 52. Background on Raffalovich is in Timothy d'Arch Smith, *Love in Earnest; Some Notes on the Lives and Writings of English 'Uranian' Poets from 1889 to 1930* (London: Routledge & Kegan Paul, 1970), p. 29–34, 53, 77, 107, 153, 186, 249 and Brian Reade, ed., *Sexual Heretics; Male Homosexuality in English Literature from 1850 to 1900* (N.Y.: Coward-McCann, 1970, p. 32–35, 38, 40, 50, 53).

9. Havelock Ellis, "Sexual Inversion in Women," *Alienist and Neurologist* (St. Louis, Mo.), vol. 16, no. 2 (April 1895), p. 158. See also: Havelock Ellis, "A Note on the Treatment of Sexual Inversion," *Alienist and Neurologist* (St. Louis, Mo.), vol. 17 (July 1896), p. 258–59.

In the mid-1890s, F. Hoyt Pilcher, the head of a Kansas institution for the feeble-minded, had four boys and fourteen girls castrated without legal authority. It was explained in his defense that castration would prevent "excessive masturbation and pervert [*sic*] sexual acts". Public outcry stopped further castration (F. C. Cave, "Report of Sterilization in the Kansas State Home for Feeble-minded," *Journal of Psycho-Asthenics*, vol. 15 [1911], p. 123–25; Arno Karlen, *Sexuality and Homosexuality; A New View* [N.Y.: Norton, 1971], p. 332).

10. E. S. Talbot and Havelock Ellis, "A Case of Developmental Degenerative Insanity, with Sexual Inversion, Melancholia, Following Removal of Testicles, Attempted Murder and Suicide," *Journal of Mental Science* (London), vol. 42, no. 177, new ser., no. 141 (April 1896), p. 341–44 (i.e., 46—erroneous pagination in original); Havelock Ellis, and John Addington Symonds, *Sexual Inversion* (London: Wilson and Macmillan, 1897; photo reprint, N.Y.: Arno, 1975), p. 73.

11. Harry Clay Sharp, "The Sterilization of Degenerates," Indiana Board of State Charities (National Christian League for Promotion of Purity, 1908), p. 1–2, 6. Reprint of a paper read before the American Prison Association, Chicago, 1909 (in the N.Y. Public Library Research Division). Also see Sharp, "Human Sterilization," *Journal of the American Medical Association*, vol. 4, no. 12 (1909). In a paper titled "Surgical Treatment as Sex Crime Prevention Measure," Marie E. Kopp says that between 1889 and 1907 Dr. Sharp of the State Reformatory for Delinquent Boys at Jefferson, Indiana, performed "several hundred" vasectomies (*Journal of Criminal Law and Criminology*, vol. 28 [Jan.–Feb. 1938], p. 687).

12. John Duncan Quackenbos, "Hypnotic Suggestion in the Treatment of Sexual Perversions and Moral Anaesthesia: A Personal Experience," *Transactions of the New Hampshire Medical Society* (Concord), 1899, p. 69, 72, 75, 78–80.

13. "The Gentleman Degenerate. A Homosexualist's Self-Description and Self-Applied Title. Pudic Nerve Section Fails Therapeutically," *Alienist and Neurologist* (St. Louis, Mo.), vol. 25, no. 1 (Feb. 1, 1904), p. 68–70. The editor of this journal, Dr. Charles H. Hughes of St. Louis, may be the anonymous physician-author of this piece.

See also R. von Krafft-Ebing, *Text Book of Insanity* (Phila.: F. A. Davis, 1904); C. E. Goodell, "Suggestive Therapy in Sexual Perversion," *American Journal of Dermatology and Genito-Urinary Disease* (St. Louis, Mo.), vol. 8 (1904), p. 104–06.

14. Edward I. Prime Stevenson (Xavier Mayne, pseud.), *The Intersexes; A History of*

Similisexualism as a Problem in Social Life ([Naples?:] Privately printed [R. Rispoli, 1908?]; photo reprint, N.Y.: Arno, 1975), p. 119–22, 549.

See also C. E. Goodell, "Sexual Perversion, Its Effects and Its Treatment," *Medical Era* (St. Louis, Mo.), vol. 19 (1910), p. 499–502; G. F. Lydston, "Sex Mutilations in Social Therapeutics, With Some of the Difficulties in the Application of Eugenics to the Human Race," *New York Medical Journal*, April 6, 1912.

15. A. A. Brill, "The Conception of Homosexuality," *Journal of the American Medical Association* (Chicago), vol. 61 (Aug. 2, 1913), p. 335–40. Footnotes omitted.

See also Isador Coriat, "Homosexuality. Its Psychogenesis and Treatment," *New York Medical Journal*, vol. 97, no. 12 (March 22, 1913), p. 589–94.

16. Magnus Hirschfeld, "Adaptionsbehandlung (Anpassungstherapie) der Homosexualität," ch. 23, p. 439–61 in *Die Homosexualität des Mannes und des Weibes*, 2nd ed. (Berlin: Louis Marcus, 1920). The same chapter appears in the first, 1914, edition. I wish to thank Richard Plant for this translation. Another translation, by Henry Gerber, the American homosexual rights pioneer, appears in *ONE Institute Quarterly* (Los Angeles), vol. 5, nos. 2-3-4, issue 17 (Spring, Summer, Fall 1962). For the works of Alexander von Gleichen-Russwurm, Élisàr von Kupffer, and Edward Carpenter see part VI, note 10.

17. Charles H. Hughes, "An Emasculated Homo-sexual. His Antecedent and Post-Operative Life," *Alienist and Neurologist* (St. Louis, Mo.), vol. 35 (1914), p. 277–80.

See also Emil Oberhoffer, "The Influence of Castration on the Libido," *American Journal of Urology and Sexology*, vol. 12 (Jan.–Dec. 1916), p. 58–60; Earl Lind, *Autobiography of an Androgyne*, ed. with an intro. by Alfred W. Herzog (N.Y.: Medico-Legal Press, 1918; photo reprint, N.Y.: Arno, 1975), p. 41–42, 74, 197–201, 230 (on his castration).

18. Sigmund Freud, "The Psychogenesis of a Case of Female Homosexuality," *International Journal of Psycho-Analysis* (London), vol. 1, no. 2 (1920), p. 129–30.

19. Freud, p. 125–27.

20. Freud, p. 131.

21. Freud, p. 133, 135.

22. Freud, p. 136.

23. Freud, p. 134.

24. Freud, p. 144.

25. Freud, p. 141–42.

26. Freud, p. 148–49.

See also Martin W. Barr, "Some Notes on Asexualization; with a Report of Eighteen Cases" (includes references to females) *Journal of Nervous and Mental Disease* (Lancaster, Pa.), vol. 51, no. 3 (March 1920), p. 231–41; J. A. Gilbert, "Homosexuality and Its Treatment," *Journal of Nervous and Mental Disease* (Lancaster, Pa.), vol. 52, no. 4 (Oct. 1920), p. 297–322 (quoted in Part III, Passing Women); Earl Lind, *The Female Impersonators . . .*, ed. with intro. by Alfred W. Herzog (N.Y.: Medico-Legal Press, 1922; photo reprint, N.Y.: Arno, 1975), p. 16, 67; Samuel Kahn, *A Study of Homosexuals and Their Education in the New York Correction Hospitals*, M. A. thesis, N.Y. University School of Education, 1923, 149 p.

27. Wilhelm Stekel, "Is Homosexuality Curable?" trans. Bertrand S. Frohman, *Psychoanalytic Review*, vol. 17 (Oct. 1930), p. 443, 447–48.

See also Albert Moll, *Perversions of the Sex Instinct* (Newark, N.J.: Julian Press, 1931).

28. Helene Deutsch, "On Female Homosexuality," authorized trans. Edith B. Jackson, *Psychoanalytic Quarterly* (N.Y.), vol. 1 (Oct. 1932), p. 484–88, 490–91. Another translation: "Homosexuality in Women," *International Journal of Psychoanalysis* (London), vol. 14 (1933), p. 34–56.

29. Nicholas Deutsch, interviewed by Jonathan Katz, N.Y.C., Oct. 17, 1974. Freud's comment is not as unambiguously pro-Gay as it may first appear. Liberal heterosexuals have for long *required* Gay people to be happy in order to legitimate their homosexual orientation, a psychological obligation experienced by Gay people as a special burden.

30. La Forest Potter, *Strange Loves: A Study in Sexual Abnormalities* (N.Y.: Robert Dodsley, 1933), p. 161–62.

31. Potter, p. 167, 173, 177–78.

32. Potter, p. 118–19.

33. Potter, p. 147.

34. Potter, p. 236–37.

See also K. Riedner, "Cure of Homosexuals," *Sexology* (N.Y.), vol. 1 (1933), p. 490–92; Ernest Bien, "Why Do Homosexuals Undergo Treatment?," *Anthropos* (N.Y.), vol. 1, no. 1 (Jan. 1934), p. 5–18; also in *Medical Review of Reviews*, vol. 40, no. 1 (Jan. 1934), p. 18–51 (includes Lesbian references); A. A. Brill, "The Psychiatric Approach to the Problem of Homosexuality," *Psychiatric Association and Student Health Association*, vol. 15 (1934), p. 31–34; reprinted in *Journal Lancet*, vol. 55 (1935), p. 249–52.

35. Louis William Max, "Breaking Up a Homosexual Fixation by the Condition Reaction Technique: A Case Study," *Psychological Bulletin* (Washington, D.C.), vol. 32 (1935), p. 734.

See also A. W. Hackfield, "Ameliorative Effects of Therapeutic Castration on Habitual Sex Offenders," *Journal of Nervous and Mental Disease*, vol. 82, no. 1 (July 1935), p. 15–29; no. 2 (Aug. 1935), p. 169–81. On April 9, 1935, Sigmund Freud answered an American mother who had written to him about treating her son's homosexuality: "Letter to An American Mother," *American Journal of Psychiatry*, vol. 107 (1951), p. 786–87; various reprints; George S. Sprague, "Varieties of Homosexual Manifestations," with discussion by Karl A. Menninger, Isador H. Coriat, Charles I. Lambert, Ernest M. Poate, and S. W. Hartwell, 1935; reprinted in *The Homosexuals As Seen by Themselves and Thirty Authorities*, ed. A. M. Krich, p. 174–87 (N.Y.: Citadel, 1954); Marie E. Kopp, "Surgical Treatment as Sex Crime Prevention Measure," *Journal of Criminal Law and Criminology*, vol. 28 (Jan.–Feb. 1938), p. 692–706; George W. Henry, *Essentials of Psychiatry* (Baltimore: Williams and Wilkins, 1938); "Criminal Law, Sex Offenders, Civil Commitment for Psychiatric Treatment," *Columbia Law Review*, vol. 39 (1939), p. 534–44; Hyman S. Barahal, "Testosterone in Psychotic Male Homosexuals," *Psychiatric Quarterly*, vol. 14, no. 2 (1940), p. 319–30.

For additional books and articles on treatment of homosexuality written or translated into English between 1940 and 1968, see Weinberg and Bell. For an additional bibliography on treatment through 1969, see Parker.

36. Newdigate M. Owensby, "The Correction of Homosexuality," *Urologic and Cutaneous Review* (St. Louis, Mo.), vol. 45, no. 8 (1941), p. 495.

37. Newdigate M. Owensby, "Homosexuality and Lesbianism Treated with Metrazol," *Journal of Nervous and Mental Disease* (N.Y.), vol. 92, no. 1 (1940), p. 65–66.

38. Owensby, (1941), p. 496.

39. George N. Thompson, "Electroshock and Other Therapeutic Considerations in Sexual Psychopathology," *Journal of Nervous and Mental Disease* (N.Y.), vol. 109, no. 6 (June 1949), p. 531–39.

40. Saul Rosenzweig and R. G. Hoskins, "A Note on the Ineffectualness of Sex-Hormone Medication in a Case of Pronounced Homosexuality," *Psychosomatic Medicine* (N.Y.), vol. 3, no. 1 (1941), p. 87–89.

For a relatively rare discussion of Lesbian treatment, see Morris Wolfe Brody, "An Analysis of the Psychosexual Development of a Female: With Special Reference to Homosexuality," *Psychoanalytic Review*, vol. 30, no. 1 (1943), p. 47–58; reprinted as

"Psychosexual Development of a Female" in *The Homosexuals As Seen By Themselves and Thirty Authorities*, ed. A. M. Krich, p. 312–24 (N.Y.: Citadel, 1954).

41. S. J. Glass and Roswell H. Johnson, "Limitations and Complications of Organotherapy in Male Homosexuality," *Journal of Clinical Endocrinology* (Phila.), vol. 4, no. 11 (1944), p. 541–43.

42. Samuel Liebman, "Homosexuality, Transvestism, and Psychosis: Study of a Case Treated with Electroshock," *Journal of Nervous and Mental Disease* (N.Y.), vol. 99, no. 6 (1944), p. 945–47.

43. Liebman, p. 950–53.

44. Liebman, p. 957.

45. Thomas V. Moore, "The Pathogenesis and Treatment of Homosexual Disorders: A Digest of Some Pertinent Evidence," *Journal of Personality* (Durham, N.C.), vol. 14 (1945), p. 57. Footnote omitted.

46. Moore, p. 72–73.

47. Ralph S. Banay and L. Davidoff, "Apparent Recovery of a Sex Psychopath after Lobotomy," *Journal of Criminal Psychopathology* (N.Y.), vol. 4, no. 1 (July 1942), p. 59–66. Here the doctors report that after lobotomy the patient's masturbation stopped, he became "complacent" and "tranquil," and "showed no sign of conflict with his environment." He "remained courteous, meek, obliging and attentive." The doctors conclude that lobotomy "might be a new and important development." A psychological dynamic here, unrecognized by the doctors, is a masochistic subject asking for a lobotomy, and the sadistic physicians obliging.

48. Joseph Friedlander and Ralph S. Banay, "Psychosis Following Lobotomy in a Case of Sexual Psychopathology; Report of a Case," *Archives of Neurology and Psychiatry* (Chicago), vol. 59 (1948), p. 303–11.

49. Friedlander and Banay, p. 315, 321.
See also Donald Webster Cory, pseud., "Can Homosexuality Be Cured?," *Sexology*, vol. 18 (Oct. 1951), p. 146–56 (an important early American homosexual emancipation movement statement, not listed in Weinberg and Bell).

50. J. Srnec and Kurt Freund, "Treatment of Male Homosexuality through Conditioning," *International Journal of Sexology* (Bombay), vol. 7, no. 2 (1953), p. 92–93.

51. Karl M. Bowman, "Sexual Deviation Research," California Assembly Judiciary Subcommittee on Sex Research, March 1952.

52. Karl M. Bowman and Bernice Engle, "The Problem of Homosexuality," *Journal of Social Hygiene* (N.Y.), vol. 39, no. 1 (1953), p. 10–11.

53. Ernest Harms, "Homo-Anonymous," *Diseases of the Nervous System* (Memphis, Tenn.), vol. 14, no. 10 (1953), p. 318–19.

54. Dolores Klaich, *Woman + Woman; Attitudes Toward Lesbianism* (N.Y.: Morrow, 1975), paperback, p. 100–01.

55. Frank S. Caprio, *Female Homosexuality; A Psychodynamic Study of Lesbianism*, Foreword Karl M. Bowman (N.Y.: Grove Press, Evergreen Black Cat, 1962), p. 299–301, 304.
See also Harold A. Abramson, "Lysergic Acid Diethylamide (LSD-25), III. As an Adjunct to Psychotherapy with Elimination of Fear of Homosexuality," *Journal of Psychology*, vol. 39 (Jan. 1955), p. 127–55. Abramson presents a verbatim recording of a four-hour interview with a forty-year-old woman, who under the influence of LSD speaks of her fear of Lesbianism. Abramson was the LSD expert, trusted by the CIA, who in Nov. 1953 twice examined Frank R. Olson—just before he committed suicide as a result of his involuntary participation in a CIA drug experiment (*New York Times*, July 11, 1975, p. 34, col. 5).
For a relatively rare Lesbian treatment reference, see Albert Ellis, "The Effectiveness of Psychotherapy with Individuals Who Have Severe Homosexual Problems" (28 males, 12 females), *Journal of Consulting Psychology*, vol. 20 (1956), p. 191–95; reprinted in

The Problem of Homosexuality in Modern Society, ed. Hendrik M. Ruitenbeek, p. 175–82 (N.Y.: Dutton, 1963); and Albert Ellis, "The Use of Psychotherapy with Homosexuals" (41 males, 12 females), *Mattachine Review*, vol. 2, no. 1 (1956), p. 14–16.

56. Samuel B. Hadden, "Attitudes Toward and Approaches to the Problem of Homosexuality," *Pennsylvania Medical Journal* (Lemoyne, Pa.), vol. 6, no. 9 (1957), p. 1195–98.

For a Lesbian treatment reference, see Albert Ellis, "New Hope for Homosexuals," 1958, reprinted in *The Third Sex*, ed. Isadore Rubin, p. 53–57 (N.Y.: New Book Co., 1961).

57. Richard C. Robertiello, *Voyage from Lesbos: The Psychoanalysis of a Female Homosexual* (N.Y.: Citadel, 1959), p. 238–47.

For a Lesbian treatment reference, see Fred Mendelsohn and Matthew Ross, "An Analysis of 133 Homosexuals Seen at A University Health Service" (109 males, 24 females), *Diseases of the Nervous System*, vol. 20, no. 6 (1959), p. 246–50.

58. Alexander B. Smith and Alexander Bassin, "Group Therapy with Homosexuals," *Journal of Social Therapy* (N.Y.), vol. 5, no. 3 (1959), p. 227, 231–32.

59. Moses Zlotlow and Albert E. Paganini, "Autoerotic and Homoerotic Manifestations in Hospitalized Male Postlobotomy Patients, *Psychiatric Quarterly* (Poughkeepsie, N.Y.), vol. 33, no. 3 (1959), p. 495.

60. Zlotlow and Paganini, p. 492–94, 496–97.

Also see Thomas Szasz, *The Myth of Mental Illness* (N.Y.: Hoeber and Harper, 1961).

61. Michael M. Miller, "Hypnotic-Aversion Treatment of Homosexuality," *Journal of the National Medical Association*, vol. 55, no. 5 (1963), p. 411–13, 415. Brief biographical information on Miller is in the *American Medical Directory*, 24th ed. (1967), part 2, p. 1503.

For Lesbian treatment references, see Richard C. Robertiello, "Clinical Notes: Results of Separation from Iposexual Parents During the Oedipal Period, [and] A Female Homosexual Panic," *Psychoanalytic Review*, vol. 51, no. 4 (1964–65), p. 670–72; M. Roman, "The Treatment of the Homosexual in the Group," *Topical Problems in Psychotherapy*, vol. 5 (1965), p. 170–75; Charles W. Socarides, "Female Homosexuality," in *Sexual Behavior and the Law*, ed. Ralph Slovenko, p. 462–77 (Springfield, Ill.: Charles C. Thomas, 1965); Cornelia B. Wilbur, "Clinical Aspects of Female Homosexuality," in *Sexual Inversion: The Multiple Roots of Homosexuality*, ed. Judd Marmor, p. 268–81 (N.Y.: Basic Books, 1965); Helga Aschaffenburg, "Relationship Therapy with a Homosexual: A Case History," *Pastoral Counselor*, vol. 4, no. 1 (1964), p. 412; John P. Kemph and Erna Schwerin, "Increased Latent Homosexuality in a Woman During Group Therapy," *International Journal of Group Psychotherapy*, vol. 16, no. 2 (1966), p. 217–24.

See also Thomas S. Szasz, *Law, Liberty, and Psychiatry: An Inquiry into the Social Uses of Mental Health Practices* (N.Y.: Macmillan, 1963); Donald Webster Cory, pseud., and John P. LeRoy, pseud., "Why Homosexuals Resist Cure," *Sexology*, vol. 30, no. 7 (1964), p. 480–82 (an early homosexual emancipationist statement); Maurice Labelle, "Laws Need to Force 'Homos' to Seek Help," *Coral Gable* [Fla.] *Times*, Feb. 4, 1965, p. 6, 8; Edwin M. Schur, *Crimes without Victims; Deviant Behavior and Public Policy: Abortion, Homosexuality, and Drug Addiction* (Englewood Cliffs, N.Y.: Prentice-Hall, 1965); Fritz A. Fluckiger, "Research Through a Glass Darkly: An Evaluation of the Bieber Study on Homosexuality," privately printed, 1966 (a homosexual emancipationist statement).

62. Harvey E. Kaye and others, "Homosexuality in Women," *Archives of General Psychiatry* (Chicago), vol. 17 (Nov. 1967), p. 626, 633–34. Footnote omitted.

63. Kaye, p. 632–33.

64. Joseph R. Cautela, "Covert Sensitization," *Psychological Reports* (Missoula, Mont.), vol. 20, no. 2 (1967), p. 464–65.

See also Donald Webster Cory, pseud., "Homosexuality," in *The Encyclopedia of Sexual Behavior*, eds. Albert Ellis and Albert Abarbanel, p. 485–93, 2nd rev. ed. (N.Y.: Hawthorn, 1967); Jerome D. Frank, "Treatment of Homosexuals," Working Paper Prepared for the National Institute of Mental Health Task Force on Homosexuality, mimeographed (Baltimore: Johns Hopkins University, 1967), 13 p.; Evelyn Hooker and others, "Final Report of the National Institute of Mental Health Task Force on Homosexuality," reprinted in SIECUS *Newsletter* (Dec. 1970).

For Lesbian treatment references, see Thomas L. Doyle, "Homosexuality and Its Treatment," *Nursing Outlook*, vol. 15, no. 8 (1967), p. 38–40; Joshua S. Golden, "Varieties of Sexual Problems in Obstetrical and Gynecological Practice," in *Sexual Problems: Diagnosis and Treatment in Medical Practice*, ed. Charles William Wahl (N.Y.: Free Press, 1967), p. 53–61; Irving C. Bernstein, "Homosexuality in Gynecologic Practice," *South Dakota Journal of Medicine*, vol. 21 (March 1968), p. 33–39. According to Blair (p. 27), a survey reported in *Modern Medicine* (April 1969, p. 20) found that only one in four Lesbians interviewed wanted to become heterosexual.

65. Ivan T. Rutner, "A Double-barrel Approach to Modification of Homosexual Behavior," *Psychological Reports* (Missoula, Mont.), vol. 26, no. 2 (1970), p. 356–58. Notes omitted.

See also Thomas Szasz, *The Manufacture of Madness* (N.Y.: Harper and Row, 1970); Chicago Gay Liberation Front, "A Leaflet for the American Medical Association," (1970), reprinted in *Out of the Closets; Voice of Gay Liberation*, eds. Karla Jay and Allen Young (N.Y.: Douglass, 1972), p. 145–47; Christopher Z. Hobson (James Coleman, pseud.), "Surviving Psychotherapy," *Radical Therapy*, vol. 2, no. 2 (Sept. 1971), reprinted in Jay and Young, p. 147–53; Radicalesbians Health Collective, "Lesbians and the Health Care System," mimeographed, 1971, reprinted in Jay and Young, p. 122–41; Franklin E. Kameny, "Gay Liberation and Psychiatry," *Psychiatric Opinion*, vol. 8, no. 1 (Feb. 1971), p. 18–27, reprinted in *The Homosexual Dialectic*, ed. Joseph A. McCaffrey (Englewood Cliffs, N.J.: Prentice-Hall, 1972); Marty Robinson, "Homosexuals & Society: The 'Cure' Is Rebellion," *Village Voice* (N.Y.), April 29, 1971; Donn Teal, *The Gay Militants* (N.Y.: Stein and Day, 1971; on treatment p. 293–301); Gary Alinder, "Gay Liberation Meets the Shrinks," in Jay and Young, p. 141–45.

66. A strikingly similar report of a female victim of shock treatment (though not involving homosexuality) is by Berton Roueché, "Annals of Medicine; As Empty As Eve," *The New Yorker*, Sept. 9, 1974, p. 84–100.

See also Charles Silverstein (review of John Bancroft's *Deviant Sexual Behavior: Modification and Assessment* [London: Oxford University, 1974] in) *Behavior Therapy*, vol. 6, no. 4 (July 1975).

67. On mental institution commitment policy and practice, see Thomas S. Szasz, *The Manufacture of Madness; A Comparative Study of the Inquisition and the Mental Health Movement* (N.Y.: Delta Books, Dell, 1970), p. 49–52, 54–56, 62, 64–67.

Bibliography

II. TREATMENT: 1884–1974

Banay, Ralph S., and Davidoff, L. "Apparent Recovery of a Sex Psychopath after Lobotomy," *Journal of Criminal Psychopathology*. Vol. 4, no. 1 (July 1942): p. 59–66.

Barlow, David H.; Leitenberg, Harold; and Agras, W. Stewart. "Experimental Control of Sexual Deviations through Manipulation of the Noxious Scene in Covert Sensitization," *Journal of Abnormal Psychology*. Vol. 74, no. 5 (1969): p. 596–601. (P. 598, 601.)

Blair, Ralph. *Etiological and Treatment Literature on Homosexuality*. Otherwise Monograph Ser., no. 5. National Task Force on Student Personnel Services and Homosexuality, 1972.

Bowman, Karl M. "Sexual Deviation Research." Report to California Assembly, Judiciary Subcommittee on Sex Research, Sacramento, Calif., March 1952, p. 80.

———, and Engle, Bernice. "The Problem of Homosexuality," *Journal of Social Hygiene*. Vol. 39, no. 1 (1953): p. 2–16. (P. 10–11.)

Brill, A. A. "The Conception of Homosexuality," *Journal of the American Medical Association*. Vol. 61 (Aug. 2, 1913): p. 335–40.

Caprio, Frank S. *Female Homosexuality; A Psychodynamic Study of Lesbianism*. Foreword by Karl M. Bowman. N.Y.: Grove Press, Evergreen Black Cat, 1962. (P. 299–301, 304.)

Cautela, Joseph R. "Covert Sensitization," *Psychological Reports*. Vol. 20, no. 2 (1967): p. 459–68. (P. 464–65.)

Chideckel, Maurice. *Female Sex Perversion*. N.Y.: Eugenics Pub. Co., 1938.

Daniel, F. E. "Castration of Sexual Perverts," *Texas Medical Journal* (Austin), Aug. 1893: p. 255–71. Reprinted in *Texas Medical Journal*. Vol. 27, no. 10 (April 1912): p. 369–85. (P. 371–72, 376–81.) Additional reprints, see footnote.

Deutsch, Helene. "On Female Homosexuality," authorized trans. Edith B. Jackson, *Psychoanalytic Quarterly*. Vol. 1 (Oct. 1932): p. 484–510. (P. 484–88, 490–91.). A second trans.: "Homosexuality in Women," *International Journal of Psychoanalysis*. Vol. 14 (1933): p. 34–56.

Deutsch, Nicholas. Interviewed by Jonathan Katz. N.Y.C., Oct. 17, 1974.

Ellis, Havelock. "A Note on the Treatment of Sexual Inversion," *Alienist and Neurologist*. Vol. 17 (July 1896): p. 257–64. (P. 258–59.)

———. "Sexual Inversion in Women," *Alienist and Neurologist*. Vol. 16, no. 2 (April 1895): p. 141–58. (P. 158.)

———, and Symonds, John Addington. *Sexual Inversion*. 1st English ed. London: Wilson and Macmillan, 1897; photo reprint, N.Y.: Arno, 1975. (P. 73.)

———, and Talbot, E. S. See Talbot and Ellis.

Freud, Sigmund. "The Psychogenesis of a Case of Female Homosexuality," *International Journal of Psycho-Analysis*. Vol. 1, no. 2 (1920): p. 125–49. (P. 125–27, 129–30, 131, 133, 134, 135, 136, 141–42, 144, 148–49.)

Friedlander, Joseph, and Banay, Ralph S. "Psychosis Following Lobotomy in a Case of Sexual Psychopathology; Report of a Case," *Archives of Neurology and Psychiatry*. Vol. 59 (1948): p. 302–21. (P. 303–11, 315, 321.)

"The Gentleman Degenerate. A Homosexualist's Self-Description and Self-Applied Title. Pudic Nerve Section Fails Therapeutically," *Alienist and Neurologist*. Vol. 25, no. 1 (Feb. 1, 1904): p. 62–70. (P. 68–70.)

Glass, S. J., and Johnson, Roswell, H. "Limitations and Complications of Organotherapy in Male Homosexuality," *Journal of Clinical Endocrinology*. Vol. 4, no. 11 (1944): p. 540–44. (P. 541–43.)

Hadden, Samuel B. "Attitudes Toward and Approaches to the Problem of Homosexuality," *Pennsylvania Medical Journal*. Vol. 6, no. 9 (1957): p. 1195–98.

Harms, Ernest. "Homo-Anonymous," *Diseases of the Nervous System*. Vol. 14, no. 10 (1953): p. 318–19.

Henry, George W. *Sex Variants; A Study of Homosexual Patterns*. 2 vols. N.Y.: Paul B. Hoeber, 1941.

Hirschfeld, Magnus. "Adaptionsbehandlung (Anpassungstherapie) der Homosexualität." Trans. Henry Gerber from *Die Homosexualität des Mannes und des Weibes*, 2nd ed. (Berlin, 1920): chap. 23, p. 439–61. In *ONE Institute Quarterly*. Vol. 5, nos. 2, 3, 4, issues 17 (Spring, Summer, Fall 1962): p. 41–54. (P. 41–46, 49-51, 54.)

Hughes, Charles H. "An Emasculated Homo-sexual. His Antecedent and Post-Operative Life," *Alienist and Neurologist*. Vol. 35 (1914): p. 277–80.

Kaye, Harvey E.; Berl, S.; Clare, J.; Eleston, M. R.; Gershwin, B. S.; Gershwin, P.; Kogan, L. S.; Torda, C.; and Wilbur, C. B. "Homosexuality in Women," *Archives of General Psychiatry*. Vol. 17 (Nov. 1967): p. 626–34. (P. 626, 632–34.)

Kiernan, James G. "Insanity. Lecture XXVI.—Perversion," *Detroit Lancet*. Vol. 7, no. 11 (May 1884): p. 481–84. (P. 483–84.)

————. "Psychical Treatment of Congenital Sexual Inversion," *Review of Insanity and Nervous Disease*. Vol. 4, no. 4 (June 1894): p. 293–95.

Klaich, Dolores. *Woman + Woman; Attitudes Toward Lesbianism*. N.Y.: Morrow, 1975, paperback. (P. 100–01.)

Liebman, Samuel. "Homosexuality, Transvestism, and Psychosis: Study of a Case Treated with Electroshock," *Journal of Nervous and Mental Disease*. Vol. 99, no. 6 (1944): p. 945–58.

LoPiccolo, Joseph. "Case Study: Systematic Desensitization of Homosexuality," *Behavior Therapy*. Vol. 2, no. 3 (July 1971): p. 394–99. (P. 396–98.)

Lydston, G. Frank. "Sexual Perversion, Satyriasis and Nymphomania," *Medical and Surgical Reporter*. Vol. 61, no. 10 (Sept. 7, 1889): p. 253–58. (P. 253.) Vol. 61, no. 11 (Sept. 14, 1889): p. 281–85. (P. 285.)

Max, Louis William. "Breaking Up a Homosexual Fixation by the Conditioned Reaction Technique: A Case Study," *Psychological Bulletin*. Vol. 32 (1935): p. 734.

Miller, Michael M. "Hypnotic-Aversion Treatment of Homosexuality," *Journal of the National Medical Association*. Vol. 55, no. 5 (1963): p. 411–15, 436. (P. 411–13, 415.)

Moore, Thomas V. "The Pathogenesis and Treatment of Homosexual Disorders: A Digest of Some Pertinent Evidence," *Journal of Personality*. Vol. 14 (1945): p. 47–83. (P. 57, 71–73.)

Owensby, Newdigate M. "The Correction of Homosexuality," *Urologic and Cutaneous Review*. Vol. 45, no. 8 (1941): p. 494–96. (P. 495, 496.)

————. "Homosexuality and Lesbianism Treated with Metrazol," *Journal of Nervous and Mental Disease*. Vol. 92, no. 1 (1940): p. 65–66.

Quackenbos, John Duncan. "Hypnotic Suggestion in the Treatment of Sexual Perversions and Moral Anaesthesia: A Personal Experience," *Transactions of the New Hampshire Medical Society*. 1899: p. 69–91. (P. 69, 72, 75, 78–80.)

Raffalovich, Marc André. "Uranism, Congenital Sexual Inversion. Observations and Recommendations . . ." Trans. C. Judson Herrick. *Journal of Comparative Neurology*. Vol. 5 (March 1895): p. 33–65. (P. 33–34, 36–37, 42, 52.)

Robertiello, Richard C. *Voyage from Lesbos: The Psychoanalysis of a Female Homosexual*. N.Y.: Citadel, 1959. (P. 238–48, 253.)

Rosenzweig, Saul, and Hoskins, R. G. "A Note on the Ineffectualness of Sex-Hormone Medication in a Case of Pronounced Homosexuality," *Psychosomatic Medicine*. Vol. 3, no. 1 (1941): p. 87–89.

Roueché, Berton. "Annals of Medicine; As Empty As Eve," *The New Yorker*. Sept. 9, 1974: p. 84–100.

Schrenck-Notzing, Albert von. *Therapeutic Suggestion in Psychopathia Sexualis with Especial Reference to Contrary Sexual Instinct*. Authorized trans. from the German by Charles Gilbert Chaddock. Phila.: F. A. Davis, 1895.

Rutner, Ivan I. "A Double-barrel Approach to Modification of Homosexual Behavior," *Psychological Reports*. Vol. 26, no. 2 (1970): p. 355–58. (P. 356–58.)

Sharp, Harry Clay. "The Sterilization of Degenerates." Indiana Board of State Charities. National Christian League for the Promotion of Purity, 1908. (P. 1–2, 6.) Reprint of paper read before the American Prison Association, Chicago, 1909. N.Y. Public Library, Research Division.

Silverstein, Charles. [Review of John Bancroft's *Deviant Sexual Behavior: Modification and Assessment*. London: Oxford University Press, 1974.] *Behavior Therapy*. Vol. 6, no. 4 (July 1975).

Smith, Alexander B., and Bassin, Alexander. "Group Therapy with Homosexuals," *Journal of Social Therapy*. Vol. 5, no. 3 (1959): p. 225–32. (P. 227, 231–32.)

Srnec, J., and Freund, Kurt. "Treatment of Male Homosexuality through Conditioning," *International Journal of Sexology*. Vol. 7, no. 2 (1953): p. 92–93.

Stekel, Wilhelm. "Is Homosexuality Curable?" Trans. Bertrand S. Frohman. *Psychoanalytic Review*. Vol. 17 (Oct. 1930): p. 443–51. (P. 443, 447–48.)

Stevenson, Edward I. Prime (Xavier Mayne, pseud.). *The Intersexes; A History of Similisexualism as a Problem in Social Life*. [Naples?:] Privately printed, [by R. Rispoli, 1908?]; photo reprint, N.Y.: Arno, 1975. (P. 119–22, 549.)

Talbot, E. S., and Ellis, Havelock. "A Case of Degenerative Insanity, with Sexual Inversion, Melancholia, following Removal of Testicles, Attempted Murder and Suicide," *Journal of Mental Science*. Vol. 42, no. 177, new ser. no. 177 (April 1896): p. 340–44 (i.e. 46—erroneous pagination in original). (P. 341–44.)

Teal, Donn. *The Gay Militants.* N.Y.: Stein and Day, 1971. (P. 293–301.)

Thompson, George N. "Electroshock and Other Therapeutic Considerations in Sexual Psycho-pathology," *Journal of Nervous and Mental Disease.* Vol. 109, no. 6 (June 1949): p. 531–39.

Zlotlow, Moses, and Paganini, Albert E. "Autoerotic and Homoerotic Manifestations in Hospitalized Male Postlobotomy Patients," *Psychiatric Quarterly.* Vol. 33, no. (1959): p. 490–97. (P. 492–97.)

NOTES

III. Passing Women: 1782–1920

1. Magnus Hirschfeld, *Die Transvestiten* . . . (Leipzig: Max Spohr 1910); Edward Carpenter, "On the Connection Between Homosexuality and Divination and the Importance of the Intermediate Sexes Generally in Early Civilizations," *American Journal of Religious Psychology and Education* (Worcester, Mass.), vol. 4 (1911), p. 228; Havelock Ellis, "Sexo-aesthetic inversion," *Alienist and Neurologist* (St. Louis, Mo.), vol. 34 (1913), p. 156–67; Havelock Ellis, "Eonism," *Medical Review of Reviews* (N.Y.), vol. 26 (1920), p. 3–12.

The OED cites a usage of "transvest" as a verb dating to 1652: "How often did she please her fancy with the imagination of transvesting herself, and by the help of a Man's disguise deceiving the eyes of those that watched her deportments?"

Hirschfeld, in the above volume, mentions several American females whose lives involved cross-dressing, cross-working, and in some cases, intimacies with other women: Frank Thompson; Loreta Velasquez from Cuba, who served in the Confederate army as a male and was involved in a love affair with a Union officer; an anonymous "girl from Brooklyn," killed in the battle of Chickamauga; Charlotte Cushman; Nicholas de Raylan; and John Wilkinson, a woman who enlisted as a sailor on the American battleship the *Vermont*, and whose sex was discovered in March 1907 while she was bathing.

2. [Herman Mann], *The Female Review: Life of Deborah Sampson, the Female Soldier in the War of the Revolution*; introduced and annotated by John Adams Vinton (Boston: J. K. Wiggin & W. P. Lunt, 1866; photo reprint, N.Y.: Arno, 1974), p. xxviii. I wish to thank Stephen W. Foster for research assistance on this document.

There are a number of similar early American women's narratives which merit investigation. One such is: Lucy Brewer West, *The Awful Beacon . . . By* [One] *Who in Disguise Served Three Years, as a Marine on Board the Frigate Constitution . . .* (Boston: Printed for N. Coverly, Jr., 1816).

3. [Herman Mann], *The Female Review: or, Memoirs of an American Young Lady, Whose Life and Character Are Peculiarly Distinguished—Being a Continental Soldier, for Nearly Three Years, in the Late American War . . .* by a Citizen of Massachusetts (Dedham, Mass.: Printed by Nathaniel and Benjamin Heaton for the author, 1797).

4. [Mann] (1866), p. 225.

5. [Mann] (1866), p. 242–43, 250.

6. NAW, vol. 3, p. 227–28 ("Sampson, Deborah").

7. Lucy Ann Lobdell, *Narrative of Lucy Ann Lobdell, the Female Hunter of Delaware and Sullivan Counties, N.Y.* (N.Y.: Published for the Authoress, 1855; copy in Rare Book Room, Library of Congress, Washington, D.C.).

8. Lobdell, p. 4.

9. Lobdell, p. 30.

10. Lobdell, p. 4–5.

11. Lobdell, p. 5–8.

12. Lobdell, p. 8–10.

13. Lobdell, p. 10, 30. Coincidentally, Alma Routsong's Lesbian novel *Patience and*

Sarah (N.Y.: McGraw-Hill, 1972) is partially set in Greene County, N.Y., and is inspired by the lives of Mary Ann Willson and a "Miss Brundidge" who lived and farmed together in that county in about 1820, some twenty years earlier than Lucy Ann Lobdell's attendance at a school in Coxsackie, in the same county. See Part V: interview with Routsong.

14. Lobdell, p. 22.
15. Lobdell, p. 15–16.
16. Lobdell, p. 16–30.
17. Lobdell, p. 30.
18. Lobdell, p. 31, 34.
19. Lobdell, p. 36–38.
20. Lobdell, p. 41–42.
21. Lobdell, p. 42–43.
22. Lobdell, p. 45.
23. Lobdell, p. 46–47.

24. Additional information about Lobdell's "wife's" background, and important details of their life together are reported by Dr. James G. Kiernan of Chicago in a medical journal article of 1884, the year following Wise's report. Referring to the mother of Lobdell's "wife," Kiernan says that she "had a neurotic ancestry, but received a fine education and was brought up in refinement. She fell in love with a young farmer, and married him much against her parents' wishes. The match proved unfortunate, she being naturally of a high spirit and of very sensitive nature and unable to help the hard-toiling farmer. He was prudent, did not give his wife the comforts of life to which she had been accustomed, and she became demonstrably insane. She finally deserted her home and was found one morning behind a pile of wood in the town of Rockland, Mass., clasping to her bosom a new-born babe. The child was taken care of by friends until the mother died. She grew up a beautiful girl, but when about 17 years old she seemed to have an inclination to wander about. She displayed a great liking for boyish games and attire, but a repugnance to suitors. She was persuaded into a marriage by a man to whom she became so repugnant that he deserted her and she sought refuge in a Pennsylvania almshouse where she met [Lucy Ann Lobdell]. . . ."

Leaving the almshouse, the two women took up life in the woods as husband and wife, Lobdell assuming the name "Joe" and providing for them by hunting and trapping. Kiernan continues: ". . . In 1876, the two returned, the wife introduced her 'husband' to her uncle. She was kindly received, and her husband was hired to work about the place.

"One day suspicion was aroused that 'Joe' was a woman in disguise, which on investigation proved to be the fact, the uncle was so indignant that he caused her arrest. She was imprisoned for four months, during which time the 'wife' visited her and carried delicacies to her. At length neighbors in the vicinity of the lawyer's home prevailed upon him to have the young woman released. When she came out of prison she lived with her 'wife' again.

"At that time the estate of the 'wife's' mother was settled, and the share that fell to her was real estate valued at several thousand dollars. This property she has not claimed, but is still in Pennsylvania, leading her curious and most remarkable life although 'Joe,' her 'husband,' is at present in the Willard asylum for the insane. She is now about 40 years old, while, 'Joe,' her curious 'husband,' is a few years her senior. . . ." Although the only source Kiernan mentions is Wise's 1883 report, Kiernan's own article contains important information not in Wise (James G. Kiernan, "Original Communications. Insanity. Lecture XXVI.—Sexual Perversion," *Detroit Lancet*, vol. 7, no. 11 [May 1884], p. 482–83).

25. P. M. Wise, "Case of Sexual Perversion," *Alienist and Neurologist* (St. Louis,

Mo.), vol. 4, no. 1 (Jan. 1883), p. 87–91. Wise's information (and asylum records stating) that Lobdell was fifty-six when she entered the Willard Asylum in Oct. 1880 means that she was born in 1824. This does not match Lobdell's own statement that she was born in 1829 (Lobdell, p. 4).

26. H. A. Gates, M.D., "Certificate of Insanity," signed Oct. 11, 1880. The other "Certificate of Insanity" is signed on the same date by John Calhoun, M.D. The "Order of Admission, No. 2680" for Lucy Ann Slater, is dated Oct. 12, 1880. The above and the doctors' logbook concerning Lucy Ann Slater (Oct. 12, 1880—March 19, 1890) are in the archives of the Willard Psychiatric Institute, Willard, N.Y.

27. An article by James G. Kiernan says that Lobdell Slater "died in the Willard Hospital for the Insane" ("Psychological Aspects of the Sexual Appetite," *Alienist and Neurologist* [St. Louis, Mo.] vol. 12 [April 1891], p. 202–03).

An unidentified, undated newspaper clipping attached to the doctors' logbook mentions Lobdell Slater's death, and her "wife." It reads:

THE HUNTERS OF LONG EDDY.

Not far from Teeple's home is the spot where Lucy Ann Lobdell Slater, the female hunter of Long Eddy, an account of whose romantic life recently appeared in the Press, lived for several years with her crazy "wife." This wife of the "female hunter" is now about forty-five years old and she still lives near here. Her hair is as white as snow, and since the death of her "female husband" she has been in poor health.

28. Lobdell, p. 15–16.

29. Lobdell, p. 29.

Three newspaper accounts of women in male attire appear in the New York *Evening Post*, Aug. 13, 1841, p. 2, col. 4; New York *Herald*, Aug. 13, 1845, p. 2, col. 3; New York *Daily Tribune*, Oct. 31, 1854, p. 7. The last tells the story of Lydia Ann Puyfer, age thirty-five, from Gowanus, Brooklyn, bound for California in her cousin's clothes. I wish to thank Charles Lockwood for these references, found in the course of his research on New York City history.

30. "A Curious Married Couple," *Fincher's Trades' Review* (Phila.), vol. 1, no. 8 (July 25, 1863), p. 29, col. 6. *Fincher's* is on microfilm; copy consulted: N.Y. University Tamiment Library. I wish to thank Carole Turbin Miller for informing me of these references.

31. "Another Female Soldier," *Fincher's*, vol. 1, no. 12 (Aug. 22, 1863), p. 46, col. 5; "Eventful History of a Soldier Woman," *Fincher's*, vol. 1, no. 19 (Oct. 10, 1863), p. 74, col. 6; "A Female Warrior," *Fincher's*, vol. 1, no. 25 (Nov. 21, 1863), p. 100, col. 3. The last two stories concern a married woman who accompanied her soldier-husband. See also "A Gallant Female Soldier—Romantic History," *Fincher's*, vol. 2, no. 17 (March 26, 1864), p. 67, col. 5 (about Frances Hook/Frank Miller, a "new protege" of Dr. Mary Walker). Two other stories of interest: "A Woman Marries A Woman," *Fincher's*, vol. 2 (April 9, 1864), p. 75, col. 6 (this story, whose source is the Green Bay, Wis., *Advocate* [n.d.], reports the arrest "in this city last week," on complaint from Manitowoc, of a woman who "had married a woman in that place, taken her money and decamped"); "A Woman-Husband," *Fincher's*, vol. 2, no. 25 (May 21, 1864), p. 100, col. 2 (includes a brief report of an eighteenth-century English case of female transvestism, involving an attempted love affair and embezzlement; it also includes a condensed version of the Mary East story, indicating that its source is an article in the *Gentleman's Magazine* [1776]).

According to the biography, *She Rode with the Generals* (N.Y.: Nelson, 1960), by Sylvia G. L. Dannett, the life of Sarah Emma Evelyn Edmonds involves transvestism and several "Lesbian" relationships (p. 34, 43–44, 48, 230). Edmonds's cross-working and cross-dressing began as a child (p. 21–26). A novel by M. M. Ballou, *Fanny Camp-*

bell, or The Female Pirate Captain . . . encouraged Edmonds to embark on an adventurous life (p. 24–25). At age fifteen she began to pass as Franklin Thompson, became a successful Bible salesman, and says she took her "lady friends out riding occasionally" (p. 34; quote from Edmonds). Edmonds says she was sent to Nova Scotia by Hurlbut and Company as a book salesman, and "came near marrying a pretty little girl . . ." (p. 43; quote from Edmonds). She moved to Flint, Mich., where, Dannett says, Edmonds "became quite a lady's man" (p. 48). In May 1861, when she was almost twenty and had passed as a man for nearly five years, she joined the army as a male nurse. She is said to have had a close friendship with "Kate B.," and, possibly, a Lesbian relationship with a nurse, Alice M. (or "Nellie," p. 175). Her military career involved activity as a spy, "posing" as a *female*. Edmonds became the only female war hero allowed to belong to the Grand Army of the Republic. She married late in life and had several children. Edmonds always continued to wear men's boots. See Lennox Strong, "To be a Man; The Story of 'Franklin Thompson'," *The Ladder*, vol. 8, no. 1 (Oct. 1963), p. 7–9. See also Edmonds's autobiography: *Nurse and Spy in the Union Army; Comprising the Adventures and Experience of a Woman in Hospitals, Camps and Battlefields* (Hartford, Conn.: W. S. Williams, 1865). Edmonds is also mentioned in Hirschfeld's *Die Transvestiten* (1910). Dannett cites other American female transvestites: Mary Hollingsworth, a Southerner, who traveled to the old West where "she became engaged to a girl" whom she jilted at the altar, and who, in turn, sued Hollingsworth, and won (p. 43); Barbara Ann Malpass, a contemporary transvestite (p. 44–45); 400 women who are said to have fought, dressed as men, in the Civil War (p. 51; the source is George Washington Adams, *Doctors in Blue; The Medical History of the Union Army* . . . [N.Y., 1952]; a suicide reported in the Louisville, Ky. *Daily Democrat*, April 16, 1863 (p. 230). An unidentified clipping (reproduced p. 160) cites female transvestites in the Civil War; the source is William F. Fox, *Regimental Losses in the American Civil War* (Albany, 1889). I wish to thank Stephen W. Foster and James Foshee for assistance with this research.

32. Philip H. Sheridan, *Personal Memoirs of Philip Henry Sheridan, General, United States Army*, 2 vols. (N.Y.: C. L. Webster, 1888), vol. 1, p. 253–55. I wish to thank Wilbur Miller for informing me of this document.

33. "Aberrations of the Sexual Instinct," *Medical Times and Gazette* (London), vol. 1 (Feb. 9, 1867), p. 142.

There is a female transvestite episode in an American novel first published in 1867, Dr. Oliver Wendell Holmes's *The Guardian Angel*. According to Jeannette H. Foster, the heroine, Myrtle Hazzard resists the efforts of two puritanical aunts to break her spirit, and at age fifteen, mature in mind and body, cuts her hair short and puts on boy's clothes, setting out for India where she had spent a happy childhood. The story, says Foster, contains no hint of any particularly intense emotional intimacy between Myrtle Hazzard and another female. That Holmes was aware of passionate attachments between women is, however, indicated in *The Guardian Angel* by a secondary female character's extremely passionate attachment to her mother (*Sex Variant Women in Literature* [N.Y.: Vantage, 1956], p. 92–93).

An episode of female transvestism, also excluding any special intimacy with other females, is reported in a New York City newspaper in 1869: "Kate Fisher, Adventures of a Girl in Male Attire," *New York World*, Jan. 12, 1869, p. 4. I wish to thank Carole Turbin Miller for informing me of this document.

34. "Aberrations," p. 143.

35. "Aberrations," p. 144.

36. "Aberrations," p. 144.

37. "Aberrations," p. 145.

38. "Aberrations," p. 145–46.

39. "Aberrations," p. 146. All the following quotations are from the same page.

40. Ironically, there is evidence suggesting that Bayard Taylor was homosexual (see J. Z. Eglinton, pseud., *Greek Love* [N.Y.: Oliver Layton, 1964], p. 364–66).

41. Ellen Coit Brown, "Yesterday," *Cornell Alumni News* (Ithaca, N.Y.), Feb. 1973, p. 27–29. I wish to thank Robert Joyce, Jr. for informing me of this document.

Other examples of passing women of this period are reported by Dr. James G. Kiernan: "The elopement of a married woman of Brandon, Wisconsin, with a young girl in 1883, led to a discovery of a similar case [involving a female–female couple]. The couple were 'married' by a minister and set up in life for themselves. A recent incarceration of a burglar in the Madison, Iowa, penitentiary, led to the revelation of a like case. The allegations which so often appear in divorce cases that a certain woman has alienated the wife's affections are an indication that cases of this type are far from infrequent" ("Sexual Perversion and the Whitechapel Murders," *Medical Standard* [Chicago], vol. 4, no. 4 [Dec. 1888], p. 171).

Dr. Kiernan also reports a case "which occurred in Belvidere, Ill., in 1883 . . ." A woman "deserted her husband (with whom sexual incompatibility existed) and abandoned her children. She donned masculine attire and obtained masculine work. While thus employed she won the affections of a young girl whom she married with the consent of her parents. Six months later the woman's husband discovered that his wife and her 'wife' were living in Waupun, Wis., in the apparent enjoyment of 'matrimonial felicity.' The husband separated his wife from her 'wife'. The sexual pervert had an enlarged clitoris two and one-half inches when erect. The girl's parents took her back but she frequently visited her late matrimonial companion, apparently with the full consent of the husband" ("Responsibility in Sexual Perversion," *Chicago Medical Recorder*, vol. 3 [May 1892], p. 208–09).

Gordon Rattray Taylor reports that the autobiography of Charlotte Clark (Mrs. C. O. Van Cleve) entitled *Three-score Years and Ten* (Minneapolis: Harrison and Smith, 1888) records how on various occasions she dressed as a man. This theme of female transvestism, says Taylor, was popular in the novels of the period ("Historical and Mythological Aspects of Homosexuality," in Judd Marmor, ed., *Sexual Inversion; The Multiple Roots of Homosexuality* [N.Y.: Basic Books, 1965] p. 161, 163).

42. "Anna Morris Given One Year," *Badger State Banner* (Black River Falls, Wis.), Jan. 18, 1894, p. 3, col. 6. I wish to thank the State Historical Society of Wisconsin for a copy of this document. This document is quoted in part by Michael Lesy in *Wisconsin Death Trip* (N.Y.: Pantheon, 1973), no pagination.

43. Havelock Ellis, *Studies in the Psychology of Sex; Sexual Inversion* (Phila.: F. A. Davis, 1901), p. 142.

44. Marian West, "Women Who Have Passed as Men," *Munzey's Magazine* (N.Y.), vol. 25 (1901), p 280; *Jahrbuch für sexuelle Zwischenstufen* . . . (Leipzig), vol. 3 (1901), p. 583. Also see p. 585–86 same volume, and p. 1186, vol. 5, part 2 (1903).

45. *New York Times*, Jan. 19, 1901, p. 2, col. 3. The previous day's *Times* carried the paper's first story on Hall ("Woman Long Posed As Man," Jan. 18, 1901, col. 2, p. 3.)

46. New York *Daily Tribune*, Jan. 20, 1901, p. 6, col. 2. A story on Hall also appeared in the *Tribune* on Jan. 24, 1901, p. 6, col. 2.

47. New York *Daily Trubune*, Jan. 29, 1901, p. 2, col. 3.

48. New York *Daily Tribune*, March 20, 1901, p. 7, col. 5. A final story on Hall appeared in the *Tribune* on March 28, 1901, p. 5, col. 6. I could not find a story which the *Times* index lists as appearing on March 29, 1901, p. 16, col. 3.

49. West, p. 273.

50. West, p. 274.

51. West, p. 274–76.

52. West, p. 277–79. West refers throughout to "Christian Davis." The correct spelling is Davies. The autobiographies of Davies, Mary Anne Talbot, Hannah Snell, and Loreta Janeta Velasquez are reprinted in *Women Adventurers*, ed. by Ménie Muriel Dowie (London: Unwin, 1893).

53. *New York Times*, Oct. 1, 1901, p. 1, col. 3. "Carolina" Hall corrected to "Caroline."

54. *New York Times*, Oct. 2, 1901, p. 10, col. 2.

55. R. W. Shufeldt, "Dr. Havelock Ellis on Sexual Inversion," *Pacific Medical Journal* (San Francisco), vol. 45 (1902), p. 201. Biographical information on Walker is in Charles McCool Snyder, *Dr. Mary Walker: The Little Lady in Pants* (N.Y.: Vantage, 1962; photo reprint, N.Y.: Arno, 1974). A summary of Walker's life is in NAW, vol. 3.

56. Mary Edwards Walker, *Hit* (N.Y.: American News Co., 1871), three first dedication pages, unpaginated.

57. Walker, *Hit*, p. 22, 38–39, 136–38, 150–53, 156.

58. Mary Edwards Walker, *Unmasked, or The Science of Immortality. To Gentlemen. By a Woman Physician and Surgeon* (Phila.: W. H. Boyd, 1878), p. 14, 107–10, 114–16, 118, 145. A later edition gives the subtitle as *The Science of Immorality* (Jersey City: Walker, 1888).

59. "Marriages Between Women," *Alienist and Neurologist* (St. Louis, Mo.), vol. 23, no. 4 (Nov. 1902), p. 497–99.

60. Edward I. Prime Stevenson (Xavier Mayne, pseud.), *The Intersexes; A History of Similisexualism as a Problem in Social Life* ([Naples?]. Privately printed [by R. Rispoli, 1908?]; photo reprint, N.Y.: Arno, 1975), p. 149–50.

Female transvestites who took up life in the American West are cited by Reggie Sigal in "The Old West," *Women; A Journal of Liberation*, vol. 1, no. 3 (Spring 1970), p. 52. One is Charlie Parkhurst, a famous stagecoach driver. The other is Joe Monahan, of Succor Creek, Idaho, whose sex was discovered when she died in Dec. 1903. Sigal's source is Vardis Fisher and Opal L. Holmes, *Gold Rushes and Mining Camps of the Early American West* (Caldwell, Idaho: Caxton Printers, 1968). I wish to thank Elizabeth Amada for this information. Additional information on Charlie Parkhurst in Mary Chaney Hoffman, "Whips of the Old West," *American Mercury*, vol. 84 (April 1957), p. 107–10.

61. Havelock Ellis, *Studies in the Psychology of Sex*, 4 vols. (N.Y.: Random House, 1936), vol. 2, part 2, *Sexual Inversion*, "3rd ed." (1915), p. 248.

62. Eugene de Savitsch, *Homosexuality, Transvestism, and Change of Sex* (Springfield, Ill.: Charles C. Thomas, 1958), p. 6–7. Savitsch cites his source as H. H. Young, *Genital Abnormalities, Hermaphroditism and Related Adrenal Diseases* (Baltimore Md.: Williams and Wilkins, 1937), but I find no mention of Nicholas de Raylan in this book.

The problem of the reliability of these early reports of Lesbian transvestism is raised by the following case cited by Havelock Ellis: "In New York in 1905 a retired sailor, 'Captain John Weed,' who had commanded transatlantic vessels for many years, was admitted to a Home for old sailors and shortly after became ill and despondent, and cut his throat. It was then found that 'Captain Weed' was really a woman. I am informed that the old sailor's despondency and suicide were due to enforced separation from a female companion" (Ellis [1936], p. 202).

The New York *Daily Tribune* in three December issues of 1905 carries news items concerning the death of a textile merchant named John Weed, said to have been caused by "a broken heart" after a dispute with a brother and co-partner, H. Frank Weed, who had the month before committed suicide. There is absolutely no indication in any of these printed news reports that either of the Weed brothers might have been a woman in disguise, and the details of John Weed's life do *not* match the details of the life of the

"Captain John Weed" cited by Ellis. It is possible that Ellis's informant had access to information about an individual whose name and history somehow became confused with that of the John Weed who died in December, 1905 (New York *Daily Tribune*, Dec. 21, 1905, p. 12, col. 3; Dec. 22, 1905, p. 14, col. 1; Dec. 30, 1905, p. 7, col. 5). Ellis's case of "Captain John Weed" illustrates the importance of substantiating evidence.

Another case of 1905 cited by Havelock Ellis follows: "Ellen Glenn, *alias* Ellis Glenn, a notorious swindler, who came prominently before the public in Chicago during 1905, was another 'man-woman,' of large and masculine type. She preferred to dress as a man and had many love escapades with women. 'She can fiddle as well as anyone in the State,' said a man who knew her, 'can box like a pugilist, and can dance and play cards'" (Ellis [1936], p. 242). Unfortunately, Ellis cites no sources, and no further information has been found on Ellen Glenn.

63. Stevenson, p. 148–49. Stevenson also describes in some detail the case of a "Mr. L. Z." or "Mrs. X." of Boston, a history reported to him by a Chicago physician. This doctor claims that the individual in question, while seeming to be of the female gender, exhibited some signs of physical hermaphroditism, which however, the individual had "no clear ideas" about until "well into adult life" (p. 140–44).

Stevenson also reports: "The second officer of an American ship, personally known to a friend of the writer of this study, is a woman. . . ." (p. 254).

64. Ellis (1936), p. 248–49.

Bram Stoker's *Famous Imposters* (N.Y.: Sturgis and Walton, 1910) contains a chapter on female transvestites titled "Women As Men." Although female–female intimacy characterizes some of the lives described, Stoker emphasizes the heterosexual aspects of most of the life histories discussed. His interpretation of female cross-dressing combines a mild feminism and a totally traditional notion of women (see espec. p. 227–28, 230, 236–39 [on the original *La Maupin*], 241–46 [on Mary East/James Howe]). Stoker's own sexual orientation merits investigation. In the early 1870s, Stoker was one of those young men who wrote what a conservative "expert" on Walt Whitman calls "semi-love letters" to the American poet (Gay Wilson Allen, *Solitary Singer* [N.Y.: N. Y. University, 1955], p. 467, 516). In 1878, the Irish-born Stoker became the manager and traveling companion of the famous English actor Henry Irving, a post Stoker occupied for twenty-seven years, until Irving's death. In 1884, Stoker and Irving visited Whitman. Stoker is now best known as author of *Dracula*, a work not without sexual undertones meriting analysis. See Stoker's brief biography in *Twentieth Century Authors* (1942), p. 1351.

65. Idah McGlone Gibson, "Amazing Double Life of Girl Who Lived for Years as a Man," datelined Milwaukee, Wis., May 13, in *The Day Book* (Chicago), vol. 3, no. 192 (May 13, 1914), no pagination; Idah McGlone Gibson, "Cora Anderson was a Good Man to Both Her Wives—How She Fooled Second One," datelined Milwaukee, Wis., May 14, in same, vol. 3, no. 193 (May 14, 1914), no pagination. Copies of the *Day Book* are in the Northwestern University Library. A copy of the marriage certificate of "Rolphero E. Kerwinies" and "Dorothy Kleinowski," dated March 24, 1914, was obtained from the Office of the Register of Deeds, Milwaukee Co., Wis. (It is in vol. 243, p. 120 of the Registration of Marriages.) The place of marriage was the City of Milwaukee; the person officiating was Edward J. Burke; the witnesses were Sophia Edwards and W. S. Edwards. Kerwinies's "Color or Race" is listed as "D[ark];" age at last birthday: 28; birthplace: So. America; occupation: clerk; name of father: Jervies Kerwinies; birthplace of father: So. America; maiden name of mother: Frances Hearst; birthplace of mother: So. America. Kleinowski's "Color or Race" is white; age at last birthday: 21; birthplace: Wis.; occupation: none listed: name of father: Michael Kleinowski; birthplace of father: Poland; maiden name of mother: Martha Speparski; birthplace of mother: Poland.

66. Cora Anderson, "Man-Woman Says Man Out In the World is a Hunter of Women," *Day Book*, vol. 3, no. 194 (May 15, 1914), no pagination.

67. Cora Anderson, "Will A Man Kiss and Not Tell?—No, Says Cora Anderson, The Man-Woman," *Day Book*, vol. 3, no. 195 (May 16, 1914), no pagination. The photos are from issues 192, 193, 194.

68. The deleted section summarizes the periods of "H's" life, and relates her grandparents', father's, and mother's histories.

69. In a sentence deleted from an earlier section (original publication, p. 317), Dr. Gilbert says of "H": "In August [1918] she underwent a complete physical examination, with subsequent laparotomy in which the uterus was removed. After the operation she assumed male attire." The excision of the uterus is now generally referred to as a hysterectomy. An oöphorectomy involves ovary removal, and hormonal effects, an even more radical operation.

70. J. Allen Gilbert, "Homosexuality and its Treatment," *Journal of Nervous and Mental Disease* (Lancaster, Pa.), vol. 52, no. 4 (Oct. 1920), p. 297–322.

71. The former Albany College is now Lewis and Clark University, Portland, Ore. *The Takenah*, the Albany College yearbook (Albany, Ore.: Albany College, 1911), includes three photographs and several written references to Lucille Hart. A brief description of Hart and two photos, one as a member of the junior class, the other a baby picture (both reproduced here), are on p. 18–19 of the *Takenah*. A description of the junior class (p. 20) says that it had dwindled from seventeen "Freshmen" to three "Juniors," all women: "[Lucille] Hart, [Eva] Cushman, [Katherine] Stuart." These women include "the most graceful dancer, the most expert mandolinist, and the finest soprano soloist in the college." Hart is said to preside over all the class meetings. "They have also decided—as a part of their duty to the world and the rising generation—to discard all rats and artificial puffs, and to adopt the dress-reform style of clothing. They have not yet worn their new costumes in public, though they contemplate doing so soon." P. 51 presents a photograph of the "Editorial Staff" of *The Takenah* (reproduced), including Lucille Hart and Eva Cushman.

Dr. Gilbert's report mentions that "H" was active at Albany College as an oratorical debator, a manager of the "College Annual," and as a leader of the Women's Mandolin Club. Dr. Gilbert's report describes "H's" sexual-affectional liaison at Albany College with a young woman "classmate" whose initials are given as "E.C." This is probably the Eva Cushman whose pictures and description appear in *The Takenah* (p. 18–19, 20, 51).

A letter to J.K. from the Stanford University registrar's office dated Dec. 3, 1975, verifies that Alberta Lucille Hart was born on Oct. 4, but not in 1892. She was in attendance at Stanford University during the first and second semesters of the academic year 1911–12.

The *Leland Stanford Junior University: Twenty-first Annual Register; 1911–12* ([Stanford], Calif.: Published by the University, 1912, p. 26) lists Alberta Lucille Hart, from Albany, Ore., as registered for Physiology 66, and living at 2 Roble (a dormitory).

"Summer School Students, 1916," *Stanford University. Department of Medicine. Annual Announcements for 1917–18*, p. 98 lists "Hart, A. Lucille, Actinography, Clinical Medicine, Portland, Ore."

The Stanford University registrar's office verified information obtained elsewhere, but did not give out additional data.

72. Vita Sackville-West's diary of 1920–21 records both her cross-dressing and her Lesbian relations with Violet Trefusis and others—readily lending itself to a feminist interpretation (Nigel Nicholson, *Portrait of a Marriage* [N.Y.: Bantam, 1973], p. 11, 107–08, 111, 114–16, 121, 141, 154, 164–65, 177).

A scrapbook, apparently kept by a Lesbian in the 1920s and 1930s, is in the collection of the Institute for Sex Research, Bloomington, Ind. It includes numbers of newspaper clippings concerning women wearing pants and reported episodes of transvestism.

Bibliography

III. PASSING WOMEN: 1782–1920

References to particular female transvestites are listed here under the individual's name.

"Aberrations of the Sexual Instinct," *Medical Times and Gazette* (London). Vol. 1, (Feb. 9, 1867): p. 141–46.

[Anderson, Cora.] Gibson, Idah McGlone, "Amazing Double Life of Girl Who Lived For Years As A Man." Dateline: Milwaukee, Wis., May 13. *The Day Book* (Chicago). Vol. 3, no. 192 (May 13, 1914): no pagination.

[Anderson, Cora.] Gibson, Idah McGlone. "Cora Anderson Was A Good Man To Both Her Wives—How She Fooled Second One." Dateline: Milwaukee, Wis., May 14. *Day Book*. Vol. 3, no. 193 (May 14, 1914): no pagination.

Anderson, Cora. "Man-Woman Says Man Out in the World Is A Hunter of Women." *Day Book*. Vol. 3, no. 194 (May 15, 1914): no pagination.

Anderson, Cora. "Will A Man Kiss And Not Tell?—No, Says Cora Anderson, The Man-Woman," *Day Book*. Vol. 3, no. 195 (May 16, 1914): no pagination.

Barahal, Hyman S. "Female Transvestism and Homosexuality," *Psychiatric Quarterly*. Vol. 27, no. 3 (1953): p. 390–438.

[Barry, James Miranda.] Clark, Ida Clyde. "First Woman Doctor," *Literary Digest*. Vol. 124, no. 23 (Aug. 7, 1937).

[Barry, James Miranda.] Niven, Vern. "The First Woman Doctor in Britain: Dr. James Barry," *The Ladder*. Vol. 8, no. 6 (March 1964): cover, p. 4–6.

[Barry, James Miranda.] Rae, Isobel. *The Strange Story of Dr. Barry*. London: Longmans Green, 1958.

[Brooks, Romaine.] Whitworth, Sarah. "Journeys in Art; Romaine Brooks—Portraits of an Epoch." *The Ladder*. Vol. 16, nos. 1–2 (Oct.–Nov. 1971): cover, p. 38–45.

Brown, Ellen Coit. "Yesterday," *Cornell Alumni News* (Ithaca, N.Y.). Feb. 1973, p. 27–29.

C., A. (N.Y.) [letter]. *The Ladder*. Vol. 1, no. 10 (July 1957): p. 27–28.

Carpenter, Edward. "On the Connection Between Homosexuality and Divination and the Importance of the Intermediate Sexes Generally in Early Civilizations," *American Journal of Religious Psychology and Education* (Worcester, Mass). Vol. 4 (1911): p. 219–43.

[Christina, Queen.] Goldsmith, Margaret. *Christina of Sweden*. N.Y.: Doubleday, 1933. (See espec. chap. 5.)

[Christina, Queen.] Grier, Barbara [Gene Damon, pseud.], and Stuart, Lee. "The Tragedy of Queen Christina," *The Ladder*. Vol. 7, no. 9 (June 1963): p. 6–8.

Edmonds, S[arah] Emma E[velyn.] *Nurse and Spy in the Union Army; Comprising the Adventures and Experiences of a Woman in Hospitals, Camps and Battlefields*. Hartford, Conn.: W. S. Williams, 1865.

[Edmonds, Sarah Emma.] Strong, Lennox. "To a Man . . . The Story of 'Franklin Thompson' [Sarah Emma Evelyn Edmonds]," *The Ladder*. Vol. 8, no. 1 (Oct. 1963): p. 7–9.

Ellis, Havelock. "Eonism," *Medical Review of Reviews* (N.Y.). Vol. 26 (1920): p. 3–12.

————. *Eonism and Other Supplementary Studies*. Phila.: F. A. Davis, 1928.

————. "Sexo-aesthetic inversion," *Alienist and Neurologist* (St. Louis, Mo.). Vol. 34 (1913): p. 156–67.

————. *Studies in the Psychology of Sex; Sexual Inversion*. "2nd ed." Phila.: F. A. Davis, 1901. (Female cross-dressing: p. 140–43; Lucy Ann Lobdell Slater: p. 141; Murray Hall: p. 142.)

————. *Studies in the Psychology of Sex*. 4 vols. N.Y.: Random House, 1936. Vol. 2, part 2, *Sexual Inversion*. "3rd ed." (1915). (Female transvestism: p. 244–51; Captain John Weed: p. 202; Lucy Ann [Lobdell] Slater: p. 246; Murray Hall: p. 246–47; Caroline Hall: p. 247; Ellen

Glenn: p. 247; Nicholai de Raylan: p. 248; "Bill": p. 248–49; Cora Anderson: p. 249; [Marriages Between Women]: p. 249–50.)

Fenichel, Otto. "The Psychology of Transvestitism." In *The Collected Papers of Otto Fenichel: First Series.* N.Y.: Norton, 1953. (P. 167–80.)

Fincher's Trades' Review; An Advocate of the Rights of the Producing Classes (Phila.).

"A Curious Married Couple." Vol. 1, no. 8 (July 25, 1963): p. 20, col. 6.

"Another Female Soldier." Vol. 1, no. 12 (Aug. 22, 1863): p. 46, col. 5.

"Eventful History of a Soldier Woman." Vol. 1, no. 19 (Oct. 10, 1863): p. 100, col. 3.

"A Gallant Female Soldier—Romantic History." Vol. 2, no. 17 (March 26, 1864): p. 67, col. 5.

"A Woman Marries A Woman." Vol. 2 (April 9, 1864), p. 75, col. 6.

"A Woman-Husband." Vol. 2, no. 25 (May 21, 1964): p. 100, col. 2.

[Fisher, Kate.] "Kate Fisher. Adventure of a Girl in Male Attire," N.Y. *World*, Jan. 12, 1869: p. 4.

"From Over the Sea" (letter), *The Ladder.* Vol. 2, no. 9 (June 1958): p. 5.

Gautier, Théophile. *Mademoiselle de Maupin; A Romance of Love and Passion; Illustrated . . . from designs by Toudouze.* Chicago: Laird and Lee, 1890. (Also later English editions.)

Gilbert, J. Allen. (See [Hart, Alberta Lucille].)

Gilbert, Oscar Paul. *Women in Men's Guise.* Trans. by J. Lewis May. London: John Lane, 1932.

Grier, Barbara [Gene Damon, pseud.], and Stuart, Lee. "Transvestism in Women," *The Ladder.* Vol. 3, no. 5 (Feb. 1959): p. 11–13.

[Hall, Caroline/Charles.] *New York Times.* "Boston Woman Posed As Man With A Wife," Oct. 1, 1901: p. 1, col. 3; " 'Mr.' Hall's Father," Oct. 2, 1901: p. 10, col. 2.

[Hall, Murray.] *New York Times.* "Woman Long Posed As Man," Jan. 18, 1901: p. 2, col. 3. "Murray Hall Fooled Many Shrewd Men," Jan. 19, 1901: p. 2, col. 3.

New York Daily Tribune. "Death Revealed Her Sex," Jan. 18, 1901: p. 1, col. 4.

"Mystery of Murray Hall," Jan. 19, 1901: p. 5, col. 1.

" 'Murray Hall' Funeral A Mystery," Jan. 20, 1901: p. 6, col. 2.

"A Letter from Murray Hall," Jan. 24, 1901, p. 7, col. 5.

"Murray Hall Inquest Closed," Jan. 29, 1901, p. 2, col. 3.

"Murray Hall's Will Filed," March 20, 1901, p. 7, col. 5.

"City Sues Murray Hall Estate," March 29, 1901, p. 5, col. 6.

"Here and There" ["David Reginald Van Rippy," bigamist, Grady, Arkansas, Cummins Prison Farm], *The Ladder.* Vol. 6, no. 6 (March 1962): p. 23.

"Here and There" ["Gary Johnson," burglar, Ohio Penitentiary], *The Ladder.* Vol. 6 no. 3 (Dec. 1961): p. 13.

[Hart, (Alberta) Lucille.] *The Takenah.* Albany, Ore.: Albany College, 1911. (References and photos of Hart: p. 18–19, 20, 51.)

[Hart, Alberta Lucille.] Gilbert, J. Allen. "Homosexuality and its Treatment." *Journal of Nervous and Mental Disease* (Lancaster, Pa.). Vol. 52, no. 4 (Oct. 1920): p. 297–322.

[Hart, Alberta Lucille.] *Leland Stanford Junior University: Twenty-first Annual Register; 1911–12.* [Stanford], Calif.; Published by the University, 1912. (Hart: p. 261.)

"Summer School Students, 1916," *Stanford University. Department of Medicine. Annual Announcements for 1917–18.* (Hart: p. 98.)

Hirschfeld, Magnus. *Die Transvestiten; eine Untersuchung über den erotischen Verkleidungsstrieb mit umfangreichem casuistischen und historischen Material* ("Transvestites; Research into the Erotic Disguise-urge, with Exhaustive Casuistics and Historical Material"). Leipzig: Max Spohr, 1910. (P. 539–43, 550.)

Holmes, Oliver Wendell. *The Guardian Angel.* Boston: Ticknor and Fields, 1867.

Kiernan, James G. (see [Lobdell Slater, Lucy Ann]).

Lesbian scrapbook. Collection of the Institute for Sex Research. (A scrapbook, apparently kept by a Lesbian in the 1920s and 1930s, including newspaper clippings, advertisements, etc., on female transvestites.)

Liechti, Robert. "Male Impersonations on the Stage; A Brief Survey of Its Past." Part 1. *The Ladder.* Vol. 7, no. 5 (Feb. 1963): p. 17–21. Part 2. *The Ladder.* Vol. 7, no. 6 (March 1963): p. 12–15.

————. (letter) *The Ladder*. Vol. 7, no. 8 (May 1963): p. 25.

Lobdell, Lucy Ann. *Narrative of Lucy Ann Lobdell, the Female Hunter of Delaware and Sullivan Counties, N.Y.* N.Y.: Published for the Authoress, 1855. Rare Book Room, Library of Congress, Washington, D.C.

[Lobdell Slater, Lucy Ann.] Kiernan, James G. "Original Communications. Insanity. Lecture XXVI.—Sexual Perversion." *Detroit Lancet*. Vol. 7, no. 11 (May 1884): p. 481–84. (Lobdell Slater: p. 482–83.)

————. "Psychological Aspects of the Sexual Appetite," *Alienist and Neurologist* (St. Louis, Mo.). Vol. 12 (April 1891): p. 188–217. (Lobdell Slater: p. 202–03.)

[Lobdell Slater, Lucy Ann.] Willard Psychiatric Institute, Willard, N.Y. Archives.
Calhoun, John. "Certificate of Insanity," Oct. 11, 1880.
Gates, H. A. "Certificate of Insanity," Oct. 11, 1880.
Doctors' Log Book: Lucy Ann Slater, Oct. 12, 1880—March 19, 1890.
"Order of Admission, No. 2680." Lucy Ann Slater. Oct. 12, 1880.

[Lobdell Slater, Lucy Ann.] Wise, P. M. "Case of Sexual Perversion," *Alienist and Neurologist* (St. Louis, Mo.). Vol. 4, no. 1 (Jan. 1883): p. 87–91.

Lyle, Dorothy. "Masquerade," *The Ladder*. Vol. 14, nos. 7–8 (April–May 1970): p. 19–22.

McMurtrie, Douglas C. "Notes on the Psychology of Sex, Sexo-esthetic Inversion," *American Journal of Urology* (N.Y.). Vol. 10 (1914): p. 91–100.

"Marriages Between Women," *Alienist and Neurologist* (St. Louis, Mo.). Vol. 23, no. 4 (Nov. 1902): p. 497–99.

[Morris, Anna.] "Anna Morris Given One Year," *Badger State Banner* (Black River Falls, Wis.). Jan. 18, 1894: p. 3, col. 6.

Philippopoulos, G. S. "A Case of Transvestism in a 17-Year-Old Girl," *Acta Psychotherapeutica et Psychosomatica*. Vol. 12, no. 1 (1964): p. 29–37.

[Raylan, Nicholai de.] Savitsch, Eugene de. *Homosexuality, Transvestism, and Change of Sex.* Springfield, Ill: Charles C. Thomas, 1958. (P. 6–7.) Also see Ellis (1936), p. 248.

Routsong, Alma (Isabel Miller, pseud.) *Patience and Sarah.* Greenwich, Conn.: Fawcett Crest, 1973. Paperback. (P. 56–85.)

Rubinstein, L. H. "The Role of Identification in Homosexuality and Transvestitism in Men and Women." In *The Pathology and Treatment of Sexual Deviation: A Methodological Approach.* Ed. Ismond Rosen, p. 163–95. London: Oxford University, 1964.

S., B. (San Leandro) (letter.) *The Ladder*. Vol. 1, no. 10 (July 1957): p. 28–29.

[Sackville-West, Vita.] Nicholson, Nigel. *Portrait of a Marriage.* N.Y.: Bantam, 1973. (Cross-dressing: p. 11, 107–08, 111, 114–16, 121, 141, 164–65, 177.)

[Sampson Gannett, Deborah.] [Mann, Herman.] *The Female Review: Life of Deborah Sampson, the Female Soldier in the War of the Revolution.* Introduced and annotated by John Adams Vinton. Boston: J. K. Wiggin & W. P. Lunt, 1866. Photo reprint, N.Y.: Arno, 1975.

[Sampson Gannett, Deborah.] [————.] *The Female Review: or, Memoirs of an Young Lady, Whose Life and Character Are Peculiarly Distinguished—Being a Continental Soldier, for Nearly Three Years, in the Late American War . . . By A Citizen of Massachusetts.* Dedham, Mass.: Printed by Nathaniel and Benjamin Heaton for the author, 1797.

Savitsch, Eugene de. (See [Raylan, Nicholai de.])

Segal, Morey M. "Transvestitism as an Impulse and as a Defence," *International Journal of Psycho-Analysis*. Vol. 46, no. 2 (1965): p. 209–17.

Sheridan, Philip H. *Personal Memoirs of Philip Henry Sheridan, General, United States Army*, 2 vols. N.Y.: C. L. Webster, 1888. (Vol. 1, p. 253–55 on two "amazons" in Union army.)

Simon, Robert I. "A Case of Female Transsexualism," *American Journal of Psychiatry*. Vol. 123, no. 12 (1967): p. 1598–1601.

Smith, Rosanne. "Women Who Wanted to be Men," *Coronet*, Sept. 1957.

Stephens, Barbara. "Transvestism—A Cross-Cultural Survey," *The Ladder*. Vol. 1, no. 9 (June 1957): p. 10–14.

Stoker, Bram. *Famous Imposters.* N.Y.: Sturgis and Walton, 1910. (Chap. VII, "Women As Men": p. 227–46.)

Stoller, Robert J. *Sex and Gender; on the Development of Masculinity and Femininity.* N.Y.: Science House, 1968.

Talmey, Bernard S. "Transvestism, A Contribution to the Study of the Psychology of Sex," *New York Medical Journal*. Vol. 99 (Feb. 21, 1914).

Thompson, C. J. S. *The Mysteries of Sex; Women Who Posed as Men and Men Who Impersonated Women.* N.Y.: Causeway, 1974.

Walker, Mary Edwards. *Hit.* N.Y.: American News Co., 1871. (Also published as *A Woman's Thought About Love And Marriage, Divorce . . .*)

———. *Unmasked, or The Science of Immortality. To Gentlemen. By a Woman Physician and Surgeon.* Phila.: W. H. Boyd, 1878.

A later edition: *Unmasked, or The Science of Immorality . . . .* Jersey City: Walker, 1888.

[Walker, Mary Edwards.] Snyder, Charles McCool. *Mary Walker: The Little Lady in Pants.* N.Y.: Vantage, 1962; photo reprint, N.Y.: Arno, 1974.

West, Marian. "Women Who Have Passed as Men. A Curious Phase of the Problem of Sex. Historical Instances of Women Who Have Fought Their Way Through the World in Masculine Disguise," *Munzey's Magazine* (N.Y.) Vol. 25 (1901): p. 273–81.

[Women in male attire: 1841–54.]

New York *Evening Post*, Aug. 13, 1841, p. 2, col. 4;

New York *Herald*, Aug. 13, 1845, p. 2, col. 3;

New York *Tribune*, Oct. 31, 1854, p. 7 (Lydia Ann Puyfer).

Wright, Richardson. *Forgotten Ladies.* Phila.: Lippincott, 1928. (American female transvestites: p. 93–104, 118–20, 301–02.)

Yawger, N. S. "Transvestism and Other Cross-sex Manifestations," *Journal of Nervous and Mental Disease.* Vol. 92 (July 1940): p. 41–48.

NOTES

IV. Native Americans/Gay Americans: 1528–1976

I wish to especially thank Stephen W. Foster for his help with the research for this section, and James Steakley for his assistance in selecting and editing these documents.

1. Francisco Guerra, *The Pre-Columbian Mind: A Study into the Aberrant Nature of Sexual Drives . . .* (London: Seminar, 1971), p. 23, 162, 206, 237, 238, 239, 256.

2. Alvar Núñez Cabeza de Vaca, "Naufragios de Alvar Núñez Cabeza de Vaca," in *Historiadores primitivos de Indias* (Vol. I), ed. Enrique de Vedia, Biblioteca de autores españoles, vol. 22 (Madrid: M. Rivadeneyra, 1852), p. 538. I wish to thank Ed Strug for translating this text.

3. Hernando de Alarcón, *The Relation of the Nauigation and Discouery which Captaine Fernando Alarchon Made, . . .* vol. 4 of *The Principal Nauigations, Voiages, Traffiqves & Discoueries of the English Nation. . .* ed. Richard Hakluyt 12 vols. (Glasgow: J. MacLehose, N.Y.: Macmillan, 1903–05), p. 286.

4. René Goulaine de Laudonnière, *A Notable Historie Containing Foure Voyages Made by Certayne French Captaynes unto Florida. . . .* trans. R[ichard] H[akluyt] (London: Thomas Dawson, 1587), p. 3 (i.e., 5).

5. Jacques Le Moyne de Morgues, *Narrative of Le Moyne, an Artist Who Accompanied the French Expedition to Florida under Laudonnière, 1564,* trans. Frederick B. Perkins (Boston: James R. Osgood, 1875), p. 7–8.

In 1566, an allegedly treasonous and sodomitical French Lutheran was murdered by Spanish Catholics in Florida. The Lutheran had lived with the local chief's two sons, and one of these sons is said to have "loved" the Frenchman "very much" (see Part I, 1566: Gonzalo Solíz de Merás . . .).

6. *Francisco Pareja's 1613 Confesionario; A Documentary Source for Timucuan Ethnolography,* ed. Jerald T. Milanich and William C. Sturtevant, trans. Emilio F. Moran (Tallahassee, Fla.: Division of Archives . . . Florida Dept. of State, 1972), p. 39, 43, 48, 75, 76. I wish to thank Stephen W. Foster for informing me of this document.

Juan de Torquemada's *Monarchía Indiana,* which he began in 1609, refers to male Indians of Florida marrying each other. These Natives he calls *mariones* (effeminate men), and says that they dress like and do the work of women. He compares these Indian customs to those of the French and Greeks (*Los veinte y un libros rituales y Monarchía Indiana*, ed. A. Gonzalez de Barcia Carballido y Zuñiga, 3 vols. [Madrid: N. Rodriguez Franco, 1723], vol. 2, p. 427); other transvestite references: vol. 1, p. 166, 307, 318, 330; vol. 2, p. 12, 13, 287, 380, 386, 392, 393, 394, 417.

Francisco Coreal's *Voyages* during the years 1666–97 included observations of the Natives of Florida, among whom he found much sodomy. He speaks of a large group of effeminate boys who take the women's role in various tribal activities, and who are allegedly held in contempt by the other Natives (*Voyages de François Coreal aux Indes occidentales . . .* 3 vols. [Amsterdam: F. Frederick Bernard, 1722], vol. 1, p. 33–34). This is a French translation of the original Spanish.

7. Jacques Marquette, "Of the First Voyage Made by Father Marquette toward New Mexico, and How the Idea Thereof Was Conceived," *The Jesuit Relations and Allied Documents*, ed. Reuben Gold Thwaites, 73 vols. (Cleveland: Burrows, 1896–1901), vol. 59, p. 129.

Father Louis Hennepin speaks of a cross-dressing, Native male teen-ager in the area of the Great Lakes and Mississippi Valley, 1678–80 (*A Description of Louisiana*, trans. John Gilmary Shea [N.Y.: John G. Shea, 1880], p. 334). A later work of Hennepin's, apparently partly plagiarized, speaks of "hermaphrodites" and boys dressed in women's clothes, kept for sodomitical practices by the Natives (*A New Discovery of a Vast Country in America*, ed. Reuben Gold Thwaites, 2 vols. [Chicago: A. C. McClurg, 1903], vol. 1, p. 167–68).

Father Zenobius Membré's narrative of the adventures of La Salle's party at Fort Crevecoeur, in Illinois, from February 1680 to June 1681, describes the customs of the Natives of the Mississippi Valley: "Hermaphrodites are numerous. . . . [The Indians] are lewd, and even unnaturally so, having boys dressed as women, destined for infamous purposes. These boys are employed only in women's work, without taking part in the chase or war" (*Discovery and Exploration of the Mississippi Valley . . .*, trans. John Gilmary Shea, 2nd ed. [Albany: Joseph McDonough, 1903], p. 155).

In "An Account of the Amours and Marriages of the Savages," Louis Armand de Lom d'Arce de Lahontan writes of his voyage to North America (1683–92): "Some Savages continue Batchelours to their Dying day, and never appear either at Hunting or in Warlike Expeditions, as being either Lunatick or Sickly: But at the same time they are as much esteem'd as the Bravest and Hailest Men in the Country, or at least if they rally upon 'em, 'tis never done where they are present. Among the Illinese there are several Hermaphrodites, who go in a Woman's Habit, but frequent the Company of both Sexes. These Illinese are strangely given to Sodomy, as well as the other Savages that live near the River Missisipi" (*New Voyages to North-America*, ed. Reuben Gold Thwaites, 2 vols. [Chicago: A. C. McClurg, 1905], vol. 2, p. 462).

Barcia Carballido y Zúñiga casually mentions La Salle's embarking on the Mississippi in the summer of 1687 with three Indian guides, "and another Indian—an hermaphrodite who invited himself to go along with them . . ." (*Barcia's Chronological History of the Continent of Florida . . .* trans. Anthony Kerrigan [Westport, Conn.: Greenwood, 1951], p. 306).

Henri de Tonti's account of La Salle's expedition, first published in 1697, the year of Tonti's return from America, says of the Illinois: "They love women with excess, and boys above women, so that they become by that horrid vice, very effeminate. 'Tis observable, however, that notwithstanding that vitious inclination, they have several laws to punish that infamous vice. For as soon as a boy has prostituted himself, he is degraded in a manner of his sex, being forbidden to wear the apparel or name of man, and to make any office or function fit for men, even not so much as to be suffered to go a hunting. They are therefore look'd upon as women, and confined to their employments, of whom they are even more slighted and hated than by men; insomuch that these wretches become, by their crime, the scorn and contempt of both sexes. Thus without any help, but natural reason, they are sensible of their crime, and have made these laws as a bridle to master their brutish sensuality, tho', as I have said before, they hate all manner of restraint. . . . Hermaphrodites are very common amongst them . . . ("An Account of Monsieur de La Salle's Last Expedition . . ." *Collections of the N.Y. Historical Society*, ser. 1, vol. 2 [1814], p. 237–38).

Buisson de St. Cosme's narrative of the American Northwest contains a reference dating to Jan. 2, 1699: "We saw . . . in the village of the Kappas one of those wretches who from their youth dress as girls and pander to the most shameful of all vices. But this infamous man was not of their nation; he belonged to the Illinois, among whom the practice is quite common" (*Early Narratives of the Northwest, 1634–1699*, ed. Louise Philips Kellogg [N.Y.: Scribner, 1917], p. 360; also see p. 244).

8. Pierre Liette, "Memoir of Pierre Liette on the Illinois Country," in *The Western Country in the 17th Century* . . . ed. Milo Quaife (N.Y.: Citadel, 1962), p. 112–13. I wish to thank Harvey Schaktman for providing this document.

John Lawson, a gentleman, and a surveyor and traveler among the American Natives, writes in his *History of North Carolina*, first published in 1709: "Although these People are called Savages, yet Sodomy is never heard of amongst them, and they are so far from the Practice of that beastly and loathsome Sin, that they have no Name for it in their Language" (*History of North Carolina* . . . ed., Frances Latham Harriss [Richmond, Va.: Garrett and Massie, 1937], p. 208).

9. Joseph François Lafitau, *Moeurs des sauvages ameriquains, comparées aux moeurs des premiers temps*, 2 vols. (Paris: Saugrain, 1724), vol. 1, p. 52. Note omitted. I wish to thank Warren Johansson for translating this text.

10. Lafitau, vol. 1, p. 603–04, 608–10. Note*: *Relation de ce qvi s'est passé de plvs remarqvable avx Missions des Pere de la Compagnie de Jesvs. En la Novvelle France, les annees 1669. & 1670* (Paris: Sebastian Mabre-Carmoisy, 1671), chap. 7, p. 246. Reference to ritual Native abductions of boys by men is also apparently made by Robert Beverley in *The History and Present State of Virginia . . . By a native and inhabitant of the place* (London: printed for R. Parker, 1705). Other notes omitted. I wish to thank Warren Johansson for translating this text.

11. Pierre François Xavier de Charlevoix, *Journal of a Voyage to North-America* . . . 2 vols. (London: R. and J. Dodsley, 1761), vol. 2, p. 80. The present text has been slightly altered, "lewdness" substituted for "lubricity," and the French "Efféminés" (from the original text) added.

12. Georg Heinrich Loskiel, *Geschichte der Mission der evangelischen Brüder unter den Indianern in Nordamerika* (Barby: Evangelische Brüdergemeine, 1789), p. 18. I wish to thank James Steakley for translating this text. An English edition is titled: *History of the Mission of the United Brethren among the Indians in North America*, trans. Christian I. LaTrobe (London: Brethren's Society for the Furtherance of the Gospel, 1794), p. 14.

Perrin du Lac's report of his travels in Louisiana and among the Natives of Missouri, Ohio, and the bordering areas (1801–03), mentions "men dressed in women's clothes," who, along with prisoners, perform the "humiliating task" of serving at Native ceremonies. He later adds: "In all the savage nations, there exist men who dress in women's clothes and who are subject to the same work as they are. They engage in neither war nor hunting, but, depending on the circumstances, are used to satisfy the brutal passion of either sex. These men, whose love of idleness and whose abominable depravity lead them to take up this kind of life, are scorned by the braves, who allow them to perform only the lowest kinds of work. Do they go hunting? If they are taken along, it is only to watch over the horses, to skin or carry the pelts of game that are killed, to carry the meat, cut the wood, light the fire, and, in the absence of women, to satisfy a brutal passion abhorrent to nature" (*Voyage dans les deux Louisianes* [Lyon: Bruyset Aîné et Buyand, 1805], p. 318, 352).

Georg Heinrich von Langsdorff was a German scientist and traveler who, employed by the Russians, visited Russian America as far as California. On his travels in 1803–07 he reported seeing homosexual male "concubines" among the Oonalashka Indians (*Voyages and Travels in Various Parts of the World . . .* 2 vols. [London: H. Colburn, 1813–14], vol. 2, p. 47–48, 64).

13. *Jean-Bernard Bossu's Travels in the Interior of North America, 1751–1762*, trans. and ed. Seymour Feiler (Norman: University of Oklahoma, 1962), p. 169.

14. Pedro Font, *Font's Complete Diary of the Second Anza Expedition*, trans. and ed. Herbert Eugene Bolton, vol. 4 of *Anza's California Expeditions* (5 vols.; Berkeley: University of California, 1930–31), p. 105.

Pedro Fages's description of California in 1775 says that the Natives of that area "are addicted to the unspeakable vice of sinning against nature, and maintain in every village their *joyas*, for common use" (*A Historical, Political, and Natural Description of California by [a] Soldier of Spain*, trans. Herbert Ingram Priestley [Berkeley: University of California, 1937], p. 48).

Captain Bernard Romans's history of Florida (first published in N.Y. in 1775), referring to the Choctaws, says: "Sodomy is also practised but not to the same excess as among the Creeks and Chicasaws, and the *Ginaedi* among the Chactwas [*sic*] are obliged to dress themselves in woman's attire, and are highly despised especially by the women" (*A Concise Natural History of East and West Florida* [New Orleans: Pelican, 1961], p. 56).

15. Francisco Palóu, *Relación histórica de la vida y apostólicas tareas del venerable Padre Fray Junípero Serra. . . .* (Mexico: Don Felipe de Zúñiga y Ontiveros, 1787), p. 222. I wish to thank Roberto Echavarren-Welker for translating this text.

16. Alexander Henry and David Thompson, *New Light on the Early History of the Greater Northwest: The Manuscript Journals of Alexander Henry and David Thompson, 1799–1814 . . .* ed. Elliott Coues, 3 vols. (N.Y.: Francis P. Harper, 1897), vol. 1, p. 163–65; see part omitted. The note in brackets appears to be by Coues. Also see p. 53, 348, 399.

17. [Nicholas Biddle], *Original Journals of the Lewis and Clark Expeditions, 1804–1806 . . .* ed. Reuben Gold Thwaites, 8 vols. (N.Y. Dodd, Mead, 1904–05), vol. 1, p. 239.

18. [Nicholas Biddle], *Letters of the Lewis and Clark Expedition, with Related Documents, 1783–1854*, ed. Donald Jackson (Urbana: University of Illinois, 1962), p. 531.

19. Claude E. Schaeffer, "The Kutenai Female Berdache: Courier, Guide, Prophetess, and Warrior," *Ethnohistory*, vol. 12, no. 3 (1965), p. 195–216. This long article contains much extraneous detail which has been deleted, as indicated in the present text. Schaeffer's source citations are included; other notes are omitted.

20. *David Thompson's Narrative of His Explorations in Western America 1784–1812*, ed. J. B. Tyrrell (Toronto: Champlain Society Publications, no. 12, 1916), pp. 512–13.

21. Gabriel Franchere, *Narrative of a Voyage to the Northwest Coast of America in the Years 1811 . . . 1814 . . .* trans. and ed. J. V. Huntington (N.Y.: Redfield, 1854), p. 118–19.

22. Alexander Ross, *Adventures of the First Settlers on the Oregon or Columbia River* (London: Smith, Elder, 1849), p. 85.

23. Franchere, p. 122.

24. David Thompson Papers, 1807–1811, Ontario Archives (Toronto).

25. David Thompson, "Narrative of the Expedition to the Kootanae and Flat Bow Indian Countries . . ." ed. T. C. Elliott, in "The Discovery of the Source of the Columbia River," *Oregon Historical Quarterly*, vol. 25 (1925), p. 512–13.

26. Ross, p. 144–49.

27. John Franklin, *Narrative of a Journey to the Shores of the Polar Seas, in the Years 1819 . . . [18]22* (London: J. Murray, 1823), p. 152.

28. O. B. Sperlin, "Two Kootenay Women Masquerading as Men? Or Were They One?" *Washington Historical Quarterly*, vol. 21 (1930), p. 127–130.

29. John Work, "Journal" [title varies], ed. T. C. Elliott, *Washington Historical Quarterly*, vol. 5 (1914), p. 190.

30. "The Unpublished Journal of William H. Gray from December 1836 to October 1837," *Whitman College Quarterly*, vol. 26 (1913), p. 46–47.

Father Geronimo Boscana, a Mallorcan cleric, left a manuscript account of the "Indians at the Missionary Establishment of St. Juan Capistrano, Alta California," where Boscana had spent the years 1814–26. His account of the Acagchemen (or Shoshonean Juaneno) tribe reports: "One of the many singularities that prevailed among these Indians was that of marrying males with males. . . . It was publicly done, but without the forms and ceremonies already described in their marriage contracts with the females. Whilst yet in infancy, they were selected and instructed as they increased in years in all the duties of the women—in their mode of dress, of walking, and dancing; so that in almost every particular, they resembled females. Being more robust than the women, they were better able to perform the arduous duties of the wife, and for this reason, they were often selected by the chiefs and others, and on the day of the wedding a grand feast was given.

"To distinguish this detested race at this mission, they were called *cuit*, in the mountains, *uluqui*, and in other parts, they were known by the name of *coias*. At the present time, this horrible custom is entirely unknown among them. I was told by a missionary from the Mission of Santo Domingo, in Lower California, that he once enquired of several Indians from the plains of the Colorado River if in their confines were to be found any of the *coias*. He replied that they were once very numerous, but a serious plague visited them many years back, which destroyed them all." (*Chinigchinich: A Revised and Annotated Version of . . . Boscana's Historical Account . . .* 1st. rev. ed. [Santa Ana, Cal.: Fine Arts, 1933], p. 54, 170–71).

31. Edwin James, *Account of an Expedition from Pittsburgh to the Rocky Mountains in the Years 1819 and '20 . . .* 2 vols. (Phila.: H. C. Carey and I. Lea, 1822–23), vol. 1, p. 129, 267.* See Hennepin's *Travels*, London, 1698, p. 133.

32. William H. Keating, *Narrative of an Expedition to the Source of St. Peter's River . . .* 2 vols. (Phila.: H. C. Carey and I. Lea, 1824), vol. 1, p. 210–11.

33. Thomas A. McKenney, *Sketches of a Tour to Lakes, of the Character and Customs of the Chippeway Indians . . .* (Baltimore: Fielding Lucas Jr., 1827), p. 315–16.

34. Isaac McCoy, *History of Baptist Indian Missions . . .* (N.Y.: H. & S. Raynor, 1840) p. 360–61.

35. John Tanner, *A Narrative of the Captivity and Adventures of John Tanner*, (U.S. Interpreter at the Sault de Saint Marie), *During Thirty Years Residence among the Indians . . .* ed. Edwin James (N.Y.: G. and C. and H. Carvill, 1830), p. 105–06.

36. George Catlin, *Illustrations of the Manners, Customs, and Condition of the North American Indians, with Letters and Notes Written during Eight Years of Travel and Adventure among the Wildest and Most Remarkable Tribes Now Existing*, 10th ed., 2 vols. (London: Henry G. Bohn, 1866), vol. 2, p. 214–15.

Catlin also speaks of a group among the Native population who observe "the strictest regard to decency, and cleanliness and elegance of dress." In this group are some "chiefs," "braves," "warriors of distinction, and their families, and dandies or exquisites." Later, writing from a Mandan village on the upper Mississippi, Catlin describes these dandies, "often seen stalking about in all Indian communities, a kind of nondescript (?), with whom I have been somewhat annoyed, and still more amused, since I came to this village. . . ." He continues: "The person I allude to [is] familiarly known and countenanced in every tribe as an Indian *beau* or *dandy*. Such personages may be seen on every pleasant day, strutting and parading around the village in the most beautiful and unsoiled dresses, without the honourable trophies however of scalp locks and claws of the grizzly bear to their costume, for with such things they deal not. They . . . generally remain about the village, to take care of the women, and attire themselves in the skins of such animals as they can easily kill. . . . They plume themselves with . . . harmless and unmeaning ornaments, which have no other merit than they themselves have, that of looking pretty and ornamental.

"These clean and elegant gentlemen, who are very few in each tribe, are held in very little estimation by the chiefs and braves; inasmuch as it is known by all, that they have a most horrible aversion to arms, and are denominated 'feint hearts' or 'old women' by the whole tribe, and are therefore but little respected. They seem, however, to be tolerably well contented with the appellation, together with the celebrity they have acquired amongst the women and children for the beauty and elegance of their personal appearance; and most of them seem to take and enjoy their share of the world's pleasures, although they are looked upon as drones in society.

"These gay and tinselled bucks may be seen in a pleasant day in all their plumes, astride their pied or dappled ponies, with a fan in the right hand . . . and underneath them a white and beautiful and soft pleasure saddle. . . ." They will spend an hour or two overlooking the "games where the braves and the young aspirants are contending in manly and athletic amusements. . . ." Catlin describes "two or three of these fops" gathering and posing around his door, while inside he paints all the "head men" of the village. When he finally asks one "beautiful" dandy to come in and be seated for his portrait, the displeasure of two or three chiefs forced him to stop painting the "worthless fellow" (vol. I, p. 96, 111–14).

Alexander P. Maximilian, Prince of Wied, who traveled in North America between 1832 and 1834, reports: "Among all the North American Indian nations there are men dressed and treated like women, called by the Canadians Bardaches; . . . but there was only one such among the Mandans, and two or three among the Manitaries." Later Maximilian says of the Crows: "They have many bardaches, or hermaphrodites among them, and exceed all the other tribes in unnatural practices" (*Travels in the Interior of North America* . . . vol. 22 of *Early Western Travels*, ed. Reuben Gold Thwaites, 32 vols. [Cleveland: A. H. Clark, 1906], p. 283–84, 354).

Victor Tixier's *Travels on the Osage Prairies* (in 1839–40) says: "In the Head Chief's lodge lived a warrior named *la Bredache*. This man, who a few years before was considered one of the most distinguished braves, suddenly gave up fighting and never left Majakita [the Head Chief] except when the latter went to war. The extremely effeminate appearance of this man, and his name, which was that of an hermaphrodite animal, gave me food for thought. Baptiste [an Osage] accused him of being the lover of the Woman-Chief; but the Osage tell only half of what they think" (trans. Albert J. Salvan, ed. John F. McDermott [Norman: University of Oklahoma, 1940], p. 234; note omitted).

In a curious chapter, "The Metamorphosis," in his *Indian Sketches Taken during an Expedition to the Pawnee Tribes* (in 1833), John Treat Irving describes the change of a once famous male warrior to the degraded status of a "squaw." Although homosexuality is not mentioned, this description seems important for the study of the related "berdache" phenomenon (ed. John Francis McDermott [Norman: University of Oklahoma, 1955], p. 93–95).

37. Pierre-Jean de Smet, *Life, Letters and Travels of Father Pierre-Jean De Smet, . . .* ed. Hiram M. Chittenden and Alfred T. Richardson, 4 vols. (N.Y.: Francis P. Harper, 1905), vol. 3, p. 1017–18.

Duflot de Mofras's *Travels on the Pacific Coast, . . .* first published in 1844, says of the East Coast tribes: "Vices found among the Indians are of a kind that usually are found only in the most corrupt circles. Every tribe has its *joyas*, men who dress like women, live with them, share in their work, and enjoy certain privileges, in return for participating in the most infamous debaucheries. These degenerates are the object of universal contempt, and are not allowed to carry weapons" (trans. and ed. Marguerite Eyer Wilbur [Santa Ana, Cal.: Fine Arts, 1937], p. 192–93; note omitted).

38. Francis Parkman, *The Oregon Trail*, ed. E. N. Feltskog (Madison: University of Wisconsin, 1969), p. 100–01, 280–82, 283. Parkman's references in the same work to Lord Byron are also relevant (see p. 30, 304–05, 458, 624, 652–53), as is his relation to the cousin with whom he traveled (see note 1, p. 415 in above ed.). Parkman's *La Salle and the Discovery of the Great West*, first published in 1879, contains a note on "licentious" practices among the Illinois: "Young men enacting the part of women were frequently to be seen among them. These were held in great contempt. Some of the early travellers . . . mistook them for hermaphrodites" (*Francis Parkman's Works*, vol. 3 [Boston: Little, Brown, 1903], p. 207).

39. George Devereux, "Mohave Ethnopsychiatry and Suicide . . ." *Smithsonian Institution, Bureau of American Ethnology Bulletin 175* (Washington, D.C.: Govt. Ptg. Ofc., 1961). Notes omitted. The above includes a revised version of the history of Sahaykwisā which originally appeared in Devereux's "Institutionalized Homosexuality of the Mohave Indians," *Human Biology*, vol. 9 (1937), p. 498–527.

One of the earliest and most often quoted medical reports on sex-role reversal and homosexuality among Native Americans is an article, "The Disease of the Scythians . . ." published in 1882 by Dr. William A. Hammond. Here Hammond mentions two *mujerados* (physically effeminized males) he had observed "over thirty years" earlier (c. 1851) among the Pueblos of New Mexico. Reading Hammond's report of the *mujerado* phenomenon, allegedly involving physical, as well as behavioral changes, it is now difficult to separate fact from fancy, to estimate the extent to which moral judgment and outmoded medical theory have influenced observation. Hammond does refer to traditional Native "pederastic ceremonies which form so important a part of their religious performances," and which are usually hidden from whites—a subject for further research. Hammond's own observations are more valuable than his historical analogies between Native American customs and those of the ancient Scythians (*American Journal of Neurology and Psychiatry*, vol. 1, no. 3 [Aug. 1882] p. 339–55).

40. Edward Thompson Denig, "Of the Crow Nation," in John C. Ewers, ed., *Anthropological Papers No. 33, U.S. Bureau of American Ethnology, Bulletin 151* (Washington, D.C.: Govt. Ptg. Ofc., 1953), p. 64–68. Reprinted in *Five Indian Tribes of the Upper Missouri . . .*, ed. John C. Ewers (Norman: University of Oklahoma, 1961), p. 195–200. A note refers to other documents concerning "Woman Chief." She is mentioned in R. F. Kurz's "Journal . . . 1846–1852" (trans. Myrtis Jarrel, ed. J. N. B. Hewitt, *Bureau of American Ethnology Bulletin 115* [Washington, D.C.: Govt. Ptg. Ofc., 1937], p. 213–14; and in Denig's "Indian Tribes of the Upper Missouri" (ed. J. N. B. Hewitt, *Forty-sixth Annual Report, Bureau of American Ethnology, 1928–29* [Washington, D.C.: Govt. Ptg. Ofc., 1930], p. 433–34). Denig says here that the success of the Crow Woman Chief "induced an imitation a few years since by an Assiniboin woman, but she was killed by the enemy on her first war excursion. . . ." J. Willard Schultz is cited as having written a fictionalized biography, *Running Eagle, The Warrior Girl*, about a famous Piegan woman warrior of a later period who may have been inspired by the story of the Crow Woman Chief.

Denig's *Five Indian Tribes*, written in 1855–56, also contains a section on "Crow [male] Hermaphrodites" (p. 187–88).

First published in London in 1875 (by Longmans, Green), Hubert Howe Bancroft's five volumes on *The Native Races of the Pacific States of North America* was one of the first large compilations of original source materials which presents, and openly discusses, "sodomy" among Native Americans. Bancroft's is a major work for the historical study of homosexuality among Native Americans.

41. H. Clay Trumbull, *Friendship the Master-Passion, or, The Nature and History of Friendship, and Its Place as a Force in the World* (Phila.: John D. Wattles, 1894), p. 165–66. Trumbull also describes a "Friendship Dance," a religious ceremony by which recognition is made of the "union" of two warriors (p. 71–72). Trumbull is the author of *The Blood Covenant* (Phila.: J. D. Wattles, 1893) about an organized, intimate brotherhood. Trumbull (1830–1903) himself had passionate friendships with Henry Ward Camp and Robert E. Speer (see Phillip E. Howard, *The Life Story of Henry Clay Trumbull* [Phila.: Sunday School Times, 1905], p. 194 ff. [to p. 230], 413). I wish to thank Stephen W. Foster for the above sources and information.

The Rev. James Owen Dorsey, in an essay on "Omaha Sociology," dating to 1881–82 quotes Native sources on homosexuality (*Third Annual Report, 1881–82, Bureau of American Ethnology, Smithsonian Institution* [Washington, D.C.: Govt. Ptg. Ofc., 1884], p. 266, 268, 365 [on "Schoopanism, or paederastia"]).

In his book on *The Lenâpé and Their Legends* . . . first published in 1884, Daniel G. Brinton includes a section on "The Lânapé as 'Women,' " and refers to Hammond's report of 1882 (Phil.: D. G. Brinton, 1885), p. 109–10.

42. A. B. Holder, "The Bote. Description of a Peculiar Sexual Perversion Found among North American Indians," *New York Medical Journal*, vol. 50, no. 23 (Dec. 7, 1889), 623–25. Also see parts omitted.

James Owen Dorsey's "Study of Siouan Cults," published in 1889–90, includes material on "Berdaches" among the Omaha, Dakota, Kansa, Teton, and Hidatsa tribes (*Eleventh Annual Report, 1889–90, U.S. Bureau of American Ethnology, Smithsonian Institution* [Washington, D.C.: U.S. Govt. Ptg. Ofc., 1894], p. 378–79, 467.

43. Matilda Coxe Stevenson, "The Zuñi Indians: Their Mythology, Esoteric Societies, and Ceremonies," *Twenty-third Annual Report of the U.S. Bureau of American Ethnology . . . 1901–1902* (Washington, D.C.: Govt. Ptg. Ofc., 1904), p. 37–38.

44. Stevenson, p. 310–13. It would be interesting to study any news reports of We'wha's trip to Washington, D.C.

In a report on "The Omaha Tribe," based in part on research dating to 1898, Alice C. Fletcher and Frances La Flesche write of dreams as harbingers of sex-role reversal (*Twenty-seventh Annual Report . . . 1905–1906, U.S. Bureau of American Ethnology, Smithsonian Institution* [Washington, D.C.: Govt. Ptg. Ofc., 1911], p. 132–33).

45. William Jones, *Fox Texts, Publications of the American Ethnological Society*, vol. 1 (Leiden: E. J. Brill, 1907), p. 151.

46. S. C. Simms, "Crow Indian Hermaphrodites," *American Anthropologist*, new Ser., vol. 5 (1903), p. 580–81. Also see part omitted.

In his anthropological report on "The Arapaho," published in 1902, A. L. Kroeber mentions "Berdaches" in that tribe, and among the Cheyenne, Sioux, Omaha, Ute, and "many" other tribes. An Arapaho story of a female who dressed and lived as a man among the Sioux is mentioned in passing (*Bulletin of the American Museum of Natural History*, vol. 18 [1902], p. 19–20).

On the basis of information obtained in 1904–09, James A. Teit reports on a few male "berdaches" among "The Salishan Tribes of the Western Plateau" (ed. Frank Boas, *Forty-fifth Annual Report, 1927–28, U.S. Bureau of American Ethnology, Smithsonian Institution* [Washington, D.C.: Govt. Ptg. Ofc., 1930], p. 292, 384).

In a report published in 1905, Roland B. Dixon says that the northern Maidu Indians "deny that there were ever any *berdaches*, or men-women among them. They were present in considerable numbers among the Achoma'wi, however, to the north" ("The Northern Maidu," *Bulletin of the American Museum of Natural History*, vol. 17 [May 1905], p. 241).

47. Robert H. Lowie, "Social Life of the Crow Indians," *Anthropological Papers of the American Museum of Natural History*, vol. 9, part 2 (1912), p. 226.

48. Edward Westermarck, *The Origin and Development of Moral Ideas*, 2nd ed., 2 vols. (London: Macmillan, 1917), vol. 2, p. 456–489.

49. Omer C. Stewart, "Homosexuality among the American Indians and Other Native Peoples of the World," *Mattachine Review*, vol. 6, no. 2 (1960), p. 17.

A few brief sentences in Dr. A. F. Hrdlička's report of 1908 on "Physical and Medical Observations Among the Indians of the Southwestern United States and Northern Mexico" reveals more about the difficulties and disinterest of a white researcher than it does about the people investigated. Beyond some marriage and pregnancy customs, says the doctor, "Further peculiarities of the sexual life of the people could not be inquired into with profitable results. From various indications the subject does not offer much of unusual interest" (*Smithsonian Institution, Bureau of American Ethnology, Bulletin 34* [Washington, D.C.: U.S. Govt. Ptg. Ofc., 1908], p. 51).

50. Robert H. Lowie, "The Assiniboine," *Anthropological Papers of the American Museum of Natural History*, vol. 4, part 1 (1909), p. 223. Also see a section on "Berdaches," p. 42.

51. Edward Carpenter, *Intermediate Types among Primitive Folk: A Study in Social Evolution*, 2nd ed. (London: Allen and Unwin, 1919; photo reprint, N.Y.: Arno, 1975).

52. Ferdinand Karsch-Haack, *Das gleichgeschlechtliche Leben der Naturvölker* (Munich: Reinhardt, 1911; photo reprint, N.Y.: Arno, 1975).

Also see Clark Wisler on "The Berdache Cult" in "Societies and Ceremonial Associations in the Oglala Division of the Teton-Dakota," *Anthropological Papers of the American Museum of Natural History*, vol. 12 (1912), p. 92.

53. Douglas C. McMurtrie, "A Legend of Lesbian Love among the North American Indians," *Urologic and Cutaneous Review* (April 1914), p. 192–93.

Also see Elsie Clews Parsons's major study of "The Zuñi la'mana" (or "men-women") in *American Anthropologist*, new ser., vol. 18 (1916), p. 521–28; A. L. Kroeber's *Handbook of the Indians of California* (preface dated 1923), *U.S. Bureau of American Ethnology Bulletin, no. 78* [Washington, D.C.: Govt. Ptg. Ofc., 1925], p. 46, 190, 497, 500–01, 647, 728–29, 748–49, 803; R. H. Lowie's "Notes on Shoshonean Ethnography," *Anthropological Papers of the American Museum of Natural History*, vol. 20, part 3 (1924), p. 282–83; R. H. Lowie, *Primitive Religion* (N.Y.: Boni and Liveright, 1924), p. 181, 243–46; E. W. Gifford's "Clear Lake Pomo Society," *University of California Publications in American Archaeology and Ethnology*, vol. 28, (1926), p. 333.

54. Leslie Spier, "Klamath Ethnography," *University of California Publications in American Archaeology and Ethnology*, vol. 27 (1930), p. 51–53.

55. C. Daryll Forde, "Ethnography of the Yuma Indians," *University of California Publications in American Archaeology and Ethnology*, vol. 28 (1931), p. 157.

56. E. W. Gifford, "The Kamia of Imperial Valley," *U.S. Bureau of American Ethnology Bulletin, no. 97* (Washington, D.C.: Govt. Ptg. Ofc., 1931), p. 12.

57. E. W. Gifford, "The Cocopa," *University of California Publications in American Archaeology and Ethnology*, vol. 31 (1933), p. 294.

Also see R. L. Beals, "Ethnography of the Nisenan," *University of California Publications in Archaeology and Ethnology*, vol. 31, no. 6 (1933), p. 376; Leslie Spier, *Yuman*

Tribes of the Gila River (Chicago: University of Chicago, 1933), p. 4, 6, 242–43; Ruth Benedict, *Patterns of Culture* (Boston: Houghton Mifflin, 1934), p. 262–65; W. W. Hill, "The Status of the Hermaphrodite and Transvestite in Navaho Culture," *American Anthropologist*, new ser., vol. 37 (1935), p. 273–79; R. H. Lowie, *The Crow Indians* (N.Y.: Farrar and Rinehart, 1935), p. viii, 48, 312–13; Ralph Linton, *The Study of Man* (N.Y.: Appleton-Century-Crofts, 1935), p. 480–81; Ruth Underhill, "The Autobiography of a Papago Woman," *Memoirs of the American Anthropological Association, no. 43* (Menasha, Wis.: Amer. Anth. Assoc., 1936), p. 43–44; W. W. Hill's brief but important "Note on the Pima Berdache," *American Anthropologist*, new ser., vol. 40 (1938), p. 338–40; May Mandelbaum, "The Individual Life Cycle," in "The Sinkaietk or Southern Okanagon of Washington," by Walter Cline and others, ed. Leslie Spier, *General Series in Anthropology, no. 6* (Menasha, Wis.: George Banta, 1938), p. 119; Ruth Benedict, "Sex in Primitive Society," *American Journal of Orthopsychiatry*, vol. 9 (1939), p. 572–73; A. L. Kroeber, "Psychosis or Social Sanction," *Character and Personality* . . . vol. 8 (1939–40), p. 209–10; E. M. Opler, *An Apache Life-Way* . . . (Chicago: University of Chicago, 1941), p. 79–80, 415–16.

58. W. W. Hill, ". . . Navaho Humor," *General Studies in Anthropology, no. 9* (Menasha, Wis.: George Banta Publishing, 1943), p. 12.

Also see Nancy Oestreich Luri, "Winnebago Berdache," *American Anthropologist* vol. 55 (1953), p. 708–12.

59. Dorothea Leighton and Clyde Kluckhohn, *Children of the People: The Navaho Individual and His Development* (Cambridge, Mass.: Harvard University, 1948), p. 78.

Also see Gladys Amanda Reichard, *Navaho Religion* . . . (N.Y.: Bollingen Foundation, Pantheon, 1950), p. 140–42.

60. Clellan S. Ford and Frank A. Beach, *Patterns of Sexual Behavior* (N.Y.: Harper & Row, 1951), p. 136–40.

61. W. Dorr Legg, "The Berdache and Theories of Sexual Inversion," *ONE Institute Quarterly*, vol. 2, no. 2 (1959), p. 59–60, 63.

62. J. J. Honigmann, "The Kaska Indians: An Ethnographic Reconstruction," *Yale University Publications in Anthropology, no. 51* (New Haven: Yale University Publications, 1964), p. 129–30. Notes omitted.

63. Bob Waltrip, "Elmer Gage: American Indian," *ONE*, no. 13 (March 1965), p. 6–10.

64. Dean Gengle, "Reclaiming the Old New World. Gay was Good with Native Americans," *The Advocate* (San Mateo, Cal.) Jan. 28, 1976, p. 40–41.

Maurice Kenny, a Gay male Mohawk from northern New York has written "Tinselled Bucks; An Historical Study in Indian Homosexuality," *Gay Sunshine*, nos. 26–27 (Winter 1975–1976), p. 15–17. Kenny is a poet who has also written a number of verses on Gay themes, among them "Winkte" (to appear in *Manroot*, 1976); "Apache" (*Mouth of the Dragon*, vol. 5 [June 1975]); "United" (*Gay Sunshine*, above issue, p. 17).

Bibliography

IV. NATIVE AMERICANS/GAY AMERICANS: 1528–1976

Alarcón, Fernando de. *The Relation of the Nauigation and Discouery which Captaine Fernando Alarchon Made.* . . . vol. 4 of *The Principal Nauigations, Voiages, Traffiqves & Discoueries of the English Nation.* . . . Ed. Richard Hakluyt. 12 vols. Glasgow: J. MacLehose; N.Y.: Macmillan, 1903–05. (P. 286.)

Angelino, Henry, and Shedd, Charles L. "A Note on Berdache," *American Anthropologist*. Vol. 55 (1955): p. 121–25.

Bancroft, Hubert Howe. *The Native Races of the Pacific States of North America*. 5 vols. London: Longmans, Green, 1875–76. (Vol. 1, p. 58, 81–82, 92, 415, 515, 773–74; vol. 2, p. 467–69, 664, 677–78; vol. 5, p. 198.)

Barcia Carballido y Zúñiga, Andres González de. *Barcia's Chronological History of the Continent of Florida . . . from 1512 . . . until the Year 1722*. Trans. Anthony Kerrigan. Westport, Conn.: Greenwood, 1951. (P. 306.)

Bastian, Adolf. *Der Mensch in der Geschichte: zur Begründung einer psychologischen Weltanschauung*. 3 vols. Leipzig: Otto Wigand, 1860. (Vol. 3, p. 314.)

Beals, Ralph L. "Ethnography of the Nisenan," *University of California Publications in Archaeology and Ethnology*. Vol. 31, no. 6 (1933). (P. 376.)

Beckwourth, James P. *The Life and Adventures of James P. Beckwourth*. Ed. T. D. Bonner. Reprint of 1856 ed., N.Y.: Knopf, 1931. (P. 133–38.)

Benedict, Ruth. "Anthropology and the Abnormal," *Journal of General Psychology*. Vol. 10 (1934): p. 59–82. (P. 59–65.)

———. *Patterns of Culture*. Boston: Houghton Mifflin, 1934. (P. 262–65.)

———. "Sex in Primitive Society," *American Journal of Orthopsychiatry*. Vol. 9 (1939): p. 570–75. (P. 572–73.)

———, and Mead, Margaret. *An Anthropologist at Work*. Boston: Houghton Mifflin, 1956. (P. 268.)

Bettleheim, Bruno. *Symbolic Wounds; Puberty Rites and the Envious Male*. Glencoe, Ill.: Free Press, 1954. (P. 109.)

[Biddle, Nicholas.] *Letters of the Lewis and Clark Expedition, with Related Documents, 1783–1854*. Ed. Donald Jackson. Urbana: University of Illinois, 1962. (P. 531.)

[———.] *Original Journals of the Lewis and Clark Expedition, 1804–1806, Printed from the Original Manuscripts in the Library of the American Philosophical Society . . .* Ed. Reuben Gold Thwaites. 8 vols. N.Y.: Dodd, Mead, 1904–05. (Vol. 1, p. 239.)

Boscana, Geronimo. *Chinigchinich: A Revised and Annotated Version of Alfred Robinson's Translation of Father Geronimo Boscana's Historical Account of Belief, Usages, Customs, and Extravagances of the Indians of this Mission of San Juan Capistrano, Called the Acagchemen Tribe*. 1st rev. ed. Santa Ana, Cal.: Fine Arts, 1933. (P. 54, 170–71.)

Bossu, Jean-Bernard. *Jean-Bernard Bossu's Travels in the Interior of North America, 1751–1762*. Trans. and ed. Seymour Feiler. Norman: University of Oklahoma, 1962. (P. 169.)

Bowers, Alfred W. *Mandan Social and Ceremonial Organization*. Chicago: University of Chicago, 1950. (P. 298–99.)

Brinton, Daniel Garrison, ed. *The Lenâpé and Their Legends . . .* Library of Aboriginal Literature, no. 5. Phila.: D. G. Brinton, 1885. (P. 109–10.)

[Buisson de St. Cosme, Jean François.] *Early Narratives of the Northwest, 1634–1699*. Ed. Louise Philps Kellogg. N.Y.: Scribner, 1917. (P. 244, 360.)

Cabeza de Vaca, Alvar Núñez. "Naufragios de Alvar Núñez Cabeza de Vaca." in *Historiadores primitivos de Indias*. Ed. Enrique de Vedia. vol. 1. *Biblioteca de autores españoles*. Vol. 22. Madrid: M. Rivadeneyra, 1852. (P. 538.)

Carr, Lucien. "The Mounds of the Mississippi Valley, Historically Considered," *Memoirs of the Kentucky Geological Survey, Vol. 2, 1883*. Smithsonian Institution. *Annual Report, 1891*. Washington, D.C.: U.S. Govt. Ptg. Ofc., 1893. (P. 531.)

Catlin, George. *Illustrations of the Manners, Customs, and Condition of the North American Indians, with Letters and Notes Written during Eight Years of Travel and Adventure among the Wildest and Most Remarkable Tribes Now Existing*. 10th ed. 2 vols. London: Henry G. Bohn, 1866. (Vol. 2, p. 214–15.)

Carpenter, Edward. *Intermediate Types Among Primitive Folk; A Study in Social Evolution*. 2nd ed. London: Allen & Unwin, 1919. Photo reprint, N.Y.: Arno, 1975.

Charlevoix, Pierre François Xavier de. *Journal of a Voyage to North-America Undertaken by Order of the French King; Containing the Geographical Description and Natural History of that Country, Particularly Canada. Together with an Account of the Customs, Characters, Religion, Manners and Traditions of the Aboriginal Inhabitants. In a Series of Letters to the Duchess of Lesdiquières*. 2 vols. London: R. and J. Dodsley, 1761. (Vol. 2, p. 80.)

Coon, Carleton. *The Hunting Peoples*. Boston: Little, Brown, 1971. (P. 270.)

[Coreal, Francisco.] *Voyages de François Coreal aux Indes occidentales, contenant ce qu'il y a vû de plus remarquable pendant son séjour depuis 1666 jusqu'en 1697* . . . 3 vols. Amsterdam: F. Frederick Bernard, 1722. (Vol. 1, p. 33–34.)

Cox, Ross. *Adventures on the Columbia River, Including the Narrative of a Residence of Six Years on the Western Side of the Rocky Mountains, among Various Tribes of Indians Hitherto Unknown: Together with a Journey Across the American Continent.* N.Y.: Harper, 1832. (P. 327 ff.)

Cushing, Frank Hamilton. "Outlines of Zuñi Creation Myths," *Thirteenth Annual Report of the [U.S.] Bureau of American Ethnology . . . 1891–92.* Washington, D.C.: U.S. Govt. Ptg. Ofc., 1896. (P. 401–03.)

Dall, William H. *Alaska and its Resources.* Boston: Lee and Shepard, 1870. (P. 402 ff.)

Debo, Angie. *The Rise and Fall of the Choctaw Republic.* Norman: University of Oklahoma, 1961. (P. 22–23.)

Denig, Edwin Thompson. *Five Indian Tribes of the Upper Missouri: Sioux, Arickaras, Assiniboines, Crees [and] Crows.* Ed. John C. Ewers. Norman: University of Oklahoma, 1961. (P. 187–88, 195–200, 535.)

———. "Indian Tribes of the Upper Missouri." Ed. J. N. B. Hewitt. *Forty-sixth Annual Report. Bureau of American Ethnology, 1928–29.* Washington, D.C.: U.S. Govt. Ptg. Ofc., 1930: p. 375–628. (P. 433–34.)

De Smet, Pierre-Jean. *Life, Letters and Travels of Father Pierre-Jan De Smith, S. J. . . .* Ed. Hiram Martin Chittenden and Alfred Talbot Richardson. 4 vols. N.Y.: Francis P. Harper, 1905. (Vol. 3, 1017–18.)

Devereux, George. "Institutionalized Homosexuality of the Mohave Indians," *Human Biology.* Vol. 9 (1937): p. 498–527.

———. "Mohave Ethnopsychiatry and Suicide: the Psychiatric Knowledge and the Psychic Disturbances of an Indian Tribe." *Smithsonian Institution. Bureau of American Ethnology. Bulletin 175.* Washington, D.C.: U.S. Govt. Ptg. Ofc., 1961.

———. "Mohave Indian Autoerotic Behavior," *Psychoanalytic Review.* Vol. 37 (1950): p. 201–20. (P. 205.)

———. "Mohave Indian Verbal and Motor Profanity," *Psychoanalysis and the Social Sciences.* Vol. 3 (1951). (P. 113.)

Dixon, Roland B. "The Northern Maidu," *Bulletin of the American Museum of Natural History.* Vol. 17 (May 1905). (P. 241.)

Dorsey, George A. and Murie, James R. "Notes on the Skidi-Pawnee Society," *Field Museum of Natural History, Anthropology Series 27.* Chicago: Field Museum Press, 1940. (P. 108.)

Dorsey, James Owen. "Omaha Sociology," *Third Annual Report, 1881–2. U.S. Bureau of American Ethnology. Smithsonian Institution.* Washington, D.C.: U.S. Govt. Ptg. Ofc., 1884: p. 205–370. (P. 266, 268, 365.)

———. "A Study of Siouan Cults," *Eleventh Annual Report, 1889–90. U.S. Bureau of American Ethnology. Smithsonian Institution.* Washington, D. C.: U.S. Govt. Ptg. Ofc., 1894: p. 351–544. (P. 378–79, 467, 516–17.)

Dragoo, Don W. "Transvestites in North American Tribes." Typescript, 13 p. Dept. of Anthropology, Indiana University, Institute for Sex Research Collection, 1950.

Driver, Harold, Edson. *Culture Element Distribution: X. Northwest California.* Berkeley: University of California, 1939. (P. 405.)

———. *Indians of North America.* Chicago: University of Chicago, 1961. (P. 535.)

Drucker, Philip. "Culture Element Distributions: XVII. Yuman-Piman," *Anthropological Records.* Vol. 6, no. 3 (1941). Berkeley: University of California, 1941. (P. 218.)

Dubois, Cora. *Wintu Ethnology.* Berkeley: University of California, 1935. (P. 50.)

Duflot de Mofras, Eugène. *Duflot de Mofras' Travels on the Pacific Coast . . .* Trans. and ed. Marguerite Eyer Wilbur. Santa Ana, Cal.: Fine Arts, 1937. (P. 192–93.)

Emory, William H. *Report of the U.S. and Mexican Boundary Survey.* 34th Cong., 1st Sess., House Ex. Doc. 135. Washington, D.C.: U.S. Govt. Ptg. Ofc., 1857. 3 vols. (Vol. 1, p. 110.)

Fages, Pedro. *A Historical, Political, and Natural Description of California by Pedro Fages, Soldier of Spain, Dutifully Made for the Viceroy in the Year 1775.* Trans. Herbert Ingram Priestley. Berkeley: University of California, 1937. (P. 48.)

Fletcher, Alice C., and La Flesche, Frances. "The Omaha Tribe," *Twenty-seventh Annual Re-*

port . . . 1905–1906. U. S. Bureau of American Ethnology. Smithsonian Institution. Washington, D.C.: U.S. Govt. Ptg. Ofc., 1911. (P. 132–33.)

Font, Pedro. *Font's Complete Diary of the Second Anza Expedition.* Trans and ed. Herbert Eugene Bolton. vol. IV of *Anza's California Expeditions.* Ed. H. E. Bolton. 5 vols. Berkeley: University of California, 1930–31. (P. 105.)

Ford, Clellan S., and Beach, Frank A. *Patterns of Sexual Behavior.* N.Y.: Harper & Row, 1951. (Chap. 7, "Homosexual Behavior," p. 136–40.)

Forbes, Jack. *Warriors of the Colorado; the Yumas of the Quechan Nation and Their Neighbors.* Norman: University of Oklahoma, 1965. (P. 57.)

Forde, C. Daryll. "Ethnology of the Yuma Indians," *University of California Publications in American Archaeology and Ethnology.* Vol. 28, no. 4 (1931): p. 83–278. (P. 157.)

Forgey, Donald G. "The Institution of Berdache Among the North American Plains Indians," *Journal of Sex Research.* Vol. 11, no. 1 (Feb. 1975): p. 1–15.

Franchere, Gabriel. *Narrative of a Voyage to the Northwest Coast of America in the Years 1811, 1812, 1813, and 1814, or The First American Settlement on the Pacific.* Trans and ed. J. V. Huntington. N.Y.: Redfield, 1854. (P. 118–19, 122.)

Franklin, John. *Narrative of a Journey to the Shores of the Polar Seas, in the Years 1819, 20, 21, and 22.* London: J. Murray, 1823. (P. 152.)

———. *Narrative of a Second Expedition to the Shores of the Polar Sea in the Years 1825, 1826, and 1827.* London: J. Murray, 1828. (P. 305–06.)

Gengle, Dean. "Reclaiming the Old New World. Gay was Good with Native Americans," *The Advocate* (San Mateo, Cal.). Jan. 28, 1976: p. 40–41.

Gifford, Edward Winslow. "Clear Lake Pomo Society," *University of California Publications in American Archaeology and Ethnology.* Vol. 28 (1926): p. 287–390. (P. 333.)

———. "The Cocopa." *University of California Publications in American Archaeology and Ethnology.* Vol. 31 (1933). (P. 277, 294.)

———. "The Kamia of Imperial Valley." *U.S. Bureau of American Ethnology Bulletin, no. 97.* Washington, D.C.: U.S. Govt. Ptg. Ofc., 1931. (P. 12.)

———. "The Northeastern and Western Yavapai," *University of California Publications in American Archaeology and Ethnology.* Vol. 34 (1936). (P. 296.)

———. "The Northfork Mono." *University of California Publications in American Archaeology and Ethnology.* Vol. 31 (1934). (P. 44.)

Gray, William H. "The Unpublished Journal of William H. Gray from December 1836 to October 1837," *Whitman College Quarterly.* Vol. 26 (1913), p. 1–79. (P. 46–47.)

Grinnell, George. *The Fighting Cheyennes.* Norman: University of Oklahoma, 1956. (P. 237.)

Guerra, Francisco. *The Pre-Columbian Mind: A Study into the Aberrant Nature of Sexual Drives, Drugs Affecting Behavior and the Attitude Towards Life and Death, with a Survey of Psychotherapy, in Pre-Columbian America.* London: Seminar, 1971. (Numerous documented references to the "bardaje" [berdache], homosexuality, Lesbianism, and sodomy.)

Hammond, William A. "The Disease of the Scythians (*Morbus Feminarum*) and Certain Analogous Conditions," *American Journal of Neurology and Psychiatry* (N.Y.). Vol. 1, no. 3 (Aug. 1882): p. 339–55.

Hallowell, A. Irving. *Culture and Experience.* Phila.: University of Pennsylvania, 1955. (P. 293–95.)

Hassrick, Royal B. *The Sioux: Life and Customs of a Warrior Society.* Norman: University of Oklahoma, 1964. (P. 121–23, 273.)

Hennepin, Louis. *A Description of Louisiana.* Trans. John Gilmary Shea. N.Y.: John G. Shea, 1880. (P. 334.)

———. *A New Discovery of a Vast Country in America.* Ed. Reuben Gold Thwaites. 2 vols. Chicago: A. C. McClurg, 1903. (Vol. 1, p. 167–68.)

Henry, Alexander, and Thompson, David. *New Light on the Early History of the Greater Northwest: The Manuscript Journals of Alexander Henry and of David Thompson, 1799–1814 . . .* Ed. Elliott Coues. 3 vols. N.Y.: Francis P. Harper, 1897. (Vol. 1, p. 53, 163–65, 348, 399.)

Herbert, Louis, gen. ed. *The Mythology of All Races.* Vol. 10, *North American.* Ed. Alexander Hartely Burr. Boston: Marshall Jones, 1916. (P. 160, 206, 308–09.)

Hill, Willard Williams. "Navaho Humor," *General Studies in Anthropology, no. 9.* Menasha, Wis.: George Banta, 1943. (P. 12.)

————. "Note on the Pima Berdache," *American Anthropologist*. New ser., vol. 40 (1938): p. 338–40.

————. "The Status of the Hermaphrodite and Transvestite in Navaho Culture," *American Anthropologist*. New ser., vol. 37 (1935): p. 273–79.

Hoebel, E. Adamson. *The Cheyennes: Indians of the Great Plains*. N.Y.: Holt, 1960. (P. 77–79, 96.)

————. *Man in the Primitive World; an Introduction to Anthropology*. N.Y.: McGraw-Hill, 1949. (P. 459.)

Hoffman, Walter James. "The Midē'wiwin or 'Grand Medicine Society' of the Ojibwa." *U.S. Bureau of American Ethnology. 7th Annual Report, 1885–86*. Washington, D.C.: U.S. Govt. Ptg. Ofc., 1891. (P. 153.)

Holder, A. B. "The Bote. Description of a Peculiar Sexual Perversion Found among North American Indians," *New York Medical Journal*. Vol. 50, no. 23 (December 7, 1889): p. 623–25.

Honigmann, John J. *Culture and Personality*. N.Y.: Harper, 1954. (P. 278.)

————. "The Kaska Indians; An Ethnographic Reconstruction," *Yale University Publications in Anthropology, no. 51*. New Haven: Yale University, 1964. (P. 129–30.)

Howard, James. "The Ponca Tribe," *Smithsonian Institution. Bureau of American Ethnology. Bulletin 195*. Washington, D.C.: U.S. Govt. Ptg. Ofc., 1965. (P. 75, 78, 143–47.)

Hrdlička, Aleš Ferdinand. "Physiological and Medical Observations among the Indians of the Southwestern United States and Northern Mexico," *Smithsonian Institution; Bureau of American Ethnology; Bulletin 34*. Washington, D. C.: U.S. Govt. Ptg. Ofc., 1908. (P. 51.)

Hyde, George. *Red Cloud's Folk; A History of the Oglala Sioux Indians*. Norman: University of Oklahoma, 1967. (P. 147.)

Irving, John Treat. *Indian Sketches Taken during an Expedition to the Pawnee Tribes [1833]*. Ed. John Francis McDermott. Norman: University of Oklahoma, 1955. (P. 93–95.)

Jacobs, Sue-Ellen. "Berdache: A Brief Review of the Literature," *Colorado Anthropologist*. Vol. 1, no. 1 (1968): p. 25–40.

James, Edwin. *Account of an Expedition from Pittsburgh to the Rocky Mountains in the Years 1819 and '20, by Order of the Hon. J. C. Calhoun, Sec'y of War: Under the Command of Major Stephen H. Long*. 2 vols. Phila.: H. C. Carey and I. Lea, 1922–23. (Vol. 1, p. 129, 267.)

Jones, William. "Fox Texts," *Publications of the American Ethnological Society*. Vol. 1. Leiden: E. J. Brill, 1907. (P. 151.)

Karsch-Haack, F[erdinand]. *Das gleichgeschlechtliche Leben der Naturvöker* ["The Same Sex Life of Primitive Peoples"]. Munich: Ernst Reinhardt, 1911. Photo reprint, N.Y.: Arno, 1975. (P. 297–362, 505–08.)

Keating, William Hypolitus. *Narrative of an Expedition to the Source of St. Peter's River, Lake Winnepeek, Lake of the Woods . . . in the Year 1823, by Order of the Hon. J. C. Calhoun, Secretary of War. . . .* 2 vols. Phila.: Carey & Lea, 1824. (Vol. 1, p. 210–11.)

Kelly, Isabel T. "Ethnology of the Surprise Valley Paiute," *University of California Publications in American Archaeology and Ethnology*. Vol. 31 (1932) p. 67–210. (P. 157–58.)

Kenny, Maurice. "Tinselled Bucks; An Historical Study in Indian Homosexuality," *Gay Sunshine*. Nos. 26–27 (Winter 1975–1976): p. 15–17.

Kiernan, James G. "Responsibility in Sexual Perversion," *Chicago Medical Recorder*. Vol. 3 (1892): p. 185–210. (P. 185–87.)

Kinietz, W. Vernon. "Chippewa Village: The Story of Katikitegon," *Cranbrook Institute of Science, Bulletin 25*. Bloomfield Hills, Mich.: Cranbrook, 1947. (P. 155–56.)

————. *The Indians of the Western Great Lakes, 1615–1760*. Ann Arbor: University of Michigan, 1965. (P. 388–89.)

Kroeber, Alfred Louis. "The Arapaho," *Bulletin of the American Museum of Natural History*. Vol. 18 (1902). (P. 19–20.)

————. "Handbook of the Indians of California," *U.S. Bureau of American Ethnology Bulletin, no. 78*. Washington, D.C.: U.S. Govt. Ptg. Ofc., 1925. (P. 46, 190, 497, 500–01, 647, 728–29, 748–49, 803.)

————. "Psychosis or Social Sanction," *Character and Personality; An International Psychological Quarterly*. Vol. 8 (1939–40): p. 204–15. (P. 209–10.)

Kurz, R. F. "Journal of Rudolph Frederick Kurz . . . 1846–1852." Ed. J. N. B. Hewitt. Trans.

Myrtis Jarrell. *Bureau of American Ethnology Bulletin 115*. Washington, D.C.: U.S. Govt. Ptg. Ofc., 1937. (P. 213–14.)

Lafitau, Joseph François. *Moeurs des sauvages ameriquains, comparées aux moeurs des premiers tempts*. 2 vols. Paris: Saugrain, 1724. (Vol. 1, p. 52, 603–10.)

Laguna, Frederica de. "Tlingit Ideas about the Indian," *Southwestern Journal of Anthropology*. Vol. 10 (1954): p. 172–79. (P. 178.)

Lahontan, Louis Armand de Lom d'Arce de. *New Voyages to North-America*. Ed. Reuben Gold Thwaites. 2 vols. Chicago: A. C. McClurg, 1905. (Vol. 2, p. 462.)

Langsdorff, Georg Heinrich. *Voyages and Travels in Various Parts of the World during the Years 1803 . . . 1809*. 2 vols. London: H. Colburn, 1813–14. (Vol. 2, p. 47–48, 64.)

Landes, Ruth. *The Mystic Lake Sioux, Sociology of the Mdewakantonwan Santee*. Madison, Wis.: University of Wisconsin, 1968. (P. 29, 31–32, 57, 66, 112–13, 127–28, 153, 193, 206–07.)

———. *The Prairie Potawatomi; Tradition and Ritual in the Twentieth Century*. Madison, Wis.: University of Wisconsin, 1970. (P. 26, 36–37, 190, 195–202, 201–02, 316.)

Laudonnière, René. *A Notable Historie Containing Foure Voyages Made by Certayne French Captaynes unto Florida . . . by Monsieur Laudonnière*. Trans. R[ichard] H[akluyt]. London: Thomas Dawson, 1587. (P. 3 [i.e. 5].)

Lawson, John. *Lawson's History of North Carolina . . .* Ed. Frances Latham Harriss. Richmond, Va.: Garrett & Massie, 1937. (P. 208.)

Legg, W. Dorr. "The Berdache and Theories of Sexual Inversion," *ONE Institute Quarterly*. Vol. 2, no. 2 (1959): p. 59–63.

Leighton, Dorothea, and Kluckhohn, Clyde. *Children of the People: The Navaho Individual and His Development*. Cambridge, Mass.: Harvard University, 1948. (P. 78.)

Le Moyne de Morgues, Jacques. *Narrative of Le Moyne, an Artist Who Accompanied the French Expedition to Florida under Laudonnière, 1564*. Trans. Frederick B. Perkins. Boston: James R. Osgood, 1875. (P. 7–8.)

Lévi-Straus, Claude. *Structural Anthropology*. N.Y.: Basic Books, 1963. (P. 233 ff.)

Liette, Pierre. *The Western Country in the 17th Century: The Memoirs of . . . Pierre Liette*. Ed. Milo Milton Quaife. N.Y.: Citadel, 1962. (P. 112–13.)

Linton, Ralph. *The Study of Man*. N.Y.: Appleton-Century-Crofts, 1936. (P. 480–81.)

Loskiel, Georg Heinrich. *Geschichte der Mission der evangelischen Brüder unter den Indianern in Nordamerika*. Barby: Evangelische Brüdergemeine, 1789. (P. 18.)

———. *History of the Mission of the United Brethren among the Indians in North America*. Trans. Christian I. LaTrobe. London: Brethren's Society for the Furtherance of the Gospel, 1794. (P. 14.)

Lowie, Robert Henry. "The Assiniboine," *Anthropological Papers of the American Museum of Natural History*. Vol. 4, part 1 (Nov. 1909). (P. 42, 223.)

———. *The Crow Indians*. N.Y.: Farrar & Rinehart, 1935. (P. viii, 48, 312–13.)

———. "Notes on Shoshonean Ethnology," *Anthropological Papers of the American Museum of Natural History* (N.Y.). Vol. 20, part 3 (1925): p. 185–315. (P. 282–83.)

———. *Primitive Religion*. N.Y.: Boni and Liveright, 1924. (P. 181, 243–46.)

———. "Social Life of the Crow Indians," *Anthropological Papers of the American Museum of Natural History* (N.Y.) Vol. 9, part 2 (1912): p. 179–248. (P. 226.)

Lurie, Nancy Oestreich. "Winnebago Berdache," *American Anthropologist*. Vol. 55 (1953): p. 708–12.

McCoy, Isaac. *History of the Baptist Indian Missions; Embracing Remarks on the Former and Present Condition of the Aboriginal Tribes; Their Settlement within the Indian Territory; and their Future Prospects*. Washington, D.C.: William M. Morrison, 1840. (P. 360–61.)

McKenney, Thomas A. *Sketches of a Tour to Lakes, of the Character and Customs of the Chippeway Indians, and of Incidents Connected with the Treaty of Fond du Lac*. Baltimore: Fielding Lucas Jr., 1827. (P. 315–16.)

McKenny, Thomas L., and Hall, James. *The Indian Tribes of North America*. Ed F. W. Hodge. 3 vols. Edinburgh: John Grant, 1933–34. (Vol. 1, p. 120–24, 326.)

McMurtrie, Douglas Crawford. "A Legend of Lesbian Love Among the North American Indians," *Urologic and Cutaneous Review*. April 1914: p. 192–93.

Mandelbaum, May. "The Individual Life Cycle." In "The Sinkaietk or Southern Okanagon of Washington" by Walter Cline and others. Ed. Leslie Spier. *General Series in Anthropology, no. 6.* Menasha, Wis.: George Banta, 1938. (P. 119.)

Marquette, Jacques. "Of the First Voyage Made by Father Marquette toward New Mexico, and How the Idea Thereof Was Conceived." Vol. 59 of *The Jesuit Relations and Allied Documents.* Ed. Reuben Gold Thwaites. 73 vols. Cleveland: Burrows, 1896–1901. (P. 129.)

Maximilian, Alexander P. *Travels in the Interior of North American: 1832–1834.* Vol. 22 of *Early Western Travels.* Ed. Reuben Gold Thwaites. 32 vols. Cleveland: A. H. Clark, 1906. (P. 283–84, 354.)

Mead, Margaret. *Male and Female: A Study of the Sexes in a Changing World.* N.Y.: Morrow, 1949. (P. 129–30.)

————. *Sex and Temperament in Three Primitive Societies.* N.Y.: New American Library, 1935. (P. 240.)

Membré, Zenobius. *Discovery and Exploration of the Mississippi Valley, with the Original Narratives of Marquette, Allouez, Membré, Hennepin, and Anastase Douay.* 2nd ed. Trans. John Gilmary Shea. Albany, N.Y.: Joseph McDonough, 1903. (P. 155.)

Morgan, Lewis Henry. *League of the Ho-dé-no-sau-nee or Iroquois.* New ed., with additional matter. Ed. and annotated by Herbert M. Lloyd. N.Y.: Dodd, Mead, 1904. (P. 329.)

Müller, J. G. *Geschichte der Amerikanischen Urreligionen.* Basel: Schweighauser, 1855. (P. 44 ff, 418.)

Murdock, George P., and others. *Outline of Cultural Materials.* vol. 1, *Behavior Science Outlines.* 4th rev. ed. New Haven: Human Resource Area Files, Inc., 1971. (P. 15, 548, 572, 588, 838.)

Olson, Ronald L. "The Quinault Indians," *University of Washington Publications in Anthropology.* Vol. 6, no. 1 (1936). (P. 99.)

O'Meara, Walter. *Daughters of the Country; the Women of the Fur Traders and Mountain Men.* N.Y.: Harcourt, Brace, and World, 1968. (P. 81, 82, 319.)

Opler, Marvin Kaufman. "Anthropological and Cross-Cultural Aspects of Homosexuality." P. 108–23 in *Sexual Inversion; The Multiple Roots of Homosexuality.* Ed. J. Judd Marmor. N.Y.: Basic Books, 1965.

————. "The Influence of Ethnic and Class Subcultures on Child Care," *Social Problems.* Vol. 3, no. 1 (1955). (P. 3, 12–21.)

Opler, Morris Edward. *An Apache Life-Way: The Economic, Social, and Religious Institutions of the Chiricahua Indians.* Chicago: University of Chicago, 1941. (P. 79–80, 415–16.)

Palóu, Francisco. *Relación histórica de la vida y apostólicas tareas del venerable Padre Fray Junípero Serra y des las Misiones que fundó en la California Septentrional.* Mexico: Don Felipe de Zúñiga y Ontiveros, 1787. (P. 222.)

Pareja, Francisco. *Francisco Pareja's 1613 Confesionario: A Documentary Source for Timucuan Ethnology.* Ed. J. T. Milanich and W. C. Sturtevant. Trans. E. F. Moran. Tallahassee, Fla.: Div. of Archives, History, and Records Management, 1972. (P. 39, 43, 48, 75, 76.)

Parkman, Francis. *Francis Parkman's Works; New Library Edition.* Vol. 3: *La Salle and the Discovery of the Great West. France and England in North America.* Boston: Little, Brown, 1903. (P. 207.)

————. *The Oregon Trail.* Ed. E. N. Feltskog. Madison: University of Wisconsin, 1969. (P. 100–01, 280–82, 283.)

Parsons, Elsie Clews. "The Zuñi la'mana," *American Anthropologist.* New ser., vol. 18 (1916): p. 521–28.

Perrin du Lac, François Marie. *Voyage dans les deux Louisianes et chez les nations sauvages du Missouri, par les États-Unis, l'Ohio et les Provinces qui bordent, en 1801, 1802 et 1803.* Lyon: Bruyset Aîné et Buyand, 1805. (P. 318, 352.)

Powers, Stephen. "Tribes of California. Contributions To North American Enthnology," *Department of the Interior. U.S. Geographical and Geological Survey of the Rocky Mountain Range.* Washington, D.C.: U.S. Govt. Ptg. Ofc., 1877. (P. 132 ff.)

Ray, Verne F. "The Sanpoil and Nespelern: Salishan Peoples of Northeastern Washington," *University of Washington, Publications in Anthropology.* Vol. 5 (1932). (P. 114–15, 148.)

Reichard, Gladys Amanda. *Navaho Religion: A Study of Symbolism.* N.Y.: Bollingen Foundation, Pantheon, 1950. (P. 140–42.)

————. "Social Life of the Navaho Indian with Some Attention to Minor Ceremonies," *Co-*

lumbia University Contributions to Anthropology. Vol. 7. N.Y.: Columbia University, 1928. (P. 150.)

Remondino, Peter Charles. *History of Circumcision from the Earliest Times to the Present.* Phila. and London: F. A. Davis, 1891. (P. 200, 333–34.)

Romans, Bernard. *A Concise Natural History of East and West Florida.* New Orleans: Pelican, 1961. (P. 56.)

Ross, Alexander. *Adventures of the First Settlers on the Oregon or Columbia River.* London: Smith, Elder, 1849. (P. 85, 144–45.)

Schaeffer, Claude E. "The Kutenai Female Berdache: Courier, Guide, Prophetess, and Warrior." *Ethnohistory.* Vol. 12, no. 3 (1965): p. 193–236.

Seligmann, Charles Gabriel. "Sexual Inversion Among Primitive Races," *Alienist and Neurologist.* Vol. 23, no. 1 (1902), p. 11–15.

Simms, S. C. "Crow Indian Hermaphrodites," *American Anthropologist.* New ser., vol. 5 (1903): p. 580–81.

Skinner, Adamson. "Notes on the Eastern Cree and Northern Sauteaux," *Anthropological Papers of the American Museum of Natural History.* Vol. 9 (1911): p. 1–77. (P. 151–52.)

Solíz de Merás, Gonsalo. *Pedro Menéndez de Avilés . . . Governor and Captain-General of Florida, Memorial . . .* Trans. Jeanette Conner. Deland, Fla.: Florida State Historical Society, 1923. (P. 180–81.)

Sonenschein, David. "Homosexuality as a Subject of Anthropological Inquiry," *Anthropological Quarterly.* Vol. 39, no. 2 (1966): p. 73–82.

Sperlin, O. B. "Two Kootenay Women Masquerading as Men? Or Were They One?" *Washington Historical Quarterly.* Vol. 21 (1930): p. 120–130.

Spier, Leslie. "Klamath Ethnography," *University of California Publications in American Archaeology and Ethnology.* Vol. 27 (1930). (P. 51–53.)

———. "The Prophet Dance of the Northwest and Its Derivatives: The Source of the Ghost Dance," *General Series in Anthropology, no. 1.* Menasha, Wis.: George Banta, 1935. (P. 27.)

———. *Yuman Tribes of the Gila River.* Chicago: University of Chicago, 1933. (P. 4, 6, 242–43.)

———, and Sapir, E. "Wishram Ethnography," *University of Washington Publications in Anthropology.* Vol. 3 (1929). (P. 220–21.)

Stevenson, Matilda Coxe. "The Zuñi Indians: Their Mythology, Esoteric Societies, and Ceremonies," *Twenty-third Annual Report. U.S. Bureau of American Ethnology . . . 1901–02. Smithsonian Institution.* Washington, D.C.: U.S. Govt. Ptg. Ofc., 1904. (P. 37–38, 150, 310–13, 374.)

Steward, Julian. *Ethnology of the Owens Valley Paiute.* Berkeley, Cal.: University of California, 1933. (P. 238, 311.)

Stewart, Omer C. "Culture Element Distributions: XVIII; Ute-Southern Paiute," *Anthropological Records.* Vol. 6, no. 4 (1941). (P. 298.)

———. "Homosexuality Among the American Indians and Other Native Peoples of the World," *Mattachine Review.* Vol. 6, no. 1 (Jan. 1960): p. 9–15; no. 2 (Feb. 1960): p. 13–19.

Stiller, Richard. "Homosexuality and the American Indian," *Sexology.* Vol. 29, no. 2 (June 1963): p. 770–72.

Swanton, John. "Early History of the Creek Indians and their Neighbors," *U.S. Bureau of American Ethnology, Bulletin 73.* Washington, D.C.: U.S. Govt. Ptg. Ofc., 1922. (P. 373.)

Tanner, John. *A Narrative of the Captivity and Adventures of John Tanner (U.S. Interpreter at the Sault de Saint Marie) During Thirty Years Residence Among the Indians in the Interior of North America.* Ed. Edwin James. N.Y.C.: G. and C. and H. Carvill, 1830. (P. 105–06.)

Teit, James A. "The Salishan Tribes of the Western Plateau." Ed. Franz Boas. *Forty-fifth Annual Report, 1927–28. U.S. Bureau of American Ethnology. Smithsonian Institution.* Washington, D.C.: U.S. Govt. Ptg. Ofc., 1930. (P. 292, 384.)

Thompson, David. David Thompson Papers, 1807–11. Ontario Archives, Toronto.

———. *David Thompson's Narrative of His Explorations in Western America 1784–1812.* Ed. J. B. Tyrrell. Toronto: Champlain Society Publications, no. 12, 1916. (P. 512–13.)

———. "Narrative of the Expedition to the Kootenae and Flat Bow Indian Countries, on the Sources of the Columbia River, Pacific Ocean by D[avid] Thompson on Behalf of the N.W. Company, 1807." Ed. T. C. Elliot. In "The Discovery of the Source of the Columbia River," *Oregon Historical Quarterly.* Vol. 25 (1925). (P. 512–13.)

Thoreau, Henry David. *A Week on the Concord and Merrimack Rivers*. Cambridge, Mass.: Riverside Press, 1961. (P. 291 ff.)

Tixier, Victor. *Tixier's Travels on the Osage Prairies*. Ed. John F. McDermott. Trans. Albert J. Salvan. Norman: University of Oklahoma, 1940. (P. 234.)

Tonti, [Henri de]. "An Account of Monsieur de La Salle's Last Expedition and Discoveries in North America," *Collections of the New-York Historical Society*. Ser. 1, vol. 2 (1814). (P. 237–38.)

Torquemada, Juan de. *Los veinte y un libros rituales y Monarchía Indiana*. Ed. A. Gonzalez de Barcia Carballido y Zuñiga. 3 vols. Madrid: N. Rodriguez Franco, 1723. (Vol. 2, p. 427.)

Trumbull, H. Clay. *Friendship the Master-Passion, or, The Nature and History of Friendship, and Its Place as a Force in the World*. Phila.: John D. Wattles, 1894. (P. 71–72, 165–66.)

Turney-High, Harry Holbert. "Ethnography of the Kutenai," *Memoirs of the American Anthropological Association, no. 56*. Menasha, Wis.: Amer. Anth. Assoc., 1941. (P. 128.)

——. "The Flathead Indians of Montana," *Memoirs of the American Anthropological Association, no. 48*. Menasha, Wis.: Amer. Anth. Assoc., 1937. (P. 85.)

Underhill, Ruth. "The Autobiography of a Papago Woman," *Memoirs of the American Anthropological Association, no. 43*. Menasha, Wis.: Amer. Anth. Assoc., 1936. (P. 43–44.)

——. *Red Man's Religion; Beliefs and Practices of the Indians North of Mexico*. Chicago: University of Chicago, 1965. (P. 65.)

——. *Social Organization of the Papago Indians*. N.Y.: Columbia University, 1939. (P. 117, 186–87.)

Vogelin, Ermine W. *Culture Element Distribution: XX. Northwestern California*. Berkeley: University of California, 1942. (P. 134.)

——. "Tubatulabal Ethnology," *University of California, Anthropological Records*. Vol. 2 (1938): p. 1–90. (P. 47.)

Waltrip, Bob. "Elmer Gage: American Indian," *ONE*. Vol. 13, no. 3 (March 1965): p. 6–10.

Weltfish, Gene. *The Lost Universe*. N.Y.: Basic Books, 1965. (P. 29.)

Westermarck, Edward. *The Origin and Development of Moral Ideas*. 2nd ed. 2 vols. London: Macmillan, 1917. (Vol. 2, chap. 43, "Homosexual Love," p. 456–89.)

Will, G. F., and Spinden, H. J. "The Mandans: A Study of their Culture, Archaeology and Language," *Papers of the Peabody Museum of American Archaeology and Ethnology*. Vol. 3 (1906): p. 79–222. (P. 128.)

Wisler, Clark. "Societies and Ceremonial Associations in the Oglala Division of the Teton-Dakota," *Anthropological Papers of the American Museum of Natural History*. Vol. 12 (1912). (P. 92.)

Work, John. "Journal" [title varies]. Ed. T. C. Elliot. *Washington Historical Quarterly*. Vol. 5 (1914). (P. 190.)

NOTES

V. Resistance: 1859–1972

1. Walt Whitman, *Leaves of Grass; Facsimile Edition of the 1860 Text*, introduction by Roy Harvey Pearce (Ithaca, N.Y.: Cornell Paperbacks, Cornell University, 1961), p. 341–42. Hereafter cited as Whitman (1860).

2. Whitman (1860), p. 347–48.

3. *Walt Whitman's Leaves of Grass; The First (1855) Edition*, ed. with an introduction by Malcolm Cowley (N.Y.: Viking, Viking Compass Edition, 1961), p. 49. See line 535 of the poem later called "Song of Myself."

4. Whitman (1860), p. 10–11.

5. Whitman (1860), p. 349–51.

6. Whitman (1860), p. 374.

7. Whitman (1860), p. 375.

8. Phyllis Grosskurth, *John Addington Symonds; A Biography* (London: Longmans, Green, 1964; photo reprint, N.Y.: Arno, 1975), p. 42–44, 119–20.

9. John Addington Symonds, *The Letters of John Addington Symonds*, eds. Herbert M. Schueller and Robert L. Peters, 3 vols. (Detroit: Wayne State University, 1967–69), vol. 1, p. 706. Hereafter cited as Symonds, *Letters*. Grosskurth, p. 120. The Symonds *Letters* contain a much greater quantity of important material than it was possible to quote here.

10. Symonds, *Letters*, vol. 1, p. 707. Grosskurth, p. 120–21.

11. Walt Whitman, *Collected Writings*, vol. 9 (in two volumes), *Prose Works*, ed. Floyd Stovall (N.Y.: N.Y. University, 1964), vol. 2, p. 414.

12. Symonds, *Letters*, vol. 2, p. 167. Note*: "F. W. H. Myer's rooms."

13. Symonds, *Letters*, vol. 2, p. 202.

14. Symonds, *Letters*, vol. 2, p. 205.

15. Grosskurth, p. 289.

16. Symonds, *Letters*, vol. 2, p. 446–47.

17. Grosskurth, p. 267.

18. Symonds, *Letters*, vol. 3, p. 301–02.

19. Horace L. Traubel, *With Walt Whitman in Camden*, vol. 1 (Boston: Small, Maynard, 1906), p. 73–77. In this letter Whitman indicates his perfectly conscious recognition of Symonds's interest and personal involvement in the "passional relations of men with men." This suggests that Whitman's "astonishment" at Symonds's question on the subject and Whitman's reply of August 19, 1890, are quite ingenuous. Whitman's awareness that he was speaking for publication and to posterity about his "Calamus" poems is also to be noted. See note 32 below.

20. Traubel, vol. 1, p. 202–05. Whitman's characterization of his "Calamus" poems as "my daughter," as feminine, is suggestive.

21. Horace L. Traubel, *With Walt Whitman in Camden*, vol. 2 (N.Y.: Appleton, 1908), p. 276–78.

22. Symonds, *Letters*, vol. 3, p. 356.

23. Symonds, *Letters*, vol. 1, p. 446. Grosskurth, p. 276–77.

24. Symonds, *Letters*, vol. 3, p. 364.

25. Symonds, *Letters*, vol. 3, p. 418–19.

26. Symonds, *Letters*, vol. 3, p. 424–25.

27. Whitman (1860), p. 354–55. Symonds, *Letters*, vol. 3, n. 3, p. 424–25. Walt Whitman, *Leaves of Grass; Comprehensive Reader's Edition,* eds. Harold W. Blodgett and Sculley Bradley (N.Y.: Norton [paperback], 1965), p. 595–96.

28. Symonds, *Letters*, vol. 3, p. 458–59.

29. Grosskurth, (p. 280), is mistaken about Symonds being in "the early stages" of preparing *A Problem in Modern Ethics* when he wrote to his friend Dakyns on July 19, 1890. Symonds had told his daughter Margaret about finishing his *Modern Ethics* manuscript in a letter to her of Dec. 6, 1889. *Modern Ethics* was not printed, however, until early in 1891, so Symonds probably wanted to incorporate Whitman's comments on homosexuality into his defense of *Modern* male–male love.

30. Symonds, *Letters*, vol. 3, p. 483–84. Note omitted.

31. Grosskurth, p. 273.

32. Whitman *Collected, The Correspondence*, ed. Edwin Haviland Miller, vol. 5, p. 72–73. See the important variant of this letter, quoted by Symonds in his letter to E. Carpenter, Feb. 13, 1893, and note 54 below. Not one of these six children has ever been reliably identified, and the present consensus is that they never existed. My purely speculative thinking on the subject is that Whitman had particular referents in mind when claiming, specifically, six offspring. Could these "children" have been the males he had most loved: (1) Peter Doyle; (2) Harry Stafford; (3) Tom Sawyer; (4) Lewis K. Brown; (5) Jack Flood; and (6) Byron Sutherland each of whom Whitman, in correspondence, referred to as "son"? (Some similar, revised combination of young men

might also be suggested—Edward Cattell is an additional likely candidate; Albert Johnston and John R. Johnston, Jr., are possible candidates.) Had any two of these men died by August, 1890? Did one have a son whom Whitman considered his "grandchild," and who wrote to him occasionally? It is noteworthy that Whitman often used familial terms in referring to his young men, and his relationships with them. See Whitman's *Collected Writings; The Correspondence*, especially his letters to Brown (vol. 1, p. 120); to Flood (vol. 2, p. 118–19); about Stafford (vol. 3, p. 67–68); to Catell (vol. 3, p. 76–77); to Sutherland (vol. 3, p. 266–67). Whitman's pathetic attempt to establish his heterosexuality by claiming paternity is ironic in light of Symonds's own three offspring. Whitman's denial of his homosexuality appears to arise from his desire to be remembered as the American poet-prophet and his recognition that homosexuality and sainthood were socially irreconcilable.

33. Whitman *Collected*, vol. 5, p. 74–75. For St. Paul's condemnation of homosexuality, see Rom. 1:26–27, 1 Cor. 6:9, 1 Tim. 1:10.

34. Symonds, *Letters*, vol. 3, p. 492–94. Note omitted.

35. Symonds, *Letters*, vol. 3, p. 508.

36. Symonds, *Letters*, vol. 3, p. 543.

37. Symonds, *Letters*, vol. 3, p. 544.

38. Symonds, *Letters*, vol. 3, p. 547–49. Note omitted.

39. Symonds, *Letters*, vol. 3, p. 533. Note omitted.

40. Symonds, *Letters*, vol. 3, p. 553, 555.

41. Symonds, *Letters*, vol. 3, p. 579. Note omitted.

42. A note in the Symonds *Letters* (vol. 3, p. 579–80) identifies the American author of the homosexual defense received by Symonds as Benjamin Osgood Pierce (*sic*—the correct spelling is Peirce). Leon Edel identifies this same individual as Charles Sanders Peirce (*Henry James; The Treacherous Years: 1895–1901* [Phila.: Lippincott, 1969] p. 124–25). In a letter to the present author, a well-informed source says "The only possible identification" for the individual in question is James Mills Peirce. See entry on J. M. Peirce in the DAB. "A Letter from Professor X" is in Havelock Ellis and John Addington Symonds, *Sexual Inversion* (London: Wilson and Macmillan, 1897; photo reprint, N.Y.: Arno, 1975), p. 273–75.

43. Symonds, *Letters*, vol. 3, p. 585–86.

44. Edel, *James: Treacherous Years*, p. 124–25, 126–27.

45. Symonds, *Letters*, vol. 3, p. 587–88.

46. Symonds, *Letters*, vol. 3, p. 642–43.

47. Symonds, *Letters*, vol. 3, p. 667–68.

48. Symonds, *Letters*, vol. 3, p. 691.

49. Symonds, *Letters*, vol. 3, p. 693–95.

50. Symonds, *Letters*, vol. 3, p. 709.

51. Symonds, *Letters*, vol. 3, p. 711.

52. Symonds, *Letters*, vol. 3, p. 797–99.

53. Symonds, *Letters*, vol. 3, p. 808–09. Notes:* "Whitman said Symonds was 'terribly literary and suspicious' in Horace L. Traubel, 'Walt Whitman's Birthday,' *Lippincott's Magazine*, XLVIII (1891), 231."† "Ellis believed that inverts are less prone than normal persons to regard caste and social position. This 'innately democratic attitude' parallels Symonds' attentiveness to gondoliers and soldiers and Carpenter's to the British peasants of Derbyshire."

54. Symonds, *Letters*, vol. 3, p. 818–19. Symonds's quotation from Whitman's letter of Aug. 19, 1890, differs significantly from the surviving draft of the same letter quoted earlier (from Whitman's published correspondence, vol. 5 [1969], the editors of which do not mention the variant). Whitman's draft says: "I at certain moments let the spirit impulse, (? demon) rage its utmost. . . ." Symonds quotes Whitman as saying: "I at

certain moments let the spirit impulse (female) rage its utmost. . . ." It is likely that Symonds, a historian, quoted Whitman accurately. The implications of the variant remain to be explored. See note 32 above.

55. Edel, *James; Treacherous Years*, p. 127.

56. Carpenter's sexual history, written by himself, appears anonymously as "Case VI" in Ellis and Symonds's *Sexual Inversion* (London: Wilson and Macmillan, 1897; photo reprint, N.Y.: Arno, 1975), p. 46–47. Carpenter's case history, beginning with the words, "My parentage is very sound," appears in post-1897 editions of *Sexual Inversion* as "Case VII." This information is from Émile Delavenay, *D. H. Lawrence and Edward Carpenter; A Study in Edwardian Transition* (N.Y.: Taplinger, 1971), p. 271.

57. G. C. Moore Smith, "Carpenter, Edward," *Dictionary of National Biography, 1922–30*, p. 159–162.

58. Traubel, vol. 1, p. 158–61. Whitman could not have avoided noticing the references in Carpenter's letter to that love "which passes the love of women," and thus must have early suspected Carpenter's homosexual orientation. It should be noted that Carpenter's letters to Whitman as quoted in Traubel contain much more pertinent material than it was possible to present here.

59. Traubel, vol. 3 (N.Y.: Mitchell Kennerley, 1914), p. 415–17.

60. Edward Carpenter, *Days with Walt Whitman: With some Notes on his Life and Work*, 2nd ed. (London: George Allen, 1906), p. 42–43.

61. Traubel, vol. 3, p. 192–94.

62. Traubel, vol. 1, p. 160.

63. Traubel, vol. 1, p. 189.

64. Traubel, vol. 3, p. 245–48.

65. Traubel, vol. 3, p. 414, 418–19.

66. Edward Carpenter, *Homogenic Love* (Manchester, England: Manchester Labour Press, [dated] 1894 [Jan. 1895]).

67. Grosskurth, p. 291.

68. Edward Carpenter, *Some Friends of Walt Whitman; A Study in Sex Psychology*, Publication No. 13 (London: British Society for the Study of Sex Psychology, 1924), p. 10. The characterization of the society as the "only official organization" formed by English male homosexuals in the early twentieth century is from Timothy d'Arch Smith, *Love in Earnest; Some Notes on the Lives and Writings of English 'Uranian' Poets from 1889 to 1930* (London: Routledge & Kegan Paul, 1970), p. 137.

69. Carpenter, *Some Friends*, p. 12.

70. Carpenter, *Some Friends*, p. 12, 15–16.

71. Carpenter, *Some Friends*, p. 16.

72. Earl Lind ("Ralph Werther"-"Jennie June"), *Autobiography of an Androgyne,* ed. with an introduction by Alfred W. Herzog (N.Y.: *Medico-Legal Journal*, 1918; photo reprint, N.Y.: Arno, 1975). Lind's sequel is titled *The Female-Impersonators . . .* ed. with an introduction by Alfred W. Herzog (N.Y.: *Medico-Legal Journal*, 1922; photo reprint, N.Y.: Arno, 1975).

73. Kate Millett, *Sexual Politics* (N.Y.: Avon Books, Equinox Edition, 1971), p. 17.

74. See the reference to "Paresis Hall" in the 1898 testimony before the N.Y. State Committee investigating conditions in N.Y.C., quoted in Part I.

75. Lind, *Female-Impersonators*, p. 146–48, 150–52.

76. Lind, *Female-Impersonators*, p. 154–57, 159–63.

77. Ellis and Symonds (1897), p. 103.

78. Ellis and Symonds (1897), p. 288–92. A footnote to this statement reads: "In the *Century Magazine*, January, 1897, there is an interesting article entitled 'The Ladies of Llangollen.' There is reason to believe that one or perhaps both of these women were

inverts. The friendship of these women was probably of the character I have mentioned. It is certainly the only kind of friendship that would prove enduring" (p. 289).

79. Ellis and Symonds (1897), p. 88.

80. Havelock Ellis, *Studies in the Psychology of Sex; Sexual Inversion* (Phila.: F. A. Davis, 1901), p. 134.

81. Ellis and Symonds (1897), p. 273–75. Professor X's identity is discussed in note 42, following Symonds's letter of May 20, 1891, above.

82. Emma Goldman, *Living My Life*, 2 vols. (N.Y.: Dover, 1971), vol. 1, p. 269. I wish to thank James Steakley for the following note: "Oskar Panizza (1853–1921) was a German psychiatrist and writer. Homoerotic themes appear in his poetry and plays, especially *Düstere Lieder* (Gloomy Songs, 1886) and *Das Liebeskonzil* (The Council of Love, 1895). His writings brought him prison sentences for blasphemy and offense to the monarchy (the King of Bavaria), and he died in a Bayreuth insane asylum to which he was committed in 1904. This enigmatic figure has received relatively little attention, although his works were recently reprinted in West Germany."

83. Goldman, vol. 2, p. 555–56. Caplan and Schmidt were alleged by the police to be active anarchist terrorists; Goldman discusses their case on p. 551, 562–63, 573.

84. Emma Goldman, "Offener Brief an den Herausgeber der Jahrbücher über Louise Michel," trans. from the English with a preface by Magnus Hirschfeld (*Jahrbuch für sexuelle Zwischenstufen* [Leipzig]), vol. 23 (1923), p. 70. Von Levetzow's "Louise Michel" appeared in the *Jahrbuch*, vol. 7 (1905), p. 307–70. I wish to thank James Steakley for retranslating this document from the German. Goldman's original letter in English is not known to be extant.

85. Goldman, "Offener," p. 73–76, 86–87, 90. Additional comments by Goldman on the subject of homosexuality and on various homosexuals appear in *Nowhere at Home: Letters from Exile of Emma Goldman and Alexander Berkman*, eds. Richard and Anna Maria Drinnon (N.Y.: Schocken, 1975). I wish to thank Martin Duberman and James Steakley for this information.

86. [Otto Spengler,] *Monatsberichte des Wissenschaftlich-humanitären Komitees*, vol. 5 (1906), p. 151. I wish to thank James Steakley for informing me of this and the following two documents, and for translating them.

87. [Georg Merzbach,] *Monatsberichte des Wissenschaftlich-humanitären Komitees,* vol. 6 (1907), p. 76–77.

88. [Anonymous, Letter from Boston,] *Monatsberichte des Wissenschaftlich-humanitären Komitees*, vol. 6 (1907), p. 98–99. Paragraphing was added and the order of the last two paragraphs is reversed for the sake of clarity. This letter was reprinted by Magnus Hirschfeld in his *Die Homosexualität des Mannes und des Weibes* (Berlin: Louis Marcus, 1914), p. 553.

In 1908, Edward I. Prime Stevenson, the American who wrote in defense of homosexuality under the pseudonym Xavier Mayne, published his major work *The Intersexes: A History of Similisexualism As A Problem In Social Life* ([Naples?], privately printed [by R. Rispoli, 1908?]; photo reprint, N.Y.: Arno, 1975). In 1906, Stevenson had published (under the alleged editorship of Mayne) his novelistic homosexual defense, the fascinating *Imre: A Memorandum* (Naples: English Book-Press: R. Rispoli, 1906; photo reprint, N.Y.: Arno, 1975). Stevenson's boys' book, *Left to Themselves, Being the Ordeal of Philip and Gerald* (N.Y.: Hunt and Eaton; Cincinnati: Cranston and Stowe, 1891) is an early homosexual "juvenile" (see Part VI, note 160). In *Left to Themselves* Stevenson writes: "To H. Harkness Flagler, This Vignette of the Beginning of an Early Lasting Friendship is Inscribed." Flagler was a financial backer of the Symphony Society of N.Y., later of the N.Y. Philharmonic. Numbers of Stevenson's other works have homosexually relevant content, and this American homosexual emancipation pioneer deserves a full and carefully researched biography. Stevenson's obituary is in the *New York Times*, Aug. 1, 1942, p. 11, col. 4. Two valuable pioneering articles on Stevenson are by Noel I. Garde [pseud.] They are "The Mysterious Father of American Homophile Literature; A Historical Study," *ONE Institute Quarterly of Homophile Studies*, vol. 1, no. 3 (Fall 1958), p. 94–98; and "The First American 'Gay' Novel," same, vol. 3, no. 2 (Spring 1960), p. 185–90.

89. The German *Jahrbuch für sexuelle Zwischenstufen* (Jan.–April, 1921, p. 8–9) mentions that Margaret Sanger and Dr. William Robinson are in touch with the British Society for the Study of Sex Psychology and are planning to form an American branch; Robinson has said he will distribute copies of the British Society's publications in the U.S. I wish to thank David Thorstad for the above information. In 1922, Magnus Hirschfeld, writing about the formation of the British Society for the Study of Sex Psychology, says: "It is of great significance that the . . . Society . . . has succeeded in establishing a branch in the United States. This branch is headed by the distinguished American sex reformer, Margaret Sanger, and our New York colleague, Dr. William Robinson, whose visits to our [Berlin] Institute [for Sexual Science] are held in the fondest memory" ("Von einst bis jetzt" [From Then 'til Now], *Die Freundschaft* [Berlin], vol. 4, nos. 51–52 [Dec. 22, 1922], p. 4). I wish to thank James Steakley for discovering and translating the above document.

Robinson was the editor of the *American Journal of Urology* (Mount Morris Park West, N.Y.) in 1914 when his article, "My Views on Homosexuality," appeared (vol. 10, p. 550–52). Robinson's "An Essay on Sexual Inversion, Homosexuality, and Hermaphroditism," appeared in *Medical Critic and Guide*, vol. 25 (1923), p. 247. Margaret Sanger's papers are deposited in the Sophia Smith Collection, Women's History Archive, Smith College, Northampton, Mass.

90. F. W. Stella Browne, "Studies in Feminine Inversion," *Journal of Sexology and Psychoanalysis* (N.Y.), vol. 1 (1923), p. 51.

91. Browne, p. 57–58. I wish to thank Robert Carter for the French translation.

In 1924, an author named Florence Berry published a defense of homosexuality in the *Medico-Legal Journal* (N.Y.), vol. 41, no. 1, p. 4–9. Titled "The Psyche of the Intermediate Sex," her essay is notable as a rare instance of an early female-authored, nonfictional defense; it is not notable for its originality, as it quotes and paraphrases heavily (without acknowledgment) from Edward Carpenter's *The Intermediate Sex*. The identity and motivation of this Carpenter disciple is an interesting subject for research.

92. Society for Human Rights, Inc., Chicago, charter signed Dec. 10, 1924; certificate no. 8018, State of Illinois, Office of the Secretary of State, Commercial Department, Springfield, Ill. I wish to thank Jim Kepner for information which led to the discovery of this document, for identifying Gerber as the author of the following letter, and for providing other information about Gerber from the Gerber letters and documents in his possession.

93. [Henry Gerber,] letter signed G.S., Washington, D.C., *ONE* (Los Angeles), vol. 1, no. 7 (July 1953), p. 22.

94. The group to which Gerber refers was the *Bund für Menschenrecht* (The Society for Human Rights), founded in 1919 by Hans Kahnert. The *Bund* was the largest of the Gay groups in Germany during the 1920s, one that aimed at being a "mass" organization, and it criticized Hirschfeld's scientistic approach. The *Bund* seems to be the particular homosexual emancipation group with which Gerber identified. Three recently discovered articles, bylined "Henry Gerber, New York," appear in German homosexual emancipation journals edited by Friedrich Radzuweit, chairman of the *Bund*. Gerber's articles are: "Englische Heuchelei" [English Hypocrisy], *Blätter für Menschenrecht* ["Journal of Human Rights"] (Berlin), vol. 6, no. 15 (Oct. 1928), p. 4–5 (the subject is the prosecution in England of Radclyffe Hall's *The Well of Loneliness*); "Die Strafbestimmungen in den 48 Staaten Amerikas und den amerikanischen Territorien für

gewisse Geschlechtsakte" ["The Penalties in the 48 American States and the American Territories for Certain Sexual Acts"], *Blätter für Menschenrecht*, vol. 7, no. 8 (Aug. 1929), p. 5–11; "Zwei Dollars oder fünfzehn Jahre Zuchthaus" ["Two Dollars or Fifteen Years in Prison"], *Das Freundschaftsblatt* ["The Friendship Journal"] (Berlin), vol. 8, no. 41 (Oct. 9, 1930), p. 4. I wish to thank James Steakley for providing the information in this and the following note.

95. A German homosexual emancipation periodical entitled *Freundschaft und Freiheit* (Friendship and Freedom) was published from 1919 until at least 1926.

96. This photo, including *Friendship and Freedom* among a selection of Gay periodicals, originally appeared in Magnus Hirschfeld's article "Die Homosexualität" in Leo Schidrowitz, ed., *Sittengeschichte des Lasters* (Vienna: Verlag für Kulturforschung, 1927), p. 301. It is reprinted in James D. Steakley's *The Homosexual Emancipation Movement in Germany* (N.Y.: Arno, 1975), opposite p. 78. I wish to thank James Steakley for providing a reproduction copy of this photo.

97. An unsuccessful attempt was made to locate the newspaper story which Gerber says was headed "Strange Sex Cult Exposed" and appeared in the Chicago *Herald and Examiner*, on the front page, probably on a Monday, probably in 1925. I am deeply grateful to Nick Patricca for voluntarily hiring a researcher who examined the front pages and skimmed the rest of (a microfilm of) this paper from Dec. 31, 1924 to Dec. 31, 1925. It is possible that the item appeared earlier in 1924, as the charter for the Society for Human Rights had been issued on Dec. 10 of that year.

98. Henry Gerber, "The Society for Human Rights—1925," *ONE Magazine* (Los Angeles), vol. 10, no. 9 (Sept. 1962), p. 5–10.

After his trouble with the law in Chicago, in 1924 (1925?), Gerber went to New York where, from 1930–39, he published a mimeographed newsletter, *Contacts*, for persons seeking penpals. The last nine issues of this newsletter are in the collection of Jim Kepner (Kepner to J.K., Jan. 2, 1974).

99. [Henry Gerber] Parisex, pseud., "In Defense of Homosexuality," *The Modern Thinker*, June 1932, p. 286–97; photo reprint in *A Homosexual Emancipation Miscellany; c. 1835–1952* (N.Y.: Arno, 1975). Gerber's authorship of this "Defense" is identified in a letter of his to Manuel Boyfrank, Jan. 4, 1945 (p. 5), now in the collection of Jim Kepner (Kepner to J.K., May 11, 1974 [p. 4]). Dr. W. Beran Wolfe's "The Riddle of Homosexuality" appeared in *The Modern Thinker*, April 1932.

100. [Gerber,] Parisex, p. 297.

101. The index for vol. 1 (1934) of *Chanticleer* (in vol. 1, no. 12 [Dec. 1934]) lists twelve articles by Henry Gerber:

"Theism and Atheism reconciled," no. 1 (Jan.)
"Recent Homosexual Literature," no. 2 (Feb.)
"What is Atheism?," no. 3 (March)
"Sterilization," no. 4 (April)
"Escape from Reality," no. 5 (May) (This issue also includes: William Chiles, "A Heterosexual looks at Homosexuality")
"A New Deal for Sex," no. 6 (June)
"A Study in Pessimism," no. 7 (July)
"Tannhauser," no. 8 (Aug.)
"Hitlerism and Homosexuality," no. 9 (Sept.)
"Moral Warfare," no. 10 (Oct.)
"Rationalism or Dogma," no. 11 (Nov.)
"More Nonsense about Homosexuals," no. 12 (Dec.).

The editor is Jacob Hauser, the circulation manager is Henry Gerber; associate editors are H. P. Seguin, William Chiles, B. G. Hagglund. No place of publication is listed. Communications are to be addressed to a post office box in N.Y.C. A complete run of vol. I of *Chanticleer* is available at the Widener Library, Harvard University. I wish to thank Warren Johansson for help in locating this document.

102. Gerber, "Recent Homosexual Literature," *Chanticleer*, vol. I, no. 2 (Feb. 1934), p. 4. In Dec. 1917, the Bolshevik government of the Soviet Union had done away with all laws against homosexual acts. Gerber had not yet heard of the rebirth of anti-homosexual persecution in the U.S.S.R. In Jan. 1934, mass arrests of homosexuals occurred in major Soviet cities. In March 1934, as a result of Stalin's personal intervention, a law punishing homosexual acts with imprisonment up to eight years was introduced (John Lauritsen and David Thorstad, *The Early Homosexual Rights Movement [1864–1935]* [N.Y.: Times Change Press, 1974], p. 68–69).

103. Henry Gerber, "Hitlerism and Homosexuality," *Chanticleer*, vol. I, no. 9 (Sept. 1934), p. 1–2.

104. Henry Gerber, "More Nonsense about Homosexuals," *Chanticleer*, vol. I, no. 12 (Dec. 1934), p. 2–3.

A group of approximately two hundred letters exchanged between Gerber and Manuel Boyfrank (about 30 percent by Gerber, c. 1935–c. 1957) is in the collection of Jim Kepner (Kepner to J.K., March 11, 1974). This is no doubt one of the most valuable collections of original Gay American history manuscripts that will ever be found. The correspondence contains references to the 1924 Chicago organizing attempt, to articles Gerber published under pseudonyms, to *four books* written by Gerber, to plans for a new homosexual emancipation organization. These letters should be carefully edited, and published in a scholarly edition—a project for which a grant is badly needed.

Between 1927 and 1930, an American art connoisseur and ex-patriot, Edward Perry Warren, published in London, under the pseudonym Arthur Lyon Raile, his three-volume *Defense of Uranian Love* (London: Cayme Press, 1928, 1930), described by Timothy d'Arch Smith as "a sixty-thousand word apologia for an acceptance of the pre-eminence of the Hellenic paederastic philosophies." Warren, says Smith, was an anglophile, who lived almost his entire life in England, and who spoke "zealously for the revival of the Greek paederastic ideal which he found embodied in the classical art works he collected." Warren's *Itamos: A Volume of Poems*, first published in 1903, is said to present the Greek pederastic ideal with "great fervor," celebrating their author's "own very real friendships, loves, and quarrels." In 1884, at Oxford, Warren had met John Marshall, the "soulmate" with whom he lived until Marshall's death in 1928. Warren's novel of Oxford life, *A Tale of Pausanian Love* (London: Cayme, 1927), is said to present a "trenchant argument in favor of Uranian affection." (Timothy d'Arch Smith, *Love in Earnest; Some Notes on the Lives and Writings of English 'Uranian' Poets from 1889 to 1930* [London: Routledge & Kegan Paul, 1970], p. 2, 114–17, 148, 253, 267–68).

105. Una [Vincenzo], Lady Troubridge, *The Life of Radclyffe Hall* (N.Y.: Citadel, 1963; photo reprint, N.Y.: Arno, 1975), p. 81–82.

106. *New York Times*, Aug. 30, 1928, p. 36, col. 2.

107. *New York Times*, Oct. 6, 1928, p. 6, col. 4.

108. Vera Mary Brittain, *Radclyffe Hall: A Case of Obscenity?* (London: Femina, 1968), p. 140.

109. *New York Times*, Jan. 12, 1929, p. 3, col. 6.

110. *New York Times*, Jan. 23, 1929, p. 7, col. 1.

111. *New York Times*, Feb. 1, 1929, p. 10, col. 2.

112. *New York Times*, Feb. 22, 1929, p. 11, col. 1.

113. *New York Times*, April 20, 1929, p. 20, col. 2.

114. Morris L. Ernst and Alan U. Schwartz, *Censorship: The Search for the Obscene* (N.Y.: Macmillan, 1964), p. 71–79.

115. Henry Gerber, "Recent Homosexual Literature," *Chanticleer* (N.Y.), vol. I, no. 2 (Feb. 1934), p. 4.

Also see Henry Gerber, "Excerpts from After-Thoughts," *The Truth Seeker*, Feb. 1944, p. 29.

116. *South Eastern Reporter* . . . vol. 200 (Jan.–March 1939), (St. Paul, Minn.: West, 1939), p. 799–800.

Legal citations: Thompson *v.* Aldredge, 200 S. E. 799; 187 Ga. 467.

From 1945 to 1954 in New York City, a group called the Veterans Benevolent Association became the first American homosexual membership organization of the post-World War II period. It incorporated in 1948. Formed by four honorably discharged veterans, it is said to have functioned primarily as a social club for its seventy-five to 100 regular members, and the as many as four or five hundred guests who sometimes attended its events. Through its officers and members, homosexual veterans and their friends were aided when in trouble with the law or an employer. Lecturers frequently spoke on some aspect of sex. After several years, conflict developed among members who wanted the group to become more active in social change. Factionalism led to the group's disbanding in 1954 (Edward Sagarin, *Structure and Ideology in an Association of Deviants; A Dissertation Presented to the Faculty of the Graduate School of Arts and Sciences, Department of Sociology and Anthropology, New York University*, 1966; photo reprint, N.Y.: Arno, 1975, p. 64–67). Sagarin's brief history of this pioneering group is "based almost entirely on private conversations and interviews with almost all the ex-leaders and many ex-members" of the Association.

The recently discovered "Certificate of Incorporation of Veterans Benevolent Association, Inc." is dated March 8, 1948, and is filed with the State of N.Y., Dept. of State, Albany. The "purposes" for which the group is formed are listed as: "To unite socially and fraternally, all veterans and their friends, of good and moral character, over the age of twenty years. To foster, create, promote, and maintain the spirit of social, fraternal, and benevolent feeling among the members and all those connected by any means and ties. To enhance the mutual welfare of its members. To promote and advance good fellowship, mutuality, and friendship, and to promote the best idealism and interests of its members. To advance the social and economic interests of its members; to provide suitable places for meeting of members and the establishment of facilities for social, fraternal, benevolent, and economic activities and functions." The names of five "Directors" are listed, along with seven witnesses. The association is also discussed in Marvin Cutler (pseud.), ed., *Homosexuals Today; A Handbook of Organization and Publications* (Los Angeles: ONE, Inc., 1956), p. 89–90. Major published sources on the early history of the American homosexual emancipation movement are Sagarin, Cutler, and Foster Gunnison's "The Homophile Movement in America," in *The Same Sex: An Appraisal of Homosexuality*, ed. Ralph W. Weltge (Phila.: United Church Press, 1969).

Nine issues of a Lesbian monthly, *Vice Versa*, were privately published (typewritten) and distributed in Los Angeles between June 1947, and Feb. 1948, by a woman who called hershelf Lisa Ben (an anagram for Lesbian). *Vice Versa* is the earliest-known American publication designed especially for Lesbians. Its 7½- by 11-inch pages included play, film, and book reviews, poetry, short stories, editorials, and an annotated bibliography of novels, all concerned with Lesbianism. The editor is said to have previously "achieved some note in the science-fiction field" (*"Vice Versa," Homosexuals Today; A Handbook of Organizations and Publication*, ed. Marvin Cutler [pseud.], [Los Angeles: ONE, Inc., 1956], p. 4, 90–91.) Excerpts (mostly poetry) from *Vice Versa* appear throughout *The Ladder* and may be found listed in the index to that Lesbian periodical (photo reprint, N.Y.: Arno, 1975). Excerpts from *Vice Versa* also appear throughout *ONE* Magazine. The library of the Homosexual Information Center in Los Angeles has copies of all but issue no. 7 of *Vice Versa*.

117. Henry Hay, taped interview by Jonathan Katz, March 31, 1974; Hay to J.K., Feb. 20, 1974. All the following quotes from Hay, unless otherwise indicated, are from the taped interview. The photos of Hay reproduced here are from his own collection.

Allen Ginsberg claims that a similar historical-sexual link exists between Edward Carpenter, Gavin Arthur, Neal Cassady, and Allen Ginsberg ("Ginsberg" [interviewed by Allen Young, Cherry Valley, N.Y., Sept. 25, 1972; transcript ed. by Winston Leyland,] *Gay Sunshine; A Newspaper of Gay Liberation* [San Francisco], Jan.–Feb., 1973, no. 16, p. 1, col. 1; p. 4, col. 4). The late Gavin Arthur left an unpublished document describing his sexual encounter with Carpenter. This document is now in the collection of Allen Ginsberg (Ginsberg to Leslie Parr, April 3, 1975; photocopy in the collection of Jonathan Katz). As described by Timothy d'Arch Smith (who does not mention Gavin Arthur's authorship), this document "claims to have been written by an American in his early twenties who went to visit Carpenter when the poet was eighty years old. Carpenter made love to the young man, expertly, 'gazing at my body rapturously between kisses and growling ecstatically. . . . I had the distinct feeling that he felt my coming as if he were coming himself—that in that moment he *was* me. Afterwards, he said 'When I was a clergyman I thought at Communion I was at one with God. But I realize now that this is a much more intimate communion. . . .'" Smith describes this source as: "Typescript document, five leaves, 4to, headed 'Anonymous: Document received from the hands of a living person and its authenticity vouched for by Allen Ginsberg,' New York, private collection" (*Love in Earnest* . . . [London: Routledge & Kegan Paul, 1970], p. 24, 43, note 84). A somewhat less explicit description of Gavin Arthur's encounter with Carpenter is found in Arthur's *The Circle of Sex* (N.Y.: University Books, 1966), p. 128–39). I wish to thank James Kepner for information about the latter source.

118. [Henry Hay,] Eann MacDonald, pseud., "Preliminary Concepts . . . (Los Angeles: privately printed [dittoed], July 7, 1950); photo reprint in *A Homosexual Emancipation Miscellany* (N.Y.: Arno, 1975). I wish to thank Henry Hay for providing an original copy of this document.

In 1950, it is said, the Knights of the Clock, an interracial group of heterosexual and homosexual men and women, was incorporated in Los Angeles, California, with the aim of promoting understanding among homosexuals, between whites and Blacks, and offering social, employment, and housing services, especially to interracial couples ([Dorr Legg] William Lambert, pseud., "Knights of the Clock, Inc.," in Cutler, p. 4, 93–94; Sagarin, p. 77–78). An attempt to locate the incorporation certificate of this group was unsuccessful (California, Secretary of State to J.K., Sacramento, April 5, 1974).

119. Three documents: "Discussion Group, Chairman, Steve, 9–6–51, Sense of Value [I]"; "Discussion Group, Chairman, Howard, 9–20–51, Sense of Value (II)"; "Discussion Group, Chairman, Harry [Henry Hay], 10–4–51, Social Directions of the Homosexual." I wish to thank Henry Hay for copies of these documents.

120. Mattachine Society, "Missions and Purposes," written April [28], 1951, ratified July 20, 1951, in Cutler, p. 14–15.

121. Hay adds: "My father and mother met and married in South Africa: they both had met Cecil Rhodes, and they knew about his life-long homophile relationship, as did most of the upper class of South African Society in those turn-of-the-century days."

122. Dale Jennings, "To Be Accused, Is To Be Guilty," *ONE* (Los Angeles), vol. 1, no. 1 (Jan. 1953), p. 10; reprinted in Cutler, p. 26–29.

"Early in 1952," in New York City, after the publication of *The Homosexual in America* by Donald Webster Cory (pseud.), Cory and several others formed a homosexual discussion group which held 15 to 20 monthly meetings (Sagarin, p. 73–74).

123. "An Anonymous Call To Arms from: The Citizens' Committee to Outlaw Entrapment to: The Community of Los Angeles," March? 1952. I wish to thank Henry Hay for providing a copy of this document. "Now Is The Time To Fight," Citizens Committee to Outlaw Entrapment, Spring (May, June?), 1952. I wish to thank James Kepner for providing a copy of this document. See also "Citizens' Committee To Outlaw Entrapment" in Cutler, p. 22–24.

124. "Invitation," letter inviting the press and public to the trial of William Dale Jennings in the city of Los Angeles on May 19, 1952. I wish to thank Henry Hay for a copy of this document.

125. Jennings, "To Be Accused," p. 13. Henry Hay recalls that ten copies were made of the trial record in the case of Los Angeles v. Wm. Dale Jennings. An unsuccessful attempt was made to locate a copy of this major document in the history of the American homosexual emancipation movement, the first legal case in which the organized movement participated.

126. "Victory" leaflet, July? 1952; photo reprint in Cutler, p. 25.

On Oct. 15, 1952, plans for the formation of ONE, Inc., began at a meeting in Los Angeles. The aim was to found a nonprofit corporation with four fields of activity: education, publicity, research, and social service. The first issue of ONE Magazine was published in Jan. 1953 (Cutler, p. 39, 55, 61–73, 84–86; Sagarin p. 80–81).

127. "The Mattachine Foundation, Inc., Official Statement of Policy on Political Questions and Related Matters," Los Angeles, Feb. 1953; photo reprint in Cutler p. 30-A.

128. "Challenge and Response," ONE (Los Angeles), vol. 1, no. 3 (March 1953), p. 9–11.

129. Paul V. Coates, "Well, Medium and Rare," Los Angeles Mirror, March 12, 1953. See also Mattachine Foundation, Inc., to Paul V. Coates, March 15, 1953, reprinted in ONE (Los Angeles), vol. 1, no. 3 (March 1953), p. 11.

130. See Cutler, p. 29–31; James Kepner, Jr., to J.K., March 19, 1974; Henry Hay to J.K. March 22, 1974.

131. It may have seemed to Hay that 500 people appeared at the 1953 convention, but another participant suggests the actual figure was between 110 and 160 persons.

132. [Henry Hay,] "Are You Now Or Have You Ever Been A Homosexual?," ONE (Los Angeles), vol. 1, no. 4 (April 1953), p. 6.

133. [Hay,] "Are You Now," p. 7.

134. [Hay,] "Are You Now," p. 10.

135. [Hay,] "Are You Now," p. 11–12.

136. [Hay,] "Are You Now," p. 13.

137. Kepner to J.K., July 27, 1974.

In June 1954 in New York City, friends and subscribers of ONE Magazine are said to have formed The League. Discussions and lectures were held twice-monthly, a meeting place was rented, a bimonthly newsletter, a constitution, and a five-page statement of purpose were issued. The group disbanded early in 1956 after rumors that it had been reported to the police (Cutler, p. 102–03; Sagarin, p. 74–76; Mikhail Itkin, "An Outline of the Stages of the Development of the Gay Movement" [Los Angeles, typescript, 1974?], p. 2–3; James Kepner to J.K., Jan. 2, 1974).

138. Biographical information about Barbara Gittings is in Kay Tobin and Randy Wicker, The Gay Crusaders (N.Y.: Paperback Library, 1972; photo reprint, N.Y.: Arno, 1975), p. 205–224.

139. Barbara Gittings, taped interview by Jonathan Katz, Phila.: July 19, 1974.

On Sept. 21, 1955, in San Francisco, Del Martin, Phyllis Lyon, and six other Lesbians met to found the secret club which, on Oct. 19, held the first meeting of the Daughters of Bilitis, the earliest Lesbian emancipation organization in America. A chapter on the formation of D.O.B., and the first publication of The Ladder, is in Martin and Lyon's Lesbian / Woman (N.Y.: Bantam, 1972; chap. 8, p. 238–79).

140. Sidonie G. Collette, Claudine à l'ecole, illus. by H. Mirande (Paris: A. Michel, n.d. [1905?]), p. 163. See also p. 249.

141. "DOB To Hold Meeting Following Mattachine Convention," The Ladder, vol. 2, no. 11 (Aug. 1958), p. 11, 15; "New York Meeting Scheduled For September 7 . . ."

The Ladder, vol. 2, no. 12 (Sept. 1958), p. 7.

142. Letter signed "L. H. N." [Lorraine Hansberry Nemiroff], *The Ladder*, vol. 1, no. 8 (Mary 1957), p. 26, 28. Barbara Grier (Gene Damon, pseud.) identifies Hansberry as the author of this and the following letter in her column "Lesbiana," *The Ladder*, vol. 14, nos. 5–6 (Feb.–March 1970), and in her introduction to the Arno Press reprint ed. of *The Ladder*, "The Ladder, Rung By Rung," dated May 1975, no pagination (in the single volume containing *The Ladder*, vols. 1 and 2 [N.Y.: Arno, 1975]).

143. Letter signed "L. N." [Lorraine (Hansberry) Nemiroff], *The Ladder*, vol. 1, no. 11 (Aug. 1957), p. 30.

144. "Purposes of the Daughters of Bilitis," *The Ladder*, vol. 3, no. 2 (Nov. 1958), p. 2.

145. Del Martin, "DOB Speaks For Lesbian," *The Ladder*, vol. 4, no. 1 (Oct. 1959), p. 18–19 (part of "Mattachine Breaks Through the Conspiracy of Silence" [report of Mattachine Convention, Denver, Sept. 1959]).

146. Dr. Beach, quoted by Sten Russell, "DOB Convention; 'A Look at the Lesbian,' " *The Ladder*, vol. 4, no. 10 (July 1960), p. 9.

147. Foster, *Sex Variant Women in Literature* (N.Y.: Vantage, 1956; reprint Baltimore, Md.: Diana Press, 1976). Marion Zimmer Bradley, *Astra's Tower: Special Leaflet No. 2* (Rochester, Tex., 1958); *Astra's Tower: Special Leaflet No. 3* (Rochester, Tex., 1959); Marion Zimmer Bradley and Barbara Grier (Gene Damon, pseud.), *Checklist 1960* (Rochester, Tex.: 1960); same authors, *Checklist 1961* (Rochester, Tex., 1961; same authors, *Checklist Supplement 1962* (Rochester, Tex., 1962); Barbara Grier (Gene Damon, pseud.) and Lee Stuart, *The Lesbian in Literature: A Bibliography* (San Francisco: Daughters of Bilitis, 1967). All except Foster are photo reprinted in *A Gay Bibliography* (N.Y.: Arno, 1975).

148. Mary Ann Wilson's Painting, "Merimaid," reproduced from the collection of the New York State Historical Association, Cooperstown. Also see Jean Lipman and Alice Winchester, *Primitive Painters in America; 1750–1950* (N.Y.: Dodd Mead, 1950), p. 53. Chap. 6 (by Lipman) is devoted to Willson: p. 50–56. Willson is referred to by Lipman and Mary C. Black, *American Folk Painting* (N.Y.: C. N. Potter, 1966).

149. Alma Routsong (Isabel Miller, pseud.), taped interview by Jonathan Katz, N.Y.C.: Jan. 20, 1975.

Bibliography

V. RESISTANCE: 1859–1972

[Anonymous. Letter from Boston.] *Monatsberichte des Wissenschaftlich-humanitären Komitees.* Vol. 6 (1907), p. 98–99. Reprinted in Magnus Hirschfeld, *Die Homosexualität des Mannes und des Weibes.* Berlin: Louis Marcus, 1914. (P. 553.)

Browne, F. W. Stella. *Sexual Variety & Variability Among Women and their Bearing upon Social Reconstruction.* London: British Society for the Study of Sex Psychology, 1915.

———. "Studies in Feminine Inversion," *Journal of Sexology and Psychoanalysis* (N.Y.). Vol. 1 (1923): p. 51–58.

Carpenter, Edward. "An Unknown People," *The Reformer.* (London), July, August 1897. Rev. and retitled "The Intermediate Sex" in *Love's Coming of Age; A Series of Papers on the Relations of the Sexes.* 5th ed. London: Swan Sonnenschein, 1906.

———. *Days with Walt Whitman: With Some Notes on his Life and Work,* 2nd ed. London: George Allen, 1906. (P. 42–43.)

———. *Homogenic Love.* Manchester, England: Manchester Labour Press, [dated] 1894, [printed Jan. 1895].

———. *Ioläus: An Anthology of Friendship.* Boston: C. E. Goodspeed, 1902.

————. *Intermediate Types Among Primitive Folk; A Study in Social Evolution*. N.Y.: Kennerley, 1914. 2nd ed. London: George Allen & Unwin, 1919; photo, reprint N.Y.: Arno, 1975.

————. *Love's Coming of Age; A Series of Papers on the Relations of the Sexes*. Manchester, England: Labour Press, 1896.

————. *My Days and Dreams; Being Autobiographical Notes*. London: George Allen & Unwin, 1916.

————. "On the Connection between Homosexuality and Divination and the Importance of the Intermediate Sexes Generally in Early Civilizations," *American Journal of Religious Psychology and Education* (Worcester, Mass.). Vol. 4 (July 1911): p. 219–43. Reprinted as part I (four chapters) of *Intermediate Types among Primitive Folk*.

————. *Some Friends of Walt Whitman: A Study in Sex Psychology*. Publication No. 13. London: British Society for the Study of Sex Psychology, 1924.

[Carpenter, Edward.] Delavenay, Emile. *D. H. Lawrence and Edward Carpenter; A Study in Edwardian Transition*. N.Y.: Taplinger, 1971.

[Carpenter, Edward.] Smith, G. C. Moore. "Carpenter, Edward." *Dictionary of National Biography, 1922–30*. London: Oxford University, 1935. (P. 159–62.)

[Carpenter, Edward.] Woolaston, Graeme. "Love's Coming of Age; Edward Carpenter on Homosexuality." London School of Economics Gay Culture Society, n.d. Reprinted in *The Body Politic; Gay Liberation Journal* (Toronto). No. 14 (July–Aug. 1974): p. 20–21, 27, 29.

Cutler, Marvin, ed. *Homosexuals Today; A Handbook of Organizations & Publications*. Los Angeles: ONE, Inc., 1956.

Edel, Leon. *Henry James; The Treacherous Years; 1895–1901*. Phila.: Lippincott, 1969. (On Charles Sanders Peirce, p. 124–25.)

Ellis, Havelock. *Studies in the Psychology of Sex; Sexual Inversion*. "2nd ed." Phila.: F. A. Davis, 1901.

————, and Symonds, John Addington. *Sexual Inversion*. 1st English ed. London: Wilson and Macmillan, 1897; photo reprint, N.Y.: Arno, 1975. (P. 46–47: E. Carpenter's sexual case history. P. 273–75: "Letter from Professor X.")

Friendship and Freedom [periodical]. Chicago: Society for Human Rights, Inc., 1924–25? (Photo in Leo Schidrowitz, ed. *Sittengeschichte des Lasters*. Vienna: Verlag für Kulturforschung, 1927, p. 301; photo reprint in James D. Steakley, *The Homosexual Emancipation Movement in Germany*. N.Y.: Arno, 1975, opposite p. 78.)

Gerber, Henry. (*Chanticleer*, vol. 1 [1934]:)
"Theism and Atheism reconciled," no. 1 (Jan.)
"Recent Homosexual Literature," no. 2 (Feb.)
"What is Atheism?" no. 3 (March)
"Sterilization," no. 4 (April)
"Escape from Reality," no. 5 (May)
"A New Deal for Sex," no. 6 (June)
"A Study in Pessimism," no. 7 (July)
"Tannhauser," no. 8 (Aug.)
"Hitlerism and Homosexuality," no. 9 (Sept.)
"Moral Warfare," no. 10 (Oct.)
"Rationalism or Dogma," no. 11 (Nov.)
"More Nonsense about Homosexuals," no. 12 (Dec.)
————. "Englische Heuchelei" ["English Hyprocrisy" (*Well of Loneliness* case)]. *Blätter für Menschenrecht* ["*Journal of Human Rights*" (Berlin)]. Vol. 6, no. 15 (Oct. 1928): p. 4–5.

Gerber, Henry. [Letters to Manuel Boyfrank. In the collection of James Kepner.]

[Gerber, Henry.] (Letter signed: G. S., Washington, D.C.) *ONE* (Los Angeles). Vol. 1, no. 7 (July 1953): p. 22.

[Gerber, Henry] Parisex, pseud. "In Defense of Homosexuality," *The Modern Thinker*. June 1932, p. 286–97; photo reprint in *A Homosexual Emancipation Miscellany; c. 1835–1952*. N.Y.: Arno, 1975.

————. (See *Friendship and Freedom*.)

————. (See Society for Human Rights, Inc.)

————. "The Society for Human Rights—1925," *ONE* (Los Angeles). Vol. 10, no. 9 (Sept. 1962): p. 5–11.

————. "Die Strafbestimmungen in den 48 Staaten Amerikas und den amerikanischen Teritorien für gewisse Geschlechtsakte" ("The Penalties in the 48 American States and the American Territories for Certain Sexual Acts"), *Blätter für Menschenrecht* ("Journal of Human Rights"). Vol. 7, no. 8 (Aug. 1929): p. 5–11.

————. "Zwei Dollars oder fünzehn Jahre Zuchthaus" ["Two Dollars or Fifteen Years in Prison"] *Das Freundschaftsblatt* ("The Friendship Journal" [Berlin]). Vol. 8, no. 41 (Oct. 9, 1930): p. 4.

Gittings, Barbara. Taped interview by Jonathan Katz. Phila.: July 19, 1974. In the collection of Jonathan Katz.

Goldman, Emma. *Living My Life.* 2 vols. N.Y.: Dover, 1971. (Vol. 1, p. 269; vol. 2, p. 555–56.)

————. "Offener Brief an den Herausgeber der Jahrbücher über Louise Michel." Trans. from English. Preface by Magnus Hirschfeld. *Jahrbuch für sexuelle Zwischenstufen* (Leipzig). Vol. 23 (1923): p. 70–92. (P. 70, 73–76, 86–87, 90.)

Grosskurth, Phyllis. *John Addington Symonds; A Biography.* London: Longmans, Green, 1964; photo reprint, N.Y.: Arno, 1975.

[Hall, Radclyffe.] Brittain, Vera Mary. *Radclyffe Hall: A Case of Obscenity?* London: Femina, 1968. (P. 140.)

[Hall, Radclyffe.] Ernst, Morris L., and Schwartz, Alan U., *Censorship: The Search for the Obscene.* N.Y.: Macmillan, 1964. (Chap. 12, "Banning a Theme," p. 71–79.)

[Hall, Radclyffe.] [Vincenzo,] Una, Lady Troubridge. *The Life of Radclyffe Hall.* N.Y.: Citadel, 1963; photo reprint, N.Y.: Arno, 1975. (P. 81–82.)

[Hansberry, Lorraine.] Letter signed "L. N." [Lorraine (Hansberry) Nemiroff]. *The Ladder.* Vol. 1, no. 11 (Aug. 1957): p. 26–30.

[Hansberry, Lorraine.] Letter signed "L. H. N." [Lorraine Hansberry Nemiroff]. *The Ladder.* Vol. 1, no. 8 (May 1957): p. 26–28.

Hay, Henry. Photos, 1938; May, 1951. Both in the collection of Henry Hay.

————. Taped interview by Jonathan Katz, March 31, 1974. In the collection of Jonathan Katz.

Hirschfeld, Magnus [Autobiographical Sketch]. *Encyclopedia Sexualis.* Ed. Victor Robinson. N.Y.: Dingwall-Rock, 1936: p. 317–321. Photo reprint in *A Homosexual Emancipation Miscellany; c. 1835–1952.* N.Y.: Arno, 1975.

[Jennings, William Dale, Case of.]

"An Anonymous Call To Arms from: The Citizens' Committee to Outlaw Entrapment to: The Community of Los Angeles." March? 1952.

"Now Is The Time To Fight," Citizens' Committee to Outlaw Entrapment. Los Angeles, May, June? 1952.

"Invitation" to Jennings's trial in Los Angeles on May 19, 1952.

"Citizens' Committee To Outlaw Entrapment." In Cutler, p. 22–24.

"Victory." Leaflet. July? 1952; photo reprint in Cutler, p. 25.

Jennings, [William] Dale. "To Be Accused, Is To Be Guilty," *ONE* (Los Angeles). Vol. 1, no. 1 (Jan. 1953): p. 10–13. Reprinted in Cutler, p. 26–29.

[Mattachine Foundation.] "Challenge and Response," *ONE* (Los Angeles). Vol. 1, no. 3 (March 1953): p. 9–11.

"Mattachine Foundation, Inc. Official Statement of Policy on Political Questions and Related Matters." Los Angeles: Feb. 1953; photo reprint in Cutler, p. 30-A.

[Mattachine Society, Los Angeles, Documents.] "Discussion Group [reports], Chairman Steve, 9-6-51, Sense of Value [I]; Howard, 9-20-51, Sense of Value (II); Harry [Henry Hay], 10-4-51, Social Directions of the Homosexual."

[Merzbach, Georg.] [Speech in New York City.] *Monatsberichte des Wissenschaftlich-humanitären Komitees.* Vol. 6 (1907), p. 76–77.

Robinson, William Josephus. "An Essay on Sexual Inversion, Homosexuality, and Hermaphroditism," *Medical Critic and Guide.* Vol. 25 (1923): p. 247.

Robinson, William Josephus. "My Views on Homosexuality," *American Journal of Urology* (Mount Morris Park West, N.Y.). Vol. 10 (1914): p. 550–52.

Routsong, Alma (Isabel Miller, pseud.). Taped interview by Jonathan Katz, N.Y.C. Jan. 20, 1975. In the collection of Jonathan Katz.

Sanger, Margaret. Papers in the Sophia Smith Collection, Women's History Archive, Smith College, Northampton, Mass.

Society for Human Rights, Inc. Chicago. Charter, signed Dec. 10, 1924. Certificate no. 8018. State of Illinois, Office of the Secretary of State. Commercial Dept., Springfield, Ill.

[Spengler, Otto.] [Speech in New York City.] *Monatsberichte des Wissenschaftlich-humanitären Komitees.* Vol. 5 (1906): p. 151.

Thompson, Ella, *v.* Aidredge, J. C. *South Eastern Reporter* . . . vol. 200 (Jan.–March 1939). St. Paul, Minn.: West, 1939. (P. 799–800.) Legal Citations: Thompson *v.* Aldredge, 200 S. E. 799; 187 Ga. 467.

Tobin, Kay, and Wicker, Randy. *The Gay Crusaders.* N.Y.: Paperback Library, 1972; photo reprint, N.Y.: Arno, 1975. (Barbara Gittings: p. 205–224.)

[Willson, Mary Ann.] Jean Lipman and Alice Winchester, *Primitive Painting in America; 1750–1950; An Anthology.* N.Y.: Dodd Mead, 1950. (Chap. 6, by Lipman: "Mary Ann Willson," p. 50–56.)

Whitman, Walt. *Collected Writings.* General Editors, Gay Wilson Allen and Sculley Bradley. *Prose Works.* Ed. Floyd Stovall. N.Y.: N.Y. University, 1964. (Vol. 9 [in two volumes], vol. 2, p. 414.)

————. *The Collected Writings. The Correspondence.* Ed. Edwin Haviland Miller. Vol. 5. (P. 72–73.)

————. *Leaves of Grass; Comprehensive Reader's Edition.* Ed. Harold W. Blodgett and Sculley Bradley. N.Y.: Norton (paperback), 1965.

————. *Leaves of Grass; Facsimile Edition of the 1860 Text.* Introduction by Roy Harvey Pearce. Ithaca, N.Y.: Cornell Paperbacks, Cornell University, 1961.

————. *Walt Whitman's Leaves of Grass; The First (1855) Edition.* Ed. with an introduction by Malcolm Cowley. N.Y.: Viking, Viking Compass Edition, 1961.

[Whitman, Walt.]

Traubel, Horace L. *With Walt Whitman in Camden.*

Vol. 1. Boston: Small, Maynard, 1906.

Vol. 2. N.Y.: D. Appleton, 1908.

Vol. 3. N.Y.: Mitchell Kennerley, 1914.

Vol. 4. Ed. Sculley Bradley. Phila.: University of Pennsylvania, 1953.

Vol. 5. Ed. Gertrude Traubel, Carbondale, Ill.: Southern Illinois University, 1964.

NOTES

VI. Love: 1779–1932

1. The early literature on masturbation unexpectedly provides an important additional source for research on social attitudes toward both male and female same-sex intimacy, and of references to physical same-sex relations that would now be called homosexual.

In a medical journal article on "Masturbation as a Cause of Insanity" (1879), Dr. Allen W. Hagenbach cites the case of an effeminate young man with "morbid" attractions to persons of his own sex (*Journal of Nervous and Mental Disease* [Chicago], vol. 6, p. 603–12. Cited by Bullough, p. 148–49, see below).

Dr. Henry N. Guernsey's *Plain Talks on Avoided Subjects* (N.Y.: 1889), p. 82, declares: "It is true that some young ladies, the sweetest and fairest of our race, play with one another in an immodest and indecent way, teaching immorality to the pure and innocent" (quoted by Milton Rugoff, *Prudery and Passion* [N.Y.: Putnam, 1971], p. 267).

Dr. James F. Scott's *The Sexual Instinct* (N.Y., 1899) contains a chapter on "Onanism" (p. 419–32) which defines this term as referring to "all forms of sexual stimulation by either sex, singly or mutually, to produce orgasm in unnatural ways—*i.e.*, otherwise than by coitus." Included among the onanistic acts are "pederasty" and " 'mutual masturbation'."

In 1905, Dr. William Lee Howard of Baltimore writes on "Masturbation in the Young

Girl [as] the Cause of Acquired Sexual Perversion [Lesbianism]" (*Buffalo Medical Journal*, vol. 61, no. 5 [Dec.], p. 290–92.)

In 1911, the same Dr. Howard, in a chapter on "Self Abuse—How to Stop It . . ." in his *Confidential Chats with Boys* (N.Y.: Clode), p. 102–04, warns: "Never sleep with another person, man or boy," describing the dire consequences of such sleeping arrangements. "Sleeping with another person . . . affects the sex organs . . . and causes a feeling of attraction towards these delicate organs. . . . many boys will be tempted to talk and play with each other. . . . in the end it means self-abuse." Dr. Howard emphasizes: "Never trust yourself in bed with a boy or man." If there is only one bed, "sleep on the floor . . . go without sleeping rather than have that 'first time' happen to you." Howard adds: "There are things in trousers called men, so vile that they wait in hiding for the innocent boy." He warns "Look out for these vermin, be suspicious of any man in trousers who . . . tries to see you alone and prefers to go in bathing with boys instead of men. Don't go to drive or walk with these things, for all the time they are only waiting to teach boys to help them in self-abuse or something far nastier." Dr. Howard concludes: "So never sleep with a man, except your father. If you . . . find yourself in bed with a man, keep awake with your eyes on something you can hit him with." I wish to thank Jeffrey Escoffier for providing the above document.

In 1914, Dr. Douglas C. McMurtrie of New York writes a "Note on Masturbation in Woman: Its Relation to Sexual Inversion" (*Cincinnati Medical News*, vol. 1, p. 287), a brief article translating parts of a work by Alibert, *La masturbation chez la femme* (Paris), n.d.

In 1973, Vern Bullough writes on the connections between "Homosexuality and the Secret Sin [Masturbation] in Nineteenth Century America" (*Journal of the History of Medicine*, vol. 28, p. 143–54). Also see note 134 below.

2. See note 9 below to Susan B. Anthony reference.

3. *New York Times*, Dec. 17, 1955, p. 16, col. 1.

4. *New York Review of Books*, Oct. 7, 1971 ("Letters. Lesbianism Never?").

5. John Eugene Unterecker, *Voyager; A Life of Hart Crane* (N.Y.: Farrar, Straus and Giroux, 1969), p. 355. See Crane's letters of April 21, Sept. 6, 23, 1924, in *The Letters of Hart Crane, 1916–1932*, ed. Brom Weber (Berkeley: University of California, 1965), p. 181, 187, 190.

6. This point is made by Martin Duberman in the *New York Times*, July 22, 1973, "Arts and Leisure," Section 2, p. 4, col. 4.

7. Mary Potter (Thacher) Higginson, *Thomas Wentworth Higginson* (Boston: Houghton-Mifflin, 1914), p. 72, 125–27, 280; Tilden G. Edelstein, *Strange Enthusiasm; A Life of Thomas Wentworth Higginson* (New Haven: Yale University, 1968), p. 64, 77–82. Higginson's autobiographical recollections, *Cheerful Yesterdays*, first published in 1896 (photo reprint, N.Y.: Arno, 1968 [p. 107–11]), refers to "Hurlbert" (the spelling later adopted), whose beauty and presence seems to have had a similar stimulating effect on others. Hurlbut is said by Higginson to be the model for the hero of his own novel *Malbone* (1869), for Charles Kingsley's *Two Years Ago* (1857), and for the title character (female!) of a novel by Theodore Winthrop, *Cecil Dreeme* (Boston: Ticknor and Fields, 1861), a curious, fascinating potboiler—about a man who falls madly in love with another man ("Cecil Dreeme")—who turns out to be a woman in disguise! The male lover's perturbance at finding himself in love with an individual who he thinks is a male is the occasion of much serious pondering. References to David and Jonathan, etc. (See espec. p. 239–44, 269–76, 281, 346–49). I wish to thank Stephen W. Foster for help with the above research.

For what it's worth, Hurlbut was one of those whom Oscar Wilde met in New York in 1882 (*Letters of Oscar Wilde*, ed. Rupert Hart-Davis [N.Y.: Harcourt, Brace & World,

1962], p. 92–93, 124). The DAB suggests that "William Henry Hurlbert" was involved in a heterosexual scandal in England.

Higginson's life suggests complicated connections between his strong attraction to another male, his concern about his physical fitness and masculinity, his ideology of "manliness," his militant, active abolitionism, his advocacy of women's emancipation, and this minister's deep, puritanical concept of sin. The latter is especially apparent in Higginson's venomous attack on the "Unmanly Manhood" of Whitman and Wilde (in the *Woman's Journal*, Feb. 4, 1882), which suggests that the two threatened Higginson's psychosexual equilibrium. (On Higginson's "manliness" see Edelstein, p. 25–26, 117–18, 148–51, 161–62, 189, 194–95, 205–06, 234–36, 242, 282–83, 316–18; on Whitman, see same, p. 352–56; on Wilde, see same, p. 354.)

Higginson was the mentor of Emily Dickinson, whom one writer has interpreted as having a central Lesbian experience (Rebecca Patterson, *The Riddle of Emily Dickinson* [Boston: Houghton-Mifflin, 1951]). Reviewers of this book denied its allegation of Lesbianism, and the book's style makes it extremely difficult to disentangle documented facts from the author's speculation. For reviews see Dickinson in bibliography. Interestingly, just one year after Higginson met Dickinson for the first time, the *Atlantic Monthly* published an essay by Higginson on an earlier woman poet—Sappho—whom Higginson is at pains to defend against the charge of being "a corrupt woman, and her school at Lesbos a nursery of sins" ("Sappho," *Atlantic*, July 1871, p. 88). Although Higginson is too puritanical to more than vaguely suggest Sappho's other than heterosexual sins, his essay indicates he was perfectly conscious of and concerned about female homosexuality! His main target of criticism is William Mure, a Scottish writer whose *Critical History of the Language and Literature of Ancient Greece* accepted all the stories of Sappho's Lesbianism (see Havelock Ellis, *Studies in the Psychology of Sex*, 4 vols. [N.Y.: Random House, 1936], vol. 2, part 2, *Sexual Inversion*, p. 197–98; and Mure's *History* [London: Longman, 1854], vol. 3, p. 272–326, 496–98). Higginson, on the other hand, denies Sappho's homosexuality—in order to defend her—in the name of women's emancipation, that cause in which Higginson had then become increasingly active.

8. William Rounseville Alger, *The Friendships of Women* (Boston: Roberts, 1868), p. 395–97. I wish to thank Stephen W. Foster for informing me of this book.

9. The intense, loving, erotically suffused relationship that might develop between females in the early women's rights movement is suggested in four letters of Anthony to Dickinson. Anthony had first been drawn into the women's rights movement in 1850. Dickinson's career as a popular lecturer in support of women's rights, against slavery, and for other social reforms, began in 1860.

In Jan. 1868, Susan B. Anthony became the publisher of the weekly women's suffrage newspaper *The Revolution*. When these letters to Anna Dickinson began a month later, Anthony was forty-eight and Dickinson was twenty-six. Anthony's letters were written on stationery boldly headed *The Revolution*.

New York, Feb. 19th, 1868

My Dear Chicky Dicky Darling

. . . I wish this tired hand could *grasp* you this very minute—Well my dear child, doesn't the world move—and don't we all move with it—

I have a world of things to say—but not a minute to begin—only this to tell you I still love you and believe in you—and at this early day went to *engage you* not to *marry* a *man*—but to speak at our Equal Rights Anniversary next May the 12th or 13th—You will surely be ready this year—But if you are not—say *no*—and still I shall wait—and still I shall believe in your heart true as steel to its own convictions—and that's all that any of us can ask of mortal man or woman.

Lovingly, lastingly yours—S. B. Anthony

A second letter reads:

New York, March 18, 1868

Dear Dicky Darling

. . . Now when are you coming to New York—Do let it be soon—then do let me see the child—I have *plain quarters*—at 44 Bond St—*double bed*—and big enough & good enough to take you *in*—So come & see me—or let me know & I'll meet you . . . any place you shall say—and let me see you—I do so long for the scolding & pinched ears & every thing I know awaits me—

I have a budget full to say to you—what worlds of experience since I last snuggled the wee child in my long arms—Well let me know when & where I am to see you— In an awful hurry—Your loving Friend

Susan

A third letter dated New York, Jan. 15, 1869, says:

Too bad the Darling Anna and sublime [George F.] Train have such a drizzly night for their meetings but the Storm God will not stay his hand for stars nor comets—Female or Male—. . . .

Lovey—I had a sad feeling to leave you alone at that dark ferry—don't never stay so late again—it is to dreary & desolate for my chicken

Anna my soul goes out to you in real mother yearnings—I don't believe you have believed the depths thereof—Good Bye

S B A

And twenty-six years later Anthony writes:

[Rochester, N.Y.] Nov. 5, 1895

My Darling Anna

It is lovely to see your hen-tracks once more—as I opened the envelope—I said— . . . this looks like Anna Dickinson's writing—& turns to the last page sure enough— there it was Anna E. Dickinson—the same dear old name—It don't matter if its contents do seem a wee bit scolding—I'm awfully glad to know you still live—and that I have a chance to tell you that my *motherly love*—my elderly sister's love—has never abated for my *first Anna*—I have had several lovely Anna girls—*"nieces"*— they call themselves now-a-days—since my *first Anna*—but none of them ever has or ever can fill the niche in my heart that you did—my dear—Now, I must see you when I get to New York. . . .

I am so glad you wrote to me—because it gives me a chance to send you the invitation to Mrs. Stanton's 80th birth day reception—and I want you to sit on the stage as the *pioneer* woman *speaker* to save the nation in its times of perils—You will come won't you? . . . I do want to take you on my arm & introduce you to the *young women* who have come among us these later years—You will come to me, or let me come to you—at the earliest moment—after my arrival in New York—Yes! Wouldn't I like to go to Del Monicos as of old!—Well my dear—we'll talk when we meet—till then—Lovingly your old & best friend—Susan B. Anthony

(Anthony's letters are in the Library of Congress, Manuscript Division, Anna Dickinson Papers, Box 5). Also see Milton Rugoff, *Prudery and Passion* (N.Y.: Putnam, 1971), p. 265–66; and Andrew Sinclair, *The Better Half* (N.Y.: Harper and Row, 1965), p. 75.

Sinclair says that late in the 1840s, at Oberlin College, Antoinette Brown, the first woman divinity student, fell in love with Lucy Stone, an older student, and an active feminist and abolitionist. After becoming a minister, Brown writes Stone, asking her "dearest little cowboy" to visit her, adding: "I love you Lucy any way, and if you would only come & take a nap with me here in my bed my head would get rested a great deal faster for it is aching now" (Sinclair, p. 155–56, quoting Brown to Stone, June 8, 1853, in the Antoinette Brown Blackwell Papers, Schlesinger Library on the History of Women in America, Radcliffe College, Cambridge, Mass.).

In the early 1900s, the Johns Hopkins Medical School, one of the first to admit women, was apparently a hotbed of Lesbianism and feminism (Richard Bridgman, *Gertrude Stein in Pieces* (N.Y.: Oxford University, 1970), p. 34–35.

10. Élisàr von Kupffer, *Lieblingsminne und Freundesliebe in der Weltliteratur; Eine Sammlung mit einer ethisch-politischen Einleitung* (Leipzig: Max Spohr, 1900); Edward Carpenter, ed. *Ioläus: An Anthology of Friendship* (London: Swan Sonnenschein, 1902); Alexander von Gleichen-Russwurm, *Die Freundschaft; eine psychologische Forschungsreise* (Stuttgart: Hoffmann, 1911); Alistair Sutherland and Patrick Anderson, eds., *Eros; An Anthology of Friendship* (London, Blond, 1961; photo reprint, N.Y.: Arno, 1975). A whole series of additional works on friendship merit investigation.

11. Carroll Smith-Rosenberg, "The Female World of Love and Ritual: Relations between Women in Nineteenth Century America," *Signs, Journal of Women in Culture and Society*, vol. 1, no. 1 (autumn 1975). This essay contains an especially important reference to the loving correspondence between Molly Hallock Foote and Helena ——— (1869–74), an intimate female relationship meriting further investigation.

A major, though controversial, work for the history and analysis of female same-sex intimacy is Elizabeth Mavor's *The Ladies of Llangollen; A Study in Romantic Friendship* (London: Joseph, 1971). Also see two reviews of this book in *The Ladder:* Ellen Gold, *The Ladder*, vol. 16, nos. 3–4 (Dec.–Jan. 1971–72), p. 38–39; anon., *The Ladder*, vol. 16, nos. 9–10 (June–July 1972), p. 19–21.

12. John Chester Miller, *Alexander Hamilton; A Portrait in Paradox* (N.Y.: Harper & Row, 1959), p. 22. I wish to thank Bill Chalson for informing me of this reference. It should be noted that Damon and Pythias are constantly referred to in homosexual literature, and that some of Plutarch's heroes were homosexual. (See John Addington Symonds, *A Problem in Greek Ethics*, many editions.)

The charge, apparently unsubstantiated, of "having taken familiarities with young boys," was "a final determining influence" in Baron Friedrich von Steuben's traveling to America and becoming a General in the American Revolutionary Army. In America Steuben was ardently admired by John Laurens, Alexander Hamilton, Nathaniel Greene, Richard Peters, Jonathan Arnold, John Mulligan, William North and Ben Walker. Steuben legally adopted North and Walker as his sons, made them his heirs, and the two men maintained intimate and tender relationships with Steuben until his death. Steuben's relationships with younger men appears to have been Greek in inspiration (John Mc-Aualey Palmer, *General Von Steuben* [New Haven: Yale University, 1937], p. 92–94, 136, 206, 208, 234–35, 271–72, 335, 362–64, 367–68, 401–04). I wish to thank Richard Plant and James Foshee for assistance with this research.

13. Alexander Hamilton, *The Papers of Alexander Hamilton*, ed. Harold C. Syrett, assoc. ed. Jacob E. Cooke (N.Y.: Columbia University, 1961), vol. 2, p. 34. The letters or words in brackets are those added by Hamilton's editors. See Hamilton *Papers* for footnotes which have been omitted from the present text. In reference to the present letter, the editors note that at some points Hamilton's words have been crossed out so that it is impossible to decipher them. At the top of the first manuscript page, a penciled note, presumably written by John C. Hamilton, an early editor, reads: "I must not publish the whole of this." J. C. Hamilton is the editor of *The Works of Alexander Hamilton* (N.Y.: 1851) which omits the part of Hamilton's letter beginning "And Now my Dear." Also see Allan McLane Hamilton, *The Intimate Life of Alexander Hamilton* (London: Duckworth, 1910), p. 241–42.

14. Hamilton, vol. 2, p. 37–38. Note* The word "intercourse" may have a double meaning.

15. Hamilton, vol. 2, p. 165.

16. Hamilton, vol. 2, p. 347–48.

17. Hamilton, vol. 2, p. 431.

18. Hamilton, vol. 3, p. 145.

19. Ralph Waldo Emerson, *The Journals and Miscellaneous Notebooks of Ralph Waldo Emerson*, eds. William H. Gilman, Alfred R. Ferguson, George P. Clark, Merrell R. Davis (Cambridge, Mass.: Belknap Press of Harvard University, 1960), vol. 1, p. 22. This volume contains background on Martin Gay.

20. Emerson, *Journals* (1960), vol. 1, p. 39.

21. Emerson, *Journals* (1960), vol. 1, p. 39–40. For information about the "eventful" week and the "accidents" mentioned by Emerson, see Emerson, *Journals* (1960), vol. 1, p. 244, note 95. Picture from *Journals of Ralph Waldo Emerson*, eds. Edward Waldo Emerson and Waldo Emerson Forbes, 10 vols. (Boston and N.Y.: Houghton Mifflin, 1909–14), vol. 1 (1909), opposite p. 70. Hereafter Emerson, *Journals* (1909–14). The editors of this 1909 edition of Emerson's *Journals* caption this picture "Memory Sketch of Martin Gay, by Emerson[.]"

22. Emerson, *Journals*, (1960), vol. 1, p. 52–53.

23. Emerson, *Journals* (1960), vol. 1, p. 54–55.

24. Emerson, *Journals* (1960), vol. 1, p. 353.

25. Emerson, *Journals* (1960), vol. 1, p. 291–92; see note 54.

26. Emerson, *Journals* (1960), vol. 1, p. 94.

27. Emerson, *Journals* (1960), vol. 1, p. 94–95.

28. Emerson, *Journals* (1960), vol. 1, p. 129–30; vol. 2, p. 59.

29. Emerson, *Journals* (1909–14), vol. 3, p. 289–90.

30. On Günderode and Brentano, see Jeannette H. Fostor, *Sex Variant Women in Literature* (N.Y.: Vantage, 1956), p. 124–27, 138, 230; and Alger, p. 306–14. Also see Margaret Fuller's *Günderode* (Boston: Peabody, 1842).

31. Margaret Fuller, *Memoirs of Margaret Fuller Ossoli*, eds. Ralph Waldo Emerson, William H. Channing, James Freeman Clarke, 2 vols. (Boston: Phillips, Sampson, 1851–52), vol. 1, p. 34–44.

32. Fuller, *Memoirs*, vol. 1, p. 127–29.

33. Fuller, *Memoirs*, vol. 2, p. 23.

34. Mason Wade, *Margaret Fuller: Whetstone of Genius* (N.Y.: Viking, 1940), p. 294–95.

35. Fuller, *Memoirs*, vol. 1, p. 304–08, 310–11. The deleted portion of this text merits investigation.

36. Fuller, *Memoirs*, vol. 2, p. 66–69.

37. Fuller, *Memoirs*, vol. 2, p. 70, 71, 72; Wade, p. 90–91.

Speculation concerning Fuller's sexual orientation is of long standing. For example, in an article in the St. Louis medical journal *Alienist and Neurologist* in 1899, Dr. James G. Kiernan defends Walt Whitman against the charge of homosexuality, but, based on Emerson's comments in the *Memoirs*, affirms it in Margaret Fuller: "Emerson had made sex a biologic subject of study from the analytic standpoint. He was thus led to detect the germ of homosexuality in Margaret Fuller. His admiration for her did not prevent him from dispassionately stating: She had a feeling that she ought to have been born a man. . . .

"Emerson who detected the sexual abnormality in Margaret Fuller would have been quick to see it in Whitman [but did not]" (James G. Kiernan, "Degeneracy Stigmata as Basis of Morbid Suspicion," *Alienist and Neurologist* [St. Louis, Mo.], vol. 20, no. 2 [April 1899], p. 184). See also: Lynn Flood, "A Life of Angels. Margaret Fuller's World," *The Ladder* (Reno, Nevada), vol. 16, nos. 9–10 (June–July 1972), p. 28–34.

Philip Van Doren Stern identifies the loving couples mentioned by Fuller (see *The Annotated Walden* . . . [N.Y.: Potter, 1970], p. 23, 25. A study, *The Passionate Exiles:*

Madam de Staël and Madame Recamier, by Maurice Levaillant, trans. from the French by Malcolm Barnes (N.Y.: Farrar, Straus and Cudahy, 1958) is reviewed by Barbara Grier (Gene Damon, pseud.) in *The Ladder*, vol. 2, no. 8 (May 1958), p. 11–12.

In 1834, Alabama Senator William Rufus De Vane King (a fifty-seven-year-old bachelor) met Pennsylvania Senator James Buchanan, and the two were inseparable until King's appointment as U.S. minister to France. Their intimate relationship caused barbed comments in Washington. Andrew Jackson called King "Miss Nancy" (effeminate); Aaron Brown (in 1844, in a private letter) called King Buchanan's "better half," referred jestingly to King and Buchanan's "divorce," and referred to King as "she," "her," and "Aunt Fancy"; King refers to his "communion" with Buchanan in a note of 1844 (Charles Sellers, *James Polk*, 2 vols. [Princeton, N.J.: Princeton University, 1966], vol. 2, p. 34). I wish to thank Jim Foshee for his assistance with this research.

38. Richard Chase, *Herman Melville; A Critical Study* (N.Y.: Macmillan, 1949) p. 6; W. Somerset Maugham, *Great Novelists and Their Novels; Essays on the Ten Greatest Novels of the World and the Men and Women Who Wrote Them* (Phila.: Winston, 1948), p. 224–25. I wish to thank George Whitmore for emphasizing to me the homosexual element in Melville's life and work.

39. Herman Melville, *Omoo; A Narrative of Adventures in the South Seas*, eds. Harrison Hayford, Hershel Parker, G. Thomas Tanselle, historical note by Gordon Ropers (Evanston & Chicago: Northwestern University and Newberry Library, 1968), p. 302, 322–25. Newton Arvin mistakenly says that a passage in *White-Jacket* on the morals of sailors is "the one occasion when [Melville] alludes to what would now be called overt homosexuality . . ." (*Herman Melville* [N.Y.: Sloan, 1950], p. 128). Pomāree II, mentioned by Melville in *Omoo*, is cited as homosexual in sources used by Melville, among them William Ellis, *Polynesian Researches . . .* 2 vols. (London: Fisher & Jackson, 1830), vol. 2, p. 432, and same, 2nd ed., 4 vols. (1831), vol. 3, p. 182.

In August 1789, about fifty years before Melville's appearance in Tahiti, an English ship, the *Mercury*, stopped there briefly for provisions. The Tahitians, according to custom, arranged entertainments for the visitors; plays and dances were performed each night in the flickering light of torches. A ship's officer, George Mortimer, reports: ". . . Attracted by the sound of drums and a great quantity of lights, I went on shore one night with two of our mates to one of these exhibitions. We seated ourselves among some of our friends, whom we found there; when one of the gentlemen who accompanied me on shore took it into his head to be very much smitten with a dancing girl, as he thought her; went up to her, made her a present of some beads, and other trifles, and rather interrupted the performance by his attentions; but what was his surprise when the performance was ended, and after he had been endeavouring to persuade her to go with him on board our ship, which she assented to, to find this supposed dancer, when stripped of her theatrical paraphernalia, a smart dapper lad" (George Mortimer, *Observations and Remarks Made During a Voyage . . .* [London, 1935], p. 47; quoted by Bengt Danielsson in *Love in the South Seas*, trans. F. H. Lyon [N.Y.: Reynal, 1956], p. 148, 236.)

In July 1799, Captain James Wilson of the missionary ship *Duff* reports another observation of a male homosexual transvestite in Tahiti: "I had desired Peter, that if a mawhoo came in our way, he should point him out; and here there happened to be one in Pomārre's train. He was dressed like a woman, and mimicked the voice and every peculiarity of the sex. I asked Pomārre what he was, who answered, 'Taata, mawhoo,' that is, a man, a mawhoo. As I fixed my eyes upon the fellow, he hid his face: this I at first construed into shame, but found it afterwards to be a womanish trick.

"These mawhoos choose this vile way of life when young: putting on the dress of a woman, they follow the same employments, are under the same prohibitions with respect to food, &c. and seek the courtship of men the same as women do, nay, are more jealous of the men who cohabit with them, and always refuse to sleep with women. We are obliged here to draw a veil over practices too horrible to mention. These mawhoos, being only six or eight in number, are kept by the principal chiefs. So depraved are these poor heathens, that even their women do not despise those fellows, but form friendships with them. This one was tayo [friend] to Iddeah.

"And here we are furnished with another impediment to population, and may ask how such a people can possibly have a numerous progeny" (James Wilson, *A Missionary Voyage to the Southern Pacific Ocean 1796 . . . 1798, in the Ship Duff, commanded by Captain James Wilson* [London: S. Gosnell for T. Chapman, 1799], p. 200–01. The old English text is modernized.)

According to Danielsson, Wilson and other early observers of Tahiti said that the transvestites they met were always attached to the chiefs' households or protected by the rulers. Wilson is said to add that in Tahiti there are a good many men who, without playing a female role, prefer homosexual relations. Danielsson also says that toward the end of the 1790s a missionary named Crook, who lived in the Marquesas Islands for a year and a half, reports in his journal that homosexuality is common, even among males who were not transvestites. In Tahiti at least, says Danielsson, the two different phenomena, homosexuality and transvestism, can be regarded as equivalent (Danielsson, p. 148–52).

Edward Handy, in his work on *The Native Culture in the Marquesas* (1923), says that there men called *mahu*, as in Tahiti, or *mahoi* "adopted the life of a woman, dressed in woman's garb, allowing their hair to grow long. They devoted themselves to all the activities and relationships of women rather than to those of men. Native informants told me that these men were not deformed physically, but that they merely preferred a woman's life and desired men" (Handy, *The Native Culture of the Marquesas* [Honolulu: The Museum, 1923], p. 103.)

Karsch-Haack, in his unsurpassed research and volume in German on homosexuality among native peoples, provides numerous, documented references to sources on both male and female homosexuality in Polynesia, particularly Tahiti and the Marquesas. Among the sources mentioned by Karsch-Haack concerning male homosexuality in Tahiti are de Bougainville, Moerenhout, Wilson, Turnbull, W. Ellis, Löhr, Schneider, Melville, Ulrichs, Jules Garnier, Beechey, Jacobus X., Cook; on male homosexuality in the Marquesas: Pinkerton, Pedro Fernandez de Quiros, Roblet, Marchand, Vincendon-Dumoulin, Desgraz, Melville, Von Hellwald (Ferdinand Karsch-Haack, *Das gleichgeschlechtliche Leben der Naturvölker* [The Same-Sex Life of Primitive Peoples: Munich: Reinhardt, 1911; photo reprint, N.Y.: Arno, 1975], p. 235–44, 491–94).

The experience of American writer Charles Warren Stoddard in the South Seas in the late 1860s, twenty years after Melville's residence there, suggests that homosexuality was not unknown at that time (see text section VI).

40. Herman Melville, *Typee; A Peep at Polynesian Life*, eds. Harrison Hayford, Hershel Parker, G. Thomas Tanselle; historical note by Leon Howard (Evanston & Chicago: Northwestern University and Newberry Library, 1968), p. 135–36.

41. Melville, *Omoo*, p. 152–53.

42. Melville, *Omoo*, p. 157.

43. Herman Melville, *White-Jacket or The World in a Man-of-War*, eds. Harrison Hayford, Hershel Parker, G. Thomas Tanselle, historical note by Willard Thorp (Evanston & Chicago: Northwestern University and Newberry Library, 1970), p. 375–76.

44. All sources mentioned are cited by Harold D. Langley, *Social Reform in the United States Navy, 1798–1862* (Urbana: University of Illinois, 1967), p. 172–74. Langley's sources are Jacob A. Hazen, *Five Years Before the Mast; or, Life in the Forecastle Aboard of a Whaler and Man-of-War* (Chicago: Belford, Clarke, 1887), p. 227; F. P. Torrey, *Journal of the Cruise of the United States Ship Ohio, Commodore*

Isaac Hull Commander, in the Mediterranean, in the Years 1839, '40, '41 (Boston: Dickinson, 1841), p. 86; Senate Executive Documents, 30th Cong., 2d Sess. (Serial 531), Doc. 23, p. 92, 97, 118, 138, 213, 219, 231, 238, 266, 291, 337; Senate Executive Documents, 30th Cong., 1st Sess. (Serial 510), Doc. 69, here and there. I wish to thank Stephen W. Foster for informing me of Langley's work.

45. See Arvin, p. 130.

46. Robert K. Martin, "Melville's Vine; The Story of a Relationship," typescript, paper delivered at the Modern Languages Association, 1975, p. 1. I wish to thank R. K. Martin for a copy of this paper. Melville's review "Hawthorne and His Mosses" appeared in two parts in *The Literary World* (N.Y.), Aug. 17, and 24, 1850.

47. Herman Melville, *Moby-Dick; An Authoritative Text; Reviews and Letters by Melville; Analogues and Sources, Criticism*, eds. Harrison Hayford and Hershel Parker (N.Y.: Norton, 1967), p. 22.

48. Melville, *Moby-Dick*, p. 24.

49. Melville, *Moby-Dick*, p. 26.

50. Melville, *Moby-Dick*, p. 27.

51. Melville, *Moby-Dick*, p. 32.

52. Melville, *Moby-Dick*, p. 33.

53. Melville, *Moby-Dick*, p. 52.

54. Melville, *Moby-Dick*, p. 53.

55. Melville, *Moby-Dick*, p. 53–54.

56. Melville, *Moby-Dick*, p. 348–49. I wish to thank Jeffrey Escoffier for reminding me of this scene, recalled from his adolescent reading. Not unrelated is the immediately following chapter 95, "The Cassock," in which Melville transubstantiates the whale's penis into the clerical garb of an "archbishoprick"—from the viewpoint of puritanical Christianity, one of the most outrageous scenes in American literature. References in *Moby-Dick* to sperm, phallicism, and erotic male-male intimacy are due for a thorough-going analysis.

57. Herman Melville, *The Letters of Herman Melville*, eds. Merrell R. Davis and William H. Gilman (New Haven: Yale University, 1960), p. 142–43. I wish to thank George Whitmore for informing me of this document.

58. Herman Melville, *Pierre or The Ambiguities*, eds. Harrison Hayford, Hershel Parker, G. Thomas Tanselle, historical Note by Leon Howard and Hershel Parker (Evanston & Chicago: Northwestern University and Newberry Library, 1971), p. 216–17.

59. Jay Leyda, *The Melville Log; A Documentary Life of Herman Melville; 1819–1891*, 2 vols. (N.Y.: Harcourt, Brace, 1951), vol. 1, p. 430. See also Arvin, p. 204.

60. Leslie A. Fiedler, *Love and Death in the American Novel*, rev. ed. (N.Y.: Laurel Edition, Dell, 1969), p. 15, 348.

61. Herman Melville, *Selected Poems of Herman Melville*, ed. Hennig Cohen (Garden City, N.Y.: Anchor Books, Doubleday, 1964), p. 141. See comment on p. 233–34. I wish to thank George Whitmore for informing me of this work.

62. Walter Sutton, "Melville's 'Pleasure Party' and the Art of Concealment," *Philological Quarterly*, vol. 30 (1951), p. 316–27. The reference to "Urania" should be explored. As Sutton notes, the term "Urning" (or "Uranian") was used in Europe for homosexual. Melville might very well have encountered the defenses of homosexuality by Karl Heinrich Ulrichs in which he coined the term.

63. Sutton, p. 316–17, 320, 326.

64. *Clarel* (II. xxxvi. 30–73); quoted in Herman Melville, *Billy Budd/ Sailor; (An Inside Narrative); Reading Text and Genetic Text, Edited from the Manuscript with Introduction and Notes* by Harrison Hayford and Merton M. Sealts, Jr. (Chicago: University of Chicago, 1962), p. 163. The notes and commentary and bibliography in

this edition provide invaluable clues for research into male–male intimacy in Melville's work.

65. Melville, *Selected Poems*, p. 69–71. See also comments p. 203–04. I wish to thank George Whitmore for informing me of this section of "Clarel," as well as the following poem, "John Marr."

66. Melville, *Selected Poems*, p. 102–03.

67. Melville, *Billy Budd*, p. 46–47.

68. Melville, *Billy Budd*, p. 51.

69. Melville, *Billy Budd*, p. 72, 73, 76–77, 78.

70. Melville, *Billy Budd*, p. 87–88. The color symbolism is striking.

71. Melville, *Billy Budd*, p. 94.

72. Melville, *Billy Budd*, p. 115.

73. Thoreau's possible homosexuality is touched on by a number of writers.

In 1948 David Kalman mentions "that there is strong evidence for latent homosexuality in Thoreau" ("A Study of Thoreau," *Thoreau Society Bulletin* 22, Jan. 1948, p. 2; this is a digest by Kalman of a longer work prepared for a course in "biographical psychology" at the University of Minnesota).

In 1957 Raymond Gozzi finds that the friendship section of Thoreau's *A Week on the Concord and Merrimack Rivers* (1849) displays "an unconscious homoerotic orientation" which may also be noted in his male friendships (Gozzi's "Tropes and Figures: A Psychological Study of Henry David Thoreau" [Ph.D. diss., N.Y. University, 1957, under Gay Wilson Allen]. Gozzi's thesis is summarized in the *Thoreau Society Bulletin 58* (Winter 1957), and in Perry Miller's *Consciousness in Concord; The Text of Thoreau's Hitherto "Lost Journal," 1840–1841, Together with Notes and a Commentary* (Boston: Houghton-Mifflin, 1958), p. 227. Gozzi's dissertation is also summarized by Carl Bode in "The Half-Hidden Thoreau" (*Massachusetts Review*, vol. 4 [Autumn 1962], p. 68–80). Two chapters of Gozzi's thesis are reprinted with revisions in Walter Harding's *Henry David Thoreau; A Profile* (N.Y.: Hill and Wang, 1971), p. 150–71.

Perry Miller in his marvelously perceptive, subtle analysis of Thoreau and New England love-friendship just skirts the issue of homosexuality (Chap. 7, "The Stratagems of Consciousness—Woman and Man," p. 80–103 [see espec. p. 96]).

Explicit, though speculative, discussion of Thoreau's homosexuality is found in J. Z. Eglinton, *Greek Love* (N.Y.: Oliver Layton, 1964, p. 366–68). Eglinton maintains that Thoreau's poem "Sympathy" is "unequivocal in both its description of [homosexual] desires and its confession of Thoreau's inability to make them known."

Although the subject of homosexuality is not indexed, it is discussed by Philip Van Doren Stern in his extraordinarily valuable notes to *The Annotated Walden* (N.Y.: Clarkson N. Potter, 1970), p. 22–23. Stern concludes: "The uncertain verdict seems to be that Thoreau had latent homoerotic tendencies. Whether they ever became overt or not may never be revealed unless some new documentation is discovered."

Leon Edel, in an essay on Thoreau, says that "his poems show that he loved [Ellen Sewall's] younger brother." Edel concludes, however, that Thoreau's character "had no room for love for anyone" save himself (*Henry D. Thoreau* [Minneapolis: University of Minnesota, 1970], p. 28–29).

In an essay of 1971, Walter Harding discusses whether Thoreau was a homosexual and concludes that he was not active, "and if he had homoerotic inclinations, he was apparently successful in suppressing or sublimating them" (Harding, *Profile*, p. 247).

George Whitmore, in a paper prepared for the Gay Academic Union conference in Nov. 1974, concludes that Thoreau was "qualifiedly homosexual" ("Friendship in New England: Thoreau, Melville," mimeographed, p. 1).

I wish to thank Dan Allen for first emphasizing to me the homosexual element in Thoreau's writings, and Walter Harding for invaluable research advice.

74. In 1832 at the Mount Pleasant Classical Institution, near Amherst, Mass., Henry Ward Beecher fell in love and signed a friendship pact with Constantine Fondolaik Newell, whose "great beauty and grace" is said to have "captivated" the young Beecher. Constantine, an orphan from the Greek island of Scio, was described by Beecher as "the most beautiful thing I had ever seen. He was like a young Greek god. When we boys used to go swimming together I would climb out on the bank to watch Constantine swim, he was so powerful, so beautiful." (William Constantine Beecher, *A Biography of Rev. Henry Ward Beecher* [N.Y.: Webster, 1888], p. 104–07. See also Paxton Hibben, *Henry Ward Beecher; An American Portrait* [N.Y.: Readers Club, 1942], espec. p. 44–48). Beecher's famous affair with the wife of his close friend Theodore Tilton may be interpreted as a repressed, transferred homosexual attraction on Beecher's part, although the subject needs more research. An amusing contemporary diary comment by George T. Strong about Beecher and Tilton kissing is relevant (*Diary of George Templeton Strong*, eds. Allan Nevins and Milton Halsey Thomas [N.Y.: Macmillan, 1952], vol. 4, p. 552). The unreliable Noel I. Garde (pseud.) in *Jonathan to Gide; The Homosexual in History* (N.Y.: Vantage, 1964), p. 605–07, cites an early pamphlet which refers to Beecher's love for Newell (J. V. Nash, *Homosexuality in the Lives of the Great* [Girard, Kan.: Little Blue Book No. 1564, n.d.], p. 57–59.) (The author and publisher of this pamphlet merit research.)

75. Stern, p. 56.

In 1838–39, the correspondence of James Thome, a young teacher at Oberlin College in Ohio, and Theodore Dwight Weld, the abolitionist leader in New York, reveals Thome's love for his idol, and Weld's less ardent response. The letters also reveal a complicated relation involving Weld's love for his future wife Angelina Grimké, and Thome's later relation to his wife. On April 5, 1838, Weld thanks Thome for a letter and adds: "You stole my heart at our first interview and you have been getting more and more of it ever since." On April 17 Thome replies, thanking Weld for his "affectionate" response, adding: "That you should ever have been led as you intimate to feel a *peculiar* attachment for me, is a fact quite as unexpected as it is gratifying. . . . I never have been able, hitherto, to satisfy myself that you reciprocated *even a little* of that affection which I have ever cherished for you, but which I have been restrained from expressing lest it might appear to your masculine, Roman nature[,] girlish and sickly. . . . my intercourse with you has been constrained and stiff. . . . I have felt that the current of my heart's affections was *dammed up* by entering your presence, and often when the gushings of my soul have prompted me to throw my arms around your neck and kiss you, I have violently quelled these impulses and affected a *manly bearing*. . . . Even now . . . I hear you saying, with ill-concealed disgust at such a strain of sentimentalism, 'well *to the docket*, Thome,—what's your business!' Thus your stern voice startles me from my maiden dreams!" (*Letters of Theodore Dwight Weld, Angelina Grimké Weld and Sarah Grimké, 1882–44*, eds. G. W. Barnes and D. L. Dumond, 2 vols. [N.Y.: Appleton-Century, 1934], see espec. vol. 2, letters of April 5, 1838; p. 620, 622; April 17: p. 642; May 2: p. 659; May 6: p. 663; May 15: p. 680; 682; Nov. 10: 712–13; May 18, 1829: 763–64). The Thome–Weld relation and letters are discussed briefly by Milton Rugoff in *Prudery and Passion* (N.Y.: Putnam, 1971), p. 267–68.

76. Henry David Thoreau, *The Journal of Henry David Thoreau*, eds. Bradford Torrey and Francis H. Allen, 14 vols. (Cambridge, Mass.: Riverside Press, Houghton Mifflin, 1906), vol. 1, p. 40–43. On Jan. 20, 1839, Thoreau writes a poem, "Love," relevant to the present history (see *Journal*, vol. 1, p. 72).

77. Thoreau, *Journal*, vol. 1, p. 80. See also Walter Harding, *The Days of Henry Thoreau* (N.Y.: Knopf, 1966), p. 77.

78. Thoreau, *Journal*, vol. 1, p. 80–81. See Harding, *Days*, p. 77–78.

79. Harding, *Days*, p. 94. On July 20 Thoreau writes a superficial ditty, "The Breeze's

Invitation," which may be about Ellen Sewall. On July 24 Thoreau writes another poem which may refer to Ellen or to Edmund Sewall (*Journal*, vol. 1, p. 86–88).

80. Thoreau, *Journal*, vol. 1, p. 88.

81. Harding, *Days*, p. 96–97.

82. Thoreau, *Journal*, vol. 1, p. 94.

83. Thoreau, *Journal*, vol. 1, p. 107–08. In early Jan. 1848 these comments on friendship were combined by Thoreau into an essay on the subject which appeared in the "Wednesday" chapter of his *A Week on the Concord and Merrimack Rivers* (see note 104 below).

84. Harding, *Days*, p. 98–99.

85. Thoreau, *Journal*, vol. 1, p. 113.

86. Thoreau, *Journal*, vol. 1, p. 115.

87. Thoreau, *Journal*, vol. 1, p. 120–21.

88. Thoreau, *Journal*, vol. 1, p. 129; Harding, *Days*, p. 99.

89. Thoreau, *Journal*, vol. 1, p. 144.

90. Thoreau, *Journal*, vol. 1, p. 154.

91. Thoreau, *Journal*, vol. 1, p. 155.

92. The complicated story of the Thoreau brothers' involvement with Ellen Sewall is detailed, as it has come down to us, by Harding (*Days*, p. 99–104). On July 19 John Thoreau returned from seeing Ellen, and Henry Thoreau wrote a cryptic entry in his *Journal* which has been interpreted as expressing his relief over Ellen's rejection of John's marriage proposal (see vol. 1, p. 170, and Harding, *Days*, p. 100–01; see also Thoreau's *Journal* entry of Aug. 7, 1840 quoted by Perry Miller, p. 148).

93. Miller, p. 176.

94. Miller, p. 176–77.

95. Miller, p. 178; Harding, *Days*, p. 101.

96. Miller, p. 181; Harding, *Days*, p. 102. Thoreau's *Journal* entries of Dec. 24 and 28, 1840, refer to the theme of friendship (Miller, p. 87).

97. Miller, p. 204. Thoreau's Jan. 4, 1841, *Journal* contains what Miller calls a love song in prose (p. 101). His Jan. 11 and 20 *Journal* entries discuss friendship (Miller, p. 87).

98. Thoreau, *Journal*, vol. 1, p. 210.

99. Thoreau, *Journal*, vol. 1, p. 220–22.

100. Thoreau, *Journal*, vol. 1, p. 223.

101. Thoreau, *Journal*, vol. 1, p. 296–97.

102. Walter Harding, *Henry David Thoreau; A Profile* (N.Y.: Hill and Wang, 1971), p. 249.

During the summer of 1841 Thoreau is said to have paid some brief attention to a young woman named Mary Russell, as is evidenced in his *Journal* for Dec. 12, 1841 (vol. 1, p. 292); see Stern, p. 62, and Harding, *Days*, p. 107–10.

The following *Journal* entries are relevant to the present history: March 2, 1842 (vol. 1, p. 324, on genius being outside morality); March 13, 1842 (vol. 1, p. 328, on friends); March 14, 1842 (vol. 1, p. 328–29, on love); March 15, 1842 (vol. 1, p. 331, on a companion); March 20, 1842 (vol. 1, p. 339–41, on a friend); March 25, 26, 27, 1842 (vol. 1, p. 348–52, on love and friendship). Thoreau's *Journal* for April 3–July 5, 1842, is missing (Stern, p. 65). In May 1843 William Ellery Channing moved to Concord and soon became a close companion of Thoreau's (Stern, p. 66).

103. The original manuscript of this sex essay is in the Berg Collection of the Research Division of the N.Y. Public Library; this manuscript will be printed for the first time in the forthcoming *Collected Works of Henry D. Thoreau* to be published by Princeton University. Seven years after writing this essay, in Sept. 1852, Thoreau gave a version of it to his friend H. G. O. Blake, with a note, on the occasion of Blake's mar-

riage. This strange wedding gift is published as "Love" and "Chastity" (F. B. Sanborn, ed., *Familiar Letters of Henry David Thoreau* [Boston: Houghton-Mifflin, 1894], p. 237–51.) A brief description of the original manuscript (in Harding, *Days*, p. 111–12) suggests that this version varies, and the later version may have been toned down.

104. Thoreau, *Journal*, vol. 1, p. 365–67.

Thoreau's *Journal* for March 13, 1846, until early in 1850 is fragmentary or missing (Stern, p. 71).

On Nov. 14, 1847, Thoreau wrote to Emerson about receiving a marriage proposition from a woman (see Walter Harding, "Thoreau's Feminine Foe," *PMLA*, vol. 69 [March 1954], p. 110–16).

In early Jan. 1848, Thoreau combined his *Journal* from the fall of 1839 into an essay on "Friendship," published in the "Wednesday" chapter of *A Week on the Concord and Merrimack Rivers* (orig. pub. in May 1849; Cambridge, Mass.: Riverside Press, 1961), p. 274–307).

On Feb. 15, 1851 [*Journal*, vol. 2, p. 161–62), Thoreau writes about the fallibility of a friend. On Oct. 10, 1851 (*Journal*, vol. 3, p. 61–62) the subject is friendship. On Nov. 13 and 14, 1851 (*Journal*, vol. 3, p. 112–16) the subject is women. On Nov. 15, 1851, Alex Therien is mentioned as being about Thoreau's area (*Journal*, vol. 3, p. 116).

105. The *Journal* of Jan. 30, 1852, uses sexual intercourse as a metaphor (vol. 3, p. 253); see also Miller, p. 94.

106. Thoreau, *Journal*, vol. 3, p. 335.

107. Thoreau, *Journal*, vol. 3, p. 406–07. See also July 5, 1852 (*Journal*, vol. 4, p. 185).

108. Thoreau, *Journal*, vol. 4, p. 92–93.

It was in Sept. 1852 that Thoreau sent his friend Blake his essay on sex. The *Journal* of Dec. 24 and 29, 1853, refers to Alex Therien (vol. 6, p. 23–24, 35–36). The *Journal* of March 4, 1856, refers to friends (vol. 7, p. 199).

109. Thoreau, *Journal*, vol. 9, p. 115–17. A note about the mushroom adds, "This is very similar to if not the same with that represented in Loudon's *Encyclopedia* and called 'Phallus impudicus, Stinking Morel, very fetid.' " It would be interesting to know if any other material was suppressed.

110. Harding, *Days*, p. 372–74.

111. *The Correspondence of Henry David Thoreau*, eds. Walter Harding and Carl Bode (N.Y.: Washington Square Press, 1958), p. 442.

112. Thoreau, *Journal*, vol. 9, p. 146. The sensuality in Whitman's *Leaves of Grass* is commented on in the *Journal* of Dec. 2, 1856 (vol. 9, p. 148). The theme of friends is discussed in the *Journal* of Dec. 5, 1856 (vol. 9, p. 160).

113. Thoreau, *Correspondence*, p. 444–45. In a letter to Thoreau of Dec. 16, 1856, his friend Thomas Cholmondeley writes: "*Forgive my English plainess of speech*. Your love for, and intimate acquaintance with, Nature is ancillary to some affection which you have not yet discovered" (Stern, p. 107).

114. Thoreau, *Journal*, vol. 9, p. 246. In his *Journal* of Oct. 10, 1858 (vol. 11, p. 203–04) Thoreau (thinking, no doubt, of himself) speaks of genius being "hermaphroditic" (see also Miller, p. 94, 227). The *Journal* of Nov. 1, 1858 (vol. 11, p. 275), contains strange and relevant musings on friendship. Friendship is also the subject of the *Journal* of Nov. 3, 1858 (vol. 11, p. 281–83). The *Journal* of Nov. 16, 1858 (vol. 11, p. 324–29), concerns religious repression and freedom of speech.

Bronson Alcott's comment that Thoreau had "no temptations" is quoted by Harding (*Days*, p. 111). Walt Whitman's comments on Thoreau are reported by Horace Traubel (*With Walt Whitman in Camden*, vol. 1 [Boston: Small, Maynard, 1906], p. 212–13; vol. 2 [N.Y.: Appleton, 1908], p. 52, 329; vol. 3 [N.Y.: Mitchell Kennerley, 1914], p. 404–05).

Walter Harding mentions that "a few years after Thoreau's death [in 1862] Concordians raised a brouhaha over the homosexual activities of one man, and ran him out of town." For the sake of American Gay history, as well as elucidating Thoreau's life, it would be most interesting to know the details and identity of the individual involved (Harding, *Profile*, p. 246–47).

115. William R. Taylor and Christopher Lasch, "Two 'Kindred Spirits': Sorority and Family in New England, 1839–1846," *New England Quarterly* (Brunswick, Me.), vol. 36, no. 1 (March 1963), p. 23–41. I wish to thank Carroll Smith-Rosenberg for informing me of this essay which is reprinted in Christopher Lasch's *The World of Nations: Reflections on History, Politics and Culture* (N.Y.: Knopf, 1973) p. 18–34; additional commentary, p. 317–18. The present text is reprinted by permission of Alfred A. Knopf, Inc.; the page references are to the original 1963 edition.

116. Taylor and Lasch, p. 23.

117. Taylor and Lasch, p. 31–32.

118. Taylor and Lasch, p. 29, 36. The use of the phrenological term "adhesiveness" is interesting. Walt Whitman would later adopt it as his own code word for intimate, erotically suffused male–male relations.

119. Taylor and Lasch, p. 36.

120. Taylor and Lasch, p. 29.

121. Taylor and Lasch, p. 38–39.

122. Taylor and Lasch, p. 38.

123. Taylor and Lasch, p. 38.

124. Taylor and Lasch, p. 39–40.

125. Taylor and Lasch, p. 40–41.

126. Taylor and Lasch, p. 27.

127. Taylor and Lasch, p. 31–32.

128. Taylor and Lasch, p. 32–33.

129. Taylor and Lasch, p. 34.

130. Taylor and Lasch, p. 35.

The life of the American actress Charlotte Cushman (1816–76) involved a series of intimate relations with other women, dating from about 1840. (It is also revelant that, as an actress, Cushman was famous for her male as well as female roles.) In her review in *The Ladder* of Joseph Leach's biography of Cushman, Lennox Strong surveys the Lesbian-relevant passages. Leach refers to Cushman's diary as "one never intended for publication," and says this diary (in Butler Library, Columbia University) records the progress of what he tactfully calls "the profound attachment" to other women. Besides her sister Susan, and the actress Fanny Kemble, among Cushman's women intimates and friends Leach lists Rosalie Kemble Sully (on whom Cushman said her "soul doted"); Eliza Cook (a young English poet who wrote [unpublished] love lyrics to Cushman, and cut her hair short, "like a man's"); Matilda Hays (an English actress-protégée with whom Cushman entered into what Elizabeth Barrett Browning called a "female marriage"); Geraldine Jewsbury (a militant English feminist writer who fell in love with Cushman and made her the model for the heroine of her scandalous novel *The Half Sisters*); Sara Jane Clarke (a popular journalist who wrote under the pen name Grace Greenwood); and three American sculptors, Harriet Hosmer, Emma Crow, and Emma Stebbins. The latter lived with Cushman for nineteen years, until Cushman's death. The first popular defense of homosexuality by an American, E. I. Prime Stevenson, mentions Cushman as "a strongly uraniadistic [Lesbian] actress (psychically)," at her best only in "almost unfeminine" roles" (Xavier Mayne, pseud., *The Intersexes; A History of Similisexualism as a Problem in Social Life* [Naples?], privately printed [by R. Rispoli, 1908?]; photo reprint, N.Y.: Arno, 1975, p. 407). See Lennox Strong, "Bright Particular Star" (review) *The Ladder*, vol. 15, nos. 4–5 (Feb.–March 1971) p. 29–31; Joseph

Leach, *Bright Particular Star; The Life and Times of Charlotte Cushman* (New Haven: Yale University, 1970); and the entries on Cushman in the DAB and NAB.

In late Feb. or early March 1860, speculates Rebecca Patterson, Emily Dickinson and Kate Scott Turner spent a "crucial night" together in Dickinson's home in Amherst, Mass. (*The Riddle of Emily Dickinson* [Boston: Houghton Mifflin, 1951], p. 143–56, 424).

131. Walt Whitman, *The Tenderest Lover; The Erotic Poetry of Walt Whitman*, ed. with an introduction by Walter Lowenfels (N.Y.: Delta, Dell, 1970), p. xx.

132. Gay Wilson Allen, *Solitary Singer; A Critical Biography of Walt Whitman* (N.Y.: N. Y. University, 1955), p. 280.

133. A parody of Walt Whitman's "Song of Myself" appeared in *Vanity Fair* on March 17, 1860, two months before the 3rd ed. of *Leaves of Grass* was published in May, with the homosexual "Calamus" poems grouped together. The parody was called "Counter-Jumps"—a counter-jumper being slang for a dry goods salesman, an occupation thought suitable only for the most effete men. The poem reads in part:

> I am the Counter-jumper, weak and effeminate.
> I love to loaf and lie about dry-goods.
> I loaf and invite the Buyer.
> I am the essence of retail. . . .
> I am the crate, and the hamper, and the yard-wand,
> And the box of silks fresh from France.
> And when I came into the world I paid duty,
> And I never did my duty.
> And never intended to do it,
> For I am the creature of weak depravities;
> I am the Counter-jumper;
> I sound my feeble yelp over the woofs of the World.

(Henry S. Saunders, comp., *Parodies on Walt Whitman* [N.Y.: American Library Service, 1923], p. 18). I wish to thank Robert Joyce Jr. for first informing me of this document.

134. Dr. James C. Jackson's home medical manual of 1864, in a section on "Bedfellows," points out the sexual "dangers" in the common practice of sisters sleeping together and older brothers sharing a bed with younger brothers, an allusion to what was called "mutual masturbation" (*The Sexual Organism and Its Healthful Management* [Boston: B. Leverett Emerson], p. 41–45). I wish to thank the Institute for Sex Research for the above information. Also see Bullough, and note 1.

135. The following extracts are from Walt Whitman "Notebook" 94 (1862) in the Library of Congress. The "Notebook" numbers are those assigned in *Walt Whitman. A Catalog Based Upon the Collections of the Library of Congress* (Washington, D.C.: Lib. of Cong., 1955). The photostat number identifies the page. I wish to thank Edward F. Grier for providing transcripts of these entries, and information concerning them. Grier is now editing the "Notebook" for publication as part of Whitman's *Collected Writings*.

From about 1862 to 1864, an Irish Confederate Army General, Patrick Ronayne Cleburne, is said to have maintained an intimate relation and slept with a fellow soldier: "Among his [Cleburne's] attachments was a very strong one for his adjutant, General Captain Irving A. Buck, a boy in years, but a man in all soldierly qualities, who for nearly two years of the [Civil] war, shared Cleburne's labours during the day and his blankets at night" (John Francis Maguire, *The Irish in America* [London: Longmans, Green, 1868; photo reprint, N.Y.: Arno, 1969], p. 651). I wish to thank Jacqueline Hunt Katz for this reference.

136. Photostat 3390. "5th av (44)" probably refers to an omnibus or "stage" line.

The last five words "slept with me Sept 3d" are written in the margin. An earlier entry reads: "Thursday evening April 17th '62 The hour or two with Henry W. Moore, evening, in Broadway, walking up—and in Bleecker street.—the brief 15 minutes, night July 18th '62, from Houston st. up from a five blocks through Bleecker street [Photostat 3389]."

137. Typed transcript made by Joseph Auslander (in the 1930s) of the original manuscript of "Notebook" 94 which has disappeared, p. 20. Just following the entry quoted is the entry: "Patrick, 7th av. always asks me about going up to 33d st" (Photostat 3385).

138. Photostat 3389. The meaning of the + sign in front of the Carr entry is not clear. It is also not clear whether Carr stayed with Whitman from Aug. 28 to Sept. 11, or simply left New York. Whitman was living with his family on Portland Ave., Brooklyn, at the time. In 1868 Whitman wrote Peter Doyle about riding on the "stage" with Carr, and had Carr's address in an 1870 notebook.

139. Photostat 3387.

140. "Notebook," 98.

A little-known German novelette by Emil Mario Vacano, *Die Helden der Reklame. Humbug, Blauer Dunst* . . . ("The Heroes of Advertisement. Humbug, Blue Haze . . ." Berlin: 1864), contains an extraordinary, completely candid "coming out" scene, set in America in which Count Alexander Althoff (disguised as "Bosco") and Kassad, two traveling circus performers, reveal their homosexuality to each other—and end up in bed. A translation of this scene and a description of its amazing author appear in Stevenson's *Intersexes* (p. 225, 314–18). The Austrian Vacano's descriptions of America are not based on personal experience; America appears in his work, as it often has in the German literature of adventure in the past two centuries, as the setting where the unusual, the exciting, even the utopian, can take place. I wish to thank James Steakley for the above information.

141. Stoddard's letters to Whitman are discussed by Edwin Haviland Miller, editor of the Whitman *Correspondence*, vol. 2, p. 81, notes 20, 21. Stoddard's brief correspondence with Herman Melville is also documented by Jay Leyda (see bibliography on Melville).

In 1868 A[nnie?] C. Wood met Irene Leache and began an intimate association lasting thirty-two years, until Leache's death in 1900. Wood commemorates this relation in *The Story of a Friendship; A Memoir* [of Irene Leache] (N.Y.: Knickerbocker, 1901). E. I. Prime Stevenson in *The Intersexes* (p. 404) calls this *Memoir* "a biographical record of a long relationship, that seems to have had a strongly psychic uranianism, an intersexual quality in it. . . ." Stevenson says Wood, an American, sketches "the personality and life of Miss Irene Leache, a Virginian lady with whom Miss Wood had been intimately associated. . . . Their companionship was of exceptional closeness, excluding approach of any counter-sentiment to interrupt its passional quality. Miss Leache had a nature of classic breadth and depth in its acceptances; was a mystic, perceptive by intuition and virile; was, in fact, one of those magnetic types whose educative currents of mind impress themselves on even casual acquaintances. . . ." I wish to thank Ed Drucker of Elysian Fields Booksellers for lending me his copy of Wood's memoir for inspection.

142. Horace Traubel, *With Walt Whitman in Camden*, vol. 1 (Boston: Small, Maynard, 1906), p. 267–69. In a section not quoted, Whitman mentions that poet Joaquin Miller "lauds" Stoddard "unreservedly."

143. Whitman, *Correspondence*, vol. 2, p. 81–82. This correct text here replaces that quoted by Traubel, which varies in minor ways.

144. Traubel, vol. 1, p. 269.

145. Whitman, *Correspondence*, vol. 2, p. 97, note 14. The author of this note is the Whitman scholar and editor of the *Correspondence*, Edwin Haviland Miller.

146. Charles Warren Stoddard, "A South Sea Idyl," *Overland Monthly; Devoted to the Development of the Country*, vol. 3, no. 3 (Sept. 1869), p. 258. This is reprinted with additional parts as "Chumming with a Savage" in *South-Sea Idyls* (Boston; Osgood, 1873), p. 2–79. An English edition of the same volume published the same year is called *Summer Cruising in the South Seas*. The story contains several references to Melville.

147. Stoddard, "South Sea Idyl," p. 258.

148. Stoddard, "South Sea Idyl," p. 259–64.

149. Traubel, vol. 3, p. 444–45. Whitman, *Correspondence*, vol. 2, p. 97, note 14, 15. Notes in the Whitman *Correspondence* indicate that the originals of Stoddard's letters are in the Charles E. Feinberg Collection; brief quotes indicate that these originals vary, in one case *significantly*, from the texts printed in Traubel. In the present text "Calamus" (Traubel) has been corrected to "CALAMUS" (*Correspondence*). Two idiosyncratic spellings, "hypocracy" and "proze *idyl*" (which are corrected in Traubel) are here left as in the original.

150. Whitman, *Correspondence*, vol. 2, p. 444–46.

151. Justin Kaplan, *Mr. Clemens and Mark Twain* (N.Y.: Simon and Schuster, 1966), p. 172. Kaplan says that Twain was giving evening lectures; he and Stoddard breakfasted on chops at midday, took long walks in the afternoon, and in the evenings before dinner, Twain sat at the piano and sang the Black jubilees he had heard as a boy. After Twain's lecture the two men returned to their rooms to smoke, sit by the fire, drink whiskey, and talk late into the night about Twain's life and their earlier days together in San Francisco. Stoddard later said he could have written Twain's biography at the end of this season. Leslie Fiedler's speculation on homoeroticism in Twain's writings takes on special interest in the context of Twain's friendship with Stoddard (*Love and Death in the American Novel*, rev. ed. [N.Y.: Dell, Laurel Ed., 1969]).

152. Stevenson, p. 383–86.
In the 1880s a number of fictional works with major or minor male homosexual themes began to be published in the U.S. The list includes: [Adolf Hausrath] George Taylor, pseud., *Antinous; A Romance of Ancient Rome* (N.Y.: Gottsberger, 1882; reprint 1884 under author's real name); Adolf von Wilbrandt, *Fridolin's Mystical Marriage* (N.Y.: Gottsberger, 1884); Caine Hall, *The Deemster* (Chicago: Rand-McNally, 1888); [Alfred J. Cohen] Alan Dale, pseud., *A Marriage Below Zero* (N.Y.: Dillingham, 1889); Howard C. Sturgis, *Tim* (London and N.Y.: Macmillan, 1891); Robert S. Hichens, *The Green Carnation* (N.Y.: Kennerley, 1894; reprint N.Y.: Appleton, 1895; Chicago: Argus, 1929); Henry B. Fuller, "At St. Judas' " (one-act poetic drama in *Puppet Show* [N.Y.: Century, 1896]); [Frederick Rolfe] Frederick Baron Corvo, pseud., *In His Own Image* (London and N.Y.: Lane, 1901); Oscar Wilde, *Portrait of Mr. W.H.* (speculation on the identity of the male to whom Shakespeare's sonnets are addressed, Portland; Me., Mosher, 1901); Paul Bourget, *A Love Crime* (N.Y.: Société des Beaux-Arts, 1905); H. A. Vachell, *The Hill; A Romance of Friendship* (N.Y.: Dodd, Mead, 1906). (List from Noel I. Garde, pseud., *The Homosexual in Literature: A Chronological Bibliography Circa 700 B.C.—1958* [N.Y.: Village Press, 1958; photo reprint in *A Gay Bibliography* (N.Y.: Arno, 1975), p. 3, 11]). Though not published in the U.S., *Imre; A Memorandum*, was authored by an American, E. I. Prime Stevenson (Xavier Mayne, pseud., Naples: The English Book-Press, R. Rispoli, 1906; photo reprint N.Y.: Arno, 1975).

153. Library of Congress, photograph collection: no. 5423 58P. I wish to thank Jacqueline Hunt Katz and William Loren Katz for providing this photo, which is not further identified.

154. Don Rickey, Jr., *Forty Miles a Day on Beans and Hay* (Norman; University of Oklahoma, 1963), p. 170–71. Rickey's sources are Brigadier General Edward S. Godfrey, "General Sully's Expedition Against the Southern Plains Indians, 1868," 3 f. in the

Charles Francis Bates Collection, Custer Battlefield National Monument, Crow Agency, Montana. Letters in the Elizabeth B. Custer Collection, same location, are said to confirm this account. I wish to thank Stephen W. Foster for discovering this reference.

155. This engraving is signed and is apparently from a painting by "A. Castaigne [18]91." The engraver is "H. Davidson." It was published in an American periodical whose name and date have unfortunately been lost.

156. Clarence Mulford, *Tex* (N.Y.: Burt, 1922), chap. 13, p. 212. I wish to thank Richard Amory for providing this document.

157. Badger Clark, *Sun and Saddle Leather*, 3rd ed. (Boston: Richard G. Badger, Gorham Press, 1919), p. 67–69. The 1st ed. was published in 1915, the second in 1917. I wish to thank Jim Kepner for information about this volume and Ed Drucker of Elysian Fields Booksellers for providing photocopies.

158. Alfred C. Kinsey, Wardell B. Pomeroy, Clyde E. Martin, *Sexual Behavior in the Human Male* (Phila.: Saunders, 1948), p. 455–57.

159. Kinsey and others, *Sexual Behavior . . . Male*, p. 630–31.

160. Mabel Ganson Dodge Luhan, . . . *Intimate Memories*, vol. 1, *Background* (N.Y.: Harcourt, Brace, 1933), p. 29–31. I wish to thank Edmund White for informing me of Luhan's autobiography.

A book of poems, *Infelicia* (Phila.: Lippincott, 1875), first published in 1868 by the American actress Adah Isaacs Menken, is said to contain verse vaguely alluding to intimate relations between women (Foster, p. 138–41). Samuel Edwards's biography, *George Sand* (N.Y.: McKay, 1972) is said to offer "fairly substantial proof" of Sand's Lesbian relation with Adah Isaacs Menken (as well as Marie Duval) (Barbara Grier [Gene Damon, pseud.], "Lesbiana," *The Ladder*, vol. 16, nos. 11–12 [Aug.–Sept. 1972], p. 34).

Close female–female relations are a theme of psychiatrist Oliver Wendell Holmes's novels, *Elsie Venner* (N.Y.: Burt, 1859), *The Guardian Angel* (Boston: Ticknor and Fields, 1867), and *A Mortal Antipathy*, first published in 1885. (See Foster, p. 91–93; Clarence P. Oberndorff, *Psychiatric Novels of Oliver Wendell Holmes* [N.Y.: Columbia University, 1943], p. 17, 42, 84, 90, 146, 170, 217, 222).

Henry James's *The Bostonians*, about a triangular relation between two feminist women and a man, was first published serially in 1885, in the *Century Magazine* (Feb. 1885–Feb. 1886), in book form, in London, in 1886. Discussion of Lesbianism and feminism in this novel may be found in Philip Rahv's introduction to it (N.Y.: Dial, 1945); Foster p. 95–96; Irving Howe's introduction (N.Y.: Modern Library, 1956); Leon Edel, *Henry James; The Middle Years* (Phila.: Lippincott, 1962), p. 137–46. The relation between Alice James (Henry's sister) and her "loyal friend and companion" Katherine Peabody Loring deserves further analysis (see *The Diary of Alice James*, ed. Leon Edel [N.Y.: Dodd, Mead, 1934; Apollo Ed., 1964]. The wife of William James (also named Alice) reportedly felt that Alice James's relationship with Katharine Loring was "Lesbian" (Barbara Grier [Gene Damon, pseud.], *The Ladder*, "Lesbiana," vol. 12, no. 3 [Feb.–March 1968], p. 15, citing the biography *William James* by Gay Wilson Allen [N.Y.: Viking, 1967], p. 227). Also see Lennox Strong, "Diary of Alice James" (review), *The Ladder*, vol. 10, no. 3 [1965], p. 23–25.

Leon Edel's five-volume biography of Henry James manages to simultaneously discuss James's homosexual attractions and to deny them much importance; the evidence of homosexuality in James's life and work and its implications remains to be carefully analyzed. There seems no doubt that Henry James had homosexual feelings—to what extent he was conscious of the character of these emotions, to what extent he acted upon them, and how they manifested themselves in his work must still be established.

Philip Rahv, in a review of the last volume of Edel's biography (*Henry James; The Master*) speaks of the elderly James's relation to three younger men: "There is the tantalizing question of James's homo-erotic tendencies that surfaced only very late in his life. It is to Edel's credit that he treats these belated 'romances' with candor, uncommon tact, and good judgment. There can be no doubt any longer that James was in love (or thought he was) with two exceedingly handsome young men: the sculptor Hendrik Andersen and the socialite Jocelyn Persse. Account must also be taken of his very ambiguous relationship with the young writer Hugh Walpole. Edel quotes extensively from the passionate letters James wrote to all three, but unfortunately their replies are mostly lost. Thus to the question of what was the exact nature of these 'affairs'—'just romantic or also physical?'—Edel can only answer that at this late date it is impossible to establish the facts on any kind of firm basis." Rahv concludes that loneliness is "decisive for our understanding of James, certainly far more so than his belated 'romances,' conducted mostly in epistolary form, which, in my effort at comprehension, appear to be no more than rather pathetic symptoms of senile sexuality, that is to say, of a sexuality so long and tenaciously suppressed that it could find an outlet only in the blessed safety of old age, when James could assure himself in good conscience that implementation was no longer a practical possibility" ("Henry James and his Cult," *New York Review of Books*, Feb. 10, 1972, p. 18–19).

Needing further exploration is James's perfectly conscious interest in John Addington Symonds's life and pioneering defense of homosexuality (see Part V, and James's short story inspired by Symonds, "The Author of Beltraffio" [1884]. Also significant is James's reaction to the works and trial of Oscar Wilde and James's relation with Edmond Gosse, who may have made a confession of homosexuality to James (Edel denies Phyllis Grosskurth's interpretation of Gosse's letter). Further research might be undertaken on James's association with Howard Sturgis, author of *Tim*, an English school novel with homosexual content, and on James's relation with the American Morton Fullerton, the bisexual lover of James's friend Edith Wharton. An essay by Mildred E. Hartsock is valuable ("Henry James and the Cities of the Plain," *Modern Language Quarterly*, vol. 29 [1968], p. 297–311). Maxwell Geismar speaks briefly of homosexuality in *Henry James and the Jacobites* (Boston: Houghton-Mifflin, 1963), p. 65, 281. James's story, "The Pupil," is also relevant.

Intimate same-sex relations are pictured in several early novels for boys. Edward I. Prime Stevenson's *The White Cockades; An Incident of the 'Forty-five'* (N.Y.: Scribner, 1887) is a novel, set at the time of the Jacobite rebellion, in which (in the words of its author) "a passionate devotion from a rustic youth toward the Prince, and its recognition are half-hinted as homosexual in essence" (Stevenson, *Intersexes*, p. 367). This is one of the earliest documented homosexual "juveniles." The same writer's *Left to Themselves, Being the Ordeal of Philip and Gerald* (N.Y.: Hunt and Eaton, 1891), also a boys' book, is described by its author as clearly conveying a "sentiment of uranian [homosexual] adolescence." This is "a romantic story in which a youth in his latter teens is irresistibly attracted to a much younger lad: and becomes, *con amore,* responsible for the latter's personal safety, in a series of unexpected events that throw them together—for life" (*Intersexes*, p. 367–68).

161. Luhan, vol. 1, p. 207–08.

162. Luhan, vol. 1, p. 235–39.

163. Luhan, vol. 1, p. 245–49.

164. Luhan, vol. 1, p. 260–66. The Shillito sisters' relationship with poet Pauline Tarn (Renée Vivien, pseud.) is also mentioned by Luhan (vol. 1, p. 250–51, 261–66) as is Natalie Barney (vol. 2, p. 214), Gertrude Stein and Alice Toklas (vol. 2, p. 324–33). Luhan's obituary is in the *New York Times*, Aug. 14, 1962, p. 31, col. 4. I wish to thank Robert Carter and Ellen Tabak for translating the French phrases in Luhan's text.

165. Willa Cather, "Three Women Poets," Lincoln, Nebraska *Journal*, Jan. 13, 1895;

reprinted in *The World and the Parish: Willa Cather's Articles and Reviews, 1893–1902*, selected and ed. with a commentary by William M. Curtin (Lincoln: University of Nebraska, 1970), p. 147. Sappho's similarity to Anacreon is mentioned by Cather. Anacreon's "delicately erotic [male] homosexual love poems" are discussed by Arno Karlen in his *Sexuality and Homosexuality* (N.Y.: Norton, 1971), p. 22, 31, 33, 50.

A questionnaire survey of adolescent psychology made at Clark University and published in 1897 asks about "Love. How did feelings about the other sex change? Was a real person loved? Was the person older, idealized, how long did the affection last, how shown? Describe the later loves." Although no question asked specifically about same-sex love, the answers of 49 persons between the ages of 16 and 25 (3 males and 46 females) "Speak of passionate love for the same sex." The author adds: "Any complete study of adolescence must needs deal with this subject. . . ." Adolescence is "the time of life when it is natural for the sexes to be attracted to each other . . . The love of the same sex is not generally known, but it is very common. Without solicitation 49 cases have been reported. It is not mere friendship. The love is strong, real and passionate. Many of the answers to the syllabus are so beautiful that if they could be printed in full no comment would be necessary." Six examples are quoted, all females speaking of love for females. A woman of 19 writes: "At 12 I was promoted to a teacher with whom I soon became infatuated. I talked of her from morning to night. Remained after school, etc. From then till 17 I adored some teacher or other all the time. At 17 I was much in love with a girl six or seven years older. I consider such love sin." A female of 21 writes: "I had an ideal lover, older than myself, it still continues. Never changed regarding the opposite sex, always had a hatred of men" (E. G. Lancaster, "The Psychology and Pedagogy of Adolescence," *Pedagogical Seminary*, vol. 5 [July 1897], p. 88–89). Havelock Ellis quotes two additional female answers in a section on "The School Friendships of Girls" (*Studies in the Psychology of Sex; Sexual Inversion* [Phila.: F. A. Davis, 1901], p. 256–57). Perhaps the original questionnaires or data for this survey still exists at Clark University, Worcester, Mass. (where a copy of Lancaster's article was located).

Diana Victrix, a novel by Florence Converse, published in 1897 (Boston: Houghton-Mifflin) is said by Nan Bauer Maglin (in her study of "Women's Activist Fiction") to focus on "the question of marriage versus selfhood. . . . Enid Spenser and Sylvia Barnett, both from New England, decide not to marry. Sylvia intends to dedicate herself to writing and Enid to radical change and teaching. They both deeply value their twelve year old relationship of love and support; nevertheless, two men from New Orleans present a serious challenge to this relationship. The struggle is not only of male love versus female love, but two different cultural definitions of female roles." At the end of this volume, says Maglin, men and marriage do *not* triumph, as they do in many other early feminist novels ("Discovering Women's Activist Fiction," *University of Michigan Papers in Women's Studies*, vol. 2, no. 2, [1976]). Maglin's research on *Diana Victrix* and author Florence Converse is continuing for another essay. Maglin points out, in a personal communication, that Converse lived for many years with Vida Scudder, a teacher at Wellesley College.

Jeannette Foster's survey of Lesbian-relevant literature mentions several early short stories. Josephine Dodge Dascom's "A Case of Interference" (in *Smith College Stories*, 1900), set in a school, is said to "just skirt" Lesbian-relevance. A Lesbian-relevant "juvenile" is Mary C. DuBois's "The Lass of the Silver Sword" (*St. Nicholas Magazine*, 1909; later book publication). Catherine Wells's "The Beautiful House (*Harper's Monthly Magazine*, March 1912; reprint, *The Ladder*, vol. 12, no. 5 [April 1968], p. 4–13) pictures a relationship between two female artists which ends tragically for one. Jeanette Lee's "The Cat and the King" (*Ladies' Home Journal*, Oct. 1919; reprint, *The Ladder*, vol. 16, nos. 7–8 [April-May 1972], p. 37–45) has a school setting (*Sex Variant Women in Literature* [N.Y.: Vantage, 1956], p. 255). "The Last Leaf" (*McClure's Magazine*, 1906), by William S. Porter (O'Henry, pseud.) is also relevant.

Among the early Lesbian-relevant volumes in English, Foster mentions *The Farrington's* (N.Y.: Appleton, 1900), by British novelist Ellen Thorncroft Fowler; *The Story of Mary MacLane* (Chicago: Stone, 1902) by a nineteen-year-old Canadian-American who purports to write her autobiography, and to continue it in *My Friend Annabel Lee* (Chicago: Stone, 1903), and *I, Mary MacLane* (N.Y.: Stokes, 1917); *Things As They Are*, Gertrude Stein's Lesbian novel (written in 1903, but not published until after her death, in 1951; later reprinted as *Q.E.D.*); *The Holland Wolves* (Chicago: McClurg, 1902) by John Breckenridge Ellis, a novel including female cross-dressing, and a close female–female relation; *Multitude and Solitude* (N.Y.: Kennerley, 1911) by John Masefield; *The Getting of Wisdom* (N.Y.: Duffield, 1910) by Henry Handel Richardson (pseud. of an Australian, Ethel F. L. R. Robertson). (Foster, p. 243–53). *Idylle Saphique* by Liane de Pougy, a French novel published in 1901 (Paris: Libraire de la Plume), is said by Foster to detail the relation of a famous, jaded courtesan and Florence, a twenty-two-year-old American who falls in love with her (Foster, p. 202–03).

The case history of an American Lesbian as reported by a physician is in Stevenson, *Intersexes* (1908?), p. 129–33. Lesbianism in American colleges is discussed in the same source, p. 181–82.

Amy Lowell's first published volume of poetry, *A Dome of Many-Colored Glass* (Boston: Houghton Mifflin, 1912), includes, according to Jeannette Foster (p. 178–79), love lyrics addressed to women, as does her *Sword Blades and Poppy Seeds* (N.Y.: Macmillan, 1914), *Pictures of the Floating World* (N.Y.: Macmillan, 1919), and *What's O'Clock* (Boston: Houghton Mifflin, 1925). Foster says the last chapter of Clement Wood's biography *Amy Lowell* (N.Y.: Vinal, 1926) is especially relevant. A recent biography, *Amy*, by Jean Gould (N.Y.: Dodd, Mead, 1976) is said to study Lowell's "early ambivalent sexual identification and later her frank love for women," including her "affection for Ada Dwyer Russell, her companion and housemate, a devotion whose warmth moved Thomas Hardy and H. D. (Hilda Doolittle)" (Grace Schulman, *N.Y. Times Book Review*, Jan. 25, 1976, p. 22).

166. Sperry's letters are in the Emma Goldman Collection, Mugar Memorial Library, Boston University. I wish to thank Rosalyn Baxandall and Alix Kates Shulman for informing me of these letters.

167. Goldman's report of her public defense of homosexuality in 1915, and the anarchist reaction, is reprinted from her autobiography in Part IV of the present book. Goldman does not mention Sperry in her autobiography. Berkman's description of prison homosexuality is reprinted from his *Prison Memoirs* in the present section, below.

168. Alexander Berkman, *Prison Memoirs of an Anarchist*, introduction by Hutchins Hapgood, new introduction by Paul Goodman (N.Y.: Schocken 1970), p. xix. Emma Goldman mentions that one commercial publisher, approached about printing Berkman's work, asked for the removal of the homosexual scenes (Goldman, vol. 1, p. 484). Goldman also says that Edward Carpenter wrote a preface to an English edition of Berkman's *Memoirs* (vol. 2, p. 983).

169. Berkman, p. 167–73.

170. Berkman, p. 318–24.

171. Berkman, p. 348.

172. Berkman, p. 433–34. Second paragraph added for clarity.

173. Berkman, p. 437–40. Berkman mentions the death of "Russell" in a letter to Emma Goldman dated July 10, 1901 (Goldman, vol. 1, p. 292).

174. Foster, p. 266–67.

175. The historical association of the color green with homosexuality is mentioned by Arno Karlen in *Sexuality and Homosexuality; A New View* (N.Y.: Norton, 1971), p. 78, 249, 250. Green carnations were associated with Oscar Wilde; *The Green Carnation,* a novel satirizing Wilde, was first published anonymously in N.Y. in 1894 (its author

was Robert Smythe Hichens). *The Green Bay Tree* (1933) was a Broadway play with a Lesbian theme.

176. Helen R. Hull, *The Labyrinth* (N.Y.: Macmillan, 1923), p. 25, 55, 59.

177. Hull, *Labyrinth*, p. 89–95.

178. Hull, *Labyrinth*, p. 103–04.

179. Hull, *Labyrinth*, p. 147–51.

180. Hull, *Labyrinth*, p. 183–87.

181. Hull, *Labyrinth*, p. 196.

182. Hull, *Labyrinth*, p. 224–39.

183. Hull, *Labyrinth*, p. 318–21.

In 1929 the "Bureau of Social Hygiene," a branch of the Rockefeller Foundation, published its report of a study of "the sex life of normal women," titled *Factors in the Sex Life of Twenty-Two Hundred Women*, by Katharine Bement Davis, a sixty-nine-year-old penologist and social worker (N.Y.: Harper; photo reprint N.Y.: Arno, 1974). The "normal" woman under study was defined as she "who was not pathological mentally or physically and who was capable of adjusting herself satisfactorily to her social group." The study was based on questionnaires answered by 1,000 married women and 1,200 single women who had graduated from college at least five years previously. Two chapters, written with Marie E. Kopp, detail the study's findings about Lesbianism among college graduates, married and unmarried.

The survey of "Homosexuality" and "The Married Woman" not surprisingly finds this group to be much more conflicted, negative, and puritanical about Lesbianism than the single college graduates—who are generally more accepting and affirmative about their Lesbian feelings.

The chapter on "Homosexuality" and "The Unmarried College Woman" reports that 605 women, or slightly over 50 percent of the 1,200 women who answered the questionnaire, said they had "at some time or other experienced intense emotional relations with other women . . ." The respondents' experience was accompanied by physical expressions recognized as sexual in 312, or slightly more than half of these 605 cases, 26 percent of the entire sample (p. 247–48, 277).

Of the above 605 women, 234 said their intense same-sex relations were "accompanied by mutual masturbation, contact of the genital organs, or other physical expressions recognized as sexual . . ." Another group of 78 women said their intense emotional relations, while without physical expression other than hugging and kissing, were "recognized at the time as sexual." These two latter groups constitute the 312 women who Davis calls "overt" homosexuals. Another group of 293 women said that their experience of intense same-sex relations were "unassociated with consciousness of a sex experience and unaccompanied by physical expression other than hugging and kissing" (p. 247).

Among the especially interesting results are the high percentage of women who found their intense emotional relation "helpful and stimulating" (p. 255). Also "only 40 of the 312 overt homosexuals regarded their homosexual relationship in the light of a sex problem requiring solution" (p. 271). Females attending coeducational schools experienced significantly fewer intense emotional relations with other women than did those attending women's schools. But the "college crush," and even "overt" homosexual relations, existed to a considerable extent at coeducational institutions (p. 258–60; 277–78). Only in the group of "social service" workers was a significant correlation found between a particular occupation and both overt Lesbian activity and intense emotional relations with other women (p. 263). The report includes selected histories of single college women and much striking firsthand testimony on the experience of female–female intimacy (see especially p. 279–80, 280–81, 281–82, 284, 285, 287–88, 289–92, 292–93, 296).

184. Mary Casal (pseud.), *The Stone Wall; An Autobiography* (Chicago: Eyncourt,

1930; photo reprint, N.Y.: Arno, 1975), p. 10, 17. The discovery of Casal's identity should not be difficult considering all the details she relates. Knowing her identity would make possible further important Lesbian history research.

185. Casal, p. 22–23, 27–28, 29.

186. Casal, p. 47, 50, 68.

187. Casal, p. 72, 77, 82, 86.

188. Casal, p. 47, 93, 94, 100, 110–11.

189. Casal, p. 139, 146, 167, 185, 190, 203, 218.

190. Casal, p. 73–74, 178–82.

191. Casal, p. 91.

192. Casal, p. 68–69, 132.

193. Casal, p. 101–02, 115–16, 131, 184, 200, 215.

194. Casal, p. 143–57.

195. Background on Thompson's relations with Christa Winsloe and on the following Thompson diaries is found in Vincent Sheean's *Dorothy and Red* (Boston: Houghton Mifflin, 1963), chap. 9, "A Rather Strange Interlude," p. 207–42. A second major source is Marion K. Sanders's *Dorothy Thompson; A Legend in her Time* (N.Y.: Avon, 1974), p. 179–81, 188–93 (on Christa Winsloe); 36–37, 39, 45, 71, 89, 155–56, 185, 349 note (on Gertrude Tone).

196. Foster, p. 300; Sanders, p. 131 note.

197. Sanders, p. 181.

198. Diary [1932–33] in Dorothy Thompson Papers, George Arents Research Library, Syracuse University. In the present text Thompson's varying punctuation marks, which look like ellipses, have been uniformly replaced by hyphens. I wish to thank James Steakley for translating the German phrases in the text.

199. Barbara Grier (Gene Damon, pseud.) and Lee Stuart, "Dorothy and Red" (review), *The Ladder*, vol. 8, no. 4 (Jan. 1964), p. 21.

200. Sanders, p. 190–93.

Bibliography

VI. LOVE: 1779–1932

Anthony, Susan B., to Anna Dickinson. Feb. 19, March 18, 1868; Jan. 15, 1869; Nov. 5, 1895; Library of Congress, Manuscript Division, Anna Dickinson Papers, Box 5 (See Rogoff, Gordon; Sinclair, Andrew.)

[Beecher, Henry Ward.] Beecher, William Constantine. *A Biography of Henry Ward Beecher*. N.Y.: Webster, 1888. Constantine Fondolaik Newell, p. 104–07.) Also Hibben, Paxton. *Henry Ward Beecher; An American Portrait*. N.Y.: Press of the Readers Club, 1942. (Constantine Fondolaik Newell, espec., p. 44–48.)

Belot, Adolphe. *Mademoiselle Giraud, My Wife*. Chicago: Laird & Lee, 1891.

Berkman, Alexander. *Prison Memoirs of an Anarchist*. Introduction by Hutchins Hapgood. New introduction by Paul Goodman. N.Y. Schocken, 1970. (P. xix, 167–73, 318–24, 348, 433–34, 437–40.)

Casal, Mary (pseud.). *The Stonewall; An Autobiography*. Chicago: Eyncourt, 1930. Photo reprint, N.Y.: Arno, 1975. (P. 143–57.)

[Case, Louella, J. B. and Edgarton, Sarah.] Taylor, William R., and Lasch, Christopher. "Two 'Kindred Spirits': Sorority and Family in New England, 1839–1846," *New England Quarterly* (Brunswick, Me.). Vol. 36, no. 1 (March 1963): p. 23–41. Reprinted in Christopher Lasch, *The World of Nations: Reflections on History, Politics and Culture*. N.Y.: Knopf, 1973. (P. 18–34; additional commentary p. 317–18.)

Cather, Willa. *The World and the Parish: Willa Cather's Articles and Reviews, 1893–1902*.

Selected and ed. with a commentary by William M. Curtin. Lincoln, Neb.: University of Nebraska, 1970. (Sappho: p. 147.)

[Dickinson, Emily.] Patterson, Rebecca. *The Riddle of Emily Dickinson.* Boston: Houghton Mifflin, 1951.

Reviews:

Chase, Richard. "Seeking a Poet's Inspiration," *Saturday Review of Literature.* Vol. 34 (Dec. 1, 1951): p. 26.

Johnson, Thomas. "Kate Scott and Emily Dickinson," *New York Times Book Review.* Nov. 4, 1951: p. 3, col. 2.

Joost, Nicholas. "The Pain That Emily Knew," *Poetry.* (Chicago) Vol. 80 (July 1952): p. 242–45.

[Edgarton, Sarah. See Case, Louella J. B.]

Emerson, Ralph Waldo. *Journals of Ralph Waldo Emerson.* Eds. Edward Waldo Emerson and Waldo Emerson Forbes. 10 vols. Boston & N.Y.: Houghton Mifflin, 1909–14. (Vol. 1, opposite p. 70.)

————. *The Journals and Miscellaneous Notebooks of Ralph Waldo Emerson.* Ed. William H. Gilman, Alfred R. Ferguson, George P. Clark, Merrell R. Davis. Cambridge, Mass.: Belknap Press of Harvard University, 1960. (Vol. 1, p. 22, 39–40, 52–55, 94–95, 129–30, 291–92, 353.)

Fiedler, Leslie. *Love and Death in the American Novel.* rev. ed. N.Y.: Laurel Edition, Dell, 1969. (P. 15, 348 [on Melville], etc.)

Foster, Jeannette Howard. *Sex Variant Women in Literature.* N.Y.: Vantage, 1956.

[Fuller, Margaret.] Flood, Lynn. "A Life of Angels. Margaret Fuller's World," *The Ladder* (Reno, Nev.) Vol. 16, nos. 9–10 (June–July 1972): p. 28–34.

[Fuller, Margaret.] *Memoirs of Margaret Fuller Ossoli.* Eds. Ralph Waldo Emerson, William H. Channing, James Freeman Clarke. 2 vols. Boston: Phillips, Sampson, 1851–52. (Vol. 1, p. 23, 34–44, 127–29, 304–08, 310–11; vol. 2, p. 66–69, 70–72.)

[Fuller, Margaret.] Stern, Philip Van Doren. *The Annotated Walden . . .* N.Y.: Potter, 1970. (P. 23, 25.)

[Fuller, Margaret.] Wade, Mason. *Margaret Fuller: Whetstone of Genius.* N.Y.: Viking, 1940. (P. 90–91, 294–95.)

Gautier, Théophile. *Mademoiselle de Maupin; A Romance of Love and Passion;* Illus. . . . from designs by Toudouze. Chicago: Laird & Lee, 1890.

Hamilton, Alexander. *The Papers of Alexander Hamilton.* Ed. Harold C. Syrett. Assoc. ed., Jacob E. Cooke. N.Y.: Columbia University, 1961. (Vol. 1, p. 34, 37–38, 164, 347, 431; vol. 3, p. 145.)

[Hamilton, Alexander.] Miller, John Chester. *Alexander Hamilton; A Portrait in Paradox.* N.Y.: Harper, 1959. (P. 22.)

Higginson, Mary Potter (Thacher). *Thomas Wentworth Higginson.* Boston: Houghton Mifflin, 1914. (Hurlbut: p. 72, 125–27, 280.)

Higginson, Thomas Wentworth. *Cheerful Yesterdays.* 1896; photo reprint, N.Y.: Arno, 1968. (Hurlbut: p. 107–11.)

————. "Sappho," *Atlantic Monthly* (Boston) July 1871: p. 83–93.

[Higginson, Thomas Wentworth.] Edelstein, Tilden G. *Strange Enthusiasm; A Life of Thomas Wentworth Higginson.* New Haven: Yale University, 1968. (Hurlbut: p. 64, 77–82; "manliness": p. 25–26, 117–18, 148–51, 161–62, 189, 194–95, 205–06, 234–36, 242, 282–83, 316–18; Whitman: p. 352–56; Wilde, p. 354; E. Dickinson, p. 342–44.)

Hull, Helen Rose. *The Labyrinth.* N.Y.: Macmillan, 1923. (P. 25, 55, 59, 88–95, 103–04, 147–51, 183–87, 196, 318–21.)

James, Henry. *The Bostonians. Century Magazine.* (Feb. 1885–Feb. 1886). Other editions: with an introduction by Irving Howe (N.Y.: Modern Library, 1956); introduction by Philip Rahv (N.Y.: Dial, 1945).

[James, Henry.] Edel, Leon. *Henry James: The Master; 1901–1916.* Phila.: Lippincott, 1972. (Dudley Jocelyn Persse: espec. p. 181–91; Hugh Walpole: espec. p. 397–409.)

[James, Henry.] Edel, Leon. *Henry James; The Middle Years, 1882–1895.* Phila.: Lippincott, 1962. (*Bostonians:* p. 137–46.)

[James, Henry.] Edel, Leon. *Henry James; The Treacherous Years; 1895–1901.* Phila.: Lippincott, 1969. (Hendrik Andersen: p. 290–91, 306–16, 335–36. See also Oscar Wilde, John Addington Symonds, Howard Sturgis.)

[James, Henry.] Grosskurth, Phyllis. *John Addington Symonds; A Biography*. London, 1964. Photo reprint, N.Y.: Arno, 1975. (P. 240, 270–71, 282, 308, 319, 321–23.)

[James, Henry.] Hartsock, Mildred E. "Henry James and the Cities of the Plain." *Modern Language Quarterly*. Vol. 29 (1968): p. 297–311.

[James, Henry.] Rahv, Philip. "Henry James and his Cult" (review of Edel's *Henry James; The Master*), *New York Review of Books*. Feb. 10, 1972: p. 18–22.

Luhan, Mabel Ganson Dodge. *Intimate Memories*. Vol. 1, *Background*. N.Y.: Harcourt Brace, 1933. (P. 29–31, 207–08, 235–39, 245–49, 260–66.)

Melville, Herman. *Billy Budd / Sailor; (An Inside Narrative): Reading Text and Genetic Text, Edited from the Manuscript with Introduction and Notes* by Harrison Hayford and Merton M. Sealts, Jr. Chicago: University of Chicago, 1962. (P. 163.)

———. "Hawthorne and His Mosses," *Literary World* (N.Y.), Aug. 17, and 24, 1850.

———. *The Letters of Herman Melville*. Eds. Merrel R. Davis and William H. Gilman. New Haven: Yale University, 1960. (P. 142–43.)

———. *Moby-Dick; An Authoritative Text; Reviews and Letters by Melville; Analogues and Sources; Criticism*. Ed. Harrison Hayford and Hershel Parker. N.Y.: Norton, 1967. (P. 22, 24, 26, 27, 32, 53–54, 348–49.)

———. *Omoo; A Narrative of Adventures in the South Seas*. Eds. Harrison Hayford, Hershel Parker, G. Thomas Tanselle. Historical note by Gordon Ropers. Evanston and Chicago: Northwestern University Press and Newberry Library, 1968. (P. 152–53, 157, 302, 322–25.)

———. *Pierre or The Ambiguities*. Eds. Harrison Hayford, Hershel Parker, G. Thomas Tanselle. Historical note by Leon Howard and Hershel Parker. Evanston & Chicago: Northwestern University and Newberry Library, 1971. (P. 216–17.)

———. *Selected Poems of Herman Melville*. Ed. Hennig Cohen. Garden City, N.Y.: Anchor Books, Doubleday, 1964. (P. 69–71, 102–03, 141, 203–04, 233–34.)

———. *Typee; A Peep at Polynesian Life*. Eds. Harrison Hayford, Hershel Parker, G. Thomas Tanselle. Historical note by Leon Howard. Evanston & Chicago: Northwestern University and Newberry Library, 1968. (P. 135–36.)

———. *White-Jacket or The World in a Man-of-War*. Eds. Harrison Hayford, Hershel Parker, G. Thomas Tanselle. Historical note by Willard Thorp. Evanston & Chicago: Northwestern University Press, 1970. (P. 375–76.)

[Melville, Herman.] Arvin, Newton. *Herman Melville*. [N.Y.:] William Sloan, 1950. (P. 128, 130.)

[Melville, Herman.] Leyda, Jay. *The Melville Log; A Documentary Life of Herman Melville; 1819–1891*. 2 vols. N.Y.: Harcourt, Brace, 1951. (Vol. 1, p. 430.)

[Melville, Herman.] Martin, Robert K. "Melville's Vine; The Story of a Relationship." Typescript. Paper delivered at the Modern Languages Association, 1975.

[Melville, Herman.] Sutton, Walter. "Melville's 'Pleasure Party' and the Art of Concealment," *Philological Quarterly*. Vol. 30 (1951), p. 316–27.

Mure, William. *A Critical History of the Language and Literature of Ancient Greece*. London: Longman, Brown, Green, and Longmans; 1853–59. 5 vols. (Sappho: vol. 3, p. 272–326, 496–98.)

Rugoff, Milton. *Prudery and Passion*. N.Y.: Putnam, 1971. (Susan B. Anthony and Anna Dickinson p. 265–66; Antoinette Brown and Lucy Stone p. 266.)

Russell, Bertrand. See [Thomas, Helen Carey, etc.]

Sinclair, Andrew. *The Better Half*. N.Y.: Harper and Row, 1965. (S. B. Anthony to Anna Dickinson p. 155; Antoinette Brown to Lucy Stone, p. 155–56.)

Smith-Rosenberg, Caroll. "The Female World of Love and Ritual: Relations between Women in Nineteenth-Century America," *Signs; Journal of Women in Culture and Society*. Vol. 1, no. 1 (Autumn 1975).

Sperry, Almeda. Letters to Emma Goldman. Emma Goldman Collection, Mugar Memorial Library, Boston University.

Stein, Gertrude. *Things As They Are*. Pawlet, Vt., Banyan Press, 1950; reprinted as *Q.E.D.* in *Fernhurst, Q.E.D., and other Early Writings*, ed. with an introduction by Leon Katz, with a note on the texts by Donald Gallup. N.Y.: Liveright, 1971.

Stevenson, Edward I. Prime. *Left to Themselves, Being the Ordeal of Philip and Gerald*. N.Y.: Hunt and Eaton; Cincinnati: Cranston and Stowe, 1891.

———. *The White Cockades; An Incident of the 'Forty-five*. N.Y.: Scribner, 1887.

[Stevenson, Edward I. Prime.] Mayne, Xavier, pseud. *The Intersexes; A History of Simili-sexualism as a Problem in Social Life*. [Naples?], privately printed [by R. Rispoli, 1908?]. (*White Cockades*: p. 367; *Left to Themselves*: p. 367–68; etc.)

Stoddard, Charles Warren. "A South Sea Idyl," *Overland Monthly; Devoted to the Development of the Country*. Vol. 3, no. 3 (Sept. 1869): p. 257–64. Reprinted with additional parts as "Chumming with a Savage" in *South-Sea Idyls* (Boston; J. R. Osgood, 1873), p. 2–79. English ed. titled *Summer Cruising in the South Seas* (1873).

[Stoddard, Charles Warren.] Kaplan, Justin. *Mr. Clemens and Mark Twain*. N.Y.: Simon and Schuster, 1966. (P. 172.)

[Stoddard, Charles Warren.] Traubel, Horace. *With Walt Whitman in Camden*. vol. 1, Boston: Small, Maynard, 1906. (P. 267–69.) Vol. 3, N.Y.: Mitchell Kennerley, 1914. (P. 444–46).

[Stoddard, Charles Warren.] Whitman, Walt. *Collected Writings*. General eds. Gay Wilson Allen, and E. Sculley Bradley. *The Correspondence*. Ed. Edwin Haviland Miller. N.Y.: N.Y. University, 1961. (Vol. 2, p. 81, 97.)

Taylor, William R. and Lasch, Christopher. (See [Case, Louella, J. B. and Edgarton, Sarah.])

[Thomas, Helen Carey, etc.] Russell, Bertrand. *The Autobiography of Bertrand Russell*. 3 vols. Vol. 1, *1872–1914*. Boston: Little, Brown, 1967. (P. 205–07.)

Thompson, Dorothy. Diary [1932–33]. Dorothy Thompson Papers. George Arents Research Library, Syracuse University.

[Thompson, Dorothy.] Grier, Barbara (Gene Damon, pseud.) and Stuart, Lee. "Dorothy and Red" (review). *The Ladder*. Vol. 8, no. 4 (Jan. 1964), p. 20–21.

[Thompson, Dorothy.] Sanders, Marion K. *Dorothy Thompson; A Legend in her Time*. N.Y.: Avon, 1974. (P. 179–81, 188–93 [on Christa Winsloe]; 36–37, 39, 45, 71, 89, 155–56, 185, 349 note [on Gertrude Tone]; 131 [on *Ann Vickers*]).

[Thompson, Dorothy.] Sheean, Vincent. *Dorothy and Red*. Boston: Houghton-Mifflin, 1963. (Chap. 9, "A Rather Strange Interlude," p. 207–42.)

Thoreau, Henry David. *Familiar Letters of Henry David Thoreau*. Ed. F. B. Sanborn. Boston: Houghton-Mifflin, 1894. (P. 238–51.)

Thoreau, Henry David. *The Journal of Henry David Thoreau*. Eds. Bradford Torrey and Francis H. Allen. 14 vols. Cambridge, Mass.: Riverside Press, Houghton-Mifflin, 1906.

[Thoreau, Henry David.] Harding, Walter, ed. *Henry David Thoreau; A Profile*. N.Y.: Hill and Wang, 1971.

[Thoreau, Henry David.] Miller, Perry. *Consciousness in Concord; the Text of Thoreau's Hitherto "Lost Journal," 1840–1841, Together with Notes and a Commentary*. Boston: Houghton Mifflin, 1958.

[Thoreau, Henry David.] Stern, Philip Van Doren, ed. *The Annotated Walden* . . . N.Y.: Potter, 1970. (P. 22–23, 56.)

[Western United States, same-sex relations in.]

Castaigne, A. "The Miner's Ball." Engraving dated 1891. (Publication data unknown.)

Clark, Badger. *Sun and Saddle Leather*. 3rd ed. Boston: Richard G. Badger, Gorham Press, 1919. (P. 67–69.)

Kinsey, Alfred C., Pomeroy, Wardell B., and Martin, Clyde E. *Sexual Behavior in the Human Male*. Phila.: Saunders, 1948. (P. 455–57, 630–31.)

[Males dancing.] Photograph. Library of Congress. No. 5423 / 58 P (not further identified).

Mulford, Clarence. *Tex*. N.Y.: Burt, 1922. (Chap. 13, p. 212.)

Rickey, Jr., Don. *Forty Miles a Day on Beans and Hay*. Norman: University of Oklahoma, 1963. (P. 170–71.)

Whitman, Walt. Diaries, 1862–63, N.Y., Brooklyn, Washington, D.C. Library of Congress.

Whitman, Walt. (See Stoddard, Charles Warren.)

Winthrop, Theodore. *Cecil Dreeme*. Boston: Ticknor & Fields, 1861. (Espec. p. 239–44, 269–76, 281, 346–49.)

INDEX